Gardner's

ART

THROUGH

THE AGES

Tenth Edition

II

RENAISSANCE
AND
MODERN ART

Gardner's

ART

THROUGH

THE AGES

Tenth Edition

II

RENAISSANCE
AND
MODERN ART

RICHARD G. TANSEY
FRED S. KLEINER

HARCOURT BRACE COLLEGE PUBLISHERS

Fort Worth Philadelphia San Diego New York Orlando Austin San Antonio
Toronto Montreal London Sydney Tokyo

PRESIDENT *Carl N. Tyson*

PUBLISHER *Ted Buchholz*

EDITOR IN CHIEF *Christopher P. Klein*

ACQUISITIONS EDITOR *Barbara J. C. Rosenberg*

DEVELOPMENTAL EDITOR *Helen Triller*

SENIOR PROJECT EDITORS *Margaret Allyson, Mark Hobbs*

SENIOR PRODUCTION MANAGER *Kathleen Ferguson*

ART DIRECTOR *Nick Welch*

PICTURE EDITORS *Peggy Cooper, Carrie Ward*

SENIOR MARKETING MANAGER *Patricia A. Murphree*

ELECTRONIC PAGE LAYOUT *Bill Maize, Duo Design Group*

FILM PREPARATION, PRINTING, AND BINDING *R. R. Donnelley & Sons, Willard, Ohio*

TIMELINE LAYOUTS *Marco Ruiz*

MAP PREPARATION *GeoSystems*

Cover Image: AUGUSTE RENOIR, *Young Woman Seated ("La Pensée")*, 1876–1877. 26″ × 21⅝″. The Barber Institute of Fine Arts, The University of Birmingham.

Address for Editorial Correspondence:
Harcourt Brace College Publishers, 301 Commerce Street, Suite 3700, Fort Worth, Texas 76102

Address for Orders:
Harcourt Brace & Company, 6277 Sea Harbor Drive, Orlando, Florida 32887
1-800-782-4479 or 1-800-433-0001 (in Florida).

Printed in the United States of America

ISBN:
0-15-501141-3 (hardbound)
0-15-501618-0 (paperbound, Vol. I)
0-15-501619-9 (paperbound, Vol. II)

Library of Congress Catalog Card Number:
95-76264 (hardbound)
95-76263 (paperbound, Vol. I)
95-76259 (paperbound, Vol. II)

8 9 0 1 2 3 4   048   9 8 7 6 5 4

PREFACE

Since its first edition, almost seventy years ago, Helen Gardner's *Art through the Ages* (1926), carried on by a succession of authors, has established a firm tradition of excellence in its presentation of art to three generations of beginning students. Helen Gardner lived long enough to see the third edition in preparation (1948). In 1958, Sumner Crosby and his colleagues in the History of Art Department at Yale University produced a fourth edition. The fifth through the ninth editions (1991) were prepared by Horst de la Croix and Richard G. Tansey of San Jose State University, the ninth with the collaboration of Diane Kirkpatrick of the University of Michigan. De la Croix's death in 1993 regrettably ended his long association with the Gardner project. His role as coauthor has been assumed by Fred S. Kleiner, Professor of Art History and Archaeology at Boston University and Editor-in-Chief of the *American Journal of Archaeology*. Herbert Cole, of the University of California, Santa Barbara, has been kind enough to contribute the chapter on the art of Africa.

The fundamental belief that guided Helen Gardner and her successors is that the history of art is essential to a liberal education. The study of art history, like its fellow humanistic studies, the history of literature and the history of music, has as its aim the opening of student perception and understanding to works of high esthetic quality and expressive significance—works that humankind has produced throughout history and around the world, and that—especially now—are cherished and conserved by the peoples of the world as representative of their cultural identities. The awareness, comprehension, and informed experience of these works are what a survey like this would encourage and hope to achieve. The art experience can only be informed, expanded, and made selective in its judgments if it is at the same time a historical experience. This means understanding works of art within the contexts of their times and places of origin and the temporal sequences of their production.

In sustaining this traditional view we are still convinced that art has its own history—within, of course, the general history of humankind—and that the discipline of art history has discernible boundaries and distinctive objects to which it attends and with which it operates. We are respectful of the fact that for a long time there has been a corpus of paintings, sculptures, buildings, and other works of art that have been considered most characteristic of the cultures that produced them, most worthy of conservation and study, and most definitive of the scope of art-historical interest. We do not reject the traditional list of "great" works or the very notion of a "canon." But we have also tried in our choice of monuments to reflect the increasingly wide range of interests of contemporary scholarship. We have included, for example, works produced for non-elite patrons alongside those of the emperors in the chapter on Roman art. The chapters on twentieth-century art cover the multitude of innovative art forms that reflect our contemporary world.

We have also taken into consideration present trends of art-historical criticism that would seem to dissolve the traditional art-historical boundaries, merging the humane studies in a kind of conglomerate that much resembles cultural anthropology. Works of art become value-free, cultural artifacts to be interpreted according to anthropological structures: sociopolitical, psychosocial, racial, ethnic, gender, and material, thought of as determined by the power and privilege enjoyed by dominant patronages. Postmodern "critical theory" would redefine the history of art, its styles, periods, and canons, in terms of contemporary ideological agendas that, for a survey of the subject, cannot help but be tendentious. There is much to be learned from these new approaches to art history, and we have ourselves profited from them. But we feel that, although art is certainly illustrative of culture, and the construction of its cultural context is most valuable in the interpretation of it, art has in fact a cross-cultural independence that makes a history of art possible at all and renders its meanings intelligible and its peculiar values accessible to all interested minds. It is to the cultivation of this interest in art in general—art from all times and places—that a survey of the history of art is dedicated.

The first task, we believe, is to present characteristic works in historical order. To bring theory about the data in before the data are presented would be, its seems to us, premature and confusing. We prefer to fix the attention of beginning students on a wide range of art-historical data, familiarizing them with the stylistic features that identify the data visually, and that differentiate one work or group of works from others within the framework of historical time. Once the distinguishing features have been mastered, special theories about their causes can be debated, although perhaps more effectively in intermediate and advanced undergraduate courses in art history than in the introductory survey courses for which this book has been designed.

The text has been thoroughly revised and in large part rewritten. We have endeavored to update it in accordance with contemporary art-historical and archeological scholarship. Specialists have reviewed each chapter, and the text has benefited. Some previous chapters have been broken down into smaller chapters in response to reviewers' suggestions and to our own feeling that they require greater emphasis: there are now separate chapters for Etruscan and Roman; for Early Christian, Byzantine, and Islamic; and for African art. And the art of Korea is a new addition to our survey of Asian art. The sequence of the chapters dealing with the Renaissance in Italy and in Northern Europe has been altered according to new interpretations of the relationship of those areas in the Renaissance. To this end, Northern art of the fifteenth and sixteenth centuries has been placed in separate chapters. The material in Part V, The Modern World, has been entirely reorganized to chronicle the many styles that characterized the art of the nineteenth century and to trace the development in the twentieth century of Modernism and its sequel, Postmodernism.

Readers of earlier editions of Gardner's classic book will note other important changes. A great effort has been made to enhance the quality of the photographs in the volume by utilizing the latest technology and a finer grade of paper. New maps and timelines open each chapter, and more works in North American collections have been included to encourage the careful study of originals.

A comprehensive package of teaching and study aids also accompanies the tenth edition of *Art through the Ages*. The pronunciation guide to artists' names, included at the end of the book, has been expanded and refined. The Study Guide by Kathleen Cohen contains chapter-by-chapter drills on the identification of geographical locations, time periods, styles, terms, iconography, major art movements, and specific philosophical, religious, and historical movements as they relate to particular works of art examined in the textbook. Self-quizzes and discussion questions enable students to evaluate their grasp of the material. Lilla Sweatt and Timothy Adams are the authors of the Instructor's Manual, which includes sample lecture topics for each chapter, a testbank of questions in formats ranging from matching to essay, studio projects, and lists of resources. A computerized testbank, consisting of questions from the Instructor's Manual, has been created for textbook users.

A work as extensive as a history of world art could not be undertaken or completed without the counsel and active participation of experts in fields other than our own. In some cases, this took the form of preparation of portions of chapters; in others, of reviews of work in progress or already prepared. For such contributions to previous editions, we offer our sincere thanks to James Ackerman, Harvard University; Majorie P. Balge, Mount Holyoke College; Colleen Bercsi, California State University, Northridge; Jacques Bordaz, University of Pennsylvania; Louise Alpers Bordaz, Columbia University; James Cahill, University of California, Berkeley; Miles L. Chappell, College of William and Mary; George Corbin, Lehman College, City University of New York; Gerald Eknoian, DeAnza College; Mary S. Ellett, Randolph-Macon Woman's College; Roger K. Elliott, Central Virginia Community College; Mary F. Francey, University of Utah; Ian Fraser, Herron School of Art, Indiana University–Purdue University; Stockton Garver, Wichita State University; Judith Paetow George, Miami University; Oleg Grabar, Institute for Advanced Study, Princeton; Hamilton Hazlehurst, Vanderbilt University; Howard Hibbard, late of Columbia University; Philancy N. Holder, Austin Peay State University; John Howett, Emory University; Joseph M. Hutchinson, Texas A & M University; Joel Isaacson, University of Michigan; R. Steven Janke, State University of New York at Buffalo; M. Barry Katz, Virginia Commonwealth University; Herbert L. Kessler, Johns Hopkins University; Robert A. Koch, Princeton University; Avra Liakos, Northern Illinois University; Elizabeth Lipsmeyer, Old Dominion University; William L. MacDonald, formerly of Smith College; A. Dean McKenzie, University of Oregon; Mary Jo McNamara, Wayne State University; Kathleen Maxwell, Santa Clara University; Milan Mihal, Vanderbilt University; Diane Degasis Moran, Sweet Briar College; Harry Murutes, University of Akron; Kristi Nelson, University of Cincinnati; Jane S. Peters, University of Kentucky; Edith Porada, late of Columbia University; Bruce Radde, San Jose State University; Gervais Reed, University of Washington; Raphael X. Reichert, California State University at Fresno; Richard Rubenfeld, Eastern Michigan University; Grace Seiberling, University of Rochester; Peter Selz, University of California, Berkeley; David Simon, Colby College; Pamela H. Simpson, Washington and Lee University; David M. Sokol, University of Illinois at Chicago; Lilla Sweatt, San Diego State University; Marcia E. Vetrocq, University of New Orleans; Richard Vinograd, Stanford University; Joanna Williams, University of California, Berkeley; and the Art History Department, Herron School of Art, Indiana University–Purdue University at Indianapolis.

For contributions to the tenth edition in the form of extended critiques of work in progress or already prepared, we wish to thank Priscilla Seabury Albright; Barbara W. Blackmun, San Diego Mesa College; Jack W. Burnham, formerly of the University of Maryland, College Park; Janet Black, College of San Mateo; Martha B. Caldwell, James Madison University; Michael Camille, University of Chicago; David Cast, Bryn Mawr College; Mark Cheetham, University of Western Ontario; Madeline L. Cohen, Community College of Philadelphia; Michael A. Coronel, University of Northern Colorado; Patricia Crane Coronel, Colorado State University; Howard Crane, Ohio State University; Anne Glenn Crowe, Virginia Commonwealth University; Tracey Cullen, Archaeological Institute of America; Walter Denny, University of Massachusetts, Amherst; Lloyd C. Engelbrecht, University of Cincinnati; Benjamin R. Foster, Yale University; Karen Polinger Foster, Connecticut College; Mark D. Fullerton, Ohio State University; Sandra C. Haynes, Pasadena City College; M. F. Hearn, University of Pittsburgh; Robert C. Hobbs, Virginia Commonwealth University; Carol Ivory, Washington State University; Christopher M. S. Johns, University of Virginia; Sandra J. Jordan, University of

Montevallo; Kumja Paik Kim, Asian Art Museum of San Francisco; Martha Kingsbury, University of Washington; Eugene Kleinbauer, Indiana University, Bloomington; Karen Koehler, Skidmore College; Laetitia La Follette, University of Massachusetts, Amherst; Jody Lamb, Ohio University; Joanne Mannell, Montana State University; Virginia Hagelstein Marquardt, Marist College; Linda F. McGreevey, Old Dominion University; Laura Meixner, Cornell University; Mary Miller, Yale University; Robert Poor, University of Minnesota; Donald Preziosi, University of California, Los Angeles; Monica Rothschild-Boros, University of California, Irvine; Charles Sable, Marquette University; Ellen C. Schwartz, Eastern Michigan University; Laurie Taylor-Mitchell, Incarnate Word College; Robert Wojtowicz, Old Dominion University. Innumerable other instructors and students have also sent us helpful reactions, comments, and suggestions for ways to improve the book. We are grateful for their interest and their insights.

We should like to acknowledge the assistance given us in innumerable ways by art and slide librarian Luraine Collins Tansey, especially for bibliographical research and for her skillful management of communications and logistics. Dr. Joel Tansey was also of assistance in compiling the bibliography. In addition, we owe a debt of gratitude to Ivy Doak, who compiled the pronunciation guide.

Among those at Harcourt Brace who have contributed their efforts to the management of an enormously detailed manuscript and have done so with consummate skill, infinite patience, and good humor are our acquisitions editors, Janet Wilhite and Barbara Rosenberg; Barbara's editorial assistant, Diane Drexler; our developmental editor, Helen Triller; our project editors, Margaret Allyson and the late Mark Hobbs; our photo editors, Peggy Cooper and Carrie Ward; our designer, Nick Welch; and our production manager, Kathleen Ferguson. We are also grateful to the marketing staff, Pat Murphree, Toni Hawkins, Patti Holland, Laura Lashley, and Mark Hatley, for their dedication to making the book successful. Recognition and thanks are also due to copy editors Joan Harlan and J. R. Peacock; proofreaders Tom Torrans, Susan Petty, and Pete Gooch; consultant Jerry Edmonson; keyboarder Norman Haskell; compositor Bill Maize; and indexer Linda Webster.

We are especially grateful to the editors at Harcourt Brace for deciding in 1992 to reach out from coast to coast and from generation to generation to bring us together for this project. Our collaboration has already resulted in a lasting friendship and, we hope, a worthy successor to the inspired text that Helen Gardner penned so many years ago.

Richard G. Tansey
Fred S. Kleiner

This volume is one of two that constitute the paperbound version of Gardner's *Art through the Ages*, Tenth Edition. The two volumes exactly reproduce the text of the one-volume version, including its pagination. The first of these volumes contains Part I, The Ancient World; Part II, The Middle Ages; and Part III, The World Beyond Europe. The second volume contains Part IV, The Renaissance and the Baroque and Rococo; and Part V, The Modern and Postmodern World. The introduction, pronunciation guide to artists' names, glossary, bibliography, copyright acknowledgments, and index appear in both volumes. The two-volume printing is intended for those who have occasion to use only half of *Art through the Ages*. The differences between the one-volume and the two-volume versions of the book are differences in form only.

A NOTE TO READERS OF THIS BOOK

The objects pictured in the images in this book vary enormously in size. The authors urge you to take note of the scales provided on all plans and all dimensions provided in captions. This will help you to appreciate the relative sizes of the objects shown.

You will notice the names of modern nations on maps illustrating areas of the world as they were in earlier times. These modern names are used merely for your ease in locating sites.

CONTENTS

V THE MODERN AND POSTMODERN WORLD   922

Gardner's

ART

THROUGH

THE AGES

Tenth Edition

II

RENAISSANCE
AND
MODERN ART

INTRODUCTION

Outside the academic world, the terms *ART* and *HISTORY* are not often juxtaposed. People tend to think of history as the record and interpretation of past human actions, particularly social and political actions. Most think of art, quite correctly, as something *present*— something that can be seen and touched—which, of course, the vanished human events that make up history are not. The fact is that a visible and tangible work of art is a kind of persisting event. It was made at a particular time and place by a particular person, even if we do not always know just when, where, and by whom. Although it is the creation of the past, art continues to exist in the present, long surviving its times; Charlemagne has been dead for a thousand years, but his chapel still stands at Aachen.

The persisting events that art history chronicles are visual and tangible objects made by human hands. These can be classified under architecture, sculpture, the pictorial arts (painting, drawing, printmaking, photography), and the craft arts, or arts of design, which produce objects of utility, like ceramic wares, metal wares, textiles, and similar accessories of ordinary living. Traditionally, machines and machine-produced objects fall outside the scope of art history, belonging rather to the history of technology (which, it is true, is currently moving into the art-historical domain, given the art-producing potential of the computer). By virtue of their function as temporal rather than spatial and static media, the performing arts—music, drama, and the dance—have their own separate histories. Today, the strict division of the arts, especially that which separates "fine" art from "craft" art and machine art from performance art, is being blurred in practice and often denied in theory.

AT LEFT: *GIOVANNI PAOLO PANNINI*, Picture Gallery with Views of Modern Rome, *1757. Oil on canvas, 67" × 96¼" (detail). Charles Potter Kling Fund, Courtesy of Museum of Fine Arts, Boston.*

In this book we shall deal primarily, but not exclusively, with architecture, sculpture, and painting and its related arts. Their monuments have long been the data with which art history has been principally concerned, in which art historians have mostly specialized, and which more immediately draw the attention of the interested public.

THE AIM OF ART HISTORY

Just as history in general seeks to understand the past through its documented events, so the history of art seeks to understand it through works of art. These works are not only "persisting events" but documents recording the times that produced them. Ultimately, art history seeks to arrive at not only as complete a picture as possible of art as it changes in time but also an explanation of those changes. Rather than attempt such an explanation, and risk premature theorizing, our survey intends only an introductory presentation of the material. It is sufficient at this point to define certain categories essential to art-historical procedure and to an understanding of its objects.

CLASSIFICATION CATEGORIES OF ART HISTORY

Art history makes use of several basic categories to identify, describe, and classify its objects, or works of art. For convenience we may call two of these categories *physical* and *esthetic.* The physical categories are the most elementary: the kind or type of object (building, statue, picture), the medium or material (brick, bronze, oil on canvas), the dimensions, the physical condition, and so forth. The esthetic categories name the visual and tactile features of the object (form, shape, line, color, mass, volume). We shall later discuss the esthetic categories in some detail (see pages 9–15).

Historical Categories

The historical categories that art history uses to arrange its objects in time sequences and time frames (*periods*) are date (*chronology*), place of origin (*provenance*), *style* and stylistic change, *iconography* and subject matter, *attribution* (assignment of a work to a maker or makers), and meaning, cause, and *context.* We shall consider them in order.

CHRONOLOGY   Before we can construct a history, we must be sure that each monument is correctly dated. Thus, an indispensable tool of the historian is chronology, the measuring scale of historical time. Without chronology, there could be no history of style—only a confusion of unclassifiable monuments.

The table of contents of this book reflects what is essentially a series of periods and subperiods arranged in chronological order—the historical sequence that embraces the sequence of art styles. Until the later eighteenth century, the history of art was really a disconnected account of the lives and works of individual artists. Now, however, we regard art history as a record of the dynamic change of styles through time and the art of individual masters as substyles of the overall period styles. Although one speaks of "change" in the history of art, the objects themselves obviously do not change, but the fact that works of art from one period look different from those of other periods leads us to infer that *something* changes. This something can only be the ways of thinking, the thought patterns of the artists and their cultures with respect to the meaning of life and of art.

PROVENANCE   Although our most fundamental way of classifying works of art is by the time of their making, classification by place of origin, or provenance, is also crucial. In many periods, a general style (Gothic, for example) will have a great many regional variations: French Gothic architecture is strikingly different from both English and Italian Gothic. Art history, then, is also concerned with the spread of a style from its place of origin. Supplementing time of origin with place of origin adds yet another dimension to our understanding of the overall stylistic development of art monuments.

STYLE AND STYLISTIC CHANGE   The time in which a work of art was made has everything to do with the way it looks—with its style. In other words, the style of a work of art is a function of its historical period. The historiography of art sorts works into stylistic classes on the bases of their similarities and the times or periods in which they were produced. It is a fundamental hypothesis of art history that works of art produced at the same time and in the same place will generally have common stylistic traits. Of course, all historiography assumes that events derive their character from the time in which they happen (and perhaps from their most prominent personages, also products of their time). Thus, we can speak of the Periclean Age, the Age of Louis XIV, or even the Age of Roosevelt. We also must know the time of a work if we are to know its meaning—to know it for what it is. We can assume that artists in every age express in their works some sort of meaning that is intelligible to themselves and others. We can discover that meaning only by comparing a particular work to other works like it that were made about the same time. By grouping works in this way, we can infer a community of meaning as well as of form; a style will then be outlined. In a chronological series of works having common stylistic features, we may find also stylistic differences between the later and the earlier works. The art historian often has tended to think of this phenomenon as reflecting an evolution, a development, and not simply a random change.

It is important to stress, however, that "development" does not mean an orderly progression of styles toward some ideal type or formal perfection, such as absolute truth to natural appearances. Although at times in the development of Western art the "imitation of nature" has been an expressed goal of the artist, photographic realism (the mechanical reporting of what the eye perceives in the visual field) has been rarely either the purpose or the result of that development. Moreover, stylistic development does not lead to ever increasing esthetic value; later phases cannot be appraised as "better" than earlier ones simply because they are presumed closer to some imagined goal of competence and achievement. Instead, we should understand stylistic development as an irregular series of steps of varying duration in which the possibilities of a given style are worked out by artists, both independently and in collaboration with others, until those possibilities are fully realized and new stylistic traits and tendencies appear and are distinguishable as such. Thus, when we talk of stylistic development in art, we do not mean artistic progress—certainly not in the sense of scientific or technological progress, whereby our knowledge appears to increase in a sequence of necessary and interdependent steps toward ever greater scope and certainty.

But even in science and technology, where "later" may be "better" with respect to scientific truth or technological efficiency of function, there is not necessarily an increase in the *quality* of the work compared with past achievement. Though new models of aircraft, automobile, and ship outdate earlier models, many of the early ones can still be admired for their "classic" design. The tall sailing ship may not be a match in speed for the modern power-driven vessel, but its beauty of design and superb performance are still appreciated. The stylistic quality remains even though the style is obsolete.

ICONOGRAPHY AND SUBJECT MATTER   Chronology, provenance, and style are supplemented by iconography in identifying, describing, and classifying works of art. *Iconography* means, literally, the "writing of" images, both the significance and the study of them. By extension it includes also the study of symbols. We experience countless images in our everyday environment as it is interpreted by the visual media, and symbols are just as familiar, not only in written, mathematical, and computer language, but in road signs, insignia, trademarks, and so forth. Symbols may be derived from images, as in the evolution of alphabets from pictographs; images may have symbolic significance, as, in Christian art, where the images of winged beasts symbolize the Gospels. The functions of image and symbol can merge, and it is the business of iconographical analysis to interpret them, whether merged or separate.

The analysis of subject matter or theme goes hand in hand with iconography. It is concerned with what the work of art is *about:* the story or narrative, the scene presented, the time and place of the action, the persons involved, the environment and its details. For different works of art some of these aspects are not present or are not relevant; but where they appear, they require identification if an understanding of the subject is to be complete. Pictorial subject matter traditionally has been broadly separated into religious, historical, mythological, genre (commonplace life), portrait, landscape, still life, and their numerous subdivisions. Even without considerations of style, and without knowledge of who the maker of a work might be, much can be determined about the period and provenance of it by iconographical and subject-matter analysis alone.

ATTRIBUTION: THE ARTIST   Worldwide, there are great works of art whose artists remain unknown to us—the pyramids at Gizeh in Egypt, Angkor Wat in Cambodia, much of the medieval architecture of Europe, and the works of a number of "masters" still not identified. The analysis of works of art by chronology, provenance, style, iconography, and subject matter gives us an account of these works that makes the identity of the artist seem at first almost irrelevant for a history of art. Art history is essentially a history of art rather than of artists; yet we feel it incomplete and inexplicable without the factor of artistic personality.

A great many artists are identified by what we call *documentary evidence*. This consists of signatures and dates on works and the artist's own writings. Where documentary evidence is lacking, the art historian attempts to assign a work to an artist on the basis of *internal evidence*. This is what can be learned by stylistic and iconographical analysis, in comparison with other works, and by analysis of the physical properties of the medium itself. This complex procedure is known as *attribution*, the assignment of a particular work to a particular artist, or artists. It requires a keen, highly trained eye and long experience to become the expert we call a *connoisseur*. Attribution is bound to be subjective and ever open to doubt. At present, international debate rages over attributions and disattributions to the famous Dutch painter Rembrandt.

It is often the case—but not always!—that artists are influenced by their masters and then influence, or are influenced by, fellow artists working somewhat in the same style at the same time and place. We designate a group of such artists as a *school*. By "school," we do not mean an academy but a chronological and stylistic classification with a stipulation of place. We speak of the Dutch school of the seventeenth century and, within it, of subschools such as those of Haarlem, Utrecht, and Leyden.

It will strike today's readers as curious that the majority of the artists recorded by art history are male. The art-historical record often has tended to exclude the contributions of women to art. Evidence from many times and places (some of it collected quite recently), however, indicates that women clearly have produced art and craftwork of extremely high quality. Women artists were known in classical antiquity and have been recognized in China, Japan, India, and many other cultures. In the Western Middle Ages, women were renowned as skilled illuminators of manuscripts and workers of textiles. With the Renaissance, women painters began to come into prominence, along with women printmakers and sculptors. The art-historical record demonstrates that artistic talent, skill, competence, inventiveness, and refinement clearly are not functions of gender.

MEANING, CAUSE, AND CONTEXT The meaning of a work of art is not completed by the categories of time, place, iconography, style, or attribution. All of these are the necessary materials of interpretation, but they are not sufficient for it. There remains the question of *cause*: Why does a particular work of art look the way it does and not some other way? What are the historical causes of its style? The answers to these specific questions enter into our explanation of works of art, the disclosure of their meaning, and the way they probably should be looked at. Of course, explanations can never be final, certain, or persuasive for all.

The iconography of a work should not be confused with its meaning. Iconography can show us what a work represents, *what* it is about, but its meaning depends upon the *way* the representation is made (its style) and the *cause* of that way of representation (the artist's purpose or intention). Works may have the same subject matter and imagery but differ markedly in style and purpose. For example, the Christian theme of the Crucifixion has been represented in different ways in different times and places (compare FIGS. 9-28, 13-35, 20-26, 23-3, and 24-38). Pious Christians will reverence these for what they represent. They are not likely to be concerned about stylistic peculiarities that might reveal levels of meaning not immediately given.

It would also seem at first that style is so bound up with meaning that it is impossible to separate them. But just as the iconography of what is represented does not exhaust the meaning of a work, so style alone does not disclose it. Nor are the procedures of attribution more than auxiliary in the elucidation of meaning. Identification of artists and the attribution to them of specific works of art constituted the history of art for centuries.

The history of art style began only in the eighteenth century. Today art history finds itself more and more engaged with *contextuality:* the causal relationships among artists, art work, and the society or culture that conditions them. The history of art has been successively a history of artists and their works, of styles and stylistic change, of images, and now contexts and cultures. Art history at its best makes use of all of these.

The cause of a particular work of art is, obviously, the artist. The purpose of the artist, the means used to fulfill that purpose, and the artist's success in doing so, should be revealed in the finished work, the effect of the artist as cause. But other factors contribute. The artist as a member of a society, as a participant in its culture, shares in a community of experience. Artists are conditioned by their culture's "styles" of seeing, perceiving and thinking, believing and knowing, speaking and acting, doing and making. This amounts to a social collaboration in the whole artistic enterprise.

Context changes in historical time just as do the art styles it conditions. Great historical changes of context cause great stylistic changes. The fall of Rome, the coming of Christianity, and the rise of Islam all had much to do with stylistic changes in architecture, sculpture, and painting in the early centuries of our era. The triumph of science and technology had everything to do with the great transformation of the Renaissance tradition that took place in what we call "modern art"—the form of our own time. The work of art, the persisting event, is, after all, a historical document. What we have to do is learn to read it as such, so that we may more perceptively "read" it as also a work of art.*

To understand the relationship of historical context and the work of art we must confront the fundamental and perhaps insoluble problem of the relation-ship of *our* historical context to the historical context we are studying. How can we comprehend a culture that is unlike our own in many respects?

For centuries, travel, migrations, cultural interchanges, and historical curios-ity have made us aware of the monuments of other cultures and those of our own. We have viewed them with interest, admiration, and awe. To make sense of them we apply the categories of art history to bring them into sharper focus. We try to reconstruct the cultural context in which they originated. In the reconstructive procedure we consult the evidence of religion, science, technol-ogy, language, philosophy, and the arts to discover the thought patterns com-mon to artists and their audiences.† Whatever our reconstructive techniques may be, we are bound to be limited by our distance from the thought patterns of the culture we are studying and by the obstructions to understanding raised by our own thought patterns—the assumptions, presuppositions, and preju-dices peculiar to our own culture. The picture of the past we are reconstructing may be distorted because of our own culture-bound blindness. At present, many art historians are insisting that this is indeed the case. For example, they claim that art history has, from the outset, been Eurocentric, viewing other cul-tures exclusively from a European perspective.

Many art historians, sympathetic to feminist aspirations and concerns, claim that the art of the West expresses the subordination and exploitation of women. Other art historians now emphasize the influence of power interests in deter-mining thought and culture patterns. They see power as the prime mover and ultimate explanation of culture and art, whether political, social, economic, psychological, or psychosexual.

To verify these various claims, art historians who make them undertake to revise traditional and conventional art history by a method of analysis called *deconstruction*. Deconstruction proceeds by "re-reading" the received art-historical picture and showing where and how it is false to the realities of the cultures it attempts to explain and to the meanings of particular works of art.

Thus, in our postmodern world reconstruction and deconstruction of context and its meaning go on together as a kind of dialogue, the outcome of which is uncertain. It may be that the discipline of art history will widen into or merge

---

*It is important to pay attention to this dual aspect of the work of art in studying art history. As a historical document, the work of art might be regarded as simply one among many documentary artifacts that define a context and enter into the interpretation of it. The work of art would then be used to explain a context, whereas, in our view, the history of art should properly use the context in the explanation of the work of art. The emphasis upon building context pulls art history in the direction of anthropology and sociology. On the other hand, to neglect context would move the work of art away from cultural conditioning as part of its explanation. It would then be part of a historically independent history of art styles. Art historians are presently experiencing this conflict of emphasis and interest.

†These cultural "constructs," as they are called, are believed by many scholars today to encode the thought patterns of a culture, and require, like any code, deciphering. The terms *code* and *encode* are borrowed from the linguistic theory of *semiotics*, which is concerned with the nature of signs—the fundamental elements in communication. All constructs, it is believed, are reducible to signs that communicate significance or meaning. The sign (the signifier) can be anything that signifies, and what it signifies (the signified) is its meaning. The semiotic approach specifically reduces words, symbols, and images to signs and the interrelationships of signs. For reconstructing contexts it is use-ful both as an extension of the category of iconography and a simplification of it. Semiotic analysis proposes to recover substrata of meaning that conventional art-historical investigation cannot reach and, perhaps, to unify all the humanistic disciplines within one explanatory theory and practice.

with a new discipline that would take in all the humanities, on the model of cultural anthropology and with the methods of semiotics.

One thing seems certain: the intermingling of many cultures today in the phenomenon of multiculturalism can make it possible for us to overcome the limits of the culture-bound and to experience the finest features of all of them. Art made by human hands can be accessible to any human subject. Its esthetic properties, whether or not we fully grasp what they signify, can be discriminated and enjoyed by those who respond to art wherever in the world they may encounter it.

The Esthetic Categories and Terms of Art History

Certain categories and terms are indispensable for describing works of art from any time and place and will be used throughout this book. They make up the vocabulary of formal analysis. Esthetic definitions, like the ones we offer here, are by no means rigid; scholars sometimes use them in slightly different ways. For the purpose of our survey they will serve as keys to a somewhat specialized language. Dictionaries will help where the meaning may seem obscure.

Form, for the purposes of art history, refers to the shape of the "object" (work) of art; in the made object, form is the shape that the expression of content takes. To create forms, to make a work of art, artists shape materials with tools. Each of the materials, tools, and processes available has its own potentialities and limitations; it is part of all artists' creative activity to select the tools most suitable to their purpose. The technical processes that artists employ, as well as the distinctive, personal ways in which they handle them, we call their *technique*. If the material that artists use is the substance of their art, then their technique is their individual manner of giving that substance form. Form, technique, and material are interrelated, as we can readily see in a comparison of a marble statue called the *Kritios Boy* (FIG. 5-37) with a bronze statue of a charioteer (FIG. 5-39). The *Kritios Boy* is firmly modeled in broad, generalized planes, reflecting the ways of shaping stone that are more or less dictated by the character of that material and by the chisel. On the other hand, the charioteer's fineness of detail, seen in the crisp, sharp folds of the drapery, reflects the qualities inherent in cast metal (compare also Verrocchio's bronze *David* [FIG. 21-50] with Michelangelo's marble *David* [FIG. 22-19]). However, a given medium can lend itself to more than one kind of manipulation. The technique of Lehmbruck's bronze *Seated Youth* (FIG. **1**), for example, contrasts strikingly with Rodin's *The Thinker* (FIG. **2**), also in bronze. The surfaces of Lehmbruck's figure are smooth, flowing, quiet; those of Rodin's figure are rough, broken, and tortuous. Here, it is not so much the bronze that determines the form as it is the sculptor's difference of purpose and of personal technique.

Space, in our commonsense experience, is the bounded or boundless "container" of collections of objects. For the analysis of works of art, we regard space as bounded by and susceptible to esthetic and expressive organization. Architecture provides our most common experience of the actual manipulation of space; the art of painting frequently projects an image (or illusion) of our three-dimensional spatial world onto a two-dimensional surface.

Area and *plane* describe a limited, two-dimensional space and generally refer to surface. A plane is flat and two-dimensional. An area is often a plane or a flat surface that is enclosed or bounded.

Mass and *volume*, in contradistinction to plane and area, describe three-dimensional space. In both architecture and sculpture, mass is the bulk, density, and weight of matter in space. Yet the mass need not be solid; it can be the exterior form of enclosed space. For example, "mass" can apply to a pyramid (FIG. 3-8), which is essentially solid, or to the exterior of a church like Hagia Sophia (FIG. 9-1), which is essentially a shell enclosing vast spaces. Volume is

1   WILHELM LEHMBRUCK, *Seated Youth*, 1918.
Bronze. Wilhelm-Lehmbruck-Museum,
Duisburg.

2   AUGUSTE RODIN, *The Thinker*, 1880.
Bronze. Metropolitan Museum of Art, New
York (gift of Thomas F. Ryan, 1910).

the space that is organized, divided, or enclosed by mass. It may be the spaces of the interior of a building, the intervals between the masses of a building, or the amount of space occupied by three-dimensional objects like sculpture, ceramics, or furniture. Volume and mass describe the exterior as well as the interior forms of a work of art—the forms of the matter of which it is composed *and* the forms of the spaces that exist immediately around that matter and interact with it. For example, in the Lehmbruck statue (FIG. 1), the expressive volumes enclosed by the attenuated masses of the torso and legs play an important part in the open design of the piece. The absence of enclosed volumes in the Rodin figure (FIG. 2) is equally expressive, closing the design, making it compact, heavy, and confined. Yet both works convey a mood of brooding introversion. These closed and open forms demonstrate the intimate connection between mass and the space that surrounds and penetrates it.

Line is one of the most important, but most difficult, terms to comprehend fully. In both science and art, line can be understood as the path of a point moving in space. Because the directions of motions can be almost infinite, the quality of line can be incredibly various and subtle. It is well known that psychological responses are attached to the direction of a line: a vertical line is active; a horizontal line, passive; and so on. Hogarth regarded the *serpentine*, or S-curve, line as the "line of beauty." Our psychological response to line is also bound up with our esthetic sense of its quality. A line may be very thin, wire-like, and delicate, as in Klee's *Twittering Machine* (FIG. 27-68, compare FIG. 3-44). Or it may alternate quickly from thick to thin, the strokes jagged, the outline broken, as in a six-hundred-year-old Chinese painting (FIG. 15-23) in which the effect is of vigorous action and angry agitation. A gentle, undulating but firm line, like that in Picasso's *Bathers* (FIG. **3**), defines a *contour* that is restful and quietly sensuous. A contour continuously and subtly contains and suggests mass and volume. In the Picasso drawing, the line can be felt as a controlling presence in a hard edge, profile, or boundary created by a contrasting area, even when its tone differs only slightly from the tone of the area it bounds. A good example of this can be seen in the central figure of the goddess in Botticelli's *The Birth of Venus* (FIG. 21-57; see also FIGS. 12-39 and 14-24).

3 PABLO PICASSO, detail of *Bathers*, 1918. Pencil drawing. Fogg Art Museum, Harvard University, Cambridge, Massachusetts (bequest of Paul J. Sachs).

An *axis* is a line along which forms are organized. The axis line itself may not be evident; several axis lines may converge (usually with one dominant), as in the layout of a city. Although we are most familiar with directional axes in urban complexes, they occur in all the arts. A fine example of the use of axis in large-scale architecture is the plan of the Palace of Versailles and its magnificent gardens (FIG. 24-65). Axis, whether vertical, horizontal, or diagonal, is also an important compositional element in painting.

Perspective, like axis, is a method of organizing forms in space, but perspective is used primarily to create an illusion of depth or space on a two-dimensional surface. Because we are conditioned by exposure to Western, single-point perspective, an invention of the Italian Renaissance, we tend to see perspective as a systematic ordering of pictorial space in terms of a single point—a point at which lines converge to mark the diminishing size of forms as they recede into the distance (FIGS. 21-31, 22-15, 24-31). Renaissance and Baroque artists created masterpieces of perspective illusionism. For example, in Leonardo's *The Last Supper* (FIG. **4**), the lines of perspective (dashed lines) converge on Christ and, in the foreground, project the picture space into the room on the wall of which the painting appears, creating the illusion that the space of the picture and the space of the room are continuous. Yet we must remember that Renaissance perspective is only one of several systems for depicting depth. Other systems were used in ancient Greece and Rome (FIG. 7-21) and still others in the East (FIGS. 10-31 and 16-9). Some of these other systems, as well as the Italian Renaissance perspective, continue to be used. There is no final or absolutely correct projection of what we "in fact" see.

Proportion concerns the relationships (in terms of size) of the parts of a work. The experience of proportion is common to all of us. We seem to recognize at once when the features of the human face or body are "out of proportion." Formalized proportion is the mathematical relationship in size of one part of a work of art to the other parts within the work, as well as to the totality of the

4   LEONARDO DA VINCI, *The Last Supper, c.* 1495-1498. Fresco. Santa Maria delle Grazie, Milan. (Perspective lines are dashed; lines indicating proportions are solid white or black.)

parts; it implies the use of a denominator that is common to the various parts. One researcher has shown that the major elements of Leonardo's *Last Supper* exhibit proportions found in harmonic ratios in music—12:6:4:3. These numbers (with the greatest width of a ceiling panel taken as one unit) are the horizontal widths, respectively, of the painting, the ceiling (at the front), the rear wall, and the three windows (taken together and including interstices); they apply to the vertical organization of the painting as well. Leonardo found proportion everywhere. The ancient Greeks, who considered beauty to be "correct" proportion, sought a *canon,* or rule, of proportion, not only in music, but also for the human figure. The famous Canon of Polykleitos (page 146) long served as an exemplar of correct proportion. But it should be noted that canons of proportion differ from time to time and culture to culture and that, occasionally, artists have used disproportion deliberately. Part of the task facing students of art history is to perceive and adjust to these differences in an effort to understand the wide universe of art forms.

Proportional relationships are often based on a *module,* a dimension of which the various parts of a building or other work are fractions or multiples. A module might be the diameter of a column, the height of a human body, or an abstract unit of measurement. For example, the famous "ideal" plan of the ninth-century monastery of St. Gall (FIG. 11-24) has a modular base of 2 1/2 feet, so that all parts of the structure are multiples or fractions of this dimension. In modern architecture, a module may be any repeatable unit that permits prefabrication (see FIGS. 28-65 and 28-66).

Scale also refers to the dimensional relationships of the parts of a work to its totality (or of a work to its setting), usually in terms of appropriateness to use or function. We do not think that a private home should be as high as an office building or that an elephant's house at the zoo should be the size of a hen coop. This sense of scale is necessary to the construction of form in all the arts. Most often, but not necessarily, it is the human figure that gives the scale to form.

Light in the world of nature is so pervasive that we often take its function for granted. Few of us realize the extraordinary variations wrought by light, either natural or artificial, on our most familiar surroundings. Daylight, for example, changes with the hour or season. The French artist Monet (pages 989–991), who realized the full extent to which light affects and reveals form, painted more than forty canvases of the facade of Rouen Cathedral revealing its changing appearance from dawn until twilight in different seasons (FIG. **5**). Light is as important for the perception of form as is the matter of which form is made.

5 CLAUDE MONET, facade of Rouen Cathedral, early 1890s. (*Right*) Museum of Fine Arts, Boston (bequest of Hanna Marcy Edwards); (*left*) National Gallery of Art, Washington, D.C. (Chester Dale Collection).

Value is one function of light. In painting, and in the graphic arts generally, value refers to lightness, or the amount of light that is (or appears to be) reflected from a surface. Value is a subjective experience (see FIG. **6**). In absolute terms (if measured, for example, by a photoelectric device), the center bar in FIG. 6 is uniform in value. Yet, where the bar is adjacent to a dark area, it *looks* lighter, and where the bar is adjacent to a lighter area, it *looks* darker. Value is the basis of the quality called, in Italian, *chiaroscuro*, which refers to the gradations between light and dark that produce the effect of *modeling*, or of light reflected from three-dimensional surfaces, as exemplified in Leonardo's superb rendering of *The Virgin and Child with St. Anne and the Infant St. John* (FIG. 22-2; compare FIG. 7-26).

In the analysis of light, an important distinction must be made for the realm of art. Natural light, or sunlight, is whole or additive light, whereas the painter's light in art—the light reflected from pigments and objects—is subtractive light. Natural light is the sum of all the wavelengths composing the visible spectrum, which may be disassembled or fragmented into the individual colors of the spectral band. Although the esthetics of color is largely the province of the artist and can usually be genuinely experienced and understood only through

6 Effect of adjacent value on apparent value. Actual value of center bar is constant.

7 Color triangle. Developed by Josef Albers and Sewell Sillman, Yale University, New Haven, Connecticut.

practice and experimentation, some aspects can be analyzed and systematized. Paint pigments produce their individual colors by reflecting a segment of the spectrum while absorbing all the rest. "Green" pigment, for example, subtracts or absorbs all the light in the spectrum except that seen by us as green, which it reflects to the eye. (In the case of transmitted, rather than reflected, light, the coloring matter blocks or screens out all wavelengths of the spectrum except those of the color we see.) Thus, theoretically, a mixture of pigments that embraced all the colors of the spectrum would subtract all light—that is, it would be black; actually, such a mixture never produces more than a dark gray.

Hue is the property that gives a color its name—red, blue, yellow. Although the colors of the spectrum merge into each other, artists usually conceive of their hues as distinct from each other, giving rise to many different devices for representing color relationships. There are basically two variables in color—the apparent amount of light reflected and the apparent purity; a change in one must produce a change in the other. Some terms for these variables are *value* and *tonality* (for lightness) and *chroma, saturation,* and *intensity* (for purity).

One of the more noteworthy diagrams of the relationships of colors is the triangle (FIG. **7**) in which red, yellow, and blue (the *primary colors*) are the vertexes of the triangle, and orange, green, and purple (the *secondary colors,* which result from mixing pairs of primaries) lie between them. Colors that lie opposite each other, such as red and green, are called *complementary* colors, because they complement, or complete, one another, each absorbing those colors that the other reflects. The result is a neutral tone or gray (theoretically, black), which is produced when complementaries are mixed in the right proportions. The inner triangles are the products of such mixing. Color also has a psychological dimension: red and yellow connote warmth; blue and green, coolness. Generally, *warm colors* seem to advance and *cool colors* to recede.

Texture is the quality of a surface (rough, smooth, hard, soft, shiny, dull) as revealed by light. The many painting media and techniques permit the creation of a variety of textures. The artist may simulate the texture of the materials represented or may create arbitrary surface differences, even using materials other than canvas, as in Picasso's *Still Life with Chair-Caning* (FIG. 27-32).

Specialized Categories and Terms

The categories and terms we have been discussing are applicable to all the visual arts. Certain observations, however, are relevant to only one category of artistic endeavor—either to architecture, or to sculpture, or to painting.

IN ARCHITECTURE   Works of architecture are so much a part of our environment that we accept them as fixed and scarcely notice them until our attention is summoned. The spatial aspect of the arts is most obvious in architecture. The architect makes groupings of enclosed spaces and enclosing masses, always keeping in mind the function of the structure, its construction and materials, and, of course, its design—the correlative of the other two. We experience architecture both visually and by moving through and around it so that we perceive architectural space and mass together. The articulation of space and mass in building is expressed graphically in several ways, including plans, sections, and elevations.

A *plan* is essentially a map of a floor, showing the placement of the masses of a structure and, therefore, the spaces they bound and enclose (FIGS. 13-6 and 27-4). A *section,* like a vertical plan, shows placement of the masses as if the building were cut through along a plane, often along a plane that is a major axis of the building (FIG. 13-7). An *elevation* is a head-on view of an external or internal wall, showing its features and often other elements that would be visible beyond or before the wall (FIG. 13-19).

The architect must have the sensibilities of a sculptor and of a painter and, in establishing the plan of a building, must be able to use the instruments of a mathematician. As architects resolve structural problems, they act as (or with) engineers who are cognizant of the principles underlying the basic structural devices used in architecture (FIG. **8**). Their major responsibilities, however, lie in the manner in which they interpret the *program* of the building. Any proposed building presents an architect with problems peculiar to it alone—problems related to the site and its surroundings, the requirements of the client, and the materials available, as well as the function of the building. A program, then, deals with more than function; it addresses all of the problems embodied in a specific building.

IN SCULPTURE   Like architecture, sculpture exists in the three-dimensional space of our physical world. But sculpture as image is closer to painting than is

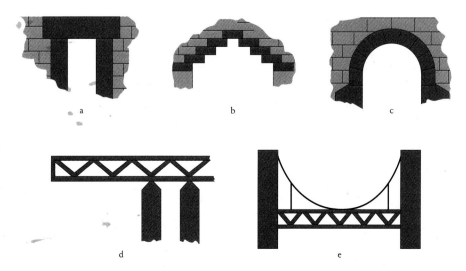

8   Basic structural devices: (a) post and lintel; (b) corbeled arch; (c) arch; (d) cantilever; (e) suspension.

architecture. Until recently, sculpture has been concerned primarily with the representation of human and natural forms in tangible materials, which exist in the same space as the forms they represent. However, sculpture also may embody visions and ideals and consistently has presented images of deities and people in their most heroic as well as their most human aspects (FIGS. 5-99, 5-100, 22-19). Today, sculpture often dispenses with the figure as image and even with the image itself, producing new forms in new materials and with new techniques (FIGS. 28-20 and 27-52).

Sculpture may be associated intimately with architecture, often to such a degree that it is impossible to dissociate the two (FIGS. 13-14, 14-33, 24-5). Sculpture is called *relief* sculpture when it is attached to a back slab or plate (FIGS. 3-43 and 23-22), *high relief,* if the figures or design project boldly (FIGS. 5-90, 21-1, 21-2), and *low relief,* or *bas-relief,* if the figures or design project slightly (FIGS. 5-54, 23-22).

Sculpture that exists in its own right, independent of any particular architectural frame or setting (FIGS. 5-42, 22-19, 22-45), is usually referred to as *free-standing* sculpture, or "sculpture in the round," although, in the art of Greece and of the Renaissance, freestanding sculpture was allied closely to architecture on many occasions. Indeed, sculpture is such a powerful agent in creating a spatial as well as an intellectual environment that its presence in city squares or in parks and gardens is usually the controlling factor in creating their "atmosphere" or general effect (FIG. 24-70).

Some statues are meant to be seen as a whole—to be walked around (FIGS. 5-98, 7-66, 22-45). Others have been created to be viewed only from a restricted angle. How a sculpture is meant to be seen must be taken into account by the sculptor and by those who exhibit the work. The effect of ignoring this is illustrated in FIG. **9.** The left figure has been photographed directly from the front, as the piece is now seen in a museum; the right figure has been

9 DONATELLO, *St. John the Evangelist,* 1412-1415. Marble. Museo del Duomo, Florence. (*Left*) as seen in museum; (*right*) as intended to be seen on facade of Florence Cathedral.

photographed from below, at approximately the same angle from which the statue was originally meant to be seen.

In sculpture, perhaps more than in any other medium, textures, or tactile values, are important. One's first impulse is almost always to handle a piece of sculpture. The sculptor plans for this, using surfaces that vary in texture from rugged coarseness to polished smoothness (FIGS. 2-5, 5-98, 21-48). Textures, of course, are often intrinsic to a material, and this influences the type of stone, wood, plastic, clay, or metal that the sculptor selects. Sculptural technique falls into two basic categories: *subtractive* and *additive*. Carving is a subtractive technique; the final form is a reduction of the original mass (FIG. **10**). Additive sculpture is built up, usually in clay around a framework, or armature; the piece is fired and used to make a mold in which the final work is cast in a material such as bronze (FIGS. 5-98 and 21-10). Casting is a popular technique today. Another common additive technique is the direct construction of forms accomplished by welding shaped metals together (FIG. 28-18).

Within the sculptural family, we must include ceramics and metalwork and numerous smaller, related arts, all of which employ highly specialized techniques described in distinct vocabularies. These will be considered as they arise in the text.

IN THE PICTORIAL ARTS   The forms of architecture and sculpture exist in actual, three-dimensional space. The forms of painting (and of its relatives, drawing, engraving, and the like) exist almost wholly on a two-dimensional surface on which the artist creates an illusion, something that replicates what we see around us or something that is unique to the artist's imagination and corresponds only vaguely to anything we can see in the optical world. Human discovery of the power to project illusions of the three-dimensional world onto two-dimensional surfaces goes back thousands of years and marks an enormous

10   MICHELANGELO, *Unfinished Bound Slave*, 1519. Marble. Accademia, Florence.

step in the control and manipulation of the things we perceive. To achieve this illusion, the artist configures images or representations drawn from the world of common visual experience. Throughout the history of art, this world has been interpreted in an almost infinite variety of ways. Undoubtedly, there is much that all people *see* in common and can agree on: the moon at night, a flying bird, an obstacle in one's path. People differ, however, in their *interpretation* of the seen. Seeing and then representing what is seen are very different matters. The difference between seeing and representing determines the variability of artistic styles, both cultural and personal. What we actually see (the optical "fact") is not necessarily reported in what we represent. In other words, in art, there is little agreement between the *likeness* of a thing and the *representation* of it. This lack of agreement makes for a persisting problem in the history of art. How are we to interpret or "read" images or replicas of the seen? Is there a "correct" vision of the "real" world?

THE PROBLEM OF REPRESENTATION

The cartoon of a life-drawing class in ancient Egypt and the actual representation of an Egyptian queen (FIGS. **11** and **12**) raise many questions: Did Egyptian artists copy models exactly as they saw them? (Did Egyptians actually see each other in this way?) Or did they translate what they saw according to some formula dictated by conventions of representation peculiar to their culture? Beginning students usually ask questions like these when they perceive deviations in styles from the recent Western realism to which they are conditioned. They wonder whether the Egyptians, or other artists, were simply unskilled at matching eye and hand and could not draw from what they saw. But such a question presupposes that the objective of the artist has always been to match appearances with cameralike exactitude. This is not the case, nor is it the case that artists of one period "see" more "correctly" and render more "skillfully" than those of another. Rather, it seems that artists represent what they *conceive* to be real, not what they *perceive*. They understand the visible world in certain unconscious, culturally agreed-on ways and thus bring to the artistic process ideas and meanings out of a common stock. They record not so much what they

11   ALAIN, Drawing from *The New Yorker*.

12   Queen Nofretari, from her tomb at Thebes, *c.* 1250 B.C. Detail of a painted bas-relief.

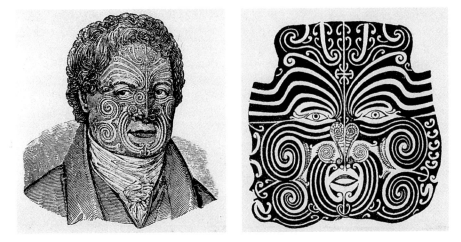

13   The Maori Chief Tupai Kupa, *c.* 1800. (*Left*) after a drawing by John Sylvester; (*right*) a self-portrait. From *The childhood of Man* by Leo Frobenius, 1909, J. B. Lippincott Company.

see as what they know or mean. Personal vision joins with the artistic conventions of time and place to decide the manner and effect of the representation. Yet, even at the same time and place (for example, nineteenth-century Paris), we can find sharp differences in representation when the opposing personal styles of Ingres and Delacroix record the same subject (FIGS. 26-8 and 26-15; compare also FIGS. 11-14 and 11-15, 19-15 and 19-16).

A final example will underscore the relativity of vision and representation that differences in human cultures produce. Although both portraits of a Maori chieftain from New Zealand (FIG. **13**)—one by a European, the other by the chieftain himself—reproduce his facial tattooing, the first portrait is a simple, commonplace likeness that underplays the tattooing. The self-portrait is a statement by the chieftain of the supreme importance of the design that symbolizes his rank among his people. It is the splendidly composed insignia that is his image of himself.

Students of the history of art, then, learn to distinguish works by scrutinizing them closely within the context of their time and provenance. But this is only the beginning. The causes of stylistic change over time are mysterious and innumerable, and neither this book nor any other can contain an outlay of facts that are incontestable. It is only through the continuing process of art-historical research that we can hope to make the picture even fragmentarily recognizable. Incomplete though the picture is and will remain, the panorama of art, changing in time, lies before students, and as their art-historical perspective gains depth and focus, they will come to perceive the continuity of the art of the past with that of the present. It will become clear that one cannot be understood without the other and that our understanding of the one will constantly change with changes in our understanding of the other. The great poet and critic T. S. Eliot has cogently expressed this truth for all art in a passage that suggests the philosophy and method of this book:

> What happens when a new work of art is created is something that happens simultaneously to all the works of art which preceded it. The existing monuments form an ideal order among themselves, which is modified by the introduction of the new (the really new) work of art among them. . . . Whoever has approved this idea of order . . . will not find it preposterous that the past should be altered by the present as much as the present is directed by the past.*

*T. S. Eliot, "Tradition and the Individual Talent," in *Selected Essays 1917–1932* (New York: Harcourt Brace, 1932), p. 5.

PART FOUR

◆

THE RENAISSANCE AND THE BAROQUE AND ROCOCO

Once did she hold the gorgeous east in fee
And was the guardian of the west...
*Venice, the eldest child of Liberty.**

THE ESSENTIALLY RELIGIOUS VIEW OF NATURE AND OF HUMANKIND, COMMON BOTH TO medieval Europe and to the great world civilizations and native cultures, begins to change dramatically in what we call the European Renaissance. The Renaissance, referred to by many historians as "early modern," extends roughly from the fourteenth through the sixteenth centuries; we anticipate it in our discussion of the late Gothic in Italy (Chapter 19). Indeed, the Renaissance should not be seen as the abrupt onset of the modern era, suddenly shining forth in the fifteenth century to illuminate medieval darkness with the rekindled light of Classical Antiquity. Much of the Renaissance has its roots in epochs that long preceded the Middle Ages, and much that is medieval continues in the Renaissance and even in later periods. Since the mid-nineteenth century, when Jacob Burckhardt wrote his influential and still highly valuable work, *The Civilization of the Renaissance in Italy,* the precise dividing line between the Middle Ages and the Renaissance and the question of whether a Renaissance ever actually took place have been disputed. Without reopening these issues, it may be useful to examine those characteristics of the Renaissance that seem to have matured and to have become influential during the period from the fourteenth through the sixteenth centuries, even though they originated during the Middle Ages.

Medieval feudalism, with its patchwork of baronial jurisdictions and sprawling, inefficient local governments, yielded slowly to the competition of strong

AT LEFT: *VITTORE CARPACCIO,* Leave-taking of the Betrothed Pair *(from the* Legend of Saint Ursula), *1495. Oil on canvas, 18' wide. Accademia, Venice.*

*From *On the Extinction of the Venetian Republic* by William Wordsworth.

cities and city-states, which increasingly were in league with powerful kings, both being the natural political enemies of the countryside barons. The outlines of the modern state, with its centralized administrations, organized armies, aggressive expansionism, and "realistic" politics, began to firm up at about this time. Encounters with the world outside Europe—especially the Western Hemisphere and Africa, themselves so dramatically expressive of Renaissance expansiveness—brought vast treasures of gold and silver into Europe, beginning its transformation into a money economy (a process already begun in the thirteenth century in the commercial cities of Italy). Religion increasingly came under the direction of the clergy of the cities. Particularly influential were the members of the Dominican and the Franciscan orders. The claims of the popes to temporal as well as spiritual supremacy were confined to the papal domains in central Italy. Eventually, with the upheaval of the Protestant Reformation, which fractured medieval religious unity, religion became almost a branch of the state, with kings and princes in control of its secular manifestations. Dramatic events in science, like Nicolaus Copernicus's enunciation of the heliocentric theory of the solar system, set the stage for the development of the first successful empirical science—mathematical physics. The opening of the heavens to the scrutiny of scientific investigation was attended by the renewed physical exploration of the globe and, until recently, by the increasing subjugation of it to the will of Europe. Technological advances in navigation, metallurgy, mechanics, and warfare helped greatly to that end.

The religious fanaticism that had launched the Crusades, Europe's first extended contact with non-European civilizations, was replaced during the Renaissance by motives of calculated economic interest mingled with the genuine and fruitful curiosity of the explorer. Indeed, the Renaissance was precisely what it often has been called—an "age of discovery"—when Europe saw before it an almost fantastic realm of possibility open to all those of merit who could perceive it.

Accompanying the great events that quite clearly set the Middle Ages and the Renaissance apart were subtler changes of human attitude. Emphasis slowly was turned away from the ideas and values of a supernatural orientation and toward those concerned with the natural world and human life. The meaning of these new concerns came to be couched in terms that were not exclusively religious. The spirit and dogma of medieval religion, and even its emotional color, were modified as the worldly philosophy of the Greco-Roman tradition revived and took on new strength. But the process of humanization had begun well before the full influence of the pagan tradition was felt; humanizing tendencies began to appear in the twelfth century. In the thirteenth century, the teaching of Saint Francis had humanized religion itself and had called attention to the beauty of the world and of all things in it. Even though Saint Francis understood the physical beauty he celebrated as a manifestation of the spiritual, his emphasis, nevertheless, was clear, and the Franciscan message calls attention to the God-made beauties of the natural order. In the Middle Ages, the focus of life was to procure the salvation of one's immortal soul through the sacred offices of the Church. In the Renaissance, however, though the obligation and concern remained and the institutions of the Church retained power, nature and the relations among human beings simply became *more interesting* than theological questions. Theology, like institutional Christianity, persisted, as did fervent Christian devotion. But these elements were affected by a new spirit—the spirit of pagan humanism—which curiously joined with and reinforced the Christian humanism of Saint Francis.

Whereas the veritable face and body of the human being emerged in the transition from Romanesque to Gothic sculpture, Renaissance art brings Western humanity rapidly into full view—a phenomenon that resembles the manifestation of the human figure in Greek art during the sixth and fifth centuries B.C. The Renaissance stresses the importance of the individual, especially individuals of merit. In life and in art, the focus is sharpened. At last, individuals are real and solid; they cast a shadow. During the Middle Ages, people saw themselves as corrupt and feeble of will, capable of acting only by the agency of God's grace. Although many thinkers, both Protestant and Catholic, insisted on this view for centuries, the Renaissance view is different: individuals may create themselves. They are assumed to have a power of agency—God-given, to be sure—that, in the greatest of achievers, becomes the divine gift of "genius." Thus, in the Renaissance, those who think may overcome the curse of original sin and, in so doing, rise above its devastating load of guilt to make themselves, if they will, what they will. In his *Oration on the Dignity of Man* (the very title of which constitutes a bold new claim), Giovanni Pico della Mirandola, an ingenious and daring Renaissance philosopher, represents God giving the following permission to every human being in a way that reflects a sharp departure from the medieval sense of humanity's natural helplessness:

> The nature of all other beings is limited and constrained within the bounds of laws prescribed by Us. Thou, constrained by no limits, in accordance with thine own free will . . . shalt ordain for thyself the limits of thy nature. We have set thee at the world's center . . . and have made thee neither of heaven nor of earth, neither mortal nor immortal, so that with freedom of choice and with honor . . . thou mayest fashion thyself in whatever shape thou shalt prefer.*

This option would have been almost unthinkable in the Middle Ages. Could one really aspire beyond the angels or debase oneself below the beasts and inanimate nature, given one's place in the carefully articulated "chain of being" that God had made permanent?

Whether or not one could indeed so rise or fall, the leaders of the Renaissance were acutely aware of the new possibilities open to their talents and did not fail to recognize, and often advertise, the powers they were confident they possessed. The wide versatility of many Renaissance artists, men like Alberti, Brunelleschi, Leonardo da Vinci, and Michelangelo, led them to experimentation and to achievement in many of the arts and sciences. Their accomplishments gave substance to that concept of the archetypal Renaissance genius—*l'uomo universale* (the universal man). Class distinctions and social hierarchies had loosened, and the ambitious and talented now could take their places even as the friends, companions, and advisers of princes. Such persons could win the award of everlasting fame, and what has been called the "cult of fame" went naturally with the new glorification of individual genius. When the painter Fra Filippo Lippi died in 1469, the town of Spoleto requested that it be allowed to keep his remains. The town fathers argued that Florence, his native city, already had many celebrated men buried within the bounds of its walls.

Petrarch, the great Italian poet and scholar of the fourteenth century, may be said to have first propounded the peculiarly Renaissance values of versatile individualism and humanism. Petrarch's eager acceptance of a new concept of Humanism encouraged the resurrection of the spirit of classical antiquity from a trove of ancient manuscripts, which were hunted eagerly, edited, and soon reproduced in books made by the new process of mechanical printing. With the help of a new interest in and knowledge of Greek (stimulated by the immigration of Byzantine refugee scholars after the fall of Constantinople to the Turks), the Humanists of the later fourteenth and fifteenth centuries recovered a large part of the Greek as well as the Roman literature and philosophy that had been lost, left unnoticed, or cast aside in the Middle Ages. The Humanists' greatest

---

*Giovanni Pico della Mirandola, *Oratio de hominis dignitate* (1485), trans. by E. L. Forbes, in Ernst Cassirer et al., eds., *The Renaissance Philosophy of Man* (Chicago: University of Chicago Press, 1956), pp. 224–25.

literary contribution was, perhaps, the translation of these works, but they also wrote commentaries on them, which they used as models for their own historical, rhetorical, poetic, and philosophical writings. What the Humanists perceived with great excitement in classical writing was a philosophy for living in *this* world, a philosophy primarily of human focus, that derived not from an authoritative and traditional religious dogma but from reason. The model for the Renaissance is thus no longer the world-despising holy man but rather the great-souled, intelligent man of the world.

The Renaissance Humanists found inspiration in the heroes of antiquity, especially in the accounts of their careers given in Plutarch's *Parallel Lives*. By the fifteenth and sixteenth centuries, even the lives of prominent contemporaries were viewed as appropriate exemplars of life's rule of reason intelligently and nobly followed. The biographies of famous men no longer dealt exclusively with the heroes of antiquity, and artists painted portraits of illustrious contemporaries. The confident, new, "modern" tone rings in Alberti's treatise *On Painting*, in which he congratulates his generation on its achievements:

> And I reveal to you, that if it was less difficult for the ancients, having as they had so very many to learn from and imitate, to rise to a knowledge of those supreme arts that are so toilsome for us today, then so much the more our fame should be greater if we, without teachers or any model, find arts and sciences unheard of and never seen.*

Almost prophetically, Alberti asserts that the moderns will go beyond the ancients, but the ancient example had first to be given—both as a model and as a point of departure.

For, not least among the leaders of the new age were the artists who, it appears to a number of modern historians, were among its most significant producers. Indeed, the products of the plastic arts may have been the most characteristic and illustrious of the Renaissance. Although we now perceive much more of the value of Renaissance literature, philosophy, and science, these branches of human creativity seem, in comparison with the plastic arts, to have been less certain, complete, and developed. But it is noteworthy that the separation of the great disciplines was not as clear-cut as it now is; mathematics and art, especially, went hand in hand, many Renaissance artists being convinced that geometry was fundamental to the artist's education and practice. In *The School of Athens* (FIG. 22-5, p. 742). Raphael places his portrait and the portraits of his colleagues among the mathematicians and philosophers, not among the poets. The medieval distinction of *ars* and *scientia* is replaced by a concept (now becoming current again) that views them as interrelated. Albrecht Dürer will insist that art without science—that is, technique without a theory relating the artist's skills and observations—is fruitless. The careful observations of the optical world made by Renaissance artists and the integration of these observations by such a mathematical system as perspective (derived from medieval optics) foreshadow the formulations of the natural sciences. The twentieth-century thinker and mathematician Alfred North Whitehead believed that the habit and temper of modern science are anticipated in the patient and careful observation of nature practiced by the artists of the Renaissance. The methodical pursuit of a system that could bring order to visual experience may necessarily precede the scientific analysis of what lies behind what we see. Thus, the art of the Renaissance may be said to be the first monument to the Western search for order in nature.

The search for order in nature continued in the seventeenth and early eighteenth centuries and was rewarded by the triumph of science in the revolu-

---

*In E. G. Holt, ed., *Literary Sources of Art History* (Princeton, NJ: Princeton University Press, 1947), p. 109.

tionary theories developed by Galileo, Kepler, and Newton—theories that stated universal laws of physical nature. In the history of human intelligence, this period has been called the Age of Reason or the Enlightenment. During the Enlightenment, answers to the age-old questions about the structure and causes of the world were sought not so much in the revelations of religion as in the deliverances of experimental science. The spiritual interpretation of nature was replaced by the mechanical, the dynamic. The world came to be seen as a magnificent machine contrived and set in motion by God, who, in the laws offered by the new physics, was thought to have revealed the secret operations that govern creation.

The Age of Reason was also the age of Europe's expansion around the globe, that period of roughly a century and a half between 1600 and 1750 in which the foundations of Europe's colonial empires were secured. It began with the last great wars of religion and closed with the world-transforming industrial, economic, social, and political revolutions that produced the secular, modern world.

For art, this period was the age of the Baroque and Rococo, when a great new surge of creativity took place. Architecture, sculpture, painting, and all the arts of design flourished magnificently throughout Europe, encouraged and patronized by sovereigns royal and aristocratic or republican. In Protestant, republican Holland, as in the lands of the Catholic dynasts of France, Spain, and papal Italy, and in the domains of the Hapsburg emperors, art reached the very highest peaks of accomplishment. The dynamism and expansiveness of the age are reflected in the very projects and principles of artistic design: in the scale and movement of composition, brilliance of color, profusion and opulence of ornament, and in stylistic variety and coherence. Rivaling the ambition and achievement of the scientists, artists in all fields—literature, drama, music, and the visual arts—created works of supreme perfection and imperishable worth. They produced and performed with a breadth of inspiration, skill, and virtuosity that emulated the great Renaissance, which indeed they continued. The Age of Reason, the Enlightenment, was also—as it has been called—the Age of Genius.

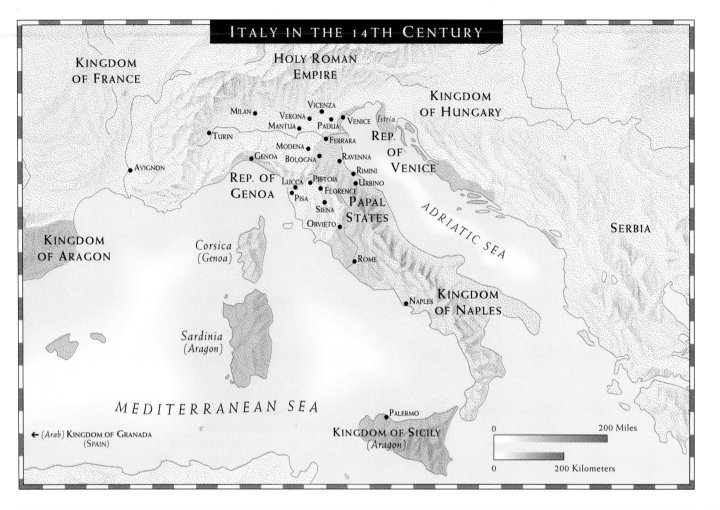

ITALY IN THE 14TH CENTURY

KINGDOM OF FRANCE

HOLY ROMAN EMPIRE

KINGDOM OF HUNGARY

MILAN
VICENZA
VERONA
MANTUA
PADUA
VENICE
Istria
TURIN
FERRARA
MODENA
REP. OF VENICE
GENOA
BOLOGNA
RAVENNA
RIMINI
REP. OF GENOA
LUCCA
PISTOIA
URBINO
PISA
FLORENCE
SIENA
PAPAL STATES
ORVIETO

ADRIATIC SEA

SERBIA

KINGDOM OF ARAGON

Corsica (Genoa)

ROME

KINGDOM OF NAPLES

NAPLES

Sardinia (Aragon)

MEDITERRANEAN SEA

PALERMO

← *(Arab)* KINGDOM OF GRANADA (SPAIN)

KINGDOM OF SICILY *(Aragon)*

0 — 200 Miles

0 — 200 Kilometers

1200	1225	1250	1275

FREDERICK II (HOLY ROMAN EMPEROR)

TRIUMPH OF THE PAPACY, FALL OF HOHENSTAUFEN HOLY ROMAN EMPERORS

Berlinghieri
St. Francis Altarpiece, 1235

N. Pisano
Pulpit, 1259-1260

Saint Dominic, 1170(?)-1221
Dominican Order founded 1215

St. Thomas Aquinas, c.1225-1274
(Scholasticism)

Saint Francis of Assisi, 1182-1226
(Christian Humanism). Franciscan Order, 1228

Political division of Italy — Guelphs (Papal Party)
vs. Ghibellines (Imperial Party), c. 1250-1400

Roger Bacon, c. 1220-1292
English Franciscan experimenter

Dante, 1265-1321, Divina Commedia

CHAPTER 19

LATE GOTHIC ART IN ITALY

1300	1325	1350	1375	1400
BABYLONIAN CAPTIVITY OF THE POPES (AVIGNON)		HUNDRED YEARS WAR BETWEEN FRANCE AND ENGLAND ▶		GREAT SCHISM IN THE CHURCH

Giotto
The Meeting of Joachim and Anna
detail c. 1305

Duccio
Maiestas Altarpiece
1308-1311

Simone Martini, The Annunciation, 1333

Lorenzetti
Birth of Virgin, 1342

Orcagna
Tabernacle, Or San Michele
1350-1360

Papacy moved to Avignon
by Philip IV of France, 1309

Hundred Years War between France and England, 1338-(1453)

William of Ockham, c. 1285-1349(?), English-Franciscan philosopher

Petrarch, 1304-1374, Humanist poet

Papacy returned to Rome, 1378

Boccaccio, 1313-1375, Humanist scholar and novelist

St. Catherine of Siena, 1347-1380

Failure of Florentine Bardi and Peruzzi banking houses, 1344

Ciompi Revolt in Florence, class strife, 1378

From the twelfth century on, the history of Western European civilization is in large part the history of the cities of Europe and the classes of people associated with them. French Gothic art developed and flourished in Paris and in the prosperous communities of northern France under the patronage of kings like Philip Augustus and (Saint) Louis IX. The story of the Italian cities is considerably different. Early on they forcibly resisted the efforts of the German emperors and the popes to bring them under imperial or papal control; from their struggle grew a confidence and self-sufficiency that led many of them to claim independence from kings, nobles, and papacy alike, and to adopt republican forms of government.

THE CITY-STATES: ECONOMICS AND POLITICS

To this end the cities of Italy had a distinct advantage—an economic one; economic life as we know it had its beginnings in Italy. The Italian peninsula held a commanding position in the Mediterranean world. Its port cities—Genoa, Pisa, and Venice—controlled the ever busier and more extended avenues of commerce that connected the West with the lands of Islam, with Byzantium and Russia, and overland with China. Italy was the natural route from the Mediterranean to the countries north of the Alps, a channel of cultural as well as commercial influence. It was economic power, along with a bold spirit of independence and political ambition, that caused the more militant of the prosperous cities to expand—at the expense of their lesser neighbors—into small territorial states, the city-states that are central to the history of Gothic Italy. The city of Milan came to dominate most of Lombardy, and Florence much of Tuscany. The city-states, whether of republican constitution or ruled by despots, were enriched by capitalist enterprise and industrial production. They became, at the same time, cultural centers favorable to patronage of the arts.

This was in spite of the political turbulence that reigned within the cities themselves and the numerous petty wars among rival cities. As we have seen, the old contest between empire and papacy was reflected in the political parties that fought for control of the cities: the Ghibellines, loyal to the imperial idea, the Guelphs, loyal to the popes. In Florence the Guelph party gained power; in neighboring Siena the citizens chose Ghibelline allegiance, to spite their bitter Florentine rivals. In the end the Ghibellines came to represent aristocratic interests, the Guelphs those of the middle classes. Most of the cities expelled the aristocrats, relics of the old barons, and adopted republican constitutions. In practice, these turned out to be oligarchic rather than democratic governments. In Lombardy, particularly, ambitious city magnates seized power and established themselves and their families as despotic princes. The Visconti of Milan ruled in Lombardy, from which they aimed to unify and control all of Italy.

Politically, the city-states were localized in Italy, but their economic influence was felt throughout the West, principally through finance. Cities like Venice, Milan, Lucca, and Florence were the bankers of Europe. Yet it was with papal Rome itself that the most profitable banking transactions were made. From all over Christendom wealth from taxes, land revenues, bequests, indulgences, spiritual fees, and services of many kinds poured into Rome. The papacy had a financial organization far more sophisticated than any elsewhere in Europe, and its managers were the bankers of Florence. For almost three centuries, except for a few brief intervals, the financial interdependency of Florence and papal Rome was a conspicuous feature of the economic history of Europe.

The financial strength of Florence, which made the gold florin the standard coin of exchange everywhere, was augmented by its industry and trade. Florence had a large share of the wool trade with England and the Netherlands and a flourishing textile industry of its own; the fine finished cloth of Florence was sold all over Europe. The social and political structure of the city reflected this. As their wealth increased, the guilds, especially the powerful wool guild, commanded ever greater political influence; eventually the city, and with it much of the patronage of art, passed into their hands. Commercial setbacks and jealousies within the guild coalitions made for unstable government with authority frequently changing hands overnight.

Yet, despite civil turbulence and the general calamities of Late Gothic Europe, which we have noted, a powerful vitality was stirring, and confusion was but one aspect of significant and beneficial change. Old ideas and institutions were being challenged and, to a degree, discredited. The reconstitution and expansion of city culture increasingly broke down the old feudal barriers, permitting the advancement of people of merit from all classes. In this age of Dante, Petrarch, Boccaccio, and Giotto, as well as of ambitious merchants and bankers, people were imbued with the sense that the times encouraged setting off in new directions.

The Florentine Republic

The Italian city-state, at least in the form it took in Florence, was itself an innovation. The claim of Florence to be a self-governing republic of free citizens on the model of the ancient Roman republic was new both as claim and ideal. The example of ancient Rome had been appealed to by emperors and popes, but not as Rome the *pagan republic.* Rather it was Rome the *Christian empire,* the empire of Constantine and Theodosius, that for a thousand years had been the ideal and inspiration of both imperial and papal authority. The Florentines appealed to the Roman republic not for its pagan religion, but for its form of government. Florence remained fervently Christian in faith, but firmly secular and anti-clerical in its political structure and policy. (Only for a few years in the next century would

Florence be governed by a priestly executive, the monk Girolamo Savonarola.)

Florence was a new kind of state: a sovereign Christian republic that severed all bonds to any feudal, royal, or ecclesiastical authority and asserted its right to defend its own, and annex additional, territory. This put it on a level of equality with states ruled by kings, princes, and popes. With this status, Florence played a shrewd hand in the complex political games of Late Gothic Italy, sometimes by war, most often by statecraft. As self-appointed champion of the genius of the Roman republic, it conceived of itself as the defender of popular liberties against the despotisms rising in other city-states, Milan in particular.

HUMANISM: THE REVIVAL OF CLASSICAL VALUES

The belief that Florence was, in the words of the early historian Villani, "the daughter and the creature of Rome" impelled Florentine intellectuals to find in the history and literature of Rome the qualities that had made it great. Ancient manuscripts were eagerly sought out, collected, and translated. From the study of the works of such Roman sages as Cicero and Seneca, a new philosophy evolved that would eventually channel the thought of the Renaissance. Humanism was not so much a philosophical system (as was, for example, Scholasticism, which it would supersede); rather it was a code of civil conduct, a theory of education, and a scholarly discipline. As the word *humanism* suggests, the chief concerns of its proponents were human values and interests as distinct from—but not opposed to—the otherworldly values of religion. The study of the Latin classics, for their practical as well as esthetic value, led to what might be called a kind of civil ethics, a guide to the conduct of life in a self-governing republic; the Roman ideal and model were always in view. The humanist enthusiasm for ancient Rome, expressed in the elegant Latin of Cicero and the Augustan age, involved a conscious emulation of what were thought to be the Roman civic virtues: self-sacrificing service to the state, participation in government, defense of state institutions (especially the administration of justice), and stoic indifference to personal misfortune in the performance of duty.

Ideally, the humanist sought no material reward for services rendered. The sole reward for the hero of civic virtue was fame, just as the reward for a leader of the holy life was sainthood. For the educated, the lives of heroes and heroines of the past became as edifying as the lives of the saints. Petrarch wrote a book on illustrious men, and his colleague Boccaccio complemented it with biographies of famous women—from Eve to his contemporary, Joanna, queen of Naples. Both Petrarch and Boccaccio were famous in their own day as poets, scholars, and men of letters—their achievements equivalent in honor to those of the heroes of civic virtue. In 1341, Petrarch was crowned in Rome with the laurel wreath, the ancient symbol of victory and merit. The humanist cult of fame emphasized the importance of the creative individual and the role of such individuals in contributing to the renown of the city-state and of all Italy.

Florentine humanism, with its revival of interest in the secular culture of antiquity, was only part of the general humanizing tendency in life and art that, as we have seen, marked the fourteenth century and foreshadowed the Renaissance. Italy, crowded as it was with the monuments and memorials of the classical past, was the natural setting for the reception of humanistic values recovered from an omnipresent influence of antiquity. Dante, the supreme poet of the age, presents in the *Inferno* a whole theater of human sin and suffering, and with passionate intensity characterizes the throngs of actors in sharp, realistic detail. Significantly, he takes as his guide through the infernal regions not a Christian saint, but Vergil, the great Roman classical poet, who is the personification of the highest attainment of human reason. Petrarch, the careful and critical scholar of classical literature, was also the poet of an ardent, personal love, freed from the conventions of the courtly kind sung by the troubadours. His verses to his loved one, Laura, are intimate, emotionally complex and psychologically insightful; they would become immensely influential in European literature in later centuries. Boccaccio, likewise the humanist scholar, projects in his *Decameron* a vivid narrative of the human scene in all variety of incident, mood, and characterization, a lasting source of inspiration and material for later novelists and playwrights.

THE HUMANIZING OF RELIGIOUS EXPERIENCE

Thus the interest in antiquity is one with the interest in human affairs and the human condition. The new conception of the sovereign, republican city-state, with its civic liberties and virtues, and the new secular view of human nature that we find in literature and art, bring actual human experience increasingly into focus and the range of human emotions into play. Individual personality and feeling are more and more taken into account, and here religion as well as philosophy expresses powerfully the humanizing current broadening in the fourteenth century.

Just as the proponents of humanism wished to reform secular life by reviving the classics and making their study the core of education in civic virtue, so the adherents to a new revivalist spirit in religion sought to reform the Church and to inspire the believer by appealing to the teachings of primitive Christianity and the example of Jesus and the martyr saints. The humanists went back to the Classical past, the religious revivalists to the Christian past. Both were reformists in spirit, who sometimes in combination, sometimes separately, would bring about the great changes we identify as the Renaissance and the Reformation.

We have noted the influence of Saint Francis and of the mendicant orders, already great in the thirteenth century. They had the effect of personalizing the religious experience, rendering it more independent of the strict observation of the dogma, decrees, and services of the Church and the official priesthood. A longing for direct experience of God led many into mysticism and away from orthodoxy altogether. The great majority of the faithful joined in the emotional rituals and excitement of popular religion, with its devotion to relics, saints, and miracles, its public celebrations, processions, and demonstrations of enthusiastic piety. Revivalist worship, often stimulated by the strident preaching of transient friars expelled from their communities, was the order of the day among the city populace, who thirsted for assurance of salvation through religious ecstasies. The established Church and the governing classes often had cause for alarm at the threat to authority posed by the unruly devout. Numerous revolts of the peasantry and uprisings of the lower classes in the cities, common in the fourteenth century, were motivated in part by religious unrest. The Great Schism, which began in 1378 and menaced the stability of the Church, caused bolder popular voices like those of John Wycliffe in England and John Hus in Bohemia to call for the abdication of popes and priests, the abolition of the mass and sacraments, and a return to the Bible. Though this radical program was too extreme for the times, it would come to have a significant role in the not-too-distant future.

Philosophy: Reason Replaced by Intuition and Experience

While revivalism sought to make the religious experience personal and direct, free of mediating agencies between the believer and God, Scholastic thinkers, mostly Franciscan, were busy with skeptical revisions of the philosophy of the Church as perfected in the system of the Dominican, Saint Thomas Aquinas. They challenged the notion, central to that system, that reason could yield knowledge of God, or demonstrate his existence. From Saint Anselm, through Abelard to Saint Thomas, this notion had been axiomatic; with the subversion of it, reason was replaced by intuition as the sole mode of knowledge of the Divine. Intuition, as a direct perceptive awareness prior to any other kind of knowing, was the philosophical equivalent of the experience of the religious, when, through prayer, sacrifice, and mystical contemplation, the soul is brought into the immediate presence of God. We can read again of that experience—long familiar in the Christian tradition—in *The Dialogue* of Saint Catherine of Siena (1347–1380), who was both a mystic and an influential activist for reform of the Church. In that work she speaks directly with God in rapturously eloquent language, praying that her "eye of understanding" (reason) be given light by divine grace, without which reason is blind.

The attack on the rationalism of Saint Thomas made by the *later* scholastics and theologians led to the discrediting of philosophy as a valid form of knowledge and to the unseating of reason, with its logical method, as the ruling faculty that produces knowledge. The unity of theology and philosophy, which Saint Thomas had achieved by bringing together Christian dogma and Aristotelian thought, was broken, theology going off in the direction of mysticism and pure faith, and philosophy yielding to skepticism and the first faint manifestation of that inquisitive bent of mind that would later mature into experimental science. If knowledge of God was impossible to achieve through philosophy and pure reason, so also was knowledge of nature and the world, God's creation. Thus, pure reason came to be despised for its failure to make intelligible the mysteries of faith or of the material world of nature. In the fifteenth century, Nicholas of Cusa would disparage philosophy as mere "learned ignorance"; in the sixteenth, Martin Luther would call reason a "whore."

A new approach was needed to understand and explain the nature of God, and it is necessary to examine the great changes in the Western view of nature that lie behind and accompany fundamental changes in art. William of Ockham (or Occam), a Franciscan friar, one of the most subtle and ingenious scholastics who attacked the rationalism of Saint Thomas, seemed to be providing such an approach when, on the verge of a great insight, he stressed the importance of the role of intuitive knowledge and individual experience in the process of knowing: "Everything outside the soul is individual . . . [and] knowledge which is simple and peculiarly individual . . . is intuitive knowledge. . . . Abstractive individual knowledge presupposes intuitive knowledge . . . , our understanding knows sensible things intuitively."

The placement of intuition before reason was common to *both* the mystical critics of Saint Thomas in the fourteenth century and, in effect, put human intuition squarely in front of individual knowledge, whether of God (for the mystic) or of the world (for the skeptic). This elevation of direct human experience constitutes a kind of exaltation of the knowing, human agent. Even in the thirteenth century, the importance of experience in acquiring knowledge had been stressed by the remarkable Roger Bacon, another Franciscan, who bore out his convictions on this point with many astonishingly precocious discoveries and inventions in what now would be called the physical sciences and technology. Calling attention to the existence and necessity of experimental science, Bacon insisted that the experimenter "*should first examine visible things* . . . without experience nothing can be known sufficiently . . . argumentation [that is, logical, rational demonstration in Saint Thomas's manner] does not suffice, but experience does" (emphasis added). In the universities of the fourteenth century (especially Oxford), the followers of men like Bacon and Ockham discussed questions in physics (the acceleration of freely falling bodies, inertia, the center of gravity, optics, and the like)—anticipating by centuries the age of Galileo.

As we have seen, many of the later thirteenth- and fourteenth-century mystical and skeptical thinkers who emphasized personal intuition and experience in seeking divine and natural knowledge were Franciscans. In view of Saint Francis's humanizing of medieval religion—making it a matter of intense personal experience and drawing attention to the handiwork of God in the beauty of natural things—it is natural that his successors should inspect nature more closely, with a curiosity that would lead to scientific inquiry. Saint Francis's independence and his critical posture toward the religious establishment were passed down to many Franciscans, the more radical of whom often were accused by the Church of association with outright heretics. The Franciscans—conspicuously, William of Ockham—challenged the papacy itself, especially its claim of secular lordship over all Christendom. In these challenges, the rebelliousness that will take mature shape in the Protestant Reformation already is being felt.

What might be called Franciscan "radicalism," then, stresses the primacy of personal experience, the individual's right to know by experiment, the futility of formal philosophy, and the beauty and value of things in the external world. It was in the stimulating intellectual and social environment created in part by the Franciscans that the painters and sculptors of Italy in the fourteenth century began a new epoch—an epoch in which the carved and painted image took its shape from experience of the visible world and what could be found of that experience in the classical antique. Individual artists, breaking with the formal traditions of centuries, now began to depend on their own inspection of the world before their eyes. Applying the Baconian principle of personal discovery through experience—in the artist's case, the experience of *seeing*—artists began to project in painting and sculpture the infinitely complex and shifting optical reticulum that we experience as the visible world.

SCULPTURE

Many imitations of the art of classical antiquity may be encountered during the Carolingian, Ottonian, Romanesque, and French Gothic periods. The statues of the *Visitation* group on the west facade of Reims Cathedral (FIG. 13-34) show an unmistakable interest in Late Roman sculpture, even though the modeling of the faces reveals their Gothic origin. However, the thirteenth-century sculpture of NICOLA PISANO (active *c.* 1258–1278), contemporary with the Reims statues, exhibits an interest in the forms of the classical antique unlike that found in the works of his predecessors. This interest was perhaps due in part to the influence of the humanistic culture of Sicily under its bril-

liant king, Holy Roman Emperor Frederick II, who, for his many intellectual gifts and other talents, was known in his own time as "the wonder of the world." Frederick's nostalgia for the grandeur that was Rome fostered a revival of Roman sculpture and decoration in Sicily and southern Italy before the mid-thirteenth century. Nicola may have received his early training in this environment, although recently scholars have suggested that his style merely continues that of Romanesque Pisa. After Frederick's death in 1250, Nicola traveled northward and eventually settled in Pisa, which was then at the height of its political and economic power and was clearly a place where a proficient artist could hope to find rich commissions.

In typically Italian fashion, Nicola's sculpture was not applied in the decoration of great portals; it is, therefore, quite unlike the French sculpture of the period. Nicola carved marble reliefs and ornament for large pulpits, the first of which he completed in 1260 for the baptistery of Pisa Cathedral (FIG. **19-1**). Some elements of the pulpit's design carry on medieval traditions (for example, the lions supporting some of the columns and the tri-lobed arches),

19-1   NICOLA PISANO, pulpit of the baptistery of Pisa Cathedral, 1259–1260. Marble, approx. 15' high.

19-2   Nicola Pisano, *The Annunciation and the Nativity* (detail of Fig. 19-1). Marble relief, approx. 34″ × 45″.

19-3   Giovanni Pisano, *The Annunciation and the Nativity*, 1297–1301, detail of the pulpit of Sant'Andrea, Pistoia. Marble relief, approx. 34″ × 40″.

but Nicola evidently is trying to retranslate a Medieval type of structure into Classical terms. The large, bushy capitals are a Gothic variation of the Corinthian capital; the arches are round rather than ogival; and the large, rectangular relief panels, if their proportions were altered slightly, could have come from the sides of Roman sarcophagi. The densely packed, large-scale figures of the individual panels also seem to derive from the compositions found on Late Roman sarcophagi. In one of these panels, representing *The Annunciation and the Nativity* (Fig. **19-2**), the Virgin reclines in the ancient fashion seen in Byzantine ivories, mosaics, and paintings. But the face types, beards, coiffures, and draperies, as well as the bulk and weight of the figures, are inspired by relief that is stronger than anything seen in several centuries.

Nicola's classicizing manner was reversed strongly by his son Giovanni Pisano (*c.* 1250–1320). Giovanni's version of *The Annunciation and the Nativity* (Fig. **19-3**), from his pulpit in Sant'Andrea at Pistoia, was finished some forty years after the one by his father in the Pisa baptistery and offers a striking contrast to Nicola's thick carving and placid, almost stolid presentation of the theme. Giovanni's figures are arranged loosely and dynamically; an excited animation twists and bends them, and their activeness is emphasized by spaces that open deeply between them, through which they hurry and gesticulate. In the Annunciation episode, which is combined with the Nativity (as in the older version), the Virgin shrinks from the sudden apparition of the angel in a posture of alarm touched with humility. The same spasm of apprehension contracts her supple body as she reclines in the Nativity scene. The principals of the drama share in a peculiar, nervous agitation, as if they all suddenly are moved by spiritual passion; only the shepherds and the sheep, appropriately, do not yet share in the

miraculous event. The swiftly turning, sinuous draperies, the slender figures they enfold, and the general emotionalism of the scene are features to be found not in Nicola's interpretation but in the Gothic art of the north in the fourteenth century. (These linear rhythms and deep currents of Gothic naturalism are evident in most sculpture in Italy throughout the fourteenth century.)

Thus, the works of Nicola and of Giovanni show, successively, two novel trends of great significance for Renaissance art: a new contract with the classical antique and a burgeoning, native Gothic naturalism.

Painting

Maniera Greca — Italo-Byzantine

Throughout the Middle Ages, Italian painting was strongly dominated by the Byzantine style. This Italo-Byzantine style, or *maniera greca*, is shown in a panel of the *St. Francis Altarpiece* (Fig. **19-4**) and is a descendant of those tall, aloof, austere figures that people the world of Byzantine art. Painted in tempera on wood panel, Saint Francis wears the cinctured canonicals of the order that he founded. He holds a large book and displays the stigmata—the wounds of Christ, imprinted as a sign of Heavenly favor—on his hands and feet. The saint is flanked by two very Byzantine angels and by scenes from his life that strongly suggest that their source is in Byzantine illuminated manuscripts. The central scene on the saint's right represents St. Francis preaching to the birds. The figures of Saint Francis and his two attendants are aligned carefully against a shallow, stage-property tower and wall, a stylized symbol of a town or city from Early Christian times. In front of the saint is another stage-scenery image of nested birds and twinkling plants. The strict formality of the composition (relieved somewhat by the sharply observed birds and the lively stippling of the plants), the shallow space, and the linear flatness in the rendering of the forms are all familiar traits of a long and august tradition, soon suddenly and dramatically to be replaced.

BONAVENTURA BERLINGHIERI (active *c.* 1235–1244), artist of the *St. Francis Altarpiece,* was one of a family of painters in the Tuscan city of Lucca. The stirrings of the new artistic movement began largely in the busy cities of Tuscany (Lucca, Pisa, Siena, Florence). Florence was destined to lead the great development toward the new pictorial manner of the Renaissance, just as politically it gradually absorbed the other cities in Tuscany to form the Florentine republic. But during the fourteenth century, its defiant rival, Siena, which had long and stubbornly resisted the encroachment of Florence, was the seat of a rich and productive school of painting of its own.

Duccio

The works of DUCCIO DI BUONINSEGNA (active *c.* 1278–1318) represent Sienese art in its supreme achievement. His immense altarpiece, the *Maestà,* was designed to replace a much smaller painting of the Virgin Mary, who, the people of Siena believed, had sponsored their victory over the Florentines at the battle of Monteperti in 1260. Sienese devotion to the Virgin was paramount in the religious life

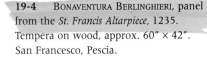

19-4   BONAVENTURA BERLINGHIERI, panel from the *St. Francis Altarpiece,* 1235. Tempera on wood, approx. 60″ × 42″. San Francesco, Pescia.

19-5   DUCCIO, *Virgin and Child Enthroned with Saints*, principal panel of the *Maestà Altarpiece*, 1308–1311. Tempera on wood, size of the panel 7' × 13'. Museo dell'Opera de Duomo, Siena.

of the city, whose citizens could boast of Siena's dedication to the Queen of Heaven as more ancient and venerable than all others.

It is important to notice in this instance how loyalty to the secular, republican city-state is joined with devotion to its favorite saint. The Virgin becomes not only protectress of each and every citizen, but of the city itself. Duccio's inscription of his name at the base of the Virgin's throne in the *Maestà* is part of a prayer for himself and for the city of Siena, the cathedral and churches of which would be filled with paintings of the Virgin by its leading masters.

The *Maestà*, a *polyptych* (four or more panels) painted front and back and composed of many panels, was commissioned for the high altar of the Cathedral of Siena in 1308 and completed by Duccio and his shop in 1311. As originally executed it consisted of a 7-foot-high central panel (FIG. **19-5**), surmounted by seven pinnacles above, and a *predella*, or raised shelf, of panels at the base, altogether some 13 feet high. Unfortunately, the work can no longer be seen in its entirety; it was dismantled in subsequent centuries, and many of its panels are now scattered as single masterpieces among the museums of the world.

The main panel of the front side represents the Virgin enthroned in majesty (*maestà*) as Queen of Heaven amidst choruses of angels and saints. The formality and symmetry of its composition are obviously drawn from Byzantine tradition, as are the figures and facial types of the principal angels and saints. But the frontality and rigidity of the figures in the typical Byzantine icon and iconostasis or apse

mosaic are considerably relaxed here; they turn to each other in quiet converse, and the four saints kneeling in the foreground are more facially individualized and perform their ceremonial gestures without stiffness. Similarly, the hard body outlines and internal patterning of drapery are much softened, the drapery falling and curving loosely, particularly that of the female saints at either end of the panel. This is a feature familiar in northern Gothic (FIG. 13-54), and is a mark of the exchange of tendency and influence between Italy and the north in the fourteenth century.

These changes from the Byzantine tradition and the Maniera Greca, along with impulses of style exchanged with the Gothic north, are part of a new naturalism that only slowly makes itself apparent in details. This is an altarpiece, and the artist respects the age-old requirement that as such it occupies the very center of the sanctuary as the focus of worship, and should be a thing holy in itself, a thing of splendor to the eye, precious in its message and its materials. As such, its function naturally impedes experiment with the depiction of narrative action and the production of illusionistic effects by the modeling of forms and their placement in pictorial space.

Instead, the Queen of Heaven panel is a miracle of color composition and manipulation of texture, unfortunately not apparent in a reproduction. Close inspection of the original reveals what the Sienese artists were learning from new media and systems of ornament. Italy in the thirteenth and fourteenth centuries was the entrepôt for the great silk trade from China and the Middle East. After processing in city-states like Lucca and Florence, the silk was exported throughout Europe to satisfy an immense market for sumptuous dress. (Dante, Petrarch, and many of the humanists decried the appetite for luxury in costume, which to them represented a decline in civic and moral virtue.) Fabrics from China, Persia, Byzantium, and the Islamic realms were universally prized, not least by artists like Duccio, who enriched with subtlest craft the real and representational surfaces of the *Maestà* panel. He created glistening and shimmering effects of textiles, adapting the motifs and design stratagems of exotic stuffs.

If on the front panel of the *Maestà* Duccio shows himself the great master of the formal altarpiece, the small accompanying panels front and back reveal his powers as a narrative painter. In the numerous panels on the back he illustrated the later life of Christ—his ministry (on the predella), his Passion (on the main panel), his Resurrection and appearances to the disciples (on the pinnacles). In the small narrative pictures, Duccio relaxed the formalism appropriate to the iconic, symbolic representation of the *Maestà* and revealed his ability not only as a narrator but as an experimenter with new pictorial ideas. In a synoptic

sequence on one of the small panels, *The Betrayal of Jesus* (FIG. **19-6**), the artist represents several episodes of the event: the betrayal of Jesus by Judas's false kiss, the disciples fleeing in terror, Peter cutting off the ear of the high priest's servant. Although the background, with its golden sky and its cheeselike rock formations, remains traditional, the figures before it have changed quite radically. They are no longer the flat, frontal shapes of earlier Byzantine art but have taken on mass; they are modeled through a range from light to dark, and their draperies articulate around them convincingly. Only their relation to the ground on which they stand remains somewhat in doubt, as they tend to sway, glide, and incline with a kind of disembodied instability. Even more novel and striking is the manner in which the figures seem to react to the central event. Through posture, gesture, and even facial expression, they display a variety of emotions, as Duccio extends himself to differentiate between the anger of Peter, the malice of Judas (echoed in the faces of the throng about Jesus), and the apprehension and timidity of the fleeing disciples. These figures have become actors in a religious drama, which, in a lively performance, is interpreted in terms of thoroughly human actions and reactions. In this and

19-6   DUCCIO, *The Betrayal of Jesus,* detail from the back of the *Maestà Altarpiece,* 1309–1311. Tempera on wood, size of detail approx. 22½" × 40". Museo dell'Opera del Duomo, Siena.

19-7 Pietro Cavallini, *Seated Apostles*, detail of *The Last Judgment*, *c.* 1291. Fresco. Santa Cecilia in Trastevere, Rome.

similar narrative panels, Duccio takes another decisive step toward the humanization of religious subject matter.

The greatness of the *Maestà* did not have to wait for modern acclaim. We learn from a Sienese chronicler that on a day declared a religious festival, the finished altarpiece was carried from the shop of Duccio (in a triumphant procession of the whole city, replete with choir, trumpets, drums, and candles) to the cathedral, where it was installed in honor of the Virgin Mary and her most favored city. The chronicler boasted that nothing like it had been done anywhere else in Italy.

Giotto

Duccio resolved his problems within the general framework of the Byzantine style, which he never really rejected. His great Florentine contemporary, Giotto di Bondone (*c.* 1266–1337), made a much more radical break with the past. The sources of Giotto's style still are debated, although one must have been the style of the Roman school of painting represented by Pietro Cavallini (active *c.* 1273–1308). As is shown in a detail from Cavallini's badly damaged fresco of *The Last Judgment* in the church of Santa Cecilia in Trastevere in Rome (Fig. **19-7**), the style is characterized by a great interest in the sculptural rendering of form. Cavallini, perhaps under the influence of Roman paintings now lost, abandons Byzantine hieratic dignity with a long-lost impression of solidity and strength.

Another, perhaps less significant, formative influence on Giotto may have been the work of the man presumed to be his teacher, Giovanni Cimabue (*c.* 1240–1302). A Florentine, Cimabue must have been an older rival of Giotto, as Dante suggests in *Il Purgatorio* (XI, 94–96): "Cimabue thought to hold the field in painting, and now Giotto has the cry, so that the fame of the other is obscured." Inspired by the same impulse toward naturalism as Giovanni Pisano and also influenced, no doubt, by Gothic sculpture, Cimabue (like Cavallini) pushed well beyond the limits of the Italo-Byzantine style. In an almost ruined fresco of the Crucifixion in San Francesco at Assisi, Cimabue's style (like Giovanni Pisano's) can be seen to be highly dramatic; the figures are blown by a storm of emotion. On the other hand, Cimabue is much more formal in his *Madonna Enthroned with Angels and Prophets* (Fig. **19-8**), as the theme here naturally calls for unmoving dignity and not for dramatic presentation. Despite such progressive touches as the three-dimensional appearance of the throne, this vast altarpiece is a final summing-up of centuries of Byzantine art before its utter transformation. Giotto's version of the same theme (Fig. 19-9) shows us what that transformation looked like in its first phase.

The art of Cimabue, the art of Cavallini and of the Roman painters like him (whom Giotto must have seen at work in San Francesco at Assisi), the art of the Gothic sculptors of France (perhaps seen by Giotto himself, but certainly received by him from the sculpture of Giovanni Pisano), and the ancient art of Rome, both sculpture and painting—all must have provided the elements of Giotto's artistic education (some believe that new developments in the contemporary art of Byzantium further influenced him).

Yet no synthesis of these varied influences could have sufficed to produce the great new style that makes Giotto the father of Western pictorial art. Renowned in his own day, his reputation has never faltered. No matter the variety of his materials of instruction, his true teacher was nature—the world of visible things.

Giotto's revolution in painting did not consist only of the displacement of the Byzantine style, the establishment of painting as a major art for the next six centuries, and the restoration of the naturalistic approach invented by the ancients and lost in the Middle Ages. He also inaugurated a firm method of pictorial experiment through observation, and, in the spirit of the experimenting Franciscans, initiated an age that might be called "early scientific." Giotto and his successors, by stressing the preeminence of the faculty of sight in gaining knowledge of the world, laid the trails that empirical science would follow. They recognized that the visual world must be observed before it can be analyzed and understood. Praised in his own and later times for his fidelity to nature, Giotto is more than an imitator of it; he *reveals* nature in the process of observing it and divining its visible order. In fact, he showed his generation a new way of seeing. With Giotto, Western artists turned resolutely toward the visible world as the source of knowledge of nature. This new *outward* vision replaced the medieval *inward* vision that searched not for the secrets of nature but for union with God.

In nearly the same great scale as the Madonna painted by Cimabue, Giotto presents her (FIG. **19-9**) in a work that offers an opportunity to appreciate his perhaps most telling contribution to representational art—sculptural solidity and weight. The Madonna, enthroned with angels, rests within her Gothic throne with the unshakable stability of a marble goddess out of antiquity. The slender Virgins of Duccio and Cimabue, fragile beneath the thin ripplings of their

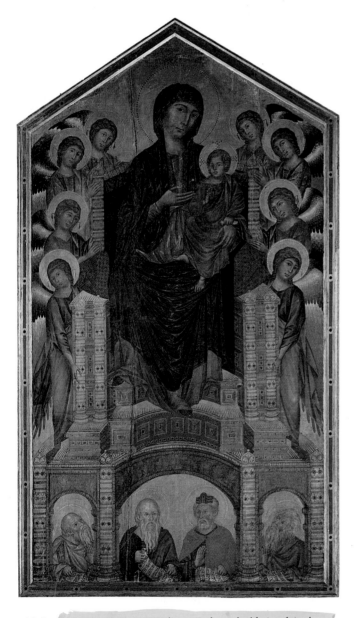

19-8   GIOVANNI CIMABUE, *Madonna Enthroned with Angels and Prophets,* c. 1280–1290. Tempera on wood, 12'7" × 7'4". Galleria degli Uffizi, Florence.

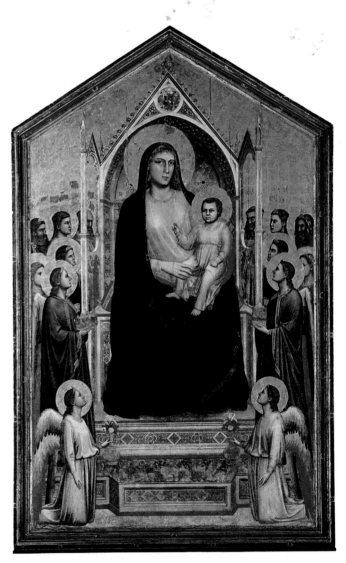

19-9   GIOTTO, *Madonna Enthroned,* c. 1310. Tempera on wood, 10'8" × 6'8". Galleria degli Uffizi, Florence.

19-10   Interior of the Arena Chapel (Capella Scrovegni), Padua, 1305–1306.

draperies, are replaced by a sturdy, queenly mother, corporeally of this world, even to the swelling of the bosom. The body is not lost; it is asserted. The new art aims, before all else, to construct a figure that will have substance, dimensionality, and bulk. Works painted in the new style portray figures, like those in sculpture, which project into the light and throw a shadow or give the illusion that they do. In this work of Giotto, the throne is deep enough to contain the monumental figure and breaks away from the flat ground to project and enclose it.

THE ARENA CHAPEL   The projection on a flat surface of an illusion of solid bodies moving through space presents a double problem. The construction of the illusion of a body requires, at the same time, the construction of the illusion of a space sufficiently ample to contain that body. In Giotto's fresco cycles (he was primarily a muralist), he constantly is striving to reconcile these two aspects of illusionistic painting. His frescoes in the Arena Chapel (Cappella Scrovegni) at Padua (FIG. **19-10**) show us his art at its finest. The Arena Chapel, which takes its name from an ancient Roman amphitheater nearby, was built for Enrico Scrovegni, a wealthy Paduan merchant, on a site adjacent to his now razed palace. This small building, intended for the private use of the Scrovegni family, was consecrated in 1305, and its design is so perfectly suited to its interior decoration that some scholars have suggested that Giotto himself may have been its architect.

The rectangular, barrel-vaulted hall has six narrow windows in its south wall only, leaving the entire north wall an unbroken and well-illuminated surface for painting. The entire building seems to have been designed to provide Giotto with as much flat surface as possible for his presentation of one of the most impressive and complete pictorial cycles of Christian Redemption ever rendered. With thirty-eight framed pictures, arranged on three levels, the artist relates the most poignant incidents from the lives of the Virgin and her parents, Joachim and Anna (*top level*), the life and mission of Christ (*middle level*), and his Passion, Crucifixion, and Resurrection (*bottom level*). These three pictorial levels rest on a coloristically neutral base on which imitation marble veneer (reminiscent of the incrustation style of ancient Roman wall decoration [see FIG. 7-18], which Giotto may have seen) alternates with representations of the Virtues and Vices, which are painted in *grisaille* (monochrome grays) to resemble sculpture. The climactic event of the cycle of human salvation, the Last Judgment, covers most of the west wall above the chapel's entrance.

The hall's vaulted ceiling is blue—an azure sky symbolic of Heaven; it is dotted with golden stars and medallions bearing images of Christ, Mary, and various prophets. The blue of the sky is the same as the color in the backgrounds of the narrative panels on the walls below and functions as a powerful unifying agent for the entire decorative scheme; it serves as visual reinforcement for the spiritual unity and the thematic continuity of the numerous pictured episodes. For the visitor to this remarkable little chapel, the formal and coloristic unity of the decorative ensemble become memorable standards against which other decorative schemes must be measured.

The individual panels are framed with decorative borders, which, with their delicate tracery, offer a striking contrast to the sparse simplicity of the figured representations they surround. Subtly scaled down to the chapel's limited space (the figures are only about one-half life size), Giotto's stately and slow-moving actors present their dramas convincingly and with great restraint. The essentials of his style are well illustrated by the *Lamentation* (FIG. **19-11**). In the presence of angels, who dart about in hysterical grief, Christ's mother, his disciples, and the holy women mourn

19-11   GIOTTO, *Lamentation,*
c. 1305. Fresco. Arena Chapel.

over the dead body of the Savior just before its entombment. Giotto has arranged a shallow stage for the figures, bounded by a thick, diagonal scarp of rock that defines a horizontal ledge in the foreground. The rocky landscape links this scene with the adjoining one. Giotto connects the framed scenes throughout the fresco cycle, much as Dante joins the cantos in his epic poem *Commedia*. Though rather narrow, the ledge provides the figures with firm visual support, while the scarp functions as an indicator of the picture's dramatic focal point at the lower left. The figures are sculpturesque, simple, and weighty, but they are not restrained by their mass from appropriate action. Postures and gestures that might have been only rhetorical and mechanical now convincingly express a broad spectrum of grief that ranges from Mary's almost fierce despair through the passionate outbursts of Mary Magdalene and John, to the philosophical resignation of the two disciples at the right and the mute sorrow of the two hooded mourners in the foreground (compare FIG. 9-29). Although Duccio makes an effort to distinguish shades of emotion in *The Betrayal of Jesus* (FIG. 19-6), he does not match Giotto in his stage management of a great tragedy. Giotto, indeed, has constructed a kind of stage, which will serve as a model for those on which many human dramas will be depicted in subsequent paintings. He is now far removed from the old isolation of episodes and actors seen in art until the late thirteenth century. In the *Lamentation*, a single event provokes a single, intense response within which degrees of psychic vibration, so to speak, are quite apparent. This integration of the formal with the emotional composition was rarely attempted, let alone achieved, in art before Giotto.

The formal design of the *Lamentation* fresco, the way the figures are grouped within the contrived space, is worth close study. Each group has its own definition, and each contributes to the rhythmic order of the composition. The strong diagonal of the rocky ledge, with its single dead tree (the tree of knowledge of good and evil, which withered at the fall of Adam), concentrates our attention on the group around the head of Christ, whose positioning is dynamically off-center. All movement beyond this group is contained, or arrested, by the massive bulk of the seated mourner in the left corner of the painting. The seated mourner to the right establishes a relation with the center group, the members of which, by their gazes and gestures, draw the viewer's attention back to the head of Christ. Figures seen from the back, which are frequent in Giotto's compositions, emphasize the foreground, helping visually to place the intermediate figures farther back in space. This device, the very contradiction of the old frontality, in effect puts the viewer behind the "observer" figures, which, facing the action as spectators, reinforce the sense of stagecraft as a model for painting.

Giotto's new devices for the depiction of spatial depth and bodily mass could not, of course, be possible without his management of light and shade. His figures are so mod-

eled (shaded) as to indicate the direction of the light that locates them and the shadows (the diminished light) that in addition to the light gives them volume. In the *Lamentation*, light falls upon the upper surfaces of the figures (note especially the two central, bending figures) and passes down to dark in the draperies, separating the volumes one from the other, pushing one to the fore, the other to the rear. The graded continuum of light and shade, directed by an even, neutral light from a single, steady source—not shown in the picture!—is the first stage in the development of chiaroscuro. We shall see a number of examples of this presently.

The stage-like settings made possible by Giotto's innovations in perspective and lighting suited perfectly the requirements of dramatic narrative now emphasized by the Franciscans as a principal method for educating the faithful in their religion. In this humanizing age the old hieratic presentations of the holy mysteries were evolving into what are called the "mystery" plays. The drama of the mass was extended into one- and two-act tableaus and scenes, and then into simple shows presented at the portals of churches and in city squares. The great increase in popular

19-12 ARNOLFO DE CAMBIO (attributed), nave of Santa Croce, Florence, *c.* 1294–1400.

sermons to huge city audiences developed a public taste for narrative, recited as dramatically as possible. The arts of illusionistic painting, of stage-play and of the rhetoric of the sermon with all its theatrical flourishes, were developing at the same time and were mutually influential. In the art of Giotto there is a masterful—perhaps unique—synthesis of dramatic narrative, holy lesson, and truth to human experience presented in a visual idiom of his own invention, now accessible to all.

SANTA CROCE   For the Franciscan church of Santa Croce in Florence, Giotto painted a Saint John cycle and frescoes of the life and death of Saint Francis. The great church of

19-13   Interior of the Bardi Chapel, Santa Croce, Florence, c. 1320.

Santa Croce, with its "stadium" (university) of the Franciscans, was second in importance only to the mother church of the order at Assisi. Intellectual center of the Franciscan order, it was founded in 1294, on a site where Saint Francis himself had built a small house, and it was not completed until about 1380. Designed, as it is believed, by ARNOLFO DE CAMBIO (c. 1245–1302), builder of the cathedral of Florence, there were no important changes in its plan during the long course of its construction. The interior (FIG. 19-12) is a masterpiece of Italian Gothic architecture. A high, unvaulted, open space, obstruction free, bright and serene, it was, and still is, an eminently public hall, inviting congregations of visitors, suiting perfectly the Franciscan ideal of a place for popular Christian worship.

Though the Franciscans quarreled bitterly among themselves about the owning of property and the building of churches—Saint Francis had sternly forbidden both—by the fourteenth century the mingling of interests of the republic of Florence, its bankers, and the Franciscan order had arrived at a kind of patriotic harmony that permitted to all of them an elevation of status through architecture and art.

In Santa Croce ten chapels flank the apse and choir. The Franciscan proprietors of the church were quite happy to have great banking families like the Bardi, Peruzzi, Alberti, and Baroncelli endow the chapels (FIG. 19-13) in honor of their special saints, making at the same time spiritual and financial investment for the salvation of themselves and their posterity, and for the honor of the order and of the city. The architectural and pictorial ornament of these richly endowed chapels symbolized the unity of state, religion, and dedicated patrons.

Our illustrations of a fresco in the Bardi Chapel of Santa Croce show the *Death of St. Francis*, as restored in the nineteenth century (FIG. 19-14, *top*) and with the restorations removed (FIG. 19-14, *bottom*).* Fortunately, despite the removal of the restorations and the resultant gaps in the composition, enough of the original *Death of St. Francis* remains to give us an idea of the later style of Giotto. Although the St. Francis painting has considerable spiritual affinity with the *Lamentation*, it also shows significant changes. The Gothic agitation has quieted, and the scene has little of the jagged emotion of the *Lamentation*. It seems, indeed, as if the artist had watched the solemn obsequies from offstage. We see the saint, at center on his bier, flanked by kneeling and standing monks; the kneeling figures are seen from behind, in Giotto's fashion. Stately processions of friars in profile come from left and right, as

*This painting exemplifies another aspect of the problem of attribution and authenticity. Until the historically sensitive twentieth century, it had long been the custom to "renew" old pictures by painting over damaged or faded areas. Some modern scholars, in their zeal to know the "real" painter, have advocated stripping even where this leaves only fragments that are perhaps esthetically unsatisfactory. The most practical restoration techniques today call for filling in the destroyed areas with fine lines of pigment so that the visual effect is not so disturbing.

19-14 GIOTTO, *Death of St. Francis, c.* 1320. Fresco. Bardi Chapel, Santa Croce, Florence. *(Top)* as restored in the nineteenth century, *(bottom)* after removal of restorations.

they would be seen in actuality—not frontally, as in a Byzantine procession like that of *Justinian and Attendants* at San Vitale (FIG. 9-9). The figures are accommodated carefully on an architecture-enclosed, stagelike space that has been widened and no longer leaves any doubt that the figures have sufficient room in which to move about. They are taller and have lost some of their former sacklike bulk; Giotto now makes a distinction between the purely form-defining function of the robes and the fact that they are draped around articulated bodies. The impressive solemnity of the procession is enhanced by the omission of the casual and incidental beauties of the world so dear to Sienese and French Gothic painters. Giotto sees and records nature in terms of its most basic facts: solid volumes resting firmly on the flat and horizontal surface of the earth. He arranges his figures in meaningful groups and infuses them with restrained emotions that are revealed in slow and measured gestures. With the greatest economy of means, Giotto achieves unsurpassed effects of monumentality, and his paintings, because of the simplicity and directness of their statements, are among the most memorable in world art.

Giotto's murals in the Bardi and Peruzzi chapels of Santa Croce served as textbooks for generations of Renaissance painters from Masaccio to Michelangelo and beyond. These later artists were able to understand the greatness of Giotto's art better than his immediate followers, who never were capable of absorbing more than a fraction of his revolutionary innovations. Their efforts usually remained confined to the emulation of his plastic figure description. Giotto's foster son and his assistant for many years, TADDEO GADDI (c. 1300–1366), is a good example of a diligent follower. The differences between the work of a great artist and that of a very good one are readily apparent if we compare Giotto's *The Meeting of Joachim and Anna* in the Arena Chapel (FIG. **19-15**) with Taddeo's version of the same subject in the Baroncelli Chapel in Santa Croce (FIG. **19-16**). Giotto's composition is simple and compact. The figures are related carefully to the single passage of architecture (the Golden Gate), where the parents of the Virgin meet in triumph in the presence of splendidly dressed ladies. The latter mock the cloaked servant who refused to believe that the elderly Anna (Saint Anne) would ever bear a child. The story, related in the Apocrypha, is managed with Giotto's usual restraint, clarity, and dramatic compactness. Taddeo allows his composition to become somewhat loose and unstructured. The figures have no clear relation to the background; the elaborate cityscape, though pleasant in itself, demands too much attention and detracts from the action in the foreground. Gestures have become weak and theatrical, and the shepherd (discreetly cut off and unobtrusive in Giotto's painting) here strides boldly toward the center of the scene—a picturesque figure, who though iconographically important as the companion of Joachim somewhat distracts from the central action. Although his figures retain much of Giotto's solidity, Taddeo's painting

weakens the dramatic impact of the story by elaborating its incidental details. Giotto stresses the essentials and, by presenting them with his usual simplicity and forceful directness, gives the theme a much more meaningful interpretation.

Yet, though Taddeo may appear, by comparison with Giotto, weak in composition and dramatic force—but who would not?—he makes an important contribution to the

19-15 GIOTTO, *The Meeting of Joachim and Anna, c.* 1305. Fresco. Arena Chapel.

19-16 TADDEO GADDI, *The Meeting of Joachim and Anna,* 1338. Fresco. Baroncelli Chapel, Santa Croce, Florence.

investigation of pictorial light. In *Joachim and Anna* he takes great pains to depict the fall of light not only on the figures, but on the architecture. A light-and-shade continuum determines the volume of the city wall and its curve into the background. Light strikes sharply on the facing planes of the arched gateway and the clustered buildings of the city (partially restored). From the low angle of the light we might even speculate as to the time of day represented, morning or evening.

Or San Michele

The catastrophes of the Black Death and the banking failures of the Bardi and the Peruzzi families divide the century. For art, the powerful influence of Giotto prevailed, and his successors worked within its limits, developing its possibilities. The tabernacle of the Virgin Mary in the Or San Michele in Florence (FIG. **19-17**) is the work of two "Giotteschi," ANDREA DI CIONE, known as ORCAGNA (active 1343–1368) and BERNARDO DADDI (c. 1290–1348). Orcagna was responsible for the architecture and sculpture of the work, Bernardo Daddi for the painted panel of the Madonna, which the tabernacle enshrines. The Or San Michele was originally a grain market, a *loggia*, or open-sided arcade, into the street; after the installation of the tabernacle it became a church and was partially walled in. The tabernacle was a kind of memorial to the great plague, in that the religious confraternity that supported it was enormously enriched by bequests of those who died in the plague and those who survived it. The bequests were made to a supposed miraculous portrait of the Virgin, which later burned and which the new image by Bernardo Daddi would replace. The tabernacle was begun and finished between 1349 and 1359 for the vast sum of 87,000 gold florins.

Orcagna, an artistic virtuoso, was an architect, sculptor, and painter; he was familiar in the styles and practice of all the arts in post-Giotto Florence. The architectural enframement of the tabernacle recalls the polygonal piers and the slender spiral colonettes of the Florence *Duomo* (cathedral) and campanile (FIG. 13-58), and the triangular pediment, fenestration, and pinnacles of a typical Italian Gothic facade (FIG. 13-61). All the planar surfaces are inlaid with gold, lapis lazuli, mosaic, and finely cut marble in geometric patterns called *Cosmato work* (from *Cosmati*, the name given to craftsmen who worked in marble and mosaic in the twelfth to fourteenth centuries, many of whom belonged to a family of that name). The effect is that of a gem-encrusted, scintillating shrine or reliquary, more the work of a jeweler than an architect. The reverse face of the tabernacle, which we do not show, is occupied by Orcagna's crowded but vivid sculptural reliefs depicting the death and Assumption of the Virgin.

This marvelous structure represents, in the splendor of its lavishly ornamented and costly fabric, the medieval association of precious material with holy things and themes, in this case with the original, miracle-working image of the Virgin, which the new Madonna and Child replaced. Bernardo Daddi's panel interprets this most popular of Gothic subjects in a manner light, delicate, and charming, a manner appropriate to the contemporary humanizing of religion and to the emotional requirements of private devotion. The Virgin is enthroned within a round arch with sculptured curtains, flanked by angels, two of whom swing censers filled with incense, while the Child playfully touches its mother's face. The composition is conventional but softened by sentiment. The architectural enframement provides an illusionistic stage for the image, composing an ensemble of architecture, painting, and sculpture in the service of Marian devotion, attesting to the versatility of Florentine artists after Giotto, as they follow the various paths suggested by his original inspiration.

Simone Martini and Siena

Duccio's successors in the Siena school display even greater originality and assurance than did Duccio himself. SIMONE MARTINI (c. 1285–1344) was a pupil of Duccio and a close friend of Petrarch, who praised him highly for his portrait of "Laura" (the woman to whom Petrarch dedicated his sonnets). Simone worked for the French kings in Naples and Sicily and, in his last years, was employed at the papal court at Avignon, where he came in contact with northern painters. By adapting the insubstantial but luxuriant patterns of the French Gothic manner to Sienese art and, in turn, by acquainting northern painters with the Sienese style, Simone became instrumental in the formation of the so-called *International Style*, which swept Europe during the late fourteenth and early fifteenth century. This style appealed to the aristocratic taste for brilliant color, lavish costume, intricate ornament, and themes involving splendid processions in which knights and their ladies, complete with entourages, horses, and greyhounds, could glitter to advantage. (Late examples of the International Style are FIG. 20-3 and FIG. 21-23.)

Simone's own style does not quite reach the full exuberance of the developed International Style, but his famous *Annunciation* altarpiece (FIG. **19-18**) is the perfect antithesis of the style of Giotto, whose work Simone certainly must have been aware of, but whose art just as certainly left him untouched. The *Annunciation* is characterized by elegant shapes and radiant color, flowing, fluttering line, and weightless figures in a spaceless setting. The complex etiquette of the chivalric courts of Europe dictates the presentation. The angel Gabriel has just alighted, the breeze of his passage lifting his mantle, his iridescent wings still beating. The white and gold of his sumptuous gown heraldically represent the celestial realm whence he bears his message. The Virgin, putting down her book of devotions, shrinks demurely from Gabriel's reverent genuflection, an appro-

19-17 ANDREA ORCAGNA, tabernacle, 1350–1360. Mosaic, gold, marble, lapis lazuli. Bernardo Daddi, *Madonna and Child with Saints*, painted panel insert, 1346–1347. Or San Michele, Florence.

priate gesture in the presence of royalty. She draws about her the deep blue, golden-hemmed mantle, the heraldic colors she wears as Queen of Heaven. Despite the Virgin's modesty and diffidence and the tremendous import of the angel's message, the scene subordinates drama to court ritual and structural experiments to surface splendor. The painted splendor is matched by the intricate tracery of the richly tooled Late Gothic frame. Of French inspiration, it replaces the more sober, clean-cut shapes that were traditional in Italy, and its appearance here is eloquent

testimony to the two-way flow of transalpine influences that fashioned the International Style.

The altarpiece is dated 1333 and signed by Simone Martini and his student and assistant, LIPPO MEMMI . Lippo's contribution to the *Annunciation* is still a matter of debate, but historians now generally subscribe to the theory that he painted the two lateral saints, Saint Ansano and his godmother, Saint Maxima (?). These figures, which are reminiscent of the jamb statues of Gothic church portals, are drawn a little more solidly and lack the linear elegance

19-18 SIMONE MARTINI, *The Annunciation*, 1333. Tempera on wood. approx. 10'1" × 8'8¾" (frame reconstructed in the nineteenth century). Galleria degli Uffizi, Florence. *INTERNATIONAL STYLE*

of Simone's central pair. Given the medieval and Renaissance workshop practices, it is often next to impossible to distinguish the master's hand from that of his assistants, especially if part of the latter's work was corrected or partially redone by the master. Generally, assistants were charged with the gilding of frames and backgrounds, the completion of decorative work, and, occasionally, the rendering of architectural settings. The present architectural enframements are almost a century later than the central panel. Figures, especially those that were central to the represented subject, were regarded as the most important and difficult parts of a painting and were the master's responsi-

bility. Assistants might be allowed to paint some of the less important, marginal figures, but only under the master's close supervision. Among the numerous contracts for paintings that have survived from this period, some are quite specific in spelling out the master's responsibilities, stipulating that the major parts of the work be executed by his hand and his alone. As we move from the anonymity of medieval art toward artists' emancipation during the Renaissance (when they rise from the rank of artisan to that of artist-scientist), the value of their individual skills—and their reputations—becomes increasingly important to their patrons and clients.

The Lorenzetti

The brothers Lorenzetti, also students of Duccio, share in the general experiments in pictorial realism that characterize the fourteenth century, especially in their seeking of convincing spatial illusions. Going well beyond his master, PIETRO LORENZETTI (active 1320–1348) achieved remarkable success in a large panel representing *The Birth of the Virgin* (FIG. **19-19**), which, like Duccio's *Maestà* and Simone Martini's *Annunciation,* was painted for the cathedral of Siena as part of a program honoring the Virgin Mary, heavenly Queen of the Republic. The wooden architectural members that divide the panel into three compartments are represented as extending back into the painted space, as if we were looking through the wooden frame (apparently added later) into a boxlike stage, where the event takes place. The illusion is strengthened by the fact that one of the vertical members cuts across one of the figures, blocking part of it from view. Whether this architecture-assisted per-

spective illusion was intentional is problematical; in any case, the full significance of the device of pictorial illusion enhanced by applied architectural parts was not realized until the next century. No precedent for it exists in the history of Western art, but a long, successful history of such visual illusions produced by a union of real and simulated architecture with painted figures was to develop during the Renaissance and Baroque periods. Pietro did not make just a structural advance here; his very subject represents a marked step in the advance of worldly realism. Saint Anne, reclining wearily as the midwives wash the child and the women bring gifts, is the center of an episode that takes place in an upper-class Italian house of the period. A number of carefully observed domestic details and the scene at the left, where Joachim eagerly awaits the news of the delivery, place the event in an actual household, as if we had moved the panels of the walls back and peered inside. The structural innovation in illusionistic space becomes one with the new curiosity that leads to careful inspection

19-19 PIETRO LORENZETTI, *The Birth of the Virgin,* 1342. Tempera on wood, approx. 6'1" × 5'11". Museo dell'Opera del Duomo, Siena.

and recording of what lies directly before our eyes in the everyday world.

Pietro's brother, AMBROGIO LORENZETTI (active 1319–1348), elaborated the Sienese advances in illusionistic representation in spectacular fashion in a vast mural in the Palazzo Pubblico. The effects of good and bad govern-

ment are allegorically juxtaposed in the *Good Government* fresco (not shown). Good Government is represented as a majestic, enthroned figure flanked by the virtues of Justice, Prudence, Temperance, and Fortitude, as well as by Peace and Magnanimity; above hover the theological virtues of Faith, Hope, and Charity. In the foreground, the citizens of

19-20   AMBROGIO LORENZETTI, *Peaceful City,* detail from the fresco *Allegory of Good Government: The Effects of Good Government in the City and the Country,* Sala della Pace, Palazzo Pubblico, Siena, 1338–1339.

19-21   AMBROGIO LORENZETTI, *Peaceful Country,* detail from the fresco *Allegory of Good Government: The Effects of Good Government in the City and the Country.*

19-22   BUONAMICO BUFFALMACCO or FRANCESCO TRAINI (?), *The Triumph of Death, c.* 1340. Fresco. Campo Santo, Pisa.

Siena advance to do homage to Good Government and all the virtues that accompany it. The turbulent politics of the Italian cities, the violent party struggles, the overthrow and reinstatement of governments would certainly have called for solemn reminders of the value of justice in high places, and the city hall would be just the place for a painting like Ambrogio's. Beyond the allegories and the dedication scene stretch the depictions of the fruits of Good Government, both in the city and the countryside. The *Peaceful City* (FIG. **19-20**) is a panoramic view of Siena itself, with its clustering palaces, markets, towers, churches, streets, and walls. The traffic of the city moves peacefully, the guildsmen ply their trades and crafts, and a cluster of radiant maidens, hand in hand, perform a graceful, circling dance. The artist fondly observes the life of his city, and its architecture gives him an opportunity to apply Siena's rapidly growing knowledge of perspective. Passing through the city gate to the countryside beyond its walls, Ambrogio's *Peaceful Country* (FIG. **19-21**) presents a bird's-eye view of the undulating Tuscan countryside—its villas, castles, plowed farmlands, and peasants going about their seasonal occupations. An allegorical figure of Security hovers above the landscape, unfurling a scroll that promises safety to all who live under the rule of the law. In this sweeping view of an actual countryside, we have the first appearance of landscape since the ancient world. The difference is that now the landscape—as well as the view of the city—is particularized by careful observation, being given almost the character of a portrait of a specific place and environment in a desire for authenticity. By combining some of Giotto's analytical powers with the narrative talent of Duccio,

Ambrogio is able to achieve more spectacular results than those of either of his two great predecessors.

The Black Death may have ended the careers of both Lorenzettis; nothing is heard of them after 1348, the year that brought so much horror to defenseless Europe. An unusual and fascinating painting relates this common late medieval theme. In *The Triumph of Death* (FIG. **19-22**) in the Campo Santo at Pisa, attributed to FRANCESCO TRAINI (active *c.* 1321–1363) and, more recently, to BUONAMICO BUFFALMACCO (active during the early fourteenth century), three young aristocrats and their ladies, mounted in a stylish cavalcade, encounter three coffin-encased corpses in differing stages of decomposition. As the horror of the confrontation with death strikes them, the ladies turn away with delicate and ladylike disgust, and a gentleman holds his nose (the animals, horses and dogs, sniff excitedly). A holy hermit unrolls a scroll that demonstrates the folly of pleasure and the inevitability of death. In another section to the right, the ladies and gentlemen, wishing to forget dreadful realities, occupy themselves in an orange grove with music, gallantries, and lapdogs, while all around them death and judgment occur, and angels and demons struggle for souls. The medieval message is as strong as ever, but gilded youth refuses to acknowledge it. The painting applies all the stock of Florentine-Sienese representational craft to present the most worldly—and mortal—picture of the fourteenth century. It is an irony of history that, as Western humanity draws both itself and the world into ever-clearer visual focus, it perceives ever more clearly that corporeal things are perishable.

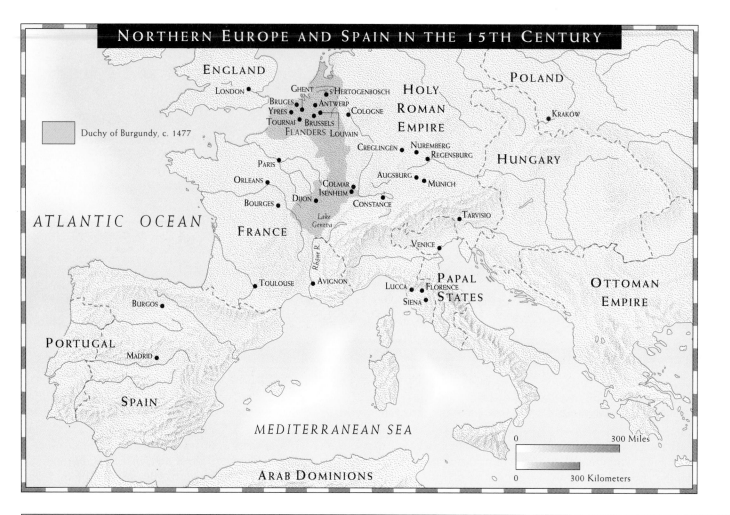

NORTHERN EUROPE AND SPAIN IN THE 15TH CENTURY

ENGLAND

POLAND

LONDON

GHENT s'HERTOGENBOSCH
BRUGES ANTWERP
YPRES COLOGNE
TOURNAI BRUSSELS
FLANDERS LOUVAIN

HOLY
ROMAN
EMPIRE

KRAKÓW

Duchy of Burgundy, c. 1477

CREGLINGEN NUREMBERG
REGENSBURG

HUNGARY

PARIS

ORLEANS

AUGSBURG
MUNICH

COLMAR
ISENHEIM

BOURGES DIJON
CONSTANCE

ATLANTIC OCEAN

Lake
Geneva

FRANCE

TARVISIO

VENICE

Rhône R.

TOULOUSE AVIGNON

LUCCA FLORENCE
SIENA

PAPAL
STATES

OTTOMAN
EMPIRE

BURGOS

PORTUGAL

MADRID

SPAIN

MEDITERRANEAN SEA

300 Miles

0   300 Kilometers

ARAB DOMINIONS

1325	1375	1425	
	PHILIP THE BOLD (BURGUNDY)	JOHN THE FEARLESS	PHILIP THE GOOD	CHARLES THE BOLD

Sluter, The Well of Moses
1395–1406

Limbourg brothers
May, c. 1413–1416

Quarton, Avignon Pietà, c. 1455

van der Weyden
Portrait of a Lady, c. 1460

Hundred Years War begins, 1337

The papacy in Avignon, 1305–1376

Chaucer The Canterbury Tales, 1387–1400

The Great Schism in the Church, 1376–1415

Nicholas of Cusa, 1401?–1464

Jacques Coeur, Merchant Banker, 1395?–1456

The Netherlands under the Dukes of Burgundy, 1384–1477

Hundred Years War ends, 1453

CHAPTER 20

FIFTEENTH-CENTURY ART IN NORTHERN EUROPE AND SPAIN

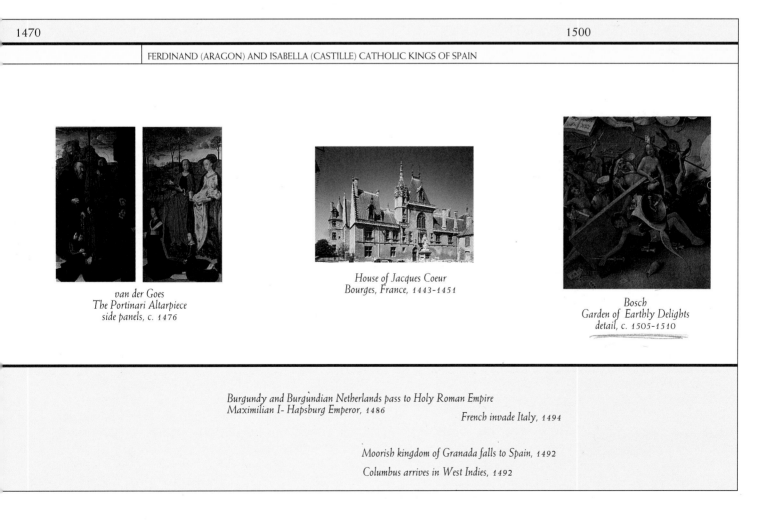

| 1470 | 1500 |

FERDINAND (ARAGON) AND ISABELLA (CASTILLE) CATHOLIC KINGS OF SPAIN

van der Goes
The Portinari Altarpiece
side panels, c. 1476

House of Jacques Coeur
Bourges, France, 1443-1451

Bosch
Garden of Earthly Delights
detail, c. 1505-1510

Burgundy and Burgundian Netherlands pass to Holy Roman Empire
Maximilian I- Hapsburg Emperor, 1486
French invade Italy, 1494

Moorish kingdom of Granada falls to Spain, 1492

Columbus arrives in West Indies, 1492

In the Late Gothic world, Western Europe beyond the Alps shared with Italy the calamities of war, plague, and the social upheavals and dislocations attendant upon dying feudalism. A new, secularizing civilization (sometimes called "early modern") was challenging the already faltering spiritual and temporal power of the Church and threatening its unity. Religious experience was intensifying; a populace impatient with the constraints imposed upon it by traditional forms, rituals, and priest-craft demanded freedom of religious expression. Forces were gathering that would produce a Christian civil war—the Protestant Reformation—early in the sixteenth century.

Politically, the long, general movement toward centralized government, begun in the twelfth century, continued apace. The authority of kings and princes overruled the scattered but still cumbersome arrangements of feudal governance. Urbanization increasingly drew the rural populations into the cities, now thriving centers of commerce, industry, and finance. Urban class struggle and peasant uprisings were evidence enough of the social displacements and economic disadvantages wrought by a profound historical change.

THE RISE OF CAPITALISM

Especially significant for art were the increasing professionalization of the artist and the passing of patronage from the Church to the great princes and princely families, in alliance with or independent of wealthy cities. We have seen this happening in the city-states of Italy. What made it possible was the acquisition and accumulation of capital.

Despite the calamities of the age, an economic system was evolving—the early stage of European capitalism. Responding to the financial requirements of trade, new systems of credit and exchange created an economic network of enterprising European cities. The trade in money accompanied the trade in commodities, and it financed industry. Both were in the hands of trading companies with central offices and international branches; the Medici of Florence were a notable example. They were influential in the powerful Netherlands city of Bruges, which by 1450 had a stock exchange and was pivotal for the integrated, economic activity of Europe.

As the city, a focus of economic energy, comes into its own, the merchant/banker stands out as a prominent occupation type, and the aristocracy, evolved from the feudal barony, plays the games of waning chivalry on the battlefield, in the tournament, and at court. The merchant/banker does not search for the Holy Grail or go on crusade; he journeys instead in search of new markets for his goods and clients for his loans; he acquires not grace but gold.

One such figure was the French trader and financier Jacques Coeur (c. 1395–1456), whose astonishing career illustrates what wealth and power could be won and lost in economic adventure. Coeur had banking houses in every city of France and many abroad; he employed over three hundred agents and could compete with the great trading republics of Italy. His merchant ships filled the Mediterranean; with the permission of the papacy, he traded widely with the Muslims of Egypt and the Levant, and gained concessions there that would benefit French commerce for centuries. He was financial adviser to King Charles VII of France, and subsidized the king's expulsion of the English from Normandy, bringing an end to the Hundred Years War. He was a friend of Pope Nicholas V and was instrumental in mending the Great Schism.

His near-monopoly of the money market in France and the animosity of hundreds of his high-born debtors and disgruntled competitors led to his downfall. He was framed on an absurd charge of having poisoned Agnes Sorel, the king's mistress, and was imprisoned; his vast wealth and property were confiscated and distributed among the king's people. He escaped from prison and made his way to Rome, where he was warmly received by the pope. He died of fever while leading a fleet of papal war galleys in the eastern Mediterranean.

Jacques Coeur's story, reading more like fiction than fact, is worth remembering when we visit the great *hôtel*, or town house, (FIG. **20-1**) he built in his native city of Bourges (we have seen this city's great cathedral, FIGS. 13-20 to 13-22). The structure is a well-preserved example of Late Gothic domestic architecture. It is of irregular plan, the units arranged around an open courtyard, a kind of municipal translation of the feudal castle. The building faces a city street and is without defensive walls or outworks, its window openings indicating little need for defense against an alien siege. The courtyard has galleries and stair towers giving access to multiple stories. The service areas—maintenance shops and storage, servants' quarters, baths—occupy the ground level. The upper stories house the great hall and auxiliary rooms that could be partitioned by paneled leaves and tapestries for offices and family living rooms. The facade is articulated by three large pavilions, the largest being the central one, with a great entrance arch, above it a deep niche for sculpture, and uppermost a mullioned window with Flamboyant tracery. Adjoining it is a polygonal stair tower with an elaborate Flamboyant spire. The steep, pyramidal, snow-shedding roofs are opened by high, narrow dormers. The lower windows, with their cross-shaped mullions, admit light from the street. The whole fabric exhibits the Gothic verticality familiar in Gothic church architecture and in its ornamental details.

The Hôtel Jacques Coeur is not only a splendid example of Late Gothic, but a monumental symbol of the new secular spirit, an expression of the triumph of city culture, of capital accumulation, and of the desire for worldly convenience and proud display.

20-1   House of Jacques Coeur, Bourges, France, 1443–1451.

THE BURGUNDIAN NETHERLANDS

The capitalist adventuring of Jacques Coeur was matched by whole cities in the Netherlands, modern Holland and Belgium. In the fifteenth century this tiny region, encircled by England, Germany, and France, was the scene of a brilliant culture contemporary with and equivalent in importance to that of Early Renaissance Florence (see Chapter 21). Indeed, it shares with Florence that immense creative activity we call "Renaissance," despite profound differences of site, circumstance, and style. Long thought of as "the last flowering of the Middle Ages," the cultural achievement in the Netherlands during the fifteenth century can just as readily—and more properly—be seen as "the dawn of a new era."

The designation "Burgundian Netherlands" signifies the union of the Netherlands (the Low Countries) with Burgundy, the fertile, east-central region of France still known for its wines. From the later fourteenth century the dukes of Burgundy, brothers and cousins of the kings of France, had acquired the counties of the Netherlands, and with them the rich, industrial, commercial, and banking cities that together were pivotal for the economic development of northern and western Europe. The capital and court of the dukes was at Dijon in Burgundy, but the source of Burgundian wealth and power was at Bruges, the city that made Burgundy an independent state and dangerous rival of royal France. Long after the fall of the House of Burgundy, the great Netherlandish cities, Bruges and then Antwerp, would continue to be the financial capitals of Europe.

Bruges derived its wealth from the wool trade and from banking. Until late in the fifteenth century, an arm of the North Sea, now silted up, reached inland to Bruges. Here, ships brought raw wool from England and Spain and carried away fine woolen cloth that became famous throughout Europe. The wool trade brought bankers, among them representatives of the House of Medici, and Bruges became the financial clearinghouse for all of northern Europe. In its streets, merchants from Italy and the Near East rubbed shoulders with traders from Russia and Spain. Despite the flourishing economies of its sister cities—Ghent, Louvain, and Ypres—Bruges so dominated Flanders (modern Belgium in large part, then the principal county of the Lowlands) that the duke of Burgundy chose to make the city his capital and moved his court there from Dijon in the early fifteenth century.

The dukes of Burgundy were probably the most powerful rulers in northern Europe during the first three-quarters of the fifteenth century. Although cousins of the French kings, they usually supported England (on which they relied for the raw materials used in their wool industry) during the Hundred Years War and, at times, were in control of much of northern France, including Paris. Through intermarriage with the House of Flanders, they annexed the Low Countries, and, at the height of their power, their lands stretched from the Rhône River to the North Sea. Only the rash policies of the last of their line, Charles the Bold, and his death at the battle of Nancy in 1477 brought to an end the Burgundian dream of forming a strong middle kingdom between France and the Holy Roman Empire. After Charles's death, the southern Burgundian lands were reabsorbed by France, and the Netherlands passed to the Holy Roman Empire by virtue of the dynastic marriage of Charles's daughter, Mary of Burgundy, to Maximilian of Hapsburg.

Philip the Bold of Burgundy, who ruled from 1364 to 1404, and his brother John, duke of Berry, were the greatest sponsors of the arts of their time in northern Europe. Their interests centered on illuminated manuscripts, *arras* tapestries (from *Arras*, a town in northeastern France famous for its fabric), and rich furnishings for their numerous castles and town houses, which were located throughout their duchies. Philip's largest artistic enterprise was the foundation of the Chartreuse (Carthusian monastery) de Champmol, near Dijon. Intended as a repository of the tombs of the grandees of the House of Burgundy, its magnificent endowment attracted artists from all parts of northern Europe.

The outstanding representative of this short-lived Burgundian school was the sculptor CLAUS SLUTER (active *c.* 1380–1406). For the cloister of the Chartreuse de Champmol, Sluter designed a symbolic well in which Moses and five other prophets surround a base that once supported a Crucifixion group. The six prophets of *The Well of Moses* (FIG. **20-2**) recall the jamb figures of the Gothic portals, but they far surpass even the most realistic of those (FIG. 13-32) in the artist's intense observation of natural appearance, in the rendering of minute detail, and in their bulk, which manages to contain a wealth of descriptive information that might otherwise be distracting. The life-size figures are swathed in heavy draperies with voluminous folds, characteristic of Sluter's style, and the artist manages to make their difficult, complex surfaces seem remarkably lifelike. This effect is enhanced by the skillful differentiation of textures, from coarse drapery to smooth flesh and silky hair, and by the paint, which still is preserved in part. This fascination with the specific and tangible in the visible world will be one of the chief characteristics of fifteenth-century Flemish painting. But despite the realism of Sluter's figures, what is still missing in the northern concept of the figure is the principle of interior movement, or weight shift.

For centuries, the characteristic painted surface in the north had been either stained glass or the illuminated manuscript page. Gothic architecture in northern Europe had eliminated solid walls and left few continuous, blank surfaces that invited painted decorations, unlike the case in Italy, where climate and architecture favored mural painting in fresco. Northern artists were accustomed to working not only in miniature but with rich, jewel-like color, which, especially in stained glass, has a profound luminosity, with light seemingly irradiating the forms. Thus, they came into the fifteenth century habituated to deep color worked into exquisitely tiny and intricate shapes and patterns. When northern miniaturists became acquainted, through the International Style, with Italian forms and ideas, they were forced to reduce to page size, or smaller, the inventions used in large compositions by Italian wall and panel painters like Duccio, Giotto, Simone Martini, and others. This development, which led to a kind of "perspective naturalism," was inconsistent with the basic function of book

20-2   CLAUS SLUTER, *The Well of Moses*, 1395–1406. Figures approx. 6′ high. Chartreuse de Champmol, Dijon, France.

illumination—page decoration and the illustration of the written text. Toward the end of the fourteenth century, illuminations began to take on the character of independent paintings, expanding on the page until they occupied it completely. By about 1400, these new forces generated in miniatures seemed to demand large surfaces, and the shift was made to panel painting.

We have seen the first steps toward the illumination's expansion within the text appear in the work of Jean Pucelle, who revitalized the stagnating Gothic manner of the Paris school. A page from the *Belleville Breviary* (FIG. 13-40) shows how the entire page has become the province of the illuminator. The borders, extended to invade the margins, include not only decorative tendrils and a profusion of spiky ivy and floral ornaments, but also a myriad of insects, small animals, and grotesques. In addition, three narrative scenes encroach on the columns of the text, the graceful postures and flowing draperies of the figures reflecting Sienese influence. One feels that any of these narratives could have been expanded into a full-page illustration or even a panel painting.

Such an expansion has occurred in the calendar pages of a gorgeously illustrated Book of Hours made for the duke of

Berry, brother of the king of France and of Philip the Bold of Burgundy. The manuscript, *Les Très Riches Heures du Duc de Berry*, was completed in 1416 by the three LIMBOURG BROTHERS—POL, HENNEQUIN, and HERMAN. Such books became favorite possessions of the northern aristocracy during the fourteenth and fifteenth centuries. As prayer books, they replaced the traditional psalters, which had been the only liturgical books in private hands until the mid-thirteenth century. The heart of the Book of Hours is the "Office of the Blessed Virgin," which contains liturgical passages to be read privately at eight set points during the day, from matins to compline. This part of these books

20-3 THE LIMBOURG BROTHERS, *May*, from *Les Très Riches Heures du Duc de Berry*, 1413–1416. Illumination, approx. 8¹/₂″ × 5¹/₂″. Musée Condé, Chantilly, France.

usually is preceded by an illustrated calendar containing local religious feast days; it is followed by penitential psalms, devotional prayers, litanies to the saints, and other offices, including those of the dead and of the Holy Cross.

The calendar pictures of *Les Très Riches Heures* are perhaps the most famous in the history of manuscript illumination. They represent the twelve months of the year in terms of the associated seasonal tasks, alternating the occupations of nobility and peasantry. Above each picture is a lunette representing the chariot of the sun as it makes its yearly round through the twelve months and signs of the zodiac; numerical notations designate the zodiacal degree passed through in the course of the year. Representative is the colorful calendar picture for the month of May (FIG. **20-3**). Here, a cavalcade of patrician ladies and gentlemen, preceded by trumpeters, rides out to celebrate the first day of May, a spring festival observed by courts throughout Europe. They are clad in springtime green, garlanded with fresh leaves, and they sparkle with ornate finery. Behind them is a woodland and the chateau of Riom. These great country estates, most of which belonged to the duke of Berry, loom in the backgrounds of most of the calendar pictures and are represented so faithfully that those still surviving today are easily recognized. The spirit of the picture is Chaucerian—lightsome, artificial, chivalric, and pleasure-loving. (*The Canterbury Tales* is hardly a generation older.) The elegant silhouettes, rich colors, and decorative linear effects again recall Sienese art. The varying scenes evidently were painted by different artists, but historians have never been able to assign specific pictures to the different Limbourg brothers. Nevertheless, although the artists' styles may differ, their main interests were the same. Within the confines of the International Style, they represented as accurately as possible the actual world of appearances and the activities of men and women, peasants and aristocrats, in their natural surroundings at specific times of the year. Thus, the traditional field of subject matter has been expanded to include genre subjects; they are given a prominent place, even in a religious book. Secular and religious subjects remain neatly separated, but they will encroach on each other increasingly during the fifteenth century to produce as thorough a humanization of religious subject matter as we will see in Italy.

Flemish Painting*

The northern painter, evolving out of the illuminator, finds, as did the artist in Italy, a new prestige and place. Although the social structure of the north in the fifteenth century adhered to the hierarchies of the Middle Ages, it coexisted with a development of commerce and wealth almost modern in tone. The nobles and clergy continued to rule,

*Flanders is one principality in the Netherlands, but has given its name generically to much of Netherlandish art—thus "Flemish art" or the art of "Flanders."

even though the true source of wealth and power was the bourgeoisie. This large middle class, in turn, still was organized and controlled by the guild system that had taken form in the Middle Ages.

In the north, the guild dominated the life of the average man to an even greater extent than in Italy. To pursue a craft, a man had to belong to the guild controlling that craft. Painters, for example, sought admission to the Guild of St. Luke, which included the saddlers, glassworkers, and mirrorworkers as well. To secure membership in the guild, the aspiring painter was apprenticed in boyhood to a master, with whom he lived as a son and who taught him the fundamentals of his craft: how to make implements; how to prepare panels with *gesso* (plaster mixed with a binding material); and how to mix colors, oils, and varnishes. Once the youth mastered these procedures and learned to work in the traditional manner of his master, he usually spent several years working as a journeyman in various cities, observing and gaining ideas from other masters. He was then eligible to become a master and was admitted to the guild. Through the guild, he obtained commissions; the guild inspected his painting for honest materials and workmanship and secured him adequate payment for his labor. The result was the solid craftsmanship that characterizes the best work of Flanders and of Italy.

We know much less about the training of women artists than we do about that of men. Certainly, far fewer women were involved in the professions of art, although a substantial number of women are recorded in the membership of the art guilds of Flemish cities like Bruges in the fifteenth century and later. Albrecht Dürer recounts women's participation in parades of the guilds as persons earning a livelihood by their art.

Women most often were tutored in art by fathers and husbands who were professionals and whom they assisted in all technical procedures of the craft. Social and moral restraints would have forbidden women's apprenticeship in the homes of male masters and would have stringently limited their freedom of movement. Moreover, from the sixteenth century on, when academic courses of training supplement and then replace guild training, women would not as a rule expect or be permitted instruction in figure painting, insofar as it involved dissection of cadavers and study of the nude, male model. Most women did not have access to the training and experience enjoyed by many male artists. Yet Lavinia Teerlinc was an accomplished professional in Bruges before she was invited to England to paint miniatures for the courts of Henry VIII and his successors. There, she was a formidable rival of some of her male contemporaries and received greater compensation for her work than they did for theirs.

The craftsmanship that gave such distinction to men and to women artists involved mastery of the new oil medium, which had such great influence on Venetian painters at the end of the fifteenth century. Traditionally, Jan van Eyck is credited with the invention of oil painting, although the facts surrounding the early history of the medium still remain mysterious; Melchior Broederlam is said to have been using oils in the 1390s. Flemish painters built up their pictures by superimposing translucent paint layers, called *glazes*, on a layer of opaque monochrome underpainting, which in turn had been built up from a carefully planned drawing made on a white-grounded panel of wood. The base of the binding medium for the pigments was a fast-drying oil that had been known and used by certain painters in the late Middle Ages. The secret of the new technique appears to have been an unidentified supplement to the usual composition of the glazes. With the new medium, painters were able to create richer colors than previously had been possible. As a result, northern painting of the fifteenth century is characterized by a deep, intense tonality, glowing light (the new colors were seemingly lit from within), and hard, enamel-like surfaces, quite unlike the high-keyed color, sharp light, and rather matte surfaces of Italian tempera.

The brilliant and versatile new medium was exactly right for the formal intentions of the northern painters, who aimed for sharply focused, hard-edged, sparkling clarity of detail in their representation of thousands of objects ranging in scale from large to almost invisible. The Italians as we shall see were interested primarily in the *structure* behind the appearances given to the eye—that is, in perspective, composition, anatomy, the mechanics of bodily motion, and proportion through measure. The northern painters were intent on rendering the *appearances* themselves—the bright, colored surfaces of things touched by light. Their traditions of stained glass and miniatures made their realism one of radiant, decorative color rather than of sculpturesque form. The differences between the painting of Italy and of northern Europe are emphasized by the fact that, when oil painting spread to Italy after the mid-century, it did not radically affect Italian sensibility to form. Although the color of Italian painting became richer, particularly in Venice, the new medium—which, in time, completely replaced tempera—was exploited in the service of the structural purposes of Italian art. On the whole, until the early sixteenth century, artistic communication between northern and southern Europe seems to have been limited to relatively few individuals, and both areas tended to develop independently of each other.

The political background against which the development of northern art took place in the fifteenth century was not unlike that of Italy. The commercial free cities that dominated the political scene at the beginning of the fifteenth century gradually fell under the rule of princes until the beginning of the sixteenth century, when powerful states like France, England, and the Hapsburg empire, comprising Spain, the Germanys, and the Netherlands, began to emerge. The wealth and leisure necessary to encourage the growth of the arts were based on commerce and on the patronage of the powerful princes and rich merchants who controlled it.

ROBERT CAMPIN   Hardly a decade after *Les Très Riches Heures*, an example of the International Style at its peak, we have a work of quite different and novel conception: *The Mérode Altarpiece* (FIG. **20-4**) by the "Master of Flémalle," now identified as ROBERT CAMPIN (c. 1378–1444), the leading painter of the city of Tournai. Here, the aristocratic taste, romantic mood, and ornamental style of the International painters are replaced with a relatively blunt, sober realism in setting and characterization. The old theme of the Annunciation occupies the central panel of the triptych, and something of the International Style remains in its decorative line play, but the donors, depicted in the left panel, set the tone. Husband and wife, they are of the grave and sedate middle class; unostentatiously prosperous, quietly attired, they kneel in a little courtyard, the man peering through the door at the mystery taking place in the central scene. Discreetly set apart from it, they take the mystery as a fact, and factualness determines the artist's whole approach.

All the objects depicted in the *Mérode Altarpiece* Annunciation scene are rendered with careful attention to their actual appearance, and the event takes place in an everyday, middle-class Flemish interior, in which all accessories, furniture, and utensils are indicated, lest the setting be incomplete. But the objects represented are not merely that; book, candle, flowers, sink (in the corner niche), fire screen, polished pot, towels, and bench symbolize, in different ways, the Virgin's purity and her divine mission. In the right panel, Joseph has made a mousetrap, symbolic of the theological tradition that Christ is bait set in the trap of the world to catch the Devil. The carpenter's shop is completely inventoried by the painter, down to the vista into a distant city street. Thus, we have a thorough humanizing of a traditional religious theme—a transformation of it in terms of a particular time and place: a middle-class house, courtyard, and shop in a fifteenth-century city of Flanders. So close is the status of the sacred actors to the human level that they are even represented without halos; this does not happen in Italy until the end of the fifteenth century.

We have been tracing the humanization of art from the thirteenth century. The distance between the sacred and the secular has now narrowed to such a degree that they become intermixed. As Johan Huizinga, renowned modern historian of the fifteenth century, describes it:

> Individual and social life, in all their manifestations, are imbued with the conception of faith. There is not an object nor an action, however trivial, that is not constantly correlated with Christ or salvation. . . . All life was saturated with religion to such an extent that the people were in constant danger of losing sight of the distinction between things spiritual and things temporal. If, on the one hand, all details of ordinary life may be raised to a sacred level, on the other hand, all that is holy sinks to the commonplace, by the fact of being blended with everyday life . . .

20-4   ROBERT CAMPIN (Master of Flémalle), *The Mérode Altarpiece* (open), *c.* 1425–1428. Tempera and oil on wood, center panel approx. 25″ × 25″. Metropolitan Museum of Art, New York (Cloisters Collection purchase).

the demarcation of the spheres of religious thought and that of worldly concerns was nearly obliterated.*

Hence, the realistically rendered, commonplace objects in a Flemish painting become suffused with religious significance and take on the nature of sacramental things. With this justification for their existence in art, the ordinary things that surround us—and we ourselves—share the realm of the saints; conversely, the saints now occupy our realm. But we, as well as our things, will remain when, with the secularization of art, the saints and sanctity have disappeared.

HUBERT AND JAN VAN EYCK   One of the largest and most admired Flemish altarpieces of the fifteenth century is *The Ghent Altarpiece* in the Cathedral of St. Bavo in Ghent (FIG. **20-5**). It also has been one of the most controversial ever since the discovery, in 1832, of a partly damaged, four-line Latin poem on the frame of one of the outside panels that translates in part: "The painter Hubert van Eyck, greater than whom no one was found, began [this work]; Jan, second in art, completed it at the expense of Jodocus Vyt." The last line of the quatrain gives the date of 1432.

For more than a century after the discovery of this inscription under a coat of greenish paint, the altarpiece was believed to be the product of a collaboration between JAN VAN EYCK (*c.* 1390–1441) and his older brother HUBERT VAN EYCK (*c.* 1370–1426). But none of the numerous attempts to assign different parts of the many-paneled work to one or the other brother found more than partial acceptance among art historians. Even Erwin Panofsky's tightly argued conclusion that the present altarpiece is the result of an artful combination of three independent works, begun by Hubert and finished by Jan, that originally were not meant to be seen together, left considerable room for doubt and argument.*

An entirely new light was thrown on the controversy with the more recent suggestion that Hubert may not have been a painter at all, but rather a sculptor, who carved an elaborate, now-lost framework for the painted panels. Lotte Brand Philip points out that the damaged word *-ictor* in the inscription, which precedes Hubert's name and had been restored to read *pictor* (painter), could also be read *fictor* (sculptor).† "Second in art" would then not mean that Jan was a less accomplished painter than his brother but would be a chronological reference to the fact that Jan worked on the altarpiece *after* Hubert. Judging from surviv-

*Johan A. Huizinga, *The Waning of the Middle Ages,* 1924. Reprint (New York: St. Martin's, 1988).

*Erwin Panofsky, *Early Netherlandish Painting* (Cambridge, MA: Harvard University Press, 1953).

†Lotte Brand Philip, *The Ghent Altarpiece and the Art of Jan van Eyck* (Princeton, NJ: Princeton University Press, 1972).

ing contracts and commissions of the period, it seems to have been fairly common practice for a painter to begin work on panels after their frames had been completed.

In 1566, the panels of the altarpiece were removed from the original frame and hidden, to protect them from Protestant iconoclasts who probably destroyed the frame. The panels were reinstalled in 1587, but without the original framework, which Lotte Brand Philip envisions to have been in the form of a richly carved, two-storied, Gothic reliquary front. Her ingenious theory and imaginative reconstruction would give sole authorship of the paintings to Jan van Eyck and solve the problem of attribution that has vexed art historians for almost a century and a half. It also would tend to explain the disparity of the scale used on the inner panels, which has disturbed some modern observers. If, indeed, the panels were originally more widely spaced and separated by richly carved, Gothic archi-

tectural elements, the formal unity of the altarpiece may have been stronger and more cohesive, especially if perspective devices in the lower level created the illusion that the smaller-scale scenes receded and were seen through, and at some distance behind, the architectural screen. On the other hand, it may well be that fifteenth-century viewers paid much less attention to formal unity than we do today and that the spiritual unity of the work was their real concern.

The Ghent polyptych remains an outstanding example of the large, folding altarpiece, typical of the north, that discloses new meanings to the observer as the unfolding panels reveal new subjects in sequence. The very form of the folding altarpiece expresses the medieval tendency to uncover truth behind natural appearances, to clothe thought in allegory, to find "essential" meaning hidden beneath layers of secondary meanings.

20-5 HUBERT and JAN VAN EYCK, *The Ghent Altarpiece* (open); completed 1432. Tempera and oil on wood, approx. 11'6" × 15'1". Cathedral of St. Bavo, Ghent, Belgium.

When opened, the altarpiece reveals a sumptuous, superbly colored representation of the medieval conception of the Redemption of man. In the upper register, God the Father—wearing the triple tiara of the papacy, with a worldly crown at his feet and resplendent in a deep-scarlet mantle—is flanked on the left by the Virgin, represented as the Queen of Heaven, with a "crown of twelve stars upon her head," and on the right by Saint John the Baptist. To either side is a choir of angels and, on the right, Saint Cecilia at her organ. Adam and Eve are in the far panels. The inscriptions in the arches above Mary and Saint John extol the virtue and purity of the Virgin and the greatness of Saint John as the forerunner of Christ. The particularly significant inscription above the head of the Lord translates: "This is God, all-powerful in his divine majesty; of all the best, by the gentleness of his goodness; the most liberal giver, because of his infinite generosity." The step behind the crown at the Lord's feet bears the inscription: "On his head, life without death. On his brow, youth without age. On his right, joy without sadness. On his left, security without fear." This inscription is a most concise and beautiful statement of the change from the concept of God as a stern, medieval judge of mankind to the benevolent Franciscan father of the human race. This Franciscan concept of the benevolent nature of God is reinforced by the pelicans embroidered on the tapestry draped over the back of his throne, for pelicans (then thought to tear open their breasts to feed their starving young with their own blood) were symbols of self-sacrificing love. The entire altarpiece ampli-

fies this central theme; though man, symbolized by Adam and Eve, is sinful, he will be saved because God, in his infinite love, will sacrifice his own son for this purpose.

The figures are rendered in a shimmering splendor of color that defies reproduction. Both Hubert and Jan van Eyck were trained miniaturists, and not the smallest detail has escaped their eyes. They amplify the beauty of the most insignificant object as if it were a work of piety as much as a work of art. The soft texture of hair, the glitter of gold in the heavy brocades, the luster of pearls, and the flashing of gems are all given with tireless fidelity to appearance. The new medium of oil paint shows its marvelous magic.

The panels of the lower register extend the symbolism of the upper. In the central panel, the community of saints comes from the four corners of the earth through an opulent, flower-spangled landscape. They move toward the altar of the Lamb, from whose heart blood flows into a chalice, and toward the octagonal fountain of life into which spills the "pure river of water of life, clear as crystal, proceeding out of the throne of God and of the Lamb" (Revelation 22:1). On the right, the Twelve Apostles and a group of martyrs in red robes advance; on the left, with minor prophets, the Four Evangelists arrive carrying their Gospels. In the right background come the holy virgins, and in the left background, the holy confessors. On the lower wings, other approaching groups symbolize the four cardinal virtues: the hermits, Temperance; the pilgrims, Prudence; the knights, Fortitude; the judges, Justice. The altarpiece celebrates the whole Christian cycle from the Fall

20-6 JAN VAN EYCK, *The Virgin with the Canon van der Paele,* 1436. Tempera and oil on wood, approx. 48″ × 62″. Musées Communaux, Bruges, Belgium.

to the Redemption, presenting the Church triumphant in heavenly Jerusalem. The uncanny naturalism and the precise rendering, in the miniaturist tradition, make the great event as concrete and credible as possible to the observer. The realism is so saturated with symbolism that we almost think of it as a kind of superreality or "surrealism," for what is given to the eye is more than the eye alone can report.

Jan van Eyck's matchless color craft also is evident in *The Virgin with the Canon van der Paele* (FIG. **20-6**), painted in 1436. The architecture, the elaborately ornamented rug, and the placement of the figures all lead the observer's eye to the Madonna and Child, who sit on a throne in the apse of a church. The rich texture of the Virgin's red robes strongly contrasts with the white surplice of the painting's donor, the kneeling Canon van der Paele. A similar contrast plays across the space between the dull glint from the armor of St. George, the patron saint of the canon, and the rich brocades of St. Donatian, the patron of the church for which the painting was commissioned. The incredibly brilliant profusion of color is controlled carefully, so that the forms are distinguished clearly in all detail. The symbolism is as profuse and controlled as the color, incorporating again the complete cycle of the Fall and the promise of Redemption. The arms of the Virgin's throne and the historiated capitals of the pilasters behind her make reference to the Old Testament prefiguration of the Coming of Christ, so well known in the Middle Ages.

Van Eyck's use of perspective is evident in the picture; he uses not a single perspective that would consistently unify the space, but several. His intention here once again appears to be accomplished indirectly, the multiple perspectives directing attention to the principal figures. For example, a projection of the line of the column base at the far right leads to the head of the canon; the orthogonals of the floor tiles converge on the midpoint of the figure of the Virgin; and the base of the throne can be projected to the infant Christ. No real spatial unification can be found here. The figures do not interrelate as we might expect. Each fills its own space with, as it were, its own perspective. Although St. George lifts his helmet to the Virgin, the direction of his gaze goes well beyond her; this disorientation is also true of the other figures. Jan van Eyck and his generation still essentially conceive the organization of the two-dimensional picture surface in terms of shape, color, and symbol; they have not yet thought of it as a window into a constructed illusion of the third dimension, as the painters of the later Flemish schools will.

The portrait head of Canon van der Paele shows the same nonstructural approach. The heavy, wrinkled visage of the canon is recorded in precise detail, almost to the pores. The artist makes a relief map of his subject, delineating every minute change of the facial surface. Unlike the Italian portraitists, who think first of the structure of the head and then draw the likeness over it, Jan van Eyck works from the outside inward, beginning with the likeness and shaping the head incidentally. This procedure is what

gives the masklike aspect to the canon's face, despite the portrait's fidelity to physiognomy; the surface is all there, but the illusion of three-dimensional mass is only implied.

We have seen three works that included painted portraits of their donors: *The Mérode Altarpiece* (FIG. 20-4), *The Ghent Altarpiece* (FIG. 20-5), and *The Virgin with Canon van der Paele* (FIG. 20-6). These portraits mark a significant revival of portraiture, a genre unknown since antiquity. A fourth portrait, Jan van Eyck's *Man in a Red Turban* (FIG. **20-7**), takes another step toward the complete secularization of the portrait. In the Mérode and Ghent altarpieces, the donors were depicted apart from the saints; in the Canon van der Paele portrait, the donor associates with the saints at the throne of the Virgin. In this portrait of a man wearing a turban (possibly a depiction of the artist himself), the image of a living individual apparently needs no religious purpose for being—only a personal one; the portrait is simply a personal record of one's features interesting to the subject himself or to someone who knows him. These private portraits now begin to multiply, as both artist and patron become interested in the reality they reveal, for the

20-7 JAN VAN EYCK, *Man in a Red Turban* (Self-portrait?), 1433. Tempera and oil on wood, approx. $10^{1}/_{4}$" × $7^{1}/_{2}$". Reproduced by courtesy of the Trustees of the National Gallery, London.

painter's close observation of the lineaments of a human face is as revealing of the real world as his observation of objects in general. As human beings confront themselves in the painted portrait, they objectify themselves as selves, as people. In this confrontation, the otherworldly anonymity of the Middle Ages must fade away. The *Man in a Red Turban* looks directly at us, or perhaps at himself in a mirror. So far as is known, this depiction is the first painted portrait in a thousand years to do so. The level, composed gaze, directed from a true three-quarter pose of the head, must have impressed observers deeply. The painter gives us the illusion that from whatever angle we observe the face, the eyes still fix us.

Another painting of this kind, by the great Rogier van der Weyden, must have inspired the writing of *The Vision of God* (1453) by Nicholas of Cusa, who says, in the preface to that work:

> To transport you to things divine, I must needs use a comparison of some kind. Now among men's works I have found no image better suited to our purpose than that of an image which is *omnivoyant* [all-seeing]—its face, by the painter's cunning art, being made to appear as though looking on all around it—for example . . . that by the eminent painter, Roger [*sic*], in his priceless picture in the governor's house at Brussels. . . . This I call the icon of God.

Nicholas goes on with a praise of sight and vision that amounts to a sanctification of them:

> Thou, Lord . . . lovest me because Thine eyes are so attentively upon me . . . where the eye is, there is love. . . . I exist in that measure in which Thou art with me, and since Thy look is Thy being, I am because Thou dost look at me, and if Thou didst turn Thy glance from me I should cease to be.
> Apart from Thee, Lord, naught can exist. If, then, Thine essence pervade all things, so also does Thy sight, which is Thine essence. . . . Thou Lord, seest all things and each thing at one and the same time.

Nicholas of Cusa was a contemporary of the great Flemish painters, and it is likely that he spoke in a sense they could understand and in a mood they could share. The exaltation of sight to divine status and the astonishing assertion that the essence of God is sight—not Being, as Saint Thomas tells us—are entirely in harmony with the new vision in painting. As sight and Being in God are essentially the same, so the painter's sight, which is instrumental in making likenesses, brings them into being. As the contemplative man achieves union with God by making himself like God, the imitation of objects in the sight of (hence, caused by) God must be a holy act on the part of the painter: seeing what God sees, he achieves the reality of God's vision and reveals it to others. The minute realism of the Flemish painters can be understood in the light of Nicholas's doctrine. God sees everything, great and small alike, and Nicholas's fundamental doctrine that all opposites and contradictions are resolved and harmonized in God makes God present in the greatest and in the smallest, in the macrocosm and in the microcosm, in the whole earth and in a drop of water. In the whole world of vision *caused* by God's sight, everything is worthwhile because it is seen by God—even the "meanest flower that blows." Nicholas's sanctification of the faculty of sight provides Flemish painters with a religious warrant to apply sight in the investigation of the given world; painters in the north will continue the investigation long after the original religious motive is gone.

Above all, an age had begun in both the Netherlands and Italy in which people gloried in the faculty of sight for what it could reveal of the world around them. Artists now began to show the Western public "what things look like," and it took extreme pleasure in recognizing a revelation. The level gaze of the *Man in a Red Turban*, in all its quiet objectivity, is not only the omnivoyant "icon of God"; in its historical destiny, it is the impartial, eternally observant face of science. It is also, significantly, humanity beginning to confront nature in terms of the human component. This step is the climax of the slow but mighty process that will bring the artist's eyes down from the supernatural to the natural world—a process that is expressed with just as much conviction and vigor in the north as it is in Italy.

The humanization of pictorial themes advances another step in Jan van Eyck's double portrait of *Giovanni Arnolfini and His Bride* (FIG. **20-8**). The Lucca financier (who had established himself in Bruges) and his lady occupy a scene that is empty of saints but charged with the spiritual. Almost every object depicted is in some way symbolic of the holiness of matrimony. Giovanni and his bride, hand in hand, take the marriage vows. Their shoes have been removed, for the sacrament of matrimony makes the room a holy place. The little dog symbolizes fidelity (the origin of the common canine name *Fido* is from the Latin *fido*, to trust). Behind the pair, the curtains of the marriage bed have been opened. The finial of the bedpost is a tiny statue of Saint Margaret, patron saint of childbirth; from the finial hangs a whisk broom, symbolic of domestic care (FIG. **20-9**). The oranges on the chest below the window may refer to the golden apples of the Hesperides, representing the conquest of death, and the presence of the omnivoyant eye of God seems to be referred to twice: once by the single candle burning in the ornate chandelier and again by the mirror, in which the entire room is reflected (FIG. 20-9). The small medallions set into the mirror's frame show tiny scenes from the Passion of Christ and represent van Eyck's ever-present promise of salvation for the figures reflected on the mirror's convex surface. These figures include not only the principals, Arnolfini and his wife, but two persons who look into the room through the door. One of these must be the artist himself, as the florid inscription above the mirror, "Johannes de Eyck fuit hic," announces that he was present. The purpose of the picture, then, is to document and sanctify the marriage of two particular per-

20-8 JAN VAN EYCK, *Giovanni Arnolfini and His Bride*, 1434. Tempera and oil on wood, approx. 32″ × 23¹/₂″. Reproduced by courtesy of the Trustees of the National Gallery, London.

20-9 Detail of *Giovanni Arnolfini and His Bride*.

sons. In this context, human beings come to the fore of their own setting; the spiritual is present, but in terms of symbol, not image.

The paintings of Jan van Eyck have a weighty formality that banishes movement and action. His symmetrical groupings have the stillness and rigidity of the symbol-laden ceremony of the Mass; each person and thing has its prescribed place and is adorned as befits the sacred occasion. The long tradition of manuscript illumination accepted that the Holy Book must be as precious as the words it contains. Jan van Eyck, himself a miniaturist and illuminator, instinctively created a rich and ornamental style in which to proclaim his optimistic message of human salvation. In their own way, the paintings of Jan van Eyck are perfect and impossible to surpass. After him, Flemish painting looked for new approaches, and van Eyck had few, if any, emulators.

VAN DER WEYDEN, CHRISTUS, AND BOUTS The art of ROGIER VAN DER WEYDEN (*c.* 1400–1464) had a much greater impact on northern painting during the fifteenth century. A

student of Robert Campin, Rogier* evidently recognized the limitations of van Eyck's style, although it had not been without influence on his own early work. By sweeping most of the secondary symbolism from his paintings, Rogier cleared his pictorial stage for fluid and dynamic compositions stressing human action and drama. He concentrates on themes like the Crucifixion and the Pietà, in which he moves the observer by relating the sufferings of Christ. For van Eyck's symbolic bleeding lamb, Rogier substitutes the tortured body of the Redeemer and his anguished mother. His paintings are filled with deep religiosity and powerful emotion, for he conceived his themes as expressions of a mystic yearning to share in the Passion of Jesus.

The great *Escorial Deposition* (FIG. **20-10**) sums up Rogier's early style and content. Instead of creating a deep landscape setting, as Jan van Eyck might have, he compresses the figures and action onto a shallow stage to

*It may help the beginning art history student to note at this point that it has become a convention among art historians to refer to some artists by their first names—hence "Rogier," "Hugo," etc.

20-10   ROGIER VAN DER WEYDEN, the *Escorial Deposition, c.* 1435. Tempera and oil on wood, approx. 7'3" × 8'7". Museo del Prado, Madrid.

concentrate the observer's attention. Here, Rogier imitates the large, sculptured shrines so popular in the fifteenth century, especially in Germany, and the device serves well his purpose of expressing maximum action within disciplined structure. The painting resembles a stratified relief carving in the crisp drawing and precise modeling of its forms. A series of lateral, undulating movements gives the group a unity, a formal cohesion, that is underlined by psychological means—by the desolating anguish common to all the figures. Few painters have equaled Rogier in the rendering of passionate sorrow as it vibrates through a figure or distorts a tear-stained face. His depiction of the agony of loss is the most authentic in religious art; in a painting as bare of secondary symbolism as the *Deposition,* the emotional impact on the observer is immediate and direct. From this single example, we can understand why

Rogier's art became authoritative for the whole fifteenth century outside of Italy.

His portraits were no less important than his altarpieces. Campin and van Eyck had established portraiture among the artist's principal tasks. Great patrons were ready to have their likenesses painted for many different reasons: to memorialize themselves in their dynastic lines; to establish their identity, rank, and station by an image far more concrete than a heraldic coat of arms; to represent themselves at occasions of state when they could not be present; even as a kind of photograph of the betrothed to be exchanged by families who had arranged their children's marriages. Royalty, nobility, and the very rich might send painters to "take" the likeness of a prospective bride or groom. It is reported that when a bride was sought for young King Charles VI of France, a painter was sent to three different royal courts to make portraits of the candidates, on the basis of which the king then made his choice.

We are not sure for what specific purpose Rogier's portrait of an unknown young lady (FIG. **20-11**) was painted. From her dress and bearing, she was probably of noble rank. The artist is at pains to realize not only a faithful likeness of her somewhat plain features, but to read, with his uncommon perception, her individual character. Her lowered eyes, tightly locked, thin fingers, and fragile physique bespeak a personality reserved, introverted, and devout. The unflattering honesty and directness, typical in the Flemish artist's approach, reveals much, despite the formality of pose and demeanor. This style contrasts with the formality of the Italian approach (FIG. 21-55), derived from the profiles common to coins and medallions, which is more stern and admits little revelation of personality. The Italian patron and portraitist will prefer the profile view throughout most of the century, rather than the full-face and three-quarter views favored by the Flemish. Rogier is perhaps chief among the Flemish in his penetrating readings of his sub-

jects, and, great pictorial composer that he is, he makes beautiful use here of flat, sharply pointed angular shapes that themselves so powerfully suggest an "angularity" (rigidity) of this subject's personality. Unlike Jan van Eyck, Rogier lays little stress on minute description of surface detail. Instead, he defines large, simple planes and volumes, achieving an almost "abstract" effect, in the modern sense, of dignity and elegance.

Although evidence that Rogier traveled to Italy is not unequivocal, some of his paintings clearly show his acquaintance with Italian pictorial devices. His religious sincerity and concern with sin and guilt, however, remained undimmed by them. The appearance of these mid-century Italian influences in Rogier's paintings was not an isolated instance in Flemish art. The work of PETRUS CHRISTUS (c. 1410–1472) shows so marked an interest in the depiction of space and cubic form that, although the idea now largely is discounted, he too was often felt to have traveled to Italy. Little is known of Christus's life, except that he may have been van Eyck's student and that he settled and worked in Bruges. His style vacillates between van Eyck's and Rogier's. Still, his interests are quite different from those of his models.

His painting of *The Legend of Saints Eligius and Godeberta* (FIG. **20-12**) seems, at first glance, to exhibit all of van Eyck's

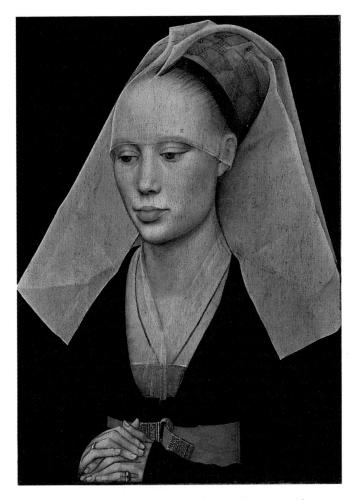

20-11   ROGIER VAN DER WEYDEN, *Portrait of a Lady, c.* 1460. Oil on wood, 14¹/₂″ × 10³/₄″. National Gallery, Washington, D.C. (Andrew W. Mellon Collection).

20-12   PETRUS CHRISTUS, *The Legend of Saints Eligius and Godeberta,* 1449. Tempera and oil on wood, approx. 39″ × 34″. Metropolitan Museum of Art, New York (the Lehman Collection).

miniaturistic traits, from the stitching on the lady's gown to the carefully enumerated attributes that identify the seated saint as a patron of the goldsmith's guild. Even the convex mirror on the table seems to have been extracted from van Eyck's portrait of Arnolfini and his bride (FIG. 20-8), and the two "witnesses" reflected in it suggest that this also may be a wedding picture. But Christus's concept of reality and his approach to it are quite different from van Eyck's; he is much more concerned with the underlying structure of an object's appearance and, in this respect, is more closely related to the Italian than to the northern approach. The three solidly constructed figures within the cubic void defined by the desk and the room corner represent an essentially southern essay in pictorial form that has been overlaid with van Eyck's surface realism. Curiously, in his effort to make the structure of his picture clear, Christus resorts to the same kind of simplification of forms seen in

the paintings of Paolo Uccello and Piero della Francesca (FIGS. 21-26 and 21-28).

Christus may have had some contact with DIRK BOUTS (*c.* 1415–1475), a slightly younger artist of similar temperament and interests. For a long time, the central panel of Bouts's *The Altarpiece of the Holy Sacrament* was believed to be the first northern painting in which the use of a single vanishing point for the construction of an interior could actually be demonstrated. Although Rogier may have known about the Italian science of linear perspective, he apparently did not use it in his paintings. Recent studies tend to give precedence in this field to Petrus Christus, from whom, in fact, Bouts may have acquired his knowledge. The setting for the altarpiece's *Last Supper* (FIG. **20-13**) is probably the refectory of the headquarters of the Louvain Confraternity of the Holy Sacrament, by which the painting was commissioned. All the orthogonals of the depicted room lead to a

20-13 DIRK BOUTS, the *Last Supper* (center panel of *The Altarpiece of the Holy Sacrament*), 1464–1468. Tempera and oil on wood, approx. 6′ × 5′. St. Peter's, Louvain, Belgium.

20-14 HUGO VAN DER GOES, *The Portinari Altarpiece,* side panels, *c.* 1476. Oil on wood. Galleria degli Uffizi, Florence.

single vanishing point in the center of the mantelpiece above the head of Christ. This painting is not only the most successful northern fifteenth-century representation of an interior, but it is also the first in which the scale of the figures has been adjusted realistically to the space they occupy. So far, however, the perspective unity is confined to single units of space only; the small side room has its own vanishing point, and neither it nor the vanishing point of the main room falls on the horizon of the landscape seen through the windows. The tentative manner with which Bouts solves his spatial problems suggests that he arrived at his solution independently and that the Italian science of perspective had not yet reached the north, except perhaps in small fragments. Nevertheless, the works of Christus and Bouts clearly show that, by mid-century, northern artists had become involved with the same scientific, formal problems that concerned Italian artists during most of the fifteenth century.

The mood of Bouts's *Last Supper* is neutral. The gathering is solemn enough, but it lacks all pathos and dramatic tension, almost as if the artist was more concerned with the solution of a difficult formal problem than with the pic-

torial interpretation, either personal or traditional, of the sacred event.

VAN DER GOES AND MEMLING   The highly subjective and introspective paintings of HUGO VAN DER GOES (*c.* 1440–1482) seem to express a discontent with the impersonal quality that the artist must have felt was a loss of religious meaning in the paintings of his older contemporaries. Hugo was dean of the painters' guild of Ghent from 1468 to 1475 and an extremely popular painter. At the height of his success and fame, he entered a monastery as a lay brother. While there, he suffered a mental breakdown, and a year later, in 1482, he died. His retirement to the monastery did not interrupt Hugo's career as a painter immediately; he continued to receive commissions and probably completed his most famous work, *The Portinari Altarpiece* (FIGS. **20-14** and **20-15**), while living in the monastery.

Hugo painted the triptych for Tommaso Portinari, an agent of the Medici, who appears on the wings of the altarpiece with his family and their patron saints. The central panel (FIG. 20-15) represents *The Adoration of the Shepherds.*

20-15   HUGO VAN DER GOES, *The Adoration of the Shepherds*, center panel, 8'3¹/₂" × 10', *The Portinari Altarpiece* (FIG. 20-14).

On this large surface, Hugo displays a scene of solemn grandeur, muted by the artist's introspective nature. The high drama of the joyous occasion is stilled; the Virgin, Joseph, and the angels seem to brood on the suffering that is to come rather than to meditate on the miracle of the Nativity. The Virgin kneels, somber and monumental, on a tilted ground that has the expressive function of centering the main actors. From the right rear enter three shepherds, represented with powerful realism in attitudes of wonder, piety, and gaping curiosity. Their lined, plebeian faces, work-worn hands, and uncouth dress and manner are so sharply characterized as to make us think of the characters in such contemporary English literature of the poor as *Piers Plowman* and the *Second Shepherd's Play.* The three panels are unified by the symbolic architecture and a continuous, wintry, northern landscape. Symbols are scattered plentifully throughout the altarpiece: iris and columbine symbolize the Sorrows of the Virgin; the fifteen angels represent the Fifteen Joys of Mary; a sheaf of wheat stands for Bethlehem (the "house of bread" in Hebrew), a reference to the Eucharist; and the harp of David, emblazoned over the portal of the building in the middle distance (just to the right of the head of the Virgin), signifies the ancestry of Christ.

To stress the meaning and significance of the depicted event, Hugo revives medieval pictorial devices and casts aside the unities of time and action so treasured by other Renaissance artists, wherein a single episode in time is confined to a single framed piece. Small scenes shown in the background of the altarpiece represent (from left to right across the three panels) the Flight into Egypt, the Annunciation to the Shepherds, and the Arrival of the Magi—the "prelude and epilogue to the Nativity." Also reflective of older traditions is the manner in which Hugo varies the scale of his figures to differentiate them according to their importance in relation to the central event. At the same time, he puts a vigorous, penetrating realism to work in a new direction, characterizing human beings according to their social level while showing their common humanity, and thus the painting becomes a plea for all to join the Brotherhood of Man.

Portinari placed his altarpiece in the church of Sant'Egidio in Florence, where it created a considerable stir among Florentine artists. Although the painting as a whole must have seemed unstructured to them, Hugo's brilliant technique and what they thought of as incredible realism in representing drapery, flowers, animals, and, above all, human character and emotion, made a deep impression on them. At least one Florentine artist, Domenico Ghirlandaio, paid tribute to the northern master by using Hugo's most

striking motif, the adoring shepherds, in one of his own Nativity paintings.

Hugo's contemporary, HANS MEMLING (c. 1430–1494), who, although like Hugo, was esteemed by all and called, at his death, the "best painter in all Christendom," was of a very different temperament. Gentle and genial, he avoided the ambitious, dramatic compositions of Rogier and Hugo, and his sweet, slightly melancholy style fits well into the twilight of the waning fifteenth century. Memling's specialty is the Madonna; the many that have survived are slight, pretty, young princesses. His depictions of the infant Christ are doll-like. A good example of his work is the center panel of a triptych representing *The Mystic Marriage of St. Catherine* (FIG. **20-16**). The composition is balanced and serene; the color, sparkling and luminous; the execution, of the highest technical quality (Memling's paintings are among the best preserved from the fifteenth century). The prevailing sense of isolation and the frail, spiritual human types contrast not only with Hugo's monumental and somber forms but also with van Eyck's robust and splendid

20-16 HANS MEMLING, *The Mystic Marriage of St. Catherine*, center panel of *The St. John Altarpiece*, 1479. Oil on wood, approx. $67^3/4'' \times 67^3/4''$. Hospitaal Sint Jan, Bruges.

ones. The century began, with van Eyck's sumptuous art, on a note of humanistic optimism. It ends with a waning strength of spirit, an erosion of confidence in the moral and religious authority of the Church. Contemporary poetry is filled with dreary pessimism and foreboding, almost in anticipation of another fall of man and the disasters that will lie ahead for Christendom in the Reformation.

HIERONYMUS BOSCH   This time of pessimistic transition finds its supreme artist in one of the most fascinating and puzzling painters in history, HIERONYMUS BOSCH (c. 1450–1516). Interpretations of Bosch differ widely. Was he a satirist, an irreligious mocker, or a pornographer? Was he a heretic or an orthodox fanatic like Girolamo Savonarola, an Italian contemporary? Was he obsessed by guilt and the universal reign of sin and death? Certainly, his art is born of the dark pessimism of his age, burdened with the fear of human fate and the conviction that man's doom is approaching. A contemporary poet, Eustache Deschamps, writes:

Now the world is cowardly, decayed and weak,
Old, covetous, confused of speech:
I see only female and male fools. . . .
The end approaches . . .
All goes badly.

Bosch's most famous work, the so-called *Garden of Earthly Delights* (FIGS. **20-17** and **20-18**), is also his most

puzzling, and no interpretation of it is universally accepted. The left wing of the triptych shows the *Creation of Eve* in the Garden of Eden. However, here Eve is not the mother of mankind, as she is in van Eyck's *Ghent Altarpiece* (FIG. 20-5), but rather the seductress whose temptation of Adam resulted in the original sin, the central theme of the main panel. Evil lurks even in Bosch's paradise: a central fountain of life is surrounded by ravens, the traditional symbol for nonbelievers and magicians; an owl, hiding in the dark hole in the center of the fountain, represents witchcraft and sorcery.

The central panel, also called the *Garden of Earthly Delights,* swarms with the frail nude figures of men and women sporting licentiously in a panoramic landscape that is studded with fantastic growths of a quasi-sexual form. Bosch seems to be showing erotic temptation and sensual gratification as a universal disaster, and the human race, as a consequence of original sin, succumbing to its naturally base disposition. The themes are derived in part from three major sources: medieval bestiaries, Flemish proverbs, dream books (then very popular), all mixed in the melting pot of Bosch's astoundingly inventive imagination. In addition, the artist includes frequent allusions to magic and alchemy and mingles animal and vegetable forms in the most absurd combinations. Symbols are scattered plentifully throughout the panel: fruit for carnal pleasure, eggs for alchemy and sex, the rat for falsehood and lies, dead fish for memories of past joys. A couple in a glass globe may illustrate the proverb "Good fortune, like glass, is easily broken." We

20-17   HIERONYMUS BOSCH, triptych of the *Garden of Earthly Delights. Creation of Eve* (left wing), *Garden of Earthly Delights* (center panel), *Hell* (right wing), 1505–1510. Oil on wood, center panel 86⅝" × 76¾". Museo del Prado, Madrid.

have lost the key to many of Bosch's symbols, but it may be assumed that they were well known to his contemporaries.

In the right wing, the fruits of license are gathered in *Hell*. There, sinful mankind undergoes hideous torments to diabolic music, while the hellish landscape burns. This symphony of damnation apparently comments on the wickedness of music, with which the Devil lures souls away from God. In this context, the ears and the musical instruments would represent the erotic, soul-destroying thoughts engendered by music. A man is crucified on a harp; another is shut up in a drum. A gambler is nailed to his own table. A girl is embraced by a spidery monster and bitten by toads. The observer must search through the hideous enclosure of Bosch's *Hell* to take in its fascinating though repulsive details. The great modern poet Charles Baudelaire catches the mood in his *Flowers of Evil*:

> Who but the Devil pulls our walking-strings!
> Abominations lure us to their side;
> Each day we take another step to hell,
> Descending through the stench, unhorrified . . .
> Packed in our brains incestuous as worms
> Our demons celebrate in drunken gangs . . .
> . . . in this den of jackals, monkeys, curs,
> Scorpions, buzzards, snakes . . . this paradise
> Of filthy beasts that screech, howl, grovel, grunt—
> In this menagerie of mankind's vice.

The triptych as a whole may represent the false paradise of this world between Eden and Hell, but this is only one interpretation. Another explanation has it that Bosch belonged to a secret, heretical sect, the Adamites, and that the central panel was thought of as a kind of altarpiece symbolically celebrating its rites and practices. A fairly strong case has been made for an interpretation in terms of contemporaneous alchemical knowledge and practice.* In this connection, it should be pointed out that alchemy, in Bosch's time, was not an illegal and occult art but a practical and legitimate science practiced to make artist's paints, women's cosmetics, herbal cooking preparations, and healing potions. The alchemical science of distillation is basic to modern chemistry, and Philippus Aureolus Paracelsus, a physician of the early sixteenth century, stated emphatically that the true and only purpose of alchemy is to heal the sick, not to make gold.

Numerous alchemical treatises circulated during Bosch's time, and some of them may well have been known to him. Many observers have noted that the triptych is punctuated by forms and shapes similar to diagrams found in distillation texts. The most striking of these, perhaps, is the beaker-shaped "fountain of life" that appears once in the center of the left wing and again in the background of

20-18 HIERONYMUS BOSCH, *Hell*, right wing of the triptych of the *Garden of Earthly Delights* (detail of FIG. 20-17).

*See Laurinda S. Dixon, "Bosch's *Garden of Delights* Triptych: Remnants of a 'Fossil' Science," *The Art Bulletin*, Vol. LXIII, No. 1 (March 1981), pp. 96–113.

the central panel. In form, this shape strongly resembles an alchemical mixing retort. Many other distillation apparatuses appear, especially in the central panel, including glass pipes and lids and transparent globes and funnels. Numerous egg shapes seem to refer to the ovoid mixing vessels in which ingredients were combined to produce the hoped-for transmutations. These vessels, called "eggs" in the symbolic language of alchemy, were considered microcosmic models of the world, which contained all the qualities of life and in which "the four elements [earth, air, fire, water] were perfectly conjoined." Egg shapes appear on all three panels of Bosch's altarpiece; the most prominent one, on the right panel, forms the body of a grotesque, human-headed monster. This creature has been called the "alchemical man," and the tiny figures inside his eggshell torso, usually interpreted as embodying the sins of gluttony and lust, are seen as gathered around a table to watch the glow of an alchemical furnace hidden by the broken shell of the egg man's body.

Bosch's message seems to become quite clear: humanity, left to its own devices, is destined for damnation. Although far from being universally accepted, this last interpretation of the *Garden of Earthly Delights* appears to conform best with the remainder of the artist's oeuvre. Neither in this, nor in Bosch's other works, does humankind appear to advantage. Abandoned to evil by the Fall, humanity merits Hell.

Bosch was a supreme narrative painter, and the visions of his bubbling imagination demanded quick release. His technique is more rapid and spontaneous than the labored traditional Flemish manner. He seems to have had no time for the customary monochrome underpaintings or careful modeling of figures. His method forecasts the *alla prima* technique (pigments laid on with little or no drawing or underpainting) of the seventeenth and eighteenth centuries, as he puts down with quick and precise strokes the myriad creatures that populate his panels. His use of *impasto* (thickly applied pigment), which did not require the traditional laborious application of numerous glazes, was ideally suited to the spinning of his morbid fantasies, and if he extends no hope of salvation for man, he only anticipates Michelangelo, who, in his *Last Judgment* fresco (FIG. 22-28), arrived at the same conclusion some thirty years later.

FRANCE, GERMANY, AND SPAIN

The bourgeoisie in France, unlike that in the Netherlands, was not wealthy, localized in strong towns, nor interested in fostering the arts, although there were exceptions, like Jacques Coeur, and his city of Bourges. In France, the Hundred Years War had wrecked economic enterprise and prevented stability. During the fifteenth century, the anarchy of war and the weakness of the kings resulted in a

group of rival duchies. The strongest of these, as we have seen, was the duchy of Burgundy; through marriage and political alliance, it occupied the Netherlands and became essentially Flemish, particularly in art commissioned by the court. In France, artists joined the retinues of the wealthier nobility, the dukes of Berry, Bourbon, and Nemours, and sometimes the royal court, where they were able to continue to develop an art that is typically French despite its regional variations. But no artist of the fifteenth century north and west of the Alps could escape the influence of the great artists of Flanders. French artists accepted it, and works of high quality were produced in all the provinces of France during the mid- and late fifteenth century.

Sculptured images of the Madonna and Child, increasingly realistic and beguiling, were produced in great numbers. The so-called *Notre-Dame de Grasse* (FIG. **20-19**), carved in Toulouse for a chapel in the church of the Jacobins, shows the merger of the older, courtly stylization of pose and facial feature, familiar in the sculpture of Paris (FIG. 13-39), with Burgundian solidity of structure and heavy drapery (FIG. 20-2). In the Virgin's face the conventional "Gothic smile" has been replaced with a softly modeled

20-19   *Notre Dame de Grasse*, 1430–1440. Painted Stone, 3'11" high. Church of the Jacobins, Toulouse, France.

expression of pathos, the pretty face seeming on the verge of tears. The pose is quite natural, as the musing young mother, her Book of Hours beneath her arm, turns for a moment from the restless child, whom she only slightly restrains. A young woman praying before this statue could easily identify with the subject; the dress was contemporary, the Book of Hours the companion of her private devotion, the girlish mother and her child could be herself and her infant. The expression of motherly love seen in the gentleness of this group is at one end of the humanized spectrum of religious emotion from the agony of the mother depicted in the German *Pietà* at the other (FIG. 13-56).

French painting cannot equal the galaxy of masters who illuminate so brilliantly the Flemish school; yet two stand out. JEAN FOUQUET (*c.* 1420–1481) worked for King Charles VII (the patron and client of Jacques Coeur), the Duke of Nemours, and for Étienne Chevalier, the king's treasurer. Fouquet's portrait of Chevalier with his patron, Saint Stephen (FIG. **20-20**), shows, in addition to Flemish influence, the effect of the two years the artist spent in Italy, between 1445 and 1447. The kneeling donor with his standing saint is familiar in Flemish art, as are the three-quarter stances and the sharp, clear focus of the portraits. The reading of the surfaces, however, is less particular than in the Flemish practice; the artist is trying to represent the forms underneath the surfaces, in the Italian manner. Also of Italian inspiration are the architectural background and its rendering in perspective. The secularizing tendency that advanced so rapidly in the fifteenth century is apparent in the familiar, comradely demeanor of the two men. Nothing whatever distinguishes them as being of different worlds, except possibly that Saint Stephen, who holds the stone of his martyrdom, is dressed as a priest.

20-20 JEAN FOUQUET, *Étienne Chevalier and St. Stephen* (from a diptych now divided), *c.* 1450. Tempera on wood, 36^1/$_2$" × 33^1/$_2$". Gemäldegalerie, Staatliche Museen, Berlin-Dahlem.

20-21   The *Avignon Pietà*, attributed to Enguerrand Quarton, *c.* 1455. Tempera on wood, approx. 5'4" × 7'2". Louvre, Paris.

The *Avignon Pietà* (FIG. **20-21**), which has both Flemish and Italian elements, is an isolated masterpiece of great power, painted in Provence, in the extreme south of France; it is attributed to Enguerrand Quarton (*c.* 1410–1466). Rogier van der Weyden's great *Escorial Deposition* (FIG. 20-10) comes to mind at once when we see the Avignon work, although the balanced, almost symmetrical massing clearly reflects the Italian Renaissance. (The subdued color scheme also has suggested Iberian influence to some writers.) The donor, now familiarly present at the sacred event, kneels at the left. His is a strikingly characteristic portrait, the face gnarled, oaken, and ascetic. The group of Christ and saints is united by the splendidly painted figure of Christ and by the angular shapes that seem deliberately simplified for graphic emphasis. As in Italian art, surface ornament is suppressed in the interest of monumental form. The luminous gold background, against which the figures are silhouetted and into which the halos are incised, is a strangely conservative feature, contrasting with the detailed background landscape reminiscent of Flemish paintings. No matter what his sources, the painter is deeply sensitive to his theme. Along with Rogier's version, the *Avignon Pietà* is one of the most memorable in the history of religious art.

Typical of the sculptural, blocky, "hard" style of southern Germany is the work of the Swiss painter CONRAD WITZ (*c.* 1400–1447). Although *The Miraculous Draught of Fish* (FIG. **20-22**) by this remarkable painter also shows Flemish

influence, particularly that of van Eyck, the painting demonstrates Witz's powerful and original sense of realism. Witz shows precocious skill in the study of water effects: the sky-glaze on the slowly moving lake surface, the mirrored reflections of the figures in the boat, and the transparency of the shallow water in the foreground. This painting is one of the first Renaissance pictures in which the landscape not only dominates the figures but is also the representation of a specific place—the shores of Lake Geneva, with the town of Geneva on the right and the ranges of the Alps in the distance.

The Late Gothic style is seen to best advantage in the works of German artists who specialized in the carving of large *retables* (altarpieces) in wood. The sculptor VEIT STOSS (1447–1533) carved a great altar for the church of St. Mary in Kraków, Poland (FIG. **20-23**), no element of which is recognizable as having been influenced by the Italian Renaissance. Typically, the altar consists of a central, boxlike space; the shrine is flanked by hinged, movable wings—an inner pair (shown here) and an outer pair. In the shrine, huge figures (some 9 feet high) represent *The Death and Assumption of the Virgin,* and, in the wings, scenes from the lives of Christ and the Virgin are portrayed. The altar expresses the intense piety of Gothic culture in its late phase, when every resource of figural and ornamental design from the vocabulary of Gothic art is utilized to heighten the emotion and to glorify the apparition of the sacred event. The disciples of Christ are gathered about the

20-22 Conrad Witz, *The Miraculous Draught of Fish,* from the *Altarpiece of St. Peter,* 1444. Tempera on wood, approx. 51″ × 61″. Musée d'Art et d'Histoire, Geneva.

20-23 Veit Stoss, *The Death and Assumption of the Virgin,* from the altar of the Virgin Mary, 1477–1489. Painted and gilded wood, triptych (wings open) 43′ × 35′. Church of St. Mary, Kraków, Poland.

Late Gothic International

Virgin, who sinks down in death. One of them supports her; another, just above her, wrings his hands in grief; others are posed in attitudes of woe and psychic shock. The sculptor strives for minute realism in every detail. At the same time, he enwraps the figures in an almost abstract pattern of restless, twisting, curving swaths of drapery, which, by their broken and writhing lines, unite the whole tableau in a vision of agitated emotion. The massing of sharp, broken, and pierced forms, which dart flamelike through the composition—at once unifying and animating it—recalls the design principles of Late Gothic Flamboyant architecture (FIG. 13-41). Indeed, in the Kraków altarpiece, sculpture and architecture are amalgamated, and their

20-24   TILMAN RIEMENSCHNEIDER, *The Assumption of the Virgin,* center panel of the *Creglingen Altarpiece, c.* 1495–1499. Carved lindenwood, 6'1" wide. Parish church, Creglingen, Germany.

union is enhanced by painting and gilding. The distinction of the different media, familiar in Italian Renaissance art and furthered by it, is as yet unknown to this Late Gothic artist, even though, like the Italian artist, his eye focuses ever more sharply on natural appearance.

In the work of TILMAN RIEMENSCHNEIDER (c. 1460–1531), we find scarcely a trace of the Italian Renaissance. The canopy of Tilman's *Creglingen Altarpiece* (FIG. **20-24**) is an intricate weaving of Flamboyant Gothic forms, and the endless and restless line is communicated to the draperies of the figures. The whole design is thus in motion and complication, and no element functions without the rest. The draperies float and flow around bodies lost within them, serving not as descriptions but as design elements that tie the figures to each other and to the framework. The spirituality of the figures, immaterial and weightless as they appear, is heightened by a look of psychic strain, a facial expression common to Tilman's figures and consonant with the age of troubles that is coming. They brood in pensive melancholy, their brows often furrowed in anxiety. A favorite theme in Late Gothic German sculpture was the *Schmerzensmann* (Man of Sorrows); for Tilman, all his actors were men of sorrow—weary, grave, and unsmiling.

The ultimate masterpiece of Late Gothic art in Spain is a large, resplendent retable (detail, FIG. **20-25**) the work of the sculptor GIL DE SILOÉ (active 1485–1501), erected over the high altar of the Cartuja (Carthusian monastery) of Miraflores near Burgos. The sculptor's origins are still a mystery; the inscriptions of his name in documents suggest he might have come from Antwerp or from Orléans in France. His style shows mingled Flemish and north German influence, but the transcendent originality of his art is owed solely to his genius as one of the greatest sculptors of the age. The iconography of the retable celebrates the mystery of the Eucharist, the Lord's Supper; its circular compartments symbolize the holy wafer of the Communion. The crucified Christ, the centerpiece of the retable, is encircled by a great halo of angels; the arms of the Cross are supported by God the Father and by the personified Holy Spirit. Mary, the mother of Jesus, and John, the Beloved Disciple, stand at the foot of the Cross; above it perches the pelican, symbol of self-sacrifice. The body of the crucified Christ, rising out of the profusion of ministering angels, is a realistically rendered icon of supreme anguish, the head expressing the pain, sorrow, and resignation of the Redeemer, who by his atonement for the sins of humanity, conquers Death.

This great work created at the end of the fifteenth century is the consummate embodiment of medieval spirituality, presenting its principal mystery with a humanistic naturalism that looks forward to a new age. The supernatural and ineffable God, Second Person of the Holy Trinity, is now definitively personified as the Man of Sorrows, the very image of suffering humanity in this world.

20-25 GIL DE SILOÉ, *Christ Crucified,* center detail of painted and gilded wooden altarpiece, Carthusian Monastery, Miraflores, Spain, 1496–1499.

Graphic Art

A new age opens in the fifteenth century with a sudden technological advance that will shape human experience henceforth; the German invention of printing with movable type. Printing had been known in China centuries before, but had never been developed, as it would be in Europe, into a revolution in written communication, in the generation and management of information. Printing provided new and challenging media for the artist, the earliest form being the *woodblock* or *woodcut* print. A block of wood, sawed along the grain, is covered with a white ground upon which a design is drawn in ink. Using a gouging instrument, the artist, following the inked lines, cuts a map of hollows and ridges; the ridges are inked and carry the design, the hollows remain dry of ink and don't print. When paper is pressed upon the inked relief, it receives the reversed impression of the design. Woodblock prints were made before movable type printing was developed; but when the requirements of book illustration were to be met on a grand scale, the trick was to bring the woodcut picture onto the same page as the letterpress.

This was efficiently achieved in the illustrations (over 650 of them!) for the so-called *Nuremberg Chronicle,* a history of the world, produced in the shop of the Nuremberg artist MICHEL WOLGEMUT (1434–1519). The page illustrated (FIG. **20-26**) represents Tarvisium, a town in the extreme northeast of Italy (modern Tarvisio), as it was in the "fourth age of the world" (the Latin inscription at top). The blunt, simple lines of the woodcut technique give a detailed

20-26 MICHEL WOLGEMUT AND SHOP, "Tarvisium," page from the so-called *Nuremberg Chronicle,* 1493. Printed by Anton Koberger.

perspective of Tarvisium, its harbor and shipping, its walls and towers, its churches and municipal buildings, the baronial castle on the hill. How faithful to the look of the actual city is its depiction here or how much was the work of the artist's imagination we do not know. But the work is a monument to a new craft, which will expand in possibility with the art of the printed book.

The woodcut medium had hardly matured when the technique of *engraving* (inscribing on a hard surface) wood or metal, begun in the 1430s and well-developed by 1450, proved a much more flexible technique, and, in the second half of the century, began to replace the woodcut, both for making book illustrations and for widely popular single prints. The reverse of the woodcut technique, which produces *relievo* (relief), metal engraving produces an *intaglio* (incised) surface for printing, the incised lines (hollows) of the design taking the ink rather than the ridges.

MARTIN SCHONGAUER (*c.* 1450–1491) was the most skilled and subtle northern master of metal engraving. His

St. Anthony Tormented by Demons (FIG. **20-27**) shows both the versatility of the medium and the artist's mastery of it. Although better known for his gentle Madonnas in a style based on that of Rogier van der Weyden, here Schongauer displays almost the same taste for the diabolical as Hieronymus Bosch; his stoic saint is caught in a revolving thornbush of spiky demons, who claw and tear at him furiously. With unsurpassed skill and subtlety, the artist makes marvelous distinctions of tonal values and textures—from smooth skin to rough cloth, from the furry and feathery to the hairy and scaly. The method of describing forms with hatching that follows the forms, probably developed by Schongauer, became standard with German graphic artists. The Italians preferred parallel hatching (compare Antonio Pollaiuolo's engraving, FIG. 21-53) and rarely adopted this method, which, in keeping with the general northern approach to art, tends to describe the surfaces of things rather than their underlying structures.

The art of the north and of Spain in the fifteenth century was sponsored by the Burgundian dukes and the Flemish merchant/bankers, as Italian art at the same time

20-27 MARTIN SCHONGAUER, *St. Anthony Tormented by the Demons,* *c.* 1480–1490. Engraving, approx. 13″ × 11″. Metropolitan Museum of Art, New York (Rogers Fund, 1920).

was sponsored by the House of Medici and the republic of Florence; we have seen the foundations laid for the leadership of the latter (Chapter 19). Both Flemish and Florentine developments in painting began in the International Style, exemplified by the *Très Riches Heures* (FIG. 20-3) and Gentile da Fabriano's *The Adoration of the Magi* (FIG. 21-22). But then they sharply diverge in style.

Italy and Florence were early touched by the presence of Classical antiquity, the monuments of which remained everywhere visible in the environment. The inspiration of Classical art and of humanist philosophy, derived from Classical learning, moved Italy in a very different direction than that taken by the north—toward the further discovery and assimilation of Classical culture. The north was not yet in possession of the Classical model; there were far fewer artistic or architectural remains of ancient Rome in the northern landscape; they were nowhere near so immediately and compellingly present as they were in Italy. Thus, Gothic principles of design lingered almost a century longer in the north than in Italy, and it would not be until the sixteenth century that the north would receive and interpret the Classical message, as delivered from Italy and in the Italian version. We have seen that fourteenth-century Florence had already identified itself with the ancient Roman Republic, and its humanist philosophers had begun the appropriation of Roman literature. By 1400 we are on the threshold of the Florentine Renaissance, which will prepare Europe for the reception of a new style of thought and art based on the Italian renovation of Classical Antiquity.

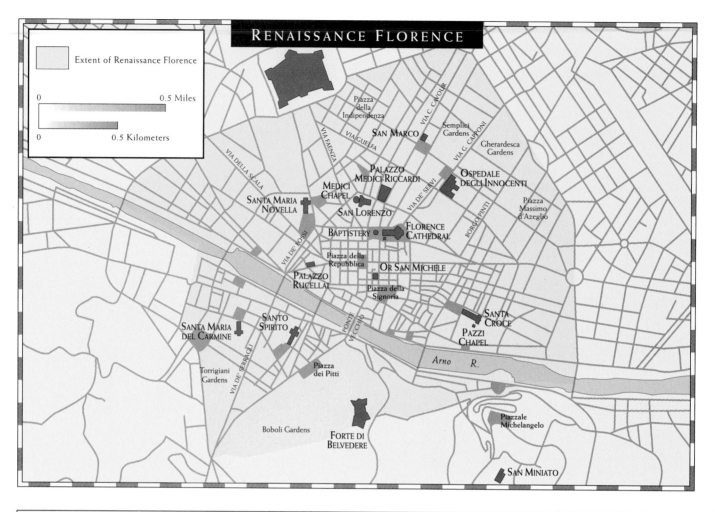

RENAISSANCE FLORENCE

Extent of Renaissance Florence

0   0.5 Miles

0   0.5 Kilometers

Piazza della Indipendenza

SAN MARCO

Semplici Gardens

Gherardesca Gardens

VIA FAENZA

VIA GUELFA

VIA C. CAVOUR

VIA G. CAPPONI

VIA DELLA SCALA

PALAZZO MEDICI-RICCARDI

OSPEDALE DEGLI INNOCENTI

MEDICI CHAPEL

VIA DE' SERVI

BORGO PINTI

Piazza Massimo d'Azeglio

SANTA MARIA NOVELLA

SAN LORENZO

BAPTISTERY

FLORENCE CATHEDRAL

VIA DE' FOSSI

Piazza della Repubblica

OR SAN MICHELE

PALAZZO RUCELLAI

Piazza della Signoria

SANTA CROCE

PAZZI CHAPEL

PONTE VECCHIO

SANTA MARIA DEL CARMINE

SANTO SPIRITO

VIA DE' SERRAGLI

Piazza dei Pitti

Arno R.

Torrigiani Gardens

Boboli Gardens

FORTE DI BELVEDERE

Piazzale Michelangelo

SAN MINIATO

1410	1420	1430	1440

EARLY RENAISSANCE

*Nanni di Banco
Quattro Santi Coronati
Or San Michele, Florence
c. 1408-1414*

*Ghiberti, Gates of Paradise
Baptistery, Florence, 1425-1452*

Masaccio, Holy Trinity, c. 1428

*Donatello
David, c. 1428-1432*

*Brunelleschi, Piazzi Chapel
Santa Croce, Florence
begun c. 1440*

Milanese armies withdraw
from Tuscany, 1402

End of Great Schism in
Catholic Church, 1417

Pisa ruled by
Florence, 1406

Cosimo de' Medici, 1389-1464

House of Medici established
early 15th century

Battle of San Romano, 1432

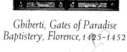

CHAPTER 21

FIFTEENTH-CENTURY ITALIAN ART: THE EARLY RENAISSANCE

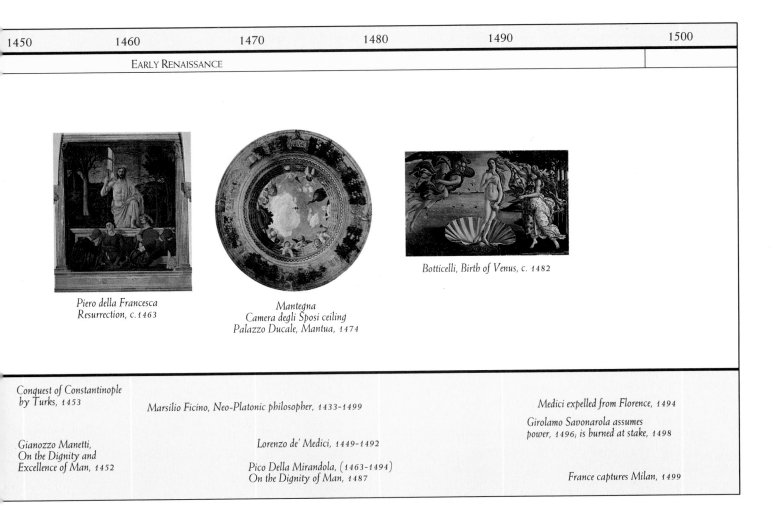

1450	1460	1470	1480	1490	1500

EARLY RENAISSANCE

Piero della Francesca
Resurrection, c. 1463

Mantegna
Camera degli Sposi ceiling
Palazzo Ducale, Mantua, 1474

Botticelli, Birth of Venus, c. 1482

Conquest of Constantinople
by Turks, 1453

Marsilio Ficino, Neo-Platonic philosopher, 1433-1499

Medici expelled from Florence, 1494

Girolamo Savonarola assumes
power, 1496; is burned at stake, 1498

Gianozzo Manetti,
On the Dignity and
Excellence of Man, 1452

Lorenzo de' Medici, 1449-1492

Pico Della Mirandola, (1463-1494)
On the Dignity of Man, 1487

France captures Milan, 1499

Florence took cultural command of Italy early in the fifteenth century, inaugurating the Renaissance and establishing itself as the intellectual and artistic capital of southern Europe—a position of dominance it was to retain until the end of the century. The power and splendor of Florence had been building for many years; the fifteenth century marked its perfection. Like the Athenians after the repulse of the Persians, the citizens of Florence (who felt a historical affinity with the Athenians) responded with conscious pride to the repulse of the dukes of Milan, who had attempted the conquest of Tuscany. The Florentines also developed a culture that was stimulated and supported by a vast accumulation of wealth, a situation much like that in Periclean Athens, except that in Athens it was the city-state, not private individuals, that commissioned the major buildings, paintings, and statues of the Classical age. In Florence a few illustrious Florentine families controlled the wealth and became the leading patrons of the Italian Renaissance.

The Medici, bankers to all Europe, became such lavish patrons of art and learning that, to this day, the name "Medici" means a generous patron of the fine arts. For centuries, the history of Florence is the history of the House of Medici. Early in the fifteenth century Giovanni de' Medici had established the family fortune. His son Cosimo secured the admiration and loyalty of the people of Florence against the noble and privileged. With this security, the Medici gradually became the discreet dictators of the Florentine republic, disguising their absolute power behind a mask of affable benevolence. Scarcely a great architect, painter, sculptor, philosopher, or Humanist scholar was unknown to the Medici. Cosimo began the first public library since the ancient world, and historians estimate that in some 30 years he and his descendants expended the equivalent of almost $20 million for manuscripts and books; such was the financial power behind the establishment of Humanism in the Renaissance. Careful businessmen that they were, the Medici were not sentimental about their endowment of art and scholarship. Cosimo declared that his good works were "not only for the honor of God but . . . likewise for [his] own remembrance." Yet the astute businessman and politician had a sincere love of learning, reading Plato in his old age and writing to his tutor, the Neo-Platonic philosopher Marsilio Ficino, "I desire nothing so much as to know the best road to happiness."

Cosimo is the very model of the cultivated, Humanist grandee. His grandson, Lorenzo, called "the Magnificent," achieved an even greater reputation for munificence than his grandfather, as his name suggests. A talented poet himself, Lorenzo gathered about him a galaxy of artists and gifted men in all fields, extending the library Cosimo had begun, revitalizing his academy for the instruction of artists, establishing the Platonic Academy of Philosophy, and lavishing funds (often the city's own) on splendid buildings, festivals, and pageants. If his prime motive was to retain the affection of the people and, thus, the power of the House of Medici, he nevertheless made Florence a city of great beauty, the capital of all the newly flourishing arts. His death, in 1492, brought to an end the golden age of Florence, and the years immediately following saw Italy invaded by France, Spain, and the Holy Roman Empire. The Medici were expelled from Florence; the reforming, fanatical Girolamo Savonarola preached repentance in the cathedral of Florence; and the Renaissance moved its light and its artists from Florence to Rome. But one of the most prominent patrons of the Roman Renaissance, Pope Leo X, benefactor of Raphael and Michelangelo, was himself a Medici, the son of Lorenzo the Magnificent. Never in history was a family so intimately associated with a great cultural revolution. We may safely say that the Medici subsidized and endowed the Renaissance.

THE FIRST HALF OF THE FIFTEENTH CENTURY

Sculpture

GHIBERTI AND BRUNELLESCHI   The spirit of the Medici and of the Renaissance was competitive and desirous of fame. But even before Medici rule, civic competitiveness and pride had motivated the adornment of Florence. The history of the Early Renaissance in art begins with an account of a competition for a design for the east doors of the baptistery of Florence (FIG. 12-20). ANDREA PISANO (c. 1270–1348), unrelated to the thirteenth-century Italian sculptors Nicola and Giovanni, had designed the south doors of the same structure between 1330 and 1335. LORENZO GHIBERTI (1378–1455), the sculptor who won the competition, describes his victory—repeatedly—in terms that reflect the egoism and the "cult of fame" characteristic of the period and of Renaissance artists in general:

> To me was conceded the palm of the victory by all the experts and by all . . . who had competed with me. To me the honor was conceded universally and with no exception. To all it seemed that I had at that time surpassed the others without exception, as was recognized by a great council and an investigation of learned men . . . highly skilled from the painters and sculptors of gold, silver, and marble. There were thirty-four judges from the city and the other surrounding countries. The testimonial of the victory was given in my favor by all. . . . It was granted to me and determined that I should make the bronze door for this church.*

This passage also indicates the esteem and importance now attached to art, with leading men of a city bestowing eagerly sought-for commissions, and great new programs of private and public works being undertaken widely.

*In E. G. Holt, ed., *Literary Sources of Art History* (Princeton, NJ: Princeton University Press, 1947), pp. 87–88.

21-1   FILIPPO BRUNELLESCHI, *Sacrifice of Isaac*, competition panel for the east doors of the baptistery of Florence, 1401–1402. Gilded bronze relief, 21″ × 17″. Museo Nazionale del Bargello, Florence.

21-2   LORENZO GHIBERTI, *Sacrifice of Isaac*, competition panel for the east doors of the baptistery of Florence, 1401–1402. Gilded bronze relief, 21″ × 17″. Museo Nazionale del Bargello, Florence.

The contestants seeking to design the doors were asked to represent the assigned subject, the sacrifice of Isaac, utilizing, it seems, the same cast of characters, and setting the composition within the same French Gothic quatrefoil frames that had been used almost three generations earlier by Andrea Pisano for the south doors of the baptistery. Only the panels by the two finalists, FILIPPO BRUNELLESCHI (1377–1446) and Ghiberti, have survived. Brunelleschi's panel (FIG. 21-1) shows a sturdy and vigorous interpretation of the theme, with something of the emotional agitation of the tradition of Giovanni Pisano (FIG. 19-3). Abraham seems suddenly to have summoned the dreadful courage needed to kill his son at God's command; he lunges forward, draperies flying, exposing Isaac's throat to the knife with desperate violence. Matching Abraham's energy, the saving angel darts in from the left, arresting the stroke just in time. Brunelleschi's figures are carefully observed and display elements of a new realism. Yet his composition is perhaps overly busy, and the figures of the two servants and the donkey are not subordinated sufficiently to the main action.

We can make this criticism more firmly when we compare Brunelleschi's panel to Ghiberti's (FIG. 21-2). In the latter, vigor and strength of statement are subordinated to grace and smoothness; little of the awfulness of the subject appears. Abraham sways elegantly in the familiar Gothic **S**-curve and seems to feign a deadly thrust rather than aim it. The figure of Isaac, beautifully posed and rendered, recalls

Greco-Roman statuary and could be regarded as the first really classicizing nude since antiquity. (Compare, for example, the torsion of Isaac's body and the dramatic turn of his head with those of the Hellenistic Greek statue of a Gaul [FIG. 5-91] thrusting a sword into his own chest). Unlike his medieval predecessors, the Early Renaissance sculptor reveals a genuine appreciation of the beauty of the nude male form and a deep interest in the muscular and skeletal structure that makes the human body move. Ghiberti's emulation of antique models may even be seen in the altar on which Isaac kneels; it is decorated with acanthus scrolls of a type that commonly adorned the friezes of Roman temples in Italy and throughout the former Roman Empire (see for example, FIG. 7-31).

Ghiberti was trained as both a goldsmith and a painter, and his skilled treatment of the fluent surfaces, with their sharply and accurately incised detail, evidences his goldsmith's craft. As a painter, he shares the painter's interest in spatial illusion. The rocky landscape seems to emerge from the blank panel toward us, as does the strongly foreshortened angel. These pictorial effects, sometimes thought alien to sculpture, are more developed in Ghiberti's later work. The execution of a second pair of doors for the baptistery (FIG. 21-8) testifies to his extraordinary skill in harmonizing the effects peculiar to sculpture and painting. Here, however, within the limits of the awkward shape of the *Isaac* panel, Ghiberti achieves a composition that is perhaps less daring than Brunelleschi's but more cohesive and unified, and the jury's choice probably was fortunate for the course of art despite accusations of collusion by Brunelleschi's biographer, Manetti. One result of the decision was, apparently, that it helped Brunelleschi to resolve his indecision about his proper calling. Subordinating sculpture to a less important role, he became the first great architect of the Renaissance. As for Ghiberti, his conservative style would be modified greatly by the discoveries of his contemporaries, and their influence on him would be visible in the set of doors he designed later for the east entrance to the baptistery.

NANNI DI BANCO   The competition for the new doors of the Florentine baptistery was sponsored by the city's wool finishers guild, and the powerful and wealthy guilds of early fifteenth-century Florence (see Chapter 19) were responsible too for the adornment of the medieval church of Or San Michele a dozen years later. Threatened by invasion by the Milanese, the citizens of Florence responded with an outburst of civic pride that manifested itself in important commissions of works of art for public display. In the case of Or San Michele, the Florentine guilds commissioned the leading sculptors of the city to create marble statues for niches in the exterior walls of the church. Each guild was represented by its patron saint; common pride in the Florentine republic mixed with a healthy competitive spirit.

NANNI DI BANCO (c. 1380–1421) was chosen to create four life-size marble statues of the martyred patron saints of the Florentine guild of sculptors, architects, and masons: four Christian sculptors who defied an imperial order to make a statue of a pagan deity and were killed for placing their Christian faith above all else. These saints were perfect role models for contemporary Florentines who were resolved to stand fast in the face of the threat from Milan. Nanni's group of the *Quattro Santi Coronati*, or *Four Crowned Saints* (FIG. **21-3**) is also an early near-solution to the Renaissance problem of integrating figures and space on a monumental scale. With these figures, we are well on the way to the great solutions of Masaccio and of the masters of the High Renaissance. The emergence of sculpture from the architectural matrix, a process that began in such works as the thirteenth-century statues of the west front of Reims Cathedral (FIG. 13-34), is almost complete in Nanni's figures, which stand in a niche that is *in* but confers some separation *from* the architecture. This spatial recess permits a new and dramatic possibility for the interrelationship of the figures. By placing them in a semicircle within their deep niche and relating them to one another by their postures and gestures, as well as by the arrangement of draperies, Nanni has achieved a wonderfully unified spatial composition. The persisting dependence on the architecture may be seen in the abutment of the two forward figures and the enframement of the niche, and in the position of the two recessed figures, each in front of an engaged half-column. Nevertheless, these unyielding figures, whose bearing

21-3   NANNI DI BANCO, *Quattro Santi Coronati, c.* 1408–1414. Marble, figures approx. life size. Or San Michele, Florence.

expresses the discipline necessary to face adversity, are joined in a remarkable psychological unity. While the figure on the right speaks, pointing to his right, the two men opposite listen and the one next to him looks out into space, pondering the meaning of the words. Such reinforcement of the formal unity of a figural group with psychological cross-references will be exploited by later Renaissance artists, particularly Leonardo da Vinci.

In his *Quattro Santi Coronati* Nanni also displays a deep respect for and close study of Roman portrait statues. The emotional intensity of the faces of the two inner saints owes much to the extraordinarily moving portrayals in stone of Roman emperors of the third century A.D. (FIG. 7-76), and the bearded heads of the outer saints reveal a familiarity with second-century A.D. imperial portraiture (FIG. 7-67). Renaissance artists have begun to comprehend what it means to portray individual personalities and physiognomies. Roman models served as inspiration, but the Roman forms have not been copied. Duplication was not the purpose of Nanni and his contemporaries; rather, they strove to interpret or offer commentary on their Classical models in the manner of the Humanist scholars dealing with Classical texts.

DONATELLO   The Humanist, Roman Classicism expressed in the sculpture of Nanni di Bianco was not exclusively of his devising. The whole city of Florence, in its last, fierce war with the Visconti of Milan at the turn of the century, modeled itself on the ancient Roman republic. The Humanist chancellor of Florence, Coluccio Salutati, whose Latin style of writing was widely influential, exhorted his fellow citizens to take as their own the republican ideal of civil and political liberty they believed to be that of Rome and to identify themselves with its spirit. To be Florentines was to be Roman; freedom was the distinguishing virtue of both.

A new realism based on the study of humanity and nature, an idealism found in the study of Classical forms, and a power of individual expression characteristic of genius are the elements that define the art and the personality of the sculptor DONATELLO (c. 1386–1466). In the early years of the century, he carried forward most dramatically the search for innovative forms capable of expressing the new ideas of the Humanistic Early Renaissance. Working side by side, Donatello and Nanni collaborated on sculpture for the cathedral of Florence and the church of Or San Michele. They shared the Humanistic enthusiasm for Roman virtue and form; their innovations in style, expressive of a new age, are parallel. Donatello's greatness lies in an extraordinary versatility and depth that led him through a spectrum of themes fundamental to human experience and through stylistic variations that express these themes with unprecedented profundity and force.

A principal characteristic of greatness is authority. Great artists produce work that their contemporaries and posterity accept as authoritative; their work becomes a criterion and a touchstone for criticism. Judgments of what is authoritative and "best" will, of course, vary with time and place, but the greatest artists seem to survive this relativity of judgment, apparently because they reveal something deeply and permanently true about human nature and broadly applicable to human experience. Shakespeare, for example, seems miraculously familiar with almost the whole world of human nature. Similarly, Donatello is at ease not only with the real, the ideal, and the spiritual, but with such diverse human forms and conditions as childhood, the idealized human nude, practical men of the world, military despots, holy men, derelict prelates, and ascetic old age. Others who follow Donatello in the school of Florence may specialize in one or two of these human types or moods, but none commands them so completely and convincingly. In the early fifteenth century, Donatello defined and claimed as his province the whole terrain of naturalistic and Humanistic art.

Early in his career, he took the first fundamental and necessary step toward the depiction of motion in the human figure—recognition of the principle of contrapposto. His *St. Mark* (FIG. **21-4**), commissioned for Or San Michele in Florence by the guild of linen drapers (fittingly, as we shall see), was completed in 1413. With it Donatello

21-4   DONATELLO, *St. Mark*, 1411–1413. Marble, approx. 7′ 9″ high. Or San Michele, Florence.

closed a millennium of medieval art and turned a historical corner into a new era. We have examined the importance of weight shift in the ancient world, when Greek sculptors, in works like the *Kritios Boy* (FIG. 5-37) and the *Doryphoros* (FIG. 5-42), grasped the essential principle that the human body is not rigid, but a flexible structure that moves by continuously shifting the weight from one supporting leg to the other with the main masses of the body moving in consonance. This concept is once again fully comprehended by the Florentine sculptor.

As the body now "moves," its drapery "moves" with it, hanging and folding naturally from and around bodily points of support, so that we sense the figure as a draped nude, not simply as an integrated column with arbitrarily incised drapery. This is what separates Donatello's *St. Mark* from all medieval portal statuary. All at once, with the same abruptness with which it appeared in ancient Greece in Early Classical art, the crucial principle of weight shift— both of the body *and* of the garment that conceals the bodily parts—has been rediscovered. Donatello's *St. Mark* is the first Renaissance figure in which the voluminous drapery (the pride of the Florentine guild that paid for the statue) does not conceal, but rather accentuates, the movement of the arms, legs, shoulders, and hips. This development further contributes to the independence of the figure from its architectural setting. We feel that Donatello's saint can and is about to move out of the deep niche in which he stands, as the stirring limbs, the shifting weight, and the mobile drapery suggest. It is easy to imagine the figure as freestanding, unframed by architecture, without loss of any of its basic qualities.

In his *St. George* (FIG. **21-5**), also designed for Or San Michele (between 1415 and 1417), Donatello provides an image of the proud idealism of youth. The armored soldier-saint, patron of the guild of armorers and swordmakers (who commissioned Donatello to carve the statue), stands with bold firmness—legs set apart, feet strongly planted, the torso slightly twisting so that the left shoulder and arm advance with a subtle gesture of haughty and challenging readiness. The figure once wore a helmet and in his right hand brandished a sword that projected outward from the niche into the street below. St. George's head is erect and turned slightly to the left; beneath the furrowed brows, the noble features of the dragon slayer are intent, concentrated, yet composed in the realization of his power, intelligence, and resolution. In its regal poise and tense anticipation, the figure, like the *St. Mark*, contrasts sharply with the facade statues of medieval churches, which, consistent with the spiritual values of the Middle Ages, seem removed from the world and unaware of their surroundings. In the *St. George* we see once again the reassertion of individual personality that is so characteristic of the Early Renaissance in Italy.

Between 1416 and 1435, Donatello carved five statues for niches on the campanile of Florence Cathedral—a project that, like the figures for Or San Michele, had originat-

ed in the preceding century. Unlike the Or San Michele figures, however, which were installed only slightly above eye level, those for the campanile were placed in niches at least 30 feet above the ground. At that distance, delicate descriptive details (hair, garments, and features), no longer can be recognized readily and become meaningless. Massive folds that can be read from afar and a much broader, summary treatment of facial and anatomical features are required for the campanile figures and are used effectively by Donatello. In addition, he takes into account the elevated position of his figures and, with subtly calculated distortions, creates images that are at once realistic and dramatic when seen from below (see Introduction, FIG. 9).

21-5   DONATELLO, *St. George*, 1415–1417, from Or San Michele. Marble (has been replaced by a bronze copy), approx. 6' 10" high. Museo Nazionale del Bargello, Florence.

7-5, 7-41, and 7-76). Their faces are bony, lined, and taut; each is strongly individualized. The *Zuccone* is also bald, a departure from the conventional representation of the prophets but in keeping with many Roman portrait heads. Donatello's prophet is dressed in an awkwardly draped and crumpled togalike garment with deeply undercut folds—a far cry from the majestic prophets of medieval portals. The head discloses an appalling personality—full of crude power, even violence. The deep-set eyes glare under furrowed brows, nostrils flaring, the broad mouth agape, as if the prophet were in the very presence of disasters that would call forth his declamation.

In a bronze relief, the *Feast of Herod* (FIG. **21-7**), on the baptismal font in the baptistery at Siena, Donatello carries his talent for characterization of single figures to the broader field of dramatic groups. Salome (to the right), still dances (no doubt because she has been closely modeled on a series of dancing maenad reliefs very popular in Roman times), even though she already has delivered the severed head of John the Baptist, which the kneeling executioner offers to King Herod. The other figures recoil in horror into two groups: at the right, one man covers his face with his hand; at the left, Herod and two terrified children shrink back in dismay. The psychic explosion that has taken place drives the human elements apart, leaving a gap across which the emotional electricity crackles. This masterful stagecraft obscures the fact that on the stage itself another drama is being played out—the advent of rationalized perspective space, long prepared for in the proto-Renaissance of Late Gothic Italy and recognized by Donatello and his

21-6   DONATELLO, prophet figure (*Zuccone*), 1423–1425, from the campanile of Florence Cathedral. Marble, approx. 6′ 5″ high. Museo dell'Opera del Duomo, Florence.

The most striking of the five figures (FIG. **21-6**) is that of a prophet, generally known by the nickname *Zuccone*, or "pumpkin-head." This figure shows Donatello's peculiar power for characterization at its most original. All of his prophets are represented with a harsh, direct realism reminiscent of some ancient Roman portraits (compare FIGS.

21-7   DONATELLO, *Feast of Herod*, from the baptismal font, *c.* 1425. Gilded bronze relief, approx. 23″ × 23″. Cathedral, Siena.

generation as a means of intensifying the reality of the action and the characterization of the actors.

Fourteenth-century Italian artists, like Duccio and the Lorenzetti brothers, used several devices to give the effect of distance, but with the invention of "true" linear perspective (a discovery generally attributed to Brunelleschi), Early Renaissance artists were given a way to make the illusion of distance mathematical and certain. In effect, they had come to understand the picture plane as a transparent window through which the observer looks *into* the constructed, pictorial world. From the observer's fixed standpoint, all orthogonals meet in a single point on the horizon (a hori-

zontal line that corresponds to the viewer's eye level), and all objects are unified within a single space system—the perspective. This discovery was of enormous importance, for it made possible what has been called the "rationalization of sight." It brought all of our random and infinitely various visual sensations under a simple rule that can be expressed mathematically.

Indeed, the discovery of perspective by the artists of the Renaissance (or, more properly, the *rediscovery* of the principles already known to the ancient Greeks and Romans) reflects the emergence of science itself, which is, put simply, the mathematical ordering of our observations of the

21-8   LORENZO GHIBERTI, east doors ("Gates of Paradise"), 1425–1452. Gilded bronze relief, approx. 17' high. Baptistery, Florence.

physical world. The artists of the Renaissance were often mathematicians, and one modern mathematician asserts that the most creative work in mathematics in the fifteenth century was done by artists. The experimental spirit that had animated many Franciscans, like Roger Bacon, now came firmly to earth; indeed, Bacon's essays on optics had considerable influence on Renaissance theorists like Leon Battista Alberti, an influential architect, mathematician, Humanist, painter, and writer on art. The position of the observer of a picture, who looks "through" it into the painted "world," is precisely that of any scientific observer fixing his gaze on the carefully placed or located datum of his research. Of course, the Early Renaissance artist was not primarily a scientist; he simply found perspective a wonderful way to order his composition and to clarify it. Nonetheless, we cannot doubt that perspective, with its new mathematical authority and certitude, conferred a kind of esthetic legitimacy on painting by making the picture *measurable* and exact. According to Plato, "the excellence of beauty of every work of art is due to the observance of measure." This dictum certainly is expressed in the art of Greece, and in the Renaissance, when Plato was discovered anew and read eagerly, artists once again exalted the principle of measure as the foundation of the beautiful in the fine arts. The projection of measured shapes on flat surfaces now influenced the character of painting and made possible scale drawings, maps, charts, graphs, and diagrams—those means of exact representation without which modern science and technology would be impossible. Mathematical truth and formal beauty became conjoined in the minds of Renaissance artists. In his *Feast of Herod* relief panel (FIG. 21-7), Donatello, using the device of pictorial perspective, opens the space of the action well into the distance, showing two arched courtyards and groups of attendants in the background. This penetration of the panel surface by spatial illusion replaces the flat grounds and backdrop areas of the medieval past. Ancient Roman illusionism (FIG. 7-19) has returned.

It is worth comparing Donatello's Siena panel with a panel from Ghiberti's famous east doors (FIG. **21-8**) of the baptistery of Florence Cathedral, which were later declared by Michelangelo to be "so fine that they might fittingly stand as the Gates of Paradise." The east doors (1425–1452) were composed differently from Ghiberti's earlier north doors. Three sets of doors provide access to the baptistery (FIG. 12-20). The first set was made by Andrea Pisano for the east doorway (1330–1335), which faces the cathedral and is the most important entrance. This set of doors was moved to the south doorway to make way for Ghiberti's first pair of doors (1403–1424), which, in turn, was moved to the north doorway so that Ghiberti's second pair of doors, the "Gates of Paradise," could be placed in the east doorway. After 1425, Ghiberti abandoned the quatrefoil pattern of the earlier doors and divided the space into ten square panels, each containing a relief set in plain mold-

ings. When gilded, the glittering movement of the reliefs created an effect of great splendor and elegance.

The individual panels of Ghiberti's doors, such as *Isaac and His Sons* (FIG. **21-9**), clearly recall painting in their depiction of space as well as in their treatment of the narrative. Some exemplify more fully than painting many of the principles Alberti formulated in his 1435 treatise *On Painting*. In his relief, Ghiberti creates the illusion of space partly by pictorial perspective and partly by sculptural means. Buildings are represented according to the painter's one-point perspective construction, but the figures (in the lower section of the relief, which actually projects slightly toward the viewer) appear almost in the full round, some of their heads standing completely free. As the eye progresses upward, the relief increasingly becomes flatter until the architecture in the background is represented by barely raised lines, creating a sort of "sculptor's aerial perspective" in which forms are less distinct the deeper they are in space. Ghiberti described the work as follows:

I strove to imitate nature as closely as I could, and with all the perspective I could produce [to have] excellent compositions rich with many figures. In some scenes I placed about a hundred figures, in some less, and in some more. I executed that work with the greatest diligence and the greatest love. There were ten stories, all [sunk] in frames because the eye from a distance measures and interprets the scenes in such a way that they appear round. The scenes are in the lowest relief and the figures are seen in the planes; those that are near appear large, those in the

21-9 LORENZO GHIBERTI, *Isaac and His Sons* (detail of FIG. 21-8). Approx. 31½" × 31½".

distance small, as they do in reality. . . . Executed with the greatest study and perseverance, of all my work it is the most remarkable I have done and it was finished with skill, correct proportions, and understanding.*

Thus, an echo of the ancient and medieval past is harmonized by the new science: "proportion" and "skill" are perfected by "understanding." Ghiberti has achieved a greater sense of depth than has ever before been possible in a relief. His principal figures, however, do not occupy the architectural space he has created for them; rather, they are arranged along a parallel plane in front of the grandiose architecture. (According to Alberti, in his *De re aedificatoria,* the grandeur of the architecture reflects the dignity of events shown in the foreground.) Ghiberti's figure style mixes a Gothic patterning of rhythmic line, Classical poses and motifs, and a new realism in characterization, movement, and surface detail. The medieval narrative method of arranging several episodes within a frame persists. In *Isaac and His Sons* (FIG. 21-9), the group of women in the left foreground attends the birth of Esau and Jacob in the left background; Isaac sends Esau and his hunting dogs on his mission in the central foreground; and, in the right foreground, Isaac blesses the kneeling Jacob as Rebecca looks on (Genesis 25–27). Yet the groups are so subtly placed that no crowding or confusion is apparent. The figures, in varying degrees of projection, gracefully twist and turn, appearing to occupy and move through a convincing stage space, which is deepened by showing some figures from behind. The Classicism derives from Ghiberti's close study of ancient art. From his biography, we know that he admired and collected Classical sculpture, bronzes, and coins, and their influence is seen throughout the panel, particularly in the figure of Rebecca, which is based on a popular Greco-Roman statuary type. The beginning of the practice of collecting Classical art in the fifteenth century had much to do with the appearance of Classicism in the Humanistic art of the Renaissance.

For a time, Donatello forgot his earlier realism under the spell of Classical Rome, the ruins and antiquities of which he studied at some length. His bronze statue of *David* (FIG. **21-10**), designed between about 1428 and 1432 for the Medici family in Florence, is the first freestanding nude statue since ancient times, and here Donatello shows himself once more to be an innovator. The nude, as such, proscribed in the Christian Middle Ages as both indecent and idolatrous, had been shown only rarely—and then only in biblical or moralizing contexts, like the story of Adam and Eve or descriptions of sinners in Hell. Donatello reinvented the Classical nude, even though, in this case, the subject is not a pagan god, hero, or athlete, but the biblical David, the young slayer of Goliath and the Old Testament ancestor and antitype of Christ, as well as symbol of the Florentine love of liberty. The statue displays Classical contrapposto—a bal-

ance of opposing axes, of tension and relaxation—and has the proportions and sensuous beauty of Praxitelean gods (FIG. 5-70), qualities unknown to medieval figures. The sculptor's admiration of the nude form is also seen in the glance of the youthful, still adolescent hero, which is not directed primarily toward the severed head of Goliath between his feet, but toward his own graceful, sinuous body, as though, in consequence of his heroic deed, he is becoming conscious for the first time of its beauty, its vitality, and its strength. This self-awareness, this discovery of self, is a dominant theme in Renaissance art.

In 1443, Donatello left Florence for northern Italy to accept a rewarding commission from the republic of Venice

21-10   DONATELLO, *David, c.* 1428–1432. Bronze, 62¼" high. Museo Nazionale del Bargello, Florence.

*In Holt, *Literary Sources of Art History,* pp. 90–91.

21-11   DONATELLO, *Gattamelata* (equestrian statue of Erasmo da Narni), *c.* 1445–1450. Bronze, approx. 11′ × 13′. Piazza del Santo, Padua.

to make a commemorative monument in honor of the recently deceased Venetian *condottiere* Erasmo da Narni, nicknamed Gattamelata ("honeyed cat," a wordplay on the name of his mother, Melania Gattelli). Donatello was asked to portray Gattamelata on horseback in a statue (FIG. **21-11**) to be erected in the square of Sant'Antonio in Padua. Although equestrian statues had occasionally been set up in Italy in the late Middle Ages, Donatello's *Gattamelata* is the first to rival the grandeur of the mounted portraits of antiquity, such as that of Marcus Aurelius (FIG. 7-66), which the artist must have seen in Rome. The reference to antiquity was not lost on Donatello's contemporaries, one of whom described *Gattamelata* as "sitting there with great magnificence like a triumphant Caesar." The figure stands high on a lofty, elliptical base to set it apart from its surroundings and becomes almost a celebration of the liberation of sculpture from architecture. Massive and majestic, the great horse bears the armored general easily for, unlike Marcus Aurelius, the Venetian commander is not represented as superhuman and over life size, and he dominates his mighty steed by force of character rather than sheer size. Together, man and horse make an overwhelming image of irresistible strength and unlimited power—an impression reinforced visually by the placement of the left forehoof of the horse on an orb, reviving a venerable ancient symbol for hegemony over the earth. The Italian rider, his face set in a mask of dauntless resolution and unshakable will, is the very portrait of the Renaissance individualist: a man of intelligence, courage, and ambition, frequently of humble origin, who, by his own resourcefulness and on his own merits, rises to a commanding position in the world.

Donatello's ten-year period of activity in Padua (he received additional commissions for statues and reliefs for the high altar of the church of Sant'Antonio) made a deep and lasting impression on the artists of the region and contributed materially to the formation of a Renaissance style in northern Italy. After Donatello's return to Florence in 1453, his style changes once more. His last period is marked by an intensely personal kind of expression, in which his earlier realism returns, but with purposeful exaggeration and distortion. He turns away from Classical beauty and grandeur toward a kind of expressionism that seems deliberately calculated to jar the sensibilities; he gives us the ugly, the painful, and the violent.

Donatello's new manner is well exemplified in his *Mary Magdalene* (FIG. **21-12**). The repentant saint in old age, after years of wasting mortification, stands emaciated, hands

21-12   DONATELLO, *Mary Magdalene, c.* 1454–1455. Polychromed and gilded wood, approx. 6′ 2″ high. Baptistery, Florence.

clasped in prayer. The sculptor, in what appears to be a rekindling of medieval piety, here rejects the body as merely the mortal shell of the immortal soul. The beautiful woman has withered, but her soul has been saved by her denial of physical beauty. Donatello's originality, independence, and insight into the meaning of religious experience are asserted here as he reinterprets medieval material in his own terms. But medieval as *Mary Magdalene* might first appear, we realize that this work also was carved by the man who created the sensuous *David*. This figure too is nude, "clothed" only in her own extraordinarily long hair, which still has traces of gold in it, and her body sways gently in a contrapposto stance that is fully in keeping with the new Renaissance spirit. Donatello again is best characterized as we first described him—a man with the vast versatility that distinguishes the great artist from the good artist.

✦Architecture

BRUNELLESCHI   FILIPPO BRUNELLESCHI, Ghiberti's final competitor for the commission to design the doors of the baptistery of Florence in 1401, was (like Ghiberti) trained as a goldsmith, but his ability as a sculptor must have been well known even at the time of the baptistery competition. Although his biographer, Manetti, tells us that Brunelleschi turned to architecture out of disappointment over the loss of the baptistery commission, he continued to work as a sculptor for several years and received commissions for sculpture as late as 1416. In the meantime, however, his interest turned more and more toward architecture, spurred by several trips to Rome (the first in 1402, probably with his friend Donatello), where he too was captivated by the Roman ruins. It may well be in connection with his close study of Roman monuments and his effort to make an accurate record of what he saw that Brunelleschi developed the revolutionary system of geometric, linear perspective that was so eagerly adopted by fifteenth-century artists and that has made him the first acknowledged Renaissance architect.

Brunelleschi's broad knowledge of the principles of Roman construction, combined with an analytical and inventive mind, permitted him to solve an engineering problem that no other fifteenth-century architect could have solved—the design and construction of a dome for the huge crossing of the unfinished cathedral of Florence (FIGS. **21-13** and 13-58). The problem was staggering; the space to be spanned (140 feet) was much too wide to permit construction with the aid of traditional wooden centering. Nor was it possible (because of the plan of the crossing) to support the dome with buttressed walls. Brunelleschi seems to have begun work on the problem about 1417; in 1420, he and Ghiberti jointly were awarded the commission. The latter, however, soon retired from the project and left the field to his associate.

With exceptional ingenuity, Brunelleschi not only discarded traditional building methods and devised new ones, but he also invented much of the machinery that was necessary for the job. Although he might have preferred the hemispheric shape of Roman domes, Brunelleschi raised the center of his dome and designed it around an ogival section, which is inherently more stable, as it reduces the outward thrust around the dome's base. To reduce the weight of the structure to a minimum, he designed a relatively thin double-shell (the first in history) around a skeleton of twenty-four ribs, the eight most important of which are visible on the exterior. Finally, in almost paradoxical fashion, Brunelleschi anchored the structure at the top with a heavy lantern, which was built after his death, but in accordance with his design. This lantern, although it added to the weight of the dome, has the effect of stabilizing the entire structure; without the pressure of its weight, the ribs had a tendency to tilt outward from the center, spreading at the top.

In spite of the fact that Brunelleschi knew of and much admired Roman building techniques, and even though the dome of Florence Cathedral is his most outstanding engineering achievement, his solution to this most critical structural problem was arrived at through what were essentially Gothic building principles. Thus, the dome,

21-13   FILIPPO BRUNELLESCHI, dome of Florence Cathedral, 1420–1436 (view from the east).

21-14   FILIPPO BRUNELLESCHI, facade of the Ospedale degli Innocenti, Piazza della S. Annunziata, Florence, 1419–1424.

which also had to harmonize in formal terms with the century-old building, does not really express Brunelleschi's own architectural style, which is shown for the first time in a project that he began shortly before he accepted the commission of the dome. The basic element of the design of that building, the Ospedale degli Innocenti (Foundling Hospital) in Florence (FIG. **21-14**), is a series of round arches supported by slender columns that carry a flat, horizontal entablature. These arches appear to have been inspired either by the baptistery of Florence Cathedral (FIG. 12-20) or by the church of San Miniato al Monte (FIG. 12-21), both Romanesque buildings. In Brunelleschi's time, the baptistery mistakenly was believed to be a Roman temple, but even if he had known that it was not Roman, Brunelleschi may well have mistaken it for an Early Christian building of the fourth or fifth century, constructed in a style that he associated closely with Classical Roman architecture and that had just as much authority for him. He modified, however, his probable Romanesque models in important ways—for example, by framing the round arches of the last bay at each end of the hospital's facade with pilasters, a venerable Roman motif that Brunelleschi would certainly have encountered often on his visits to Rome in such ancient monuments as the Colosseum (FIG. 7-39). The hospital also expresses quite a different style from that of the Florence baptistery and San Miniato. The stress on horizontals, the clarity of the articulation (the height of each column is the same as the distance between the columns and also equal to the depth of each bay), and the symmetry of the design, combined with the use of Corinthian capitals and fluted pilasters, as well as second-story windows topped by Classically inspired pediments, create an impression of rationality and logic that, in spirit at least, relates the Ospedale degli Innocenti more to the architecture of Imperial Rome than to that of Romanesque Florence.

The same clarity of statement is to be found in San Lorenzo and Santo Spirito, the two basilican churches that Brunelleschi built in Florence. Of the two, the later Santo Spirito shows the architect's mature style (FIGS. **21-15** and **21-16**). Begun around 1436 and completed, with some changes, after Brunelleschi's death, this cruciform building is laid out on the basis of either multiples or segments of the dome-covered crossing square, in a manner reminiscent of Romanesque planning. But this segmentation is not reflected in the nave, which is a continuous, unbroken space in the tradition of Early Christian basilicas. The aisles, subdivided into small squares covered by shallow, saucer-shaped vaults, run all the way around the flat-roofed central space and have the visual effect of compressing the longitudinal design into a centralized one, because the various aspects of the interior resemble each other, no matter where the observer stands. Originally, this effect of centralization would have been even stronger; Brunelleschi had planned to extend the aisles across the front of the nave as well, as shown on the plan (FIG. 21-16, left). Because of the modular basis of the design, adherence to it would have demanded four entrances in the facade, instead of the traditional and symbolic three, a feature that was hotly debated during Brunelleschi's lifetime and that was changed after his death. The appearance of the exterior walls also was changed later, (compare the two plans in FIG. 21-16) when the recesses between the projecting, semicircular chapels were filled in to convert an originally highly plastic wall surface into a flat one.

The major features of the interior (FIG. 21-15), however, are much as Brunelleschi designed them. Compared with those of the Ospedale degli Innocenti, the forms have gained in volume. The moldings project more boldly, and the proportions of the columns more closely approach the Classical ideal. Throughout the building, proportions in a

21-15 FILIPPO BRUNELLESCHI, interior of Santo Spirito, Florence, begun *c.* 1436 (view facing east).

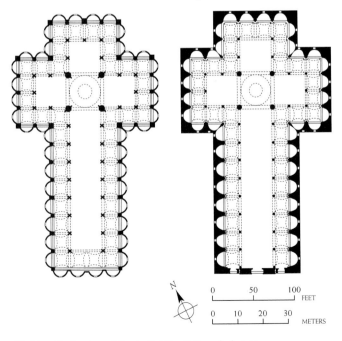

21-16 Early plan of Santo Spirito (*left*) and plan as constructed (*right*).

ratio of 1:2 have been used with great consistency. The nave is twice as high as it is wide; arcade and clerestory are of equal height, which means that the height of the arcade equals the width of the nave; and so on. These basic facts about the building have been delineated for the observer by crisp articulations, so that they can be read like mathematical equations. The cool logic of the design contrasts sharply with the soaring drama and spirituality of the vaults and arcades of the naves of Gothic churches—even those in Italy, like that of Florence Cathedral (FIG. 13-60), whose verticality is restrained in comparison to that of their northern counterparts—and fully expresses the new Renaissance spirit that places its faith in reason rather than in the emotions.

Brunelleschi's evident effort to impart a centralized effect to the interior of Santo Spirito suggests that he was intrigued by the compact and self-contained qualities of earlier central-plan buildings, such as the Pantheon and medieval baptisteries. In the chapel (FIGS. **21-17** to **21-19**) that was the Pazzi family's gift to the church of Santa Croce in Florence, Brunelleschi was able to explore his interest in the central plan in a structure much better suited to such a design than a basilican church. The Pazzi Chapel was begun around 1440 and completed in the 1460s, long after Brunelleschi's death. The exterior (FIG. 21-17) probably does not reflect Brunelleschi's original design; the narthex, admirable as it is, seems to have been added as an afterthought, perhaps by the sculptor-architect GIULIANO DA MAIANO (1432–1490). Behind the narthex stands one of the first independent buildings of the Renaissance to be conceived basically as a central-plan structure. Although the plan (FIG. 21-18) is rectangular, rather than square or round, all emphasis has been placed on the central, dome-covered space. The short, barrel-vault sections that brace the dome on two sides appear to be no more than incidental appendages. Articulations and trim in the interior (FIG. 21-19) are done in gray stone, the so-called *pietra serena* ("serene stone"), which stands out against the white, stuccoed walls and crisply defines the modular relationships of plan and elevation. Medallions with glazed terracotta reliefs representing the Four Evangelists in the dome's pendentives and the Twelve Apostles on the pilaster-framed wall panels provide the tranquil interior with striking color accents. Alberti was to praise the central plan in one of his treatises and instill a taste for it in generations of later architects.

MICHELOZZO   It seems curious that Brunelleschi, the most renowned architect of his time, did not participate in the upsurge of palace-building that Florence experienced in the 1430s and 1440s and that testified to the soundness of the Florentine economy and the affluence and confidence of the city's leading citizens. His efforts in this field were confined to work on the Palazzo di Parte Guelfa and to a rejected model for a new palace that Cosimo de' Medici intended to build. Cosimo evidently felt that Brunelleschi's

21-17 FILIPPO BRUNELLESCHI, west facade of Pazzi Chapel, Santa Croce, Florence, begun *c.* 1440.

21-19 Interior of Pazzi Chapel (view facing northeast).

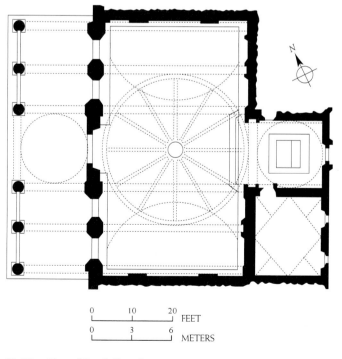

21-18 Plan of Pazzi Chapel.

project was too imposing and ostentatious to be politically wise. Although the Medici were in actuality the rulers of Florence, the city was nominally still a republic, and Cosimo did not want his private residence to resemble the domicile of an emperor or king. Instead, he awarded the commission to MICHELOZZO DI BARTOLOMMEO (1396–1472), a young architect who had been Donatello's collaborator in several sculptural enterprises. Michelozzo's architectural style was influenced deeply by Brunelleschi, and, to a limited extent, the Palazzo Medici-Riccardi (FIG. **21-20**) may reflect Brunelleschian principles.

Later bought by the Riccardi family, who almost doubled the length of the facade in the eighteenth century, the palace, both in its original and extended form, is a simple, massive structure. Heavy rustication on the ground floor accentuates its strength. The building block is divided into stories of decreasing height by long, unbroken stringcourses (horizontal bands), which give it articulation and coherence. The severity of the ground floor is modified in the upper stories by dressed stone, which presents a smoother surface with each successive story, so that the building appears progressively lighter as the eye moves upward. This effect is dramatically reversed by the extremely heavy cornice, which Michelozzo related not to the top

21-20   MICHELOZZO DI BARTOLOMMEO, facade of Palazzo Medici-Riccardi, Florence, begun 1444.

21-21   Interior court of the Palazzo Medici-Riccardi.

story but to the building as a whole. Like the ancient Roman cornices that served as Michelozzo's models (compare, for example, FIGS. 7-35, 7-43, and 7-52), the cornice of the Palazzo Medici-Riccardi is a very effective lid for the structure, clearly and emphatically defining its proportions. Michelozzo may also have been inspired by the many extant examples of Roman rusticated masonry, and there are even Roman precedents for the juxtaposition of rusticated and dressed stone masonry on the same facade (FIG. 7-37). There is, however, nothing precisely comparable to Michelozzo's design in the ancient world; the Palazzo Medici-Riccardi is an excellent example of the simultaneous respect for and independence from the antique that characterizes the Early Renaissance in Italy.

Michelozzo's Palazzo Medici-Riccardi is built around an open, colonnaded court (FIG. **21-21**) that clearly shows its architect's debt to Brunelleschi. The round-arched colonnade, although more massive in its proportions, closely resembles that of the Ospedale degli Innocenti (FIG. 21-14); however, Michelozzo's failure to frame each row of arches with piers and pilasters, as Brunelleschi might have,

causes the structure to look rather weak at the angles. Nevertheless, this *cortile,* or internal court surrounded by an arcade, was the first of its kind and was to have a long line of descendants in Renaissance domestic architecture.

Painting

The three leading innovators of the early fifteenth century were Donatello, Brunelleschi, and the young painter Tommaso Guidi, known as MASACCIO (1401–1428). To understand the almost startling nature of Masaccio's innovations, we should look again at the International Style in painting, which was the dominant style around 1400 and one that persisted well into the fifteenth century. The International Style developed side by side with the grand new style of Masaccio and his followers. GENTILE DA FABRIANO (c. 1370–1427), who was working in Florence at the same time as Masaccio, produced what may be the masterpiece of the International Style, the *Adoration of the Magi* (FIG. **21-22**), the altarpiece of the church of Santa Trinità in Florence. Gentile's patron was Palla Strozzi, the wealthiest Florentine of his day, and the altarpiece, with its elaborate gilded Gothic frame, is a testimony to Strozzi's lavish tastes. So, too, is the painting itself, with its gorgeous surface and sumptuously costumed kings, courtiers, captains, and retainers accompanied by a menagerie of exotic and ornamental animals. All of these elements were portrayed by Gentile in a rainbow of color with much display of gold. The painting presents all the pomp and ceremony of chivalric etiquette in a picture that proclaims the sanctification of aristocracy in the presence of the Madonna and Child. The stylistic apparatus used by Gentile differs only slightly from that used in the century following the

21-22 GENTILE DA FABRIANO, *Adoration of the Magi,* altarpiece from Santa Trinità, Florence, 1423. Tempera on wood, approx. 9′ 11″ × 9′ 3″. Galleria degli Uffizi, Florence.

International Style

junction of Gothic and Sienese painting. Into this traditional framework, however, Gentile inserts striking bits of radical naturalism. Animals are seen from a variety of angles and are foreshortened convincingly, as are tilted human heads and bodies (note the man removing the spurs from the standing magus in the center foreground). On the right side of the predella, Gentile shows the Presentation scene in a "modern" architectural setting (the arcade in the right background looks much like Brunelleschi's Ospedale degli Innocenti, FIG. 21-14.) And on the left side of the predella, he paints what may be the very first nighttime Nativity in which the light source—the radiant Christ child—is introduced into the picture itself. Although dominantly conservative, Gentile shows that he is not oblivious to contemporary experimental trends, and that he is able to blend naturalistic and inventive elements

skillfully and subtly into a traditional composition without sacrificing Late Gothic coloristic splendor.

MASACCIO Masaccio was much less compromising. Although his presumed teacher, MASOLINO DA PANICALE, had worked in the International Style, Masaccio moved suddenly, within the short span of only six years, into wide-open and unexplored territory. No other painter in history is known to have contributed so much to the development of a new style in so short a time as Masaccio, whose creative career was cut short by his death at age twenty-seven. Masaccio is the artistic descendant of Giotto, whose calm, monumental style he revolutionized through a whole new repertoire of representational devices that generations of Renaissance painters would later study and develop. Masaccio also knew and understood the innovations of his

21-23   MASACCIO, *Tribute Money, c.* 1427. Fresco, 8′ 1″ × 19′ 7″. Brancacci Chapel, Santa Maria del Carmine, Florence.

great contemporaries, Donatello and Brunelleschi, and he introduced new possibilities for both form and content.

Masaccio's innovations are seen best in the frescoes he painted in the Brancacci Chapel of Santa Maria del Carmine in Florence. In the *Tribute Money* (FIG. **21-23**), painted shortly before his death, Masaccio groups three episodes. In the center, Christ, surrounded by his disciples, tells Saint Peter that in the mouth of a fish he will find a coin to pay the imperial tax demanded by the collector who stands in the foreground, his back to the spectator. At the left, in the middle distance, Saint Peter struggles to extract the coin from the fish's mouth, while at the right, with a disdainful gesture of great finality, he thrusts the coin into the tax collector's hand. Masaccio's figures recall Giotto's in their simple grandeur, but they stand before us with a psychological and moral self-realization that is entirely new. Masaccio realizes the bulk of the figures not through generalized modeling with a flat, neutral light lacking an identifiable source, as Giotto does, but by means of a light that comes from a specific source outside the picture. This light strikes the figures at an angle, illuminating the parts of the solids that obstruct its path and leaving the rest in deep shadow. This chiaroscuro gives the illusion of deep sculptural relief. Between the extremes of light and dark, the light is a constantly active but fluctuating force, almost a tangible substance independent of the figures. In Giotto's frescoes, light is merely the modeling of a mass; in Masaccio's, light comes to have its own nature, and the masses we see are visible only because of the direction and intensity of the light. We imagine the light as playing over forms—revealing some and concealing others, as the artist directs it. In the creation of a space filled with atmosphere, Masaccio anticipates the achievements of the High Renaissance; few painters between Masaccio and Leonardo da Vinci have so realistically created the illusion of space as a substance of light and air existing between our eyes and what we see.

The individual figures in the *Tribute Money* are solemn and weighty, but they also express bodily structure and function, as do Donatello's statues. We feel bones, muscles, and the pressures and tensions of joints. Each figure conveys a maximum of contained energy. Both the stately stillness of Nanni di Banco's *Quattro Santi Coronati* (FIG. 21-3) as well as the weight-shifting figures of Donatello (FIG. 21-4) are here. The figure of Christ and the two appearances of the tax collector make us understand what the biographer Vasari* meant when he said: "Masaccio made his figures stand upon their feet."

The arrangement of the figures is another important innovation or invention. They no longer appear as a stiff screen in the front planes. Here, they are grouped in circular depth around Christ, and the whole group is shown in a spacious landscape, rather than in the confined stage space of Giotto's frescoes. The foreground space is generated by the group itself, as well as by the architecture on the right, shown in a *one-point perspective* construction in which the location of the *vanishing point*, where all the orthogonals

---

*Giorgio Vasari, a versatile painter and architect, is best known for his *Lives of the Most Eminent Italian Architects, Painters, and Sculptors* (1550), a series of biographies that, although not always reliable, remains one of the most important art-historical sources for the Italian Renaissance.

of the perspective converge, coincides with the head of Christ. The foreground is united with the distance by *aerial perspective,* which employs the diminution in light and the blurring of outlines that come with distance. This device, used by ancient Roman painters, was forgotten during the Middle Ages and rediscovered by Masaccio and his contemporaries, apparently independently. They came to realize that light and air interposed between ourselves and what we see are parts of the visual experience we call "distance." With this knowledge, the world as given to ordinary sight can become for the painter the vast pictorial stage of human action.

In an awkwardly narrow space at the entrance to the Brancacci Chapel, Masaccio painted the *Expulsion of Adam and Eve from Eden* (FIG. **21-24**), another fresco in which the representational innovations of the *Tribute Money* are present: the sharply slanted light from an outside source, creating deep relief by the placement of lights and darks side by side and acting as a strong unifying agent; the structurally correct motion of the figures; their bodily weight and substantial contact with the ground; the hazed, atmospheric background that gives no locale but suggests a space around and beyond the figures. Masaccio's *Expulsion* is one of the supreme masterpieces of Renaissance art and an interpretation of the tragic scene of humanity's fall that is perhaps unsurpassed even by Michelangelo's Sistine Chapel ceiling. Adam's feet, clearly in contact with the ground, mark man's presence on earth, and the cry issuing from Eve's mouth voices the anguish of humanity deprived of God. Adam and Eve do not resist; there is no physical contact with the angel, nor are the figures crowded against the frame. Rather, they stumble on blindly, driven by the will of the angel and their own despair. The composition is starkly simple, its message incomparably eloquent.

In the *Holy Trinity* fresco (FIG. **21-25**) in Santa Maria Novella, the dating of which is still in dispute, Masaccio gives a brilliant demonstration of the organizing value of Brunelleschi's perspective; indeed, this work is so much in the Brunelleschian manner that some historians have suggested that Brunelleschi may have directed Masaccio. The composition is painted on two levels of unequal height. Above, in a coffered, barrel-vaulted chapel reminiscent of a Roman triumphal arch as well as the pilaster-framed bays of Brunelleschi's Ospedale degli Innocenti (FIG. 21-14), the Virgin Mary and Saint John are represented on either side of the crucified Christ, whose arms are supported by God the Father. The Dove of the Holy Spirit rests on Christ's halo. The donors of the painting, husband and wife, are portrayed kneeling just in front of the pilasters that enframe the chapel. Below the altar—a masonry insert in the depicted composition—the artist has painted a tomb containing a skeleton, said to represent Adam. An inscription in Italian painted above the skeleton reminds the spectator that "I was once what you are, and what I am you will become."

21-24   MASACCIO, *Expulsion of Adam and Eve from Eden, c. 1425.* Fresco, 7' × 2' 11". Brancacci Chapel, Santa Maria del Carmine, Florence.

Masaccio places the vanishing point at the center of the masonry altar. With this point at eye level, the spectator looks up at the Trinity and down at the tomb. About 5 feet above the floor level, the vanishing point pulls the two

21-25   MASACCIO, *Holy Trinity, c.* 1428. Fresco, 21′ × 10′ 5″. Santa Maria Novella, Florence.

views together, creating the illusion of an actual structure that transects the vertical plane of the wall. While the tomb projects, the chapel recedes visually behind the wall and takes on the appearance of an extension of the space in which the spectator is standing. This adjustment of the pictured space to the position of the viewer is a first step in the development of illusionistic painting, which fascinated many artists of the Renaissance and the later Baroque period. Masaccio has been so exact in his metrical proportions that we can actually calculate the numerical dimensions of the chapel (for example, the span of the painted vault is 7 feet; the depth of the chapel, 9 feet). Thus, he achieves not only successful illusion, but a rational, metrical coherence that, by maintaining the mathematical proportions of the surface design, is responsible for the unity and harmony of this monumental composition.

Masaccio's *Holy Trinity,* a work created at the very beginning of the history of Renaissance painting, embodies two principal Renaissance interests: realism based on observation and the application of mathematics to pictorial organization in the new science of perspective. But the function of so much of the art of the preceding Middle Ages has not been rejected. Masaccio's fresco in the church of Santa Maria Novella still serves to instruct the faithful through didactic images: in an ascending pyramid of figures we move from the Old Testament Adam to the New Testament Christ, from the despair of death to the hope of resurrection and eternal life.

UCCELLO AND CASTAGNO   Masaccio's discoveries, like Donatello's, led to further experiments by his contemporaries and successors in the use of perspective to render pictorial space and in the representation of weighty, volumetric figures within that illusionistic world that the painter had created. PAOLO UCCELLO (1397–1475), a Florentine painter trained in the International Style, discovered perspective well along in his career and became obsessed with it. In the *Battle of San Romano* (FIG. **21-26**), one of three wood panels painted for the Palazzo Medici to commemorate the Florentine victory over the Sienese in 1432, Uccello creates a composition that recalls the processional splendor of Gentile da Fabriano's *Adoration of the Magi* (FIG. 21-22). But the world portrayed by Uccello, in contrast with the surface decoration of the International Style, is constructed of immobilized, solid forms; broken spears and lances and a fallen soldier are foreshortened and carefully placed along the converging orthogonals of the perspective to create a base plane like a checkerboard, on which the volumes are then placed in measured intervals. All this works very well as far back as the middle ground, where the horizontal plane is met abruptly by the up-tilted plane of an International Style background. Beyond that, Uccello's sense of design is impeccable. The careful rendering of three-dimensional form, used by other painters for representational or expressive purposes, became for Uccello a

21-26 PAOLO UCCELLO, *Battle of San Romano*, c. 1455. Tempera on wood, approx. 6' × 10' 5". National Gallery, London. Reproduced by courtesy of the Trustees.

preoccupation; for him, it had a magic of its own, which he exploited to satisfy his inventive and original imagination. His fascination with perspective had little in common with the rationality in Masaccio's concern for defining the dimensionality of space.

ANDREA DEL CASTAGNO (c. 1421–1457) interested himself both in perspective and in the representation of imposing, strong, structurally convincing human figures. He is seen at his best in the group of nine famous people—notably, three of them are women, but they are not historical personages—he painted in the Villa Pandolfini near Florence around 1448. One figure, a portrait of the general called *Pippo Spano* (FIG. **21-27**), is the very image of the swaggering commander—his feet firmly planted, "powerful among peers," and bristling with insolent challenge. The figure is meant to be seen as standing in a loggia, the space of which is continuous with that occupied by the spectator. The illusion is reinforced by the heavy, armored, foreshortened foot that seems to protrude over a sill of the opening. If Masaccio first "made his figures stand upon their feet," then Andrea followed him faithfully and made the point more emphatically in this splendid figure, which is alive with truculent energy. And by having parts of the figure appear to project into the space of the viewer, Andrea, doubtless influenced also by the grand niche statues of Donatello and others on the exterior of Or San Michele (FIGS. 21-3 through 21-5), takes a step beyond Masaccio's *Holy Trinity* in the direction of Baroque illusionism (see Chapter 24).

PIERO DELLA FRANCESCA The leading Florentine painter at mid-century was PIERO DELLA FRANCESCA (c. 1420–1492). Piero's art is the projection of a mind cultivated by mathematics and convinced that the highest beauty is found in forms that have the clarity and purity of

21-27 ANDREA DEL CASTAGNO, *Pippo Spano*, from the Villa Pandolfini, Florence, c. 1448. Fresco, 8' × 5' 5". Galleria degli Uffizi, Florence.

geometric figures. Toward the end of his long career, Piero, who was a skilled geometrician, wrote the first theoretical treatise on systematic perspective, after having practiced the art with supreme mastery for almost a lifetime. His association with the architect Alberti at Ferrara and at Rimini around 1450–1451 probably turned his attention fully to perspective (a science in which Alberti was an influential pioneer) and helped to determine his later, characteristically architectonic compositions. One can fairly say that Piero's compositions are determined almost entirely by his sense of the exact and lucid structures defined by mathematics. Within this context, however, he handled light and color with considerable sophistication, and color became the matrix of his three-dimensional forms, lending them a new density as well as fusing them with the surrounding space.

A damaged but still beautiful panel, Piero's *Flagellation of Christ* (FIG. **21-28**), is almost a painted exposition of the rules of linear perspective and its inherent pictorial possibilities. The painting has been designed with such precision that modern architects, using the division of the brick floor paneling along the painting's baseline as a module, have been able to reconstruct accurately the floor plans of the depicted court and building and the positions of the figures within them. However, as exact as the architectural rendering of the portico appears to be, its structure has been modified for pictorial reasons. Stalactite-shaped forms at the beam crossing denote the positions from which two interior columns have been removed in order to create a continuous space that encloses the martyrdom scene and

permits a full view of Pontius Pilate, who watches impassively as the executioners raise their whips to chastise Christ. The column to which Christ is tied is topped by a golden statue of a nude man holding an orb in his extended left hand, a motif frequently employed in antiquity for portraits of Roman emperors. Freestanding columns topped by honorary statues were also commonplace in Roman times. The grandest of them all, the Column of Trajan (FIG. 7-48), originally bore a gilded, heroically nude statue of the emperor (today the Column is capped by a statue of Saint Peter). The meaning of this statue within Piero's panel has been debated by scholars, but it may simply underscore that Christ's flagellation was ordered by an official of the Roman state and remind the spectator of the all-powerful pagan empire that Christianity had to confront and overcome.

The lighting is not as clearly legible as the perspective rendering. All outdoor forms are illuminated from the left, but the interior of the loggia receives its light from the right, either reflected from the buildings across the court or from a stipulated secondary light source behind the second column of the right colonnade. Even more ambiguous are the identities of the three figures in the right foreground and their relation to the central event; none of many tentative identifications, nor their meanings in relation to the central event, have found universal acceptance. Perhaps we should be content with viewing and experiencing the formal aspects of a masterful painting. In a composition that is at once clear, complex, and marvelously subtle, the perspective design is reinforced by visual cross-references that cre-

21-28 Piero della Francesca, *Flagellation of Christ, c.* 1455–1460. Tempera on wood, 32³/₄″ × 23¹/₃″. Palazzo Ducale, Galleria Nazionale delle Marche, Urbino.

ate a compact, pictorial unity. In the foreground figure group, which, at first glance, seems to have little relation to the depicted event, the pose of the central figure is almost identical to that of Christ. In addition, the relation of the turbaned man with his back to us (Herod?) to the flagellation scene is the same as that of the viewer of the painting to the foreground figure group. Thus, in a unique and ingenious manner, the artist draws the spectator past the foreground triad toward the main subject in the middle ground. By manipulating perspective and the disposition of volumes and voids, Piero creates pictorial tension using forms that are essentially static, in a composition that is firmly contained within its frame and, at the same time, highly dynamic. By placing the massed volumes of his three foreground figures off-center into a relatively restricted space, Piero poses the question of how much mass balances how large an empty space. The proportional relationships Piero shows us in this painting provide one possible (and certainly most satisfying) answer.

Piero's most important work is the fresco cycle in the apse of the church of San Francesco in Arezzo, which represents ten episodes from the legend of the True Cross (the cross on which Christ died). Painted between 1452 and 1456, the cycle is based on a thirteenth-century popularization of the scriptures, the *Golden Legend* by Jacobus de Voragine. In the climactic scene of Piero's Arezzo cycle, the *Proving of the True Cross* (FIG. **21-29**), Saint Helena, mother of Constantine, accompanied by her retinue, witnesses how the True Cross miraculously restores a dead man (the nude figure) to life. The grouping of the figures is controlled by the architectural background; its medallions, arches, and rectangular panels are the two-dimensional counter-

parts of the ovoid, cylindrical, and cubic forms placed in front of it. One feels the careful planning behind the placement of each shape and volume; it is almost the procedure of an architect, certainly that of a man entirely familiar with compass and straightedge. As the architectonics of the abstract shapes controls the grouping, so does it impart a mood of solemn stillness to the figures— a quiet rapture shown by unindividualized and emotionless faces, the slow gestures like those of a priest at an altar. The concourse of all these solid forms yet yields an impression of an otherworldly, mystical, and eternally celebrated rite that knows nothing of the passing facts and accidents of this world. We see a union of the unchanging mathematical form with the calm silences of the contemplative spirit.

Piero's work shows, in addition, an unflagging interest in the properties of light and color. He suspects that one is the function of the other; he observes that colors turn cool (bluish) in shadow and that they lose intensity with increasing distance from the observer. In his effort to make the clearest possible distinction between forms, he floods his pictures with light, imparting a silver-blue tonality. To avoid heavy shadows, he illumines the dark sides of his forms with reflected light. By moving the darkest tones of his modeling toward the centers of his volumes, he separates them from their backgrounds. As a result, Piero's paintings lack some of Masaccio's relief-like qualities but gain in spatial clarity as each shape becomes an independent unit, surrounded by an atmospheric envelope and movable to any desired position, like a figure on a chessboard.

In the *Resurrection* fresco in the chapel of the town hall of Borgo San Sepolcro (FIG. **21-30**), Piero utilizes the

21-29   PIERO DELLA FRANCESCA, *Proving of the True Cross, c.* 1455. Fresco (detail), San Francesco, Arezzo.

the rules of linear perspective, but the fact that the vault is too low to allow the Virgin to stand would have been unacceptable to Piero della Francesca and other less conservative artists. However, such considerations were secondary to Fra Angelico; what he wanted above all was to stress the religious content of his paintings, and he did so by using the means, past and present, that he felt were most appropriate. In our example, the simplicity of the statement recalls Giotto, as does the form of the kneeling, rainbow-winged angel; the elegant silhouette of the sweetly shy Madonna descends from Sienese art, and the flower-carpeted, enclosed garden (symbolic of the virginity of Mary) is a bit of International Style Gothic. All these elements have been combined with lyrical feeling and a great sense for decorative effect, so that nothing seems incongruous. Like most of Fra Angelico's paintings, the naive and tender charm of the

Annunciation still has an almost universal appeal and fully reflects the character of the artist, who, as Giorgio Vasari tells us, "was a simple and most holy man . . . most gentle and temperate, living chastely, removed from the cares of the world . . . humble and modest in all his works."

The lingering popularity of the International Style may still be seen in the work of Fra Angelico's most important pupil, BENOZZO GOZZOLI (1420–1497), especially in the frescoes he painted for the Medici on three walls of the chapel in their Florentine palace. The subject of the commission was the *Journey of the Magi* (FIG. **21-33**), a venerable theme that had special meaning for the Medici, who were members of a Florentine religious group called the Company of the Magi. Benozzo set his scene in a landscape that recalls the Tuscan hills around Florence, and, it has been said, he incorporated portraits of the Medici in the retinue of the

21-33   BENOZZO GOZZOLI, *Journey of the Magi, c.* 1459. Fresco, approx. 12' 4" long. Chapel, Palazzo Medici-Riccardi, Florence.

Magi (on horseback in the lower-left corner of our illustration). Benozzo's treatment of the theme is reminiscent of that of Gentile da Fabriano nearly forty years before (FIG. 21-22)—the winding procession and castle on a hill in the background of Benozzo's fresco and the foreshortened horses seen from the front in the foreground are almost interchangeable with those of Gentile's altarpiece—although the use of gold is not quite so lavish and the Gothic frame is nowhere to be seen. Still, Benozzo's style is that of an earlier generation. There could hardly be a greater contrast between the work of master and pupil than that between the simplicity and spirituality of Fra Angelico and the action-packed surfaces and worldly pageantry of Benozzo Gozzoli.

FRA FILIPPO LIPPI   Older than Benozzo and a younger contemporary of Fra Angelico was FRA FILIPPO LIPPI (c. 1406–1469), who was also a friar—but there all resemblance ends. From reports, Fra Filippo seems to have been a kind of amiable scapegrace quite unfitted for monastic life, who indulged in misdemeanors ranging from forgery and embezzlement to the abduction of a pretty nun, Lucretia, who became his mistress and the mother of his son, the painter FILIPPINO LIPPI (1457–1504). Only the Medici's intervention on his behalf at the papal court preserved Fra Filippo from severe punishment and total disgrace. An orphan, Fra Filippo was raised in a monastery adjacent to the church of Santa Maria del Carmine, and, when about eighteen, he must have met Masaccio there and witnessed the decoration of the Brancacci Chapel. Fra Filippo's early work survives only in fragments, but these show that he tried to work with Masaccio's massive forms. Later, probably under the influence of Ghiberti's and Donatello's relief sculptures, he developed a linear style that emphasizes the contours of his figures and permits him to suggest movement through flying and swirling draperies.

A fresh and inventive painting from Fra Filippo's later years, *Madonna and Child with Angels* (FIG. **21-34**) shows his skill in manipulating line. Beyond noting its fine contours and modeling, we soon become aware of the wonderful flow of line throughout the picture; the forms are precisely yet smoothly delineated, whether they are whole figures or the details within them. Even without the reinforcing modeling, the forms would look three-dimensional and plastic, as the line is handled in a sculptural rather than in a two-dimensional sense. Fra Filippo's skill in the use of line is rarely surpassed; in the immediate future, only his most famous pupil, Botticelli, will use it with greater subtlety. Fra Filippo has interpreted his subject here in a surprisingly worldly manner. The Madonna, a beautiful young mother, is not at all spiritual or fragile, and neither is her plump bambino, the child Christ, who is held up to her by two angels, one of whom turns toward us with the mischievous, puckish grimace of a boy refusing to be subdued by the pious occasion. Significantly, all figures reflect the

21-34   FRA FILIPPO LIPPI, *Madonna and Child with Angels*, c. 1455. Tempera on wood, approx. 36" × 25". Galleria degli Uffizi, Florence.

use of models (that for the Madonna may even have been Lucretia). Fra Filippo plainly relishes the charm of youth and beauty as he finds it in this world. He prefers the real in landscape also, and the background, seen through the window, has, despite some exaggerations, recognizable features of the Arno River valley. Compared with the earlier Madonnas by Duccio (FIG. 19-5) and Giotto (FIG. 19-9), this work shows how far the humanization of the theme has been carried. Whatever the ideals of spiritual perfection may have meant to artists in past centuries, those ideals now are realized in terms of the sensuous beauty of this world.

THE SECOND HALF OF THE FIFTEENTH CENTURY

In the early fifteenth century, Florence led all of Italy in the development of the new Humanism; later, the city shared its leadership role with other Italian cities. Under the sponsorship of local rulers, important cultural centers developed in other parts of Italy and began to attract artists and scholars: Urbino under the Montefeltri, Mantua under the Gonzaga, Milan under the Sforza, Naples under the kings of Aragon, and so forth.

This later period of Humanism is marked by a new interest in the Italian language and literature, the beginnings of literary criticism (parallel to the development of theory in art and architecture), the foundation of academies (especially the Platonic Academy of Philosophy in Florence), and the introduction of the printing press—and all that these elements could mean for the dissemination of culture.

The conquest of Constantinople by the Turks in 1453 caused an exodus of Greek scholars, many of whom fled to Italy, bringing with them knowledge of ancient Greece to feed the avid interest in Classical art, literature, and philosophy. That same conquest closed the Mediterranean to Western shipping, making it necessary to find new routes to the markets of the East. Thus began the age of navigation, discovery, and exploration.

In art and architecture, a theoretical foundation could now be placed under the more or less "intuitive" innovations of the earlier generation of artists. We must emphasize again the high value that Renaissance artists placed on theory. In their view, if any occupation or profession were to have dignity and be worthy of honor, it must have an intellectual basis. Renaissance artists strove to associate themselves with princes and the learned in order to rise above the long-standing ancient and medieval prejudice that saw them as mere artisans.

Beginning with Alberti's treatises on painting and architecture, theoretical studies multiplied. The rediscovered text of the ancient Roman architect and theoretician Vitruvius became the subject of exhaustive examination and interpretation (partly because the recovered text was only a copy, which, unlike the original, was not illustrated, rendering passages that referred to illustrations obscure and subject to varying interpretations). Brunelleschi's reinvention of perspective and Alberti's and Piero's treatises on the subject provided the Renaissance artist with the opportunity to demonstrate the scientific basis of the visual arts.

The genius and creative energy required to achieve the new social and intellectual status claimed by the artist were available in abundance. The Renaissance ideal of *l'uomo universale* (the universal man—or what we have, tellingly, come to call the Renaissance man or woman) here finds its full realization; indeed, in Leon Battista Alberti (1404–1472), it finds one of its first personifications. Writing of himself in the third person, Alberti gives us a most revealing insight into the mind of the brilliant Renaissance man—his universal interests, broad capabilities, love of beauty, and hope of fame:

In everything suitable to one born free and educated liberally, he was so trained from boyhood that among the lead-

ing young men of his age he was considered by no means the last. For, assiduous in the science and skill of dealing with arms and horses and musical instruments, as well as in the pursuit of letters and the fine arts, he was devoted to the knowledge of the most strange and difficult things. And finally he embraced with zeal and forethought everything which pertained to fame. To omit the rest, he strove so hard to attain a name in modeling and painting that he wished to neglect nothing by which he might gain the approbation of good men. His genius was so versatile that you might almost judge all the fine arts to be his. . . . He took extraordinary and peculiar pleasure in looking at things in which there was any mark of beauty. . . . Whatever was done by man with genius and with a certain grace, he held to be almost divine.*

It is probably no accident that this autobiography sounds like a funeral oration for a great man.

Architecture

Alberti   Alberti scarcely mentioned architecture as a prime interest. He entered the profession rather late in life, but today we know him chiefly as an architect. He was the first to study seriously the treatise of Vitruvius (*De architectura*), and his knowledge of it, combined with his own archeological investigations, made him the first Renaissance architect to understand Roman architecture in depth. Alberti's most important and influential theoretical work, *De re aedificatoria* (*On Architecture*), published before 1450, although inspired by Vitruvius contains much new and original material. Alberti advocated a system of ideal proportions, and argued that the central plan was the ideal form for a Christian church. He also considered the combination of column and arch (which had persisted from Roman times [Figs. 7-58 and 7-83] to Brunelleschi in the fifteenth century) to be incongruous. By arguing that the arch is a wall opening that should be supported only by a section of wall (a pier), not by an independent sculptural element (a column), Alberti (with a few exceptions) disposed of the medieval arcade for centuries. The early impact of Alberti's ideas may already be seen in the architectural backdrop in Ghiberti's *Isaac and His Sons* (Fig. 21-9) on the "Gates of Paradise" of Florence's baptistery, although the older, Brunelleschian manner was still favored by Michelozzo (Fig. 21-21) and Fra Angelico (Fig. 21-32).

Alberti's own architectural style represents a scholarly application of Classical elements to contemporary buildings. His Palazzo Rucellai in Florence (Fig. **21-35**) probably dates from the mid-1450s. The facade, built over a group of three medieval houses, is much more severely organized

*In J. B. Ross and M. M. McLaughlin, eds., *The Portable Renaissance Reader* (New York: Viking, 1953), pp. 480ff.

meshed, linear net that, stretched tightly across the front of his building, not only unifies its three levels but also emphasizes the flat, two-dimensional qualities of the wall.

The design for the facade of the fourteenth-century Gothic church of Santa Maria Novella in Florence (FIGS. **21-36** and **21-37**) also was commissioned by the Rucellai family. Here, Alberti takes his cue (just as Brunelleschi did occasionally) from a pre-Gothic medieval design—that of San Miniato al Monte (FIG. 12-21). Following his

21-35   LEON BATTISTA ALBERTI, Palazzo Rucellai, Florence, *c.* 1452–1470.

21-36   LEON BATTISTA ALBERTI, west facade of Santa Maria Novella, Florence, *c.* 1458–1470.

than that of the Palazzo Medici-Riccardi (FIG. 21-20). Each story of the Palazzo Rucellai is articulated by flat pilasters, which support full entablatures; the whole is crowned by a Classical cornice. The rustication of the wall surfaces between the smooth pilasters is subdued and uniform, and the suggestion that the structure becomes lighter toward its top is made in an adaptation of the ancient Roman manner by using different articulating orders for each story: Tuscan (the Etruscan variant of the Greek Doric order) for the ground floor, Composite (the Roman combination of Ionic volutes with the acanthus leaves of the Corinthian) for the second story, and Corinthian for the third floor. Alberti's model for the facade was certainly the most imposing Roman ruin of all, the Colosseum (FIG. 7-39), but he is no slavish copyist; on the facade of the Colosseum the orders employed are, from the bottom up, Tuscan, Ionic, and Corinthian. Moreover, Alberti has adapted the articulation of the Colosseum to a flat facade, which does not allow the deep penetration of the building's mass that is so effective in the Roman structure. By converting the plastic, engaged columns of his ancient model into shallow pilasters that barely project from the wall, Alberti has created a large-

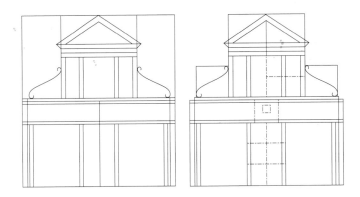

21-37   Diagrams of west facade, Santa Maria Novella.

Romanesque model, he designs a small, pseudo-Classical, pediment-capped temple front for the upper part of the facade and supports it with a broad base of pilaster-enframed arcades that incorporate the six tombs and three doorways of the extant Gothic building. (One is reminded of the problem Brunelleschi faced earlier in the century when he was asked to design the dome for the medieval cathedral of Florence [FIG. 21-13].) But in the organization of these elements (FIG. 21-37), Alberti takes a long step beyond the Romanesque planners. The height of Santa Maria Novella (to the tip of the pediment) equals its width, so that the entire facade can be inscribed in a square. The upper structure, in turn, can be encased in a square one-fourth the size of the main square; the cornice of the entablature that separates the two levels halves the major square, so that the lower portion of the building becomes a rectangle that is twice as wide as it is high; and the areas outlined by the columns on the lower level are squares with sides that are about one-third the width of the main unit. Throughout the facade, Alberti defines areas and relates them to each other in terms of proportions that can be expressed in simple numerical ratios (1:1, 1:2, 1:3, 2:3, and so on). In his treatise, Alberti uses considerable space to propound the necessity of such harmonic relationships for the design of beautiful buildings.

Alberti shares this conviction with Brunelleschi, and it is basically this dependence on mathematics—a belief in the eternal and universal validity of numerical ratios as the source of beauty—that distinguishes the work of these two architects from that of their medieval predecessors. In this respect, Alberti and Brunelleschi are reviving the true spirit of the High Classical age of fifth-century Greece, as epitomized by the sculptor Polykleitos and the architect Iktinos, whose canons of proportions for the perfect statue and the perfect temple Alberti would have known secondhand through the architectural treatise of Vitruvius. But it was not only a desire to emulate Vitruvius and the Classical masters that motivated Alberti to turn to mathematics in his quest for beauty. His contemporary, the Florentine Humanist Giannozzo Manetti, had argued that Christianity itself possessed the order and logic of mathematics by insisting in his 1452 treatise, *On the Dignity and Excellence of Man,* that the religious truths of Christianity were as self-evident as the axioms of mathematics.

The facade of Santa Maria Novella is an ingenious solution to a difficult design problem. On one hand, it adequately expresses the organization of the structure to which it is attached; at the same time, it subjects preexisting and quintessentially medieval features like the large round window on the second level to a rigid geometrical order that instills a quality of Classical calm and reason. This facade also introduces a feature of great historical consequence: the scrolls that simultaneously unite the broad lower and narrow upper level and screen the sloping roofs over the aisles. With variations, such spirals will appear in

literally hundreds of church facades throughout the Renaissance and Baroque periods.

At San Francesco in Rimini (FIG. **21-38**), Alberti again modernized a Gothic church—in this case, at the behest of one of the more sensational figures of the Early Renaissance, Sigismondo Pandolfo Malatesta, Lord of Rimini. Malatesta wanted a "temple" in which to enshrine the bones of great Humanist scholars like Gemistus Pletho, who dreamed of a neopagan religion that would supersede Christianity and whose remains Malatesta had brought from Greece. He intended his temple also to memorialize his mistress, Isotta. Alberti's thoroughly Roman design is a monument both to Malatesta's love of Classical learning and to his arrant paganism. Alberti redesigned the exterior shell of San Francesco, making a cubic structure, complete within itself, and fronting it with a facade modeled after the Roman triumphal arch (FIG. **21-39**) erected at Rimini in 27 B.C. in honor of the emperor Augustus. Alberti's Augustan model also has tondi (sing. *tondo,* circular painting or relief) in the spandrels—a motif employed earlier by Brunelleschi for the facade of the Ospedale degli Innocenti in Florence (FIG. 21-14) and one that may also be seen in the painted triumphal arch that frames Masaccio's *Holy Trinity* fresco inside the old church of Santa Maria Novella (FIG. 21-25). Alberti would, of course, have had ample time to study Masaccio's three-decade-old mural painting when he designed a new facade for the Florentine church after 1458. In Alberti's design for the facade of San Francesco, four massive engaged columns frame three recessed arches and carry a flat entablature that projects sharply, making a *ressaut,* or "projection," above each capital—exactly as on the Augustan arch at Rimini. Alberti intended the second

21-38 Leon Battista Alberti, San Francesco, Rimini, begun 1451 (view from the northwest).

the facade to the small square in front of it, even at the expense of continuity with the body of the building, is frequently manifest in Renaissance architecture, where considerations of visual appeal are of first importance. On the other hand, structural correspondences do exist in the Sant'Andrea facade. The facade pilasters are the same height as those on the interior walls of the nave, and the central barrel vault over the main entrance, from which smaller barrel vaults branch off at right angles, introduces

21-39   Arch of Augustus, Rimini, 27 B.C.

story, which remains incomplete, to have an arched window framed by pilasters. The heavy relief of this facade contrasts with the flat, bandlike elements in most of Alberti's other buildings. The deep, arched niches, rhythmically deployed along the flanks of the building, which contain sarcophagi for the remains of famous men, are in keeping with Alberti's conviction that arches should be carried on piers, not columns. These niches, along with the elements of the facade, provide an effect of monumental scale and grandeur that approaches ancient Roman architecture.

Adjusting the Classical orders to facade surfaces occupied Alberti throughout his career. In 1470, in his last years, he designed the church of Sant'Andrea in Mantua (FIGS. **21-40** to **21-42**) to replace an older eleventh-century church. In the ingeniously planned facade, which illustrates the culmination of Alberti's experiments, he locks together two complete Roman architectural motifs—the temple front and the triumphal arch. (The combination was already a feature of Classical architecture; many Roman triumphal arches incorporate a pediment over the arcuated passageway, including the Augustan arch at Rimini.) His concern for proportion made him equalize the vertical and horizontal dimensions of the facade, which leaves it considerably lower than the church behind it. This concession to the demands of a purely visual proportionality in the facade and to the relation of

21-40   LEON BATTISTA ALBERTI, west facade of Sant'Andrea, Mantua, designed c. 1470.

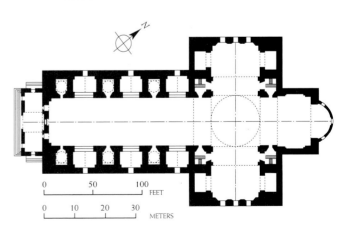

21-41   Plan of Sant'Andrea.

21-42   Interior of Sant'Andrea.

with a Christian building tradition that had endured for a thousand years was extremely influential in later Renaissance and Baroque church planning.

For many Renaissance architects and theoreticians, the circle was the ideal geometric figure; without a beginning or an end and with all points equidistant from a common center, it seemed to reflect the nature of the universe. This is one reason why the central plan was felt to be so appropriate for religious architecture. (Figures that approached the circle, such as polygons, were considered adequate.) But as firm as this conviction of the architects may have been, the clergy was almost as firm in its demands for traditional longitudinal churches, which, of course, are much more practical for Christian religious services. In addition to the question of how to accommodate the congregation in central-plan churches, architects were confronted with the question of where to put the main altar, and they were permitted to realize their ideal relatively rarely.

A compromise solution, suggested first in Alberti's San Sebastiano in Mantua (his one, abortive attempt at building a central-plan church), was realized by GIULIANO DA SANGALLO (c. 1443–1516) in Santa Maria delle Carceri in Prato (FIGS. **21-43** to **21-45**). This building was erected according to the plan of a Greek cross, with the cross arms so short that the emphasis is on the central, dome-covered

(in proportional arrangement but on a smaller scale) the system used in the interior. The facade pilasters, becoming part of the wall, run uninterrupted through three stories in an early application of the "colossal" or "giant" order that will become a favorite motif of Michelangelo.

The interior of Sant'Andrea (FIG. 21-42) suggests that Alberti may have been inspired by the tremendous vaults of the ruined Basilica Nova of Constantine in Rome (FIG. 7-90)—erroneously thought in the Middle Ages and Renaissance to be a Roman temple. The medieval columned arcade, still used by Brunelleschi in Santo Spirito (FIG. 21-15), now is forgotten, and the huge barrel vault, supported by thick walls alternating with vaulted chapels and interrupted by a massive dome over the crossing,* returns us to the vast interior spaces and dense enclosing masses of Roman architecture. In his treatise, Alberti calls the traditional basilican plan (in which continuous aisles flank the central nave) impractical, because the colonnades conceal the ceremonies from the faithful in the aisles; for this reason, he designed a single, huge hall, from which independent chapels branch off at right angles. This break

*No one knows what kind of dome Alberti planned for the crossing; the present dome was added by Filippo Juvara in the eighteenth century.

21-43   GIULIANO DA SANGALLO, Santa Maria delle Carceri, Prato, 1485 (view from the northwest).

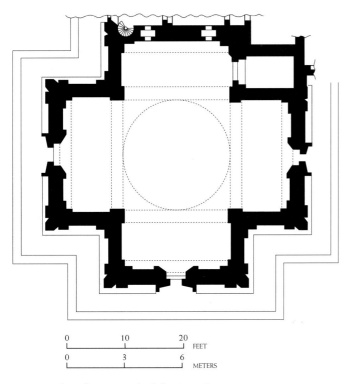

21-44   Plan of Santa Maria delle Carceri.

square, very closely approaching the central-plan ideal. Blocklike, the structure is as high as it is wide, the cross arms are twice as wide as they are deep, and the Ionic second story is two-thirds the height of the Tuscan first floor. The whole building can be read in terms of the simple numerical relationships that Alberti advocates. Interior articulation, however, is much closer to Brunelleschi and resembles that of the Pazzi Chapel (FIG. 21-19). The building seems to be a hybrid of the styles of Giuliano's two great predecessors, but it is also a neat and compact near-realization of an ideal central-plan Renaissance church.

Sculpture

Like the work of Alberti in the latter half of the fifteenth century, the sculpture of the Florentine school realizes new triumphs of Humanist Classicism. Donatello's successors refined his innovating art and each specialized in one of its many forms and subjects.

BERNARDO AND ANTONIO ROSSELLINO   No monument made by the next generation expresses more beautifully and clearly this dedication to the values of pagan antiquity than the tomb of Leonardo Bruni in Santa Croce in

21-45   Interior of Santa Maria delle Carceri (view facing northeast).

Florence (FIG. **21-46**). Its sculptor, BERNARDO ROSSELLINO (1409–1464), like the man whose tomb he built, was at one time a resident of Arezzo. Rossellino strove mightily to immortalize his fellow citizen. The wall tomb has a history that reaches back into the Middle Ages, but Rossellino's version is new and definitive and the expression of an age deliberately turning away from the medieval past.

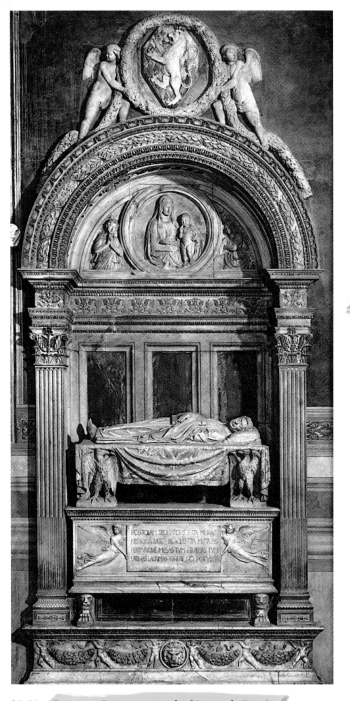

21-46   BERNARDO ROSSELLINO, tomb of Leonardo Bruni, *c.* 1445–1450. Marble, approx. 20' high to top of arch. Santa Croce, Florence.

Leonardo Bruni was one of the most distinguished men of Italy, and his passing was mourned widely. As an erudite scholar in Greek and Latin, a diplomat and apostolic secretary to four popes, and a member of the chancery of the city of Florence, Bruni's career sums up the Humanistic ideal. The Florentines particularly praised him for his *History of Florence*. In his honor, the practice of the funeral oration was revived, as was the ancient custom of crowning the deceased with laurel. The historic event of the crowning of the dead Humanist may have given Rossellino his theme and the tomb may have been intended as a kind of memorialization of the laureate scene.

The deceased lies on the *catafalque* (framework supporting the deceased) in a long gown, the *History of Florence* on his breast, the drapery of his couch caught up at the ends by imperial Roman eagles. Winged genii at the summit of the arch above the catafalque hold a great *escutcheon* (an emblem bearing a coat of arms); on the side of the sarcophagus, other genii support a Latin inscription that describes the Muses' grief at the scholar's passing. Roman funeral garlands are carved on the narrow platform at the base of the niche. The only unmistakably Christian reference is a Madonna and Child with angels in the tympanum. The selection of motifs reveals an intimate familiarity with the art of ancient Italy, for the motifs chosen are not generic evocations of Classical art; all of them have specific sources in Etruscan and Roman funerary monuments. Rossellino would not have had to travel far to study examples of sculptured marble figures on the lids of their sarcophagi (FIG. 7-69) and the conceit of having the deceased hold a book (or a scroll) attesting to his achievements in life also comes directly from antiquity (FIG. 6-17). Winged Victories displaying engraved epitaphs, putti bearing garlands, and eagles (who carry the deceased to a heavenly afterlife) are also staples on Roman sarcophagi—which, like Bruni's, were usually set into niches in walls. As in Alberti's "temples," a Humanist and pagan Classicism controls the mood of the design in an evocation of the ancient Greco-Roman world.

Few could hope for a funeral and tomb like those given Leonardo Bruni, but in a Humanistic age, many people wanted to see their memory, if not their fame, perpetuated. In addition, Renaissance patrons probably enjoyed seeing likenesses of themselves. Roman portrait busts were being found and preserved in ever-greater numbers during the latter half of the fifteenth century, and, given this model, it was almost inevitable that the Renaissance would develop a similar portrait type. The form may have originated in the workshop of ANTONIO ROSSELLINO (*c.* 1427–1479), the younger brother of Bernardo. The portrait bust of *Matteo Palmieri* (FIG. **21-47**), apostolic delegate of Pope Sixtus IV, is an example of Antonio's work. Palmieri, who held high rank in Florence, was a learned man and author of a theological poem, *City of Life,* based formally on Dante's writing. After Palmieri's death, parts of the poem were declared

21-47 ANTONIO ROSSELLINO, *Matteo Palmieri*, 1468. Marble, 21″ high. Museo Nazionale del Bargello, Florence.

planes, so that the light will be modulated softly and the impression of living, tender flesh conveyed. The subtlety of Desiderio's surfaces and the consequent effect of life they give have long been admired by the Italians, as is evident in their phrase, *"il vago Desiderio, si dolce bello"* (the charming Desiderio, so sweetly beautiful). A whole school of sculptors worked in this manner, and attributions, often quite uncertain, range from Desiderio to the young Leonardo da Vinci. The soft, misty, shadow effects certainly point ahead to the *sfumato* ("smoky" light and shade) in Leonardo's paintings.

LUCA DELLA ROBBIA   Since the thirteenth century, the Madonna and Child theme had become increasingly humanized, until, in the fifteenth century, we might almost speak of a school of sweetness and light in which many sculptors attempt to outdo each other in rendering the theme ever gentler and prettier, especially in relief. In the latter half of the fifteenth century, increasing demand for devotional images for private chapels and shrines (rather than for large public churches) contributed to an increasing secularization of traditional religious subject matter. LUCA DELLA ROBBIA (1400–1482), a sculptor in the generation of Donatello and a leader of the trend toward sweetness and light, discovered a way to multiply the images of the

heretical because the souls of men were originally represented as fallen angels. However, at the time of his death, Palmieri received a state funeral like Bruni's; his book was placed on his breast, and a funeral oration was delivered. Like the best portraits of the Roman Republic, Antonio's likeness of Palmieri goes beyond the careful cataloguing of individual features to communicate something of the character of the man. Head held high, this proud portrait of a man with an enormous nose and endless mouth is filled with a bright, intelligent animation, and the fine eyes seem those of a man engaged in a quick and subtle dialogue.

Donatello had shown the sternly real and the gently idealized in his forms; indeed, realism and idealism are parallel tendencies in the later fifteenth century. DESIDERIO DA SETTIGNANO (1428–1464) specialized in the sensitive reading of the faces of women and children, which he idealized without diminishing character, as we may see in his bust of a little boy (FIG. **21-48**). The proportions and soft contours of the head are wonderfully understood, as is the psychological set—a wondering innocence—captured by Desiderio in the ambiguous pout and in the uplifted brows and large eyes directed wide at an adult world. The marble has been carved to give a remarkable smoothness to the

21-48   DESIDERIO DA SETTIGNANO, Bust of a little boy, *c.* 1455–1460. Marble, 10¹/₂″ high. National Gallery of Art, Washington, D.C. (Andrew W. Mellon Collection).

Madonna so that they would be within the reach of persons of modest means. His discovery (around 1430), involving the application of vitrified potters' glazes to sculpture, led to his production, in quantity, of the glazed terracotta reliefs for which he is best known. Because they were inexpensive, durable, and decorative, these works became extremely popular and provided the basis for a flourishing family business. The tradition was carried on by Luca's nephew Andrea della Robbia (1435–1525), whose colors tend to become a little garish, and by the latter's sons, Giovanni della Robbia (1469–1529) and Girolamo della Robbia (1488–1566), whose activity extends well into the sixteenth century, when the product tends to become purely commercial; we still speak today of "della Robbia ware."

An example of Luca's specialty is the *Madonna and Child* set into a wall of Or San Michele (FIG. **21-49**). The figures are composed within a tondo, a format that will become popular with both sculptors and painters in the later part of the century—it was used also, for example, by Bernardo Rossellino for the Madonna and Child of Leonardo Bruni's tomb (FIG. 21-46) and by Brunelleschi in the interior of the Pazzi Chapel (FIG. 21-19), where most of the roundels are the work of Luca della Robbia himself. In Luca's tondo for Or San Michele, the introduction of high-key color into sculpture adds a certain worldly gaiety to the Madonna and Child theme, and his customary light blue grounds (and here the green and white of lilies and the white architecture) suggest the festive season of Easter and the freshness

21-49 Luca della Robbia, *Madonna and Child,* c. 1455–1460. Terracotta with polychrome glaze, diameter approx. 6'. Or San Michele, Florence.

of May, the month of the Virgin. Of course, the somber majesty of the old Byzantine style has long since disappeared. The young mothers who prayed before images like this new form easily could identify with the Madonna and doubtless did. The distance between the observed and the observer has vanished.

VERROCCHIO   The most important sculptor during the second half of the century was ANDREA DEL VERROCCHIO (1435–1488). A painter as well as a sculptor, with something of the versatility and depth of Donatello, Verrocchio directed a flourishing *bottega* (studio-shop) in Florence that attracted many students, among them Leonardo da Vinci. Verrocchio, like Donatello, also had a broad repertoire. He too made a figure of *David* (FIG. **21-50**), one that contrasts strongly in its narrative realism with the quiet, esthetic Classicism of Donatello's *David* (FIG. 21-10). Verrocchio's *David*—made for Lorenzo de' Medici to exhibit in his Florentine palace—is a sturdy, wiry young apprentice clad in a leathern doublet, who stands with a jaunty pride, the head of Goliath at his feet. He poses like any sportsman who has just won a game, or a hunter with his kill. The easy balance of the weight and the lithe, still thinly adolescent musculature, in which the veins are prominent, show how closely Verrocchio read the text and how clearly he knew the psychology of brash and confident young men. Although the contrast with Donatello's interpretation need hardly be labored, we might note the "open" form of the Verrocchio *David*, the sword and pointed elbow sharply breaking through the figure's silhouette and stressing the live tension of the still alert victor. Donatello's *David*, on the other hand, has a "closed" silhouette that emphasizes its Classical calm and relaxation. The description of the anatomy of the two figures—specific in the former, generalized in the latter—puts further accent on the difference between them. Both statues are masterpieces and show how two skillful and thoughtful artists can approach the same theme very differently.

Verrocchio competes with Donatello again in an equestrian statue of another *condottiere* of Venice, *Bartolommeo Colleoni* (FIG. **21-51**), who, eager to emulate the fame and the monument of Donatello's *Gattamelata* (FIG. 21-11), provided for the statue in his will. Both Donatello's and Verrocchio's statues were made after the deaths of their subjects, so that neither artist knew the person being portrayed. The result is a fascinating difference of interpretation (like that between the two *Davids*) as to what a professional captain of armies would look like. On a pedestal even higher than that used in Donatello's *Gattamelata*, Verrocchio's statue of the bold equestrian general is placed so that the dominating, aggressive figure can be seen above the rooftops from all major approaches to the piazza (the Campo dei Santi Giovanni e Paolo), silhouetted against the sky, its fierce authority unmistakably present.

In contrast with the near repose of the *Gattamelata*, the Colleoni horse moves in a prancing stride, arching and curving its powerful neck, while the commander seems suddenly to shift his whole weight to the stirrups and, in a fit of impassioned anger, to rise from the saddle with a violent twist of his body. The figures are charged with an exaggerated tautness; the bulging muscles of the animal and the fiercely erect and rigid body of the man unify brute strength and rage. The commander, represented as delivering the battle harangue to his troops before they close with the enemy, has worked himself into a frenzy that he hopes to communicate to his men. In the *Gattamelata*,

21-50 ANDREA DEL VERROCCHIO, *David*, c. 1465–1470. Bronze, approx. 49¹/₂" high. Museo Nazionale del Bargello, Florence.

21-51   ANDREA DEL VERROCCHIO, *Bartolommeo Colleoni, c.* 1483–1488. Bronze, approx. 13' high. Campo dei Santi Giovanni e Paolo, Venice.

Donatello gives us a portrait of grim sagacity; Verrocchio's *Bartolommeo Colleoni* is a portrait of savage and merciless might. Machiavelli wrote in his famous political treatise of 1513, *The Prince,* that the successful ruler must combine the traits of the lion and the fox; one feels that Donatello's *Gattamelata* is a little like the latter and that Verrocchio's *Bartolommeo Colleoni* is much like the former.

POLLAIUOLO   Closely related in stylistic intent to the work of Verrocchio is the work of ANTONIO POLLAIUOLO (*c.* 1431–1498). Pollaiuolo, who is also important as a painter and engraver, infuses the nervous movement and emotional expressiveness of Donatello's late style with a new linear mobility, spatial complexity, and dramatic immediacy. He has a realistic concern for movement in all its variety and for the stress and strain of the human figure in violent action. These qualities are apparent in Pollaiuolo's small-scale group of *Hercules and Antaeus* (FIG. **21-52**), which dramatically departs from the rule of frontality that had dominated the art of statuary during the Middle Ages and the Early Renaissance. Not quite 18 inches high, *Hercules and Antaeus* embodies the ferocity and vitality of elemental, physical conflict. The group illustrates the Greek myth of a wrestling match between Antaeus (Antaios), a giant and son of the earth, and Hercules (Herakles). We already have seen this story represented by

21-52 ANTONIO POLLAIUOLO, *Hercules and Antaeus, c.* 1475. Bronze, approx. 18" high with base. Museo Nazionale del Bargello, Florence.

Euphronios on an ancient Greek vase (FIG. 5-25). Each time Hercules threw him down, Antaeus sprang up again, his strength renewed by contact with the earth. Finally, Hercules held him aloft, so that he could not touch the earth, and strangled him around the waist. Here, the artist strives to convey the final, excruciating moments of the struggle—the straining and cracking of sinews, the clenched teeth of Hercules, the kicking and screaming of Antaeus. The figures are interlocked in a tightly wound coil, and the flickering reflections of light on the dark, gouged surface of the bronze contribute to the effect of agitated movement and a fluid play of planes. Pollaiuolo's *Hercules and Antaeus* is a very early Renaissance instance in which nudity and Classical subject matter are combined; Pollaiuolo is also thought to be responsible for adding bronze statues of Romulus and Remus to one of the most

famous ancient statues in Renaissance times, the Etruscan *Capitoline Wolf* (FIG. 6-11).

Painting and Engraving

The twisting of figures through space shows the growing interest in realistic action among artists during the second half of the century. Now an enthusiasm, this interest is further revealed in Pollaiuolo's *Battle of the Ten Nudes* (FIG. **21-53**). Pollaiuolo belongs to the second generation of experimentalists, who, in their pursuit of realism, were absorbed in the study of anatomy. The problem of rendering human anatomy had been rather well solved by earlier artists like Donatello and Andrea del Castagno, but their figures usually are shown at rest or in restrained motion. As we can see in his *Hercules and Antaeus,* Pollaiuolo takes delight in showing violent action and finds his opportunity in subjects dealing with combat. He conceives the body as a powerful machine and likes to display its mechanisms; knotted muscles and taut sinews activate the skeleton as ropes pull levers. To show this to best effect, Pollaiuolo developed a figure so lean and muscular that it appears *écorché* (as if without skin), with strongly accentuated articulations at the wrists, elbows, shoulders, and knees. His *Battle of the Ten Nudes* shows this figure type in a variety of poses and from numerous points of view. The composition has no specific mythological or historical subject; rather it is an excuse for Pollaiuolo to demonstrate his prowess in rendering the nude male figure. In this, he is a kindred spirit of those late sixth-century Greek vase painters, like Euthymides (FIG. 5-27), who were experimenting with foreshortening for the first time in history. If Pollaiuolo's figures, even though they hack and slash at one another without mercy, seem somewhat stiff and frozen, it is because Pollaiuolo shows *all* the muscle groups at maximum tension. The fact that only part of the body's muscle groups are involved in any one action, while the others are relaxed, was to be observed only several decades later by an even greater anatomist, Leonardo da Vinci.

Pollaiuolo's *Battle of the Ten Nudes* is an engraving, a new medium that, as we have seen, was probably developed around the middle of the fifteenth century in northern Europe. But whereas German graphic artists, like Martin Schongauer (FIG. 20-28), described their forms with hatching that follows the forms, Italian engravers, like Pollaiuolo, preferred parallel hatching. The former method is in keeping with the general northern approach to art, which tends to describe the surfaces of things rather than their underlying structures, while the latter was better suited for the anatomical studies that preoccupied Pollaiuolo and his Italian contemporaries.

GHIRLANDAIO   DOMENICO GHIRLANDAIO (1449–1494) differs in character from Pollaiuolo. Neither an innovator nor an experimenter, Ghirlandaio is rather a synthesizer who,

21-53 ANTONIO POLLAIUOLO, *Battle of the Ten Nudes, c.* 1465. Engraving, approx. 15″ × 23″. Metropolitan Museum of Art, New York (bequest of Joseph Pulitzer, 1917).

21-54 DOMENICO GHIRLANDAIO, *Birth of the Virgin,* 1485–1490. Fresco. Cappella Maggiore, Santa Maria Novella, Florence.

profiting from everything done before, summarizes the state of Florentine art by the end of the century. His works express his times to perfection, and, for this, he enjoyed great popularity among his contemporaries. Ghirlandaio's paintings also show a deep love for the city of Florence, its spectacles and pageantry, its material wealth and luxury. His most representative pictures, a cycle of frescoes representing scenes from the lives of the Virgin and Saint John the Baptist, are found in the choir of Santa Maria Novella and were commissioned by Giovanni Tornabuoni, one of the wealthiest Florentines of his day. In our illustration, the *Birth of the Virgin* (FIG. **21-54**), Mary's mother, Saint Anne, reclines in a palace room embellished with fine *intarsia* (wood inlay) and sculpture, while midwives prepare the infant's bath. From the left comes a grave procession of women, led by a young member of the Tornabuoni family, probably Ludovica, Giovanni's daughter. This splendidly dressed beauty holds as prominent a place in the composition (close to the central axis) as she must have held in Florentine society; her appearance in the painting (a different female member of the house appears in each of the frescoes) is conspicuous evidence of the secularization of sacred themes commonplace in art by this time. Living persons of high rank now are not only represented as present at biblical dramas but, as here, often steal the show from the saints. The display of patrician elegance absorbs and subordinates the devotional tableau.

The composition epitomizes the achievements of Early Renaissance painting: clear spatial representation; statuesque, firmly constructed figures; and rational order and logical relation among these figures and objects. If anything of earlier traits remains, it is in the arrangement of the figures, which still somewhat rigidly cling to layers parallel to the plane of the picture.

Another aristocratic young woman, probably Giovanna Tornabuoni, is the subject of a portrait by Ghirlandaio (FIG. **21-55**), the cool formality of which recalls the portrait of Ludovica Tornabuoni in the fresco. Although the profile pose is not intended primarily to convey a reading of character, this portrait reveals the proud bearing of a sensitive and beautiful young woman and tells us much about the high state of human culture achieved in Florence, the value and careful cultivation of beauty in life and art, the breeding of courtly manners, and the great wealth behind it all. It is also a record of the powerful attraction that Classical literature held for Italian Humanists: in the background is an epitaph (Giovanna Tornabuoni died in childbirth in 1488) that is a quotation from the ancient Roman poet Martial.

BOTTICELLI   The profile pose was customary in Florence until about 1470, when three-quarter and full-face portraits began to replace it. In about the last decade of the fifteenth century, SANDRO BOTTICELLI (1444–1510) painted

21-55   DOMENICO GHIRLANDAIO, *Giovanna Tornabuoni* (?), 1488. Oil and tempera on wood, approx. 30" × 20". Sammlung Thyssen-Bornemisza, Lugano, Switzerland.

the nearly full-face *Portrait of a Young Man* (FIG. **21-56**). Three-quarter and full-face views were made common earlier in the century by the painters of northern Europe (FIG. 20-7). The Italian painters now adopt them, perceiving that they increase the viewer's information about the subject's appearance and allow the artist to reveal the subject's character, although Italian artists will long prefer an impersonal formality that conceals the private, psychological person. An apparent exception, Botticelli's young man is highly expressive psychologically. The delicacy of the pose, the graceful tilt of the head, the sidelong glance, and the elegant gesture of the hand compose an equivocal expression half musing and half insinuating. Feminine and masculine traits are merged to make an image of rarefied, epicene beauty.

21-56 SANDRO BOTTICELLI, *Portrait of a Young Man, c.* 1489–1490. Tempera on panel, 16¹/₈″ × 12¹/₄″. National Gallery of Art, Washington, D.C. (Andrew W. Mellon Collection).

21-57   SANDRO BOTTICELLI, *Birth of Venus, c.* 1482. Tempera on canvas, approx. 5′ 8″ × 9′ 1″. Galleria degli Uffizi, Florence.

Botticelli was the pupil of Fra Filippo Lippi, from whom he must have learned the method of "drawing" firm, pure outline with light shading within the contours. The effect clearly is apparent in the explicit and sharply elegant form of the portrait. In the hands of Botticelli, this method will be refined infinitely, and he is known as one of the great masters of line.

No discussion of Botticelli can be fully meaningful without some reference to the environment that peculiarly encouraged him—the circle of Lorenzo de' Medici and the Platonic Academy of Philosophy. Here, he studied the philosophy of Plato, or rather of Neo-Platonism, for scholars had not yet developed the critical sense that would distinguish between Plato and the Neo-Platonic mystics of Alexandria. It was this spiritualized and mystical Platonism that Botticelli absorbed, believing that it was close to Christianity in essence and that the two could be reconciled. He must have heard the Humanists gathered around Lorenzo discoursing on these new mysteries in one of the Medici villas—surroundings highly conducive to reflection.

For one of these villas Botticelli painted his famous *Birth of Venus* (FIG. **21-57**), inspired by a poem on that theme by Angelo Poliziano, one of the leading Humanists

of the day. Botticelli is of his generation in his enthusiasm for themes from Classical mythology, as well as in his suiting of the ancient pagan materials to a form prepared by the Early Renaissance, a form realistic yet still modified by something of the medieval past. Competent in all the new representational methods, he seems deliberately to sacrifice them in the interest of his own original manner, rarefying the realism of the Early Renaissance into an inimitable decorative and linear system that generates its own kind of figure and space.

Venus, born of the sea foam, is wafted on a cockle shell, blown by Zephyrus (the west wind), to her sacred island, Cyprus, where the nymph Pomona, runs to meet her with a brocaded mantle. The lightness and bodilessness of the winds move all the figures without effort. Draperies undulate easily in the gentle gusts, perfumed by rose petals that fall on the whitecaps stirred by Zephyrus's toes. The presentation of the figure of Venus nude was, in itself, an innovation; as we have seen, the nude, especially the female nude, had been proscribed during the Middle Ages. Its appearance on such a scale and the use of an ancient Venus statue of the *Venus pudica* (modest Venus) type— a Hellenistic variant of Praxiteles's famous *Aphrodite of*

Knidos (FIG. 5-68)—as a model could have drawn the charge of paganism and infidelity. But under the protection of the powerful Medici, a new world of imagination could open freely with the new Platonism.

In Botticelli's hands, the pagan myth is transmuted into a Neo-Platonic allegory of the human soul. The high priest of the Neo-Platonic cult (for which the *Birth of Venus* almost could have been an altarpiece) was the Humanist philosopher Marsilio Ficino, certainly known to Botticelli through Lorenzo de' Medici's circle. Ficino taught that God had created the universe as a hierarchy of descending orders of being that extended from the perfection of the angelic spheres down to the inert being of base matter. The human soul, before its birth, had perfect existence; coming into the world of matter, it had become corrupt. Now it occupied the central place in the great chain of being. It could regain its original perfection and ascend to fullest being only by the love of God as manifested in the beauty of creation. By the contemplation of beauty, the soul could progress from the love of the material to the love of the abstract and then to the love of the spiritual. The goal of the quest is the vision of God—Dante's experience at the end of the *Commedia*. Venus, the pagan goddess of beauty and love, is transformed into the Heavenly Venus, purged of all mundane sensuality; it is she whom the soul must contemplate.

Botticelli gives us the Heavenly Venus. Her lovely figure, strangely weightless and ethereal, is the intellectual and spiritual apparition of beauty; at the same time, she personifies the human soul. The *Birth of Venus* is an allegory of the primal innocence and truth of the soul, before its birth into gross matter, its fall into lesser being. Here, the soul—naked as truth is naked—is blown upon by the winds of passion but is soon to be clothed in the robe of reason. The pagan myth of the goddess is conflated with the Neo-Platonic account of the journey of the soul to God through the contemplation of beauty. The ascent of the soul to the ultimate ecstasy, the vision of God, is the main theme of Christian mysticism; the concept that the ascent is made possible by the contemplation of beauty is Neo-Platonic. The beauty of the pagan goddess becomes the beauty of the perfected soul.

This kind of mystical approach, so different from the earnest search of the early fifteenth century to comprehend humanity and the natural world through a rational and empirical order, finds expression in Botticelli's strange and beautiful style, which seems to ignore all of the scientific ground gained by experimental art. His style parallels the allegorical pageants in Florence, which were staged as chivalric tournaments but revolved completely around allusions to Classical mythology; the same trend is evident in the poetry of the 1470s and 1480s. Artists and poets at this time did not directly imitate Classical antiquity, but used the myths, with delicate perception of their charm, in a way still tinged with medieval romance.

A decade after Botticelli painted the *Birth of Venus,* Florence would undergo a political, cultural, and religious upheaval. Lorenzo de' Medici died in 1492 and two years later the Medici were expelled from the city. Florentine artists and their fellow citizens now were responding not only to the Humanist and Neo-Platonic ideas of Lorenzo's intellectual circle, but to the incursion of the French armies and especially to the preaching of the Dominican monk Girolamo Savonarola, the reforming priest-dictator who denounced the paganism of the Medici and their artists, philosophers, and poets. Savonarola called on the people of Florence to repent their iniquities, and, when the Medici fled, he prophesied the doom of the city and of Italy and took absolute power over the state. Together with a large number of citizens, Savonarola believed that the Medici had been a political, social, and religious influence for the worse—corrupting Florence and inviting the scourge of foreign invasion. Modern scholars still debate the significance of Savonarola's brief span of power. Apologists for the undoubtedly sincere monk deny that his actions played a role in the decline of Florentine culture at the end of the century. But he did rail at the Neo-Platonist Humanists as heretical gabblers, and his banishing of the Medici, Tornabuoni, and other noble families from Florence deprived local artists of some of their major patrons. Florence lost its position of cultural leadership at the end of the century and never regained it. Certainly, the puritanical spirit that moved Savonarola must have dampened considerably the neopagan enthusiasm of the Florentine Early Renaissance.

SIGNORELLI AND PERUGINO   Outside Florence, the fiery passion of the sermons of Savonarola finds its pictorial equal in the work of the Umbrian painter, LUCA SIGNORELLI (*c.* 1445–1523), who further developed the interest of Antonio Pollaiuolo in the depiction of muscular bodies in violent action in a wide variety of poses and foreshortenings. In the San Brizio Chapel in Orvieto Cathedral, Signorelli's painted scenes depicting the end of the world include the *Damned Cast into Hell* (FIG. **21-58**). Few figure compositions of the fifteenth century have the same awesome psychic impact. Saint Michael and the hosts of Heaven hurl the damned into Hell, where, in a dense, writhing mass, they are tortured by vigorous demons. The horrible consequences of a life of sin have not been so graphically depicted since Gislebertus carved his vision of the Last Judgment in the west tympanum of St. Lazare at Autun (FIGS. 12-30 and 12-31) around 1130. The figures—nude, lean, and muscular—assume every conceivable posture of anguish. Signorelli's skill at foreshortening the human figure is one with his mastery of its action, and although each figure is clearly a study from a model, he fits his theme to the figures in an entirely convincing manner. Terror and rage pass like storms through the wrenched and

PROPHETARVM LAVDABILIS NVMERVS

21-58   LUCA SIGNORELLI, *Damned Cast into Hell*, 1499–1504. Fresco, approx. 23' wide. San Brizio Chapel, Cathedral, Orvieto.

twisted bodies. The fiends, their hair flaming and their bodies the color of putrefying flesh, lunge at their victims in ferocious frenzy. Not even Pollaiuolo achieves such virtuosity in the manipulation of anatomy for dramatic purpose. Doubtless, Signorelli influenced Michelangelo, who makes the human nude his sole and sufficient expressive motif. In the *Last Judgment* in the Sistine Chapel (FIG. 22-28), Michelangelo shows that he was much aware of Signorelli's vision of the theme.

Signorelli's fellow Umbrian, Pietro Vannucci, known as PERUGINO (*c.* 1450–1523), was concerned not with the human figure in violent action, as Signorelli was, but with the calm, geometric ordering of pictorial space. Between 1481 and 1483, Perugino, Botticelli, Ghirlandaio, and

Signorelli were among a group of artists summoned to Rome to decorate with frescoes the walls of the newly completed Sistine Chapel. Perugino painted *Christ Delivering the Keys of the Kingdom to St. Peter* (FIG. **21-59**), the event on which the papacy had, from the beginning, based its claim to infallible and total authority over the Church. Christ hands the keys to Saint Peter, standing at the center of solemn choruses of saints and citizens, who occupy the apron of a great stage space that marches into the distance to a point of convergence in the doorway of a central-plan temple. (The intervening space is stepped off by the parallel lines of the pavement.) Figures in the middle distance complement the near group, emphasizing its density and order by their scattered arrangement. At the corners of the

21-59 PERUGINO, *Christ Delivering the Keys of the Kingdom to St. Peter,* 1481–1483. Fresco, 11′ 5¹/₂″ × 18′ 8¹/₂″. Sistine Chapel, Vatican, Rome.

great piazza, duplicate triumphal arches mark the base angles of a compositional triangle having its apex in the central building. (The arches are modeled very closely on the Arch of Constantine in Rome [FIG. 7-86], an anachronism in a painting depicting a scene from the life of Christ, but their presence is a reminder of the close ties between Constantine and Saint Peter and the great basilica the first Christian emperor built over Saint Peter's tomb in Rome.) Christ and Peter are placed on the central axis, which runs through the temple's doorway, within which is the vanishing point of the perspective. Thus, the composition interlocks both two-dimensional and three-dimensional space, and the central actors are integrated carefully with the axial center. This spatial science provides a means for organizing the action systematically. Perugino, in this single picture, incorporates the learning of generations. His coolly rational, orderly style and the uncluttered clarity of his compositions left a lasting impression on his best-known student, Raphael.

MANTEGNA   Many Florentine artists worked in northern Italy: Donatello in Padua; Paolo Uccello, Andrea del Castagno, and Fra Filippo Lippi in Venice. Gradually, the International Style, which lingered long in the north, yield-

ed to the new Florentine art. Around mid-century, one of the most brilliant talents of the entire Renaissance, ANDREA MANTEGNA (c. 1431–1506) of Padua, appeared in northern Italy; there he must have met Donatello, who greatly stimulated and influenced his art. Mantegna's frescoes in the Ovetari Chapel in the Church of the Eremitani in Padua (largely destroyed in World War II) bring northern Italian painting into line with the Humanist art of Florence. *St. James Led to Martyrdom* (FIG. **21-60**) depicts the sad-countenanced saint stopping, even on the way to his own death, to bless a man who has rushed from the crowd and kneels before him (while a Roman soldier restrains others from coming forward). Yet narrative does not seem to be Mantegna's primary concern in this fresco in which he reveals the breadth of his literary, archeological, and pictorial learning. The motifs that appear on the barrel-vaulted triumphal arch are taken from the Classical ornamental vocabulary. The soldiers' costumes are studied from antique models; the painter strives for historical authenticity, much as did the antiquarian scholars of the University of Padua. Mantegna sets up for himself difficult problems in perspective for the joy of solving them. Here, the observer views the scene from a very low point, almost as if looking up out of a basement window at the vast arch looming above. The lines of the building to the right plunge down dramatically. Several significant deviations from true perspective are apparent, however, and establish that Mantegna does not view the scientific organization of pictorial space as an end in itself. Using artistic license, he ignores the third vanishing point (seen from below, the buildings should converge toward the top). Disregarding the facts of perspective, he prefers to work toward a unified, cohesive composition in which pictorial elements are related to the picture frame. The lack of perspective logic is partly compensated for by the insertion of strong diagonals in the right foreground (the staff of the banner, for example).

From about 1460 onward, Mantegna worked predominantly for the Gonzaga family of Mantua, who were great patrons like the Medici. Unlike the Medici, however, who were the most powerful members of a merchant oligarchy, the Gonzaga were hereditary dukes. In the ducal palace at Mantua, Mantegna performed a triumphant feat of pictorial illusionism, producing the first completely consistent illusionistic decoration of an entire room—the so-called Camera degli Sposi (Room of the Newlyweds). Utilizing actual architectural elements, Mantegna paints away the walls of the room in a manner that forecasts later Baroque decoration—and recalls the efforts of Italian painters over fifteen centuries earlier at Pompeii and elsewhere to integrate mural painting and actual architecture in frescoes of the so-called Second Style of Roman painting (FIGS. 7-18 and 7-19). Mantegna's *trompe l'oeil* (literally "deceives the eye") design, however, goes far beyond anything preserved

21-60   ANDREA MANTEGNA, *St. James Led to Martyrdom, c.* 1455. Fresco, 10′ 9″ wide. Ovetari Chapel, Church of the Eremitani, Padua (largely destroyed, 1944).

from ancient Italy. The Renaissance painter's daring experimentalism leads him to complete the room's decoration with the first *di sotto in sù* ("from below upwards") perspective of a ceiling (FIG. **21-61**). This technique was broadly developed later by the northern Italian painter, Correggio, and the Baroque ceiling decorators. In the Room of the Newlyweds, we look directly up at figures looking down at us. Italians traditionally have a great deal of fun with newlyweds; spying on them is part of the fun. The dome of the room is positioned directly over the marriage bed. The oculus is itself an "eye" looking down. Cupids (the sons of Venus), strongly foreshortened, set the amorous mood, as the painted spectators (who are not identified) smile down on the scene. The peacock is an attribute of Juno, the bride

21-61   ANDREA MANTEGNA, ceiling of the Camera degli Sposi, 1474. Fresco, 8′ 9″ in diameter. Palazzo Ducale, Mantua.

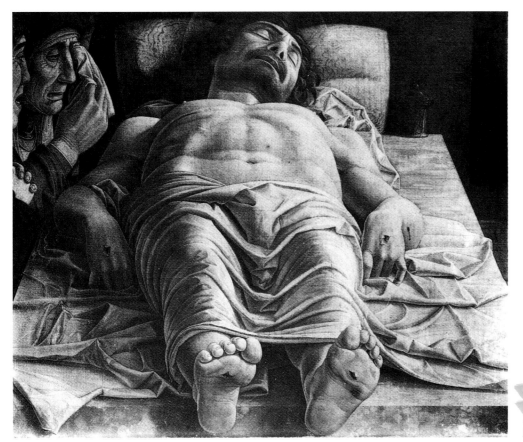

21-62   ANDREA MANTEGNA, *Dead Christ*, c. 1501. Tempera on canvas, 26³/₄″ × 31⁷/₈″. Pinacoteca di Brera, Milan.

of Jupiter, who oversees lawful marriages. This tour de force of illusionism climaxes almost a century of experiment in perspective.

One of Mantegna's later paintings, the *Dead Christ* (FIG. **21-62**), is a work of overwhelming power, despite the somewhat awkward insertion of the two mourning figures on the left. What seems to be a strikingly realistic study in foreshortening, however, is modified by a reduction in the size of the figure's feet, which, as every photographer knows (and as Mantegna must have known), would cover the body if properly represented. Thus, tempering naturalism with artistic license, Mantegna presents both a harrowing study of a strongly foreshortened cadaver and an intensely poignant presentation of a cosmic tragedy. The harsh, sharp line seems to cut the surface as if it were metal and conveys, by its grinding edge, the corrosive emotion of the theme; the observer thinks immediately of Ernest Hemingway's "the bitter nail holes in Mantegna's Christ."

Mantegna's presentation is unrelievedly bitter, an unforgiving reproach to guilty humankind. What is remarkable is that all the science of the fifteenth century here serves the purpose of devotion. A Gothic religious sensitivity of great depth and intensity still lingers in northern Italy at the end of the Middle Ages and is embodied in an image created by a new science.

Mantegna's work was highly influential in northern Italy, especially in the school of Ferrara—but also in Venice, where his style had a strong, formative influence on Giovanni Bellini, who may be viewed as the progenitor of Venetian painting. Mantegna's influence went even further, however, for he was a great engraver (the line in the *Dead Christ* certainly suggests engraving), and his prints found their way across the Alps to where they influenced Albrecht Dürer, German father of the Northern Renaissance.

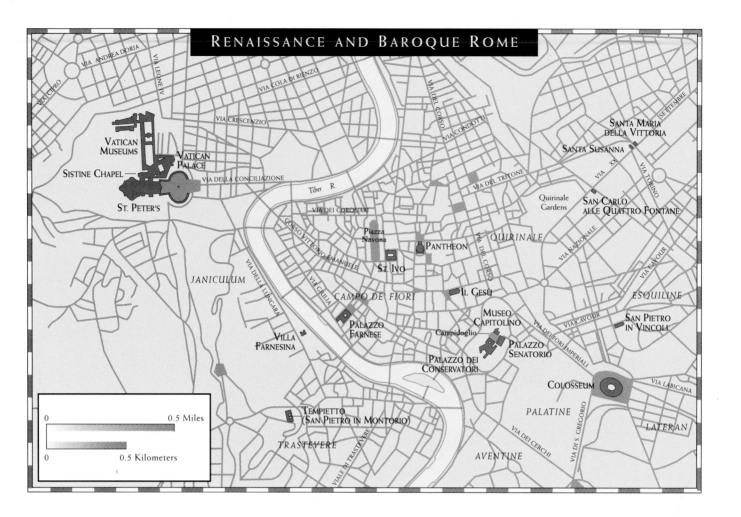

RENAISSANCE AND BAROQUE ROME

VIA ANDREA DORIA · VIA LEONE IV · VIA CIPRO · VIA COLA DI RIENZO · VIA CRESCENZIO · VIA DEL CORSO · VIA CONDOTTI · SETTEMBRE · SANTA MARIA DELLA VITTORIA · SANTA SUSANNA · VIA DEL TRITONE · VIA XX · VIA TORINO · Quirinale Gardens · SAN CARLO ALLE QUATTRO FONTANE · VATICAN MUSEUMS · VATICAN PALACE · SISTINE CHAPEL · VIA DELLA CONCILIAZIONE · ST. PETER'S · Tiber R. · VIA DEI CORONARI · QUIRINALE · VIA DEL CORSO · VIA NAZIONALE · VIA CAVOUR · Piazza Navona · PANTHEON · CORSO VITTORIO EMANUELE · ST. IVO · JANICULUM · VIA DELLA LUNGARA · VIA GIULIA · CAMPO DE' FIORI · IL GESÙ · ESQUILINE · VILLA FARNESINA · PALAZZO FARNESE · MUSEO CAPITOLINO · Campidoglio · PALAZZO SENATORIO · VIA DEI FORI IMPERIALI · SAN PIETRO IN VINCOLI · VIA CAVOUR · PALAZZO DEI CONSERVATORI · COLOSSEUM · VIA LABICANA · TEMPIETTO (SAN PIETRO IN MONTORIO) · PALATINE · LATERAN · VIA DI S. GREGORIO · TRASTEVERE · VIALE DI TRASTEVERE · VIA DEI CERCHI · AVENTINE

0 — 0.5 Miles
0 — 0.5 Kilometers

1500	1525
HIGH RENAISSANCE	LATE RENAISSANCE

Bramante, Tempietto
San Pietro in Montorio
Rome. c. 1502

Leonardo da Vinci
Mona Lisa, c. 1503–1505

Michelangelo, Creation of Adam
(detail of Sistine Chapel ceiling), 1508–1512

Titian, Venus of Urbino, 1538

Pope Alexander VI (Borgia), 1492–1503

Niccolò Machiavelli, 1469–1527
The Prince, 1532

Protestant Reformation begins, 1517

Pope Clement VII (Medici), 1523–1534

Pope Julius II (della Rovere), 1503–1513

Baldassare Castiglione, 1478–1529
The Courtier, 1528

Pope Leo X (Medici), 1513–1521

CHAPTER 22

SIXTEENTH-CENTURY ITALIAN ART: THE HIGH RENAISSANCE AND MANNERISM

1550	1575	1600

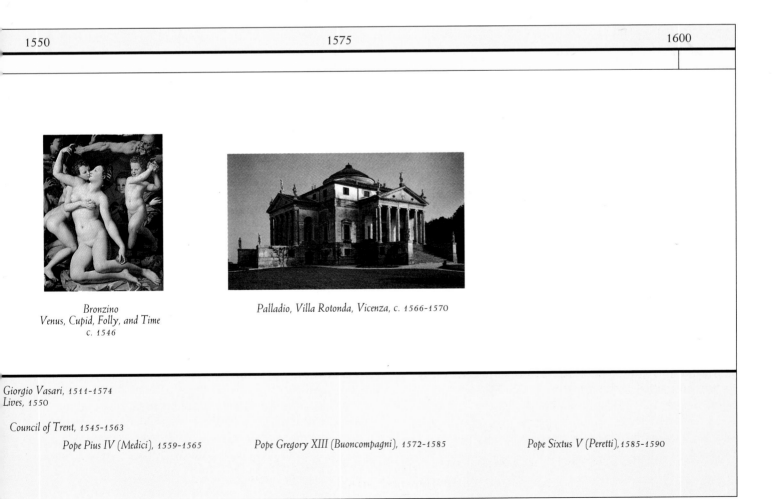

Bronzino
Venus, Cupid, Folly, and Time
c. 1546

Palladio, Villa Rotonda, Vicenza, c. 1566-1570

Giorgio Vasari, 1511-1574
Lives, 1550

Council of Trent, 1545-1563

Pope Pius IV (Medici), 1559-1565   Pope Gregory XIII (Buoncompagni), 1572-1585   Pope Sixtus V (Peretti), 1585-1590

Before the end of the fifteenth century, Florence had lost its unique position of leadership in the arts, and the innovations of its artists had become the property of Italian artists, regardless of local political boundaries. We do not mean to suggest that Florence no longer produced the artistic giants of an earlier age. Leonardo da Vinci and Michelangelo called themselves Florentines even though they spent a great part of their lives outside the city, and the turning point in Raphael's artistic education occurred as a result of his experience of Florentine art. In addition, Florence, with the early work of Leonardo, already had become the source of sixteenth-century style and later shared with Rome the beginnings and growth of Mannerism, a style that was to dominate Western European art during much of the sixteenth century. But Florence was faced with a time of crisis that began with the expulsion of the Medici and the brief and stormy dictatorship of Girolamo Savonarola and ended with the subversion of the Florentine republic by the Spanish and the return of the Medici (a collateral line of the original family) as tyrants under Spanish protection. Finally, in the 1530s, Florentine independence became a thing of the past when the state was made into a grand duchy under the crown of the Hapsburgs.

THE HIGH RENAISSANCE

Between about 1495 and the date of its own invasion and sack in 1527, Rome took the place of Florence and laid claim to its artistic preeminence. A series of powerful and ambitious popes—Alexander VI (Borgia), Julius II (della Rovere), Leo X (Medici), and Clement VII (Medici)—created a new power in Italy: a papal state, with Rome as its capital. At the same time, Rome became the artistic capital of Europe. The popes, living in the opulent splendor of secular princes, embellished the city with great works of art, inviting artists from all over Italy and providing them with challenging tasks. Artists during the short duration of the High Renaissance produced works of such authority that generations of later artists were instructed by them. The art of Leonardo, Raphael, Michelangelo, and Titian belongs to no school but is, in the case of each, something unique. The masters had of course inherited the pictorial science of the fifteenth century, and they learned from one another. Yet they made a distinct break with the past, occupying new ground—ground so lofty as to discourage emulation by their successors.

The High Renaissance produced a cluster of extraordinary geniuses and found in divine inspiration the rationale for the exaltation of the artist-genius. The Neo-Platonists found in Plato's *Ion* his famous praise of the poet: "All good poets compose their beautiful poems not by art, but because they are inspired and possessed . . . for not by art does the poet sing, but by power divine." And what the poet could claim, the Renaissance artist claimed also, raising visual art to the status formerly held only by poetry. Thus, painters, sculptors, and architects came into their own, successfully claiming for their work a high place among the fine arts. In the High Renaissance, the masters in a sense created a new profession, having its own rights of expression, its own venerable character, and its own claims to recognition by the great. The "fine" artist today lives, often without realizing it, on the accumulated prestige won by preceding artists, beginning with those who made the first great gains of the High Renaissance.

Leonardo da Vinci

A man who is the epitome of the artist-genius as well as of the "universal man," LEONARDO DA VINCI (1452–1519) has become a kind of wonder of the modern world, standing at the beginning of a new epoch like a prophet and a sage, mapping the routes that art and science are to take. The scope and depth of his interests were without precedent—so great as to frustrate any hopes he might have had of realizing all that his feverishly inventive imagination could conceive. We still look with awe on his achievements and, even more, on his unfulfilled promise. His mind and personality seem to us superhuman; the man himself was mysterious and remote.

Although we are concerned here primarily with Leonardo as an artist, we scarcely can hope to do his art credit in isolation from his science; his scientific drawings are themselves works of art, as well as models for that exact delineation of nature that is one of the aims of science. Leonardo's unquenchable curiosity is revealed best in his voluminous notes, liberally interspersed with sketches dealing with matters of botany, geology, zoology, hydraulics, military engineering, animal lore, anatomy, and aspects of physical science, including mechanics, perspective, light, optics, and color. Leonardo's great ambition in his painting, as well as in his scientific endeavors, was to discover the laws underlying the flux and processes of nature. With this end in mind, he also studied the human body and contributed immeasurably to our knowledge of physiology and psychology. Leonardo believed that reality in an absolute sense is inaccessible and that we can know it only through its changing images. He considered the eyes to be the most vital organs and sight the most essential function, as, through these, the images of reality could be grasped most directly and profoundly. He stated many times in his notes that all his scientific investigations merely were aimed at making himself a better painter.

Leonardo was born in the small town of Vinci, near Florence, and was trained in the studio of Andrea del Verrocchio, but he left Florence around 1481, offering his services to Ludovico Sforza, duke of Milan. The political situation in Florence was uncertain, and the Neo-Platonism of Lorenzo de' Medici and his brilliant circle may have proved uncongenial to the empirical and pragmatic Leonardo. It also may be that Leonardo felt that the artistic scene in Milan would be less competitive. He devoted most of a letter to the duke of Milan to advertising his competence and his qualifications as a military engineer, mentioning only at the end his supremacy as a painter and sculptor:

> And in short, according to the variety of cases, I can contrive various and endless means of offence and defence. . . . In time of peace I believe I can give perfect satisfaction and to the equal of any other in architecture and the composition of buildings, public and private; and in guiding water from one place to another. . . . I can carry out sculpture in marble, bronze, or clay, and also I can do in painting whatever may be done, as well as any other, be he whom he may.*

The letter illustrates the new relation of the artist to his patron, as well as Leonardo's breadth of competence. That he should select military engineering and design to interest a patron is an index of the dangerousness of the times. Weaponry now had been developed to the point, especially in northern Europe, that the siege cannon was a threat to the feudal castles of those attempting to resist wealthy and aggressive new monarchs. When, in 1494, Charles VIII of France invaded Italy, his cannon easily smashed the fortifications of the Italian princes. By the turn of the century, when Italy's liberties and unity were being trampled by the aspiring kingdoms of Europe, not only soldiers and architects, but artists and Humanists, were deeply concerned with the problem of designing a system of fortifications that might withstand the terrible new weapon.

During his first sojourn in Milan, Leonardo painted the *Virgin of the Rocks* (FIG. **22-1**) as the central panel of an altarpiece for the Confraternity of the Immaculate Conception's chapel in San Francesco Grande. The painting, although it may derive ultimately from Fra Filippo Lippi (FIG. 21-34), is well on its way out of the older tradition. The old triangular composition now broadens out into three dimensions, making a weighty pyramid. The linear approach, with its musical play of undulating contours and crisp edges, is abandoned, as Leonardo journeys back through the generations of the fifteenth century to Masaccio's great discovery of chiaroscuro, the subtle play of light and dark. What we see is the result of the moving together and interpenetration of lights and darks. "Drawn" representations, consisting of contours and edges, can be beautiful, but they really are not true to the optical facts. Moreover, a painting must embody not only physical chiaroscuro but the lights and darks of human psychology as well. Modeling with light and shadow and the expression of emotional states were, for Leonardo, the heart of painting:

22-1 LEONARDO DA VINCI, *Virgin of the Rocks, c.* 1485. Oil on wood (transferred to canvas), approx. 6′ 3″ × 3′ 7″. Louvre, Paris.

> A good painter has two chief objects to paint—man and the intention of his soul. The former is easy, the latter hard, for it must be expressed by gestures and the movement of the limbs. . . . A painting will only be wonderful for the beholder by making that which is not so appear raised and detached from the wall.*

The figures in the *Virgin of the Rocks* are knit together not only as a pyramidal group but as figures sharing the same atmosphere, a method of unification first seen in Masaccio's *Tribute Money* (FIG. 21-23). The Madonna, Christ Child, infant John the Baptist, and angel emerge through subtle gradations and nuances of light and shade from the

*In E.G. Holt, ed., *Literary Sources of Art History* (Princeton, NJ: Princeton University Press, 1947), p. 170.

*In Anthony Blunt, *Artistic Theory in Italy, 1450–1600* (London: Oxford University Press, 1964), p. 34.

half-light of the cavernous, visionary landscape. Light simultaneously veils and reveals the forms of things, immersing them in a layer of atmosphere between them and our eyes. The ambiguity of light and shade (familiar in the optical uncertainties of dusk) functions here in the service of the psychological ambiguity of perception. The group depicted, so strangely wrapped in subtle light and shade, eludes our precise definition and interpretation. The figures pray, point, and bless, and these acts and gestures, although their meanings are not certain, visually unite the individuals portrayed. The angel points to the infant John and, through his outward glance, involves the spectator in the tableau. John prays to the Christ Child and is blessed in return. The series of interlocking gestures is completed by the Virgin herself, whose left hand lovingly shelters the Christ Child and whose right hand protectively rests on John's shoulder. The melting mood of tenderness, enhanced by the caressing light, is compounded of yet other moods. What the eye sees is fugitive, as are the states of the soul, or, in Leonardo's term, its "intentions."

The style of the High Renaissance fully emerges in a *cartoon* (a full-size, preliminary drawing) for a painting of the *Virgin and Child with St. Anne and the Infant St. John* (FIG. **22-2**). The glowing light falls gently on the majestic forms and on a tranquil grandeur, order, and balance. The figures are robust and monumental, moving with a stately grace reminiscent of the Phidian statues of goddesses in the pediments of the Parthenon (FIG. 5-50)—statues that Leonardo and his contemporaries never saw, their acquaintance with Classical art being confined to Etruscan and Roman monuments and Roman copies of Greek masterpieces unearthed in Italy. Every part of Leonardo's cartoon is ordered by an intellectual, pictorial logic into a sure unity. The specialized depiction of perspective, anatomy, light, and space is a thing of the past. Leonardo has assimilated the learning of two centuries and applies it wholly, in a manner that is Classical and complete. This High Renaissance style, as Leonardo authoritatively presents it here, is stable without being static, varied without being confused, and dignified without being dull. As was the case in Greece, this brief, Classical moment inaugurated by Leonardo unifies and balances the conflicting experiences of an entire culture. This style will prove difficult to maintain. In a rapidly changing world, the artist may either repeat the compositions and forms of the day in a sterile, academic manner or revolt against the practices of the time by denying or exaggerating their principles. For these reasons, the High Renaissance was of short duration—even shorter than the brief span of the golden age of Athens in the fifth century B.C.

LAST SUPPER For the refectory of the church of Santa Maria delle Grazie in Milan, Leonardo painted the *Last Supper* (FIG. **22-3**). Despite its ruined state (in part the result of the painter's own unfortunate experiments with his

22-2 LEONARDO DA VINCI, cartoon for the *Virgin and Child with St. Anne and the Infant St. John*, 1498 (?). Charcoal heightened with white on brown paper, approx. 54″ × 39″. National Gallery, London.

materials), and although it has often been ineptly restored, the painting is both formally and emotionally his most impressive work.* It is the first great figure composition of the High Renaissance and the definitive interpretation of its theme. Christ and his twelve disciples are seated at a

*Since 1977, the painting has undergone painstaking, scientifically controlled restoration (a square inch at a time!). Although much of it is lost permanently, enough already has been recovered and repaired to reveal Leonardo's actual intentions and performance. The restored portions, freed from five hundred years' dark accumulation of dirt, mold, glue, and overpainting, reveal bright and strong colors and firm and elegant contours. Restoration also shows that Leonardo's style is rooted firmly in the practice of fifteenth-century Italian painting. Beneath the many mistaken overpaintings, the true characters of the disciples emerge from the blurred, murky, out-of-focus forms of the damaged picture. They are vividly realized individuals, of the kind we find in Leonardo's preserved preparatory drawings. Through their attitudes, gestures, personal traits, and facial expressions, they compellingly play the roles Leonardo designed for them, consistent with his own highly personal conception of this drama and its protagonists.

long table set parallel to the picture plane in a simple, spacious room. The highly dramatic action of the painting is made still more emphatic by the placement of the group in the austerely quiet setting. Christ, with outstretched hands, has just said, "One of you will betray me." A wave of intense excitement passes through the group, as each disciple asks himself and, in some cases, his neighbor, "Is it I?" Leonardo has made a brilliant conjunction of the dramatic "One of you will betray me" with the initiation of the ancient liturgical ceremony of the Eucharist, when Christ, blessing bread and wine, said "This is my body and this is my blood: do this in remembrance of me." The force and lucidity with which this dramatic moment is expressed are due to the abstract organization of the composition.

In the center, Christ is in perfect repose, the still eye of the swirling emotion around him. Isolated from the disciples, his figure is framed by the central window at the back, the curved pediment of which arches above his head. The pediment is the only curve in the architectural framework, and it serves here as a halo. Christ's head is the focal point of all perspective lines in the composition. Thus, the still, psychological focus and cause of the action is, at the same time, the perspective focus as well as the center of the two-dimensional surface. One could say that the two-dimensional, the three-dimensional, and the psycho-dimensional focuses are one and the same. The agitated

disciples, registering a broad range of rationally ordered, idealized, and proportionate responses, embracing fear, doubt, protestation, rage, and love, are represented in four groups of three, united among and within themselves by the gestures and postures of the figures. Leonardo sacrifices traditional iconography to pictorial and dramatic consistency by placing Judas on the same side of the table as Jesus and the other disciples. His face in shadow, Judas clutches a money bag in his right hand and reaches his left forward to fulfill the Master's declaration: "Behold, the hand of him that betrayeth me is with me on the table." The two disciples at either end of the table are more quiet than the others, as if to enclose the overall movement, which is more intense closer to the figure of Christ, whose calm at the same time halts and intensifies it.

We know from numerous preparatory studies that Leonardo thought of each figure as carrying a particular charge and type of emotion. Like a skilled stage director (perhaps the first, in the modern sense), he has read the gospel story carefully and scrupulously cast his actors as their roles are described. With him begins that rhetoric of Classical art that will direct the compositions of generations of painters until the nineteenth century. The silence of Christ is one such powerful rhetorical device. Indeed, Heinrich Wölfflin saw that the Classical element is precisely here, for in the silence following Christ's words, "the

22-3   LEONARDO DA VINCI, *Last Supper, c.* 1495–1498. Fresco (Oil and tempera on plaster), 29' 10" × 13' 9". Refectory, Santa Maria delle Grazie, Milan.

original impulse to the emotional excitement continues to echo, and the action is at once momentary, eternal and complete."* The two major trends of fifteenth-century painting—monumentality and mathematically ordered space at the expense of movement, and freedom of movement at the expense of monumentality and controlled space—are here harmonized and balanced. The *Last Supper* and Leonardo's career leading up to it are at once a synthesis of the artistic developments of the fifteenth century and a first statement of the High Renaissance style in Italy during the early sixteenth century.

If Leonardo's *Last Supper* is the world's most famous religious picture, the *Mona Lisa* (FIG. **22-4**) is probably the world's most famous portrait. The identity of the sitter is still the subject of scholarly debate, but Vasari states that

*Heinrich Wölfflin, *Classic Art: An Introduction to the Italian Renaissance,* 4th ed. (Ithaca: Cornell University Press, 1980), p. 27.

she is Lisa di Antonio Maria Gherardini, the wife of Francesco del Giocondo, a wealthy Florentine—hence "Mona (an Italian contraction of *ma donna,* my lady) Lisa"—and that Leonardo took three years to complete the portrait after he returned to Florence from Milan. This was one of his favorite pictures—one with which he could not bear to part and which was still in his possession at the time of his death. Originally Mona Lisa was represented in a loggia with columns that have been cut from the painting (the remains of the column bases may still be seen to the left and right of her shoulders). She is shown in half-length view, her hands quietly folded and her gaze directed at the observer. The ambiguity of the famous "smile" is really the consequence of Leonardo's fascination and skill with atmospheric chiaroscuro, which we have seen in his *Virgin of the Rocks* and *Virgin and St. Anne* groups, and which here serve to disguise rather than reveal a human psyche. The light is adjusted subtly enough, but the precise planes are blurred—Leonardo's famous smoky *sfumato*—and the facial expression is hard to determine.

A useful comparison may be made between the *Mona Lisa* and the earlier portraits we have examined by Domenico Ghirlandaio (FIG. 21-55) and Sandro Botticelli (FIG. 21-56), from which Leonardo's panel differs not only in the handling of light and dark and in the facial expression of the sitter but also in the very format of the portrait. Although Leonardo's *Mona Lisa* and Botticelli's *Young Man* are both represented facing the spectator, the latter is set against a dark, neutral background, and Ghirlandaio's *Giovanna Tornabuoni* is seen in left profile against an interior bookshelf. The appeal of the *Mona Lisa* over the centuries is due in no small part to Leonardo's decision to set his subject against the backdrop of a mysterious uninhabited landscape with roads and bridges that seem to lead nowhere, a solution reminiscent of his *Virgin of the Rocks* and one that recalls Fra Filippo Lippi's "portrait" of the Madonna (his mistress Lucretia?) and Child (FIG. 21-34) seated in front of a window through which we look out into a distant landscape.

Leonardo completed very few paintings; his perfectionism, restless experimentalism, and far-ranging curiosity scattered his efforts. Yet an extensive record of his ideas is preserved in the drawings in his notebooks. Science interested him increasingly in his later years, and he took knowledge of all nature (given first to the eye) as his proper province. His investigations in anatomy yielded drawings of great precision and beauty of execution. The *Embryo in the Womb* (FIG. **22-5**), although it does not meet twentieth-century standards for accuracy (the shape of the uterus, for example, has been regularized to that of a sphere and the characterization of the lining is incorrect), is an astounding achievement for its day. Analytical anatomical studies such as this one epitomize the scientific spirit of the Renaissance, establishing that era as the prelude to the modern world and setting it apart so sharply from the pre-

22-4 LEONARDO DA VINCI, *Mona Lisa, c.* 1503–1505. Oil on wood, approx. 30" × 21". Louvre, Paris.

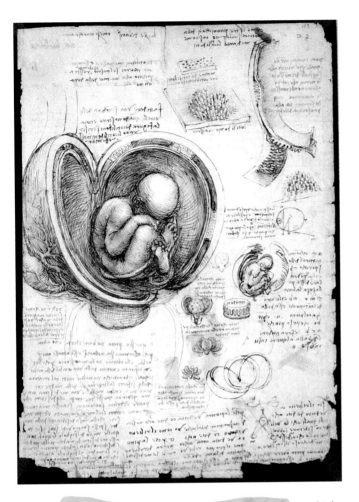

22-5 LEONARDO DA VINCI, *Embryo in the Womb, c.* 1510. Pen and ink on paper. Royal Library, Windsor Castle.

ceding Middle Ages. Although Leonardo may not have been the first scientist of the modern world (at least not in the modern sense of "scientist"), he certainly originated the method of scientific illustration, especially cutaway and exploded views. The importance of this has been stressed by Erwin Panofsky: "Anatomy as a science (and this applies to all the other observational or descriptive disciplines) was simply not possible without a method of preserving observations in graphic records, complete and accurate in three dimensions."*

Leonardo was well known in his own time as both architect and sculptor, though no actual buildings can be attributed to him and no sculpture that is certainly by him has survived. From his many drawings of central-plan buildings, it appears that he shared the interest of other Renaissance architects in this building type. In Milan, Leonardo must have been in close contact with the architect Bramante, who may well have remembered a drawing

*Erwin Panofsky, "Artist, Scientist, Genius," in *The Renaissance,* ed. Wallace K. Ferguson (New York: Harper & Row, 1962), p. 147.

by Leonardo when he prepared his original designs for the great church of St. Peter's in Rome (FIG. 22-7). As for sculpture, Leonardo left numerous drawings of monumental equestrian statues, one of which ripened into a full-scale model for a monument to the Sforza; used as a target, it was shot to pieces by the French when they occupied Milan in 1499. Leonardo left Milan outraged at this treatment of his work and was employed for a while as a military engineer for Cesare Borgia, who, with the support of his father, Pope Alexander VI, tried to conquer the cities of the Romagna and create a Borgia duchy. At a later date, Leonardo returned to Milan in the service of the French. At the invitation of King Francis I, he then went to France, where he died at the chateau of Cloux in 1519. Although born only eight years after Botticelli at the mid-point of the fifteenth century (his *Virgin of the Rocks* is almost exactly contemporary to the *Birth of Venus* [FIG. 21-57]), we always think of Leonardo da Vinci as the first great artistic personality of the sixteenth century; that alone is ample testimony to the extraordinary genius of the man.

Bramante and His Circle

The most important artist with whom Leonardo came into contact in Milan was DONATO D'ANGELO BRAMANTE (1444–1514). Born in Urbino and trained as a painter (perhaps by Piero della Francesca), Bramante went to Milan in 1481 and, like Leonardo, stayed there until the arrival of the French in 1499. In Milan, he abandoned painting to become the greatest architect of his generation. Under the influence of Filippo Brunelleschi, Leon Battista Alberti, and perhaps Leonardo, all of whom had been influenced strongly by the art and architecture of Classical antiquity, Bramante developed the High Renaissance form of the central-plan church. But it was not until after his arrival in Rome in 1499 that Bramante built what was to be the perfect prototype of Classical, domed architecture for the Renaissance and subsequent periods. This building—the Tempietto (FIG. **22-6**)—received its name because, to contemporaries, it had the aspect of a small pagan temple from antiquity. "Little Temple" is, in fact, a perfectly appropriate sobriquet for the structure, for its lower story was directly inspired by the round temples of Roman Italy that Bramante would have known in Rome itself and in its environs (FIG. 7-2). The building's traditional date of 1502 has been disputed, but Bramante seems to have been asked to undertake the project in that year, and construction of the Tempietto was certainly begun during the first decade of the sixteenth century. It was commissioned by the king of Spain to mark the conjectural location of St. Peter's crucifixion. Standing inside the cloister alongside the church of San Pietro in Montorio, the Tempietto resembles a sculptured reliquary and would have looked even more like one inside the circular, colonnaded courtyard that was planned for it but never executed.

22-6   BRAMANTE, Tempietto, 1502 (?). San Pietro in Montorio, Rome.

All but devoid of ornament, this little building relies for its effect on the composition of volumes and masses and on a sculptural handling of solids and voids that set it apart from anything built in the preceding century. If one of the main differences between the Early and High Renaissance styles of architecture is the former's emphasis on the articulation of flat wall surfaces and the latter's sculptural handling of architectural masses, then the Tempietto certainly breaks new ground and stands at the beginning of a new era.

At first glance, the structure may seem overly formalistic and rational with its sober, circular stylobate and the cool Tuscan order of the colonnade, neither of which gives any indication of the placement of an interior altar or of the location of the entrance. However, Bramante achieved a truly wonderful balance and harmony in the relationship of the parts (dome, drum, and base) to each other and to the whole. The balustrade echoes, in shorter beats, the rhythm of the colonnade and averts a too-rapid ascent to the drum, while the pilasters of the drum itself repeat the ascending motif and lead the eye past the cornice to the exposed ribs of the dome. The play of light and shade around columns and balustrade and across alternating deep-set, rectangular windows and shallow, shell-capped niches in cella walls

and drum enhances one's experience of the building as an articulated sculptural mass. Although the Tempietto, superficially at least, may resemble a Classical tholos (compare FIGS. 5-81 and 7-2), and although all of its details have been studied closely from antique models, the combination of parts and details is new and original (Classical tholoi, for instance, had neither drum nor balustrade). Conceived as a tall, domed cylinder projecting from the lower, wider cylinder of its colonnade, this small building incorporates all the qualities of a sculptured monument.

The significance of the Tempietto was well understood in the sixteenth century. The architect Andrea Palladio, an artistic descendant of Bramante, included it in his survey of ancient temples because "Bramante was the first who brought good and beautiful architecture to light, which from the time of the ancients to his day had been forgotten." Round in plan, elevated on a base that isolates it from its surroundings, the Tempietto conforms with Alberti's and Palladio's strictest demands for an ideal church, demonstrating "the unity, the infinite essence, the uniformity, and the justice of God."

The same architectural concept guided Bramante's plans for the new St. Peter's, which was commissioned by Pope Julius II in 1505 to replace the Constantinian basilica, Old St. Peter's (FIG. 8-8). The earlier structure had fallen into considerable disrepair and, in any event, did not suit this ambitious and warlike pope's taste for the colossal; Julius wanted to gain sway over the whole of Italy and to make the Rome of the Popes more splendid than the Rome of the Caesars. As originally designed by Bramante, the new St. Peter's (FIG. 22-7) was to have consisted of a cross with

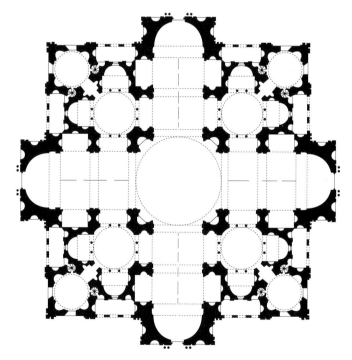

22-7   BRAMANTE, plan for the new St. Peter's, the Vatican, Rome, 1505.

22-8 CHRISTOFORO FOPPA CARADOSSO, medal showing Bramante's design for the new St. Peter's, 1506. British Museum, London.

arms of equal length, each terminated by an apse. The new building was intended as a martyrium to mark St. Peter's grave; Julius also hoped to have his own tomb in it. The crossing would have been covered by a large dome, and smaller domes over subsidiary chapels would have covered the diagonal axes of the roughly square plan. Bramante's ambitious plan called for a boldly sculptural treatment of the walls and piers under the dome. The interior space is complex in the extreme, with the intricate symmetries of a crystal. It is possible to detect in the plan some nine interlocking crosses, five of which are domed. The scale was titanic; Bramante is said to have boasted that he would place the dome of the Pantheon (FIG. 7-55) over the Basilica of Constantine (FIG. 7-90).

A commemorative medal by CHRISTOFORO FOPPA CARADOSSO (FIG. **22-8**) shows how Bramante's scheme would have attempted to do just that. The dome is hemispherical, like the Pantheon's, but otherwise the exterior, with two towers and a medley of domes and porticoes, breaks the massive unity, resulting in a still essentially anthropometric design scaled down to human proportions in the Early Renaissance manner. The commemoration of Bramante's design for the new St. Peter's on a medal is in itself significant. Such medals were already being struck in the fifteenth century; we know, for example, Alberti's plans for the unfinished "temple" of San Francesco at Rimini (FIG. 21-38) from a contemporary medal. The Renaissance practice is a revival of the ancient Roman habit of placing images of important imperial building projects on the reverses of Roman coins. These coins were much prized in Renaissance Italy and were avidly collected; the collection

of the Medici family still forms the core of the numismatic cabinet of Florence's Archeological Museum.

During Bramante's lifetime, the actual construction of the new St. Peter's basilica did not advance beyond the building of the piers of the crossing and the lower walls of the choir. With his death, the work passed from one architect to another and finally to Michelangelo, who was appointed by Pope Paul III in 1546 to complete the building.

After Bramante's Tempietto, the closest realization of the High Renaissance Classical ideals—order, clarity, lucidity, simplicity, harmony, and proportion—is found in the pilgrimage church of Santa Maria della Consolazione at Todi (FIG. **22-9**), begun in 1508. This church's hillside site outside the town makes it visible from far away, and its sturdy, carefully proportioned silhouette offers an attractive goal for the faithful approaching through the valley below. Although the identity of its designer is uncertain, it is quite clearly in the manner of Bramante, and we can call it "Bramantesque."

In its plan, the church takes the form of a domed cross, with its lobelike arms ending in polygonal apses. The interior space, showing a Classical purity of arrangement in which the layout is immediately open to the eye and volumes and spaces are in exquisite adjustment, finds its exact

22-9 Santa Maria della Consolazione, Todi, begun 1508 (view from the south).

expression on the exterior. Here, each level is carefully marked off by projecting cornices, and the rhythm increases steadily from bottom to top. The unfenestrated first story, marked off into blank panels by pilasters, provides a firm base for the upper structure. The second story is fenestrated, the windows topped by alternating triangular and segmental pediments. The attic story makes a transition to the half-domes, and the half-domes serve the same function in relation to the balustraded platform that sets off drum and dome as it makes a transition to them. The rhythm of fenestration of the second floor reappears in the drum, where it is quickened by the interpolation of round-headed niches between the windows, like the appearance of a second voice in a fugue.

Regardless of the side from which it is seen, the building presents a completely balanced and symmetrical aspect. Like a three-dimensional essay in a rational order, all of its parts are in harmonious relation to each other and to the whole, yet each is complete and independent. In both scale and complexity, Santa Maria della Consolazione stands between the Tempietto and the design for the new St. Peter's. More amply than the former, with greater purity than the latter, it expresses the architectural ideals of the High Renaissance. Its spirit is that of Classical antiquity, and, though it is modern, it speaks only the Classical language.

The palaces designed by Bramante have been preserved only in drawings or engravings. His Palazzo Caprini (FIG. **22-10**), bought by Raphael in 1517, was torn down during the rebuilding of the area around St. Peter's. Still, it was one of the most important and influential palace designs of the sixteenth century. In it, Bramante reduced the typical three-story facade of the fifteenth century to two stories, with the strongly rusticated first story serving as a robust support for the elegantly articulated *piano nobile* (main story). This arrangement not only differentiates the two stories, but emphatically puts the residential level of the building above the commercial. (The ground floor was occupied by shops and offices, in accordance with an Italian tradition that goes back to the townhouses and apartment blocks of ancient Pompeii and Ostia and continues to the present day.) The pedimented windows of the second story are flanked by pairs of engaged Tuscan columns supporting an entablature in which some of the metopes of the Doric frieze are pierced by the windows of an attic story. The total aspect of the building is one of rugged plasticity, and its influence on contemporary and later architects, including Palladio and Inigo Jones, was lasting. With Baroque modifications, Bramante's scheme can be recognized in Claude Perrault's Louvre facade (FIG. 24-63), erected in Paris almost two centuries later.

Less plastic, perhaps, than Bramante's design, but equally imposing, is the Palazzo Farnese in Rome (FIG. **22-11**), designed by ANTONIO DA SANGALLO THE YOUNGER (1483–1546), which fully expresses the Classical order, reg-

22-10 . BRAMANTE, Palazzo Caprini (House of Raphael), Rome, *c.* 1510. (Drawing attributed to ANDREA PALLADIO.)

ularity, simplicity, and dignity of the High Renaissance. Antonio, the youngest of a family of architects, received his early training from his uncles Giuliano, the designer of Santa Maria delle Carceri in Prato (FIG. 21-43), and Antonio the Elder. Antonio the Younger went to Rome around 1503 and became Bramante's draftsman and assistant. As the favorite architect of Pope Paul III, he received many commissions that might have gone to Michelangelo. He is the perfect example of the professional architect, and his family constituted an architectural firm, often working up the plans and doing the drafting for other architects. Antonio built fortifications for almost the entire papal state and received more commissions for military than for civilian architecture. Although he may not have invented it, Antonio certainly developed to a high degree the modern method of bastioned fortifications.

The Palazzo Farnese, built for Cardinal Farnese (later Pope Paul III), sets a standard for the High Renaissance palazzo. The sixteenth century was the beginning of the age of the great dynasties that would dominate Europe until the French Revolution in the late eighteenth century. It was an age of royal and princely pomp, of absolute monarchy rendered splendid by art. The broad, majestic front of the Palazzo Farnese asserts to the public the exalted station of a great family. This proud frontispiece symbolizes the aristocratic epoch that followed the stifling of the nascent,

22-11 ANTONIO DA SANGALLO THE YOUNGER, Palazzo Farnese, Rome, *c.* 1530–1546 (view from the northwest).

middle-class democracy of European cities (especially the Italian cities) by powerful kings heading centralized states. It is thus significant that the original, rather modest palace was greatly enlarged to its present form after Paul's acces-

22-12 ANTONIO DA SANGALLO THE YOUNGER, courtyard of the Palazzo Farnese. Third story and attic by MICHELANGELO, 1548.

sion to the papacy in 1534, reflecting the ambitions of the pope both for his family and the papacy. Unfinished at the time of Antonio's death in 1546, the building was completed by Michelangelo.

The facade is the very essence of princely dignity in architecture. Facing a spacious paved square, the rectangle of the smooth front is framed and firmly anchored by the *quoins* (rusticated building corners) and cornice, while lines of windows (with alternating triangular and segmental pediments, in Bramante's fashion) mark a majestic beat across it. The window casements are no longer flush with the wall, as in the Palazzo Medici-Riccardi (FIG. 21-20), but project from its surface, so that instead of being a flat, thin plane, the facade becomes a spatially active, three-dimensional mass. Each casement is a complete architectural unit, consisting of a *socle* (a projecting under-member), engaged columns, and pediment. The variations in the treatment of these units prevent the symmetrical scheme from becoming rigid or monotonous. The rusticated doorway and second-story balcony, surmounted by the Farnese coat of arms, emphasize the central axis and bring the horizontal and vertical forces of the design into harmony. This centralizing feature, not present in the palaces of Alberti or Michelozzo di Bartolomeo, is the external opening of a central-corridor axis that runs through the whole building and continues in the garden beyond; around this axis, the rooms are disposed with strict regularity. The interior courtyard (FIG. **22-12**) displays stately column-enframed arches, as in the Roman Colosseum (FIG. 7-39), on the first two levels. On the third level is Michelangelo's sophisticated variation on that theme (itself based in part on the Corinthian pilasters of the fourth story of the Colosseum), with overlapping pilasters replacing the weighty columns of Antonio's design.

Raphael

The artist most typical of the High Renaissance is Raffaello Sanzio, known as RAPHAEL (1483–1520). The pattern of his growth recapitulates the sequence of artistic tendencies of the fifteenth century, and although strongly influenced by Leonardo and Michelangelo, Raphael developed an individual style that, in itself, clearly states the ideals of High Renaissance art. His powerful originality prevailed while he learned from everyone; he assimilated what he best could use and rendered into form the Classical instinct of his age. Goethe, the renowned German poet and critic, said of Raphael that he did not have to imitate the Greeks, for he thought and felt like them. But Raphael's acquaintance with Classical art was, like all his contemporaries', with Roman rather than with Greek art. He was among a large group of Renaissance painters in Rome who explored the "grottoes" of the Domus Aurea of Nero, the then-underground frescoed vaulted chambers of the Roman emperor's fabulous Golden House (FIG. 7-23), which had been discovered around 1480. The signatures of these painters may still be seen on the ancient walls, and the Neronian *grotteschi,* as the Fourth Style frescoes of the Domus Aurea came to be called, had a profound influence on sixteenth-century mural design.

Born in a small town in Umbria near Urbino, Raphael probably learned the rudiments of his art from his father, Giovanni Sanzio, a provincial painter connected with the court of Federigo da Montefeltro. While still a child, Raphael was apprenticed to Perugino, who had been trained in Verrocchio's shop with Leonardo. We have seen in Perugino's *Christ Delivering the Keys of the Kingdom to St. Peter* (FIG. 21-59) that the most significant formal quality of his work is the harmony of spatial composition. While Raphael was still in the studio of Perugino, the latter painted a panel of the *Marriage of the Virgin* (not shown), which, in its composition, very closely resembles the central portion of his Sistine Chapel fresco. Perugino's panel probably served as the model for Raphael's *Marriage of the Virgin* (FIG. **22-13**), which was painted for the Chapel of St. Joseph in the church of San Francesco in Città di Castello. The subject is a fitting one. According to the *Golden Legend* (a thirteenth-century collection of stories about the lives of the saints), Joseph competed with other suitors for Mary's hand. The Virgin was to be given by the high priest to whichever suitor presented to him a rod that had miraculously bloomed. Joseph is here shown with his flowering rod while Mary receives her wedding ring. Other virgins are grouped at the left and the unsuccessful suitors are to the right; one of them breaks his rod in half over his knee in frustration—giving Raphael an opportunity to demonstrate his mastery of foreshortening as well as of the perspective system that he learned from Perugino. The temple in the background is Raphael's version of a centrally

planned structure. The painting is almost exactly contemporary to Bramante's Tempietto (FIG. 22-6), but Raphael employs Brunelleschian arcades rather than Bramante's more "modern" classicizing post-and-lintel system.

Raphael spent the four years from 1504 to 1508 in Florence. Here, in the home of the Renaissance, he discovered that the style of painting he had learned so painstakingly from Perugino already was, like the architectural style of Brunelleschi, outmoded. The two archrivals, Leonardo and Michelangelo, were engaged in an artistic battle. Crowds flocked to Santissima Annunziata to see the recently unveiled cartoon for Leonardo's *Virgin and Child with St. Anne and the Infant St. John* (FIG. 22-2), the original version of which was done about 1498. Michelangelo responded with the *Doni Madonna.* Both artists were commissioned to decorate the council hall in the Palazzo Vecchio with pictures memorializing Florentine victories of the past. Although only Leonardo completed this task, and although only some small preparatory sketches and small copies sur-

22-13 RAPHAEL, *Marriage of the Virgin,* 1504. Oil on wood, 67″ × 46¹/₂″. Pinacoteca di Brera, Milan.

22-14   RAPHAEL, *Madonna with the Goldfinch*, 1505–1506. Oil on wood, 42" × 29¹/₂". Galleria degli Uffizi, Florence.

dering of this sublime theme of grace and dignity, sweetness and lofty idealism.

VATICAN STANZE   Had Raphael painted nothing but his Madonnas, his fame still would be secure. But he was also a great muralist, a master in the grand style begun by Giotto and carried on by Masaccio and other artists of the fifteenth century. In 1508, Raphael was called to the court of Pope Julius II in Rome, perhaps on the recommendation of his fellow townsman, Bramante. There, in competition with older artists like Perugino and Luca Signorelli, Raphael received one of the largest commissions of the time: the decoration of the papal apartments in the Vatican. Of the several rooms (*stanze*) of the suite, Raphael painted the first, the Stanza della Segnatura; the others were done mostly by his pupils, following his sketches. On the four walls of the Stanza della Segnatura, under the headings of *Theology, Law, Poetry,* and *Philosophy,* Raphael deploys a host of magnificent figures that symbolize and sum up Western learning as it was understood in the Renaissance. His intention was to indicate the four branches of human knowledge and wisdom, while pointing out the virtues and the learning appropriate to a pope.

The iconographic scheme is most complex, and Raphael probably received advice from the brilliant company of Classical scholars surrounding Julius. On one wall, in his *Philosophy* mural, the so-called *School of Athens* (FIG. **22-15**), the artist presents a composition that, in and of itself, constitutes a complete statement of the High Renaissance in its artistic form and spiritual meaning. The setting is not a "school" but rather a concourse of the great philosophers and scientists of the ancient world, who—rediscovered by the Renaissance—hold a convention, where they teach one another once more and inspire a new age. In a vast hall covered by massive vaults that recall Roman architecture (and approximate the appearance of the new St. Peter's in the year the painting was executed [1509]), the figures are arranged ingeniously around the central pair, Plato and Aristotle, in the presence of colossal statues of Apollo and Athena, patron gods of the arts and of wisdom. The ancient philosophers, men concerned with the ultimate mysteries that transcend this world, stand on Plato's side; on Aristotle's side are the philosophers and scientists concerned with nature and the affairs of men. At the lower left, Pythagoras writes as a servant holds up the harmonic scale. In the foreground, Heraclitus (probably a portrait of Michelangelo) broods alone. Diogenes sprawls on the steps. At the right, students surround Euclid, who demonstrates a theorem. This group is especially interesting; Euclid may be a portrait of the aged Bramante. At the extreme right, Raphael includes his own portrait. The groups move easily and clearly, with eloquent poses and gestures that symbolize their doctrines and are of the greatest variety. Their self-assurance and natural dignity bespeak the very

vive, the effect on artists in Florence, especially on one as gifted as Raphael, must have been considerable.

Under the influence of Leonardo, Raphael began to modify the Madonna compositions he had learned in Umbria. In the *Madonna with the Goldfinch* (FIG. **22-14**) of 1506, Raphael uses the pyramidal composition of Leonardo's *Virgin of the Rocks* (FIG. 22-1). The faces and figures are modeled in subtle chiaroscuro, and Raphael's general application of this technique is based on Leonardo's cartoon for the *Virgin and Child with St. Anne and the Infant St. John* (FIG. 22-2). At the same time, the large, substantial figures are placed in a Peruginesque landscape, with the older artist's typical feathery trees in the middle ground. Although Raphael experimented with Leonardo's dusky modeling, he tended to return to Perugino's lighter tonalities. Raphael preferred clarity to obscurity, not being, as Leonardo was, fascinated with mystery. His great series of Madonnas, of which this is an early example, unify Christian devotion and pagan beauty; no artist ever has rivaled Raphael in his definitive rendering

22-15   RAPHAEL, *Philosophy (School of Athens)*, 1509–1511. Fresco, approx. 19′ × 27′. Stanza della Segnatura, Vatican Palace, Rome.

nature of calm reason, that balance and measure so much admired by the great minds of the Renaissance as the heart of philosophy.

Significantly, in this work, Raphael places himself among the mathematicians and scientists, and certainly the evolution of pictorial science comes to its perfection in the *School of Athens*. A vast perspective space has been created, in which human figures move naturally, without effort—each according to his own intention, as Leonardo might say. The stage setting, so long in preparation, is finally complete; the Western artist knows now how to produce the human drama. That this stagelike space is projected onto a two-dimensional surface is the consequence of the union of mathematics with pictorial science, here mastered completely.

The artist's psychological insight has matured along with his mastery of the problems of physical representation. Each character in Raphael's *School of Athens*, like those in Leonardo's *Last Supper* (FIG. 22-3), is intended to communicate a mood that reflects his beliefs, and each group is uni-

fied by the sharing of its members in the mood. The design devices by which individuals and groups are related to each other and to the whole are wonderfully involved and demand close study. From the center, where Plato and Aristotle stand, silhouetted against the sky within the framing arch in the distance, the groups of figures are rhythmically arranged in an elliptical movement that swings forward, looping around two forward groups to either side, and then back again to the center. Moving through the wide opening in the foreground along the perspective pattern of the floor, we penetrate the assembly of philosophers and are led, by way of the reclining Diogenes, up to the here-reconciled leaders of the two great opposing camps of Renaissance philosophy (the vanishing point of the perspective is between their heads, making neither Plato nor Aristotle, but the two together, the focus of attention). In the Stanza della Segnatura, Raphael reconciles and harmonizes not only the Platonists and Aristotelians, but paganism and Christianity, in the same kind of synthesis manifest in his Madonnas.

Pope Leo X, the son of Lorenzo de' Medici, succeeded Julius II as Raphael's patron. During Leo's pontificate, Rome achieved a splendor it had not known since ancient times. Leo was a worldly, pleasure-loving prince, who spent huge sums on the arts, of which, as a true Medici, he was a sympathetic connoisseur. Raphael moved in the highest circles of the papal court, the star of a brilliant society. He was young, handsome, wealthy, and adulated, not only by his followers but by the city of Rome and all Italy. His personality contrasts strikingly with that of the aloof, mysterious Leonardo or the tormented and intractable Michelangelo. Genial, even-tempered, generous, and high-minded, Raphael was genuinely loved. The pope was not his only patron. His friend, Agostino Chigi, an immensely wealthy banker who managed the financial affairs of the papal state, commissioned Raphael to decorate his palace on the Tiber with scenes from Classical mythology. Outstanding among the frescoes painted by Raphael in the small but splendid Villa Farnesina is the *Galatea* (FIG. **22-16**), which takes its theme from the popular Italian

22-16 RAPHAEL, *Galatea*, 1513. Fresco, 9′ 8″ × 7′ 5″. Sala di Galatea, Villa Farnesina, Rome.

poem "La giostra" by Poliziano. Botticelli took the theme for his *Birth of Venus* (FIG. 21-57) from the same work.

In Raphael's fresco, Galatea flees from her uncouth lover, the Cyclops Polyphemus, on a shell drawn by leaping dolphins. She is surrounded by sea creatures and playful cupids. The painting erupts in unrestrained pagan joy and exuberance, an exultant song in praise of human beauty and zestful love. The composition artfully wheels the sturdy figures around Galatea in bounding and dashing movements that always return to her as the energetic center. The cupids, skillfully foreshortened, repeat the circling motion. Raphael's figures are sculpturally conceived, and the body of Galatea—supple, strong, and vigorously in motion—should be compared with Botticelli's delicate, hovering, almost dematerialized Venus—and with the spiraling compositions of Hellenistic statuary (for example, FIG. 5-91). Pagan myth presented in monumental form, in vivacious movement, and in a spirit of passionate delight brings back the seminal substance of which the naturalistic art and poetry of the Classical world was made. Raphael revives the gods and heroes and the bright world they populated, not to venerate them but to make of them the material of art. From Raphael almost to the present, Classical matter will hold as prominent a place in art as religious matter. So completely does the new spirit embodied in the *Galatea* take control that it is as if the Middle Ages had never occurred.

Raphael was also an excellent portraitist. His subjects were the illustrious scholars and courtiers who surrounded Pope Leo X, among them Count Baldassare Castiglione, a close friend of Raphael and the author of a handbook on High Renaissance criteria of genteel behavior. In the *Book of the Courtier*, Castiglione portrays an ideal type of the High Renaissance, a courageous, sagacious, truth-loving, skillful, and cultivated man—in a word, the completely civilized man, a culmination of the line that runs from the rude barbarian warriors who succeeded to the Roman Empire through the half-literate knights and barons of the Middle Ages. Castiglione goes on to describe a way of life based on cultivated rationality in imitation of the ancients. In Raphael's portrait of him (FIG. **22-17**), Castiglione, splendidly yet soberly garbed, looks directly at us with a philosopher's grave and benign expression, clear-eyed and thoughtful. The figure is in half-length and three-quarter view, in the pose made popular by the *Mona Lisa* (FIG. 22-4), and we note in both portraits the increasing attention paid by the High Renaissance artist to the personality and psychic state of the subject. The tones are muted and low-keyed, as would befit the temper and mood of this reflective middle-aged man; the background is entirely neutral, without the usual landscape or architecture. The head and the hands are both wonderfully eloquent in what they report of the man, who himself had written so eloquently in the *Courtier* of the way to enlightenment by the love of beauty. Raphael, Castiglione, and other artists of

22-17   RAPHAEL, *Baldassare Castiglione, c.* 1514. Oil on wood transferred to canvas, approx. 30¼" × 26½". Louvre, Paris.

their age were animated by such love, and we know from his poetry that Michelangelo shared in this widely held Neo-Platonic belief that the soul rises to its enlightenment by the progressively rarefied experience of the beautiful.

Michelangelo

MICHELANGELO BUONARROTI (1475–1564) is a far more complex personality than Raphael, and his art is not nearly so typical of the High Renaissance as that of his somewhat younger contemporary. Frequently irascible, Michelangelo was as impatient with the shortcomings of others as he was with his own. He was jealous of Raphael, disliked Leonardo, and had almost continuous difficulties with his patrons. Perhaps these personal problems arose out of his strong and stern devotion to his art, for he was always totally absorbed in the work at hand. He identified himself completely with the task of artistic creation, and his reactions to his rivals often were impulsive and antagonistic. In this respect, Michelangelo's character often has been compared to Beethoven's, but the personal letters of both reveal a deep sympathy and concern for those close to them, and a profound understanding of humanity informs their works.

Whatever his traits of character, Michelangelo's career realizes all those Renaissance ideals that we conceptualize as being characteristic of an "inspired genius" and a "universal man." His work has the authority of greatness we already have attributed to Donatello. His confidence in his genius was unbounded; the demands of that genius determined his choices absolutely, often in opposition to the demands of his patrons. His belief that nothing worth preserving could be done without genius was attended by the conviction that nothing could be done without perservering study.

Although he was an architect, a sculptor, a painter, a poet, and an engineer, Michelangelo thought of himself first as a sculptor, regarding that calling as superior to that of a painter because the sculptor shares in something like the divine power to "make man." In Platonic fashion, he believed that the *image* produced by the artist's hand must come from the *idea* in the artist's mind; the idea is the reality that has to be brought forth by the genius of the artist. But artists are not the *creators* of the ideas they conceive; rather they find their ideas in the natural world, reflecting the absolute idea, which, for the artist, is *beauty*. In this way, the strongly Platonic strain makes the Renaissance theory of the imitation of nature a *revelation* of the high truths hidden within nature. The theory that guided Michelangelo's hand, though never complete or entirely consistent, appears in his poetry:

> Every beauty which is seen here below by persons of perception
> resembles more than anything else that celestial source from
> which we all are come . . .
> My eyes longing for beautiful things
> together with my soul longing for salvation
> have no other power
> to ascend to heaven than the contemplation of beautiful things.*

One of the best-known observations by Michelangelo is that the artist must proceed by finding the idea—the image, locked in the stone, as it were—so that, by removing the excess stone, he extricates the idea, like Pygmalion bringing forth the living form:

> The best artist has no concept which some single marble
> does not enclose within its mass, but only the hand which
> obeys the intelligence can accomplish that . . . Taking
> away . . . brings out a living figure in alpine and hard
> stone, which . . . grows the more as the stone is chipped
> away.†

*In Robert J. Clements, *Michelangelo's Theory of Art* (New York: New York University Press, 1961), p. 9. © 1961 by Robert J. Clements. Reprinted by permission of the publisher.

†Ibid., p. 16.

The artist, Michelangelo felt, works through many years at this unceasing process of revelation and "arrives late at lofty and unusual things and . . . remains little time thereafter."

Michelangelo did indeed arrive "at lofty and unusual things," for he broke sharply from the lessons of his predecessors and contemporaries in one important respect: he mistrusted the application of mathematical methods as guarantees of beauty in proportion. Measure and proportion, he believed, should be "kept in the eyes." Giorgio Vasari quotes Michelangelo as declaring that "it was necessary to keep one's compass in one's eyes and not in the hand, for the hands execute, but the eye judges." Thus, Michelangelo would set aside Vitruvius, Alberti, Leonardo, Albrecht Dürer, and others who tirelessly sought the perfect measure, being convinced that the inspired judgment could find other pleasing proportions and that the artist must not be bound, except by the demands made by the realization of the idea. This insistence on the artist's own authority is typical of Michelangelo and anticipates the modern concept of the right of talent to a self-expression limited only by its own judgment. The license thus given to genius to aspire far beyond the "rules" led Michelangelo to create works in architecture, sculpture, and painting that depart from High Renaissance regularity and put in its stead a style of vast, expressive strength with complex, eccentric, often titanic forms that loom before us in tragic grandeur. His self-imposed isolation, his creative furies, his proud independence, and his daring innovations led Italians to speak of the dominating quality of the man and his works in one word: *terribilità*, the sublime shadowed by the awesome and the fearful.

EARLY WORKS   As a youth, Michelangelo was apprenticed to the painter Domenico Ghirlandaio, whom he left before completing his training. He soon came under the protection of Lorenzo the Magnificent and must have been a young and thoughtful member of the famous Neo-Platonic circle. He studied sculpture under one of Lorenzo's favorite artists, Bertoldo di Giovanni, a former collaborator of Donatello who specialized in small-scale bronzes. When the Medici fell in 1494, Michelangelo fled from Florence to Bologna, where he was impressed by the sculpture of Jacopo della Quercia, a Sienese sculptor who competed with Ghiberti and Brunelleschi for the commission to fashion the doors of the Florentine baptistery. Besides his study of Jacopo's works, although he claimed that in his art he owed nothing to anyone, Michelangelo made studious drawings after the great Florentines Giotto and Masaccio, and his consuming interest in representing the male nude both in sculpture and painting in all likelihood was much stimulated by Signorelli (FIG. 21-58).

Michelangelo's wanderings took him to Rome, where, at age twenty-three, he produced his first masterpiece, a *Pietà*

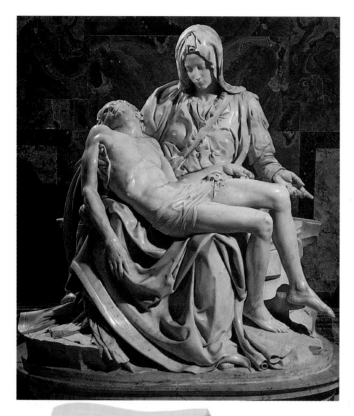

22-18   MICHELANGELO, *Pietà*, 1498–1500. Marble, 5′ 8¹/₂″ high. St. Peter's, Vatican, Rome.

(FIG. **22-18**), for the French cardinal Jean de Bilhères Lagraulas. The statue was destined to adorn the chapel in St. Peter's where the cardinal was to be buried. The theme—Mary cradling the dead body of Christ in her lap—was all but unknown in Italy before Michelangelo made it famous in this statue, but it was a staple in the repertoire of French and German sculptors and painters (FIGS. 13-56 and 20-21) and was doubtless dictated to Michelangelo by his French patron. The Italian, however, rendered the Northern theme in an unforgettable manner. Here, Michelangelo transforms marble into flesh, hair, and fabric with a sensitivity for texture that is almost without parallel; the polish and luminosity of the exquisite marble surface cannot be captured in photographs and can be fully appreciated only in the presence of the original. Breathtaking too is the tender sadness of the beautiful and youthful Mary as she mourns over the death of her son. In fact, her age—seemingly less than that of Christ—was a subject of controversy from the moment the statue was unveiled. Mary's ageless beauty was explained by the artist as an integral part of the Madonna's purity and virginity. Beautiful too is the son whom she holds. He seems less to have died than to have drifted off into peaceful sleep in Mary's maternal arms; his wounds are barely visible.

Michelangelo returned to Florence in 1501, partly because the city might permit him to work a great block of

marble, called the Giant, left over from an earlier, abortive commission. With his sure insight into the nature of stone and a proud, youthful confidence that he could perceive its idea, Michelangelo added to his already great reputation by carving his *David* (FIG. **22-19**), the defiant hero of the Florentine republic. This colossal figure again takes

22-19   MICHELANGELO, *David*, 1501–1504. Marble, 14′ 3″ high. Galleria dell'Accademia, Florence.

up the theme that Donatello (FIG. 21-10) and Verrocchio (FIG. 21-50) had used successfully, but it reflects Michelangelo's own highly original interpretation of the subject. David is represented not after the victory, with the head of Goliath at his feet, but rather turning his head to his left, sternly watchful of the approaching foe. His whole muscular body, as well as his face, is tense with gathering power. The ponderated pose, suggesting the body at ease, is misleading until we read in the tightening sinews and deep frown what impends.

Here is the characteristic representation of energy in reserve that gives the tension of the coiled spring to the figures of Michelangelo's mature period. The anatomy plays an important part in this prelude to action. The rugged torso and sturdy limbs of the young David and the large hands and feet, giving promise of the strength to come, are not composed simply of inert muscle groups, nor are they idealized by simplification into broad masses. They serve, by their active play, to make vivid the whole mood and posture of tense expectation. Each swelling vein and tightening sinew amplifies the psychological vibration of the monumental hero's pose.

Michelangelo doubtless had the Classical nude in mind—Greco-Roman statues, which were being found everywhere, were greatly admired by Michelangelo and his contemporaries for their skillful and precise rendering of heroic physique. In his David, Michelangelo, without strictly imitating the Antique, captures the tension of Lysippan athletes (FIG. 5-74) and the psychological insight and emotionalism of Hellenistic statuary (FIGS. 5-91 and 5-92). This David differs from those of Donatello and Verrocchio in much the same way that later Greek statues depart from their Classical predecessors. The self-contained compositions of the fifteenth-century David statues have been broken open by Michelangelo with the abrupt turn of David's head toward his gigantic adversary. Michelangelo's David is compositionally and emotionally connected to an unseen presence beyond the statue; this too we have observed in Hellenistic sculpture (FIG. 5-98). As early as the David, then, Michelangelo's genius, unlike the classicizing Raphael's, is dedicated to the presentation of towering, pent-up passion rather than to calm, ideal beauty. His own doubts, frustrations, and torments of mind passed easily into the great figures he created or planned. He is the spiritual heir, not of Polykleitos and Phidias, but of the masters of the Laocoön group (FIG. 5-101).

The tomb of Julius II, a colossal structure that would have given Michelangelo the room he needed for his superhuman, tragic beings, became one of the great disappointments of Michelangelo's life when the pope, for unexplained reasons, interrupted the commission, possibly because funds had to be diverted for Bramante's rebuilding of St. Peter's. The original project called for a freestanding, two-story structure with some twenty-eight statues. After the pope's death in 1513, the scale of the project was reduced step by step until, in 1542, a final contract specified a simple wall tomb with fewer than one-third of the originally planned figures.

The spirit of the tomb may be summed up in the figure of *Moses* (FIG. **22-20**), which was completed during one of the sporadic resumptions of the work in 1513. Meant to be seen from below, and balanced with seven other massive forms related in spirit to it, the *Moses* now, in its comparatively paltry setting, can hardly have its full impact. The leader of Israel is shown seated—the tables of the Law under one arm, his other hand gripping the coils of his beard. We may imagine him pausing after the ecstasy of receiving the Law on Mount Sinai, while, in the valley below, the people of Israel give themselves up once more to idolatry. Here again, Michelangelo uses the turned head, which concentrates the expression of awful wrath that now begins to stir in the mighty frame and eyes. One must study the work closely to appreciate Michelangelo's sense

22-20 MICHELANGELO, *Moses, c.* 1513–1515. Marble, approx. 8' 4" high. San Pietro in Vincoli, Rome.

22-21   Michelangelo, *Dying Slave*, 1513–1516. Marble, approx. 7' 5" high. Louvre, Paris.

22-22   Michelangelo, *Bound Slave*, 1513–1516. Marble, approx. 6' 10½" high. Louvre, Paris.

of the relevance of each detail of body and drapery in forcing up the psychic temperature. The muscles bulge, the veins swell, the great legs begin slowly to move. If this titan ever rose to his feet, says one writer, the world would fly apart. The holy rage of *Moses* mounts to the bursting point, yet must be contained, for the free release of energies in action is forbidden forever to Michelangelo's passion-stricken beings. To find such pent-up energy—both emotional and physical—in a seated statue, we must turn once again to Hellenistic statuary (FIGS. 5-97 and 5-98). The Classical repose and quiet sadness of the earlier *Pietà* (FIG. 22-18) is nowhere to be found in this "portrait" of the tormented Old Testament prophet.

Two other figures, the *Dying Slave* (FIG. **22-21**) and the *Bound Slave* (FIG. **22-22**), believed to have been intended for the Julius tomb (although this is now doubted by some), may represent the enslavement of the human soul by matter when the soul falls from Heaven into the prison house of the body. With the imprisoned soul slumbering, our actions, as Marsilio Ficino says, are "the dreams of sleepers and the ravings of madmen." Certainly, the dreams and ravings are present in these two figures. Originally, some twenty slaves, in various attitudes of revolt and exhaustion, were to have been designed for the tomb. In the two slaves shown, as in the *David* and the *Moses*, Michelangelo makes each body a total expression of the idea, so that the human figure serves not so much as a representation of a concept, as in medieval allegory, but as the concrete realization of an intense feeling. Indeed, Michelangelo's own powerful imagination communicates itself in every plane and hollow of the stone. The beautiful lines of the swooning captive present—in their slow, downward pull—the weight of exhaustion; the violent contrapposto of the defiant captive is the image of frantic, impotent struggle. Once more we must turn to Hellenistic art to find sculptors who share Michelangelo's vision of the human form. (Compare, for example, the upper part of Michelangelo's *Dying Slave* with that of the fitfully sleeping *Barberini Faun* [FIG. 5-97] or the spiral composition of his *Bound Slave* with that of the suicidal Gallic chieftain [FIG. 5-91].) The influence of the *Laocoön* group [FIG. 5-101], discovered in Rome in 1506, is especially clear in the struggling *Bound Slave*. Michelangelo's whole art depends on his conviction that whatever can be said greatly through sculpture and painting must be said through the human figure.

A group of four unfinished slaves, one of which is illustrated in the Introduction (FIG. 10), was probably meant for one of the later versions of the Julius tomb. These figures serve not only as object lessons in the subtractive method of sculpture, but also as revelations of the creative process in which abstract ideas—in effect, encased in blocks of stone—are converted into dynamically expressive, concrete forms. If Michelangelo's slaves indeed symbolize the struggle of the human soul to find release from the bonds of its material body, then this idea can find no fuller expression than in these partly finished figures that, with superhuman effort, struggle to cast off the inert masses of stone that imprison them.

SISTINE CHAPEL CEILING   With the failure of the tomb project, Julius II gave the bitter and reluctant Michelangelo the commission to paint the ceiling of the Sistine Chapel (FIGS. **22-23** and **22-24**). The artist, insisting that painting was not his profession (a protest that rings hollow after the fact, but Michelangelo's major works until then had been in sculpture, and painting was of secondary interest to him), assented in the hope that the tomb project could be revived. The difficulties facing Michelangelo were enormous: his relative inexperience in the fresco technique; the dimensions of the ceiling (some 5,800 square feet); its height above the pavement (almost 70 feet); and the complicated perspective problems presented by the height and curve of the vault. Yet, in less than four years, Michelangelo produced an unprecedented work—a one-man masterpiece without parallel in the history of art. Taking the most august and solemn themes of all, the Creation, Fall, and Redemption of humanity, Michelangelo spread a colossal decorative scheme across the vast surface, weaving together more than three hundred figures in an

22-23   Interior of the Sistine Chapel (view facing east). The Vatican, Rome.

22-24   MICHELANGELO, ceiling of the Sistine Chapel, 1508–1512. Fresco, approx. 128' × 45'.

ultimate grand drama of the human race. A long corridor of narrative panels describing the creation recorded in Genesis runs along the crown of the vault, from God's *Separation of Light and Darkness* (above the altar) to the *Drunkenness of Noah* (nearest the entrance). The Hebrew prophets and pagan sibyls who foretold the coming of Christ are seated on either side, where the vault curves down. At the four corner pendentives Michelangelo placed four Old Testament scenes with David, Judith, Haman, and the Brazen Serpent. Scores of lesser figures also appear: the ancestors of Christ in the triangular compartments above the windows, the nude youths who punctuate the corners of the central panels, and the small pairs of putti in grisaille, who support the painted cornice surrounding the whole central corridor. The conception of the whole design is astounding in itself; the articulation of it in its thousand details is a superhuman achievement.

Unlike Andrea Mantegna's decoration of the Camera degli Sposi in Mantua (FIG. 21-61), the strongly marked unifying architectural framework in the Sistine Chapel is not used to construct "picture windows" through which we may look up into some illusion just above. Rather, our eyes seize on figure after figure, each sharply outlined against the neutral tone of the architectural setting or the plain background of the panels. Here, as in his sculpture, Michelangelo relentlessly concentrates his expressive purpose on the human figure. To him, the body is beautiful not only in its natural form but also in its spiritual and philosophical significance; the body is simply the man-ifestation of the soul or of a state of mind and character. Michelangelo represents the body in its most simple, elemental aspect: in the nude or simply draped, with no background and no ornamental embellishment, and always with a sculptor's sense that the figures could be tinted reliefs or full-rounded statues.

One of the central panels of the ceiling will evidence Michelangelo's mastery of the drama of the human figure. The *Creation of Adam* (FIG. **22-25**) is not the traditional representation but a bold, entirely Humanistic interpretation of the primal event. God and Adam, members of the same race of superbeings, confront each other in a primordial, unformed landscape of which Adam is still a material part, heavy as earth, while the Lord transcends it, wrapped in a billowing cloud of drapery and borne up by his genius powers. Life leaps to Adam like an electric spark from the extended and mighty hand of God. The communication between gods and heroes, so familiar in Classical myth, is here concrete: both are made of the same substance; both are gigantic. This blunt depiction of the Lord as ruler of Heaven in the Olympian, pagan sense is an indication of how easily the High Renaissance joined pagan and Christian traditions; we could imagine Adam and the Lord as Prometheus and Zeus. Yet the essential Christian message is not obscured by the Classical trappings. Beneath the Lord's sheltering left arm is a female figure, apprehensively curious but as yet uncreated, who was long held to represent Eve, but recently has been interpreted as the Virgin Mary (with the Christ Child at her knee). If the new

22-25   MICHELANGELO, *Creation of Adam* (detail of FIG. 22-24). Fresco, approx. 18′ 8″ × 9′ 2″.

identification is correct, Michelangelo has incorporated into his fresco one of the essential tenets of Christian faith: that Adam's original sin leads ultimately to the sacrifice of Christ, which in turn makes possible the redemption of all humankind. As God reaches out to Adam, our eyes move from right to left, but Adam's extended left arm also sends our eyes back to the right, through the Lord's right arm, shoulders, and left arm to his left forefinger, which points to the Christ Child's face. The focal point of this right-to-left-to-right movement—the fingertips of Adam and the Lord—is dramatically off-center. The straight, architectural axes we find in the compositions of Leonardo and Raphael

are replaced by curves and diagonals (the bodies of the two great figures are complementary—the concave body of Adam fitting the convex body and billowing "cloak" of God); thus, motion directs not only the figures but the whole composition. The reclining poses, the heavy musculature, and the twisting contrapposto are all a part of Michelangelo's stock, which he will show again later in the sculptured figures of the Medici tombs.

The *Creation of Adam*, along with the rest of the Sistine Chapel ceiling, is newly cleaned and restored—the result of twelve years of painstaking work. Centuries of accumulated grime, overpainting, and protective glue have been

22-26   Detail of the left side of the *Azor-Sadoch* lunette over one of the windows of the Sistine Chapel at various stages of the restoration process.

removed, and the restorers have uncovered much of the artist's original craft in form, color, style, and procedure. Four stages of the restoration process are illustrated here in before-and-after details of one of the lunettes over the windows (FIG. **22-26**). In these semicircular spaces, Michelangelo painted figures representing the ancestors of Christ (Matthew 1:1–17). These figures, once thought to be purposefully dark, now show brilliant colors of high intensity, brushed on with an astonishing freedom and verve. Our details (of the *Azor-Sadoch* lunette) reveal the startling product of the restorers' procedure, as the original work emerges from the dark film laid down by time and faulty repair. The fresh, luminous hues, boldly joined in unexpected harmonies, seem uncharacteristically dissonant to some experts and have aroused brisk controversy. Some believe the restorers removed Michelangelo's work along with the accumulated layers and that the apparently strident coloration cannot possibly be his. Others insist that the artist's real intentions and effects only now are being revealed to modern eyes—and that in the Sistine Chapel Michelangelo has already paved the way for the Mannerist reaction to the High Renaissance that we will examine in detail later. In any event, as a result of the restoration, the pictorial art of Michelangelo and its influence are now being restudied and reassessed.

LATER WORKS Following the death of Julius II, Michelangelo went once again into the service of the Medici popes, Leo X and Clement VII. These pontiffs were not interested in perpetuating the fame of their predecessor by letting Michelangelo complete Julius's tomb; instead, they commissioned him to build a funerary chapel, the New Sacristy, in San Lorenzo in Florence. Brunelleschi's Old Sacristy was off the left transept of San Lorenzo, and Michelangelo was given responsibility for completing the chapel off the right transept. He attempted a unification of architecture and sculpture, designing the whole chapel as well as the tombs. This relationship between the two arts (and, in this case, painting as well) was a common medieval feature; we think of the sculptured portals and stained glass of the Gothic cathedral. But the relationship had been broken in the fifteenth century, when sculpture fought free of its architectural matrix and asserted its independence— so much so that Brunelleschi could complain that Donatello's architectural and sculptural additions to his Old Sacristy spoiled the purity of his design. This new integration by Michelangelo, though here unfinished, pointed the way to Baroque art, in which the architectural-sculptural-pictorial ensemble again will become an effective standard.

At opposite sides of the New Sacristy stand the tombs of Giuliano, duke of Nemours, and Lorenzo, duke of Urbino, son and grandson of Lorenzo the Magnificent. The tomb of Giuliano (FIG. **22-27**) is compositionally the twin of Lorenzo's. Both are unfinished; scholars believe that pairs of recumbent river gods were to be placed at the bottom of the sarcophagi, balancing the pairs of figures that rest on the sloping sides. The composition of the tombs has been a long-standing puzzle. How were they ultimately to look? What is their relationship to one another? What do they signify? The present arrangement seems quite unstable. Were the sloping figures meant to recline on a flat surface, or were they to be partly supported by the river gods below them? We can do little more here than to state some of the questions; we cannot answer them in full.

Art historians have suggested that the arrangement planned by Michelangelo, but never completed, can be interpreted as the ascent of the soul through the levels of the Neo-Platonic universe. The lowest level, represented by the river gods, would have signified the underworld of brute matter, the source of evil. The two statues on the sarcophagi would then symbolize the realm of time: the specifically human world of the cycles of dawn, day, evening, and night. Humanity's state in this world of time is one of pain and anxiety, frustration and exhaustion. At left, the female figure of Night and, at right, the male figure of Day appear to be chained into never-relaxing tensions. Both

22-27 MICHELANGELO, tomb of Giuliano de' Medici, 1519–1534. Marble, central figure approx. 71" high. New Sacristy (Medici Chapel), San Lorenzo, Florence.

exhibit that anguished twisting of the masses of the body in contrary directions seen in the *Bound Slave* (FIG. 22-22) and in the Sistine Chapel paintings. This contrapposto is the signature of Michelangelo. Day, with a body the thickness of a great tree and the anatomy of Hercules (or one of the reclining Greco-Roman river gods that may have inspired Michelangelo's statue), strains his huge limbs against each other, his unfinished visage rising menacingly above his shoulder. Night, the symbol of rest, twists as if in troubled sleep, her posture wrenched and feverish. The artist has surrounded her with an owl, poppies, and a hideous mask symbolic of nightmares.

On their respective tombs, the figures of Lorenzo and Giuliano, rising above the troubles of the realm of time, represent the two ideal human types: the contemplative man (Lorenzo) and the active man (Giuliano). They thus become symbols for the two means by which human beings might achieve union with God: meditation or the active life fashioned after that of Christ. Michelangelo disdained to make portraits of the actual persons; who, he asked, would care what they looked like in a thousand years? What counted was the contemplation of what was beyond the corrosion of time. Giuliano, the active man (FIG. 22-27), his features quite generalized, sits clad in the armor of a Roman emperor, holding the baton of a commander, his head turned alertly, as if in council (he looks toward the statue of the Virgin at one end of the chapel). Across the room, Lorenzo, the contemplative man, sits wrapped in thought, his face in deep shadow. In these works, as in many others, Michelangelo suggests powerful psychic forces that cannot be translated into action but are ever on the verge of it. His prevailing mood is tension and constraint, even in the figures that seem to aspire to the ideal, to the timeless, perfect and unmoving. Michelangelo's style was born to disturb. It brings the serene, brief High Renaissance to an end.

While Michelangelo endured the tribulations of age and the long frustrations of art, his soul was further oppressed by the events that had been erupting around him from the time he fled Florence as a young man after the fall of the Medici. The liberties of Florence were destroyed; the Medici had returned as tyrants, and Michelangelo felt himself an exile, even while he worked for them. Italy was laid to waste by the French and Spanish invasions, and the Protestant Reformation divided Christendom into warring camps. The Catholic Counter-Reformation gained force, and Europe was to be racked by religious war for more than a century. The glories of the High Renaissance faded, and the philosophy of Humanism retreated before the resurgence of a religious spirit that was often pessimistic, moralizing, and grimly fanatical, whether Protestant or Catholic. Michelangelo himself turned from his Humanist beginnings to a deep religious preoccupation with the fate of humanity and of his own soul. His sense that the world had gone mad and that humankind, forsaking God, was

doomed must have been sharpened by his still vivid memory of Savonarola's foreboding summons of sinners to repent and by his very close reading of Dante.

In this spirit, Michelangelo undertook the great *Last Judgment* fresco (FIG. **22-28**) on the altar wall of the Sistine Chapel (also newly cleaned and restored). The change in this fresco from the mood of the ceiling paintings of twenty years before is radical. In the ceiling frescoes, fallen humanity was to have been exalted by the coming of the Redeemer, announced everywhere in the thronging figures of the ceiling panels. Now, on the altar wall, Christ indeed has come, but as the stern judge of the world—a giant whose mighty right arm is lifted in a gesture of damnation so broad and universal as to suggest he will destroy all creation, Heaven and earth alike. The choirs of Heaven surrounding him pulse with anxiety and awe. The spaces below are crowded with trumpeting angels, the ascending figures of the just, and the downward-hurtling figures of the damned. On the left, the dead awake and assume flesh; on the right, the damned are tormented by demons whose gargoyle masks and burning eyes revive the demons of Romanesque tympana (FIG. 12-31). Michelangelo's terrifying vision of the fate that awaits sinners goes far beyond even the gruesome images of Signorelli (FIG. 21-58). Martyrs who suffered especially agonizing deaths crouch below the Judge. One of them, Saint Bartholomew, who was skinned alive, holds the flaying knife and the skin, in which hangs a grotesque self-portrait of Michelangelo. We cannot find any trace of the old Neo-Platonic aspiration to beauty anywhere in this fresco. The figures are grotesquely huge and violently twisted, with small heads and contorted features. The expressive power of ugliness and terror in the service of a terrible message reigns throughout the composition.

ARCHITECTURE   The restive genius of Michelangelo was rarely content to grapple with a single commission. While the *Last Judgment* fresco was being executed, Michelangelo received another flattering and challenging commission from Pope Paul III. In 1537, he undertook to reorganize the Capitoline Hill (the Campidoglio) in Rome (FIG. **22-29**). The pope wished to transform the ancient hill, which once had been the spiritual capitol of the Roman Empire, the site of the greatest temple to Jupiter in the Roman world, into a symbol of the power of the new Rome of the popes. The great challenge of the project was that Michelangelo was required to incorporate into his design two existing buildings—the medieval Palazzo dei Senatori (Palace of the Senators), on the east, and the fifteenth-century Palazzo dei Conservatori (Palace of the Conservators), on the south. These buildings formed an 80-degree angle. Such preconditions might have defeated a lesser architect, but Michelangelo converted what seemed to be a limitation into the most impressive design for a civic unit formulated during the entire Renaissance.

22-28   MICHELANGELO, *Last Judgment*, fresco on the altar wall of the Sistine Chapel, 1534–1541. The Vatican, Rome.

instead of upward (in the Minoan-Mycenaean manner that the Greeks had rejected). In short, Michelangelo disposes willfully and abruptly of Classical architecture as it was valued by other artists of the High Renaissance and points the way toward the ensuing Mannerist reaction to High Renaissance Classicism. And, in the vast, flowing stairway (the last element of the vestibule to be designed and executed) that protrudes, tongue-like, into the room from the "mouth" of the doorway to the library, Michelangelo foreshadows the dramatic movement of seventeenth-century Baroque architecture. With his usual trailbreaking independence of mind, Michelangelo has sculptured an interior space that conveys all the strains and tensions we find in his statuary and in his painted figures.

Michelangelo's art began in the manner of the fifteenth century, rose to an idealizing height in the High Renaissance, and, at the end, moved toward Mannerism and the Baroque. Like a colossus, he bestrides three centuries. He became the archetype of the supreme genius who transcends the rules by making his own. Few artists could escape his influence, and variations of his style will constitute much of artistic experiment for centuries.

Andrea del Sarto and Correggio

The towering achievements of Raphael and Michelangelo in Rome tend to obscure everything else that was done during their time. Nevertheless, aside from the flourishing Venetian school, some excellent artists were active in other parts of Italy during the first part of the sixteenth century. One of these, the Florentine ANDREA DEL SARTO (1486–1531), expresses, in his early paintings, the ideals of the High Renaissance with almost as much clarity and distinction as does Raphael.

Andrea's *Madonna of the Harpies* (FIG. **22-35**) shows the Madonna standing majestically on an altarlike base decorated with sphinxes (figures misidentified by Vasari as harpies—hence, the name of the painting). The composition is based on a massive and imposing figure pyramid, the static qualities of which are relieved by the opposing contrapposto poses of the flanking saints—a favorite and effective High Renaissance device to introduce variety into symmetry. The potentially rigid pyramid is softened further by the skillful coordination of the figures' poses into an organic movement that leads from Saint Francis (on the left) to the Virgin, to Saint John the Evangelist, and downward from him toward the observer. This main movement is either echoed or countered by numerous secondary movements brought into perfect formal balance in a faultless compositional performance. The soft modeling of the forms is based on Leonardo but does not affect the colors, which are rich and warm. Andrea's sense of and ability to handle color set him apart from his central Italian contem-

22-35 ANDREA DEL SARTO, *Madonna of the Harpies*, 1517. Oil on wood, approx. 6′ 9″ × 5′ 10″. Galleria degli Uffizi, Florence.

poraries; he is perhaps the only Renaissance artist to transpose his rich color schemes from panels into frescoes. Andrea's later compositions tend to be less firmly knit and his color schemes move toward the cool harshness that will become typical of Mannerist painting. Although he was greatly admired in the sixteenth and seventeenth centuries, Andrea's fame has waned; today, he seems to be remembered primarily as the teacher of Jacopo da Pontormo, Rosso Fiorentino, and Vasari and, thus, as one of the forerunners of Mannerism.

Andrea del Sarto may still be placed firmly in the High Renaissance, but his northern Italian contemporary, ANTONIO ALLEGRI DA CORREGGIO, (c. 1489–1534), of Parma, is almost impossible to classify. A solitary genius, Correggio brings together many stylistic trends, including those of Leonardo, Raphael, and the Venetians. Yet he developed a unique personal style, which, if it must be labeled, might best be called "proto-Baroque." Historically, his most enduring contribution was the development of illusionistic ceiling perspectives to a point seldom surpassed by his Baroque emulators. At Mantua, Mantegna had painted a hole into the ceiling of the Camera degli Sposi (FIG. 21-61); some fifty years later, Correggio painted away the entire dome of the cathedral of Parma (FIG. **22-36**). Opening up

22-36 CORREGGIO, *Assumption of the Virgin*, 1526–1530. Fresco. Dome of Parma Cathedral.

the cupola, the artist shows his audience a view of the sky, with concentric rings of clouds among which hundreds of soaring figures perform a wildly pirouetting dance in celebration of the *Assumption of the Virgin*. These angelic creatures will become permanent tenants of numerous Baroque churches in later centuries. Correggio was also an influential painter of religious panels, in which he forecast many other Baroque compositional devices.

As a painter of erotic mythological subjects, Correggio had few equals. *Jupiter and Io* (FIG. **22-37**) depicts a suavely sensual vision out of the pagan past. The painting is one of a series on the loves of Jupiter that Correggio painted for the duke of Mantua, Federigo Gonzaga. The god, who assumed many disguises to hide his numerous liaisons from his wife, Juno, appears here as a cloud that embraces the willing nymph. The soft, smoky modeling (sfumato), derived from Leonardo, is fused with glowing color and renders the voluptuous moment with exquisite subtlety. Even Titian, in his mythological paintings, rarely was able to match the sensuous quality expressed here by Correggio.

Unlike Andrea del Sarto, Correggio was little appreciated by his contemporaries; later, during the seventeenth century, Baroque painters recognized him as a kindred spirit.

22-37   CORREGGIO, *Jupiter and Io, c.* 1532. Oil on canvas, approx. 64¹/₂″ × 29³/₄″. Kunsthistorisches Museum, Vienna.

MANNERISM

The term *Mannerism* refers to certain tendencies in the art of the Late Renaissance—the period from the death in 1520 of Raphael (who was laid to rest in the ancient Roman Pantheon) to the end of the sixteenth century. In its broadest sense, the word means excessive or affected adherence to a distinctive manner, especially in art and literature. In its early application to these tendencies, it also carried the pejorative connotation of the term when applied to a description of individual behavior. Today, we view these styles in art and literature more objectively and appreciate much that is excellent in them.

The artists of the Early Renaissance and the High Renaissance developed their characteristic styles from the studious observation of nature and the formulation of a pictorial science. By the time Mannerism matured, all the representational problems had been solved; a vast body of knowledge had been accumulated. In addition, an age of antiquarianism and archeology now was bringing to light thousands of remnants of Classical art. The Mannerists, instead of continuing the earlier research into nature and natural appearance, turned for their models to the masters of the High Renaissance (especially Michelangelo) and to Roman sculpture (especially relief sculpture). Instead of nature as their teacher, they took art. One could say that whereas their predecessors sought nature and found their style, the Mannerists looked first for a style and found a manner.

Following Michelangelo's example in one respect, the Mannerists declared each artist's right to a personal interpretation of the rules, looking for inspiration to the Platonic Idea, which they referred to as the *disegno interno* (inner design) and with which they fired their creative fervor. They saw a roughness in nature that needed refining, and they turned to where it had already been refined in art.

From the Antique and the High Renaissance, Mannerist artists, to the limits of their own ingenuity and skill, abstracted forms that they idealized further, so that the typical Mannerist picture or statue looks like an original essay in human form somewhat removed from nature. As *maniera* (the name given the style by Mannerist theorists) is almost exclusively an art of the human figure, its commonest expression is in paintings of numerous figures performing what appears to be a complicated dance and pantomime, in which the compositions, as well as the fanciful gestures and attitudes, are deliberately intricate. The movements are so studied and artificial that they remind us not of the great stage dramatics of the High Renaissance but of an involved choreography for interpretive dancers. Where the art of the High Renaissance strives for balance, Mannerism seeks instability. The calm equilibrium of the former is replaced by a restlessness that leads to distortions, exaggerations, and affected posturings on the one hand and sinuously graceful, often athletic attitudes on the other. The

Mannerist requirement of "invention" leads its practitioner to the maniera, a self-conscious stylization involving complexity, caprice, fantasy (the "conceit"), elegance, preciosity, and polish. Mannerism is an art made for aristocratic patrons by artists who sense that their profession is worthy of honor and the admiration of kings. This was an age when monarchs and grandees would plead for anything from the hands of Raphael and Michelangelo, if only a sketch. The concepts of "classic" and "old master" are abroad, and artists are being called *divino*. Artists become conscious of their own personalities, powers of imagination, and technical skills; they acquire learning and aim at virtuosity. They cultivate not the knowledge of nature but the intricacies of art.

Painting

The *Descent from the Cross* (FIG. **22-38**) by JACOPO DA PONTORMO (1494–1557) exhibits almost all the stylistic features characteristic of the early phase of Mannerism in painting. The figures crowd the composition, pushing into the front plane and almost completely blotting out the setting. The figure masses are disposed around the frame of the picture, leaving a void in the center, where High Renaissance artists had concentrated their masses. The composition has no focal point, and the figures swing around the edges of the painting without coming to rest. The representation of space is as strange as the representation of the human figure. Mannerist space is ambiguous; we are never quite sure where it is going or just where the figures are in it. We do not know how far back the depicted space extends, although its limit is defined by the figure at the top. But we do know that the space is really too shallow for what is taking place in it. For example, Pontormo does not provide any space for the body belonging to the head, seen in a three-quarter rear view, that appears immediately over Christ's.

The centrifugal effect of the positions of the figures is strengthened by the curiously anxious glances that the actors cast out of the picture in all directions. Many figures are characterized by an athletic bending and twisting, with distortions (a torso cannot bend at the point at which the foreground figure's does), an elastic elongation of the limbs, and a rendering of the heads as uniformly small and oval. The composition is jarred further by clashing colors, which are unnatural and totally unlike the sonorous primary color chords used by painters of the High Renaissance—except for those of Michelangelo's Sistine Chapel frescoes in their newly cleaned state. The mood of the painting is hard to describe; it seems the vision of an inordinately sensitive soul, perhaps itself driven, as are the actors, by nervous terrors. The psychic dissonance of the composition would indeed appear out of tune to a Classical artist.

ROSSO FIORENTINO (1494–1540), who was, like Pontormo, a pupil of Andrea del Sarto, compresses space in a manner

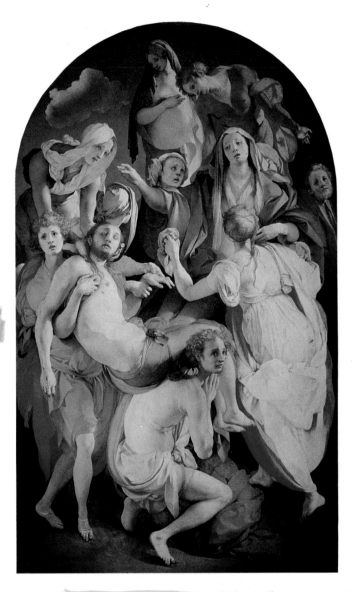

22-38 PONTORMO, *Descent from the Cross*, 1525–1528. Oil on wood, approx. 10′ 3″ × 6′ 6″. Capponi Chapel, Santa Felicità, Florence.

similar to that used by Pontormo but fills it with turbulent action. Rosso's painting of *Moses Defending the Daughters of Jethro* (FIG. **22-39**) recalls the titanic struggles and powerful musculature of Michelangelo's figures of the Sistine Chapel ceiling, but Rosso's purpose is not so much expressive as it is inventive of athletic poses. At the same time, although the figures are modeled for three-dimensional effect (note the way the painter leads us into his canvas by placing two boldly foreshortened figures—with hidden heads—in the foreground), they are compressed within a limited space, so that surface is emphasized as a two-dimensional pattern. Indeed, the fact that Rosso has cut off his figures on all four sides of the painting causes the eye to wander the surface and move beyond the edges of the frame instead of into the distance. The scientific perspective of the fifteenth

22-39 Rosso Fiorentino, *Moses Defending the Daughters of Jethro*, 1523. Oil on canvas, approx. 63' × 46¹/₂". Galleria degli Uffizi, Florence.

century—and the underlying assumption that spatial recession could and should be depicted by employing a rational, mathematical system of converging orthogonals—has been firmly rejected.

Correggio's pupil Girolamo Francesco Maria Mazzola, known as Parmigianino (1503–1540), in his best-known work, *Madonna with the Long Neck* (FIG. **22-40**), achieves the elegance that is a principal aim of Mannerism. He smoothly combines the influences of Correggio and Raphael in a picture of exquisite grace and precious sweetness. The small, oval head of the Madonna; her long, slender neck; the unbelievable length and delicacy of her hand; and the sinuous, swaying elongation of her frame are all marks of the aristocratic, gorgeously artificial taste of a later phase of Mannerism. Here is Raphael distilled through Correggio. On the left stands a bevy of angelic creatures, melting with emotions as soft and smooth as their limbs (the left side of the composition is quite in the manner of Correggio). On the right, the artist has included a line of columns without

capitals—an enigmatic setting for an enigmatic figure with a scroll, whose distance from the foreground is immeasurable and ambiguous.

The Mannerists sought a generally beautiful style that had its rules, but rules, as we have seen, that still permitted artists the free play of their powers of invention. Thus, although all Mannerist paintings share common features, each artist, as it were, has an individualized, recognizable signature.

All the points made thus far about Mannerist composition are recognizable in *Venus, Cupid, Folly, and Time*, also called the *Exposure of Luxury* (FIG. **22-41**), by Agnolo di Cosimo, called Bronzino (1503–1572). A pupil of Pontormo, Bronzino was a Florentine and painter to Cosimo I, first Grand Duke of Tuscany. In this painting, he

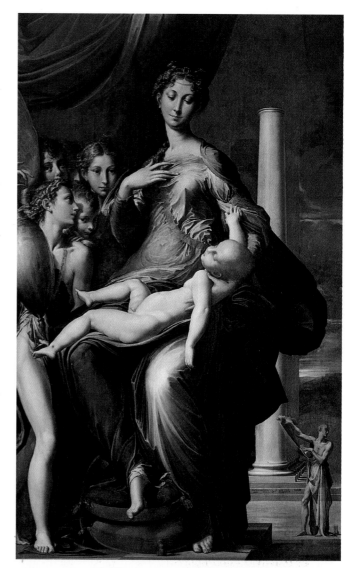

22-40 Parmigianino, *Madonna with the Long Neck*, c. 1535. Oil on wood, approx. 7' 1" × 4' 4". Galleria degli Uffizi, Florence.

22-41   BRONZINO, *Venus, Cupid, Folly, and Time (Exposure of Luxury)*, *c.* 1546. Oil on wood, approx. 61″ × 56³/₄″. National Gallery, London.

manifests the Mannerist fondness for extremely learned and intricate allegories that often have lascivious undertones; we are now far from the simple and monumental statements and forms of the High Renaissance. Venus, fondled by her son Cupid, is uncovered by Time, while Folly prepares to bombard them with roses; other figures represent Hatred and Inconstancy. The masks, a favorite device of the Mannerists, symbolize falseness. The picture seems to convey that love—accompanied by its opposite, hatred, and plagued by inconstancy—is foolish, and that its folly will be discovered in time. But, as in many Mannerist paintings,

the meaning is ambiguous, and interpretations vary. The figures are drawn around the front plane and almost entirely block the space, although there really is no space. The contours are strong and sculptural, the surfaces, of enamel smoothness. Of special interest are the heads, hands, and feet, for the Mannerists considered the extremities to be the carriers of grace and the clever depiction of them evidence of skill in maniera.

The sophisticated elegance sought by the Mannerist painter most often was achieved in portraiture, in which the Mannerists excelled. Bronzino's *Portrait of a Young Man*

22-42 BRONZINO, *Portrait of a Young Man, c.* 1550. Oil on wood, approx. 37¹/₂″ × 29¹/₂″. Metropolitan Museum of Art, New York (H. O. Havemeyer Collection, bequest of Mrs. H. O. Havemeyer, 1929).

(FIG. **22-42**) is exemplary of Mannerist portraiture. The subject is a proud youth—a man of books and intellectual society, rather than a man of action or a merchant. His cool demeanor is carefully affected, a calculated attitude of nonchalance toward the observing world. This austere and incommunicative formality is standard for the Mannerist portrait. It asserts the rank and station of the subject but not his personality. The haughty poise, the graceful, long-fingered hands, the book, the masks, and the severe architecture all suggest the traits and environment of the high-bred disdainful patrician. The somber Spanish black of the young man's doublet and cap (this is the century of Spanish etiquette), and the slightly acid olive-green walls of the room make for a deeply restrained color scheme—a muted background for the sharply defined, busily active Manneristic silhouette that contradicts the subject's impassive pose.

The aloof formality of Bronzino's portrait is much relaxed in the portraiture of SOFONISBA ANGUISSOLA (1527–1625). A northern Italian from Cremona, Anguissola uses the strong contours, muted tonality, and smooth finish familiar in Mannerist portraits. But she introduces, in a group portrait of irresistible charm (FIG. **22-43**),

an informal intimacy of her own. Like many of her other works done before 1559, this is a portrait of members of her family. Against a neutral ground, she places her two sisters and her brother in an affectionate pose meant not for official display but for private showing, much as they might be posed in a modern photo-studio portrait. The sisters, wearing matching striped gowns, flank their brother, who caresses a lap dog. The older sister (at the left) has summoned up the dignity required for the occasion, while the boy looks quizzically at the portraitist with an expression of naive curiosity, and the other girl's attention has been diverted toward something or someone to the painter's left.

The naturalness of poses and expressions, the sympathetic, personal presentation, and the graceful treatment of the forms did not escape the attention of famous contemporaries. Vasari praised Anguissola's art as wonderfully lifelike, and declared that she "has done more in design and more gracefully than any other lady of our day." She was praised, moreover, for her "invention," and, though the word does not now have quite the meaning it had then, Anguissola can be considered to have introduced the intimate, anecdotal, and realistic touches of *genre painting* (the painting of scenes from ordinary life) into formal portraiture. This group portrait could be simply a good-natured portrayal of the members of any happy, middle-class family; names, titles, and elegance of dress are not flourished to gain public respect. Anguissola lived long and successfully. She knew and learned from the aged Michelangelo, was court painter to Phillip II of Spain, and, at the end of her life, gave advice on art to a young admirer of her work, Anthony Van Dyck, the great Flemish master.

Sculpture

With Bronzino, Florentine Mannerism in painting passed its high-water mark. But a remarkable person, as Mannerist in his action as in his art, has left us, in his sculpture, the mark of the prevailing style. To judge by his fascinating *Autobiography*, BENVENUTO CELLINI (1500–1571) had an impressive proficiency as an artist, statesman, soldier, lover, and many other things. He was, first of all, a goldsmith. The influence of Michelangelo led him to attempt larger works, and, in the service of Francis I, he cast in bronze the *Genius of Fontainebleau* (FIG. **22-44**), which sums up Italian and French Mannerism. The female *Genius*, or spirit, is a composite of Diana, the Greco-Roman goddess of the hunt, here embracing her animal, the deer, and a Classical personification of a spring leaning on an urn from which water spews forth (compare FIG. 8-26). She is derived also from the reclining figures in the Medici Chapel tombs (FIG. 22-27) and from the female nudes, both Venuses and courtesans, that had only recently become popular subjects for Renaissance paintings (FIG. 22-61), but Cellini exaggerates their characteristics. The head is remarkably small, the

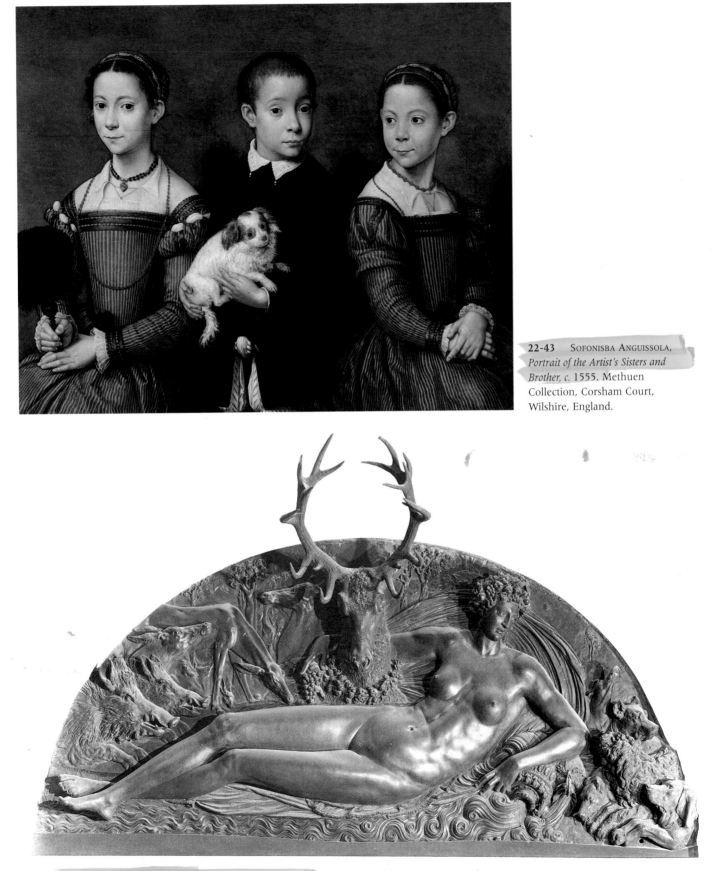

22-43 SOFONISBA ANGUISSOLA, *Portrait of the Artist's Sisters and Brother, c.* 1555. Methuen Collection, Corsham Court, Wilshire, England.

22-44 BENVENUTO CELLINI, *Genius of Fontainebleau,* 1543–1544. Bronze, over life size. Louvre, Paris.

torso stretched out, and the limbs elongated. The contrapposto is more apparent than real, for it is flattened out almost into the forward plane, as Mannerist design sense dictates. This almost abstract figure, along with Mannerist works by Rosso and others, greatly influenced the development of French Renaissance art, particularly in the school of Fontainebleau.

Italian influence, working its way into France, had strength enough to draw a brilliant, young French sculptor, Jean de Boulogne, to Italy, where he practiced his art under the equivalent Italian name of GIOVANNI DA BOLOGNA (1529–1608). Giovanni is the most important sculptor in sixteenth-century Italy after Michelangelo, and his work provides the stylistic link between the sculpture of that great master and that of the Baroque sculptor Gianlorenzo Bernini. Giovanni's *Abduction of the Sabine Women* (FIG. 22-45) wonderfully exemplifies the Mannerist principles of figure composition and, at the same time, shows an impulse to break out of the Mannerist formulas of representation.

The title—drawn from the legendary history of early Rome, which relates how the Romans abducted wives for themselves from their neighbors, the Sabines—was given to the group only after it was raised; Giovanni probably intended to present only an interesting figure composition involving an old man, a young man, and a woman, all nude in the tradition of ancient statues portraying mythological figures. The amateurs who flocked around works of art in this age of Mannerism, naming groups in any way they found appropriate, serve to indicate how important and how valued the visual arts had become. The artist himself is learned in his artistic sources. Giovanni would have known the century-earlier group of *Hercules and Antaeus* by Pollaiuolo (FIG. 21-52), in which the Greek hero lifts his opponent off the ground, but here, unlike his fifteenth-century predecessor, he turns directly to Classical sculpture for inspiration. Giovanni twice adapts the *Laocoön* (FIG. 5-101)—once in the figure of the crouching old man and again in the gesture of the woman with one arm flung up. The three bodies interlock on an axis, along which a spiral movement runs; significantly, the figures do not break out of this vortex but remain as if contained within a cylinder. The viewer must walk around the sculpture to appreciate that, despite its confinement, the aspect of the group changes radically according to the point from which it is viewed. One reason is that the open spaces that pass through the masses (for example, the space between an arm and a body) have as great an effect as the solids. This sculpture is the first large-scale group since Classical antiquity composed to be seen from multiple points of view, in striking contrast to Pollaiuolo's group, which was designed to be seen from the angle shown in our illustration. Giovanni's figures do not, however, yet reach freely out into space and relate to the environment. The fact that they remain "enclosed" prevents our calling them Baroque. Yet the

22-45   GIOVANNI DA BOLOGNA, *Abduction of the Sabine Women*, completed 1583. Marble, approx. 13′ 6″ high. Loggia dei Lanzi, Piazza della Signoria, Florence.

Michelangelesque potential for action and the athletic flexibility of the figures are there. The Baroque period will see sculptured figures released into full action.

Architecture

Mannerism in painting and sculpture has been studied fairly extensively since the early decades of this century, but only in the 1930s was it discovered that the term also could be applied to much of sixteenth-century architecture. The corpus of Mannerist architecture that has been compiled since then, however, is far from homogeneous and includes many works that really do not seem to fit the term "Mannerist." The fact that Michelangelo was using Classical architectural elements in a highly personal and unorthodox manner does not necessarily make him a Mannerist architect. In his designs for St. Peter's, he certainly was striving for those effects of mass, balance, order, and stability that are the very hallmarks of High Renaissance design, and even in the Laurentian Library (FIG. 22-34), Michelangelo never really aimed to baffle or to confuse. This, however, was the precise goal of GIULIO ROMANO (c. 1492–1546) when he designed the Palazzo del Tè in Mantua (FIG. **22-46**) and, with it, formulated almost the entire architectural vocabulary of Mannerism.

Giulio Romano became Raphael's chief assistant in the decoration of the Vatican stanze. After Raphael's premature death in 1520, Giulio became his master's artistic executor, completing Raphael's unfinished frescoes and panel paintings. In 1524, Giulio went to Mantua, where he found a patron in Federigo Gonzaga, for whom he built and decorated the Palazzo del Tè between 1525 and 1535.

The Palazzo del Tè was intended to combine the functions of a suburban summer palace with those of a stud farm for the duke's famous stables. Originally planned as a relatively modest country villa, Giulio's building so pleased the duke that he soon commissioned his architect to enlarge the structure. In a second building campaign, the villa was expanded to a palatial scale by the addition of three wings, which were placed around a square central court. This once-paved court, which serves both as a passage and as the focal point of the design, has a near-urban character and, with its surrounding buildings, forms a self-enclosed unit to which a large, stable-flanked garden has been attached on the east side.

Giulio's Mannerist style is best exhibited in the facades that face the interior courtyard of the palace (FIG. 22-46), where the divergences from architectural convention are so pronounced that they constitute an enormous parody on the Classical style of Bramante. In a building laden with structural surprises and contradictions, the design of the interior courtyard facades is the most unconventional of all. The *keystones* (central voussoirs), for example, either have not fully settled or seem to be slipping from the arches— and, more eccentric still, Giulio has even placed voussoirs in the pediments over the rectangular niches, where there

22-46 GIULIO ROMANO, interior courtyard facade of the Palazzo del Tè, Mantua, 1525–1535.

are no arches. The massive Tuscan columns that flank these niches carry incongruously narrow architraves whose structural insufficiency is stressed by the fact that they break midway between the columns, evidently unable to support the weight of the triglyphs above, which threaten to crash down upon the head of anyone foolish enough to stand below them. To be sure, the appreciation of Giulio's joke requires a highly sophisticated audience, and the recognition of some quite subtle departures from the norm presupposes a thorough familiarity with the established rules of Classical architecture. It speaks well for the duke's sophistication that he accepted Giulio's form of architectural humor.

If the architectural chaos of the facades of the Palazzo del Tè did not suffice to shock the visitor, Giulio delivered the coup de grâce in the Sala dei Giganti within (FIG. **22-47**). In a panoramic sequence that covers the ceiling and all the walls of this room, Giulio represented Jupiter destroying the palaces of the rebellious giants with thunderbolts. Viewers cringe involuntarily as the entire universe appears to be collapsing around them in a tour de force of pictorial illusionism and wild Mannerist convulsion.

In short, in the Palazzo del Tè most of the Classical rules of order, stability, and symmetry have been flouted deliberately, and every effort has been made to startle and shock the beholder. This desire to create ambiguities and tensions is as typical of Mannerist architecture as it is of Mannerist painting, and many of the devices invented by Giulio Romano for the Palazzo del Tè became standard features in the formal repertoire of later Mannerist building.

Acceptance of the Mannerist style in architecture was by no means universal, either on the part of architects or patrons. Indeed, later sixteenth-century designs more in keeping with the ideals of the High Renaissance proved to have a greater impact on seventeenth-century architecture

in Italy than the more adventurous, yet eccentric, works by Giulio Romano and the other Mannerists.

Probably the most influential building of the latter half of the sixteenth century was the mother church of the Jesuit order, founded in 1534, in the pontificate of Paul III. Because Michelangelo was dilatory in providing the plans, the church, called Il Gesù, or Church of Jesus (FIGS. **22-48** and **22-49**), was designed and built between 1568 and 1584 by GIACOMO DA VIGNOLA (1507–1573), who designed the ground plan, and Giacomo della Porta, who is responsible for the facade. Chronologically and stylistically, the building belongs to the Late Renaissance, but its enormous influence on later churches marks it as one of the seminal monuments for the development of Baroque church architecture. Its facade (FIG. 22-48) is an important model and point of departure for the facades of Roman Baroque churches for two centuries, and its basic scheme is echoed and re-echoed throughout the Catholic countries, especially in Latin America. The design of the facade is not entirely original; the union of the lower and upper stories, effected by scroll buttresses, goes back to Alberti's Santa Maria Novella in Florence (FIG. 21-36); its Classical pediment is familiar in Alberti as well as in the Venetian architect Andrea Palladio, whose work we shall examine presently; and its paired pilasters appear in Michelangelo's design for St. Peter's (FIG. 22-33). But the facade is a skillful synthesis of these already existing motifs; the two stories are well unified, the horizontal march of the pilasters and columns builds to a dramatic climax at the central bay, and the bays of the facade snugly fit the nave-chapel system behind them. The many dramatic Baroque facades of Rome will be architectural variations on this basic theme.

In plan (FIG. 22-49), a monumental expansion of Alberti's scheme for Sant'Andrea in Mantua (FIG. 21-41), the nave takes over the main volume of space, so that the structure becomes a great hall with side chapels. The approach to the altar is emphasized by a dome. The wide acceptance of the Gesù plan in the Catholic world, even until modern times, seems to attest that it is ritually satisfactory. The opening of the church building into a single great hall provides an almost theatrical setting for large promenades and processions (that seemed to combine social with sacerdotal functions) and, above all, a space adequate to accommodate the great crowds that gathered to hear the eloquent preaching of the Jesuits. The Jesuits had a strong, indirect influence on art and architecture through the teachings of Saint Ignatius of Loyola, their Spanish founder. Loyola, in his *Spiritual Exercises,* advocated that the spiritual experience of the mysteries of the Catholic faith be intensely imagined, so much so as to be visible to the eye. The content of faith was to be visualized, and the sacred objects of the Church were to be venerated as defenses against false doctrine and the powers of Hell. This is still the function and warranty of religious art throughout the Roman Catholic world.

22-47 GIULIO ROMANO, *Fall of the Giants* (detail), 1532–1534. Fresco. Sala dei Giganti, Palazzo del Tè, Mantua.

22-48 GIACOMO DELLA PORTA, facade of Il Gesù, Rome, c. 1575–1584.

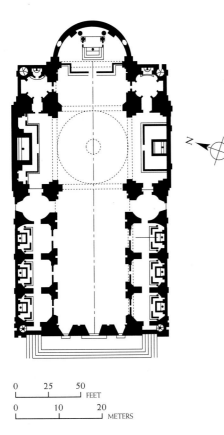

0 25 50 FEET

0 10 20 METERS

22-49 GIACOMO DA VIGNOLA, plan of Il Gesù, Rome, 1568.

VENETIAN ART AND ARCHITECTURE

In the sixteenth century, Venetian art became a strong, independent, and influential school in its own right, touched only very slightly (if at all) by the fashions of Mannerism sweeping Western Europe. Venice had been the proud maritime monarch of the Mediterranean and its coasts for centuries; as the gateway to the Orient, it "held the gorgeous east in fee; and was the safeguard of the west." At the height of its commercial and political power during the fifteenth century, Venice saw its fortunes decline in the sixteenth century. Even so, Venice and the papal state were the only Italian sovereignties to retain their independence during the century of strife; all others were reduced to dependency on either France or Spain. Although the fundamental reasons for the decline of Venice were the discoveries in the New World and the economic shift from Italy to Hapsburg Germany and the Netherlands, other even more immediate and pressing events drained its wealth and power. Venice was constantly embattled by the Turks, who, after their conquest of Constantinople, began to contest with Venice for control of the eastern Mediterranean. Early in the century, Venice also found itself attacked by the European powers of the League of Cambrai, formed and led by Julius II, who coveted Venetian holdings on the mainland. Although this wearing, two-front war sapped its strength, Venice's vitality endured, at least long enough to overwhelm the Turks in the great sea battle of Lepanto in 1571. This time, Europe was on Venice's side.

Architecture

SANSOVINO Venice was introduced to the High Renaissance style of architecture by a Florentine called JACOPO SANSOVINO (Jacopo Tatti, 1486–1570). Originally trained as a sculptor under Andrea Sansovino (c. 1467–1529), whose name he adopted, Jacopo went to Rome in 1518, where, under the influence of Bramante's circle, he increasingly turned toward architecture. When he arrived in Venice as a refugee from the sack of Rome in 1527, he quickly established himself as that city's leading and most admired architect; his buildings frequently inspired the architectural settings of the most prominent Venetian painters, including Titian and Veronese.

Sansovino's largest and most rewarding public commissions were the Mint (la Zecca) and the adjoining State Library (FIG. **22-50**) in the heart of the island city. The Mint, begun in 1535, faces the Canale San Marco with a stern and forbidding three-story facade. Its heavy rustication gives it an intended air of strength and impregnability. This fortresslike look is emphasized by a boldly projecting, bracket-supported cornice reminiscent of the machicolated galleries of medieval castles.

22-50   JACOPO SANSOVINO, The Mint (la Zecca), 1535–1545 (*left*) and the State Library, begun 1536, Piazza San Marco, Venice.

A very different spirit is expressed by the neighboring State Library of San Marco, begun a year after the Mint, which Palladio referred to as "probably the richest and most ornate edifice since ancient times." With twenty-one bays (only sixteen of which were completed during Sansovino's lifetime), the library faces the Gothic Doge's Palace (FIG. 13-64) across the Piazzetta, a lateral extension of Venice's central Piazza San Marco. The relatively plain ground-story arcade has Tuscan columns attached to the arch-supporting piers in the manner of the Roman Colosseum (FIG. 7-39); it is capped by a Doric frieze of metopes and triglyphs—none of which slides out of place as in the frieze of the contemporary Palazzo del Tè in Mantua (FIG. 22-46). The lower story serves as a sturdy support for the higher, lighter, and much more decorative Ionic second story, which housed the reading room, with its treasure of manuscripts, keeping them safe from not-uncommon flooding. On this second level, the stern system of the ground story has been softened by the introduction of Ionic colonnettes that flank the piers and are paired in depth, rather than in the plane of the facade. Two-thirds the height of the main columns, they rise to support the springing of arches, the spans of which are two-thirds those of the lower arcade, accentuating the verticality of the second story. The main columns carry an entablature with a richly decorated frieze on which, in strongly projecting relief, putti support garlands. This favorite decorative motif of the ancient Romans, which we already have seen in Bernardo Rossellino's tomb of Leonardo Bruni (FIG. 21-46), is punctuated by the oval windows of an attic story. Perhaps the most striking feature of the building is its roofline, where Sansovino replaces the traditional straight and unbroken cornice with a balustrade (reminiscent of the one on Bramante's Tempietto, FIG. 22-6) interrupted by statue-bearing pedestals. The spacing of the latter corresponds to that of the orders below, so that the sculptures become the sky-piercing finials of the building's vertical design elements. The deft application of sculpture to the massive framework of the building (no walls are visible) mitigates the potential severity of its design and gives its aspect an extraordinary plastic richness.

One feature rarely mentioned is the subtlety with which the library echoes the design of the lower two stories of the Doge's Palace (FIG. 13-64) opposite it. Although he uses a vastly different architectural vocabulary, Sansovino manages admirably to adjust his building to the older one. Correspondences include the almost identical spacing of the lower arcades, the rich and decorative treatment of the second stories (including their balustrades), and the dissolution of the rooflines (by use of decorative battlements in the palace and a statue-surmounted balustrade in the library). It is almost as if Sansovino set out to translate the Gothic architecture of the Doge's Palace into a "modern" Renaissance idiom. If so, he was eminently successful; the two buildings, although of different spiritual and stylistic worlds, mesh and combine to make the Piazzetta one of the most elegantly framed urban units in Europe.

PALLADIO   When Jacopo Sansovino died, he was succeeded as chief architect of the Venetian Republic by ANDREA PALLADIO (1508–1580). Beginning as a stonemason and decorative sculptor, at the age of thirty Palladio turned to architecture, the ancient literature on architecture, engineering, topography, and military science. Unlike the universal scholar Alberti, Palladio became more of a specialist. He made several trips to Rome to study the ancient buildings at firsthand. He illustrated Daniele Barbaro's edition of *Vitruvius* (1556), and he wrote his own treatise on architecture, *I quattro libri dell'architettura* (*Four Books on Architecture*), originally published in 1570, which had a wide-ranging influence on succeeding generations of architects throughout Europe. Palladio's influence outside Italy,

most significantly in England and in colonial America, was stronger and more lasting than that of any other architect.

Palladio is best known for his many villas built on the Venetian mainland, of which nineteen still stand; the villas were especially influential on later architects. The same Arcadian spirit that prompted the ancient Romans to build villas in the countryside, and that will be expressed so eloquently in the art of the Venetian painter Giorgione, motivated a similar villa-building boom in the sixteenth century. One can imagine that Venice, with its very limited space, must have been more congested than any ancient city. But a longing for the countryside was not the only motive; declining fortunes prompted the Venetians to develop their mainland possessions with new land investment and reclamation projects. Citizens who could afford it were encouraged to set themselves up as gentlemen farmers and to develop swamps into productive agricultural land. Wealthy families could look on their villas as providential investments. The villas were thus gentleman farms (like the much later American plantations, which were architecturally influenced by Palladio) surrounded by service out-buildings that Palladio generally arranged in long, low wings branching out from the main building and enclosing a large, rectangular court area.

Although it is the most famous, Villa Rotonda (FIG. **22-51**), near Vicenza, is not really typical of Palladio's villa style. It was not built for an aspiring gentleman farmer but for a retired monsignor who wanted a villa for social

22-51   ANDREA PALLADIO, Villa Rotonda (formerly Villa Capra), near Vicenza, *c.* 1566–1570.

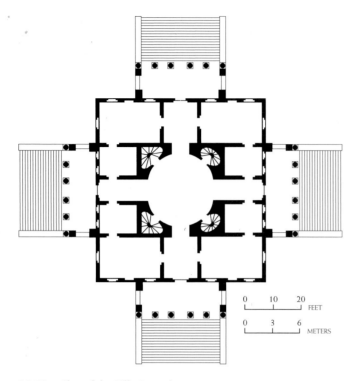

22-52   Plan of the Villa Rotonda.

22-53   Andrea Palladio, west facade of San Giorgio Maggiore, Venice, 1565.

events. Located on a hilltop, Villa Rotonda was planned and designed as a kind of belvedere, without the usual wings of secondary buildings. Its central plan (FIG. **22-52**), with four identical facades and projecting porches, is therefore both sensible and functional; each of the porches can be used as a platform from which to enjoy a different view of the surrounding landscape. In this design, the central dome-covered rotunda logically functions as a kind of revolving platform, from which the visitor can turn in any direction for the preferred view. The result is a building with parts that are functional and systematically related to one another in terms of calculated mathematical relationships. Villa Rotonda, like Santa Maria della Consolazione at Todi (FIG. 22-9), thus embodies all the qualities of self-sufficiency and formal completeness that most Renaissance architects sought. In his formative years, Palladio was influenced by Alberti, by Bramante, and by the remains of Classical architecture he studied in Rome (each facade of his Villa Rotonda resembles a Roman temple, and in placing a traditional temple porch in front of a dome-covered interior, Palladio doubtless had the Pantheon [FIG. 7-55] ever in his mind as a model), as well as, briefly, by Giulio Romano. By 1550, however, he had developed his own personal style, which mixes elements of Mannerism with the clarity and lack of ambiguity that characterizes Classicism at its most "correct."

One of the most dramatically placed buildings in Venice is San Giorgio Maggiore (FIG. **22-53**), directly across a broad canal from the Piazza San Marco. Dissatisfied with earlier solutions to the problem of integrating a high central nave

22-54   Interior of San Giorgio Maggiore (view facing east).

and lower aisles into a unified facade design, Palladio solved it by superimposing a tall, narrow, Classical porch on a low, broad one. This solution reflects the interior arrangement of the building, and in that sense is coolly logical, but the intersection of two temple facades is irrational and ambiguous at the same time, in the Mannerist fashion. Palladio's design also introduces the illusion of three-dimensional depth, an effect that is intensified by the strong projection of the central columns and the shadows they cast. The play of shadow across the building's surfaces, its reflection in the water, and its gleaming white against sea and sky create a remarkably colorful effect, looking forward to the Baroque. The interior of the church (FIG. **22-54**) lacks the ambiguity of the facade and is firmly rooted in High Renaissance architectural style. It is flooded with light, which crisply defines the contours of the rich wall articulations (pedestals, bases, shafts, capitals, entablatures), all beautifully and "correctly" profiled—the exemplar of what Classical architectural theory means by "rational" organization.

Painting

BELLINI AND GIORGIONE   The soft, colored light of Venice, which relaxes the severe lines of Palladio's architecture, lives at its fullest in Venetian painting. In the career of GIOVANNI BELLINI (*c.* 1430–1516), we find the history of that style. In his long productive life, Bellini, always alert to what was new, never ceased to develop artistically and, almost by himself, created what is known as the Venetian style, which will be so important to the subsequent course of painting. Trained in the tradition of the International Style by his father, a student of Gentile da Fabriano, Bellini worked in the family shop and did not develop his own style until after his father's death in 1470. His early independent works show him to be under the dominant influence of his brother-in-law, Andrea Mantegna. But in the late 1470s, he was impressed by the work of the Sicilian-born painter Antonello da Messina, (*c.* 1430–1479) the only major artist of the fifteenth century to be born south of Rome. Antonello received his early training in Naples, where he must have come in close contact with Flemish painting and mastered the use of mixed oil—a more flexible medium that is wider in coloristic range than tempera or fresco (see page 655). Antonello arrived in Venice in 1475 and during his two-year stay introduced his Venetian colleagues to the possibilities offered by the new oil technique. As a direct result of his contact with Antonello, Bellini abandoned Mantegna's harsh, linear style and developed a sensuous, coloristic manner that was to become characteristic of Venetian painting.

Bellini is best known for his many Madonnas, which he painted both in half-length (with or without accompanying saints) on small devotional panels and on large, monumental altarpieces of the *sacra conversazione* (holy conversation)

type. In the *sacra conversazione*, which enjoyed great popularity as a theme for religious paintings from the middle of the fifteenth century on, saints from different epochs are joined in a unified space and seem to be conversing either with each other or with the audience. (Raphael had employed much the same conceit in his *School of Athens* [FIG. 22-15], where he gathered together Greek philosophers of different eras.) Bellini carries on the tradition in two of his large altarpieces, the *San Giobbe Altarpiece* (FIG. **22-55**) and the *San Zaccaria Altarpiece* (FIG. **22-56**), which illustrate not only two stages in the artist's stunning development but also the essential differences between the Early and the High Renaissance treatments of the same subject. The earlier work, the *San Giobbe Altarpiece*, painted for the chapel of the Venetian Hospital of St. Job, groups the enthroned Madonna and Child with Saints Francis, John

22-55   GIOVANNI BELLINI, *San Giobbe Altarpiece, c.* 1490. Oil on wood, 15' 4" × 8' 4". Galleria dell'Accademia, Venice.

22-56 GIOVANNI BELLINI, *San Zaccaria Altarpiece*, 1505. Oil on wood transferred to canvas, approx. 16′ 5″ × 7′ 9″. San Zaccaria, Venice.

the Baptist, Job, Dominic, Sebastian, and Louis of Toulouse. Although the space is large, airy, and clearly defined, the figures seem to be crowded. They cling to the foreground plane and are seen in a slightly forced, Mantegnesque, "worm's-eye" perspective. The drawing remains sharp and precise, particularly in that charming Venetian trademark, the group of angel-musicians at the foot of the Madonna's throne. The figures already are arranged in the pyramidal grouping preferred by the High Renaissance, but they tend to exist as individuals rather than as parts of an integrated whole. Seen by itself, the *San Giobbe Altarpiece* is an orderly, well-balanced painting that can hold its own with any produced during the Early Renaissance, but, side by side with the subsequent *San Zaccaria Altarpiece*, it suddenly seems cluttered and overly busy.

In the *San Zaccaria Altarpiece,* Bellini takes the long step into the High Renaissance. In contrast to his earlier treat-

ment of the theme, Bellini raises the observer's viewpoint and deemphasizes the perspective. The number of figures is reduced, and they are more closely integrated with each other and with the space that surrounds them. Combined into a single, cohesive group, the figures no longer cling to the front of the painting; disposed in depth, they now move in and out of the apse instead of standing before it. Their attitudes produce a rhythmic movement within the group, but all obvious gestures have been eliminated and the former busyness has changed to serene calm. In addition, Bellini's method of painting has become softer and more luminous. Line is no longer the chief agent of form but has been submerged in a sea of glowing color—a soft radiance that envelops the forms with an atmospheric haze and enhances their majestic serenity.

The San Zaccaria Madonna is the mature work of an old man whose paintings spanned the development of three artistic generations in Florence. Departing from the Gothic, Bellini moved through the Early Renaissance and arrived in the High Renaissance even before Raphael and Michelangelo. At the very end of his long life, this astonishingly apt artist was still willing and able to make changes in his style and approach to keep himself abreast of his times; he began to deal with pagan subjects.

The *Feast of the Gods* (FIG. **22-57**) was influenced by one of Bellini's own students, Giorgione, who developed his master's landscape backgrounds into poetic, Arcadian reveries. After Giorgione's premature death, Bellini embraced his student's interests and, in the *Feast of the Gods,* developed a new kind of mythological painting. Although some of the figures—most notably the nymph carrying a vase on her head and the sleeping nymph in the lower right corner of the canvas—are drawn from the standard repertoire of Greco-Roman art, in Bellini's painting the Olympian gods appear as peasants enjoying a heavenly picnic in a shady northern glade. Bellini's source is Ovid's *Fasti,* which describes a banquet of the gods. The figures are spread across the foreground: satyrs attend the gods, nymphs bring jugs of wine, a child draws from a keg, couples engage in love play, and the sleeping nymph with exposed breast receives amorous attention. The mellow light of a long afternoon glows softly around the gathering, touching the surfaces of colorful draperies, smooth flesh, and polished metal. Here, Bellini announces the delight the Venetian school will take in the beauty of texture revealed by the full resources of gently and subtly harmonized color. Behind the warm, lush tones of the figures, a background of cool, green, tree-filled glades reaches into the distance; at the right, a screen of trees makes a verdant shelter. The atmosphere is idyllic, a lush countryside making a setting for the never-ending pleasure of the immortal gods. The poetry of Greece and Rome, as well as that of the Renaissance, is filled with this pastoral mood, and the Venetians make a specialty of its representation. Its elements include the smiling landscape, eternal youth, and song and revelry, always with a touch of the sensual.

22-57 GIOVANNI BELLINI, *Feast of the Gods*, 1514. Oil on canvas, approx. 5′ 7″ × 6′ 2″. National Gallery of Art, Washington, D.C. (Widener Collection).

Thus, with Bellini, Venetian art becomes the great complement of the schools of Florence and Rome. The Venetians' instrument is color; that of the Florentines and Romans is sculpturesque form. These two schools run parallel—sometimes touching and engaging—through the history of Western art from the Renaissance on. Their themes are different. Venice paints the poetry of the senses and delights in the beauty of nature and the pleasures of humanity. Florence and Rome attempt the sterner, intellectual themes—the epic of man, the masculine virtues, the grandeur of the ideal, the lofty conceptions of religion as

they involve the heroic and sublime. Much of the history of later Western art can be broadly understood as a dialogue between these two traditions.

The inspiration for Bellini's late Arcadianism is to be found in paintings like the so-called *Pastoral Symphony* (FIG. **22-58**) by his illustrious student GIORGIONE DA CASTELFRANCO (*c.*1477–1510), a work held by some to be an early Titian. Out of dense color shadow emerge the soft forms of figures and landscape. The theme is as mysterious as the light. Two nude females, accompanied by two clothed young men, occupy the rich, abundant landscape through which a

22-58   GIORGIONE (and/or TITIAN ?), *Pastoral Symphony, c.* 1508. Oil on canvas, approx. 43" × 54". Louvre, Paris.

shepherd passes. In the distance, a villa crowns a hill. The pastoral mood is so eloquently evoked here that we need not know (as we do not) the precise meaning of the picture; the mood is enough. The shepherd is symbolic of the poet; the pipes and the lute symbolize his poetry. The two women accompanying the young men may be thought of as their invisible inspiration, their muses. One turns to lift water from the sacred well of poetic inspiration. The great, golden bodies of the women, softly modulated by the smoky shadow, become the standard Venetian type. It is the Venetian school that resurrects the Venus figure from antiquity, making her the fecund goddess of nature and of love. The full opulence of the figures should, of course, not be read according to modern preferences in womanly physique but as poetic personifications of the abundance of nature.

As a pastoral poet in the pictorial medium and one of the greatest masters in the handling of light and color, Giorgione praises the beauty of nature, music, woman, and pleasure. Vasari reports that Giorgione was an accomplished lutist and singer, and adjectives from poetry and music seem best suited to describe the pastoral air and muted chords of his painting. He casts a mood of tranquil revery and dreaminess over the whole scene, evoking the landscape of a lost but never forgotten paradise. Arcadia and its happy creatures persist in the subconscious memory and longing of humankind. Among the Italians, the Venetians were foremost in expressing a love of nature and a realization of its potentialities for the painter, although they never represent it except as humanly inhabited. The ancient spirits, the deities of field and woodland, still inhabit it too, and landscape—manifesting the bounty of Venus and sanctified by her beauty—as yet simply provides the inspiring setting for the poet, without whom it would be incomplete.

TITIAN   Giorgione's Arcadianism passed not only to his much older yet constantly learning master, Bellini, but also to Tiziano Vecelli, whose name we anglicize into TITIAN (c. 1490–1576). Titian is the most prodigious and prolific of the great Venetian painters. He is among the very greatest painters of the Western world—a supreme colorist and, in a broad sense, the father of the modern mode of painting. An important change that took place in Titian's time was the almost universal adoption of canvas, with its rough-textured surface, in place of wood panels for paintings. The works of Titian establish oil color on canvas as the typical medium of our pictorial tradition. According to a contemporary of Titian, Palma Giovane:

> Titian [employed] a great mass of colors, which served . . . as a base for whatever he was going to paint over it. . . . I myself have seen his determined brushstrokes laden with color, sometimes a streak of pure earth-red which served him (one might say) as a half-tone, other times with a brushstroke of white lead; and with the same brush colored with a red, black, and yellow, he formed a highlight; and with these rules of technique made the promise of an excellent figure appear in four brushstrokes.
> After having laid these important foundations, he then used to turn the pictures to the wall, and leave them— sometimes for as long as several months—without looking at them; and when he wanted to apply his brush to them again, he [examined] them most rigorously . . . whether he could find any defects in them or discover anything which would not be in harmony with the delicacy of his

intentions. . . . Working thus, and redesigning his figures, Titian brought them into a perfect symmetry which could represent the beauty of Art as well as of Nature. After this was done, he put his hand to some other picture until the first was dry, working in the same way with this other; thus gradually he covered those quintessential outlines of his figures with living flesh. . . . He never painted a figure all at once, and used to say that he who improvises his song can form neither learned nor well-turned verses. But the final polish . . . was to unite now and then by a touch of his fingers the extremes of the light areas, so that they became almost half-tints . . . at other times, with a stroke he would place a dark streak in a corner; to reinforce it he would add a streak of red, like a drop of blood . . . in the final phase [he] painted more with his fingers than with his brushes.

Trained by both Bellini and Giorgione, Titian learned so well from them that even today no general agreement exists as to the degree of his participation in their later works. He completed several of Bellini's and Giorgione's unfinished paintings. One of his own early works, *Sacred and Profane Love* (FIG. **22-59**), is very much in the manner of Giorgione, with its Arcadian setting, its allegory, and its complex and enigmatic meaning. Two young women, one draped, the other nude, flank a sarcophagus into which a cupid reaches. Behind them is a screen of trees and, to the left and right, deep vistas into different landscapes. The two figures may represent the different levels of Neo-Platonic love: the sumptuously draped woman is a kind of allegory of vanity and the love of this world; the nude who holds aloft her lamp represents the highest level of love that can be reached (love of the divine, nudity being symbolic of truth). Titian's figures are not suffused with Giorgione's

22-59   TITIAN, *Sacred and Profane Love,* c. 1515. Oil on canvas, approx. 3′ 11″ × 9′ 2″. Galleria Borghese, Rome.

glowing, mysterious tones; they are drawn firmly and boldly and brilliantly colored, and the artist manifests his chief interest in the play of light over the rich satins and the smooth volumes of the body and glossy flesh. The world given to the eye is a world of color before it is a world of solid forms, and this truth is one that the Venetians were the first to grasp.

On the death of Giovanni Bellini in 1516, Titian was appointed painter to the republic of Venice. Shortly there-

after, he painted the *Madonna of the Pesaro Family* (FIG. **22-60**) for the church of the Frari. This great work, which furthered Titian's reputation and established his personal style, was presented to the church by Jacopo Pesaro, bishop of Paphos in Cyprus and commander of the papal fleet, in thanksgiving for a successful expedition in 1502 against the Turks during the Venetian–Turkish war. In a stately, sunlit setting, the Madonna receives the commander, who kneels dutifully at the foot of her throne. A soldier (Saint George?)

22-60   TITIAN, *Madonna of the Pesaro Family,* 1519–1526. Oil on canvas, approx. 16′ × 9′. Santa Maria dei Frari, Venice.

22-61 TITIAN, *Venus of Urbino*, 1538. Oil on canvas, approx. 48″ × 66″. Galleria degli Uffizi, Florence.

behind the commander carries a banner with the arms of the Borgia (Pope Alexander VI); behind him is a turbaned Turk, a captive of the Christian forces. Saint Peter occupies the steps of the throne, and Saint Francis introduces other members of the Pesaro family (all male—women and children were typically not thought worthy of inclusion among the donors in Italian paintings of this era), who kneel solemnly in the right foreground.

The massing of monumental figures, singly and in groups, within a weighty and majestic architecture is, as we have seen, characteristic of the High Renaissance. But Titian does not compose a horizontal and symmetrical arrangement, as Leonardo did in the *Last Supper* (FIG. 22-3) or Raphael in the *School of Athens* (FIG. 22-15). Rather, he places the figures in occult balance on a steep diagonal, positioning the Madonna, the focus of the composition, well off the central axis. Attention is directed to her by the perspective lines, by the inclination of the figures, and by the directional lines of gaze and gesture. The design is beau-

tifully brought into poise by the banner that inclines toward the left, balancing the rightward and upward tendencies of the main direction.

This kind of composition is more dynamic than what we have seen so far in the High Renaissance. The forces already moving in it promise a new kind of pictorial design—one built on movement rather than rest. In his rendering of the rich surface textures, Titian gives a dazzling display of color in all its nuances. The human—especially the Venetian—scene is one with the heavenly, as the Madonna and saints find themselves honoring the achievements of particular men in this particular world. A quite worldly transaction is taking place (albeit beneath a heavenly cloud bearing angels) between a queen, her court, and her loyal servants; the tableau is constructed in terms of Renaissance protocol and courtly splendor.

In 1538, at the height of his powers, Titian painted the so-called *Venus of Urbino* (FIG. **22-61**) for Guidobaldo II, duke of Urbino. The title (given to the painting only later) elevates what was probably merely a representation of a courtesan in her bedchamber to the status of Classical mythology, but there is no evidence that when the work was commissioned it was intended as anything more than a female nude for the private delectation of the duke. Whether the subject is divine or mortal, in this canvas Titian gives us the compositional essentials for the representation of a theme that will be popular for centuries. Titian's version, based on an earlier (and pioneering) painting of Venus by Giorgione, was to become official for paintings of the reclining female nude, regardless of the many variations that would later ensue. Titian's "Venus" reclines on a gentle slope made by her luxurious, pillowed couch, the linear play of the draperies contrasting with the sleek, continuous volume of her body. At her feet is a *pendant* (balancing) figure—in this case, a slumbering lapdog. Behind her, a simple drape serves both to place her figure emphatically in the foreground and to press a vista into the background at the right half of the picture. In the vista, two servants bend over a chest; beyond them, a smaller vista opens into a landscape. The steps backward into space and the division of the space into progressively smaller units are beautifully contrived. All of the resources of pictorial representation are in Titian's hands, and he uses them here to create original and exquisite effects of the sort that will inspire generations of painters in Italy and the north.

Deep Venetian reds set off against the pale, neutral whites of the linen and the warm ivory-gold of the flesh are echoed in the red tones of the matron's skirt, the muted reds of the tapestries, and the neutral whites of the matron's sleeves and the kneeling girl's gown. One must study the picture carefully to realize what subtlety of color planning is responsible, for example, for the placing of the two deep reds (in the foreground cushions and in the background skirt) that function so importantly in the composition as a gauge of distance and as terminals of an implied diagonal opposed to the real one of the reclining figure. Here, color is used not simply for the tinting of preexisting forms but as a means of organization that determines the placement of forms.

Titian was also a highly esteemed portraitist and one of the very best. Of the well over fifty portraits by his hand to survive, an early example, *Man with the Glove* (FIG. **22-62**), will suffice to illustrate his style. The portrait is a trifle more than half-length. The head is turned slightly away from the observer; the right hand gathers the drapery of a mantle, and the gloved left hand holds another glove. The V-shaped shirtfront directs attention to the face as well as to the right hand, which points in the direction of the gloved hand. These dexterous compositional arrangements, creating a kind of "three-spot" relationship among head and hands, had already been made by Leonardo in his *Mona Lisa* (FIG. 22-4). Titian's portraits, as well as those of many of the Venetian and subsequent schools, generally make much of the psychological reading of the most expressive parts of

22-62   TITIAN, *Man with the Glove, c.* 1519. Oil on canvas, approx. 39″ × 35″. Louvre, Paris.

the body—the head and the hands. We are not immediately aware that these subtle placements influence our response to the portrait subject. In fact, a portrait must be as skillfully composed as a great figure composition. The mood of this portrait is Giorgionesque—one of dreamy preoccupation. The eyes turn away from us, as if, in conversation, the subject has recalled something that sets him musing in silence. Titian's *Man with the Glove* is as much the portrait of a cultivated state of mind as of a particular individual. It is the meditative, poetic youth, who is at the same time Baldassare Castiglione's ideal courtier, perfectly poised and self-assured, handsome, gallant, debonair, the "glass of fashion and the mold of form." No portrait gives us so much of the Renaissance manner in a single individual, unless it be Raphael's *Castiglione* (FIG. 22-17).

Honor and glory attached to Titian as he grew older. He was known and sought after by all the great of Europe. He was painter to and close friend of Emperor Charles V, who made him a knight of the Holy Roman Empire; afterward, he painted numerous pictures for Charles's son, Phillip II of Spain. The great Hapsburg painting collections centered around Titian's works, and his fame and wealth recall the success of Raphael. He was the master of all themes, whether the Virgin Mary or a sensuous courtesan, an elegant courtier or a suffering Christ. The last is the subject he took up in a painting that he made toward the end of his life. In his *Christ Crowned with Thorns* (FIG. **22-63**), Titian

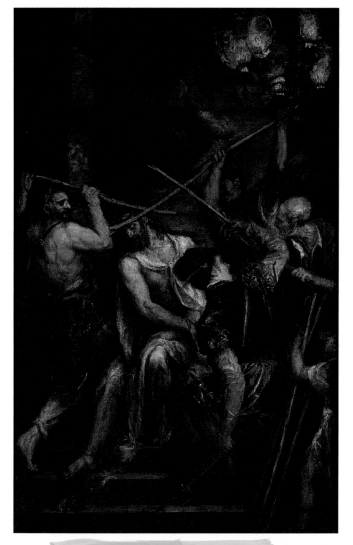

22-63   TITIAN, *Christ Crowned with Thorns, c.* 1573–1575. Oil on canvas, approx. 9′ × 6′. Alte Pinakothek, Munich.

shows Christ tormented by the soldiers of Pilate, who twist a wreath of thorns around his head. The drama is achieved by the limited number of figures, the emphasis on the figure of Christ, and the muted, flickering light that centers the action. The color scheme is almost monochromatic; the light and color play freely within and beyond the contours, making a patchy, confused mixture of lights and darks, in which it is difficult to read the forms with precision. But this effect only enhances the mystery, the gloomy environment, and the mood of torment. Titian's intention is not so much to stage the event as to present his religious and personal response to it. His very brushstroke—broad, thick, and freely applied—bespeaks the directness of his approach. It melts and scatters solid form to produce the wavering, supernatural glow that encircles spiritual vision. Here Titian's art looks forward to the painting of Rembrandt in the next century.

TINTORETTO AND VERONESE   JACOPO ROBUSTI, known as TINTORETTO (1518–1594), claimed to be a student of Titian and aspired to combine the color of Titian with the drawing of Michelangelo. He usually is referred to as the outstanding Venetian representative of Mannerism. He adopts many Mannerist pictorial devices, but his dramatic power, depth of spiritual vision, and glowing Venetian color schemes do not seem to fit the Mannerist mold. We need not settle here the question of whether or not Tintoretto is a Mannerist; we need only mention that he shares some common characteristics with central Italian Mannerism and that, in other respects, his work really anticipates the Baroque.

The art of Tintoretto is always extremely dramatic. In his *Miracle of the Slave* (FIG. **22-64**), we find some of his typical stageplay. Saint Mark hurtles downward to the assistance of a Christian slave, who is about to be martyred for the faith, and shatters the instruments of torture. These are held up by the executioner to the startled judge as the throng around the central action stares. The dynamism of Titian is greatly accelerated, and the composition is made up of contrary and opposing motions; for any figure leaning in one direction, another figure counters it. At the extreme left, a group of two men, a woman, and a child winds contrapuntally about a column, resembling the later Mannerist twisting of Giovanni da Bologna's *Abduction of the Sabine Women* (FIG. 22-45). The main group curves deeply back into space, but the most dynamic touch of all is made by the central trio of the slave, the executioner, and the inverted Saint Mark. The three figures sweep together in a great, upward, serpentine curve, the motion of which is checked by the plunging figure of Saint Mark, moving in the opposite direction. The entire composition is a kind of counterpoint of motion characteristic of Mannerism. The motion, however, is firmly contained within the picture frame, and the robustness of the figures, their solid structure and firm movement, the clearly composed space, and the coherent action have little to do with Manneristic presentation. There is nothing hesitant or ambiguous in the depiction of the miraculous event, which is dramatized forcefully and with conviction. Tintoretto's skillful theatricality and sweeping power of execution set him apart from the Mannerists and make him a forerunner of the Baroque, the age of theater and opera. And the tonality—the deep golds, reds, and greens—is purely Venetian.

Toward the end of his life, Tintoretto's art, like Titian's, becomes spiritual, even visionary, as solid forms melt away into swirling clouds of dark, shot through with fitful light. In Tintoretto's *Last Supper* (FIG. **22-65**), painted for the interior of Palladio's church of San Giorgio Maggiore (FIG. 22-54), the actors take part in a ghostly drama; they are as insubstantial as the shadows cast by the faint glow of their halos and the flame of a single lamp that seems to breed phosphorescent spirits. All are moved by an intense, psychic commotion. The space speeds away into an unearthly darkness peopled by phantoms. Only the

22-64   TINTORETTO, *Miracle of the Slave*, 1548. Oil on canvas, approx. 14′ × 18′. Galleria dell'Accademia, Venice.

incandescent nimbus around his head identifies Jesus as he administers the Sacrament to his disciples.

The contrast with Leonardo's *Last Supper* (FIG. 22-3) is both extreme and instructive. Leonardo's composition, balanced and symmetrical, parallels the picture plane in a geometrically organized and closed space; Christ's figure is the tranquil center of the drama and the focus of the perspective. In Tintoretto's painting, Christ is above and beyond the converging perspective lines that race diagonally away from the picture surface, creating disturbing effects of limitless depth and motion. Tintoretto's Christ is located by light flaring beaconlike out of darkness; Leonardo's is placed by geometric and perspectival centralization. The contrast of the two expresses the direction Renaissance painting takes in the sixteenth century, as it moves away from architectonic clarity of space and neutral lighting toward the dynamic perspectives and dramatic chiaroscuro of the coming Baroque.

The last of the great Venetian masters was Paolo Cagliari of Verona, called PAOLO VERONESE (1528–1588). Where Tintoretto glories in monumental drama and deep perspectives, Veronese specializes in splendid pageantry painted in superb color and set within a majestic, Classical architecture. Like Tintoretto, Veronese painted on a huge scale, with canvases often as large as 20 by 30 feet or more. His usual subjects, painted for the refectories of wealthy monasteries, afforded him an opportunity to display magnificent companies at table.

Christ in the House of Levi (FIG. **22-66**), originally called the *Last Supper,* is a good example. Here, in a great open loggia framed by three monumental arches (the style of the architecture closely resembles the upper arcades of Jacopo Sansovino's State Library [FIG. 22-50]), Christ is seen seated at the center of splendidly garbed grandees of Venice, while with a courtly gesture, the very image of gracious grandeur, the chief steward welcomes guests. The spacious

22-65 TINTORETTO, *Last Supper*, 1594. Oil on canvas, 12′ × 18′ 8″. Chancel, San Giorgio Maggiore, Venice.

22-66 VERONESE, *Christ in the House of Levi*, 1573. Oil on canvas, approx. 18′ 6″ × 42′ 6″. Galleria dell'Accademia, Venice.

loggia is crowded not only with robed magnificoes but with their colorful retainers, clowns, dogs, and dwarfs. The Holy Office of the Inquisition accused Veronese of impiety in painting such creatures so close to the Lord, and he was ordered to make changes at his own expense. Reluctant to do so, he simply changed the painting's title, converting the subject to a less solemn one. As Palladio looks to the example of Classical architecture of the High Renaissance, so Veronese returns to High Renaissance composition, its symmetrical balance, and its ordered architectonics. His shim-

22-67   VERONESE, *Triumph of Venice, c.* 1585. Oil on canvas, approx. 29′ 8″ × 19′. Ceiling of the Hall of the Grand Council, Palazzo Ducale, Venice.

mering color is drawn from the whole spectrum, although he avoids solid colors for half shades (light blues, sea greens, lemon yellows, roses, and violets), creating veritable flower beds of tone.

Tintoretto and Veronese were employed by the republic of Venice to decorate the grand chambers and council rooms of the Doge's Palace. A great and popular decorator, Veronese shows himself to be a master of imposing, illusionistic ceiling compositions like the *Triumph of Venice* (FIG. **22-67**), where, within an oval frame, he presents Venice, crowned by Fame, enthroned between two great, twisted columns in a balustraded loggia, garlanded with clouds, and attended by figures symbolic of its glories. This work represents one of the very first modern, pictorial glorifica-tions of a state—a subject that will become very popular during the Baroque period. Veronese's perspective is not, like Mantegna's or Correggio's, projected directly up from below; rather, it is a projection of the scene at a forty-five-degree angle to the spectator, a technique that will be used by many later Baroque decorators, particularly the Venetian Tiepolo in the eighteenth century.

It is fitting that we close our discussion of Italian art in the sixteenth century with a scene of triumph, for, indeed, the century witnessed the triumph of architecture, sculpture, and painting. They achieve the status of fine arts, and a tradition is established by these masters of prodigious genius, whose works inspire all artists who follow but never surpass them.

WESTERN EUROPE IN THE SIXTEENTH CENTURY

ENGLAND
NETHERLANDS
HAARLEM · · AMSTERDAM
LONDON
BRUGES · ANTWERP
FLANDERS
GHENT · BRUSSELS
Rhine R.
GERMANY
HOLY
WITTENBERG
HALLE
PRAGUE

ATLANTIC
OCEAN

PARIS
MAINZ
ROMAN
NUREMBERG
REGENSBURG
Danube R.
VIENNA

FONTAINEBLEAU
COLMAR · AUGSBURG
MUNICH

CHAMBORD
ISENHEIM
BASEL
EMPIRE
HUNGARY

FRANCE
GENEVA
LOMBARDY
MILAN · VENICE
REP.
OF
VENICE
Danube R.

GENOA
FLORENCE
PAPAL
STATES
ADRIATIC SEA

BURGOS
VALLADOLID
GRAND DUCHY
OF TUSCANY
ITALY

PORTUGAL
MADRID
ROME
KINGDOM
OF
NAPLES
TOLEDO

SPAIN

GRANADA
MEDITERRANEAN SEA

0   300 Miles

0   300 Kilometers

1475	1500	1525
		◀ AGE OF EUROPEAN EXPLORATION AND COLONIZATION OVERSEAS AN
	MAXIMILIAN I OF HAPSBURG, HRE	CHARLES V (HAPSBURG), HRE, KING OF SPAIN AND
	HENRY VIII OF ENGLAND (TUDOR)	
	FRANCIS I OF FRANCE (VALOIS)	

Grünewald
The Isenheim Altarpiece,
c. 1510-1515

Chateau de Chambord,
France, begun 1519

HRE - Holy Roman Emperor

Duchy of Burgundy and the Netherlands absorbed by Holy Roman Empire, 1477.

Valois/Bourbon dynasty, 1498-1589/1589-(1830)   Spanish conquest of Muslim Granada. 1492.   John Calvin, (1509-1564)

Hapsburg dynasty, 1493-(1918)   Sir Thomas More (1477-1535).   Spread of Calvinist Protestantism in France and Switzerland, 1536

Martin Luther posts theses against Indulgences. Beginning of Protestant Reformation, 1517.

Netherlands House of Orange/Nassau 1584-20th Century   Spanish conquest of Mexico and Peru, (1518-36)

House of Tudor 1485-1603   Erasmus of Rotterdam (c.1466- 1536).

CHAPTER 23

SIXTEENTH-CENTURY ART IN NORTHERN EUROPE AND SPAIN

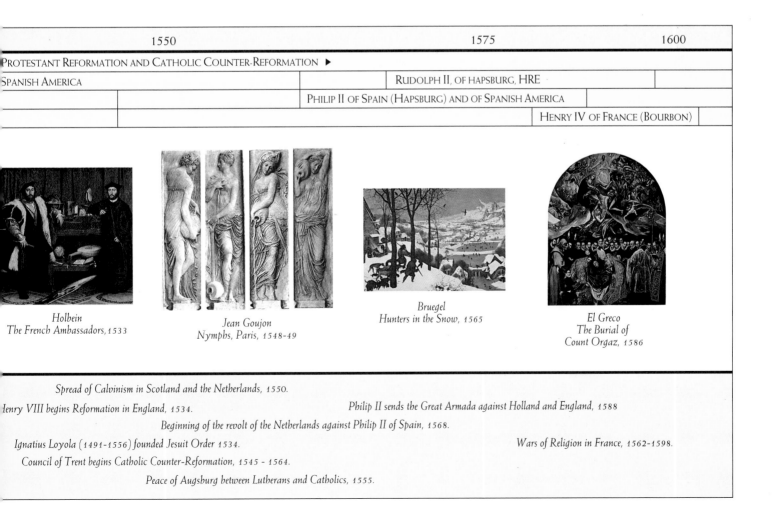

1550	1575	1600

PROTESTANT REFORMATION AND CATHOLIC COUNTER-REFORMATION ▶

SPANISH AMERICA

RUDOLPH II, OF HAPSBURG, HRE

PHILIP II OF SPAIN (HAPSBURG) AND OF SPANISH AMERICA

HENRY IV OF FRANCE (BOURBON)

Holbein
The French Ambassadors, 1533

Jean Goujon
Nymphs, Paris, 1548-49

Bruegel
Hunters in the Snow, 1565

El Greco
The Burial of
Count Orgaz, 1586

Spread of Calvinism in Scotland and the Netherlands, 1550.

Henry VIII begins Reformation in England, 1534.

Philip II sends the Great Armada against Holland and England, 1588

Beginning of the revolt of the Netherlands against Philip II of Spain, 1568.

Ignatius Loyola (1491-1556) founded Jesuit Order 1534.

Wars of Religion in France, 1562-1598.

Council of Trent begins Catholic Counter-Reformation, 1545 - 1564.

Peace of Augsburg between Lutherans and Catholics, 1555.

THE PROTESTANT REFORMATION

The most fateful event of the sixteenth century was the so-called Protestant Reformation. Beginning with the preaching and the writings of Martin Luther, a German theologian, the "reformation" was a revolution that split Christendom in half and produced a hundred years of civil war between Protestant and Catholic. The Reformation culminated centuries of reform movements within the Church and decided the long struggle between Church and state in favor of the state once and for all. The medieval world of the priest mediating between people and God was largely replaced by the modern world of the laity and religious individualism.

The Reformation aimed not at the age-old objective of reform—the worldliness and corruption of the clergy—but at a redefinition of Christianity itself. According to Luther and other great reformers like Zwingli and Calvin, the whole ecclesiastical structure of the Catholic Church needed to be cast out, for it had no basis in scripture whatsoever. The Bible and nothing else could serve as the foundation for Christianity. Luther declared the pope to be the Antichrist (for which the pope excommunicated him), the Church the "whore of Babylon," and ordained priests, along with the sacramental systems they administered, the pagan obstacles to salvation (Luther accepted only two sacraments, baptism and the Eucharist, the Lord's Supper). Christianity needed to be cleansed of all the impurities of doctrine that had collected through the ages and to have its original purity restored.

Central to the reformers' creed was the question of salvation—how it was to be achieved. Their answer was twofold: (1) by faith alone, and (2) by faith in the sole authority of scripture, the Bible. This was the word of God, not the councils, law, and ritual of the Church. Humankind was hopelessly depraved, and, by virtue of original sin, unworthy of being saved from eternal damnation. No ecclesiastical machinery with all its miraculous rites and indulgent forgivenesses could save the sinner face to face with God. Before the just anger of God even a life of good works was of no avail. Only absolute faith in Christ could justify the sinner and insure salvation. Justification by faith alone, with the guidance of scripture, was the fundamental doctrine of Protestantism.

If scripture alone, and not the Church, was the Christian's guide to salvation, then each Christian was obliged to read and interpret the scripture for himself. It soon became evident that Christians could differ in their interpretations of the sacred texts, and this gave rise to serious differences among the reformers themselves. Luther clashed with Zwingli over the meaning of the sixth chapter of John, Calvin went his own way to set up a God-ruled state in Geneva, and Anabaptists, radicals of Protestantism, founded a sect despised by all the others, almost as much as they all despised the Catholics.

This Protestant sectarianism and the Catholic opposition were inextricably linked with the territorial and state politics of the time. Lutherans were located mostly in Germany and Scandinavia, Zwinglians in Switzerland, Calvinists in Geneva, France, the Netherlands, and Scotland. In England, Henry VIII declared himself head of a church still Catholic, but no longer Roman.

Personal religious loyalty, whether Protestant or Catholic, could come into conflict with loyalty to the religion of the ruler of the city, county, duchy, principality, or kingdom where one lived. By mid-century the legal principle was emerging that one either accepted the religion of one's sovereign or emigrated to a territory where the sovereign's religion and one's own were the same.

Religion followed class distinction, especially in the cities; the religion of the rich was very seldom the religion of the poor. In wealthy cities like Augsburg in Germany, the merchant/bankers, publishers, printers, artists—the bourgeois masters of the city—might be Catholic, the lower levels Lutheran, and the workers Anabaptists. The German peasants, victims of a pitiless repression of their uprising in 1525, saw scripture as a liberating manifesto against feudal serfdom; they chanted

When Adam delved and Eve span,
Who was then the gentleman?

Their Lutheran masters who put them down were urged on by Luther to "smite, stab, slay, and burn" [them], for nothing can be more poisonous, hateful, or devilish than a rebel." The Catholics as well as Protestants took this tone, and the story of the Reformation and Counter-Reformation is one of cruel repression of dissenting voices.

The European powers, Protestant and Catholic, played it all ways wherever their interest was at issue. Spain, at the greatest height of imperial power, was captain of the Catholic world as it battled the Reformation on the soil of the Netherlands, where the Protestant powers focused their resistance, and where the Dutch republic made its Protestant appearance and defiant stand. The Lutheran princes of Germany fought against—and sometimes with—their Catholic emperor; Calvinist Huguenots and Catholics devastated France in half a century of civil war.

This widespread and grueling civil war of Christianity went on through wholesale murdering of populations, burning of heretics, dislocation of petty states, and aggrandizement of greater states, whose kings and princes now asserted themselves to be heads of their sovereign churches in place of Rome. The slogan became "one religion, one state." The old unity of the Church was broken forever, but a hundred years of religious war and fanaticism were at last succeeded by a period of religious tolerance. The intellectual shakeup of age-old faiths and opinions prepared the way for a new and nonreligious outlook on the world—the Enlightenment—when the rise of a scientific view of nature would challenge forever the dogmatisms of the past.

Interestingly, throughout all the religious conflict that agonized sixteenth-century Europe, the exchange of intellectual and artistic ideas continued and thrived. Catholic Italy and (mostly) Lutheran Germany shared in a lively commerce—economic and cultural—and the art of the sixteenth century in the north manifests the benefit of that exchange.

GERMANY

The art of northern Europe during the sixteenth century is characterized by a sudden awareness of the advances made by the Italian Renaissance and by a desire to assimilate this new style as rapidly as possible. Many artists traveled to Italy to study the new art firsthand; others met it either directly, in the form of Italian artists who came to the north, or indirectly, through the numerous Italian engravings that circulated throughout northern Europe. One of the most prolific Italian engravers, Marcantonio Raimondi, rarely invented his own compositions but copied those of other artists, particularly Raphael. In this way, many panel paintings and frescoes by Italian Renaissance artists became the common property of all Europe. Naturally, the impact of Italian art varied widely, according to the artist, the time, and the place. Many artists never abandoned existing local traditions; others frequently were content to borrow only single motifs or the general form of a composition. In Germany, the wealthy merchant class maintained close commercial relations with Venice, and German Humanists were in contact with the Platonic Academy of Philosophy in Florence. As a result, Albrecht Dürer often illustrated Florentine thought clothed in Venetian and German forms.

During the fifteenth century, painting in the wealthy towns of southern Germany developed along its own expressionistic lines under the dominant influences of Flemish art. Around the turn of the century, it suddenly burst into full bloom. By 1528, with the deaths of its two greatest exponents, Dürer and Matthias Grünewald, it had spent itself. Thus, its most brilliant period corresponds almost exactly to the High Renaissance in Italy. Its decline around 1530 was just as abrupt as its rise; the reason for this is uncertain. The almost incessant religious wars devastated the German lands, and puritanism, which accompanied the triumph of Protestantism in the north, may have opposed Humanistic paganism in the figurative arts. With the exception of Hans Holbein the Younger, the main representatives of the German school were born within ten years of one another and were contemporaries of Michelangelo, Raphael, Giorgione, and Titian.

ALTDORFER AND CRANACH   ALBRECHT ALTDORFER (c. 1480–1538) is the primary representative of the *Donaustil* (Danube style), which flourished along the Danube River from Regensburg (Altdorfer's hometown) eastward into Austria. The style formed around the depiction of landscape and stresses mood, sometimes heightened to passion. Altdorfer's own style is highly personal and only occasionally modified by the influence of Dürer. As a gifted colorist and observer of atmospheric and light effects, Altdorfer loved to paint forests and ruins, in which his figure groups are half-submerged. He painted at least one landscape without figures, making *Danube Landscape, Near Regensburg* (*c.* 1522; not shown) perhaps the first landscape in Western art since antiquity painted entirely for its own sake.

His most renowned work, *The Battle of Issus* (FIG. **23-1**), bears little resemblance to a Danube setting, although it does give a bird's-eye view of an Alpine landscape. Here, Altdorfer spreads out in awesome detail the battle in which Alexander the Great overthrew the Persian king, Darius; a huge inscription hanging in the clouds relates this. Swarms of warriors from both sides contest on a plain backed by cities, mountains, seas, and the opposed forces of nature: the sun and the moon in an illuminated sky. This sudden opening up of space, with its subordination of the human figure to the cosmic landscape, bespeaks a new view of nature—a view that will see human beings as insignificant motes in an infinite universe.

We need not suppose that German artists knew of the work of the contemporary astronomer, Copernicus, who was about to revise the age-old view that the earth is fixed and to suggest instead that the earth and the other "fixed" planets revolve about the sun. Such high-horizoned, "topographical" landscapes (we might better call them "cosmographical") anticipate, interestingly, the coming cosmic view that the sciences of physics and physical astronomy will open to the Western world. Altdorfer's technique is still that of the miniaturist, yet his setting is no longer a page but a world, one in which his insectlike combatants are all but lost. In this first vision of the immense space and power of the cosmos, Altdorfer seems to suggest a theme that all subsequent philosophers, scientists, and clergymen, as well as artists, will confront—the insignificance of human life.

The early works of LUCAS CRANACH THE ELDER (1472–1553) are close to the Donaustil, which immerses human beings in the breadth of nature. At Wittenberg, Cranach became a friend and follower of Luther, and he has been called the outstanding representative of German Protestant painting. His later works are marked by a shift from religious to humanistic subject matter: mythology, history, and portraits. Best known are his figure compositions featuring the nude, which he renders with a charming, provincial naiveté. A good example is *The Judgment of Paris* (FIG. **23-2**). Here, Paris and Mercury consult, while three spindly little goddesses show off their pretty contours. One of them coyly turns her head toward us, another instructs Paris as to the conditions of the contest, a third—Venus—stands by wearing a fashionable hat and pointing upward to her son, Cupid, ready with his arrow. Cranach

23-1 ALBRECHT ALTDORFER, *The Battle of Issus*, 1529. Oil on wood., 52¼″ × 47¼″. Alte Pinakothek, Munich.

Revolt in 1525, and, after its collapse, had to flee to northern Germany, where he settled at Halle in Saxony. The sources of Grünewald's style are not certain. He may have been to Italy, but few indications of Renaissance Classicism appear in his art. He knew the work of Dürer (FIGS. 23-5 to 23-11) and perhaps of Bosch. A brilliant colorist, he was not interested in the construction of the monumental, idealized figure in the Italian manner. His color is characterized by subtle tones and soft harmonies on the one hand and shocking dissonance on the other. Uninterested in natural landscape, Grünewald shows us either the celestial or the infernal.

In his appalling *Crucifixion* from *The Isenheim Altarpiece* (FIG. **23-3**), Grünewald gives us perhaps the most memorable interpretation of the theme in the history of art. The altar is composed of a carved wooden shrine with two pairs of movable panels, one directly in back of the other. Painted by Grünewald between 1510 and 1515 for the monastic hospital order of St. Anthony of Isenheim, the panels show three scenes, with the *Crucifixion* outermost, when the altar is closed. The dreadful aspect of the painting, it has been suggested, may be due in part to its placement in the house of the sick, where it may have admonished the inmates that Another has suffered more. It also may have had a therapeutic function, in that it offered some hope to the afflicted. Two saints are represented on the wings flanking the central panels: on the left, Saint Sebastian, whose intercession was invoked to ward off disease (especially the plague); on the right, Saint Anthony, the patron saint of the order, who was identified with miraculous cure. Together, the saints establish the theme of disease and healing that is reinforced by the paintings on the inner wings.

One of the main illnesses treated at the hospital was ergotism (called "Saint Anthony's Fire"), a disease caused by ergot, a fungus that grows especially on rye. Although the cause of this disease was not discovered until about 1600, its symptoms (convulsions and gangrene) were well known. The gangrene often compelled amputation, and it has been noted in this connection that the two movable halves of the predella of the altarpiece, if slid apart, make it appear as if the legs of Christ have been amputated. The same observation can be made of the two main panels. Due to the off-center placement of the cross, the opening of the left center panel would "sever" one arm from the crucified figure.

Much of this symbolism may have been dictated by his patrons, but Grünewald's own inflamed imagination produced the terrible image of the suffering Christ. Against the pall of darkness lowered on the earth, the devastated body looms—dead, the flesh already discolored by decomposition and studded with the thorns of the lash. In death, the strains of the superhuman agony twist the blackening feet, tear at the arms, wrench the head to one side, and turn the fingers into crooked spikes. One has only to tense one's fingers in the position of Christ's to experience the shuddering

23-2 LUCAS CRANACH THE ELDER, *The Judgment of Paris, c.* 1528. Tempera and oil on wood, 40½″ × 28″. Metropolitan Museum of Art, New York.

makes no effort to dress his gods after the Antique manner. They wear the functional armor of German knights attached to provincial courts. Doughty and square-faced, they could have just come in from the field of honor. The background landscape reflects Cranach's earlier Donaustil in its meticulous description of foliage. And so far, only Dürer's approach to the nude (FIG. 23-6) is tutored by Italian art.

MATTHIAS GRÜNEWALD   One of the greatest individualists of the Renaissance and an artist of highly original genius is Matthias Neithardt, known conventionally as MATTHIAS GRÜNEWALD (*c.* 1480–1528). Forgotten until our time, he appears to have had the wide interests of the individualistic Renaissance artists. Working for the archbishops of Mainz from 1511 on as court painter and decorator, he also served them as architect, hydraulic engineer, and superintendent of works. Undoubtedly, he had Lutheran sympathies. He participated in the Peasant

23-3 MATTHIAS GRÜNEWALD, *The Isenheim Altarpiece* (closed), *Crucifixion* (center panel), *c.* 1510–1515. Oil on wood, center panel 9'9^{1}/$_{2}$" × 10'9", each wing 8'2^{1}/$_{2}$" × 3'1^{1}/$_{2}$", predella 2'5^{1}/$_{2}$" × 11' 2". Musée d'Unterlinden, Colmar, France.

tautness of nerves expressed in every line of the figure. No other artist has produced such an image of the dreadful ugliness of pain. The sharp, angular shapes of anguish appear in the figures of the swooning Virgin and Saint John and in the shrill delirium of Mary Magdalene. On the other side, the gaunt, spectral form of John the Baptist stands in ungainly pose, pointing with a finger sharp as a bird's beak to the dead Christ and indicating in a Latin inscription Christ's destiny as Redeemer and his own as mere precursor: "It is fitting that he increase and I diminish." The bright, harsh, dissonant colors—the black, blood-red, acid-yellow, and the dreadful green of death—suit the flat, angular shapes. Placed in a wilderness of dark mountains, the scene is relieved by a flood of glaring light that holds the figures in a tableau of awful impact.

Death and suffering seem to be the dominant themes shown by the altarpiece in its closed state. Yet they are

combined with symbols offering hope and comfort to the viewer. Behind Saint John is a body of water (the river Jordan?), which signifies baptism—the healing action of water, which symbolically washes away sin (it may also refer to the growing contemporary interest in hydrotherapy, as numerous handbooks advertising local thermal and mineral baths were being published at the beginning of the sixteenth century). The wine-red sky behind the cross evokes the blood of Christ and may symbolize the Eucharist. These references to the sacraments of baptism and the Eucharist offer the viewer the hope of salvation through the sacrifice of Christ, should earthly cures fail.

When we turn from the Good Friday of the *Crucifixion* to the Easter Sunday of the *Resurrection* (FIG. **23-4**), an inner panel of *The Isenheim Altarpiece,* the mood changes from disaster to triumph. Christ, in a blazing aureole of light so incandescent that it dissolves his form and overwhelms the guards, rises like a great flame into the starlit heavens. The fluttering Gothic line prevails in the ascending Christ, and something of the awkward angularity of the *Crucifixion* scene shapes the fallen soldiers. The highly expressive light in both scenes is supernatural, not the light of common day. It is certainly not the even, flat light that models Piero della Francesca's *Resurrection* fresco (FIG. 21-30). Indeed, in these two pictures, we find the fundamental differences that set the German school apart from the Italian school in the Renaissance. Piero's *Resurrection* typically represents the event in terms of a static grouping of solidly rendered figures in a completely balanced, measured composition; the central figure of Christ stands solid as a column, with one foot placed weightily on the edge of the sarcophagus. Grünewald converts everything into flowing motion; his

23-4 MATTHIAS GRÜNEWALD, *Resurrection,* detail of the inner right panel of the first opening of *The Isenheim Altarpiece.* Approx. 8'8³/₈" × 4'6³/₄".

Christ is disembodied, almost formless, and the composition has the irregularity and free form of a flaming cloud. Color determines everything here—not sculpturesque form and geometric composition, as with Piero's works. Moreover, Grünewald's intention is to render the supernatural in a bodiless way appropriate to it. Piero makes Christ as massive and corporeal as the stone sarcophagus on which he stands. From the Italian point of view, the visionary flashing and flickering of Grünewald's *Resurrection* must have appeared crude, formless, and utterly devoid of the order that theory, based on the study of nature and measurement, could confer.

Albrecht Dürer

We know that Grünewald's great contemporary, ALBRECHT DÜRER (1471–1528), felt that much of the art of the north was crude and devoid of order, and that, in comparison with Italian art, it appeared to him old-fashioned, clumsy, and without knowledge. In the introduction to an unfinished and unpublished treatise on painting, Dürer wrote:

> Now, I know that in our German nation, at the present
> time, are many painters who stand in need of instruction,
> for they lack all real art theory. . . . For as much as they
> are so numerous, it is very needful for them to learn to
> better their work. He that works in ignorance works more
> painfully than he who works in understanding; therefore
> let all learn to understand art aright.

While still a journeyman under Michael Wolgemut in his native Nuremberg, where he learned the technique of the woodcut, Dürer became acquainted with, and began to copy, prints by Mantegna and Pollaiuolo (FIG. 21-53). Fascinated with Classical ideas, as transmitted through Italian Renaissance artists, he was the first northern artist to travel to Italy expressly to study Italian art and its underlying theories at their source. After his first journey in 1495 (he made a second trip in 1505 to 1506), it became his life mission to bring the modern—the Italian Renaissance— style north and establish it there. Although Dürer did not always succeed in fusing his own native German style with the Italian manner, he was the first northern artist who fully understood the basic aims of the southern Renaissance.

Dürer was also the first artist outside of Italy to become an international art celebrity. Well traveled and widely admired, he knew many of the leading Humanists and artists of his time, among them Erasmus of Rotterdam and Giovanni Bellini. A man of wide talents and tremendous energy; he became the "Leonardo of the North," achieving fabulous fame in his own time and a firm reputation ever since. Like Leonardo da Vinci, Dürer wrote theoretical treatises on a variety of subjects, such as perspective, fortification, and the ideal in human proportions. Through his prints, he exerted strong influence throughout Europe, especially in Flanders, but also in Italy. Moreover, he was the first northern artist to make himself known to posterity through several excellent self-portraits, through his correspondence, and through a carefully kept, quite detailed, and eminently readable diary.

In his own time, Dürer's fame and influence depended on his mastery of the graphic arts, and we still think that his greatest contribution to Western art lies in this field. Trained as a goldsmith by his father before he took up painting and printmaking, he developed an extraordinary proficiency in the handling of the *burin*, the engraving tool. This technical ability, combined with a feeling for the form-creating possibilities of line, enabled him to create a corpus of graphic work in woodcut and engraving that has seldom been rivaled for quality and number. In addition to illustrations for books, Dürer circulated and sold prints in single sheets, which people of ordinary means could buy and which made him a "people's artist" quite as much as a model for professionals. It also made him a rich man.

An early and very successful series of woodblock prints on fourteen large sheets illustrates the Apocalypse, or the Revelation of Saint John the Divine, the last book of the Bible. With great force and inventiveness, Dürer represents terrifying visions of doomsday and of the omens preceding it. The fourth print of the series, *The Four Horsemen* (FIG. **23-5**), represents, from foreground to background, Death trampling a bishop, Famine swinging scales, War wielding a sword, and Pestilence drawing his bow. The human race, in the last days of the world, is trampled by the grim quartet.

Technically, the virtuosity of Dürer's woodcuts never has been surpassed. By adapting to the woodcut the form-following hatching from Schongauer's engravings (FIG. 20-28), Dürer converts the former's primitive contrasts of black and white into a gliding scale of light and shade, achieving a quality of luminosity never before seen in woodblock prints. *The Four Horsemen* retains some Late Gothic characteristics in the angularity of shapes and the tendency of forms to merge into one another. On the other hand, Mantegna's influence can be found in the plastic and foreshortened poses of the trampled victims in the right foreground and in the head of Famine. But despite such Italicisms, the dramatic complexity of the composition remains essentially northern.

From 1500 on, Dürer increasingly became interested in the theoretical foundations of Italian Renaissance art. An engraving of *The Fall of Man (Adam and Eve)* (FIG. **23-6**) represents the first distillation of his studies of the Vitruvian theory of human proportions. Clearly outlined against the dark background of a northern forest, the two idealized figures of Adam and Eve stand in poses reminiscent of the *Apollo Belvedere* (FIG. 5-71) and the *Medici Venus* (not shown)—two Hellenistic statues probably known to Dürer through graphic representations. Preceded by numerous

23-5 ALBRECHT DÜRER, *The Four Horsemen,* from the Apocalypse series, *c.* 1498. Woodcut, approx. 15¹/₄″ × 11″. Metropolitan Museum of Art, New York (gift of Junius S. Morgan, 1919).

geometric drawings, in which he tried to systematize sets of ideal human proportions in balanced contrapposto poses, the final print presents Dürer's 1504 concept of the "perfect" male and female figures. Adam does, in fact, approach the southern ideal quite closely, but the fleshy Eve remains a German matron, her individualized features suggesting the use of a model. The elaborate symbolism of the background "accessories" to the main figures is also a northern trait. The choleric cat, the melancholic elk, the sanguine rabbit, and the phlegmatic ox represent the four humors of man, and the relation between Adam and Eve at the crucial moment of *The Fall of Man* is symbolized by the tension between cat and mouse in the foreground.

Dürer's *The Fall of Man* shows idealized forms and strongly naturalistic ones in a close combination that, depending on the viewer's attitude, may be regarded as complementary or conflictive elements—closely allied ingredients in most of Dürer's works. Dürer agreed with Aristotle (and the new critics of the Renaissance) that "sight is the noblest faculty of man" and that "every form brought before our vision falls upon it as upon a mirror." "We regard," said Dürer, "a form and figure out of nature with more pleasure than any other, though the thing itself is not necessarily altogether better or worse." This idea is a new and important one for artists. Nature holds the beautiful, said Dürer, for him who has the insight to extract it. Thus, beauty lies even in humble, perhaps ugly things, and the ideal, which bypasses or improves on nature, may not be the truly beautiful in the end: uncomposed and ordinary nature might be a reasonable object of the artist's interest, quite as much as its composed and measured aspect.

With an extremely precise watercolor study of a piece of turf, Dürer allies himself to the scientific studies of Leonardo; for both artists, observation yields truth. Sight, sanctified by mystics like Nicholas of Cusa and artists like Jan van Eyck, becomes the secularized instrument of modern knowledge. The "mirror" that is our "vision" will later become telescope, microscope, and television screen. The remarkable *The Great Piece of Turf* (FIG. **23-7**) is as scientifically accurate as it is poetic; the botanist can distinguish

23-7 ALBRECHT DÜRER, *The Great Piece of Turf,* 1503. Watercolor, approx. 16″ × 12¹/₂″. Graphische Sammlung Albertina, Vienna.

23-6 ALBRECHT DÜRER, *The Fall of Man (Adam and Eve),* 1504. Engraving, approx. 10″ × 7¹/₂″. Courtesy Museum of Fine Arts, Boston, centennial gift of Landon T. Clay.

each springing plant and variety of grass: dandelions, great plantain, yarrow, meadow grass, heath rush. "Depart not from nature in your opinions," said Dürer, "neither imagine that you can invent anything better. . . . for art stands firmly fixed in nature, and he who can find it there, he has it." The exquisite still life one finds in the northern paintings of the fifteenth century is irradiated with religious symbolism. Dürer's still life is of and for itself; he has found it in nature, and its representation no longer requires religious justification.

As Dürer's floral studies reveal the natural world, so he makes his portraits readings of character. The fifteenth-century portrait, like van Eyck's *Man in a Red Turban* (FIG. 20-7) or his *Canon van der Paele* (FIG. 20-6), is a graphic description of features; Dürer's portraits, like that of *Hieronymus Holzschuher* (FIG. **23-8**), are interpretations of personality. It may be, however, that they are as much projections of Dürer's own personality as they are readings of his subjects', for his portraits of men all show the subject as bold and virile, square-jawed, flashing-eyed, and truculent. All the subjects appear intense and intently aware of the observer. This strong psychic relationship to the external world, when the features are precisely particularized,

23-8 ALBRECHT DÜRER, *Hieronymus Holzschuher*, 1526. Oil on wood, approx. 19″ × 14″. Gemäldegalerie, Staatliche Museen, Berlin-Dahlem.

makes for an extremely vivid presence. Holzschuher, a friend of Dürer's and town councilor of Nuremberg, fairly bristles with choleric energy and the burly belligerence of Nuremberg citizens, who, on many an occasion, had defended the city against all comers, including the emperor himself. Leaving the background blank, except for an inscription, the artist achieves a remarkable concentration on the forceful personality of his subject. The portrait in Italy never really brings the subject into such a tense personal relationship with the observer.

Dürer always found it quite difficult to reconcile his northern penchant for precise naturalism with his intellectual, theoretical pursuits and with the demands of southern High Renaissance art for simplified monumentality. This life-long dilemma seems to be expressed in *Melencolia I* (FIG. **23-9**), one of three so-called master prints Dürer made between 1513 and 1514. These works (the other two are *Knight, Death, and the Devil* [FIG. 23-10] and *St. Jerome in His Study*) were probably intended to symbolize the moral, theological, and intellectual virtues. They clearly carry the art

of engraving to the highest degree of excellence. Dürer used his burin to render differences in texture and tonal values that would be difficult to match even in the much more flexible medium of *etching* (corroding a design into metal), which was developed later in the century (later in life Dürer experimented with the medium).

The complex symbolism of *Melencolia I* is based primarily on concepts derived from Florentine Neo-Platonism. The instruments of the arts and sciences lie strewn in idle confusion about the seated, winged figure of Melancholy; she is the personification of knowledge that, without divine inspiration, lacks the ability to act. According to then current astrological theory, the artist, or any individual engaged in creative activity, is the subject of Saturn. Such a person is characterized by a melancholia bordering on madness that either plunges one into despondency or raises one to the heights of creative fury; Michelangelo was regarded as subject to this humor. Dürer and Michelangelo both conceived of artists (and thus of themselves) as geniuses who struggle to translate the pure idea in their minds into gross but visible matter. Thus, the monumental image of the winged genius, with burning eyes in a shaded face and wings that do not fly, becomes the symbol for divine aspira-

23-9 ALBRECHT DÜRER, *Melencolia I*, 1514. Engraving, approx. 9³⁄₈″ × 6⁵⁄₈″. Fogg Museum of Art, Harvard University, Cambridge, Massachusetts (bequest of Francis Calley Gray).

23-10 ALBRECHT DÜRER, *Knight, Death, and the Devil,* 1513. Engraving, 9⅝" × 7⅜". Metropolitan Museum of Art, New York.

Leonardo's sketches for the Sforza monument in Milan; and doubtless he knew the *Gattamelata* of Donatello (FIG. 21-11) and the *Colleoni* of Verrocchio (FIG. 21-51). His highly developed feeling for the real and his meticulous rendering of it are evident in the myriad details: the Knight's armor and weapons, the anatomy of the horse, the textures of the loathsome features of Death and the Devil, the forms of rock and rugged foliage. All are realized with densely gathered yet supple hatching of engraved line that rivals the tonal range of painting. Erasmus could rightly compliment Dürer as the "Apelles [the ancient Greek master of painting] of black lines."

Only toward the very end of his life, and in one of his very last paintings, was Dürer finally able to reconcile the two opposing tendencies of northern naturalism and southern monumentality that had struggled for dominance in his entire *oeuvre.* He painted *The Four Apostles* (FIG. **23-11**) without commission and presented the two panels to the city fathers of Nuremberg in 1526 to be hung in the city hall. The work has been called Dürer's religious and political testament, in which he expresses his sympathies for the Protestant cause and warns against the dangerous times, when religion, truth, justice, and the virtues all will be threatened. The four apostles (John and Peter on the left panel; Mark and Paul on the right) stand on guard for the city. Quotations from each of their books, in the German of Luther's translation of the New Testament, are written on the frames. They warn against the coming of perilous times and the preaching of false prophets who will distort the word of God. The figures of the apostles summarize Dürer's whole craft and learning. Representing the four temperaments, or humors, of the human soul, as well as the four ages of man and other quaternities, these portraitlike characterizations of the apostles have no equal in the idealized representations of Italian saints. At the same time, the art of the Italian Renaissance is felt in the monumental grandeur and majesty of the figures, which are heightened by vivid color and sharp lighting. Here, Dürer unites the northern sense of minute realism with the Italian tradition of balanced forms, massive and simple. The result is a vindication of the artist's striving toward a new understanding—a work that stands with the greatest of the masterpieces of Italian art.

tions defeated by human frailty and, in a way, is a "spiritual self-portrait of Albrecht Dürer."

Knight, Death, and the Devil (FIG. **23-10**), in sharp contrast with the immobilized *Melencolia I,* is an image of the *vita activa,* the active life, and a metaphor of the Christian soul marching resolutely through a sinful, threatening world. The soul, as mounted, armored knight, ignores the menaces of Death and Devil, as it makes its way to its destination, the citadel of Virtue on the distant mountaintop. The Knight is accompanied by his faithful retriever; alert and eager, the dog symbolizes right reason in pursuit of elusive truth. Death, a crowned, mouldering cadaver, wreathed with snakes, holds up an hourglass, a reminder of time and mortality. The Devil, almost pathetically hideous, carries a pickax. These grisly phantoms inhabiting the desolate wilderness through which the Knight passes cannot terrify him, armored as he is with Christian fortitude.

The theme, symbolism, and characters are all medieval: the Knight in search of the Holy Grail, and Death and the Devil are conventional Gothic grotesques. But the monumental figure of the Knight and his mount have the strength, movement, and proportions of the Renaissance equestrian statue. Dürer was probably familiar with

HANS HOLBEIN THE YOUNGER   What Dürer had struggled all his life to formulate and construct was achieved almost effortlessly by his younger contemporary, HANS HOLBEIN THE YOUNGER (*c.* 1497–1543). Holbein's specialty was portraiture, in which he displayed a thorough assimilation of all that Italy had to teach of monumental composition, bodily structure, and sculpturesque form. He retains the northern traditions of close realism elaborated in fifteenth-century Flemish art. The color surfaces of his paintings are as lustrous as enamel; his detail, exact and exquisitely drawn; and his contrasts of light and dark, never heavy.

23-11   ALBRECHT DÜRER, *The Four Apostles*, 1526. Oil on wood, each panel 7'1" × 2'6". Alte Pinakothek, Munich.

Holbein was first active in Basel, where he knew Erasmus of Rotterdam. Because a religious civil war was imminent in Basel, Erasmus suggested that Holbein leave for England and gave him a recommendation to Thomas More, chancellor of England under Henry VIII. Holbein did leave and became painter to the English court. While there, he painted a superb double portrait of the French ambassadors to England, Jean de Dinteville and Georges de Selve (FIG. **23-12**). The two men, both ardent Humanists, stand at either end of a side table covered with an oriental rug and a collection of objects reflective of their interests: mathematical and astronomical models and implements, a lute with a broken string, compasses, a sundial, flutes, globes, and an open hymnbook with Luther's translation of *Veni,*

Creator Spiritus and of the Ten Commandments. The still-life objects are rendered with the same meticulous care as the men themselves, the woven design of the deep emerald curtain behind them, and the floor tiles, constructed in faultless perspective. The stable, balanced, serene composition is interrupted only by a long, gray shape that slashes diagonally across the picture plane. This form is an *anamorphic* image that when viewed by some special means (for example, reflected in a cylindrical mirror) is recognizable. In this case, the image is of a death's-head, for Holbein, like Dürer, was interested in symbolism as well as in radical perspectives. The color harmonies are adjusted in symphonic complexity and richness. The grave, even somber portraits indicate that Holbein follows the Italian portrait tradition, which gives the face a neutral expression, rather than Dürer's practice of giving it an expression of keen intensity. *The French Ambassadors* exhibits Holbein's peculiar talents: his strong sense of composition, his subtle linear patterning, his gift for portraiture, his marvelous sensitivity to color, and his faultlessly firm technique. This painting may have been Holbein's favorite; it is the only one signed with his full name.

Holbein died prematurely in 1543 and with him died the great German school of the Renaissance. But in 1532, when he left Basel for England, he already had taken the Renaissance with him. He had no significant successors, and German art faded in the uproar of a century of religious war.

THE NETHERLANDS

The resurgence of France and the eclipse of the House of Burgundy robbed the Flemish schools of their precedence. The tremendous acclaim of Albrecht Dürer, when he visit-ed Antwerp in 1520, indicates a reverse for Flanders; Germany, which had followed Flanders, now led developments in the north. The decay of the old Flemish tradition, both in form and content, left a void that was filled by the confusing appearance of Italian ideas, received second-hand through Dürer. As with any new, inspiring, but ill-understood fashion, a number of conflicting mannerisms arose, which, if anything, had in common only their misunderstanding of the principles behind the novel forms. This period is characterized by a great delight in decorative extravagance, in which pedantic allusion to the classics is combined with exotic settings made of piled-up fragments of Italianate ornament. For a generation or so, the north, as it has been said, "simply could not get its Renaissance on straight."

But from all this confusion, new and confident movements could begin. In a first step toward new beginnings, remnants of the medieval tradition had to be swept away. The dominance of religious conventions yielded to experiments in subject matter and form; although religious material persisted, it no longer prevailed in art. We have seen

23-12 HANS HOLBEIN THE YOUNGER, *The French Ambassadors*, 1533. Oil and tempera on wood, approx. 6′8″ × 6′9½″. Reproduced by courtesy of the Trustees of the National Gallery, London.

23-13   QUENTIN METSYS, *The St. Anne Altarpiece*, center panel, 1507–1509. Oil on wood, 7′4¹/₂″ × 7′2¹/₄″. Musée Royaux des Beaux-Arts de Belgique, Brussels.

how religious themes were modified by humanization over a period of more than a century; now they had to share the artist's interest in portraiture, mythology, landscape, and genre. The structural basis for a new, Humanistic realism had been introduced by the great German painters. It was on this foundation that an international, European art, dealing primarily with human interests, had to be built.

Changing views and attitudes were accompanied by a geographical shift in the region's commercial center. Partly as a result of the silting-up of the Bruges estuary, traffic was diverted to Antwerp, which became the hub of economic activity in the Low Countries after 1510. By mid-century, a jealous Venetian envoy had to admit that more business was transacted in Antwerp in a few weeks than in a year in Venice. As many as five hundred ships a day passed through Antwerp's harbor, and large trading colonies from England, Germany, Italy, Portugal, and Spain established themselves in the city.

QUENTIN METSYS   Antwerp's growth and prosperity, along with the propensity of its wealthy merchants for col-

lecting and purchasing art, attracted artists to the city. Among them was QUENTIN METSYS (*c.* 1466–1530), who became Antwerp's leading master after 1510. Son of a Louvain blacksmith, Metsys may have been largely self-taught, which would explain, in part, his susceptibility to outside influences and his willingness to explore the styles and modes of a variety of models, from van Eyck to Bosch, and from van der Weyden to Dürer and Leonardo. Yet his eclecticism was subtle and discriminating and enriched by an inventiveness that gave a personal stamp to his paintings and made him a popular as well as important artist. Quentin Metsys represents both the bad and the good aspects of early sixteenth-century Flemish art in its struggle to shed fifteenth-century traditions in favor of a more "modern" Renaissance mode of expression.

Metsys painted *The St. Anne Altarpiece* for the Louvain Brotherhood of Saint Anne between 1507 and 1509. Its central panel (FIG. **23-13**) shows a stable and orderly grouping of figures before a triple-vaulted loggia, through which a finely painted distant landscape can be seen. The round-arched architecture, complete with *tie-rods* (beams, bars, or rods that tie parts of a building together) and a central dome, seems functional enough (except for the rectangular window, which intrudes illogically into the hemispheric dome), but it has little to do with Italian Renaissance architecture, which Metsys evidently tried to emulate. In this respect, he was no more successful than his Romanist contemporaries, whose attempts to provide their paintings with "modern" (Italian Renaissance) settings produced little more than architectural fantasies. On the other hand, the triple loggia effectively unifies the solemn, softly draped figures, whose heads are grouped in three inverted triangles. The compression of the composition may have been inspired by one of the late paintings of Hugo van der Goes, and the calm serenity of the scene evokes memories of Hans Memling's paintings (FIG. 20-16). But these and other possible sources of inspiration are thoroughly assimilated and synthesized by Metsys into a personal style. The regularized composition and the light coloration of his forms produce a tapestry-like effect that is decorative and memorable.

Metsys's explorations of the past are liberally mixed with forward-looking genre and moralizing subjects to give his *oeuvre* a highly diversified aspect. The variety of his inventions provides a bridge from the fifteenth into the sixteenth century and makes him an influential inspiration to many of his contemporaries.

JAN GOSSAERT   More single-minded, although no more successful than Metsys in his assimilation of Italian Renaissance art, was JAN GOSSAERT (*c.* 1478–1535), who worked for the later Philip of Burgundy, associated with Humanist scholars, and visited Italy. There, Gossaert (who adopted the name MABUSE, after his birthplace of Maubeuge) became fascinated with the Classical Antique and its mythological subject matter. Giorgio Vasari, the Italian historian and Gossaert's contemporary, wrote that "Gossaert was almost the first to bring the true method of representing nude figures and mythologies from Italy to the Netherlands," although it is obvious that he derived much of his Classicism from Dürer.

The composition and poses in Gossaert's *Neptune and Amphitrite* (FIG. **23-14**) are borrowed from Dürer's *Adam and Eve* (FIG. 23-6), although Gossaert's figures have been inflated, giving an impression of ungainly weight. The artist approximates the Classical stance but seems to have been more interested in nudity than in a Classical, ideal canon of proportions. The setting for the figures is a carefully painted architectural fantasy that illustrates a lack of understanding of the Classical style. Yet the painting is executed with traditional Flemish polish, and the figures are skillfully drawn and modeled. Although Gossaert also painted religious subjects in the traditional style, attempting unsuccessfully to outshine the fifteenth-century Flemish masters, his *Neptune and Amphitrite* aligns him firmly with the so-called *Romanists*, in whose art Italian Mannerism joins with fanciful native interpretations of the Classical style to form

23-14 JAN GOSSAERT (MABUSE), *Neptune and Amphitrite, c.* 1516. Oil on wood, 7′2″ × 4′1″. Gemäldegalerie, Staatliche Museen, Berlin-Dahlem.

a highly artificial, sometimes decorative, and often bizarre and chaotic style.

BARTHOLOMEUS SPRANGER   Much more the Romanist than Jan Gossaert, the later Netherlandish painter BARTHOLOMEUS SPRANGER (1546–1611) exaggerates the stylistic peculiarities of Italian Mannerism almost to the point of caricature. Spranger traveled widely in Italy and France, studying a variety of pictorial styles that ranged from those of Jacopo da Pontormo and Parmigianino to the painters of the school of Fontainebleau (FIG. 23-19). What he learned from them merged with his earlier training in the Netherlands to form a highly sophisticated and imaginative style.

For the connoisseur Emperor Rudolph II, whose court painter he became at Prague, Spranger fashioned such classically learned, intricately composed, and suggestively erotic pictures as *Salmacis and Hermaphroditus* (FIG. **23-15**), based on a mythological story from the ancient Roman poet Ovid. Ovid's *Metamorphoses* was a thesaurus of mythological material for the poets and artists of the Renaissance and a favorite reading of their learned patrons. In this instance Ovid relates, and Spranger illustrates, the love of the naiad Salmacis, personification of the river of that name, for the beautiful youth Hermaphroditus, whose name combines those of his parents Hermes and Aphrodite. Salmacis's embrace of the youth is so passionate, and his attempt to escape so insistent, that she prays to the gods that they may never separate.

> The gods heard her prayer. For their two bodies, joined together as they were, were merged in one, with one face and form for both. . . . They were no longer two but one.
> (*Metamorphosis* IV: 370–380)

In Spranger's painting, Salmacis, disrobing, slowly advances with a voluptuous undulation toward Hermaphroditus, who bathes his feet in the stream.

23-15 BARTHOLOMEUS SPRANGER, *Salmacis and Hermaphroditus, c. 1585.* Oil on canvas, approx. 44″ × 32¼″. Kunsthistorisches Museum, Vienna.

Her emphatically sensual body and pose powerfully exaggerate the conventional Mannerist elongation, torsion, and contrapposto. Worldly, lascivious, thoroughly pagan, Spranger's work expresses a luxurious, courtly taste that contrasts markedly with the reverent art of the bourgeois towns in which the Netherlandish master artists worked.

PIETER BRUEGEL THE ELDER   An interest in the interrelationship of human beings and nature is expressed in the works of the greatest and most original Flemish painter of the sixteenth century, PIETER BRUEGEL THE ELDER (c. 1525–1569), whose early, high-horizoned, "cosmographical" landscapes probably were influenced by Patinir (not shown). But in Bruegel's paintings, no matter how huge a slice of the world he shows, human activities remain the dominant theme. Bruegel was apprenticed to a Romanist, Pieter Coecke, and, like many of his contemporaries, traveled to Italy, where he seems to have spent almost two years, going as far south as Sicily. Unlike his contemporaries, however, Bruegel was not overwhelmed by Classical art, and his Italian experiences are reflected only incidentally in his paintings, usually in the form of Italian or Alpine landscape features that he recorded in numerous drawings made during his journey. On his return from Italy, Bruegel was exposed to Bosch's works, and the influence of that strange master, strongly felt in Bruegel's early paintings, must have swept aside any Romanist inclinations he may have had.

Hunters in the Snow (FIG. **23-16**) is one of five surviving paintings of a series of six in which Bruegel illustrated seasonal changes in the year. It shows human figures and landscape locked in winter cold. The weary hunters return with their hounds, wives build fires, skaters skim the frozen pond, the town and its church huddle in their mantle of snow, and beyond this typically Flemish winter scene lies a bit of alpine landscape. Aside from this trace of fantasy, however, the landscape is realistic. It develops smoothly from foreground to background and draws the viewer diagonally into its depths. The artist's consummate skill in the use of line and shape and his subtlety in tonal harmony make this one of the great landscape paintings in history and an occidental counterpart of the masterworks of classical Chinese landscape.

Bruegel, of course, is not simply a landscapist. In his series of the months, he presents—in a fairly detached manner, occasionally touched with humor—human activities at different times of the year. And he chooses for his purpose the social class that is most directly affected by seasonal changes, the peasantry. But usually Bruegel is much more personal as he makes satirical comments on the dubious human condition. His meaning in specific cases is often as obscure as Bosch's, and he seems to delight in leading us into his pictures through devious paths and confronting us with mystery, with an appalling revelation. As a vehicle for his sarcasm, he again chooses the peasant, whom he sees as

23-16 PIETER BRUEGEL THE ELDER, *Hunters in the Snow,* 1565. Oil on wood, approx. 46" × 64". Kunsthistorisches Museum, Vienna.

an uncomplicated representative of humanity—a member of society whose actions and behavior are open, direct, and unspoiled by the artificial cultural gloss that disguises but does not alter the city dweller's natural inclinations.

These good countryfolk are shown enjoying themselves in *The Peasant Dance* (FIG. **23-17**), which is no mincing quadrille, but a boisterous, whirling, hoedown in which plenty of sweat is shed. One can almost hear the feet stomping to the rhythm of the bagpipe. With an eye much more incisive than any camera lens, the artist grasps the entire scene in its most characteristic aspect and records it in a broad technique that discards most of the traditional Flemish concern for detail. Strong but simplified modeling emphasizes the active, solidly drawn silhouettes, which, combined with strong local colors, give the painting the popular robustness so suited to its subject. From the hilltop that he shared with the *Hunters,* Bruegel descends into the village to look more closely at its life and amusements, and he finds that all is not well in this rustic paradise. A fight is brewing at the table on the left; everyone's back is turned

to the church in the background; nobody is paying the least attention to the small picture of a Madonna tacked to the tree on the right; the man next to the bagpiper is wearing the feather of a peacock (a symbol of vanity) in his cap; and what about the young couple kissing unashamedly in public in the left middle ground? Is Bruegel telling us, like Bosch in his *Hell* (FIG. 20-18), that music is an instrument of the Devil and a perverter of morals? A closer inspection of the painting reveals that Bruegel is telling much more than the simple story of a country festivity. He is showing that a *kermess,* a festival celebrating a saint, has become a mere pretext for people to indulge their lust, anger, and gluttony.

Toward the end of his life, Bruegel's commentary on the human condition takes on an increasingly bitter edge. The Netherlands, racked by religious conflict, had become the seat of cruel atrocities, made even more cruel by the coming of the power of Catholic Spain to put down the Reformation. We do not know whether Bruegel took sides; like the great satirist he was, he may have preferred

23-17 PIETER BRUEGEL THE ELDER, *The Peasant Dance*, 1567. Oil on wood, approx. 45″ × 65″. Kunsthistorisches Museum, Vienna.

to make all mankind, not just partisans, the object of his commentary. His secret meanings may be explained partly by the danger of too much outspokenness. His biographer, Karel van Mander,* writes:

> Many of Bruegel's strange compositions and comical subjects one may see in his copper engravings . . . he supplied them with inscriptions which, at the time, were too biting and too sharp, and which he had his wife burn during his last illness, because of . . . fear that most disagreeable consequences might grow out of them.

Bruegel knew well how to disguise his intent—so well that in his day he was called "Peter the Droll," because, as van Mander writes, "there are very few works from his hand that the beholder can look at seriously, without laughing."

*Karel van Mander's *Het Schilderboeck (The Painter's Book)* was published in Haarlem in 1604. It contains a section with biographies of Netherlandish and German painters that is the northern equivalent of Giorgio Vasari's *Lives of the Most Eminent Italian Architects, Painters, and Sculptors.*

FRANCE

Divided and harried during the fifteenth century, France was reorganized by decisive kings and was strong enough to undertake an aggressive policy toward its neighbors by the end of the century. Under the rule of Francis I, the French held a firm foothold in Milan and its environs. The king eagerly imported the Renaissance into France, bringing Leonardo da Vinci and Andrea del Sarto to his court, but they left no permanent mark on French art. It was Florentine Mannerists like Rosso Fiorentino and Benvenuto Cellini who implanted the Italianate style that replaced the Gothic in France. Francis's attempt to glorify the state and himself meant that the religious art of the Middle Ages finally was superseded, for it was the king and not the Church who now held power.

A portrait of *Francis I* (FIG. **23-18**), painted by JEAN CLOUET (c. 1485–1541) in the Franco-Italian manner, shows a worldly prince magnificently bedecked in silks and brocades, wearing a gold chain, and caressing the pommel of a dagger. One would not expect the king's talents to be

23-18 JEAN CLOUET, *Francis I, c.* 1525–1530. Tempera and oil on wood, approx. 38" × 29". Louvre, Paris.

directed to spiritual matters, and legend has it that the "merry monarch" was a great lover and the hero of hundreds of "gallant" situations. The flat light and suppression of modeling give equal emphasis to head and costume, so that the king's finery and his face enter equally into the effect of royal splendor. Yet, despite this Mannerist formula for portraiture, the features are not entirely immobile; the faintest flicker of an expression that we might read as "knowing" lingers on the king's features.

The personal tastes of Francis and his court must have run to an art at once suave, artificial, elegant, and erotic. The sculptors and painters working together on the decoration of the new royal palace at Fontainebleau, under the direction of Florentines Rosso Fiorentino and FRANCESCO PRIMATICCIO (1504–1570), are known as the school of Fontainebleau. Rosso became the court painter of Francis I shortly after 1530. In France, his style no longer showed the turbulent harshness of *Moses Defending the Daughters of Jethro* (FIG. 22-39) but became consistently more elegant and graceful. When Rosso and Primaticcio decorated the Gallery of Francis I at Fontainebleau, they combined painting, fresco, imitation mosaic, and stucco sculpture in low and high relief (FIG. **23-19**). The abrupt changes in scale and texture of the figurative elements are typically Mannerist, in compressed Mannerist space with elongated grace and mannered poses. The artificial grace of the paintings can be seen in the stucco relief figures and caryatids, yet the viewer is jarred by the shift in scale between the painted and the stucco figures. However, the combination of painted and stucco relief decorations became extremely popular from

23-19 ROSSO FIORENTINO and FRANCESCO PRIMATICCIO, ensemble of architecture, sculpture, and painting, *c.* 1530–1540. Gallery of King Francis I, Fontainebleau, France.

this time on and remained a favorite decorative technique throughout the Baroque and Rococo periods.

It has been said of Francis I that, besides women, his one obsession was building. During his reign, which lasted from 1515 to 1547, several large-scale chateaux were begun, among them the Chateau de Chambord (FIG. **23-20**), on which construction was started in 1519. Reflecting the more peaceful times, these chateaux, developed from the old countryside fortresses, served as country houses for royalty and usually were built near a forest, for use as hunting lodges. The plan of Chambord, originally drawn by a pupil of Giuliano da Sangallo, imposes Italian concepts of symmetry and balance on the irregularity of the old French fortress. A central square block with four corridors, in the shape of a cross, leads to a broad, central staircase that gives access to groups of rooms—ancestors of the modern suite of rooms or apartments. The square plan is punctuated at each of the four corners by a round tower, and the whole is surrounded by a moat. From the exterior, Chambord presents a carefully contrived horizontal accent on three levels, its floors separated by continuous moldings. Windows are placed exactly over one another. This matching of horizon-

tal and vertical features is, of course, derived from the Italian palazzo, but above the third level, the lines of the structure break chaotically into a jumble of high dormers, chimneys, and lanterns that recall soaring, ragged, Gothic silhouettes on the skyline.

The architecture of Chambord is still essentially French. During the reign of Francis's successor, Henry II (r. 1547–1559), however, treatises by Italian architects were translated and Italian architects came to work in France; at the same time, the French turned to Italy for study and travel. This interchange brought about a more thoroughgoing revolution in style, although it never eliminated certain French elements that persisted from the Gothic tradition. Francis began the enlargement of the Louvre in Paris (FIG. **23-21**) to make a new royal palace, but he died before the work was well begun. His architect, PIERRE LESCOT (1510–1578), continued under Henry II and, with the aid of the sculptor JEAN GOUJON (c. 1510–1565), produced the Classical style of the French Renaissance.

Although Chambord incorporated the formal vocabulary of the Early Renaissance, particularly from Lombardy, Lescot and his associates were familiar with the High

23-20   Chateau de Chambord, France, begun 1519.

23-21 PIERRE LESCOT, west facade of the Square Court of the Louvre, Paris, begun 1546.

Renaissance of Bramante and his school. Each of the stories of the Louvre forms a complete order, and the cornices project enough to furnish a strong horizontal accent. The arcading on the ground story reflects the ancient Roman arch-order and is recessed enough to produce more shadow than in the upper stories, strengthening the visual base of the design. On the second story, the pilasters rising from bases and the alternating curved and angular pediments supported by consoles have direct antecedents in several Roman High Renaissance palaces. On the other hand, the decreased height of the stories, the proportionately much larger windows (given the French weather!), and the steep roof are northern. Especially French are the pavilions that jut from the wall. These are punctuated by a feature that the French will long favor—double columns framing a niche. The vertical lines of the building remain strong. The wall is deeply penetrated by openings and (in un-Italian fashion) profusely sculptured. This French Classical manner—double-columned pavilions, tall and wide windows, profuse statuary, and steep roofs—will be imitated widely in other northern countries, with local variations. The mannered Classicism produced by the French will be the *only* Classicism to serve as a model for northern archi-

tects through most of the sixteenth century. The west courtyard facade of the Louvre is the best of French Renaissance architecture; eventually, the French will develop a quite native Classicism of their own, cleared of Italian Mannerist features.

The statues of the Louvre courtyard facade, now much restored, are the work of Goujon. We can appreciate the quality of Goujon's style best by examining his *Nymphs* reliefs from the Fountain of the Innocents in Paris (FIG. **23-22**). Like the architecture of the Louvre, Goujon's nymphs are intelligent and sensitive French adaptations of the Italian Mannerist canon of figure design. Certainly, they are Mannerist in their ballet-like contrapposto and in their flowing, clinging draperies, which recall the ancient "wet" drapery of Hellenic sculpture—the figures on the parapet of the Temple of Athena Nike (FIG. 5-62), for example. Goujon's slender, sinuous figures perform their steps within the structure of Mannerist space, and it is interesting that they appear to make one continuous motion, an illusion produced by reversing the gestures, as they might be seen in a mirror. The style of Fontainebleau, and ultimately of Primaticcio and Cellini, guides the sculptor here, but Goujon has learned the manner so well that he can create

23-22   Jean Goujon, *Nymphs*, from the dismantled Fountain of the Innocents, Paris, 1548–1549. Marble reliefs. Louvre, Paris.

originally within it. The nymphs are truly French master-pieces, with lightness, ease, grace, and something of a native French chic that saves them from being mere lame derivatives of the Italian Mannerist norm.

SPAIN

In some respects, the sixteenth century is the Spanish century. Under Charles V of Hapsburg and his son, Philip II, the Spanish Empire dominated a territory greater in extent than any ever known: a large part of Europe, the western

Mediterranean, a strip of North Africa, and vast expanses in the newly conquered Western Hemisphere. The Hapsburg Empire, enriched by the plunder of the New World, supported the most powerful military force in Europe, which backed the ambitions and the ventures of the "Most Catholic Kings." Spain defended and then promoted the interests of the Catholic Church in its battle against the inroads of the Protestant Reformation. What we call the Catholic Counter-Reformation was funded, directed, fought for, and then enforced by Spain. By force and influence—by the preaching and the propaganda of the newly founded Spanish order of the Society of Jesus (the

Jesuits)—Spain drove Protestantism from a large part of Europe and sponsored the internal reform of the Catholic Church at the great Council of Trent. The Spaniards humbled France; trampled the Netherlands; reclaimed much of Germany, Poland, and Hungary for Catholicism; and held England at bay (until the end of the century), while they converted the native empires of the New World to the Catholic faith and destroyed them in a relentless search for treasure. The material and the spiritual exertions of Spain—the fanatical courage of Spanish soldiers and the incandescent fervor of the great Spanish mystical saints—coalesced. The former became the terror of the Protestant and pagan worlds, while the latter served as the inspiration of the Catholic faithful. The crusading spirit of Spain, nourished by centuries of war with Islam, engaged body and soul in the formation of the most Catholic civilization of Europe and the Americas. In the sixteenth century, for good or for ill, Spain left the mark of Spanish power, religion, language, and culture on two hemispheres.

Yet Spain, like all of Europe at this time, came under the spell of Renaissance Italy; Spanish architecture especially shows that influence, but not all at once. During the fifteenth century and well into the sixteenth, a Late Gothic style of architecture, the Plateresque, prevailed side by side with buildings influenced by Italy. (*Plateresque* is derived from the Spanish word *platero*, meaning silversmith, and is applied to the style because of the delicate execution of its ornament.) The Colegio de San Gregorio (FIG. **23-23**) in the Castilian city of Valladolid handsomely exemplifies the Plateresque manner. The Spanish were particularly fond of great carved retables, like the German altar screens that influenced them (FIGS. 20-23 and 20-24)—so much so that they made them a conspicuous decorative feature of their exterior architecture, dramatizing a portal set into an otherwise blank wall. The Plateresque entrance of San Gregorio is a lofty, sculptured stone screen that bears no functional relation to the architecture behind it. On the entrance level, ogival, flamboyant arches are hemmed with lacelike tracery reminiscent of Moorish design. A great screen, paneled into sculptured compartments, rises above the tracery; in the center, the coat of arms of Ferdinand and Isabella is wreathed by the branches of a

23-23   Portal, Colegio de San Gregorio, and detail, Valladolid, Spain, *c.* 1498.

23-24   PEDRO MACHUCA, courtyard of the palace of Charles V, Alhambra, Granada, Spain, c. 1526–1568.

huge pomegranate tree (symbolizing Granada, the Moorish capital of Spain, captured by the "Most Catholic Kings" in 1492). Cupids play among the tree branches, and, flanking the central panel, niches enframe armed pages of the court, heraldic wildmen, and armored soldiers, attesting to the new, proud militancy of the united kingdom of Spain. In typical Plateresque and Late Gothic fashion, the whole design is unified by the activity of a thousand intertwined motifs, which, in sum, create an exquisitely carved panel greatly expanded in scale.

A sudden and surprising Italianate Classicism makes its appearance in the unfinished palace of Charles V in the Alhambra in Granada (FIG. **23-24**), which is the work of the painter-architect PEDRO MACHUCA (active 1520–1550). The circular central courtyard is ringed with superposed Doric and Ionic orders, which support continuous horizontal entablatures rather than arches. Ornament consists only of the details of the orders themselves, which are rendered with the simplicity, clarity, and authority we find in the work of Bramante and his school. The lower story recalls the ring colonnade of the Tempietto (FIG. 22-6); although here, of course, the curve is reversed. This pure Classicism, entirely exceptional in Spain at this time, may be a reflection of Charles V's personal taste, acquired on

one of his journeys to Italy. (It should be remembered that the emperor was an enthusiastic patron of Titian.) Machuca himself had sojourned in Italy, and the courtyard may be the consequence of his endeavor to revive this feature of the ancient Classical palace.

But the Spanish spirit of the time seemed to disdain the ideal purity of feature and correctness of proportion sought in Classical design. Spanish builders seemed to feel a need to do something different with what was received from Italy. What could be done is visible in the great complex called the Escorial (FIGS. **23-25** and **23-26**), which was constructed for Philip II by JUAN BAUTISTA DE TOLEDO (d. 1567) and JUAN DE HERRERA (c. 1530–1597), principally the latter. The king, perhaps the greatest in Spanish history, must have had much to do with the design. Certainly Philip and his architects collaborated closely. The whole vast structure is in keeping with his austere and conscientious character, his passionate Catholic religiosity, his proud reverence for his dynasty, and his stern determination to impose his will worldwide. Philip wrote to Herrera to outline what he expected from him: "Above all, do not forget what I have told you—simplicity of form, severity in the whole, nobility without arrogance, majesty without ostentation." The result is a Classicism of Doric severity, ultimately derived from Italian architecture and with the grandeur of St. Peter's implicit in the scheme, but unique in Spanish and European architecture—a style inimitably of itself, even though later structures will reflect it.

In his will, Charles V stipulated that a "dynastic pantheon" be built to house the remains of past and future monarchs of Spain. Philip II, obedient to his father's wishes, chose a site some 30 miles northwest of Madrid, in rugged terrain with barren mountains. Here, he built the Escorial, not only a royal mausoleum, but a church, a monastery, and a palace. Legend has it that the gridlike plan for the enormous complex, 625 feet wide and 520 feet deep, was meant to symbolize the gridiron on which Saint Lawrence, patron of the Escorial, was martyred.

The long sweep of the severely plain walls of the complex is broken only by the three entrances, with the dominant central portal framed by superposed orders and topped by a pediment in the Italian fashion. The corners of the wall are punctuated by massive square towers. The stress on the central axis, with its subdued echoes in the two flanking portals, forecasts the three-part organization of later Baroque palace facades. Like the whole complex of buildings, the domed-cross church, with similarly heavy towers, is constructed of granite, expressing, in its grim starkness of mass, the obdurate quality of a material most difficult to work. The massive facade of the church and the austere geometry of its interior, with its blocky walls and ponderous arches (FIG. 23-26), dominate the Classical forms, producing an effect of overwhelming strength and weight that contradicts the grace and elegance we associate with much of the Renaissance architecture of Italy.

23-25 JUAN DE HERRERA, *The Escorial, near Madrid, Spain, c. 1563–1584* (bird's-eye view after an anonymous eighteenth-century painting).

The Escorial is a monument to the collaboration of a great king and a remarkably understanding architect, who made of it an original expression of a unique idea and personality—the embodiment of the stern virtues of a monarch, a realm, and an age conscious of their peculiar power and purpose. The visitor to the Escorial is awed by the overpowering architectural expression of the spirit of Spain in its heroic epoch and of the character of Philip II, the extraordinary monarch who directed it.

EL GRECO   There appear to be two sides to the Spanish genius in the period of the Counter-Reformation: fervent religious faith and ardent mysticism, on the one hand, and an iron realism on the other. Saint Theresa of Ávila and Saint John of the Cross can be considered representative of the first; the practical Saint Ignatius of Loyola, founder of the Jesuit order, represents the latter. It is possible for the two tempers to be found in the same persons and works of art, but it is more common to find them separately. Interestingly enough, a painter of foreign extraction was able to combine them in a single picture.

DOMÉNIKOS THEOTOKÓPOULOS (*c.* 1547–1614), called EL GRECO, was born on Crete but emigrated to Italy as a young man. In his youth, he was trained in the traditions of Late Byzantine frescoes and mosaics. While still young, El Greco went to Venice, where he was connected with the shop of Titian, although Tintoretto's painting seems to have made a

23-26 The Escorial, interior of church.

23-27   EL GRECO, *The Burial of Count Orgaz*, 1586. Oil on canvas, approx. 16′ × 12′. Santo Tomé, Toledo, Spain.

stronger impression on him. A brief trip to Rome explains the influences of Roman and Florentine Mannerism on his work. By 1577, he had left for Spain to spend the rest of his life in Toledo.

El Greco's art is a strong, personal blending of Late Byzantine and Late Italian Mannerist elements. The intense emotionalism of his paintings, which naturally appealed to the pious fervor of the Spanish, the dematerialization of form, and a great reliance on color bind him to sixteenth-century Venetian art and to Mannerism. His strong sense of movement and use of light, however, prefigure the

Baroque. El Greco's art is not strictly Spanish (although it appealed to certain sectors of that society), for it had no Spanish antecedents and little effect on later Spanish painters. Nevertheless, the paintings of this hybrid genius interpret Spain for us in its Catholic zeal and yearning spirituality. This statement is especially true of the artist's masterpiece, *The Burial of Count Orgaz* (FIG. **23-27**), painted in 1586 for the church of Santo Tomé in Toledo. The theme illustrates the legend that the Count of Orgaz, who had died some three centuries before and who had been a great benefactor of the church of Santo Tomé, was buried in the church by Saints Stephen and Augustine, who miraculously descended from heaven to lower the count's body into its sepulcher. The earthly scene is irradiated by the brilliant heaven that opens above it, as El Greco carefully distinguishes the terrestrial and celestial spheres. The terrestrial is represented with a firm realism; the celestial, in his quite personal manner, is shown with elongated, undulant figures, fluttering draperies, cold highlights, and a peculiar kind of ectoplasmic, swimming cloud. Below, the two saints lovingly lower the count's armor-clad body, the armor and heavy draperies painted with all the rich sensuousness of the Venetian school. The background is filled with a solemn chorus of black-clad Spanish grandees, in whose carefully individualized features El Greco shows us that he was also a great portraitist. These are the faces that looked on the greatness and glory of Spain when it was the leading power of Europe—faces like those of the *conquistadores,* who, earlier in the century, brought Spain the New World and who, two years after this picture was completed, would lead the Great Armada against both Protestant England and Holland.

The lower and upper spheres of the painting are linked by the upward glances of the figures below and by the flight of an angel above, who carries the soul of the count in his arms as Saint John and the Virgin intercede for it before the throne of Christ. El Greco's deliberate change in style to distinguish between the two levels of reality gives the viewer the opportunity to see the artist's early and late manners in the same work, one above the other. The relatively sumptuous and realistic presentation of the earthly sphere is still strongly rooted in Venetian art, but the abstractions and distortions that El Greco uses to show the immaterial nature of the Heavenly realm will become characteristic of his later style. Pulling Heaven down to earth, he will paint worldly inhabitants in the same abstract manner as celestial ones. His elongated figures will exist in undefined spaces, bathed in a cool light of uncertain origin. For this, El Greco has been called the last and greatest of the Mannerists, but it is difficult to apply that label to him without reservations. Although he used Manneristic formal devices, El Greco was not a rebel, nor was he aiming for elegance in his work. He was concerned primarily with emotion and with the effort to express his own religious fervor or to arouse the observer's. To make the inner meaning of his paintings forceful, he developed a highly personal style in which his attenuated forms become etherealized in dynamic swirls of unearthly light and color. Some ambiguity may be found in El Greco's forms, but none exists in his meaning, which is mystical, spiritual, ecstatic devotion.

Toward the end of his life, El Greco painted a portrait of his friend, the theologian, poet, and Trinitarian priest, *Fray*

23-28 El Greco, *Fray Hortensio Félix Paravicino,* 1609. Oil on canvas, 44½″ × 33¾″. Isaac Sweetser Fund, Museum of Fine Arts, Boston.

Hortensio Félix Paravicino (FIG. **23-28**). It is one of the most distinguished portraits of the age. Father Hortensio, clad in the black-and-white vesture of his order, is represented seated, which, since the time of Raphael, was the customary pose used in portraits of ecclesiastics of high rank. In his left hand, he holds books, attributes of intellectual dedication and accomplishment. The vividly contrasting black and white of his canonicals and the square-backed leather chair, with its gilt bronze studs and finials, magnificently set off the pale, ascetic face, accented by the dark hair, eyebrows, and beard. El Greco renders the character of a man given wholly to otherworldly concerns as a kind of apparition not quite of this world. The likeness fades into the image of a typical El Greco saint. As is often the case when a great painter creates the likeness of a great-souled subject, the latter becomes more than an individual person. He becomes, as here, generalized into a type, that of the spiritually exalted priest, protagonist in the drama of Spanish history in its great century.

BAROQUE EUROPE

ATLANTIC OCEAN

SCOTLAND
GLASGOW • • EDINBURGH

SWEDEN

BALTIC SEA

NORTH SEA

DENMARK
COPENHAGEN •

IRELAND
DUBLIN •

ENGLAND
HOLLAND
HAARLEM AMSTERDAM
LEIDEN • UTRECHT
LONDON • ROTTERDAM
ANTWERP
FLANDERS

Thames R.

BERLIN •

POLAND

Weser R.

Elbe R.

Vistula R.

Oder R.

HOLY ROMAN
EMPIRE
NUREMBERG •

ROUEN
PARIS •
VERSAILLES

Seine R.

Meuse R.

Rhine R.

MUNICH •
Danube R.

VIENNA •

0 — 500 Miles

0 — 500 Kilometers

Loire R.

BLOIS •

FRANCE

SWITZERLAND

AUSTRIA

HUNGARY

TRENT •

Garonne R.

Rhône R.

TURIN •

MANTUA •
Po R.

VENICE •

GENOA •

ITALY

FLORENCE •

Tiber R.

PORTUGAL

Duero R.

Ebro R.

MADRID •

ROME •

NAPLES •

LISBON •

Tagus R.

SPAIN

Guadiana R.

SEVILLE • Guadalquivir R.

GRANADA •

MEDITERRANEAN SEA

1600	1610	1620	1630	1640	165

PHILIP III OF SPAIN			PHILIP IV OF SPAIN		
HENRY IV OF FRANCE	LOUIS XIII OF FRANCE (DOMINATED BY CARDINAL RICHELIEU; MARIE DE' MEDICI, REGENT 1610-1614)				
	JAMES I OF ENGLAND		CHARLES I OF ENGLAND		

Caravaggio
Conversion of St. Paul
c. 1601

Rubens, Abduction of the
Daughters of Leucippus, 1617

Hals, Archers of St. Hadrian (detail)
c.1633

Bernini
Ecstasy of St. Theresa
1645-1652

William Shakespeare, 1564-1616

Galileo Galilei invents telescope, 1609

Pope Paul V, 1605-1621

Johannes Kepler's laws of planetary motion, 1609-1619

Thirty Years War begins, 1618

William Harvey discovers blood circulation, 1628

René Descartes, Discourse on Method, 1637

Galileo's laws of falling bodies, projectile motion, 1638

French Royal Academy of Painting and Sculpture founded, 1648

Thirty Years War ends, 1648

Pope Urban VIII, 1623-1644

CHAPTER 24

BAROQUE ART

1660	1670	1680	1690	1700

CHARLES II OF SPAIN

LOUIS XIV OF FRANCE (DOMINATED BY CARDINAL MAZARIN UNTIL 1661)

ENGLAND UNDER CROMWELL	CHARLES II OF ENGLAND	JAMES II	WILLIAM AND MARY

Velázquez
Las Meninas
1656

Rembrandt
Self-portrait, c.1659

Palace at Versailles
begun 1669

Wren, new St. Paul's Cathedral
London, 1675-1710

Pope Innocent X, 1644-1655   Great fire of London, 1666

"Glorious Revolution" — movement toward
parliamentary government begins in England, 1688

Pope Alexander VII, 1655-1667

Royal Society founded in London, 1662

Blaise Pascal, 1623-1662   Jean Baptiste Racine, 1639-1699

The wars of Louis XIV begin, 1667   Sir Isaac Newton's laws of motion, gravitation, 1687

John Milton, Paradise Lost, 1667

The general period we have labeled "Renaissance" continues without any sharp stylistic break (except for the interrupting episode of Mannerism) into the seventeenth and eighteenth centuries. We call the art of this later period *Baroque,* although no one Baroque style or set of stylistic principles actually has been defined. The origin of the word is not clear. It may come from the Portuguese word *barroco,* meaning an irregularly shaped pearl. Certainly, the term originally was used in a disparaging sense, especially in connection with post-Renaissance architecture, which nineteenth-century critics perceived as decadent Classical: unstructural, overornamented, theatrical, and grotesque. The use of "Baroque" as a pejorative has faded, however, and the term has been included in the art-historical vocabulary for many years as a blanket designation for the art of the period roughly covering 1600 to 1750 and encompassing the careers of some of the greatest painters, sculptors, and architects the Western world has ever produced.

Scholars gradually came to see that the Baroque styles were quite different from those of the Renaissance. The Baroque, for example, looks dynamic; Renaissance styles are relatively static. This basic difference led to the claim that the two are fundamentally in opposition; scholars still disagree about the historical and formal relation of the two stylistic periods, especially since it is clear that the Classicism of the High Renaissance is restored and flourishes in the Baroque. The historical reality lies in the flow of stylistic change, and Baroque art is a useful classification for isolating the tendencies and products of stylistic change. We shall designate here as Baroque those traits that the styles of the seventeenth and early eighteenth centuries seem to have in common. We have earlier applied the adjective *baroque* retrospectively to examples of ancient sculpture and architecture that appear to modern art historians to have strong stylistic affinities with seventeenth- and eighteenth-century monuments, for example, the Hellenistic sculpture of Pergamon and Samothrace (FIGS. 5-90 to 5-93, 5-97) and certain Roman buildings erected during the second and third centuries A.D. (FIGS. 7-58, 7-59, 7-80).

Like the art it produced, the Baroque era was manifold—spacious and dynamic, brilliant and colorful, theatrical and passionate, sensual and ecstatic, opulent and extravagant, versatile and *virtuoso.* It was an age of expansion following on an age of discovery, and its expansion led to still further discovery. The rising national powers colonized the globe. Wars between Renaissance cities were supplanted by wars between continental empires, and the history of Europe was influenced by battles fought in the North American wilderness and in India. The art of the Baroque period reflects this growing nationalism. In France, for example, it centers around the powerful monarchy; in Italy, it is the Catholic art of the popes, in opposition to the art of the Protestant North.

Baroque expansiveness extended well beyond the earth in the conceptions of the new astronomy and physics proposed by Galileo, Kepler, and Newton. The same laws of mechanics were found to govern a falling apple and a celestial body moving at great velocity. Humanity's optical range was expanding to embrace the macroscopic spaces of the celestial world and the microscopic spaces of the cellular. The Baroque is almost obsessively interested in the space of the unfolding universe. Descartes makes extension (space and what occupies it) the sole physical attribute of being; only mind and extension exist, the former proving the reality of the latter in Descartes's famous phrase *Cogito, ergo sum* (I think, therefore I am). Pascal confesses in awe that "the silence of these infinite spaces frightens me." Milton expresses the Baroque image of space in a phrase: "the vast and boundless deep."

The Baroque scientist comes to see physical nature as matter in motion through space and time; the latter two are thought of as the conditions of the first. The measurement of motion is made possible by the new mathematics of analytical geometry and the infinitesimal calculus, and experiment comes to be accepted as the prime method for getting at the truth of physical nature. Time, like space and motion, is a preoccupation of the creative Baroque mind, in art as well as in science. The age-old sense of time, rich with religious, philosophical, psychological, and poetic import, persists alongside the new concept of it as a measurable property of nature. Time, "the subtle thief of youth" that steals away the lives of all of us; that, in the end, reveals the truth, vindicates goodness, and rescues innocence; that demolishes the memory of great empires; and that points to the ultimate judgment of humankind by God—this sense of time pervades the art and literature of the Baroque. The sonnets of Shakespeare dwell on the mutability and brevity of life and on time's destruction of beauty ("that time will come/and take my love away"). The great landscapes of van Ruisdael (FIG. 24-55) suggest the passage of time in hurrying clouds, restless sea, and ever-changing light. Painters and sculptors, eager to make action explicit and convincing, depict it at the very moment it is taking place, as in Bernini's *David* (FIG. 24-8). Countless allegorical representations portray time as the fierce old man carrying his scythe or devouring his children. For the Baroque artist, then, time has acquired its new "scientific" connotations of the instantaneous and the infinite, yet without any loss of its significance for each human life.

Scarcely less fascinating to the Baroque mind is light. Light, which for thousands of years was thought of and worshiped as the godlike sun or the truth of the Holy Spirit, now becomes a physical entity, propagated in waves (or corpuscles) through Pascal's "infinite spaces," capable of being refracted into color by a prism. But, as with time, the new-found materiality of light by no means diminishes its ancient association with spirituality in the religion, poetry, and art of the Baroque. It still stands for inspiration, truth of dogma, the mystical vision of the transcendental world, the presence of the Divine, the "inner light" (FIG. 24-10). And it can have these associations in a commonplace setting or in one of splendor and magnificence (FIG. 24-7). Yet the age of the new science, adapting the old metaphor of light to the dawn of a new day, would be called the "Enlightenment," signifying that the old, dark, mythical way of reading the world has been given up and that the light of knowledge brings a new day. Alexander Pope, expressing the enthusiasm of his day for the discoveries of Newton, makes them out to be a kind of second revelation:

Nature, and Nature's laws lay hid in night.
God said: "Let Newton be!" and all was Light!

The elements of perception in naturalistic Baroque art are the elements of nature described by Baroque science: matter in motion through space, time, and light. And the ingredients of an increasingly precise method for the scientific study of nature—observation and measurement, representation and experimental testing—are analogous to the naturalistic artist's careful study and reproduction of natural appearances.

Although the exclusive and exacting report of these elements is a most important enterprise in the age of the Baroque, the mechanical simulation of appearances for its own sake is by no means the naturalistic artist's intention. Although each artist obviously delights in the achievement of astonishing illusion, the images that are rendered embody spiritual and metaphysical meanings of nature so persuasively real and present that their significance and truth are strongly reinforced. In this way, the artist brings before us the reality of the unseen world by means of the seen, the visible objects that are regarded as symbolic or emblematic of invisible and unchanging truth. Baroque naturalism remains largely religious in content.

While naturalism thrived in Baroque art, Classicism was revised and further developed, and the two styles divided the taste of the age with a third: the dynamic, colorful, sensuous style characteristic of Rubens and Bernini. The differences among these three styles were not so definitive as to disallow exchanges of influence or even occasional collaboration, although the esthetic doctrines or presuppositions of naturalism were fundamentally opposed to those of the other two, and the members of the Royal Academy of Painting and Sculpture in France could debate the virtues of the Classical (formalistic) Poussin over the coloristic Rubens. Art theory flourished, and most of it was on the side of Classicism. The cause of Classicism also was favored by a growing antiquarian literature, the fruit of an expanding enthusiasm for ancient civilization and art and an increasingly sophisticated and systematic study of it. The Classical masters of the Baroque took as their models the great artists of the High Renaissance, Antique statuary, and nature; artists of whatever stylistic bent often were learned in Classical literature and antiquities. Although the

Classical masters' philosophy of art proclaimed the ideal rather than the real as the only worthy subject and form for painting and sculpture, they believed that study of nature was essential to the full and valid realization of the ideal in its purity and perfection. This concept was manifest in their insistence on the careful observation and depiction of the human figure from life.

Nevertheless, the opposition of Classicism to the dramatic dynamism of painters like Rubens becomes conscious and fixed in the Baroque. This dualism will hold well into the nineteenth and even the twentieth century. Indeed, it reaches through the entire Western tradition, exclusive of the Middle Ages; an ancient statement of it may be seen in the art of Greece and Rome (compare FIGS. 5-42 and 5-91). Classicism in art and thought amounts to calm rationality; we see it in the landscapes of Poussin (FIG. 24-60). Its opposite—turbulent action stirred by powerful passions—(later, we shall call it "Romanticism") appears in the painting of Rubens (FIG. 24-40) and in the sculpture of Bernini (FIG. 24-10). A central theme of Baroque art and literature is the conflict of reason with passion. The representation of that conflict is, of course, as ancient as Plato and survives as a great dualism in Western thinking about human nature.

The exploration of the elementary structure of physical nature is accompanied, quite consistently, by the exploration of human nature, the realm of the senses and the emotions. The function of the representational arts is to open that realm to full view. The throwing open to human scrutiny of the two physical universes of macrocosm and microcosm did not distract Baroque humanity from the age-old curiosity about the nature of humankind. After all, it was now perceived that if we are one with nature, the knowledge of ourselves must be part of the knowledge of nature. The new resources given to Baroque artists allow them to render, with new accuracy and authority, the appearances of the world and of the beings that people it. Painting and sculpture, equipped with every device of sensuous illusion now available, provide a stage for the enactment of the drama of human life in all its variety.

Baroque is preeminently the age of theater. Art shares with the actor's stage the purpose (as Shakespeare puts it in *Hamlet*)

to hold, as 'twere, the mirror up to nature, to show
virtue her own feature, scorn her own image, and the
very age and body of the time his form and pressure.

(III:2)

Shakespeare urges us to present and analyze the spectrum of human actions and passions in all its degrees of lightness, darkness, and intensity. In this great era of the stage, tragedy and comedy are reborn. At the same time, the resources of music greatly expand, creating the opera and refining the instruments of the modern orchestra.

All the arts approve the things of the senses and the delights of sensuous experience. Although here and there the guilty fear of pleasure lingers from the times of Hieronymus Bosch, poetry and literature in all countries acquire a richly expressive language capable of rendering themes that involve the description, presentation, conflict, and resolution of human emotions. In the Catholic countries, every device of art is used to stimulate pious emotions—sometimes, to the pitch of ecstasy. Luxurious display and unlimited magnificence and splendor frame the extravagant life of the courts, cost notwithstanding; the modes of furniture and dress are perhaps the most ornate ever designed. Even in externals, a dramatic, sensuous elaborateness is the rule. However, what people wear and what they do must approach perfection, with the added flourish of seeming effortless. Courtiers, at one end of Baroque society, and brigands and pirates at the other, are brilliant performers, as are those who fashion the arts and the sciences. All are virtuosi, proud of their technique and capable of astonishing quantities of work.

ITALY

The age of the Baroque has been identified with the Catholic reaction to the advance of Protestantism. Although it extends much more widely in time and place than seventeenth-century Italy and is by no means only a

24-1 CARLO MADERNO, Santa Susanna, Rome, 1597–1603.

manifestation of religious change, Baroque art doubtless had papal Rome as its birthplace. Between the pontificates of Paul III from 1534 to 1549 and of Sixtus V in the 1580s, the popes led a successful military, diplomatic, and theological campaign against Protestantism, wiping out many of its gains in central and southern Europe. The great Council of Trent, which met in the early 1540s and again in the early 1560s, was sponsored by the papacy in an effort to systematize and harden orthodox Catholic doctrine against the threat of Protestant persuasion. The Council firmly resisted Protestant objection to the use of images in religious worship, insisting on their necessity in the teaching of the laity. This implied separation of the priest from an unsophisticated congregation was to be reflected in architecture as well, the central type of church plan being rejected in favor of the long church and of other plans that maintained the distinction between clergy and laity.

Interrupted for a while, the building program begun under Paul III (with Michelangelo's Capitoline Hill design, FIG. 22-29) was taken up again by Sixtus V, who had augmented the papal treasury and who intended to construct a new and more magnificent Rome, an "imperial city that had been subdued by Christ and purged of paganism." Sixtus was succeeded by a number of strong and ambitious popes—Paul V, Urban VIII, Innocent X, and Alexander VII—the patrons of Bernini and Borromini and the builders of the modern city of Rome, which bears their Baroque mark everywhere. The energy of the Catholic Counter-Reformation, transformed into art, radiated throughout Catholic countries and even into Protestant lands, which found a response to it in their own art.

Architecture and Sculpture

MADERNO   One of the earliest manifestations of the Baroque spirit in architecture is found in the facade designed at the turn of the century by CARLO MADERNO (1556–1629) for the Roman church of Santa Susanna (FIG. 24-1 and Chapter 22 map). In its general appearance, Maderno's facade resembles Giacomo della Porta's immensely influential design for Il Gesù (FIG. 22-48), the seat of the Jesuit order. But the later facade has a greater verticality, concentrating and dramatizing the major features of its model. The tall central section of the facade projects forward from the horizontal lower story, and the scroll buttresses that connect the two levels are narrower and set at a sharper angle. The vertical thrust of the design is further enhanced by the elimination of the arch framing the pediment over the doorway. Strong shadows cast by the vigorously projecting columns and pilasters of Santa Susanna mount dramatically toward the emphatically stressed central axis; the sculptural effect is enhanced by the recessed niches, which contain statues.

Maderno was also involved in the greatest Baroque project in Rome, the completion of St. Peter's. Bramante's and

Michelangelo's central plan was unsatisfactory to the clergy of the seventeenth century, who thought it smacked of paganism and who felt it was inconvenient for the ever-growing assemblies. Paul V commissioned Maderno to add three bays of a nave to the earlier nucleus (compare FIGS. 22-7 and 24-4) and to provide the building with a facade (FIG. **24-2**). In many ways the facade of St. Peter's is a gigantic expansion of the elements of Santa Susanna's first level, but Maderno overextends his theme, and the compactness and verticality of the smaller church's facade is lost. The elements are spread so far apart that the quickening rhythm of pilasters and columns from the sides toward the center—one of the keys to the success of the earlier design—becomes slack. The central pediment, for example, now serves only as a cap to a temple-like front rather than as the first of several vertical elements in a coherent design. In fairness to Maderno, it must be pointed out that he had to work with the preexisting core of an incomplete building and did not have the luxury of formulating a grand new concept for St. Peter's; moreover, his design for the facade was also never fully executed. The two outside bays were meant to be the first stages of two flanking towers, which never were built; their vertical accents might have visually compressed the central part of the facade. As it stands, the unfinished frontispiece of St. Peter's is neither the realization of Maderno's wishes nor of those of Michelangelo and Bramante. Lengthening the nave moved the facade outward and away from the dome, and the effect that Michelangelo had planned—a structure pulled together

and dominated by its dome—is seriously impeded. When viewed at close range, the dome hardly emerges above the soaring cliff of the facade; seen from farther back (FIG. 24-2), it appears to have no drum. One must go back beyond the piazza to see the dome and drum together and to experience the effect that Michelangelo intended. Today, to see the structure as it was envisioned by the sixteenth-century architect, it must be viewed from the back (FIG. 22-32).

BERNINI The design of St. Peter's, which had been evolving since the days of Bramante and Michelangelo and had engaged all of the leading architects of the Renaissance and Baroque periods, was completed (except for details) by GIANLORENZO BERNINI (1598–1680). Bernini was an architect, a painter, and a sculptor—one of the most brilliant and imaginative artists of the Baroque era and, if not the originator of the Baroque style, probably its most characteristic and sustaining spirit. Bernini's largest and most impressive single project was the design for a monumental piazza in front of St. Peter's (FIGS. **24-3**, **24-4** and Chapter 22 map). In much the way that Michelangelo was forced to reorganize the Capitoline Hill, Bernini had to adjust his design to some preexisting structures on the site: an ancient obelisk brought from Egypt by the Romans and a fountain designed by Maderno. He used these features to define the long axis of a vast oval embraced by colonnades that are joined to the facade of St. Peter's by two diverging wings. Four files of huge Tuscan columns make up the two colonnades, which

24-2 CARLO MADERNO, facade of St. Peter's, the Vatican, Rome, 1606–1612.

24-3   Aerial view of St. Peter's.

terminate in severely Classical temple fronts. The dramatic gesture of embrace made by the colonnades symbolizes the welcome given its communicants by the Roman Catholic church. Thus, the compact, central designs of Bramante and Michelangelo are expanded by a Baroque transformation into a dynamic complex of axially ordered elements that reach out and enclose spaces of vast dimension. Where the Renaissance building stood in self-sufficient isolation, the Baroque design expansively relates to its environment.

The wings that connect St. Peter's facade with the oval piazza flank a trapezoidal space also reminiscent of the Campidoglio (FIG. 22-29), but here the latter's visual effect is reversed; as seen from the piazza, the diverging wings counteract the natural perspective and tend to bring the facade closer to the observer. Emphasizing the facade's height in this manner, Bernini subtly and effectively compensates for its excessive width.

The Baroque delight in illusionistic devices is expressed again in the Vatican in the Scala Regia or Royal Stairway

24-5   GIANLORENZO BERNINI, Scala Regia, the Vatican, Rome, 1663–1666.

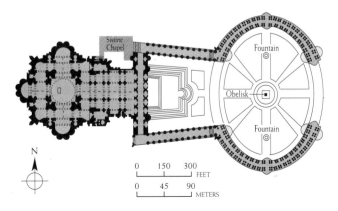

24-4   Plan of St. Peter's, with adjoining piazza designed by GIANLORENZO BERNINI.

(FIG. **24-5**), the monumental corridor of steps connecting the papal apartments and the portico and narthex of the church. Because the original passageway was irregular, dark, and dangerous to descend, Pope Alexander VII commissioned Bernini to replace it. Bernini, like Michelangelo at the Campidoglio, here makes architectural virtue of necessity by using illusionistic techniques characteristic of stagecraft. The stairway, its entrance crowned by a sculptural group of trumpeting angels and the papal arms, is covered by a barrel vault (in two stages) carried on columns that form aisles flanking the central corridor. By gradually reducing the distance between the columns and walls as the stairway ascends, Bernini actually eliminates the aisles on the upper levels, while creating an illusion of uniformity of width and continuity of aisle for the whole stairway. At the same time, the space between the colonnades also narrows with ascent, reinforcing the natural perspective and making the stairs appear to be longer than they actually are. To minimize this effect, Bernini made the lighting at the top of the stairs brighter, exploiting the natural human inclination to move from darkness toward light. To make the long ascent more tolerable, he provided an intermediate goal in the form of an illuminated landing that promises a midway resting point. The result is a highly sophisticated design, both dynamic and dramatic, which repeats on a smaller scale, but perhaps even more effectively, the processional sequence found inside St. Peter's.

Long before the planning of the piazza and the completion of the Scala Regia, Bernini had been at work decorating the interior of St. Peter's. His first commission, completed between 1624 and 1633, called for the design and erection of the gigantic bronze *baldacchino* (FIG. **24-6**) above the main altar under the great dome, which was built to mark and memorialize the tomb of Saint Peter.

24-6 GIANLORENZO BERNINI, baldacchino, St. Peter's, Rome, 1624–1633. Gilded bronze, approx. 100' high.

Almost 100 feet high (the height of an average eight-story building), this canopy serves as a focus of the church's splendor; and it is at once in harmony with the tremendous proportions of the new church and a visual bridge between human scale and the lofty vaults and dome above. Its four spiral columns recall those of the ancient baldacchino over the same spot in Old St. Peter's. Partially fluted and wreathed with vines, they seem to deny the mass and weight of the tons of bronze (stripped from the portico of the Pantheon) resting on them. At the same time, the columns communicate their Baroque energy to the four colossal angels standing guard at the upper corners and to

24-7 GIANLORENZO BERNINI, *Cathedra Petri* (Chair of St. Peter), St. Peter's, Rome, 1656–1666. Gilded bronze, marble, stucco, and stained glass.

the four serpentine brackets that elevate the orb and the cross, symbols of the triumph of the Church since the time of the emperor Constantine (FIG. 7-93, right), builder of the original St. Peter's basilica.

Indeed, it is this theme of triumph that dictates the architectural as well as the sculptural symbolism both inside and outside the new St. Peter's. Suggesting a great and solemn procession, the main axis of the complex traverses the piazza (marked but slowed by the central obelisk, FIG. 24-4) and enters Maderno's nave. It comes to a temporary halt at the altar beneath the baldacchino, but it continues on toward its climactic destination at another great altar in the apse, the *Cathedra Petri*, or chair of St. Peter (FIG. **24-7**), also the work of Bernini. In this explosively dramatic composition, the seat of the founder of the papacy is exalted in a burst of light, in which the Dove of the Holy Ghost appears amid flights of angels and billowing clouds. Four colossal figures in gilded bronze seem to support the chair miraculously, for they scarcely touch it. The two in the foreground represent two fathers of the Latin church, Saints Ambrose and Augustine. Behind them, less conspicuously, stand Saints Athanasius and Chrysostom, representing the Greek church. The grouping of the figures consitutes an appeal for unity within Christianity but, at the same time, suggests the subservience of the Eastern church to the Western. (Directly above St. Peter's throne, two cherubs hold up the papal tiara like Classical Victories about to crown a victor.) The Cathedra Petri is the quintessence of Baroque composition. Its forms are generated and grouped not by clear lines of structure but by forces that unfold from a center of violent energy. Everything moves, nothing is distinct, light dissolves firmness, and the effect is visionary. The vision asserts the triumph of Christianity and the papal claim to doctrinal supremacy.

Much of Bernini's prolific career was given to the adornment of St. Peter's, where his works combine sculpture with architecture. Although Bernini was a great and influential architect, his fame rests primarily on his sculpture, which, like his architecture, expresses the Baroque spirit to perfection. It is expansive and dramatic, and the element of time usually plays an important role in it. Bernini's version of *David* (FIG. **24-8**) aims at catching the split-second action of the figure and differs markedly from the restful and tense figures of *David* portrayed by Donatello (FIG. 21-10), Verrocchio (FIG. 21-50), and Michelangelo (FIG. 22-19). Bernini's *David*, his muscular legs widely and firmly planted, is beginning the violent, pivoting motion that will launch the stone from his sling. A moment before, his body was in one position; the next moment, it will be in a completely different one. Unlike Myron, the fifth-century B.C. Greek sculptor whose *Discus-Thrower* (FIG. 5-41) is temporarily and uncharacteristically frozen in inaction, Bernini selects the most dramatic of an implied sequence of poses, so that the observer has to think simultaneously of the continuum and of this tiny fraction of it. The implied continu-

um imparts a dynamic quality to the statue that suggests a bursting forth of the energy one sees confined in Michelangelo's figures (FIGS. 22-19 and 22-20). Bernini's statue seems to be moving through time and through space. This is not the kind of statue that can be inscribed in a cylinder or confined in a niche; its implied action demands space around it. Nor is it self-sufficient in the Renaissance sense, as its pose and attitude direct the observer's attention beyond itself and to its surroundings (in this case, toward an unseen Goliath). For the first time since antiquity (FIG. 5-93), a sculptured figure moves out into and partakes of the physical space that surrounds it and the observer.

The expansive quality of Baroque art and its refusal to limit itself to firmly defined spatial settings are encountered

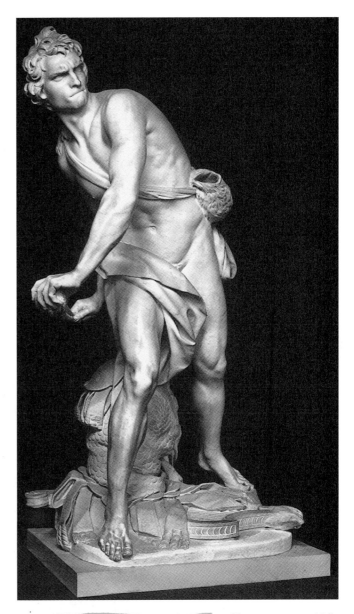

24-8 GIANLORENZO BERNINI, *David*, 1623. Marble, approx. 5' 7" high. Galleria Borghese, Rome.

again in the *Ecstasy of St. Theresa* in the Cornaro Chapel (FIG. **24-9**) of the church of Santa Maria della Vittoria. In this chapel, Bernini draws on the full resources of architecture, sculpture, and painting to charge the entire area with crosscurrents of dramatic tension. Saint Theresa was a nun of the Carmelite order and one of the great mystical saints of the Spanish Counter-Reformation. Her conversion took place after the death of her father, when she fell into a series of trances, saw visions, and heard voices. Feeling a persistent pain in her side, she came to believe that its cause was the fire-tipped dart of Divine love, which an angel had thrust into her bosom and which she described as making her swoon in delightful anguish. The whole chapel becomes a theater for the production of this mystical drama. The niche in which it takes place is a *proscenium* (the part of the stage in front of the curtain) crowned with a broken Baroque pediment and ornamented with polychrome marble. On either side of the chapel, portraits of

24-9 GIANLORENZO BERNINI, interior of the Cornaro Chapel, Santa Maria della Vittoria, Rome, 1645–1652. Eighteenth-century painting, Staatliches Museum, Schwerin, Germany.

the Cornaro family in sculptured opera boxes represent an audience watching the denouement of the heavenly drama with intent piety. Bernini shows the saint in ecstasy (FIG. **24-10**), unmistakably a mingling of spiritual and physical passion, swooning back on a cloud, while the smiling angel aims his arrow. The group is of white marble, and the artist goes to extremes of virtuosity in his management of textures: the clouds, rough monk's cloth, gauzy material, smooth flesh, and feathery wings are all carefully differen-

tiated, yet harmonized in visual and visionary effect. Light from a hidden window of yellow glass pours down bronze rays that are meant to be seen as bursting forth from a painting of Heaven in the vault (FIG. 24-9). Several tons of marble seem to float in a haze of light, the winds of Heaven buoying draperies as the cloud ascends. The remote mysteries of religion, taking on recognizable form, descend to meet the human world halfway, within the conventions of Baroque art and theater. Bernini had much to do with

24-10 GIANLORENZO BERNINI, *Ecstasy of St. Theresa*, Cornaro Chapel, Santa Maria della Vittoria, Rome. 1645–1652. Marble, height of group 11′ 6″.

the establishment of the principles of visual illusion that guided both. He was perfectly familiar with the writing of plays, theatrical production, and stagecraft. The young English traveler, John Evelyn, sojourning in Rome in 1644, wrote that

> Bernini, a Florentine sculptor, architect, painter, and poet, gave a public opera . . . wherein he painted the scenes, cut the statues, invented the engines, composed the music, writ the comedy, and built the theater.

The community of the Baroque arts is reflected in the universal genius of Bernini.

BORROMINI   It seems curious that Bernini, whose sculpture expresses the very essence of the Baroque spirit, should remain relatively conservative in his architecture. Frequently planning on a vast scale and employing striking illusionistic devices, Bernini tends to use the Classical orders in a fairly sober and traditional manner, except, notably, when the architecture is inextricably bound up

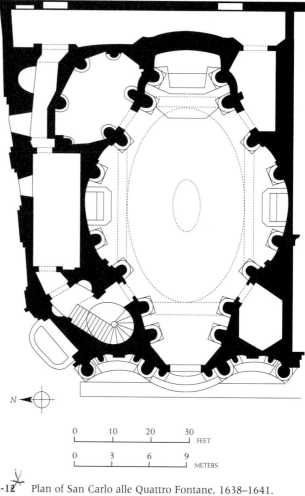

24-12   Plan of San Carlo alle Quattro Fontane, 1638–1641.

with sculpture, as in his baldacchino in St. Peter's (FIG. 24-6) and the St. Theresa altar (FIG. 24-9). One might call his architectural style academic, at least in comparison with the unorthodox and quite revolutionary manner of his contemporary FRANCESCO BORROMINI (1599–1667). A new dynamism appears in the little church of San Carlo alle Quattro Fontane (FIG. **24-11** and Chapter 22 map), where Borromini goes well beyond any of his predecessors or contemporaries in the plastic handling of a building. Maderno's facades of Santa Susanna (FIG. 24-1) and St. Peter's (FIG. 24-2) are deeply sculptured, but they develop along straight, lateral planes. Borromini, perhaps thinking of Michelangelo's apse wall in St. Peter's (FIG. 22-32), sets his whole facade in serpentine motion forward and back, making a counterpoint of concave and convex on two levels (note the sway of the cornices), and emphasizes the sculptured effect with deeply recessed niches. This facade is no longer the traditional, flat frontispiece that defines a building's outer limits; it is a pulsating membrane inserted between interior and exterior space, designed not to separate but to provide a fluid transition between the two. This functional interrelation of the building and its environment is underlined by the curious fact that it has not

24-11   FRANCESCO BORROMINI, facade of San Carlo alle Quattro Fontane, Rome, 1665–1676.

one but two facades. The second, a narrow bay crowned with its own small tower, turns away from the main facade and, following the curve of the street, faces an intersection. (The upper facade was completed seven years after Borromini's death, and we cannot be sure to what degree the present supplemented and complex structure reflects his original intention.)

The interior is not only an ingenious response to an awkward site, but also a provocative variation on the theme of the centrally planned church. In plan (FIG. **24-12**) it looks like a hybrid of a Greek cross and an oval, with a long axis between entrance and apse. The side walls move in an undulating flow that reverses the motion of the facade. Vigorously projecting columns articulate the space into which they protrude just as much as they do the walls to which they are attached. This molded interior space is capped by a deeply coffered, oval dome that seems to float on the light entering through windows hidden in its base. Rich variations on the basic theme of the oval, dynamic relative to the static circle, create an interior that appears to flow from entrance to altar, unimpeded by the segmentation so characteristic of Renaissance buildings.

The unification of interior space is carried even further in Borromini's Chapel of St. Ivo in the courtyard of the College of the Sapienza (Wisdom) in Rome (FIG. **24-13** and

Chapter 22 map). In his characteristic manner, Borromini plays concave against convex forms on the upper level of the exterior of his chapel. The lower stories of the court, which frame the bottom facade, were already there when Borromini began work. Above the inward curve of the facade—its design adjusted to the earlier arcades of the court—rises a convex, drumlike structure that supports the lower parts of the dome. Powerful pilasters restrain the forces that seem to push the bulging forms outward. Buttresses above the angle pilasters curve upward to brace a tall, plastic lantern topped by a spiral that seems to fasten the structure, screwlike, to the sky. The striking similarity between Borromini's St. Ivo lantern, with its scalloped entablature and platform, and the third-century A.D. Roman temple of Venus at Baalbek (FIG. 7-80)—the ruins of which were already known in the sixteenth century—underscores the commonality of approach to structural design on the part of the Baroque architects of both eras.

The centralized plan of the St. Ivo Chapel (FIG. **24-14**) is that of a star, having rounded-off points and apses on all sides. Indentations and projections along the angled, curving walls create a highly complex plan, all the elements of which are fully reflected in the interior elevation. From

24-13 FRANCESCO BORROMINI, Chapel of St. Ivo, College of the Sapienza, Rome, begun 1642.

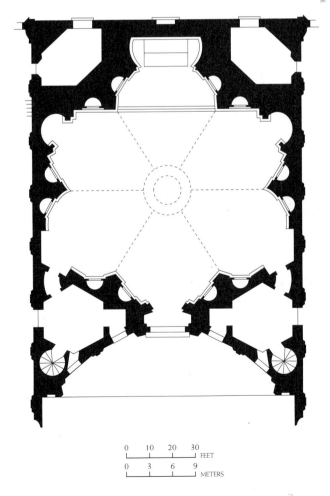

24-14 Plan of the Chapel of St. Ivo.

24-15   View into the dome of the Chapel of St. Ivo.

floor to lantern, the wall panels rise in a continuously tapering sweep that is halted only momentarily by a single, horizontal cornice (FIG. **24-15**). The dome is thus not, as in the Renaissance, a separate unit placed on the supporting block of a building; rather it is an organic part that evolves out of and shares the qualities of the supporting walls, from which it cannot be separated. The complex, horizontal

motion of the walls is transferred fully into the elevation, creating a dynamic and cohesive shell that encloses and energetically molds a scalloped fragment of universal space. Few architects have matched Borromini's ability to translate extremely complicated designs into such masterfully unified and cohesive structures as that of St. Ivo.

GUARINI AND LONGHENA   The heir to Borromini's sculptured architectural style was GUARINO GUARINI (1624–1683), a priest, mathematician, and architect who spent the last seventeen years of his life in Turin, converting that provincial Italian town into a fountainhead of architectural theories that would sweep much of Europe. In his Palazzo Carignano (FIG. **24-16**), Guarini effectively applies Borromini's principle of undulating facades. He divides his long facade into three units, the central one of which curves much like the facade of San Carlo alle Quattro Fontane (FIG. 24-11) and is flanked by two blocklike wings. This lateral, three-part division of facades, characteristic of most Baroque palazzos, probably is based on the observation that the average person instinctively can recognize up to three objects as a unit; a greater number would require the observer to count each object individually. A three-part organization of extended surfaces thus allows the artist to introduce variety into the design without destroying its unity. It also permits emphasis to be added on the central axis, which Guarini has done here most effectively by punching out deep cavities in the middle of his convex central block. The variety of his design is enhanced by richly textured surfaces (all executed in brick) and by pilasters, which further subdivide his units into three bays each. High and low reliefs create shadows of different intensities and add to the decorative effect, making this one of the finest facades of the late seventeenth century.

24-16   GUARINO GUARINI, Palazzo Carignano, Turin, 1679–1692.

24-17 GUARINO GUARINI, Chapel of the Santa Sindone, Turin, 1667–1694 (view into dome).

24-18 Dome of Sant'Eligio degli Orifici, Rome, attributed to BRAMANTE and RAPHAEL, c. 1509; reconstructed c. 1600 (view into dome).

Guarini's mathematical talents must have been guiding him when he designed the extraordinarily complex dome of the Chapel of the Santa Sindone (Holy Shroud), a small, central-plan building attached to the cathedral of Turin. A view into this dome (FIG. **24-17**) reveals a bewildering display of geometric figures that appear to wheel slowly in kaleidoscopic fashion around a circular focus that contains the bright Dove of the Holy Ghost. Here, the traditional dome has been dematerialized into a series of figures that seem to revolve around each other in contrary motion; they define it, but they no longer limit the interior space. A comparison of Guarini's dome with that of the church of Sant'Eligio degli Orifici in Rome (FIG. **24-18**), attributed both to Bramante and to Raphael and reconstructed about 1600, indicates that a fundamental change has taken place. The static "dome of heaven" of Renaissance architecture and philosophy (which here, in the pristine clarity of its unmodified circular shape, immediately recalls the dome of the cosmos in the Classical Pantheon, FIG. 7-57) has been converted into the dynamic Baroque apparition of a mathematical heaven of calculable motions.

The style of Borromini and Guarini will move across the Alps to inspire architecture in Austria and southern Germany in the late seventeenth and early eighteenth centuries. Popular in the Catholic regions of Europe and the New World (especially in Brazil), it will exert little influence in France, where the more conservative style of Bernini will be favored.

In Venice, something of the Late Renaissance Classicism of Andrea Palladio survives, paradoxically, in the very Baroque church of Santa Maria della Salute (FIG. **24-19**), often called simply the "Salute" (health). Built by BALDASSARE LONGHENA (1598–1682), the church was commissioned by the Venetian republic in thanksgiving to the

24-19 BALDASSARE LONGHENA, Santa Maria della Salute, Venice, 1631–1648 (consecrated 1687).

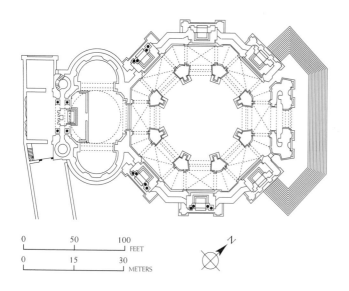

24-20   Plan of Santa Maria della Salute. (After Christian Norberg-Schulz.)

Virgin Mary for ridding the city of plague. Standing at the head of the Grand Canal, the main thoroughfare of Venice, the Salute has for centuries dominated it like a gorgeous crown, the admiration of generations of travelers and artists and the setting for countless splendid spectacles of the kind depicted a half century earlier by VITTORIO CARPACCIO (c. 1465–1525). (The locale of Carpaccio's *Leavetaking of the Betrothed Pair,* page 618, is invented but based on the waterways and buildings of his beloved Venice.) Longhena was well aware of the architectural value of the site; the two domes of the Salute harmonize with the family of domes in its vicinity, among them those of St. Mark's (FIG. 9-24) and of the Palladian churches of San Giorgio Maggiore (FIG. 22-53) and Il Redentore (The Redeemer). Together, they make a skyline of surpassing beauty, floating above the city or reflected in its waters in ever-changing groupings as the admiring visitor moves.

Central plans were largely foreign to Venice, and it may be that the domes and central plan of St. Mark's suggested the design of the Salute, although Longhena insisted his design had not been done before. The plan of the building (FIG. **24-20**) is an octagon with an auxiliary choir. The greater of the two domes is over the octagon; the lesser is over the choir and is flanked by campaniles. Both in plan and elevation, the grouping of the masses and spaces is essentially Renaissance, without the intricacies of Bernini, Borromini, or Guarini. This observation is especially true of the interior, which has the clear arrangement, the correct orders, and the steady gray-white color of Palladio's wall-and-column features, as in San Giorgio Maggiore (FIG. 22-54). But the exterior elevation is dramatic. The facade-like faces of the octagon play counterpoint with the main facade, and the highest excitement of Baroque invention is

apparent in the great scroll buttresses that seem to open organically from the main body and to sprout statuary (FIG. 24-19). The Salute is a splendid example of an architecture rooted in a native (Venetian) tradition, yet flowering successfully in a new stylistic climate.

The style of Palladio and the Venetian Renaissance could be and was transplanted into a widely different environment. While Longhena was building the Salute, the Palladian style was already being naturalized in the distant north, in England (FIG. 24-71).

Painting

Italian painters of the seventeenth century, with the possible exception of Caravaggio and the later decorators, were somewhat less adventurous than the sculptors and architects. The painters of the High Renaissance had bequeathed to them an authoritative tradition as great as that of classical antiquity. After the sixteenth century, European artists drew from both sources, and the history of painting well into the nineteenth century is an account of the interpretation, development, and modification of these two great traditions. The three most influential stylistic bequests of the High Renaissance were the styles of Raphael, Michelangelo, and Titian, with an additional subdominant trend inspired by Correggio. Baroque painting is the consequence of the many varied interchanges among these styles, with the Antique sometimes supplementing them and sometimes used against them. A style that seems hostile to both authorities and that is based on the assumption that the artist should paint what he sees, without regard for either the Antique or the Renaissance masters, might be called "native naturalism." This native naturalism appears as a minority style in Italy and France but plays an important role in Spain and a predominant one in the Dutch school.

THE CARRACCI   The Baroque gets well under way in Italian painting around the year 1600, with the decoration of the gallery of the Palazzo Farnese by ANNIBALE CARRACCI (1560–1609). His generation, weary of the strained artifice of Mannerism, returned for a fresh view of nature, but only after they had studied the Renaissance masters carefully. Annibale had attended an academy of art in his native city of Bologna. Founded cooperatively by members of his family, among them Lodovico Carracci (1555-1619) and Agostino Carracci (1557-1602), the Bolognese academy is the first significant institution of its kind in the history of Western art. It was founded on the premises that art can be taught—the basis of any academic philosophy of art—and that the materials of instruction must include the Antique and the Renaissance traditions, in addition to the study of anatomy and life drawing. The Bolognese painters were long called academics, and sometimes eclectics, for they appeared to assume that the development of a correct style

24-21 ANNIBALE CARRACCI, *Loves of the Gods*, ceiling frescoes in the Gallery, Palazzo Farnese, Rome, 1597–1601.

in painting is learned and synthetic. In any event, we can tell from the Gallery of the Palazzo Farnese that Annibale was familiar with Michelangelo, Raphael, and Titian, and also that he could make clever, illusionistic paintings. The Farnese ceiling (FIG. **24-21**) is a brilliant and widely influential revision of High Renaissance painting. It restores the Renaissance interest in human themes and emotions, renouncing the artificialities of Mannerism to return to the study of nature, and forming a firm bridge between the Renaissance and the Baroque. The style is a vigorous, sensuous, and adroit naturalism, modified by the Classical form inherited from the masters.

The iconographical program of the ceiling is the *Loves of the Gods*, interpretations of the subtle and various stages and degrees of earthly and Divine love (see Raphael's *Galatea*, FIG. 22-16, and Titian's treatment of the theme in *Sacred and Profane Love*, FIG. 22-59). Despite the apparent paganism of the subjects here, we find them to have Christian overtones. The human nude is the principal motif, as it is in Michelangelo's frescoes and in much of Venetian art. Luxuriantly pagan images from Classical literature, especially Ovid's *Metamorphoses*, throng the vault, binding the composition together and filling it with exuberant and passionate life.

The scenes are arranged in panels resembling framed easel paintings on a wall, but here they are on the surfaces of a shallow, curved vault; the Sistine Chapel ceiling (FIG. 22-24), of course, comes to mind, although it is not an

24-22   GUIDO RENI, *Aurora*, 1613–1614. Ceiling fresco in the Casino Rospigliosi, Rome.

exact source. This type of simulation of easel painting for ceiling design is called *quadro riportato* (transferred framed painting). The great influence of the Carracci will make it fashionable for more than a century. The framed pictures are flanked by polychrome seated nude youths, who turn their heads to gaze at the scenes above them, and by standing Atlas figures resembling marble statues—motifs taken directly from Michelangelo's Sistine Chapel ceiling. It is noteworthy that the chiaroscuro is not the same for both the pictures and the painted figures surrounding them. The figures inside the *quadri* are modeled in an even, sculptured light; the outside figures are lit from beneath, as if they were actual three-dimensional beings or statues illuminated by torches in the gallery below. This interest in illusion, already manifest in the Renaissance, will continue in the grand ceiling compositions of the seventeenth century. In the crown of the vault, a long panel representing the *Triumph of Bacchus* is a quite ingenious mixture of Raphael and Titian and represents Annibale's adroitness in adjusting their authoritative styles to make something of his own.

Another artist trained in the Bolognese academy, GUIDO RENI (1575–1642), selected Raphael for his inspiration, as we see in his *Aurora* (FIG. **24-22**), a ceiling painting conceived in quadro riportato. Aurora (Dawn) leads the chariot of Apollo, while the Hours dance about it. The fresco exhibits a suave, almost swimming motion, soft modeling, and sure composition, without Raphael's sculpturesque strength. It is an intelligent interpretation of the master's style, as well as of Classical antiquity, for the ultimate sources of the composition are Roman reliefs (FIG. 7-45) and coins depicting emperors in triumphal chariots accompanied by flying Victories and other personifications. The painting is in every sense learned, or "academic."

However, "academic" should not be burdened here with the unfortunate connotation it will later acquire as art that is mechanical, imitative, dull, and uninspired. The *Aurora* is a masterpiece of the Bolognese style and of its age. Guido was so much admired in his own day and well into the nineteenth century that he was known as "the divine Guido."

Another member of the Bolognese school, Giovanni Francesco Barbieri, called IL GUERCINO (1591–1666), also painted a ceiling *Aurora* (FIG. **24-23**), but with a very different effect. Guercino abandons the method of quadro riportato to emulate that of Veronese, whose figures are seen from below at a forty-five-degree angle (FIG. 22-67). By this method, the subject of the picture is painted as if happening above our heads and seen from beneath; it is not simply a transfer of a painting from wall to ceiling. Taking his cue from the illusionistic figures in the Farnese Gallery and from its central ceiling panel (FIG. 24-21), Guercino converts the ceiling into a limitless space, through which the procession sweeps past. The observer's eye is led toward the celestial parade (in which Aurora herself is now the charioteer) by converging, painted extensions of the room's architecture. While the perspective may seem a little forced, Guercino's *Aurora* inspired a new wave of enthusiasm for illusionistic ceiling paintings that culminated in some of history's most stupendous decorations.

CARAVAGGIO   Although the Bolognese painters were willing to imitate nature as directly as possible, they believed that the Renaissance and Antique masters already had captured much of nature's essence and that the earlier masters would prepare them for the study of nature. MICHELANGELO MERISI, known as CARAVAGGIO (1573–1610) after the northern Italian town from which he came, thought very much otherwise. His outspoken disdain for the Classical masters (probably more vocal than real) drew bitter criticism from many painters, one of whom denounced him as the "anti-Christ of painting." Giovanni Pietro Bellori, the most influential critic of the age and an admirer of the Carracci, felt that Caravaggio's refusal to emulate the models of his distinguished predecessors threatened the whole Classical tradition of Italian painting that had reached its climax in Raphael and that was the philosophical basis of the Bolognese academy. Yet many paid Caravaggio the genuine compliment of borrowing from his innovations, and his influence on later artists, as much outside Italy as within, was immense.

The unconventional life of this great painter was consistent with the defiant individualism of his art. We know almost as much about Caravaggio from police records as from other documents. Violent offenses and assaults reaching to murder trace his tragic, antisocial career through restless, tormented wanderings, which, nevertheless, did not prevent him from producing a large number of astonishing works. His very association with lowlifes and outcasts may help to account for his unglorified and

unfashionable view of the great themes of religion, as well as his indifference to the Renaissance ideals of beauty and decorum. In his art, he secularizes both religion and the classics, reducing them to human dramas that might be played out in the harsh and dingy settings of his time and place. He employs a cast of unflattering characters selected from the fields and the streets; these, he was proud to declare, were his only teachers—to paint from them gave him sufficient knowledge of nature.

We easily can appreciate how startling Caravaggio's methods must have been for his contemporaries when we look at the *Conversion of St. Paul* (FIG. **24-24**), which he painted for the Roman church of Santa Maria del Popolo. The scene illustrates the conversion of the Pharisee Saul by a light and a voice from Heaven (Acts 9:3–9). The saint-to-be is represented flat on his back, his arms thrown up, while an old ostler appears to maneuver the horse away from its fallen master. At first inspection, little here suggests the awful grandeur of the spiritual event that is taking place. We seem to be witnessing a mere stable accident, not a man overcome by a great miracle. The protagonist is not specifically identified; he could be anyone. The ostler is a swarthy, bearded old man, who looks well acquainted with stables.

24-23 IL GUERCINO, *Aurora*, 1621–1623. Ceiling fresco in the Villa Ludovisi, Rome.

The horse fills the picture as if it were the hero, and its explicitness and the angle from which it is viewed might betray some irreverence on the part of the artist for this subject. Although Caravaggio found numerous sympathetic patrons in both church and state, a number of his works were refused on the ground that they lacked propriety (that is to say, decorum). He sometimes appears to pay no attention to the usual dignity appointed to scenes from scripture and to go too far in dismissing the formal graces of Renaissance figure composition and color.

The fact is that, above all, Caravaggio seeks to create a convincing copy of the optical world as a vehicle of spiritual meanings; his intention in this respect is like Bernini's in the *St. Theresa* (FIG. 24-10). To this end, he uses a perspective and a chiaroscuro designed to bring viewers as close as possible to the space and action of the scene, almost as if they were participating in it. The *Conversion of St. Paul* is placed on the chapel wall and is composed with an extremely low horizon or eye level; the painting is intended to be on the viewers' line of sight as they stand at the entrance of the

24-24   CARAVAGGIO, *Conversion of St. Paul, c.* 1601. Oil on canvas, approx. 7′ 6″ × 5′ 9″. Cerasi Chapel, Santa Maria del Popolo, Rome.

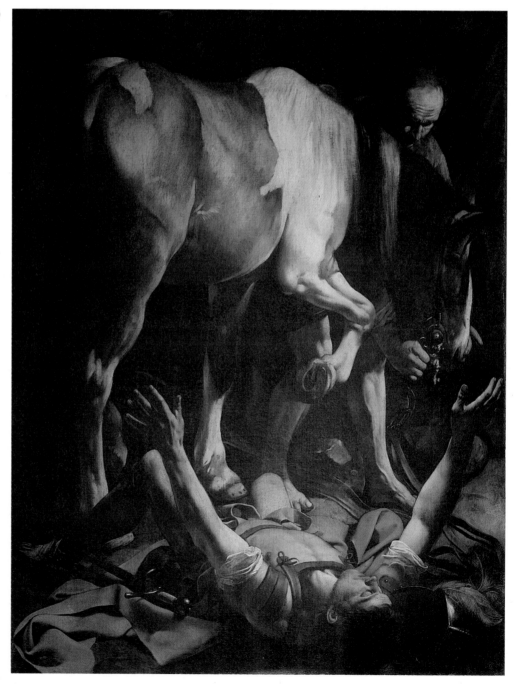

24-25   CARAVAGGIO, *Calling of St. Matthew,* c. 1597–1601. Oil on canvas, 11' 1" × 11' 5". Contarelli Chapel, San Luigi dei Francesi, Rome.

chapel. The sharply lighted figures are meant to be seen as emerging from the dark of the background. The actual light from windows outside the chapel functions as a kind of stage lighting for the production of a vision, analogous to the rays in Bernini's *St. Theresa.* Thus, Caravaggio, like Bernini, makes use of the world of optical experience to stage the visionary one. In the *Conversion of St. Paul,* what we see first as merely commonplace is in fact the elevation of the commonplace to the miraculous.

The stark contrast of light and dark was the feature of Caravaggio's style that first shocked and then fascinated his contemporaries. The sharp and sudden relief it gives to the forms and the details of form emphasizes their reality in a way than an even or subtly modulated light never could. Dark next to light is naturally dramatic; we do not need a director of stage lighting to tell us this. Caravaggio's device, a profound influence on European art, has been called *tenebrism,* from the Italian word *tenebroso,* or "dark manner." Although tenebrism is widespread in Baroque art, it will have its greatest consequences in Spain and the Netherlands. This technique goes quite well with material

that is realistic and is another mode of Baroque illusionism by which the eye is almost forced to acknowledge the visual reality of what it sees. In the hands of Caravaggio, tenebrism also contributes mightily to the essential meaning of his pictures. In the *Conversion of St. Paul,* the dramatic spotlight shining down upon the fallen Pharisee is the light of divine revelation that brings about Paul's conversion to Christianity.

A piercing ray of light illuminating a world of darkness and bearing a spiritual message is also a central feature of one of the early masterpieces of Caravaggio, the *Calling of St. Matthew* (FIG. **24-25**), one of two large canvases honoring the saint that Caravaggio painted for the side walls of the Contarelli Chapel in San Luigi dei Francesi in Rome. The setting is typical of Caravaggio: a dingy tavern of the sort that the artist frequented himself. Into this mundane environment, cloaked in mysterious shadow and almost unseen, Christ, identifiable initially only by his indistinct halo, enters from the right. With a commanding gesture that recalls that of the Lord in Michelangelo's *Creation of Adam* on the Sistine Chapel ceiling (FIG. 22-25), he summons Matthew to a higher calling. The astonished tax collector, whose face is highlighted for the viewer by the beam of light emanating from an unspecified source above the head of Christ and outside the picture, points to himself in disbelief: "Can it be I that you call?" he seems to say. Never before had this New Testament theme been rendered in such a fashion, and its worldly, genre quality, regarded as irreverent by many, caused the church to refuse the work at first.

Caravaggio's unorthodox realism finds full orchestration in his *Death of the Virgin* (FIG. **24-26**), which was also refused by the clergy—but, on the recommendation of the great Flemish painter Peter Paul Rubens, was purchased by the duke of Mantua for his own collection. The painting, which depicts the disciples and friends of Christ mourning over the dead Virgin Mary, was meant to serve as an altarpiece for Santa Maria della Scala in Rome. In Caravaggio's unique

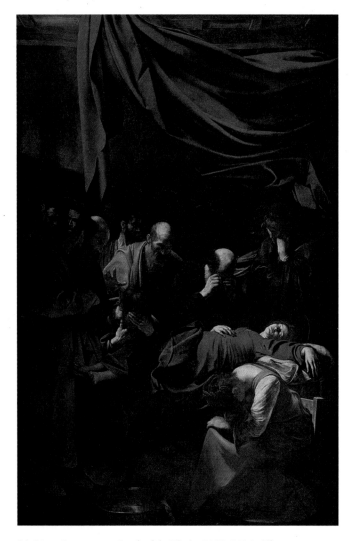

24-26   CARAVAGGIO, *Death of the Virgin,* 1605–1606. Oil on canvas, approx. 12′ × 8′. Louvre, Paris.

realization of the theme, the Virgin is unceremoniously laid out in the awkward stiffness of death, her body swollen, limbs uncomposed, and feet uncovered (the last feature considered indecent at the time). Contemporaries complained that Caravaggio had used as his model for the mother of Christ the corpse of a young woman who had drowned. Around the dead woman, in attitudes of genuine if uncouth grief, without rhetoric or declamation, Caravaggio portrays the customary plebeian types that he usually casts in his pictorial dramas of reality. The drawn curtain emphasizes the stagelike setting into which the grouping of figures invites the viewer as participant. The harsh light plunges into the space from a single source, shattering the darks into broken areas of illumination that reveal the coarse materialities of the scene. But, again (as in the *Conversion of St. Paul* and the *Calling of St. Matthew,* although in a different way), we can read the artist's interpretation not as diminishing the spiritual import of the theme but rather as informing it with a simple, honest, unadorned piety that is entirely sincere—the very piety that moves the humble watchers of the dead to tears.

DOMENICHINO AND GENTILESCHI   One would think that Annibale and Lodovico Carracci and their colleagues at the Bolognese academy would have carefully avoided the dangerous art of Caravaggio. To the contrary, many borrowed from it (some more than others), unconsciously integrating it into the tradition and into their own work. The *Last Communion of St. Jerome* (FIG. **24-27**) is a painting so typical of the Catholic Baroque—so expressive of the Counter-Reformation and its ideals—that we can hardly find its equal as a document of the times. The artist is another Bolognese disciple, DOMENICO ZAMPIERI, called DOMENICHINO (1581–1641). In a Renaissance loggia that opens into a Venetian landscape background, Saint Jerome, propped up to receive the Eucharist, is surrounded by sorrowing friends. The realism of Caravaggio stamps the old man's sagging features, his weakened, once-rugged body, and the faces of at least three of his attendants and of the grave old priest. The sharpened darks and lights are also out of Caravaggio; the general composition, the architecture, the floating putti, and the turbaned spectator echo Titian, Correggio, and the mood of the High Renaissance. A painting like this would seem to be, of necessity, an academic pastiche, but all of its borrowed elements are synthesized successfully in a rare, effective unity. Domenichino's *St. Jerome* is a successful "school" picture, nourished as it is by all the sources, traditional and contemporary, available to him.

We already have mentioned the spread of Caravaggio's style outside Italy. Of course, he had many followers within its borders also, and they were artists more directly in tune with his message than eclectics like Domenichino. One of the best is ARTEMISIA GENTILESCHI (c. 1593–1653).

Gentileschi was instructed by her artist father, Orazio, who was himself strongly influenced by Caravaggio. Her successful career, pursued in Florence, Venice, Naples, and Rome, helped to propagate Caravaggio's manner throughout the peninsula.

In her *Judith and Maidservant with the Head of Holofernes* (FIG. **24-28**), we find the tenebrism and what might be called the "dark" subject matter favored by the "Caravaggisti," the painters of "night pictures." The heroism of Judith, often a subject in Italian painting and sculpture, is depicted here. The story, which is told in an Apocryphal work of the Old Testament, the Book of Judith, relates the delivery of Israel from its enemy, Holofernes. Having succumbed to the charms of Judith, Holofernes invites her to his tent for the night. When he has fallen

24-28   ARTEMISIA GENTILESCHI, *Judith and Maidservant with the Head of Holofernes, c.* 1625. Oil on canvas, approx. 6' × 4' 8". Detroit Institute of the Arts (gift of Leslie H. Green).

asleep, Judith cuts off his head. Here, the act performed, her maidservant is putting the severed head in a sack, but the tension is not yet relaxed, for the two daring women must now face another danger—their escape from the enemy camp. The action takes place in a curtained, oppressively closed space. The atmosphere of menace and horror is thickened by the heavy darks, scarcely relieved by the feeble candle, the sole source of light. Yet the light falls on the courtly splendor of the women's raiment and exhibits forms and characters intended by the artist to be convincingly real. The light is interrupted dramatically by Judith's hand, which casts a shadow on her face. This device is a favorite of the "night painters": a single source of illumination within the painting—partly or wholly concealed by an object in front of it or, as in this case, intercepted by an object—casting an abrupt shadow. The effect is like opening the shutter of a lantern for a brief moment in a pitch-black cellar where unspeakable things are happening.

24-27   DOMENICHINO, *Last Communion of St. Jerome,* 1614. Oil on canvas, approx. 13' 9" × 8' 5". Vatican Museums, Rome.

LANDSCAPE   The Carracci and Caravaggio powerfully influenced the art of figure painting for two centuries,

24-29 ANNIBALE CARRACCI, *Flight into Egypt*, 1603–1604. Oil on canvas, approx. 4′ × 7′ 6″. Galleria Doria Pamphili, Rome.

but the Carracci largely determined the dominant course taken by landscape painting over the same period. In his *Flight into Egypt* (FIG. **24-29**), Annibale Carracci created the "ideal" or "Classical" landscape. Adopted and developed in France by Nicolas Poussin (FIG. 24-60) and Claude Lorrain (FIG. 24-61), this kind of landscape would come to prevail as the accepted pictorial representation of nature ordered by Divine law and human reason. The roots of the style are in the landscape backgrounds of Venetian paintings of the Renaissance (compare FIGS. 24-29 and 22-58). Tranquil hills and fields, quietly gliding streams, serene skies, unruffled foliage, shepherds with their flocks—all the props of the pastoral scene and mood—expand to fill the picture space. They are introduced regularly by a screen of trees in the foreground, dark against the even light of the sky. Attenuated streams or terraces, carefully placed one above the other, make a compositional direction left or right through the terrain. In the middle ground, many landscape artists place compositions of architecture (as in Annibale's *Flight into Egypt*)—walled towns or citadels, towers, temples, monumental tombs, villas—the constructed environment of idealized antiquity and the idyllic life, undisturbed by the passions. The subjects are drawn from religious or heroic story; here, Mary, with the Christ Child, and Saint Joseph wend their slow way to Egypt, after having been ferried across a stream (Matthew 2:13–14). The figures shrink in scale and importance, relative to the landscape,

and are sometimes simply its excuse. Now, in the seventeenth century, landscape comes fully into its own as a major subject for the painter.

But there are landscape types other than the Classical during the seventeenth century. A landscape by SALVATOR ROSA (1615–1673), *St. John the Baptist in the Wilderness* (FIG. **24-30**), contrasts dramatically with Carracci's *Flight into Egypt*. Rosa's painting also has a sacred theme, and the figures in it are subordinate to the landscape, but the two paintings obviously have nothing else in common. Instead of the calm of idealized nature in Annibale's landscape, in Rosa's we have nature in a violent mood, a savage wilderness abandoned by Heaven. A ragged tree, blasted by generations of thunderbolts, writhes before a chaos of barren rocks. For Rosa, nature appears malevolent, the home only of wild beasts, of holy or of desperate men. The broken surfaces, jagged contours, and harsh textures in confused arrangement here should be compared with the smooth volumes and contours and regular placement of forms that characterize the Classical landscape. The alternative style of Rosa will exercise a great deal of influence on the next century's taste for the "picturesque"—sublime and awesome scenes, filled with terror and foreboding, which will indulge the Romantic temperament and fuel its enthusiasm.

PERSPECTIVE ILLUSIONISM   The development of landscape painting was contemporary with that of ceiling painting, the latter form being stimulated anew by the large, new churches of Baroque Rome. The problems associated with ceiling painting are, of course, special. Looking *up* at a painting is different from simply looking *at* a painting. The experience of looking at what is above us carries with it an element of awe, particularly when we are viewing something located at considerable height. Guercino recognized this when he painted his *Aurora* (FIG. 24-23), but Guido Reni apparently did not. In his *Aurora* fresco (FIG. 24-22), he either did not realize the special power of ceiling painting or perhaps preferred or was required to use the quadro riportato method. The Baroque artist found a ceiling surface high above the ground a natural field for the projection of visual illusion. The devout Christian, thinking of Heaven as "up," must be overwhelmed with emotion when, looking up, he sees its image before his eyes. In the Sistine Chapel ceiling (FIG. 22-24), Michelangelo made no attempt to project an image of the skies opening into Heaven; rather, he represented an epic narrative of events of no physical place or time that could be read almost as well from walls as from ceilings. The *illusion* of bodies actually soaring

above was of no interest to him; the truth of certain events in the history of Genesis was, and these events and figures could be shut off in their own compartments, self-contained.

A Baroque master of ceiling decoration like FRA ANDREA POZZO (1642–1709) takes an entirely different approach. A lay brother of the Jesuit order and a master of perspective, on which he wrote an influential treatise, Pozzo designed and executed the vast ceiling fresco depicting the *Glorification of St. Ignatius* (FIG. **24-31**) for the church of Sant'Ignazio in Rome. This fresco is indeed the culmination of the *di sotto in sù* experiments of Mantegna (FIG. 21-61) and Correggio (FIG. 22-36). The artist intends to create the illusion that Heaven is opening up above the heads of the congregation—indeed, of the very congregation that fills this church of Sant'Ignazio. For, in painted illusion, Pozzo continues the actual architecture of the church into the vault, so that the roof seems to be lifted off, as Heaven and earth commingle and Saint Ignatius is carried to the waiting Christ in the presence of figures personifying the four corners of the world. A metal plate in the nave floor marks the

24-30 SALVATOR ROSA, *St. John the Baptist in the Wilderness, c.* 1640. Oil on canvas, approx. 5′ 8″ × 8′ 6″. Art Gallery and Museum, Glasgow.

24-31   FRA ANDREA POZZO, *Glorification of St. Ignatius*, 1691–1694. Ceiling fresco in the nave of Sant'Ignazio, Rome.

standpoint for the whole perspective illusion. Looking up from this point, the observer takes in the celestial-terrestrial scene as one, for in Pozzo's design the two are meant to fuse without the interruption of a boundary. To achieve his visionary effects, the artist employs all means offered by architecture, sculpture, and painting and unites them in a fusion that surpasses even the Gothic effects of total integration.

Sound, as well as light, is a vehicle of ecstasy and vision in the Baroque experience. We know that churches were designed with acoustical effect in mind, and, in a Baroque church filled with Baroque music, the power of both light and sound would be vastly augmented. Through simultaneous stimulation of both the visual and auditory senses, the faithful might be transported into a trancelike state that would, indeed, in the words of Milton, "bring all Heaven before [their] eyes." But this transport always would have to be effected by physical means; although the devout in the Middle Ages were able to find the vision within, in the Baroque period they demanded that that mystery be made visible to the outward sight. To be credible, Heaven must more and more visually resemble the domain of earth. Dante could see Heaven in a dream, but Pozzo wanted to see it unfold above him while he was awake and walking

in a church. Medieval humanity aspired to Heaven; Baroque humanity wanted Heaven to come down to their station, where they might see it, or even inspect it. Optical vision is the supreme faculty in seventeenth-century art and science.

SPAIN

In Spain, as in the other countries of Europe, Italianate Mannerism was adopted in the sixteenth century and cast off in the Baroque period. But along with Mannerism, Spain seemed to reject most of what the Italian Renaissance stood for, just as it would reject, for a long time, the scientific revolution and the Enlightenment. Although centrally involved in the political affairs of Europe, the Spanish cultivated in character and custom a proud, "quixotic" isolationism.

Painting

In the art of El Greco (FIG. 23-28), we have seen the mystical side of the Spanish character. The hard, unsentimental realism that is the other side appears in the painting of JOSÉ DE RIBERA (c. 1588–1652), who, because he emigrated to Naples as a young man and settled there, is sometimes called by his Italian nickname, Lo Spagnoletto, "the little Spaniard." The realism of his style, a mixture of a native Spanish strain and the "dark manner" of Caravaggio, gives shock value to Ribera's often brutal themes, which express at once the harsh times of the Counter-Reformation and a Spanish taste for the representation of courageous resistance to pain. His *Martyrdom of St. Bartholomew* (FIG. **24-32**) is grim and dark in subject and form. Saint Bartholomew, who suffered the torture of being skinned alive, is being hoisted into position by his executioners. The saint's rough, heavy body and swarthy, plebeian features express a kinship between him and his tormentors, who are members of the same cast of characters we found in the painting of Caravaggio and the Neapolitan school he so strongly influenced. In this painting, Ribera scorns idealization of any kind, and we have the uncomfortable feeling that he is recording rather than imagining the grueling scene. In an age of merciless religious fanaticism, torture, as a means of saving stubborn souls, was a common and public spectacle.

FRANCISCO DE ZURBARÁN (1598–1664) softens realism with an admixture of the mystical. His principal subjects are austere saints, represented singly in devotional attitudes and usually sharply lighted from the side. He shows us *St. Francis in Meditation* (FIG. **24-33**), his uplifted face almost completely shadowed by his cowl, clutching a skull to his body. The skull is the *memento mori,* a constant reminder to the contemplative individual of his own mortality. The bare, unfurnished setting and the stark light and somber dark are the bleak environment of this entranced soul. We

24-33 FRANCISCO DE ZURBARÁN, *St. Francis in Meditation, c.* 1639. Oil on canvas, approx. 60" × 30". National Gallery, London. Reproduced by courtesy of the Trustees.

see enough to read this as an image of rapt meditation—the parted lips, the tensely locked fingers, the rigid attitude of a devotee utterly unaware of his surroundings and mystically in contact with God. Here, Zurbarán gives us a personification of the fierce devotion of Catholic Spain.

VELÁZQUEZ In the Baroque age, visions and the visual go together. DIEGO VELÁZQUEZ (1599–1660), an artist who set aside visions in the interest of what is given to the eye in the optical world, stands among the great masters of visual realism. Although he painted religious pictures, he shunned idealism or high-flown rhetoric, and his sacred subjects are bluntly real. Velázquez, who trained in Seville, as a young man came to the attention of King Philip IV, and became the court painter at Madrid, where, save for two extended trips to Italy and a few excursions, he remained for the rest of his life. His close personal relationship with Philip and his high office of marshal of the palace gave him prestige and a rare

24-32 JOSÉ DE RIBERA, *Martyrdom of St. Bartholomew, c.* 1639. Oil on canvas, approx. 92" × 92". Museo del Prado, Madrid.

24-34   DIEGO VELÁZQUEZ, *Los Borrachos, c.* 1628. Oil on canvas, approx. 5' 6" × 7' 6". Museo del Prado, Madrid.

opportunity to fulfill the promise of his genius with a variety of artistic assignments.

In an early work, *Los Borrachos,* The Drinkers (FIG. **24-34**), Velázquez shows his cool independence of the ideals of Renaissance and Baroque Italy in a native naturalism that has the strength and something of the look of Caravaggio. Commissioned to paint Bacchus among his followers, presenting them with the liberating gift of wine, Velázquez seems to mock Classical conventions in both theme and form. He burlesques the stately, Classical Bacchic scenes, making the god a mischievous young *bravo,* stripped to the waist, crowning a wobbly tippler who kneels before him. (Caravaggio had painted a similar, although half-length and more elegant, *Bacchus* around 1595—a painting considered by many to be a self-portrait in mythological guise.) The rest of the company is of the same type: weather-beaten, shabby roisters of the tavern crowd, who grin and jape at the event uncouthly, enjoying the game for what it is. Painting the crude figures in strong light and dark that is evenly distributed so as not to obscure them, Velázquez makes sharp characterizations of each person, showing not only his instinct for portraiture but a Baroque interest in human "types." And, typically Spanish, he caricatures, through realism, an Italianate subject that ordinarily would be idealized. Enrique Lafuente, a twentieth-century critic, states the Spanish attitude, as he perceives it:

Spain refuses to accept the basic ideas which inspire the Italian Renaissance because they are repugnant to its sense of the life of the Spanish man. The Spaniard knows that reality is not Idea, but Life. . . . The supreme value of life is linked with experience and the moral values that are based on personality. Idea, beauty, formal perfection are abstractions and nothing more. Art, in its turn, is bound to concern itself with realities and not with dreams.*

To Velázquez, as to many Spanish artists, the academic styles of Baroque Italy must have seemed pretentious and insincere, not to say pagan. He turned away from them to concentrate instead on the world before his eyes.

One could hardly find in art a better example of Lafuente's dictum that "reality is not Idea, but Life" than Velázquez's portrait of *Juan de Pareja* (FIG. **24-35**). At the height of his powers, Velázquez painted his assistant when they were in Rome together in 1650. He was intending to paint a portrait of Pope Innocent X, a patron of Bernini, and he did the study of Pareja as a kind of trial run. The work was exhibited in the Pantheon and drew the admiration of the many artists in Rome, Italian and foreign alike. They perceived in it an almost incredible knowledge of the structure of appearance, a matchless technique of execution,

*Enrique Lafuente, *Velázquez* (New York: Oxford University Press, 1943), p. 6.

and an eloquent simplicity of composition that rejected conventional Baroque props and rhetoric. The apparent simplicity of the formal means matches the simplicity of presentation. Placed before an entirely neutral ground, Pareja looks directly at us with a calm dignity and quiet pride, a man perfectly self-contained. His character gives him a natural poise, utterly without arrogance or affectation. His level gaze, the easy gesture of arm and hand, and his erect carriage place him directly in front of us, and Velázquez introduces him.

Most of Velázquez's portraits are of members of the Spanish nobility or of attendants of the royal family, and even the artist's likeness of *Juan de Pareja* was conceived as a preparatory study for a papal portrait. Much rarer are Velázquez's portraits of ordinary people, especially if the sitter was a woman, but one of these, *Woman with a Fan* (FIG. **24-36**), painted before Velázquez's departure for Rome, is among the artist's finest portraits. The woman has never been identified (some have suggested that she is Velázquez's wife or daughter), but the date of the painting is secure. In April 1639 a royal decree concerning dress codes was published and it forbade women (other than licensed prostitutes) from wearing, among other things, just the sort of low-cut French-inspired bodice that Velázquez's *Woman with a Fan* displays in this portrait. She also wears a dark veil and gloves and, in addition to the fan,

24-36 DIEGO VELÁZQUEZ, *Woman with a Fan*, 1638–1639. Oil on canvas, 37¼" × 27½". Wallace Collection, London.

24-35 DIEGO VELÁZQUEZ, *Juan de Pareja*, 1649–1650. Oil on canvas, approx. 33" × 28". Metropolitan Museum of Art, New York.

her attributes include a golden rosary chain and a blue ribbon from which a religious medal hangs. In this sensitive and informal portrait set against a neutral ground, Velázquez has here achieved a difficult and delicate balance between sensual beauty and fashionable dress on the one hand, and modesty and religious piety on the other.

Velázquez's uncanny power of penetration of the form and meaning before him, though in some ways unique, was not entirely untaught. He had studied the works of other artists carefully and was fully aware of the achievements of the great masters like Michelangelo and the Venetians. He knew the latter from the king's collections, of which he had charge, and he also studied them in Italy, where he journeyed at the suggestion of Peter Paul Rubens, whom he met when the older Rubens was copying the Venetians in the collections at the Madrid court. His studies in Italy did not make a "Romanist" of Velázquez, however. Their most notable effects were a softening of his earlier, somewhat heavy-handed realism (seen in *Los Borrachos*) and a lighter palette, which gave his paintings brighter and subtler tonality.

Velázquez's greatest masterpiece, *Las Meninas*, The Maids-in-waiting (FIG. **24-37**), was painted after his return to Spain from Rome. In it Velázquez shows himself to be the master of a brilliant optical realism that seldom has been approached and never has been surpassed. The painter represents himself in his studio standing before a large canvas, on which he may be painting this very picture or, perhaps, the portraits of King Philip and Queen Mariana, whose reflections appear in the mirror on the far wall. The little Infanta, Margarita, appears in the foreground with her two maids-in-waiting, her favorite dwarfs, and a large dog. In the middle ground are a duenna and a male escort; in the background, a gentleman is framed in a brightly lit open doorway. The personages present have been identified, though we need not enumerate them here. What is worthy of note is the way Velázquez has extended the pictorial depth of his composition in both directions; the open doorway and its ascending staircase lead the eye beyond the artist's studio, and the device of the mirror and the outward glances of several of the figures serve to incorporate the space in which the viewer stands into the picture as well. (Compare the way the mirror in Jan van Eyck's *Giovanni Arnolfini and His Bride* [FIG. 20-8] also incorporates the area in front of the canvas into the picture, although less obviously and without a comparable extension of space beyond the rear wall of the room.)

On the wall above the doorway and mirror in *Las Meninas*, two faintly recognizable pictures represent the immortal gods as the source of art. There is thus a duality of theme in the Velázquez painting: it is both an informal family group, seemingly casually arranged and miraculously lifelike, and it is a genre painting—"A Visit to the Artist's Studio" would be an equally apt title. As first painter to the king and as chief steward of the palace, Velázquez was conscious not only of the importance of his court office but of the honor and dignity belonging to his profession as a painter. In this painting, he appears to bring the roles together, asserting their equivalent value. A number of pictures from the seventeenth century show painters with their royal patrons, for painters of the time continually sought to aggrandize their profession among the arts and to achieve by it appropriate rank and respect. Throughout his career, Velázquez hoped to be ennobled by royal appointment to membership in the ancient and illustrious Order of Santiago, from which, he must have expected, his profession as painter would not disqualify him. Because some of the required patents of nobility were lacking in his background, he achieved this only with difficulty at the very end of his life, and then only through a dispensation from the pope. In the painting, he wears the red cross of the order on his doublet, painted there, legend tells us, by the king himself; the truth is that the artist painted it. In Velázquez's mind, *Las Meninas* might have embodied the idea of the great king visiting his studio, as Alexander the Great visited the studio of the painter Apelles in ancient times. We now know that the room represented in the painting was in the palace of the Alcázar in Madrid. After the death of Prince Baltasar Carlos in 1646, his chambers were partly converted into a studio for Velázquez. *Las Meninas* was designed to hang in the personal office of King Philip, in another part of the palace. It was intended for the king as private viewer and was not to be displayed in a gallery for a general audience. The figures in the painting all acknowledge the royal presence. Placed among them in equal dignity is Velázquez, face-to-face with his sovereign. The art of painting, in the person of the painter, is elevated to the highest status. Velázquez sought ennoblement not for himself alone, but for his art.

Although Velázquez intends an optical report of the event, authentic in every detail, he also seems to intend a pictorial summary of the various kinds of images in their different levels and degrees of reality—the reality of canvas image, of mirror image, of optical image, and of the two imaged paintings. This work—with its cunning contrasts of mirrored spaces, "real" spaces, picture spaces, and pictures within pictures—itself appears to have been taken from a large mirror reflecting the whole scene, which would mean the artist has not painted the princess and her suite, but himself in the process of painting them. In the Baroque period, when artists were taking Leonardo's dictum that "the mirror is our master" very seriously, it is not surprising to find mirrors and primitive cameralike devices used to achieve optimum visual fidelity in painting. *Las Meninas* is a pictorial summary as well as a commentary on the essential mystery of the visual world and on the ambiguity that results when we confuse its different states or levels.

How does Velázquez achieve this stunning illusion? He opens the spectrum of light and the tones that compose it. Instead of putting lights abruptly beside darks, as Caravaggio, Ribera, and Zurbarán would do or as he himself had done in earlier works like *Los Borrachos* (FIG. 24-34), Velázquez allows a great number of intermediate values of gray to come between the two extremes. Thus, he carefully observes and records the subtle gradations of tone, matching with graded glazes what he sees in the visible spread of light and dark, using strokes of deep dark and touches of highlight to enliven the neutral tones in the middle of the value scale. This essentially cool, middle register of tones is what gives the marvelous effect of daylight and atmosphere to the painting. Velázquez's matching of tonal gradations approaches effects that the age of the photograph later will discover. His method is an extreme refinement of Titian's. Velázquez does not think of figures as first drawn, then modeled into sculptural effects, and then colored. He thinks of light and tone as the whole substance of painting—the solid forms being only *suggested*, never really constructed. Observing this reduction of the solid world to purely optical sensations in a floating,

24-37 DIEGO VELÁZQUEZ, *Las Meninas*, 1656. Oil on canvas, approx. 10′ 5″ × 9′. Museo del Prado, Madrid.

fugitive skein of color tones, one could say that the old, sculpturesque form has disappeared. The extreme thinness of Velázquez's paint and the light, almost accidental touches of thick pigment here and there destroy all visible structure; we examine his canvas closely, and everything dissolves to a random flow of paint. As a wondering Italian painter exclaimed of a Velázquez painting, "It is made of nothing, but there it is!" And viewing *Las Meninas,* the artist's biographer, Palamino, exclaimed, "It is truth, not painting!" Painters three hundred years later will realize that Velázquez's optical realism constitutes a limit. Their attempts to analyze it and to take it further will lead in an opposite direction to the one taken by the great Spanish master—to the abstract art of our own time.

FLANDERS

In the sixteenth century, the Netherlands came under the crown of Hapsburg Spain when the emperor Charles V retired, leaving the Spanish throne and his Netherlandish provinces to his only son, Philip II. Philip's repressive measures against the Protestants led the northern provinces to break away from Spain and to set up the Dutch republic under the House of Orange. The southern provinces remained with Spain, and their official religion continued to be Catholic. The political distinction between modern Holland and Belgium more or less reflects this original separation, which, in the Baroque period, signalized not only religious but also artistic differences. The Baroque art of Flanders (the Spanish Netherlands) remained in close contact with the Baroque art of the Catholic countries, while the Dutch schools of painting developed their own subjects and styles, consonant with their reformed religion and the new political, social, and economic structure of the middle-class Dutch republic.

Painting

RUBENS   The brilliant Flemish master PETER PAUL RUBENS (1577–1640) preceded Bernini in the development and dissemination of the Baroque style. The influence of Rubens was international; he drew together the main contributions of the masters of the Renaissance (Michelangelo and Titian) and of the Baroque (the Carracci and Caravaggio) to synthesize in his own style the first truly European manner. Thus, Rubens completes the work begun by Albrecht Dürer in the previous century. The art of Rubens, even though it is the consequence of his wide study of many masters, is no weak eclecticism but an original and powerful synthesis. From the beginning, his instinct was to break away from the provincialism of the old Flemish Mannerists and to seek new ideas and methods abroad.

His aristocratic education, his courtier's manner, diplomacy, and tact, as well as his Classical learning made him the associate of princes and scholars. He became court painter to the dukes of Mantua (descended from the patrons of Mantegna), friend of the king of Spain and his adviser on art collecting, painter to Charles I of England and Marie de' Medici, queen of France, and permanent court painter to the Spanish governors of Flanders. Rubens also won the confidence of his royal patrons in matters of state, and he often was entrusted with diplomatic missions of the highest importance. In the practice of his art, he was assisted by scores of associates and apprentices, turning out large numbers of paintings for an international clientele. In addition, he functioned as an art dealer, buying and selling works of contemporary art and Classical antiquities. His numerous enterprises made him a rich man, with a magnificent town house and a chateau in the countryside. Wealth and honors, however, did not spoil his amiable, sober, self-disciplined character. We have in Rubens, as in Raphael, the image of the successful, renowned artist, the consort of kings, and the shrewd man of the world, who is at the same time the balanced philosopher. Rubens more than makes good the Renaissance claim for the preeminence of the artist in society.

Rubens became a master in 1598 and went to Italy two years later, where he remained until 1608. During these years, he formulated the foundations of his style. Shortly after his return from Italy, he painted for Antwerp Cathedral the *Elevation of the Cross,* a triptych of which we reproduce the central panel (FIG. **24-38**). This work shows the result of his long study of Italian art, especially of Michelangelo, Tintoretto, and Caravaggio. The scene is a focus of tremendous straining forces and counterforces, as heavily muscled giants strain to lift the cross. Here, the artist has the opportunity to show foreshortened anatomy and the contortions of violent action—not the bound action of Mannerism, but the tension of strong bodies meeting resistance outside themselves. The body of Christ is a great, illuminated diagonal that cuts dynamically across the picture and, at the same time, inclines back into it. The whole composition seethes with a power that we feel comes from genuine exertion, from elastic human sinew taut with effort. The tension is emotional as well as physical, as reflected not only in Christ's face but also in the features of his followers in the wings of the triptych (not shown). Strong modeling in dark and light, which heightens the drama, marks Rubens's work at this stage of his career; it gradually will give way to a much subtler, coloristic style.

The vigor and passion of Rubens's early manner never leave his painting, although the vitality of his work is modified into less strained and more subtle forms, depending on the theme. Yet Rubens has one general theme—the human body, draped or undraped, male or female, freely acting or free to act in an environment of physical forces and other interacting bodies. Rubens's conception of the human scene does not contain profoundly tragic elements nor anything manneristically intellectual, enigmatic, or complex. His forte is the strong animal body described in the joyful, exuberant motion natural to it. His *Abduction of the Daughters of Leucippus* (FIG. **24-39**) describes the capture of two young mortal women by the gods Castor and Pollux, who have fallen in love with them. The sensual theme permits departures from realism, especially in the representation of movement and exerted strength. The gods do not labor at the task of sweeping up the massive maidens—descendants of the opulent Venuses of Giorgione (FIG. 22-58) and Titian (FIG. 22-61)—nor do the maidens struggle fiercely. The figures are part of a highly dynamic, yet slowly revolving composition that seems to turn on an axis; they form a diamond-shaped group that defies stability and the logic of

24-38 PETER PAUL RUBENS, *Elevation of the Cross*, 1610. Oil on canvas, 15′ 2″ × 11′ 2″. Cathedral, Antwerp.

statics. The surface pattern, organized by intersecting diagonals and verticals, consists of areas of rich, contrasting textures: the soft luminous flesh of the women, the bronzed tan of the muscular men, lustrous satins, glinting armor, and the taut, shimmering hides of the horses (the reins of which are held by small Cupids, under whose spell the divine cavaliers act). All around this surface pattern, a tight massing of volumes moves in space. The solid forms are no

24-39 ✸ Peter Paul Rubens, *Abduction of the Daughters of Leucippus,* 1617. Oil on canvas, approx. 7′ 3″ × 6′ 10″. Alte Pinakothek, Munich.

longer described simply in terms of the dark-light values of Florentine draftsmanship but are now built up in color and defined by light, as in Venetian painting.

The impact of Rubens's hunting pictures lies in their depiction of ferocious action and vitality. In the *Lion Hunt* (FIG. **24-40**), a cornered lion, three lances meeting in its body, tears a Berber hunter from his horse. A fallen man still grips his sword, while another, in a reversed position, stabs at a snarling cat. Horsemen plunge in and out of the picture space, and the falling Berber makes a powerful, diagonal cut across the canvas—a compositional device that we have already seen Rubens use with great success in his *Elevation of the Cross* (FIG. 24-38). The wild melee of thrusting, hacking, rearing, and plunging is almost an allegory of the confined tensions of Mannerism exploding into the extravagant activity that characterized the Baroque.

Rubens shared heartily in the Baroque love of magnificent pomp, especially as it set off the majesty of royalty, in which Rubens, born courtier that he was, heartily believed. The Baroque age saw endless, extravagant pageants and festivals produced whenever the great or even lesser dynasts moved. Their authority and right to rule were for-

ever being demonstrated by lavish display. We have seen that the popes themselves, the princes of the Church, made of St. Peter's a permanently festive monument to papal supremacy. And Marie de' Medici, a member of the famous Florentine house, commissioned Rubens to paint a cycle memorializing and glorifying her career and that of her late husband, the first of the Bourbon kings, Henry IV. Between 1622 and 1626, Rubens, working with amazing creative energy, produced by his own hand twenty-one huge historical-allegorical pictures, designed to hang in the queen's new palace, the Luxembourg, in Paris.

Perhaps the most vivacious and dexterously composed of the series is the *Arrival of Marie de' Medici at Marseilles* (FIG. **24-41**); it can be taken as exemplary of the mood and style of the others. Marie has arrived in France after the sea voyage from Italy. Surrounded by her splendid ladies, she is welcomed by an allegory of France, a figure draped in the fleur-de-lis. The sea and sky rejoice at her safe arrival; Neptune and the Nereids salute her, and a winged, trumpeting Fame swoops overhead. Conspicuous in the opulently carved stern-castle of the Baroque galley, under the coat of arms of the Medici, stands the imperious

24-40   PETER PAUL RUBENS, *Lion Hunt,* 1617–1618. Oil on canvas, approx. 8′ 2″ × 12′ 5″. Alte Pinakothek, Munich.

24-41   PETER PAUL RUBENS, *Arrival of Marie de' Medici at Marseilles*, 1622–1625. Oil on canvas, approx. 5′ 1″ × 3′ 9¹/₂″. Louvre, Paris.

commander of the vessel. In black and silver, his figure makes a sharp accent in the midst of the swirling tonality of ivory, gold, and red. He wears the cross of a Knight of Malta, which may identify this as a ship belonging to that order. The only immobile figure in the composition, he could be director of and witness to the boisterous ceremonies. Broad and florid compliments, in which Heaven and Earth join, are standard in Baroque pageantry, where honor is done to royalty. (We already have met the collaboration of the celestial and earthly spheres in the glorification of religious themes in Italian Baroque art.) The artist enriches his surfaces here with a decorative splendor that pulls the whole composition together, and the audacious vigor that customarily enlivens Rubens's figures, beginning with the monumental, twisting sea creatures, vibrates through the entire design.

Rubens's imposing, dynamic figure compositions were not his only achievement; he also produced rich landscapes and perceptive portraits. His portrait of *Thomas Howard, Earl of Arundel* (FIG. **24-42**) is a painting of singular power. This great English nobleman played a leading role in the complicated diplomacy and statecraft of the age of Charles I,

when England was on the verge of a tragic civil war between the Stuart king and Parliament. Arundel is best remembered, however, as a lover of art, who built a collection of ancient statuary and other works of art unsurpassed in the Europe of his time. Rubens was a friend of Arundel and an admirer of his taste and learning. The artist's admiration for the man himself, regarded by contemporaries as the bringer of "true virtu"—knightly gallantry and magnanimity—to England, is clearly expressed in the portrait. The earl is posed in an attitude of regal majesty. He directs a sharp, stern, haughty glance over his shoulder, creating instant distance between *his* rank and that of the observer. The look given by the aquiline features is that of a commander of armies silencing a subordinate; it is full of an authority not to be questioned. Rubens gives us not the sensitive lover of art but the fearless captain. We realize that the earl himself must have stipulated that this aspect of his character and career be shown. To this end, Rubens has garbed him in magnificent ceremonial armor. His gauntleted hand rests on the commander's staff; his plumed helmet sits on a table at his side. Behind him, a curtain is drawn aside, revealing a severe Classical monument, probably a triumphal arch, a fitting backdrop for the portrait of the fearless conqueror. Rubens lavishes all of his rich resources

24-42   PETER PAUL RUBENS, *Thomas Howard, Earl of Arundel,* c. 1630. Oil on canvas, approx. 4′ 6″ × 3′ 9″. Isabella Stewart Gardner Museum, Boston.

of color tone in the rendering of the splendid accoutrements of high rank and latter-day chivalry. This imperious image speaks for an autocratic age—for the great dynasts of the Baroque, whom Rubens knew well and who were his patrons.

VAN DYCK   Most of Rubens's successors in Flanders had been his assistants. The most famous, ANTHONY VAN DYCK (1599–1641), probably worked with his master on the canvas of the *Abduction of the Daughters of Leucippus* (FIG. 24-39). Quite early, the younger man, unwilling to be overshadowed by the undisputed stature of Rubens, left his native Antwerp for Genoa and then London, where he became court portraitist to Charles I. Although Van Dyck created dramatic compositions of high quality, his specialty became the portrait, and he developed a courtly manner of great elegance that would be influential internationally. His style is felt in English portrait painting into the nineteenth century. In one of his finest works, *Charles I Dismounted* (FIG. **24-43**), he shows the ill-fated Stuart king standing in a Venetian landscape (with the river Thames in the background), attended by an equerry and a page. Although the king impersonates a nobleman out for a casual ride in

24-43 ANTHONY VAN DYCK, *Charles I Dismounted, c.* 1635. Oil on canvas, approx. 9' × 7'. Louvre, Paris.

his park, no one can mistake the regal poise and the air of absolute authority that his Parliament resented and was soon to rise against. Here, in a pose reminiscent of Rubens's *Earl of Arundel,* King Charles turns his back on his attendants as he surveys his domain. The composition is exceedingly artful in the placement of the king. He stands off-center, but balances the picture with a single keen glance at the observer. The full-length portraits by Titian and the cool composure of the Mannerists both contribute to Van Dyck's sense of pose and arrangement of detail. For centuries to come, artists who make portraits of the great—Thomas Gainsborough, Joshua Reynolds, and John Singer Sargent, among them—will keep Van Dyck very much in mind.

HOLLAND

For all intents and purposes, the style of Peter Paul Rubens is the style of Baroque Flanders; he had few rivals of significance and held a monopoly on commissions. The situation is so completely different in Holland that it is difficult to imagine how, within such a tiny area, two such opposite artistic cultures could flourish. The Dutch Protestants and the Flemish Catholics went their separate ways after the later sixteenth century. Although closer in outlook to the Germans, the Dutch were ethnically the same as the Flemish, who were, in turn, closer in viewpoint to their neighbors to the south—the French. A Catholic, aristocratic, and traditional culture reigned in the Flanders of Rubens. In Holland, severe Calvinistic Protestantism was puritanical toward religious art, sculptural or pictorial, although many of the Dutch were Catholics, including a number of painters. The churches were swept clean of images, and any recollection of the pagan myths, the material of Classicism, or even historical subjects, was proscribed in art.

During the Middle Ages and the Renaissance, religious subjects and, later, Classical and historical subjects had been the major stimuli for artistic activity. Divested of these sources, what remained to enrich the lives of wealthy Hollanders? For they *were* wealthy! During the early part of Spanish rule, the Dutch, like the Flemish, prospered. The East India Company was formed, and the discovery of the New World opened up further opportunities for trade and colonization. The wars of independence from Spain made Holland the major maritime country of Europe; its closest rival was England, another Protestant power in the times of the Spanish decline. The great Dutch commercial cities, such as Haarlem and Amsterdam, had been stimulated and enriched, and civic pride was strong. Although it was not internationally recognized until the Peace of Westphalia in 1648, Holland in fact had been independent from Spain since about 1580 and was extremely proud of its hard-won freedom.

Painting

We have followed the secularization and humanization of religious art since the thirteenth century. In the Dutch school of the seventeenth century, the process is completed. A thousand years and more of religious iconography are dismissed by a European people who ask for a view of the world from which angels, saints, and deities have been banished. The old Netherlandish realism remains, but it no longer serves religious purposes. The Dutch artists rise to the occasion, matching the open, competitive, Dutch society, which is thoroughly middle-class, with an equally open arrangement of their own, in which the painter works not for a patron but for the market.

Dutch painters increasingly pried into the pictorial possibilities of everyday life and kept an eye on their customers, the middle-class burghers, who wanted paintings to hang on their walls as evidence of their growing wealth and social position.

Dutch artists become specialists in any one of a number of subjects—genre, landscape, seascape, cattle and horses, table still life, flower still life, interiors, and so on. In short, they paint subjects that they feel will appeal to the public and therefore be marketable. This independence from the patron gives the Dutch painter a certain amount of freedom, even if it is only the freedom to starve on the free-picture market. With respect to the artist-market relationship, the contrast between Flanders and Holland in the seventeenth century is poignantly reflected in the careers of Rubens and Rembrandt. The former *is* the market in Flanders; his genius determines it. The latter, after finding a place in the market, is rejected by it when his genius is no longer marketable.

The realism of Dutch art is made up of the old tradition, which goes back to Hubert and Jan van Eyck, and of the new "realism of light and dark," brought back to Holland by Dutch painters who had studied Caravaggio in Italy. One of these "night painters" (as they were called), GERRIT VAN HONTHORST (1590–1656) of Utrecht, spent several years in Italy absorbing Caravaggio's style. He is best known for merry genre scenes like the *Supper Party* (FIG. **24-44**), in which unidealized human figures are shown in an informal gathering. In this painting, while a musician plays, his companions delight in the scene of a young woman feeding a piece of chicken to a friend whose hands are both occupied; one holds a jug and the other a glass with which to wash down the meat and to clear his mouth for another portion. These canvases owe much to Caravaggio's religious paintings set in taverns (compare the *Calling of St. Matthew*, FIG. 24-25, with the *Supper Party*), and although these Dutch "merry companies," naturalistically rendered in night settings, were popular and widely produced in the Baroque period, they were not necessarily taken simply as pictures of people enjoying themselves. We must remember the Baroque mental habit of allegorizing and symbolizing even the most realistic images. Here, for example, we may be expected to witness the loose companions of the Prodigal Son (Luke 15:13)—panderers and prostitutes, drinking, singing, strumming, laughing. Perhaps, at the same time, we have an allegory of the Five Senses, through which sin can enter the soul: taste, touch, sight, sound, scent. Fascinated by nocturnal effects, van Honthorst fre-

24-44 GERRIT VAN HONTHORST, *Supper Party*, 1620. Oil on canvas, approx. 7′ × 4′ 8″. Galleria degli Uffizi, Florence.

quently places a hidden light source (two, in this case) in his pictures and uses it as a pretext to work with dramatic and violently contrasted dark-light effects. Without the incisive vision of Caravaggio, van Honthorst nevertheless is able to match, and sometimes to surpass, Caravaggio's tenebristic effects.

HALS   The Dutch schools were centered in various cities (Utrecht, Haarlem, Leiden, Amsterdam), but all had in common the lesson of Caravaggio as interpreted by Dutch Caravaggisti like van Honthorst. FRANS HALS (*c.* 1581–1666) was the leading painter of the Haarlem school and one of the great realistic painters of the Western tradition. Hals appropriates what he needs from the new lighting to make portraiture (his specialty) an art of acute psychological perception as well as a kind of comic genre. The way

light floats across the face and meets shadow can be arranged by the artist, as can the pose and the details of costume and facial expression. Hals shows himself to be a master of all the devices open to a portraitist who no longer needs to maintain the distance required by the strictly formal portrait.

The relaxed relationship between the portraitist and his subject is apparent in the engaging portrait of *Willem Coymans* (FIG. **24-45**), dated 1645. Although the subject is a young man of some importance, the artist seems to be taking a great many liberties with his portrait. The young man leans on one arm with a jaunty air of insolence, his hat cocked at a challenging angle. The illusion of life is such that we take cues from the subject's expression as if we were face to face with him. Hals's genius lies in capturing the minute, expressional movements by which we appraise

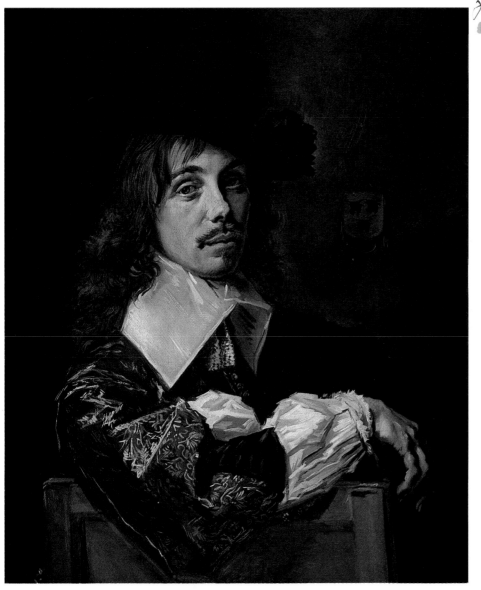

24-45   FRANS HALS, *Willem Coymans,* 1645. Oil on canvas, approx. 30¼″ × 25″. National Gallery of Art, Washington, D.C. (Andrew W. Mellon Collection).

the man across from us in everyday life. Until now, this kind of intimate confrontation rarely had been seen in painting. It is a kind of contradiction of the masks of formal portraiture created in the Renaissance. We are in the presence of an individual without formal introduction; the gap between us and the subject is reduced until we are almost part of his physical and psychological environment. The casualness, immediacy, and intimacy are intensified by the manner in which the painting is executed. The touch of the painter's brush is as light and fleeting as the moment in which the pose is caught; the pose of the figure, the highlights on the sleeve, the reflected lights within face and hand, and the lift of the eyebrow are all the instant prey of time. Thus, the evanescence of time that Bernini caught in his *David* (FIG. 24-8) is recorded far to the north a few years later in a different subject and medium. Both are Baroque.

Frans Hals is a genius of the comic. He had precedents in the gargoylism and grotesquerie of the northern Middle Ages and, in later times, in the works of Hieronymus Bosch and Pieter Bruegel. But Hals's comedy is that of character rather than situation. He shows us people as they are and somewhat less than they are; this puts us at ease, out of superiority, so that we can laugh at others and at ourselves. Hals takes his comic characters, as did Shakespeare, his contemporary, from the lower levels of society.

Good-humored stageplay also brightens Hals's great canvases of units of the Dutch civic guard, which played an important part in the liberation of Holland. The companies of archers and musketeers met on their saints' days in dress uniform for grand banquets, some of which lasted an entire week, prompting an ordinance limiting the celebrations to "three, or at the most four days." These occasions gave Hals the opportunity to attack the problem of adequately representing each subject of a group portrait while retaining action and variety in the composition. Earlier group portraits in the Netherlands represent the sitters as so many jugs on a shelf. Hals undertook to correct this and, in the process, produced dramatic solutions to the problem, like that found in his *Archers of St. Hadrian* (FIG. **24-46**). Here, each man is both a member of the troop and an individual with a distinct personality as well as physiognomy. Some engage us directly, others look away or at a companion; where one is stern, another may be animated. As a stage director, Hals has few equals. In quite Baroque fashion, he balances direction of glance, pose, and gesture, making compositional devices of the white ruffs, broad-brimmed hats, and banners. Although the instantaneous effect—the preservation of every detail and facial expression—is, of course, the result of careful planning, Hals's vivacious brush seems to have moved spontaneously, directed by a plan in

24-46   FRANS HALS, *Archers of St. Hadrian, c.* 1633. Oil on canvas, approx. 6' 9" × 11'. Frans Halsmuseum, Haarlem.

the artist's mind but not traceable in any preparatory scheme on the canvas. The bright optimism of this early period of Dutch freedom is caught in the swaggering bonhomie of the personalities, each of whom plays his particular part within the general unity of mood. This gregariousness goes with the new democracy, as well, perhaps, as with the fellowship that grows from a common experience of danger.

REMBRANDT   With Hals, Baroque realism concentrates on the human subject so intimately that we are forced to relate it to ourselves. We and the subject look at each other, as if in a sharing of mood; Hals purposely attempts to set up a confrontation of personalities. Yet most subjects still prefer to present only a public image, and even Hals has not entirely broken away from the tradition of formal portraiture that goes back to the fifteenth century. The first deep look into the *private* person will be made by Hals's younger contemporary, REMBRANDT VAN RIJN (1606–1669).

Rembrandt's way was prepared spiritually by the Protestant Reformation and the Dutch aspiration to freedom, and formally by the Venetian painters, Rubens, and Caravaggio and his Dutch imitators. The richness of this heritage alone, however, cannot account for the extraordinary achievement of this artist, one of the very greatest among those geniuses who excel in revealing Western humanity to itself. Rembrandt used painting as a method for probing the states of the human soul, both in portraiture and in his uniquely personal and authentic illustrations of the scriptures. The abolition of religious art by the reformed Church in Holland did not prevent him from making a series of religious paintings and prints that synopsize the Bible from a single point of view. His art is that of a believing Christian, a poet of the spiritual, convinced that the biblical message must be interpreted for human beings in human terms. In Rembrandt, the humanization of medieval religion is now completed in the vision of a single believer.

Rembrandt's pictorial method involves refining light and shade into finer and finer nuances, until they blend with one another. (Caravaggio's "absolute" light has, in fact, many shadows; his "absolute" dark is brightened by many lights.) We have seen that Velázquez renders optical reality as a series of values—a number of degrees of lightness and darkness. The use of abrupt lights and darks gives way, in the works of men like Rembrandt and Velázquez, to gradation, and, although the dramatic effects of violent chiaroscuro may be sacrificed, the artist gains much of the truth of actual appearances. This happens because the eye perceives light and dark not as static but as always subtly changing. Changing light and dark can suggest changing human moods; we might say that the *motion* of light through a space and across human features can express *emotion*, the changing states of the psyche.

The Renaissance represents forms and faces in a flat, neutral, modeling light (even Leonardo's shading is of a standard kind), just as it represents action in a series of standard poses. The Renaissance painter represents the *idea* of light and the *idea* of action, rather than the actual *look* of either. Light, atmosphere, change, and motion are all concerns of Baroque art, as well as of mathematics and physics in the Baroque age. The difference between the Baroque view and what went before lies largely in the new desire to *measure* these physical forces. For example, as the physicist in the seventeenth century is concerned not just with motion but with acceleration and velocity—degrees of motion—so Baroque painters discover degrees of light and dark, of differences in pose, in the movements of facial features, and in psychic states. They arrive at these differences *optically,* not conceptually or in terms of some ideal. Rembrandt found that by manipulating light and shadow in terms of direction, intensity, distance, and texture of surface, he could render the most subtle nuances of character and mood, of persons, or of whole scenes. Rembrandt discovered for the modern world that differences of light and shade, subtly modulated, could be read as emotional differences. In the visible world, light, dark, and the wide spectrum of values between the two are charged with meanings and feelings that sometimes are independent of the shapes and figures they modify. The lighted stage and the photographic arts have accepted this for many decades as the first assumption behind all their productions. What Masaccio and Leonardo began, the age of Rembrandt completed.

In his early career in Amsterdam, Rembrandt's work was influenced by Rubens and by Dutch Caravaggesque painters like van Honthorst. Thus, in a work like his early *Supper at Emmaus* (FIG. **24-47**), which dates from about 1630, he represents the subject with high drama—in sharp

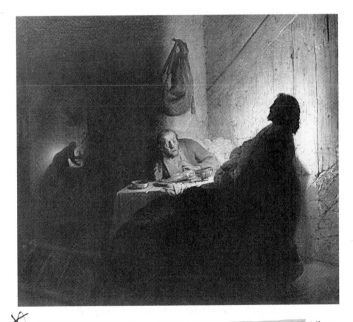

24-47   REMBRANDT VAN RIJN, *Supper at Emmaus,* c. 1628–1630. Oil on canvas, 14$\frac{1}{2}$" × 16$\frac{1}{8}$". Musée Jacquemart-André, Paris.

light and dark contrast—even using the device, familiar among his contemporaries, of placing the source of illumination behind an obstructing form (in this case, the head of Christ). This placement puts the darkest shadow in front of the brightest light, creating an emphatic, if obvious, dramatic effect. The poses of the two alarmed disciples to whom the risen Christ reveals himself are likewise a studied stage maneuver.

Some eighteen years later, in another painting of the same subject (FIG. **24-48**), the mature Rembrandt forsakes the earlier melodramatic means for a serene and untroubled setting. Here, with his highly developed instinct for light and shade, he gives us no explosive contrasts; rather, a gentle diffusion of light mellows the whole interior, condensing just slightly to make an aureole behind the head of Christ. The disciples only begin to understand what is happening; the servant is unaware. This Christ is Rembrandt's own interpretation of the biblical picture of the humble Nazarene—gentle, with an expression both loving and melancholy.

The spiritual stillness of Rembrandt's religious painting is that of inward-turning contemplation, far from the choirs and trumpets and the heavenly tumult of Bernini or Pozzo. Rembrandt gives us not the celestial triumph of the Church, but the humanity and humility of Jesus. His psychological insight and his profound sympathy for human affliction produce, at the very end of his life, one of the most moving pictures in all religious art, the *Return of the*

24-49   Rembrandt van Rijn, *Return of the Prodigal Son, c.* 1665. Oil on canvas, approx. 8′ 8″ × 6′ 9″. Hermitage Museum, St. Petersburg.

Prodigal Son (FIG. **24-49**). Tenderly embraced by his forgiving father, the son crouches before him in weeping contrition while three figures, immersed in varying degrees in the soft shadows, note the lesson of mercy. The scene is determined wholly by the artist's inward vision of its meaning. The light, everywhere mingled with shadow, controls the arrangement of the figures, illuminating the father and son and largely veiling the witnesses. Its focus is the beautiful, spiritual face of the old man; secondarily, it touches the contrasting, stern face of the foremost witness. There is no flash or glitter of light or color; the raiment is as sober as the characters are grave. Rembrandt, one feels, has put the official Baroque style far behind him and has developed a personal style completely in tune with the simple eloquence of the biblical passage. One could not help but read the Bible differently, given the authority of Rembrandt's pictorial interpretations of it.

Rembrandt carries over the spiritual quality of his religious works into his later portraits by the same means— what we might call the "psychology of light." Light and dark are not in conflict in his portraits; they are reconciled, merging softly and subtly to produce the visual equivalent of

24-48   Rembrandt van Rijn, *Supper at Emmaus, c.* 1648. Oil on canvas, approx. 27″ × 26″. Louvre, Paris.

quietness. The prevailing mood is that of tranquil meditation, of philosophical resignation, of musing recollection—
indeed, a whole cluster of emotional tones heard only in
silence.

In a late self-portrait (FIG. **24-50**), the light from above
and from the artist's left pitilessly reveals a face ravaged by
anxiety and care. The pose is that of Raphael's *Baldassare
Castiglione* (FIG. 22-17), which Rembrandt had sketched in
Amsterdam in 1639 and emulated in an earlier self-portrait.
The difference between Raphael's and Rembrandt's portraits tells us much about the difference between the
approaches of the artists and the philosophies of their
times. In Raphael's subject, the ideal has modified the real.
Rembrandt, on the other hand, shows himself as he
appears to his own searching and unflattering gaze. Here,
an elderly man is not idealized into the image of the courtly philosopher; he is shown merely as he is, a human being
in the process of dwindling away. For some, the portrait
and the self-portrait, which began as a medium for the
recording of likeness, came to be painted out of motives of
vanity. With Rembrandt, they are the history of Everyman's
painful journey through the world.

24-50 REMBRANDT VAN RIJN,
Self-Portrait, c. 1659. Oil on canvas,
approx. 33" × 26". National Gallery
of Art, Washington, D.C. (Andrew
W. Mellon Collection).

24-51   REMBRANDT VAN RIJN, *Syndics of the Cloth Guild*, 1662. Oil on canvas, approx. 6′ 2″ × 9′ 2″. Rijksmuseum, Amsterdam.

In the group portrait, an area of painting in which Frans Hals excelled, Rembrandt shows himself to be the supreme master. In *Syndics of the Cloth Guild* (FIG. **24-51**), representing an archetypal image of the new businessmen, Rembrandt applied all that he knew of the dynamics and the psychology of light, the visual suggestion of time, and the art of pose and facial expression. The five syndics, or board of directors, are going over the books of the corporation, while a bare-headed attendant looks on. It would appear that someone has entered the room and they are just at the moment of becoming aware of him, each head turning in his direction. Rembrandt gives us the lively reality of a business conference as it is interrupted; the air of surprise is greatly enhanced by the artist's decision to portray the group at a sharp angle from below. Yet, despite the fact that Rembrandt has here striven to capture a fleeting moment, he renders each portrait with great care and a studied attention to personality that one would expect to be possible only from a long studio sitting for each man. Although we do not know how Rembrandt proceeded, this harmonizing of the instantaneous action with the permanent likeness seems a work of superb stage direction that

must have needed long rehearsal; X-rays have revealed that Rembrandt shifted the position of the six figures several times before settling on the final composition. The result, a superb harmony of light, color, movement, time, and pose has few rivals in the history of painting.

Rembrandt's virtuosity also extends to the graphic media—in particular, to etching. Here, again, he ranks at the summit, alongside the original master, Dürer, who was actually an engraver. *Etching*, perfected early in the seventeenth century, rapidly was taken up by many artists; it was far more manageable than engraving and allowed greater freedom in drawing the design. In etching, a copper plate is covered with a layer of wax or varnish in which the design is drawn with an etching needle or any pointed tool, exposing the metal below but not cutting into its surface. The plate is then immersed in acid, which etches, or eats away, the exposed parts of the metal, acting in the same capacity as the burin in engraving. The softness of the medium gives the etcher greater freedom than the woodcutter and the engraver, who work directly in their more resistant media of wood and metal. Thus, prior to the invention of the lithograph in the nineteenth century, etching was the most

24-52 REMBRANDT VAN RIJN, *Three Crosses*, 1653. Fourth-state etching, approx. 15″ × 18″. British Museum, London.

facile of the graphic arts and the one that offered the greatest subtlety of line and tone.

If Rembrandt had never painted, he still would be renowned, as he principally was in his lifetime, for his prints. Prints were a major source of income for him, and he often reworked the plates so that they could be used to produce a new issue or edition. The illustration here shows the fourth state, or version, of his *Three Crosses* (FIG. **24-52**). In the earlier states, he represented only the hill of Calvary in a quite pictorial, historical way, with crowds of soldiers and spectators, all descriptively and painstakingly rendered. In this last state, not the historical but the symbolic significance of the scene comes to the fore. As if impatient with the earlier detail, Rembrandt furiously eliminated most of it—even virtually all of the third cross at the right—with hard, downward strokes of the needle, until what appears like a storm of dark lines pours down from Heaven, leaving a zone of light on the lonely figure of the crucified Christ. These heavenly spikes remind us of the golden rays of light in Bernini's *Ecstasy of St. Theresa* (FIG. 24-10), but here they are dark and foreboding, communicating a very different mood, if by similar means.

The art of Rembrandt's later years was not really acceptable to his contemporaries (although he occasionally received important commissions, like that for the *Syndics of the Cloth Guild*). It was too personal, too eccentric. Many,

like the Italian biographer Filippo Baldinucci, thought Rembrandt was a tasteless painter, concerned with the ugly and ignorant of color. This prejudice lasted well into the nineteenth century, when Rembrandt's genius finally was acknowledged. We see him now as one of the great masters of the whole tradition, an artist of great versatility, and the unique interpreter of the Protestant conception of scripture.

At the same time, modern scholarship and connoisseurship are revising our notion of Rembrandt's uniqueness and our view of him as an isolated and courageous master, who found his own way to new heights of expression, no matter the barriers of misunderstanding raised against him. Though his greatness is still conceded, Rembrandt now is understood to have been very much a part of his time, society, and stylistic school. He had numerous colleagues and pupils, with whom he shared stylistic traits and technical methods—so much so that it is often difficult and sometimes impossible to determine which of the many paintings attributed to him are actually his. For decades, a team of Dutch scholars, the Rembrandt Research Project, has been carefully examining paintings attributed to Rembrandt in museums and private collections throughout the world. The results of their investigation, which still continues, have raised vehement debate, controversy, and consternation among art historians, museum curators, collectors, and dealers. Millions of dollars are at stake. The Rembrandt research team does not seem willing to allow more than 350 pictures to be credited with certainty to Rembrandt; at one time, twice that number had been so attributed. None of this subtracts, of course, from the esthetic value of Rembrandt's contribution, which certainly is inestimable; nor does it in any way diminish his stature in the history of art. It *does* remind us once again that the "facts" of art history are always open to review, and our interpretations of them to revision.

VERMEER, HEDA, AND VAN RUISDAEL   The Dutch masters of the seventeenth century seem to have surpassed all others in their comprehensiveness of subject, taking all that is given to the eye as their province. The whole world of sight is explored, but especially the things of ordinary use and aspect with which human beings surround themselves. In some ways, the old Netherlandish tradition of Jan van Eyck lives on in the rendering of things in the optical environment with a loving and scrupulous fidelity to their appearances. Dutch painters came to specialize in portraiture, genre, interiors, still life, landscape and seascape, and even in more specialized subdivisions of these. With many, the restriction of their professional interest is all to the good; they may not create works of grand conception, but, within their small compass, they produce exquisite art.

The best-known and most highly regarded of these painters, once referred to as the "little Dutch masters," is JAN VERMEER (1632–1675) of Delft, who was rediscovered in the nineteenth century. Vermeer's pictures are small, few, and perfect within their scope. While the fifteenth-century Flemish artists usually painted interiors of houses occupied by persons of sacred significance, Vermeer and his contemporaries composed neat, quietly opulent interiors of Dutch middle-class dwellings, in which they placed men, women, and children engaged in household tasks or some little recreation—totally commonplace actions, yet reflective of the values of a comfortable domesticity that has a simple beauty.

Vermeer usually composed with a single figure, but sometimes with two or more. His *Young Woman with a Water Jug* (FIG. 24-53) can be considered typical, although we cannot be sure of the precise action being depicted or the precise moment of action. The woman may be opening the window to water flowers in a window box outside. This action is insignificant in itself and only one of hundreds performed in the course of a domestic day. Yet Vermeer, in his lighting and composing of the scene, raises it to the level of some holy, sacramental act. The old Netherlandish symbolism that made every ordinary object a religious sign is gone, but this woman's slow, gentle gesture is almost liturgical. The beauty of humble piety, which Rembrandt found in human faces, is extended here to a quite different context. The Protestant world, renouncing magnificent churches, finds a sanctuary in a modest room illuminated by an afternoon sun. Yet the light is not the mysterious,

spiritual light that falls on the face in a Rembrandt portrait as an outward manifestation of the "inner light" of grace stressed in Protestant mysticism; it is instead ordinary daylight, observed with a keenness of vision unparalleled in the history of art, unless we think of Velázquez.

Vermeer was master of pictorial light and so comprehended its functions as to place it completely in the service of the artist's intention, which is to render a lighted depth so faithfully that the picture surface is but an invisible glass through which we look immediately into the constructed illusion. We know that Vermeer made use of mirrors and of the *camera obscura,* an ancestor of the modern camera in which a tiny pinhole, acting as a lens, projects an image on a screen or the wall of a room. (In later versions, the image was projected on a ground-glass wall of a box, the opposite wall of which contained the pinhole.) This does not mean that Vermeer merely copied the image; these aids helped him to obtain results that he reworked compositionally, placing his figures and the furniture of the room in a beautiful stability of quadrilateral shapes that gives his designs a matchless Classical calm and serenity. This quality is enhanced by a color so true to the optical facts and so subtly modulated that it suggests Vermeer was far ahead of his time in color science. Close examination of the original painting shows, for one thing, that Vermeer realized that shadows are not colorless and dark, that adjoining colors affect one another,* and that light is composed of colors. Thus, the blue drape is caught as a dark blue on the side of the brass pitcher, and the red of the carpet is modified in the low-intensity gold hue of the basin. It has been suggested that Vermeer also perceived the phenomenon modern photographers call *circles of confusion,* which appear on out-of-focus negatives; Vermeer could have seen them in images projected by the primitive lenses of the camera obscura. He approximates these effects in light dabs and touches that, in close view, give the impression of an image slightly "out of focus"; when we draw back a step, however, as if adjusting the lens, the color spots cohere, giving an astonishingly accurate illusion of a third dimension.

All of these technical considerations reflect the scientific spirit of the age, but they do not explain the exquisite poetry of form and surface, of color and light, that could come only from the sensitivity of a great artist. In Marcel Proust's *Swann's Way,* the connoisseur hero, trying unsuccessfully to write a monograph on Vermeer, admits that no words could ever do justice to a single patch of sunlight on one of Vermeer's walls.

The "little Dutch masters" treat the humblest objects, which receive their meaning by their association with human uses, as reverently as if they were sacramentals. The Dutch painters of still life isolate these objects as profoundly interesting in themselves, making of their representation

*This is due to the phenomenon of *complementary afterimage,* in which, for example, the eye retains briefly a red image of a green stimulus; thus, a white area adjoining a green will appear slightly pink, and a blue adjoining the same green will shift toward violet (blue plus the afterimage of red).

both scientific and poetic exercises in the revelation of the functions and the beauties of light. Many fine examples of Dutch still life have come down to us, each painted with the expertness of the specialist in analytical seeing. A still life (FIG. **24-54**) by WILLEM CLAESZ HEDA (*c.* 1599–1680), depicting, typically, the remnants of an incompletely consumed meal, can serve as exemplary of the school. Here, against a stark background variegated only by light, the artist arranges oysters, fruit, costly Venetian glass goblets, and elegant silverware on a plain wooden table covered in part by an equally plain cloth, focusing our attention on the precious table service and the food and drink. The painter delights in rendering the textural counterpoint of the absorptive and reflective surfaces. The tall, transparent goblet sparkling with multiple reflections of light from an

unseen source, the duller skin of the lemon and its juicy core, the soft and malleable oyster in its hard shell, the overturned, gleaming silver cup with its intricate design—nothing has escaped the eye of the Dutch painter, who has lovingly recorded the textural gradation from the glass to the silver to the food to the tablecloth. He has also chosen and composed his objects with the intent of creating a dynamic interplay of abstract shapes. The large, half-empty rum glass serves as a central, vertical anchor for the composition; the table provides its stable horizontal base. Relieving this severe perpendicularity and animating the inanimate are the diagonals of the silver goblet and the rolled paper between the circular plates, and the cascading spiral of the partially peeled lemon. This little masterpiece shows how this age of seeing must have taken pleasure in

24-53 JAN VERMEER, *Young Woman with a Water Jug, c.* 1665. Oil on canvas, approx. 18″ × 16″. Metropolitan Museum of Art, New York (gift of Henry G. Marquand, 1889).

24-54 WILLEM CLAESZ HEDA, *Still Life with Oysters, Rum Glass, and Silver Cup*, 1634. Oil on wood, approx. 17" × 22". Museum Boymans-van Beuningren, Rotterdam.

24-55 JACOB VAN RUISDAEL, *View of Haarlem from the Dunes at Overveen*, *c.* 1670. Oil on canvas, approx. 22" × 25". Royal Picture Gallery (Mauritshuis), The Hague.

the infinite variety of the play of light in the small universe as well as the large. Such work is not dull imitation; it is revelation of what can be seen if the eye will learn to see it. And in the concern for composing geometric shapes within a rectilinear frame, these Dutch still lifes presage the abstract designs of many twentieth-century canvases.

The Baroque world discovers the infinite, whether it is the infinitely small or the infinitely great. The minute spark of light that lifts the rim of a glass out of darkness becomes, when expanded, the sunlit heavens. The globule of dew on a leaf in a Dutch flower becomes the aqueous globe of Earth itself. The space that began to open behind the figures of Giotto now, in Dutch landscape, takes flight into limitless distance, and the human being dwindles to insignificance— "his time a moment, and a point his place."

In some of the works of JACOB VAN RUISDAEL (*c.* 1628–1682), the human figure does not appear at all or appears only minutely. In *View of Haarlem from the Dunes at Overveen* (FIG. **24-55**), van Ruisdael gives us almost a portrait of the newly discovered, infinite universe, allowing the sky to take up almost three-quarters of the picture space. One of the great landscape painters of all time, the artist turns to the vast and moody heavens that loom above the flat dunelands of Holland. His sullen clouds, in great droves never quite scattered by the sun, are herded by the winds that blew the fortunes of Holland's fleets as well as the disasters of the invading sea. Storms always are breaking up or gathering; the earth always is drenched or about to be. As Rembrandt reads the souls of men in their faces, so van Ruisdael reads the somber depths of the heavens. No angels swoop through his skies or recline on his clouds. Like Rembrandt's, his is a "Protestant" reading of nature. The difference between northern and southern Baroque is evident at once in a comparison of Pozzo's *Glorification of St. Ignatius* (FIG. 24-31) and van Ruisdael's *View of Haarlem.* It is the difference between the heavens of Jesuit vision and the heavens seen as one element of the natural world that engulfs humankind.

FRANCE

In the second half of the seventeenth century, France began a slow recovery from the anarchy of the religious wars. While Cardinals Richelieu and Mazarin painfully rebuilt the power and prestige of the French throne, French art remained under the influence of Italy and Flanders. Even so, artists of originality emerged.

Painting

Among them was the painter GEORGES DE LA TOUR (1593–1652), who learned of Caravaggio possibly through the Dutch school of Utrecht. Much as La Tour uses the devices of the northern Caravaggisti, his effects are strikingly different from theirs. His *Adoration of the Shepherds*

24-56 GEORGES DE LA TOUR, *Adoration of the Shepherds,* 1645–1650. Oil on canvas, approx. 42″ × 54″. Louvre, Paris.

(FIG. **24-56**) shows us the night setting favored by that school, much as we have seen it in van Honthorst (FIG. 24-44). But here, the light, its source shaded by the hand of an old man, falls upon a very different company in a very different mood. We see a group of humble men and women, coarsely clad, gathered in prayerful vigil around a luminous infant. If we did not know that this is a representation of the sacred event of the Nativity, we would consider it a genre piece, a narrative of some happening from peasant life. Nothing in the environment, placement, poses, dress, or attributes of the figures might distinguish them as the scriptural Virgin Mary, Joseph, Christ Child, or shepherds. The artist has not portrayed haloes, choirs of angels, stately architecture, or resplendent grandees (FIGS. 20-14, 21-22). The light is not spiritual but material; it comes from a candle. La Tour's scientific scrutiny of the effects of material light, as it throws precise shadows on surfaces that intercept it, has, nevertheless, religious intention and consequence. It illuminates a group of ordinary people, held in a mystic trance induced by their witnessing the miracle of the Incarnation. The dogmatic significance and traditional iconography of the Incarnation are absorbed without trace in this timeless tableau of simple people, who are in reverent contemplation of something they regard as holy. As such, the painting is readable to the devout of any religious persuasion, whether or not they know of this central mystery of the Christian faith. Yet the effect of rapt religiosity is created by essentially the same devices of composition, chiaroscuro, and commonplace subject that we find in the worldly art of the Dutch Caravaggisti.

The supernatural calm that pervades this picture is characteristic of the mood of the art of Georges de La Tour. It is achieved by the elimination of motion and emotive gesture (only the light is dramatic), by the suppression of surface detail, and by the simplification of body volumes. These

24-57   LOUIS LE NAIN, *Family of Country People, c.* 1640. Oil on canvas, approx. 44" × 62". Louvre, Paris.

traits of style we associate with art of Classical substance or tendency—for example, that of Piero della Francesca (FIG. 21-30). Several apparently contrary elements meet in the work of La Tour: Classical composure, fervent spirituality, and genre realism.

LOUIS LE NAIN (*c.* 1593–1648) and his contemporary, La Tour, bear comparison with the Dutch. Subjects that in Dutch painting are an opportunity for boisterous good humor are managed by the French with cool stillness. *Family of Country People* (FIG. **24-57**) expresses the grave dignity of a family close to the soil, one made stoic and resigned by hardship. Obviously, Le Nain sympathized with his subjects and seems here to want to emphasize their rustic virtue, far from the gorgeous artificiality of the courts. Stress on the honesty, integrity, and even innocence of uncorrupted country folk became sentimentality in the fol-

lowing century. However, Le Nain's objectivity permitted him to record a group of such genuine human beings that the picture rises above anecdote and the picturesqueness of genre. These still, somber country folk could have had little reason for merriment. The lot of the peasant, never easy, was miserable during the time Le Nain painted. The terrible conflict we call the Thirty Years War (1618–1648) was raging. The last and most devastating of the wars of religion between Protestants and Catholics, which had begun a century before, spread atrocity and ruin throughout France, Italy, and Germany. The anguish and frustration of the peasantry, suffering from the cruel depredations of unruly armies living off the country, often broke out in savage revolts that were savagely put down.

A record of the times appears in a series of etchings by JACQUES CALLOT (*c.* 1592–1635) called *Miseries of War.* Callot, the first great master of the art of etching, a medium to which he confined himself almost exclusively, was widely influential in his own time and since; Rembrandt was among those who knew and learned from his work. Callot perfected the medium and the technique of etching, developing a very hard surface for the copper plate, to permit fine and precise delineation with the needle. In one small print, he may assemble as many as twelve hundred figures, which only close scrutiny can discriminate. His quick, vivid touch and faultless drawing produce a panorama sparkling with sharp details of life—and death. In the *Miseries of War* series, he observes these coolly, presenting without comment things he himself must have seen in the wars in his own country, Lorraine.

In one etching, he depicts a mass execution by hanging (FIG. **24-58**). The unfortunates may be war prisoners or defeated peasant rebels. The event takes place in the presence of a disciplined army, drawn up on parade, with banners, muskets, and lances, their tents in the background.

24-58   JACQUES CALLOT, *Hanging Tree,* from the *Miseries of War* series, 1621. Etching, 3³/₄" × 7¹/₄". Bibliothèque Nationale, Paris.

Hanged men sway in clusters from the branches of a huge, cross-shaped tree. A monk climbs a ladder, holding up a crucifix to a man, around whose neck the noose is being adjusted. At the foot of the ladder, another victim kneels to receive absolution. Under the crucifix-tree, men roll dice on a drumhead for the belongings of the executed. (This may be an allusion, in the Baroque manner, to the soldiers who cast lots for the garments of the crucified Christ.) In the right foreground, a bound man is consoled by a hooded priest. Callot's *Miseries of War* are the first realistic, pictorial record of the human disaster of armed conflict. They foreshadow Goya's great paintings (FIG. 26-10) and prints on the same theme.

POUSSIN   The brisk animation of Callot's manner contrasts with the quiet composure in the art of La Tour and Le Nain, his exact contemporaries. Yet, although calm simplicity and restraint characterize the latter two, in comparison with other northern painters inspired by Caravaggio, and although these qualities suggest the Classical, it remained for another contemporary, NICOLAS POUSSIN (1594–1665), to establish Classical painting as peculiarly expressive of French taste and genius in the seventeenth century. Poussin, born in Normandy, spent most of his life in Rome. There, inspired by its monuments and countryside, he produced his grandly severe and regular canvases and carefully worked out a theoretical explanation of his method. He worked for a while under Domenichino but shunned the exuberant Italian Baroque; Titian and Raphael were the models that he set for himself.

Of his two versions of a single theme titled *Et in Arcadia Ego* (*I, too, in Arcadia* or *Even in Arcadia, I* [am present]), the earlier (not illustrated) is strikingly Titianesque, with all the warm, rich tonality of the Venetian master and the figure types familiar in Titian's idyllic "bacchanals." But, in the end, the rational order and stability of Raphael proved more appealing to Poussin. His second version of *Et in Arcadia Ego* (FIG. **24-59**) shows what he learned from Raphael, as well as from Antique statuary. Landscape, of which Poussin became increasingly fond, expands in the picture, reminiscent of Titian but also indicative of Poussin's own study of nature. But the foreground is dominated by

24-59   NICOLAS POUSSIN, *Et in Arcadia Ego, c.* 1655. Oil on canvas, approx. 34" × 48". Louvre, Paris.

three shepherds living in the idyllic land of Arcadia, who spell out an enigmatic inscription on a tomb as a statuesque female figure quietly places her hand on the shoulder of one of them. She may be the spirit of death, reminding these mortals, as does the inscription, that death is found even in Arcadia, where naught but perfect happiness is supposed to reign. Her figure is loosely based on the countless draped female statues surviving in Italy from Roman times, and the youth with one foot resting on a boulder is modeled on Greco-Roman statues of the sea god, Neptune, leaning on his trident. The compact, balanced grouping of these figures, the even light, and the thoughtful, reserved, elegiac mood set the tone for Poussin's art in its later, Classical phase.

In notes for an intended treatise on painting, Poussin outlined the "grand manner" of Classicism, of which he became the leading exponent in Rome. One must first of all choose great subjects: "The first requirement, fundamental to all others, is that the subject and the narrative be grandiose, such as battles, heroic actions, and religious themes." Minute details should be avoided, as well as all "low" subjects, like genre ("Those who choose base subjects find refuge in them because of the feebleness of their tal-

ents"). This dictum rules out a good deal of both the decorative and realistic art of the Baroque, and it would lead to a doctrinaire limitation on artistic enterprise and experiment in the rules of the French Royal Academy of Painting and Sculpture, which, under Charles Le Brun in the 1660s, would take Poussin as its greatest modern authority. Although Poussin could create with ease and grandeur within the scope of his rather severe maxims, his method could become wooden and artificial in the hands of academic followers.

Poussin represents that theoretical tradition in Western art that goes back to the Early Renaissance and that asserts that all good art must be the result of good judgment—a judgment based on sure knowledge. In this way, art can achieve correctness and propriety, two of the favorite categories of the Classicizing artist or architect. Poussin praised the ancient Greeks for their musical "modes," by which, he said, "they produced marvelous effects." He observed that "this word 'mode' means actually the rule or the measure and form which serves us in our production. This rule constrains us not to exaggerate by making us act in all things with a certain restraint and moderation." "Restraint" and "moderation" are the very essence of French Classical doc-

24-60   NICOLAS POUSSIN, *Burial of Phocion*, 1648. Oil on canvas, approx. 47" × 70". Louvre, Paris.

trine; in the age of Louis XIV, we find this doctrine preached as much for literature and music as for art and architecture. Poussin tells us further that

> the Modes of the ancients were a combination of several things . . . in such a proportion that it was made possible to arouse the soul of the spectator to various passions. . . . The ancient sages attributed to each style its own effects. Because of this they called the Dorian Mode stable, grave, and severe, and applied it to subjects which are grave and severe and full of wisdom.*

Poussin's finest works, like the *Burial of Phocion* (FIG. **24-60**), are instances of his obvious preference for the "Dorian Mode." His subjects are chosen carefully from the literature of antiquity, where his age would naturally look for the "grandiose," and it is with Poussin that the visual arts draw closer to literature than ever before. Here, he takes his theme from Plutarch's *Life of Phocion,* a biography of the distinguished Athenian general who was unjustly put to death by his countrymen but then given a public funeral and memorialized by the state. In the foreground, Poussin represents the body of the hero being taken away, his burial on Athenian soil having at first been forbidden. The two massive bearers and the bier are starkly isolated in a great landscape that throws them into solitary relief, eloquently expressive of the hero abandoned in death. The landscape is composed of interlocking planes that slope upward to the lighted sky at the left, carefully arranged ter-

*In E. G. Holt, ed., *Literary Sources of Art History* (Princeton, NJ: Princeton University Press, 1947), p. 380.

races that bear slowly moving streams, shepherds and their flocks, and, in the distance, whole assemblies of solid geometric structures (temples, towers, walls, villas, and a central grand sarcophagus). The skies are untroubled and the light is even and form-revealing. The trees are few and carefully arranged, like curtains lightly drawn back to reveal a nature carefully cultivated as a setting for a single human action. Unlike van Ruisdael's *View of Haarlem* (FIG. 24-55), this scene is not intended to represent a particular place and time; it is the construction of an *idea* of a noble landscape to frame a noble theme, much as we have seen it in Annibale Carracci's Classical landscape (FIG. 24-29). The *Phocion* landscape is nature subordinated to a rational plan, much like the gardens of Versailles (FIG. 24-65); it is eminently of the Age of Reason.

CLAUDE LORRAIN   The disciplined, rational art of Poussin, with its sophisticated revelation of the geometry of landscape, is modulated in the softer style of CLAUDE GELLÉE, called CLAUDE LORRAIN (1600–1682). Unlike Poussin's pictures, Claude's are not "Dorian." The figures in his landscapes tell no dramatic story, point out no moral, and praise no hero; indeed, they often appear added as mere excuses for the radiant landscape itself. For Claude, painting involves essentially one theme: the beauty of a broad sky suffused with the golden light of dawn or sunset that makes its glowing way through a hazy atmosphere and reflects scintillatingly from the rippling water.

In one realization of Claude's landscape ideal the setting is a seaport, where the Queen of Sheba is embarking for home (FIG. **24-61**). Servants are loading boats with the rich

24-61   CLAUDE LORRAIN, *Embarkation of the Queen of Sheba,* 1648. Oil on canvas, approx. 58″ × 76″. National Gallery, London.

gifts bestowed upon the queen by King Solomon (1 Kings 10:1–10, 13). The queen, with her stately entourage, descends to the quay from a majestic palace, the style of which is familiar in the Classicizing architecture of the seventeenth century. Occupying the dark left foreground is a lofty fragment of a Roman ruin. The ships, their sails still furled, await their cargoes. A tower, arched bridge, and tall trees are grouped in the distance. These are the stage properties invented by Claude to set off his theme; they are not to be thought of as authentic representations of the time and place of his narrative. The Roman ruin, for example, is an unorthodox composite of a temple colonnade and a triumphal arch and is as anachronistic in an Old Testament story as the Baroque palace but effective in conjuring up a romantic ancient past. The firm architectural shapes, the busy diagonals of the ships' rigging, and the perfunctory, small figures are meant solely to frame (like the wings of a stage) the central actor and the pictorial focus, which is the effulgent sun and the trail of sparkling accents it leaves upon the sea. The dark foreground, lighter middleground, and dim background recede in serene orderliness, until all form dissolves in a luminous mist. Atmospheric and linear perspective reinforce one another to turn a vista into a typical Claudian vision, an ideal Classical world bathed in sunlight in infinite Baroque space.

In formalizing nature with balanced groups of architectural masses, screens of trees, and sheets of water, Claude is working in the great tradition of Classical landscape that opens in the backgrounds of Venetian painting (FIGS. 22-57 and 22-58) and continues in the art of Annibale Carracci (FIG. 24-29) and Poussin (FIG. 24-60). At the same time, Claude, like the Dutch painters, studied the actual light and the atmospheric nuances of nature, making a unique contribution. He recorded carefully in hundreds of sketches the veritable look of the Roman countryside, its pellucid air, its gentle terrain variegated by stone-pines, cypresses, and poplars, and by ever-present ruins of ancient aqueducts, tombs, and towers. He made these the fundamental accessories of his compositions; travelers could learn of and could recognize the picturesque beauties of the outskirts of Rome in Claude's landscapes.

His marvelous effects of light were achieved by painstaking placement of infinitesimally small value gradations, which imitated, though on a very small scale, the actual range of values of out-of-door light and shade. Avoiding the problem of high noon, Claude preferred, and could convincingly represent, the disc of the sun as it gradually radiates the morning sky, or with its dying glow sets the pensive mood of evening. Thus he matched the moods of nature and of the human subject. Claude's infusion of nature with human feeling, while re-composing it in a calm equilibrium, would have great appeal to the landscape painters of the eighteenth and earlier nineteenth centuries, especially Turner, whose lifelong admiration of Claude's art was almost obsessive.

The softening of Poussin's stern manner in Claude parallels the reaction of other painters of the time against the severe rules and regulations of the French Royal Academy of Painting and Sculpture under the dictatorial administration of Charles Le Brun. Established in 1648, the Academy had been intended to free artists from the constraints of the old guild system of art training, to improve the social status of painters and sculptors, so that they would be seen as more than mere handicraftsmen, to regularize instruction in the arts, and to centralize art production in the interest of the absolute monarchy. Above all, the Academy was to develop and propagate a Classical taste, based on the study and imitation of ancient works of art and such classicizing modern masters as Raphael, the Carracci, and Poussin himself. Students were taught the supremacy of drawing over coloring, of sculpturesque form over painterly tonality, of symmetrical and closed composition over the dynamic and open—in short, the superiority of Poussin over Rubens. Yet, well before the end of the century, the painting of Rubens was increasingly admired, and his influence would weaken the doctrine of the Academy and shape the taste of eighteenth-century Rococo.

Architecture

In architecture, as in painting, France maintained an attitude of cautious selectivity toward the Italian Baroque. The Classical bent asserted itself early in the work of FRANÇOIS MANSART (1598–1666), as seen in the Orléans wing of the Chateau de Blois (FIG. **24-62**), built between 1635 and 1638. The polished dignity and sobriety evident here will become the hallmarks of French "Classical-Baroque," contrasting with the more daring, excited, and fanciful styles of the Baroque in Italy and elsewhere. The strong, rectilinear organization and a tendency to design in terms of repeated units remind us of Italian Renaissance architecture, as does the insistence on the purity of line and sharp relief of the wall articulations. Yet the emphasis on a focal point—achieved through the curving colonnades, the changing planes of the walls, and the concentration of ornament around the portal—is characteristic of Baroque architectural thinking in general.

The formation of the French Classical style accelerated with the foundation of the Royal Academy of which Poussin was a director, and with the determination of King Louis XIV and his principal adviser, Jean-Baptiste Colbert, to organize art and architecture in the service of the state. No pains were spared to raise great symbols and monuments to the king's absolute power and to regularize taste under the academies.

The first project undertaken by the young monarch and Colbert was the closing of the east side of the Louvre court, left incomplete by Lescot in the sixteenth century. Bernini, as the most renowned architect of his day, was summoned from Rome to submit plans, but he envisioned an Italian palace on a monumental scale that would have involved the demolition of all previous work. His plan rejected, Bernini returned to Rome in high indignation. The east facade of the Louvre (FIG. **24-63**) is the result of a collaboration between CLAUDE PERRAULT (1613–1688), LOUIS LE VAU (1612–1670), and CHARLES LE BRUN (1619–1690), with Le Vau probably playing a preponderant role. The design is a brilliant adjustment of French and Italian Classical elements, culminating in a new and definitive formula. The French pavilion system is retained; the central pavilion is in

the form of a Classical temple front, and a giant colonnade of paired columns, resembling the columned flanks of a temple folded out like wings, is contained by the two salient pavilions at either end. The whole is mounted on a stately basement, or podium. An even roof line, balustraded and broken only by the central pediment, replaces the traditional French pyramidal roof. All memory of Gothic verticality is brushed aside in the emphatically horizontal sweep of this facade. Its stately proportions and monumentality are both an expression of the new official French taste and a symbol for centrally organized authority.

24-62 FRANÇOIS MANSART, Orléans wing of the Chateau de Blois, 1635–1638.

24-63 CLAUDE PERRAULT, LOUIS LE VAU, and CHARLES LE BRUN, east facade of the Louvre, Paris, 1667–1670.

24-64   Palace at Versailles, begun 1669, and a small portion of the surrounding park (aerial view). The white trapezoid in the lower part of the plan (FIG. 24-65) outlines the area shown here.

VERSAILLES   Work on the Louvre hardly had begun when Louis XIV decided to convert a royal hunting lodge at Versailles, a few miles outside Paris, into a great palace. A veritable army of architects, decorators, sculptors, painters, and landscape architects was assembled under the general management of former Poussin student Le Brun, the king's impresario of art and dictator of the Royal Academy of Painting and Sculpture. In their hands, the conversion of a simple hunting lodge into the Palace of Versailles (FIGS. 24-64 and 24-65) became the greatest architectural project of the age.

Planned on a gigantic scale, the project called not only for a large palace flanking a vast park but also for the construction of a satellite city to house court and government officials, military and guard detachments, courtiers, and servants. This town is laid out to the east of the palace along three radial avenues that converge on the palace structure itself; their axes, in a symbolic assertion of the ruler's absolute power over his domains, intersect in the king's bedroom. (As the site of the king's morning levee, this bedroom was actually an audience room, a state chamber.) The palace itself, over a quarter of a mile long, is placed at right angles to the dominant east-west axis that runs through city and park.

Careful attention was paid to every detail of the extremely rich decoration of the palace's interior; every-thing from wall paintings to doorknobs was designed in keeping with the whole and was executed with the very finest sense of craftsmanship. Of the literally hundreds of rooms within the palace, the most famous is the Galerie des Glaces, or Hall of Mirrors (FIG. 24-66), which overlooks the park from the second floor and extends along most of the width of the central block. Although deprived of its original sumptuous furniture, which included gold and silver chairs and bejeweled trees, the Galerie des Glaces retains much of its splendor today. Its tunnel-like quality is alleviated by hundreds of mirrors, set into the wall opposite the windows, which illusionistically extend the width of the room. The mirror, that ultimate source of illusion, was a favorite element of Baroque interior design; here, it must have harmonized as it augmented the flashing splendors of the great festivals of which Louis XIV was so fond.

The enormous palace might appear unbearably ostentatious, were it not for its extraordinary setting in the vast park to which it becomes almost an adjunct. The Galerie des Glaces, itself a giant perspective, is dwarfed by the sweeping vista (seen from its windows) down the park's tree-lined central axis and across terraces, lawns, pools, and lakes toward the horizon. The park of Versailles (FIG. 24-65), designed by ANDRÉ LE NÔTRE (1613–1700), must rank among the world's greatest works of art, not only in size but also in concept. Here, an entire forest has been transformed into a park. Although the geometric plan may appear stiff and formal, the park, in fact, offers an almost unlimited variety of vistas, as Le Nôtre utilized not only the multiplicity of natural forms but also the slightly rolling contours of the terrain with stunning effectiveness.

A rational transition from the frozen forms of the architecture to the living ones of nature is provided by the formal gardens near the palace. Here, tightly designed geometric units are defined by the elegant forms of trimmed shrubs and hedges, each one different from its neighbor and having a focal point in the form of a sculptured group, a pavilion, a reflecting pool, or perhaps a fountain. Farther away from the palace, the design loosens as trees, in shadowy masses, screen or frame views of open countryside. All vistas are composed carefully for maximum effect. Dark and light, formal and informal, dense growth and open meadows—all are played against each other in unending combinations and variations. No photograph or series of photographs can reveal the full richness of the design; the park unfolds itself only to the person who actually walks through it. In this respect, it is a temporal work of art; its aspects change with time and with the relative position of the observer.

24-66   Jules Hardouin-Mansart and Charles Le Brun, Galerie des Glaces (Hall of Mirrors), Palace of Versailles, *c.* 1680.

As a symbol of the power of absolutism, Versailles is unsurpassed. It also expresses, in the most monumental terms of its age, the rationalistic creed, based on the mathematical philosophy of Descartes, that all knowledge must be systematic and all science must be the consequence of the imposition of the intellect on matter. The whole stupendous design of Versailles proudly proclaims the mastery of human intelligence over the disorderliness of nature.

After Le Vau's death, Jules Hardouin-Mansart (1646–1708), a great-nephew of François Mansart, completed the garden facade of the Versailles palace and in 1698 was commisioned to add a Royal Chapel to the complex. The chapel's interior (FIG. **24-67**) is a masterful synthesis of Classical and Baroque elements. It is essentially a rectangular building with an apse as high as the nave, which gives the fluid central space a curved Baroque quality. But the light entering through the large clerestory windows lacks the directed, dramatic effect of the Italian Baroque and illuminates the precisely chiseled details of the interior brightly and evenly. Pier-supported arcades carry a majestic row of Corinthian columns that define the royal gallery, the back of which is occupied by the royal pew, accessible directly from the king's apartments. The decoration is restrained and, in fact, only the illusionistic ceiling decorations, added in 1708 to 1709 by Antoine Coypel

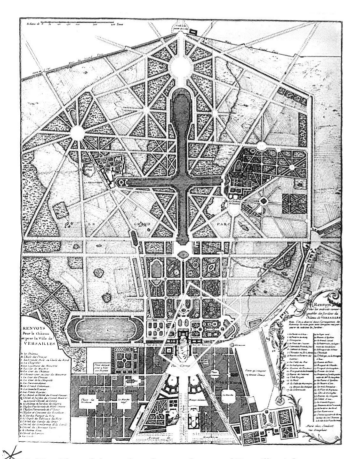

24-65   Plan of the park, palace, and town of Versailles (after a seventeenth-century engraving by François Blondel). The area outlined in the white trapezoid (lower center) is shown in FIG. 24-64.

24-67   JULES HARDOUIN-MANSART, Royal Chapel of the Palace of Versailles, 1698–1710. (Ceiling decorations by ANTOINE COYPEL.)

24-68   JULES HARDOUIN-MANSART, Église de Dôme, Church of the Invalides, Paris, 1676–1706.

(1661–1722), can be called Baroque without reservation. Throughout the architecture, Baroque tendencies are severely checked by Classicism.

Although checked, such tendencies are not suppressed entirely in Hardouin-Mansart's masterwork, the Église de Dôme, Church of the Invalides in Paris (FIG. **24-68**). An intricately composed domed square of great scale, the church is attached to the veterans' hospital set up by Louis XIV for the disabled soldiers of his many wars. The frontispiece is composed of two firmly separated levels, the upper pedimented. The grouping of the orders and the bays they frame is not unlike that in Italian Baroque. The compact facade is low and narrow in relation to the vast drum and dome, for which it seems to serve simply as a base. The overpowering dome, conspicuous on the skyline of Paris, is itself expressive of the Baroque love for dramatic magnitude. The way that its design aims for theatrical effects of light and space is especially Baroque. The dome is built of three shells, the lowest cut off so that the visitor looks up through it to the one above, which is painted illusionisti-

cally with an apotheosis of Saint Louis, patron of France. This second dome, filled with light from hidden windows in the third, outermost dome, creates an impression of the open, limitless space and brightness of the heavens. Below, the building is only dimly illuminated and is designed in a Classicism only less severe than that of the Escorial (FIG. 23-25). The rapid vertical gradation from the austerely membered masses below to the ethereal light and space above is entirely Baroque. Yet we feel here the dominance of the Classical style in substance, despite the soaring illusion for which it serves as a setting.

Sculpture

The stylistic dialogue between Classicism and the Italian Baroque in seventeenth-century French sculpture also ends with a victory for Classicism. The strained dramatic and emotional qualities in the work of PIERRE PUGET (1620–1694) were not at all to the court's taste. His *Milo of Crotona* (FIG. **24-69**) represents the powerful ancient hero, his hand trapped in a split stump, helpless before the attacking lion. With physical and psychic realism, Puget presents a study of immediate and excruciating agony—an attitude that ran counter to the official taste for heroic design dictated by the king and Le Brun. Although Puget was very briefly in vogue, the most original French sculptor of his time never found acceptance at the French court.

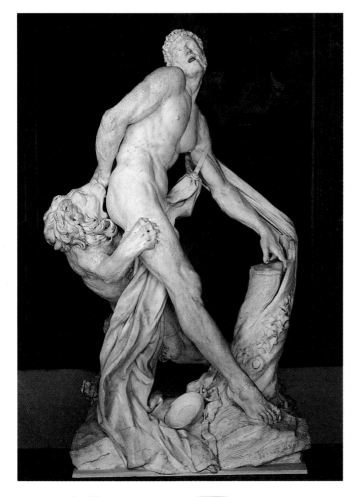

24-69   PIERRE PUGET, *Milo of Crotona*, 1671–1682. Marble, approx. 8′ 10″ high. Louvre, Paris.

Much more fortunate was FRANÇOIS GIRARDON (1628–1715), who admirably adjusted his style to the taste of his sponsors. His *Apollo Attended by the Nymphs* (FIG. **24-70**) was designed as a tableau group for the Grotto of Thetis in the gardens of Versailles. (The three nymphs in the backgound are the work of THOMAS REGNAUDIN, 1622–1706.) Both stately and graceful, the nymphs have a compelling charm as they minister to the god at the end of the day. The style of the figures is heavily conditioned by the artist's close study of Greco-Roman sculpture, the central figure imitating the much-admired Apollo Belvedere (FIG. 5-71) in the Vatican. The arrangement is inspired by Poussin's figure compositions (FIG. 24-59). And if this combination did not suffice, the group's rather florid reference to Louis XIV as the "god of the sun" was bound to assure its success at court. Girardon's style and symbolism were well suited to the glorification of royal majesty.

ENGLAND

English art has been mentioned little since the Middle Ages because, except for its architecture, England stands outside the main artistic streams of the Renaissance and Baroque periods—just as it stands apart from continental Europe in religious matters. It is as if the English genius were so occupied with its prodigious creation in dramatic literature, lyric poetry, and music, that it did not find itself particularly suited to the purely visual arts. Not until the eighteenth century did England develop an important native school of painting and extend its distinguished architectural tradition.

24-70   FRANÇOIS GIRARDON and THOMAS REGNAUDIN, *Apollo Attended by the Nymphs, c.* 1666–1672. Marble, life size. Park of Versailles.

24-71 INIGO JONES, Banqueting House at Whitehall, London, 1619–1622.

Architecture

Gothic practices lived on in English, as in French, building, long after Renaissance architects in Italy struck out in new directions. During the seventeenth century, the English made minor concessions to Italian architectural ideas. Classical ornament appeared frequently in the decoration of buildings, and a distinct trend developed toward more regular and symmetrical planning. But not until the early seventeenth century did England wholeheartedly accept the principles that govern Italian architectural thinking.

JONES AND WREN   The revolution in English building was primarily the work of one man, INIGO JONES (1573–1652), architect to James I and Charles I. Jones spent considerable time in Italy. He greatly admired the Classical authority and restraint of Palladio's structures and studied his treatise on architecture with great care. From Palladio's villas and palaces, Jones took many motifs, and he adopted Palladio's basic principles of design for his own architecture. The nature of his achievement is evident in the buildings he did for his royal patrons, among them the Banqueting House at Whitehall (FIG. **24-71**). In this structure, a symmetrical block of great clarity and dignity, Jones superimposed two orders, using columns in the center and pilasters near the ends. The balustraded roof line, uninterrupted in its horizontal sweep, anticipated the facade of the Louvre (FIG. 24-63) by more than forty years. There is almost nothing here that Palladio would not have recognized and approved, but the building as a whole is not a

copy. While working within the architectural vocabulary and syntax of the revered Italian, Jones retained his own independence as a designer; for two centuries his influence was almost as authoritative in English architecture as Palladio's. In a fruitful collaboration recalling the combination of painting by Veronese and architecture by Palladio in northern Italian villas, Jones's interior at Whitehall is adorned with several important paintings by Rubens.

Until almost the present day, the dominant feature of the London skyline was the majestic dome of St. Paul's (FIG. **24-72**), the work of England's most renowned architect, CHRISTOPHER WREN (1632–1723). A mathematical genius and skilled engineer, whose work won the praise of Isaac Newton, Wren was appointed professor of astronomy in London at the age of twenty-five. Mathematics led to architecture and, when asked by Charles II to prepare a plan for the restoration of the old Gothic church of St. Paul, Wren proposed to remodel the building "after a good Roman manner" rather than "to follow the Gothic rudeness of the old design." Within a few months, the Great Fire of London, which destroyed the old structure and many churches in the city in 1666, gave Wren his opportunity. He built not only the new St. Paul's but numerous other churches as well.

Wren was a Baroque virtuoso of many talents, the archetype of whom we see in Bernini. He was strongly influenced by the work of Jones, but he also traveled in France, where he must have been much impressed by the splendid palaces and state buildings being created in and around Paris at the time of the competition for the Louvre

24-72 CHRISTOPHER WREN, new St. Paul's Cathedral, London, 1675–1710.

design. Wren also must have closely studied prints illustrating Baroque architecture in Italy, for Palladian, French, and Italian Baroque features are harmonized in St. Paul's.

In view of its size, the cathedral was built with remarkable speed—in a little over thirty years—and Wren lived to see it completed. The form of the building was constantly refined as it went up, and the final appearance of the towers was not determined until after 1700. The splendid skyline composition, with the two foreground towers acting effectively as foils to the great dome, must have been suggested to Wren by similar schemes devised by Italian architects to solve the problem of the facade-dome relation of St. Peter's in Rome (FIGS. 22-32 and 24-2). Certainly, the upper levels and lanterns of the towers are Borrominesque (FIG. 24-13), the lower levels are Palladian, and the superposed,

paired columnar porticoes remind us of the Louvre facade (FIG. 24-63). Wren's skillful eclecticism brings all of these foreign features into a monumental unity.

Wren's designs for the city churches are masterpieces of Baroque planning and ingenuity. His task was never easy, for the churches often had to be fitted into small, irregular areas. Wren worked out a rich variety of schemes to meet awkward circumstances. In designing the exteriors of the churches, he concentrated his attention on the towers, the one element of the structure that would set the building apart from its crowding neighbors. The skyline of London, as left by Wren, is punctuated with such towers, which will serve as prototypes for later buildings both in England and in colonial America.

EUROPE AFTER 1720

RUSSIA

KINGDOM OF SWEDEN

SCOTLAND

NORTH SEA

KINGDOM OF DENMARK

BALTIC SEA

PRUSSIA

KINGDOM OF POLAND

GREAT BRITAIN

IRELAND

MANCHESTER

WALES · DERBY

COALBROOKDALE

ENGLAND

OXFORD · LONDON

Severn R.

BATH

BRANDENBURG

Vistula R.

ATLANTIC OCEAN

UNITED NETHERLANDS

HOLY ROMAN EMPIRE

SAXONY

FLANDERS · BRUSSELS

AMIENS

Seine R. · PARIS

VERSAILLES

STAFFELSTEIN

ROHR ·

Rhine R.

BOHEMIA

AUSTRIA

BAVARIA

· MUNICH

KINGDOM OF HUNGARY

0   300 Miles

0   300 Kilometers

Loire R.

KINGDOM OF FRANCE

Garonne R.

SWITZERLAND

TYROL

Danube R.

SAVOY   LOMBARDY

Po R.

TURIN

PIEDMONT

VENICE

· STRA

REP. OF VENICE

Rhône R.

REP. OF GENOA

TUSCANY

PAPAL STATES

ADRIATIC SEA

OTTOMAN EMPIRE

Ebro R.

KINGDOM OF PORTUGAL

KINGDOM OF SPAIN

ROME ·

NAPLES ·

KINGDOM OF THE TWO SICILIES

KINGDOM OF SARDINIA

MEDITERRANEAN SEA

Sicily

1700	1710	1720	1730	1740	1750

| QUEEN ANNE OF ENGLAND | | GEORGE I OF ENGLAND | | GEORGE II OF ENGLAND | |

| LOUIS XIV OF FRANCE | | LOUIS XV OF FRANCE | | | |

Rigaud, Louis XIV, 1701

Watteau
Return from Cythera (detail)
1717-1719

Chardin
Grace at Table, 1740

Alexander Pope, 1688-1744

Bach, 1686-1750

First copyright act
passed in England, 1735

Excavation of Pompeii, 1748

Voltaire, 1694-1778

Diderot, 1713-1784
Encyclopedia

Winckelmann, 1717-1768

Buffon, 1707-1778

Rousseau, 1712-1778

CHAPTER 25

THE EIGHTEENTH CENTURY: LATE BAROQUE AND ROCOCO, AND THE RISE OF ROMANTICISM

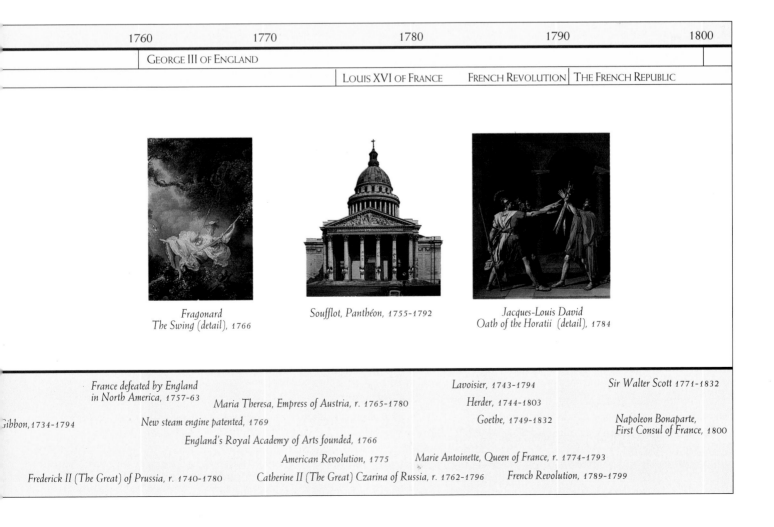

1760	1770	1780	1790	1800

GEORGE III OF ENGLAND

LOUIS XVI OF FRANCE   FRENCH REVOLUTION   THE FRENCH REPUBLIC

Fragonard
The Swing (detail), 1766

Soufflot, Panthéon, 1755-1792

Jacques-Louis David
Oath of the Horatii (detail), 1784

France defeated by England
in North America, 1757-63

Maria Theresa, Empress of Austria, r. 1765-1780

Gibbon, 1734-1794

New steam engine patented, 1769

England's Royal Academy of Arts founded, 1766

American Revolution, 1775

Frederick II (The Great) of Prussia, r. 1740-1780   Catherine II (The Great) Czarina of Russia, r. 1762-1796

Lavoisier, 1743-1794

Herder, 1744-1803

Goethe, 1749-1832

Marie Antoinette, Queen of France, r. 1774-1793

Sir Walter Scott 1771-1832

Napoleon Bonaparte,
First Consul of France, 1800

French Revolution, 1789-1799

The eighteenth century had a dual character; its two parts corresponded chronologically to an earlier and a later stage. The earlier stage was a continuation of the Baroque seventeenth century, with a number of distinctive differences; the later stage was the period during which the foundations of the modern world were laid. The present chapter, in its title and arrangement, reflects this bipartite division. However, a brief view of the century as a whole also can be useful.

The political world took new shapes in the eighteenth century. The maritime British Empire achieved great power and pursued disputes with France over the continent of North America and the subcontinent of India. Most of Europe was divided into small political units governed by princes, by high-ranking priests, or, in a few cases, by democratic councils. Once-powerful Spain was crippled by war and corrupt rule. Italy and much of Germany, as we now know them, were patchworks of principalities, duchies, and other small governing bodies. Against the awkward and shaky Holy Roman (later Austrian) Empire rose the small but aggressive state of Prussia, soon to become a significant military power, and, in the next century, the political foundation of the German Empire. Farther to the east loomed the still dormant might of half-Asiatic Russia, accelerating its slow turn toward the West under Peter the Great.

Scientifically and commercially inspired voyages opened the world to European knowledge, continuing the expansion begun in the age of the Baroque. The South Seas of the Pacific were explored and charted by Bougainville and Captain Cook; in the north, Danish navigator Bering charted the strait that separates Siberia from Alaska; in Africa, Mungo Park navigated the great Niger River far into the interior; and James Bruce, searching for the sources of the Nile, found in Ethiopia the confluence of its distant tributaries, the White Nile and the Blue Nile. These voyages of exploration were emblematic of the many that in the eighteenth century brought Europeans into contact with the native peoples inhabiting the great land-masses and archipelagos of the globe, laying the foundations of colonial empires that for good and for ill would dominate the world until well into the twentieth century.

THE ENLIGHTENMENT: PHILOSOPHY AND SOCIETY

The global expansion of European influence was matched by the extension of the boundaries of European knowledge that marks what has been called the Age of Enlightenment. We have observed its beginnings in the seventeenth century, with the mathematical and scientific achievements of Descartes, Pascal, Newton, and Leibnitz. The Enlightenment was in essence a new way of thinking critically about the world and about humankind, independently of revealed religion, of myth, and of tradition.

Ideally, the new critical method would proceed by the use of reason reflecting upon the results of physical experiment and critical analysis of texts. The German critic Lessing declared that the real power of reason is to be found not in the possession of truth but in its acquisition. All received truths should be open to scientific questioning, which must reject unfounded beliefs about the nature of humankind and of the world. The enlightened mind must be skeptical of doctrines and theories for which no verifiable evidence can be found. Thus the Enlightenment encouraged and stimulated that habit and application of mind that we know as the scientific method.

England and France were the principal centers of the Enlightenment, though its dictums influenced the thinking of intellectuals throughout Europe and in the American colonies; Franklin, Jefferson, and other American notables were educated in its principles. In England, Newton's theories of the mechanical structure of physical reality and John Locke's empiricism gave form and direction to the Enlightenment.

England had already pointed the way to great changes, providing the political environment for the freedom of opinion favorable to the enlightened intelligence. Its parliamentary form of government, free press, and a high degree of religious tolerance all tempered the power of the monarchy. Throughout the century, England enjoyed great material prosperity generated by inventions in industry and agriculture and by international trade. The middle-class, democratic values nurtured by these favorable conditions were summed up in the writings of the immensely influential Locke, whose works became almost the gospel of the Enlightenment. What we know, wrote Locke, comes to us through sense perception of the material world and is imprinted upon the mind as upon a blank tablet. From these perceptions alone we form ideas. Our ideas are not innate or God-given; it is only from experience that we can know (this is called the "doctrine of empiricism"). Human beings are born good, not cursed by original sin. The law of Nature grants them the natural rights of life, liberty, and property, as well as the right to freedom of conscience. Government is by contract, and its purpose is to protect these rights; if and when government abuses these rights, we have the further natural right of revolution. Happiness is to be gained by the rational pursuit of pleasure, which involves regard for the good of others. The founding documents of the United States clearly reflect these principles, and these beliefs form the credo of American democracy.

The work of Newton and Locke inspired the intellectuals of France. After a visit to England in 1726, Voltaire, enthusiastic about the free institutions he found there, "discovered" England for France and for the rest of Europe. His *Philosophical Letters on the English* (1734) advertised their thought, science, and government, which became the subjects of international discussion and debate. These were to inspire campaigns to reform the abuses and limit the privileges of royalty, the aristocracy, and the Church. The

English poet Alexander Pope, a contemporary of Voltaire, had declared: "The proper study of mankind is Man!" New philosophies of human beings and of society as part of physical nature were advanced by thinkers in France, who are still known by their French appellation—*philosophes*. They shared the conviction that the ills of humanity could be remedied by the application of reason and common sense to human problems. They criticized the powers of church and state as irrational limits placed upon political and intellectual freedom. They believed that, by the accumulation and propagation of knowledge, humanity could advance by degrees to a happier state than it had ever known. This conviction matured into the characteristically modern "doctrine of progress" and its corollary doctrine of the perfectibility of humankind. By the end of the century, the Marquis de Condorcet, in his *Historical Picture of the Progress of the Human Mind*, could make of the doctrine of progress a kind of religion of utopia.

Animated by their belief in human progress and perfectibility, the philosophes went about the task of gathering knowledge and making it accessible to all who could read; their program was in effect the democratization of knowledge. Diderot, a genius whose brilliant, critical intelligence greatly influenced the rationalistic and materialistic thinking of the Enlightenment, became editor of the pioneering *Encyclopedia* (1745), enlisting the contributions of the leading philosophes. The *Encyclopedia* proposed to include all available knowledge—historical, scientific, technical, as well as religious, moral—and political theory. Diderot's contemporary, Buffon, undertook a kind of encyclopedia of the natural sciences. His *Natural History*, a monumental work of forty-four volumes, was valuable especially for its zoological study and had the general effect of inspiring in the reading public an interest in the world of nature.

Scientific investigation and technological invention opened up great new possibilities for human understanding of the world and control of its material forces. Research into the phenomena of electricity and combustion, and the discovery of oxygen and the power of steam had enormous consequences. Steam power as an adjunct to, or replacement for, human labor began a new era in world history. The invention of steam engines in England for industrial production and, later, their use for transportation began what we know historically as the technological and industrial revolutions, which took place from about 1740 onward. England and all of Europe were destined to be transformed within a century by the harnessed power of steam, coal, oil, iron, steel, and electricity working in concert.

The political, economic, and social consequences of these changes were tremendous. The era of industrial capital and labor was born, as people flocked to cities to take jobs in the new steam-powered factories. The growth of the urban working class was so swift that social services could not evolve fast enough to serve new city residents. A split between employer and employee widened. The merchant rich became captains of industry, demanding that production and trade be free from government regulation and, at the same time, that the heads of industry participate in the fiscal decisions of government. Antagonisms between the powerful wealthy few and the workers helped to fuel political revolutions organized under the banners of democracy and free trade later in the century. All of these developments helped to initiate the era we call "modern," and many of the ideas and institutions that originated in the mid-eighteenth century are still with us today.

The ruling aristocracies, as if conscious of their waning historical significance, gradually abandoned their administrative and executive functions to members of the increasingly wealthy and influential middle class. Without fully realizing it, royalty and the nobility were slowly becoming obsolete. Stubbornly insisting on their ancient privileges, the nobility helped precipitate the French Revolution. Still, earlier in the century, these patrons of the arts and sciences followed with great interest news of the theories and discoveries exchanged by scholars in official groups like England's Royal Society and Royal Academy of Arts and France's academies of science and painting, and they joined intellectuals and members of the wealthy middle class in "salons" to discuss the latest ideas.

But with the increasing political and cultural influence of the middle classes, the later century witnessed a reaction to the rationalism, skepticism, materialism, and sometimes atheism of the philosophes. Their concern for humanity only in the abstract sense rather than with the facts of everyday living and the feelings of ordinary people, led the reading public to turn instead to the narratives of the newly popular novel, rather than to the philosophical essay, for a true account of the human scene. This accompanied the rejection of the "Rococo" style in art as an artificial and aristocratic taste untrue to the experience of plain people, who now demanded "naturalness" in art as well as in literature.

"Naturalness" was not simply truth to visual perception; it meant truth to human emotions—"sensibility" in the language of the day—which involved sensitivity and sincerity of feeling, rather than cynical rationality. It meant moral fervor in place of licentiousness, modest domestic settings in place of the glitter of courts and salons. Again, in the language of the day, one should listen to the dictates of the "heart" rather than the to reasonings of the "head." This new emotionalism, which would gradually replace the rationalism of the Enlightenment, we presently shall see as the first manifestation of Romanticism and of the modern spirit. Yet, for the great revolutions that usher in and characterize the modern age, the Enlightenment provided the ideas and the aims, Romanticism the passions and the action. The immensely influential thinker Rousseau would write in *Émile* (1762): "It is one of the faults of our age to rely on cold reason, as if man were all mind . . . small minds have a mania for reason. Strong souls speak a very different language, and it is by this language that men are persuaded and driven to action."

THE EARLY EIGHTEENTH CENTURY: LATE BAROQUE AND ROCOCO

Older patterns of life and society continued and obscured for a time the emergence of the new forces of change. On the continent, the decades between the death of Louis XIV in 1715 and the middle of the century were a period of relative relaxation after the exhausting "world" wars conducted by the great kings. Wars still were fought, but they were more often balancing maneuvers among the various states, waged by professional soldiers, with a kind of chess-board formality. In the arts, the wealthy remained eager to follow the royal taste for Baroque splendor, but this eagerness was modified everywhere by changes in society. Members of the aristocracy continued to be the primary patrons of the arts in many countries, and much of the century's art made before the French Revolution expressed their philosophy. The art that won aristocratic favor was luxurious, frivolous, sensual, and clever. The great religious and Classical themes and the grand manner of the Baroque gradually were overshadowed. Intricate and witty artifice now became the objective in all the arts—drama, music, painting, sculpture, architecture. The French were leaders in creating this art. In France, members of the court increasingly lived more in Paris than at Versailles, and they surrounded themselves with objects created in a delicately elegant Late Baroque variant called the *Rococo* style. Something of the quality of the Rococo also spread to the rest of Europe, competing in Italy with a lingering enjoyment of the heavier monumen-

tality of the Classical Baroque, and being transformed in Germany and Austria by a distinctively buoyant and festive air.

Late Baroque and Palladian Classicism in England

In England, early in the century, the monumentality of the Baroque inspired one vast palace, Blenheim (FIG. **25-1**), which was commissioned by the government to commemorate the British victory over the French led by John Churchill, Duke of Marlborough. Designed by JOHN VANBRUGH (1664–1726), Blenheim was one of the largest of the splendid country houses built during the period of prosperity that resulted from Great Britain's expansion into the New World. During this period, a small group of architects associated with the aging Sir Christopher Wren were responsible for a brief return to favor of the Baroque over the Palladian Classicism of Inigo Jones. Vanbrugh was the best known of this group. The picturesque silhouette he created for Blenheim, with its massing and its inventive architectural detail, is thoroughly Baroque. The design demonstrates his love of variety and contrast, tempered by his ability to create areas of focus like those found so frequently in the Baroque architecture of the seventeenth century. The tremendous forecourt, the hugely projecting pavilions, and the extended colonnades simultaneously recall St. Peter's and Versailles (FIGS. 24-3 and 24-64). Perhaps because Vanbrugh had begun his career as a

25-1 JOHN VANBRUGH, Blenheim Palace, Oxfordshire, England, 1705–1722.

writer of witty and popular comedies and as the builder of a theater in which to produce them, all of his architecture tended toward the theatrical on a mighty and extravagant scale. Like many Baroque architects, he even sacrificed convenience to dramatic effect, as in the placement of the kitchen at Blenheim some 200 feet from the majestic dining salon. Vanbrugh's architecture pleased his patrons in the beginning, but even before Blenheim was completed, critics were condemning what they considered its ponderous and bizarre qualities.

The criticism of buildings like Blenheim gradually was broadened to encompass the defects of the Baroque style in general. Soon, preference swung from the "irrationality" and "artificiality" of Baroque pomp, vast scale, theatrical effects, irregular forms, exuberant details, and grandiose rhetoric toward the "good sense" found in simple, harmonious, and useful Palladian designs. The British may also have come to connect the Baroque style with the showy rule of absolute monarchy—something to be played down in parliamentary England. In English architecture, the instinct for an unostentatious and commonsensical style led straight from the authority of Vitruvius, through the work of Andrea Palladio (FIG. 22-51), and on to that of Inigo Jones (FIG. 24-71). As Alexander Pope, in his *Fourth Moral Epistle* (1731), advised his friend, the statesman and architectural amateur RICHARD BOYLE, Earl of Burlington (1695–1753):

> You, too, proceed! make falling arts your care,
> Erect new wonders, and the old repair;
> Jones and Palladio to themselves restore
> And be whate'er Vitruvius was before.

Lord Burlington took the advice and strongly restated the Palladian doctrine of Inigo Jones in a new style in Chiswick House (FIG. **25-2**), which he built on the outskirts of London with the help of the talented professional WILLIAM KENT (c. 1686–1748). The way had been paved for this shift in style by, among other things, the publication of Colin Campbell's *Vitruvius Britannicus* (1715), three volumes of engravings of ancient buildings in Britain, prefaced by a denunciation of Italian Baroque and high praise for Palladio and Inigo Jones.

Chiswick House is a free variation on the theme of Palladio's Villa Rotonda (FIG. 22-51). The exterior design provided a clear alternative to the colorful splendors of Versailles. In its simple symmetry, unadorned planes, right angles, and stiffly wrought proportions, Chiswick looks very Classical and "rational," but, like so many Palladian villas in England, the effect is modified by its setting within informal gardens, where a charming irregularity of layout and freely growing, uncropped foliage dominate the scene. The development of the "English garden" as a rival to the formality of the continental garden is an important chapter in the history of eighteenth-century taste, about which we will say more later. Just as irregularity was cultivated in the landscaping surrounding English Palladian villas, so the interiors of buildings sometimes were ornamented in a style more closely related to the Rococo decoration fashionable on the continent than to the severity of the Classical Palladian exteriors. At Chiswick, the interior design creates a luxurious Late Baroque foil to the stern symmetry of the exterior and the plan. Despite such "lapses," Palladian Classicism prevailed in English architecture until about 1760, when it began to evolve into Neoclassicism.

At just about this time of change, John Wood the Elder (c. 1704–1754) and his son, JOHN WOOD THE YOUNGER (1728–1782), father and son, laid out, for the fashionable resort town of Bath in Somersetshire, a magnificent complex of buildings, grouped around simple, geometrical spaces, the square, circle, and semi-circle: thus, Queen's

25-2 RICHARD BOYLE (Earl of Burlington) and WILLIAM KENT, Chiswick House, near London, begun 1725.

25-3 JOHN WOOD THE YOUNGER, The Royal Crescent, 1769–1775, Bath, England.

Square, the Circus, and the Royal Crescent (FIG. **25-3**), the last being exclusively the work of John Wood the Younger. These early, ingenious solutions to the problems of urban design were intended not for royalty but for the well-to-do members of society who came "to take the waters" at the city's hot springs, which, restored and operating in the eighteenth century, had been famous since Roman times and had given the city of Bath its name. In both the Circus and the Royal Crescent the houses are linked into rows behind a single, continuous Palladian facade, which transforms the joined units into one palatial edifice. The Royal Crescent joins thirty residences in a great semi-ellipse, originally intended to have a matching semi-ellipse facing it across an intersecting roadway, so as to suggest the ancient Roman Colosseum (FIGS. 7-39 and 7-40). Bath, with its ancient Roman associations, prompted the younger John Wood to refer to Rome, not only for the Colosseum-like plan, but for the imperial scale and majesty of the elevation of the building. Especially "Roman" is the sweeping parade of colossal Ionic columns along the lofty, curving basement; the roofline, punctuated regularly with clusters of chimney pots, is traditionally English. The Bath designs will, with many variations, be a standard for British urban architecture for a century. Here, they announce a new Roman Classical presence in what is still a Palladian edifice.

Late Baroque in Italy and Germany

ARCHITECTURE   The titled grandees of Europe were still under the spell of Versailles when they planned their palaces, and the builders of churches sought to emulate

the glories of Counter-Reformation Baroque in the modes of Bernini, Borromini, and Guarini. Yet the restraining example of the Classical is felt in one of the finest early eighteenth-century ecclesiastical structures, the Superga (FIG. **25-4**), located near Turin in northwestern Italy. This church was designed by FILIPPO JUVARA (1678–1736) for Victor Amadeus II, king of Savoy, to commemorate Savoy's victory over the French in 1706 during the War of the Spanish Succession. Juvara had begun his career as

25-4   FILIPPO JUVARA, the Superga, near Turin, Italy, 1715–1731.

royal architect at Turin by practicing the lavish Baroque style of his predecessor, Guarini (FIG. 24-16), but a period of study in Rome turned Juvara toward a more Classical approach. The style of the Superga reflects this shift, although the building's setting is entirely Baroque. The layout of the church and the monastery, of which the Superga is the frontispiece, is similar to that of the Church of the Invalides in Paris (FIG. 24-68). The great dome and drum of the Superga are close to the dimensions of the Invalides and may reflect Juvara's knowledge of that building. At the same time, the Superga's deep, four-columned portico, surmounted by a balustrade that continues around the building, echoes Palladian Classicism, and the relation of the portico to the rotunda-like structure behind it recalls the ancient Pantheon (FIG. 7-55). The severity of the portico and of the colossal orders that articulate the walls is offset by the light, fanciful bell towers that flank the dome. In its adroit adjustment of Classical features and Baroque grouping, the building is an impressive example of Juvara's intelligent eclecticism.

The influence of Borromini and Guarini was most strongly felt in the ecclesiastical architecture of southern Germany and Austria, an area that had lain dormant artis-

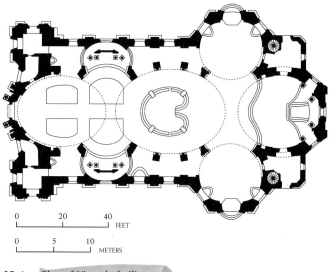

25-6   Plan of Vierzehnheiligen.

tically through most of the seventeenth century. One of the most splendid of the German buildings is the pilgrimage church of Vierzehnheiligen (Fourteen Saints), designed by BALTHASAR NEUMANN (1687–1753). Born in the German part of Bohemia, Neumann traveled in Austria and northern Italy and studied in Paris before returning home to become one of the most active architects working in his native land. Numerous large windows in the richly articulated but continuous walls of Vierzehnheiligen flood the interior with an even, bright, and cheerful light. The pilgrimage church sanctuary (FIG. **25-5**) exhibits a vivacious play of architectural fantasy that retains the dynamic energy but banishes all the dramatic qualities of Italian Baroque.

The complexity of Vierzehnheiligen is readable in its ground plan (FIG. **25-6**), which has been called "one of the most ingenious pieces of architectural design ever conceived." The straight line deliberately seems to have been banished. The composition is made up of tangent ovals and circles, so that, within the essential outlines of the traditional Gothic church (apse, transept, nave, and western towers), a quite different interior effect is achieved, one of undulating space in continuous motion, creating unlimited vistas bewildering in their variety and surprise effects. The features of the structure pulse, flow, and commingle as if they were ceaselessly in the process of being molded. The fluency of line, the floating, hovering surfaces, the interwoven spaces, and the dematerialized masses of the design combine to suggest a "frozen" counterpart to the intricacy of voices in a fugue by Bach. We must think of this kind of church as a brilliant ensemble of architecture, sculpture, music, and painting, in which the boundaries of the arts dissolve in a visionary unity.

SCULPTURE   Pictorial embellishment of German and Austrian churches was supplemented by sculpture conceived to produce entirely pictorial effects. The group of the

25-5   BALTHASAR NEUMANN, interior of the pilgrimage chapel of Vierzehnheiligen, near Staffelstein, Germany, 1743–1772.

Assumption of the Virgin (FIG. **25-7**) was created by EGID QUIRIN ASAM (1692–1750) for the space above the altar in the monastery church at Rohr, Germany. The church was designed in collaboration with his brother COSMAS DAMIAN ASAM (1686–1739). The brothers were influenced in their building designs by the Late Baroque architecture they saw on a trip to Rome. What they brought home was a feeling for illusionistic spectacle. In Egid Quirin Asam's *Assumption of the Virgin*, as in Bernini's *Ecstasy of St. Theresa* (FIG. 24-10), the miraculous is made real before our eyes, a spiritual vision materially visible. The Virgin, effortlessly borne aloft by angels, soars to the glowing paradise above her, while the apostolic witnesses below gesticulate in astonishment around her vacant tomb. The figures ascending to Heaven have gilded details that set them apart from those that remain on earth. The setting is a luxuriously ornamented theater; the scene itself, pure opera—an art that was perfected and became very popular in the eighteenth century. One can imagine the Virgin as the protagonist in an oper-

25-7 EGID QUIRIN ASAM, *Assumption of the Virgin*, monastery church at Rohr, Germany, 1723.

atic production, singing the climactic aria, with all appropriate gestures, to the excited accompaniment of a chorus, while a virtuoso designer directs the stagecraft. Here, sculpture dissolves into painting, theater, and music, its mass rendered weightless, its natural compactness of composition broken up and diffused. In this instance, the art of the sculptor was used, paradoxically, to disguise substance and function, weight and tactility in the interest of eye-deceiving mystical illusion.

PAINTING   Illusion in painting, particularly for the ceilings of churches and palaces, was already a venerable tradition in the Late Baroque. The ceilings of Late Baroque palaces sometimes became painted festivals for the imagination. The master of such works, GIAMBATTISTA TIEPOLO (1696–1770), was the last great Italian painter to have an international impact until the twentieth century. Of Venetian origin, Tiepolo worked for patrons in Austria, Germany, and Spain, as well as in Italy, leaving a strong impression wherever he went. His bright, cheerful colors and his relaxed compositions are ideally suited to Rococo architecture. *The Apotheosis of the Pisani Family* (FIG. **25-8**), a ceiling fresco in the Villa Pisani at Stra in northern Italy, shows airy populations fluttering through vast sunlit skies and fleecy clouds, their figures making dark accents against the brilliant light of high noon. As the word *apotheosis* indicates, members of the Pisani family are elevated here to the rank of the gods in a heavenly scene that recalls the ceiling paintings of Correggio (FIG. 22-36) and Pozzo (FIG. 24-31). While retaining the illusionistic tendencies of the seventeenth century, Tiepolo discards all rhetoric to create gay and brightly colored pictorial schemes of great elegance and grace, which, for sheer effectiveness as decor, are unsurpassed.

Rococo: The French Taste

The death of Louis XIV in 1715 brought many changes in French high society. The court of Versailles was at once abandoned for the pleasures of town life. The *hôtels* (town houses) of Paris soon became the centers of a new, softer style we call Rococo. The sparkling gaiety cultivated by the new age, associated with the Regency that followed the death of Louis XIV and with the reign of Louis XV, found perfectly harmonious expression in this new style. Rococo appeared in France in about 1700, primarily as a style of interior design. The French Rococo exterior was most often simple, or even plain, but Rococo exuberance took over the interior. The word *Rococo* came from the French word *rocaille*, which literally means "pebble," but the term referred especially to the small stones and shells used to decorate the interiors of grottoes. Such shells or shell forms were the principal motifs in Rococo ornament.

The feminine look of the Rococo style suggests that the age was dominated by the taste and the social initiative of

25-8 GIAMBATTISTA TIEPOLO, *The Apotheosis of the Pisani Family,* 1761–1762. Ceiling fresco in the villa Pisani, Stra, Italy.

women—and, to a large extent, it was. Women—Madame de Pompadour in France, Maria Theresa in Austria, Elizabeth and Catherine in Russia—held some of the highest positions in Europe, and female influence was felt in any number of smaller courts. The Rococo salon was the center of early eighteenth-century Parisian society, and Paris was the social capital of Europe. Wealthy, ambitious, and clever society hostesses competed to attract the most famous and the most accomplished people to their salons. The medium of social intercourse was conversation spiced with wit, repartee as quick and deft as a fencing match. The masculine heroics and rhetoric of the Baroque era were replaced by dainty gallantries and pointed sallies of humor. Artifice reigned supreme, and it was considered in bad taste to be enthusiastic or sincere.

A typical French Rococo room is the Salon de la Princesse (FIG. **25-9**) in the Hôtel de Soubise in Paris, designed by GERMAIN BOFFRAND (1667–1754). If we compare this room with the Galerie des Glaces at Versailles (FIG. 24-66), we see the fundamental difference at once. The strong architectural lines and panels of the earlier style were softened here into flexible, sinuous curves luxuriant-

25-9   GERMAIN BOFFRAND, Salon de la Princesse, Hôtel de Soubise, Paris, 1737–1740. Painting by NATOIRE, sculpture by J. B. LEMOINE.

ly multiplied in mirror reflections. The walls melt into the vault; the cornices are replaced by irregular painted shapes, surmounted by sculpture and separated by the typical shells of rocaille. Painting, architecture, and sculpture make a single ensemble. The profusion of curving tendrils and sprays of foliage combine with the shell forms to give an effect of freely growing nature and to suggest that the Rococo room is permanently decked for a festival.

Rococo was a style preeminently evident in small art; furniture, utensils, and accessories of all sorts were exquisitely wrought in the characteristically delicate, undulating Rococo line. French Rococo interiors were designed as lively, total works of art in which the architecture, relief sculptures, and wall paintings were complemented by elegant furniture, enchanting small sculpture, ornamented mirror frames, delightful ceramics and silver, a few "easel" paintings, and decorative tapestry. As we see them today, French Rococo interiors, like that of the Salon de la Princesse, have lost most of the moveable "accessories" that once adorned them. We can imagine, however, how such rooms, with their alternating gilded moldings, vivacious relief sculptures, and daintily colored ornament of flowers and garlands, must have harmonized with the chamber music played in them, with the elaborate costumes of satin and brocade, and with the equally elegant etiquette and sparkling wit of the people who graced them.

By the second quarter of the century, the grandeur of the Late Baroque was being modified by French Rococo overtones in much of Germany and Austria. A brilliant example of French Rococo in Germany is the Amalienburg (FIGS. **25-10** and **25-11**), a small lodge built by FRANÇOIS DE CUVILLIÉS (1695–1768) in the park of the Nymphenburg Palace in Munich. Although we have seen that the Rococo was essentially a style of interior design, the Amalienburg beautifully harmonizes the interior and exterior elevations through the curving flow of lines and planes that cohere in a plastic unity of great elegance. The *bombé* (outward-bowed) shape of the central bay of the Amalienburg facade was a common feature of Rococo furniture design; indeed, the compactness, diminutive scale, graceful lines, and exquisite detail invest the Amalienburg with the appearance of a kind of precious furnishing set down on the manicured greensward of its park setting. The most spectacular interior room in the lodge is the circular Hall of Mirrors (FIG. 25-11), a silver and blue ensemble of architecture, stucco relief, silvered-bronze mirrors, and crystal that dazzles the eye with myriad scintillating motifs, forms, and figurations borrowed from the full Rococo repertoire of ornament. This is the zenith of the style. Facets of silvery light, multiplied by windows and mirrors, sharply or softly delineate the endlessly proliferating shapes and contours that weave rhythmically around the upper walls and the coves of the ceiling. Everything seems organic, growing, and in motion, an ultimate rarefaction of illusion created with virtuoso flourishes by the assemblage of architect,

25-10 FRANÇOIS DE CUVILLIÉS, the Amalienburg, Nymphenburg Park, Munich, Germany, 1734–1739.

25-11 Hall of Mirrors, the Amalienburg.

25-12 Hyacinthe Rigaud, *Louis XIV*, 1701. Oil on canvas, approx. 9'2" × 6'3". Louvre, Paris.

25-13 Antoine Watteau, *L'Indifférent, c.* 1716. Oil on canvas, approx. 10" × 7". Louvre, Paris.

artists, and artisans, all magically in command of the resources of their varied media.

The painter above all others whom we associate with the French Rococo is Antoine Watteau (1684–1721). The differences between the age of the Baroque and the age of Rococo can be seen clearly if we contrast the portrait of Louis XIV (FIG. **25-12**) by Hyacinthe Rigaud (1659–1743) with one of Watteau's paintings, *L'Indifférent* (FIG. **25-13**). Rigaud portrays pompous majesty in slow and stately promenade, as if the French monarch were reviewing throngs of bowing courtiers at Versailles. The other painting represents a languid, gliding dancer, whose mincing minuet might be seen as mimicking the monarch's solemn pacing. In Rigaud's portrait, stout architecture, bannerlike curtains, flowing ermine, and fleur-de-lis exalt the king, while fanfares of trumpets blast. In Watteau's painting, the dancer moves in a rainbow shimmer of color, emerging onto the stage of the intimate comic opera to the silken sounds of strings. The portrait of the king is very large, the "portrait"

of "the indifferent one," quite small. The first painting is Baroque; the second is Rococo.

Watteau's masterpiece (of which he painted two different versions) is *Return from Cythera* (FIG. **25-14**), completed between 1717 and 1719 as the artist's acceptance piece for admission to the French Royal Academy. Watteau was Flemish, and his style was a beautiful derivative of the style of Rubens—a kind of rarefaction and refinement of it.

At the turn of the century, the French Royal Academy was rather sharply divided between two doctrines. One doctrine upheld the ideas of Le Brun (the major proponent of French Baroque under Louis XIV), who followed Nicolas Poussin in teaching that form was the most important element in painting, while "colors in paintings were . . . blandishments to lure the eyes," something added for effect and not really essential. The other doctrine, with Rubens as its model, proclaimed the supremacy of color as natural and the coloristic style as the proper guide to the artist. Depending on which side they took, members of the Academy were called "Poussinistes" or "Rubénistes." With Watteau, the Rubénistes carried the day, and the Rococo

25-14 ANTOINE WATTEAU, *Return from Cythera*, 1717–1719. Oil on canvas, approx. 4'3" × 6'4". Louvre, Paris.

style in painting was established on the colorism of Rubens and the Venetians.

Watteau's *Return from Cythera* represents a group of lovers preparing to depart from the island of eternal youth and love, sacred to Aphrodite. Young and luxuriously costumed, they perform, as it were, an elegant, tender, graceful ballet, moving from the protective shade of a woodland park peopled with amorous cupids and voluptuous statuary, down a grassy slope to an awaiting golden barge. The attitudes of the figures were studied carefully; Watteau has never been equaled for his distinctive poses, which combine elegance and sweetness. He composed his generally quite small paintings from albums of superb drawings that have been preserved and are still in fine condition. In these, we find him observing slow movement from difficult and unusual angles, obviously with the intention of finding the smoothest, most poised, and most refined attitudes. As he sought nuances of bodily poise and movement, Watteau also strove for the most exquisite shades of color difference, defining in a single stroke the shimmer of silk at a bent knee or the iridescence that touches a glossy surface as it emerges from shadow.

Art historians have noted that the theme of love and Arcadian happiness (which we have seen since Giorgione and which Watteau may have seen in works by Rubens) in Watteau's pictures is slightly shadowed with wistfulness, or even melancholy, as if Watteau, during his own short life, meditated on the swift passage of youth and pleasure. The haze of color, the subtly modeled shapes, the gliding motion, and the air of suave gentility were all to the taste of the Rococo artist's wealthy patronage. The unifying power of that taste drew the arts together. The titles, as well as the mood of many musical compositions by Watteau's contemporary Jean Philippe Rameau are perfectly suited to Watteau's pictures. The mood is also wonderfully echoed in a passage from Alexander Pope's *Rape of the Lock* (1714), showing that Rococo taste touched even the English arts on occasion:

> *But now secure the painted vessel glides,*
> *The sunbeams trembling on the floating tides;*
> *While melting music steals upon the sky,*
> *And softened sounds along the waters die.*
> . . . .
> *The lucid squadrons round the sails repair:*
> *Soft o'er the shrouds aërial whispers breathe,*
> *That seemed but zephyrs to the train beneath.*
> *Some to the sun their insect wings unfold,*
> *Waft on the breeze, or sink in clouds of gold;*
> *Transparent forms too fine for mortal sight,*
> *Their fluid bodies half dissolved in light,*
> *Loose to the wind their airy garments flew,*
> *Thin glittering textures of the filmy dew.*

Watteau's successors never quite matched his taste and subtlety. Their themes were concerned with love, artfully and archly pursued through erotic frivolity and playful intrigue. After Watteau's untimely death at 37, his follower, FRANÇOIS BOUCHER (1703–1770), painter to Madame de

Pompadour, rose to the dominant position in French painting. Although he was an excellent portraitist, Boucher's fame rests primarily on his gay and graceful allegories, in which Arcadian shepherds, nymphs, and goddesses cavort in shady glens, engulfed in pink and sky-blue light. *Cupid a Captive* (FIG. **25-15**) presents the viewer with a rosy pyramid

25-15   FRANÇOIS BOUCHER, *Cupid a Captive*, 1754. Oil on canvas, approx. 66" × 34". Reproduced by permission of the Trustees of the Wallace Collection, London.

of infant and female flesh, set off against a cool, leafy background, with the nudity of the figures both hidden and revealed by fluttering draperies. Boucher used the full range of Baroque devices to create his masterly composition: the dynamic play of crisscrossing diagonals, curvilinear forms, and slanting recessions. But powerful Baroque curves in his work were dissected into a multiplicity of decorative arabesques, and Baroque drama dissipated into sensual playfulness. Gay and superficial, Boucher's artful Rococo fantasies became mirrors in which his patrons, the wealthy French, could behold the ornamental reflections of their cherished pastimes.

JEAN-HONORÉ FRAGONARD (1732–1806), Boucher's student, was a first-rate colorist whose decorative skill almost surpassed his master's. An example of his manner can stand as characteristic not only of him, but of the later Rococo in general. *The Swing* (FIG. **25-16**) is a typical "intrigue" picture. A young gentleman has managed an arrangement by which an unsuspecting old bishop swings the young man's pretty sweetheart higher and higher, while her lover stretches out to admire her ardently from a strategic position on the ground. The young lady flirtatiously and boldly kicks off her shoe at the little statue of the god of discretion, who holds his finger to his lips. The landscape setting is out of Watteau—a luxuriant, perfumed bower in a park that very much resembles a stage scene for the comic opera. The glowing pastel colors and soft light convey, almost by themselves, the sensuality of the theme.

The Rococo mood of sensual intimacy also permeated much of the small sculpture designed for the salons of the day. Artists like Claude Michel, called CLODION (1738–1814), specialized in small, lively sculptures that combined the sensuous fantasies of the Rococo with lightened echoes of Bernini's dynamic Baroque figures. Perhaps we should expect such influence in the works of Clodion; he lived and worked in Rome for some years after discovering the charms of the city during his tenure as the recipient of the cherished Prix de Rome. Clodion's small group, *Nymph and Satyr* (FIG. **25-17**), has an open and vivid composition suggestive of its dynamic Baroque roots, but the artist has overlaid that source with the erotic playfulness of Boucher and Fragonard to energize his eager nymph and the laughing satyr into whose mouth she pours a cup of wine. Here, the sensual exhilaration of the Rococo is caught in diminutive scale and fragile terracotta; as with so many Rococo artifacts, and most of Clodion's best work, this group was designed for a tabletop.

In pictorial art the eighteenth century witnesses a new specialty—the small, intimate portrait rendered in pastels rather than in oil paint. The medium of pastel is especially associated with the art of the Rococo, although it will be popular again with the Impressionists of the late nineteenth century. *Pastels* are chalk-like crayons, made of ground color pigments mixed with water and a binding medium. They lend themselves to quick execution and sketching, particularly of portraits, and provide the artist with a very wide range of colors and subtle variations of tone, suitable for rendering nuances of value and fleeting facial expressions. Typically, the colors are high-keyed and luminous, shading is minimal, and the forms are modulated by a slightly hazed soft focus suggestive of sunlit atmosphere.

Introduced into France by the talented and popular Venetian painter Rosalba Carriera (1675–1757), the pastel portrait becomes almost the monopoly of QUENTIN DE LA TOUR (1704–1788), who gives us in his self-portrait (FIG. **25-18**) the very type of the Enlightenment personality. In

his own features and expression, in the sidelong glance and almost jaunty pose, we find the kind of poise and suave elegance characteristic of the cultivated society of the age— the *esprit* of the Enlightenment personality. The face is open and lively, with a bright look of amiable and active intelligence. Here is the optimistic (if slightly sardonic) believer in progress, a man of good taste, conversant with the ideas of the Age of Reason. He is critical of ancient privilege, prejudice, and superstition, a reader of Locke, Voltaire, Montesquieu, Diderot, Rousseau, and the other thinkers whose principles will rationalize the American and

25-16   JEAN-HONORÉ FRAGONARD, *The Swing*, 1766. Oil on canvas, approx. 35″ × 32″. Reproduced by permission of the Trustees of the Wallace Collection, London.

specialists in an entirely different discipline. In this respect it becomes a technological device, an art or craft applied to a science. The technological applications of draftsmanship and model building would be indispensable to the development of science well into the age of the computer.

Technological advance depended on the new enthusiasm for mechanical explanation of the wonders of the clockwork cosmos. The fascination it had for ordinary people as well as for the learned is the subject of *A Philosopher Giving a Lecture at the Orrery (in which a lamp is put in place of the sun)* (FIG. **25-21**), by the English painter JOSEPH WRIGHT OF DERBY (1734–1797). Wright specialized in the dramatic lighting of candlelight and moonlit scenes. He loved subjects like the orrery demonstration, which could be illuminated by a single light from within the picture. The effect recalls Gerard van Honthorst's *Supper Party* (FIG. 24-44), but Wright's subject is thoroughly one from the Age of Reason. A scholar uses a special technological model (called an *orrery*) to demonstrate the theory that the universe operates

like a gigantic clockwork mechanism. Light from the lamp used to represent the sun pours forth from behind the figure of the boy silhouetted in the foreground to create dramatic light and shadows that heighten the drama of the scene. Awed children crowd close to the tiny metal orbs that represent the planets within the arcing bands that symbolize their orbits. An earnest listener makes notes, while the lone woman seated at the left and the two gentlemen at the right look on with rapt attention. Everyone in Wright's painting is caught up in the wonders of scientific knowledge; an ordinary lecture takes on the qualities of a grand "history painting." Wright has scrupulously rendered with careful accuracy every detail of the figures, the mechanisms of the orrery, and even the books and curtain in the shadowy background. The mood created by the lighting and the intensity of the poses, however, suffuse this realistic rendering with an aura of larger-than-life energy that is linked to the sense of emotional drama underlying much of the evolving vision of Romanticism. Wright's realism appealed

25-21   JOSEPH WRIGHT OF DERBY, *A Philosopher Giving a Lecture at the Orrery (in which a lamp is put in place of the sun), c.* 1763–1765. Oil on canvas, 58" × 80". Derby Museums and Art Gallery, Derby, England.

25-22 ABRAHAM DARBY III and THOMAS F. PRITCHARD, iron bridge at Coalbrookdale (first cast-iron bridge over the Severn River), 1776–1779.

to the great industrialists of his day. Works like *Orrery* often were purchased by scientific-industrial innovators like Josiah Wedgwood (who pioneered many techniques of mass-produced pottery) and Sir Richard Arkwright (whose spinning frame revolutionized the textile industry). To them, Wright's elevation of the theories and inventions of the Industrial Revolution to the plane of history painting was excitingly and appropriately in tune with the future.

Eighteenth-century engineering, especially, foreshadowed the future, particularly in its use of industrial materials. The first use of iron in bridge design came when a cast-iron bridge was built in England over the river Severn, near the site at Coalbrookdale where ABRAHAM DARBY III (1750–1789) ran his family's cast-iron business. The Darby family had spearheaded the evolution of the iron industry in England, and they vigorously supported the investigation of new uses for the material. The fabrication of cast-iron rails and bridge elements inspired Darby to work with architect THOMAS F. PRITCHARD (1723–1777) in designing the Coalbrookdale Bridge (FIG. **25-22**). The utilitarian shapes in this structure are still breathtakingly beautiful. The cast-iron armature that supports the roadbed springs from stone pier to stone pier until it leaps the final 100 feet across the Severn River gorge. The style of the graceful center arc echoes the grand arches of Roman aqueducts (FIG. 7-36). At the same time, the exposed structure of the cast-iron parts of the bridge prefigures the skeletal use of iron and steel in the nineteenth century, when visible structural armatures will be expressive factors in the design of buildings like the Crystal Palace (FIG. 26-94) and the Eiffel Tower (FIG. 26-95).

REACTION AGAINST THE ROCOCO: THE TASTE FOR THE "NATURAL"

Earlier we have mentioned the immense influence of Rousseau. His name is traditionally joined with that of Voltaire as representative of the French Enlightenment and instrumental in preparing the way ideologically for the French Revolution. Yet Voltaire, as we have seen, thought the salvation of mankind to be in the advancement of science and in the rational improvement of human society, while Rousseau declared that the arts, sciences, society, and civilization in general had corrupted "natural man"—man in the primitive state—and that humanity's only salvation was a return to something like "the ignorance, innocence and happiness" of its original condition. According to Rousseau, human feeling, sensibility, and emotions are prior to reason: "To exist is to feel; our feeling is undoubtedly earlier than our intelligence, and we had feelings before we had ideas." Nature alone must be the guide: "all our natural inclinations are right,"—and, "What I feel to be right is right, what I feel to be wrong is wrong. . . . Too often does reason deceive us . . . but conscience never deceives us." Rousseau's basic point: "Man by nature is good . . . he is depraved and perverted by society." As against progress, he insists: "Our minds have been corrupted in proportion as the arts and sciences have improved."

These, and like sentiments of Rousseau, shocked Voltaire, who responded to them with acid sarcasm in a letter to Rousseau, that expresses their fundamental difference of outlook.

I have received, sir, your new book against the human race [*Dissertation on the Origin of Inequality*, 1755]. The horrors of human society have never been painted in such striking colors . . . no one has ever been so witty as you are in trying to turn us into brutes: to read your book makes one long to go on all fours. Since, however, it is now some sixty years since I gave up the practice, I feel that it is unfortunately impossible for me to resume it.

The society that Rousseau attacked and Voltaire defended in general terms was in fact the one they both knew and moved in; its center was Paris, ornamented by the Rococo. For Rousseau its "statues and pictures" were "representations of vice, every perversion of heart and mind." The views of Rousseau, widely read and popular, were largely responsible for the turning away from the Rococo and the formation of a taste for the "natural," as opposed to the artificial.

Taste and good taste were favorite topics of discussion in the eighteenth century; leading thinkers gave them much attention and came up with many definitions. For our purpose, *taste* is the habit of discerning, judging, and preferring the qualities of things (*good taste* would be judging "correctly"). Although taste is subjective and relative in its selections, and often subject to fashion, we can readily observe when it is widely shared (we have already spoken of the Rococo as the "French taste,"—the preference of French society for the Rococo style in art). *Style* might be defined as the esthetic expression of a culture or society to changes in science, technology, philosophy, historical development, and the like. What people like or dislike is a certain style, which we say "suits" their taste or does not. Thus, style refers to the art object and taste to the response. Of course, the artist or artists, who are creators of the style, can be judged to have good or bad taste, as can the artists' audience. In this book we have been concerned primarily and necessarily with the description of style; but as we get close to the modern age we become more acquainted with preferences decided by the individual as well as by the community—the tastes of the artist's public audience.

Taste, both the artist's and the public's, becomes more and more subjective; we find rapid changes of taste and different tastes existing at the same time. Personal preference takes the place of the old, academic system that established rules for good taste. The taste for the "natural" in art, which we consider first, is a preference for themes that are simple, honest, unaffected, showing people as they are in their natural settings and particular occupations. (We shall find that these "natural" themes need not be depicted in only one style!) Ornament is largely eliminated, as are mythological subjects with their erotic overtones. Aristocratic rank and its pompous attributes are dismissed. Rousseau urges us to "have respect for human kind; remember that it consists essentially of the people; if all the kings . . . were removed they would scarcely be missed,

and things would go on none the worse." This is the rationale of the taste for the "natural."

We find "naturalness" in sharp focus in a portrait of Paul Revere (FIG. **25-23**) by the American artist JOHN SINGLETON COPLEY (1738–1815). Copley had matured as a painter in the Massachusetts Bay Colony and later emigrated to England, where he absorbed the fashionable English portrait style. But here he shows something of the hard, provincial precision of his colonial masters. *Paul Revere*, painted before Copley left Boston, conveys a sense of directness and faithfulness to visual fact that marked the taste for "downrightness" and plainness noticed by many visitors to America during the eighteenth and nineteenth centuries. At the time the portrait was painted, Revere was not yet the familiar hero of the American Revolution. In the picture, he is working at his everyday profession of silversmithing. The setting is plain, the lighting clear and revealing. The subject sits in his shirtsleeves, bent over a teapot in progress; he pauses and turns his head to look the observer straight in the eye. The artist has treated the reflections in the polished wood of the tabletop with as much care as Revere's figure, his tools, and the teapot resting on its leather graver's pillow. Special prominence was

25-23 JOHN SINGLETON COPLEY, *Paul Revere, c.* 1768–1770. Oil on canvas, 35″ × 28¹/₂″. Museum of Fine Arts, Boston (gift of Joseph W., William B., and Edward H. R. Revere).

25-24   THOMAS GAINSBOROUGH, *Mrs. Richard Brinsley Sheridan, c.* 1785. Oil on canvas, approx. 7' 2" × 5'. National Gallery of Art, Washington, D.C. (Andrew W. Mellon Collection).

given to the figure's eyes by means of the intense reddish light that reflects onto the darkened side of the face and hands. The informality and the sense of the moment link this painting to contemporaneous English and European portraits, but the spare style and the emphasis on the sitter's down-to-earth character differentiate this American work from its British and continental counterparts (FIGS. 25-18 and 25-30).

A contrasting blend of "naturalistic" representation and Rococo setting is found in the portrait of *Mrs. Richard Brinsley Sheridan* (FIG. **25-24**) by the British painter THOMAS GAINSBOROUGH (1727–1788). This portrait shows the lovely woman, dressed informally, seated in a rustic landscape faintly reminiscent of Watteau in its soft-hued light and feathery brushwork. Gainsborough intended to match the unspoiled beauty of the natural landscape with the natural beauty of the subject, whose dark brown hair blows freely in the slight wind and whose clear, unassisted "English" complexion and air of ingenuous sweetness con-

trast sharply with the pert sophistication of continental Rococo portraits. The artist originally had planned to give the picture "an air more pastoral than it at present possesses" by adding several sheep, but he did not live long enough to paint them in. Even without this element, we can sense Gainsborough's deep interest in the landscape setting; although he won greater fame in his time for his portraits, he had begun as a landscape painter and always preferred painting scenes of nature to the depiction of human likenesses.

The *Self-portrait* (FIG. **25-25**) by ÉLISABETH LOUISE VIGÉE-LEBRUN (1755–1842) is another variation of the "naturalistic" impulse in eighteenth-century portraiture. In the new mode, Vigée-Lebrun looks directly at the viewer like Paul Revere; like Revere, she pauses in her work to return our gaze. Although her mood is more lighthearted than that of Revere and details of her costume echo the serpentine curve beloved by Rococo artists and wealthy patrons, nothing about Vigée-Lebrun's pose or her mood speaks of Rococo frivolity. Hers is the self-confident stance of a woman whose art has won her an independent role in her society. Like many of her contemporaries, Vigée-Lebrun

25-25   ÉLISABETH LOUISE VIGÉE-LEBRUN, *Self-portrait,* 1790. Oil on canvas, 8' 4" × 6' 9". Galleria degli Uffizi, Florence.

lived a life of extraordinary personal and economic independence, working for the nobility throughout Europe. She was famous for the force and grace of her portraits, especially those of high-born ladies and royalty. Although she was successful during the age of the late monarchy in France, she survived the fall of the French aristocracy through her talent, her wit, and her ability to forge connections with those in power in the post-revolutionary period. In her self-portrait, Vigée-Lebrun shows herself to us in a close-up, intimate view at work on one of the portraits that won her renown, that of Queen Marie Antoinette. The naturalism and intimacy of her expression are similar to those in Gainsborough's portrait of Mrs. Sheridan, which reflects the ideals of independence and self-reliance she exhibits as a woman.

"Naturalness" was also sought after in the depiction of the human setting, the peopled landscape. Documentation of particular places became popular, both to serve the needs of the many scientific expeditions mounted during the century and to satisfy the desires of genteel tourists for mementos of their journeys. By this time, a "grand tour" of the major sites of Europe was considered part of every well-bred person's education. Naturally, those on tour wished to bring home things that would help them remember their experiences and would impress those at home with the wonders they had seen.

The English were especially eager collectors of pictorial souvenirs. Certain artists in Venice specialized in painting the most characteristic scenes, or *vedute*, of that city to sell to British visitors. The veduta paintings of ANTONIO

CANALETTO (1697–1768) were eagerly acquired by English tourists, who hung them on the walls of great houses like Chiswick and Blenheim as visible evidence of their visit to the city of the Grand Canal. It must have been very cheering in the midst of a gray winter afternoon in England to look up and see a sunny, panoramic view like that in Canaletto's *Basin of San Marco from San Giorgio Maggiore* (FIG. 25-26), with its cloud-studded sky, calm harbor, varied water traffic, picturesque pedestrians, and well-known Venetian landmarks all picked out in scrupulous perspective and minute detail.

Canaletto had trained as a scene-painter with his father, but his easy mastery of detail, light, and shadow soon made him one of the most popular "vedutista" in Venice. Occasionally, he painted his scenes directly from life, but usually he made drawings "on location" to take back to his studios as sources for canvases to be painted there. To help make the on-site drawings true to life, he often used a camera obscura. Like van Ruisdael (FIG. 24-55), Canaletto was interested in painting the visible facts of the scene he had chosen, but unlike the Dutch painter, the Venetian artist's main subject was the architectural setting and the space it created. His paintings give the impression of capturing every detail, with no "editing." Actually, he presented each site within the rules of Renaissance perspective and exercised great selectivity about which details to include and which to omit to make a coherent and engagingly attractive picture. In addition, the mood in each of his works was carefully constructed to be positive and alluring. Everything in the world presented by Canaletto is clean, orderly, and

25-26 ANTONIO CANALETTO, *Basin of San Marco from San Giorgio Maggiore, c.* 1740. Oil on canvas. Wallace Collection, London.

tidy. The sun always shines, and every aspect of the weather is serene.

Adherents to the taste for the "natural" preferred narratives that would teach a moral lesson, dismissing the frivolities and indecent gallantries of the Rococo. In the painting of JEAN-BAPTISTE-SIMÉON CHARDIN (1699–1779), his audience was gratified to find moral values in quiet scenes of domestic life, wherein the artist seems to praise the simple goodness of ordinary people, especially mothers and young children, who, in spirit, occupation, and environment live far from corrupt society. (In the eighteenth century, taste could also mean the appreciation of moral as well as esthetic qualities.) Rousseau measured human quality in terms of the degree to which it was out of reach of society's bad influence and found it in people of the countryside or, as here, in the unpretentious houses of the urban middle class. In *Grace at Table* (FIG. **25-27**), Chardin shows us a modest room in which a mother and her small daughters are about to dine. The mood of quiet attention is at one with the hushed lighting and mellow color and the closely studied still-life accessories, with worn surfaces that tell their own humble domestic history. We are witnesses to a moment of social instruction, when mother and older sister

25-27   JEAN-BAPTISTE SIMÉON CHARDIN, *Grace at Table,* 1740. Oil on canvas, 19" × 15". Louvre, Paris.

supervise the younger sister in the simple, pious ritual of giving thanks to God before a meal. In his own way, Chardin was the poet of the commonplace and the master of its nuances. A gentle sentiment prevails in all of his pictures, an emotion not contrived and artificial but born of the painter's honesty, insight, and sympathy. (It is interesting that this picture was owned by King Louis XV, the royal personification of the Rococo in his life and tastes.)

The taste of the newly prosperous and confident middle class was expressed in the art of WILLIAM HOGARTH (1697–1764), who satirized contemporary life with comic zest and with only a modicum of Rococo "indecency." With Hogarth, a truly English style of painting emerged. England had had few painters or sculptors who could match the accomplishments of English architects; traditionally, painters (such as Holbein, Rubens, and Van Dyck) were imported from the continent. Hogarth waged a lively campaign throughout his career against the English feeling of dependence on, and inferiority to, continental artists. Although Hogarth himself would have been the last to admit it, his own painting owed much to the work of his contemporaries across the channel in France, the artists of the Rococo. Yet his subject matter, frequently moral in tone, is distinctively English. It was the great age of English satirical writing, and Hogarth (who knew and admired this genre and included Henry Fielding, the author of *Tom Jones,* among his closest friends) clearly saw himself as translating satire into the visual arts:

> I therefore turned my thoughts to . . . painting and engraving modern moral subjects. . . . I have endeavored to treat my subjects as [would] a dramatic writer; my picture is my stage, and men and women my players, who by means of certain actions and gestures, are to exhibit a dumb show.

Hogarth's favorite device was to make a series of narrative paintings and prints, in a sequence like chapters in a book or scenes in a play, that follow a character or group of characters in their encounters with some social evil. He is at his best in pictures like the *Breakfast Scene* (FIG. **25-28**) from *Marriage à la Mode,* in which the marriage of a young viscount, arranged through the social aspirations of one father and the need for money of the other, is just beginning to founder. The anglicized Rococo style is admirably suited to the scene, but we must read the situation carefully from its large inventory of naturalistic detail if we are to enjoy it fully. The moment portrayed is just past noon; husband and wife are tired after a long night spent in separate pursuits. The music and the musical instrument on the overturned chair in the foreground and the disheveled servant straightening the chairs and tables in the room at the back indicate that the wife has stayed at home for an evening of cards and music making. She stretches with a mixture of sleepiness and coquettishness, casting a glance toward her young husband, who clearly has been away from the house

25-28 WILLIAM HOGARTH, *Breakfast Scene*, from *Marriage à la Mode*, *c.* 1745. Oil on canvas, approx. 28" × 36". Reproduced by courtesy of the Trustees of the National Gallery, London.

for a night of suspicious business. Still dressed in hat and social finery, he slumps in discouraged boredom on a chair near the fire. His hands are thrust deep into the empty money-pockets of his breeches, while his wife's small dog sniffs inquiringly at a lacy woman's cap protruding from his coat pocket. A steward, his hands full of unpaid bills, raises his eyes to Heaven in despair at the actions of his noble master and mistress. The house is palatial, but Hogarth has filled it with witty clues to the dubious taste of its occupants. The mantelpiece is crowded with tiny statuettes and a classical bust, which hide everything in the architecturally framed painting on the wall behind except a winged Eros figure. Paintings of religious figures hang on the upper wall of the distant room, contradicted by the curtained canvas at the end of the row (partially hidden by the columnar supports of the arched doorway). The curtain undoubtedly covers a canvas with an erotic subject, discreetly hidden from the eyes of casual visitors and ladies, according to the custom of the day, but available at the pull of a curtain cord for the gaze of the master and his male guests. In this composition, as in all his work, Hogarth proceeded as a novelist might, elaborating on his subject with carefully chosen detail, which, as we continue to discover it, heightens the comedy. This scene is one in a sequence of six paintings that satirize the immoralities practiced within marriage by the moneyed classes in England. Hogarth designed the marriage series to be published as a set of engravings. The prints of this and his other moral narratives were so popular that

unscrupulous entrepreneurs produced unauthorized versions almost as fast as the artist created his originals.*

Rousseau, in placing feelings above reason as the most primitive, hence most "natural," of human expressions, called for the cultivation of sincere, sympathetic, and tender emotion. This led him to exalt the simple life of the peasant, with its honest and unsullied emotions, as ideal, and to set it up as a model to be imitated. The joys and sorrows of uncorrupted, "natural" people, now described everywhere in novels (for example, Goldsmith's *Vicar of Wakefield*, 1766, or Bernardin de Saint-Pierre's *Paul and Virginia*, 1787), soon drowned Europe in floods of tears. It became fashionable to weep, to fall to one's knees, and to languish in hopeless love. Hopelessly in love, Goethe's hero in *The Sorrows of Young Werther* (1774) kills himself under the moon.

The sentimental narrative in art became the specialty of JEAN BAPTISTE GREUZE (1725–1805), whose most popular work, *The Village Bride* (FIG. 25-29), sums up the characteristics of the genre. The setting is an unadorned room in a rustic dwelling. In the presence of a notary, the elderly

*To protect himself against the loss of revenue from such theft, Hogarth helped write and win support for a proposal to include prints in the protections provided by the Copyright Act, which finally was passed by the British Parliament in 1735. Unfortunately, the act could not prevent rival printers from sending spies to memorize details of Hogarth's latest paintings and rush them into mimicking versions before he had a chance to issue them as prints.

25-29   JEAN-BAPTISTE GREUZE, *The Village Bride*, 1761. Oil on canvas, 36" × 46½". Louvre, Paris.

father has passed his daughter's dowry to her youthful husband-to-be and now blesses the pair, who gently take each other's arms. The old mother tearfully gives her daughter's arm a farewell caress, while the youngest sister melts in tears upon the shoulder of the demure bride. An envious older sister broods behind her father's chair. Rosy-faced, healthy children play around the scene. The story of the picture is simple: the happy climax of a rural romance. The moral of the picture is just as clear: happiness is the reward of "natural" virtue.

The audience—as we say—loved it. They carefully analyzed each gesture and each nuance of sentiment and reacted with tumultuous enthusiasm. At the Salon of 1761, Greuze's picture received enormous attention. The great compiler of the *Encyclopedia*, Diderot, who reviewed the picture for the press, declared that it was difficult to get near it because of the throngs of admirers. What he felt then is significant: it was a "pathetic subject," conveying a "sweet emotion. . . . There is decency and reverence, and a charming innocence." After a long and specific description of the picture, Diderot concluded: "this will do him honor as a painter skilled in his art and as a man of intelligence and taste. His work is full of understanding and delicacy. His choice of subjects is a mark of sensibility and morality."

Morality of a very different tone, yet in harmony with "naturalness," included the virtues of honor, valor, and love of country, the virtues that, it was thought, produced great men and great deeds, like those of the ancient Romans. "If

there is no such thing as morality in man's heart," asked Rousseau, whose hero was the ancient Roman Cato, "what is the source of his rapturous admiration of noble deeds, his passionate devotion to great men? . . . Take from our hearts this love of what is noble, and you rob us of the joy of life." The "nobility" lauded by Rousseau was understood to refer to character, not to aristocratic birth; and as the century aged and the tremors of coming revolutions were felt, sensibility was directed toward the virtues of courage and resolution, patriotism, and self-sacrifice. The modern military hero, risen from humble origins, not the decadent aristocrat, brought the excitements of war into the company of the "natural" emotions.

In England, SIR JOSHUA REYNOLDS (1723–1792) specialized in portraits of contemporaries who participated in the great events of the latter part of the century. Not least among them was *Lord Heathfield* (FIG. 25-30). Reynolds was at his best with a subject like this burly, brandy-flushed English officer, commandant of the fortress of Gibraltar during the American Revolution. Heathfield had doggedly defended the great rock against the Spanish, for which he was later honored with the title Baron Heathfield of Gibraltar. His victory is symbolized here by the huge key to the fortress, which he holds thoughtfully. He stands in front of a curtain of dark smoke rising from the battleground, flanked by one cannon that points ineffectively downward and another whose tilted barrel indicates that it lies uselessly on its back. The features of the general's heavy,

25-30   Sir Joshua Reynolds, *Lord Heathfield,* 1787. Oil on canvas, approx. 56″ × 45″. Reproduced by courtesy of the Trustees of the National Gallery, London.

honest face and his uniform are portrayed with a sense of unidealized realism, but his posture and the setting dramatically suggest the heroic theme of battle and also refer to the actual revolutions (American, French) then taking shape in deadly earnest, as the old regime faded into the past.

The "death in battle of a young military hero" theme, familiar in art and literature since the ancient Greeks, was brought up to date in *The Death of General Wolfe* (FIG. **25-31**) by the expatriate American artist Benjamin West (1738–1820). Born in Pennsylvania, on what was then the colonial frontier, West was sent to Europe early in life to study art and then went to England, where he had almost immediate success. He was a cofounder of the Royal Academy of Arts and succeeded Sir Joshua Reynolds as its president. He became official painter to King George III and retained that position during the strained period of the American Revolution. In *The Death of General Wolfe,* West depicted the mortally wounded young English commander just after his defeat of the French in the decisive battle of Quebec in 1759, which gave Canada to Great Britain. Unlike Renaissance, Baroque, and Rococo artists, West chose to portray a contemporary historical subject, and his

characters wear contemporary costume (although the military uniforms are not completely accurate in all details). However, West blended this realism of detail with the grand tradition of history painting by arranging his figures in an essentially Baroque composition, and his modern hero dies among grieving officers on the field of victorious battle in a way that suggests the death of a great saint. West wanted to present this hero's death in the service of the state as a martyrdom charged with religious emotions, and his innovative combination of the conventions of traditional heroic painting with a look of modern realism was so effective that it won the hearts of viewers in his own day and continued to influence history painting well into the nineteenth century.

THE RISE OF ROMANTICISM

"Man is born free, but is everywhere in chains!"—so exclaims Rousseau in the opening line of his *Social Contract* (1762), a book carefully read and pondered by the radicals of the French Revolution and many revolutions since then. With these words he supplies a lasting slogan: in one word, *freedom.* Romanticism has as its prime motive the desire for freedom—not only political freedom, but freedom of thought, of feeling, of action, of worship, of speech, of taste, and all the other freedoms. Freedom is the right and property of one and all, though for each one, each living subject, it may be a different kind or in different degree. In the opening paragraph of his *Confessions* (published posthumously 1781 to 1788), Rousseau makes the following claim for each Romantic soul, in making it for himself: "I am like no one in the whole world. I may be no better, at least *I am different.*" The freedom and unique subjectivity of each individual is the first principle of Romanticism and key to the understanding of much that has happened and is believed in the modern world.

The faculty of mind that opens all experience to the free subject is *imagination* rather than reason, and it functions through *feeling* rather than through thinking. The late eighteenth century was increasingly a period under the spell of Romanticism. For almost two centuries, scholars have debated the definition and the historical scope of Romanticism; to this day, the controversy has not ended. The very widest definition would equate Romanticism and Modernism, making Romanticism the mood of the modern world and coextensive with its history. More narrowly, Romanticism was a phenomenon that began around 1750 and ended about 1850. Still more narrowly, Romanticism was just another among a miscellany of styles that rose and declined in the course of modern art, flourishing from about 1800 to 1840 and coming between Neoclassicism and Realism. In this book, we take the middle position, defining *Romanticism* as a way of perceiving the world, above all, with strong feelings. This attitude influenced art most strongly between 1750 and 1850.

Romantic

25-31 BENJAMIN WEST, *The Death of General Wolfe,* 1771. Oil on canvas, approx. 5′ × 7′. National Gallery of Canada, Ottawa (gift of the Duke of Westminster, 1918).

Though Rousseau was the prophet of Romanticism, he never knew it as such. The term *Romanticism* originated toward the end of the eighteenth century among German literary critics, who aimed to distinguish peculiarly "modern" traits from the Neoclassical traits that already had displaced elements of Baroque and Rococo design. "Romance," which could refer as much to the novel, with its sentimental hero, as it does to the old medieval tales of fantastic adventure written in the "romance" languages, never quite fit with the broader term "romantic," nor has "romantic" ever comfortably covered all that might be understood by it.

Romanticism was preceded and prepared for by the so-called Age of Sensibility, roughly 1750 to 1780, when thinkers like Rousseau preached the value of sincere feeling and natural human sympathy over artful reason and the cold calculations of courtly societies. The slogan of sensibility was "Trust your heart rather than your head," or, as Goethe put it, "Feeling is all!" Werther, the young Goethe's

tragic hero in *The Sorrows of Young Werther* and an archetype of Romantic sensibility, cried: "We desire to surrender our whole being, that it may be filled with the perfect bliss of one glorious emotion!" All that was false and artificial was to be banished as the enemy of honest emotion. In art, sensibility joined with the idea of Enlightenment thinkers that paintings with a moral theme could move the hearts of viewers toward correct social behavior.

Sensibility was swiftly overtaken by the heroic emotions of the revolutionary age. Archeological discoveries of ancient Roman cities in the early and mid-eighteenth century helped to reinforce a rising belief that people in the days of ancient Greece and Rome had lived by a splendid moral code, which had governed their behavior and their allegiance to the wider society. Eighteenth-century thinkers were quick to link models of self-sacrificing virtue from the Greek and Roman past with some from the rebellious present—heroes like Cato and Washington, Regulus and Marat—to touch the hearts of viewers and readers and to inspire thoughts and deeds of civic idealism. A revived Classical style was developed in architecture, painting, and sculpture to help encourage modern citizens toward exemplary acts of behavior.

Contemporary with both the sentimental and the heroic came the taste for the sublime in art and nature. The sublime inspired feelings of awe mixed with terror—the feelings we experience when we look on vast, impassable mountain peaks or great storms at sea. Accompanying the taste for the sublime was the taste for the fantastic, the occult, the grotesque, the macabre—for the adventures of the soul voyaging into the dangerous reaches of consciousness. Images of the sublime and the terrible often combined something of Baroque dynamism with natural details in their quest for the presentation of grippingly convincing visions.

Everything that moved the emotions of artists and their audience—the sentimental, the heroic, the sublime, the "Gothick," or combinations of them—was marked by a shift in emphasis from reason to feeling, from calculation to intuition, from objective nature to subjective emotion. Here, that attitude of the modern mind we call Romanticism first emerges.

J. P. Eckermann's *Conversations with Goethe* throws a strong, revealing light on the emotional side of Romanticism, especially on its supposed opposition to Classicism. Goethe is recorded as declaring:

> The distinction between Classical and Romantic poetry, which is now spread over the whole world and occasions so many quarrels and divisions, came originally from Schiller and myself. [Goethe was looking back some forty years in time.] I laid down the maxim of objective treatment in poetry, and would allow no other; but Schiller, who worked quite in the subjective way, deemed his own fashion right, and to defend himself against me, wrote the treatise upon *Naïve and Sentimental Poetry*. He proved to me that I, against my will, was romantic, and that my *Iphigenia*, through the predominance of sentiment, was by no means so much in the Antique spirit as some people supposed. The Schlegels took up this idea, and carried it further, so that it has now been diffused over the whole world; and everybody talks about Classicism and Romanticism—of which nobody thought fifty years ago.*

Goethe wanted his drama *Iphigenia* to be in the Antique spirit and, "against his will," discovered that he had been romantic all the time. This discovery was probably made by many artists throughout the era of Romanticism. The break with tradition forced the artist to look at tradition historically; if Classical art was preferred, then a "classic" bent of mind must be assumed or affected, but the artist would

still be representing Classical form, not *creating* it. In the end, it was the emotional response to Classical form that counted, and the emotional response to Classical form was precisely Romantic!

Romanticism: The "Gothick" Taste

If, as Rousseau insisted, humankind had been more human at the primitive level, and if the ancient Classical world could provide models of high moral action, then the historical past was worth reviewing for what it could provide the present by way of inspiration or example. While retaining much of the "natural" taste for themes of the here and now, one could develop a taste for history. This is what happened. While already recovering and surveying the Classical world, the Romantic imagination was discovering the Middle Ages, the "Gothick" world, as it was then known and spelled. (We here use the eighteenth-century spelling of *Gothick* to identify a specific period within the century and to avoid confusion with the actual, medieval Gothic.) For people living in the eighteenth century the Middle Ages were the "dark ages," a time of barbarism, superstition, dark mystery, and miracle. The Gothick imagination stretched its apparition of the Middle Ages into all the worlds of fantasy open to it, touching the sublime, the infernal, the terrible, the nightmarish, the grotesque, the sadistic, and all the remaining imagery that comes from the chamber of horrors when reason is asleep.

The Gothic Revival in architecture reflects the "Gothick" taste. Beginning with a penchant for haunted castles and mouldering ruins, English gentlemen undertook to build in the "Gothick manner." HORACE WALPOLE (1717–1797), a novelist and wealthy architectural dilettante, renovated Strawberry Hill, his "villa" at Twickenham (FIG. **25-32**), in the rising "Gothick" fashion, converting it into a sprawling "castle" with turrets, towers, battlements, galleries, and corridors. Sir Walter Scott was captivated by the effect and wrote that the structure's "fretted roofs, carved panels, and illuminated windows were garnished with the appropriate furniture of escutcheons, armorial bearings, shields, tilting lances, and all the panoply of chivalry." At Strawberry Hill, the master (and any visitor) could fully enjoy Walpole's favorite pastime, which was "to gaze on Gothic toys through Gothic glass." The features of the structure are, of course, pseudo-Gothic, but Walpole's version of Gothic architecture would be as influential for later architecture as his gothic novels would be for subsequent literature. Walpole was the author of the first and most influential Gothick novel, the *Castle of Otranto* (1764). Scott enumerated the ghostly and ghastly details of the lurid work: supernatural thunders and howling winds, giant helmets that fall from the skies, bleeding skeletons, clanking chains, huge apparitions of the dead, pictures that step out of their frames—all the eerie machinery that will thrill generations of sensation-seeking readers from that time to this.

*John Oxenford, trans., and J. K. Moorehead, ed., *Conversations of Goethe with Eckermann* (New York: Dutton, 1935), p. 366.

25-32   HORACE WALPOLE, Strawberry Hill, Twickenham, near London, 1749–1777.

Edmund Burke, the noted British philosopher and statesman, attempted an explanation of this ghastly aspect of the Gothick taste in his *A Philosophical Enquiry into the Origin of Our Ideas of the Sublime and the Beautiful* (1757). For Burke, the sublime was related to our instinct for self-preservation:

> The passions which concern self-preservation turn mostly on *pain* or *danger*. The ideas of *pain, sickness,* and *death* fill the mind with strong emotions of horror; but *life* and *health,* though they put us in a capacity of being affected with pleasure, they make no such impression. . . . The passions therefore which are conversant about the preservation of the individual, turn chiefly on *pain* and *danger,* and they are the most powerful of all the passions. . . . Whatever is fitted in any sort to excite the ideas of pain and danger . . . is a source of the *sublime.* The passions which belong to self-preservation . . . are simply painful when their causes immediately affect us; they are delightful when we have an idea of pain and danger, without being actually in such circumstances. . . . Whatever excites this delight, I call *sublime.**

Strawberry Hill provided a setting that encouraged romantic flights of fancy about damsels in distress, ghouls, and other imaginings of the darker side of the psyche. These things were part of the sensibility for sublime terror that would become an important part of nineteenth-century Romanticism. The thrill produced by contemplating the supposed remains of a vanished past was cultivated by garden designers in England, who inserted replicas of period architecture amid the random copses of trees, rustic

*In J. T. Boulton, ed., (Oxford, UK: Basil Blackwell Ltd., 1987), pp. 38–39, 51ff.

bridges, and winding streams that filled the stately gardens of the time. Sometimes a single garden would boast structures in four or five different styles. Typical are the gardens at Hagley Park, where a sham Gothic ruin erected in 1747 (FIG. **25-33**) stands near a Doric portico built in 1758 (FIG. 25-38).

A work that could illustrate Burke's theory of the sublime, laced with the infernal, is an etching by GIOVANNI BATTISTA PIRANESI (1720–1778). A series of prints of imaginary prisons, the *Carceri,* shows Piranesi conjuring up awe-inspiring visions of bafflingly complicated architectural

25-33   SANDERSON MILLER, sham Gothic ruin, Hagley Park, Worcestershire, England, 1747.

25-34   GIOVANNI BATTISTA PIRANESI, *Carceri 14, c.* 1750. Etching, second state, approx. 16″ × 21″. Ashmolean Museum, Oxford.

masses, piled high and spread out through gloomy spaces. In such pictures, vistas are multiplied and broken by a seeming infinity of massive arches, vaults, piers, and stairways, through which small, insectlike human figures move stealthily. Despite wandering, soaring perspectives, the observer is overwhelmed by a suffocating sense of enclosure; the spaces are locked in, and no exit is visible. These grim places are filled with brooding menace and hopelessness. Within this series of etchings, Piranesi often darkened subsequent editions to make them even more sinister. Our picture, *Carceri 14* (FIG. **25-34**), is one of these. It reminds us that the gaiety of the Rococo and the rationality of the Enlightenment coexisted with an eighteenth-century sensibility for the sublime, the "Gothick," that returned to haunt the night imaginings of many a Romantic artist and poet in the nineteenth century.

Like Piranesi, many artists at the end of the eighteenth century worked in more than one mode; we shall presently see Piranesi's other interest. The Englishman GEORGE STUBBS (1724–1806) won a reputation for his naturalistic paintings of horses, but he also enjoyed creating scenes of natural struggle and horror. Stubbs began his career painting human portraits to support himself while he studied his lifelong passion, anatomy. Soon, he was specializing in the anatomy of horses and using this knowledge to create "portraits" of the mares, stallions, and foals owned by the English gentry. These were naturalistic images linked in

spirit to the works of Canaletto (FIG. 25-26), but Stubbs was not content to remain tied always to a careful rendering of visual facts. He also invented a new type of picture, the "animal history painting," which depicted dramatic episodes from the lives of wild animals. This type of subject fit well with the teachings of Rousseau and others who idealized life far from any taint of civilization, which, as we have seen, they believed distorted the innate "goodness" of the natural order. *Horse Being Devoured by a Lion* (FIG. **25-35**) shows the violent side of nature in the raw. A flash of light illuminates the struggle of a terrified horse, trying in vain to shake off a hungry lion that is already biting deeply into the horse's vulnerable back. The composition of *Horse Being Devoured by a Lion* may seem a "wilder" version of the lion attack on a man in Puget's *Milo of Crotona* (FIG. 24-69), but Stubbs's animal struggle also resembles an ancient Classical sculpture of a lion on the back of a horse, which the artist could have seen in Rome during a visit there. The scene also may have been inspired in part by an attack Stubbs witnessed in North Africa on his way back to England after studying Classical and Renaissance art in Italy. Whatever the source, the subject was so popular that Stubbs did nine versions of this Romantic scene. For the eighteenth-century viewer, the emotional shudders aroused by the horse–lion confrontation would have sharpened philosophical thoughts about the nobility of the natural state and the inevitable connections between life and death. In the nine-

25-35 GEORGE STUBBS, *Horse Being Devoured by a Lion*, 1763. Enamel on metal, 27¹/₂″ × 40³/₄″. Tate Gallery, London.

teenth century, the emotions in such sublime Romantic themes will be fused into a fuller exploration of the qualities of the sublime in nature.

HENRY FUSELI (1741–1825) attempted to arouse delectable terror of a different sort. He specialized in night moods of horror and in "Gothick" fantasies—in the demonic, the macabre, and often the sadistic. Swiss by birth, Fuseli settled in England and eventually became a member of the Royal Academy and an instructor there. Largely self-taught, he contrived a distinctive manner compounded of the influence of Michelangelo, the Antique style, and his own extravagant invention to express the fantasies of his vivid imagination. The twisted poses and frantic gestures of his figures go well beyond exaggeration and often suggest the influence of Italian Mannerism. *The Nightmare* (FIG. **25-36**) was the first of four versions of this terrifying theme. The beautiful young woman, tormented by some terrible dream and still not awake, has thrown herself partly from her couch. She lies helpless beneath the incubus that squats malignantly on her body, as a horse with flaming eyes bursts into the scene from beyond the curtain.

The sublime vein of violent emotion and of perverse and tragic action in this composition will be heavily mined in the nineteenth century. Fuseli's art was among the first that attempted to depict the dark terrain of the human subconscious.

In his art the visionary English poet, painter, and engraver WILLIAM BLAKE (1757–1827) combined a calm Neoclassicism with the storm and stress of late eighteenth-century "Gothick" Romanticism. Blake greatly admired both the art of ancient Greece and Gothic art. "Gothick" for him was the style best suited to the expression of personal religious emotions, while Classical Greek art exemplified the mathematical, and thus eternal, in a different way. Yet Blake joined neither the prominent figures of the Enlightenment nor any organized religious group. He would have been an uneasy member of any group because he treasured the fact that the compositions of many of his paintings and poems were given to him by spirit visitors in dreams. The importance he attached to these experiences led him to believe that rationalism's search for material explanations of the world stifled the spiritual side of human

25-36 Henry Fuseli, *The Nightmare*, 1781. Oil on canvas, 40″ × 50″. The Detroit Institute of the Arts (gift of Mr. and Mrs. Bert L. Smokler and Mr. and Mrs. Lawrence A. Fleishman).

nature, while the stringent rules of behavior imposed by orthodox religions killed the individual creative impulse. Blake's vision of the Almighty in *Ancient of Days* (FIG. **25-37**) combines his ideas and interests in a highly individual way. For Blake, this figure combined the concept of the Creator with that of Wisdom as a part of God. The *Ancient of Days,* printed as the frontispiece for Blake's book *Europe: A Prophesy,* was published with a quote ("When he set a compass upon the face of the deep") from Proverbs (8:22–23, 27–30) in the Old Testament. Most of that chapter is spoken by Wisdom, identified as a female, who tells the reader how she was with the Lord through all the time of the Creation:

The Lord possessed me in the beginning of his way,
before his works of old.
I was set up from everlasting,
from the beginning,
or ever the earth was. . . .
When he prepared the heavens, I was there:
when he set a compass upon the face of the depth:
when he established the clouds above:
when he strengthened the fountains of the deep:
when he gave to the sea his decree,
that the waters should not pass his commandment:
when he appointed the foundations of the earth:
then I was by him,
as one brought up with him:
and I was daily his delight,
rejoicing always before him. . . .

Energy fills this composition. The Ancient of Days leans forward from a fiery orb, peering toward earth and unleashing power through his outstretched left arm into twin rays of light, which emerge between his spread fingers like an architect's measuring instrument. A mighty wind surges through his thick hair and beard. Only the strength of his Michelangelesque physique keeps him firmly planted within his heavenly perch. Here, Baroque vigor and ideal Classical anatomy merge with the inner, dark dreams of "Gothick" Romanticism, which we will meet often in the nineteenth century. In his independence and in the individuality of his artistic vision, Blake was very much a man of the modern age.

The world of dreams and visions provided wonderful sublime materials for artists who yearned to escape the rules of reason. Blake wrote: "I will not reason and compare, my business is to create. . . . The road of excess leads to the palace of wisdom." Yet, grave risks imperiled such an approach. Raw feeling could lead the soul astray, perhaps beyond the limits of sanity. The Romantic imagination, challenged by sublimity and terror of sensation, would eagerly explore the limitless world of "Gothick" fantasy, willing to take those risks.

Romanticism: The Neoclassical Taste

Depending upon what was meant by "nature," the taste for the "natural" could develop into several different tastes—including even a taste for the supernatural. Though

25-37 WILLIAM BLAKE, *Ancient of Days,* frontispiece of *Europe: A Prophecy,* 1794. Metal relief etching, hand-colored, approx. 9^1/$_2$" × 6^3/$_4$". Whitworth Art Gallery, University of Manchester, England.

naturally; there was no such thing as "natural man" in the abstract, and no one set of unchanging principles by which a people could be represented in art or in literature; each culture is unique. For art, this position led to a number of almost simultaneous "revival" styles, each regarded as being as "natural" as another.

This Romantic eclecticism emerged first in garden design. In England, a revolt against the "regularity" of French Classical architecture had begun as early as the late seventeenth century, with the growth of an enthusiasm for Chinese art, especially the Chinese garden (FIG. 15-41). An English critic of the time, Sir William Temple, described the Chinese garden as "without . . . order or disposition of parts that shall be commonly or easily observed," clearly unlike the carefully ordered gardens of France and other European countries. Within a generation of Temple's observation, gardens in England were being designed along informal, "naturalizing," Oriental lines. In the eighteenth century, the "English" garden became a vogue throughout Europe, while the formality of such gardens as those at Versailles was now thought unnatural. Similarly, "naturalness" was soon prized over formal order in architecture, and "natural" styles, like the Gothic, which had never entirely died out in England, became very popular.

We have noted the "Gothick" taste of Horace Walpole's Strawberry Hill (FIG. 25-32), as well as Sanderson Miller's sham "Gothic" ruin in the gardens of Hagley Park (FIG. 25-33), where it exists in the neighborhood of a stage-set Doric portico (FIG. **25-38**). Here on the same grounds the "Gothick" and the Classical tastes, both Romantic, meet— the owner of the estate doubtless thought of them as equally picturesque. That Romantic sentiment made him indifferent to their apparent stylistic contradiction.

Rousseau described quite thoroughly what *he* meant by "natural man," he and other Enlightenment figures were not in general agreement about the definition of "nature" and "natural." *What* was "nature," and *where* was the "natural man" to be found? People who lived "according to nature" were found both near and far, among the sober citizens of the town, the peasants of the countryside, the natives of the American forests, the wise men of China, Persia, and India, the populations of ancient Greece and republican Rome, the chivalric nobility of the Middle Ages. All of these had been brought into view by local observation, geographical exploration, and now by historical investigation and archeological discovery. It was a matter of taste which or how many of these should be taken as models for the "natural" in correcting the "unnatural" or artificial conditions of contemporary European civilizations.

With Johann Gottfried von Herder, a philosopher, philologist, and leader of the Romantic movement in Germany, it came to be understood that *all* peoples and their cultures, their customs, languages, poetry, and song have evolved

25-38 JAMES STUART, Doric portico, Hagley Park, 1758.

The portico is of special interest as the work of JAMES STUART (1713–1788), a British painter and architect, who, with Nicholas Revett (1720–1804), also a painter and architect, introduced to Europe the splendor and originality of Greek art in the enormously influential *Antiquities of Athens,* the first volume of which appeared in 1762. These volumes firmly distinguished Greek art from the "derivative" Roman style that had served as the model for Classicism since the Renaissance. Stuart's efforts, as shown in the Doric portico at Hagley Park (FIG. 25-38), were greeted with enthusiasm by those who had no use for the Rococo or any of the later "irregular" styles in art. A contemporary journal voiced the hope that the writings of Stuart and Revett and Robert Wood's magnificently illustrated *Ruins of Palmyra* (1753) and *Ruins of Baalbek* (1757) would "expel the littleness and ugliness of the Chinese and the barbarity of the Goths, that we may see no more useless and expensive trifles; no more dungeons instead of summer houses." Instead, the journal's author hoped that all eyes would rest only on the tantalizing echoes of proper Classical civilization.

As the presence of the Doric building in the gardens at Hagley Park indicates, a renewed interest in the style of ancient art developed side by side with the Gothick and other exotic styles. By mid-century, the rediscovery of Greek art and architecture had inspired a renewed taste for a serenely Classical style. The expanding desire for things connected with ancient Greece and Rome sparked the style we call *Neoclassicism,* which is based on the idea of a changeless generality that transcends the accidents of time. Neoclassicism, once thought of as a style in opposition to Romanticism, is now understood as simply one of the many fashions within that general movement but opposed to the "irregularity" of styles like Neo-Gothic, Neo-Baroque, and Chinese. By the late eighteenth and early nineteenth centuries, a Neoclassical taste for the more or less exact replication of Greek and Roman buildings spread rapidly throughout Europe and America.

The enthusiasm for classical antiquity permeated much of the scholarship of the time. More and more in the late eighteenth century attention turned toward the ancient world. Edward Gibbon was stimulated on a visit to Rome to begin his monumental *Decline and Fall of the Roman Empire,* which appeared between 1776 and 1788. Earlier, in 1755, Johann Winckelmann, the first modern historian of art, published his *Thoughts on the Imitation of Greek Art in Painting and Sculpture,* in which he uncompromisingly designated Greek art as the most perfect to come from the hands of man and a model that, if followed, would confer "assurance in conceiving and designing works of art, since they [the Greeks] have marked for us the utmost limits of human and divine beauty." Winckelmann characterized Greek sculpture as manifesting a "noble simplicity and quiet grandeur." In his *History of Ancient Art* (1764), he undertook to describe each monument as an element in the development of a single grand style. Before Winckelmann, the his-

tory of art had been a matter of biography, as with Giorgio Vasari. Winckelmann thus initiated one modern method thoroughly in accord with Enlightenment ideas of ordering knowledge; his was clearly a method that undertook the classification and description of art on the basis of general stylistic traits that change over time. Strangely enough, Winckelmann did not know much about original Greek art—at least not much beyond the Laocoön group (FIG. 5-101) and other late Greek works in the Vatican collections, of which he was custodian. For the most part, he had only late Roman copies for study, and he never visited Greece, where he might have seen the genuine thing. Despite the obvious defects of his work, however, its pioneering character cannot be overlooked. Winckelmann had wide influence, and his writings laid a theoretical and historical foundation for the enormously widespread taste for Neoclassicism that was to last well into the nineteenth century.

The Romantic fascination with ruins, constructed or genuine, was combined with an Enlightenment curiosity about archeology to sharpen a taste for images like Piranesi's etching *Temple of Saturn* (FIG. **25-39**) from his *Views of Rome.* We have already met this versatile artist's awe-inspiring "Gothick" prints, the *Carceri* series (FIG. 25-34), which were, in a sense, relaxation of the imagination after the meticulous depictions of the innumerable monuments of the ancient city. Piranesi's early experience as an architect in Venice may have provided the inspiration and technical mastery for his project, begun shortly after he moved to the "Eternal City," to record in etchings the monuments of Rome. His dramatic, "picturesque" presentations of the majestic, Classical ruins enthralled his Romantic audience and have served for generations as the standard image of Roman grandeur.

25-39 GIOVANNI BATTISTA PIRANESI, the *Temple of Saturn, c.* 1774. Etching from the *Views of Rome.* The Metropolitan Museum of Art, New York (Rogers Fund, 1941)

THE NEOCLASSIC TASTE IN ARCHITECTURE   In architecture, the Roman ruins at Baalbek in Syria, especially a titanic colonnade, provided much of the inspiration for the Neoclassical portico of the church of Ste.-Geneviève (FIG. **25-40**), now the Panthéon, in Paris, designed by JACQUES-GERMAIN SOUFFLOT (1713–1780). The columns, reproduced with studied archeological exactitude, are the first revelation of Roman grandeur in France. The walls are severely blank, except for a repeated garland motif in the attic level. The colonnaded dome, a Neoclassical version of the domes of St. Peter's in Rome, the Church of the Invalides in Paris, and St. Paul's in London (FIGS. 22-32, 24-68, 24-72), rises above a Greek-cross plan. Both dome and vaults rest on an interior grid of splendid, freestanding Corinthian columns, as if the colonnade of the portico were continued within. Although the whole effect, inside and out, is Roman, the structural principles employed are essentially Gothic. Soufflot was one of the first eighteenth-century builders to suggest that Gothic engineering was highly functional structurally and could be applied in modern building. In his work, we have the curious, but not unreasonable conjunction of Gothic and Classical in a structural integration that foreshadows nineteenth-century admiration of Gothic engineering.

Eighteenth-century Neoclassical interiors were directly inspired by new discoveries of "the glory that was Greece / And the grandeur that was Rome," and summarized the conception of a noble Classical world. The first great archeological event of modern times, the discovery and initial excavation of the ancient buried Roman cities of Pompeii (page 20 and FIG. 7-10) and Herculaneum in the 1730s and 1740s, startled and thrilled all of Europe. The excavation of these cities was the veritable resurrection of the ancient world, not simply a dim vision of it inspired by a few moldering ruins; historical reality could now replace fancy with fact. The wall paintings and other artifacts of Pompeii inspired the slim, straight-lined, elegant "Pompeian" style that, after mid-century, almost entirely displaced the curvilinear Rococo.

In France, the new Pompeian manner was associated with Louis XVI; in England, it took the name of its most artful practitioner, ROBERT ADAM (1728–1792), whose interior architecture was influential throughout Europe. The Etruscan Room in Osterley Park House (FIG. **25-41**) was begun in 1761. If compared with the Rococo salons of the Hôtel de Soubise (FIG. 25-9) and the Amalienburg (FIG. 25-11), this room shows how completely symmetry and rectilinearity have returned, but this return is achieved with great delicacy and none of the massive splendor of the style of Louis XIV. The decorative motifs (medallions, urns, vine scrolls, sphinxes, and tripods) were taken from Roman

25-40   JACQUES-GERMAIN SOUFFLOT, the Panthéon (Ste.-Geneviève), Paris, 1755-1792.

25-41   ROBERT ADAM, Etruscan Room, Osterley Park House, Middlesex, England, begun 1761. By courtesy of the Board of Trustees of the Victoria and Albert Museum, London.

art and, as in Roman stucco work, are arranged sparsely within broad, neutral spaces and slender margins (FIG. 7-23). Adam was an archeologist as well as an architect, and he had explored and written accounts of the ruins of the palace of Diocletian at Split (FIG. 7-82). Kedleston House in Derbyshire, Adelphi Terrace in London, and a great many other structures that he designed also show the influence of Split on his work.

In architecture, Neoclassicism proved to be such an expressively versatile style that it continued well into the nineteenth century. By the end of the eighteenth century, however, in architecture, as in painting and sculpture, Neoclassicism was being used to symbolize moral and heroic links with the ancient past. Napoleon supported its use as appropriate for new buildings in his imperial state. In the new American republic, Thomas Jefferson (1743–1826) spearheaded a movement for the adoption of a symbolic Neoclassicism (a style he saw as representative of the democratic qualities of the United States) as the national architecture.

Scholar, economist, educational theorist, statesman, and gifted amateur architect, Jefferson was, by nature, attracted to Classical architecture. He worked out his ideas in his design for his own home, Monticello (FIG. **25-42**), which was begun in 1769. Jefferson admired Palladio immensely and read carefully the Italian architect's *Four Books of Architecture*. While minister to France, Jefferson studied French eighteenth-century Classical architecture and city planning and visited Maison Carrée, the Roman temple at Nîmes (FIG. 7-35). After his European trip, Jefferson completely remodeled Monticello, which had first been designed in an English Georgian style. In his remodeling, he emulated the manner of Palladio, with a facade inspired by the work of Robert Adam. The final version of Monticello is somewhat reminiscent of the Villa Rotonda (FIG. 22-51) and of Chiswick House (FIG. 25-2), but its materials are the local wood and brick used in Virginia. Its hilltop setting was originally designed to open onto a garden facade designed in a less Classical style and to provide an extended view over the surrounding countryside, linking people and nature in a manner that anticipated nineteenth-century ideas of the sublime in the picturesque.

Turning from the private domain to that of public space, Jefferson began to carry out his dream of developing a Classical style for the official architecture of the United States. Here, his Neoclassicism was an extension of the Enlightenment belief in the perfectibility of human beings and in the power of art to help bring about that perfection. As secretary of state to George Washington, Jefferson supported the logically ordered city plan for Washington, D.C., created in 1791 by the French-American architect Major Pierre L'Enfant (1724–1825), which extended earlier

25-42 Thomas Jefferson, Monticello, Charlottesville, Virginia, 1770–1806.

25-43   View of Washington, 1852, showing BENJAMIN LATROBE's Capitol and Major L'Enfant's plan of the city.

ordered designs for city sections, like Wood's designs for Bath (FIG. 25-3), to an entire community. As an architect, Jefferson also incorporated the specific look of the Maison Carrée into his design for the Virginia State Capitol building in Richmond. He approved William Thornton's initial Palladian design for the federal Capitol building in 1793, and in 1803, as president, he selected BENJAMIN H. LATROBE (1764–1820) to take over the design of the structure (FIG. **25-43**), with the goal of creating "a building that should . . . stand out as a superb visible expression of the ideals of a country dedicated to liberty." Jefferson's choice of a Roman-Classical style was influenced partly by his admiration for its beauty and partly by his associations of it with an idealized Roman republican government and, through that, with the democracy of ancient Greece. Latrobe wrote that in his design for the Capitol he wanted to recreate "the glories of the Greece of Pericles in the woods of America." To that end, in the architecture of the Capitol, the symbol of the Roman eagle became the American bald eagle, a special new Corinthian order was devised in which corn plants replaced acanthus leaves, and the sculptured representation of Liberty was designed to abandon traditional trappings and to hold a liberty cap in one hand and rest her other hand on the Constitution.

THE NEOCLASSIC TASTE IN PAINTING, ENGRAVING, AND SCULPTURE   As Greek and Roman art were gradually

brought into the view of artists by archeological finds and historical criticism, the impulse to approximate them as closely and as authentically as possible could not be resisted. The sculptor and engraver JOHN FLAXMAN (1755–1826), who was a friend of Blake, and knew Fuseli well, illustrates in his severe Neoclassicism how much one could associate with, and even agree with, colleagues working within different shades of taste, yet stubbornly express his own. Already, the multiplicity of tastes that would characterize the next century are apparent in the English school of Flaxman, Fuseli, and Blake.

Flaxman represents the extreme limit of withdrawal from the intricacy and sensuality of the Rococo, which he loathed. He reduces his forms to bare, linear outlines, without color or chiaroscuro, and his subject matter to themes of an almost ascetic purity and severity in *Electra Leading the Procession to Agamemnon's Tomb* (FIG. **25-44**). His models were taken from Greek and Etruscan vase painting (FIGS. 5-25 and 5-26) and Greek sculpture (FIGS. 5-56 and 5-60). He chose his subjects from Homer, Hesiod, Aeschylus, Dante, and the other great classics of the West, and his illustrations of them were immensely popular, both in England and America.

Shown here is the opening scene of *The Choephoroe (The Libation Bearers)* by Aeschylus, in which Electra and her mourning women move slowly to the tomb of her murdered father, Agamemnon. There she will meet her

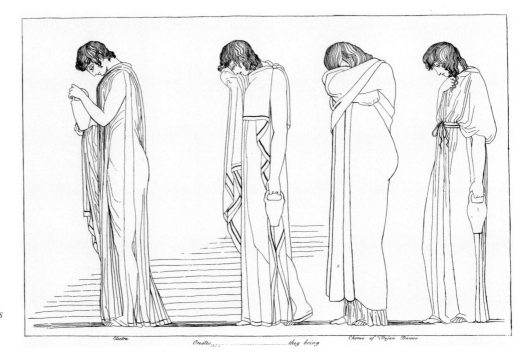

25-44 JOHN FLAXMAN, *Electra Leading the Procession to Agamemnon's Tomb* (from the *Choephoroe*), 1795. Engraving, approx. 8½" × 11¾".

brother, Orestes, and swear him to avenge their father's death on their hated mother, Clytemnestra, Agamemnon's murderer. Flaxman renders the procession with epic sparseness; indeed, his interpretations of the Classical themes were thought worthy of Homer. The drooping figures of the sorrowing women lose nothing of majesty; they have a columnar strength reminiscent of the caryatids of the Erechtheion (FIG. 5-60). At the same time there is a slow, steady, rhythmic motion, as of some solemn dance interpretive of grief. The disciplined delineation in pure, unaccented line loses nothing of this sense of movement; it does not become immobilized into rigidity. Flaxman's art, inspired by ancient Greek vase ornament, found ready application in the great Wedgwood ware, and for more than a generation was considered the perfection of the Neoclassical ideal.

Flaxman's Neoclassicism is at a point of final definition of what the taste should accept as its best expression, which is a doctrinaire, almost unapproachable ideal. Earlier, the Neoclassical taste found itself in harmony with the easier taste for the "natural," and later it came about that the "natural" and the "classical" were identified as the same thing.

In the art of ANGELICA KAUFFMANN (1741–1807), the simple figure types, homely situations, and contemporary settings of Greuze's moral, "natural" pictures were transformed by a Neoclassicism that still contained elements of the Rococo style. Born in Switzerland and trained in Italy, Kauffmann spent many of her productive years in England. A protégée of Sir Joshua Reynolds, and the decorator of the interiors of many houses built by Robert Adam, she was a founding member of the British Royal Academy of Arts and enjoyed a fashionable reputation. Her *Cornelia, Pointing to Her Children as Her Treasures,* or *Mother of the Gracchi* (FIG. **25-45**), is a kind of "set piece" of early Neoclassicism. Its subject is an *exemplum virtutis* (example or model of virtue) of the didactic kind, drawn from the history and literature of Greece and Rome. The moralizing pictures of Hogarth and Greuze had already marked a change in taste, but the modern setting of their works was replaced by Kauffmann, who clothed her actors in ancient Roman garb and posed them in classicizing Roman attitudes within Roman interiors. The theme in this painting is the virtue of Cornelia, mother of the future political leaders Tiberius and Gaius Gracchus, who, in the second century B.C., attempted to reform the Roman republic. Cornelia's character is revealed in this scene, which takes place after a lady visitor has shown off her fine jewelry and then haughtily requested that Cornelia show hers. Instead of rushing to get her own precious adornments, Cornelia brings her sons forward, saying, "*These* are my jewels!" The architectural setting is severely Roman, with no Rococo motif in evidence, and the composition and drawing have the simplicity and firmness of low relief carving. Only the charm and grace of the Rococo style linger—in the arrangement of the figures, the soft lighting, and in Kauffmann's own tranquil manner.

Within a few years, Kauffmann's sentimental Neoclassicism had hardened into the public, programmatic stoicism of JACQUES-LOUIS DAVID (1748–1825), the painter-ideologist of the Neoclassical art of the French Revolution and the Napoleonic empire. David was a distant relative of Boucher and followed Boucher's style until a period of

25-45 ANGELICA KAUFFMANN, *Cornelia Pointing to Her Children as Her Treasures,* or *Mother of the Gracchi, c.* 1785. Oil on canvas, 40″ × 50″. Virginia Museum of Fine Arts, Richmond (the A. D. and W. C. Williams Fund).

study in Rome won the younger man over to the tradition of Classical art and to the academic teachings about the elements of art based on rules taken from the ancients and from the great masters of the Renaissance. In his own quite individual and often non-Classical style, David reworked the Classical and academic traditions. He rebelled against the Rococo as an "artificial taste" and exalted Classical art as, in his own words, "the imitation of nature in her most beautiful and perfect form." He praised Greek art enthusiastically, although he, like Winckelmann, knew almost nothing about it firsthand: "I want to work in a pure Greek style. I feed my eyes on ancient statues; I even have the intention of imitating some of them." David's doctrine of the superiority of Classical art was not based solely on an isolated esthetic, however. Believing that "the arts must . . . contribute forcefully to the education of the public," he was prepared both as an artist and as a politician when the French Revolution offered him the opportunity to create a public art—an art of propaganda.

David played many roles in the French Revolution: he was a Jacobin friend of the radical Maximilien Robespierre, a member of the National Convention that voted for the death of King Louis XVI, and the quasi dictator of the Committee on Public Education. David joined scholars and artists in persuading the revolutionary government to abolish the old French Royal Academy and to establish in its

place panels of experts charged with reforming public taste. His position of power made him dominant in the transformation of style, and his own manner of painting was the official model for many years.

Although painted in 1784, before the French Revolution, David's *Oath of the Horatii* (FIG. **25-46**) reflects his politically didactic purpose, his doctrine of the educational power of Classical form, and his method of composing a Neoclassical picture. David agreed with the Enlightenment belief that subject matter should have a moral and should be presented so that the "marks of heroism and civic virtue offered the eyes of the people will electrify its soul, and plant the seeds of glory and devotion to the fatherland." The *Oath of the Horatii* depicts a story from pre-republican Rome, the heroic phase of Roman history that had been pushed to the foreground of public interest by the sensational archeological discoveries at Pompeii and Herculaneum. The topic was not an arcane one for David's audience. This story of conflict between love and patriotism, first recounted by the ancient Roman historian Livy, had been retold in a play by Pierre Corneille that was performed in Paris several years earlier, making it familiar to David's viewing public. According to the story, the leaders of the Roman and Alban armies, poised for battle, decided to resolve their conflicts in a series of encounters waged by three representatives from each side. The Roman

25-46   JACQUES-LOUIS DAVID, *Oath of the Horatii*, 1784. Oil on canvas, approx. 11' × 14'. Louvre, Paris.

champions, the three Horatius brothers, would face the three sons of the Curatius family, the Alban warriors. A sister of the Horatii, Camilla, was the bride-to-be of one of the Curatius sons.

David's painting shows the Horatii as they swear on their swords to win or die for Rome, oblivious to the anguish and sorrow of their sisters. In its form, *Oath of the Horatii* is a paragon of the Neoclassical style. The theme is stated with admirable force and clarity. In a shallow picture box, defined by a severely simple architectural framework, the statuesque and carefully modeled figures are deployed across the space, close to the foreground, in a manner reminiscent of ancient relief sculpture. The rigid and virile forms of the men effectively eclipse the soft, curvilinear shapes of the mourning women in the right background. Such manly virtues as courage, patriotism, and unwavering loyalty to a cause are emphasized over the less heroic emotions of love, sorrow, and despair symbolized by the women. The message is clear and of a type with which the prerevolutionary French public could readily identify. The picture created a sensation when it was exhibited in Paris in 1785, and, although it had been painted under royal patronage and was not at all revolutionary in its original intent, its Neoclassical style soon became the

semiofficial voice of the revolution. David may have been painting in the academic tradition, but he made something new of it; he created a program for arousing his audience to patriotic zeal. From David's *Oath of the Horatii* onward, art became increasingly political—if not often in the strict sense of serving a state or party, then at least in its passionate adherence to selected trends, movements, and ideologies.

We have seen that the taste for "naturalness" includes the moral as a higher "naturalness"; this is the case with Greuze's *Village Bride* (FIG. 25-29) and Kauffmann's *Mother of the Gracchi* (FIG. 25-45). They praise respectively the virtues of rustic matrimony and the mother-love of heroes-to-be. David's *Horatii* is within the taste for "naturalness," praising the moral virtues of heroism, patriotism, and self-sacrifice. The Classical settings and accessories of the Kauffmann and the David simply locate virtue in antiquity rather than in the contemporary world. At this point David is not committed to the kind of exclusive, thoroughgoing Classicism we find in Flaxman (whose *Electra*, after all, is ten years later than the *Horatii*).

David's double portrait of the Lavoisiers (FIG. **25-47**) is quite in accord with the taste for the "natural." It is contemporary and represents a husband and wife of the privileged classes, with the accessories of their occupation: the chemical apparatus that symbolizes the scientific achievement of Antoine-Laurent Lavoisier, founder of quantitative chemistry and discoverer of the role of oxygen in combustion and in the respiration of plants and animals, and the portfolio of drawings made by Mme. Lavoisier to illustrate her husband's treatises on chemistry. At the same time, the painting celebrates the virtue of conjugal affection (compare the young couple in Greuze's picture). There are Classical touches: Mme. Lavoisier is not only the loyal and affectionate wife and secretary, she is his muse, his inspiration. The architecture and furniture are in the early Neoclassical style of the reign of Louis XVI. A pathos attaches to this great picture from the circumstance that Lavoisier perished on the guillotine during the Reign of Terror in the French Revolution, some five years after the picture was painted. His reputation as a great scientist could not preserve him from fanatical, political enmity.

The Revolution, in which, as we have noted, David played a considerable part, gave him the painful opportuni-

25-48   JACQUES-LOUIS DAVID, *The Death of Marat*, 1793. Oil on canvas, approx. 63" × 49". Musées Royaux des Beaux-Arts de Belgique, Brussels.

25-47   JACQUES-LOUIS DAVID, *Antoine-Laurent Lavoisier and Wife, Marie-Anne Pierrette Paulze*, 1788. Oil on canvas. 102" × 76⁵/₈". Metropolitan Museum of Art, New York (gift of Mr. and Mrs. Charles Wrightsman).

ty to paint one of his greatest pictures, indeed, one of the masterpieces of Western art: *The Death of Marat* (FIG. **25-48**). Marat, a revolutionary radical and a personal friend of David, had been stabbed to death in his bath by Charlotte Corday, a political enemy. David depicted the aftermath of the fatal attack with the directness and simple clarity of Zurbarán's painting of St. Francis (FIG. 24-33). The cold, neutral space above Marat's figure, slumped in the tub, makes for a chilling oppressiveness. Narrative details—the knife, the wound, the blood, the letter by which the young woman gained entrance—are vividly placed to sharpen the sense of pain and outrage and to confront the viewer with the scene itself. David's depiction was shaped by historical fact, not Neoclassical theory, but his stele-like composition reveals his close study of Michelangelo, especially the Renaissance master's Christ in the *pietà* in St. Peter's in Rome (FIG. 22-18). *The Death of Marat* is convincingly real, yet it is masterfully composed to present Marat to the French people as a tragic martyr who died in the service of their state. In this way, the painting was meant to function as an "altarpiece" for the new civic "religion"; it was

25-49 JACQUES-LOUIS DAVID, *The Sabine Women*, 1799. Oil on canvas, approx. 12′ 5″ × 16′ 9″. Louvre, Paris.

designed to inspire viewers with the saintly dedication of their slain leader. This depiction is a more severe version of modern martyrdom than West's *The Death of General Wolfe* (FIG. 25-31), which was imbued with the grandeur of spectacle in a way that foreshadowed the dramatic and demonstrative side of nineteenth-century history painting. David's *Marat* has been stripped to a severe Neoclassical spareness like that of the compositions of Flaxman.

At the fall of the French revolutionist Robespierre and his party in 1794, David barely escaped with his life. He was tried and imprisoned, and during his years in and out of prison worked hard at what was to be his monumental statement and the standard of Neoclassical taste, *The Sabine Women* (FIG. **25-49**). This immense picture represented the ancient story of the quarrel between the Romans and the Sabines, their neighbors; it is not the traditionally pictured scene of the Romans carrying away the Sabine women (the "rape of the Sabines"), but the peace brought by the Sabine women between their Roman husbands and Sabine kinsmen. Against the background of a fortress, very much resembling the Bastille, the actors are deployed, like bas-relief sculptures in a frieze, upon a stage parallel to the plane of the picture surface, just as in the *Horatii*. The composition is symmetrical, its axis defined by the figure of Romulus's wife, the beautiful Hersilia, who, with wide-flung arms parts Tatius and his Sabines from the shield-

bearing Romulus and the Roman host. Women with their children surround and obstruct the hostile men. The women and children are quite "natural" in their poses and gestures; the healthy infants in the foreground recall the cherubs in Greuze's cottage (FIG. 25-29).

David takes his figures from Classical statuary, though he mixes them with references to Raphael, the Baroque, and, for the figure of Romulus, possibly Flaxman. David's younger pupils and assistants criticized him for not being "classical" enough and for taking too much from the non-Classical past. The representation of the heroes nude— in the preliminary sketches they were clothed—caused a noisy scandal, though David in his catalog for the exhibition of the *Sabines* vigorously defended nudity of heroes as properly antique. One way or another, the picture established the Neoclassical standard that would guide the practice of a generation of painters loyal to that taste and would provide a target for criticism from the opposing "Romantic" school.

The rise to power of Napoleon Bonaparte in France found enthusiastic approval from David and many of his old Jacobin friends who had survived the fate of Robespierre. After the young Napoleon's dramatic victory over the Austrians at Marengo (in northern Italy) in 1801, David was commissioned by the king of Spain, Charles IV, to do a portrait of the victorious general in his bold crossing of the Alps

Here David glorifies the modern conquering hero as a secular saint. He gave us the martyr of the revolution, Marat, and here Bonaparte, the success-sanctified evangelist who will reveal the new political dispensation to the modern world. It is curious that the same artist could produce the *Marat,* the *Sabines,* and the *Napoleon* within ten years, the first a powerful realism, the second a manifesto of Neoclassicism, and the third Neo-Baroque. These apparently conflicting styles will vie for prominence in the nineteenth century.

We close our narrative of eighteenth-century art with a work of sculpture that sums it up, joining the taste of the earlier century with that coming to the foreground at the end of it. We have met the artist before: Houdon, who carved the bust of Voltaire (FIG. 25-19). Houdon's mastery of the three-dimensional portrait brought him fame and many commissions to portray the great men of his time. In addition to Voltaire, Houdon completed busts of Rousseau, Buffon, Franklin, Washington, Jefferson, Lafayette, and John Paul Jones. In all his portraits Houdon's strong, perceptive "naturalness" penetrates at once to personality, catching the most subtle shade of character.

But the same versatile sculptor could turn his hand to an utterly different yet age-old theme. The elegant bronze *Diana* (FIG. **25-50**) brings together the traditional subject, the ancient goddess, with innovating form. As such, the work stands at the crossroads of a great tradition and a future that will challenge it. The subject is ancient and Renaissance and continues into the Baroque and Rococo, where it fades: Diana, the moon goddess, patron of the hunt, carrying her bow and pursuing her quarry through the forests. She is also goddess of chastity, and is seldom represented nude, as she is here. Her image graces the gardens of royalty and aristocracy, in the company of the mythological personages who do not belong to Rousseau's "nature." Houdon, master of the "natural" in his portraits, here works within the aristocratic taste, which trifles with "nature" or does without it; this goddess disdains the claims of the "natural." Her fleet body, almost flying, is caught in one swift movement of supernatural balance, delicately poised on a single point of support, the toes of her left foot. Here is the lightness and grace of the Rococo and an echo of Renaissance Mannerism. But she has the new simplification of form—and the nudity—favored by Neoclassical taste. The suavely modeled volumes, the supple contours, the compact silhouette, all contribute to her cool simplicity and dignity. No Rococo sensuality, but also no doctrinaire, Neoclassical rigidity and dryness.

Houdon's *Diana* closed the age when the gods were still honored in art. She appeared only once more "and then fleetingly," at the opening of an age that would declare the gods dead. Her Neoclassical appearance would be her last.

25-50 JEAN-ANTOINE HOUDON, *Diana,* 1790. Bronze, 6′ 11″ high. Louvre, Paris.

at the pass of St. Bernard. With characteristic switching of style—as he could switch his politics—David produced not a Neoclassical vision of the event, but a quasi-Baroque one. Except for the parallellism of figure and picture plane, the *Napoleon* (page 922) has all the dramatically swirling forms and vivid coloration of the Baroque. Whipped by the Alpine winds, his cloak whirling, the young general on his ramping steed gestures his troops forward. Beneath, on the foreground rock surfaces, are engraved the names of Napoleon's illustrious predecessors in the Alpine crossing, the ancient Carthaginian Hannibal, the almost conqueror of Rome, and the Holy Roman Emperor, the legendary Charlemagne.

Romanticism

PART FIVE

✦

THE MODERN AND POSTMODERN WORLD

What, then, was the force that moved the nations? …
Power. What then is power? Power is the sum total
*of will as expressed by one person.**

OUR MODERN ERA EMERGES ABOUT THE MIDDLE OF THE EIGHTEENTH CENTURY WITH THE Industrial Revolution, which introduced the age of the machine. In just two and a half centuries—an extremely short span of historical time—we have created a universe of machines that replace physical labor and extend the powers of the brain enormously. Control of nature is now widespread and tenacious, and the application of science in technology and industry has become the characteristic activity or ambition of modern societies.

The picture of the world of physical nature, and of humankind within it, changed radically during this short period. Religion no longer played the dominant role. Soon, eighteenth-century Enlightenment thought was replacing spiritual forces with the mechanical forces described by Newton, later extended and outmoded by Einstein's physics of relativity and space-time. Darwin's theory of evolution altered traditional and religious accounts of the origin of living species and would lead to the science of genetics. The dialectical materialism of Marx purported to show the dynamics of evolutionary social change and the meaning of history. Freud's psychological theory of the irrational unconscious would largely determine modern interpretations of human behavior.

As science and technology challenged old views of the physical world, so political revolution challenged the old absolutisms of church and monarchy and the privileges of a social structure that had originated in the Middle Ages. Following the upheaval of the French Revolution of 1789, a chain of revolutions, counter-revolutions, and civil wars in Europe and America continued the assault upon established power.

AT LEFT: *JACQUES-LOUIS DAVID,* Napoleon Crossing the Alps, *1800. Oil on canvas, 8'10" × 7'7".*
National Museum, Versailles.

*From the epilogue to *War and Peace,* Leo Tolstoy.

Replacing the ancient dogmas of religion, new, secular ideologies—capitalism, liberalism, conservatism, socialism, communism, populism, and their variants—advertised the doctrines, virtues, and aims of the forces fighting to change the world or to defend the status quo. The most powerful and persuasive of the modern ideologies has been nationalism, the secular religion of the nation-state.

The great European nations, enriched by the Industrial Revolution, pursued the aims of empire. Imperial competition and national jealousies, made audacious by technologically perfected armaments, brought about the European civil war we know as World War I. Successful postwar revolutions like the fascist ones in Germany, Italy, and Spain, brought about confrontations that occasioned the even more destructive World War II. Europe was devastated, and by 1960 all the European empires were liquidated. America's defeat in Vietnam brought to an end the old imperial drama. The Cold War between the United States and the Soviet Union ended with the collapse of the Soviet empire and its disintegration into independent states.

The clamor of conflicting ideologies, the restless agitation for political, social, and economic change that aimed to replace worn-out institutions with modern ones, could not help but be reflected in the development of modern art. The aims, definitions, and declarations of the artists and critics who named and propagated the various movements of modern art, have the polemical tone of modern political ideologies, and, like them, are classified by the suffix "-ism"—Romanticism, Realism, Naturalism, Impressionism, Symbolism, Cubism, and the like.* The militancy of political activism is expressed in the term *avant garde*—the vanguard of an army—applied to artists thought to be progressive in creating a new, *modern* art; progressive versus conservative, the modern artist against the traditional, academic artist. This opposition is fundamental for the ideology of Modernism. And, as in political discourse, it is the way one recognizes one's party.

Thus, Modernism as a progressive force harmonized with the doctrine of progress that the achievements of modern science and technology seemed to validate and proclaim. Indeed, modern art not only shared with science and technology the spirit of progress, but it was directly influenced by many of their innovations. The new medium of photography enabled artists to create images in a new way. New theories of color and optics, synthetic pigments, primed canvas, and packaged paints allowed artists to paint more easily and rapidly, as well as to analyze their color perceptions. Advanced metal-casting and welding techniques facilitated the work of the sculptor and suggested new kinds of form. Ferro-concrete, concrete braced with steel, became standard in architectural construction, affecting ambitious experiments in architectural design. Latterly, electronic tools have made possible new kinds of expression in all the traditional media and have pointed the way to still more novel media and types of artistic experience. The printed media largely have been supplanted by radio, television, and telecommunication networks, strongly influencing our percep-

---

*Terms like these, which we will now encounter more frequently, designate stylistic trends, movements, philosophies, and periods. Where they are so used, we will capitalize them as nouns and also as adjectives. When such terms are used in their broader senses, they will not be capitalized. Realism, for example, can be, on the one hand, the narrower, specific reference to the nineteenth-century movement of that name and, on the other, the wider, more general reference to art that emphasizes the literal reproduction of the facts of appearance, no matter the period, as in the painting of Velázquez, Vermeer, and many others (in the latter case, our choice is "realism" and "realistic"). Any rule for capitalization is arbitrary and sometimes inconsistent; it can, however, be useful in defining trends and influences and as a mnemonic device.

tion of reality. At present, computer simulation has created a *virtual* reality nearly indistinguishable from *actual* reality.

The credibility of the doctrine of progress, sustained since the late eighteenth century by the successes of science and technology, has been damaged by their misuse. The destruction spread by mechanized warfare, the irreparable pollution inflicted on the environment, and the threats posed to the biosphere by chemicals and radiation have convinced thoughtful people that the very survival of the planet could be at risk. In this view the benefits of science and technology are accompanied by balancing damage. Deteriorating human conditions (crime, poverty, social alienation) have also called attention to the defects in Western values and institutions.

The modern era and its "post-modern" sequel have witnessed, along with the praise of progress, an insistent criticism of progress as an illusion that means a better life for few, a marginal existence for many. This criticism has denounced the Western establishment and its history and has sharpened into a critical attack upon Western culture in general. The most cherished beliefs of the West have come into question. Political, social, and legal institutions are seen—in the post-modern perspective—as facades that conceal hidden agendas by which the dominant powers of Western society have subordinated women, minorities, and races declared to be inferior. The mores of the West are only the masks of selfish privilege; they must be "deconstructed" to be shown up for what they are. Equal rights for all must be acknowledged and assured and discriminating prejudices abandoned.

These critical and accusatory sentiments have been widespread in the "Postmodern" sequel to Modernism. Modernist art, with its avant garde exclusivism, and its severely formalist definitions of art, has been declared to be elitist and in the tradition of "fine" art (Postmodernists deny the distinction between "fine" art and popular art). Modernism is accused of being intolerant of the artist's right to unlimited freedom of expression. As Modernism attacked traditional definitions of art, so Postmodernism declares the obsolescence of Modernism; and the age-old question "what is art?" becomes a matter of individual or group decision.

For the student, all this means confrontation with a bewildering plurality of personalities, movements, doctrines, opinions, and styles. In the following chapters we attempt to find some order in complexity and confusion, to outline sequences and connections, and to describe what we think to be significant art monuments of a feverish, contradictory, yet intensely exciting era—our own.

INDUSTRIALIZATION OF EUROPE AND THE UNITED STATES ABOUT 1850

ATLANTIC OCEAN

Percent of population residing in cities of 100,000 or more*

- 20%
- 6–10%
- 5% or less

*No countries with 11–19% of the population residing in cities of 100,000 or more.

0   500 Miles

0   500 Kilometers

PARIS   Cities > 1,000,000
CONSTANTINOPLE   Cities 500,000 - 1,000,000
MOSCOW   Cities 200,000 - 500,000

EXPLANATION OF FIGURES

27,700,000   Population in 1850
(240)   Railroad mileage per million of population
3,500,000   Pig iron production in long or metric tons

Cities with less than 500,000 not shown

NORWAY 1,400,000
SWEDEN 3,480,000 *157,000*
FINLAND 1,637,000
St. Petersburg
Moscow
DENMARK 1,415,000 *(13)*
NETHERLANDS 3,057,000 *(35)*
Amsterdam
Berlin
RUSSIA (IN EUROPE) 57,200,000 *(6)* 300,000
POLAND 4,850,000 *(40)*
GLASGOW
UNITED KINGDOM 27,700,000 *(240)* 3,500,000
Dublin
Liverpool
Manchester
Birmingham
LONDON
Brussels
BELGIUM 4,337,000 *(125)* 235,000
GERMAN STATES 34,300,000 *(106)* 600,000
AUSTRIA 17,535,000 *(49)* 200,000
Vienna
HUNGARY 13,192,000 *(11)*
PARIS
FRANCE 35,800,000 *(52)* 650,000
SWITZERLAND 2,393,000 *(6)*
PORTUGAL 3,500,000
Madrid
Lisbon
SPAIN 15,674,000 27,000
ITALIAN STATES 24,348,000 *(16)* 72,000
Naples
OTTOMAN EMPIRE
Constantinople
GREECE 1,035,000
UNITED STATES 23,000,000 *(530)* 1,000,000
New York

ATLANTIC OCEAN
NORTH SEA
BALTIC SEA
MEDITERRANEAN SEA

1800	1810	1820	1830	1840	1850
GEORGE III OF ENGLAND		GEORGE IV		WILLIAM IV	VICTORIA	
FIRST REPUBLIC	NAPOLEON I (THE EMPIRE)	LOUIS XVIII	CHARLES X	LOUIS PHILIPPE		SECOND REPUBLIC

Goya, *The Third of May, 1808* (detail), *1814*

Delacroix, *Liberty Leading the People, 1830*

Courbet, *Burial at Ornans* (detail), *1849*

Chateaubriand, *Genius of Christianity, 1802*

Napoleon crowned emperor, *1804*

Napoleon abdicates, *1814*

Battle of Waterloo, *1815*

Restoration of the Bourbons, *1815*

Death of Napoleon, *1821*

Constitutional monarchy begins in France, *1830-(1848)*

Daguerreotype presented, *1839*

Marx, *1816-1883* Communist Manifesto, *1848*

Revolution in Europe *1848-52*

CHAPTER 26

THE NINETEENTH CENTURY: PLURALISM OF STYLE

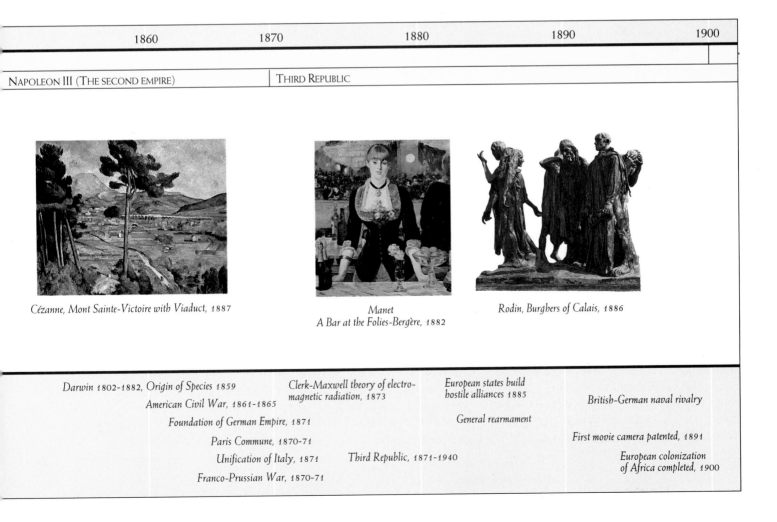

| 1860 | 1870 | 1880 | 1890 | 1900 |

NAPOLEON III (THE SECOND EMPIRE) | THIRD REPUBLIC

Cézanne, Mont Sainte-Victoire with Viaduct, 1887

Manet
A Bar at the Folies-Bergère, 1882

Rodin, Burghers of Calais, 1886

Darwin 1802-1882, Origin of Species 1859
American Civil War, 1861-1865
Foundation of German Empire, 1871
Paris Commune, 1870-71
Unification of Italy, 1871
Franco-Prussian War, 1870-71

Clerk-Maxwell theory of electromagnetic radiation, 1873

Third Republic, 1871-1940

European states build
hostile alliances 1885

General rearmament

British-German naval rivalry

First movie camera patented, 1891

European colonization
of Africa completed, 1900

For Europe, the nineteenth century was an age of radical change during which the modern world took shape. In a world that was experiencing a population explosion of unparalleled magnitude, revolution followed revolution, a pattern punctuated by counterrevolution and conservative reaction. This was the era in which the modern nation-state and accompanying ideas of nationalism were born. European governments extended their rule to virtually every part of the globe, spreading the influence of European culture into colonies in Africa, the Americas, India, Asia, and Australasia, and clearing the way for influences from those areas to flow back to Europe. The formation of empires abroad was supported by the enthusiasm of popular nationalism at home, and patriotism and imperialism went hand in hand.

SCIENCE AND TECHNOLOGY

Behind these great changes, and propelling them onward with ever greater speed, were the scientific, technological, and industrial revolutions that originated in the eighteenth-century Enlightenment and would change the human environment forever. The powers of steam, petroleum, and electricity were harnessed to industrial production, transportation, and communication. The revolution in industrial materials produced cast-iron buildings; and iron, converted by new methods into steel and its alloys, was the elementary stuff of heavy industry and its products: ships, locomotives, and big guns; bridges, tunnels, and dynamos—and an endless variety of machines. Light industry flooded the expanding markets with machine-made commodities, from textiles to typewriters. Steam-powered ships and railway trains foreshortened time and distance. Oil, the life-fluid of the machine age, was first drilled in 1859 and was soon indispensable to modern life. The electric generator furnished power to whole cities. The petroleum fueled internal-combustion engine-powered automobiles, which made their appearance toward the end of the century. Power-driven farm vehicles and implements encouraged agricultural expansion and enormously increased harvests. The telegraph, telephone, and wireless (radio) turned sound into information transmitted across vast distances.

The eighteenth century had seen the physical world as mechanical, simply as matter in motion, regulated by fixed laws. Scientists in the nineteenth century, observing closely the physical forces that drove the new technology, analyzed the properties of motion, light, heat, electricity, magnetism and chemical reaction, and found that they could be converted into one another, all of them being manifestations of a single entity, energy. At the end of the century, the discovery of radioactivity prepared the way for the great physical discoveries leading to atomic particle theory and relativity.

Scientific experiments in chemistry, progressing from the eighteenth-century discovery of oxygen, isolated more and more of the chemical elements that compose organic and inorganic matter and this, in turn, permitted scientists to predict accurately the existence of still others. Biologists discovered that the cell is the elementary unit of all living tissue, that genetic inheritance explains hybrid species, and that micro-organisms ("germs") are the sources of disease and fermentation. The germ theory of disease led to antisepsis and sanitation. It influenced food technology, leading to methods for the preservation of food through refrigeration and pasteurization.

Scientific psychology began with the experimental study of human thought processes—the analysis and measurement of perception and learning as reflexes and responses to the physical stimuli of the environment. The brain was dissected, and its speech centers localized. Mental disorders were described and theorized; "hysteria" and "neuraesthenia" were the common terms for what has come to be known as neurosis. The century closed with Freud's trailblazing theory of the unconscious, which led to the therapeutic technique called psychoanalysis.

The public rejoiced in the achievements of technology and called it progress. "The most striking and palpable evidence of progress in the reign [of Queen Victoria]," wrote a journalist in 1897,

> is the ever increasing speed which the discoveries of physical science have forced into everyday life. Steam and electricity have conquered time and space to a greater extent in the last sixty years than all the preceding six hundred years witnessed; so that a man can now cram into ten years as much experience as his grandfather could have done in fifty.*

The tempo of modern life, as noted a century ago, has continued—as we are all aware—with ever-increasing acceleration.

The public may have rejoiced in the manifestations of progress that the achievements of science and technology afforded, but two closely related scientific theories, one geological, the other biological, deeply troubled many observers. Geologists claimed that the physical features of the earth pointed to the planet's age, millions of years, and that the geological processes still slowly going on were uniform and continuous with those at work from the beginning. This contradicted the biblical account of the Creation and substituted natural for supernatural cause. With Charles Darwin's *Origin of Species* (1859), the doctrine of Evolution propounded the theory (though it was vehemently rejected by many) that life on earth evolved through variations determined by natural selection favoring the best adapted species—in effect, that humankind evolved from pre-human, simian ancestors. This doctrine

*Asa Briggs, *The Nineteenth Century: The Contradictions of Progress* (New York: 1970), p. 12.

countered Christian teaching, as well as the Enlightenment view of humanity as a completed species not subject to change in time. In the new view, human nature was not a constant, but an organic variable, subject to natural forces and indefinite change.

Still, although these theories set off a war between science and religion, evolution and the doctrine of progress easily could be reconciled; social and economic progress, through free competition, would come to be seen by many as simply a matter of "survival of the fittest."

Industrial Society and Ideology

Science and technology were in the hands of the middle class, as were the social, political, and economic management of society, which the middle class had won by their victory over the Old Regime in the French Revolution of 1789. Middle-class entrepreneurs and financiers put science and technology to work in creating the Industrial Age, which, though it raised the living conditions of many and added conveniences to life, caused severe dislocation and deprivation among the vast, property-less majority, the new class of industrial laborers and urban poor, known as the proletariat. The main industrial institution, the factory system, took manufacturing out of the hands of cottage industry and relocated it in dismal factories and factory towns, where throngs of workers were required to live, rent, and labor twelve or more hours a day. An unregulated capitalism exploited an unorganized laboring population; labor bid against labor in the market, so that wages rarely rose above the subsistence level. The expanding metropolises of Europe swarmed with the perennially destitute unemployed.

The plight of the proletariat inspired new social and political movements: Socialism, Communism, Anarchism, Syndicalism were ideologies and calls for the proletariat to organize and to change the system either by democratic participation in it or by forcible subversion. At the same time, middle-class liberals sought to reform by extending the voting franchise to "the people"; and conservatives, many capitalists, surviving landholders, aristocrats, and monarchists fought against all threats, real or imagined, to privilege, property, and the accumulation of untaxed wealth. To them the word *socialism* was anathema, much as the word *Jacobinism,* the ideology of the radicals like Robespierre, was to the aristocracy in the French Revolution.

The French Revolution was the first modern event that showed that a militant ideology could succeed in changing the world. An ideology is a set of ideas on the march, not ideas passively held and open to debate, but ideas that, from the ideologue's point of view, are no longer debatable; becoming firmly, even fanatically, held beliefs, these ideas supply the motives of action. The name of the ideology carries the suffix *ism;* thus, *communism, capitalism, nationalism, imperialism, populism,* and so on. The name of a subscriber to

an ideology, and thus a member of its movement, carries the suffix *-ist: anarchist, syndicalist, irredentist,* and so forth.

The French Revolution and the advent of industrial democracy stimulated a movement of prime importance in the modern world: feminism. Still a powerful force, feminism asserts the right of women to equal status with men—intellectual, moral, political, legal, social, and economic. For centuries the subordination of women had made them ineligible to hold property in their own names, to dispose of their own children, or even their own bodies. The "weaker sex"—as they were defined by religion, custom, and law—were shut out from public office, denied higher education, and undercompensated in the new world of industrial labor, where they were assigned backbreaking tasks, inhuman working hours, and starvation wages.*

Modern feminism early declares itself in Mary Wollstonecraft's *Vindication of the Rights of Women,* published in 1792 at the height of the French Revolution. Acknowledging the revolutionary government's proclamation of the *Rights of Man,* the *Vindication* is a kind of preamble to any feminist manifesto, for it first demands recognition of the right of women to intellectual and moral equality with men. Wollstonecraft accuses male-dominated society of having kept women in subordination by denying them education and reducing them to childishness. She protests the double standard, intellectual and moral, by which men have kept women in bondage.

> Many are the causes that, in the present corrupt state of society, contribute to enslave women by cramping their understandings. . . . The instruction which women have hitherto received has only tended . . . to render them insignificant objects of desire—mere propagators of fools! The illegitimate power [over men], which [women] obtain by degrading themselves, is a curse, and they must return to nature and equality. . . . I here throw down my gauntlet and deny the existence of [separate] sexual virtues. For man and women, truth, if I understand the meaning of the word, must be the same.†

Wollstonecraft does not expect immediate legal and political emancipation of women, though she guesses that it will come, The feminist program leading to that end, and prominently demanding female suffrage, would evolve in the nineteenth century, especially in Great Britain and the United States.

In 1848, echoing the enthusiasm and resolve of the European revolutionaries of that year, women held a

---

*A poignant ballad of the early nineteenth century, *Song of the Shirt,* records the distressful conditions of early industrial labor and paints the misery of a female garment worker. Some of its telling lines:
Stitch! Stitch! Stitch!/ In poverty, hunger and dirt,/ A woman sat in unwomanly rags / Singing the song of the shirt /. . . Why do I talk of death? / Because of the fasts I keep / O God that bread should be so dear, / And flesh and blood so cheap!

†In Janet M. Todd, *A Wollstonecraft Anthology,* Bloomington/London, Indiana University Press, 1977. pp. 84–114.

convention at Seneca Falls, New York. They declared women's independence—equality before the law, married women's right to property, acceptance in institutions of higher learning, admission to all trades and professions, equal pay for equal work, and, of course, the right to vote. The movement spread rapidly in the United States and overseas. After the American Civil War the demand for women's suffrage, backed by many men, became insistent. Wyoming granted women the vote in 1869, soon followed by Utah. Though most of the states held out against women's suffrage, women were not deterred from taking prominent part in public life and politics, in literature and the arts, and in education. Women were active in promoting reform movements like midwest Populism and led the moral crusade for Prohibition. The early twentieth century would see the success of American feminism's struggle for the vote and for the abolition (briefly) of the traffic in alcohol. The late twentieth century would see a radical broadening of feminist politics and ideology.

But ideology is not exclusively social, political, and economic. The art of the nineteenth and twentieth centuries, created very much in the midst of and influenced by the movements of the time, has been classified by historians, critics, and often by the artists themselves in much the same way: the critic and novelist Gautier, a member of the Romantic circle in France, wrote a history of Romanticism (*Histoire de Romantisme*) in 1874. Today we still use ideological terms to classify the many styles in modern (now "modernist"!) art. We will find that the adherents and promoters of modern art, critics and artists alike, represent themselves as being in disagreement and conflict with other styles and tastes, and, what is most significant, that they maintain that they are, unlike their opponents, representatives of progress. They lead the march into the modern world. They are its *avant-garde*.

Ideology and Progress

A profound sense of history pervaded the nineteenth century. The past was rapidly receding, and a unique present was asserting its originality as decisively as the early Christian world had asserted *its* values against the defeated and devalued pagan past. The new age, created by the great revolutions, was *modern*, and modern, for many, was good. What was not modern was rejected, for what was to come would be better. These concepts constituted the "doctrine of progress"—which we have seen developing in the eighteenth century—whose supporters maintained the permanency of change for the better. As early as 1750, Turgot had predicted that the doctrine of progress would replace that of the will of God.

Many in the nineteenth century, of course, did not accept the doctrine of progress; others did so with reservations or with grave misgivings. Such critics saw much of value being lost through change and feared for the traditions, institutions, customs, and mores that knit society together and give meaning to life. They could accept neither the depreciation of human value implicit in scientific explanations of human nature like Darwin's, nor the alienation and degradation of human beings by a mechanized and impersonal industry. They had a special distaste for the type of modern society built by new wealth, with all its ostentatious materialism. Many of those who objected to the vulgarity and banality of taste predominant in such a society were artists—some of them, the best artists of the century.

The liberal belief in progress is a belief that the course of history can be changed by thought and action, as long as people are not impeded by repressive authority—the questions of what should be believed, respected, defended, and conformed to. Revolutionary shake-ups of authority reverberated throughout the century, carrying people's hopes for something newer, better, truer, and purer. Humanity was thought to be perfectible, and the principle of utility, calling for the greatest good for the greatest number, was advocated for law, government, and economic life. Confusion arose, however, over the means to these ends, a confusion that produced a wide variety of philosophies rationalizing change and the reactions to change. These ideologies, as we have seen, provided the maxims and slogans of the countless movements that agitated the nineteenth century and remain current today.

The element that all of these ideologies had in common was dissatisfaction with a status quo in which the past lingered and disagreement about how it should be corrected—that is, modernized. For the arts, this meant continuing debate over the relative values of the "traditional" and the "modern"—a debate restimulated as each new style was itself rapidly superseded by yet a newer one. This rapid appearance and obsolescence of a variety of artistic styles (analogous to the concurrent rapid turnover in types of mechanically produced commodities and to the quick progression of scientific and technological discoveries and inventions) transformed painting, the graphic arts, sculpture, and architecture so radically that the transformations amounted to a dismantling of tradition altogether and the appearance of something utterly novel in the early twentieth century. This process was the reverse of the development of science, which built on its tradition in largely unbroken continuity within the expanding language of mathematics.

THE ARTIST: TRADITIONAL OR MODERN?

The nineteenth-century artist had to face formidable changes on all sides. The Church and the secular nobility were replaced as sources of artists' commissions by the triumphant middle class, the national state, and national academies. The uncultivated taste of a vast new audience, concerned, above all, with money and property and guided and manipulated by professional critics writing in the press, created an uncertain and risky market for the artist working alone. Competition forced crowds of artists, whose numbers had more than doubled since the end of the previous century, to bid for the public's attention by flattering its taste. Like small, independent capitalists with their own stocks and stores, artists took chances in the market, aiming to please. If they were unwilling to take such chances, they risked the suspicion and the hostility of the public. These developments contributed to the gradual alienation of artists and the emergence of their often isolated and difficult situation in modern society.

Artists who were dissatisfied with standards of public taste and the kind of art designed to satisfy it used their own work and the writings of friendly critics to protest what they viewed as the degeneration of art into shallow entertainment. Imbued with the romantic ideals of self-expression, they called for a new, highly individualistic vision, one that was original and sincere, free from the sentimentalities, trivialities, and hypocrisies of conventional taste. Rejecting the authority of prevailing taste and of the institutions backing it, these artists claimed the right to an authority of their own, often with a sense of mission not unlike that of the seer and prophet; they would restore or re-create art. These artists tended to group or be grouped into parties or "movements" analogous to those in political life and recognizable by their opposition in the complex, stylistic dialogues that took place; they were, in fact, debating in a new way the very nature of art and the function of the artist. As it turns out, they were dealing with the question of a *modern* art, one fundamentally different from that of the past, even though it might be constructed out of the "tradition" of the past to a greater or lesser degree.

The *Tradition,* as we will refer to it, was the whole corpus, or canon, of art acknowledged to be good or great: the art of Greece and Rome, of the Renaissance, and of the Baroque. Such art spanned a stylistic spectrum from "classical idealism" to "optical realism" and seemed to exhaust the physical possibilities of the media as well as their thematic content. The Tradition was first challenged and, by the end of the century, rejected for an art "of our own times," a modern art. In the course of the century, challenge was met by response, and response by new challenge, so that the modes of traditional and modern were interwoven, recombined, and separated by independent artists, producing a bewildering plurality of individual styles not easily categorized. Although we will use the conventional categories of art history—Romanticism, Realism, Impressionism, and so on—as markers, these terms cannot help but be indefinite and often misleading. What we *do* perceive by mid-century is a bifurcation of emphasis and purpose: one branch, optical realism, is linked to scientific discoveries about the physical world and to the development of photography and the motion picture; the other branch is connected with psychological and spiritual investigations leading to the abstract art of the twentieth century. The former is directed to the public and popular taste; the latter is aimed, for the most part, at a select, specially trained audience.

Various factors contributed to this historical division. Artists in the nineteenth century were confronted by three innovations that fatefully affected their craft: the camera, the mass-produced print, and the printed reproduction. The almost infinite proliferation of the products of these new media flooded the world with images that became formidable rivals of the unique work made by hand. In a way, the nineteenth-century artist was technologically displaced, much as the manuscript scribe of the sixteenth century had been displaced by the printer. Moreover, the collective techniques of an industrial age forced nineteenth-century artists, as individual craftspeople, to analyze their function and to study closely the physical nature of their medium. Photographic images challenged the iconic function of traditional art by accurately capturing the optical world of human experience. Toward the end of the century, artists found themselves using the elements of line, shape, and color to represent their private world, the realm of imagination and feeling. The functions of the artist and of the artist's medium were decisively transformed by the modern world, and the art of that world broke firmly away from the Tradition.

THE EARLY NINETEENTH CENTURY: THE ROLE OF ROMANTICISM

In art, stylistic change never occurs neatly at the beginning of a new century. The revolutions that ushered in the modern world were accompanied by a widespread agitation of spirit, a kind of collective mental revolution—the emotional response to accelerating change. We already have been introduced to Romanticism in the eighteenth century and have examined its onset, its rise, and the problems of defining its period. In the nineteenth century, Romanticism continued to center around the concerns for the abrogation of traditions, institutions, and privileges that were seen to have impeded human progress. Romanticism as a view of life, as well as a state of mind, inherited the Enlightenment's admiration of nature and "the natural" over convention and artifice, and it continued to uncover history as a storehouse of natural lessons for correcting the defects of the present.

The emphasis on human rights in the public sphere was accompanied by the assertion of the value of feeling and emotion in private experience. Truth could be sought and found inwardly more surely than in doctrines of religion or rules of reason; Romanticism's orientation was subjective, and the intensity of the religious and mystical emotions associated with traditional Christianity could live on in the individual, with or without reference to specific creeds. The ardor of Romanticism was also religious, as were its soul-searching and truth-seeking through feeling and vision. The pantheistic union of the soul with nature—nature, for many, replacing the Christian God—was part of the Romantic ritual and excitement. T. E. Hulme defined Romanticism as "spilled religion": the old doctrinal vessels were broken, and their volatile contents spread widely and indefinitely.

The contents spread indefinitely, because no fixed doctrines for Romanticism could really be identified. How could such doctrines be defined in a world of decisive change in which all that was fixed, dogmatic, and categorical was challenged? On issues of the day, we can find Romantic spirits on opposing sides: progressive and conservative, democratic and monarchistic, religious and agnostic, hoping and despairing, satanic and angelic. The world of history, for example, in the process of being systematically recovered, could be valued as serving the hopes of new nations by showing them the heroic past, by supplying them with an identity. Or it could be regarded as a nightmare from which the present was trying to wake: "The world," wrote Percy Bysshe Shelley, "is weary of the past / Oh, might it die, or rest at last!"

Romanticism, protean as the modern world it reflected, and, like the modern mind, incorrigibly romantic, had one firm conviction at its center. That belief was the identification of reality as rooted in the self, not in the external, manmade world. The search for this identity—the revelation and expression of it in art and life—was the objective and meaning of personal existence. We have heard Rousseau preach the religion of the value of the individual in a single assertion: "I may be no better than anyone else; at least I am different." For the Romantic, it was the difference that counted.

Despite the plurality of styles and tastes in the nineteenth century, the artist's claim of autonomy was a constant, and this individualism sometimes resulted in alienation. The right to be an individual authority justified this procedure, even when an artist chose to accept the authority of, say, the academies. The broad right to select a mode of expression was then matched by the broad range of materials supplied by the Tradition, which the artists would either adopt or turn aside. The artist's motives might be various: to stir an audience with drama or melodrama; to reconstruct historical incident; to exhibit the beauty of the human figure, a landscape, a still life, or other traditional subjects; to present the genre of modern life; to paint the inventions of a fertile imagination; to externalize dreams as images, private and strange. The subjects, modes of representation, and techniques of the artists of the nineteenth century, various as they may have been, were all derived from a common attitude and claim of autonomy.

In this earlier century of the modern era, then, much of the subject matter in art was mainly romantic, in that the artist stressed dramatic emotion or ideal beauty, or combinations of these with other material. Romantic artists discovered their themes in history, literature, nature and religion, the exotic, and the esoteric, and they drew on the pictorial modes of the Tradition—the Classical, the Renaissance, and the Baroque. Romantic architects recovered the historical styles of Western architecture and those of the non-European world and paraded them dramatically. Historical and literary material, often produced with a photographic realism, predominated. It is this retrospective subject matter, seeming separate or escaping from the specifically modern scene, that, in part, invites the use of the term *Romanticism*. Yet we will see that some aspects of Romanticism survived into the twentieth century and that much contemporary art has been, in essence, subjective—an intellectual and emotional reflection of challenging and continual change.

Continuation of the Neoclassical Style

The romantic Neoclassical taste for the more or less exact replication of Greek and Roman buildings spread throughout Europe and America. From Virginia to Munich, from Paris to St. Petersburg, Neoclassicism was associated with everything from revolutionary aspirations for democratic purity to imperial ambitions for unshakable authority.

In France, the early years of the century were dominated by Napoleon Bonaparte, a figure of romantically enlightened temperament and enormous ego, who embraced all links with the Classical past as sources of symbolic authority for his short-lived imperial state. La Madeleine (FIG. **26-1**) was briefly intended to be a "temple of glory" for Napoleon's armies and a monument to the newly won glories of France. Begun as a church in 1807, at the height of Napoleon's power (some three years after he proclaimed himself emperor), the structure reverted again to a church after his defeat and long before its completion in 1842. Designed by PIERRE VIGNON (1763–1828) as an octastyle peripheral temple, its high podium and the broad flight of stairs leading to a deep porch simulate the buildings of the time of the first caesars, making La Madeleine a symbolic link between the Napoleonic and the Roman empires. Curiously, the building's Classical shell surrounds an interior that is covered by a sequence of three domes, a feature found in Byzantine and Aquitanian Romanesque churches, as though this Christian church had been clothed in the costume of pagan Rome.*

Under Napoleon, Classical models were apparent in all the arts. The emperor's favorite sculptor was ANTONIO CANOVA (1757–1822), who somewhat reluctantly left a successful career in Italy to settle in Paris and serve the emperor. Once in France, Canova became an admirer of Napoleon and made numerous portraits, all in the neo-Classical style,

---

*Karl Marx neatly described the change from the Neoclassicism of the Revolutionary age to the Neoclassicism of the Napoleonic empire: "The Revolution of 1789 to 1814 draped itself alternately as the Roman Republic and the Roman Empire." *The Eighteenth Brumaire of Louis Bonaparte* (1852).

of the emperor and his family. Perhaps the best known of these works is the portrait of Napoleon's sister, *Pauline Borghese as Venus* (FIG. **26-2**). The sensuous pose and form of Canova's figure recall Greek sculpture, while the sharply detailed rendering of the couch and drapery echo a later Hellenistic style. With remarkable discretion, Canova created a daring image of seductive charm, generalized enough to personify the goddess of love, yet still suggestive of the

26-1   PIERRE VIGNON, La Madeleine, Paris, 1807–1842.

26-2   ANTONIO CANOVA, *Pauline Borghese as Venus,* 1808. Marble, life size. Galleria Borghese, Rome.

Neo Classical

26-3   HORATIO GREENOUGH, *George Washington*, 1832–1841. Marble, approx. 11′4″ high. National Museum of American Art, Smithsonian Institution, Washington, D.C.

living person. Despite a lingering Rococo charm, this work shows the artist to have been firmly Neoclassical in his approach. Canova was considered to be the greatest sculptor of his time but suffered greatly in reputation later. Current criticism has restored him somewhat, although he still carries, as the most typical of the Neoclassicists, something of the burden of negative criticism leveled against this often doctrinaire style.

The defects of the Neoclassical style are apparent in a statue of George Washington (FIG. **26-3**), by the American sculptor HORATIO GREENOUGH (1805–1852). Here, the Neoclassical style Jefferson had championed so successfully for the architecture of the new democracy (FIG. 25-42) turned out to be less suitable for commemorative portraits. Commissioned by the United States Congress to honor Washington as the country's first president, the sculptor used as a model for the head a popular bust of Washington by Houdon (a work with the same lively realism as Houdon's *Voltaire* [FIG. 25-19]). In the body of the statue, Greenough aimed at the monumental majesty inspired by a lost, but famous, sculpture by Phidias of the Greek god Zeus. The sheathed sword, offered hilt forward, was intended to symbolize "Washington the peacemaker," rather than

"Washington the revolutionary war general." The representation of the "father of his country," deified as a half-naked pagan god, however, was, at the time, beyond the taste of the American public. The statue was considered to be a failure in Greenough's time precisely because it manifested, more than many sculptures of the Neoclassical style, the contradictions that sometimes develop when idealistic and realistic illusion meet. Canova appeared to harmonize these two trends; Greenough put them in opposition. Although Greenough's statue was never thrown into the Potomac River, "to hide it from the world," as one congressman suggested, it also was never placed in its intended site beneath the Capitol dome. Today, the work is more highly regarded and is displayed at the National Museum of American History in Washington, D.C. While to some, it may seem stiff, cold, or simply unconvincing, it does have an imperious majesty appropriate to the national memory of its subject.

The Search for Ideal Form

Painting in the early nineteenth century proved to be an extraordinarily sensitive medium for the romantically subjective, personal expression of the time. In France, David demanded that his pupils select their subjects from Plutarch, the ancient author of *Lives of the Great Greeks and Romans* and a principal source of standard Neoclassical subject matter. David's pupils, however, often found their subjects elsewhere, and it was this distinction in subject matter that divided his art from that of many of his successors.

Whatever their subject matter, some of David's pupils shared his preference for ideal form, based on what they could learn from Classical sculpture. The ideal, as opposed to the real, was to be found, according to those who sought it, in the Greek statue; there, they believed, the idea of perfect human beauty had been embodied. They felt it should be the artist's purpose to capture that beauty once again. Painting should learn from sculpture simplicity and smoothness of surface, flowing contour, minimal chiaroscuro, and color, which only distract from the sense of form. The nude figure was seen as best expressing the ideal (FIG. 25-49). Compositions made of nude or partly draped figures should emulate bas-relief sculpture and should be in symmetrical balance. The prevailing mood should be tranquil, permitting a contemplative calm, appropriate in the presence of beauty. Few painters could avoid mixing the ideal with the real, or refrain from mixing ideal form with exciting subjects and with realistic touches in the description of action and setting.

One of David's students, ANNE-LOUIS GIRODET-TRIOSON (1767–1824), turned to a popular novel by Chateaubriand (*Atala*) for the subject of his *Burial of Atala* (FIG. **26-4**). This painting could be a set piece for Romanticism. Atala, sworn

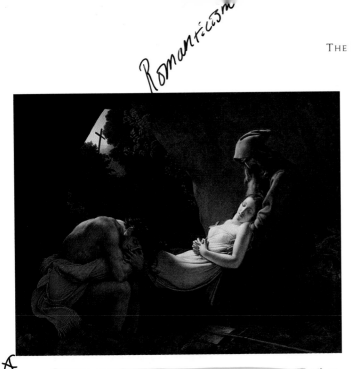

26-4   ANNE-LOUIS GIRODET-TRIOSON, *The Burial of Atala*, 1808. Oil on canvas, approx. 6′11″ × 8′9″. Louvre, Paris.

to lifelong virginity, falls passionately in love with a wild, young savage of the Carolina wilderness. Rather than break her oath, she commits suicide and is buried in the shadow of a cross by her grief-stricken lover. By representing the holy church in the person of the cloaked priest, Girodet daringly puts religion and sexual passion side by side, binding them with the theme of death and burial. Hopeless love, perished beauty, the grave, the purity of primitive life, and the consolation of religion are some of the Romantic themes Girodet successfully showed in this work. The picture's composite style combines classicizing contours and modeling with a dash of the erotic sweetness of the Rococo and the dramatic illumination of the Baroque. Unlike David's appeal to the feelings that manifest themselves in public action in the *Oath of the Horatii* (FIG. 25-46), the appeal here is to the viewer's private world of fantasy and emotion. If David's purpose was to "electrify the soul," Girodet's was, in the language of Rousseau, to "wring the heart." The artist speaks here to emotions, rather than inviting philosophical meditation or revealing some grand order of nature and form. The Romantic artists, above all else, wanted to excite the emotions of the audience.

INGRES   But JEAN-AUGUSTE-DOMINIQUE INGRES (1781–1867) shunned excitement in his painting and became the most renowned artistic representative of the nineteenth century romantic taste for ideal form. Ingres arrived at David's studio after Girodet-Trioson had left to establish an independent career of his own. Ingres's study there was to be short-lived, however, as he soon broke with David on matters of style. This difference of opinion involved Ingres's adoption of a manner based on what he believed to be a truer and purer Greek style than that employed by David.

The younger man adopted flat and linear forms approximating those found in Greek vase painting and in the work of Flaxman (FIG. 25-44). In a good deal of Ingres's work, the figure is placed in the foreground, much like a piece of low-relief sculpture. The value Ingres placed on the flow of the contour is a characteristic of his style throughout his career. Contour, which is simply shaded line, was everything for Ingres, and drawing was the means of creating contour. Ingres has been credited with the famous slogan that became the battle cry of his school: "Drawing is the probity of art." In content, Ingres first adopted David's Neoclassical subjects, but he later also traversed the complete range of other Romantic sources.

It was this rather strange mixture of artistic allegiances—the precise adherence to Classical form conveyed in Romantic content—that provoked one critic to ridicule Ingres's work as the vision of "a Chinaman wandering throughout the ruins of Athens." In both form and content, Ingres initially was seen by critics as a kind of rebel; they did not cease their attacks until the mid-1820s, when another enemy of the official style, Eugène Delacroix, appeared. Then they suddenly perceived that Ingres's art, despite its innovations and deviations, still contained many elements that adhered to the official Neoclassicism—the taste for the ideal. Ingres soon was to become the leader of the academic forces in their battle against the "barbarism" of Géricault, Delacroix, and their "movement." Gradually, Ingres warmed to the role in which he had been cast by the critics, and he came to see himself as the conservator of good and true art, a protector of its principles against its would-be "destroyers."

While Ingres's *Grande Odalisque* (FIG. **26-5**) drew acid criticism when first shown in 1814 ("She has three vertebrae too many," "No bone, no muscle, no life"), the painting seems today to sum up the painter's artistic intentions. Ingres treats the figure in his own "sculpturesque style"—polished surfaces and simple, rounded volumes controlled by rhythmically flowing contours. The smoothness of the planes of the body is complemented by the broken, busy shapes of the drapery. Ingres's subject, the reclining nude figure, is traditional enough and goes back to Giorgione and Titian (FIG. 22-61), but by converting the figure to an odalisque (a member of a Turkish harem) the artist made a strong concession to the contemporary Romantic taste for the exotic. The work also shows his admiration for Raphael in his borrowing of that master's type of female head, but Ingres did not draw only from the period of the High Renaissance. His figure's languid pose, her proportions (small head and elongated limbs), and the generally cool color scheme also reveal his debt to such Mannerists as Parmigianino (FIG. 22-40). Often criticized for not being a colorist, Ingres, in fact, had a superb color sense. It is true that he did not seem to think of his paintings primarily in terms of their color, as did Delacroix, but he did

26-5   JEAN-AUGUSTE-DOMINIQUE INGRES, *Grande Odalisque*, 1814. Oil on canvas, approx. 35″ × 64″. Louvre, Paris.

26-6   JEAN-AUGUSTE-DOMINIQUE INGRES, *Apotheosis of Homer*, 1827. Oil on canvas, approx. 12′8″ × 16′10³/₄″. Louvre, Paris.

Apotheosis
— Perfect example of

far more than simply tint his drawings for emphasis, as recommended by the Academy. In his best paintings, Ingres created color and tonal relationships so tastefully as to render them unforgettable.

The huge composition, the *Apotheosis of Homer* (FIG. **26-6**), which Ingres exhibited at the Salon of 1826, presented in a single statement the doctrine of ideal form, of Neoclassical taste, to which generations of academic painters would remain loyal. Enthroned before an Ionic temple, the epic poet Homer is crowned by a winged victory. At his feet are two statuesque women, who personify the *Iliad* and the *Odyssey,* the offspring of his imagination. Symmetrically grouped about him is a company of the "sovereign geniuses"—as Ingres called them—who expressed the highest ideals of humanity in philosophy, poetry, music, and art. To the left of Homer is Anacreon with his lyre, Phidias with his sculptor's hammer, and Plato, Socrates, and other ancient worthies. To his far right are Horace, Vergil, Dante, and, conspicuously, Raphael, the painter Ingres most admired. Among the forward group to the left are Poussin (pointing) and Shakespeare (half concealed); and at the right Racine, Molière, Voltaire, and Fénelon. Ingres had planned a much larger and more inclusive group, but the project was never completed; for years he agonized over whom to admit to and whom to exclude from this select company of heroes of the humanities.

It is obvious that the idea for the *Apotheosis,* and, to a degree, the composition, were inspired by Raphael's *School of Athens* (FIG. 22-15). As Ingres developed as an artist, he turned more and more to Raphael, perceiving in his art the essence of Classicism and disdaining, in proportion, the new "modern" styles (the "romantic" and the "realistic" as they were then called) as destructive of true art. "We must ever turn to the past," he said.

> Let me hear no more of that absurd maxim: "We need the new, we must follow our century, everything changes, everything is changed." All that is sophistry! Does nature change, do the light and air change, have the passions of the human heart changed since the time of Homer? "One must follow one's century" . . . but what if my century's wrong?

This is the cry of the great conservative, rejecting the modern. It expresses precisely the Classicist's resistance to the new school of Romantic color and passion, that would change the school of ideal form, of which Ingres had become high priest and first master.

In his many portraits, Ingres mingled the real and the ideal. He always insisted that he painted exactly what he saw, despite what one critic declared to be his "genius for idealizing." An exquisite example of Ingres's method is to be seen in his portrait of the *Princess de Broglie* (FIG. **26-7**). The princess was the wife of an aristocrat of a famous family, active in both literature and politics in the time of Napoleon III. The painter represents her as elegantly

26-7   JEAN-AUGUSTE-DOMINIQUE INGRES, *Princess de Broglie,* 1853. Oil on canvas, approx. 47³/₄″ × 35³/₄″. The Metropolitan Museum of Art, New York, Robert Lehman Collection.

dressed for an imperial reception or ball. With an air of aristocratic nonchalance, she leans gracefully on the crest of a sumptuously upholstered chair. The ice-blue of her gown and lace, and the golden hue of the satined chair, compose the simple yet brilliant color scheme, a harmony that sets off the ivory of her bare arms and shoulders, the pale lustre of the pearls, and the faint blush of warm tone in her cheeks and in the auburn highlights of her hair. With a minimum of shading, and a matchless precision in the rendering of shapes and textures, Ingres yet centers the composition on the lovely head. He gives us a likeness, but a likeness idealized, a likeness modified by an ideal of serene beauty that he has absorbed from the art of Raphael and of the Greeks.

Through the painted forms of Ingres's portraits, one always senses the meticulous drawing. Ingres drew a number of portraits that are entirely complete and satisfying in themselves; one could agree with him that often the color is something super-added, almost an afterthought. His pencil portrait of the great violin virtuoso Niccoló Paganini (FIG. **26-8**), speaks to this. Ingres was a creditable amateur

26-8 JEAN-AUGUSTE-DOMINIQUE INGRES, *Paganini*, 1819. Pencil drawing, approx. 12″ × 8½″. Louvre, Paris.

violinist, passionately fond of music (he wanted to include Mozart among the immortals surrounding Homer), and he knew Paganini personally. The portrait, executed with that marvelously crisp, clean descriptive line that we find in all of Ingres's portraits, painted or drawn, is entirely literal in its report of Paganini's features and demeanor. He gives us the musician's appearance as a kind of official likeness, enhanced by a suggestive likeness and sense of setting. Paganini, sharing a certain fragility and suppleness with his violin and bow, seems about to make his introductory obeisance to his audience. The portrait is *formal*—a graceful, not a stiff, formality. It is the musician face to face with the public world, rising as always to the familiar occasion, which he knows he can command. The ideal of the great musician rises through the faithfully real likeness of Paganini.

Dramatic Action, Emotion, and Color

So far we have dealt almost exclusively with French art and artists, who worked within the Neoclassical style and the search for Ideal Form into which it was resolved. When we move to a consideration of the opposing Romantic use of dramatic color, we must first step outside of the French milieu to encounter the work of a lonely, titanic genius, who almost is impossible to classify.

FRANCISCO JOSÉ DE GOYA Y LUCIENTES (1746–1828), Spanish by birth and culture, was a contemporary of David, but one could scarcely find two artists living at the same time and in adjacent countries who were so completely unlike. Goya, the great independent, disdained the Neoclassical and the model of classical antiquity, acknowledging only Velázquez, Rembrandt, and "nature" as his teachers. Goya was a great traditional figure who changed the Tradition while he manifested the present and prophesied the future. In his long life, he produced masterworks in a variety of artistic styles, and, from a higher vantage point than most of his contemporaries, he often depicted humanity's capacity for evil in bitter and unsparing revelation. Great Spanish painting has rarely been sentimental; it has insisted, often with ruthless honesty, on the cruel facts of life.

Little of the grim account of humanity can be seen in Goya's early, vivacious manner, which was brilliantly adapted from Tiepolo. At the royal court in Madrid, his precocious talent produced a series of genre paintings (not illustrated) designed to serve as models for tapestries. Their prevailing mood of gaiety was the mood of the Rococo, but the blitheness of Goya's early mood soon waned. His experiences as painter to Charles IV, at whose sensationally corrupt court he lived, must have fostered the unsentimental, hard-eyed realism of his later style. In his large painting of *The Family of Charles IV* (FIG. **26-9**), certainly inspired by Velázquez's *Las Meninas* (FIG. 24-37), Goya presented, with a straight face, a menagerie of human grotesques who, critics have long been convinced, must not have had the intelligence to realize that the artist was presenting them with unflinching and unflattering truth. This superb revelation of stupidity, pomposity, and vulgarity, painted in 1800, led a later critic to summarize the subject as the "grocer and his family who have just won the big lottery prize." The painter, behind his canvas, is dimly discernible at the left; his features impassively ironical, he looks beyond his subjects to the observer. In this work, Goya exhibited his extraordinary skill as a colorist and manager of the oil medium. The colors float with a quiet iridescence across the surface, and the paint is applied with deft economy. Great solidarity is suggested by the most transparent tones. A magician of optical pictorialism, Goya used the methods of his great predecessor, Velázquez.

The Third of May, 1808 (FIG. **26-10**) is perhaps the most compelling of all Goya's works. The subject is an incident that took place in 1808 during Napoleon's intervention in Spain when a French firing squad executed a "token" number of civilians in Madrid in retaliation for the murder of some of Napoleon's troops by Spanish troops the day before. Here, Goya showed the horrors of war without

26-9 FRANCISCO GOYA, *The Family of Charles IV*, 1800. Oil on canvas, approx. 9'2" × 11'. Museo del Prado, Madrid.

Romante

26-10 FRANCISCO GOYA, *The Third of May, 1808*, 1814. Oil on canvas, approx. 8'8" × 11'3". Museo del Prado, Madrid.

Romantic

national bias (although he was a patriot) and without mercy for the viewer's sensibilities. Goya was in Madrid at the time the execution took place and visited the site later to make sketches of it to ensure the accuracy of his depiction of the bleak hillside and distant city. His main concern, however, was not the accurate recording of fact, but the expression of empathetic horror for the psychological agonies of men facing execution. Unlike the subtle, even suave realism of *The Family of Charles IV,* Goya's method here is coarse and extreme in its departure from optical fact. The postures and gestures of the figures are shockingly distorted to signal defiance and terror. The French firing squad has become an anonymous, murderous wall, while the victims are portrayed as separate individuals, each facing the moment of death in his own way. The intense psychological reality is modern in its stress on the experience of the individual as one among many (quite different from the more traditional, carefully choreographed Baroque staging in Callot's "Hanging Tree," from the *Miseries of War* series (FIG. 24-58), and foreshadows Picasso's *Guernica* (FIG. 27-80), a twentieth-century masterpiece on a related theme.

Toward the end of his life, the follies and brutalities he had witnessed and his own increasing infirmities, including deafness, combined to depress Goya's outlook further, as evidenced in his so-called "black paintings," done for the walls of his own home. In ominous midnight colors, he created whole populations of subhuman monsters who worship the devil and swarm in nightmares. *Saturn Devouring His Children* (FIG. **26-11**) was one product of this pessimistic and misanthropic style. Saturn (Time) glares in lunatic frenzy while devouring part of a small body clutched in his hands. The forms are torn and jagged, the colors raw. This appalling late work is not only a savage expression of man's inhumanity to man, but a recognition of the desperate conditions of life itself. Life is in time, and time devours all.

Goya's art is a powerful, independent example of the Romanticism of expressive color and passionate action, fired by an imagination that could sharpen reality, or depart from it into the realm of appalling fantasy and "Gothick" visions. (Goya was, after all, the contemporary of Fuseli [FIG. 25-36] and Blake [FIG. 25-37].) The French painters of the Romantic coloristic taste never attempted the tremendous expressive gestures of Goya, nor did they come quite in contact with bruising reality, as he did.

Another pupil of David, the baron ANTOINE-JEAN GROS (1771–1835), deviated, like Girodet, from the master's teachings, but even though his art was influential in the development of French dramatic narrative, it maintained a certain French reserve. In his *Pest House at Jaffa* (FIG. **26-12**) Gros took a then radically independent tack, sorting through and selecting numerous Baroque pictorial devices of light, shade, and perspective to create a dramatic tableau testifying to the superhuman power and glory of Napoleon. This work is similar to David's *Oath of the Horatii* in that both

26-11   FRANCISCO GOYA, *Saturn Devouring His Children,* 1819–1823. Detail of a detached fresco on canvas, full size approx. 57″ × 32″. Museo del Prado, Madrid.

artists stage the action within an architectural enframement, deploying the figures in front of the arcade. Where David's arcade is Roman, however, Gros's is Moorish. The vista through Gros's arcade is that of a distant landscape dominated by a fortress flying the French tricolor. Time has changed the setting, and the painter's means have changed to suit the present. In *Pest House,* Gros dismissed theoretical considerations of Classical balance and modeling by depicting Napoleon as a stage director might and making the fullest use of stage lighting and dramatic darkness to center attention on the figure of the chief protagonist. The result is the elevation of history painting to an art of almost religious

26-12   ANTOINE-JEAN GROS,
Pest House at Jaffa, 1804.
Oil on canvas, approx.
17′5″ × 23′7″. Louvre, Paris.

Romantic
— Napoleon — Jaffa port in Israel
troops dying — went in & sick
house & touch sick men

significance and solemnity—one in which Napoleon, the messiah of democracy, simultaneously plays the roles of Alexander, Christ, and Louis XIV.

Napoleon, portrayed here as general of the army of Egypt and not yet as Emperor Napoleon I, is at the end of the disastrous Egyptian campaign and in the process of retreating with his troops up the coast of Palestine (modern Israel). His army is stricken with the plague. He is shown visiting his sick and dying soldiers in the hospital in the ancient city of Jaffa. In the midst of the dead and dying, the fearless genius of the New Order touches the plague sores of a sick soldier, who stares at him in awe, as if he were the miracle-working Christ. Napoleon's staff officers cover their noses against the stench of the place, but the general is calm and unperturbed, like the king curing by the "King's Touch." In the left foreground, men brood, crouch, and sprawl in a gloom of misery and anguish; these figures will be of special interest to later Romantic artists like Théodore Géricault and Eugène Delacroix. The entire scene is wrapped in the glamour of its Near Eastern setting. As in the work of Girodet, identifiable Romantic themes are evident—suffering and death and personal heroism, the allure of distant places, patriotism. All of these held a certain appeal to the modern need for emotional stimulation.

THÉODORE GÉRICAULT (1791–1824) studied with an admirer of David (P. N. Guérin, 1774–1833), but in the pupil the rigid Neoclassicism of the Davidian school receded to allow David's use of sharp light and shade to come to the fore.

Géricault's work is also characterized by a maturing of the naturalistic element and further movement toward the dramatic presentation of contemporary events on huge canvases. For Géricault (unlike his predecessors), these events did not always demand a central hero. His masterpiece, *Raft of the Medusa* (FIG. **26-13**), shows these influences as well as those of Michelangelo and Rubens. Géricault took for his subject the ordeal of the survivors of the French ship *Medusa,* which had foundered off the west coast of Africa in 1816, laden with Algerian immigrants. This incident was the result of tragic mismanagement and provoked scandal in France when the survivors were able to tell their stories. Géricault's depiction of the anguish of the event also was construed by the government as an outright political attack. The artist avoided showing the most horrific aspects of the tragedy—murder, cannibalism, and immense hardship—in choosing to depict the dramatic moment when the frantic castaways attempt to attract the attention of the distant ship that was eventually to rescue them. Fifteen survivors and several corpses are piled onto one another in every attitude of suffering, despair, and death (recalling Gros's *Pest House*) and are arranged in a powerful **X**-shaped composition. One light-filled diagonal axis stretches from bodies at the lower left up to the figure of the black man, raised on the shoulders of his comrades and waving a piece of cloth toward the horizon. The cross-axis descends from the storm clouds and dark, wind-filled sail at the upper left to the shadowed upper torso of the body trailing in the open sea.

26-13   Théodore Géricault, *Raft of the Medusa*, 1818–1819. Oil on canvas, approx. 16′ × 23′. Louvre, Paris.

Although Baroque devices abound, Géricault's use of shock tactics, stunning the viewer's sensibilities, amounted to something new—a new tone and intention that distinguished the "high" phase of Romanticism. In this phase, an instinct for the sublime and the terrible, qualities celebrated in the esthetic theory and art of the eighteenth-century nature (see, for example, Fuseli's *Nightmare* [FIG. 25-36]), found sharpest expression in a method of reportorial accuracy far more stringent than that found in certain works by David. The value Géricault placed on accuracy in *Raft of the Medusa* is indicated by the fact that he carried out prodigious research and completed numerous preliminary studies for the work, even going so far as to interview survivors of the wreck.

An interest in mental aberration, which contributed to the development of modern psychopathology later in the nineteenth century, was part of another Romantic fascination—an interest in the irregular and the abandoned. The inner storms that overthrow rationality could hardly have failed to be of interest to the rebels against the Enlightenment. Géricault, like many of his contemporaries, examined the influence of mental states on the human face and believed, as others did, that a face accurately revealed character, especially in madness and at the instance of death. He made many studies of the inmates of hospitals and institutions for the criminally insane (indeed, he spent some time as a patient in such places), and he studied the severed heads of victims of the guillotine. Scientific and artistic curiosity were not easily separated from the morbidity of the Romantic interest in derangement and death. Géricault's *Insane Woman (Envy)* (FIG. **26-14**)—her mouth

tense, her eyes red-rimmed with suffering—is one of several "portraits" of insane subjects that have a peculiar, hypnotic power and present the psychic facts with astonishing authenticity. *Insane Woman* is only another example of the increasingly realistic core of Romantic painting. The more the Romantics became involved with nature, sane or mad, the more they hoped to get at the truth. For painting, this increasingly came to mean the *optical* truth, as well as the truth of "the way things are." Meanwhile, for the Romantic, the real was nature, wild and untamed. In Géricault's paintings, suffering, death, and madness amounted to nature itself, for nature, in the end, is formless and destructive.

The history of nineteenth-century painting in its first sixty years has often been interpreted as a contest between two major artists—Ingres, the draftsman, and Eugène Delacroix (1798–1863), the colorist. Their dialogue reached back to the end of the seventeenth century in the quarrel between the Poussinistes and the Rubénistes. As we have seen, the Poussinistes were conservative defenders of academism who held drawing to be superior to color, while the Rubénistes proclaimed color's importance over line (the quality of line being more intellectual and thus more restrictive than color). While their differences were clear, Ingres and his great rival Delacroix, in the end, complemented rather than contradicted each other, their work being a part of the great Romantic dialogue.

A comparison of Ingres's pencil portrait of the great violin virtuoso Paganini (FIG. 26-8) with Delacroix's painted version of the same personality (FIG. **26-15**) discloses the difference in approach that separated the two artists. We have seen Ingres's objective, formal, public portrait of Paganini, a faithful likeness of the subject, we believe, yet heightened into a kind of ideal image—"the Virtuoso." Delacroix's *Paganini* presents a likeness not of the virtuoso's form but of his performance. Forgetting his audience, no longer in formal confrontation with his listeners, Paganini yields himself completely to the whirlwind of his own inspiration, which envelops his reedlike frame, making it vibrate in tune to the quivering strings of his instrument. Delacroix tries to suggest the portrait, as it were, of Paganini's music, as it plays to his own ear and spirit. Where Ingres gave us the outside aspect of his subject and tried to perfect the form as presented to the eye, Delacroix represented the inner substance—the musician transformed by his music—in an attempt to realize the truth as given to the imagination.

While critics now regard both masters as equally great, it was this celebration of the imagination, the faculty that captures the essential in life and transforms mundane experience, that defined the fundamental difference between Ingres and Delacroix. Delacroix called the art of Ingres "the complete expression of an incomplete intellect," incomplete because it was unleavened with imagination. In a passage from his famous *Journal,* Delacroix wrote: "Baudelaire . . . says that I bring back to painting . . . the feeling which delights in the terrible. He is right."* Delacroix, who knew and admired Géricault, greatly

*In *Journal of Eugène Delacroix,* trans. Walter Pach (New York: Grove Press, 1937, 1948). Charles-Pierre Baudelaire, one of the nineteenth century's finest and most influential poets, was also a perceptive art critic.

26-14   THÉODORE GÉRICAULT, *Insane Woman (Envy),* 1822–1823. Oil on canvas, approx. 28" × 21". Musée des Beaux-Arts, Lyons.

Romantic
, Forshadow Freud

26-15   EUGÈNE DELACROIX, *Paganini, c.* 1832. Oil on canvas, approx. 17" × 11¹/₂". The Phillips Collection, Washington. D.C.

expanded the expressive possibilities of Romantic art by developing its themes and elaborating its forms in a direction of ever-greater emotional power—in Romantic parlance, of "sublimity." While Delacroix denigrated Ingres's art, he also found much to admire in his rival's work, especially the drawings. The two artists continued to go their separate ways, Ingres even being instrumental in preventing Delacroix's election to the Académie des Beaux Arts until 1857.*

Although the faculty of mind most valued by the Romantic was imagination (to be intensely imaginative was to be intensely alive), Delacroix realized that skill and

---

*The personal antagonisms between the two artists may have softened eventually. Of an accidental encounter between them later in their careers on the steps of the French Institute, the painter Paul Joseph Chenevard recounted that, after an awkward pause, Ingres impulsively extended his hand to Delacroix, who shook it sincerely.

restraint must accompany it. Baudelaire, writing of Delacroix, observed that "in his eyes imagination was the most precious gift, the most important faculty, but [he believed] that this faculty remained impotent and sterile if it was not served by a resourceful skill which could follow it in its restless and tyrannical whims." Nevertheless, Delacroix's works were products of his view that the artist's powers of imagination would in turn capture and inflame the imagination of the viewer.

Literature of similar imaginative power served Delacroix (and many of his contemporaries) as a useful source of subject matter. Since David, literature and the other arts had been developing in ever more intimate association. Baudelaire remarked that Delacroix

> inherited from the great Republican and Imperial school [of David] a love of the poets and a strangely impulsive spirit of rivalry with the written word. David, Guérin, and Géricault kindled their minds at the brazier of Homer, Virgil, Racine, and Ossian. Delacroix was the soul-stirring translator of Shakespeare, Dante, Byron, and Ariosto.

The prominent Romantic critic and novelist, Théophile Gautier, recalled:

> In those days painting and poetry fraternized. The artists read the poets, and the poets visited the artists. We found Shakespeare, Dante, Goethe, Lord Byron and Walter Scott in the studio as well as in the study. There were as many splashes of color as there were blots of ink in the margins of those beautiful books which we endlessly perused. Imagination, already excited, was further fired by reading those foreign works, so rich in color, so free and powerful in fantasy. Our enthusiasm reached the delirious. It seemed that we had discovered poetry, and that it was in fact truth.*

The relationship between the arts went back as far as the Renaissance, with its famous slogan *ut pictura poesis,* "as painting, so poetry"; but in the Romantic age, the association became so close that the paintings produced almost could be said to be programmed by literature (recall the "program" of Ingres's *Apotheosis of Homer*). The same held for music, as attested by Hector Berlioz's *Harold in Italy,* patterned after Lord Byron's *Childe Harold.* This trend that began with David culminated with Delacroix in the literature-inspired staging of exciting and disturbing human events, real or imaginary, and is a concern for the most accurate visual means of conveying them. The belief inherent in this practice was that the purpose of art was to stir, to "electrify," and to render the modern spirit with a modern look, accurately and sympathetically. It was an art also meant to appeal to the new, rapidly expanding democratic society. The "story picture" resulting from the painter's translation of literature into art, when further

---

Histoire de Romantisme (Paris: Charpentier, 1874), p. 204.

26-16   EUGÈNE DELACROIX, *Death of Sardanapalus*, 1826. Oil on canvas, approx. 12'1" × 16'3". Louvre, Paris.

merged with the dramatic and musical theater, would evolve into the new medium of the motion picture—a composite of drama, narrative, sound, and pictures.

Delacroix's *Death of Sardanapalus* (FIG. **26-16**), which should be compared with FIG. 26-6, is an example of pictorial grand opera on a colossal scale. Undoubtedly, Delacroix was inspired by Lord Byron's narrative poem *Sardanapalus*, but the painting does not illustrate that text. Instead, Delacroix depicts the last hour of the ancient king in a much more tempestuous and crowded setting than Byron described, with orgiastic destruction replacing the sacrificial suicide found in the poem. In the painting, on hearing of the defeat of his armies and the enemies' entry into his city, the king orders all of his most precious possessions—his women, slaves, horses, and treasure—destroyed in his sight while he watches gloomily from his funeral pyre, soon to be set alight. The king presides like a genius of evil over the panorama of destruction, most conspicuous in which are the tortured and dying bodies of his women, the one in the foreground dispatched by an ecstatically murderous slave. This carnival of suffering and death is glorified by superb drawing and color, by the most daringly difficult and tortuous poses, and by the richest intensities of hue and contrasts of form and color. It is a testament to Delacroix's genius that his center of meaning is placed away from the central action yet entirely controls it as the psychological focus of attention.

Delacroix's composition in *Death of Sardanapalus* is an early example in painting of the newly invented Romantic picture type called the *vignette, an image with a strong center that becomes less defined at its edges*. In *Death of Sardanapalus*, everything swirls around the empty foot of the bed, but details fade toward the edge of the canvas. Similarly vortical compositions were common in painters of the dynamic Baroque (FIG. 24-39) but in Delacroix's work this device extended its efforts to a then unknown, and not entirely appreciated, degree (the work pleased none of the critics of the day). The Romantic vignette first appeared in book illustrations in which Romantic artists attempted to recapture the kind of total unity of text and illustration that they admired in medieval illuminated manuscripts. Cultural historians Charles Rosen and Henri Zerner offer an explanation for the vignette's eager adoption by painters:

The vignette, by its general appearance, presents itself both as a global metaphor for the world and as a fragment. Dense at its center, tenuous on the periphery, it seems to disappear into the page: this makes it a naive but powerful metaphor of the infinite, a symbol of the universe; at the same time, the vignette is fragmentary . . . incomplete, mostly dependent upon the text for its meaning. . . . The vignette launches a powerful attack on the classical definition of representation, a window on the world. The vignette is not a window because it has no limit, no frame. The image, defined from its center rather than its edges, emerges from the paper [or canvas] as an apparition or a fantasy.*

Generally, Delacroix chose his subjects from either non-Classical or post-Classical periods and literature, but sometimes he dealt with a Greek subject that moved him. Other sources of subjects were the events of his own time, notably popular struggles for freedom: the ill-fated revolt of the Greeks against Turkish rule in the 1820s; the Parisian revolution of 1830, which overthrew the restored Bourbons and placed Louis Philippe on the throne of France. In *Liberty Leading the People* (FIG. **26-17**), Delacroix makes no attempt to represent a specific incident seen in actuality. Instead, he gives us a full-blown allegory of revolution itself, teeming with unidealized and carefully presented details. Liberty, a majestic, partly nude woman, whose beautiful features wear an expression of noble dignity, waves the people forward to the barricades, the familiar

*Charles Rosen and Henri Zerner, *Romanticism and Realism: The Mythology of Nineteenth-century Art* (London: Faber and Faber, 1984), p. 81.

revolutionary apparatus of Paris streets. She carries the tricolor banner of the republic and a musket with a bayonet and wears the cap of liberty. Her advance is over the dead and dying of both sides—the people and the royal troops. Arrayed around her are bold Parisian types: the street boy brandishing his pistols, the menacing *prolétaire* with a cutlass, the intellectual dandy in plug hat with sawed-off musket. In the background, the towers of Notre-Dame rise through the smoke and clamor, witnessing the tradition of liberty that has been cherished by the people of Paris throughout the centuries.

In terms of form, *Liberty Leading the People* still reflected the strong impression made on Delacroix by the art of Géricault, especially *Raft of the Medusa* (FIG. 26-13); the fact that Delacroix made an allegory of Liberty shows that he was familiar with traditional conventions. The clutter of sprawling bodies in the foreground provides a kind of base for the pyramid of figures in the center, which builds from the heavy, inert forms of the dead and dying to the frantic energy of Liberty and the citizens still engaged actively in the struggle. The flashes of light suggest gunfire, while the intermingling of light and shadow echoes the confusion of battle and the dense atmosphere stirred up by the conflict. The forms were generated from the Baroque, as they were in Géricault, but Delacroix's sharp agitation of them created his own special brand of tumultuous excitement.

26-17 Eugène Delacroix, *Liberty Leading the People,* 1830. Oil on canvas, approx. 8′6″ × 10′8″. Louvre, Paris.

Delacroix's early use of the vignette shows him to have been an innovator. He was always studying the problems of his craft and always searching for fresh materials to supply his imagination. These were conscious efforts on his part; he said, "style can only result from great research." He made numerous studies for each of his projects and even worked with the photographer Eugène Durieu (see page 958) to create photographic studies for paintings.

A camera study was a supremely practical tool, if only because a photographic model would pose untiringly for just the cost of making the initial print. More important to the Romantic (and later Realist) interest in the depiction of nature was the camera's ability to record, with absolute fidelity, the physical facts of what was before it. *Draped Model* (FIG. 26-30) is an early example of the photographic nudes Delacroix used for this purpose. On one occasion, Delacroix shared some of the photographic studies he had made with visitors and then showed some engravings by the famous Renaissance artists Marcantonio Raimondi. Writing of this event in his *Journal,* Delacroix recorded that

[After] they had studied these photographs of nude models, some of whom were poorly built, oddly shaped in places and not very attractive generally, I put before their eyes engravings by Marcantonio. We all experienced a feeling of revulsion, almost disgust, for their incorrectness, their mannerisms, and their lack of naturalness, despite their quality of style. . . . Truly, if a man of genius should

use the daguerreotype as it ought to be used, he will raise himself to heights unknown to us.*

An enormously influential event in Delacroix's life, and one that affected his art in both subject and form, was his visit to North Africa in 1832. Things he saw there shocked his imagination with fresh impressions that would last throughout the rest of his life. He discovered, in the sun-drenched landscape and in the hardy and colorful Arabs dressed in robes reminiscent of the Roman toga, new insights into a culture built on proud virtues—a culture that he believed to be more Classical than anything European Neoclassicism could conceive. "The Greeks and the Romans," he wrote to a friend, "they are here, within my reach. I had to laugh heartily about the Greeks of David." The gallantry, hardihood, valor, and fierce love of liberty made the Arabs, in Delacroix's eyes, "nature's noblemen"— unspoiled heroes, uninfected by European decadence.

The Moroccan journey renewed Delacroix's Romantic conviction that there is beauty in the fierceness of nature, natural processes, and natural beings, especially animals. After Morocco, more and more of Delacroix's subjects involved combats between beasts and between beasts and men (FIG. **26-18**). He painted snarling tangles of lions and tigers, battles between horses, and clashes of Arabs with great cats in swirling hunting scenes. In these, what he had

*In Aaron Scharf, *Art and Photography* (Baltimore: Penguin, 1974), p. 122.

26-18 EUGÈNE DELACROIX, *Tiger Hunt*, 1854. Oil on canvas, approx. 29" × 36". Louvre, Paris.

learned from the hunting pictures of Rubens (FIG. 24-40) mingles in explosive combination with his own visions, reinforced by his memories of the North African scene.

Delacroix's African experience also further heightened his already considerable awareness of the expressive power of color and light. What Delacroix knew about color he passed on to later painters of the nineteenth century, particularly to the Impressionists. He observed that pure colors are as rare in nature as lines, that color appears only in an infinitely varied scale of different tones, shadings, and reflections, which he tried to recreate in his paintings. He recorded his observations in his *Journal,* which became a veritable corpus of pre-Impressionistic color theory and was acclaimed as such by the Post-Impressionist painter Paul Signac. Delacroix anticipated the later development of Impressionist color science, but that art-science had to await the discoveries by Michel Eugène Chevreul and Hermann von Helmholtz of the laws of light decomposition and the properties of complementary colors before the problems of color perception and juxtaposition in painting could be properly formulated. Nevertheless, Delacroix's observations were significant: "It is advisable not to fuse the brushstrokes," he wrote, "as they will [appear to] fuse naturally at [a] . . . distance. In this manner, color gains in energy and freshness." This observation, suggested to him by his examination of a group of landscapes by John Constable, the great English landscape painter (FIG. 26-23), had strongly impressed Delacroix even before his color experiences in Morocco.

No other painter of the time explored the domain of Romantic subject and mood as thoroughly and definitively as Delacroix, and none matched his style and content. Delacroix's technique—impetuous, improvisational, and instinctive, rather than deliberate, studious, and cold—epitomizes Romantic-colorist painting, catching the impression at the very beginning and developing it in the process of execution. We know how furiously Delacroix worked once he had an idea, keeping the whole painting progressing at once. The fury of his attack matched the fury of his imagination and his subjects; he was indeed the artist of passion. Baudelaire sums him up as "passionately in love with passion . . . an immense passion, reinforced with a formidable will—such was the man." In the end, his friend Silvestre, in the language of Romanticism, delivered a eulogy that amounts to a definition of the Romantic artist:

> Thus died, almost with a smile on August 13, 1863, that painter of great race, Ferdinand Victor Eugène Delacroix, who had a sun in his head and storms in his heart; who for forty years played upon the keyboard of human passions and whose brush—grandiose, terrible, or suave—passed from saints to warriors, from warriors to lovers, from lovers to tigers, and from tigers to flowers.

The dispute between the Romantics who favored ideal form, with Ingres as their hero (after David), and the Romantics who favored color and drama, with Delacroix as theirs, made a considerable, almost political, uproar in the journals and salons, the theaters and boulevards of earlier nineteenth-century Paris. Gautier gives a brief and amusing account of their open hostility: "You could scarcely imagine how pallid and insignificant literature had become [before the arrival of Victor Hugo and his 'Young Romantics']." The last pupils of David laid out their flat, insipid colors within the hackneyed Greco-Roman outlines. Neoclassical people thought them perfectly beautiful; but, standing before these masterpieces, their admiration could not prevent them from trying to stifle a yawn. This, however, did not make them more indulgent to the artists of the young ("Romantic") school, whom they called "tattooed savages," and whom they accused of painting "with a drunken broom. . . . We didn't let these insults pass. We called them 'mummies,' when they called us 'savages.' We despised each other thoroughly."*

Imagination and Mood in Landscape Painting

Landscape painting, though never quite matching the prestige of history painting (sacred or secular narrative), came into its own in the nineteenth century as a fully independent and respected genre. Briefly eclipsed at the beginning of the century by the taste for ideal form, which favored figure composition and history, landscape painting flourished as leading painters made it their profession.

The eighteenth century had regarded the pleasurable, esthetic mood inspired by natural landscape as making the landscape itself "picturesque," that is, worthy of being painted. Early on, it was the "natural" English garden that was considered picturesque; later, landscape vistas, colored by the mood of the viewer who gazed upon them, were transmuted by the sensitive Romantic into esthetic form, poetry, or painting. Wordsworth, in a reflective mood, responded to a sunset: "The clouds that gather round the setting sun / Do take a sober coloring from an eye / That hath watched over man's mortality." Rather than provide simple descriptions of nature, poets and artists represented nature as an extension of their own subjectivity. Nature and the artist became one being.

Early in the century, most landscape painting to some degree expressed this Romantic, pantheistic view (first extolled by Rousseau) of nature as a "being" that included the totality of existence in organic unity and harmony. It was in nature—"the living garment of God," as Goethe called it—that the artist found an ideal subject to express the Romantic theme of the soul in union with the natural world. Romanticism in the arts, it could be said, made a kind of personal religion of nature, a religion based in profound esthetic emotion—of mystery and beauty, to recall

*Histoire de Romantisme, op cit., p. 2.

the ideas of Chateaubriand. If nature was akin to religion, the artist could be likened (in the thought of the Idealist philosopher Schelling) to a priest, who in the act of creation duplicates or becomes one with the creative powers of nature itself, thus resolving the contradictions of the inner (subjective) and the outer (objective) worlds. The landscape would reveal the divine being of nature to the artist who was prepared by innocence, sincerity, and intuitive insight to receive the revelation. As all nature was mysteriously permeated by "being," the landscape artist had the task of interpreting the signs, symbols, and emblems of universal "spirit" disguised within visible material things. The artist was no longer a mere beholder of the landscape but a participant in its spirit, no longer a painter of mere things but the translator of nature's transcendent meanings, arrived at through feelings inspired by the landscape.

Artists in northern Europe were the first to depict the Romantic transcendental landscape. One, PHILIPP OTTO RUNGE (1777–1810), declared that true art could be understood only through the deepest mystical experience of religion. In words, as well as images, he celebrated

> The feeling of the whole universe with us; this united chord which in its vibrations touches every string of our heart; the love which keeps us and carries us through life . . . each leaf and each blade of grass teems with life and stirs beneath me, all resounds together in a single chord . . . I hear and feel the living breath of God who holds and carries the world, in whom all lives and works; here is the highest that we divine—God!*

Considering nature to be a part of God, and human beings to be part of nature, Runge said, "Once we see in all of nature only our own life, then it follows clearly, the right landscape can come about." Runge designed a four-part series, *The Times of Day,* as sacred pictures for a chapel dedicated to a new religion of nature. In *Morning* (FIG. **26-19**) from this series, he created an allegory of dawn enriched with his personal flower and color symbolism. In this work, all plants are descended from Paradise and are emblematic of the states of the human soul, as are colors and musical harmonies. The image of the great lily floating in the sky is the floral manifestation of light and the symbol of Divine knowledge and purity. The morning star, Venus, glows above, under the arc of the earth; below it, on the central axis, is the graceful figure of the goddess herself in the guise of Aurora. On the ground below, the supine figure of an infant is an allusion to the Christ Child, as well as a symbol of regeneration and redemption and all the promise of the newborn day. The composition has the symmetry and formality of traditional religious painting and the mood of supernatural mystery, but the careful, objective study of color tone—the actual hues of dawn with its tincture of

26-19   PHILIPP OTTO RUNGE, *The Times of Day: Morning* (large version), 1809. Oil on canvas, approx. 60″ × 45″. Kunsthalle, Hamburg.

rose turning to radiance—shows Runge's concern for the truth of appearance as the vehicle of symbolic truth. Fusing the empirical world with the transcendental, he gives us an apparition of the supernatural in a natural sky. Like Blake, whose work he must have known (FIG. 25-37), Runge was a religious visionary who believed in angels; unlike Blake, Runge revered nature as given to the eye.

Runge's ideas are believed to have influenced the art of his great contemporary, CASPAR DAVID FRIEDRICH (1774–1840); in the work of both, as art historian Robert Rosenblum has remarked, "the experience of the supernatural has . . . been transposed from traditional religious imagery to nature."* Nature, as immanent God, requires no personifications other than its organic and inorganic subjects and objects, things visible to the eye, which symbolically express through their forms the truth of nature, which is to say, Divine truth. For Friedrich, landscapes were temples; his paintings themselves were altarpieces. His reverential mood demands from the viewer the silence

---

*From letters translated in R. M. Bisanz, *German Romanticism and Philipp Otto Runge* (De Kalb: Northern Illinois University Press, 1970), pp. 48–51.

*Robert Rosenblum, *Modern Painting and the Northern Romantic Tradition: Friedrich to Rothko* (New York: Harper & Row, 1975), p. 22.

✗ 26-20   CASPAR DAVID FRIEDRICH, *Cloister Graveyard in the Snow,* 1810. Oil on canvas, approx. 47″ × 70″. (Painting destroyed during World War II)

appropriate to sacred places filled with a divine presence. *Cloister Graveyard in the Snow* (FIG. **26-20**) is like a solemn requiem. Under a winter sky, through the leafless oaks of a snow-covered cemetery, a funeral procession bears a coffin into the ruins of a Gothic chapel. The emblems of death are everywhere: the desolation of the season, leaning crosses and tombstones, the black of mourning worn by the grieving and by the skeletal trees, the destruction wrought by time on the chapel. The painting is a kind of meditation on human mortality, as Friedrich himself remarked: "Why, it has often occurred to me to ask myself, do I so frequently choose death, transience, and the grave as subjects for my paintings? One must submit oneself many times to death in order some day to attain life everlasting."* The sharp-focused rendering of details demonstrates the artist's keen perception of everything in the physical environment relevant to his message. In the work of Friedrich, we find a balance of inner and outer experience. "The artist," he wrote "should paint not only what he sees before him, but also what he sees within him. If, however, he sees nothing within him, then he should also refrain from painting that which he sees before him."

A very different kind of natural symbolism is found in the widely influential school of English landscape painting. Just as literature and history are keys to the art of the French Romantics, English Romantic poetry is key to the paintings of the English landscapists. In the works of

*In H. Borsch-Supan, *Caspar David Friedrich* (New York: Braziller, 1974), p. 7.

JOSEPH MALLORD WILLIAM TURNER (1775–1851), we find readings of nature in its terror and grandeur somewhat more often than in its peace and serenity, although the artist was capable of realizing all of nature's emotions. The critic John Ruskin wrote of Turner's *The Slave Ship* (FIG. **26-21**) in *Modern Painters* (1846):

> But I think the noblest sea that Turner has ever painted, and if so, the noblest certainly ever painted by man, is that of *The Slave Ship,* the chief Academy picture of the exhibition of 1840 . . . I believe, if I were reduced to rest Turner's immortality upon any single work, I should choose this.

The full title of the painting is S*lavers Throwing Overboard the Dead and Dying—Typhoon Coming On.* Its subject is an incident that took place in 1783 in which the captain of a slave ship threw sick and dying slaves overboard in hopes of collecting insurance on the claim that they were "lost at sea." The horror of the event is matched by Turner's turbulently emotional depiction of it. The sun is transformed into an incandescent comet amid flying, scarlet clouds that swirl above a sea choked with the bodies of slaves jettisoned from the ship by its ruthless master. The particulars of the event are almost lost in the boiling colors of the work. Turner was a great innovator whose special invention in works like *The Slave Ship* was to release color from any defining outlines in order to express the forces of nature, as well as the painter's emotional response to them. In works like this, the reality of color is one with the reality of feeling. Turner's methods had an incalculable effect on the development of modern art. His discovery of the esthetic and emotive power of pure color (the most fundamental element of the painting medium), and his pushing of the fluidity of the medium to a point at which the subject is almost manifest through the paint itself, were important steps toward twentieth-century abstract art, which dispenses with shape and form altogether.

The American painter of English birth, THOMAS COLE (1801–1848), was less concerned with pioneering advances in color and technique, and his work typified the landscape of reflection and mood so romantically appealing to the public, especially in the English-speaking world. Best known as the leading painter of the Hudson River school, whose members drew their subjects from the uncultivated regions of the Hudson River valley, Cole celebrated the wonders of the North American landscape in many of his works. He wrote:

Whether he [the American] beholds the Hudson mingling waters with the Atlantic, explores the central wilds of this vast continent, or stands on the margin of the distant Oregon, he is still in the midst of American scenery—it is his own land; its beauty, its magnificence, its sublimity—all are his; and how undeserving of such a birthright, if he can turn towards it an unobserving eye, an unaffected heart!*

In *The Oxbow (Connecticut River near Northampton)* (FIG. **26-22**), the viewer looks out from a high promontory over a peaceful plain dotted with signs of human habitation and dominated by the lazy oxbow turning of the Connecticut River. Our hilly perch is densely forested; at the near left is

*In John W. McCoubrey, *American Art 1700–1960: Sources and Documents* (Englewood Cliffs, NJ: Prentice-Hall, 1965), pp. 98, 106 and passim. Cole's sensitivity for the sublime quality of landscape also inspired him to produce heroic symbolic landscape cycles with themes like "The Voyage of Life."

26-21 JOSEPH MALLORD WILLIAM TURNER, *The Slave Ship,* 1840. Oil on canvas, 35³⁄₄″ × 48¹⁄₄″. Courtesy Museum of Fine Arts, Boston (Henry Lillie Pierce Fund).

✳26-22 THOMAS COLE, *The Oxbow (Connecticut River near Northampton),* 1836. Oil on canvas, 76" × 51¹/₂". The Metropolitan Museum of Art, New York (gift of Mrs. Russell Sage, 1908).

an ancient, craggy tree. In contrast with the valley below, this high realm seems still part of the untouched wilderness. Just below, on a rock to the right, are the artist's stool and parasol; nearby, (below and to the left of the parasol), we see the artist himself at work on a painting. The broad vista suggests the public fascination with the panorama, which Cole shared. Originally, "panoramas" were specially designed buildings that housed colossal circular murals; the buildings' curved walls surrounded spectators who stood on a central platform to view vast paintings of historical scenes or landscapes. Soon, the panorama experience was translated outdoors in Europe and America to viewing platforms overlooking spectacular landscape vistas. In his affection for his adopted country, the artist may have combined the natural drama of the panoramic view with the widely held notion that America was a new Eden, which, in its unspoiled and pristine virtue, might avoid the fateful cycle of European decay and decadence that had doomed earlier empires. This thoroughly Romantic myth of the innocence of America in contrast to the corruption of Europe was widely believed on both sides of the Atlantic in the nineteenth century.

The sublimity and passion, the hectic color and dissolving forms of Turner's paintings were avoided by JOHN CONSTABLE (1776–1837), his great contemporary in the English school of Romantic landscape. Constable turned from mountain vastness, stormy seas, and flaming sunset to the studious observation of quiet nature, recording the optical facts of the rustic environment, which he believed could be rendered "picturesque" and "poetical" as well as "scientific" by the artist's refined sensibility. Acknowledging the influence of Rubens and of the great

Dutch masters of landscape, Constable undertook to lighten their visions of nature with airiness and sun-shot atmosphere.

Constable's landscapes—for the most part placid, untroubled views of the English (Suffolk) countryside—are careful studies of nature rendered in the local colors of woodland, meadow pond and stream, hill and sky, interspersed with the architecture of mill, cottage, and country church. Constable portrayed these, his favorite subjects, as lighted by a mild sun or shadowed briefly by a changing cloud, bathed in an atmosphere fresh with dew or rain, moved by soft winds. He did not depict heroic action, nor has the landscape been constructed to stage it. In *The Haywain* (FIG. **26-23**), which was a great success at the Paris Salon of 1824, a farmer in a cart fords a stream. Living nature includes him as it does the dog, the cottage, the stream, the copse, the distant park, the scudding clouds. Constable portrayed the oneness with nature sought by the Romantic poets; man is not the observer, but a participant in the landscape's being. The image is not a dream vision. The artist has insisted on the reality of the landscape as given to the eye and rendered with the brush: "I hope to show that our profession as painters is *scientific* as well as poetic; that imagination never did, and never can, produce works that are to stand by comparison with *realities*" (emphasis added). Constable made countless studies from nature for each of his canvases, which produced the convincing sense of reality in his works that was praised by his contemporaries. In his quest for the reality of landscape, Constable studied it like a meteorologist (which he was by avocation). His special gift was for capturing the texture given to landscape by atmosphere (the climate and the weather, which delicately veil what is seen) and for revealing that atmosphere as the key to representing the ceaseless process of nature, which changes constantly through the hours of the day and through shifts of weather and season. Constable's use of tiny dabs of local color, stippled with white, created a sparkling shimmer of light and hue across the surface of the canvas—the vibration itself suggestive of movement and process. In speaking of the qualities he intended in his pictures, Constable mentioned "light—dews—breezes—bloom—and freshness, not one of which . . . has yet been perfected on the canvas of any painter in the world." These are the qualities that we sense in the fleeting states of changing nature—the qualities that startled the young Delacroix when he saw *The Haywain* in the Paris Salon. Constable's certainty that the painting of nature partook of science was his challenge and his bequest to the Impressionists.

In the landscape painting of JEAN-BAPTISTE-CAMILLE COROT (1796–1875), a late Romantic artist in France, Romantic colorism is subdued and, to a degree, neutralized, by the advancing spirit of Realism, especially as it is felt in the artist's management of tonality. In Corot's *The Harbor of La Rochelle* (FIG. **26-24**), the moist clouds and sparkling atmosphere in Constable's pictures have given way to a still, cloudless, limpid, almost airless dimension, in which objects retain a near-Classical firmness of definition (his critics complained that Corot "Ingres-ized" the landscape!). Corot, in his earlier style (his later work became much hazier and mood-filled), achieved his effects of super-clarity by carefully attending to the full tonal spread—the careful arrangement of dark and light values—which the new medium of photography was achieving automatically. Corot's method was to be as faithful as possible to the scale of light to dark. His procedure was interesting. He wrote in his notebooks:

> The first two things to study are form and values. For me, these are the bases of what is serious in art. Color and finish put charm into one's work. In preparing a study or a picture, it seems to me very important to begin by an indication of the darkest values . . . and continue in order to the lightest value. From the darkest to the lightest I would establish twenty shades.

26-23 JOHN CONSTABLE, *The Haywain*, 1821. Oil on canvas, 4′3″ × 6′2″. National Gallery, London.

26-24 JEAN-BAPTISTE-CAMILLE COROT, *The Harbor of La Rochelle*, 1851. Oil on canvas, approx. 20″ × 28″. Yale University Art Gallery, New Haven, Connecticut (bequest of Stephen Carlton Clark, B.A., 1903).

Both Constable and Corot point toward the Impressionists, but in different ways. Constable foreshadowed their work in his brilliant freshness of color and divided brush stroke, while Corot prefigures their concern for the rendering of outdoor light and atmosphere in terms of values.

The Dramatic in Sculpture

As we might expect, the differences between idealizing Romanticism and dramatizing Romanticism are reflected in sculpture as well. Yet, a combination of ideal traits and dramatic tumult appears in the colossal group *La Marseillaise* (FIG. **26-25**), mounted on one face of Chalgrin's Arc de Triomphe in Paris. The sculptor, FRANÇOIS RUDE (1784–1855), carves here an allegory of the national glories of revolutionary France, the volunteers of 1792 departing to defend the nation's borders against foreign enemies of the Revolution. The Roman goddess of war, Bellona (who here personifies Liberty, as well as the revolutionary hymn, now the national anthem of France), soars above patriots of all ages, exhorting them forward with her stentorian battle cry. The figures recall David's classically armored or nude heroes (FIGS. 25-46 and 25-49), as do the rhetorical gestures of the wide-flung arms and the striding poses. The densely packed, overlapping masses, the jagged contours, and violence of motion agree with the compositional method of dramatic Romanticism, as we find in Gros, Géricault, and Delacroix (FIGS. 26-12, 26-13, and 26-17). The allegorical figure of *La Marseillaise* is the spiritual sister of Delacroix's *Liberty* (FIG. 26-17); they share the same Phrygian cap, the

26-25 FRANÇOIS RUDE, *La Marseillaise*, Arc de Triomphe, Paris, 1833–1836. Approx. 42′ × 26′.

26-26 ANTOINE-LOUIS BARYE, *Jaguar Devouring a Hare*, 1850–1851. Bronze, approx. 16″ × 37″. Louvre, Paris.

badge of liberty. But, though the works are almost exactly contemporary, the figures in the sculpted group are represented in Classical costume, while those in Delacroix's painting wear the costumes of modern Paris. Both works are allegorical, but one looks to the past, the other to the present.

Delacroix's fascination with brute beauty is echoed in *Jaguar Devouring a Hare* (FIG. **26-26**), a much smaller group in bronze by ANTOINE-LOUIS BARYE (1795–1875). Painful as the subject is, Barye draws us irresistibly to it by the work's fidelity to brute nature. The belly-crouching cat's swelling muscles, hunched shoulders, and tense spine—even the switch of the tail—tells of the sculptor's long sessions observing the animals in the Jardin des Plantes in Paris. This work shows the influence of the vast new geographies opening before the naturalistic eyes and temper of the nineteenth century, while demonstrating Romanticism's obsession with strong emotion and untamed nature. Nineteenth-century sensibility generally prevented animal ferocity from being shown in human beings but enthusiastically accepted its portrayal in Romantic depictions of wild beasts. Barye's portrayal of a beast with its dead prey contrasts with the more sublime depiction by Stubbs of a ferocious struggle to the death between two more equal natural enemies (FIG. 25-35).

Various Revivalist Styles in Architecture

While Romantic Neoclassicism flourished, the Romantic Gothic taste begun in the eighteenth century by Walpole and others, in places like Strawberry Hill (FIG. 25-32), was by no means extinguished. On the contrary, its development paralleled that of Romantic Neoclassicism and took on new significance in connection with religious meanings and the century's rising tide of nationalism. In 1802, the eminent French writer François René de Chateaubriand published his influential *Genius of Christianity,* a defense of religion on the grounds not of its truth, but of its beauty and mystery. A work such as this was in direct opposition

to the skeptical rationalism of the Enlightenment and many of the ideals of the French Revolution. In this treatise, Chateaubriand says, "There is nothing of beauty, sweetness, or greatness in life that does not partake in mystery." (How different this statement is from the Age of Reason's injunction, "Be thou clear!") Christian ritual and Christian art, born of mystery, could move adherents by their strange and ancient beauty. Gothic cathedrals, according to Chateaubriand, were translations into stone of the sacred groves of the Druidical Gauls and must be cherished as manifestations of France's holy history. In his view, the history of Christianity and of France merged in the Middle Ages. As the nineteenth century gathered the documentary materials of European history in stupendous historiographic enterprises, each nation came to value its past as evidence of the validity of its ambitions and claims to greatness. The art of the remote past was now appreciated as a product of racial and national genius. In 1773, Goethe, praising the Gothic cathedral of Strasbourg in *Of German Architecture,* announced the theme by declaring that the German art scholar "should thank God to be able to proclaim aloud that it is German architecture, our architecture"; he also bid the observer, "approach and recognize the deepest feeling of truth and beauty of proportion emanating from a strong, vigorous German soul."

Modern nationalism thus helped to bring about a new evaluation of the art in each country's past. In London, when the old Houses of Parliament burned in 1834, the Parliamentary Commission decreed that designs for the new building be either "Gothic or Elizabethan." CHARLES BARRY (1795–1860), with the assistance of A. W. N. PUGIN (1812–1852), submitted the winning design (FIG. **26-27**) in 1835. By this time, style had become a matter of selection from the historical past. Barry had traveled widely in Europe, Greece, Turkey, Egypt, and Palestine, studying the architecture in each place. He preferred the Renaissance Classical styles, but he had designed some earlier Neo-Gothic buildings, and Pugin influenced him successfully in the direction of English Late Gothic. Pugin was one of a group of English artists and critics who saw moral purity and spiritual authenticity in the religious architecture of the Middle Ages and glorified the careful medieval craftsmen who had produced it. The Industrial Revolution was now flooding the market with cheaply made and ill-designed commodities. Handicraft was being replaced by the machine. Many, like Pugin, believed in the necessity of restoring the old craftsmanship, which had honesty and quality. The design of the Houses of Parliament, however, is not genuinely Gothic, despite its picturesque tower groupings (the Clock Tower, containing Big Ben, at one end, and the Victoria Tower at the other). The building

has a formal axial plan and a kind of Palladian regularity beneath its Tudor detail. Pugin himself is reported to have said of it: "All Grecian, Sir. Tudor details on a classical body."*

While the Neoclassical and Neo-Gothic styles were dominant in the early nineteenth century, exotic new styles of all types soon began to appear, in part as a result of European imperialism. Great Britain's forays into all areas

*In Nicholas Pevsner, *An Outline of European Architecture* (Baltimore, MD: Penguin, 1960), p. 627.

26-27 CHARLES BARRY and A. W. N. PUGIN, Houses of Parliament, London, designed 1835.

26-28 JOHN NASH, Royal Pavilion, Brighton, England, 1815–1818.

of the world, particularly India, had exposed English culture to a broad range of non-Western artistic styles. The Royal Pavilion (FIG. **26-28**), designed by JOHN NASH (1752–1835), exhibits a wide variety of these styles. Nash was an established architect, known for Neoclassical buildings in London, when he was asked to design a royal pleasure palace in the seaside resort of Brighton for the prince regent (later King George IV). The structure's fantastic exterior is a confection of Islamic domes, minarets, and screens that has been called "Indian Gothic," while the decor of the interior rooms was influenced by sources ranging from Greece and Egypt to China. Underlying the exotic facade is a cast-iron skeleton, an early (if hidden) use of this material in non-commercial building. Nash also put this metal to fanciful use in its own right, creating life-size, cast-iron palm-tree columns to support the Royal Pavilion's kitchen ceiling. The building, an appropriate enough backdrop for gala throngs pursuing pleasure by the seaside, served as the prototype for numerous playful architectural exaggerations still to be found in European and American resorts.

The Baroque was also adapted in architecture, to convey a grandeur worthy of the riches acquired during this age of expansion by those who heeded the advice of the French historian and statesman François Guizot to "get rich." The opulence reflected in the lives of these few was mirrored in the Paris Opéra (FIG. **26-29**), designed by J. L. CHARLES GARNIER (1825–1898). The Opéra parades a festive and spectacularly theatrical Neo-Baroque front that should be compared with the facade of the Louvre (FIG. 24-63), which it mimics to a degree. The interior is ingeniously planned for the convenience of human traffic. Intricate arrangements of corridors, vestibules, stairways, balconies, alcoves, entrances, and exits facilitate easy passage throughout the

building and provide space for entertainment and socializing at intermissions. The Baroque grandeur of the layout and of the ornamental appointments of the opera house proclaims and enhances its function as a gathering place for glittering audiences in an age of conspicuous wealth. The style was so attractive to the moneyed classes who supported the arts that theaters and opera houses continued to reflect the design of the Paris Opéra until World War I transformed society.

MID-CENTURY REALISM: THE REACTION AGAINST ROMANTICISM

While Romanticism dominated the early decades of the century with its goals of expressing dramatic emotion or ideal beauty and its subject matter, taken for the most part from scenes outside common, everyday experience, another vein of expression also was beginning to address the century's growing appreciation of the representation of optical fact in art. Increasingly during this period, largely due to the powerful influence of the example set by positivist science, real events were becoming subjects for artists who were willing to report or reconstruct scenes in visual modes faithful to appearance. These artists produced images that invited comparison to everyday optical experience in life, using simple recognition as a new criterion for judgment. Although it came into being slowly and at first was combined with some of the qualities of Romanticism, Realism eventually became the dominant style of art during the middle part of the nineteenth century.

The Beginnings of Photography

A technological device of immense consequence for the modern experience was invented at precisely this time: the *camera,* with its attendant art of photography. We are all familiar with what the camera equips us to do—report and record optical experience at will. We assume that a very close correlation exists between the photographic image and the fragment of the visual world it records. The evidence of the photograph is proof that what we think we see is really there. In other words, the camera can be a check on what is "real," "true," or "factual" in our visual experience.

Photography was celebrated as embodying a kind of revelation of visible things from the time Louis J. M. Daguerre and Henry Fox Talbot announced the first practical photographic processes in 1839. The medium, itself a product of science, was an enormously useful tool for recording the discoveries of the century. The relative ease of the process seemed a dream come true for scientists and artists, who for centuries had grappled with less satisfying methods for capturing accurate images of their subjects. Photography was also perfectly suited to an age that saw artistic patronage

26-29   J. L. CHARLES GARNIER, the Opéra, Paris, 1861–1874.

continue to shift away from the elite few toward a broader base of support, away from noble patronage and toward that of the growing and increasingly powerful middle class, who embraced the comprehensible images of the new medium and also its lower cost.

For the traditional artist, photography suggested new answers to the great debate about what is real and how to represent the real in art; but it also presented a challenge to the place of traditional modes of pictorial representation that had originated in the Renaissance. Artists as diverse as Delacroix, Ingres, Courbet, and Degas welcomed photography as a helpful auxiliary to painting and were increasingly intrigued by the manner in which photography translated three-dimensional objects onto a two-dimensional surface. Other artists, however, saw photography as a mechanism capable of displacing the painstaking work of a skilled painter dedicated to representing the truth of a chosen subject. The challenge of photography to painting, both historically and technologically, seemed to some an expropriation of the realistic image, until then the exclusive property of painting. As one painter, Maurice de Vlaminck, declared at the end of the century: "We [painters] hate everything that has to do with the photograph." But just as some painters looked to the new medium of photography for answers on how best to render an image in paint, so some photographers looked to painting for suggestions about ways to imbue the photographic image with qualities beyond simple reproduction—the near symbiotic relationship already discussed in connection with collaborative efforts of Delacroix and the photographer Eugene Durieu (1800–1874). Durieu's *Draped Model (back view)* (FIG. **26-30**) demonstrates that although such images were often sought for their accuracy of detail, photographers sometimes also attempted, as here, to create a mood through careful lighting and the draping of cloth.

In any event, at this time, painting and photography, whether in collaboration or opposition, were destined to replace the Tradition altogether—a tradition still very much alive in Romanticism. In substance and direction, in subject matter, and in form and technique, painting and photography were to topple the conventions of the Tradition through visual means faithful to Realism's new concerns with the optically real.

"Reality," "truth," "fact"—that elusive quality sought by artists throughout time with painstaking effort in the traditional media of paint, crayon, and pen-and-ink—could be captured readily and with breathtaking accuracy in the new mechanical medium of photography. Artists themselves were instrumental in the development of this new technology. As early as the seventeenth century, as we saw with Vermeer (FIG. 24-53), artists had used an optical device called the camera obscura (literally, dark room) to help them render the details of their subjects more accurately. These instruments were darkened chambers (some virtually portable closets) with optical lenses fitted into a hole in

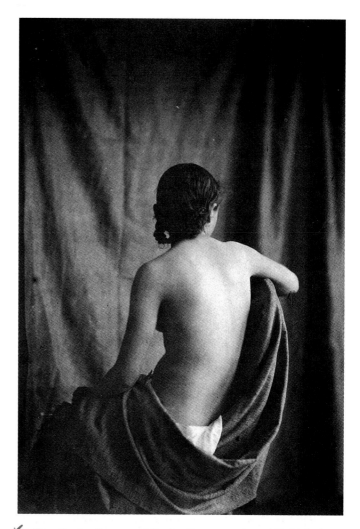

26-30 Eugène Durieu and Eugène Delacroix, *Draped Model (back view)*, c. 1854. Albumen print, 7⁵/₁₆″ × 5¹/₈″. The J. Paul Getty Museum, Malibu, California.

one wall through which light entered to project an inverted image of a subject onto the chamber's opposite wall. The artist could trace the main details from this image for later reworking and refinement. In 1807, the invention of the *camera lucida* (lighted room) replaced the enclosed chamber with an arrangement in which a small prism lens, hung on a stand, projected the image of the object at which it had been "aimed" downward onto a sheet of paper. Artists using these two devices found this preliminary stage of the artistic process long and arduous, no matter how accurate the resulting work. All yearned for a better way of capturing the image of a subject directly. Two very different scientific inventions that accomplished this were announced, almost simultaneously, in France and England in 1839.

The first new discovery was the development of the *daguerreotype* process, named for Louis-Jacques-Mandé Daguerre (1789–1851), one of its two inventors. Daguerre had trained as an architect before becoming a set painter and designer in the theater. This background led him to open (with a friend) a popular entertainment called the Diorama, in which audiences witnessed performances of "living paintings" created by changing the lighting effects on a "sandwich" composed of a painted backdrop and several layers of painted, translucent front curtains. Daguerre used a camera obscura for the Diorama, but he wanted to find a more efficient and effective procedure. Through a mutual acquaintance, he was introduced to Joseph Nicéphore Nièpce who, in 1826, had successfully made a permanent picture of the cityscape outside his upper-story window by exposing, in a camera obscura, a metal plate covered with a light-sensitive coating. Although the eight-hour exposure time needed to record Nièpce's subject hampered the process, Daguerre's excitement over its possibilities led to a partnership between the two men to pursue its development. Nièpce died in 1833, but Daguerre continued to work on his own. His contributions to the process consist of the discovery of latent development (in which the image is brought out through chemical solutions, considerably shortening the length of time needed for exposure) and the discovery of a better way to "fix" the image (again, chemically) by stopping the action of light on the photographic plate, which otherwise would continue to darken until the image could no longer be discerned.

The French government presented the new daguerreotype process at the Academy of Science in Paris on January 7, 1839, with the understanding that the details of the process would be made available to all interested parties without charge (although the inventor received a large annuity in appreciation). Soon, people all over the world were taking pictures with the daguerreotype "camera" (a name shortened from camera obscura) in a process almost immediately christened *photography*, from the Greek *photos* (light) and *graphos* (writing). From the start, painters were intrigued with the possibilities of the process as a new art medium. Paul Delaroche, a leading painter of the day, wrote in an official report to the French government:

> Daguerre's process completely satisfies all the demands of art, carrying certain essential principles of art to such perfection that it must become a subject of observation and study even to the most accomplished painters. The pictures obtained by this method are as remarkable for the perfection of the details as for the richness and harmony of the general effect. Nature is reproduced in them not only with truth, but also with art.*

Each daguerreotype is a unique work, possessing amazing detail and finely graduated tones from black to white. Both qualities are evident in *Still Life in Studio* (FIG. **26-31**), which is one of the first successful plates Daguerre produced after perfecting his method. The process captured every detail—the subtle shapes, the varied textures, the diverse tones of light and shadow—in Daguerre's carefully constructed tableau. The three-dimensional forms of the

*Letter from Delaroche to François Arao, in Helmut Gernsheim, *Creative Photography* (New York: Bonanza Books, 1962), p. 24.

26-31 LOUIS-JACQUES-MANDÉ DAGUERRE, *Still Life in Studio*, 1837. Daguerreotype. Collection Société Française de Photographie, Paris.

sculptures, the basket, and the bits of cloth spring into high relief and are convincingly *there* within the image. The composition of this work was clearly inspired by seventeenth-century Dutch still lifes such as those of Heda (FIG. 24-54). Like Heda, Daguerre arranged his objects to reveal clearly their textures and shapes. Unlike a painter, however, Daguerre could not alter anything within his arrangement to effect a stronger image. However, he could suggest a symbolic meaning within his array of objects. Like the peeled lemon and half-filled glasses of wine in Heda's painting, Daguerre's sculptural and architectural fragments and the framed print of an embrace suggest that even art is *vanitas* and will not endure forever.*

In the United States, where the first daguerreotype was taken within two months of Daguerre's presentation in Paris, two particularly avid and resourceful advocates of the new medium were JOSIAH JOHNSON HAWES (1808–1901), a painter, and ALBERT SANDS SOUTHWORTH (1811–1894), a pharmacist and teacher. Together, they ran a daguerreotype studio in Boston that specialized in portraiture, now popular due to the shortened exposure time required for the process (although it was still long enough to require a head brace to help the subject remain motionless while the photograph was being taken).

*Evidently Daguerre was well satisfied with the artistic merit of *Still Life in Studio,* because he presented it to the curator of the Louvre, who accepted it for the state collections.

The partners also, however, took their equipment outside of the studio to record places and events of particular interest to them. One such image is *Early Operation under Ether, Massachusetts General Hospital* (FIG. **26-32**). This daguerreotype was taken from the vantage point of the gallery of a hospital operating room, putting the viewer in the position of a medical student looking down on a lecture-demonstration of the type common through the nineteenth century. An image of historic record, this early daguerreotype gives the viewer a glimpse into the whole of Western medical practice. The focus of attention in *Early Operation* is the white-draped figure of the patient, who is surrounded by a circle of darkly clad doctors. The details of the figures and the furnishings of the room are recorded clearly, but the slight blurring of several of the figures betrays motion during the exposure. The concentration of the action in the center of the work creates an image reminiscent of the vignette composition favored by the Romantics, while the elevated viewpoint flattens the spatial perspective and emphasizes the relationship of the figures in ways that will be of immense interest to the Impressionists, especially Degas.

The daguerreotype reigned supreme in photography until the 1850s, but the second major photographic invention—the ancestor of the modern negative-print system—was announced less than three weeks after Daguerre's method was unveiled in Paris, and eventually replaced it. On January 31, 1839, William Henry Fox Talbot

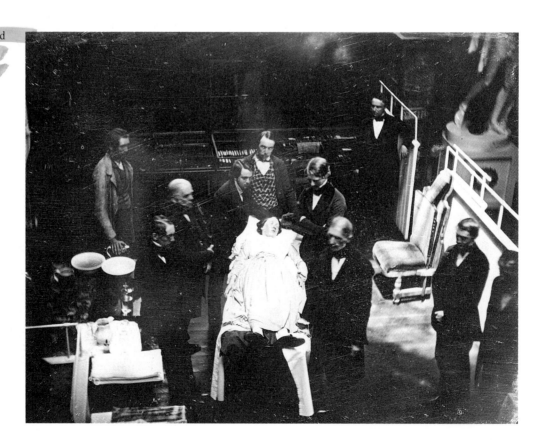

26-32 JOSIAH JOHNSON HAWES and ALBERT SANDS SOUTHWORTH, *Early Operation under Ether, Massachusetts General Hospital, c.* 1847. Daguerreotype. Massachusetts General Hospital, Boston.

(1800–1877) presented a paper on his "photogenic drawings" (not illustrated) to the Royal Institution in London. As early as 1835, Talbot made "negative" images by placing objects on sensitized paper and exposing the arrangement to light, creating a design in which white silhouettes recorded the places where opaque or translucent objects had blocked light from darkening the emulsion on the paper. However, Talbot's process was limited both by the size of the subjects it could record and by the fact that its images incorporated the texture of the paper on which they were recorded, producing a slightly blurred effect very different from the crisp detail and wide range of tones available with the daguerreotype.

Talbot's efforts to improve on his early work led to the photographic process its inventor named the *calotype,* a term he derived from the Greek term *kalos,* meaning beautiful. Although the calotype image still retained a grainy and shadowy effect due to the texture of the papers used, its widespread adoption was precluded primarily by the stiff licensing and equipment fees charged for many years after Talbot patented his new process in 1841. As a result of both the look and the cost of the calotype, many photographers elected to stay with the daguerreotype until photographic technology could overcome these problems.

Portraiture was an important economic component in the work of most photographers, as we have seen with Daguerre and Southworth and Hawes, but the greatest of the early portrait photographers was undoubtedly the Frenchman GASPAR-FÉLIX TOURNACHON (1820–1910), who adopted the name NADAR for his professional career as novelist, journalist, enthusiastic balloonist, and caricaturist. Photographic studies for his caricatures, which followed the tradition of Honoré Daumier's (see p. 966) most satiric lithographs (not illustrated), led Nadar to open a portrait studio. So talented was he at capturing the essence of his subjects that the most important people in France, including Delacroix, Daumier, Courbet, and Manet, flocked to his studio to have their portraits made. Nadar said he sought in his work "that instant of understanding that puts you in touch with the model—helps you sum him up, guides you to his habits, his ideas, and character and enables you to produce . . . a really convincing and sympathetic likeness, an intimate portrait."*

Nadar's skill in the genre can be seen in *Eugène Delacroix* (FIG. **26-33**), which shows the painter at the height of his career. In this photograph, the artist appears with remarkable presence; even in half-length, his gesture and expression create a revealing mood that seems to tell us much about him. Perhaps Delacroix responded to Nadar's famous gift for putting his clients at ease by assuming the pose that best expressed his personality. The rich range of tones in Nadar's images were made possible by new photographic materials. The glass negative and albumen printing paper could record finer detail and a wider range of light and shadow than Talbot's calotype process.

The new "wet-plate" technology almost at once replaced both the daguerreotype and the calotype and became the universal way of making negatives up to 1880. However, wet-plate photography had drawbacks. The plates had to be prepared and processed on the spot. To work outdoors meant taking along a portable darkroom of some sort: a wagon, or tent, or a box with light-tight sleeves through which the operator could thrust his arms. Yet, with the wet plate, remarkable photographs were made of battlefields, the Alps, and even of the flow of traffic in crowded streets (FIG. 26-68).

The documentary power of the photograph was immediately realized; thus began the story of the influence of the medium on modern life and the immense changes that it brought to communication and the management of information. For the historical record it was of unrivaled importance. For the first time great events could be recorded on the spot and the views preserved. The photographs taken of the Crimean War (1856) by Roger Fenton (1819–1869),

26-33 NADAR (GASPARD FÉLIX TOURNACHON), *Eugène Delacroix, c.* 1855. Modern print from original negative in the Bibliothèque Nationale, Paris.

*In Naomi Rosenblum, *A World History of Photography* (New York: Abbeville Press, 1984), p. 69.

26-34 ALEXANDER GARDNER, *Carnage at Antietam,* September 1862. Wet-plate photograph. (Culver Service, N.Y.)

and of the American Civil War by Matthew B. Brady (1823–1896) and ALEXANDER GARDNER (1821–1882) are still unsurpassed as incisive accounts of military life, unsparing in their truth to detail, poignant as expressions of human experience.

Of the Civil War photographs, the most moving are the inhumanly objective records of combat deaths—corpses strewn, "in death's extreme decrepitude," beside their wrecked cannon (FIG. **26-34**); in this view by Alexander Gardner (1821–1882), the unburied slaughtered have fallen in the bloodiest engagement of the war, fought at Antietam Creek, near Sharpsburg, Maryland (1862). Though it would be years before photolithography could reproduce photographs like this in newspapers, they were publicly exhibited and made an impression that newsprint engravings never could.

Painting of History and of Modern Life

We already have seen realism in the art of Constable and of Corot, and we have seen realistic images mechanically produced by the camera. Actually, realism, in different degrees of focus, has been an ingredient in Western art for centuries, from van Eyck to Velázquez and Vermeer and beyond. Nineteenth-century realism can be described technically and iconographically. Technically, realism deals with the replication of an optical field achieved by matching its color tones on a flat surface, whether or not the subject matter has or could have been seen by the artist. Iconographically, nineteenth-century Realism can be described as the subject matter of everyday, contemporary life as seen or seeable by the artist, whether recorded photographically or by other modes of visual report. The quarrel between Realism and Romanticism at mid-century was primarily over subject matter. Realists disapproved of traditional and fictional subjects on the grounds that they were not real and visible and were not of the present world. These artists argued that only the things of one's own times, the things one can see, are "real." The Realist vision and method resulted in a *modern* style—one, by definition, cut off from the past.

The Realist position in art and literature was strengthened by the scientific and technological achievements of the nineteenth century. Proponents of scientific positivism asserted that only scientifically verified fact was "real" and that the scientific method was the only legitimate means of gaining knowledge; all other means—religion, revelation, intuition, imagination—produced only fictions and illusions. Science was the most prestigious of all nineteenth-century intellectual enterprises; its authority rose from its triumphs. Its rigorous practicality and its search for the facts necessarily served as an example to artists searching for a modern truth and a modern style free from fable and fantasy. Realism stood for what the eye could see in the modern world—for actuality in all subject matter and verisimilitude in all images. Works of imagination based on subjects from myths and history were believed false.

Yet historical research and historiography in the nineteenth century were also concerned with fact, and historians claimed to be scientific in their method of gathering facts and drawing conclusions from them. This transformed the tradition of "history" painting, and seemed to validate a new approach. "History painting," as it had been known since the Renaissance, was supposed to depict elevating scenes from Christian and Classical story, with settings, costumes, poses, and accessories left in a more or less indefinite and conventional mode. Though actual historical events had been depicted before, notably by Velázquez, it was West's *General Wolfe* (FIG. 25-31) that headed a series of history paintings that, unlike those of the Tradition, aimed at reporting actual historical events in more or less authentic circumstances of time and place.

This new kind of history painting matures in the nineteenth century, at a time when the foundations are being laid and the materials gathered for the modern science of historiography. The aim of historical scholarship is to recover and present the past in all accurate detail. Not only the scholars, but poets, artists, and the educated public read history; the period is obsessed with it. We have already seen this in architecture; and, as in architecture, so also in art and literature (this is the century of the historical novel), reconstruction of the past can be imaginary, arbitrary, often inaccurate, often simply wrong.

On the other hand, there are painters as careful as scholars about the truth of the historical events they describe (although, being concerned with the dramatic essence of an event, painters may exaggerate in the interest of excitement). For it now becomes the history painter's function to produce, as on a stage, a convincing reenactment of an incident out of the past that will appeal both to the audience's sense of drama and its knowledge of history. This is a new genre, unknown to the Tradition, born of the age of West and David, and developing well beyond the limits they may have appeared to set for it.

HIPPOLYTE-PAUL DELAROCHE (1797–1856) specialized in this type of nineteenth-century painting. Delaroche was a pupil of Delacroix, who himself painted many historical pictures, but in his own, quite personal manner. In Delaroche's painting we sense that the artist is intent on neutralizing the intrusion of his personality in order to produce effects entirely independent of it. He is after an illusion so objective, complete, and immediate that the spectator will think: "It might have looked this way—it might *not* have looked this way—but it *could* have looked this way." The value of the picture lies in its presumptive truth, not simply to life, but to life at a particular time and place and as once lived.

This new approach to history painting can be seen in Delaroche's *Death of the Duc de Guise* (FIG. **26-35**). The visitor to the Salon in 1835 would have known the story and would have responded to the picture as if it were a scene from a stage production of the event. The third Duke of Guise, leader of the Catholic party in the religious wars in France during the later sixteenth century, aspired to the

26-35 HIPPOLYTE-PAUL DELAROCHE, *Death of the Duc de Guise*, 1835. Oil on canvas, Musée Condé, Chantilly.

throne held by Henry III. On Christmas Day, 1588, he was summoned to the king's chamber at the royal chateau of Blois (FIG. 24-62) and there murdered by assassins in the pay of the king. Delaroche gives us a careful inventory of all the particulars of the event, of the action, and of the setting. The composition is uncentered; the dead duke lies at the right, the excited murderers crowd across from him at the left. The slain man, in falling, has pulled down the curtain of the royal bed, revealing, ironically, the rich covering embroidered with the monogram of his murderer, Henry III. One assassin puts up his sword, the other's is still drawn; a cape has fallen on the floor. The description of the action could go on. The architecture of the room is exactly that of the period. Delaroche has researched the scene with the care of a historian. He achieves the illusion by exactly matching on his canvas the total, optical spread of tone before him; the effect is photographic. The surface has a glassy smoothness, a finish in which the brush stroke is intended to be invisible. In this way the artist reduces to the barest minimum interference by his own imagination or feeling or even by the agent of that feeling—his "hand." Like a director in the theater, he expects to be judged on his interpretation—manifest in the characterizations he elicits, in the species of action, scene design, and authenticity of detail. His insistence upon a particular event, a particular time, place, and action, realized by an untraditional technique, puts Delaroche outside the Tradition even while he appears to continue it.

The same may be said of Delaroche's pupil JEAN-LÉON GÉRÔME (1824–1904). In his painting *Thumbs Down! (Pollice Verso)* (FIG. **26-36**), Gérôme moves even farther from the Tradition than Delaroche; the inherited formulas have been almost entirely transformed. The time and place specifications are as exact as they can be. Although we do not know the day, month, and year of the event, nor the names of the principals involved, we recognize it for what it is and where it is happening; we can even guess the time of day. Gladiatorial combats were part of the Roman imperial games held regularly in great arenas or amphitheaters like the one pictured—the Colosseum at Rome (FIG. 7-39). The incident represented must have happened countless times, and, though it does not have the uniqueness of the Duc de Guise's murder, it is this very ordinariness that makes it equally dramatic and equally factual. A triumphant gladiator bestrides his fallen opponent and looks toward the box where the Vestal Virgins are seated. The fallen man gestures for mercy. The Vestals deny his appeal by turning their thumbs down; he will be killed on the spot. Gérôme authenticates the scene to the last detail: the Vestals, the emperor's party (in the box fronted with columns and trophies), the streaks of light (clue to the time of day) thrown upon the tapestried barrier walls by chinks in the great awnings overhead, the texture of the blood-stained sand and, conspicuously, the fantastic garb of the gladiators, their splendid helmets replicating originals found at Pompeii. The scenic illusion is produced, as in Delaroche, by a smooth continuum of tone that runs through the whole scale of values. There is scrupulous fidelity to optical fact. Evidence of brush strokes is suppressed in a glassy surface exquisitely finished. But there is a significant difference from Delaroche in the composition. The figures in the *Duc de Guise* are uncentered within the frame—that is, placed right and left, leaving a void in the middle, a natural enough distribution given the action. The frame controls

26-36 JEAN-LÉON GÉRÔME, *Thumbs Down! (Pollice Verso), c.* 1872. Oil on canvas, 39$\frac{1}{2}$″ × 58$\frac{1}{2}$″. Phoenix Art Museum (museum purchase).

26-37   JEAN-FRANÇOIS MILLET, *The Gleaners*, 1857. Oil on canvas, approx. 33" × 44". Louvre, Paris.

the figures so as to give the whole the appearance of a stage upon which actors are playing a scene. This makes us an audience at a play; what we see is play-acting and not the *real* murder of the duke. Gérôme, on the other hand, making use of a similar off-centered, dynamic placement of his figures, makes us spectators at a *real* event, which we witness from *within* the framed space of the action. The curving wall sweeps toward us, and we can feel that our own point of vantage is continuous with that of the Vestal Virgins. Gérôme thus brings us onto the stage, while with Delaroche we are still out in front of it. This radical narrowing of the space between the spectator and the event being watched is a device of great importance in nineteenth-century pictorial technique.

MILLET   In sharp contrast with the historical painters, Realist painters of contemporary life found their subjects in the persons and occupations familiar in the everyday world. This is where Realism finds its proper exercise, the practice of its own theory: that the business of the artist is to depict the factual and the commonplace, plainly and simply, as given to the eye. As we have seen, the eighteenth-century taste for the "natural" had idealized country people and country life; "nature," yes, but "nature" viewed through sentiment (FIG. 25-29). Something of that idealization lingers in the work of JEAN-FRANÇOIS MILLET (1814–1878), though it does not weaken the authority of his realistic statement.

Millet was one of a group of painters of landscape and figure, who, to be close to their rural subjects, settled near the village of Barbizon in the forest of Fontainebleau. The "Barbizon" school specialized in detailed pictures of forest and countryside; Corot was in close association with them. Millet, perhaps their most prominent member, was of peasant stock and identified with the hard lot of the country

poor. In *The Gleaners* (FIG. **26-37**), he shows three peasant women, two of them performing the back-breaking task of gleaning the last scraps of grain after the harvest. Millet characteristically places his monumental figures in the foreground, against a broad sky. Here the field stretches back to a rim of haystacks, cottages, trees, and distant workers and flat horizon. The quiet design of Millet's painting shares the careful arrangement and calm mood of Corot's *Harbor of La Rochelle* (FIG. 26-24); but Millet concentrates on the figures looming against the sky, fronting their dull, featureless, and tired landscape. His scrupulous truth to detail of figure and setting shows him intent on revealing the dignity of these eternal labors.

The solemn grandeur with which Millet invested the poor did not meet with the approval of the prosperous classes. Socialism was a growing movement, and its views on property and its call for social justice, not to say economic equality, frightened the bourgeoisie. Millet's glorification of the poor seemed like a political manifesto.

DAUMIER   The political and social agitation that accompanied the violent revolutions in France and the rest of Europe in the earlier century made the arts suspect of subversive intention. One could be jailed for too bold a statement in the press, in literature, in art—even in music and the drama. An artist who was imprisoned for boldly confronting authority with social criticism and political protest was HONORÉ DAUMIER (1808–1879). Daumier, painter, sculptor, and, like Goya, one of the world's great masters of the graphic (print) medium, was a defender of the urban working classes, as Millet was a defender of the farming poor. He was early known for the satirical lithographs he contributed to the liberal French Republican journal *Caricature*. In these, he mercilessly lampooned the foibles and misbehavior of politicians, lawyers, doctors, and the rich bourgeoisie in general. He was ever in close touch with the acute political and social unrest in Paris at the time of the revolutions of 1830 and 1848.

His lithograph, *Rue Transnonain* (FIG. **26-38**) depicts an atrocity with the same shocking impact as Goya's *Third of May* (FIG. 26-10). The title names a street in Paris where a civil guard, part of a government force trying to repress a worker demonstration, was killed by a sniper. Because the fatal shot had come from a workers' housing block, the remaining guards immediately stormed the building and massacred all of its inhabitants. With the power of Goya, Daumier created a view of the atrocity from a sharp, realistic angle of vision. We see not the dramatic moment of execution, but the terrible, quiet aftermath. The broken, scattered forms, lying in the midst of violent disorder, are reported as if newly found. Daumier used every available device of his skill to make the situation real. The harsh facts speak for themselves; the artist did not have to interpret them for us. The print's significance lies in its factualness. What we find here is an example of an increasing artistic bias toward using facts as subject, if not always with the

Realism

26-38 HONORÉ DAUMIER, *Rue Transnonain*, 1834. Lithograph, approx. 12″ × 17½″. Philadelphia Museum of Art. Bequest of Fiske and Marie Kimball.

optical realization of fact as method. Daumier's manner is rough and spontaneous; the way it carries expressive exaggeration is part of its remarkable force. Daumier is true to life in content, but his style is uniquely personal.

Daumier brought the same concerns to the paintings he did, especially after 1848. His unfinished *The Third-Class Carriage* (FIG. **26-39**) gives us a glimpse into the rude railway compartment of the 1860s. The inhabitants are poor and can afford only third-class tickets. The disinherited masses of nineteenth-century industrialism were Daumier's indignant concern, and he made them his subject over and over again. He shows them to us in the unposed attitudes and unplanned arrangements of the millions thronging the modern city—anonymous, insignificant, dumbly patient with a lot they cannot change. Daumier saw people as they ordinarily appeared, their faces vague, impersonal, blank—unprepared for any observer. He tried to achieve the real by isolating a random collection of the unrehearsed details of human existence from the continuum of ordinary life, a vision that paralleled the spontaneity and candor of scenes being captured by the end of the century with the modern snapshot camera.

COURBET   From fragmentary observations like the following, made by JEAN DÉSIRÉ GUSTAVE COURBET (1819–1877), we learn of Realism as the Realists and their friendly critics understood it.

> To be able to translate the customs, ideas, and appearances of my time as I see them—in a word, to create a living art—this has been my aim. . . . The art of painting can

consist only in the representation of objects visible and tangible to the painter . . . , [who must apply] his personal faculties to the ideas and the things of the period in which he lives . . . I hold also that painting is an essentially *concrete* art, and can consist only of the representation of things both *real* and *existing*. . . . An *abstract* object, invisible or nonexistent, does not belong to the domain of painting. . . . Show me an angel, and I'll paint one.*

Courbet has long been regarded as the father of the Realist movement in nineteenth-century art; certainly, he used the term "realism" in exhibiting his own works, even though he shunned labels. "The title of Realist," he insisted, "was thrust upon me, just as the title of Romantic was imposed upon the men of 1830. Titles have never given a true idea of things."

In and since Courbet's time, confusion about what Realism is has been widespread. Writing in 1857, Champfleury, one of the first critics to recognize and appreciate Courbet's work, declared: "I will not define Realism. . . . I do not know where it comes from, where it goes, what it is. . . . The name horrifies me by its pedantic ending; . . . there is enough confusion already about that famous word." Confusion, or at least disagreement, about Realism still exists among historians of nineteenth- and, for that matter, twentieth-century art. Yet from Courbet's own brief statements, we gather that he wished to be only of his time and to paint only what it made visible to him.

*In Robert Goldwater and Marco Treves, eds., *Artists on Art*, 3rd ed. (New York: Pantheon, 1958), pp. 295–97.

REALISM

26-39   HONORÉ DAUMIER, *The Third-Class Carriage, c.* 1862. Oil on canvas, 25³/₄″ × 35¹/₂″. The Metropolitan Museum of Art, New York (Havemeyer Collection, bequest of Mrs. H. O. Havemeyer, 1929).

Born into a wealthy family in the primarily rural area of Franche-Comté, Courbet became an anticlerical painter who took as his subjects the working-class people and ordinary landscapes around him. Although his early career was distinguished by self-portraits displaying a wildly Romantic mood, in most of his works he made a sharp break with the Tradition; all mythological, religious, and purely imaginative subjects were ruled out as not visible to the modern eye. The critic Jules Antoine Castagnary, writing in 1863, said of Courbet: "[His] great claim is to represent what he sees. It is, in fact, one of his favorite axioms that everything that does not appear upon the retina is outside the domain of painting." At this time, critics looking for an expressly modern art could find their hero in Courbet.

A man of powerful personality, Courbet was cut out to be the truculent champion of the Realist cause, defying both public taste and the art juries that rejected two of his major works for the Paris International Exhibition in 1855 on the grounds that his subjects and figures were too coarsely materialistic (so much so as to be plainly "socialistic") and too large. Plain people of the kind Courbet shows us in his work were considered by the public to be unsuitable for artistic representation and were linked in the middle-class mind with the dangerous, newly defined working class, which was finding outspoken champions in men like Marx, Engels, Proudhon, Balzac, Flaubert, Zola, and Dickens. Rejected by the exhibition jury, Courbet set up his own gallery outside the grounds, calling it the Pavilion of Realism. Courbet's pavilion and his utterances amounted

to the manifestoes of the new movement. Although he maintained that he founded no school and was of no school, he did, as the name of his pavilion suggests, accept the term "realism" as descriptive of his art. With the unplanned collaboration of Millet, Daumier, and other artists, Courbet challenged the whole iconographic stock of the Tradition and called public attention to what Baudelaire termed the "heroism of modern life," which Courbet felt should replace all the heroism of traditional subject matter. For the public, it was a contest between the painters of the "ugly" (Courbet) and the painters of the "beautiful" (those who opposed Courbet), as the public understood those qualities.

Representative of Courbet's work is *Burial at Ornans* (FIG. **26-40**), which depicts a funeral in a bleak, provincial landscape, attended by obscure persons "of no importance," the type of people presented by Balzac and Flaubert in their novels. While an officious clergyman reads the Office of the Dead, those in attendance cluster around the excavated gravesite, their faces registering all degrees of response to the situation.

Although the painting has the monumental scale of a traditional history painting, contemporary critics were horrified not only by the ordinariness of the subject matter, but also by the starkly antiheroic composition. Arranged in a wavering line extending across the broad widths of the canvas, the figures are portrayed in groups—the somberly clad women at the back right, a semicircle of similarly clad men by the open grave, and assorted churchmen at the left. The

26-40   GUSTAVE COURBET, *Burial at Ornans,* 1849. Oil on canvas, approx. 10' × 22'. Louvre, Paris.

observer's attention, however, is wholly on the wall of figures, seen at eye-level, that blocks any view into deep space. The faces of the figures are portraits; some of the models were friends of Courbet. Behind and above the figures are bands of overcast sky and barren cliffs. The dark pit of the grave opens into the viewer's space in the center foreground. Despite the unposed look of the figures (which in conjunction with the cut-off figures at the edges of the canvas, may owe something to Courbet's interest in photography), the artist has controlled the composition in a masterful way by his sparing use of bright color. Patches of white carry the eye across the bank of figures. The strong red of the lawyers' robes appears in the caps and skirts of the acolytes to the left; the red is then countered by its complement in the green-blue stockings of the mourner whose hand is extended toward the grave. The long, narrow rectangle of the canvas has something of panoramic effect; the viewer's eyes cannot take in the whole with one glance but must scan across the composition from group to group. The heroic, the sublime, and the terrible are not found here— only the drab facts of undramatized life and death. In 1857, Champfleury wrote of *Burial at Ornans,* "It represents a small-town funeral and yet reproduces the funerals of *all* small towns." Unlike the superhuman or subhuman actors on the grand stage of the Romantic canvas, this Realist work moves according to the ordinary rhythms of contemporary life.

Beyond his new subject matter, Courbet's intentionally simple and direct methods of expression in composition and technique seemed to many of his more traditional contemporaries to be unbearably crude, and he was called a primitive. Although his bold, somber palette was essentially traditional, Courbet often used the palette knife, with which he could quickly place and unify large daubs of paint, producing a roughly wrought surface. His example inspired the young men who worked for him (and later impressionists like Claude Monet and Auguste Renoir), but the public accused him of carelessness and critics wrote of his "brutalities."

Although often embattled with critics over the spirit and form of Realism, Courbet had secure official backing from the late 1850s onward, and, in his later years, painted with greater intention to please the public. Indeed, the mode of these later pictures recalls traditional methods, with dark underpainting, heavy chiaroscuro, and subject matter familiar in the popular Salon. This conservatism disappointed younger artists who had come to rely strongly on Courbet's vigorous style and technique, as well as on his courageous individualism. Most of the Impressionists had associated and exhibited with him in their early years, but Courbet failed to catch the spirit of the new style that was emerging in their work. Despite this, neither the Impressionists, nor history itself, could deny the impetus Courbet's art had given the movement toward a modern style based on observations of the modern environment.

Variations in Realism: Realism Outside France

Although French artists took the lead in promoting Realism, lending especially strong support to the idea that Realism should be the depiction of the realities of modern life,

Realism was not exclusively French. Often influenced by the appearance of photography and almost always inspired by the optical truth of the physical world, Realism appeared in all countries in a variety of forms and was taken for granted by the end of the century.

In the United States, a dedicated appetite for showing the realities of the human experience made THOMAS EAKINS (1844–1916) a master Realist portrait and genre painter. Eakins studied both painting and medical anatomy in Philadelphia before undertaking further study under Gérôme (FIG. 26-36). He was resolutely a Realist; his ambition was to paint things as he saw them rather than as the public might wish them to be portrayed. This attitude was very much in tune with nineteenth-century American taste, which was said to combine an admiration for accurate depiction with a hunger for truth. These twin attributes are reflected in Ralph Waldo Emerson's observations that "Our American character is marked by a more than average delight in accurate perception," and Henry David Thoreau's declaration: "Let us not underrate the value of a fact. It will one day flower in a truth."

Eakins's early masterpiece, *The Gross Clinic* (FIG. **26-41**), was rejected for its too-brutal Realism by the art jury for the exhibition in Philadelphia that celebrated the centennial of

American independence. The work represents the renowned surgeon Dr. Samuel Gross in the operating amphitheatre of the Jefferson Medical College in Philadelphia, where the painting now hangs. The surgeon is accompanied by colleagues, all of whom have been identified, and by the patient's mother, who covers her face. Dr. Gross, with bloody fingers and scalpel, lectures on his procedure. The painting is indeed an unsparing description of a contemporary event, with a good deal more reality than many viewers could endure: "It is a picture," said one critic, "that even strong men find difficult to look at long, if they can look at it at all." It was true to the program of "scenes from modern life," as Southworth and Hawes had been in their daguerreotype of a similar setting (FIG. 26-32). Each image records a particular event at a particular time.

Eakins believed that knowledge—and where relevant, scientific knowledge—was a prerequisite to his art. As a scientist (in his anatomical studies), Eakins preferred a slow, deliberate method of careful invention based on his observations of the perspective, the anatomy, and the actual details of his subject. His concern for anatomical correctness led him to investigate the human form and the human form in motion, both with regular photographic apparatus and with a special camera devised by the French kinesiologist (scholar of motion) Étienne-Jules Marey. Eakins's later collaboration with Eadweard Muybridge in the photographic study of animal and human action of all types drew favorable attention in France, especially from Degas, and anticipated the motion picture.

The Realist photographer and scientist EADWEARD MUYBRIDGE (1830–1904) came to the United States from England in the 1850s and settled in San Francisco, where he established a prominent international reputation for his photographs of the western United States. (His large-plate landscape images of the Yosemite region won him a gold medal at the Vienna Exposition of 1873.) In 1872, the governor of California, Leland Stanford, sought Muybridge's assistance in settling a bet about whether, at any point in a stride, all four feet of a horse galloping at top speed are off the ground. Through his photography, Muybridge was able to prove that they were. This experience was the beginning of Muybridge's photographic studies of the successive stages in human and animal motion—detail too quick for the human eye to capture. These investigations culminated in 1885 at the University of Pennsylvania with a series of multiple camera motion studies that recorded separate photographs of each progressive moment in a single action. The results of this research were widely publicized in Muybridge's book *Animal Locomotion* (1887).

Handspring, a flying pigeon interfering (FIG. **26-42**) is a typical plate from the book. Taken with two batteries of cameras placed at right angles to one another, this photograph combines the side and front views of the successive instants in an athletic stunt. At the top is the series of twelve images shot from the side view, split into two rows to match in

26-41 THOMAS EAKINS, *The Gross Clinic*, 1875. Oil on canvas, 8′ × 6′6″. Jefferson Medical College of Thomas Jefferson University, Philadelphia.

26-42   EADWEARD MUYBRIDGE, *Handspring, a flying pigeon interfering, June 26, 1885,* Plate 365 of *Animal Locomotion,* 1887. Print from original master negative. International Museum of Photography at George Eastman House, Rochester, New York.

width the twelve narrower front views that are spread across the bottom. With our Western habit of reading type in books, we begin at the upper left and scan along the top two rows to reconstruct the hand-spring, perhaps wondering as we do so where the pigeon mentioned in the title comes in. The drama is revealed at the bottom, where we see the strolling pigeon startled into flight as the handspring unfolds, almost upsetting the athlete in the process. Muybridge's motion photographs earned him a place in the history of science as well as art. His sequential studies of motion, along with those of Eakins and Marey, influenced many other artists, including their contemporary, the painter and sculptor Edgar Degas, and twentieth-century artists like Marcel Duchamp.

Muybridge presented his work to scientists and general audiences by means of a device called the *zoopraxiscope,* which he invented to project his sequences of images (mounted on special glass plates) onto a screen. The result was so lifelike that one viewer said it "threw upon the screen apparently the living, moving animals. Nothing was wanting but the clatter of hoofs upon the turf."* The illusion of motion here was created by a physical fact of human eyesight called "persistence of vision," which, stated simply, means that whatever the eye sees is held in the brain for a fraction of a second after the eye stops seeing it, causing a rapid succession of different images to merge one into the next and producing the illusion of continuous change.† This illusion lies at the heart of the "realism" of all cinema.

*Scientific American, May 1888, cited in Kenneth MacGowan, *Behind the Screen* (New York: A Dell Book, Delta Publishing Co., 1965), p. 49.

†News of Muybridge's zoopraxiscope spread rapidly. One interested person was the inventor Thomas Alva Edison, who had just perfected the phonograph and wanted to add sound to Muybridge's moving images. Edison and his assistant, William Kennedy Laurie Dickson, eventually developed a true motion-picture camera (patented in 1891) that used strips of photographic film newly invented by George Eastman. Innovations such as these helped lay the foundations of the art of cinema.

The expatriate American artist JOHN SINGER SARGENT (1856–1925) was a younger contemporary of Eakins and Muybridge. In contrast to Eakins's carefully rendered details, Sargent developed a looser, more dashing Realist portrait style. Sargent studied art in Paris before settling in London, where he was renowned as a cultivated and cosmopolitan gentleman, and as a facile and fashionable painter of portraits. His fluent brushing of paint in thin films and his effortless achievement of quick and lively illusion were learned from his study of Vélazquez, whose masterpiece, *Las Meninas* (FIG. 24-37), may have influenced Sargent's family portrait *The Daughters of Edward Darley Boit* (FIG. **26-43**). The four girls (the children of one of Sargent's close friends) are grouped casually within a hall and small drawing room in their Paris home. The informal, eccentric arrangement of their slight figures suggests how much at ease they are within this familiar space and with objects like the monumental Japanese vases, the red screen, and the fringed rug, whose scale subtly emphasizes the diminutive stature of the children. Sargent must have known the Boit daughters well and liked them. Relaxed and trustful, they gave the artist an opportunity to record a gradation of young innocence in which he sensitively captures the naive, wondering openness of the little girl in the foreground, the grave artlessness of the ten-year-old child, and the slightly self-conscious poise of the adolescents. From the positioning of the figures and the continuity of the space of hall and drawing room (conveyed by the lighting), we sense how spontaneously they function within this setting. They seem to be attending momentarily to an adult who has asked them to interrupt their activity and "look this way." Here is a most effective embodiment of the Realist belief that the business of the artist is to record the modern being in modern context. Through devices like the cut-off vase and rug, we see the beginnings of the way in which Realist painters increasingly will move into the space of their works, regulating the distance of the artist's (and viewer's) standpoint from the objects represented, so that the action and environment in the painting seem one with those outside it.

As Realism spread throughout the world, Realist artists expanded and diversified their subject matter to embrace all classes and levels of society, all types of people and environments: the urban and rural working class, the denizens of the big city, the burghers of the small town, the leisure class at its resorts, the rustics of the provinces. Added to the social sympathies we found in Daumier, Courbet, and Millet were motives of an anthropological kind, reflecting interest in national and regional characteristics, folk customs and culture, and the quaintness and picturesqueness of local color.

WILHELM LEIBL (1844–1900), perhaps the most important German Realist painter in the later nineteenth century, is a master of the quaint and picturesque detail of country life. Influenced by Courbet, but lacking his breadth and depth, Leibl exemplified the Realist credo. His masterpiece, *Three*

Women in a Village Church (FIG. **26-44**), is the record of a sacred moment—the moment of prayer—in the life of three country women of different generations. Dressed in rustic costume, their Sunday best, they pursue their devotions unselfconsciously, their prayer books held in big hands roughened by work. Their manners and their dress proclaim them innocent of the affectations and refinements of the metropolis, which they probably have never seen. Leibl chose to show their natural virtues: simplicity, honesty, steadfastness, patience. He could subscribe, doubtless, to the words of a poet from another country and another time: "Far from the madding crowd's ignoble strife / . . . / they kept the noiseless tenor of their way."* Leibl himself wrote in a letter: "Here in the open country and among those who live close to nature, one can paint naturally."

For three years, he worked from his peasant models in the little church, often under impossible conditions of

*Thomas Gray, *Elegy Written in a Country Churchyard,* 1751.

26-43 JOHN SINGER SARGENT, *The Daughters of Edward Darley Boit,* 1882. Oil on canvas, 7'3" × 7'3". Courtesy Museum of Fine Arts, Boston (gift of Mary Boit, Florence D. Boit, Jane H. Boit, and Julia O. Boit, in memory of their father).

lighting and temperature. The light in *Three Women* is hard and neutral, without cast shadows and with only the slightest modeling. The focus is sharp, the forms and space flattening out into pattern. We are aware of the documentary power of the photograph-like approach. Yet, for all its objectivity, the picture is a moving expression of the artist's intelligent sympathy for his subjects, a reading of character without a trace of sentimentality, rare for a subject like this.

Unlike the literature of nineteenth-century Russia, which has received a great deal of attention, nineteenth-century Russian art has been little known outside that nation. The Realist impulse was prized in Russia, and the painting *A Religious Procession in the Kursk District* (FIG. **26-45**), by ILYA YEFIMOVICH REPIN (1844–1930), is a Realist work of extraordinary power. Simultaneously drama and document, this work makes us witness to a dense throng of people traveling along a road past us. They move in measured procession behind a shrine carried on the shoulders of monks and beneath religious banners held proudly on

high. Priest, peasants, burghers, students, soldiers, police, provincial officials, and bureaucrats all join in this homage to a saint on his feast day. Alongside the procession straggle beggars and cripples, perhaps hoping for a healing miracle. It is a multitude that, in itself, characterizes the society of "Holy Russia" before the revolutions of the twentieth century. The throng tramps along a country road, raising clouds of dust in the heat of noon as it crosses a featureless Russian landscape where trees recently have been hacked down. Closer inspection reveals two files of mounted riders—some in uniform, some priestly in appearance—coming slowly forward through the crowd. Their way is being cleared by men who savagely ply whips and cudgels to open a path. In the left foreground, a boy on a crutch has just been struck heavily with a staff wielded by the priest behind him. We can read in the crowded details of Repin's *Procession* the sullen poverty and misery of the people; the dogged, almost primitive religion; the officials' arrogance; and the pitiless harshness of the old Russian scene. These elements are much as they have been described in the novels of Dostoevsky (*Procession* and *The Brothers Karamazov* are contemporaneous works). One need suspect no interinfluence; painter and novelist are simply confronting the same realities.

Repin's painting expands the program of Realism formulated in his time. He records a scene taken directly from modern life, at a particular place and time, objectively recorded with little of the artist's comment, unless it be a touch of sad irony or protest. The artist reconstructs the scene using his acute visual memory. He may have used sketches but certainly portrayed the event close to the way he saw it, in a manner similar to Eakins's method. The space is fluent and is assumed to continue, along with the action, beyond the frame. The light is out-of-doors, rather than of the studio, and the color, with its myriad modulations and accents, is suited to the time of day and the local color of landscape and costume.

Repin's crowd scene is unusual for Realist painting, which more often emphasized the dignity of individuals. Typical of the Realist painter's desire to depict the lives of ordinary people is the early work of the American artist HENRY OSSAWA TANNER (1859–1937). Tanner studied art with Eakins before moving to Paris, where he combined Eakins's belief in careful study from nature and reverence for the light and mood in Rembrandt's portraiture with a desire to portray with dignity the life of the ordinary people among whom he had been raised as the son of an African-American minister in Pennsylvania. The mood of quiet devotion in *The Thankful Poor* (FIG. **26-46**) is as intense as that in Leibl's *Three Women in a Village Church* (FIG. 26-44), but Tanner's lighting is softer (more Rembrandtesque), and his style incorporates a selective focus different from, but linked to, the Realism of Millet (FIG. 26-37) and to photography. In Tanner's painting, the grandfather, grandchild, and main objects in the room

26-44   WILHELM LEIBL, *Three Women in a Village Church*, 1878–1881. Oil on canvas, approx. 29″ × 25″. Kunsthalle, Hamburg.

26-45   ILYA REPIN, *A Religious Procession in the Kursk District, c.* 1880. Oil on canvas, approx. 5'8" × 9'2". Tretyakov Gallery, Moscow.

26-46   HENRY OSSAWA TANNER, *The Thankful Poor*, 1894. Oil on canvas, 49" × 35$^1/_2$". Private collection.

—AFRICAN AMERICAN ARTIST

REALISM

26-47 WINSLOW HOMER, *The Fox Hunt*, 1893. Oil on canvas, 38″ × 68¹/₂″. The Pennsylvania Academy of the Fine Arts, Philadelphia (Joseph E. Temple Fund).

are painted with the greatest detail, while everything else dissolves into loose strokes of color and light that owe something to Impressionism but here remain more tied to the surface of things. Expressive lighting reinforces the reverent spirit of the painting, with deep shadows intensifying the devout concentration of the man and golden light pouring in the window to illuminate the quiet expression of thanksgiving on the younger face. The deep sense of sanctity that is expressed here in terms of everyday experience became increasingly important for Tanner. Within a few years of completing *The Thankful Poor,* he was painting biblical subjects, grounded in direct study from nature and the love of Rembrandt that had inspired him from his days as an art student in Philadelphia.

A very different mood fills *The Fox Hunt* (FIG. **26-47**) by Tanner's contemporary, WINSLOW HOMER (1836–1910), a leading American painter. Homer began his career making newspaper illustrations of daily life and of soldiers in the Civil War and went on to become famous for his painting of unspoiled nature—especially the turbulent sea—and of individual human beings caught up in the natural world. *The Fox Hunt* is rare among his works, both for its subject and for its composition. A fox, bogged down in heavy winter snow, is attacked by crows made fierce by starvation. The fox is trapped and its fate is certain. The figure of the fox is silhouetted against the flat white of the snowy ground; above, the dark shapes of the crows fill the sky, overshadowing and overwhelming the fox.

Homer's method is objective and simple, conveying with Realist directness the mood of struggle and death in nature. Form and color convey the grim mood of the scene in reinforcement of what the images literally depict. The artist is "present" but powerless to intervene. In any event, this is a

fact of nature. The color areas are sharp-edged and icy cold, except for the faintly warm tonality of the fox's coat and the spangle of red berries against the snow. The broad, short rectangle of the composition presents a low, panoramic view similar to that in Courbet's *Burial at Ornans,* but Homer has filled most of his picture with the field of white snow, which pushes the action of fox and crows so close to the foreground (and the space of the viewer) that parts of the bodies of the leading attackers are cut off by the frame. This spacing emphasizes the double irony of the title: in the uneasy world of man and nature, where a fox is often hunted by mounted human beings for sport, it is now hunted by hungry crows in a morbid reversal of the process of nature that usually finds the fox hunting birds for food. Homer expresses with Realist intensity the impersonal, cruel competition of natural species asserted as a rule of life in the Darwinian-Spencerian theory of the survival of the fittest.

Romantic Responses to Realism

Realism stood for what the eye could see in the here and now—for actuality in all subject matter and verisimilitude in all images. Reflecting the Realist credo of art, philosopher Friedrich Nietzsche wrote, "We do not demand beautiful, illusory lies from it. . . . Brutal positivism reigns, recognizing facts without becoming excited." Like the positivists of science, the Realists believed in the supremacy of cold fact and made it the basis of esthetic truth and personal honesty. Some artists who subscribed to the Realist view, however, found Realist doctrine arbitrary and too restrictive of that play of artistic imagination long honored in the Tradition. While using Realist techniques scrupulous to

Realism

26-48   MARIE-ROSALIE (ROSA) BONHEUR, *The Horse Fair*, 1853. Oil on canvas, 8'1/4" × 16'7 1/2". The Metropolitan Museum of Art, New York (gift of Cornelius Vanderbilt, 1887).

truth and detail, these artists gave full play to their imaginative faculties in idea and content in order to render their subject Romantically.

MARIE-ROSALIE (ROSA) BONHEUR (1822–1899) was a painter who could merit membership in both parties: she was a Realist in her scientific study of her favorite subject, and a Romantic in her idealization of its natural beauty, in her dynamic composition, and in her pictorial lighting and colorism. Trained as an artist by her father, Bonheur founded her career on his belief that, as a woman and an artist, she had a special role to play in creating a new and perfect society. In her work, she combined a naturalist's knowledge of equine anatomy and motion with an honest love and admiration for the brute strength of wild and domestic animals. Driven by a Realist passion for accuracy in painting, she observed the anatomy of living horses at the great Parisian horse fair, where the animals were shown and traded, and also spent long hours studying the anatomy of carcasses in the Paris slaughterhouses. For her best-known work, *The Horse Fair* (FIG. **26-48**), she adopted a panoramic composition similar to that in Courbet's *Burial at Ornans*, painted a few years earlier. In contrast to the still figures in *Burial*, Bonheur filled her broad canvas with the sturdy farm animals and their grooms seen on parade at the annual Parisian horse sale. Some horses, not quite broken, rear up; others plod or trot, guided on foot or ridden by their keepers. The uneven line of the march, the thunderous pounding, and the seemingly overwhelming power of the

Percherons were clearly based on close observation from life, even though Bonheur acknowledged some inspiration from the Classical model of the Parthenon frieze (FIG. 5-54). The dramatic lighting, loose brushwork, and rolling sky also reveal her admiration of the style of Géricault. Bonheur's depiction of equine drama in *The Horse Fair* captivated viewers, who eagerly bought engraved reproductions of the work, making it one of the most well-known paintings of the century.

In England, JOHN EVERETT MILLAIS (1829–1896) was among a group of artists who refused to be limited to the contemporary scenes portrayed by the strict Realist. These artists chose instead to represent fictional, historical, and fanciful subjects, but to do so using the techniques of Realism; in this respect, of course, they parallel Delaroche and Gérôme. So painstakingly careful in his study of visual facts closely observed from nature that Baudelaire called him "the poet of meticulous detail," Millais was a founder of the so-called Pre-Raphaelite Brotherhood. This group of artists, organized in 1848, wished to create fresh and sincere art, free from what they considered to be the tired and artificial manner propagated by the successors of Raphael in the academies.

Millais's method is seen to advantage in his *Ophelia* (FIG. **26-49**), which he exhibited in the Universal Exposition in Paris in 1855, where Courbet set up his Pavilion of Realism. The subject, from Shakespeare's *Hamlet*, is the drowning of Ophelia, who, in her madness, is unaware of her plight:

26-49   JOHN EVERETT MILLAIS, *Ophelia*, 1852. Oil on canvas, 30" × 44". Tate Gallery, London.

Her clothes spread wide,
And mermaidlike awhile they bore her up—
Which time she chanted snatches of old tunes,
As one incapable of her own distress.
(IV.vii.176–79)

Attempting to make the pathos of the scene visible, Millais became a faithful and feeling witness of its every detail, reconstructing it with a circumstantial stagecraft worthy of the original poetry. While Millais's technique is Realistic, the orthodox Realist would complain that the subject is not—that it is playacting. Yet it is unlikely that an impartial observer of the painting familiar with Hamlet would object that, as the subject is not of the artist's time and place, it is, of necessity, deficient in truth. It is certainly not deficient in truth to appearance. It may be that this conflict between the seen (in everyday experience) and the seeable (implausible reconstructions of fictitious or past events) is resolved in modern cinema. The kind of picture drama we have in *Ophelia,* which brings the fictive action of a nonpictorial medium before our eyes with all optical fidelity, anticipates the dramatic motion pictures in which fictions and facts are presented to the eye as equally real. Nineteenth-century Realists might have objected that the picture-drama was not painting, but stage production, and could only be judged as such.

A younger member of the Pre-Raphaelite Brotherhood, EDWARD BURNE-JONES (1833–1898) was one of the many painters during this period who did not accept Realism in terms of either subject or technique. A friend and protégé of John Ruskin and an associate of William Morris and Dante Gabriel Rossetti, (who, as we shall see in our discussion of Manet, slurred the work of the Realists), Burne-Jones agreed with their distaste for the materialism and ugliness of the contemporary, industrializing world and shared their appreciation for the spirituality and idealism (as well as the art and craftsmanship) of past times, especially the Middle Ages and the Early Renaissance. Like Millais, Burne-Jones drew his subjects from literature, but he chose to depict them in a soft, languid style much influenced by Sandro Botticelli (FIG. 21-57). Burne-Jones's *King Cophetua and the Beggar Maid* (FIG. **26-50**) illustrates a poem of the same name, written by Alfred Tennyson in 1842, which itself was a modern reworking of an ancient and popular ballad. The situation is given in the last lines:

> *So sweet a face, such angel grace,*
> *In all that land had never been:*
> *Cophetua sware a royal oath:*
> *"This beggar maid shall be my queen!"*

The king, in grave reverie, contemplates the maiden, who sits serenely above him, like some pedestaled perfection oblivious to mortal presence. Although Burne-Jones insisted that he wanted the maid to resemble a beggar, she does not. Like the atmosphere, she belongs to the world of trance and dream, in which images arise from some lost age of beauty and innocence. The composition, planar and still, recalls the mural tableau of the Renaissance, the suspended action of stained glass and tapestry. Burne-Jones's dreamy, decorative manner was perfectly suited to the somewhat precious, estheticizing taste of the later nineteenth century. How far we are here from Realism, as well as the great diversity of style at the time, can be appreciated if we compare Burne-Jones's beggar maid with Manet's barmaid (FIG. 26-56) especially if we consider that the two paintings were completed only two years apart.

In the age of Courbet and of the Romanticism of ideal form, the authority of the Tradition could still command artistic obedience. Only slightly touched by the influence of Courbet in Paris, ANSELM FEUERBACH (1829–1880) found in Italy, as did so many of his German compatriots, the age-old inspiration of Renaissance and Classical antiquity. A longtime resident of Rome, he was under the spell of Raphael when he painted the *Medea* (FIG. **26-51**). Here, Feuerbach gives us not the climax of the tragedy but its quiet prologue. Jason and his argonauts set out to find the Golden Fleece, while Medea, not foreseeing his faithlessness, embraces the children whom she will later kill. The grieving nurse has a premonition of the disaster to come. Yet nothing disturbs the calm of the composition, in which the Classicism of Raphael is enhanced by Feuerbach's study of ancient sculpture. The conception of the figure of Medea is in the spirit of the reclining goddess from the east pediment of the Parthenon (FIG. 5-53). In this picture, more than in any of his others, Feuerbach realizes his stated ideal: a "truly majestic, forbidding tranquillity," a Classicism aristocratic and aloof.

In the painting of ADOLPHE-WILLIAM BOUGUEREAU (1825–1905), Realism was blended with a very different kind of Classicism. Bouguereau depicted Classical, mythological subjects with a dynamic Rococo exuberance of composition and an optical Realism that achieved a startling illusionism, as in his *Nymphs and Satyr* (FIG. **26-52**), where the playful and ideally beautiful nymphs strike graceful poses, yet seem based as closely on nature as are the details of their leafy surroundings. The painter even created the figure of his mythical beast-man by combining Realist

26-50 EDWARD BURNE-JONES, *King Cophetua and the Beggar Maid,* 1884. Oil on canvas, approx. 9′7″ × 4′5″. Tate Gallery, London.

26-51 ANSELM FEUERBACH, *Medea*, 1870. Oil on canvas, 6'6" × 13'. Bayerische Staatsgemäldesammlungen, Munich.

depictions of a goat's hind quarters and horns and a horse's ears and tail with the upper body of a man.

A painting like this presses the question of whether the subjects of myth, fancy, and fiction could be painted with the techniques of Realism without evoking incredulity and, perhaps, a sense of absurdity in the observer. For the Classicist, Bouguereau's *Nymphs and Satyr* would fail to fulfill a longing "for nothing more than the moment in which conception and representation will flow together." The Realist would find the picture false due to the incongruence of its form and content and the unrealistic nature of its subject. The obvious conflict of conception and representation in many of Bouguereau's pictures, as well as in those of other recognized artists of the time, did not displease the public. Bouguereau was immensely popular, enjoying the favor of state patronage throughout his career. His reputation has fluctuated violently; the moderns of his century damned him as the very archetype of the official painter, but critics of our own day acknowledge his love of beauty and his undeniable painterly skills, if not always his esthetic wisdom and taste.

In a balance of Realist style and Romantic subjects, JULES BASTIEN-LEPAGE (1848–1884) makes the perfect compromise. His *Joan of Arc* (FIG. **26-53**) represents the inspired heroine of France in the garden of her parents' humble cottage. She hearkens, entranced, to her hovering saints, Michael, Katherine, and Margaret—who announce her mission to save her country from the English enemy. The saints appear as dim apparitions in the trees at the upper left; Joan is off-center at the right. The informal arrangement—the continuing, inclusive space cropped accidentally by the frame—is, as we shall presently see, characteristic of Impressionistic composition, which seeks to catch the casual, the informal, the unposed "snapshot." It is as if we

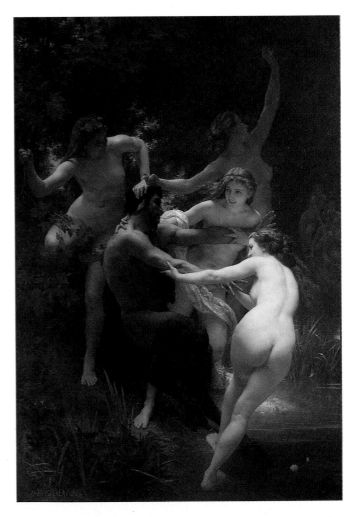

26-52 ADOLPHE WILLIAM BOUGUEREAU, *Nymphs and Satyr*, 1873. Oil on canvas, approx. 8'6" high. Clark Institute, Williamstown, Massachusetts.

have come on the saint suddenly and unannounced. Although the figure is farther away from us and the optical manifold (all the details within the frame) is more sharply focused than in Manet's *Bar at the Folies-Bergère* (FIG. 26-56), the profusion of evenly stressed detail, spread flatly across the picture plane, is closely comparable. If the saints were eliminated and the situation and dress made contemporary, the Realist could have little to complain of. In Bastien-Lepage's *Joan of Arc,* the stylistic paths of Romanticism and Realism run together; the disagreement could only be about the subject: is it "modern" or not? Here, the dialogue-like exchanges between Romanticism and Realism seem to end, at least, in an agreement about form. But do they? We have seen that many artists rejected Realism altogether, and some compromised with it. Still others will follow the Realist premise to its conclusion. These are the Impressionists, whom we shall examine shortly, and their point of departure is the art of Manet.

Photography, the artificial eye, the medium created to serve the taste for visual fact, for realistic report of the world, was itself the creator of a new realism. But it could also be manipulated by talented photographers to produce quite Romantic effects. After the first great breakthroughs, which bluntly showed what was before the eye, photographers imitated Romantic arrangements of nature, filtering natural appearance through sentiment—soft-focusing it, as it were. In the later century, with much public approval, photography had a Romantic-Realist school of its own. The photographers thought of it as a "pictorial" method.

One of the leading practitioners of the *Pictorial* style in photography was the American GERTRUDE KÄSEBIER (1852–1934). Käsebier took up photography in 1897 after raising a family and working as a portrait painter. She soon became famous for photographs with symbolic themes, such as *Blessed Art Thou among Women* (FIG. **26-54**). The title repeats the phrase used in the New Testament by the angel Gabriel to announce to the Virgin Mary that she will be the mother of Jesus. In the context of Käsebier's photography, the words suggest a parallel between the biblical "Mother of God" and the modern mother in the image, who both protects and sends forth her daughter. The white setting and the mother's pale gown shimmer in soft focus behind the

26-53 JULES BASTIEN-LEPAGE, *Joan of Arc,* 1880. Oil on canvas, 8'4" × 9'2". The Metropolitan Museum of Art, New York (gift of Erwin Davis, 1889).

Realism

serious figure of the girl, who is dressed in darker tones and captured with sharper focus. Here, as in her other works, Käsebier was influenced by Peter Henry Emerson's ideas about naturalism in photography, but deliberately ignored his teachings about different focus in favor of achieving an "expressive" effect by blurring the entire image slightly. In *Blessed Art Thou,* the whole scene is invested with an aura of otherworldly peace by the soft focus, the appearance of the centered figures, the vertical framing doors, and the relationship between the frontally posed girl and her gracefully bending mother. As one contemporary critic wrote: "The manner in which modern dress was handled, subordinated, and made to play its proper part in the composi-

tion . . . evidenced great artistic feeling."* *Blessed Art Thou* is a superb example of Käsebier's moving ability to invest scenes from everyday life with a sense of their connection to the realm of the spirit and the divine.

Impressionists: Optical Reality and Color Functions

The Realism of Courbet and his followers had hardly established one kind of Realism before a different version, leading away from Courbet, took its place. In the fall of 1864, the English painter Dante Gabriel Rosetti wrote home describing French Realism as he had seen it in visits to the studios of Courbet and Manet: "There is a man named Manet . . . whose pictures are for the most part mere scrawls, and who seems to be one of the lights of the Realist school. Courbet, the head of it, is not much better." This somewhat priggish dismissal of Courbet and Manet linked the differences between them. Courbet, himself, said of Manet's work in 1867: "I myself shouldn't like to meet this young man. . . . I should be obliged to tell him I don't understand anything about his paintings, and I don't want to be disagreeable to him."

Manet   It was with Édouard Manet (1832–1883), however, that the course of modern painting shifted into a new phase, one that, in addition to recording with accuracy the appearance of the physical world, had as its aim the authentic representation of the color and light that reveal that world to the eye. In his work, Manet, the Realist, became the point of departure for the later Impressionist transformation of the tradition in painting that had begun with Giotto.

Although the term *Impressionism* was first used in 1874 by a journalist ridiculing a landscape by Monet called *Impression—Sunrise,* the battle over the merits of Impressionist painting began eleven years earlier with Manet's *Le Déjeuner sur l'herbe,* or *Luncheon on the Grass,* (FIG. **26-55**). In 1863, Manet exhibited this then-controversial painting at the Salon des Refusés (Salon of the Rejected) in Paris. As the name suggests, the exhibit consisted of a large number of works rejected by the jury for the major Academy Salon that year. The Academy Salons were government-subsidized arbiters of French art—"warehouses," as Émile Zola called them—where the artists of France annually exhibited thousands of canvases. Prizes or recognition at the Salon could ensure professional success; refusal or rejection often led to neglect or failure. The Salon, at least until the 1880s, was the field of intense pro-

*Joseph T. Keiley, "Mrs. Käsebier's Prints," *Camera Notes* (July, 1899), in Robert A. Sobieszak, *Masterpieces of Photography from the George Eastman House Collection* (Rochester, NY: International Museum of Photography, 1985), p. 214.

fessional competition among artists and the battleground of "modern" versus "traditional." Ironically, it was a public seeking the avant-garde at the Salon des Refusés that was shocked by Manet's *Le Déjeuner sur l'herbe,* originally titled simply *The Bath.*

Manet may have been "a child of the century," as Zola called him in praise of his daring modernity, but he did not care to isolate himself as such. Instead, he wished to shine in the Salon with works (preferably figure paintings) as strong as the masterpieces of the Tradition. In *Le Déjeuner,* Manet does not attempt to revive "great painting," but tries to speak in a new voice and with an authority equal to that of his celebrated predecessors. The source of the work is proper enough; it takes as its theme the pastoral paradise familiar in paintings from Giorgione to Watteau. We know that at first Manet had Giorgione's (and Titian's?) *Pastoral Symphony* (FIG. 22-58) in mind as the source for *Le Déjeuner,* but for the actual composition, he used an engraving by Marcantonio Raimondi, a pupil of Raphael. Manet also may have been mindful of Baudelaire's observation (made as early as 1845) that "we are surrounded by the heroism of modern life, [but there is as yet no painter] who will know how to tear out of life its epic side and make us see, with color or drawing, how grand we are in our neckties and varnished boots!"

Nothing about the foreground figures in *Le Déjeuner* is very heroic. In fact, the foreground figures were all based on living, identifiable people. The seated nude was Victorine Meurend (Manet's favorite model at the time) and the gentlemen were his brother Eugène (with cane) and the sculptor Ferdinand Leenhof. The two men wear fashionable Parisian attire of the 1860s, and the foreground nude is not only a distressingly unidealized figure type, but she seems disturbingly unabashed and at ease, looking directly at the viewer without shame or flirtatiousness.

This outraged the public—the pastoral brought up to date in a manner that seemed merely to represent the promiscuous in a Parisian park. One hostile critic, no doubt voicing public opinion, said:

> A commonplace woman of the demimonde, as naked as can be, shamelessly lolls between two dandies dressed to the teeth. These latter look like schoolboys on a holiday, perpetrating an outrage to play the man. . . . This is a young man's practical joke—a shameful, open sore.*

Manet's work would have been accepted had he shown men and women as nymphs and satyrs in Classical dress or

*In G. H. Hamilton, *Manet and His Critics* (New Haven, CT: Yale University Press, 1954), p. 45.

26-55 ÉDOUARD MANET, *Le Déjeuner sur l'herbe (Luncheon on the Grass),* 1863. Oil on canvas, approx. 7′ × 8′10″. Musée d'Orsay, Paris.

undress, as did his contemporary Bouguereau (FIG. 26-52). In *Le Déjeuner,* Manet raised the veils of allusion and reverie, and bluntly confronted the public with reality.

The public and the critics disliked Manet's subject matter only slightly less than the method he used to present his figures. The landscape and the background pool, in which the second woman bathes, are rendered in soft focus and broadly painted compared to the clear forms of the harshly lit trio of figures in the foreground and the pile of discarded female attire and picnic foods at the lower left. The lighting displays the strong contrasts between darks and highlighted areas found in many contemporaneous photographs. In the main figures, the middle values, so carefully observed and recorded by Corot, and even Courbet, are blotted out; in a "crowding of the lights" and a compensating "crowding of the darks," many values are summed up in one or two lights or darks. The effect is both to flatten the form and to give it a hard, snapping presence,

similar to that in early photographs. Manet's use of broadly painted tones was a method that he learned primarily from Velázquez and Frans Hals. The paint directly reports what is given to the eye, without any presuppositions of form, structure, or contour. Form, here no longer a matter of line, is only a function of paint and light. Manet himself declared that the chief actor in the painting is the light. The public and the critics, guardians of public taste, knew nothing of this. They saw only a crude sketch without the customary "finish."

Manet's masterpiece, *A Bar at the Folies-Bergère* (FIG. **26-56**), was painted in 1882, after the artist had become associated with the Impressionists. This work shows both an impersonality toward the subject and Manet's fascination with the effects of light spilling from the gas globes onto the figures and the objects around them. In this study of artificial light (both direct light and that reflected in the mirrored background), the artist tells us little about the bar-

26-56 ÉDOUARD MANET, *A Bar at the Folies-Bergère,* 1882. Oil on canvas, approx. 37" × 51". The Courtauld Institute Galleries, London.

maid* and less about her customers, but much about the optical experience of this momentary pattern of light, in which the barmaid is only another motif—another still life amid the bottles on the counter. The painting tells no story, and has no moral, no plot, and no stage direction; it is simply an optical event, an arrested moment, in which lighted shapes of one kind or another participate. One is reminded of the novels of Manet's friend Zola, especially of *Nana,* whose heroine is nothing but a meaningless human consequence of the intersecting of social forces that create and destroy her. The barmaid in Manet's painting is primarily a compositional device—automatic and nonpersonal. (Some contemporary art historians would argue this.)

The *Folies-Bergère* illustrates another quality that first made its appearance in *Le Déjeuner sur l'herbe* and was to loom with increasing importance in the works of later paintings. Although the effect was perhaps unplanned, Manet's painting made a radical break with the Tradition by redefining the function of the picture surface. Ever since the Renaissance, the picture had been conceived as a "window" through which the viewer looked at an illusory space developed behind it. By minimizing the effects of modeling and perspective, Manet forced the viewer to look at the painted surface and to recognize it once more as a flat plane covered with patches of pigment. This "revolution of the color patch," combined with Manet's cool, objective approach, pointed painting in the direction of abstraction, with its indifference to subject matter and its emphasis on optical sensations and the problems of organizing them into form. In most nonobjective twentieth-century work, not only the subject matter, but even its supposed visual manifestation in the external world, will disappear.

Throughout his career, Manet suffered the hostility of the critics as surrogates of the public. This attitude wounded him deeply. He never understood their animosity and continued to seek their approval, but the doses of the real that he administered in art were too harsh. His contemporary, the philosopher and historian Ernest Renan, expressed the real moral threat some of the public feared from the new realism in art:

> It is possible, then, that the ruin of idealistic beliefs is destined to follow the destruction of supernatural beliefs, and that a real abasement of human morality dates from *the day it saw the reality of things* [emphasis added].†

Though Manet was much admired by the Impressionist painters, whom we shall presently be considering, he remained aloof from them, and refused to take part in their exhibitions, preferring to take his chances at the Salon, where he was now coming to have some success. But

he would likely have been in agreement with the views of Edmund Duranty, who defended the Impressionists' second exhibition in 1876. In his review entitled "The New Painting . . ." Duranty observed that the first "idea, was to take away the partition separating the studio from everyday life. . . . Farewell to the human body treated like the vase. . . . What we need is the particular note of the modern individual in his clothing, in the midst of his social habits, at home or in the street."*

MORISOT AND CAILLEBOTTE   Duranty's concept of the "New Painting" could hardly be better realized than in the work of BERTHE MORISOT (1841–1895), the sister-in-law of Manet (and granddaughter of Fragonard!). Though she was a pupil of Corot and responsive to his respect for "values," she was principally influenced by Manet, though, unlike him, she regularly exhibited with the Impressionists. The open brushwork and the *plein-air* (out-of-doors) lighting characteristic of Impressionism appear in her *Villa at the Seaside* (FIG. **26-57**), in which she answers the "New Painting"'s call for an image of everyday life separate from the studio. The setting is the shaded veranda of a summer hotel at a fashionable shore resort. A woman elegantly but quietly dressed sits gazing out across the railing to a sunlit beach with its umbrellas and bathing cabins. Her child, its discarded toy boat a splash of red, is attentive to the passing sails on the placid sea. The railing makes a compositionally important downward diagonal, framing people casually ascending the stair. The figures fall informally into place, as they would in a random snapshot taken by someone who shares their intimate space. Whether at the seaside, the park, the racetrack, the café, or on the boulevard, well-to-do people at their leisure are the subjects of the "New Painting."

Morisot's brushwork is telegraphic in its report of her quick perceptions; everything is suggested by swift, sketchy strokes, and nowhere is there a lingering on contours or enclosed details. It is all in a slightly filmy soft focus that conveys a feeling of airiness quite distinct from the atmosphere of the studio, which still lingers in the painting of Manet. Among the Impressionists she is unsurpassed in catching the instantaneous pictorial moment and in her spontaneous rendering of it.

Another member of the Impressionist group, GUSTAVE CAILLEBOTTE (1849–93), snaps yet another scene in his *Paris: A Rainy Day* (FIG. **26-58**). His setting is a junction of spacious boulevards of the kind that Baron Haussmann (a French administrator who inaugurated and carried through huge municipal improvements in Paris) built. These great avenues, for the construction of which thousands of ancient buildings and streets were demolished, transformed

---

*Or is it *barmaids*? A lively debate currently rages about whether Manet has depicted two different girls or just one girl and her reflection.

†In J. C. Sloane, *French Painting between the Past and the Present* (Princeton, NJ: Princeton University Press, 1951), p. 57.

*In Linda Nochlin, *Impressionism and Post-Impressionism 1874–1904* (Englewood Cliffs, NJ: Prentice-Hall, 1966). *Sources and Documents in the History of Art*, ed., H. W. Janson, p. 5.

26-57 BERTHE MORISOT, *Villa at the Seaside*, 1874. Oil on canvas, approx. 20″ × 24″. Norton Simon Art Foundation, Los Angeles.

26-58 GUSTAVE CAILLEBOTTE, *Paris: A Rainy Day*, 1877. Oil on canvas, approx. 6′9″ × 9′9″. The Art Institute of Chicago, Worcester Fund.

medieval Paris into the present modern city, with its superb vistas, and wide, uninterrupted arteries for the flow of vehicular and pedestrian traffic.

The composition of the picture is deliberately informal and asymmetrical, the figures randomly placed, with the frame cropping them arbitrarily as they would be if caught momentarily by a camera's shutter. Well-dressed Parisians of the leisure class share the space of the viewer. Viewer and subjects all participate in the same weather, which the painter carefully indicates, not only by the umbrellas, but by the wet cobblestones, puddles, and faint reflections that blend into the monochromatic tonality of a gray day. This is the outdoor painting of everyday life that Duranty and the leading progressive spirits of the time called for. Caillebotte has not yet dissolved the camera-like impression into the broken color and brushwork characteristic of Impressionist practice, but in the apparently chance arrangement of his figures, their motion suspended in a moment already passed, Caillebotte's picture is certainly an "impression."

Caillebotte was independently wealthy and was able to purchase many works from his sometimes penniless colleagues. On his death in 1893 he embarrassed the government by bequeathing it his collection of Impressionist paintings. This caused great indignation among the academic painters. Gérôme, speaking to the École des Beaux Arts, declared it immoral of the government to accept "such filth." That was indeed a Romantic response to Realism, at least to Realism in Impressionist development!

DEGAS In any discussion of Impressionism, the name of EDGAR DEGAS (1834–1917) is usually included. Although actively sympathetic with the Impressionists, he stood somewhat apart from them, an independent talent of great power. More than any of his contemporaries, Degas studied the infinite variety of particular movements and, even more, the kinesthetic qualities of bodies in motion—especially racehorses, bathers, laundresses, milliners, and ballet dancers.

Like Caillebotte, he took to the boulevards to watch the pedestrians, to catch the chance arrangements, the shifting patterns of their motion, which the frame crops as they pass. His *Viscount Lepic and His Daughters* (FIG. **26-59**), summarizes what the artist had learned from photography, from his own painstaking research, and from what his generation in general absorbed from the Japanese print: the clear, flat pattern; the unusual point of view; the informal glimpse of contemporary life. Whatever his subject, Degas saw it in terms of clear line and pattern, observed from a new and unexpected angle. In the divergent movements of the father and his small daughters, of the man entering the picture at the left, and of the horse and carriage passing across the background, we have a vivid pictorial account of a moment in time at a particular position in space, much as Monet, in his own way, would define such space and time in landscape painting. In another instant, this picture would disappear, for each of the figures would move in a different direction, and the group would dissolve. Here again, Degas, like Caillebotte, makes clever use of the street to integrate the viewer into the space containing the figures. Actually, the painter seems to have taken into account the range of the sweep of our glance—everything that we would see in the single split-second inspection; indeed, the

26-59 EDGAR DEGAS, *Viscount Lepic and His Daughters*, 1873. Oil on canvas, approx. 32" × 47". The Hermitage, St. Petersburg.

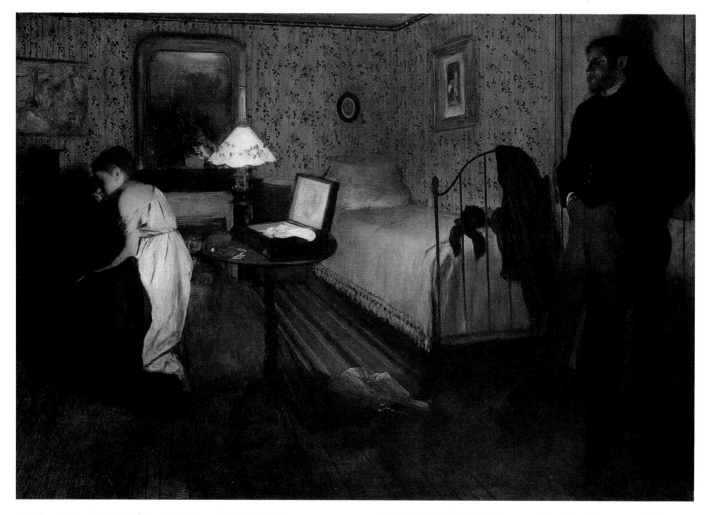

26-60 EDGAR DEGAS, *Intérieur (Le Viol), c.* 1868–1870. Oil on canvas, approx. 32″ × 45″. Philadelphia Museum of Art: The Henry P. McIlhenny Collection.

picture resembles a snapshot made with a hastily aimed camera.

A painting of his early middle period, *Interieur (Le Viol)* (FIG. **26-60**), invades a bedroom with penetrating realism, where a man and woman appear in unhappy conflict. This is a picture from a time when literature and drama, as well as art, are seeking to analyze and present the peculiarly modern view of human relationships, especially the tensions between the sexes: the novels and stories of Flaubert, de Maupassant, Zola, and Henry James, the plays of Ibsen and Chekhov. Some believe that a novel by Zola, *Thérèse Racquin* (1867), provided the program for Degas's painting. The picture has been said to be deliberately ambiguous in its refusal to admit of any single meaning or "story," and at least one critic has concluded that, if anything, it is meant to force the viewer to enter it, and suffer voyeuristic guilt for witnessing, and intruding upon, a very private affair. At this point, narrative painting is supposed to shed its "subject," and leave itself forever open to interpretation. In any event, it is one thing to introduce us to the public world

of the boulevard and to share its space with the citizens, as do both Caillebotte and Degas; it is quite another to make us witness and take us into the space of a painful scene. More than a century later, the modern moving picture will do precisely that.

Whatever art historians believe the "subject" is (*le viol* means rape), the picture manifests Degas's awareness of contemporary science in its studies of human behavior. Like Manet, Degas was a member of the upper class and a cultivated man of the world, conversant with the ideas of the day; like both Manet and Zola—who championed the Impressionists—he would be interested in the causes that positivist science now saw as determining the way we behave—biological, sociological, and psychological forces in the heredity and environment of every human individual. Human emotions in Zola's, and presumably, in Degas's view, are akin to physiological or even pathological symptoms: love, hate, desire, anxiety, frustration, alienation, and despair are the results of hidden, psychic mechanisms within an irrational or subrational nature. In light of these con-

26-61 EDGAR DEGAS, *Ballet Rehearsal (Adagio)*, 1876. Oil on canvas, 23″ × 33″. Glasgow Museum: The Burrell Collection.

cepts, which foreshadow the work of Freud, the Realist-as-Degas studies human behavior—as movement—dispassionately, like a clinician in a laboratory. The persons of *Interieur* are entirely unaware that they are being observed by us. This is the case in almost all of Degas's work.

Degas's fascination with the patterns of motion brought him to the Paris Opéra and its school for ballet. Here his great power of observation took in the formalized movements of the classical ballet, one of his favorite subjects. In *Ballet Rehearsal (Adagio)* (FIG. **26-61**), Degas used several devices to bring the observer into the pictorial space: the frame cuts off the spiral stair, the windows in the background, and the group of figures in the right foreground; the figures are uncentered and "accidental" in arrangement; the rapid diagonals of the wall bases and floorboards carry us into and along the directional lines of the dancers; and, as is customary in Degas's ballet pictures, a large, off-center, empty space creates the illusion of a continuous floor that connects us with the pictured figures. By seeming to stand on the same surface with them, we are drawn into their space. The often arbitrarily cutoff figures in this and other works by Degas reveal his fascination with photography. He not only studied the photography of others, but he used the camera consistently himself to make preliminary studies for his own works, particularly with figures in interiors. The cunning spatial projection in *Ballet Rehearsal* probably derived not only from careful observation and the artist's interest in photography, but was also undoubtedly inspired by eighteenth-century Japanese woodblock prints, such as this one by SUZUKI HARUNOBU (1724–1778) (FIG. **26-62**), in which diverging lines not only organize the

26-62 SUZUKI HARUNOBU, *The Evening Glow of the Ando*, c. 1766. Woodblock print, 11¼″ × 8½″. The Art Institute of Chicago (Clarence Buckingham Collection).

flat shapes of the figures but also function to direct the viewer's attention into the picture space. The Impressionists, familiar with these prints as early as the 1860s, greatly admired their spatial organization, the familiar and intimate themes, and the flat, unmodeled color areas, and drew much instruction from them. These popular Japanese prints, "discovered" by European artists in the mid-nineteenth century, were the first definitive non-European influence on European pictorial design. Earlier borrowings from China, India, and Arabia had been superficial.

When Degas was a very young man and about to enter into a career as a painter, he met Ingres, whose work he greatly admired and who advised him to "draw lines . . . many lines, from memory or from nature; it is this way that you will become a good painter." Degas, faithful to the old linearist's advice, became a superb master of line, so much so that his identification as an Impressionist, in the sense that, as we shall see, Monet, Pissarro, and Renoir are Impressionists, seems a mistake to many critics. Certainly, Degas's designs do not cling to the surface of the canvas, as do Manet's and Monet's; they are developed in depth and take the viewer well behind the picture plane. We are always aware of the elastic strength of his firmly drawn contours. However, Degas did specialize in studies of figures in rapid and informal movement, recording the quick impression of arrested motion, and he did use the spectral color—the fresh, divided hues of the Impressionists—especially when he worked in his favorite medium, pastel. These dry sticks of powdered pigment cannot be "muddied" by mixing them on a palette, so they produce, almost automatically, those fresh and bright colors so favored by the Impressionists. All of these qualities are seen in *The Morning Bath* (FIG. **26-63**), which is like Renoir's treatment of the same subject (not illustrated) in its informality and intimacy, but unlike Renoir's work in its indifference to either formal or physical beauty. Degas's concern was with the unplanned realism of the purely accidental attitude of the human figure, seen in an awkward yet natural enough moment. The broken volume of the nude body twists across "Japanese" angles, flat planes, and patterns (FIG. 26-62). The informality and spontaneity of the pose again suggest snapshot photography, but photographic materials available at the time (including those of the motion picture, then just in its infancy) could not capture the range of light and the verity of motion that Degas sought to depict above all else.

In the Salon of 1874, Degas admired a painting by a young American artist, MARY CASSATT (1844–1926), the daughter of a Philadelphia banker. "There," he remarked, "is a person who feels as I do." Cassatt was befriended and influenced by Degas and exhibited regularly with the Impressionists. She had trained as a painter before moving to Europe to study masterworks in France and Italy. Her

26-63   EDGAR DEGAS, *The Morning Bath, c.* 1883. Pastel on paper, 27³/₄″ × 17″. The Art Institute of Chicago (Potter Palmer Collection).

choice of subject matter was limited by the facts that, as a woman, she could not easily frequent the cafés with her male artist friends, and that she was responsible for the care of her aging parents, who had moved to Paris to join her. Because of these restrictions, Cassatt's subjects were principally women and children, whom she presented with an inimitable conjunction of objectivity and genuine sentiment. Works like *The Bath* (FIG. **26-64**) show the tender relationship between a mother and child. The mother's torso shelters the child against the diagonal slope of her lap. Color binds mother, child, and wash basin into one central form that is pushed against the flattened space of the darker-hued rug, wallpaper, and bureau by placement of the remarkably solid jug at the lower right. Cassatt's style in this work owed much to the compositional devices of Degas and of Japanese prints, but the painting's design has an originality and strength all its own.

OTHER IMPRESSIONISTS   After the mid-1860s, Impressionist painters such as Monet, Pissarro, and Renoir followed Manet's lead in depicting scenes of contemporary middle-class Parisian life and landscape. Their desire for a more modern expression led them to prize the immediacy of visual impression and persuaded the landscapists, especially Monet, to work out-of-doors. From this custom of painting directly from nature came the spontaneous representation of atmosphere and climate so characteristic of Impressionist painting. The rejection of idealistic interpretation and literary anecdote was paralleled by an intense scrutiny of color and light. Scientific studies of light and the invention of chemical pigments increased artistic sensitivity to the multiplicity of colors in nature and gave artists new colors with which to work.* Most of the eight cooperative Impressionist exhibitions held between 1874 and 1886 irritated the public. However, Impressionist technique was actually less radical than it seemed at the time; in certain respects, these artists were simply developing the color theories of Leonardo and the actual practice of Rubens, Delacroix, Constable, and Turner.

The Impressionists sought to create the illusion of forms bathed in light and atmosphere. This goal required an intensive study of outdoor light as the source of our experience of color, which revealed the important truth that local color—the actual color of an object—is usually modified by the quality of the light in which it is seen, by reflections from other objects, and by the effects produced by juxtaposed colors. Shadows do not appear gray or black, as many earlier painters thought, but seem to be composed of colors modified by reflections or other conditions. (One earlier artist, Vermeer, evidently observed this.) In painting, if complementary colors are used side by side over large enough areas, they intensify each other, unlike the effect of small quantities of mixed pigments, which blend into neutral tones. Furthermore, the juxtaposition of colors on a canvas for the eye to fuse at a distance produces a more intense hue than the mixing of the same colors on the palette. Although it is not strictly true that the Impressionists used only primary hues, juxtaposing them to create secondary colors (blue and yellow, for example, to create green), they did achieve remarkably brilliant effects with their characteristically short, choppy brush strokes, which so accurately caught the vibrating quality of light.

*Special luminance was achieved by using new pigment colors like viridian green and cobalt violet (both invented in 1859) and cerulean blue (invented in 1860). These pigments, applied with newly available flat-bound brushes, often were placed on the canvases covered with a base of white pigment (white ground), rather than with the brown or green tones favored by earlier artists.

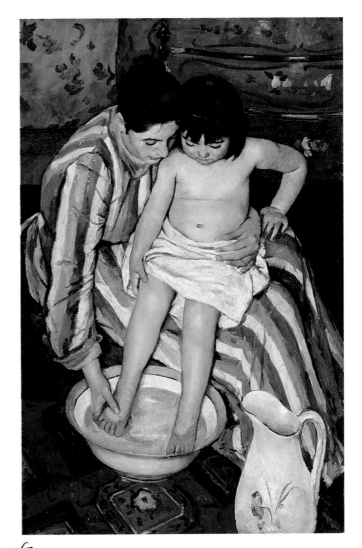

26-64   MARY CASSATT, *The Bath, c.* 1892. Oil on canvas, 39" × 26". The Art Institute of Chicago, Robert A. Walker Fund.

The fact that the surfaces of their canvases look unintelligible at close range and their forms and objects appear only when the eye fuses the strokes at a certain distance accounts for much of the early adverse criticism leveled at their work, such as the conjecture that the Impressionists fired their paint at the canvas with pistols.

Of the Impressionists, CLAUDE MONET (1840–1926), whose *Impression—Sunrise* was mentioned earlier, carried the color method furthest. Monet called color his "day-long obsession, joy and torment." One among many successful results of his obsession with color is the huge canvas *Luncheon (Decorative Panel)* (FIG. **26-65**). A blaze of light, vibrating with granules of spectral color, transmute a suburban garden into a sunburst, the picture giving off its own light. The radically eccentric composition places two ladies at the extreme upper right, and a small boy (the artist's son Jean), at the extreme lower left, almost invisible in the

26-65   CLAUDE MONET, *Luncheon (Decorative Panel)*, 1874. Oil on canvas, approx. 5'3" × 6'7". Musée d'Orsay, Paris.

bright glow from the tea-table cloth. The luminous space that opens up between the figures is a field for the play of color particles, seeming to gather into light, then dissipate. That spacious area joins the space of the observer, placing us in the garden; we have seen this framing device used by Caillebotte and Degas, but it is a constant in all Impressionist design. The space is continuous beyond the frame, and time is framed into this very moment. Monet is like a scientist, eagerly experimenting with the properties of some newly discovered phenomenon; for Monet the phenomenon is color, and his laboratory is out-of-doors (*plein-air*). In this instance, it is his garden at Argenteuil, where he often painted in the company of Manet and Renoir.

But the apparition of color challenged him everywhere: gardens, fields in bloom, cloud-mottled skies, rivers with sailboats, seaside resorts, rocky coasts. For him these are not things but color aggregates that have to be perceived, their relationships understood, and then recreated by the artist's brush. Lila Cabot Perry, a student of Monet's late in his career, gave this description of his approach:

I remember his once saying to me: "When you go out to paint, try to forget what objects you have before you—a tree, a house, a field, or whatever. Merely think, here is a little square of blue, here an oblong of pink, here a streak of yellow and paint it just as it looks to you, the exact color and shape, until it gives your own naïve impression of the scene before you." He said he wished he had been born blind and then had suddenly gained his sight so that he could have begun to paint in this way without knowing what the objects were that he saw before him.*

Monet's contribution was especially evident in several series of paintings of the same subject. He painted sixteen views of Waterloo Bridge in London and some forty views of Rouen Cathedral (FIG. **26-66** and Introduction FIG. 5). In each canvas in the latter series, the cathedral was observed from the same point of view but at different times of the day or under various climatic conditions. Monet, with a scientific precision, created an unparalleled and unexcelled

*In Linda Nochlin, *Impressionism and Post-Impressionism 1874–1904* (Englewood Cliffs, NJ: Prentice-Hall, 1966), p. 35.

26-66 CLAUDE MONET, *Rouen Cathedral: The Portal (in Sun)*, 1894. Oil on canvas, approx. 39" × 26". The Metropolitan Museum of Art, New York (Theodore M. Davis Collection, bequest of Theodore M. Davis, 1915).

record of the passing of time as seen in the movement of light over identical forms. Later critics accused Monet and his companions of destroying form and order for the sake of fleeting atmospheric effects, but we may feel that light is properly the "form" of Monet's finest paintings, rather than accept the narrower definition that recognizes "formal" properties only in firm, geometric shapes. The Impressionist artists ignored much that was prized by the Realists—the world of Corot's "values," of graduated tones of lights and darks; rather, the Impressionists recorded their own sensations of color, and the outlines and solidities of the world as interpreted by common sense melt away.

The Impressionist emphasis on the prime reality of sensation in the process of apprehending nature or the world had its parallel in the work of contemporaneous scientists, philosophers of science, and psychologists who asserted that reality is sensation and that knowledge could be based only on the analysis of our sensations. Artists who shared the belief that a single, accepted model of unchanging optical truth no longer existed—just as a standard way of seeing could not be mandated—considered "nature," in the broadest sense of whatever the world reveals, to be the source of all sensation. In the *Place du Théâtre Français* (FIG. **26-67**), CAMILLE PISSARRO (1830–1903) records a panorama of blurred, dark accents against a light ground that represents clearly the artist's visual sensations of a crowded Paris square, viewed from several stories above street level. Like Monet, Pissarro sought to depict the fugitive effects of light at a particular moment, but the moment in Pissarro's *Place du Théâtre*, unlike those in Monet's work, is not so much one of light itself as of the life of the street, achieved through a deliberate casualness in the arrangement of his figures that is related to that in early photographs of street scenes. When Pissarro wrote in a letter to his son Lucien, "we have to approach nature sincerely, with our own modern sensibilities," he spoke of the Impressionist belief that what was real in nature was the light and color stimuli it revealed to the analytic eye of the modern painter.

Like many of his fellow Impressionists, Pissarro sometimes used the amazing "reality" of photography to supplement work directly from a model. Although he may not have known this particular example, the effect of Pissarro's *Place du Théâtre* is remarkably similar to that in the *stereo photograph** *The Pont Neuf, Paris* (FIG. **26-68**) by HIPPOLYTE JOUVIN (active mid-1800s). In this stereograph, we look from the upper story of a building along the roadway of the "New Bridge," which stretches diagonally from lower left to upper right. Hurrying pedestrian figures become dark silhouettes, and the scene moves from sharp focus in the foreground to soft focus in the distance. These qualities, plus

Stereo photographs were made with special twin-lensed cameras and viewed with special apparatus to recreate the illusion of seeing the world with two eyes (in three dimensions).

26-67   CAMILLE PISSARRO, *Place du Théatre Français*, 1895. Oil on canvas, approx. 28^1/$_2$″ × 36^1/$_2$″. Los Angeles County Museum of Art (the Mr. and Mrs. George Gard De Sylva Collection).

26-68   HIPPOLYTE JOUVIN, *The Pont Neuf, Paris, c.* 1860–1865. Albumen stereograph. Collection, The Museum of Modern Art, New York.

the arbitrary cutting off of figures at the edge of the frame and the curious flattening spatial effect caused by the high viewpoint, were of special interest to Pissarro and the other Impressionists.

Although the Impressionist artists were linked by what we might call "color sensationism" and fugitive effects of light and motion, each had very much an individualistic manner. PIERRE-AUGUSTE RENOIR (1841–1919), for example,

was a specialist in the human figure, a sympathetic admirer of what was beautiful in the body and what was pleasurable in the simple round of human life. The bright gaiety of his *Le Moulin de la Galette* (FIG. **26-69**), where a Sunday throng enjoys a popular Paris dance hall, is characteristic of his celebration of vivacious charm. Some people crowd the tables and chatter, while others dance energetically. The whole scene is dappled by sunlight and shade, artfully blurred into the figures themselves to produce just that effect of floating and fleeting light so cultivated by the Impressionists. The casual, unposed placement of the figures and the suggested continuity of space, spreading in all directions and only accidentally limited by the frame, introduce us, as observers, into the very scene. We are not, as with the Tradition, observing a performance on a stage set; rather, we ourselves are part of the action. Renoir's subjects are quite unconscious of the presence of an observer; they do not pose but merely go about the business of the moment. As Classical art sought to express universal and timeless qualities, so Impressionism attempted to depict just the opposite—the incidental, momentary, and passing aspects of reality.

JAMES ABBOTT MCNEILL WHISTLER (1834–1903) was an American expatriate artist, who worked on the Continent before settling finally in London. In Paris, he knew many of the Impressionists, and his art is an interesting mixture of

some of their concerns and his own. He shared their interests in the subject matter of contemporary life and the sensations produced on the eye by color. To these influences he added his own interest in creating harmonies paralleling those achieved in music:

> Nature contains the elements, in color and form, of all pictures, as the keyboard contains the notes of all music. But the artist is born to pick, and choose, and group with science, these elements, that the result may be beautiful—as the musician gathers his notes, and forms his chords, until he brings forth from chaos glorious harmony.*

To underscore his artistic intentions, Whistler began calling his paintings "arrangements" or "nocturnes." *Nocturne in Blue and Gold (Old Battersea Bridge)* (FIG. **26-70**) is a daring

*In Harold Spencer, *American Art: Readings from the Colonial Era to the Present* (New York: Scribners, 1980), pp. 154–55.

26-69   AUGUSTE RENOIR, *Le Moulin de la Galette*, 1876. Oil on canvas, approx. 51" × 68". Louvre, Paris.

26-70 JAMES ABBOTT MCNEILL WHISTLER, *Nocturne in Blue and Gold (Old Battersea Bridge)*, 1877. Oil on canvas, 23³/₄″ × 18³/₈″. Tate Gallery, London.

I did not intend it to be a "correct" portrait of the bridge. It is only a moonlight scene and the pier in the center of the picture may not be like the piers at Battersea Bridge as you know them in broad daylight. *As to what the picture represents, that depends upon who looks at it. To some persons it may represent all that is intended: to others it may represent nothing* [emphasis added].*

Although Whistler won the case, his victory had sadly ironic consequences for him. The judge in the case, showing where his sympathies—and perhaps those of the public—were, awarded the artist only one farthing (less than a penny) in damages and required him to pay all of the court costs, which ruined him financially. He continued to produce etchings and portraits for two decades after his bankruptcy.

Numerous Realist painters (foremost among them, Courbet and Manet) recorded the life of their times in factual images of it, yet their styles had little in common. At the same time, many artists embodied imaginative subject matter in strikingly realistic forms. Indeed, a dialogue between Realism and Romanticism went on throughout the century, and although technical Realism seemed predominant during the latter half of the century, Romantic subject matter and arbitrary formal experiment persisted, and by the end of the century, appeared to carry the day for pure artistic subjectivity.

The realism of Manet, which became the realism of the Impressionists, reveals the striking paradox in Realism. To capture the entire optical field spread before them, artists must paint it just as they see it. To record this instantaneous impression, however, painters must work swiftly in a sketchlike execution that blurs the visual field as it increasingly emphasizes the brush stroke and the blot of color. The wholeness of the field disintegrates into a plurality of color functions. Scientists would say that these artists were not painting the world, but only individual sensations of it. As those sensations belong to each artist's private world, the Realist artists found that the external reality they sought so avidly was *really* determined by their own inescapable subjectivity.

composition in which evening light simplifies shapes into hazy silhouettes. We are so close to the bridge that all we see is the thick **T**-shape made by a single buttress-support, the silhouette of a lone boat near its base, a band of distant shore, and the cropped section of the bridge roadway high overhead. Blue tones fill the canvas, relieved only by touches of yellow and red, indicating shore lights and the effects of the setting sun on the heavy clouds in the sky. The artist was clearly more interested in creating an elegantly simple color harmony for this spare arrangement of shapes than he was in giving details of the actual scene. In works like *Nocturne,* Whistler has taken the "impression" of what our eye sees in nature further than any of the Impressionists. His emphasis was on creating a harmonious arrangement of shapes and colors on the rectangle of his canvas, an approach that will interest many twentieth-century artists.

Such works angered many viewers. The British critic John Ruskin accused Whistler of "flinging a pot of paint in the public's face" with his style. In reply, Whistler sued Ruskin for libel. During the trial, Whistler defended his artistic methods by describing his approach in *Nocturne:*

THE LATER NINETEENTH CENTURY: REACTIONS AGAINST REALISM IN PAINTING

Post-Impressionism: The Search for More Expressive Form and Color

By 1886, the Impressionists were accepted as serious artists by most critics and by a large segment of the public. Just at the time when their gay and colorful studies of contemporary life no longer seemed crude and unfinished, however,

*In McCoubrey, *American Art 1700–1960*; p. 184.

some of the painters themselves and a group of younger followers came to feel that too many of the traditional elements of picture making were being neglected in the search for momentary sensations of light and color. In a conversation with the influential art dealer Ambroise Vollard in about 1883, Renoir commented: "I had wrung Impressionism dry, and I finally came to the conclusion that I knew neither how to paint nor how to draw. In a word, Impressionism was a blind alley, as far as I was concerned." By the 1880s, a much more systematic examination of the properties of three-dimensional space, the expressive qualities of line, pattern and color, and the symbolic character of subject matter was being undertaken by four artists in particular: Georges Seurat, Paul Cézanne, Vincent van Gogh, and Paul Gauguin. Because their art diverged so markedly from earlier Impressionism (although each of these painters at first accepted Impressionist methods and never rejected the new and brighter palette), these four artists and others sharing their views have come to be know as the *Post-Impressionists,* a classification that simply signifies their chronological position in nineteenth-century French painting.

SEURAT   At the eighth and last Impressionist exhibition in 1886, GEORGES SEURAT (1859–1891) showed his *Sunday Afternoon on the Island of La Grande Jatte* (FIG. **26-71**), which set forth the Impressionist interest in urban holiday themes and the analysis of light in a new and monumental synthesis that seemed strangely rigid and remote. Seurat's system of painting in small dots that stand in relation to each other was based on the color theories of Delacroix and the color

scientists Hermann von Helmholtz and Michel Chevreul.* Seurat's system was a difficult procedure, as disciplined and painstaking as the Impressionist method had been very spontaneous and exuberant. Seurat also developed a theory of expressive composition in which emotions were conveyed by the deliberate orchestration of the action of color and the emotional use of lines in a composition. For example, "gaiety of tone" would be created by using warm, luminous colors and placing the most active lines and shapes in the composition above the perspective horizon line.

Seurat was less concerned with the recording of immediate color sensations than he was with their care and systematic organization into a new kind of pictorial order. The free and fluent play of color in his work was disciplined into a calculated arrangement by prior rules of design accepted and imposed by the artist. The apparent formlessness of Impressionism has hardened into severe regularity. The pattern in *La Grande Jatte* is based on the verticals of the figures and trees, the horizontals in the shadows and the distant embankment, and the diagonals in the shadows and shoreline, each of which contributes to the pictorial effect. At the same time, by the use of meticulously calculated values, the painter has carved out a deep rectangular space. In creating both flat pattern and suggested spatial depth,

---

*This method, called *divisionism* by Seurat, was often confused with *pointillism,* in which dots of color were distributed systematically on a white ground that remained partially exposed and hence visually functional. In one respect—the breaking of mass into discrete particles (and color into dots of the component colors)—Seurat's *La Grande Jatte* may be said to have been the forerunner of the modern techniques of photoengraving and color reproduction, as well as television and digital imaging.

26-71   GEORGES SEURAT, *La Grande Jatte,* 1884–1886. Oil on canvas, approx. 6'9" × 10'. The Art Institute of Chicago (Helen Birch Bartlett Memorial Collection).

26-72   PAUL CÉZANNE, *Mont Sainte-Victoire with Viaduct,* 1885–1887. Oil on canvas, approx. 25⅝″ × 31⅞″. The Metropolitan Museum of Art, New York (Havemeyer Collection).

Seurat played on repeated motifs: the profile of the female form, the parasol, and the cylindrical forms of the figures, each placed in space so as to set up a rhythmic movement in depth as well as from side to side. The picture is filled with sunshine, but not broken into transient patches of color. Light, air, people, and landscape are fixed in an abstract design in which line, color, value, and shape cohere in precise and tightly controlled organization.

Seurat's art is a severely intellectual art, of which he himself said, "They see poetry in what I have done. No, I apply my method, and that is all there is to it." His work reveals something of the scientific attitude we have found manifesting itself throughout nineteenth-century painting and also recalls Renaissance geometric formalism; Seurat's stately stage space, with its perspective and careful placement of figures, is descended from the art of Uccello and Piero della Francesca and, like theirs, moves us by its serene monumentality. Seurat, in *La Grande Jatte,* turned traditional pictorial stage space into pattern by applying a color formula based on the belief that our optical experience of space can only be a function of color, which makes space a fairly unimportant variable. In the tradition of Giotto and Raphael, the reality was space, with color something added, but now with Seurat (and, as we shall see, with Cézanne),

color is the reality and spaces and solids are merely illusion. Having found the formula of color relationships, the artist need no longer rely on the dubious evidence of his impressions. Paul Signac, Seurat's collaborator in the design of the "neo-impressionist" method, described their discovery:

> By the elimination of all muddy mixtures, by the exclusive use of the optical mixture of pure colors, by a methodical divisionism and a strict observation of the scientific theory of colors, the Neo-Impressionist ensures a maximum of luminosity, of color intensity, and of harmony—a result that has never yet been obtained.*

CÉZANNE   Like Seurat, PAUL CÉZANNE (1839–1906) turned from Impressionism to the development of a newer style. Although a lifelong admirer of Delacroix, Cézanne allied himself, early in his career, with the Impressionists, especially Pissarro, and at first accepted their theories of color and their faith in subjects chosen from everyday life. Yet his own studies of the old masters in the Louvre persuaded him that Impressionism lacked form and structure. He said: "I want to make of Impressionism something solid and lasting like the art in the museums."

*In Goldwater and Treves, eds., *Artists on Art,* p. 378.

The basis of Cézanne's art was his unique way of studying nature in works like *Mont Sainte-Victoire with Viaduct* (FIG. **26-72**). His aim was not truth in appearance, especially not photographic truth, nor was it the "truth" of Impressionism, but rather a lasting structure behind the formless and fleeting screens of color the eyes take in. If all we see is color, then color gives us every clue about structure, and color must fulfill the structural purposes of traditional perspective and light and shade; color alone must give depth and distance, shape and solidity. Rather than employ the random approach of the Impressionists when he was face to face with nature, Cézanne attempted to bring an intellectual order into his presentation of the colors that comprised it by constantly and painfully checking his painting against the part of the actual scene—he called it the "motif"—that he was studying at the moment. When he said, "We must do Poussin over again, this time according to nature," he apparently meant that Poussin's effects of distance, depth, structure, and solidity must be achieved not by perspective and chiaroscuro but entirely in terms of the color patterns provided by an optical analysis of nature.

With special care, Cézanne explored the properties of line, plane, and color, and their interrelationships: the effect of every kind of linear direction, the capacity of planes to create the sensation of depth, the intrinsic qualities of color, and the power of colors to modify the direction and depth of lines and planes. Through the recession of cool colors and the advance of warm ones, he controlled volume and depth. Having observed that saturation (or the highest intensity of a color) produces the greatest effect of fullness of form, he painted objects chiefly in one hue—apples, for example, in green—achieving convincing solidity by the control of color intensity alone, in place of the traditional method of modeling in light and dark.

Mont Sainte-Victoire with Viaduct is one of many views that Cézanne painted of this mountain near his home in Aix-en-Provence. In it, we can see how the transitory effects of changing atmospheric conditions, effects that occupied Monet, have been replaced by a more concentrated, lengthier analysis of the colors in large, lighted spaces. The main space stretches out behind and beyond the plane of the canvas (emphasized by the pattern of the pine tree in the foreground) and is made up of numerous small elements, such as roads, fields, houses, and the viaduct at the far right, each seen from a slightly different point of view. Above this shifting, receding perspective rises the largest mass of all, the mountain, with an effect—achieved by stressing background and foreground contours equally—of being simultaneously near and far away. This portrayal is close to the actual experience a person observing such a view might have if the forms of the landscape were apprehended piecemeal so that the relative proportions of objects vary, rather than being fixed by a strict one- or two-point perspective, such as that normally found in a photograph.

Cézanne immobilized the shifting colors of Impressionism into an array of clearly defined planes that compose the objects and spaces in his scene. Describing his method in a letter to a fellow painter, he wrote:

> Treat nature by the cylinder, the sphere, the cone, everything in proper perspective so that each side of an object or a plane is directed towards a central point. Lines parallel to the horizon give breadth, that is a section of nature. . . . Lines perpendicular to this horizon give depth. But nature for us men is more depth than surface, whence the need of introducing into our light vibrations, represented by reds and yellows, a sufficient amount of blue to give the impression of air.*

In his *Still Life with Peppermint Bottle* (FIG. **26-73**), the individual forms have lost something of their private character as bottles and fruit and approach the condition of cylinders and spheres. The still life was another good vehicle for Cézanne's experiments, as a limited number of selected objects could be arranged by the artist to provide a well-ordered point of departure. A sharp clarity of planes and of their edges set forth the objects as if they had been sculptured. Even the highlights of the glassware are as sharply defined as the solids. The floating color of the Impressionists has been arrested, held, and analyzed into interlocking planes. Cézanne created here what might be called, paradoxically, an architecture of color.

The Boy in a Red Vest (FIG. **26-74**) shows Cézanne's application of his method to the human figure. Here, the

*Letter from Cézanne to Émile Bernard, April, 15, 1904, in Herschel Chipp, *Theories of Modern Art* (Berkeley: University of California Press, 1968), p. 19.

26-73   PAUL CÉZANNE, *Still Life with Peppermint Bottle, c.* 1894. Oil on canvas, approx. 26″ × 32³⁄₈″. National Gallery of Art, Washington, D.C. (Chester Dale Collection).

26-74   PAUL CÉZANNE, *Boy in a Red Vest*, 1888–1890. Oil on canvas, 35¼" × 28½". Collection of Mr. and Mrs. Paul Mellon, Upperville, Virginia.

breaking up of the pictorial space, the volumes of the figure, and the drapery into emphatic planes is so advanced that the planes almost begin to take over the picture surface. The geometric character of the color areas pushes to the fore, and we at once become aware of the egglike shape of the head and the flexible, almost metallic shapes of the prominent planes of the body and drapery. The disproportionately long left arm is obvious, for the distortions and rearrangement of natural forms that may go unnoticed in landscape and still-life paintings are immediately apparent in the human figure and often disturbing to the viewer. Still, we may be sure that Cézanne's distortions—and they occur in most of his figure paintings—were not accidental. What Cézanne did, in effect, was to rearrange the parts of his figure, shortening and lengthening them in such a way as to make the pattern of their representation in two dimensions conform to the proportions of his picture surface. Like the Impressionists, Cézanne de-emphasized subject matter. Although the depicted object was primarily a light-reflecting surface to the Impressionists, to Cézanne it became a secondary aid in the organization of the picture plane. By reducing the importance of the subject matter, Cézanne automatically enhanced the value of the picture

he was making, which has its own independent existence and must be judged entirely in terms of its own inherent pictorial qualities. In Cézanne's works, the simplification of shapes and their sense of sculptural relief and weight give a peculiar look of stable calm and dignity that is reminiscent of the art of the fifteenth-century Renaissance and has led modern critics to find in Cézanne some vestige of that ancient Mediterranean sense of monumental and unchanging simplicity of form that produced Classical art.

VAN GOGH   Unlike Seurat and Cézanne, who, in different ways, sought, by almost scientific investigation, new rules for the ordering of the experience of color, VINCENT VAN GOGH (1853–1890) exploited new colors and distorted forms to express his emotions as he confronted nature. The son of a Dutch Protestant pastor, van Gogh believed that he had a religious calling and did missionary work in the slums of London and in the mining districts of Belgium. Repeated failures exhausted his body and brought him close to despair. Only after he turned to painting did he find a means of communicating his experience of the sun-illuminated world in landscapes, which he represented pictorially in terms of his favorite color, yellow. His insistence on the expressive values of color led him to develop a corresponding expressiveness in his application of the paint. The thickness, shape, and direction of his brush strokes create a tactile counterpart to his intense color schemes. He moved the brush vehemently back and forth or at right angles, giving a textile-like effect, or squeezed dots or streaks onto his canvas from his paint tube. This bold, almost slapdash attack might have led to disaster had it not been controlled by sensibility.

A rich source of van Gogh's thought on his art is left in the letters he wrote to his brother, Theo. In one of these, this minister's son who had once wanted to be a pastor wrote: "In life and in painting too I can easily do without God, but I cannot—I who suffer—do without something that is bigger than I, that is my life: the power to create." For van Gogh, the power to create involved the expressive use of color. As he wrote to Theo: "Instead of trying to reproduce exactly what I have before my eyes, I use color more arbitrarily so as to express myself forcibly." In another letter, he explained that the color in one of his paintings was "not locally true from the point of view of the stereoscopic Realist, but color to suggest any emotion of an ardent temperament." This particular comment sounds like Delacroix, and, indeed, van Gogh wrote: "And I should not be surprised if the Impressionists soon find fault with my way of working, for it has been fertilized by the ideas of Delacroix rather than by theirs," by which he seemed to mean that he took his color method from Delacroix directly rather than from the Impressionists.

The Night Café (FIG. **26-75**), as van Gogh described it, was meant to convey an oppressive atmosphere of evil, through every possible distortion of color. The scene, a café interior

26-75 VINCENT VAN GOGH, *The Night Café*, 1888. Oil on canvas, approx. 28¹/₂″ × 36″. Yale University Art Gallery, New Haven, Connecticut (bequest of Stephen Carlton Clark, B.A., 1903).

in a dreary provincial town, is supposed to be felt, not simply observed. Van Gogh described it in a letter to Theo:

> I have tried to express the terrible passions of humanity by means of red and green. The room is blood red and dark yellow with a green billiard table in the middle; there are four citron-yellow lamps with a glow of orange and green. Everywhere there is a clash and contrast of the most disparate reds and greens in the figures of little sleeping hooligans, in the empty, dreary room, in violet and blue. The blood-red and the yellow-green of the billiard table, for instance, contrast with the soft, tender Louis XV green of the counter, on which there is a pink nosegay. The white coat of the landlord, awake in a corner of that furnace, turns citron-yellow, or pale luminous green.*

The proprietor, the pale demon who rules over the place, rises like a specter from the edge of the billiard table, which is depicted in a steeply tilted perspective that suggests the spinning, vertiginous world of nausea.

Even more illustrative of van Gogh's "expressionist" method is *The Starry Night* (FIG. **26-76**), which was painted in 1889, the year before the artist's death. In this work, the artist did not represent the sky as we see it when we look up on a clear, dark night—filled with twinkling pinpoints of light against a deep curtain of blue. Rather, he felt the vast-

ness of the universe, filled with whirling and exploding stars and galaxies of stars, beneath which the earth and men's habitations huddle in anticipation of cosmic disaster. Mysteriously, a great cypress is in the process of rapid growth far above the earth's surface and into the combustion of the sky. The artist did not seek or analyze the harmony of nature here. Instead, he transformed it by projecting on it a vision that was entirely his own. This painting, more than any of his others, seems to carry the meaning of a particularly poignant passage from a letter to his brother:

> Is the whole of life visible to us, or isn't it rather that this side of death we see only one hemisphere?
>
> Painters—to take them alone—dead and buried, speak to the next generation or to several succeeding generations through their work.
>
> Is that all, or is there more to come? Perhaps death is not the hardest thing in a painter's life.
>
> For my own part, I declare I know nothing whatever about it, but looking at the stars always makes me dream, as simply as I dream over the black dots representing towns and villages on a map. Why, I ask myself, shouldn't the shining dots of the sky be as accessible as the black dots on the map of France? Just as we take the train to get to Tarascon or Rouen, we take death to reach a star.*

Van Gogh: A Self-portrait, Letters Revealing His Life as a Painter, selected by W. H. Auden (New York: Dutton, 1963), p. 320.

*Ibid. p. 299

26-76 VINCENT VAN GOGH, *The Starry Night,* 1889. Oil on canvas, approx. 29″ × 36¹/₄″. The Museum of Modern Art, New York (acquired through the Lillie P. Bliss Bequest).

GAUGUIN Like van Gogh, PAUL GAUGUIN (1848–1903) rejected objective representation in favor of subjective expression. Gauguin wrote disparagingly of Impressionism:

> The Impressionists study color exclusively, but without freedom, always shackled by the need of probability. For them the ideal landscape, created from many entities, does not exist. Their edifice rests upon no solid base and ignores the nature of the sensations perceived by means of color. They heed only the eye and neglect the mysterious centers of thought, so falling into merely scientific reasoning.*

Gauguin used color in new and unexpected combinations, but his art was very different from van Gogh's. It was no less tormented, perhaps, but more learned in its combination of rare and exotic elements and more broadly decorative. Gauguin had painted as an amateur, but after taking lessons with Pissarro, he resigned from his prosperous brokerage business in 1883 to devote his time entirely to painting. Although his work did not sell and he and his family were reduced to poverty, he did not abandon his art, for he felt that, despite ridicule and neglect, he was called to be a great artist. In his search for provocative subjects, as well as for an economical place to live, he stayed for some time in small villages in Brittany and visited Martinique in the West

*In Goldwater and Treves, eds., *Artists on Art,* p. 373.

Indies. Thus, even before he settled in Tahiti in 1891, tropical color and subjects drawn from his primitive life had entered his art. In his attitude toward color, Gauguin broke with the Impressionistic studies of minutely contrasted hues because he believed that color above all must be expressive and that the power of the artist to determine the colors in a painting is an important part of creativity: "Art is an abstraction; derive this abstraction from nature while dreaming before it, but think more of creating than of the actual result. The only way to rise towards God is by doing as our divine Master does, create." The influence of Gauguin's art and ideas was felt especially by members of the younger generation, such as Parisian artist Maurice Denis, who wrote in *Definition of Neo-Traditionalism* in 1890:

> Gauguin freed us from all the restraints which the idea of copying nature had placed upon us. For instance, if it was permissible to use vermilion in painting a tree which seemed reddish . . . why not stress even to the point of deformation the curve of a beautiful shoulder or conventionalize the symmetry of a bough?

Gauguin's first stop on his flight from the plague of civilization was at Pont-Aven in Brittany, the remotest province of France. There he painted a work decisive for the modern rejection of Realism and Impressionism, *The Vision after the Sermon,* or *Jacob Wrestling with the Angel* (FIG. **26-77**). Gauguin was attracted to Brittany by its unspoiled culture, its ancient Celtic folkways, the still medieval

26-77   PAUL GAUGUIN, *The Vision after the Sermon* or *Jacob Wrestling with the Angel*, 1888. Oil on canvas, 28³/₄" × 36¹/₂". The National Galleries of Scotland, Edinburgh.

Catholic piety of its people. These were indeed "natural" men and women, perfectly at ease in their unspoiled peasant environment. The story of Jacob's encounter with the Angel (the Lord) is told in Genesis 32: 24–30. The painting shows Breton women, wearing their starched white Sunday caps and black dresses, visualizing a sermon they have just heard at church, which was on the theme of Jacob's encounter with the Holy Spirit. They pray devoutly before the apparition, as they would before the roadside crucifix-shrines that are familiar features of the Breton countryside.

Gauguin composes the elements of the picture so as to concentrate the idea and intensify its message. The images are not what the impressionist eye would see and replicate, but what memory would recall and imagination would re-work for the expression of what they mean. Thus the perspective is twisted, and the space allotted so as to emphasize the innocent faith of the unquestioning women, while the figures of Jacob and the Angel, wrestling in a ring enclosed by a Breton stone fence, dwindle to the size of fighting cocks. The women are spectators at a contest, which, like a cockfight, is for them perfectly real.

The picture is not unified by horizon perspective, light and shade, or by a fine-meshed screen of shimmering color. Instead, Gauguin abstracts the scene into pattern: flat planes and shapes are filled by pure, unmodulated color and bounded by firm line. Here there are the white caps, black dresses, and the red field of combat. The shapes are angular, even harsh: the caps and lappets, the sharp fingers and profiles, the hard contours, suggest the austerity of peasant ritual and peasant life. Gauguin was receptive to the influences of Japanese prints, stained glass, and cloisonné enamels (FIGS. 11-2 and 11-3). These contributed to his own daring experiment to transform traditional painting and Impressionism into abstract patterns of line, shape, and pure color. His revolutionary method finds its first authoritative expression in *Jacob Wrestling with the Angel.*

After a brief period of association with van Gogh in Arles, Gauguin, in his restless search for the unspoiled primitive, reached his goal in the South Pacific. He spent the last years of his life in Tahiti, where his Breton manner flowered in the color-drenched environment of the tropical islands. There, Gauguin expressed his love of primitive life and brilliant color in a series of magnificent, decorative canvases. The design was often based, although indirectly, on native motifs, and the color owed its peculiar harmonies of lilac, pink, and lemon to the tropical flora of the islands. Nevertheless, the mood of such works is that of a sophisticated, modern man interpreting an ancient and innocent way of life.

Although the figure and setting in *Spirit of the Dead Watching* (FIG. **26-78**) are Tahitian, the theme of a reclining nude with a watching figure as a matching or balancing element belongs to the Renaissance and later periods. The simplified linear pattern and broad areas of flat color recall Byzantine enamels and Gothic stained glass, which

26-78 PAUL GAUGUIN, *Spirit of the Dead Watching*, 1892. Oil on burlap mounted on canvas, 28¹/₂″ × 36³/₈″. Albright-Knox Art Gallery, Buffalo, New York (A. Conger Goodyear Collection, 1965).

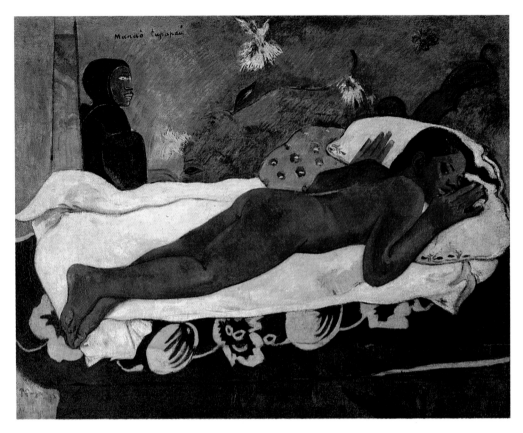

26-79 HENRI DE TOULOUSE-LAUTREC, *At the Moulin Rouge*, 1892–1895. Oil on canvas, approx. 48″ × 55″. The Art Institute of Chicago (Helen Birch Bartlett Memorial Collection).

Gauguin admired, and the slight distortion of the flattened forms is not unlike similar effects in Egyptian sculpture. Romantic art begins with the admiration of "exotic" lands (and peoples) peripheral to Europe; with Gauguin, a kind of adaptation of non-European artistic styles was initiated. He represented a new rebelliousness, not just against the artistic tradition, but against the whole of European civilization. According to Gauguin, "civilization is what makes you sick." The search for vitality in new peoples and new life styles, launched in the eighteenth century, now quickened, prefiguring the twentieth-century interest in drawing artistic inspiration not only from the Orient, but from the Pacific Islands, and from much of the world beyond Europe.

TOULOUSE-LAUTREC   A dissatisfaction with civilization, an anxious awareness of the psychic strains it imposed, and a perception of the banality and degradation it can bring with it colored the mood of many artists toward the end of the century and during the years before World War I. This period is the *fin de siècle* (end of the century), when art and literature languished in a kind of malaise compounded of despondency, boredom, morbidity, and hypersensitivity to the esthetic. In a switch from recording the contemporary scene, with all its variety and human interest, as the Impressionists had done, painters influenced by Gauguin and van Gogh often interpreted it in bitter commentary communicated in harsh distortion of both form and color.

In the work of HENRI DE TOULOUSE-LAUTREC (1864–1901), who deeply admired Degas, the older master's cool scrutiny of modern life was transformed into grim satire and mordant caricature. Toulouse-Lautrec's art was, to a degree, the expression of his life. Self-exiled by his odd stature and crippled legs from the high society that his ancient, aristocratic name would have entitled him to enter, he became a denizen of the night world of Paris, consorting with a tawdry population of entertainers, prostitutes, and other social outcasts. His natural environment became the din and nocturnal colors of cheap music halls, cafés, and bordellos. In *At the Moulin Rouge* (FIG. **26-79**), the influences of Degas, of the Japanese print, and of photography can be seen in the oblique and asymmetrical composition, the spatial diagonals, and the strong patterns of line to which Toulouse-Lautrec added dissonant color. But each element, although closely studied in actual life and already familiar to us in the work of the older Impressionists, has been so emphasized or exaggerated that the tone is new. Compare, for instance, the mood of this painting with the relaxed and casual atmosphere of Renoir's *Le Moulin de la Galette* (FIG. 26-69). Toulouse-Lautrec's scene is night life, with its glaring, artificial light, brassy music, and assortment of corrupt, cruel, and masklike faces. (He included himself in the background: the tiny man with the derby accompanying the very tall man, his cousin.) Such distortions by simplification of the figures and faces anticipated the later Expressionism, when artists would become ever more arbitrary in altering

what they saw to increase the impact of their images on the observer.

Symbolism: Freedom of Imagination, Expression, and Form

We could argue that what seemed to be antagonistic movements—Realism, Impressionism, and Post-Impressionism—were only so many permutations of Romanticism, changing its earlier iconography, but always putting artistic autonomy at the center of the argument, no matter the subject or the technique. Nature, as given to the eye, was transformed by the artist's emotion and sensation until, by the end of the century, its representation came to be completely subjectivized, to the point that the artist did not imitate nature but created free interpretations of it. The optical world as given was rejected in favor of a world of fantasy, of forms conjured up and produced by the artist's free imagination, with or without reference to things conventionally seen. Technique and ideas were individual to each of these artists; color, line, and shape, separated from conformity to the optical image, might be used as symbols of personal emotions in response to the world. No requirement was recognized other than expressing reality in accord with the artist's spirit and intuition. Deliberately choosing now to stand outside of conventional meanings and conventional images, such artists spoke like prophets, in signs and symbols.

Many of the artists following this path adopted an approach to subject matter and form that associated them with a general European movement called *Symbolism*. The term had application to both art and literature, which, as critics in both fields noted, were in especially close relation at this time. A manifesto of literary Symbolism appeared in Paris in 1886, and, in 1891, the critic Albert Aurier applied the term to the painting of Gauguin and van Gogh. Symbolists disdained the "mere fact" of Realism as trivial and asserted that fact must be transformed into a symbol of the inner experience of that fact. Fact was thus nothing in itself; mentally transformed, it was the utterance of a sensitized temperament responding in its own way to the world. In Symbolism, the subjectivity of Romanticism became radical; it would continue to be so in much of the art of the twentieth century. The task of Symbolist visual and verbal artists was not to *see* things but to see *through* them to a significance and reality far deeper than what is given in superficial appearance. In this function, as the poet Rimbaud insisted, the artist became a being of extraordinary insight. (One group of Symbolist painters, influenced by Gauguin, called itself *Nabis*, the Hebrew word for *prophet*.) Rimbaud, whose poems had great influence on the artistic community, went so far as to say, in his *Lettre du Voyant*, that to achieve the seer's insight, the artist must become deranged—in effect, systematically unhinging and confusing the everyday faculties of sense and reason, which served only to blur artistic vision. The objects given us in our commonsense world must be converted by the artist's mystical vision into symbols of a reality beyond that world, and, ultimately, a reality from within the individual.

The extreme subjectivism of the Symbolists led them to cultivate all the resources of fantasy and imagination, no matter how recondite and occult. Moreover, it led them to urge the exclusiveness, even the elitism, of the artist against the vulgar materialism and conventional mores of industrial and middle-class society. Above all, by their philosophy of estheticism, the Symbolists wished to purge literature and art of anything utilitarian, to cultivate an exquisite esthetic sensitivity, and to make the slogan "art for art's sake" into a doctrine and a way of life. As early as 1856, Théophile Gautier wrote: "We believe in the autonomy of art; art for us is not the means but the end; any artist who has in view anything but the beautiful is not an artist in our eyes." Walter Pater, an English scholar and esthete, advanced the same point of view in 1868 in the conclusion to his work *The Renaissance:*

> Our one chance lies in expanding that interval [of our life], in getting as many pulsations as possible into the given time. Great passions may give us this quickened sense of life. . . . Of such wisdom, the poetic passion, the desire of beauty, the love of art for its own sake has most. For art comes to you proposing frankly to give nothing but the highest quality to your moments as they pass.*

The subject matter of the Symbolists, determined by this worshipfulness toward art and exaggerated esthetic sensa-

The Renaissance: Studies in Art and Poetry. (London: Macmillan, 1910), p. 238–9.

tion, became increasingly esoteric and exotic, weird, mysterious, visionary, dreamlike, fantastic. (Perhaps not coincidentally, contemporary with the Symbolists, Sigmund Freud, the founder of psychoanalysis, began the new century and the age of psychiatry with his *Interpretation of Dreams,* an introduction to the concept and the world of unconscious experience.)

Elements of Symbolism appeared in the works of both Gauguin and van Gogh, but their art differed from mainstream Symbolism in their insistence on showing unseen powers as linked to the surface of physical reality, instead of attempting to depict an alternate, wholly interior life. The artists who participated in the actual Symbolist movement were less important than the writers, but two great French artists—Gustave Moreau and Odilon Redon—had a strong influence on the movement, and a number of other painters followed the Symbolist-related path of imagination, fantasy, and inner vision in their works. Prominent figures in this group were the Frenchman Henri Rousseau, the Belgian James Ensor, the Norwegian Edvard Munch, and the American Albert Pinkham Ryder. All of these artists were visionaries who anticipated the strong twentieth-century interest in creating art that expressed psychological truth.

Rejecting Realism and the modern taste that called for it was an artist who went his own way in the nineteenth century, who is hard to classify, and who spanned the time separating Romantic ideal formalism from Symbolism, serenely unaffected by anything in between; and, though he never identified himself with that taste, he became the "prophet" of Symbolism. PUVIS DE CHAVANNES (1824–1898) sought to adopt a Classical mood and form to his own

26-80 PIERRE PUVIS DE CHAVANNES, *The Sacred Grove,* 1884. Oil on canvas, 2′11¹/₂″ × 6′10″. The Art Institute of Chicago (Potter Palmer Collection).

esthetic ends, an art that was ornamental and reflective, and removed from the noisy world of Realism. In *The Sacred Grove* (FIG. **26-80**), he deployed statuesque figures in a tranquil landscape with a Classical shrine. Their motion has been suspended in timeless poses, their contours are simple and sharp, their modeling as shallow as bas-relief. Primarily a mural painter, Puvis was obedient to the requirements of the wall surface, neutralizing and restraining color, and banishing pictorial illusionism with its perspective and tone matching. The calm, almost bland atmosphere suggests some consecrated place, where all movements and gestures, undisturbed by the busyness of life, have a perpetual, ritual significance. The stillness and simplicity of the forms, the linear patterns created by their rhythmic contours, and the suggestion of their symbolic import amount to a kind of program of anti-Realism that impressed younger painters like Paul Gauguin and the Symbolists, who saw in Puvis the prophet of a new style that would replace Realism. Puvis had a double reputation: he was accepted by the Academy and the government for his Classicism, and he was revered by the avant-garde for his vindication of imagination and his artistic independence from the world of materialism and the machine. He asked a question significant for artists of his time and later: "What will become of artists in the face of the invasion of engineers and mechanics?"

GUSTAVE MOREAU (1826–1898) sought a form to suit the content of his fantasies that would incorporate reference to the facts of the optical world when he needed them. An influential teacher, Moreau expanded his natural love of sensuous design to embrace gorgeous color, intricate line, and richly detailed shape. He preferred subjects inspired by dreaming solitude and as remote as possible from the everyday world—subjects that could be submerged in all the glittering splendor that imagination could envision and painterly ingenuity could supply.

Jupiter and Semele (FIG. **26-81**) is one of Moreau's rare finished works. The mortal girl Semele, one of Jupiter's loves, begged the god to appear to her in all his majesty, a sight so powerful that she dies from it. The theme is presented within an operalike setting, a towering, opulent architecture. (Moreau was a lover of the music of Wagner and, like that great composer, dreamed of a grand synthesis of the arts.) The painter depicted the royal hall of Olympus as shimmering in iridescent color, with tabernacles filled with the glowing and flashing shapes that enclose the figure of Jupiter like an encrustation of gems. In this painting, the color of Delacroix is harmonized with the exotic hues of medieval enamels, Indian miniatures, Byzantine mosaics, and the designs of exotic wares then influencing modern artists. Semele, in the lap of Jupiter, is overwhelmed by the apparition of the god, who is crowned with a halo of thunderbolts. Her languorous swoon and the suspended motion of all the entranced figures show the "beautiful inertia" that Moreau said he wished to render with all "necessary richness." His cherishing of the enigmas of fable, myth, vision,

and dream caused Manet to remark of him: "I have a lively sympathy for him, but he is taking a bad road . . . he takes us back to the incomprehensible, while we wish that everything be understood"; and, said Degas, "He puts watch-chains on the gods."

The sharp differences of artistic intention expressed in these comments are even more striking in any comparison of the work of ODILON REDON (1840–1916) and Monet, who were born in the same year. Redon used the Impressionist palette and stippling brush stroke for a very different purpose. Like Moreau, Redon was a visionary. He had been aware of an intense inner world from childhood

26-81 GUSTAVE MOREAU, *Jupiter and Semele*, *c.* 1875. Oil on canvas, approx. 7' × 3'4". Musée Gustave Moreau, Paris.

26-82 ODILON REDON, *The Cyclops*, 1898. Oil on canvas, 25″ × 20″. State Museum Kröller-Müller, Otterlo, The Netherlands.

and later wrote of "imaginary things" that haunted him. In *The Cyclops* (FIG. **26-82**), Redon did not record a fleeting impression of a one-eyed giant in love; rather, he projected a figment of the imagination as if it were seeable, coloring it whimsically with a rich profusion of fresh, saturated hues that were in harmony with the mood he felt fitted the subject. The fetal head of the shy, simpering Polyphemus, with its huge, loving eye, rises balloonlike above the sleeping Galatea. The image born of the dreaming world and the color analyzed and disassociated from the waking world come together here at the will of the artist. As Redon himself observed: "My originality consists in bringing to life, in a human way, improbable beings and making them live according to the laws of probability, by putting—as far as possible—the logic of the visible at the service of the invisible." To evoke his world of fantasy, Redon developed a broadly brushed and suggestive style very different from the careful naturalism in Bouguereau's mythical images on which the imagination of the viewer could project additional details.

Symbolism had a wide appeal for the so-called decadents of the fin de siècle, who shunned action for esthetic passivity and who sought escape in art from the ugliness and bru-

tality of a materialistic world on the way to war. Although not strictly speaking a Symbolist, AUBREY BEARDSLEY (1872–1898) was one of a circle of English esthetes that included the brilliant wit Oscar Wilde, whose close friend he was and whose controversial books and plays he illustrated. For one of them, *Salomé*, Beardsley drew *The Peacock Skirt* (FIG. **26-83**), a dazzlingly decorative composition perfectly characteristic of his style. The influence of the Japanese print is obvious, although Beardsley has assimilated it into his own unique manner. Banishing Realism, he confines himself to lines and to patterns of black and white, eliminating all shading. His tense, elastic line encloses sweeping, curvilinear shapes that lie flat on the surface—some left almost vacant, others filled with swirling complexes of mostly organic motifs. His mastery of calligraphic line is supported by his unfailing sense of linear rhythms and harmonies. In his short lifetime—he died at 26—he expressed in both his life and art the esthete's ideal of "art for art's sake." Beardsley's work exhibits its own beauty; it has no other message. It reflects and will strongly influence the design principles of Art Nouveau (see Horta's Hotel von Eetvelde, FIG. 27-1).

26-83 AUBREY BEARDSLEY, *The Peacock Skirt*, 1894. Pen-and-ink illustration for Oscar Wilde's *Salomé*.

26-84 HENRI ROUSSEAU, *The Sleeping Gypsy*, 1897. Oil on canvas, 4′3″ × 6′7″. The Museum of Modern Art, New York (gift of Mrs. Simon Guggenheim).

The imagination of the French artist HENRI ROUSSEAU (1844–1910) engaged a different but equally powerful world of personal fantasy. Gauguin had journeyed to the South Seas in search of primitive innocence; Rousseau was a "primitive" without leaving Paris—an untrained amateur painter who held a post as a customs collector (hence, his sobriquet, *le douanier*). Rousseau produced an art of dream and fantasy in a style that had its own sophistication and made its own departure from the artistic currency of the fin de siècle. His apparent visual, conceptual, and technical naiveté was compensated by a natural talent for design and an imagination teeming with exotic images of mysterious, tropical landscapes. In perhaps his best-known work, *The Sleeping Gypsy* (FIG. **26-84**), in a desert world, silent and secret, dreams beneath a pale, perfectly round moon. In the foreground, a lion that resembles a stuffed but somehow menacing animal doll sniffs at the Gypsy. A critical encounter impends, one that is not possible for most of us in the waking world but is all too common when our vulnerable, subconscious selves are menaced in uneasy sleep. Rousseau mirrored the landscape of the subconscious, and we may regard him as the forerunner of the Surrealists in

the twentieth century, who will attempt to represent the ambiguity and contradiction of waking and dreaming experiences taken together.

As Goya proved earlier, a fantastic and horrifying image of human decadence and depravity may be revealed when imagination turns a critical eye toward society. The Belgian painter JAMES ENSOR (1860–1949) created a spectral and macabre visionary world in his paintings and filled it with grotesques, masked skeletons, and hanged men populating sideshows, carnivals, and city streets. His best-known work, which was severely criticized for blasphemy, is *Christ's Entry into Brussels in 1889* (FIG. **26-85**). In spirit, it recalls the demonizing, moralizing pictures of Hieronymus Bosch (FIG. 20-17). In Ensor's work, however, the human creatures are masked "hollow men" who have no real substance or genuine identity; they are only "images," a theme often sounded in criticism of modern civilization. Ensor's color is hard, strident, and spotted—a tonal cacophony that matches the sound of his repulsive crowd.

Linked in spirit to Ensor was the Norwegian painter and graphic artist EDVARD MUNCH (1863–1944), another moralizing critic of modern man. Munch felt deeply the pain of

26-85 JAMES ENSOR, *Christ's Entry into Brussels in 1889*, 1888. Oil on canvas, approx. 8'5" × 14'1". The J. Paul Getty Museum, Malibu. California.

human life. His Romantic belief that humans were powerless before the great natural forces of death and love became the theme of most of his art. Specific ideas came to him spontaneously.

> I painted picture after picture after the impressions that my eye took in at moments of emotion—painted lines and colors that showed themselves on my inner eye. . . . I painted only the memories without adding anything— without details I could no longer see. . . . By painting colors and lines and shapes that I had seen in an emotional mood I wanted to make the emotional mood ring out again as happens on a gramophone.*

Like his friend, the dramatist August Strindberg, Munch presented almost unbearable pictures of the tensions and psychic anguish that besiege human beings and the ultimate loneliness that, according to the philosophy of existentialism, is the inescapable lot of humanity.

Such is his picture *Puberty* (FIG. **26-86**) intended as an early subject in his great series *The Dance of Life*. A nude, adolescent girl has become rigid with apprehension, either from the sudden appearance of an intruder, or her own just-as-sudden awareness of herself in a mirror. She shrinks into the center of her new-found womanhood, her tense arms and legs lock in defensively in the gesture of Eve. Looking directly at us, the face with its enormous eyes is the very mask of threatened and frightened maidenhood. Her own great shadow looming behind her amplifies the menace she feels.

*In Johan H. Langaard and Reidar Revold, *Edvard Munch: Masterpieces from the Artist's Collection in the Munch Museum in Oslo* (New York: McGraw-Hill, 1964), p. 53.

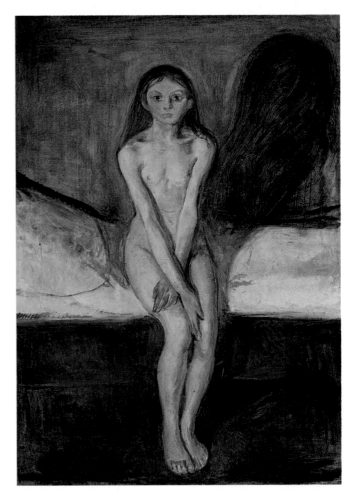

26-86 EDVARD MUNCH, *Puberty*, 1895. Oil on canvas, approx. 5' × 3^1/$_2$'. National Gallery, Oslo.

26-87 ALBERT PINKHAM RYDER, *Death on a Pale Horse (The Racetrack),* c. 1906–1908. Oil on canvas, approx. 28¼″ × 35¼″. The Cleveland Museum of Art (purchase from the J. H. Wade Fund).

It would be a mistake to view this with the bias of Realism, as the visual record of the traumatic experience of some trapped young girl. Rather, in the spirit of Symbolism, it should be understood as an allegory of adolescence, a natural stage in the development from child to woman, as the title *Puberty* indicates, a dramatic moment mixed with wonder, fear, and the shock of self-discovery. It is the genius of Munch to take the abstract idea and personify it so poignantly.

Munch had been influenced by Gauguin's work, not only his paintings but the woodblocks he produced from them. The later artist also made prints that carried the same high emotional charge as his painted works, and both his intense images and the print medium that carried them would be major sources of inspiration for the German Expressionists in the early twentieth century.

The art of the American painter ALBERT PINKHAM RYDER (1847–1917) is filled with personal visions, most of which are based in literary or religious themes. His work is the very essence of Romantic inwardness and is witness to the persistence of Romanticism and its seemingly endless variety of utterance. A recluse, shut away by choice from the world, Ryder found a depthless reservoir of subject matter in his own imagination, from which arose images uniquely private yet often universal. The power of Ryder's interior world was as strong as that of Munch, Redon, or Rousseau.

Although he studied drawing and made several trips abroad, Ryder's improvisational style was deeply rooted in his highly creative spirit. As he commented: "It is the first vision that counts. The artist has only to remain true to his dream, and it possesses his work in such a manner that it will resemble the work of no other man—for no two visions are alike. . . . Imitation is not inspiration, and inspiration only can give birth to a work of art."*

Inspiration guided his *Death on a Pale Horse,* or *The Racetrack,* (FIG. **26-87**). The scythe-bearing specter speeds on its ceaseless round through a dead landscape that supports only the withered stalk of a tree. In the foreground, a malignant serpent with glowing eyes undulates. No one remains on earth but Death and the snake, the symbol of primordial evil. The utter simplicity of the conception and execution require none but the barest reference to things outside the mind. Blank zones of dark and somber light are traced through by the faint streaks of the fence rails, which remain undisturbed by the passage of the phosphorescent wraith. Ryder's indifference to the material world unfortunately extended to his material medium and technique. He painted in thick layers with badly prepared or unstable pigments, and many of his works have suffered serious deterioration.

*In McCoubrey, *American Art 1700–1960,* p. 187.

SCULPTURE IN THE LATER NINETEENTH CENTURY

The three-dimensional art of sculpture was not readily adaptable to the optical realism favored by many painters and the public in the nineteenth century. Its very nature requires the sense of its permanence as an enduring form, a palpable mass sufficient unto itself. The timeless ideal, not the evanescent real, best suits it. The space it occupies is abstract—if the work is free-standing—not descriptive of some particular locale it does not occupy; certainly, sculpture is not the apt medium for representing the passing season or time of day, fleetingly observed and fleetingly recorded. Thus, sculpture is not really suitable for the description either of historical events or of scenes from contemporary life, although it was often required to do both in the nineteenth century. But Rude's *La Marseillaise* (FIG. 26-25) is an allegory of an event, and Barye's *Jaguar* (FIG. 26-26), though realistic enough, is the imaginative evocation of a *possible* event.

In sculpture, JEAN-BAPTISTE CARPEAUX (1827–1875) combines his Realist intention with a love of Baroque and Antique sculpture and of the work of Michelangelo. Carpeaux's group *Ugolino and His Children* (FIG. **26-88**) is based on a passage from Dante's *Inferno* and shows Count Ugolino with his four sons shut up in a tower to starve to death. In Hell, Ugolino relates to Dante how, in a moment of extreme despair,

> *I bit both hands for grief. And*
> *they, thinking I did it for hunger,*
> *suddenly rose up and said, "Father" . . .*
> *[and offered him their own flesh as food.]*
> *(XXXIII, 58–75)*

The powerful forms—twisted, intertwined, and densely concentrated—suggest the self-devouring torment of frustration and despair that wracks the unfortunate Ugolino. A careful student of the male figures of Michelangelo, Carpeaux also said that he had the *Laocoön* group (FIG. 5-101) in mind. Certainly the storm and stress of the *Ugolino* recall the Hellenistic "baroque" of that group and others, like the battling gods and giants on the frieze of the Pergamon altar (FIG. 5-90). Regardless of such influences, the sense of vivid reality about the anatomy of the *Ugolino* figures shows Carpeaux's interest in study from life.

For the leading sculptors of the nineteenth century, the influence of Michelangelo was decisive. ANTOINE-AUGUSTE PRÉAULT (1809–1879) supplemented his study of that great artist with close reference to sculptors of the French Renaissance. Baudelaire heard him say: "I am a connoisseur of Michelangelo, of Jean Goujon, of Germain Pilon" (see FIG. 23-22). Certainly, the influence of Goujon visibly commingled in Préault's superb *Ophelia* (FIG. **26-89**). Taking the same Shakespearean theme as did Millais for his painting (FIG. 26-49), Préault creates a pattern of swirling,

26-88 JEAN-BAPTISTE CARPEAUX, *Ugolino and His Children*, 1865–1867. Marble, 6′ 5″ high. The Metropolitan Museum of Art, New York (Josephine Bay Paul and C. Michael Paul Foundation and the Charles Ulrick and Josephine Bay Foundation gifts and Fletcher Fund, 1967).

rippling line that simulates both the clinging, drenched drapery and the rushing water. The body of the drowning heroine makes a beautiful, buoyant curve, expressive of the undulating current in which she is suspended and which is sucking her down. She is one of Goujon's fountain nymphs, tragically overwhelmed by the flooding waters she has poured. The sweep and play of curving line are both passionate and decorative; they look forward to the intricate, abstract style of Art Nouveau and its esthetic ideal of graceful, curvilinear ornament. (FIG. 27-1)

AUGUSTUS SAINT-GAUDENS (1848–1907), an American sculptor trained in France, used realism effectively in a number of his portraits, where realism was highly appropriate. For a design of a memorial monument of Mrs. Henry Adams (FIG. 26-90) Saint-Gaudens chose, instead, a Classical mode of representation, which he modified freely. Of course, he had no need to specify a particular character; he wanted to represent a generality outside of time and place. The resultant statue is that of a woman of majestic bearing sitting in mourning, her classically beautiful face

26-89   ANTOINE-AUGUSTE PRÉAULT, *Ophelia*, 1876 (original 1843). Bronze, 6'7" long. Musée de Longchamps, Marseille.

26-90   AUGUSTUS SAINT-GAUDENS, Adams Memorial, 1891. Bronze, 70" high. Rock Creek Cemetery, Washington, D.C.

partly shadowed by a sepulchral drapery that voluminously enfolds her body. The immobility of her form, set in an attitude of eternal vigilance, is only slightly stirred by a natural, yet mysterious and exquisite gesture. Saint-Gaudens's masterpiece is a work worthy of the grave stelae of Classical Athens (FIG. 5-63).

In the work of the French artist AUGUSTE RODIN (1840–1917), however, a modified Realism found its sculptural counterpart and regained the artistic preeminence it had lost to the pictorial media in the nineteenth century. Primarily a Realist by impulse, Rodin ably assimilated and managed the century's other concurrent esthetic styles— Romanticism, Impressionism, and Symbolism, generating in the process a unique personal style that anticipated twentieth-century Expressionism. Avoiding the stilted formulas of the Academy, Rodin looked carefully at the sculpture of Michelangelo and Puget (FIG. 24-69), learning from them to appreciate the unique possibilities of the human body for emotional expression. Rodin wanted to express the "existential situation of modern man, his inability to communicate, his despair." His goal, as he put it, was "to render inner feelings through muscular movement." He achieved this aim by joining his profound knowledge of anatomy and movement with special attention to the body's surfaces, saying, "The sculptor must learn to reproduce the surface, which means all that vibrates on the surface, soul, love, passion, life. . . . Sculpture is thus the art of hollows and mounds, not of smoothness, or even polished planes." Primarily a modeler of pliable material rather than a carver of hard wood or stone, Rodin worked his surfaces with fingers sensitive to the subtlest variations of plane, catching the fugitive play of living motion as it changed fluidly under light, a kind of "expressionist realism." Like Muybridge and Eakins, Rodin was fascinated by the human body in motion. Often in his studio, he would have a model move around in front of him, while he modeled sketches with coils of clay. *Walking Man* (FIG. **26-91**) was the first major sculpture in which he captured the sense of a body in motion. Headless and armless, the figure is caught in mid-stride at the moment when weight is transferred across the pelvis from the back leg to the front. As with many of his other early works, Rodin executed *Walking Man* with such careful attention to details of muscle, bone and tendon, that it is filled with forceful reality, despite the sketchy modeling of the torso. Rodin conceived this figure as a study for his sculpture of *St. John the Baptist Preaching*, part of the process by which he built his conception of how the human body would express the symbolism of the larger theme.

Similarly, he made many nude and draped studies for each of the figures in the life-size group *Burghers of Calais* (FIG. **26-92**). This monument was commissioned to commemorate a heroic episode in the Hundred Years' War, in which, during the English siege of Calais in 1347, six of the city's leading citizens agreed to offer their lives in return for the English king's promise to lift the siege and spare the rest of the populace. Each of the individual figures is a convincing study of despair, resignation, or quiet defiance. The psychic effects were achieved through the choreographic placement of the members of the group and through the manipulation of a few simplified planes in each figure, so that the rugged surfaces catch and disperse the light. Rodin designed the monument without the traditional high base in the hope that modern-day citizens of Calais would be

26-91   AUGUSTE RODIN, *Walking Man*, 1905. Bronze, 83³/₄″ high. Hirshhorn Museum and Sculpture Garden, Smithsonian Institution, Washington, D.C. (gift of Joseph H. Hirshhorn, 1966).

26-92   AUGUSTE RODIN, *Burghers of Calais*, 1886. Bronze, 6′10¹/₂″ high, 7′11″ long, 6′6″ deep. Hirshhorn Museum and Sculpture Garden, Smithsonian Institution, Washington, D.C. (gift of Joseph H. Hirshhorn, 1966).

inspired by the sculptured representations of their ancestors standing in the city center and preparing eternally to set off on their sacrificial journey. The government commissioners found the Realism of Rodin's vision so offensive, however, that they banished the monument to an out-of-the-way site and modified the impact of the work by placing it high on an isolating pedestal.

Many of Rodin's projects were left unfinished or were deliberate fragments. See, for example, *The Thinker* (p. 10), a figure from the group *The Gates of Hell*. Seeing the esthetic and expressive virtue of these works, modern viewers and modern sculptors have developed a taste for the way in which the sketch, the half-completed figure, the fragment, and the vignette lifted out of context, all have the power of suggestion and understatement. Characteristically, although we feel the power of Rodin's art, we cannot quite describe which traits make us feel it. His methods, grounded in Realism, achieve an overwhelmingly moving effect through emphasis and distortion.

26-93   HENRI LABROUSTE, reading room of the Bibliothèque Ste.-Geneviève, Paris, 1843–1850.

ARCHITECTURE IN THE LATER NINETEENTH CENTURY: THE BEGINNINGS OF A NEW STYLE

The epoch-making developments in architecture that paralleled mid-century Realism in the other arts were rational, pragmatic, and functional. Toward the end of the nineteenth century, architects gradually abandoned sentimental and Romantic designs from the historical past and turned to a presentation of the honest expression of a building's purpose. Since the eighteenth century, bridges had been built of cast iron (FIG. 25-22), and most other utility architecture—factories, warehouses, dockyard structures, mills, and the like—had long been built simply and without historical ornament. Iron, along with other materials of the Industrial Revolution, permitted engineering advancements in the construction of larger, stronger, and more fire-resistant structures. The tensile strength of iron (and especially of steel, available after 1860) permitted architects to create new designs involving vast enclosed spaces, as in the great train sheds of railroad stations and in exposition halls.

The Bibliothèque Ste.-Geneviève (1843–1850), built by HENRI LABROUSTE (1801–1875), shows an interesting adjustment of the revived Romantic style—in this case, Renaissance—to a Realistic interior, the skeletal elements of which are cast iron (FIG. **26-93**). The row of arched windows in the facade recalls the flank of Alberti's San Francesco at Rimini (FIG. 21-38), yet the division of its stories distinguishes the levels of its interior—the lower, reserved for stack space and the upper, for the reading rooms. The latter consists essentially of two tunnel-vaulted halls, roofed in terracotta, and separated by a row of slender cast-iron columns on concrete pedestals. The columns,

recognizably Corinthian, support the iron roof arches, which are pierced with intricate vine-scroll ornament out of the Renaissance architectural vocabulary. One could scarcely find a better example of how the forms of traditional masonry architecture are esthetically transformed by the peculiarities of the new structural material. Nor could one find a better example of how reluctant the nineteenth-century architect was to surrender traditional forms, even when fully aware of new possibilities for design and construction. Architects would scoff at "engineers' architecture" for many years to come and would continue to clothe their steel and concrete structures in the Romantic "drapery" of a historical style.

Completely "undraped" construction first became popular in the conservatories (greenhouses) of English country estates. JOSEPH PAXTON (1801–1865) built several such structures for his patron, the duke of Devonshire; in the largest—300 feet long—he used an experimental system of glass-and-metal roof construction. Encouraged by the success of this system, Paxton submitted a winning glass-and-iron building plan to the design competition for the hall that was to house the Great Exhibition of 1851, which was organized to gather "Works of Industry of All Nations" together in London. Paxton's exhibition building, the Crystal Palace (FIG. **26-94**) was built with prefabricated parts, which allowed the vast structure to be erected in the then unheard-of time of six months and dismantled at the closing of the exhibition to avoid permanent obstruction of the park.* The plan borrowed much from ancient Roman

---

*The public admired the building so much that when it was dismantled, it was reerected at a new location on the outskirts of London, where it remained until it was destroyed by fire in 1936.

26-94 JOSEPH PAXTON, Crystal Palace, London, 1850–1851. Iron and glass. Courtesy of the Board of Trustees, Victoria and Albert Museum.

and Christian basilicas, with a central, flat-roofed "nave" and a barrel-vaulted crossing "transept," which allowed ample interior space to contain displays of huge machines as well as to accommodate such decorative touches as large working fountains and giant trees.

The iron structural supports used by Labrouste and Paxton were steps on the way to the twentieth-century skyscraper. The elegant metal skeleton structures of the French engineer-architect ALEXANDRE-GUSTAVE EIFFEL (1832–1923) constituted an equally important contribution. A native of Burgundy, Eiffel trained in Paris before beginning a distinguished career designing exhibition halls, bridges, and the interior armature for France's anniversary gift to the United States—Bartholdi's *Statue of Liberty*. Eiffel's best-known work, the Eiffel Tower (FIG. **26-95**), was designed for a great exhibition in Paris in 1889. Originally seen as a symbol of modern Paris, and still considered a symbol of nineteenth-century civilization, the elegant metal tower thrusts its needle shaft 984 feet above the city, making it at the time of its construction (and for some time to come) the world's highest structure. The tower's well-known configuration rests on four giant supports, connected by gracefully arching open-frame skirts that provide a pleasing mask for the heavy horizontal girders needed to strengthen the legs. Visitors can take two elevators to the top, or they can use the internal staircase. Architectural historian Siegfried Giedion described the sense of the tower well when he wrote:

> The airiness one experiences when at the top of the tower makes it the terrestrial sister of the aeroplane. . . . To a previously unknown extent, outer and inner space are

interpenetrating. This effect can only be experienced in descending the spiral stairs from the top, when the soaring lines of the structure intersect with the trees, houses, churches, and the serpentine windings of the Seine. The interpenetration of continuously changing viewpoints create, in the eyes of the moving spectator, a glimpse into four-dimensional experience.*

This interpenetration of inner and outer space would become a hallmark of twentieth-century art and architecture. At the time of their construction, however, Eiffel's metal skeleton structures and the iron skeletal frames designed by Labrouste and Paxton jolted some in the architectural profession into a realization that the new materials and new processes might contain the germ of a completely new style, a radically innovative approach to architectural design, something that picturesque, historical romanticism had failed to produce.

The desire for greater speed and economy in building, as well as for a reduction in fire hazards, encouraged the use of cast and wrought iron for many building programs, especially commercial ones. Designers in both England and the United States enthusiastically developed cast-iron architecture until a series of disastrous fires in the early 1870s in New York, Boston, and Chicago demonstrated that cast iron by itself was far from impervious to fire. This discovery led to the practice of encasing the metal in masonry, combining the strength of the first material with the fire-resistance of the second.

*Siegfried Giedion, *Space, Time, and Architecture* (Cambridge, MA: Harvard University Press, 1965), p. 282.

26-95 ALEXANDRE GUSTAVE EIFFEL, Eiffel Tower, Paris, 1889. Wrought iron, 984' high.

In cities, convenience required that buildings be closely grouped, and increased property values forced architects literally to raise the roof. Even an attic could command high rentals if the building were provided with one of the new elevators, used for the first time in the Equitable Building in New York (1868–1871). Metal could support such tall structures, and the American skyscraper was born. It was with rare exceptions, however, as in the work of Louis Sullivan (FIGS. 26-97 and 26-98), that this innovative type of building was treated successfully and produced distinguished architecture.

Sullivan's predecessor, HENRY HOBSON RICHARDSON (1838–1886), frequently used heavy round arches and massive masonry walls, and because he was particularly fond of the Romanesque architecture of the Auvergne in France, his work was sometimes thought of as a Romanesque revival. This designation does not do credit to the originality and quality of most of the buildings Richardson designed during the brief eighteen years of his

practice. Although Trinity Church in Boston and his smaller public libraries, residences, railroad stations, and courthouses in New England and elsewhere best demonstrate his vivid imagination and the solidity (the sense of enclosure and permanence) so characteristic of his style, his most important and influential building was the Marshall Field wholesale store (now demolished) in Chicago (FIG. **26-96**), which was begun in 1885. This vast building, occupying a city block and designed for the most practical of purposes, recalled historical styles without being at all in imitation of them. The tripartite elevation of a Renaissance palace or of the aqueduct near Nîmes, France (FIG. 7-36), may have been close to Richardson's mind, but he used no Classical ornament, made much of the massive courses of masonry, and, in the strong horizontality of the windowsills and the interrupted courses that defined the levels, stressed the long sweep of the building's lines, as well as its ponderous weight. Although the structural frame still lay behind and in conjunction with the masonry screen, the great glazed arcades, in opening up the walls of a large-scale building, pointed the way to the modern, total penetration of the wall and the transformation of it into a mere screen or curtain that serves both to echo the underlying structural grid and to protect it from the weather.

LOUIS HENRY SULLIVAN (1856–1924), who has been called the first truly modern architect, recognized Richardson's architectural innovations early in his career and worked

26-96 HENRY HOBSON RICHARDSON, Marshall Field wholesale store, Chicago, 1885–1887.

LOUIS SULLIVAN, Guaranty (Prudential) Building, Buffalo, New York, 1894–1895.

forward from them in designing his "tall buildings," especially the Guaranty (Prudential) Building in Buffalo, New York (FIG. **26-97**), built between 1894 and 1895. Here, the subdivision of the interior is expressed on the exterior, as is the skeletal (as opposed to the bearing-wall) nature of the supporting structure, with nothing more substantial than windows occupying most of the space between the terracotta-clad vertical members. In Sullivan's designs, one can be sure of an equivalence of interior and exterior design, not at all the case in Richardson's wholesale store (FIG. 26-96) or in Labrouste's Library (FIG. 26-93). Yet something of old habits of thought hung on; the Guaranty Building has a base and a cornice, even though the base is penetrated in such a way as to suggest the later free supports of twentieth-century architecture.

The form of the building, then, was beginning to express its function, and Sullivan's famous dictum that "form follows function," long the slogan of early twentieth-century architects, found its illustration here. Sullivan did not mean by this slogan that a functional building is automatically beautiful, nor did he advocate a rigid and doctrinaire correspondence between exterior and interior design. Rather, he espoused a free and flexible relationship—one that his great pupil, Frank Lloyd Wright, would later describe as similar to that between the bones and tissue of the hand.

Sullivan took a further step in the unification of exterior and interior design in his Carson, Pirie, Scott Building in Chicago, Illinois (FIG. **26-98**), built between 1899 and 1904. A department store, this building required broad, open, well-illuminated display spaces. The structural steel skeleton, being minimal, permitted the singular achievement of this goal. The relation of spaces and solids here is so logical that nothing in the way of facing had to be added, and the skeleton is clearly revealed on the exterior. The deck-like stories, faced in white ceramic slabs, seem to sweep freely around the building and show several irregularities (notably the stressed bays of the corner entrance) that help the design to break out of the cubical formula of Sullivan's older buildings. The lower two levels of the Carson, Pirie, Scott Building are given over to an ornament in cast iron (of Sullivan's invention) made of wildly fantastic motifs that bear little resemblance to anything traditional architecture could show. In the general search for a new style at the end of the century, Sullivan was a leader. He gave as much attention to finding new directions in architectural ornament as in architecture itself. In this respect, he was an important figure in the movement called Art Nouveau, whose adherents sought an end to all traditional ornamental styles—indeed, to the whole preoccupation with historical style that had been postponing the true advent of a modern method of representing form in the arts.

LOUIS SULLIVAN, Carson, Pirie, Scott Building, Chicago, 1899–1904.

26-99 RICHARD MORRIS HUNT, *The Breakers,* Newport, Rhode Island, 1892.

But the reader must not be left with the impression that these great innovations were accepted everywhere and all at once. Well into the twentieth century the historical styles would determine public taste and architectural design. Especially in the last decades of the nineteenth century, huge accumulations of wealth in the hands of industrialists and railway magnates permitted the construction of lavishly expensive villas, mansions, and palatial town houses. Historical styles seemed appropriate to the newly rich who would live like medieval barons or Renaissance princes. They were overwhelming evidence that their owners, as the millionaires boasted, could buy up European noblemen by the dozen. Indeed, it was a time when many an American aristocrat by wealth could buy a title for his daughter by marrying her to a European aristocrat by birth.

RICHARD MORRIS HUNT (1827–1895) specialized in serving the building ambitions of America's new aristocracy. He brought Renaissance and Baroque form to the design of their ostentatious plans. Hunt had studied architecture in Switzerland and Paris and was happy to combine the historical styles arbitrarily to suit the taste of his patrons. The Breakers (FIG. **26-99**), built by Hunt for Cornelius Vanderbilt II, the railroad king, is a splendid private palace in Newport, Rhode Island, a favorite summer vacation spot for the affluent, who competed with one another in the magnitude and majesty of their mansions. Occupying a glorious promontory above the sea, with a splendid view of the incoming "breakers," the residence resembles more a sixteenth-century Italian palazzo (with touches of French style) than a large summer cottage. The interior rooms are grand in scale and sumptuously rich in decor, each having its own variation of Classical columns, painted ceilings, lavish fabrics, and sculptured furbelows. The entry hall, rising some 45 feet above the majestic main stairway, signals the opulence of the rooms beyond. This hall and most of the main rooms of the house offer a magnificent view over the grounds and the ocean, a view assured by Hunt's siting of the building. As Garnier's Opèra influenced theater design well into the twentieth century, so the grandeur and lavishness of Hunt's palatial domestic style were to remain popular with the ultrarich until World War I shattered the bright period known as *la belle époque.*

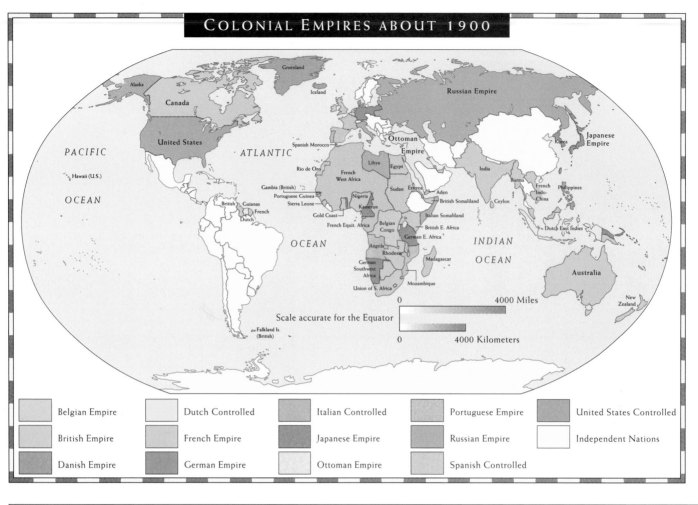

COLONIAL EMPIRES ABOUT 1900

Greenland

Alaska

Canada

Iceland

Russian Empire

PACIFIC

United States

ATLANTIC

Spanish Morocco

Ottoman Empire

Japanese Empire

Korea

Hawaii (U.S.)

OCEAN

Rio de Oro

Libya

Egypt

India

Burma

French Indo-China

Philippines

Gambia (British)

French West Africa

Portuguese Guinea

Sudan

Eritrea

Aden

British Somaliland

Ceylon

Sierra Leone

Nigeria

Gold Coast

Kamerun

British Guianas

French

Dutch

OCEAN

French Equit. Africa

Belgian Congo

Italian Somaliland

British E. Africa

German E. Africa

INDIAN

Dutch East Indies

Angola

Rhodesia

OCEAN

Madagascar

German Southwest Africa

Australia

Mozambique

Union of S. Africa

New Zealand

Falkland Is. (British)

0 ——— 4000 Miles

Scale accurate for the Equator

0 ——— 4000 Kilometers

Belgian Empire	Dutch Controlled	Italian Controlled	Portuguese Empire	United States Controlled
British Empire	French Empire	Japanese Empire	Russian Empire	Independent Nations
Danish Empire	German Empire	Ottoman Empire	Spanish Controlled	

1900   1910   1920

Matisse
Red Room (Harmony in Red), 1908-1909

Braque
The Portuguese, 1911

First trans-Atlantic radio signal, *1901*   Queen Victoria's reign ends, *1901*

Die Blaue Reiter, 1911

Russian Revolution, *1917-* Communist Regime

Sigmund Freud, *1856-1939*
The Interpretation of Dreams, 1900

Les Fauves, *1906*

Die Brücke, *1905*   Futurist Manifesto, *1909*

Carl Jung, *1875-1961*
(Analytical psychology)

Wright brothers' first flight, *1903*

World War I, *1914-1918*

Bauhaus founded, *1919*

Max Planck (Quantum theory, *1900*)

Niels Bohr (Atomic Theory, *1913*)

Treaty of Versailles, *1919-1921*

Realistic Manifesto, 192
("Constructivism")

Albert Einstein, *1879-1955 (Theory of Relativity) 1905-1915*

League of Nations, *1921-1939*

CHAPTER 27

◆

THE EARLY
TWENTIETH CENTURY:
THE ESTABLISHMENT OF
MODERNIST ART

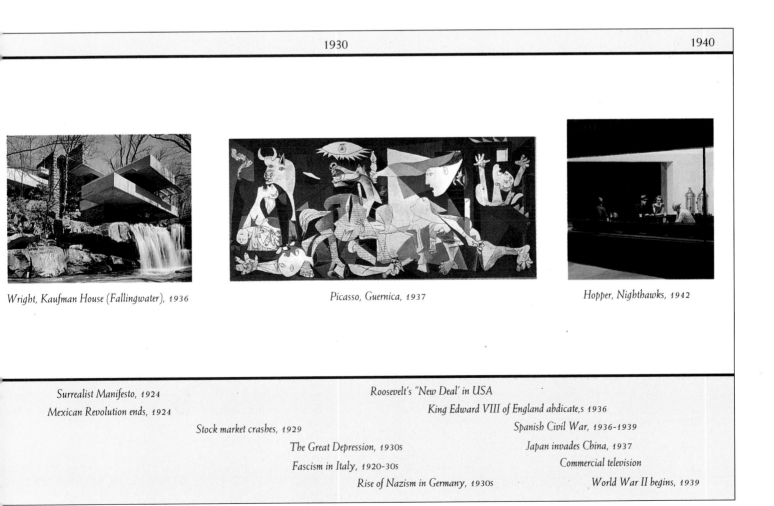

1930   1940

Wright, Kaufman House (Fallingwater), 1936   Picasso, Guernica, 1937   Hopper, Nighthawks, 1942

Surrealist Manifesto, 1924   Roosevelt's "New Deal' in USA

Mexican Revolution ends, 1924   King Edward VIII of England abdicate,s 1936

Stock market crashes, 1929   Spanish Civil War, 1936-1939

The Great Depression, 1930s   Japan invades China, 1937

Fascism in Italy, 1920-30s   Commercial television

Rise of Nazism in Germany, 1930s   World War II begins, 1939

Imperialism, Racism, Nationalism, and War

By the beginning of the twentieth century the European powers had established colonial empires throughout most of the world, completing a process that had begun in the Renaissance. The continent of Africa was partitioned by Britain, France, Germany, Belgium, Italy, Spain, and Portugal. In Asia, Britain ruled India, the Dutch ruled the vast archipelago of Indonesia, the French ruled Indochina, the Russians ruled Central Asia and Siberia. Japan was rising as a new and formidable Pacific power that would stake its claims to empire in the 1930s. Various European powers had Pacific colonies and the United States held sway over the Philippines and Hawaii. Australia and Canada were British dominions. The islands of the Caribbean were alternately French and British, and Puerto Rico was an American annex. The United States would create the Republic of Panama out of a section of Colombia. It was inevitable that these imperialistic interests would clash, and clash they did—in two great world wars that in the end closed down the empires and liberated the colonial people.

Imperialism was not only capitalist and expansionist, establishing colonies as sources of raw material, as markets for European manufactures, and as territorial acquisitions; it had, it was believed, a missionary function, to bring the light of Christianity and civilization to "backward peoples" and to educate "inferior races."* Along with racism, nationalism was party to the ideology and practice of imperialism. On the European continent the industrialized nations watched anxiously over the balance of power among them, and by 1900 they had forged alliances guaranteed to resist by war any attempt to upset it. Patriotic nationalism in each country proclaimed the superiority of that country above the others and the willingness to fight to prove it. Thus, nationalism upheld the superiority of one European nation to another, while racism upheld the superiority of Europe to the rest of the world; as the poet Tennyson put it: "better fifty years of Europe, than a cycle of Cathay [China]."

The interlaced ideologies of imperialism, racism, and nationalism were instrumental in motivating both world wars. In the first war, colonial peoples fought in the armies of their imperial masters on either side. But the war was mostly a conflict between white peoples. The second war was fought in the lands of the colonial races as well as in Europe, and racial motivation played a decisive role.

The devastation of World War I brought widespread misery, social disruption, and economic collapse. The Great Depression of the 1930s was a consequence of it. So also was the rise of new and aggressive social forces. The collapse of the Russian army in 1917 and the defeat of Germany and Austria-Hungary in 1918 had already produced revolutions; the Bolshevik revolution in Russia was successful. New ideologies took hold: Communism, in what was now the Soviet Union, became an international, subversive political movement; National Socialism (Nazism) became dominant in Germany under Hitler; Fascism triumphed in Italy, Spain, Portugal, and various nations of central Europe. Japan developed a militaristic ideology and a nationalist imperialism of its own.

Whatever the differences among these new movements and regimes, they all shared in a hatred of democratic institutions, civil rights, the personal autonomy of citizens, and competitive capitalism. They agreed in their hostility to the victors of World War I, the "free" nations of Western Europe, and the United States. Each of the new systems, however, like the ones they had replaced, felt superior to its neighbors, was imperialist and expansionist, and turned the resources of the state into rearmament for military adventure. The old entrepreneurial capitalism that had fueled colonialism was replaced by state capitalism; the imperialist instinct remained the same.

With the failure of post-war treaties and the League of Nations to keep the peace, the cynical and brutal aggression of Hitler's Germany in Europe and of Tojo's Japan in the Pacific brought World War II. Readers will be familiar enough with the main events of that catastrophe. What is important to notice is that, as we have just mentioned, the war was fought not only in Europe, but throughout the world and especially in the colonial territories. Japan defended its conquests in China, Southeast Asia, Indonesia, and the Philippines as a liberation of the ethnic populations from their white oppressors; it wished to establish a "southeast Asian co-prosperity sphere." Hitler intended and largely achieved the obliteration of the "inferior Jewish race," and attempted but failed to enslave the "inferior" Slavic peoples of the Soviet Union, Poland, and the Balkans. Thus, the ideology of race inflamed nationalism, "excused" imperialism and, at the same time, unintentionally aroused the erstwhile colonial millions of the world to self-awareness, to the injustice of their plight, and to revolt.

Science and Technology

The two great wars, with their apocalyptic destruction of life and property, could not have been waged without the instrumentality of science and technology. At the same time, the advance of science and technology was powerfully stimulated by the wars, though enormous progress had already been made before the first one, and independently

---

*Kipling referred to them as "lesser breeds without the law." The ideology of imperialist racism rings loudly in a speech in the U.S. Senate by Senator Albert J. Beveridge urging occupation of the Philippines, January 9, 1900: "Mr. President, God has not been preparing the English-speaking and Teutonic peoples for nothing but vain and idol self-contemplation and self-admiration. No! He has made us the master-organizers of the world to establish system where chaos reigns. . . . He made us adept in government that we may administer government among savage and senile peoples. . . . He has marked the American people as his chosen nation to finally lead in the regeneration of the world. This is the divine mission of America. . . . We will not renounce our part in the mission of our race, trustee under God, of the civilization of the world."

of military necessity. A brief review of that progress will be useful.

The early century witnessed an astounding burst of scientific activity that amounted to what has been called "the second scientific/technological revolution" (the first being the achievements of the Age of Newton). The "heroic" phase of this revolution took place just before and during World War I. The Quantum Theory of Max Planck (1900), the Special Theory (1905) and the General Theory of Relativity (1915) proposed by Albert Einstein, and the Rutherford-Bohr descriptive model of the nuclear atom (1913) constituted a new view of physical nature and raised the curtain on the Atomic Age. The discovery of radioactivity opened the way for world-transforming electronic technology. Energy was now shown to be not distinct from matter but its equivalent, as demonstrated by Einstein's famous equation $E=mc^2$, where E stands for energy, m for mass, and c^2 for the speed of light, a new limiting factor for the events of the physical universe. Both energy and matter are atomic. The absolute, continuous, three-dimensional space and time of Newton became the four-dimensional space-time of Einstein. Newton's continuum becomes discrete and atomistic. All motion is relative, depending upon the relative velocities of the systems observing and measuring it. Radically oversimplified, the complicated theory of relativity was reduced to the popular slogan: "everything is relative."

Advances in chemistry, biology, biochemistry, microbiology, and medicine in the earlier century yielded knowledge of polymers, plastics, fertilizers, enzymes, viruses, vitamins, hormones, and antibiotics. The structure of cells and tissues and the electrical nature of the brain and nervous system were analyzed and described. The new science of molecular biology began with the study of proteins and nucleic acids, leading to an understanding of the genetic structure of life.

The most conspicuous technological achievements, which largely depended upon the scientific, were in communication and transportation, elaborating on the technological achievements of the later nineteenth century: radio, radar, television, the talking motion picture; the automobile, the airplane—from propeller-driven to jet—electrified railway and municipal transit systems, electrification of street lighting and home appliances. Large-scale building was facilitated by the use of reinforced and pre-stressed concrete.

Chemical technology became an industry as important as electrical technology. It presided over the world of materials; mining, metals, oil refining, textiles, pharmaceuticals, agriculture, food production and food processing. It stood guard against disease and famine, though at this time its ecological effects for good or for ill were not yet suspected. In the dawn of the Nuclear Age the perils of atomic power in peacetime application had not yet appeared.

Mass-production and the assembly line became indispensable to industry. Scientific instruments like the electron microscope became essential to chemical and biological research. The requirements of calculation, vastly expanded by war and the new complexities of the machine environment, demanded electronic instrumentation and control mechanisms. Cybernetic theory and early models of the computer were in place by mid-century.

Science and Technology as Models of Progress: The Ideology of Modernism

No one could doubt what was obvious, that science and technology represented progress. This had long been noticed, almost since the time of Newton. Now, in the twentieth century, science and technology were controlling the very conditions of life, and it could be believed that they would improve those conditions increasingly and indefinitely. But it was also obvious, from the great wars, that science could destroy as well as create, depending upon whose hands manipulated it. Science obviously progressed, but it was just as obvious that the moral and social nature of humankind did not keep up with it. The leading philosophers of the Enlightenment had thought that reason and knowledge, open to all, would automatically lead to human moral improvement. Yet this conviction had led imperialism to enslave human populations in order to improve and uplift them—in the name of progress. In the name of progress great social revolutions promised emancipation to exploited classes, but in the end incarceration became the norm in totalitarian political and social systems. Biological evolution had seemed to make progress itself a law of nature, but evolution was being used to justify cutthroat economic competition and to demonstrate the natural inferiority of certain human races and societies to others.

Nevertheless, science and its achievements are understood to be the manifestation of progress. Science has made the modern world, and to acknowledge this and to live accordingly is to be authentically progressive, which, in its very broadest sense, means modern. This is the core idea of *Modernism*. Modernity, the condition of being modern, rejects the past as having been passed by. To live by past ideas and values is to regress; those still living in pre-modern conditions are in a stage of underdevelopment and of immaturity. The centuries-old contest between the "ancients" and the "moderns" is now decided in favor of the moderns—once and for all. The past may have produced great theories of reality and great works of art, but the theories are now obsolete, and the great works of art cannot be done over again. Even if they could, the result would be mere imitation, incapable of expressing the modern experience.

A corollary idea of Modernism derives from the scientific worldview. According to that view, our commonsensical world, the world of everyday perception, is not "real." It is reducible by scientific analysis to the reality of subatomic particles, or expandable to the atomic universe of stars, galaxies, gas clouds, matter, and anti-matter investigated by astrophysics. To take as "real" the world as we see it is a fundamental error. The analytical reduction of the world to energy systems, and the synthesis of it by scientific construction of theories, make up the as yet incomplete world-picture accepted by Modernism.

The media by which scientific reduction and construction take place are abstractions, mathematical and graphic. These control the experimental instruments by which science operates and through which the results of those operations are secured. Modern science abstracts and operates instrumentally without making judgments about "reality" as such.

Similarly, Modernism for the visual arts repudiates the notion that representation of the optical world correctly reports "reality." The appearances of things are not the way things are; the representation of appearances even less so (Plato!). Thus, the representational art of the Western Tradition is false and misguided and should be fundamentally altered or dismissed. The way we actually experience things is much more complicated than our visual information gives us to believe; a table seen in perspective, and represented as such, is neither the whole nor the "real" table. We sit at it, walk around it, bump into it, move it out of the way, and may see it at different times in different lighting and from different angles. What counts is the way we feel and think about it; and to express this in visual art we need to abstract from it its characteristic features as differently perceived, to distort its many appearances for expression's sake, or to abandon making images of it as an object altogether, in favor of nonobjective lines, shapes, and colors. The ultimate "reality" is the medium itself and its physical elements.

Moreover, since our feelings are necessarily subjective, that is, uniquely our own, they will be expressed in uniquely subjective terms. And since, as the adherents of modern Freudian psychology theorize, our "real" selves are unconsciously defined and moved, we must allow the unconscious to rise into our conscious experience and to affect the kind of art we make. The true and the "real" must be found within ourselves, and must not submit to repression or distortion by the conditioning of institutions, social convention, tradition, education, and other sources of fallacious stereotypes.

In our account of Modernist art we permit artists to speak for themselves. Despite their individual differences of viewpoint there is a remarkable agreement about what Modernism should be and what it is driving at.

THE ESTABLISHMENT OF MODERNIST ART

"Establishment" here is to be taken in both its senses, as the process of establishing, and as the institution that is estab-

lished. The pluralism of styles that distinguished the nineteenth century was succeeded by twentieth-century Modernism, which established both a modern taste and a modern style. Though there are a variety of modern styles, their differences are the result of specialization in one artistic problem or another, whether of medium or form or both; they all satisfy a single, exclusive taste for what is modern.

We have seen that by the time of Courbet, Manet, and the Impressionists, demand was rising for art that would be of its own time, that would express the modern experience. Artists responding to this demand—often sharing in the initiation of it—became increasingly independent of the traditional art favored by the bourgeois public, by academies, and by governments. In the early decades of the twentieth century, encouraged by sympathetic critics, art dealers, and collectors, artists formed groups and movements to advance the cause of artistic innovation and engage in a running battle with a largely unsympathetic public and hostile authorities.

Their struggle, protests, language, organization, and party divisions resemble those of the political and social movements of the time. They held independent exhibitions and conferences, published their own journals, issued manifestoes and proclamations. Numerous disagreements arose among them, with groups seceding from one another to form new groups and these seceding once again. The militancy of the more radical groups is expressed in the tactical term *avant-garde* (literally, the vanguard of a column of troops); they advocated a complete break with traditional, representational art, and with the institutions that supported it. They wanted total reform of the art situation, a new visual order "purified" of all representational traits, an art "true" to the elementary functions of artistic materials, and honestly expressive of the artist's feelings and free imagination. The prophet of the Modernist doctrine was Cézanne, and the principal heroes of the movement were Seurat, van Gogh, and Gauguin.

Modernist exhibitions, the art equivalent of political demonstrations, successively challenged the public's taste for the traditional. We have noticed this as early as the Impressionists. There followed the "Secessionist" exhibitions in Germany and Austria, which introduced Art Nouveau to a wide audience between 1897 and 1905. The "Fauve" (literally, "wild beast") painters of Paris, in two salons in 1905 and 1907, startled the public with expressionistic distortions of shape and color. In 1913 the Armory Show in New York marked the first appearance of Modernist art in the United States. Futurist and Surrealist shows in the 1920s and 1930s attracted public attention and critical review of a positive kind.

In addition to public exhibitions, Modernist art was shown in the privately owned galleries of professional art dealers, who were, the best of them, genuinely interested in the new work and willing to contract with the artists, often at considerable risk to themselves, in order to sell and advertise it. This three-way relationship of artist, dealer, and collector was, and still is, of fundamental importance in establishing Modernist art, promulgating its values, and furthering the educational process. By the 1930s and 1940s, art schools and the art departments of colleges and universities were teaching the practice, theory, and history of Modernist art as thoroughly serious disciplines.

The Museum of Modern Art in New York was organized in 1929 by a group of wealthy and converted collectors. By the very title of the organization and by its building designed especially to house and exhibit modernist art, the new art was conspicuously and officially recognized as both distinct from and on a par with the art of other historical periods. In Paris, Rome, Brussels, and Berlin similar institutions marked the establishment, recognition, and acceptance of the art of the twentieth century and of its nineteenth-century forerunners.

Modernist art could now boast the authority of a respected institution, which had won its way through a revolutionary process to a position of powerful and determining influence upon the taste of the public, as well as to a legitimate place in the history of world art.

The transition from the nineteenth to the twentieth century can best be shown in architecture, where the decorative style associated with fin de siècle symbolism in painting, Art Nouveau, yields to the new "purified" architecture of the International Style.

ARCHITECTURE

Art Nouveau

*Art Nouveau** was a movement whose proponents tried to synthesize all the arts, in a determined attempt to create art based on natural forms that could be mass-produced by the technologies of the industrial age. The Art Nouveau style emerged at the end of the nineteenth century and adapted the twining plant form to the needs of architecture, painting, sculpture, and all of the decorative arts. Foliate patterns, rendered in cast iron, had adorned the ground floor of Louis Sullivan's Carson, Pirie, Scott building in Chicago (FIG. 26-98). The mature Art Nouveau style, however, was first seen in houses designed in Brussels in the 1890s by VICTOR HORTA (1861–1947). The staircase in the Hotel van Eetvelde (FIG. **27-1**), which Horta built in Brussels in 1895, is a good example of his Art Nouveau work. Every detail functions as part of a living whole. Furniture, drapery folds, veining in the lavish stone panelings, and the patterning of

*The international style of *Art Nouveau* took its name from a shop in Paris dealing with *"L'Art Nouveau"* (new art) and was known by that name in France, Belgium, Holland, England, and the United States. In other places, it had other names: *Jugendstil* in Austria and Germany (after the magazine *Der Jugend,* youth), *Modernismo* in Spain, and *Floreale* or *Liberty* in Italy.

the door moldings join with real plants to provide graceful counterpoints for the metallic tendrils that curl around the railings and posts, the delicate metal tracery that fills the glass dome, and the floral and leaf motifs that spread across the fabric panels of the screen (left background).

A number of influences can be identified in Art Nouveau; they range from the rich, foliated, two-dimensional ornament and craftsman's respect for materials of the "Arts and Crafts" movement in late nineteenth-century England to the free, sinuous, whiplash curve of designs inspired by Japanese prints (FIG. 26-62). Art Nouveau also borrowed from the expressively patterned styles of Vincent van Gogh (FIG. 26-76), Paul Gauguin (FIG. 26-77), and their Post-Impressionist and Symbolist contemporaries.

Art Nouveau achieved its most personal expression in the work of the Spanish architect ANTONIO GAUDI (1852–1926). Before becoming an architect, Gaudi had trained as an ironworker. Like many young artists of his time, he longed to create a style that was both modern and appropriate to his country. Taking inspiration from Moorish-Spanish architecture and from the simple architecture of his native Catalonia, Gaudi developed a personal esthetic in which he conceived a building as a whole and

27-1 VICTOR HORTA, staircase in the Hotel van Eetvelde, Brussels, Belgium, 1895.

molded it almost as a sculptor might shape a figure from clay. Although work on his designs proceeded slowly under the guidance of his intuition and imagination, Gaudi was a master who invented many new structural techniques that facilitated the actual construction of his visions. His apartment house, Casa Milá (FIG. **27-2**), is a wondrously free-form mass wrapped around a street corner. Lacy iron railings enliven the swelling curves of the cut-stone facade, while dormer windows peep from the undulating tiled roof, which is capped by fantastically writhing chimneys that poke energetically into the air above. The rough surfaces of the stone walls suggest naturally worn rock. The entrance portals look like eroded sea caves, but their design also may reflect something of the excitement that swept Spain following the 1879 discovery of Paleolithic paintings at Altamira cave. Gaudi felt that each of his buildings was a symbolically living thing, and the passionate naturalism of his Casa Milá is the spiritual kin of early twentieth-century Expressionist painting and sculpture.

The New Architecture

FRANK LLOYD WRIGHT   One of the most striking personalities in the development of early twentieth-century architecture was FRANK LLOYD WRIGHT (1867–1959). Born in Wisconsin, Wright attended a few classes at the University of Wisconsin in Madison before moving to Chicago where he eventually joined the firm headed by Louis Sullivan. Wright set out early to create "architecture for democracy."

27-2   Antonio Gaudi, Casa Milá, Barcelona, Spain, 1907.

Early influences were the volumetric shapes in a set of educational blocks designed by the German educator Friedrich Froebel (from Wright's childhood), the organic unity of a Japanese building he saw at the Columbian Exposition in Chicago in 1893, and a Jeffersonian belief in individualism and the common man. Always a believer in architecture as "natural" and "organic," Wright saw it in the service of free individuals who have the right to move within a "free" space, which he envisioned as a nonsymmetrical design that interacted spatially with its natural surroundings. He sought to develop an organic unity of planning, structure, materials, and site. He identified the principle of continuity as fundamental to the understanding of his view of organic unity:

"Classic architecture was all fixation. . . . Now why not let walls, ceilings, floors become seen as component parts of each other? . . . You may see the appearance in the surface of your hand contrasted with the articulation of the bony structure itself. This ideal, profound in its architectural implications . . . I called . . . continuity.*

Wright's ideas were not unique to architecture. The concepts of flux, of constant change, of evolution and progress are inherent in Wright's principle of continuity and also appeared in the work of the poet Walt Whitman and in the writings of the greatly influential philosopher Henri Bergson, a contemporary of Wright, who stressed the reality of vitalism—living process—above any other.

*In Edgar Kaufmann, ed., *American Architecture* (New York: Horizon, 1955), pp. 205, 208.

Wright's vigorous originality was manifested early and, by 1900, he had arrived at a style entirely his own; in his work during the first decade of this century, his cross-axial plan and his fabric of continuous roof planes and screens defined a new domestic architecture.* Although the skeleton frame made a significant appearance in the works of Sullivan and others, Wright attacked the concept in his studies of other systems. He rejected both posts and columns: "In my work, the idea of plasticity may now be seen as the element of continuity . . . the new reality that is space instead of matter." As for architectural interiors, he declared that he "came to realize that the reality of a building was not the container but the space within."

These elements and concepts are fully expressed in Wright's Robie House (FIG. 27-3), which was built between 1907 and 1909. Like others in the Chicago area designed by Wright at about the same time, this building was called a "prairie house." The long, sweeping, ground-hugging lines, unconfined by abrupt limits of wall, were conceived to reach out toward and to express the great flatlands of the Midwest. All symmetry was abandoned. The facade disappeared, the roofs were extended far beyond the walls, and the entrance was all but concealed. Wright filled the "wandering" plan of the Robie House (FIG. 27-4) with intricately articulated spaces (some, large and open; others, closed), grouped freely around a great central fireplace. (He felt strongly the age-old domestic significance of the hearth.)

*Wright's designs for roofs, planes, and screens were inspired by so-called shingle-plan resort houses designed in the late nineteenth century by H. H. Richardson.

27-3 FRANK LLOYD WRIGHT, Robie House, Chicago, 1907–1909.

Enclosed patios, overhanging roofs, and strip windows were designed to provide unexpected light sources and glimpses of the outdoors as one moved through the interior space. These elements, together with the open ground plan, created a sense of space-in-motion inside and out. Wright's new and fundamental spatial arrangement of the interior was matched by his treatment of the exterior. Masses and voids were set in equilibrium; the flow of interior space determined the placement of the exterior walls. The exterior, with its sharp, angular places meeting at apparently odd angles, matches the complex play of interior solids that function not as inert, containing surfaces but as elements equivalent in role to the spaces in the design.

The Robie House is a good example of Wright's "naturalism" in the adjustment of building to site, although, in this particular case, the confines of the city lot constrained the building to site relationship more than did the sites of some of Wright's more expansive suburban and country homes. The Kaufmann House, nicknamed "Fallingwater" (FIG. 27-5), which was designed as a weekend retreat at Bear Run near Pittsburgh, is a prime example of the latter. Perched on a rocky hillside over a small waterfall, this structure extends the blocky masses of the Robie House in all four directions. Its shapes are enlivened by the contrast in textures between concrete, painted metal, and natural stones in its walls, and by the way in which Wright used full-length strip windows to create a stunning interweaving of interior and exterior space. The implied message of Wright's new architecture was space, not mass—a space designed to fit the life of the patron, being enclosed and

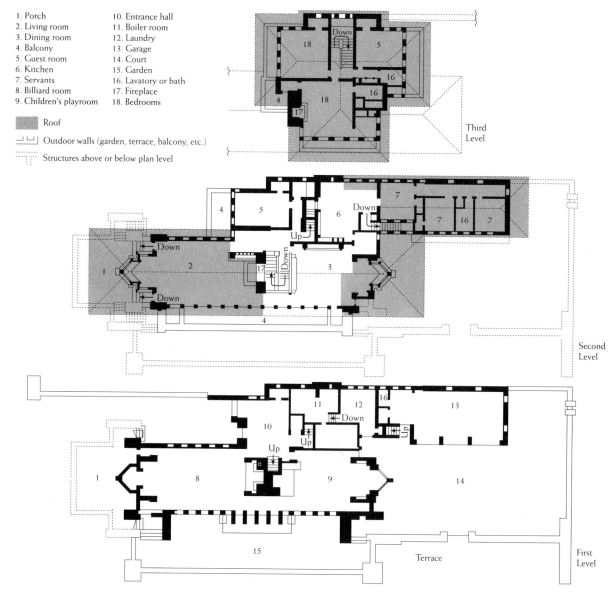

1. Porch
2. Living room
3. Dining room
4. Balcony
5. Guest room
6. Kitchen
7. Servants
8. Billiard room
9. Children's playroom
10. Entrance hall
11. Boiler room
12. Laundry
13. Garage
14. Court
15. Garden
16. Lavatory or bath
17. Fireplace
18. Bedrooms

Roof

Outdoor walls (garden, terrace, balcony, etc.)

Structures above or below plan level

27-4 Plan of the Robie House.

[handwritten margin notes:]
Chicago 1875-1900
Art Nouveau 1900-10
Wright 1910-36
Art Deco 1929
Int Sty 1920

27-5 FRANK LLOYD WRIGHT, Kaufmann House (Fallingwater), Bear Run, Pennsylvania, 1936–1939.

divided as required. Wright took special pains to meet the requirements of his clients, often designing all the accessories of a house himself (including, in at least one case, gowns for his client's wife!). In the late 1930s, he acted on a cherished dream to provide good architectural design for less well-to-do people by adapting the ideas of his prairie house to plans for smaller, less-expensive dwellings called "Usonian" houses.

The publication of Wright's plans brought him a measure of fame in Europe, especially in Holland and Germany. The issuance of a portfolio of his work in Berlin in 1910 and an exhibition of his designs the following year hastened the death of Art Nouveau and stimulated younger architects to adopt some of his ideas about open plans and the freedom they afforded clients. Some forty years before the end of his career, his work was already of revolutionary significance. Another great modern architect, Ludwig Mies van der Rohe, wrote in 1940 that the "dynamic impulse from [Wright's] work invigorated a whole generation. His influence was strongly felt even when it was not actually visible."*

DE STIJL   In 1917, a group of young artists in Holland formed a new movement and began publishing a magazine; both movement and magazine were called *De Stijl* (the

Style). The group was cofounded by the painters Piet Mondrian (see page 1061) and Theo van Doesburg (1883–1931). Group members believed that a new age was being born in the wake of World War I—that it was a time of balance between individual and universal values, when the machine would assure ease of living: "There is an old and a new consciousness of the age. The old one is directed toward the individual. The new one is directed toward the universal."* The goal would be a total integration of art and life:

> We must realize that life and art are no longer separate domains. That is why the "idea" of "art" as an illusion separate from real life must disappear. The word "art" no longer means anything to us. In its place we demand the construction of our environment in accordance with creative laws based upon a fixed principle. These laws, following those of economics, mathematics, technique, sanitation . . . are leading to a new, plastic unit.†

One of the masterpieces of De Stijl architecture is the Schröder House in Utrecht, Holland (FIG. **27-6**), built in 1924 by GERRIT THOMAS RIETVELD (1888–1964). Rietveld came to the group as a cabinetmaker and made De Stijl furnishings throughout his career. His architecture carries the

*In Philip Johnson, *Mies van der Rohe,* rev. ed. (New York: Museum of Modern Art, 1954), pp. 200–201.

*In Kenneth Frampton, *A Critical History of Modern Architecture* (London: Thames & Hudson, 1985), p. 142.

†Ibid., p. 147.

27-6 GERRIT RIETVELD, Schröder House, Utrecht, Netherlands, 1924.

same spirit into a larger, integrated whole. The main living rooms of the Schröder House are on the second floor, with more private rooms on the ground floor. However, Rietveld's house has an open plan and a relationship to nature more like the houses of Frank Lloyd Wright (FIGS. 27-3 and 27-5). The entire second floor is designed with sliding partitions that can be closed to define separate rooms or pushed back to create one open space broken into units only by the arrangement of the furniture. This shifting quality appears also on the outside, where railings, free-floating walls, and long rectangular windows give the effect of cubic units breaking up before our eyes. The Schröder House is the perfect expression of van Doesburg's definition of De Stijl architecture:

> The new architecture is anti-cubic, i.e., it does not strive to contain the different functional space cells in a single closed cube, but it throws the functional space (as well as canopy planes, balcony volumes, etc.) out from the centre of the cube, so that height, width, and depth plus time become a completely new plastic expression in open spaces. . . .The plastic architect . . . has to construct in the new field, time-space.*

The link between all the arts in De Stijl is clear in Rietveld's design, where the rectangular planes, which seem to slide across each other on the facade of the Schröder House like movable panels, make this structure a kind of three-dimensional projection of the rigid but carefully proportioned flat places in Mondrian's paintings (FIG. 27-50).

*In Hans L. Jaffé, *De Stijl* (New York: Harry N. Abrams, n.d.), pp. 185–188.

ART DECO The new architecture, in theory and practice, repudiated ornament of any kind. Pure form emerged from functional structure and required no appliqué. Yet popular taste still favored the decorative, especially in public architecture. The 1920s and 1930s saw a movement to upgrade industrial design in competition with "fine art," and to work new materials into decorative patterns that could be either machined or handcrafted and that could, to a degree, reflect the simplifying trend in architecture. A remote descendant of Art Nouveau, this movement came to be known as *Art Deco*. (Like its predecessor, it was an event in the history of industrial design, not in the history of architecture.) But it did have universal application—to buildings, interiors, furniture, utensils, jewelry, fashions, illustration, and commercial products of every sort. Art Deco products have a "streamlined," elongated, symmetrical aspect; simple flat shapes alternate with shallow volumes in hard patterns simulating mainline modern architecture. In fact, Art Deco was often described contemptuously as "modernistic," though it was a quite distinctive taste and style contemporary in time with early modern architecture. As a cultural phenomenon, it is associated with Jazz Age flair, flippancy, and elegance, and with the gorgeous salons of the great ocean liners that ferried the carefree rich in the days of the "lost generation."

Art Deco's exemplary masterpiece is the stainless steel spire of the Chrysler Building in New York City (FIG. **27-7**), designed by WILLIAM VAN ALEN (1882–1954). The building and spire are monuments to the fabulous twenties, when American millionaires and corporations competed with one another to raise the tallest skyscrapers in the biggest cities. The spire, built up of diminishing fan shapes, glitters triumphantly in the sky, a resplendent oriental crown honoring the business achievements of the great auto manufacturer. As a temple of commerce, the Chrysler Building is dedicated to the principles and success of American business, before its chastening in the Great Depression.

Art Deco was not taken seriously by the major architects of its time, but it reminds us of a perennial popular taste for the ornamental and how large a part it plays in the history of world architecture.

THE BAUHAUS The De Stijl group dreamed of harnessing the machine to create whole environments. In reality, De Stijl architects actually built more private than public buildings. In Europe, German architects pioneered new industrial techniques for commercial and factory buildings, often under the inspiration of American silos, warehouses, and the early highrise structures of Richardson and Sullivan (FIGS. 26-96 and 26-97). A particular vision of "total architecture" was developed by the German architect WALTER GROPIUS (1883–1969), who made this concept the foundation not only of his own work but also of the work of generations of pupils who came under his influence.

27-7 WILLIAM VAN ALEN, Chrysler Building, New York, 1928–1930. Spire of stainless steel, overall height 1048'.

Gropius's revolutionary ideas about the nature of architecture and architects developed during his early career in designs for objects and structures intended to serve large sections of the population: group farm dwellings, diesel locomotives, and model factories. In 1919 he had a chance to broaden his sphere of influence and to gain additional exposure for his ideas when he became the director of an art school in Weimar, Germany. Founded in 1906 as the Weimar School of Arts and Crafts, with an educational program that emphasized craftsmanship, free creativity, and experimentation, under Gropius the school was renamed Das Staatliche Bauhaus (roughly translated as "State School of Building"), and referred to as the *Bauhaus*, and its mission was transformed to fit his ideas about the training of the modern architect:

> The complete Building is the final aim of the visual arts. . . . The objective of all creative effort in the visual arts is to give form to space. . . . But what is space, how can it be understood and given form? . . . True creative work can be done only by the man whose knowledge and mastery of the physical laws of statics, dynamics, optics, acoustics, equip him to give life and shape to his inner vision. In a work of art, the laws of the physical world, the intellectual world, and the world of the spirit function and are expressed simultaneously. . . . We want to create a clear, organic architecture, whose inner logic will be radiant and naked, unencumbered by lying facades and trickeries; we want an architecture adapted to our world of machines, radios, and fast motor cars, an architecture whose function is clearly recognizable in the relation of its form. . . . A new esthetic of the horizontal is beginning to develop which endeavors to counteract the effect of gravity. At the same time the symmetrical relationship of parts of the building and their orientation toward a central axis is being replaced by a new conception of equilibrium which transmutes this dead symmetry of similar parts into an asymmetrical but rhythmical balance.*

Gropius reorganized the various departments of the original Weimar school and redesigned its curriculum to stress the search for solutions to contemporary problems in such areas as housing, urban planning, and high-quality, utilitarian mass production—all vital needs in impoverished post–World War I Germany. Under the guidance of teachers like Kandinsky, Klee, and László Moholy-Nagy (all of whom are discussed later in this chapter), the Bauhaus offered courses not only in architecture, but also in music, drama, painting, typography, and most crafts. In design, the study of handicraft was considered the natural way for artists to master the qualities of materials and form so that they could design well for mass production. In these respects, and in the minimizing of philosophy and other "verbal" disciplines, the Bauhaus was the earliest working example of much contemporary design education. Gropius worked actively to make the Bauhaus into a "consulting center for industry and the trades." By the time he designed new quarters for the school in 1925, in preparation for its

*In Herbert Bayer, Walter Gropius, Ise Gropius, et al., *Bauhaus: 1919–1928* (Boston: Branford, 1959), *passim*.

27-8 WALTER GROPIUS, Shop Block, the Bauhaus, Dessau, Germany, 1925–1926.

move to a new location in Dessau, Germany, a new generation of teachers had been trained as artists-craftsmen-industrial designers, and Bauhaus students and faculty were designing buildings, stained-glass windows, furniture, lighting, fabrics, pottery, metal objects of every kind, advertising, books, and commercial displays—all for mass production.

Gropius's design for the Bauhaus buildings included a glass-walled workshop (FIG. **27-8**), a block of studio-bedrooms for students, and a building for technical instruction. Linking these three main blocks were other units, such as the administrative offices, which were located on the bridge that spans the road in our illustration. Gropius also designed houses nearby for himself and six major Bauhaus teachers. Planned as a series of units, each with its own specific function, the Bauhaus design is the direct expression in glass, steel, and thin concrete veneer, of the technical program it housed. The forms are clear, cubic shapes—the epitome of classicizing purity. The workshop/block is a cage of glass that extends beyond and encloses its steel supports. The transparent block makes an equilibrium of inner and outer space. The whole fulfilled Gropius's original dream for the kind of architecture that should be created by the Bauhaus. Bauhaus style spread rapidly as its students and faculty fled the rise of Nazi power, firmly establishing the principles of the Bauhaus throughout much of the industrialized world during the next three decades.* The buildings were torn

down by the Nazi government, but the main buildings were later reconstructed.

One of the most important ex-Bauhaus teachers to carry its style abroad was the Hungarian-American LÁSZLÓ MOHOLY-NAGY (1895–1946), who taught at the Bauhaus during Gropius's directorship and later extended the school's ideas of total architecture to embrace the concept of the total artist as an individual who puts personal talent at the service of humanity in any way possible. Moholy-Nagy was a visionary who saw clearly the nature of the modern age and believed that society in this period was

> heading toward a kinetic, time-spatial existence; toward an awareness of the forces plus their relationships which define all life and of which we had no previous knowledge and for which we have as yet no exact terminology. . . . Space-time stands for many things: relativity of motion and its measurement, integration, simultaneous grasp of the inside and outside, revelation of the structure instead of the facade. It also stands for a new vision concerning materials, energies, tensions, and their social implications.*

Moholy-Nagy believed that artists should create works to help ordinary people develop this "vision in motion . . . seeing, feeling, and thinking in relationship and not as a series of isolated phenomena." Such art would capture the ways our space-time perceptions have been expanded as our eyes, ears, and senses of balance and equilibrium increasingly have functioned from within speeding cars, trains, and planes, and through X-ray cameras, telescopes, and microscopes. Moholy-Nagy experimented with light and color in painting, sculpture, prints, photograms, pho-

*The ideals of the Bauhaus were taken to the United States when its artists were forced to emigrate to escape the effects of Nazi power. Gropius headed the architecture program at Harvard University. In Chicago, Moholy-Nagy founded the New Bauhaus (later, the Institute of Design) and Mies van der Rohe shaped the architecture department at Illinois Institute of Technology.

*László Moholy-Nagy, *Vision in Motion* (Chicago: Paul Theobald, 1969), p. 268.

27-9   LÁSZLÓ MOHOLY-NAGY, *From the Radio Tower Berlin*, 1928, Gelatin silver print. The Art Institute of Chicago.

tography, experimental cinema, typography, advertisements, stage sets, and special effects for movies. Photography was an especially important medium for expressing his ideas. The bird's-eye view that he took from the top of the Radio Tower in Berlin (FIG. **27-9**) is an exercise in his "new vision" of "seeing, feeling, and thinking in relationship and not as a series of isolated phenomena." The abrupt shift from normal, eye-level viewing reveals new patterns of reality, unexpected formal associations, and a refreshingly different way of looking at the world.

THE INTERNATIONAL STYLE   Of the architectural purists—perhaps, puritans—of the style we have come to call "International," the first and most persuaded was Le Corbusier. Wright believed that people lived better when their houses allowed them easy contact with nature, and he designed his buildings accordingly. The Swiss architect CHARLES-ÉDOUARD JEANNERET (1887–1965), called LE CORBUSIER, had a rather different idea about the ideal architectural setting for people. Trained as an architect in Paris

and Berlin, Le Corbusier settled in Paris in 1917, where he became a painter, using his birth name, Jeanneret, for his work in this medium. With another artist, Amadée Ozenfant (1886–1966), Le Corbusier practiced painting in a style known as *Purism,* in which he attempted to perfect Cubism (see page 1045) by reducing it to patterns inspired by machine forms. However, Le Corbusier was best known as an influential architect and theorist on modern architecture. As such, he applied himself to the design of a "functional" living space, which he described as a "machine for living."

The drawing for his Domino House project (FIG. **27-10**) shows the skeleton of his ideal dwelling. Every level can be used. Reinforced concrete slabs serve the double function of ceiling and floor, supported by thin steel posts, or *pilotis,* that rise freely inside the perimeter of the interior spaces of the structure. The whole structure is raised above ground on short blocks. The space underneath, as well as that on the roof, was utilized. As Le Corbusier later wrote: "The house is in the air, far from the soil; the garden spreads under the house, the garden is also on top of the house, on the roof." Exterior walls can be suspended from the projecting edges of the concrete slabs in this model, like free-hanging curtains. Because the skeleton is self-supporting, an architect using this plan has complete freedom to subdivide the interior, wherever desired, with light walls that bear no structural load.

The scheme allowed the architect to provide for what Le Corbusier saw as the basic physical and psychosomatic needs of every human being—sun, space, and vegetation combined with controlled temperature, good ventilation, and insulation against harmful and undesired noise. He also believed that human scale must be the measure of dwelling design, because the house is the assertion of man within nature. The main principles of the Domino House system had been anticipated about half a decade earlier in the designs of the German architects Walter Gropius and Peter

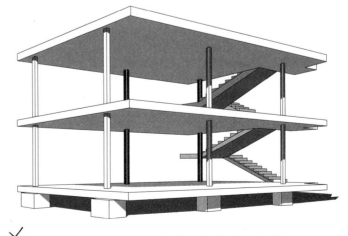

27-10   LE CORBUSIER, perspective drawing for Domino House project, Marseilles, France, 1914.

International Styl

27-11 LE CORBUSIER, Villa Savoye, Poissy-sur-Seine, France, 1929.

Behrens (with whom Le Corbusier worked early in his career). However, Le Corbusier's drawing stated their ideas with such elegant simplicity that his image had enormous influence as the primary statement of the design concepts governing the structural principles used in many modern office buildings and skyscrapers, concepts practiced by so many architects (including Gropius and Mies van der Rohe [FIG. 27-12]) that the "look" was eventually named the *International Style.*

Le Corbusier used the basic ideas of the Domino House project in many single-family dwellings, the most elegant of which is the Villa Savoye (FIG. **27-11**), located at Poissy-sur-Seine, near Paris. The Villa Savoye is set conspicuously within its site, tending to dominate it, and has a broad view of the landscape. In this way, it resembles a Palladian villa and contrasts sharply with Frank Lloyd Wright's dwellings, which hug and adjust to the landscape, almost as if they were intended to be part of it and concealed by it. The Villa Savoye is a cube of lightly enclosed and deeply penetrated space. The ground floor (containing a three-car garage, some bedrooms, a bathroom, and some utility rooms) is only partially enclosed. Much of the house's interior is open space, with the main living floor and the roof garden area supported by the thin pilotis. Here one sees a parallel with Wright's open floor plans. The major living rooms in the Villa Savoye are on the second floor, wrapping around an open central court and lighted by strip windows that run along the membranelike exterior walls. From the second floor court, a ramp leads up to a flat roof-terrace and garden, protected by a curving windbreak along one side. The approach does not define an entrance; the building has no traditional facade. One must walk around and through the building to comprehend its layout. Spaces and masses interpenetrate so fluently that "inside" and "outside" space intermingle. The machine-planed smoothness of the surfaces, entirely without adornment, the slender "ribbons" of continuous windows, the buoyant lightness of the whole fabric—all present a total effect that is the

reverse of the traditional country house (compare Andrea Palladio's Villa Rotunda, FIG. 22-51, and John Vanbrugh's Blenheim, FIG. 25-1).

Le Corbusier inverted the traditional design practice that placed light elements above and heavy ones below by refusing to enclose the ground story of the Villa Savoye with masonry walls, creating the effect that the "load" of the Villa Savoye's upper stories hovers lightly on the slender piloti supports. His use of color in this building—originally, dark-green base, cream walls and rose-and-blue windscreen—was a deliberate analogy for that in the contemporary, machine-inspired Purist style of painting, in which he was actively engaged.

The Villa Savoye was a marvelous house for a single family, but like the De Stijl architects, Le Corbusier also dreamed of extending his ideas of the house as a "machine for living" to designs for efficient and humane cities. He believed that "great cities are the spiritual workshops in which the work of the world is done," and proposed to correct the deficiencies caused by poor traffic circulation, inadequate living "cells," and the lack of space for recreation and exercise in existing cities by replacing them with three types of new communities. Vertical cities would house workers and the business and service industries. Linear-industrial cities would run as belts along the routes between the vertical cities and would serve as centers for the people and processes involved in manufacturing. Finally, separate centers would be constructed for those people involved in intensive agricultural activity. Le Corbusier's cities would provide for human cultural needs in addition to serving every person's physical and psychosomatic comfort needs. The Domino House project was a key part of Le Corbusier's thinking because the design was a module that could be repeated almost indefinitely, both horizontally and vertically. Its volumes could be manipulated and interlocked to provide interior spaces of different sizes and heights. It was not site-specific and could stand comfortably in any setting. Later in his career, Le Corbusier was able to design a few of his vertical cities, most notably the Unité d'Habitation in Marseilles (1945–1952). He also created the master plan for the entire city of Chandigarh, the capital city of the Punjab, India (1950–1957). He would end his career with a personal expressive style in the Chapel of Notre Dame du Haut at Ronchamp (FIGS. 28-62 and 28-63).

When Walter Gropius resigned as head of the Bauhaus in 1930, LUDWIG MIES VAN DER ROHE (1886–1969) became its director, moving it to Berlin before political pressures forced it to close in 1933. In his architecture and furniture, he made such a clear and elegant statement of the International Style that his work had enormous influence on modern architecture. Taking as his motto, "less is more" and calling his architecture "skin and bones," his esthetic was already fully formed in the model for a glass skyscraper building he conceived in 1921 (FIG. **27-12**). Working with

glass provided him with new freedom and many new possibilities:

> I discovered by working with glass models that the important thing is the play of reflections and not the effect of light and shadow as in ordinary buildings. . . . At first glance the curved outline . . . seems arbitrary. These curves, however, were determined by three factors: sufficient illumination of the interior, the massing of the building viewed from the street, and lastly, the play of reflections."*

In the glass model, three irregularly shaped towers flow outward from a central court designed to hold a lobby, a porter's room, and a community center. Two cylindrical entrance shafts rise at the ends of the court, each containing elevators, stairways and toilets. The perimeter walls are wholly transparent, revealing the regular horizontal patterning of the cantilevered floor planes and their thin, vertical supporting elements. The weblike delicacy of the lines of the glass model, its radiance and the illusion of movement created by reflection and by light changes seen through it prefigure many of the glass skyscrapers found in major cities throughout the world today.

PAINTING AND SCULPTURE

Expressionism: "Les Fauves" in France

In 1905, the first signs of a specifically twentieth-century movement in painting appeared in Paris. In that year, at the third Salon d'Automne, a group of younger painters under the leadership of Henri Matisse exhibited canvases so simplified in design and so shockingly bright in color that a startled critic described the artists as *fauves* (wild beasts). The *Fauves* were totally independent of the French Academy and the "official" Salon, and their works were heavily influenced by the art of non-European cultures. They were among the first twentieth-century artists to be inspired by non-Western art. In African fetishes, in Polynesian decorative wood carvings, and in the sculptures and textiles of the ancient cultures of Central and South America, Fauve artists saw unexpected shapes and colors that suggested new ways of communicating emotion. These discoveries led them individually into paths of free invention and away from the traditions of the Renaissance. The Fauves produced portraits, landscapes, still lifes, and nudes of great spontaneity and verve, with rich surface textures, lively linear patterns, and boldly clashing primary colors. They were also inspired by the works of van Gogh and Gauguin (shown in retrospective exhibitions in Paris in 1901 and 1903), but the Fauves went further than any earlier artist by bringing color to a new intensity with startling discords of vermilion and emerald green, cerulean blue and

27-12 LUDWIG MIES VAN DER ROHE, model for a glass skyscraper, 1920–1921. Present location of model unknown.

*In A. James Speyer with Frederick Koeper, *Mies van der Rohe* (Chicago: The Art Institute of Chicago, 1968), p. 16.

27-13 ANDRÉ DERAIN, *London Bridge,* 1906. Oil on canvas, approx. 26″ × 39″. The Museum of Modern Art, New York (gift of Mr. and Mrs. Charles Zadok).

vivid orange held together by sweeping brush strokes and bold patterns.

Typical of their vibrant vision is *London Bridge* (FIG. **27-13**) by ANDRÉ DERAIN (1880–1954). In this work, Derain rejects the harmonies of Impressionism, so expressive of atmospheric and light conditions, in favor of a distorted perspective emphasized by the contrast of the non-naturalistic colors—clashing yellows, blues, greens, reds, and oranges—against the black accents of the arches. Derain, like the Fauves, believed that an artist's goal should be to make the strongest possible presentation of his emotional reaction to a subject by using bold color and strong linear patterns. In Fauve works, color no longer describes the local tones of an object; instead, it creates the expressive content of the picture, foreshadowing later nonobjective works whose entire content is the interaction of color and form.

The Fauve group was never an official organization of painters and it lasted only a short time. Within five years, most of the artists had modified their violent colors and found their own, more personal styles. The artist who remained most faithful to Fauve principles, while trans-

forming them through his extraordinary sensitivity for color, was HENRI MATISSE (1869–1954). Throughout his long life, Matisse's gifts for combining colors in unexpected ways and for inventing new combinations never flagged. He had trained as a lawyer, was employed as a designer for tapestry and textiles, and began painting as a pupil of Moreau (FIG. 26-81), working his way through a variety of earlier styles before beginning to follow Cézanne's idea that light could not be reproduced in painting, but must be represented there by color. *Red Room (Harmony in Red)* (FIG. **27-14**) shows Matisse's mature style, one in which bold Fauve color is controlled by wonderful curving lines, partly inspired by the artist's strong interest in works as diverse as those of Duccio (FIG. 19-6) and Ingres (FIG. 26-5), as well as Japanese prints (FIG. 26-62), and Near Eastern textiles, pottery, and paintings (FIG. 10-31). The composition is a festive, lyrical arrangement of simplified interlocking shapes. The space of the room is suggested by the perspective view of the chair seat and the window's frame, but it is simultaneously transformed into a flat pattern of colored shapes and the patterned red-pink fields shared by the tablecloth and the wallpaper. The work is a harmonious whole. Even the figure of the woman at the right is constructed from the same kind of forms as the other objects in the painting. Matisse himself said that his procedure was one of continuous adjustment—color to color, shape to shape, and color to shape—until he had achieved exactly the right "feel" and the painting was completed.

Composition for Matisse involved drawing on every element of color, shape, and arrangement to create a harmonious unity; he sought to soothe the mind and emotions of viewers in the midst of a demanding and often troubling world.

> The whole arrangement of my picture is expressive. The place occupied by figures or objects, the empty spaces around them, the proportions, everything plays a part. Composition is the art of arranging in a decorative manner the various elements at the painter's disposal for the expression of his feelings. . . . A work of art must be harmonious in its entirety; for superfluous details would, in the mind of the beholder, encroach upon the essential elements. . . . What interests me most is neither still life nor landscape but the human figure. It is through it that I best succeed in expressing the nearly religious feeling that I have towards life. . . . What I dream of is an art of balance, or purity and serenity devoid of troubling or depressing subject matter, an art which might be for every mental worker, be he businessman or writer, like an appeasing influence, like a mental soother, something like a good armchair in which to rest from physical fatigue.*

*In Herschel B. Chipp, ed., *Theories of Modern Art* (Berkeley: University of California Press, 1973), pp. 132, 135.

27-14 HENRI MATISSE, *Red Room (Harmony in Red)*, 1908–1909. Oil on canvas, approx. 5'11" × 8'1". State Hermitage Museum, St. Petersburg, Russia.

27-15 GEORGES ROUAULT, *The Old King,* 1916–1936. Oil on canvas, 30¼″ × 21¼″. The Carnegie Museum of Art, Pittsburgh (Patrons' Art Fund, 1940).

In a vein very different from that of Matisse, GEORGES ROUAULT (1871–1958) treats themes of grave social and religious import. His studies of sad clowns and broken prostitutes and his long series of religious paintings are Fauve in their simplified designs. They are constructed with black outlines like the leading in medieval stained glass, which Rouault, who had worked as a glassmaker's apprentice in his youth, had always admired. These strongly effective, black bar-like divisions and the somber tonalities he preferred—the deep glowing reds, greens, and midnight blues of stained glass—are harmonized in Rouault's powerful evocation of *The Old King* (FIG. **27-15**). The fierce aquiline features, dark complexion, and thick black hair recall some ancient Assyrian despot in brooding reverie, almost an icon of absolute and pitiless authority. The sharp and rugged simplification of the forms and harsh, hacked-out edges convey with blunt force an aspect of monarchic vengeance. Paradoxically, the figure appears to clutch flowers in one hand.

From Symbolism to Expressionism in Austria and Germany

We have discussed Symbolism, the pictorial equivalent of Art Nouveau, as dominant at the end of the nineteenth century. We saw that the Symbolists carried the subjectivity of Romanticism to new extremes. In doing so, they turned away from the common stock of historical, mythological, and anecdotal narrative to new, extremely personal visions. To express these in appropriate form, they searched unfamiliar artistic territory,—Asia (other than Japan), Oceania, Byzantium, Persia, and other exotic places. From these uncommon sources they derived novel principles of design. Of course, they did not ignore the lessons of post-Impressionism, which they had already assimilated. The picture-box of the pictorial tradition came to be replaced by flat surfaces, decoratively embellished with figures that are not modeled or, if modeled, that are often contrasted with flat patterns.

An example of this experimental adjustment of planar shapes and plastic forms is the painting *Death and Life* (FIG. **27-16**), executed in the first decade of the new century by the Viennese artist GUSTAV KLIMT (1862–1918). In 1903, Klimt visited Ravenna and saw its great mosaics. Although Byzantine art had begun to be appreciated in the early nineteenth century, Klimt approaches it here not as critic, historian or connoisseur, but as an artist open to fresh inspiration, ready and competent to assimilate form from outside his own tradition to express a modern mood. The painting is quite typically *Symbolist* in both content and form. Bright colors, mosaic-like or enamel-like, stud the surfaces that enwrap the voluptuously somnolent figures in the *Life* group, in which intertwined images of infancy, youth, maturity, and old age celebrate life as bound up with love. Outlined shapes are modeled to the extent needed to show the softness of flesh and the firmness of sinew. It is characteristic of Klimt to contrast often quite realistically modeled forms with flat patterns. The tableau of defenseless sleep is set off against the specter of Death, the nocturnal assassin, who advances threateningly upon it. The shroud of the fleshless Death is appropriately dark as night, only dimly decked with funereal black crosses and chiromantic symbols. While Life, sated with love, sleeps, its enemy, Death, wakes. The grim interval between Life and Death will soon be crossed. In this and other Symbolist works, the ornamental flatness of the drapery, the organic, undulating contours, and the arbitrary placement of the figures, so that they seem to float and hover as they would in a dream, contradict the presuppositions of realistic representation.

But the flat, decorative patterning, linear description of shape, suave technique, and occult allusions of the Symbolist painter Klimt had little appeal for German artists. Alerted to the French Fauvists, they preferred immediate, bold, personal expression in terms of wrenching distortions

Symbolist

27-16 GUSTAV KLIMT, *Death and Life,* 1908 and 1911. Oil on canvas, 5'10" × 6'6". Collection of Marietta Preleuthner, Salzburg.

of form, ragged outline, and dissonances of intense color. German expressionists, convinced they had a message, organized into movements: *Die Brücke* (the Bridge) at Dresden, and *Der Blaue Reiter* (the Blue Rider) at Munich. These painters carried even further the tendencies in the work of Derain and Matisse. In Germany, there was less concentration than in France on purely formal problems. German Expressionism was a manifestation of subjective feeling toward objective reality and the world of imagination. With bold, vigorous brushwork, emphatic lines, and bright color, the German painters produced splendid, almost savagely powerful canvases, particularly expressive of intense human feeling.

A striking example is *The Bride of the Wind* (FIG. **27-17**) by OSKAR KOKOSCHKA (1886–1980), a Viennese painter early influenced by Klimt. The theme of the painting has its roots far back in the peak of the Romantic period and (even farther back) in the pathetic story of Paolo and Francesca told by Dante in his *Inferno* (V, 73–142), although it may also be Kokoschka's response to a poignant love affair. Two lovers are swept by turbulent winds through a nightmare landscape, neither they nor the winds ever to be at rest. The

anguish of love—its lacerating power, not its delight and ecstasy—is expressed in the violence of shredded contours, alternating cold and lurid color, and painfully agitated brushwork. The painting is a passionate expression of the state of two souls who embrace not in joy but in unmitigated sorrow. Here, Kokoschka gives us a clear instance of the transition from Symbolism to *Expressionism.*

German Expressionism is in the direct line of descent from earlier German painting and engraving, especially in its strong color, rough pattern, emphasis on subject matter of a highly emotional character, and frequent transcendental overtones. These elements appear most effectively in the work of EMIL NOLDE (1867–1956), and an especially good example is *St. Mary of Egypt Among Sinners* (FIG. **27-18**). Although he learned much from the masks of Ensor and the color of Matisse, Nolde's painting has an original force of its own, reminiscent of Grünewald (FIG. 23-3) in its expressive violence. Mary, before her conversion, entertains lechers whose brutal ugliness is magnified by their lust. The distortions of form and color (especially the jarring juxtapositions of red and green) work to the same end—an appalling tableau of subhuman and depraved passion in which evil

27-17 Oskar Kokoschka, *The Bride of the Wind* 1914. Oil on canvas, 5'11 1/2" × 7'2$^{1}/_{2}$". Kunstmuseum, Basel.

27-18 Emil Nolde, *St. Mary of Egypt Among Sinners*, 1912. Left panel of a triptych, oil on canvas, approx. 34" × 39". Kunsthalle, Hamburg.

wreaks its visible consequences in the repulsive faces and gestures.

DIE BRÜCKE   Nolde, a very independent artist, was for a while associated with the first group of artists to follow Expressionist ideas who gathered in Dresden in 1905, under the leadership of ERNST KIRCHNER (1880–1938). The group's members thought of themselves as preparing the way for a more perfect age by forming a bridge from the old age to the new—a concept that gave them their name: Die Brücke. Kirchner's early studies in architecture, painting, and the graphic arts had instilled in him a deep admiration for German medieval art, which stirred the group to model themselves on their ideas of medieval craft guilds by living together and practicing all the arts equally. Kirchner described their lofty goals in a ringing statement:

> With a profound belief in growth, a belief in a new genera-
> tion of creators and appreciators, we summon the entire
> younger generation—and as the youth which carries with-
> in it the future, we wish to provide ourselves with a sphere
> of activity opposed to the entrenched and established ten-
> dencies. Everyone belongs to us who portrays his creative
> impulses honestly and directly.*

Borrowing ideas from van Gogh, Munch, the Fauves, and the art of Africa and Oceania, Die Brücke artists created landscapes, cityscapes, genre scenes, portraits, and still lifes in which harsh colors, aggressively brushed paint, and distorted form expressed their feelings about the injustices of society or their belief in a healthful union of human beings and nature. After only a few years, many of the group, including Kirchner, moved to Berlin, where the tensions preceding World War I divided them further. By 1913, the group dissolved and each of them was working independently.

In Berlin, Kirchner retained some of the energy and interest of Die Brücke in social breakdown in paintings like *Street, Berlin* (FIG. **27-19**), where steep perspective, jaggedly angular forms, acrid colors, and haunted people suggest the brittleness and fragility of life in the German metropolis as Europe moved closer to war. Kirchner's later painted and sculptured figures continue to show his interest in medieval German woodcuts and in the fiercely emotive qualities of African and Oceanic art, which he and the members of Die Brücke had discussed in their magazine *Die Brücke.*

DER BLAUE REITER   For the most part, German Expressionism represents the human race as degenerate and society as corrupt. Kirchner's people are caricatures recalling Ensor's (FIG. 26-85) unpleasant marionettes who parade the fashionable avenues—wingless, malignant fowl with beaks and feathers. FRANZ MARC (1880–1916) goes so far in his distaste for humanity as to replace it with animals in

*In Bernard S. Myers, *The German Expressionists: A Generation in Revolt* (New York: Praeger, 1956), pp. 111–112.

27-19   ERNST KIRCHNER, *Street, Berlin*, 1913. Oil on canvas, 47¹/₂″ × 35⁷/₈″ The Museum of Modern Art, New York (purchase).

his pictures, finding the animal superior in beauty, strength, innocence, and naturalness. This modern striving away from society toward nature is, of course, as old as Rousseau (actually, much older!) In the years just before World War I, it becomes a passion with painters and poets, who seem to sense the coming calamity, and who lay the blame for it on the sins of reprobate humanity. Marc's horses (FIG. **27-20**) are blue or red, unharnessed and wild, happily curvetting through some idyllic, tropical world far from human habitation. Their great curves billow like massive, swiftly moving clouds through a rainbow atmosphere.

Marc's later works moved even farther away from natural forms and colors to become completely nonobjective. His disgust for the very image of humanity ended, with tragic irony, in his death in action on a battlefield of World War I.

Marc's friend and co-founder of the Der Blaue Reiter group was WASSILY KANDINSKY (1866–1944), a cosmopolitan artist born in Russia, who shows in his work what Marc might have arrived at had he lived: a full-blown, Nonobjective Expressionism. Kandinsky carried his research into the emotional and psychological properties of color, line, and shape to the point that subject matter and

27-20 FRANZ MARC, *The Great Blue Horses,* 1911. Oil on canvas, 40″ × 63″. Walker Art Center, Minneapolis, Minnesota (gift of the T. B. Walker Foundation, Gilbert M. Walker Fund, 1942).

27-21 WASSILY KANDINSKY, *Improvisation 28* (second version), 1912. Oil on canvas, approx. 44″ × 63³/4″ Solomon R. Guggenheim Museum, New York.

even representational elements are entirely eliminated. Now that abstract art has become so much a part of our experience, we tend to forget the courage such a step required and the creative imagination needed to undertake such a completely new direction in the art of painting. By 1914, Kandinsky had perfected his methods and established, in two groups of works, two principal kinds of paint-

ing. He called one kind "Compositions," the title for this group implying that such arrangements of geometric shapes were consciously planned and intellectually ordered; on the other hand, in his "Improvisations" (an example of which is shown in FIG. **27-21**), he approaches the canvas with no preconceived theme but allows the colors to come as they will, prompted by subconscious feelings. In these works, the brilliant colors flow across the canvas with as little conscious order or control as possible on the artist's part. In utilizing subconscious sensations, Kandinsky uncovered an area soon to be exploited by other artists, notably the Surrealists.

Kandinsky describes his methods and the philosophical connotations of his art in his influential treatise *Concerning the Spiritual in Art* (1912),* in which he proclaims the independence of color and the spiritual value inherent in it. In Kandinsky's view, colors have deep-seated, psychic correlations, and the artist's being is revealed in the prerational, utterly uninhibited expression of them. The "rational" world, given to ordinary vision, is hopelessly deceptive, and we must set aside reasoned "seeing" and planning so that the deeper reality of ourselves, living in the instinctual world of the subconscious, may rise into sight. This view harmonizes with Freud's conclusions concerning the subconscious and with the poet Rimbaud's claim that the true artist is a visionary.

The emotional range of German Expressionism extends widely, from passionate protest and satirical bitterness to the poignantly expressed pity for the poor in the woodblock prints of the independent artist KÄTHE KOLLWITZ (1867–1945). The graphic art of Gauguin and Munch stimulated a revival of the print medium in Germany, especially the woodcut, and the forceful block prints cut in the days of the German Reformation, like those of Holbein, proved

*In M. T. Saddler, trans., *Concerning the Spiritual in Art* (Mineola, NY: Dover, 1977).

inspiring models. The harsh, black, splintered lines of the woodblock print were ideal for the stark forms and blunt emphasis of message prized by the modern Expressionists. In her *Memorial to Karl Liebknecht* (FIG. **27-22**), Kollwitz represents the sorrowing poor gathered around the bier of the assassinated leader of the 1919 socialist revolution, a man on whom they had pinned their hopes for leadership in building a new German social order. This is a classic of Expressionism, a masterful presentation of the theme of mourning for the lost leader, and a strong political protest. We have seen to what effective political use Daumier put the graphic medium (FIG. 26-38). Regrettably, modern methods of pictorial reproduction have largely taken over the public role of the woodblock print.

The brutality of life in post-war Europe and hope for a mythic escape from the despair and disillusionment of the period became the central themes in the works of MAX BECKMANN (1884–1950). Beckmann's early work was linked to a development of German Expressionism in the 1920s called *New Objectivity (Neue Sachlichkeit)*, a movement whose members tried to build a new reality to replace the one that had been shattered by the disasters of the war. Beckmann fills his paintings with figures and objects stripped to a basic, almost sculptural simplicity. Their solidarity, he said, provided a bulwark against the echoing void of space, which yawned threateningly everywhere. By the 1930s, Beckmann had evolved a more personal Expressionist style. He spoke of using a "transcendental realism" that would link "the real love for the things outside of us and the deep secrets of events within us." His

27-22   KÄTHE KOLLWITZ, *Memorial to Karl Liebknecht*, 1919. Woodcut. (Location unknown.)

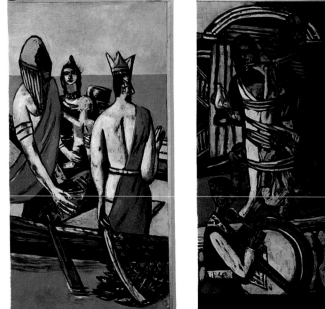

27-23 MAX BECKMANN, *Departure* 1932–1933. Oil on canvas, center panel of triptych 7' ³/4" × 3' ³/8", side panels each 7' ³/4" × 3'3 ¹/4". The Museum of Modern Art, New York (given anonymously by exchange).

was a world that mixed physical reality and the realm of the spirit:

> What I want to show in my work is the idea which hides itself behind so-called reality. I am seeking for the bridge which leads from the visible to the invisible, like the famous cabalist who once said: "if you wish to get hold of the invisible you must penetrate as deeply as possible into the visible.". . . What helps me most in this task is the penetration of space. Height, width, and depth are the three phenomena which I must transfer into one plane to form the abstract surface of the picture, and thus to protect myself from the infinity of space. . . . When spiritual, metaphysical, material, or immaterial events come into my life, I can only fix them by way of painting. It is not the subject which matters but the translation of the subject into the abstraction of the surface by means of painting.*

Beckmann's art was elicited by some of the darkest moments of the twentieth century, when the rise of Nazi tyranny threatened European civilization. While his message was bitter, its reference was not specific to one time or place but concerned human cruelty and suffering in general. Works like *Departure* (FIG. 27-23) hauntingly show both Beckmann's primary themes and the powerful tension he creates between objects and space in his paintings. He uses the three panels of *Departure* in the same way a filmmaker might use *jump cuts* (cinematic technique used to disrupt flow by omitting chunks of film from long continuous shots) to move between scenes that lack clear transitions. The side panels in the painting show bondage and torture. On the left, victims are mutilated by their tormenter; on the

*In Myers, *The German Expressionists*, p. 307.

right, captive figures are helplessly bound together in a mysterious rite overseen by a blindfolded attendant, while a strange figure passes by in the foreground, beating a bass drum. These side panels are claustrophobic; the space is crammed with figures, walls, curtains, balustrades, and other objects. The central panel is more tranquil, with a still sea, empty sky, and mysterious boat carrying the richly symbolic figures of a fisher-king, a hooded oarsman, and a queenly woman hugging a child close to her. The meaning may allude to Beckmann's own flight from Nazi Germany after his work (along with that of most of the German Expressionists and other avant-garde German artists) had been condemned and banned by Hitler as "degenerate." However, the power of *Departure* lies not so much in any moving personal references as in its expressions of universals in the human condition.

Expressionism in Sculpture

Expressionist sculptors sought maximum significance through three-dimensional form, as Expressionist painters sought it through line, color, and manipulation of shape and texture. Both groups of artists attempted to let the esthetic features stand by themselves, without the aid of psychological, historical, or literary reference. Thus the sculptor ARISTIDE MAILLOL (1861–1944), who was also an accomplished painter and print maker, admired Rodin, but thought his emotionalism, taste for narrative, and the impressionistic, roughly irregular surfaces of his statues were basically unsculptural. He observed: "There is something to be learned from Rodin, yet I felt I must return to more stable and self-contained forms. Stripped of all psychological details, forms yield themselves up more readily

27-24 ARISTIDE MAILLOL, *The Mediterranean, c.* 1902–1905. Bronze, approx. 41" high, base 45" × 24³/₄". The Museum of Modern Art, New York (gift of Stephen C. Clark).

to the sculptor's intentions." Maillol preferred and produced figures—exclusively the female nude—in settled, quiet poses, stressing massive, simple volume and smooth planes. Stress is banished, tranquillity is all. One of his first and most important works, the seated *Mediterranean* (FIG. **27-24**) shows his conscious adaptation of pre-Classical Greek art, the influence of Gauguin, and his stylistic relationship to the ideal formalism of painters like Ingres (FIG. 26-5).

The same quiet mood is achieved through completely different sculptural means and effect in the work of WILHELM LEHMBRUCK (1881–1919). Lehmbruck studied sculpture, painting, and the graphic arts in Dusseldorf before moving (in 1910) to Paris, where he developed the style of his *Standing Youth* (FIG. **27-25**). His sculpture combines the expressive qualities he much admired in the work of two fellow sculptors—the Classical idealism of Maillol (FIG. 27-24) and the psychological energies of Rodin (FIGS. 26-91 and 26-92). In Lehmbruck's *Standing Youth*, the tense pose, the poignant elongation of human proportions, and the rippling hair all impart an undertone of anguish to the rather Classical figure. The *Youth* stands in quiet introspection, his head bowed in thought and his right hand raised toward his shoulder, as if in silent debate with himself. Lehmbruck's figure communicates by pose and gesture alone; it has no specific historical or symbolic significance. Its extreme proportions may recall medieval (FIG. 12-28) and even Mannerist (FIG. 22-44) attenuation, but its distortions announce a new freedom in the interpretation of the human figure. Lehmbruck wrote that "sculpture is the essence of things, the essence of nature, that which is eter-

nally human." For him, as for Rodin, the human figure could express every human condition and emotion. The introspection of *Standing Youth* reflects the bittersweet yearnings of an individual. *Seated Youth,* which we saw in the Introduction (FIG. 1), carries a broader symbolism, having been designed in grieving memory as a monument to all who gave their lives in World War I.

A work more mystical in its expression is the *War Monument* (**FIG. 27-26**) by the German sculptor ERNST BARLACH (1870–1938), created for the cathedral in his hometown. As the son of a country doctor in northern

27-25 WILHELM LEHMBRUCK, *Standing Youth*, 1913. Cast stone, approx. 7'8" high, base dimensions 36" × 26³/₄". The Museum of Modern Art, New York (gift of Abby Aldrich Rockefeller).

27-26 Ernst Barlach, *War Monument*, Güstrow Cathedral, 1927. Bronze. Schildergasse Antoniterkirche, Cologne.

27-27 Ernst Barlach, *Head*, study for *War Monument*, separately cast. Bronze, approx. 13½" high. The Museum of Modern Art, New York (gift of Edward M. M. Warburg).

Germany, Barlach found natural symbolism in the people and forms of the rural areas of his native land: "Country life lends the smallest thing a noble shape. . . .My mother tongue is the human body to the milieu, the object, through which or in which man lives, suffers, enjoys himself, feels, thinks."*

Working often in wood, Barlach sculptured single figures, usually dressed in flowing robes and portrayed in strong, simple poses that embody deep human emotions and experiences such as grief, vigilance, or self-comfort. Much influenced by medieval carving, Barlach's works combine sharp, smoothly planed forms with intense action and keen expression. The hovering figure of his *War Monument* is one of the poignant memorials of World War I. Unlike traditional war memorials, which depict heroic military figures, often engaged in battle, Barlach created a hauntingly symbolic figure that speaks to the experience of all who have been caught in the conflagration of war.

*In Carl Dietrich Carls, *Ernst Barlach* (London: Pall Mall Press, 1969), pp. 8, 9.

The floating human form suggests a dying soul at the moment when it is about to awaken to everlasting life—the theme of death and transfiguration. The rigid economy of surfaces concentrates attention on the superb head (FIG. **27-27**). The spiritual anguish evoked by the disaster of war and the release from that anguish through the hope of salvation have rarely been expressed as movingly as they are in *War Monument*.

Another artist used powerfully expressive distortion of the human figure to signify the wasting travail of the human spirit. The Swiss sculptor Alberto Giacometti (1901–1966) turned in the 1940s from his earlier Cubist and Surrealist work to the roughly modeled, emaciated figures for which he is best known. Giacometti found that his sculptured figures seemed most real when they represented a human form at the distance from which one would be able to recognize an approaching person as an acquaintance. To achieve this effect, Giacometti covers basic wire figures with rough blobs of clay or plaster to create the impression of individual faces and body details, but these do not materialize as one moves closer.

27-28   ALBERTO GIACOMETTI, *La Place* (or *City Square*), 1948. Bronze, approx. 6³/₄" high, 23¹/₂" wide, 16" deep. The Museum of Modern Art, New York (purchase).

In sculptures like *La Place* or *City Square* (FIG. **27-28**), Giacometti's pencil-thin, elongated figures stride abstractedly through endless space; they never meet. At certain angles, the forms are so attenuated that they almost disappear, just as in the human condition, people often fade noiselessly out of sight. Such figures suggest to many viewers the modern experiences of bewilderment, loss, and alienation—the increased sense of strangeness and loneliness felt by people in contemporary urban society. Giacometti denied that this was his theme; he insisted that he was merely trying to render the effect of great space as it presses around a figure and nothing more. He was apparently unwilling to recognize the way in which such a representation might echo the modern individual's awareness of the distance in physical and psychic space that separates one human being from another. If we compare Giacometti's figures with those in Rodin's *Burghers of Calais* (FIG. 26-92), we can readily appreciate the changes wrought during the first half of the twentieth century in the interpretation of the human form in art.

Abstract Art: Cubism and Futurism

Abstract art in its first manifestation, called *Cubism*, represents a radical turning-point in the history of Western art, nothing less than a dismissal of the pictorial illusionism of the Tradition. Optical pictorialism is rejected for compositions of forms "abstracted" from the world we conventionally perceive and reproduce within the picture frame. The continuous optical spread is shattered into its many constituent features, which are then recomposed, by a new logic of design, without reference to the original optical unit. Cézanne began the procedure by a reductive analysis of the optical world into color planes. The founders of the new method, the Spanish artist PABLO PICASSO (1881–1973) and the French painter GEORGES BRAQUE (1882–1963), adopted Cézanne's suggestion that artists use the simple forms of cylinders, spheres, and cones to represent nature in art. The Cubists then expanded on his idea that each object could be depicted from a shifting point of view, as if seen from several markedly different angles at once. The central concepts of Cubism were beautifully summarized in 1913 by the French writer and theorist Guillaume Apollinaire:

> Authentic Cubism [is] the art of depicting new wholes with formal elements borrowed not from the reality of vision, but from that of conception. This tendency leads to a poetic kind of painting which stands outside the world of observation; for, even in a simple cubism, the geometrical surfaces of an object must be opened out in order to give a complete representation of it. . . . Everyone must agree that a chair, from whichever side it is viewed, never ceases to have four legs, a seat and back, and that if it is robbed of one of these elements, it is robbed of an important part.*

The new style received its name after Matisse described some of Braque's work to a critic, Louis Vauxcelles, as having been painted "*avec des petits cubes*" (with little cubes), and the critic went on in his review to speak of "cubic oddities." Thus this original and trailbreaking method of design was greeted facetiously with a belittling label, as were Impressionism and Fauvism.

ANALYTIC CUBISM   The first Cubist style developed jointly by Picasso and Braque has been designated *Analytic*

---

*In Edward Fry, ed., *Cubism* (London: Thames & Hudson, 1966), pp. 112–113, 116.

Cubism. Since the kind of total view described by Apollinaire could not be achieved by the traditional method of drawing or painting a model from one position, these artists began to analyze the forms of their subjects from every possible vantage point and to combine the various views into one pictorial whole.

The first steps toward this new style were taken by Picasso in a large painting, *Les Demoiselles d'Avignon* (FIG. **27-29**), which broke decisively with the art of the past. Picasso was a precocious student who had mastered all aspects of late nineteenth-century Realist technique by the time he entered the Barcelona Academy of Fine Art in the

27-29 Pablo Picasso, *Les Demoiselles d'Avignon*, Paris (begun May, reworked July 1907). Oil on canvas, 8′ × 7′8″. The Museum of Modern Art, New York (acquired through the Lillie P. Bliss Bequest).

late 1890s. His prodigious talent led him to experiment with a wide range of visual expression, first in Spain and then in Paris, where he settled in 1904. Throughout his career, Picasso remained a traditional artist in the way he made careful studies in preparation for each major work. He was characteristic of the modern age, however, in his constant experimentation, in his sudden shifts from one kind of painting to another, and in his startling innovations in painting, graphic art, and sculpture. Inspired by Michelangelo, Rodin, and El Greco, Picasso explored the ways in which the human body could express emotion. By the time he settled permanently in Paris, his work had evolved from the sober Realism of Spanish painting, through a brightening of color in an Impressionistic manner (for a time, influenced by the early works of Toulouse-Lautrec), and into the so-called Blue Period (1901–1905), in which he used primarily blue colors to depict worn, pathetic, alienated figures in the pessimistic mood of the end of the nineteenth century.

By 1906, Picasso was searching restlessly for new ways to depict form. He found clues in African sculpture (the expansion of colonial empires in the late nineteenth and early twentieth centuries resulted in wider exposure of European artists to art from Africa, India, and other faraway locales), in the sculpture of ancient Iberia, and in the late paintings of Cézanne. The three sources come together in *Les Demoiselles d'Avignon* (FIG. 27-29), which opened the way for a radically new method of representing form in space. Picasso began the work as a symbolic picture to be titled "Philosophical Bordello," in which male clients intermingled with women in the "receiving" room of a brothel. By the time the artist began the final canvas, he had eliminated the male figures and simplified the details of the room to a suggestion of drapery and a schematic foreground still life; Picasso had become wholly absorbed in the problem of finding a new way to represent the five female figures in their interior space.* Instead of representing the figures as continuous volumes, Picasso fractures their shapes and interweaves them with the equally jagged planes that represent drapery and empty space. The treatment of form and space used by Cézanne is pushed here to a new tension between the representation of three-dimensional space and a statement of painting as a two-dimensional design lying flat on the surface of a stretched canvas. The radical nature of *Les Demoiselles* is extended even further by the disjunctive styles of the heads of the figures and by the pose of the figure at the bottom right. The calm, ideal features of the three young women at the left were inspired by the sculpture of ancient Iberia, which Picasso saw during summer visits to Spain. The energetic, violently striated features of the two heads to the right came late in the making of the work and grew directly out of the artist's increasing fascination with the power of African sculpture (see, for example, FIG. 27-46). As if in response to the energy of these two new heads, Picasso also revises their bodies, breaking them into more ambiguous planes that suggest a combination of views, as if the figures are being seen from more than one place in space. The woman seated at the lower right shows these multiple views most clearly, seeming to present the viewer simultaneously with a three-quarter back view from the left, another from the right, and a front view of the head that adds the suggestion that we see the figure frontally as well. Gone is the traditional concept of an orderly, constructed, unified pictorial space that mirrors the world. In its place are the rudimentary beginnings of a new representation of the world as a dynamic interplay of time and space.

From the time of Masaccio, painting had been assumed to give, in one- or two-point perspective, a fixed and complete "view," in which everything in all planes, forward and back, appears simultaneously with everything else. But this is true only if we the observers are stationary; our view of the picture, as well as the scene pictured, is the result of a great number of eye movements. In essence, this is the basis of Cézanne's innovation with respect to a shifting viewpoint. The Cubists, however, go beyond this purely optical reason for using multiple viewpoints. They wish to present the total essential reality of forms in space, and because objects do not appear only as they are seen from one viewpoint at one time, it becomes necessary to introduce multiple angles of vision and simultaneous presentations of discontinuous planes. This, of course, shatters the old continuity of single-viewpoint composition imposed by the Renaissance. The Cubist painter believes that "in order to discover one true relationship it is necessary to sacrifice a thousand surface appearances."*

The concept of reality thus becomes separated from that of appearance, and the resemblance of essential form to ordinary vision is no longer important. The assumption, beginning in the Renaissance, that what we see in nature should find correspondence in the forms that the artist paints, is given up, and the epoch that began with Giotto and Masaccio comes to an end in the twentieth century.

Cubism's break with the world of ordinary vision was not simply a matter of esthetic fashion, random experiment, or quixotic exhibitionism, although it has been denounced as all these things and worse: "Cubists," claimed the *New York Times* on the occasion of the 1913 Armory Show, an exhibition that introduced modern art to the general public in the United States in that city, "are making insanity pay." However, affinities of thought and imagination give a certain coherence to historical periods; seen within the context of the new Einsteinian vision of the physical world, the new art seems less strange. It has been said that Cubist pictorial space suggests the addition of the

---

*The artist did keep a sly reference to the original subject in his final title— "Avignon" was the name of a well-known street in Barcelona's red-light district.

*In Albert Gleizes and Jean Metzinger, "Cubism," in R. L. Herbert, *Modern Artists on Art* (Englewood Cliffs, NJ: Prentice-Hall, 1964), p. 3.

dimension of time to spatial dimensions, because objects are represented in temporal sequence, not as they are seen at any one moment. To perceive the many views of the object as given would require movement by the viewer (or at least the viewer's eyes) through some temporally sequential positions. In Einstein's description of the physical world, there is a similar merger of space and time, especially when astronomical distances are involved; they are functions of each other and are never independent. This is decisively different from the Baroque, Newtonian concept of space and time, where both are absolute and independent and where, no matter the distance between two events, it is possible for them to be simultaneous. By extension, simultaneous events presuppose a continuous space that is invariant with respect to them. But in the space-time of Einstein's relativity, it is impossible to prove that two physical events at an astronomical distance are actually simultaneous, because time elapses in the very process of their measurement.

Perspective space in Western painting since Masaccio assumes a continuous, unbroken space fixed from a single point of view. We can say of this rigid, geometric space that all the represented objects in it are *simultaneous;* the single *scene* constitutes a single *event.* Cubism, with its new kind of simultaneity—the simultaneity of different viewpoints—destroys consistency of image and appearance and replaces it with "abstract" form. This process is well begun in Picasso's *Les Demoiselles d'Avignon.*

Thus, the recognition and involvement of time in the very pictorial process destroys the structure of appearance constructed with the unlimited possibilities of form. No longer restricted to a single viewpoint, the artist may see any given object in the world not as a fixed appearance or shape, but as a universe of possible lines, planes, and colors. The world of appearance can be analyzed into a world of patterns that is open to endless exploration and adjustment. The shattering of the rigid Renaissance structure of appearance comes to be regarded by the abstract artist as a means by which art can be returned to its fundamental functions.

For many years, Picasso showed *Les Demoiselles* only to other painters. One of the first to see it was Georges Braque, a Fauve painter, who was so agitated and challenged by it that he began reinventing his own painting style in response. One of Braque's paintings, *The Portuguese* (FIG. **27-30**), is a striking example of Analytic Cubism. The subject is derived from the artist's memories of a Portuguese musician seen years earlier in a bar in Marseilles. In this painting, all of Braque's energy has been concentrated on dissecting the form and placing it in dynamic interaction with the space around it; color is reduced to a monochrome of brown tones. The process of analysis has been carried so far that the viewer must work diligently to discover clues to the subject. The construction of large, intersecting planes suggests the forms of a man and

27-30 GEORGES BRAQUE, *The Portuguese,* 1911. Oil on canvas, 46⅛" × 32". Kunstmuseum, Basel, Switzerland (Emanuel Hoffmann-Stiftung).

a guitar. Smaller shapes interpenetrate and hover in the large planes. Light and dark passages suggest both chiaroscuro modeling and transparent planes that allow us to see through from one level to another. As we look, solid forms emerge only to be canceled almost immediately by a different reading of the subject. The stenciled letters and numbers add to the painting's complexity. Letters and numbers are flat shapes; on the page of a book they exist outside of three-dimensional space, but as shapes in a Cubist painting like *The Portuguese,* they allow the painter to play with our perception of two- and three-dimensional space. The letters and numbers lie flat on the painted canvas surface, yet because the shading and shapes of the image seem to flow behind and underneath them, they are pushed forward into our space. Occasionally, they may seem to be attached to the surface of some object within the painting, but the combination of multiple views of each object causes such a perception to slide away in the next instant.

While Picasso and Braque were investigating the possibilities of released shape and volume in painting, they suppressed color; Analytical Cubism as they managed it is mostly monochromatic. Their contemporary, ROBERT DELAUNAY (1885–1941), experimented with the shape and motion functions of color, inventing a kind of color Cubism (which Apollinaire called *Orphism*). In *Champs de Mars,* or *The Red Tower* (FIG. **27-31**), Delaunay breaks the perceptual unity of the monument into a kaleidoscopic array of colored shards, which variously leap forward or pull back according to the relative hues and values of the broken shapes; the structure ambiguously rises and collapses. Delaunay's experiments with color dynamics strongly influenced the Futurists (see page 1054) and the German Expressionists (he exhibited with Der Blaue Reiter group as well as with the Cubists), who found in his art means for intensifying expression by suggesting violent motion through shape and color.

SYNTHETIC CUBISM   In 1912, Cubism entered a new phase during which the style no longer relied on a decipherable relation to the visible world. In this new phase, called *Synthetic Cubism,* paintings and drawings were constructed from objects and shapes cut from paper or other materials to represent parts of a subject. The work marking the point of departure for this new style was Picasso's *Still Life with Chair-Caning* (FIG. **27-32**), a painting done on a piece of oilcloth imprinted with the pattern of a cane chair seat and framed with a piece of rope. This work provided

27-31 ROBERT DELAUNAY, *Champs de Mars* or *The Red Tower,* 1911. Oil on canvas, 63" × 51". Art Institute of Chicago.

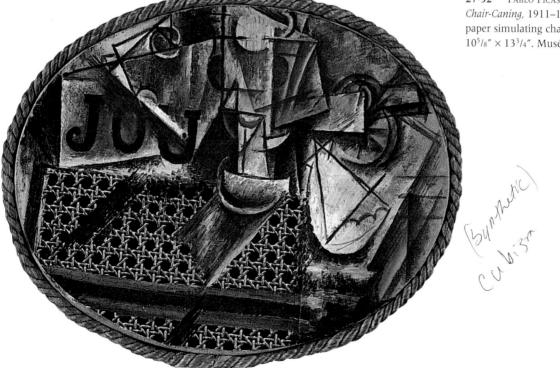

27-32 PABLO PICASSO, *Still Life with Chair-Caning,* 1911–1912. Oil and pasted paper simulating chair-caning on canvas. 10⁵/₈" × 13³/₄". Musée Picasso, Paris.

the means with which to play visual games with variations of illusion and reality. The photographically replicated chair-caning seems so "real" that one expects any brushstrokes laid upon it to be broken by the holes. The painted passages seem to hover magically in the air in front of the cane seat, lending the painted objects a visual tangibility that suggests relief sculpture more than painting. The visual play is extended in the way in which the letter escapes from the space of the accompanying *J* and *O*, yet it is partially covered by a painted cylindrical shape that pushes across its left side. The letters *JOU* appear in many cubist paintings; these letters formed part of the masthead of the daily newspapers (journals) that were often found among the objects represented. Picasso and Braque especially delighted in the punning references to *jouer* and *jeu*—the French words for "to play" and "game."

After *Still Life with Chair-Caning,* both Picasso and Braque continued to explore the new medium introduced in that work. The new possibilities offered by *collage* (from the French word meaning "to stick") can also be seen in Braque's *Fruit Dish and Cards* (FIG. **27-33**), done in a variant of collage called *papier collé* (stuck paper), in which assorted paper shapes are glued to a drawing or painting. Charcoal and pencil lines and shadows provide us with clues to the Cubist multiple views of table, dishes, playing cards, and fruit. Roughly rectangular strips of wood-grained, gray, and black paper run vertically up the composition, overlapping each other to create a layering of unmistakably flat planes that both echo the space suggested by the lines and establish the flatness of the surface of the work. All shapes in the image seem to oscillate between pushing forward and dropping back in space. Shading seems to carve space into flat planes in some places and to turn them into transparent surfaces in others. The bottom edge of the ace of clubs seems to extend forward over a strip of wood-grained paper, while its top corner appears to slip behind a filmy plane.

The viewer is always aware that this is a work of art created by an artist and that each observer must enter the visual game to decipher all levels of representation. Braque is no longer analyzing the three-dimensional qualities of the physical world; here, objects and space alike are constructed or synthesized from the materials used to make the work. Picasso stated his views on Cubism at this point in its development:

> Not only did we try to displace reality; reality was no longer in the object. . . . In the *papier collé* . . . we didn't any longer want to fool the eye; we wanted to fool the mind. . . . If a piece of newspaper can be a bottle, that gives us something to think about in connection with both newspapers and bottles, too.*

*In François Gilot and Carlton Lake, *Life with Picasso* (New York: McGraw Hill, 1964), p. 77.

27-33 Georges Braque, *Fruit Dish and Cards*, 1913. Oil, pencil, paper collage, and charcoal on canvas, 31^7/$_8$″ × 23^5/$_8$″. Musée Nationale d'Art Moderne, Centre Georges Pompidou, Paris (gift of Paul Rosenberg).

Cubism's papier collé was essentially a formalist activity. Like all collage, the technique was modern in its medium—mass-produced materials never before found in "high" art—and modern in the way the "message" of the art became the imagery and nature of these everyday materials.

The use of found materials in collages allowed Braque and Picasso to reintroduce color into their work. By the 1920s, both were going their separate ways as artists, and Picasso had developed a very colorful version of Synthetic Cubism into a highly personal painting style that mimicked the look of the earlier pasted works. In paintings like *Three Musicians* (FIG. **27-34**), Picasso constructs figures from simple flat shapes that interlock and interpenetrate in a composition that whimsically combines a Modernist statement of the flat plane of the canvas with traditional modes of representation. The floor and walls of the room in which this lively musical trio performs suggest Renaissance perspective gone only a little awry, while the table, with an

27-34   PABLO PICASSO, *Three Musicians,* Fontainebleau, summer 1921. Oil on canvas, approx. 6′7″ × 7′3³/4″. The Museum of Modern Art, New York (gift of Mrs. Simon Guggenheim).

unlikely still life in its middle, is presented in reverse perspective. A jumble of flat shapes materializes into the figures of Pierrot on clarinet, Harlequin on guitar, and a mysterious masked monk as vocalist. Miraculously, the flat, syncopated shapes give each musician a different personality and simultaneously suggest the sprightly tune they are performing. Careful inspection reveals an alert dog sprawled behind the troupe, apparently beating its tail vigorously in time to the music.

In contrast to the vivacious movement and vivid color of Picasso's *Musicians,* Braque's *The Table* (FIG. **27-35**) is a subdued composition, with a kind of traditional French formalism moderating the exuberant play of Cubist shapes and restraining their color intensities. The Cubist collage-like motifs are present: the fruit bowl, the guitar, the lettered fragment, the tablecloth, the "pasted" linoleum pattern. The bowl-shaped table post and the table legs are subtly rendered more objectively, though they share the

27-35 GEORGES BRAQUE, *The Table*, 1928. Oil on canvas, approx. 70³/₄" × 28³/₄". The Museum of Modern Art, New York (bequest of Lillie P. Bliss).

transparent, intersecting planes of the paneled wainscot and the other color areas in the overall stability and harmony of the design. Picasso's Cubism leads to powerfully expressionistic composition (FIG. 27-80), while Braque's is directed toward formal order, elegantly contrived and classically restrained. Braque is the undisputed master/composer of the formal, idiomatic elements of Cubism. A work like *The Table* can be taken as representative and exemplary of the ideals of the whole movement.

Synthetic Cubism influenced many American artists. Two American painters created especially personal versions of the style. STUART DAVIS (1894–1964) tried to create what he believed was a modern American art style by combining the flat shapes of Synthetic Cubism with his own sense of jazz rhythms and his perception of the dynamism of the modern, urban industrial scene. Davis's long professional career began with the inclusion of some of his works in the 1913 Armory Show. By the 1920s, Davis was investigating Synthetic Cubism.

To master the style, he made repeated drawings, collages, and paintings of a single still life, gradually simplifying the shapes of its objects into compositions of flat, colored forms. As he described the process, he "brought drawings of different places and things into a single focus. The necessity to select and define the spatial limits of these separate drawings, in relation to the unity of the whole picture, developed an objective attitude toward size and shape."* Davis used his new style in paintings of street scenes in Manhattan and Paris. *House and Street* (FIG. **27-36**) is a simple combination of two views of New York City— one, a detail of a building facade seen head-on and the second, a more distant view of a city street presented as if seen through a window placed at an angle to the picture surface. All details are constructed from flat, colored shapes that interlock more than they overlap. Although the play of angular and rectilinear forms and flat, hard colors does not toy as obviously with our perception of two and three dimensions as do the Synthetic Cubist works of Braque and Picasso, the details in Davis's work create an intriguing ambiguity of figure and ground in which "forward" and "backward" alternate as convincingly as in the European examples. In addition to being a double scene, the whole visual field in *House and Street* sets up a lively vibration of colors and shapes.

The personal Synthetic Cubism of the American painter AARON DOUGLAS (1898–1979) was filled with more symbolism and emotion than anything Davis painted. Douglas used the style to represent symbolically the historical and cultural memories of African Americans. Born in Kansas, he studied in Nebraska and Paris before settling in New York City, where he became part of the flowering of art and literature in the 1920s known as the Harlem Renaissance. Encouraged by the German artist Winold Reiss to create an

*In Chipp, ed., *Theories of Modern Art*, p. 526.

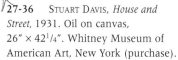

27-36 STUART DAVIS, *House and Street*, 1931. Oil on canvas, 26″ × 42¼″. Whitney Museum of American Art, New York (purchase).

27-37 AARON DOUGLAS, *Noah's Ark, c.* 1927. Oil on masonite, 48″ × 36″. Afro-American Collection of Art, The Carl Van Vechten Gallery of Fine Arts, Fisk University, Nashville.

art that would express the cultural history of his race, Douglas incorporated motifs from African sculpture into compositions painted in a version of Synthetic Cubism that stressed angular, transparent planes. *Noah's Ark* (FIG. **27-37**) was one of seven paintings based on a book of poems by James Weldon Johnson called *God's Trombones: Seven Negro Sermons in Verse.* Rather than combining different viewpoints in space, Douglas used the flat planes of Synthetic Cubism to evoke a sense of mystical space and miraculous happenings. In *Noah's Ark,* lightning strikes and rays of light crisscross the area in which pairs of animals enter the ark, while men load supplies in preparation for departure across the heaving seas. Deep space is suggested by the difference in scale between the huge human head and shoulders of the worker in the foreground and the small person at work on the distant rear deck of the ship. At the same time, the unmodulated color shapes of the composition create a pattern on the surface of the masonite panel that cancels any illusion of three-dimensional depth. Here, Douglas used the formal language of Cubism to express a powerful religious vision.

PURISM   We have briefly noted that the architect Le Corbusier, who was also a painter, had founded a movement called Purism (1918), which opposed Synthetic Cubism on the grounds that it was becoming merely an esoteric, decorative art out of touch with the machine age. Purists maintained that the clean, functional lines of machinery, the pure forms of its parts, should direct the artist's experiments in design, whether in painting, architecture, or industrially produced objects. FERNAND LÉGER (1881–1955), a French painter, who had early on painted with the Cubists, was inspired by the "machine esthetic" of

27-38 FERNAND LÉGER, *The City,* 1919. Oil on canvas, approx. 7′7″ × 9′9¹/₂″. Philadelphia Museum of Art (A. E. Gallatin Collection).

Purism. He devised an effective compromise of tastes, bringing together meticulous Cubist analysis of form with Purist broad simplification and machine-like finish of the design components. He retained from his Cubist practice a preference for cylindrical and tube-like motifs, suggestive of machined parts like pistons and cylinders.

His works have the sharp precision of the machine, the beauty and quality of which Léger was one of the first to discover. A modern composer, George Antheil, composed a score for a Léger film, *Ballet Méchanique;* it is significant that the work included the sound of an airplane engine. Léger is preeminently the painter of modern urban life, incorporating into his work the massive effects of modern posters and billboard advertisements, the harsh flashing of electric lights, the noise of traffic, the robotlike movements of mechanized people. An early work in which these effects

appear—modulated, however, by the esthetic of Synthetic Cubism—is *The City* (FIG. **27-38**). Its monumental scale proves that Léger, had he been given the opportunity, would have been one of the great mural painters of our age. In a definitive way, he presents the mechanical commotion of the contemporary city.

FUTURISM   MARCEL DUCHAMP (1887–1968), a French painter and influential theorist, attempted to reconcile Analytical Cubism with the representation of motion; in this respect he shared the program of the "Futurists." In his painting *Nude Descending a Staircase, no. 2* (FIG. **27-39**), which was exhibited at the Armory Show and caused an uproar of negative criticism, he sets the dislocated planes of a single figure into a time continuum, suggesting the effect of a primitive motion-picture technique. The stuttering rhythm of the bundled, monochromatic planes resembles more the effect produced by a stroboscope. The arcs made of lines and dots indicate the sway of the body's main masses. Not only is form analyzed into its planar components, but also into the motion that carries it through space and time. In Léger's art, motion is *suggested* by the staccato action of the various mechanical forms. Duchamp attempts a *description* of a single form in motion, analyzed into a succession of movements and intervals.

Though Duchamp's *Nude* manifests the essential features of *Futurism,* the Futurist label is conventionally assigned to a militant group of Italian poets, painters, and sculptors, who regularly signed and issued manifestoes declaring rev-

27-39 MARCEL DUCHAMP, *Nude Descending a Staircase,* 1912. Oil on canvas, approx. 58″ × 35″. Philadelphia Museum of Art (Louise and Walter Arensberg Collection).

olution in art. These declarations, with their strong political overtones, are the first of the many that would announce the avant-garde movements of Modernism. The Italian poet Marinetti, in a manifesto of 1909, inaugurated Futurism and gave the movement its name. He called for radical innovation in the arts, rejection of all traditional tastes, values, and styles, and the unconstrained liberty of the artist to create. Marinetti praised the modern age of steel and speed and the virtues of violence and war. For him the new phenomenon of speed enhanced the splendor of the universe; he insisted that "a speeding automobile. . . is more beautiful than the *Nike of Samothrace*" (FIG. 5-93). The sculptor Umberto Boccioni, whose work we shall soon examine, exalted modern dynamism, as well as velocity; he praised great ocean liners, submarines, airplanes, battleships, and armored cars as the irresistible engines of modern power in its most conspicuous forms. Art must exhibit motion in time and space; it should reveal the simultaneously present perceptions that comprise any given event in any given place.

This requirement is met by GINO SEVERINI (1883–1966), another signatory of Futurist manifestoes, who made a veritable manifesto of his *Dynamic Hieroglyph of the Bal Tabarin* (FIG. **27-40**). Severini declared that the method used by Cubists for apprehending an object is to walk around it, while the Futurists believe one must get inside it. The kaleidoscopic composition illustrated here represents a momentary storm of perceptions, immediate and remembered, that make up the mental happenings of a visitor to a large, crowded, noisy Parisian dance hall, the Bal Tabarin. The visitor's eyes rapidly and randomly take in flashes and fragments of swirling shapes. There is no fixed location of things, nor any direction of attention to them. Actually, for Severini, there are no "things," only symbols, or "hieroglyphs," of things. A Cubist device, the printed word suggests the kinds of events, "valse" and "polka" for the dancing, or "bowling" for that game. The shapes are scattered throughout the picture: the spheres of the bowling balls, the fluttering skirt hems of dancing women, the conic and cylindrical shapes of their trousered male partners. Everything is happening simultaneously, and everything is part of the happening. Simultaneity of shapes-in-motion is Futurism's principal value, and the convincing representation of it is the Futurist's principal objective.

A more obvious method for rendering simultaneity of things in motion is evident in *Dynamism of a Dog on a Leash* (FIG. **27-41**) by GIACOMO BALLA (1871–1958). Here the observer is stationary, and his gaze is focused on a passing dog and its owner, the skirts of the latter placed just within the visual range of the viewer. The forms are not fragmented but easily read for what they appear to be. The effect of motion is achieved by repetition of shape, as in the legs and tail of the dog, and in the swinging line of the leash. These simple devices are familiar in the modern cartoon, where

27-40 GINO SEVERINI, *Dynamic Hieroglyph of the Bal Tabarin*, 1912. Oil on canvas, 63" × 61". The Museum of Modern Art, New York.

27-41 GIACOMO BALLA, *Dynamism of a Dog on a Leash*, 1912. Oil on canvas, 35³/₈" × 43¹/₄". Albright-Knox Art Gallery, Buffalo, New York (bequest of A. Conger Goodyear, gift of George F. Goodyear.

they are most often used for the same comic effect that we find in Balla's painting.

Abstract Sculpture

As we might expect, sculpture invited abstraction as did painting; many Cubists and Futurists were both sculptors and painters, and their abstractive methods, allowing for the physical differences of the media, were much the same. UMBERTO BOCCIONI (1882–1916) applied to sculpture the representational technique of Balla. What we want, he claimed, is not fixed movement in space, but the sensation of motion itself: "Owing to the persistence of images on the retina, objects in motion are multiplied and distorted, following one another like waves in space. Thus, a galloping horse has not four legs, it has twenty." Though Boccioni in this instance was talking about painting, his observation helps us to comprehend what is perhaps the definitive work of Futurist sculpture, his *Unique Forms of Continuity in Space* (FIG. 27-42).

Unique Forms calls attention to the formal and spatial effects of motion rather than to the fact that the source for

futurist

27-42 UMBERTO BOCCIONI, *Unique Forms of Continuity in Space,* 1913 (cast 1931). Bronze, approx. 43¹/₃" high. The Museum of Modern Art, New York, (acquired through the Lillie P. Bliss Bequest).

these is the striding human figure. The "figure" is so expanded, interrupted, and broken in plane and contour that it disappears, as it were, behind the blur of its movement; only the blur remains. Boccioni's search for plastic means with which to express dynamic movement reaches a monumental expression here. In its power and sense of vital activity, this sculpture surpasses similar efforts in painting (by Boccioni and his Futurist companions) to create images symbolic of the dynamic quality of modern life. To be convinced by it, we need only reflect on how details of an adjacent landscape appear in our peripheral vision when we are traveling at great speed on a highway or in a low-flying airplane. Although Boccioni's figure bears a curious resemblance to the ancient *Nike of Samothrace* (FIG. 5-93), a cursory comparison reveals how far the modern work departs from the ancient one.

But the representation of motion in sculpture reaches a limit here with Boccioni. After all, the piece itself does not move. (It would be the motion picture, operating by rapid changes of fixed images, that would produce convincing illusions of movement.) Sculpture composed of actually moving parts, like a machine, would be designed by Alexander Calder (FIG. 27-52) and would make no pretense

of "representing" any movement other than its own. Thus the field of experiment with abstraction was left to the Analytic Cubist sculptors, whose work assumed the observer to be in motion around an essentially stationary object, rather than the object itself being in motion.

Analytic Cubism did not just open new ways of representing form on two-dimensional surfaces; it also inspired new approaches to sculpture. Picasso tested the possibilities of Cubism in sculpture throughout the years he and Braque were developing the style, but one of the most successful sculptors to adapt the spatial feeling of Analytic Cubist painting into three dimensions was JACQUES LIPCHITZ (1891–1973). Lipchitz was born in Latvia but resided for many years in France and the United States. His ideas for many of his sculptures were worked out in clay before being transferred into bronze or into stone. *Bather* (FIG. 27-43) is typical of his Cubist style. The continuous form in this work is broken down into cubic volumes and planes.

27-43 JACQUES LIPCHITZ, *Bather,* 1917. Bronze, 34³/₄" × 13¹/₄" × 13". The Nelson-Atkins Museum of Art, Kansas City, Missouri (gift of the Friends of Art F70-12).

Cubist

As with Cubist painting, there is no single point of view, no continuity or simultaneity of image contour. Lipchitz was part of the "second generation" of Cubists—artists who invested the innovations of Braque and Picasso with theory and a more consistent technical approach. Proportion and mathematics were important analytical tools for these artists. Like many of them, Lipchitz based a considerable number of his sculptures on the Golden Mean, which had been used in antiquity to suggest the perfection of ideal proportion and order. Lipchitz combined this Classical mathematical formula with a modern energy to create what he called "the sense of twisting movement, of the figure spiraling around its axis." The spiraling movement in *Bather* recalls both the energy of El Greco's painted figures (FIG. 23-28), which Lipchitz much admired, and the twisting tension of Mannerist works like Giovanni de Bologna's *Abduction of the Sabine Women* (FIG. 22-45). Yet these qualities are modified by the way in which the cubic shapes of *Bather* seem to slip and slide before our eyes, presenting first one view of the body parts and then another; Lipchitz has fully invested this figure with the qualities of space-time so important to the Cubist vision.

An even more decisive break with the long tradition of Western sculpture than this analysis of mass into planes is the piercing of the mass. An early example of this new turn can be seen in *Woman Combing Her Hair* (FIG. **27-44**) by the Russian sculptor ALEKSANDR ARCHIPENKO (1887–1964). This statuette, recalling in its graceful contrapposto something of Renaissance Mannerism, introduces in place of the head a void with a shape of its own that figures importantly in the whole design. Enclosed spaces have always existed in figure sculpture—for example, the space between the arm and the body when the hand rests on the hip, as in Verrocchio's *David* (FIG. 21-50). But here there is penetration of the continuous mass of the figure, and shaped space (often referred to as *negative space*) occurs with shaped mass in the same design. Archipenko's figure shows the same slipping of the planes that we have seen in pictorial Cubism, and the relation of the planes to each other is similarly complex. Thus, in painting and sculpture, the traditional limits are broken through and the medium transformed. Archipenko's figure is still quasi-representational, but sculpture (like painting) executed within the Cubist orbit tends to cast off the last vestiges of representation.

A friend of Picasso, JULIO GONZÁLEZ (1876–1942), shared his interest in the artistic possibilities of new materials and new methods borrowed from both industrial technology and traditional metalworking. Constructed or "direct" shapes (using ready-made bars, sheets, rods, or the like) of welded or wrought iron and bronze can produce, in effect, simple or incredibly complex sculptured spaces in a kind of fluent openwork, in which the solids function only as contours, boundaries, or dividing planes. In *Woman Combing Her Hair* (FIG. **27-45**) by González (compare with Archipenko's version of the same subject; FIG. 27-44), fan-

tasy is restrained by no traditional convention of representation, and the actual constructive process is unimpeded by the more demanding methods of carving and casting. Sculptors in the 1960s and 1970s would fully exploit the advantages of this method: linear effects impossible for other modes, flexibility in construction, speed of execution,

27-44 ALEKSANDR ARCHIPENKO, *Woman Combing Her Hair,* 1915. Bronze, approx. 13³⁄₄" high. The Museum of Modern Art, New York (bequest of Lillie P. Bliss).

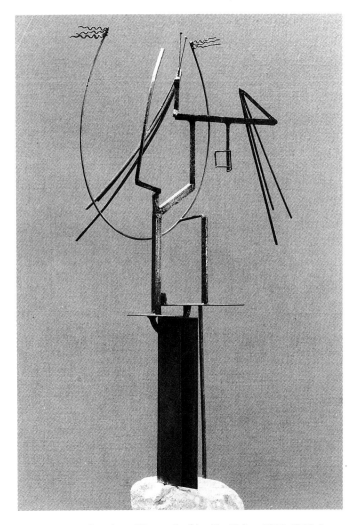

27-45 JULIO GONZÁLEZ, *Woman Combing Her Hair, c.* 1930–1933. Iron, 57" high. Moderna Museet, Stockholm.

essentially independent painter and sculptor AMEDEO MODIGLIANI (1884–1920), however, steps outside the tradition altogether. Modigliani, who was only loosely related to Cubism, takes as his model the carved African mask (FIG. **27-46**), which already has been "analyzed" into geometrical pattern by the abstracting formal instinct and practice of a native tradition. We have seen the influence of the African mask in Picasso's *Les Demoiselles* (FIG. 27-29). There it is only one exotic motif among several. Modigliani's *Head*

and easy correction of errors or changes in intention. The direct-metal method in the hands of contemporary sculptors parallels the methods used by the so-called Abstract Expressionist painters. It should be noted that although González innovates in material and method, he still thinks (as the title of this piece indicates) of the human figure as a point of departure for abstraction, even though the forms could stand without external reference to the natural world. After years as an unsuccessful painter, González was asked by Picasso for technical help in constructing metal sculpture. From that time, his influence has been continuous, with a special impact on today's sculptors.

Lipchitz, Archipenko, and González dismantle the traditional, sculptured figure by—respectively—reducing it to planes and volume, piercing its mass with open space, and transforming it into an open work of spaces, lines, bars, and rods. Yet they take the traditional figure as their point of departure and make reference to it by labels such as "dancer" or "woman combing her hair." One work by the

27-46 Mask, Fang peoples, Oyem Region, Gabon, Africa, nineteenth to twentieth centuries. Wood with white clay pigment, 26" high. Musee de l'Homme, Paris.

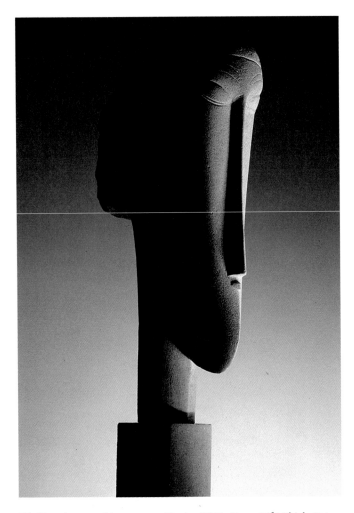

27-47   AMEDEO MODIGLIANI, *Head, c.* 1913. Stone 24³/₄″ high. Tate Gallery, London (Courtesy of the Trustees).

(FIG. **27-47**) is an adaptation of the African mode of representation. Through it Modigliani rejects the Western tradition totally, accepting the exclusive authority of African art as its modern and entirely appropriate replacement. In his painting, also, Modigliani derives his characteristic shapes and volumes from the same African source, but he adapts them to Western themes, composition, and setting. From the Cubist point of view, his painting is conservative.

Nonobjective Art: Geometric and Organic Formalism, and Constructivism

Modigliani's dismissal, in one instance, of the Western tradition, is contemporary with painting and sculpture that dismiss representation entirely, no matter to what tradition they belong. The creators of such works strive—not always successfully—to eliminate even the slightest reference to the world of perceived objects; they want to have nothing to do with images, even fragments and traces of them

as in the residues of Cubist analysis. Rather than abstract forms from an image, they prefer an entirely fresh start, inventing and constructing forms of the most elemental kind: geometrical—angular, rectilinear, circular; mechanical—machined parts; organic—rounded, soft-contoured, cellular, like living organisms. According to those artists who think this way, art must be pure form, unsullied by any taint of representation, since representation is, in essence, deceitful.

We have met this purism in reference to Le Corbusier and the Bauhaus. It belongs to the esthetic doctrine of the new architecture and to machine design; unconcealed function is a virtue. It also belongs to the esthetic doctrine of nonobjective form as expressed by the Russian painter KAZIMIR MALEVICH (1878–1935). Malevich studied art in Germany early in his career, but then returned to Russia, where he developed an *Abstract Formalist* style to convey his belief that the supreme reality in the world is pure feeling, which attaches to no object and thus calls for new, nonobjective forms in art—shapes not related to objects in the visible world. Malevich had studied painting, sculpture, and architecture, and had worked his way through most of the avant-garde styles of his youth before deciding that none was suited to the expression of the subject he found most important—"pure feeling." He christened his new artistic approach *Suprematism* and said of it:

> Under Suprematism I understand the supremacy of pure feeling in creative art. To the Suprematist, the visual phenomena of the objective world are, in themselves, meaningless; the significant thing is feeling, as such, quite apart from the environment in which it is called forth. . . . The Suprematist does not observe and does not touch—he feels.*

The basic form of his new Suprematist nonobjective art was the square. Combined with its relatives, the straight line and the rectangle, the square soon filled paintings like *Suprematist Composition: Aeroplane Flying* (FIG. **27-48**), in which the brightly colored shapes float against and within a white space and are placed in dynamic relationship to one another. Malevich believed that his new art would be easily understood by all peoples, because it required no special education to comprehend its symbols. It used the pure language of form and color that everyone could understand intuitively. Having formulated his artistic approach, Malevich welcomed the Russian Revolution as a political act that would wipe out past traditions and begin a new culture in which his art could play a major role. In actuality, after a short period in which avant-garde art was heralded by the new regime, the political leaders of post-Revolution Russia decided that the new society needed a more "practical" art that would teach citizens about

*In Chipp, ed., *Theories of Modern Art*, pp. 341, 345.

27-48 KAZIMIR MALEVICH, *Suprematist Composition: Aeroplane Flying,* 1915 (dated 1914). Oil on canvas, approx. 22⁷/₈″ × 19″. The Museum of Modern Art, New York (purchase).

their new government or produce goods that would help make their lives better. Malevich was horrified; to him, true art was forever divorced from such practical connections with life:

> Every social idea, however great and important it may be, stems from the sensation of hunger; every art work, regardless of how small and insignificant it may seem, originates in pictorial or plastic feeling. It is high time for us to realize that the problems of art lie far apart from those of the stomach or the intellect.*

Disappointed and unappreciated in his own country, Malevich eventually stopped painting and turned his attention to other things, such as mathematical theory.

Like Malevich, the Russian-born sculptor NAUM GABO (1890–1977) wanted to create a new art to express a new reality, and, like Malevich, Gabo believed that such art would spring from sources separate from the everyday world. For Gabo, the new reality was the space-time world described by early twentieth-century advances in science. As he wrote in *Realistic Manifesto,* published with his broth-

er Anton Pevsner in 1920: "Space and time are the only forms on which life is built and hence art must be constructed." Later he explained:

> We are realists, bound to earthly matters. . . . The shapes we are creating are not abstract, they are absolute. They are released from any already existent thing in nature and their content lies in themselves. . . . It is impossible to comprehend the content of an absolute shape by reason alone. Our emotions are the real manifestation of this content.*

According to Gabo, he called himself a "Constructivist" partly because he built up his sculptures piece by piece in space, instead of carving or modeling them in the traditional way. This method freed the Constructivists to work with "volume of mass and volume of space" as "two different materials" in creating compositions filled with the "kinetic rhythms" by which humans perceive "real time."

The name *Constructivism* may have originally come from the title "*Construction,*" which had been used by the Russian artist Vladimir Tatlin for some relief sculptures he made in 1913 to 1914. Tatlin shared some ideas and goals with Gabo, but soon after the Revolution, Tatlin allied himself with a variant of Constructivism—*Productivist Constructivism*—that was devoted to using artists' talents in practical ways for the good of society (see page 1062). Like Malevich, Gabo believed that pure art was apart from life, and he and Tatlin parted company. Although Gabo experimented briefly with real motion in his work, most of his sculptures relied on the relationship of mass and space to suggest the nature of space-time. To indicate the volumes of mass and space more clearly in his sculpture, Gabo used some of the new synthetic plastic materials, including celluloid, nylon, and lucite, to create constructions in which space seems to flow through as well as around the transparent materials. In works like *Column* (FIG. **27-49**), the depth through the sculpture is visible, because the circular mass of the column has been opened up so that the viewer can experience the volume of space it occupies. Two transparent planes extend through its diameter, crossing at right angles at the center of the implied cylindrical column shape. The opaque colored planes at the base and the inclined open ring set up counter rhythms to the crossed upright planes, establishing the sense of dynamic kinetic movement that Gabo always sought to express as an essential part of reality.

Malevich desired to express "pure feeling" in his paintings, and Gabo sought to convey in his sculpture the reality of the newly revealed world of space and time. The Dutch artist PIET MONDRIAN (1872–1944), loosely associated with De Stijl, went even further in representing hidden realities than any of these other artists by creating a style

---

*In Herbert, ed. *Modern Artists on Art*, pp. 140–141, 145–146.

*In Chipp, ed., *Theories of Modern Art*, pp. 341, 345.

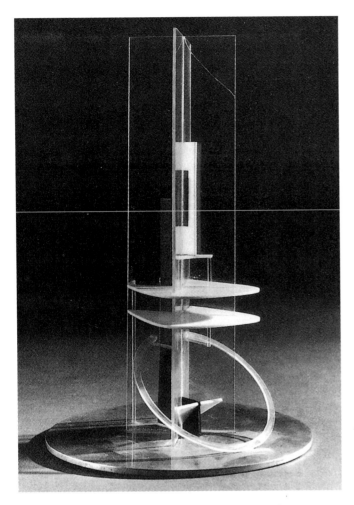

27-49 NAUM GABO, *Column*, 1922–1923. Perspex, on aluminum base, approx. 11¹⁄₈″ high. Family collection.

that he believed reflected the underlying eternal structure of existence. Inspired by the work of van Gogh, Mondrian began in an Expressionist style. He was keenly interested in conveying mystical and spiritual ideas in his art. Study in Paris, just before World War I, introduced him to modes of abstraction in avant-garde modern art such as Cubism. However, as his attraction to contemporary theological writings (especially the teachings of Theosophy) grew, Mondrian sought to purge his art of every overt reference to individual objects in the external world. He turned toward a conception of nonobjective or pictorial design—"pure plastic art"—that he believed expressed universal reality. He stated his credo with great eloquence in 1914:

> What first captivated us does not captivate us afterward (like toys). If one has loved the surface of things for a long time, later on one will look for something more. . . . The interior of things shows through the surface; thus as we look at the surface the inner image is formed in our soul. It is this inner image that should be represented. For the natural surface of things is beautiful, but the imitation of it

is without life. . . . Art is higher than reality and has no direct relation to reality. Between the physical sphere and the ethereal sphere there is a frontier where our senses stop functioning. . . . The spiritual penetrates the real . . . but for our senses these are two different things. To approach the spiritual in art, one will make as little use as possible of reality, because reality is opposed to the spiritual. We find ourselves in the presence of an abstract art. Art should be above reality, otherwise it would have no value for man.*

Caught by the outbreak of hostilities while on a visit to Holland, Mondrian remained there during the war, developing his theories for what he called *Neoplasticism*—the new "pure plastic art." He believed that all great art has polar but coexistent goals: the attempt to create "universal beauty" and the desire for "esthetic expression of oneself." The first goal is objective in nature, while the second is subjective, existing within the mind and heart of the individual. To create such a universal expression, an artist must discover and work with laws of perfect equilibrium that lie beyond the disharmonies and unhappiness that occur daily, because life in the world cannot achieve this balance. To express his vision of the true balance that lies beyond the physical world, Mondrian eventually limited his formal vocabulary to the three primary colors (red, blue, and yellow), the three primary values (black, white, and gray), and the two primary directions (horizontal and vertical). Basing his ideas on a combination of teachings, he concluded that primary colors and values were the purest colors and therefore were the perfect tools to help an artist to construct a harmonious composition. In *Composition in Blue, Yellow, and Black* (FIG. **27-50**), Mondrian used the elements of his Neoplastic style very sparingly, adjusting the design so that every portion of the composition engages in a static-dynamic play of color and form. The power of the colors and lines to hold the viewer's attention is subtly equivalent to the attraction exerted by the larger blank areas. The proportions of each of these areas are cunningly varied to avoid an inert mechanical uniformity of the general equilibrium of the grid. The whole painting resonates with the calm external order that we saw in ideal Classical works such as Raphael's *School of Athens* (FIG. 22-15), Poussin's *Burial of Phocion* (FIG. 24-60), and Ingres's *Apotheosis of Homer* (FIG. 26-6).

Following the revolution in 1917, the Soviet Union was the home of a new art movement whose members were activist counterparts of the Bauhaus utopian dream of an artist-craftsman-engineer who would devote every talent to designing a better environment for human beings. The Russians called their movement *Productivism*; it developed, as we have seen, as an arm of the Constructivist movement and one of its most gifted leaders

*In Michel Seuphor, *Piet Mondrian: Life and Work* (New York: Harry N. Abrams, 1956), p. 177.

27-50   PIET MONDRIAN, *Composition in Blue, Yellow, and Black,* 1936. Oil on canvas, approx. 17″ × 13″. Kunstmuseum, Basel, Switzerland (Emanuel Hoffmann-Stiftung).

was VLADIMIR TATLIN (1885–1953), a painter and sculptor who had been a sailor before turning to art. Influenced by the formal analysis of Cubism, the dynamism of Futurism, and the rhythmic compositions of flat, curved planes in traditional Russian icon paintings (FIG. 9-32), Tatlin turned to abstract relief constructions and models for stage sets after a brief period as a Cubo-Futurist painter. He experimented with every kind of material—glass, iron, sheet metal, wood, plaster—to lay the basis for what he called the "culture of materials."

The revolution had been the signal to Tatlin and other avant-garde artists in Russia that the hated old order was ending, and they determined to play a full role in the creation of a new world, one that would fully use the power of industrialization for the benefit of all the people. Initially, like Malevich and Gabo, Tatlin believed that non-objective art was ideal for the new society, free as such art was from any symbolism from the past. For a few years, all Russian avant-garde artists worked together, designing public festivals and demonstrations, presenting plays and exhibitions designed to help educate the public about their new government and the possibilities for their future. The

Russian Futurist-Constructivist poet Vladimir Mayakovskii proclaimed their new goal: "We do not need a dead mausoleum of art where dead works are worshiped, but a living factory of the human spirit—in the streets, in the tramways, in the factories, workshops, and workers' homes." Art schools like the College of Painting, Sculpture, and Architecture in Moscow were reorganized and combined with craft schools to form new educational programs—the one in Moscow was renamed the *Vkhutemas* (Higher Technical-Artistic Studios). Tatlin, Malevich, and Gabo's brother, Pevsner, had studios there, and Gabo (a frequent visitor) described the school's activities, which were much like those of Germany's *Bauhaus:*

> [It was] both a school and a free academy where not only the current teaching of special professions was carried out (. . . painting, sculpture, architecture, ceramics, metalwork, and woodwork, textile, and typography) but general discussions were held and seminars conducted amongst the students on diverse problems where the public could participate, and artists not officially on the faculty could speak and give lessons. . . . During these seminars . . . many ideological questions between opposing artists in our abstract group were thrashed out.*

As Gabo's statement indicates, a split was developing between members of the avant-garde. On one side were Malevich, Gabo, Kandinsky, and all the other artists who believed that art was an expression of humanity's spiritual nature. On the other side were the Productivist Constructivists—Tatlin and other artists who felt the artist must direct art toward the creation of useful products for the new society. The position of the Productivist Constructivists was connected to that of a group called Proletkult (Organization for Proletarian Culture), which had been founded in 1906, but became free to follow its primary doctrine ("Art is a social product, conditioned by the social environment") only after the 1917 revolution. Tatlin enthusiastically abandoned abstract art for functional art by designing such things as an efficient stove and a "functional" set of worker's clothing; for a time, he even worked in a metallurgical factory near Petrograd (after 1989 once again St. Petersburg).

Tatlin's most famous work is his design for a *Monument to the Third International* (FIG. **27-51**), commissioned early in 1919 to honor the Russian Revolution. His concept was for a huge glass and iron symbol-building that would have been twice as high as the Empire State Building. On its proposed site in the center of Moscow, it would have served as a propaganda and news center for the Soviet people. Within a dynamically tilted spiral cage, three geometrically shaped chambers were to rotate around a central axis, each chamber housing facilities for a different type of

*In Camilla Gray, *The Russian Experiment in Art 1863–1922* (New York: Harry N. Abrams, 1970), pp. 232–233.

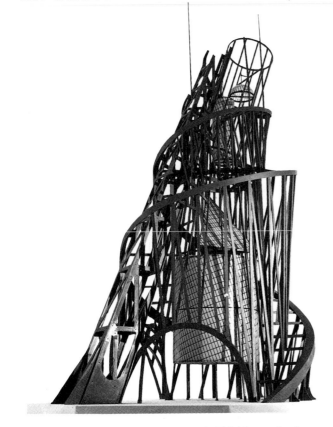

27-51   VLADIMIR TATLIN, *Monument to the Third International,*
1919–1920. Model in wood, iron, and glass. Re-created in 1968 for
exhibition at the Moderna Museet, Stockholm.

governmental activity and rotating at a different speed.
At the bottom, a huge, cylindrical glass structure, meant
to house lectures and meetings, was to revolve once a
year. The next highest chamber was to be a cone-shaped
structure assigned to administrative functions and rotating
once a month. At the top, a cubic information center would
revolve daily, issuing news bulletins and proclamations via
the most modern means of communication, including an
open-air news screen (illuminated at night) and a special
instrument designed to project words on the clouds on any
overcast day. Tatlin envisioned the whole complex as a
dynamic communications center, perfectly suited to the
exhilarating pace of the new age. Due to the desperate economic situation in Russia during these years, Tatlin's ambitious design was never realized as a building; it existed only
in models in metal and wood, which were exhibited on
various official occasions before disappearing. The only
record of the model in our illustration is to be found in a
few drawings, photographs, and recent reconstructions.

Moholy-Nagy's belief that modern experience is spa-
tiotemporal and aware of "relativity of motion and its measurement, integration, simultaneous grasp of the inside and
outside, . . . [and] a new vision concerning materials, energies, tensions," could have served as a program for the
American sculptor ALEXANDER CALDER (1898–1976). Calder
used non-objective organic forms and a thorough knowledge of engineering techniques in a new kind of sculpture

that utilized motion to express the innate dynamism of
reality. Both the artist's father and grandfather were sculptors, but Calder initially studied to be a mechanical engineer. He was fascinated all his life by motion, and much of
his sculpture explored that phenomenon and its relationship to three-dimensional form.

As a young artist in Paris in the late 1920s, Calder
invented a circus full of miniature performers that were
activated by the artist into realistic analogues of the motion
of their counterparts in life. After a visit to Mondrian's studio in the early 1930s, Calder was filled with a desire to
set the brightly colored rectangular shapes in the Dutch
painter's compositions into motion. (It was Marcel
Duchamp, intrigued by early motorized and hand-cranked
examples of Calder's moving, abstract pieces, who named
them *mobiles.*) Calder's engineering skills soon helped him
to fashion a series of balanced structures hanging from
rods, wires, and colored biomorphic-shaped plates. *Hanging
Spider* (FIG. **27-52**) was designed to perform in response to
air currents and to suggest natural patterns like those of
clouds, leaves, or waves blown by the wind. The initial
inspiration for the mobiles may have come from the work
of Mondrian, but the organic shapes in the mobiles resemble those in the Surrealist paintings of Joan Miró (FIG.

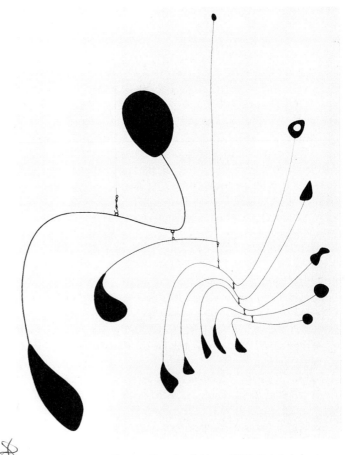

27-52   ALEXANDER CALDER, *Hanging Spider, c.* 1940. Painted sheet
metal, wire, 51″ high. Private collection.

27-70) and were actually generated by Calder's love of nature. The compositions of each of Calder's nonmechanized mobiles were carefully planned so that any air current would set the parts moving within a pattern to create a constantly shifting dance in space, an effect splendidly described by the sculptor's friend, the British painter Ben Nicholson (1894–1981):

> The first time I encountered a Calder was in Paris some years ago when I borrowed one and hung it from the center of the ceiling of a white room overlooking the Seine, and at night, with the river glistening outside, this mobile object turned slowly in the breeze in the light of an electric bulb hung near its center—a large black, six white, and one small scarlet, balls on their wires turned slowly in and out, around, above and below one another, with their shadows chasing, round the white walls in an exciting interchanging movement, suddenly hastening as they turned the corners and disappearing, as they crossed the windows, into the night—it was alive like the hum of the city, like the passing river, but it was not a work of art—imprisoned in a gold frame or stone-dead on a pedestal in one of our marble-pillared mausoleums. It was "alive" and that, after all, is not a bad qualification for a work of art.*

Calder's forms can be read either as geometrical or organic: geometrically, the lines suggest circuitry, and rigging, the shapes, irregular sections of the cone; organically, the lines suggest nerve axons and the shapes are cells, leaves, fins, wings, and other bioforms. *Hanging Spider,* helped by its title, does indeed suggest (*not* represent) that ingenious creature, and illustrates exactly the description of it in Pope's lines: "The spider's touch, how exquisitely fine! / feels at each thread, and lives along the line." At the same time, the piece is animated not only by air flow, but by subtle mechanical engineering. We can take the art of Calder as mediating between *Geometric* and *Organic Formalism.*

In this respect he belongs in the company of the Romanian sculptor CONSTANTIN BRANCUSI (1876–1957), who, in his own words, sought in nature "what is real . . . not the outward form, but the idea, the essence of things." Works like *Bird in Space* (FIG. **27-53**) were created at the end of a long process in which Brancusi began with a sculpture closer in detail to the shape of something in the world—in this case, a bird standing at rest with its wings folded at its sides. Gradually, he simplified the bird's shape until its feet and body merged, the final form suggesting that it is about to leave the ground to soar in free flight

*In Michel Seuphor, *The Sculpture of This Century* (New York: George Braziller, 1960), p. 85.

†Many people have noted a resemblance between Brancusi's *Bird in Space* and the appearance of the streamlined *moderne* style being developed by industrial designers during the 1930s. The resemblance is fortuitous, but not surprising, as both artist and designers each based their concept on a careful study of birds in flight.

through the heavens.† Brancusi envisioned many of his works, including this one, enlarged to monumental scale. The subtitle for this work was *Project of bird which, when enlarged, will fill the sky,* and the sculptor spoke of the work's ability on that scale to fill viewers with comfort and peace. The polished bronze was intended to catch and reflect light. Brancusi always paid special attention to the intrinsic qualities in the materials he used. He made sculptures in wood, marble, stone, and bronze. In each, he tried to create forms that respected and worked with the nature of the material itself, extracting from it—whether marble, metal, or wood—its maximum effect. It may be that it was with Brancusi's scrupulous attention to the nature of his materials that the pervading doctrine and mystique of modernist art—"truth to the material"—arose. This doctrine demands that the artist respect the material, that formal intentions never abuse its particular nature. What is appropriate for bronze is not so for marble; what is appropriate for marble is not so for wood; and so on. Respect for the function of the material is also a necessity in industrial production. This

27-53 CONSTANTIN BRANCUSI, *Bird in Space,* 1928(?). Bronze, unique cast, approx. 54" high. The Museum of Modern Art, New York (given anonymously).

truth to material goes along with the modernist quest for purity or "reality" of form. As Mondrian found rectilinear form to be most "real," so Brancusi visualized an extended ovoid structure as the most "natural" shape and simplified the most complex natural forms and even natural movements to variations on this fundamental shape. In *Bird in Space*, everything accidental is eliminated or compressed into the most direct and economical expression, yet the form as a whole suggests the essence of a bird's sudden upward movement through air. Even more, there is a remarkable suggestion of airflow, as delineated by modern aerodynamics, and Brancusi's means of conveying flight are not unrelated to those used by the modern engineer in designing "streamlined" industrial forms. There is the same study of the nature of the material—the same meticulous attention to proportions, contour, and surface finish. Here, the coming together of art and technology is evident. At the same time, despite the technological connection, the artist derives forms from living and growing things.

JEAN (HANS) ARP (1887–1966), painter, sculptor, and poet, was a kind of maverick who associated with all the major movements (Expressionist, Constructivist, Dada, and Surrealist), yet a free spirit, not definitely committed to any of their doctrines. He exhibited with *Der Blaue Reiter* in Germany, with the first Surrealists, and was in early contact with the Paris avant-garde. His biomorphic forms mediate between the Constructivists and Organic Formalists on the one hand, and the Surrealists on the other. In *Human Concretion* (FIG. **27-54**) he suggests the natural processes that generate the shapes of the physical world. Borrowing a term from geology, Arp called many of his Surrealist sculptures "concretions:" "Concretion signifies the natural process of condensation, hardening, coagulating, thickening, growing together. . . . Concretion designates solidification. . . . Concretion is something that has grown."* *Human Concretion* was designed so that it could be placed in a number of positions. The way in which its forms twist and push forward in many directions creates the effect that the piece is still in the process of growing toward its final state. Arp's definition and the title of this piece both reflect his deep belief that the whole earth is alive and that all living things share in the same vital forces. The biomorphic organism of *Human Concretion* links Arp's Surrealism with the abstract forms created by Barbara Hepworth (FIG. 27-55) and Henry Moore (FIG. 27-56) in England.

BARBARA HEPWORTH (1903–1975) developed her own kind of essential sculptural form, combining pristine shape with a sense of organic vitality. The rugged landscape of Yorkshire, in the north of England, helped to shape her sculptural vision. She had vivid childhood memories of driving there with her father; reflecting on these drives years later, she wrote: "the sensation of moving physically

27-54 JEAN ARP, *Human Concretion*, 1935. Original plaster, 19¹/₂″ × 25¹/₂″. Collection, The Museum of Modern Art, New York (gift of the Advisory Committee).

over the contours of fulnesses and concavities, through hollows and over peaks—feeling, touching, seeing, through mind and hand and eye . . . has never left me. I, the sculptor, am the landscape. I am the form and I am the hollow, the thrust and the contour." This feeling led her ever deeper into a search for forms that would express her sense both of the landscape and of the person who is in and observes it:

> The forms which have had special meaning for me since childhood have been the standing form (which is the translation of my feeling towards the human being standing in landscape); the two forms (which is the tender relationship of one living thing beside another); and the closed form, such as the oval, spherical, or pierced form (sometimes incorporating colour) which translates for me the association and meaning of gesture in the landscape. . . . In all these shapes the translation of what one feels about man and nature must be conveyed by the sculptor in terms of mass, inner tension, and rhythm, scale in relation to our human size, and the quality of surface which speaks through our hands and eyes.*

Three Forms (FIG. **27-55**) was the first in a series of works that Hepworth began soon after she became the mother of triplets in 1934, an experience that apparently stimulated her to explore the relationship in size, shape, and position in space between three elements arranged on a thin base. In this piece, a small ovoid form nestles close to a larger form, a kind of inflated relative of it. A petite sphere rests on the corner of the base farthest from them. The artist has gathered here the basic organic forms that had special

---

*In Herbert Read, *The Art of Jean Arp* (New York: Harry N. Abrams, 1968), p. 93.

*Barbara Hepworth, *A Pictorial Autobiography* (London: The Tate Gallery, 1978), pp. 9, 53.

ABSTRACT

27-55 BARBARA HEPWORTH, *Three Forms,* 1935. Marble. Tate Gallery, London.

meaning for her. The shapes and the impeccably smooth surfaces suggest both the cellular elements of life and the perfection of things made by human hands and tools. Like those in all of her mature works, the shapes in Hepworth's *Three Forms* are contained and classical, expressing a sense of the timelessness of eternity.

The English sculptor HENRY MOORE (1898–1986) shared Brancusi's profound love of nature and knowledge of natural forms and materials. Moore maintained that every "material has its own individual qualities" and that these qualities could play a role in the creative process. "It is only when the sculptor works direct, where there is an active relationship with his material, that the material can take part in the shaping of an idea." Moore combined this insight with memories of the shapes of the hilly Yorkshire

countryside he had known as a boy to express the ways in which the shapes of landscape and the human figure echo one another in a marvelous unity of form: "The human figure is what interests me most deeply, but I have found principles of form and rhythm from the study of natural objects." One great recurring theme in Moore's work is the reclining female figure, whose simplified and massive forms originally were inspired by a tiny photograph of a Chacmool figure from pre-Columbian Mexico.*

Although one can recognize a human figure in most of Moore's works, the artist pushed always toward an Abstract Symbolism that would express a universal truth beyond the physical world. He summarized his feelings about abstract figurative form in two passages from essays written in the 1930s:

Because a work does not aim at reproducing natural appearances, it is not, therefore, an escape from life—but may be a penetration into reality. . . . My sculpture is becoming less representational, less an outward visual copy . . . , but only because I believe that in this way I can present the human psychological content of my work with greatest directness and intensity.†

Reclining Figure (FIG. **27-56**) is a wonderful example of Moore's handling of his particular Abstract Symbolism.

*Chacmool figures are thought perhaps to represent a god or a worshiper bearing an offering. Usually carved in stone, each figure characteristically reclines on its back with the knees bent and its torso bent upright, head turning abruptly toward one side.

†In Herbert, ed. *Modern Artists on Art,* pp. 140–141, 145–146.

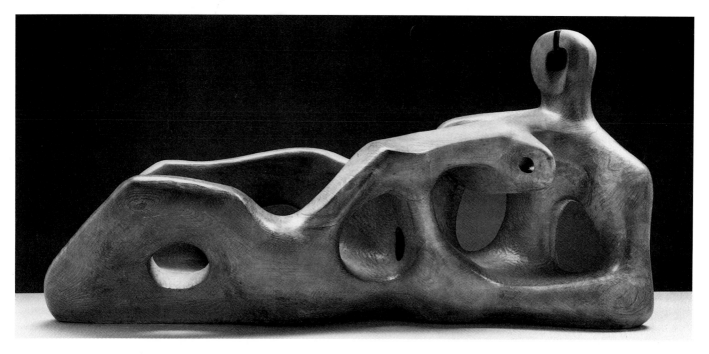

27-56 HENRY MOORE, *Reclining Figure,* 1939. Elmwood, 37" × 6'7" × 30". Detroit Institute of the Arts (gift of Dexter M. Ferry, Jr., Trustee Corporation).

The massive shapes of the figure suggest the biomorphic forms of Surrealism, but Moore's recumbent woman is also a powerful earth mother, whose undulant forms and hollows suggest nurturing human energy and at the same time evoke the contours of Yorkshire hills and the wind-polished surfaces of weathered wood and stone. Allusions in Moore's work to landscape and to biomorphic Surrealist form are heightened by the interplay of mass and void, which the sculptor based on the intriguing qualities of cavities in nature: "The hole connects one side to the other, making it immediately more three-dimensional. . . . The

mystery of the hole—the mysterious fascination of caves in hillsides and cliffs." The contours and openings of *Reclining Figure* follow the grain of the wood. Above all, *Reclining Figure* is filled with a tightly coiled, dynamic energy that seems to radiate from its innermost core outward through the breasts, the jutting knees, and the upthrust head.

Artists working in other media also valued the goals espoused by these sculptors. The American painter GEORGIA O'KEEFFE (1887–1986) was especially inspired by light and by the patterns of nature, stripping her subjects to their purest forms and colors to heighten their expressive power.

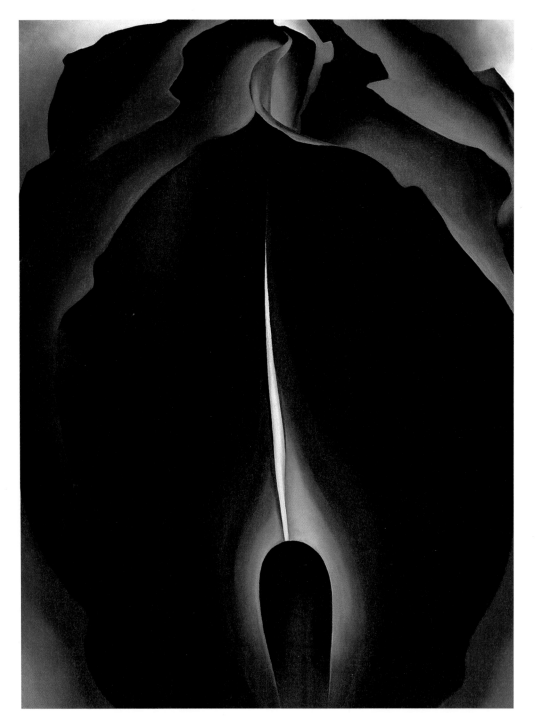

27-57 GEORGIA O'KEEFFE, *Jack-in-the-Pulpit IV,* 1930. Oil on canvas, 40″ × 30″. Formerly in the collection of Georgia O'Keeffe.

Born in rural Wisconsin, O'Keeffe worked as a commercial artist and an art teacher as she developed a personal style that incorporated the ideas of the art theorist Arthur Wesley Dow and his follower, the artist-theorist-teacher Alon Bement, both of whom stressed "the idea of filling a space in a beautiful way," especially a space created with the simple flat shapes characteristic of Japanese paintings and prints. The look of things in the world inspired O'Keeffe's paintings of flowers, landscape, objects, and the sun in Texas and New Mexico (the spiritual home in which she lived much of each year), and scenes in upstate New York and Manhattan, where she made her home for the rest of the year with her husband, Alfred Stieglitz, until his death. In all her works, O'Keeffe reduced the incredible details of her subject to a symphony of basic colors, shapes, textures, and vital rhythms. Her style is fully realized in the painting *Jack-in-the-Pulpit IV* (FIG. **27-57**), an expanded, sharply focused, close-up view of the handsome plant. Exhibiting the natural flow of curved planes and contour, O'Keeffe reduces the form almost to the limit of the flower's identity; it might, at first sight, be something exfoliating on some distant star, or in the cellular world beneath the microscope. The fluid planes unfold like undulant petals from a subtly placed axis—the white, jet-like streak—in a vision of the slow, controlled motion of growing life. O'Keeffe's painting, in its graceful, quiet poetry, reveals the organic reality (Brancusi would say its "essence") of the object by strengthening its characteristic features, in striking contrast with either Kandinsky's explosions (FIG. 27-21) or Mondrian's rectilinear absolutes (FIG. 27-50).

Dada, Surrealism, and Fantastic Art

DADA In the late nineteenth century, Impressionism, Post-Impressionism, and Symbolism began the dismantling of the Renaissance tradition necessary for the establishment of Modernism; in the early twentieth century, the process was quickened with Expressionism, Cubism, and Futurism. World War I did not interrupt this process, though it did for a while stimulate a movement, called *Dada*, which protested against all art, modern or traditional, as well as the civilization that had produced it.

Dada was born of the war itself, and of the social, economic, and political calamities that followed it. Humanity had never before witnessed such wholesale slaughter on so grand a scale over such an extended period of time; millions were killed, wounded, or missing (blown to bits) in great battles: in 1916 the battle of Verdun, lasting five months, left five hundred thousand casualties; in the same year, and on a single day, the British lost sixty thousand men in the opening battle of the Somme. The new technology of armaments, bred of the age of steel, made it a "war of the guns." In the face of massed artillery hurling millions of tons of high explosives and gas shells, and in the sheets of fire from thousands of machine guns, attack was

suicidal, and battle movement congealed into the stalemate of trench warfare, stretching from the English Channel almost to Switzerland. The mud, filth, and blood of the trenches, the pounding and shattering of incessant shell fire, the terrible deaths and mutilations, were a devastating psychological as well as physical experience for a generation brought up with the doctrine of progress and a belief in the fundamental values of civilization.

It was against this madness that the banner of Dada was raised in disgust and protest—not by the soldiers themselves, but by men who had escaped the war by fleeing to neutral territory. The city of Zurich in Switzerland hosted crowds of "deserters, anarchists, and revolutionaries," poets, painters, actors, musicians, who were united in their horror of the war and disgust for the society that had produced it. Some of these formed a group that they named "Dada," a nonsense word picked at random from a French dictionary; actually, *dada* is French for a child's hobbyhorse, but the word was sufficiently insignificant to satisfy the Dadaists' contempt for significance.

The nihilism of Dada, its disdain for all traditional and modern values, and its derisive iconoclasm can be read at random from its numerous manifestoes and declarations of intent:

> Dada knows everything. Dada spits on everything. Dada says "knowthing," Dada has no fixed ideas. Dada does not catch flies. Dada is bitterness laughing at everything that has been accomplished, sanctified. . . . Dada is never right. . . . No more painters, no more writers, no more religions, no more royalists, no more anarchists, no more socialists, no more police, no more airplanes, no more urinary passages. . . . Like everything in life, Dada is useless, everything happens in a completely idiotic way. . . . We are incapable of treating seriously any subject whatsoever, let alone this subject: ourselves. [Dadaists, describing their own movement, said] Dada was a phenomenon bursting forth in the midst of the post-war economic and moral crisis, a savior, a monster, which would lay waste to everything in its path. [It was] a systematic work of destruction and demoralization. . . . In the end it became nothing but the act of sacrilege.*

Duchamp painted a moustache on a reproduction of Leonardo's *Mona Lisa;* the French painter Francis Picabia (1879–1953), Duchamp's collaborator in setting up Dada in New York, nailed a toy monkey to a board, and labeled it *Portrait of Cézanne.*

The Dada movement actually began independently in both New York and Zurich during the war and soon spread throughout Europe. It was more a mind-set than a single, identifiable style; wherever it arose, its artists were committed to questioning everything about artistic expression.

*All of these passages are to be found, *passim,* in Robert Motherwell, ed., *The Dada Painters and Poets: An Anthology,* 2nd ed. (Cambridge, MA: Belknap Press of Harvard University, 1989).

Much Dada work was intentionally ephemeral. Yet it had important consequences for later art—reinforcing a tendency toward a spontaneous, intuitive expression of the whimsical, fantastic, humorous, sardonic, and absurd. A whole new realm of artistic possibility opened in which the remnants of the optical world, shattered by scientific and compositional analysis, emerged to play expressive new roles determined by the different contexts in which they drew on materials lying deep within human consciousness; the artistic act of expression became the proclamation of new realities that were no less real because they were psychic. Dada work paralleled the psychoanalytic views of Sigmund Freud, Carl Jung, and others, and Dada artists believed that art was a powerfully practical means of self-revelation and catharsis, and that the images that arose out of the subconscious mind had a truth of their own, independent of the world of conventional vision. The attitude of the European Dadaists was summed up by Hans Richter, a Dada filmmaker:

> Possessed, as we were, of the ability to entrust ourselves to "chance," to our conscious as well as our unconscious minds, we became a sort of public secret society. . . . We laughed at everything. . . . But laughter was only the *expression* of our new discoveries, not their essence and not their purpose. Pandemonium, destruction, anarchy, anti-everything of the World War? How could Dada have been anything but destructive, aggressive, insolent, on principle and with gusto?*

Perhaps the most influential of all the Dadaists, and somewhat independent of them, was Marcel Duchamp, the central artist of New York Dada and active in Paris at the end of the Dada movement (we have already seen him as a Futurist [FIG. 27-39]). Raised as a member of an artistic Parisian family (an older brother was a painter and a younger brother a sculptor), Duchamp made an early reputation for Futurist paintings before becoming fascinated simultaneously with the world of ideas (including a topsy-turvy pseudophysics called "pataphysics") and that of machines and their representation in the language of mechanical drawing. Soon he was producing paintings in which figures were rendered as mechanized forms. In 1913, he exhibited his first "ready-made" sculptures, which were mass-produced objects selected by the artist and sometimes "rectified" by modification of their substance or combination with another object. *Bicycle Wheel* (FIG. **27-58**) was Duchamp's first ready-made. In *Bicycle Wheel*, he combines two ordinary mass-produced objects and displaces them from their expected, everyday locations by mounting a single bicycle wheel atop the seat of an ordinary wooden kitchen stool. Such works, he insisted, were created free from any consideration of either good or bad taste, qualities shaped by a society that he and other Dada artists found

27-58 MARCEL DUCHAMP, *Bicycle Wheel*, 1951 (third version after lost original of 1913). Metal wheel mounted on painted wooden stool, 50$\frac{1}{2}$" high, 25$\frac{1}{2}$" wide; stool, 23$\frac{3}{4}$" high. The Museum of Modern Art, New York (gift of the Sidney and Harriet Janis Collection).

esthetically bankrupt. In place of "taste," Duchamp gave ideas. As he wrote in a "defense" published in 1917, after the exhibition committee for an unjuried show failed to exhibit his ready-made *Fountain* (a detached urinal, set on its side and signed visibly with a witty pseudonym derived from the Mott plumbing manufactory's name and that of the short half of the Mutt and Jeff comic-strip team): "Whether Mr. Mutt with his own hands made the fountain or not has no importance. He *chose* it. He took an ordinary article of life, placed it so that its useful significance disappeared under the new title and point of view—created a new thought for that object."* Among the ideas in *Bicycle*

---

*Hans Richter, *Dada: Art and Anti-Art* (London: Thames & Hudson, 1961), pp. 64–65.

*In Arturo Schwarz, *The Complete Works of Marcel Duchamp* (London: Thames & Hudson, 1965), p. 466.

Wheel are those connected with optical illusion and with motion (separated from usefulness). Spinning the wheel introduces the viewer to the visual illusions of strobing spokes, which seem to rotate forward or backward, or even to disappear completely into a shimmering blur, depending on the speed of rotation. Duchamp's interest in motion had first appeared early in his career in his Futurist paintings, partially inspired by the multiple-exposure, motion-study photographs of the nineteenth-century French kinesiologist Étienne-Jules Marey. Duchamp explored this interest in paintings, cinema, and various experiments in optical illusions throughout the rest of his career.

Many of Duchamp's ideas appeared in a large, two-panel painting on glass, *The Bride Stripped Bare by Her Bachelors, Even* (FIG. **27-59**), whose complex iconography he began developing as early as 1912. Intrigued by the suggestions of space with four and more dimensions in the work of mathematician Edward Abbey, Duchamp chose to paint on glass because he felt the shapes he created there in rigorous Renaissance perspective would appear to float free of their support, suggesting "the projection of a four-dimensional shape in a three-dimensional world." Unlike traditional diptychs, the two panels in this painting are placed one above the other. Each plate of glass represents a separate realm. The artist's fascination with machines led him to invent a symbolism based on mechanical forms.

The upper plate of glass contains the region of the bride, whose mechanized form is seen at the far left. Next to her is a cloud shape—the "Milky Way"—designated by Duchamp as the place of "blossoming." The bottom plate of glass contains the realm of the bachelors, represented at the left in a circle of nine "malic molds," whose shapes were based on the silhouettes of uniformed Frenchmen—among them a policeman, a bellboy, and a messenger. An admirer of the wacky machines devised by the American cartoonist Rube Goldberg, Duchamp here imagined an elaborate setup by which the bachelors could attempt to disrobe the bride. At the same time, however, the artist also introduced elements that would forever prevent that desired consummation. Duchamp made careful studies for each section of the composition, but he also employed methods of chance to determine many details. For example, the shapes of the "draft pistons" within the area of blossoming at the top were determined by having Duchamp's friend, the American artist Man Ray, take three photographs of a meter-square piece of dotted net fabric as it blew in the breeze coming through an open window. The three different contours determined the shapes of the three "openings" in the cloud, and the double meaning for "draft" (work and breeze) is a good example of the verbal puns Duchamp loved to include in his work. He found the operation of chance so intriguing that he even employed it in some of the innovative techniques with which he applied color to the glass. The most unusual of these probably occurred in the series of multiple cones (or "sieves") in the lower half, which were created by allowing dust to accumulate on the

surface of the glass for several weeks and then using varnish to fix the dust in place, creating a translucent, mottled, warm brown hue within these shapes.*

According to Duchamp (and the generations of artists after him who were profoundly influenced by his art and especially his attitude), life and art were matters of chance and choice freed from the conventions of society and tradition. Within his approach to art and life, each act was

*Although Duchamp worked on painting the glass panels intermittently between 1915 and 1925, he had not added all planned details when the work was returned damaged to his studio after an exhibition. Regarding the pattern of diagonal cracks with some satisfaction, he declared the piece "incompleted" and did no further work on it. We know his intentions from voluminous notes he made for the painting (nicknamed "The Large Glass"), which he published in facsimile in two special "boxes," and we know the planned look of the final composition from a diagrammatic etching the artist made late in his career.

27-59 MARCEL DUCHAMP, *The Bride Stripped Bare by Her Bachelors, Even (The Large Glass)*, 1915–1923. Oil, lead wire, foil, dust, and varnish on glass, 8'11" × 5'7". The Philadelphia Museum of Art (bequest of Katherine S. Dreier).

individual and unique: every person's choice of found objects would be different, each person's throw of the dice would be at a different instant and probably would yield a different number. This philosophy of utter freedom for the artist is fundamental to the history of art in the twentieth century. In addition, the viewer of a Duchamp work must decipher the meaning of the work in a way that makes the experience an intellectual exercise that yields different and continually shifting "meanings" for each individual. All of these factors cause Duchamp's influence to continue to be as strong for Postmodernist art late in the twentieth century as it was for Modernism.

Duchamp spent much of World War I in New York, inspiring a group of American artists and collectors with his radical rethinking of the role of the artist and of the nature of art. By 1916, another group of young European artists had gathered in neutral Zurich, filled with a similar but more boisterous reaction against the norms of the society of their day. Collectively (and idealistically), this European group set out to use their art as a weapon to shock viewers into self-awareness and to stimulate action that would change civilization into something better. This is the group that, as we have noted, actually called their anti-art "Dada" and themselves "Dadaists." They challenged people in their gathering place, the Cabaret Voltaire, through aggressive performances based on provocative insults, nonsense speeches, and a variety of outlandish pranks, or *gestes*, which they described as "cerebral revolver shots." As one of the Zurich group, Hans Richter, later wrote:

> Dada invited, or rather defied, the world to misunderstand it, and fostered every kind of confusion. . . .Dada has reaped the harvest of confusion that it sowed. However, the harvest of confusion was only a facade. Our provocations, demonstrations, and defiances were only a means of arousing the bourgeoisie to rage and through rage to shame-faced self-awareness.*

Like Duchamp, the Zurich Dadaists sought ways to stop relying on the operation of reason, which they saw as conditioned by upbringing and education. Many of their methods involved either "automatism" or the operations of chance.

Automatism was the process of yielding oneself to instinctive actions after establishing a set of conditions (such as size of paper and medium), within which a work would be carried out. One of the Zurich Dadaists, Jean Arp, whose biomorphic art we have described (FIG. 27-54), specialized in automatic drawings made in a two-step process that he began by letting his pencil wander over a sheet of paper with as little intellectual control as possible. Then he scrutinized the patterns made for shapes that seemed to have significance to him and filled those contours with ink to create a final design. Arp also was a leader in the use of

chance in making art. Tiring of the look of some Cubist-related collages he was making at the time, he took some sheets of paper, tore them into roughly shaped squares, haphazardly dropped them to a sheet of paper on the floor, and glued them into the arrangement that resulted; the rectilinearity of the shapes guaranteed a somewhat regular design, but chance had introduced an imbalance that seemed to Arp to restore to his work a special mysterious vitality that he wanted to preserve. The operations of "chance" were for Dadaists a crucial part of this kind of improvisation. As Richter stated:

> For us chance was the "unconscious mind" that Freud had discovered in 1900. . . . Adoption of chance had another purpose, a secret one. This was to restore to the work of art its primeval magic power and to find a way back to the immediacy it had lost through contact with . . . classicism.*

From Zurich, Dada spread throughout much of Western Europe, arriving as early as 1917 in Berlin, where it soon took on an activist political edge, partially in response to the economic, social, and political chaos in that city in the years at the end of and immediately after World War I. The Berlin Dadaists developed to a new intensity a technique used earlier in popular art postcards. Pasting parts from many pictures together into one image, the Berliners christened their version of the technique *photomontage*. The technique of creating a composition by pasting together pieces of paper had been used in private and popular arts long before the twentieth century. In the early decades of the century, the process was named "collage" by the Cubists (see page 1045). Unlike Cubist collage, the parts of a Dada collage were made almost entirely of "found" details, usually combined into deliberately anti-logical compositions. Collage lent itself well to the Dada desire to use chance in the creation of art and anti-art, but not all Dada collage was as savagely aggressive as that of the Berlin photomontagists.

The Hanover Dada artist KURT SCHWITTERS (1887–1948) followed a gentler muse. Inspired by Cubist collage, but working in a nonobjective way, Schwitters found visual poetry in the cast-off junk of modern society and scavenged in trash bins for materials, which he pasted and nailed together into designs like *Merz 19* (FIG. **27-60**). He borrowed the term *merz* from a word fragment in one of his collages (part of *kommerz*, "commerce"). His compositions are nonobjective, yet they still resonate with the "meaning" of the fragmented found objects they contain. Like the readymades of Duchamp, the recycled elements of Schwitter's collages are invested with new meanings through their new uses and locations.

The American artist MAN RAY (1890–1976), who worked closely with Duchamp through the 1920s, incorporated

*Richter *Dada: Art and Anti-Art*, p. 9.

*Ibid., p. 57.

ready-mades into many of his paintings, sculptures, movies, and photographs. Trained as an architectural draftsman and engineer, Man Ray earned his living as a graphic designer and portrait photographer, and he brought to his personal work an interest in mass-produced objects and technology and a committed dedication to exploring the psychological realm through which we perceive the exterior world. Like Schwitters, Man Ray used chance and the dislocation of ordinary things from their everyday settings to surprise his viewers into new awareness. His displacement of found objects was particularly effective in works like *Gift* (FIG. **27-61**), in which he equips a laundry iron with a row of wicked-looking spikes, contravening its proper function of smoothing and pressing. The malicious humor of *Gift*—seen throughout Dada and, indeed, in much of contemporary art—gives it a characteristic edge that can cut the unwary. Contradiction, paradox, irony, even blasphemy are the bequest of Dada. They are, in the view of Dada and its successors, the free and defiant artist's weapons in what has been called the "hundred years war with the public."

27-61 MAN RAY, *Gift, c.* 1958 (replica after destroyed original of 1921). Painted flatiron with metal tacks, 6$^{1}/_{8}$" high, 3$^{5}/_{8}$" wide, 4$^{1}/_{2}$" deep. The Museum of Modern Art, New York (James Thrall Soby Fund).

27-60 KURT SCHWITTERS, *Merz 19*, 1920. Paper collage, approx. 7$^{1}/_{4}$" × 5$^{7}/_{8}$". Yale University Art Gallery, New Haven, Connecticut (collection, Société Anonyme).

Surrealism and Fantastic Art

The exuberant aggression and anti-esthetic activity of the Dadaists, however, only sustained their sharp spirit for a short time; after that, most of the Dada group's practitioners were absorbed into the Surrealist movement and its determined exploration of ways to express in art the world of dreams and the unconscious. The Surrealists borrowed many of the improvisational techniques of the Dadaists, believing these to be important methods for engaging the elements of fantasy and activating the unconscious forces that lie deep within every human being. The Dadaists found a kindred spirit in the work of the Greco-Italian painter GIORGIO DE CHIRICO (1888–1978), whose emphatically ambiguous works also make him a precursor of Surrealism. De Chirico's paintings of cityscapes and shop windows were part of a movement called *pittura metafisica*, or *Metaphysical Painting*. As the son of a railroad engineer, his childhood was flavored by the continual arrival and departure of his father's trains. Returning to Italy after study in Munich, de Chirico found inspiration in the writings of Nietzsche, who saw hidden reality revealed through strange juxtapositions, like those seen on late autumn afternoons in the city of Turin, when its vast open squares and silent public monuments were transformed by the long shadows of the setting sun into "the most metaphysical of Italian towns." De Chirico translated this vision into paint in works like *The Soothsayer's Recompense* (fig. **27-62**), where the squares and palaces of Roman and Renaissance Italy are visualized in a mood of intense and mysterious melancholy. A strangely displaced reality is evoked by the clock, the distant train, the blank sky, the tilted perspective, the blank facade broken by a yawning arcade, and the empty piazza with its mysteriously alive sculpture and slanting shadows. This image is a perfect illustration of the world of Metaphysical Painting, which de Chirico described:

> In the construction of cities, in the architectural forms of houses, in squares and gardens and public walks, in gateways and railway stations . . . are contained the initial foundations of a great metaphysical esthetic. . . . We who know the signs of the metaphysical alphabet are aware of the joy and the solitude enclosed by a portico, the corners of a street, or even in a room, on the surface of a table, between the sides of a box. The limits of these signs constitute for us a sort of moral and esthetic code of representation, and more than this, with clairvoyance we construct in painting a new metaphysical psychology of objects.*

De Chirico's paintings were reproduced in periodicals almost as soon as he completed them, and his works quick-

*In Massimo Carrá, Ewald Rathke, Caroline Tisdall, and Patrick Waldberg, *Metaphysical Art* (New York: Praeger, 1971), p. 90.

ly influenced artists outside Italy, including both the Dadaists and Surrealists. The disjunctive reality in his work intrigued the Dadaists, while the eerie mood and visionary quality of paintings like *The Soothsayer's Recompense* excited and influenced those Surrealist artists who sought to portray the world of dreams.

By 1924, much of the spirit of Dada had faded, and the energies of many of its adherents were turned toward the new movement of *Surrealism* (the chance association of things and events, the dislocation of images and meanings, the scrambling of conventional contexts, the exploration of the subconscious, and the radical freedom of artistic choice). The Surrealists were determined to explore the inner world of the psyche, the realm of fantasy and the unconscious. Inspired in part by the ideas of the psychoanalysts Jung and Freud, the Surrealists were especially interested in the nature of dreams. They viewed dreams as occurring at the level at which all human consciousness connects and as constituting the arena in which people could move beyond the constricting forces of their environment to re-engage with the deeper selves that society had long suppressed. In 1924, these Surrealist beliefs were presented in the form of a dictionary definition of Surrealism formulated by one of its leading thinkers, the young Parisian writer André Breton:

> Pure psychic automatism, by which one intends to express verbally, in writing, or by any other method, the real functioning of the mind. Dictation by thought, in the absence of any control exercised by reason, and beyond

27-62 Giorgio de Chirico, *The Soothsayer's Recompense*, 1913. 53³/₈" × 71". Philadelphia Museum of Art (The Louise and Walter Arensberg Collection).

any esthetic or moral preoccupation. . . . Surrealism is based on the belief in the superior reality of certain forms of association heretofore neglected, in the omnipotence of dreams, in the undirected play of thought. . . . I believe in the future resolution of the states of dream and reality, in appearance so contradictory, in a sort of absolute reality, or surreality.*

Thus, the dominant motivation of Surrealist art was to bring the aspects of outer and inner "reality" together into a single position, in much the same way that seemingly unrelated fragments of life combine in the vivid world of dreams. The projection in visible form of this new conception required new techniques of pictorial construction. The Surrealists adapted some Dadaist devices and invented new techniques like automatic writing and various types of planned "accidents" not so much to reveal a world without meaning as to provoke reactions closely related to subconscious experience.

Originally a Dada activist in Cologne, Germany, MAX ERNST (1891–1976) became one of the early adherents of the Surrealist circle surrounding Breton. As a child living in a small community near Cologne, Ernst had found his existence to be fantastic and filled with marvels. In autobiographical notes, written mostly in the third person, he said of his birth: "Max Ernst had his first contact with the world of sense on the 2nd April 1891 at 9:45 A.M., when he emerged from the egg which his mother had laid in an eagle's nest and which the bird had incubated for seven years." Early success as an Expressionist was swept away by Ernst's service in the German army during World War I; in his own words:

Max Ernst died on 1st August 1914. He returned to life on 11th November 1918, a young man who wanted to become a magician and find the central myth of his age. From time to time he consulted the eagle which had guarded the egg of his prenatal existence. The bird's advice can be detected in his work.†

Ernst explored every means to achieve the sense of the psychic in his art. Like other Dadaists, he set out to incorporate found objects and chance into his works. Using a process called *frottage,* he created some works by combining the patterns achieved by rubbing a crayon or another medium across a sheet of paper that was placed over a surface with a strong and evocative texture pattern. In other works, he joined fragments of images he had cut from old books, magazines, and prints to form one hallucinatory collage.

Ernst soon began making paintings that shared the mysterious dreamlike effect of his collages. In the early 1920s,

*In William S. Rubin, *Dada, Surrealism, and Their Heritage* (New York: Museum of Modern Art, 1968), p. 64.

†In Richter, *Dada: Art and Anti-Art,* pp. 155, 159.

his works brought him into contact with Breton, who instantly recognized Ernst's affinity with the Surrealist group. Many of the creative bases of Surrealism are manifest in Ernst's *Two Children Are Threatened by a Nightingale* (FIG. **27-63**). Here, Ernst displayed a private dream, which challenged the post-Renaissance idea that a painting should resemble a window looking into a "real" scene that is rendered illusionistically three-dimensional through the use of mathematical perspective. In *Two Children,* the landscape, the distant city, and the tiny flying bird are traditionally painted; the artist followed all of the established rules of aerial and linear perspective. The three sketchily rendered figures, however, clearly belong to a world of dreams, and the literally three-dimensional miniature gate, the odd button-knob, and the strange, closed building "violate" the space of the bulky frame. Additional dislocation occurs in the traditional museum identification label, which has been displaced into a cutaway part of the frame. Handwritten, it announces the title of the work (taken from a poem written by Ernst before this work was painted), adding another note of irrational mystery.

Like the title of many Surrealist works, that of *Two Children* is ambiguous and has an uneasy relation to what

27-63 MAX ERNST, *Two Children Are Threatened by a Nightingale,* 1924. Oil on wood with wood construction, 22$\frac{1}{4}$" high, 22$\frac{1}{2}$" wide, 4$\frac{1}{4}$" deep. The Museum of Modern Art, New York (purchase).

the spectator sees. The viewer must struggle to decipher connections between image and words. When Surrealists (and Dadaists and Metaphysical artists before them) used such titles, they intended for the seeming contradiction between title and picture to act like a "blow to the mind," knocking the spectator off balance, with all expectations challenged. Much of the impact of Surrealist works begins with the viewer's sudden awareness of the incongruous and the absurd in what is pictured.

SALVADOR DALI (1904–1989), an established Surrealist painter, also explored his own psyche and dreams in his paintings, sculptures, jewelry, and designs for furniture and movies. Dali probed a deeply erotic dimension through his work, studying the writings of Freud and Richard von Krafft-Ebing and inventing what he called the "paranoiac-critical method" to assist his creative process. As he described it, his aim in painting was "to materialize the images of concrete irrationality with the most imperialistic fury of precision . . . in order that the world of imagination and of concrete irrationality may be as objectively evident . . . as that of the exterior world of phenomenal reality."* All of these aspects of Dali's style can be seen in *The Persistence of Memory* (FIG. **27-64**). Here, he creates a haunting allegory of empty space in which time is at an end. The barren landscape, without horizon, drifts to infinity, lit by some eerie, never-setting sun. An amorphous creature sleeps in the foreground; it is based on a figure in the *Paradise* section of Bosch's *Garden of Earthly Delights* (FIG.

20-17). Dali has draped his creature with a limp pocket watch. Another watch hangs from the branch of a dead tree that springs surprisingly from a blocky, architectonic form. A third watch hangs half over the edge of the rectangular form, beside a small timepiece resting dial-down on the block's surface. Ants swarm mysteriously over the small watch, while a fly walks along the face of its large neighbor, almost as if this assembly of watches were decaying organic life—soft and viscous. Dali rendered every detail of this dreamscape with precise control, striving to make the world of his paintings as convincingly real as the most meticulously rendered landscape based on an actual scene from nature.

The Belgian painter RENÉ MAGRITTE (1898–1967) also expresses in exemplary fashion the Surrealist idea and method: the dreamlike dislocation of image and meaning, and the putting together of images and meanings that are totally unalike. This administers a distinct shock to our conventional, commonsensical expectations. In *Le Viol* (FIG. **27-65**) Magritte reinforces the shock by combining two images into one: a female head and female torso sharing a single anatomical feature, the extended phallic neck—which belongs to the head and not the torso. We are confronted simultaneously by a bewigged head registering pop-eyed alarm (the breasts), sealed mouth (the pubic area), and a perfectly tranquil body. This disturbing chimera

*In Rubin, *Dada, Surrealism, and Their Heritage*, p. 111.

27-64 SALVADORE DALI, *The Persistence of Memory*, 1931. Oil on canvas, 9¹/₂" × 13". The Museum of Modern Art, New York (given anonymously).

27-65   RENÉ MAGRITTE, *Le Viol*, 1934. Oil on canvas, 28³/₄″ × 21¹/₄″.
Menil Foundation, Houston.

thin artery that stretches between them, joining their
exposed hearts and culminating on one side in surgical
forceps and on the other in a miniature portrait of her
husband, the artist Diego Rivera (1886–1957), as a child.
Breton found Kahlo to be a natural Surrealist. He recognized that her deeply personal double self-portrait touches
sensual and psychological memories in each of us.

Loosely associated with Dada and Surrealism but sharing
their philosophy of the primacy of the subconscious in
artistic creation were three major painters—Marc Chagall,
Paul Klee, and Joan Miró, who maintained a more or less
independent stance, producing their personal worlds of
free fantasy.

A dynamic union of symbol and fantasy was employed
by the Russian artist MARC CHAGALL (1887–1985) to create
works filled with the extremes of visionary joy and despair.
Chagall studied and worked in Paris and Berlin and incorporated into his work elements of Expressionism, Cubism,
and Fauvism. However, he never forgot his early years in
an obscure Russian village, and themes from his childhood
returned as if in dreams and memories. Some, gay and fanciful, suggest the simpler pleasures of folk life, others,
somber and even tragic, recall the trials and persecutions of
the Jewish people. Through all of his work runs a sense of
the deep religious experience that was an inextricable part
of his early life. In *The Falling Angel* (FIG. **27-67**), Chagall
combines his themes to symbolize the suffering of all ordinary people as Europe slid toward and into World War II. A
flaming angel plummets across a moonlit night sky, one

rises before us in broad daylight, like some obsessive
image out of the suppressed, deranged subconscious. The
title, which translates as "rape," does not relieve the stress
of ambiguity nor the impact of the irrational masked as
the real. Like Dali, Magritte renders his grotesque images
with entirely literal representational technique.

Perhaps the most autobiographical of all artists connected with Surrealism is the Mexican painter FRIDA KAHLO
(1907–1954), who used the details of her life as powerful
symbols for the psychological pain of human existence.
Kahlo began painting seriously as a young student, during
convalescence from a tragic accident that left her in constant pain. Her life became a heroic and tumultuous battle
for survival against illness and stormy personal relationships. *The Two Fridas* (FIG. **27-66**), one of the few large-scale
canvases she ever produced, is typical of Kahlo's long series
of unflinching self-portraits. The twin figures sit side by side
on a low bench in a barren landscape under a stormy sky.
One figure wears a simple Mexican costume, while the
other is dressed in what might be an elaborate wedding
dress. The figures suggest different sides of the artist's personality, inextricably linked by the clasped hands and by the

27-66   FRIDA KAHLO, *The Two Fridas*, 1939. Oil on canvas, 67″ × 67″.
Collection of the Museo de Arte Moderno, Mexico City.

27-67 MARC CHAGALL, *The Falling Angel*, 1923, 1933, 1947. Kunstmuseum, Basel, Switzerland (Emanuel Hoffmann-Stiftung).

wing stretched upward and the other pointing toward the earth. A mother and child, floating over a slumbering village, mingle with the earthside wing. To the right is a crucifix. To the left, a bearded peasant holds a Torah scroll. Above him, a workman tumbles through the air. From a central position at the bottom of the composition, a strange yellow beast looks directly at the viewer. This enigmatic creature is placed beside a mysteriously floating violin. A lighted candle recalls the sacred light in both Christian and Jewish ritual. The terrors of war and pogroms are suggested by the pitiful little figure trudging along the path leading from the village, while resignation and hope are expressed in other symbols. The work is a moving portrayal of the artist's feeling that faith is important in a world of war and brutality. Clearly, Chagall was a highly individual artist who intuitively used diverse avant-garde styles to help him transform the personal themes of his Jewish childhood into symbols that suggest human experience.

Perhaps the most inventive artist using abstract figuration to express the world of the spirit was the Swiss-German painter PAUL KLEE (1879–1940). The son of a professional musician and an accomplished violinist in his own right, Klee thought of painting as similar to music in its expressiveness and in its ability to touch the spirit of its viewers through a studied use of color, form, and line:

Art does not reproduce the visible; rather it makes visible. . . . The formal elements of graphic art are dot, line, plane and space—the last three charged with energy of various kinds. . . . Formerly we used to represent things visible on earth, things we either liked to look at or would have liked to see. Today we reveal the reality that is behind visible things. . . . By including the concepts of good and evil, a moral sphere is created. . . . Art is a simile of the Creation.*

To penetrate the reality that is behind visible things, Klee studied nature avidly, taking special interest in analyzing processes of growth and change. He coded these studies in diagrammatic form in notebooks, and the knowledge he gained in this way became so much a part of his consciousness that it influenced the "psychic improvisation" he used to create his art.

Klee's works, like *Twittering Machine* (FIG. **27-68**), are small and intimate in scale. A viewer must draw near to decipher the delicately rendered forms and enter this mysterious dream world. The ancient world of nature and the modern world of machines are joined in this picture, where four diagrammatic birds appear to be forced into twittering action by the turning of a crank-driven mechanism. We

*Chipp, ed., *Theories of Modern Art,* pp. 182–185.

Klee shared the widespread modern apprehension concerning the rationalism behind a technological civilization that could be as destructive as it was constructive. As do some psychologists, he sought clues to man's deeper nature in primitive shapes and symbols. Like Jung, Klee seems to have accepted the existence of a collective unconscious that reveals itself in archaic signs and patterns and that is everywhere evident in the art of primitive peoples. Toward the end of his life, Klee suffered from a debilitating and painful illness. Its effects heightened his depression over the worsening of world conditions. *Death and Fire* (FIG. **27-69**) expresses the dark mood of his last years in the style of an *ideogram*—a simple, picturelike sign filled with implicit meaning. A stick figure moves left toward three vertical bars. A white death's-head, heavily outlined, dominates the work and seems to rise toward a glowing sun. The features of the skull may also be letters, perhaps *tod* (the German word for death). The pale green, harmonized with the chords of red, may suggest the element of water reconciled with fire in the ever-changing alternation of life and death. The eerie color, the primitive starkness of the images, and the mysterious arrangement convey an almost religious sense of awe, as if one were in the presence of a totem having magical powers. Enigmatic as the subject is, we feel its sources, as definitely as those of Chagall, in the human religious experience.

27-68   PAUL KLEE, *Twittering Machine*, 1922. Watercolor and pen and ink, approx. 16¼″ × 12″. The Museum of Modern Art, New York (purchase).

customarily associate birds with life and machines with man's ability to control nature. (Indeed, a 1921 drawing by Klee called *Concert on a Twig* shows these four birds with their double-curved perch clearly attached to a tree.) In *Twittering Machine*, however, Klee has linked the birds inextricably to the machine, creating an ironic vision of existence in the modern age. Each bird responds in such an individual way that we may see all of them as metaphors for ourselves—beings trapped by the operation of the industrial society we've created. Some observers see an even darker meaning in *Twittering Machine:* the individual birds are said to represent the four temperaments of the medieval and Renaissance periods, while their loony appearance also features avian shapes capable of luring real birds into a trap in the rectangular trough at the bottom of the image. Perhaps no other artist of the twentieth century matches the subtlety of Klee as he adroitly plays with sense, creating an artistic device of ambiguity and understatement that draws each viewer into finding a unique or markedly individualistic interpretation of the work.

27-69   PAUL KLEE, *Death and Fire*, 1940. Oil drawing in black paste on jute burlap, mounted on stretched jute. Approx. 18″ × 17⁵⁄₁₆″. Paul Klee Foundation, Kuntsmuseum, Berne, Switzerland.

27-70   JOAN MIRÓ, *Painting*, 1933. Approx. 5'8¹/₂" × 6'5¹/₄". The Museum of Modern Art, New York (Loula D. Lasker Bequest by exchange).

Like the Dadaists, the Surrealists used many methods to free their creative process from reliance on the kind of conscious control they believed had been too much shaped by society. Dali used his paranoiac-critical approach to encourage the free play of association as he worked. Other Surrealists used automatism and various types of planned "accidents" to provoke reactions closely related to subconscious experience. The Catalan artist JOAN MIRÓ (1893–1983) was a master of this approach. From the beginning, his work contained an element of fantasy and

hallucination. Introduced to the use of chance in the creation of art by Surrealist poets in Paris, the young Spaniard devised a new painting method that allowed him to create works like *Painting* (FIG. 27-70). Miró began this painting by making a scattered collage composition with assembled fragments cut from a catalogue for machinery. The shapes in the collage became motifs that the artist freely reshaped to create biomorphic black silhouettes—solid or in outline, with dramatic accents of white and vermilion—that suggest, in the painting, a host of amoeba-like organisms, or constellations in outer space, floating in an immaterial background space filled with soft reds, blues, and greens. Miró described the creative process he used as switching back and forth between unconscious and conscious image making: "Rather than setting out to paint something, I begin painting and as I paint the picture begins to assert itself, or suggest itself under my brush. The form becomes a sign for a woman or a bird as I work. . . . The first stage is free, unconscious. . . . The second stage is carefully calculated."* Even the artist could not always explain the meanings of pictures like *Painting*. They are, in the truest sense, spontaneous and intuitive expressions of the little-understood, submerged, unconscious part of life.

We have already noted the curious resemblance of Miró's motifs to those in the mobiles of Calder (FIG. 27-52). Though they were of very different cultures and training, though they worked in different media, and had apparently very different ways of conceiving and realizing their objects, the finished projects have strikingly similar effect. Floating biomorphic shapes, hovering, vibrating, advancing, and retreating, they are suggestive of musical tones made visible. The tempo is light and graceful, the mood playful and humorous. The nonobjective approach coincides with the Surrealistic; both do perfectly well without images.

Objective Art and Social Subject

Of course, Surrealism makes use of images, but images as metamorphosed by the operation of the subconscious and inconsistent with what conscious perception reports of the visual world. The untransformed image of reality is the substance of objective art, as it always has been; and it coexists in the twentieth century with expressionist, abstract, and nonobjective kinds of imagery that we have been examining. The photographic medium is also coexistent with the others, and it exhibits a wide range of possibilities for achieving similar effects. We can use a photograph as a bridge from Surrealist to Objective art.

The Surrealists found hallucinatory magic in the strangely disconcerting photographs of Paris and its environs made by the French artist JEAN EUGÈNE AUGUSTE ATGET (1856–1927). Atget earned a precarious living as a photographer, having set for himself the goal of recording on film everything in Paris or its suburbs that was artistic or "picturesque." He was especially eager to photograph buildings slated for demolition to make way for modern structures. Each day he set out early in the morning with a large view camera to capture subjects before many people were in the streets. Even his most straightforward shot of a Paris street or a corner of the garden at Versailles often had an aura

*In William S. Rubin, *Miró in the Collection of The Museum of Modern Art* (New York: The Museum of Modern Art, 1973), p. 32.

27-71 JEAN EUGÈNE AUGUSTE ATGET, *Avenue de Gobelins*, Paris, 1925. Albumen silver print, 8¹/₄″ × 9⁹/₁₆″. The Museum of Modern Art, New York (Abbott-Levy Collection. Partial gift of Shirley C. Burden.)

of mysterious life. His gift for seeing strangeness in the everyday, however, was most clearly expressed in pictures of shop windows, such as *Avenue des Gobelins* (FIG. 27-71). In these pictures, the everyday banality of ordinary objects is transformed into a dreamlike reality. The viewer is transported into an unusual world where store mannequins seem to be participating in some strange ritual and objects merge with the fuzzy reflections of distant buildings and trees (Dada artists regularly used dress dummies as characters in their productions). Atget's almost metaphysical photographs of Parisian shop windows, buildings, and gardens were known only to a few Parisian artists until the 1920s, when they were discovered by Man Ray and soon after praised by the Surrealists as the work of a genuine kindred spirit who believed in the world of dreams as strongly as they did themselves.

We surface from the subterranean and limitless sea of the unconscious into the light of common day with photographers and painters who were content to document

27-74 CHARLES SHEELER, *The Upper Deck,* c. 1928. Vintage silver print 8″ × 10″. Collection, Gilman Paper Company.

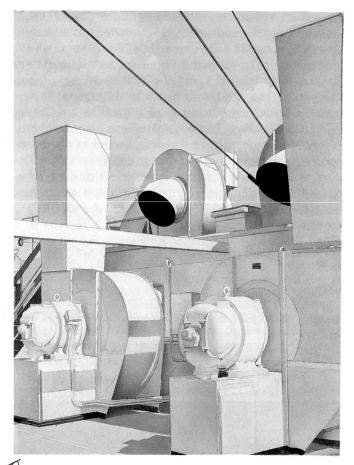

27-75 CHARLES SHEELER, *The Upper Deck,* 1929. Oil on canvas, 29$^1/_8$″ × 22$^1/_8$″. Courtesy of the Fogg Art Museum, Harvard University, Cambridge, Massachusetts (Louise E. Bettens Fund).

rivets and rust and modifying the shadow patterns into a symphony of tawny and rosy whites. This painting was special for Sheeler; it signaled the attainment of an artistic goal: "This is what I have been getting ready for. I had come to feel that a picture could have incorporated in it the structural design implied in abstraction and be presented in a wholly realistic manner."* Inspired by the power of this work, Sheeler continued to use photographs as studies for his paintings of the shapes of man-made environments, emptied of human beings and symbolic of the beauty of the new world of perfect and precise machine forms. The clarity of the scenes he painted and the precise manner of his style linked Sheeler to a group of American artists whom the critics called the *Precisionists* because of their loving depiction of the new industrial environment.

Within the limits of objectivity that, by its very nature, define the photographic medium, we find variations that reflect the interests of Modernism: the surrealistic tone of Atget, the descriptive and analytic realism of Stieglitz, the expressionistic realism of Lange, the purely formalistic

*In Carol Troyen and Erica E. Hirshler, *Charles Sheeler: Paintings and Drawings* (Boston: Museum of Fine Arts, 1987), p. 116.

realism of Sheeler. In Sheeler's art the boundaries of the photographic medium and of objective painting are exactly congruent, defining one and the same image.

Almost from its beginnings photography had interested painters as a way to record with fidelity the life of modern society at the moment of its happening. The hope to capture it "as it really is" motivated not only photographers and painters, but a whole school of novelists and playwrights. The lives of ordinary people, in all variety of circumstance and shades of mood, were the subjects of the ubiquitous motion picture; and painters could compose scenes that resembled "stills" from a movie reel, with or without the original's precision of detail.

We find this kind of objective realism, disciplined by lessons in Modernist formalism, in the painting of EDWARD HOPPER (1882–1967), who took as his subject the awesome loneliness and echoing isolation of modern life in the United States. Trained as a commercial artist, Hopper studied painting and printmaking in New York and Paris before returning to the United States and concentrating on scenes of contemporary city and country life in which the buildings, streets, and landscapes he chose to paint are curiously muted, still, and filled with empty spaces. Motion is stopped and time is suspended, as if the artist has recorded the major details of a poignant personal memory. From the darkened streets outside a restaurant in *Nighthawks* (FIG. **27-76**), we glimpse the lighted interior through huge plate-glass windows, which lend the inner space the paradoxical sense of being both a safe refuge and a vulnerable place for the three customers and the counterman. The interplay between small figures and empty space recalls the compositions of Poussin, but the seeming indifference of Hopper's characters to one another and the echoing spaces that surround them evoke the unmitigated loneliness of modern humans—a very different expression from the stately interplay of humans and environment in Poussin's *The Burial of Phocion* (FIG. 24-60). Hopper invested works like *Nighthawks* with the straightforward mode of representation valued by Americans, creating a kind of realist vision that recalls that of nineteenth-century artists like Eakins and Tanner.

The objective artist, sensitive to social conditions and events, could escape from the constraints of the noncommittal photograph or the traditional techniques of pictorial realism when the occasion or subject demanded a personal, critical response. In that case, all the expressionistic and formalistic devices of Modernism were available. The

American painter BEN SHAHN (1898–1969) used photographs as a point of departure for semi-abstract figures he felt would express the emotions and facts of social injustice that were his main subject throughout his career. Shahn came to the United States from Lithuania in 1906 and trained as a lithographer before broadening the media in which he worked to include easel painting, photography, and murals. In France in 1929, he found his life's direction in art: "If I am to be a painter, I must show the world how it looks through my eyes." He focused on the lives of ordinary people and the injustices often done to them by the structure of an impersonal society. In the early 1930s, he completed a cycle of twenty-three paintings and prints inspired by the trial and execution of the two Italian anarchists Nicola Sacco and Bartolommeo Vanzetti, whom many people considered to be unjustly convicted of killing two men in a holdup in 1920. Shahn felt he had found in this story a subject the equal of any in Western art history: "Suddenly I realized . . . I was living through another crucifixion." Basing many of the works in this cycle on newspaper photographs of the events, Shahn devised a style that adapted his knowledge of Synthetic Cubism and his training in commercial art to an emotionally expressive use of flat, intense color in figural compositions filled with sharp, dry, angular forms. The major work in the series was called

27-76   EDWARD HOPPER, *Nighthawks*, 1942. Oil on canvas, 30" × 56¹¹⁄₁₆". The Art Institute of Chicago. Friends of American Art Collection.

simply *The Passion of Sacco and Vanzetti* (FIG. **27-77**). This tall, narrow painting compresses time as well as space in a symbolic representation of the trial and its aftermath. The two executed men lie in coffins at the bottom of the composition. Presiding over them are the three members of the commission chaired by Harvard University president A. Laurence Lowell, who declared the original trial fair and cleared the way for the executions to take place. Behind, on the wall of a schematized government building, is the framed portrait of Judge Webster Thayer, who pronounced

27-77 BEN SHAHN, *The Passion of Sacco and Vanzetti,* 1931–1932. Tempera on canvas, 84¹/₂″ × 48″. Whitney Museum of American Art, New York (gift of Edith and Milton Lowenthal in memory of Juliana Force).

the initial sentence. The gray pallor of the dead men, the stylized mask-faces of the mock-pious mourning commissioners, and the sanctimonious, distant judge all contribute to the mood of anguished commentary that makes this image one of Shahn's most powerful works.

Like Shahn, the American artist JACOB LAWRENCE (b. 1917) found his subjects in modern history, but, unlike Shahn, Lawrence concentrated on the culture and history of African Americans. Lawrence moved to Harlem in 1927 at about the age of ten. There, he came under the spell of the African art and the African-American history he found in lectures and exhibitions and in the special programs sponsored by the 125th Street New York Public Library, which had outstanding collections of African-American art and archival data. Inspired by the politically committed art of Goya (FIG. 26-10), Daumier (FIG. 26-38), and Orozco (FIG. 27-79), Lawrence found his subjects in the everyday life of Harlem and the history of his people. He interpreted his themes in rhythmic arrangements of bold, flat, strongly colored shapes, using a style that drew equally from his interest in the push-pull effects of Cubist space and his memories of the patterns made by the colored scatter rugs that had brightened the floors of his childhood homes. His first historical subject was a series of forty-one paintings showing key incidents from the life of Toussaint L'Ouverture, a slave who led a revolution in the late eighteenth and early nineteenth century, winning independence from French rule for Haiti and establishing the first black Western republic. *No. 36: During the truce Toussaint is deceived and arrested by LeClerc. LeClerc led Toussaint to believe that he was sincere, believing that when Toussaint was out of the way, the Blacks would surrender* (FIG. **27-78**) is typical of Lawrence's masterful compositions and the way in which he added long narrative titles to make the series a kind of history text for younger viewers. Everything is arranged to draw the viewer's attention to the figure of Toussaint, who is held prisoner by his captors in the center of the picture space behind a wall of criss-crossed swords. The steep perspective of the walls of the room and the foreground rug, the thrusting figures of the captors, and the outspread legs of the hero dramatically draw the viewer into empathy with Toussaint's heroic defiance of foreign authority in the face of overwhelming odds. Like every other subject Lawrence painted during his long career, he believed this story had important things to teach viewers:

> I didn't do it just as a historical thing, but because I believe these things tie up with the Negro today. We don't have a physical slavery, but an economic slavery. If these people, who were so much worse off than the people today, could conquer their slavery, we certainly can do the same thing.*

*In Ellen Harkins Wheat, *Jacob Lawrence: American Painter* (Seattle: University of Washington Press, 1986), p. 40.

27-78 JACOB LAWRENCE, *No. 36: During the truce Toussaint is deceived and arrested by LeClerc. LeClerc led Toussaint to believe that he was sincere, believing that when Toussaint was out of the way, the Blacks would surrender,* 1937–1938. Tempera on paper, 11″ × 19″. The Amistad Research Center's Aaron Douglas Collection, New Orleans.

Lawrence found inspiration for his early art in the example of JOSÉ CLEMENTE OROZCO (1883–1949), one of a group of Mexican artists determined to base their art on the indigenous history and culture that existed in Mexico before the arrival of Europeans. The movement formed by these artists was part of the idealistic rethinking of society that took place during the political turmoil of the period of the Mexican Revolution between 1910 and the 1920s. Among the projects undertaken by these politically motivated artists were vast mural cycles placed in public buildings to dramatize and validate the history of Mexico's native peoples. Orozco worked on one of the first major cycles, painted in 1922 on the walls of the National Training School in Mexico City. He carried the ideas of this mural revolution to the United States, completing many commissions for wall paintings between 1927 and 1934. From 1932 to 1934, he worked on one of his finest mural cycles in the Baker Library at Dartmouth College, partly in honor of its superb collection of books in Spanish. The choice of subject was left up to him. What he depicted, in fourteen large panels and ten smaller ones, was a panoramic and symbolic history of ancient and modern Mexico, from the early mythic days of the feathered-serpent god Quetzalcóatl to a contemporary and bitterly satiric vision of modern education.

The imagery in our detail, *Epic of American Civilization: Hispano-America* (FIG. **27-79**), revolves around the monumental figure of a heroic Mexican peasant armed to participate in the Mexican Revolution. Looming on either side of him are mounds crammed with symbolic figures of his oppressors—bankers, government soldiers, officials, gangsters, and the rich. Money-grubbers pour hoards of gold at the feet of the incorruptible peon, cannon threaten him, and a bemedaled general raises a dagger to stab him in the back. Orozco's training as an architect gave him a sense of the framed wall surface, which he easily commanded, projecting his quickly grasped figures onto the solid mural plane in monumental scale.

In addition, Orozco's early training as a maker of political prints and as a newspaper artist had taught him the

27-79   JOSÉ CLEMENTE OROZCO, *Epic of American Civilization: Hispano-America,* c. 1932–1934. Fresco. Baker Memorial Library, Dartmouth College, Hanover, New Hampshire.

rhetorical strength of graphic brevity and simplicity, which he used here to assure that his allegory was easy to read. His special merging of the effects of the graphic and mural media give his work an originality and force rarely seen in mural painting after the Renaissance and Baroque periods.

Modern artists who have sought to stir the emotions of viewers about specific incidents of human injustice have found it difficult to record or symbolize enough information in a single image to accomplish their purpose. Paintings like David's *Death of Marat* (FIG. 25-48), Géricault's *Raft of the Medusa* (FIG. 26-13), Goya's *Third of May, 1808* (FIG. 26-10), and Daumier's *Rue Transnonain* (FIG. 26-38), are rare. The greatest twentieth-century painting inspired by outrage directed toward brutal human behavior is *Guernica* (FIG. **27-80**), created by Pablo Picasso in 1937 in response to the saturation bombing of an ancient Basque city by German forces acting for the rebel general Francisco Franco during the Spanish Civil War.

Throughout his career Picasso had never been content to work for long in any one style. While still painting Synthetic Cubist pictures, he also made "Ingres-like" drawings and painted figure subjects in a broadly Realistic manner often influenced by Antique sculpture. He frequently moved back and forth between creating works with symbolic significance, like those of his Blue Period, and works in which he explored esthetic problems of style, like *Les Demoiselles d'Avignon* (FIG. 27-29) and *Three Musicians* (FIG.

27-34). In the latter work, he had also bent Synthetic Cubism to express irony and whimsy. In the late 1920s and early 1930s, Picasso's Cubism took on a Surrealistic quality; the forms became more biomorphic and the interweaving of planes began to suggest the qualities of a dreamy metamorphosis from one state of being to another. As Franco's forces assumed power in Spain, Picasso began using motifs from bullfighting and mythology to symbolize the struggles in his homeland. His political commitment, his feelings, and his role as an artist were painfully united in a new and powerful way: "Painting is not done to decorate apartments. It is an instrument of war for attack and defence against the enemy."

In January 1937, the Spanish Republican government in exile in Paris asked Picasso to do a work for their pavilion at the Paris International Exposition to be held that summer. He agreed but had done nothing when he received word that the Basque capital, Guernica, had been almost totally destroyed in an air raid on April 26 by German planes acting on behalf of General Franco. The event jolted Picasso into action; by the end of June, the mural-sized canvas of *Guernica* was complete. Picasso uses a fluid, expressive Synthetic Cubist style to organize his figures into a three-part composition with a triangular middle and two flanking rectangular wings; with this he conjures up an overpowering Surrealist nightmare. Forms bend and stretch in response to the emotional stress of the characters.

Surrealism —of Social Subject

27-80 PABLO PICASSO, *Guernica*, 1937. Mural painting, approx. 11'6" × 25'8". Museo del Prado, Madrid.

Borrowed from the picador's mount in the bullfight, the horribly wounded dying horse at the center stands for all innocent victims, while (according to the artist) the bull represents "brutality and darkness." A slain soldier stretches awkwardly across the ground at the lower left, in front of a shrieking woman who holds her dead child in helpless agony. A searching head balloons from an upper window, accompanied by an eerily elongated arm holding an oil lamp. A woman falls in flames from a building, while, beneath, another woman attempts to run in fright; her suddenly swollen and weighted legs and feet refuse to move. The black, white, and gray colors, the patterns of light and dark, and the action of the figures lead the viewer's eyes relentlessly back to the upthrust head of the central victim-horse and to its open mouth, exposed teeth, and agonizedly pointed tongue—the unforgettable emblem of helpless terror and suffering.

The stupendous talent of Picasso invented, or absorbed and exploited to capacity, all the revolutionary movements that broke the Tradition and established Modernist art. It was that talent alone that could supply and focus the power of expression necessary to embody in the imagery of *Guernica* the prelude to the greatest catastrophe of the twentieth century, the Second World War.

THE POST-COLONIAL WORLD TODAY

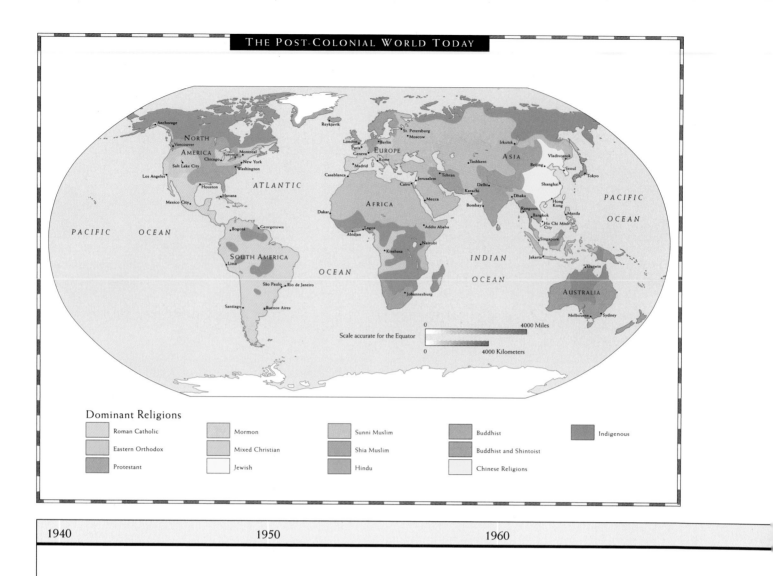

Dominant Religions

- Roman Catholic
- Eastern Orthodox
- Protestant
- Mormon
- Mixed Christian
- Jewish
- Sunni Muslim
- Shia Muslim
- Hindu
- Buddhist
- Buddhist and Shintoist
- Chinese Religions
- Indigenous

1940	1950	1960

Le Corbusier, Notre Dame du Haut, 1950-1955

Jasper Johns, Painted Bronze, 1960

Frank Stella, Nunca Pasa Nada, 1964

Commercial television begins

People's Republic of China established, 1949

State of Israel created, 1948

Existentialism, 1930-50's   Republic of India begun, c. 1949

Crick and Watson,
Structure and function of DNA, 1954

United Nations organized, 1945   Korean Conflict, 1950-1953

Atomic bomb devastates Hiroshima and Nagasaki, 1945

Transistor invented, 1948

Sputnik I launched, 1957

Computer chip invented, 1959

Lasers invented, 1960

First manned space flight, 1961

John F. Kennedy
assassinated, 1963

Corporation for Public
Broadcasting formed, 1967

Martin Luther King
and Robert Kennedy
assassinated, 1968

Moon landing, 1969

CHAPTER 28

THE LATER
TWENTIETH CENTURY

1970   1980   1990

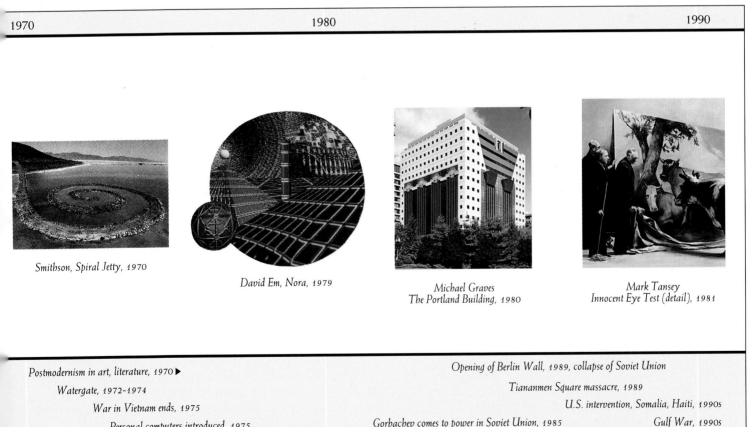

Smithson, *Spiral Jetty*, 1970

David Em, *Nora*, 1979

Michael Graves
The Portland Building, 1980

Mark Tansey
Innocent Eye Test (detail), 1981

Postmodernism in art, literature, 1970 ▶

Watergate, 1972-1974

War in Vietnam ends, 1975

Personal computers introduced, 1975

Islamic Revolution in Iran, 1978-1979

Opening of Berlin Wall, 1989, collapse of Soviet Union

Tiananmen Square massacre, 1989

U.S. intervention, Somalia, Haiti, 1990s

Gorbachev comes to power in Soviet Union, 1985

Gulf War, 1990s

Breakup of Yugoslavia, 1990s

The "Cybernetic Revolution", 1990s

Post-Imperialism: Questions of Culture

The word *culture* as used here refers to the collective characteristics by which a community identifies itself and by which it expects to be recognized and respected. Race, religion, nationality, and language have a place in a culture's identity, though they by no means complete its definition. Americans of the Civil War era shared the same races, religions, language, and nationality, though the mercantile culture of New England was markedly different from the plantation culture of the South. In the United States are communities whose members are American citizens, Roman Catholics, and who speak English, but whose cultures are recognizably Irish-German-Polish-Asian-Italian-Hispanic-African-American. In Bosnia live Muslims of different nationality, race, and language from the Muslims of the Sudan or Somalia, and their cultures also differ. What seems to count most in the definition of culture today is its perceived heritage and its customs, folkways, and lifestyles, and, of course, its art. In this book we have been presenting world cultures primarily in terms of the art they have produced.

A central and compelling issue in the contemporary world involves the status that each of many distinctive cultures should have within the secular civilization of the developed nations; this is the issue of *multiculturalism*. The Western world, during the last five centuries, has witnessed in succession wars of religion, wars between dynastic states, wars among nations, and wars among classes of people. We are now seeing what amount to ethnic conflicts among cultures making territorial claims, as in the former Yugoslavia and the former Soviet Union, or seeking political recognition and accommodation within the ethnically divergent countries to which they have migrated or fled. How did this most conspicuous feature of our time arise? And what are its consequences for art?

Triumph and Tragedy

World War II was the most atrocious war in the history of humankind, and its far-reaching consequences still trouble the world. It is forever memorable not only for genocide—the deliberate massacre of whole groups of people such as the European Jews, who were annihilated by the millions in the Holocaust—but also for the leveling of whole cities and the displacing of millions of the populations of whole countries. Paradoxically, it led to the liquidation of the colonial empires built by Europe in all parts of the world. In Winston Churchill's words, the defeat of Nazi Germany and Imperial Japan was a "triumph," but the "cold war," which ensued almost immediately between the victors, the Allies on the one hand, the Soviet Union on the other, was a "tragedy." The tragedy was played out over a period of forty years, from 1949 until 1989 and the collapse of the Soviet Union. For those forty years peoples of the world lived with the dread of nuclear war. The two superpowers, the United States and the Soviet Union, divided the world into spheres of influence, and each regularly intervened politically, economically, and militarily wherever it considered its interests to be at stake. Uprisings in nations subject to the Soviets—East Germany, Poland, Hungary, and Czechoslovakia—were brutally suppressed. The United States intervened in the political imbroglios of Central and South America. After fifteen years of bitter war in Southeast Asia, the United States was defeated in Vietnam. Somewhat later, after a similar war, the Soviets were driven from Afghanistan.

Throughout the world, disruption and dislocation were taking place. Hardly had they won their independence than the newly independent nations of Africa were devastated by civil wars—Kenya, Uganda, Nigeria, the Congo, Angola, Mozambique, the Sudan, and, presently, Rwanda. In Indonesia civil war left over a hundred thousand dead. The world was appalled by brutal massacres in Cambodia. After a catastrophic war the Communists came to power in China, and North Korea tested the fledgling United Nations by invading South Korea and fighting a grim war with the United States and its UN allies. The British left India to blow up behind them in a murderous Hindu-Muslim war that divided the sub-continent into the new, still hostile, nations of India and Pakistan. France was expelled from Algeria after a prolonged and peculiarly vicious war with its Muslim natives. Arab nations, their armaments financed by oil wealth, fought three wars with Israel. A revitalized Islam rose in the Arab world, inspired a fundamentalist religious revolution in Iran, and encouraged "holy war" with the West, using a new weapon—international terrorism. In 1991, West clashed with East in the Persian Gulf.

Thus, the "tragedy" has been far more devastating than Churchill could have guessed, and it has been international in scope—it is a world full of wars, with no simple alignment and confrontation of great powers. However we account for them, these wars have displaced millions of people and sent them away from the countries of their birth, seeking refuge from mounting miseries.

International Migration

Refugees worldwide, fleeing from war, famine, and political persecution, or simply seeking a better way of life in the developed nations, enacted the international drama of migration and resettlement that began after World War II. This movement was especially true of the post-colonial peoples who looked for security in the lands of their erstwhile imperial masters. West Indians, Hindus, and Pakistanis emigrated to Britain; Algerians to France, Indonesians to Holland. The United States absorbed many thousands of Vietnamese, Cambodians, Pacific islanders,

Filipinos, Cubans, and Central Americans; Mexican nationals still cross American borders in great numbers. Jews from Europe, the Soviet Union, and North Africa moved to Israel. Turkish laborers were imported by an economically restored Germany. Chinese fleeing the Communist revolution of 1949 settled throughout Southeast Asia, where they have achieved great economic power. Recently, there has been heavy immigration of prosperous Chinese, anticipating the communist government's takeover of the former British colony of Hong Kong.

Migrations on this grand scale are nothing new in the history of the world. We have described in earlier chapters the Germanic invasions that conquered and settled the provinces of the Roman Empire; the Islamic conquests and settlement of the Near East, North Africa, and Spain. More than a century ago the immigration of European and Asian industrial labor helped build nineteenth-century America. The millions displaced by World War II crossed borders in all directions. Today, many thousands wait for visas to enter Europe and the United States.

Traditional Cultures and the New Cultures of Protest

The movement of millions of people criss-crossing the globe might be expected to bring increasingly rapid global acculturation, that is, cultural exchange. Acculturation on a global scale had begun slowly in the centuries of European expansion. In the nineteenth century it quickened with the opening of the East and the colonization of Africa. In the twentieth century it has greatly accelerated. The collisions of ethnically diverse peoples in war, and the exchange of ethnic cultures as the result of communication and commerce, have gone on at the same time. Western civilization has colored world civilization, but in the process it has itself become significantly modified. What has hastened the transformation of the West has been not only its transactions with the non-West (whether in war or in peace) but also internal questioning of the validity of Western culture. The indigenous cultures that migrating peoples bring with them are not so much competitive with Western culture as they are complementary and cooperative, or at least so it would appear at this time. Insofar as they are not eroded in acculturation, and insofar as they seek only to be recognized and to have some degree of political representation, the traditional cultures of the many migrant groups retain their visibility and integrity, offering no significant opposition. On the other hand, as we have just remarked, some voices have been raised in the West that protest against certain fundamental features of Western culture, demanding that they be changed.

In the 1960s and 1970s, certain well-defined movements challenged the cultural status quo. In the United States, the struggle for civil rights for the African Americans, for free speech in the universities, and against the war in Vietnam brought about a near-rebellion of young Americans, who took to the streets in often violent demonstrations. The prolonged ferment produced a new system of values, a "youth culture," expressed in radical rejection not only of national policies, but often also of the society that had sponsored them. The young derided the lifestyles of their elders as mendacious and hypocritical ("Trust no one over thirty!"), and adopted unconventional dress (long hair, beards, and workers' jeans), manners, habits, and morals deliberately subversive of conventional social standards. The youth era witnessed the sexual revolution, the widespread use and abuse of drugs, and the development of an exclusively youthful art-form: rock music. Young people "dropped out" of regulated society, read mystical literature, and despised the irrelevancy of "Western" university curricula.

The "youth movement" had considerable political impact. It closed the career of President Lyndon Johnson, harassed President Richard Nixon, and helped turn national opinion against the Vietnam War. In Paris, a student uprising threatened for a while to bring down the government. The youth culture has had influence far beyond its political phase. Youthful design in dress and lifestyle has been marketed in these last decades of the century to make a popular consumer culture.

Contemporary with the youth culture, but maintaining and increasing its political power, has been the Feminist movement. Taking advantage of the shakeup of society's patterns of convention, Feminists have argued the right of women to freedom from a male-dominated culture that has long denied them an equal share in political power and economic opportunity. Feminists charge that the institutions of Western society, particularly the patriarchal family, are designed to perpetuate male power and the subordination of females. According to the ideology of Feminism, the monuments of Western culture, its arts and sciences, as well as its political, social, and economic institutions, simply mask the realities of male power, as "deconstructive" analysis of them can show. (We shall presently look more closely at "deconstruction.")

Feminists have in common with minority cultures the struggle against discrimination. One of these minorities, the homosexual community, a large subculture that traditionally has been discriminated against, has in recent years made public its claim to be recognized, respected, and protected by the law and to fight discrimination with political action. The homosexual culture demands the same rights as heterosexual citizens and the public acknowledgment of the legitimacy of its lifestyle. The African-American community, with its own rich subculture, is a minority that has long fought in the battle against discrimination. For them the fight has been bitter and prolonged, with only a modicum of success. African-American demands for full equality and their protests against social and economic exclusion have, to all intents and purposes, gone unheard. Though they have some political representation, it is not in proportion to their numbers or their need. The acceptance they have long sought has not been forthcoming. All these protesting subcultures, though they have different ideologies and agendas, agree that the institutions of Western culture are defective and need restructuring. They are all agreed that political power is the answer, power that will remedy the inequality and discrimination built into the established mainstream culture. In this they are joined by ethnic minorities like Hispanic and Asian, and others not native-born but immigrant.

Political Equality and Cultural Equivalence

In the reasoning of the aggrieved subcultures it is but a step from the proposition that in a democracy like ours all persons are politically equal (or should be) to the proposition that their cultures are politically equal. As no person should be discriminated against, so no culture should be discriminated against. No person and no culture, moreover, should be privileged above another. This applies to the established, mainstream culture as well as to the subcultures. Value judgments about the *quality* of persons or cultures are irrelevant as well as illegal, insofar as they prompt discrimination. All cultures are politically equal, or should be, and they are entitled to legal and legislative remedy when they are not—that is, when they are discriminated against. Judgments of good, better, best are prejudicial and unjust, and arise from the elitist interests of those who make them. Religious, ethical, moral, sexual, and social preferences must not be allowed to justify discrimination against persons or cultures.

The reasoning goes a step further. Value judgments as to good and bad being eliminated, one person or one culture is as "good" as any other person or culture. Political equality translates into cultural equivalence, "equivalence" meaning of equal value. This is the root assumption of multiculturalism. All cultures, as equivalent, should be recognized *and* respected. Recognition and respect for a culture, as for a person, forbid the disparagement of it, which amounts to a form of discrimination. Given multiculturalism, we are asked to observe undiscriminating respect for the sensitivities of persons and the cultures by which they identify themselves.

Egalitarianism, the theory within the theory of multiculturalism, demands not only political equality, but also economic opportunity and equal social access. These demands have only partly been met in the United States by arrangements like affirmative action, originally intended to redress the injustices of discrimination. Egalitarianism also extends its demands into the educational system, calling for multilingual instruction in the lower grades, and for adjustment of the curricula of universities to include studies, with

equal emphasis, of cultures other than Western. For courses in literature, works by women and non-Western authors have been introduced to correct what is seen as an imbalance in favor of the Western literary tradition. And some universities have instituted rules against the use of politically incorrect language by professors and students.

The political issue of egalitarianism/multiculturalism has also entered into the intellectual sphere of the studies of the humanities and the arts. Teaching, writing, and making art have become political acts, not precisely by their subject matter, but by virtue of what they exclude from it, what they seem to favor or privilege ("privilege" is a key concept in egalitarian ideology).

Rankings of scholarly achievement or of artistic quality are suspect as value judgments determined by cultural preferences and prejudices; and, as we have seen, egalitarianism would eliminate all value judgment as inherently unfair, wherever it may appear.

EGALITARIAN MULTICULTURALISM IN POSTMODERN ART

(We shall be considering Postmodernism in more detail later in this chapter. Here, by way of preliminary, we suggest that the ideology of egalitarianism/multiculturalism is the most widespread and significant of those ideologies that comprise Postmodernist thinking.)

As a model for the arts, egalitarian/multicultural ideology would supply the popular electronic and print media as exactly meeting the requirements of value-free communication. Even though their programming and features imply preferential judgments of all sorts, the media themselves *as* media are intellectually accessible to all, unlike the art of the museum and galleries, or the reading lists drawn up in universities. They offer entertainment—and instruction of a sort—to the whole public and are the authentic expression of popular culture. No critical apparatus is necessary to explain what they present, and no special capacity is required of their consumers. What they offer is either interesting or boring, and its "value" does not depend upon any presumed intrinsic value of the offering but is judged only by audience ratings, box-office receipts, or sales of commodities. The media give people what they want. From a critical point of view, programs and features may be "good" or "bad," "high" culture or "low"; the media offer both, without respect to a definition or standard by which one might complain, for example, that "That's not TV!"

Criticism of art, on the other hand, has long appealed to certain standards in declaring "That's not art!" *Postmodernism* is in reaction against just such standards. Modernist criticism, especially in the writings of the late Clement Greenberg, was rigorously, if not rigidly, formalist in its definition of what art is and should be. With its egalitarian bent, Postmodernism denounces Modernism and

Modernist criticism as elitist, through and through, for its contempt for everything but avant-garde formalism. Postmodernism draws upon culture and its iconography for inspiration and encourages unlimited stylistic diversity. (Of course, there are art critics who deplore or evade this egalitarian approach and artists who still practice Modernist formalism.)

Postmodernism would depose "fine art" from its privileged position and simply include it among the visual artifacts of a culture. The media themselves are merged in practice. The labels "architecture," "sculpture," and "painting" are used simply for convenience of reference and are given no superior status to other media, like ceramics, textiles, furniture, basketwork, or computer graphics and holograms. The old distinction between arts and crafts is abolished, and the boundary that separates art from technology is blurred.

The materials of sculpture range from traditional marble and bronze through plastics and nylon to junk. Forms are carved, cast, welded, wired, sewn, glued, painted, and lighted. They are pierced with space, reduced to filaments, set in motion by air currents or electrical means. The framed picture loses its illusionistic picture-perspective space and becomes a two-dimensional object. The frame itself is discarded, the wall takes its place, and, eventually, the gallery or the spaces of physical nature become the setting for the object. The relation of the artist to the viewer through the object becomes problematical, as does the status of the object within the space it occupies with the viewer. Finally, focus moves from the object to the process of its production and to the idea of the object as conceived, described, recorded. The making of the object, an incomplete and temporary process, is followed by its elimination and by the elimination of the artist as the determiner of its effect on audience or environment. The physical media are replaced by act, performance, and then by the record of these. Like vapor trails, the arts leave an ephemeral trace.

As the traditional boundaries of the media of painting and sculpture are being erased, science and technology are providing new materials and techniques that may or may not be thought of as "art" (unless we wish to define "art" as "what artists do") and that may or may not be the media of the future. We have video art, recording on magnetic tape a continuum of images that can be instantly combined, recombined, and replayed in an infinite variety of ways; computer-generated art, programming abstract or figural shapes and colors to appear on a display terminal, as on a television screen; light "sculpture" and projection and reflection, having a purity and intensity comparable to laser beams; and holograms, producing perfect illusions of objects in three dimensions, so that they can be "walked around." At this time, advanced computer technology is giving us a new medium and message, "virtual reality," which produces so thorough an illusion that we can "walk through" it and experience perceptions and—perhaps eventually—sensations indistinguishable from the real ones. With virtual-reality devices, and with digital imaging replacing the photographic arts, it may be that hand-manipulated representational art is obsolescent.

While the media are being democratically diversified, no one of them privileged above another, and as "fine" art has been demoted to cultural artifact, the unique status of the artist has come to be questioned. The prestige of the artist's profession, inherited from the admiration bestowed upon the Renaissance artist, is considerably leveled by egalitarianists on the grounds of elitism. The egalitarian objection to "fine" art is carried over to the "fine" artists—artists who work for galleries rather than for magazines. The cultural and social elevation of the artist is decried because of presumed "talent," "genius," "originality," "mastery," "inspiration," and other gifts and virtues not generally distributed. Egalitarians especially reject the "fame" that attaches to artistic "achievement," or "greatness." The artist should be considered only a worker among workers, as anonymous as the masons who shaped stone for the medieval cathedrals; to attribute "greatness" to an artist is to belittle the unadvertised labors of the mass of humankind.

What, then, about the artist's work, the individual piece? Adherents of Egalitarian/Multicultural ideology assert that the artifact must be free of all value judgments of it, most certainly free of all censorship, for value judgments cannot fail to be exclusive and discriminatory. Moreover, standards of judgment are unacceptable, whether of esthetic quality, craftsmanship, moral value, or interpretation of meaning. Esthetic and moral judgments are relative and conventional, as are the meanings of words, symbols, and images. *Deconstructive* philosophy, born of linguistic study, and strongly influential on Egalitarian/Multicultural ideology, declares the permanent and incorrigible ambiguity of language. Meanings will differ within different contexts and for different persons. The declared or inferred intention of the artist is irrelevant to explanation of the work, since the artifact is comprehensible only in relation to the family of artifacts that make up a given culture and can be understood only within the cultural framework.

Though artists, critics, dealers, buyers, and the public continue to explain and to judge, or seek explanation or methods of judging, the pervasive effects of the Egalitarian/Multicultural ideology can be felt everywhere in today's art world. There is widespread fear of *ethnocentrism*, the tendency to explain and to judge artifacts from the perspective of one's own culture and to the detriment of other cultures. This fear prevails in the field of art history, which now, tending to follow the model of anthropology, increasingly would make the study of works of art an account of the ways different cultures, European and non-European alike, produce art and the ways that their peoples receive and make use of it. The nature of the cultures that produced them, not the judgment of the value of the works of art themselves, is increasingly the art historian's concern. The art of no one culture, certainly not that of the West, is to be privileged above another, in the way we view it or the attention we give to it. This approach seems to work for the art of the later twentieth century, though readers will readily notice that up till now, in our descriptions, explanations, judgments, and emphasis, we have made little use of it.

POSTWAR EXPRESSIONISM IN EUROPE

World War II left not only devastated cities; millions dead, disabled, and displaced; ruptured economies and broken governments, but a general sense of desolation and despair at yet another colossal human failure. The widely accepted philosophy of existentialism preached the absurdity, the meaninglessness, of human existence. Nothing was left to the individual but a pointless freedom and an all-pervasive dread of choosing to act, one choice being no better than another, where authentic value had ceased to exist.

The existential spirit of hopelessness and desolation led the French artist BERNARD BUFFET (b. 1928) to recall the medieval theme of the *pietà* (FIGS. 13-56 and 20-21) in somber tonality, with the flattened, angular shapes and gaunt elongations of medieval figure types (FIG. **28-1**). Buffet's composition is also a kind of continuation of the woodcut manner of earlier German Expressionism (FIG. 27-22) and can be thought of as a somewhat conventional statement of that mood.

Far more forceful and original is the work of the British artist FRANCIS BACON (1910–1992), which expresses a disgust for humanity in uniquely repulsive forms. In his appalling *Painting* (FIG. **28-2**), a humanoid monster sits under an umbrella, imprisoned by a railing, in the blood-dimmed corner of a slaughterhouse. Behind it hangs the flayed and eviscerated carcass of an ox; the railing is threaded through chunks of meat and vertebra, while bones form the arms of the chair. The monster is without a head, the stump of the neck is a bloody mouth with a row of white teeth. This is the hostile vision of an artist bitterly reflecting on the butchery of war and the monstrous nature of the human animals that bring it about.

Another French artist, JEAN DUBUFFET (1901–1985), attacks contemporary values not by creating hideous images of depraved humanity, but by subverting art and the materials of art as they are conventionally understood. In works like *Vie Inquiète,* or *Uneasy Life,* (FIG. **28-3**), he builds up a thick impasto of plaster, glue, asphalt, or other common materials, upon which he paints or incises crude images of the kind produced by small children, the insane, or the scrawlers of graffiti. The images are interspersed with random scribblings, which heighten the effect of the smeared and gashed surfaces of moldering walls and worn pavements, upon which naive, untaught experience in the raw leaves its mark. Dubuffet would raise despised and discarded junk to the level of fine art or refuse to recognize a distinction between art and the relics of ordinary touch. The beautiful and the ugly, form and the formless, the planned effect and the random are all the same. The artist, who was also a prosperous businessman, founded a company for the advancement of what he called *Art Brut,* that is, untaught, coarse, brutish. He accumulated and exhibited a large collection of the works of children, the mentally unbalanced, prisoners, outcasts, whose art he believed was

28-1 BERNARD BUFFET, *Pietà,* 1946. Oil on canvas, approx. 5′7″ × 8′3″. Musée National d'Art Moderne, Paris.

genuine, since it was produced without thought from the depth of experience, unspoiled by conventional standards of art and esthetic response. His refusal to separate art from life links him with Dada and the Pop artists we shall presently consider.

MODERNIST FORMALISM

The New York School: Abstract Expressionism

Sometime during World War II the center of the Western art world shifted from Europe to the United States—specifically, from Paris to New York. Émigré artists arrived and their influence merged with native American traditions to create new ideas and styles. Abstraction was the main stylistic vehicle, and Abstract Expressionism, centered in New York, spread through the postwar world.

Abstract Expressionist artists turned, as had the Dadaists before them, and later, Dubuffet, against conventional definitions and techniques. They tried to broaden their artistic processes to express what Jung called the "collective unconscious" by adopting the methods of Surrealist improvisation and using their creative minds as open channels through which the forces of the unconscious could make themselves visible. The Abstract Expressionists saw themselves as leaders in the quest to find the path to the future. These New York artists viewed their art as a weapon in the struggle to maintain their humanity in the midst of the world's increasing insanity. To create, they turned inward. Their works had a look of rough spontaneity and exhibited a refreshing energy; their content was intended to be grasped intuitively by each viewer, in a state free from structured thinking. Abstract Expressionist artists believed

28-2 FRANCIS BACON, *Painting*, 1946. Oil and pastel on linen, approx. 6'5" × 4'4". The Museum of Modern Art, New York.

28-3 JEAN DUBUFFET, *Vie Inquiète*, 1953. Oil on canvas, approx. 4'3" × 6'4"'. Tate Gallery, London.

their work could help to counter the forces of dislocation by reawakening in people a sense of interconnectedness with all living things. As the painter Robert Motherwell eloquently wrote:

> The emergence of abstract art is a sign that there are still men of feeling in the world. . . . From their perspective, it is the social world that tends to appear irrational and absurd. . . . Nothing as drastic as abstract art could have come into existence save as the consequence of a most profound, relentless, unquenchable need. The need is for felt experience—intense, immediate, direct, subtle, unified, warm, vivid, rhythmic. If a painting does not make a human contact, it is for nothing. But the audience is also responsible. Through pictures our passions touch. Pictures are vehicles of passion, of all kinds and orders, not pretty luxuries like sports cars. In our society, the capacity to give and receive passion is limited. For this reason, the act of painting is a deep human necessity, not the production of a hand-made commodity.*

JACKSON POLLOCK (1912–1956) was the artist most often associated with the Abstract Expressionist or *Gestural Abstractionist* approach, and the power of his works influenced artists throughout the world. Pollock brought to his paintings his memories of the vast open spaces of the southwestern United States, where he grew up, and of the sand painting techniques of the Native American medicine men he had seen there. After a brief period as a Social Realist, Pollock transformed his interest in dynamic rhythms into a free, abstract style that had him working

with his whole body in swirling gestures as he poured or flung paint onto the surface of his canvases. As a rationale for his method, Pollock commented that "new needs need new techniques. . . . The modern painter cannot express this age . . . in the old forms of the Renaissance or of any other past culture."*

For a work like *Lucifer* (FIG. **28-4**), Pollock unrolled a large section of canvas directly onto the floor of his studio and dripped and splattered paint on it while moving energetically along its edge or across it. On the floor, he felt more comfortable: "I feel nearer, more a part of the painting, since this way I can walk around it, work from the four sides, and internally be in the painting." Like Miró, Pollock alternated between periods of spontaneous improvisation and periods of careful scrutiny of his developing composition. However, his methods also had roots in Kandinsky's automatic and spontaneous nonobjectivity (FIG. 27-21),† and even in the improvisation used by jazz musicians admired at the time by most of the New York Abstract Expressionists. The random fall and scatter of the paint in *Lucifer* emphasizes the liquid nature of the medium itself, but the gestures of the artist have turned the paint into loose skeins of color that loop back and forth across the canvas, thickening in some places and falling in almost straight lines in others. No easily identifiable shapes help

*In Francis V. O'Connor, *Jackson Pollock* (New York: Museum of Modern Art, 1967), pp. 40, 79.

†The label "abstract expressionism" was attached to Kandinsky's art as early as 1919. A large retrospective exhibition of the Russian artist's works in 1945 at the Museum of Non-Objective Painting (now the Solomon H. Guggenheim Museum) in New York City impressed many young artists, including Pollock.

*In Frank O'Hara, *Robert Motherwell* (New York: Museum of Modern Art, 1965), pp. 45, 50.

non objective or non Representational

Abstract Expressionism

28-4 JACKSON POLLOCK, *Lucifer*, 1947. Oil, aluminum paint, and enamel on canvas, approx. 3′5″ × 8′9″. Collection of Harry W. and Mary Margaret Anderson.

the viewer to establish the familiar depth of a normal, figure-ground relationship; instead, the rhythmic layers of line spread far beyond its edges. As he worked, Pollock looked not *out* (as from a viewpoint) but *down*, seeing his "landscape" unfold. When the works were exhibited, this "plane of action" on which they were created was transformed into a "plane of confrontation" on a vertical wall, lending the compositions a sense of floating, gravity-less space. The overall pattern of interweaving lines may suggest the patterns of motion and energy found in micro- and macro-photographs of the basic structures of the physical world, but the artists intended no direct reference to nature. Instead, the painting becomes almost a record of Pollock's actions in making it. Indeed, in works like *Lucifer,* the sense of the process of painting is stronger than the awareness of the painted surface itself.

Gestural Abstract Expressionism, as it has also been called, had many possible methods of approach. In the work of FRANZ KLINE (1910–1962), it was a vehicle of very personal psychic revelation, possibly as mysterious to the artist as to the observer. Kline trained in Boston and London before settling in New York City. His early work was expressive and realistic, but gradually he concentrated on abstract form. He used a special opaque projector to enlarge designs onto a wall as a means of achieving simplification and abstraction in his paintings. His mature works include many large black-and-white canvases, like *Painting* (FIG. **28-5**), which are filled with ragged bars and stripes of black that play against white slablike areas as sharp-edged as broken panes of glass. These configurations suggest Chinese characters boldly brushed and greatly magnified, a kind of ideogram of the artist's psychic state. As hieratic and quasi-magical shapes, the forms can be interpreted as the observer pleases; as purely nonobjective forms in a wide

28-6 WILLEM DE KOONING, *Woman I,* 1950–1952. Oil on canvas, approx. 6'4" × 4'10". The Museum of Modern Art, New York (purchase).

variety of arrangements, they are expressive in their blunt esthetic force and bold, free execution.

The Dutch-born painter WILLEM DE KOONING (b. 1904) has used the techniques of New York *Action Painting* to make both abstract works and the energetic images of massive women for which he is best known. De Kooning embraced Gestural Abstract Expressionism after an early career in commercial art and as a figure and portrait painter—experience that gave him a special command of fluid line and subtle color. His series of huge women, like *Woman I* (FIG. **28-6**), was inspired in part by female models on advertising billboards, but the forms also suggest fertility figures and a satiric inversion of the traditional image of Venus, goddess of love. In *Woman I,* the figure is defined with manic excitement, apparently slashed out at full speed with a brush held at arm's length. Shapes and colors play through, over, and across one another with no definable order. The brazen and baleful mask of the face mixes a toothpaste smile (inspired by an ad for Camel cigarettes) with the grimace of a death's head. The effect is one of simultaneous delineation and defacement, of construction and cancellation—a conflict between sketch and finished picture. As with other Action

28-5 FRANZ KLINE, *Painting,* 1952, 1955–1956. Oil on canvas, approx. 6'5" × 8'4". Present location unknown.

Painting, the image seems to be eternally coming into being before the eyes of the viewer, but the tension between flat design and lines in space, between image and process, is heightened by the recognizable figure whose violent power demands recognition. It is for such qualities that de Kooning has been called an "artist who makes ambiguity a hypothesis on which to build."*

The Russian-French painter NICOLAS DE STAEL (1914–1955) created figurative works in the 1950s with the direct painterliness of the Abstract Expressionist mode imbued with a static, timeless mood, somewhat like a Classicism based on style rather than subject. De Stael's early nomadic life took him from his native Russia to Poland, Belgium, Morocco, and Algeria. He settled in Paris in the late 1930s. Like Matisse, de Stael used figures, objects, and their settings as the source for harmonious

*Thomas B. Hess, *Willem de Kooning* (New York: Museum of Modern Art, 1968), p. 25.

28-7 NICOLAS DE STAEL, *Musicians*, 1953. Oil on canvas, 5'6⁷/₈" × 3'9". The Phillips Collection, Washington, D.C.

arrangements of colors and shapes. *Musicians* (FIG. **28-7**) is typical of his work, presenting an image in which mosaiclike color shapes resolve themselves into a group of performing music makers. Simpler in composition and less involved with the character of each figure than Picasso's *Three Musicians* (FIG. 27-34), de Stael's *Musicians* focuses attention instead on the process of painting, and the viewer is most aware of the way that light, color, and space fill the canvas in a serenely orchestrated manner.

Post-Painterly ("Color-Field") Abstraction

The work of Pollock and the other Abstract Expressionists is often termed "painterly" abstraction. Very different in approach from the improvisation and spontaneity of Abstract Expressionism was painting in which evocative fields of color hinted at myth, ritual, and the themes of psychology—especially Freud's ideas of sexuality and Jung's ideas concerning universal archetypes. The links with universal imagery were extremely important to artists working in this mode. Painters with expansive vision expressed a sense of limitless space by covering canvases with fields of color. Critics termed these artists *Color-Field* painters or *Post-Painterly Abstractionists*. Among the earliest artists working in this way were Barnett Newman and Mark Rothko, who each explored a quieter esthetic than that followed by their contemporary associates, the New York Abstract Expressionists.

In the works of BARNETT NEWMAN (1905–1970), such "fields" of color suggest space of an almost purely perceptual kind. Newman's early works were organic abstractions inspired by his study of biology and his fascination with Native American art. Soon, however, he simplified his compositions so that each canvas is filled with a single, modulated color split by narrow bands the artist called "zips," which run from one edge of the painting to the other. As the artist explained it, "The streak was always going through an atmosphere; I kept trying to create a world around it." Newman had a special feeling for scale, proportion, and the absolute quality of each particular hue, and he used these elements in large paintings to express his feelings about the tragic condition of modern life and the human struggle to survive. He said, "The artist's problem is the idea complex that makes contact with mystery—of life, of men, of nature, of the hard black chaos that is tragedy." The title of his huge painting *Vir Heroicus Sublimis* (the exalted heroic man) (FIG. **28-8**) suggests the epic nature of these themes. Newman used the vast color field as a way to engage even the peripheral vision of his viewers, to create a particular sense of sublime and infinite space.

The best-known of the Color-Field painters was probably MARK ROTHKO (1903–1970), who, like Newman, used the Color-Field approach to represent the sublime. Rothko was

Color Field Abstracto

28-8 BARNETT NEWMAN, *Vir Heroicus Sublimis,* 1950–1951. Oil on canvas, 7'11³/₈" × 17'9¹/₄". The Museum of Modern Art, New York (gift of Mr. and Mrs. Ben Heller).

born in Russia but grew up in the United States and studied liberal arts before becoming a painter. His early paintings were figurative works, but he soon came to believe that references to anything specific in the physical world conflicted with the sublime idea of the universal, supernatural "spirit of myth," which he saw as the core of meaning in art. In a statement co-written with Newman and another artist, Rothko articulated his beliefs about art:

> We favor the simple expression of complex thought. We are for the large shape because it has the impact of the unequivocal. We wish to reassert the picture plane. . . . We assert that . . . only that subject matter is valid which is tragic and timeless. That is why we profess spiritual kinship with primitive and archaic art.*

Rothko gradually reduced his compositions to two or three large rectangles composed of layers of color with hazily brushed contours, spreading almost to the edges of the canvas. Subtle tonal variations in his works transcend the essentially monochromatic effect and create a mysterious sense of forms or images hovering in an ambiguously defined space. Works like *Four Darks in Red* (FIG. **28-9**) are perceived at once as a whole. Their still, shimmering veils of color encourage a calm and contemplative mood in the viewer, and, to maximize this effect, Rothko preferred that they be exhibited either in isolation or with other paintings by him.

*In Diane Waldman, *Mark Rothko, 1903–1970: A Retrospective* (New York: Solomon R. Guggenheim Museum, 1978), p. 39.

Pushing toward the limit of color-field abstraction, and of painting itself, ELLSWORTH KELLY (b. 1923), in *Red Blue Green* (FIG. **28-10**), rigidly excludes all reference, whether to subject or to any signature-like gestures left by the motion of the brush. The work is a perfectly even placement of three hues of unequal saturation within knife-edged fields (leading to the later identification of Kelly and related artists as *Hard-Edge Abstractionists*). The title declares clearly enough what the artist considers to be the painter's "meaning"—simply, the names of the hues. The fundamental modernist purism, stressed in formalist and constructivist theory and practice, that the "subject" of the painting should be its form and nothing else, is here bluntly expressed.

The reduction of painting to nothing but the painted surface logically leads to its becoming simply a painted object, no more, no less; as Frank Stella describes his work, "what you see is what you see." FRANK STELLA (b. 1936) exhibits the result in early works, like *Nunca Pasa Nada* (FIG. **28-11**), an enormous monochrome of chevron stripes following the indented outlines of the canvas support. The forces of the single motif are perfectly steady, and even as they move across the field, there is no centralizing focus, no balancing relationships, no painterly or expressive touches or clues. The painting could be a fragment of a much larger surface, like a wall, that carried the chevron figure overall. Or it could be the forward plane of a painted "minimal" sculpture, the other sides of which are not visible. Indeed, it has the abstraction of architectural ornament in its assertion of mural presence.

28-9 MARK ROTHKO, *Four Darks in Red*, 1958. Oil on canvas, 8'6" × 9'8". The Whitney Museum of American Art (gift of the Friends of the Whitney Museum of American Art, Mr. and Mrs. Eugene M. Schwartz, Mrs. Samuel A. Seaver, Charles Simon, and purchase).

28-10 ELLSWORTH KELLY, *Red Blue Green*, 1963. Oil on canvas, approx. 7' × 11'4". Museum of Contemporary Art, San Diego. Gift of Dr. and Mrs. Jack M. Farris.

28-11 FRANK STELLA, *Nunca Pasa Nada,* 1964. Metallic powder in polymer emulsion on canvas, approx. 8'9" × 17'6". Collection of the Lannan Foundation.

For the reduction of the pictorial surface to a painted object there is a complementary abstraction, the reduction of the pictorial surface to the texture of color-stained canvas. Newman stretched one color to fill a vast canvas field and Rothko created radiant clouds of color that seem to float within the rectangular shape of his canvases; in the works of both artists, the paint lies on the surface of the canvas. The American painter HELEN FRANKENTHALER (b. 1928) was one of the first artists to explore the effects of drenching the fabric of the canvas with fluid paint. This technique, called *soak-stain,* was inspired by a series of paintings Pollock made in the early 1950s by pouring thinned black paint onto raw canvas—bare fabric that had not been treated with the traditional protective coating of glue sizing nor covered with the traditional layer of colored or white primer paint.

Frankenthaler's early work was influenced by the spatial complexity of Cubism and the free expressive abstraction of Kandinsky; these influences helped her to understand the implications for her personal style when she saw pictures of Pollock painting one of his works on raw canvas. Inspired by his method, Frankenthaler thinned her oil paint and choreographed the flow of liquid shapes over huge areas of raw canvas laid on her studio floor. However, she ignored Pollock's swinging lines in favor of fluid, flowing shapes, and she replaced Pollock's black-and-white color scheme with elegantly varied hues.

In the 1960s, Frankenthaler began using water-soluble acrylic paint, which gave her a greater range of color and allowed a different degree of control over the creation of her shapes, a control evident in *Bay Side* (FIG. **28-12**). The medium now soaked into the canvas support and dried without forming any of the "halo" silhouettes that occurred

with the oil-based paints she used for her early soak-stain works. The method made her works look spontaneous, almost as if they had been conceived in the inspiration of a single moment. This quality is prized by the artist, but as she admits, it is not achieved without some effort, however masked that effort may seem to be in the final work:

> A really good picture looks as if it's happened at once. It's an immediate image. For my own work, when a picture looks labored and overworked, and you can read in it—

28-12 HELEN FRANKENTHALER, *Bay Side,* 1967. Acrylic on canvas, 6'2" × 6'9". André Emmerich Gallery, New York.

Color field

28-13 MORRIS LOUIS, *Alpha-Pi*, 1961. Acrylic on canvas, approx. 8′6″ × 14′8″. The Metropolitan Museum of Art, Arthur H. Hearn Fund.

well, she did this and then she did that, and then she did that—there is something in it that has not got to do with beautiful art to me. And I usually throw those out, though I think very often it takes ten of those over-labored efforts to produce one really beautiful wrist motion that is synchronized with your head and heart, and you have it, and therefore it looks as if it were born in a minute.*

Frankenthaler's technique of staining had a decisive influence on MORRIS LOUIS (1912–1962), who, in his work, accommodated the free improvisation of the Abstract Expressionists to the careful management of color, which occupied the Color-Field painters. His work has been termed "breakthrough" because of its ultimate reduction of painting to the concrete fact of the paint-impregnated canvas. His intricate, painstaking pouring of water-soluble acrylic paint on the unsized canvas duck support allowed color to enter the canvas weave rather than cling to the surface. Color purity was maintained in the process, transforming the canvas into an object like a woven textile. Louis produced sets of paintings, which varied according to the nature of his experiments. His *Alpha-Pi* (FIG. **28-13**) belongs to the set he described as "unfurleds," perhaps from their suggestion of wind-rippled flags. Varicolored streamlets gather into triangle clusters on either side of a broad white void, exhibiting both the untouched textural nature of the canvas and the nature of color as it streams into the canvas weave making one integrated fabric. Louis's work may be regarded as the definitive statement of Modernist Purism in painting. One could go no farther in the reduction of painting to its physical essence.

*In Barbara Rose, *Frankenthaler* (New York: Harry N. Abrams, 1975), p. 85.

Optical ("Op") Art

Formally related to the geometrical, hard-edged approach, but very different in purpose, so-called *Optical* or *Op Art* produces precisely drafted patterns that directly, even uncomfortably, affect visual perception. Using numerous devices illustrative of visual ambiguity (familiar in the science of perceptual psychology), the Op artist designs surfaces that vibrate, pulsate and flicker, advance and retreat, creating the illusion of movement. VICTOR VASARELY (b. 1908), an admirer of the art of De Stijl, the Bauhaus and Constructivism, and founder of the Op method, summarizes it in his *Orion* (FIG. **28-14**). The eye is first attracted by the regular order and brightly colored shapes. A longer look reveals that the rows of flat squares filled with circles and ellipses do not lie flat on the surface of the canvas. Instead, the eye reads one square in relation to the next so that the darkening or lightening of the ground, any shifts from warm to cool hues, and all changes in the size or shape of the central form create illusions of movement in space as the eye travels along a row of squares. In the 1950s and 1960s, especially, Vasarely dreamed of filling whole cities with buildings whose walls would vibrate with his patterns, echoing in pure abstraction what he viewed as the dynamism of modern urban life. His theories inspired a number of younger artists in Paris to form the *Groupe de Recherché d'Art Visuel* (Research Group for Visual Art) to explore similar ideas.

Unlike its abstractionist relatives, Op Art does not find its objects in the painted canvas itself, but in the optical illusion, which has its seat in the brain; we might call Op Art "perceptual abstraction." The pattern reaches out and

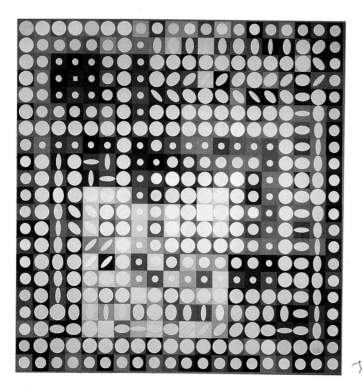

28-14 VICTOR VASARELY, *Orion*, 1956. Paper on paper mounted on wood, 6'10¹/₂" × 6'6³/₄". Hirshhorn Museum and Sculpture Garden, Smithsonian Institution, Washington, D.C. (gift of Joseph H. Hirshhorn, 1966).

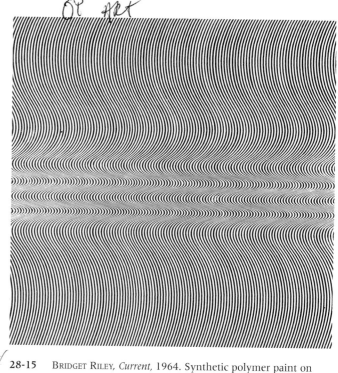

28-15 BRIDGET RILEY, *Current*, 1964. Synthetic polymer paint on composition board, approx. 58³/₈" × 58⁷/₈". The Museum of Modern Art, New York (Philip Johnson Fund).

"abstracts" our actual setting into perceptual illusions. In *Current* (FIG. **28-15**), the British artist BRIDGET RILEY (b. 1931) presents a pattern of lines that seem to swim in contrary motion. If we stare at it long enough its vibrations seem to penetrate the eye and cause some discomfort. It is noteworthy that the elements in *Current* stand in a definable mathematical relation to one another, and patterns like this can be generated by computer; here the pattern repeats a sinusoidal curve, with a linearly increasing period, giving an overwhelming impression of motion. Thus, the perceptual abstraction of vision can correspond to mathematical abstraction, and we have in Op Art an anticipation of computer-generated art.

Sculpture: Kinetic, Assemblage, Organic

It is a logical step from Op Art's production of the perception of motion by visual stimulus to the presentation of objects actually moving. This *Kinetic Art* appears already in the work of Calder (FIG. 27-52) and the Constructionists, such as Tatlin (FIG. 27-51). Vasarely called his work *"cinétisme,"*—that is, "kineticism," and the two movements are closely related.

In sculpture, advances in technology provided the means for representing the effects of change in a new kind of Kinetic Art. One of the most engaging of the sculptors of Kinetic works is JEAN TINGUELY (b. 1925), who creates machines that are as cranky and unpredictable as human beings. Trained as a painter in his native Switzerland, Tinguely turned to motion sculpture as the result of his growing belief that "the only stable thing is movement." In the 1950s, he made a series of "metamatic" machines, programmed electronically to act with an antimechanical unpredictability when viewers inserted felt-tipped marking pens into a pincer and pressed a button to initiate motion of the pen across a small sheet of paper clipped to an "easel." Different colored markers could be used in succession, and the viewer could stop and start the device to achieve some degree of control over the final image; the results of these operations were a series of small works that resembled Abstract Expressionist paintings.

In 1960, Tinguely expanded the scale of his work with a piece designed to "perform" and then destroy itself in a large area of the courtyard at the Museum of Modern Art in New York City. *Homage to New York* (FIG. **28-16**) was created with the aid of engineer Billy Klüver*, who helped Tinguely scrounge wheels and other objects from a dump near Manhattan. The completed structure, painted white to show up against the dark night sky, included a player piano

*Klüver was later involved with Robert Rauschenberg and others in the establishment of EAT (Experiments in Art and Technology), a group of artists and engineers, mostly from the New York area, who fostered interactions between art and technology in the 1960s and early 1970s.

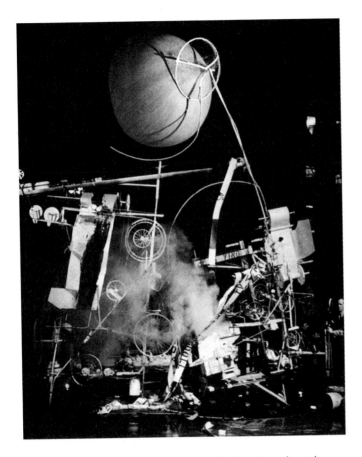

28-16 JEAN TINGUELY, *Homage to New York,* 1960, just prior to its self-destruction in the garden of the Museum of Modern Art, New York.

modified into a "metamatic" painting machine, a weather balloon that inflated during the performance, vials of colored smoke, and a host of gears, pulleys, wheels, and other found machine parts. Like Tinguely's other Kinetic sculptures, *Homage to New York* shared something of the satiric, Dadaist spirit of Duchamp (FIG. 27-58) and the droll import of Klee's *Twittering Machine* (FIG. 27-68). But the wacky behavior of *Homage to New York* was deliberately more playful and more endearing. Having been given a "freedom" of eccentric behavior unprecedented in the mechanical world, Tinguely's creations often seem to behave with the whimsical individuality of human actors.

Just as Kinetic art had its sources in Constructivism, so *Assemblage* ("assembled" art) continued and expanded procedures familiar in Cubism (FIG. 27-32) and Dada (FIG. 27-60). LOUISE NEVELSON (1899–1988) created sculpture that combined a sense of the architectural fragment with the power of Dada and Surrealist found objects to express her personal sense of the underlying meanings of life. Multiplicity of meaning was important to Nevelson. She sought "the in-between place . . . the dawns and the dusks" where one could sense the transition between one state of being and another. By the late 1950s, she was making Assemblages of found wooden objects and forms, enclosing smaller sculptural compositions in boxes of varied sizes, and joining the boxes to one another to form "walls," which she then painted in a single hue—usually black, white, or gold.

The monochromatic color scheme unifies the diverse parts of pieces like *Tropical Garden II* (FIG. **28-17**) and also creates a mysterious field of shapes and shadows. The struc-

28-17 LOUISE NEVELSON, *Tropical Garden II,* 1957–1959. Wood painted black, 5'11 1/2" × 10'11 3/4" × 1'. Musée National d'Art Moderne, Centre Georges Pompidou, Paris.

tures suggest magical environments that resemble the treasured secret hideaways dimly remembered from childhood. Yet, the boxy frames and the precision of the manufactured found objects create a rough geometrical structure over

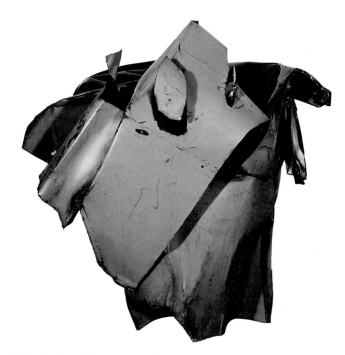

28-18 JOHN CHAMBERLAIN, *Miss Lucy Pink,* 1963. Painted steel, 3'11" × 3'6" × 3'3". Photograph courtesy of The Pace Gallery.

which the viewer's eye roams freely, lingering on some details before moving on. The parts of a Nevelson sculpture and their interrelation recall the *Merz* constructions of Kurt Schwitters (FIG. 27-60). The effect is also rather like viewing the side wall of an apartment building from a moving elevated train or looking down on a city from the air.

Using very different materials and techniques to achieve markedly different effects, JOHN CHAMBERLAIN (b. 1927) assembles the broken and jagged fragments of junked cars—twisting, bending, and welding them together. To these compositions he assigns whimsical, Dada-like titles, such as *Miss Lucy Pink* (FIG. **28-18**). At the same time, the work, in its apparent spontaneity of execution, its vivid color contrast and collisions of shape, is a kind of three-dimensional Abstract Expressionism. Though Chamberlain is obviously concerned with purely formal effects, his allusive title and his material, the salvaged remnants of discarded automobiles, are ironic comments upon a principal end-product of our industrial age, metallic junk. This is the subject and substance of what is called "junk art."

In striking contrast to Assemblage, a continuing preoccupation with Organic Abstraction appears in the sculpture of the French-American artist LOUISE BOURGEOIS (b. 1911), who is heir to the evocative biomorphic Surrealist forms of Jean Arp (FIG. 27-54). In her sculpture her subject has been "groups of objects relating to each other . . . the drama of one among many." *Cumul I* (FIG. **28-19**) is a collection of round-headed units huddled within a collective cloak

28-19 LOUISE BOURGEOIS, *Cumul I,* 1969. Marble, 22³/₈" × 50" × 48". Musée National d'Art Moderne, Centre Georges Pompidou, Paris.

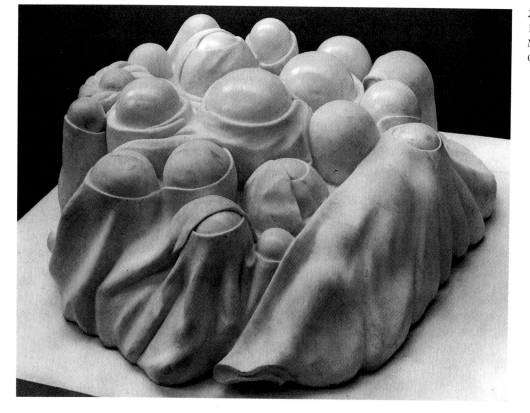

dotted with holes, through which the tops of the individual units protrude. The units differ in size, and their position within the group lends a distinctive personality to each. Although the shapes remain abstract, the reference to human figures is strong. Bourgeois uses a wide variety of materials in her works, including wood, plaster, latex, and plastics, in addition to alabaster, marble, and bronze. She exploits the qualities of the material to suit the expressiveness of the piece.

In *Cumul I,* the fact that marble can take either a high gloss or a matte finish increases the sensuous distinction between the group of swelling forms and the soft folds that swaddle them. Like Hepworth (FIG. 27-55), Bourgeois connects her sculpture with the multiple relationships of the body to landscape: "[My pieces] are anthropomorphic and they are landscape also, since our body could be considered from a topographical point of view, as a land with mounds and valleys and caves and holes." However, Bourgeois's pieces are more personal and more openly sexual than those of Hepworth. *Cumul I* represents perfectly the allusions Bourgeois seeks: "There has always been sexual suggestiveness in my work. Sometimes I am totally concerned with female shapes—characters of breasts like clouds—but often I merge the activity—phallic breasts, male and female, active and passive."*

Sculpture: Abstract and Minimal

Formal sculpture, like formalist painting, seeks always more complete abstraction. The oldest and most influential formalist sculptor, DAVID SMITH (1906–1965), whose mastery of spatial composition was widely admired by younger artists like Chamberlain, began as a painter associated with the Abstract Expressionists. When he took up sculpture he explored the possibilities of expressive line; his early sculptures were done in a linear, open style influenced by the work of Julio González (FIG. 27-45). In his later work, Smith used the metal-fabrication techniques he had learned earlier as a factory worker in Indiana: "The equipment I use, my supply of material comes from factory study, and duplicates as nearly as possible the production equipment used in making a locomotive." Sculptures like *Cubi XXVI* (FIG. **28-20**) are monumental constructions in stainless steel in which Smith arranged solid, geometric masses in remarkable equilibriums of strength and buoyancy. Smith was at ease in the age of the machine: "What associations the metal possesses are those of this century: power, structure, movement, progress, suspension, destruction, brutality." His welded compositions were tough enough to allow the remarkably free balancing in space that is characteristic of his last style. Here, as in all Smith's work, the viewer has a sharp awareness of the lin-

28-20 DAVID SMITH, *Cubi XXVI,* 1965. Steel, approx. 10′ × 12′6″ × 2′3″. National Gallery of Art, Washington, D.C. (Ailsa Mellon Bruce Fund, 1978).

ear outlines of the planes that make up the composition and help to create and reinforce the rhythms of the piece, including the kinesthetic sense of motion created by a strong axis and the thrusting of elements at angles against and away from the axis. Like much of the work of the Abstract Expressionists, Smith's work addresses the viewer's sense of gesture in space; his sculptures always seem poised on the edge of moving between one position in space and another.

Along with David Smith, the British artist ANTHONY CARO (b. 1924) inaugurated the move toward definitive abstraction in sculpture. For two years, Caro served as an assistant to Henry Moore (FIG. 27-56), and on a visit to New York in the late fifties, he met David Smith and admired the work of Morris Louis. Like Smith's, Caro's material is scrap steel—plates, girders, boiler-tops, propeller blades, and the like. His technique is welding, and his forms, as seen in *Midday* (FIG. **28-21**), exhibit the blunt, elemental geometry of industrial metal. Caro does not provide a base or pedestal; the horizontally oriented piece lies flat upon the ground; some of his works are below eye-level. He paints the metal a color suggestive of the mood indicated by the caption; in this example, a saturated orange hue that brightly says "Midday!" Analogous to the radical abstraction of the work of painters like Morris Louis (FIG. 28-13), Caro's sculpture asserts the essential fact of the material as its sole and sufficient "meaning," despite his assignment to it of a mood-suggestive title.

The faintly gestural positioning of components in David Smith's compositions, and the "moods" assigned by Caro to

*In Deborah Wye, *Louise Bourgeois* (New York: Museum of Modern Art, 1982), pp. 22, 25, 27.

28-21 ANTHONY CARO, *Midday,* 1960. Steel, 7′7³/4″ × 37³/8″ × 12′1³/4″. The Museum of Modern Art, New York. Mr. and Mrs. Arthur Wieserberger Fund.

his, were too referential for certain purist sculptors, who produced work that banished *all* reference beyond itself. Their severe reduction of form to single, homogenous units has been called *Minimalism,* and the units themselves have been termed "primary structures." One of the most rigorous practitioners of the Minimalist approach in sculpture was DONALD JUDD (1928–1994). To his sculpture, Judd brings his study of art history and his experience as a painter and critic. He aspired to create sculpture so unified in effect that even if a piece had more than one part, the parts would be seen as a whole rather than in relation to one another. To Judd and the other Minimalists, this unity is the basic and true statement of form in space; anything else is a distortion. Against all two-dimensional space that invites illusionistic figuration, including even Mondrian's paintings (FIG. 27-50), the Minimalist sculptors insist that only the spatial wholeness of the third dimension in the simple reductive shapes of solid geometry contains the truth of art.

In the untitled work illustrated here (FIG. **28-22**), Judd aligned eight identical, brightly machined stainless-steel cubes in the center of a gallery floor. Even though this grouping includes a series of distinct box forms, no single shape stands out. The only real difference among the cubes is one of placement within the group. The cubes' identical repetitiveness creates, for Judd, the sense of wholeness he sought. As in Post-Painterly Abstract painting, little trace of the artist can be seen in this work; the surfaces of the cubes exhibit, in their superhuman precision and exacti-

tude, the depersonalized technological order that produced them. Although none of Judd's structures is intended to carry an allusion to anything outside itself, he is interested in making us aware of how we see form in space. The scale of the whole work is huge, but the modules of each box are comprehensible in terms of human size. This characteristic can help us to sharpen our ability to perceive three-dimensional forms because the identical units serve as visual markers for measuring an area of wall space and the

28-22 DONALD JUDD, Untitled, 1968. Stainless steel, each box 4′ square. Collection of Miles Fiterman, Minneapolis.

section of air before it. Our viewing of form in space, however, is also complicated by the playful way in which these clear, Minimal shapes appear to dissolve as their polished sides reflect their neighbors and the environment around them.

By the end of the 1960s, some Minimalist artists tired of Minimal art's restrictive, reductive forms and reintroduced a sense of visible process in their work. Eva Hesse (1936–1970), a Minimalist in the early part of her career, was a leading figure in this approach, called *Post-Minimalism* by the critics. Using nontraditional sculptural materials like fiberglass, cord, and latex, Hesse created sculpture in which the pure forms of Minimal art appear to crumble, sag, and warp under the pressures of atmospheric force and gravity. Born a Jew in Hitler's Germany, as a child Hesse was hidden with a Christian family when her parents and elder sister had to flee the Nazis, and was not reunited with them until the early 1940s, just before her parents divorced. This complex set of extraordinary circumstances helped to give her a lasting sense that the central qualities of modern life are strangeness and absurdity. Struggling to express these qualities in her art, she created informal sculptural arrangements in which units often hung from the ceiling, leaned against the walls, or spilled out along the floor. She said she wanted her pieces to be "non art, non connotive, non anthropomorphic, non geometric, no nothing, everything, but of another kind, vision, sort." Amazingly, *Hang-Up* (FIG. **28-23**) fulfills these requirements. The piece looks like a carefully made, empty frame sprouting a strange feeler that extends out into the viewer's space. Hesse wrote that in this work, for the first time, her "idea of absurdity or extreme feeling came through." In her words, "[*Hang-Up*] has a kind of depth I don't always achieve and that is the kind of depth or soul or absurdity of life or meaning or feeling or intellect that I want to get."* Absurd and nontraditional the piece certainly is, but it also possesses a disquieting and touching presence, suggesting the fragility and grandeur of life amidst the pressures of the modern age.

EARTH AND SITE ART

Minimalism moves out of the galleries, sculpture gardens, and city plazas into the more extensive settings of nature, there to construct with natural or artificial materials monuments of great scale and minimal form. Permanent or impermanent, these works are intended to transform some sector of the environment so as to assert its presence and importance as reworked by the hand of the artist. The enterprise, much like architecture, requires not only the design talents of the artist, but managerial, logistic, and engineering skills, plus the cooperation of teams of workers

*In Linda Shearer, *Eva Hesse: A Memorial Exhibition* (New York: Solomon R. Guggenheim Museum, 1972), unpaginated.

28-23 Eva Hesse, *Hang-Up*, 1965–1966. Acrylic on cloth over wood and steel, 6′ × 7′ × 6′6″. The Art Institute of Chicago (gift of Arthur Keating and Mr. and Mrs. Edward Morris by exchange).

capable of carrying out the artist's plan. Depending upon the artist's approach, this kind of construction has been called variously *Earth Art, Environmental Art,* or *Site Art.*

A leading site artist was Robert Smithson (1938–1973), who used industrial construction equipment to manipulate vast quantities of earth and rock on isolated sites. Beginning with early works based on the structure and behavior of crystals, Smithson moved to a series of *Site/Nonsite* pieces. In these, he transported materials from specific distant locations to museum settings and displayed the collected material (with accompanying topographical maps and photographs) in constructed metal bins, establishing a dialogue for the viewer between the original site and the museum location. He then did a series of temporary on-location pieces in which he modified the landscape physically (through processes such as pouring asphalt down a rock face) or visually (through placement of mirrored plates throughout the space). In seeking to do a more permanent Site piece, Smithson was attracted to a site on the Great Salt Lake in Utah. He built *Spiral Jetty* (FIG. **28-24**), a vast coil of earth and stone that symbolized the reality of time, on a monumental scale, so that it extended out into the lake. The idea grew from Smithson's first impression of the location:

Earn-Environm

28-24 ROBERT SMITHSON, *Spiral Jetty,* April 1970. Black rocks, salt crystal, earth, red water, algae, 1,500′ long, 15′ wide. Great Salt Lake, Utah.

As I looked at the site, it reverberated out to the horizons only to suggest an immobile cyclone while flickering light made the entire landscape appear to quake. A dormant earthquake spread into the fluttering stillness, into a spinning sensation without movement. The site was a rotary that enclosed itself in an immense roundness. From that gyrating space emerged the possibility of the *Spiral Jetty.**

Smithson tried in this piece for an indissoluble unity of art and nature, much like the suspension of the boundaries between "self" and "nonself" that he hoped to instill in his viewers. As was the case with many other Earth Art works, *Spiral Jetty*'s location made it difficult for viewers to see in person. People know of such works mostly through photographs, and artists are increasingly self-conscious about how they document their work visually. Smithson not only recorded *Spiral Jetty* in photographs, but he filmed its construction in a movie that describes the forms and life of the whole site, including its relative inaccessibility. The photographs and film have become increasingly important because shifts in the water level of the Great Salt Lake have placed *Spiral Jetty* underwater for several years.

CHRISTO and JEANNE-CLAUDE (b. 1935) intensify the viewer's awareness of the space and features of natural and urban sites by modifying parts of them with cloth. Their pieces also incorporate the relationship between human social/political action, art, and the environment. Study of

art in Christo's native Bulgaria and in Vienna was followed by a period in Paris, where he began to encase objects in clumsy wrappings, in this way appropriating bits of the real world into the mysterious world of the unopened package whose contents can be dimly seen in silhouette under the wrap.

Settling in New York City in 1964, Christo and Jeanne-Claude made storefronts like strange stage sets surrounded with windows wrapped in paper and cloth, and constructed ambitious temporary installations, wrapping sections of buildings or even entire buildings. Turning their attention to the environment, they created giant "air packages" in Minneapolis and Germany. Then they dealt with the land itself, carrying out projects like wrapping over a million square feet of Australian coast and hanging a vast curtain across a valley at Rifle Gap, Colorado. The land pieces required years of preparation, research, and scores of meetings with local authorities and interested groups of local citizens. The artists have always considered that their Site pieces include the lobbying activity and the visual documentation that goes into them as well as the actual short-lived physical pieces themselves. *Surrounded Islands* (FIG. **28-25**), created in Biscayne Bay in Miami, Florida, for only two weeks in May of 1983, is typical of the Site work. For this project, eleven small man-made islands in the bay were surrounded with specially fabricated pink polypropylene fabric. This required two years of preparation to gain the required permissions, to assemble the necessary troop of unskilled and professional workers, and to raise the $3.2 million cost of the project (accomplished through the sale of preliminary drawings, collages, and models). Huge crowds

*In Nancy Holt, ed., *The Writings of Robert Smithson* (New York: New York University Press, 1975), p. 111. Smithson was tragically killed in 1973 when the airplane in which he was surveying a site for a new Earth sculpture crashed near Amarillo, Texas.

28-25 CHRISTO, *Surrounded Islands*, Biscayne Bay, Greater Miami, Florida, 1980–1983. Pink woven polypropylene fabric, 6¹/₂ million sq. ft.

watched as crews stripped accumulated trash from the islands (to assure maximum contrast between their dark colors, the pink of the cloth, and the blue of the bay), then unfurled the fabric "cocoons" toward the islands to form magical "skirts" around each tiny bit of land. Because each Site piece has the quality of spectacle, some critics have compared these works to Happenings (see page 1121) but Christo disagrees: "All Happenings are make-believe situations. Everything in my work is strongly literal. If three hundred people are used, it is not because we want three hundred people to play roles, but because we have work for them. . . . My work may look very theatrical, but it is a very professional activity."* Despite its short actual life, *Surrounded Islands* lives on in the host of photographs, films, and books that document the piece.

POP ART AND POSTMODERN TRENDS

While Modernist formalism was at its height, a new movement, called *Pop Art*, appeared in Britain and America; it contradicted the premises of Modernism and introduced the Postmodernist decades that close the twentieth century. The name *Pop* was coined by the British critic Lawrence Alloway to refer to the popular mass culture and vernacu-

*In David Bourbon, *Christo* (New York: Harry N. Abrams, 1972), p. 25.

lar imagery of the contemporary urban environment. Pop culture is manifest in our everyday experience through photography, movies, billboards, commodity packaging, and all the commercial "visuals" that are so commonplace we hardly notice them though we absorb them totally.

Pop adherents declared this popular media worthy of notice and worthy of notice as art—quite the equal of "fine" art when skillfully managed; indeed, for Pop artists there is no distinction. Pop Art reintroduces all the instrumentalities of meaning that purist Modernism had banished from its abstract and minimal forms—signs, symbols, metaphors, allusions, illusions, images—and selected these from the infinitude of artifacts that make up the context of our daily experience. Rather than disdain the cheap, vulgar, and banal, Pop artists confer value upon them as real and present, and the selection and presentation of them as legitimate art. Pop Art owes much to Duchamp and the tradition of Dada, though it makes art out of what the latter would regard as non-art, or would exhibit as an anti-art statement.

Pop Art emerged in the early 1950s with a group of young British artists, architects, and writers who joined Alloway to form the *Independent Group* at the Institute of Contemporary Art in London. This group's members sought to initiate fresh thinking in art, in part by sharing their fascination with the symbol and content of American advertising, comic books, and popular movies. In America, artists used Pop images to give art the immediacy of life.

Some Pop artists mixed mass-media images with gestural paintings and found objects, some rendered advertising images with commercial art techniques, and some used Pop motifs to pose questions about the nature of verbal and visual symbols. By the early 1960s, Pop Art was an important force in England, New York, California, and Europe, especially France and Italy. Its success with the public was due in large measure to its use of easily recognizable images, an iconography of commerce and culture as widely known in the modern world as earlier symbols tied to religion and government had been in premodern society.

Discussions at the Independent Group in London probed the role and meaning of symbols from mass culture and the advertising media. In 1956, a group member, RICHARD HAMILTON (b. 1922), made a small collage, *Just What Is It That Makes Today's Homes So Different, So Appealing?* (FIG. **28-26**), that symbolized many of the attitudes of British Pop Art. Trained as an engineering draftsman, exhibition designer, and painter, Hamilton was very interested in the way advertising shapes our attitudes. Long intrigued by the ideas of Duchamp, Hamilton has consistently combined elements of popular art and fine art, seeing both as belonging to the whole world of visual communication. *Just What Is It* was created for the poster and catalogue of one section of an exhibition entitled *This Is Tomorrow*—an environment/installation filled with images from Hollywood cinema, science fiction, the mass media, and one reproduction

28-26   RICHARD HAMILTON, *Just What Is It That Makes Today's Homes So Different, So Appealing?*, 1956. Collage, 10¼″ × 9¾″. Kunsthalle Tübingen, Germany.

of a van Gogh painting to represent popular fine art works. The fantasy interior in Hamilton's collage reflects the values of modern consumer culture through figures and objects cut from glossy magazines by Hamilton's wife, Terry, and his friend, the artist Magda Crodell McHale, who followed a list of themes he gave them. *Just What Is it* reconstructs the found images into a new whole, wittily transforming an Abstract Expressionist painting into a rug, and turning a comic book and an automobile logo into paintings on the wall (or is the logo intended to serve as a lampshade?). Much has been written about the possible deep meaning of this piece, and few would deny the work's sardonic effect, whether or not the artist intended to make a pointed comment. Although *Just What Is It* has none of the dialogue between lushly illusionistic painting and popular iconography found in much of Hamilton's other work, the way in which this collage suggests the contents of a mass mind stimulates wide-ranging speculation by viewers about society's values, and this kind of intellectual toying with mass-media meaning and imagery typifies British and European Pop Art.

Pop brings representation back via the informal photograph and advertising illustration, or what would appear to be a crossing of both, in *American Collectors* (FIG. **28-27**) by DAVID HOCKNEY (b. 1937), which shows friends of the artist in the opulent setting of their Southern California residence. The subjects pose with prized items of their art collection on the patio of their California-Bauhaus home, making a tableau instantly recognizable as standard for its affluent locale and conspicuous consumerism. The composition is cleanly rectilinear, the color flat and bright as the Sunland milieu, the shadows sharply defined. We sense the influence of Hard-Edged Abstraction as well as the crisp shapes in real-estate advertising art. At the same time, a trance-like stillness and frozen action suggest Surrealism. The characterization is slightly sardonic, verging on caricature. The rigid stance of the husband is like that of a butler on call, the monumental figure of the wife a symbol of imperious reign over the household. Hockney is quite aware of and well-versed in the formalist experiments of his time, and uses them adroitly in producing both a convincingly realistic effect and a sly social comment.

The American artist JASPER JOHNS (b. 1930) inaugurated the Pop trend in New York in the mid-1950s with paintings of numbers, flags, and targets, common shapes that are seldom examined closely. In his view they are simple fact, entirely conventional, without allusion of any sort, needing no comment other than their own; this is not far from the Minimalist thinking we have already noted. Viewers cannot ignore the presence of one of Johns's painted targets (FIG. 28-28); such images fill the entire canvas and are rendered with the unmistakable texture of a hand-applied art medium—in this case, encaustic. As a representation of a target, a Johns target has no reference beyond the design

28-27 DAVID HOCKNEY, *American Collectors,* 1968. Acrylic on canvas, 7' × 10'. Art Institute of Chicago. Restricted gift of Mrs. Frederick Pick.

and the fact that it "represents" a target. Such a painted target remains the replica of a target, but it has also become an art object—by the artist's designation of it as such—with no clear significance, because it cannot be used as a target and remain a painting. The puzzle of the relationship between the painting and its design was set down by Johns as a formula: "*A = B, A is B, A* represents *B.*"* In *Target with Four Faces* (FIG. **28-28**) the artist has complicated the situation by adding, above the flat painted target, four boxes (with a single hinged lid), each containing a cast of the lower portion of a human face. These casts are not portraits. They seem to be the same face, although slight differences between them are evident (they were cast at four distinct but successive moments). Unlike the target, the faces *represent* actual faces: they are not *themselves* real flesh-and-blood faces. In the faces, as with the target, Johns has picked a part of life—nose and mouth—that we generally see but do not examine; it is the eyes that usually capture our attention in the human face. In Johns's work, such simple, appropriated things acquire a haunting "presence" that forces us to wrestle with the relationship between the thing and its representation. As the artist himself said: "Meaning is determined by the use of the thing, the way an audience uses a painting once it is put in public."

Also paradoxical, Johns's *Painted Bronze* (FIG. **28-29**) is not quite so puzzling as *Target.* Though the two ale cans were originally useful as such, they no longer have that use, although the target could still conceivably be used as a target even though painted. Yet, being cast in bronze

*This is a paradox that haunts much of Pop Art: the thing is the same as its representation! When we have painted numbers, are the numbers themselves, or replicas of themselves? Consider the sign that reads: "Ignore this sign."

28-28 JASPER JOHNS, *Target with Four Faces,* 1955. Assemblage of encaustic and collage on canvas with objects, 26" × 26", surmounted by four tinted plaster faces in wood box with hinged front, overall dimensions with box open, 33⁵/₈" × 26" × 3". The Museum of Modern Art, New York (gift of Mr. and Mrs. Robert C. Scull).

28-29 JASPER JOHNS, *Painted Bronze*, 1960. Approx. 5¹/₂" high, 8" wide, 4³/₄" deep. Wallraf-Richartz-Museum, Cologne (Sammlung Ludwig).

appear, sit down at the piano, raise the keyboard cover to mark the beginning of the piece, remain motionless at the instrument for "four minutes and twenty-two seconds" (during which time all ambient sounds "become" the music), and then close the keyboard cover, rise, and bow to signal the end of the work.

Rauschenberg set out to create works that would be as open and indeterminate as Cage's pieces, and he began by making "combine paintings," in which the parts coexisted equally and simultaneously. In the 1950s, such works contained an array of art reproductions, magazine and newspaper clippings, and segments painted in an Abstract Expressionist style. In the early 1960s, Rauschenberg adopted the commercial medium of *photoscreen*, first in black and white and then in color, and began filling entire canvases with appropriated news images and anonymous photographs of city scenes. *Estate* (FIG. **28-30**) is typical of his color photoscreen paintings. A jumble of images sprawls across the canvas. Familiar sights, like traffic signs, the Statue of Liberty, and a view of the Sistine Chapel in Rome showing the *Last Judgment* by Michelangelo (FIG. 22-28), are

and bereft of their use, the cans are still cans, and representations of cans. Johns's purpose, like that of Pop Art in general, is manifest. Through art, what is customarily discarded as junk can be reconstituted and re-situated as something worthy of the attention we rarely give it. Johns solemnly exalts the banal by preserving it in durable bronze, faithfully preserving its commercial logo, and firmly mounting it upon a base. There the flimsy and disposable container is monumentalized as a profoundly symbolic artifact of our material culture. As has been the case with so many ancient cultures, it is by our commonplace artifacts that we are and will be known. The irony of Johns's work echoes the poet T. S. Eliot's prediction that nothing will survive us but a thousand lost golf balls. And, we might add, bronzed beer cans and baby shoes!

Johns's colleague ROBERT RAUSCHENBERG (b. 1925) was called a "father of Pop" because he began using mass-media images in his work in the mid-1950s. For him, as an admirer of the ideas of the composer John Cage, such images were important bits of the world that could be used in an attempt to narrow the gap between art and life. Cage was a charismatic and widely influential teacher, who encouraged his students to link their art directly with life. He brought to his music composition an interest in the thoughts of Duchamp and in Eastern philosophy. In his own work, Cage used methods like chance and indeterminacy to avoid the closed structures that marked traditional music and, in his view, separated it from the unpredictable and multilayered qualities of daily existence. For example, the score for one of Cage's piano compositions instructs the performer to

28-30 ROBERT RAUSCHENBERG, *Estate*, 1963. Oil and printer's ink, 8' × 5'10". Philadelphia Museum of Art (given by the Friends of the Philadelphia Museum of Art).

intermixed with abstract painted shapes, and "anonymous" pictures of city buildings, human legs, a clock face, a mysterious group of objects, and a "palette" of color patches containing the tonal values and the colors red, blue, and yellow—the basic vocabulary of painting. Some of the images tilt or turn sideways; each overlays or is invaded by part of its neighbor. The compositional confusion may resemble that in a Dada collage, but the parts of Rauschenberg's combine paintings retain their individuality more than those in a Schwitters piece (FIG. 27-60). The eye scans a Rauschenberg canvas much as it might survey the environment on a walk through the city. As John Cage perceptively noted: "There is no more subject in a *combine* [by Rauschenberg] than there is in a page from a newspaper. Each thing that is there is a subject. It is a situation involving multiplicity."* Individually, Rauschenberg's works resist precise memorization. Collectively, they represent the experience of day-to-day life in modern cities.

The new universe of shapes and colors produced by mass culture and its visual explosion supplied Pop Art with its material, its new fact. But as Rauschenberg shows us, instant fact can be made fantasy simply by shattering factual contexts and realigning and regrouping the elements that compose the conventional aggregates of fact. The effect of this process is to surprise and defeat expectation—the old Dada aim to shake up conventional minds. The sympathetic neutrality of the Pop attitude toward mass culture could, under the impact of the mischievous Dada impulse, quickly yield to making fun of that culture through fantastic exaggeration and paradox; we have seen the paradox working in the art of Johns (FIGS. 28-28 and 28-29).

The exaggeration appears in the art of CLAES OLDENBURG (b. 1929), where the good-humored cynicism of Duchamp seems to be influential. With Oldenburg, simple domestic utensils, like his colossal *Clothespin* (FIG. **28-31**), are expanded to giant scale; this piece dominates a city square in Philadelphia, like a pedestalled obelisk in a Roman piazza (FIG. 24-3). That insignificant, homely attachment of the clothesline takes on the proportions of a civic monument by mocking the pretentious, official architecture that is now merely a foil for it. It is as if Bach were to write an oratorio in honor of a square nail.

The incongruity of scale and significance is matched in a different medium by ROY LICHTENSTEIN (b. 1923), who reconstructs on a giant scale the thudding clichés and ear-splitting rhetoric of comic strips devoured daily by millions. His *Blam!* (FIG. **28-32**) is a tongue-in-cheek commentary on the taste and the fantasy life of the public. Trivially familiar as the form and iconography are, they create a powerful effect when written large and out of context. The new landscape and still life of Pop offer us views of the garish artifice that surrounds us and reflects us all too clearly.

*John Cage, *Silence* (Middletown, CT: Wesleyan University Press, 1961), p. 101.

28-31 CLAES OLDENBURG, *Clothespin*, 1976. Cor-Ten and stainless steel, approx. 45′ × 6′3″ × 4′4″. Centre Square, Philadelphia.

28-32 ROY LICHTENSTEIN, *Blam!*, 1962. Oil on canvas, approx. 5′8″ × 6′8″. Collection of Richard Brown Baker, New York.

The quintessential New York Pop artist was undoubtedly ANDY WARHOL (1925–1987). Like Rauschenberg, whom he greatly admired, Warhol found his subjects in mass media, but mostly in commercial design, mass advertising, and news photos of ordinary people rather than in images of fine art, famous events, or anonymous buildings. After producing a few works in which he carefully mimicked the look of commercial printing, Warhol began using photoscreen to create paintings of subjects like Campbell's soup can labels, sheets of stamps, ads for dance lessons and other self-improvement courses, and news photos of disaster, wanted criminals, and famous people. An early career as a commercial artist and illustrator may have helped interest Warhol in the expressive force of the harsh colors and simplified shapes to be found in labels and publicity photos, which he used to powerful effect in his celebrity series.

The initial work in the celebrity series was inspired by the suicide of Marilyn Monroe in 1962. *Marilyn Diptych* (FIG. **28-33**) contains fifty reproductions of a well-known publicity photo of the actress, twenty-five in a color panel and twenty-five in a black-and-white panel. For the color side, Warhol simplified the areas of Monroe's hair and face into stark color patches that suggest both a mask and the high-key look of a publicity poster. The images on the black-and-white side have been screened unevenly, with one row almost obliterated by smeared paint and another so faintly imprinted as to create a ghostly effect. Although it is hard not to try to read symbolic meaning into such manipulation, Warhol denied any such intention. Yet the artist remained fascinated all of his life with the idea of fame, especially its fragility and the way in which those in its limelight can suffer from a double life of public glamour and private sorrow. Warhol predicted that the age of mass media would enable everyone to become famous for fifteen minutes at some time in the future, and he became a renowned public figure himself, as did some of those who worked with him in his studio, the Factory.

Paralleling Warhol's use of the impersonality of mass-media techniques to heighten the effect of his work, California artist EDWARD RUSCHA (b. 1937) has utilized

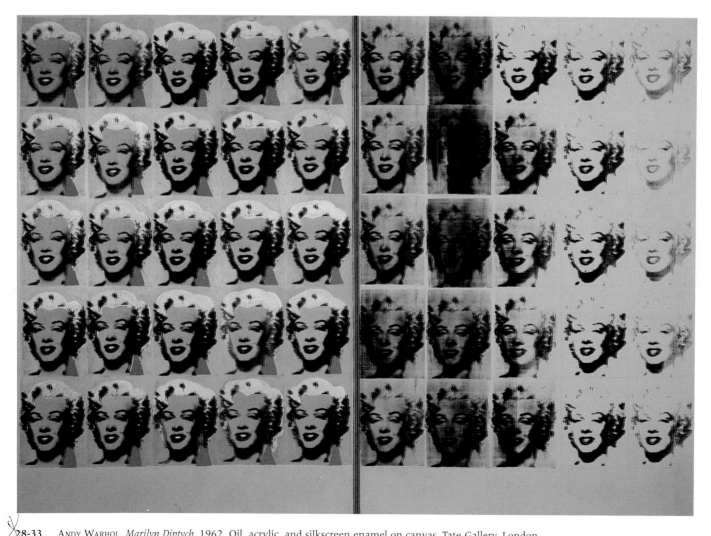

28-33   ANDY WARHOL, *Marilyn Diptych,* 1962. Oil, acrylic, and silkscreen enamel on canvas. Tate Gallery, London.

the impersonality of billboard advertising to provide an almost philosophical consideration of the arbitrariness and mystery of painted and printed representation. *Noise, Pencil, Broken Pencil, Cheap Western* (FIG. **28-34**) illustrates Ruscha's approach. At the extreme edge of this composition, the artist placed four things: a real pulp-western magazine, two illusionistically painted pencils, and letters· spelling the word *noise*. The title is a literal list of the painting's contents, but the artist also is playing with levels of representation and "reality" in the work. The main field of the canvas is a dark blue, which reads as infinite space. Against it float the pulp magazine and the two painted pencils. Part of each pencil disappears beyond the edge of the canvas, and the broken one can be seen either as in the process of breaking (with chips flying from the fracture) or as lying on a solid plane amid the flakes of its ruin. The word *noise* is similarly equivocal. Letters of the alphabet, as the Cubists knew, usually emphasize the flatness of the surface, but modern graphic design often energizes them into dynamic, three-dimensional shapes. Here, the word blares forth as a series of bright red letters against the face of a white, three-dimensional block drawn in steep perspective. Like Warhol's work, Ruscha's paintings exemplify American Pop Art; he takes as subjects the thematic clichés and appearance of advertising and popular culture and reshapes the way we see the commercially oriented world immediately around us.

28-34 EDWARD RUSCHA, *Noise, Pencil, Broken Pencil, Cheap Western*, 1963. Collage and painted canvas, 5'11¼" × 5'7". Virginia Museum of Fine Arts, Richmond (gift of Sydney and Frances Lewis).

Postmodernism: Art Since the 1970s

Readers will notice that in the course of narrating the stylistic changes of twentieth-century art we have been shifting from labeling it "Modern" to "Modernist"; and its ideology, the set of ideas by which it explains itself, we now call "Modernism." The complex of Modernist styles originating at the end of the nineteenth century is now identified as a distinct period; its art-historical development seems to be reaching a conclusion or, at least, a bewildered pause—perhaps a transition to something new. Modernist art and ideology are being revised and reacted against. The revisions and reaction go by the name Postmodernism.

In Chapter 27 we sorted out the Modernist styles and traced their development; in passing, we have touched on some of the ideas behind them. In simple summation, the most important axioms of Modernism will be examined here.

Modern art, according to Modernist ideology, is the consequence of a successful and continuing revolution led by an avant-garde of artists and critics who overthrew the Tradition that began in the Renaissance and exhausted itself in the nineteenth century. Their formal method is abstraction, by which images referring to objects in the world of sight are progressively distorted or eliminated, leaving the particular painting or sculpture to refer only to itself as a unique thing. The mission and triumph of the avant-garde is the "liberation" of the pictorial and sculptural object from any obligation to mean something other than itself. This liberation of the plastic media from all but self-reference makes for a "purification" of visual art, which had been corrupted by its bondage to subject matter drawn from myth, religion, history, or literature. The only "truth" for art is to be found not in something extraneous to it, like the forms of nature, but in its own materials, techniques, and forms. All reference otherwise is a lie; the truth of the object is simply *that,* and *what,* it is. The main avenue, up which the avant-garde march forever, is abstraction. The truly modern styles all branch from abstraction; all others run counter to it in anachronistic, retrograde reaction. Abstract art and its relatives constitute the only authentic art for our times; this art is always revolutionary and progressive—in a word, "modern." In the search for truth of statement, the Modern artist strives for the ever more abstractive reduction of the art object, until nothing is left but its minimal elements and the *process* of composing them.

This Modernist ideology, hardened into inflexible doctrine, has exercised considerable control over both artistic procedure and critical judgment. (We are reminded of the influence of the French Royal Academy in the time of Louis XIV; see Chapter 24.) Against this Modernism, Postmodernism seems to be in uncertain revolt.

The value and method of abstraction are still acknowledged, even as its absolute claims are being rejected; indeed, it seems still dominant at the very moment it is being sharply challenged. For the referential, mediating function of art—its age-old purpose—is being appealed to once more. The importance of content and meaning is being reaffirmed, and traditional subject matter is being reintroduced: report of optical fact, the human figure, the human environment, narrative, social commentary, imaginative transformation of the commonplace. Increasingly, the world of the photograph is yielding vast quantities of materials for the expression and representation of human experience. One thing is certain: artists, searching in all directions for fresh inspiration, feel that abstraction has reached its limit of invention, that it is a dead end, and that they wish to escape from a stern and doctrinaire formalism that has narrowed into academic precept. But thus far, the revisionism is incoherent; it has no central theme, no certain direction.

Meanwhile, the play of the art market, with its urgent demands for novelty, stimulates the feverish exploration for innovation at any cost and the rapid turnover of fads and fashions—adding to the confusion of the scene. Old paths are being sought out once more, and old modes are being restored with superficial changes. We find Neo-Primitivism, Neo-Symbolism, Neo-Abstract Expressionism, Neo-Formalism, Neo-Social Realism, even Neo-Impressionism—and hybrids of all of them. Side-by-side with these persist elements of Pop, Op, Minimalism, Conceptualism, Photo Realism and the like.

It is difficult for us to find a way through what, at present, seems to be both the recapitulation and the deconstruction of Modernism to locate firm evidence of an emerging style that could replace it. Nevertheless, some description can be made of the present situation by pointing to a small selection of artists whose work is Postmodern by date, if not by agreed-upon definition. Many characteristics of art after 1945 remain in evidence: the pieces are very large; the broad, monochrome areas of Color-Field painting persist; the pictorial and sculptural media are often combined; experiment with both Formalistic and Expressionistic modes goes on.

Superrealism

While avant-garde Modernism was dominant, many artists still continued to paint realistically, even though they were not admitted by the critic gatekeepers to the orthodox, formalist school. Pop Art gave new respectability to realism, if it dealt with the Pop environment; we have seen this Pop realism in the work of David Hockney (FIG. 28-27). A group of artists we call *Superrealists* expanded the iconography of Pop in both sculpture and painting by making images of persons and things with scrupulous, photographic fidelity to optical fact. Superrealism reproduces in minute and unsparing detail the commonplace facts and artifacts to which Pop Art called attention.

DUANE HANSON (b. 1925) casts three-dimensional figures that are startling illusions of actual—or possible—persons,

and at the same time comments satirically on the banality of our consumer culture. His *Supermarket Shopper* (FIG. **28-35**) is an unflattering portrait of an obese female bulging out of her undersized sweater and miniskirt, her hair in curlers, her cigarette dangling jauntily. She is utterly indifferent to her appearance, to the significance of her overflowing shopping cart, and to the fact that for an observer she could be a living allegory of the deadly sin of gluttony. She is more than an instantly identifiable Pop presence; she is a symbol of "the excess sugar of a diabetic culture."

Hanson's *Shopper,* though totally factual in representation, points to a broader meaning beyond itself, a social and a moral meaning. More often the Superrealist aims to render fact alone. This is the case with PHILIP PEARLSTEIN (b. 1924), whose masterful restatement of the Renaissance theme of the nude (FIG. 22-61) in *Female Model on Platform Rocker* (FIG. **28-36**) is entirely acceptable in the permissive atmosphere of Postmodernism. The figure is casually placed within a composition that crops the head and part of a leg, a device, familiar in Impressionism (FIGS. 26-58 and 26-59), that marks the range of the visual field at an instant when the observer enters the space of the subject. This enhances the effect of immediacy and of the flexibility of the unposed. Also, it may simply indicate the arbitrary limits of the artist's intention and the decision that the composition is satisfactorily complete as is. The play of studio spotlights creates numerous high and reflected lights and luminous shadows that suggest a sun-drenched space and the bright

28-35 DUANE HANSON, *Supermarket Shopper,* 1970. Polyester resin and fiberglass, polychromed in oil, with clothing, steel cart, groceries, life size. Nachfolgeinstitut, Neue Galerie, Sammlung Ludwig, Aachen, Germany.

28-36 Philip Pearlstein, *Female Model on Platform Rocker,* 1977-78. Oil on canvas, approx. 6′ × 8′. The Brooklyn Museum (Woodward, Healy, Ramsay, and other funds).

tonality of the model's body. The glossy surface and smooth finish, without visible brushwork, are photographic, as are the minutely recorded, fugitive shadow patterns that give the sense of a moment in time. Though the subject is traditional, its uncompromisingly realistic presentation is in accord with the value Postmodernism places on what is in front of us now—at this time and no other.

Along with the traditional theme of the nude, Postmodernism accepts the theme of the portrait, which had been disintegrated by Cubist analysis in the early twentieth century (FIG. 27-30). A self-portrait (FIG. **28-37**) by Chuck Close (b. 1940) confronts us with the blown-up features of a photograph on an enormous scale, demanding attention to the least detail of a quite ordinary face as it might be picked out of the crowd. We could scarcely find a more forceful expression of the Postmodern theory of egalitarianism, which obviously the artist shares; just as all persons are or should be equal, so everything in our environment has equivalent artistic value, and one face is as good as another for the artist's purpose. That purpose is to proclaim the commonness of the face, no matter whose. Thus, the magnified mirror image of a face, frontal and rigid as a police mugshot, without makeup, all blemishes recorded by harsh lighting, becomes a masklike icon of human ordinariness. It confronts us with the Postmodern paradox of the importance of the unimportant in a faceless culture that is full of faces. The photographic technique and effect reinforce the message as we receive it daily through the media.

The theme of landscape also returns with Postmodernism, though the Superrealists for the most part choose—appropriately enough—the "landscape" shaped by the popular culture, the city. The city views of Richard Estes (b. 1936) are sharply excised visual sectors that make inventory of the Pop items of which they are collections. In *Nedick's* (FIG. **28-38**), he gives us the image of a familiar fast-food restaurant and fountain with all the optical fidelity of a photograph taken through a pristine plate-glass window with the latest-model camera. The glassy essence of the urban scene, with its myriad reflecting and refracting surfaces, and flat, sparkling patterns of light and dark, confuses the eye as to what is light or surface, shadow or substance; the artist "multiplies variety in a wilderness of mirrors." In Estes's pictures the human figure is eliminated, so that we can contemplate the Pop artifacts in isolation, as if they were exhibited in a gallery setting. We are invited to concentrate on the information they give about the popular culture; the human presence among them is superfluous.

Estes takes numerous photographs of the sites that interest him, with different angles and exposures. He develops these and arranges them in a collage, shifting the photographs about until he finds a promising combination. After integrating them into a compositional unity, eliminating, correcting, and reworking details, Estes renders the images carefully in the oil medium.

The value of the photograph as auxiliary to painting has long been appreciated by artists. In the Postmodern restoration of realism it plays a leading part, sometimes, as we shall see, in painting that is "realistic" in appearance, but far from realistic in subject and content (FIG. 28-53).

Happenings, Performance Art, Conceptual Art

The permissiveness of Postmodernism has encouraged so wide a latitude of experiment and invention that we can move from Superrealism, which after all is grounded in a long tradition of representational painting, to art events that go well beyond the limits of the media of painting or of sculpture. There we encounter activities like Happenings—or Performance, which Happenings anticipate—where the physical work is replaced by the movements, gestures, and sounds of persons communicating with an audience whose members may or may not be participants in the event. Whatever the message conveyed in this kind of discourse, the medium is essentially that of the drama or the dance and deliberately avoids the fixity and definition of the painted or sculpted work. It is calculated to convey a sense of the randomness, impermanence, and contradiction of contemporary life, and often of its absurdity.

A precursor of Performance artists, Allan Kaprow (b. 1927), was instrumental in developing the art form for which he is best known—the *Happening*. Influenced heavily by his knowledge of art history, his study of music composition with John Cage, and a belief that Jackson Pollock's actions in making a painting were more important than the

28-37 Chuck Close, *Self-Portrait*, 1968. Acrylic on canvas, 9′ × 7′. Walker Art Center, Minneapolis.

28-38 Richard Estes, *Nedick's*, 1969–1970. Oil, 4′ × 5′6″. Collection of Mrs. Donald Pritzker.

painting itself, Kaprow's Happenings were loosely structured performances presented in varied public indoor and outdoor sites. Generally, they combined ordinary and pseudo-ritualistic actions. Kaprow's first Happening took place in 1958 at the Reuben Gallery in New York City, and the art form soon spread throughout the United States, Europe, and Japan. Happenings occurred in lofts and studios, in department stores, in auditoriums, on college campuses, and on private estates. Usually Happenings lacked specific plots, but they always contained a collage of actions that suggested a narrative or ritual reflecting the contemporary human condition. Their mood often recalled that of Dada and Futurist performances or events, but rather than taking the role of onlookers, as had the viewers of the earlier works, the audience at a Happening often participated fully in the action.

Performance art usually centers on a single actor/artist, who signalizes and symbolizes some special message through body motion and gesture, declamatory speech, costume and accessories, or stage properties and sound.

The social and political concerns of German artist JOSEPH BEUYS (1921–1986), were directed at the whole condition of modern human beings, especially those in Western developed nations. Beuys strongly believed that the spiritual nature of humans is expressed through creativity and ability, in vigorous opposition to the negative forces of what he called "the principle of Auschwitz." After narrowly escaping death as a Nazi pilot shot down in a remote part of the Crimea, Beuys dedicated himself to working for the future of humanity. First, he studied natural science but left that field to take up sculpture. He wanted to make a new kind of sculptural object that would include "Thinking Forms: how we mould our thoughts . . . Spoken Forms: how we shape our thoughts into words . . . [and] Social Sculpture: how we mould and shape the world in which we live."

Believing that all art belongs to the same sphere of human activity, no matter what medium the creator uses, Beuys accepted sculptors, musicians, and writers into his classes at the Düsseldorf Art Academy. Beuys's objects and installations seem to be connected with mysterious rites. Charismatic in person, he also created one-person performances in which his stylized actions evoked a sense of mystery, profound human meaning, and sacred ritual. *Iphigenia/Titus Andronicus* (FIG. **28-39**) was developed from an invitation to create modern performances of two historic theatrical masterpieces—Goethe's *Iphigenia* and Shakespeare's *Titus Andronicus*. Beuys contrived a divided setting, incorporating a spotlighted, tethered white horse standing on a metal plate that resounded every time the horse moved. In this dual setting, the artist read from each play and performed mysterious actions using objects positioned near a microphone, including a pair of cymbals, which he clashed when necessary to quiet boisterous behavior in the audience. In such performance, Beuys considered himself as a shaman carrying out actions to help

28-39 JOSEPH BEUYS, *Iphigenia/Titus Andronicus*, 1969. Performance art.

"revolutionize human thought," so that each human being could become a truly free and creative person. As was fitting for the actions of a shaman, most of Beuys's performances were not public events, but were witnessed only by small audiences. Through the effect on the viewers, and even more, through the efficacy of the acts themselves, the artist believed that the world could be changed.

Conceptual art communicates message and meaning through the more permanent media, two dimensional or three dimensional or both, often in combination with printed text. The primary purpose is to get across an idea, a concept, with whatever visual means are available. In this respect, Conceptual art resembles advertising art and display, which no doubt have strongly influenced it. Since the 1960s, a preoccupation with the primacy of language in human experience has persuaded philosophers, psychologists, sociologists, and anthropologists, as well as critics of literature and the arts, that all cultural artifacts are "texts," from which can be read the value structures of a society and the systems of interrelation that make it function. The conceptual artist fastens upon the "textuality" of the work first. It does not have to *represent* anything; it *says* something. It is simply the *idea* physically presented; the sign of the broken cigarette says "No smoking!"

The Conceptual artist SYLVIA PLIMACK MANGOLD (b. 1938) demonstrates the paradox of illusionistic painting by presenting the paradox; she shows us how the eye is fooled by fooling the eye. *Two Exact Rules on Dark and Light Floor* (FIG. **28-40**) is a meticulously rendered painting of a section of black-and-white tiled floor, seen from above in subtle perspective, sloping away from us. This illusion is canceled wittily and abruptly by what appear to be two identical metal "Exact Rule" yardstick fragments fastened to the surface of the canvas. These rulers suggest the precise measuring tools used to create the straight perspective lines in the painting; at the same time, they appear to lie outside the illusionistic painted space, on our side of the painted canvas surface. However, the realization that the top one is actually smaller in scale than the bottom one, making it seem to rest farther back in space, reveals that each ruler is in fact a painted replica of a ruler. Mangold has toyed here with contradictory visual cues and the paradoxes they ·establish about the relationship between illusion and reality.

Perhaps the boldest of all Conceptual art is that produced by the British team of GILBERT AND GEORGE (Gilbert Proesch, b. 1943 in Italy, and George Passmore, b. 1942 in England), who question every aspect of traditional art and assert that they are "living sculpture" and that their entire "proper English lives" together contributed to their art. Adopting the respectable, middle-class "uniform" of conservatively cut suits, shirts, and ties, Gilbert and George have given varied forms to the ongoing artwork of their lives together through postcard collages, drawings, and most recently, giant "sculpture" pieces in which collages of hand-colored photographs use a personal iconography to express the pair's response to their life in London's working-class East End and to their experiences with religion, sex, and the

28-40 SYLVIA PLIMACK MANGOLD, *Two Exact Rules on Dark and Light Floor,* 1975. Acrylic on canvas, 24″ × 30″. Brooke Alexander, Inc.

vision of the volatile connection between youthful vigor and the life of the urban poor in contemporary England. *We Are* (FIG. **28-41**) is typical of their large-scale photo-sculptures, with the sculptors themselves standing frontally, in identical poses a short distance from one another, their legs spread apart and their hands clasped. Their forms are lit from each side, throwing a band of shadow down the middle of their faces. George wears glasses; Gilbert does not. The paired figures alternate, one pair above the other in increasing size at each stage. Each set fits neatly between the spread legs of the next largest to form two hieratic human columns that frame the central "window," in which we see a confused scene of road repair and an enigmatic

28-41 GILBERT AND GEORGE, *We Are,* 1985. Panel photo-piece, . 7′ 10⁷/₈″ × 6′ 7¹/₈″. Robert Miller Gallery.

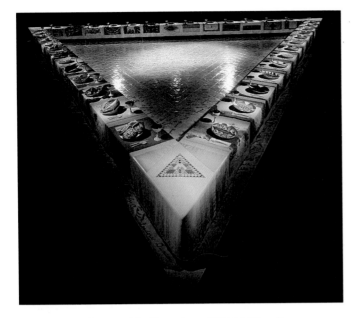

28-42 JUDY CHICAGO, *The Dinner Party,* 1979 Multimedia, 48′ × 48′ × 48′ installed.

disembodied head, lit from the bottom to create eerie highlights and shadows. Sprouting from the figure-columns like wings are a pair of giant hands with palms facing us and fingers spread wide, The clear, formal arrangement, the bold transparent colors, and the stiff black outlines and grid lines suggest devotional stained-glass windows, but the images convey a sense of ritual bestowed upon the whole messy range of everyday life, echoing the simple declarative words of the title—"We are."

Conceptualism can bring into focus a single idea to advertise the social and political concerns of special-interest groups, as it does in Feminist art. The idea is that women have long been subordinate in a patriarchal society and now demand equal power with men. The Conceptual approach in art can here be the most effective one in expression and promotion of Feminist activism.

In the 1970s, the Feminist movement focused the attention of women on their history and their place in society. In art, the feminist movement was given shape by two women—Judy Chicago and Miriam Schapiro—under the auspices of the Feminist Art Program, which they founded at the California Institute of the Arts in Valencia, California. As part of this program, teachers and students joined to create projects like *Womanhouse,* for which they completely converted an abandoned house in Los Angeles in 1972 into a suite of "environments," each based on a different aspect of women's lives and fantasies.

In her own work, JUDY CHICAGO (born Judy Cohen in 1939) wanted to educate viewers about women's role in history and the fine arts. Inspired early in her career by the work of Hepworth (FIG. 27-55), O'Keeffe (FIG. 27-57), and Nevelson (FIG. 28-17), Chicago developed a personal painting style that consciously included abstract floral vaginal images. In the early 1970s, Chicago became interested in the expressive possibilities of china painting, and she began planning an ambitious piece, *The Dinner Party* (FIG. **28-42**), which used "crafts" techniques traditionally practiced by women (china painting and stitchery) to depict the roles played by women throughout history. The work was originally conceived as a Feminist "Last Supper" attended by thirteen women (the "honored guests"), in a selection embodying both the positive and negative meanings associated with the number thirteen (the number or persons present at the Christian Last Supper and the number of witches in a coven). Research uncovered so many worthy women that Chicago expanded the number of guests threefold to thirty-nine and placed them around a triangular table 48 feet long on a side that symbolizes both the traditional sign for woman and for the "Goddess." The piece's assembly was carried out by a team of nearly four hundred workers under Chicago's supervision and to her designs.

28-43 MIRIAM SCHAPIRO, *Anatomy of a Kimono* (section) 1976. Fabric and acrylic on canvas, 6′8″ × 11′11″. Collection of Bruno Bishofberger, Zurich.

The Dinner Party rests on a white tile floor inscribed with the names of 999 additional "women of achievement" to signify that the accomplishments of the thirty-nine honored guests rest on a foundation laid by the other women. Among the "invited" women at the table are Georgia O'Keeffe, the Egyptian pharaoh Hatshepsut, the British writer Virginia Woolf, the Native American guide Sacajawea, and the American suffragist Susan B. Anthony. Each guest was given a place setting with identical eating utensils and goblet. All of the guests also have an individual, oversized, porcelain plate and a long place mat or table runner filled with symbols that reflect significant facts about their lives. The plates range from simple concave shapes with china-painted designs to dishes from which sculptured three-dimensional designs almost seem to be trying to fly away. Each table runner is worked with a combination of traditional needlework techniques, including needlepoint, embroidery, crochet, beading, patchwork, and appliqué. The rigorous arrangement of *The Dinner Party* and its sacramental qualities draw visitors in and let them experience the importance of forgotten details in the history of women.

Pursuing a somewhat different path than that undertaken by Chicago, MIRIAM SCHAPIRO (b. 1923) tries in her work to rouse her viewers to a new appreciation of the beauty in humble materials and techniques used by women artists throughout art. Schapiro was in the midst of a thriving career as a Hard-Edge Abstract Formalist painter when she moved to California, co-founded the Feminist Art Program, and became fascinated with the hidden metaphors for womanhood she now saw in her Abstract Formalist paintings. Intrigued by the materials she had used to create a doll's house for her part in *Womanhouse,* Schapiro began to make huge sewn collages (which she called *femmages*), assembled from fabrics, quilts, buttons, sequins, lace trim, and rickrack collected at antique shows and fairs. *Anatomy of a Kimono* (FIG. **28-43**) is one of a series of monumental femmages based on the patterns of Japanese kimonos, fans, and robes. This vast composition repeats the kimono shape in a sumptuous array of fabric fragments.

Schapiro is not alone in finding magic in pattern, and her femmages were part of a movement in the 1970s called *Pattern and Decoration Painting,* because its members were dedicated to making decorative pattern the content of their works. However, Schapiro's femmages are not solely *Formalist Abstractions,* as are many other Pattern and Decorations works; instead, her materials carry references to the whole history of women's crafts and needlework and call attention to the often complex abstract compositions in handwork hitherto considered beyond the arena of fine art. Viewing her works encourages observers to rethink traditional ideas about media, subject matter, and the artistic energies of women.

Creating a broader social awareness, often with a Feminist twist, is the goal of the American artist BARBARA KRUGER (b. 1945), whose best-known subject has been the manipulation of attitudes by modern mass media. Kruger's serious art career began with fiber sculpture inspired by the works of Magdalena Abakanowicz (FIG. 28-46) but she soon began creating pieces that drew on her early training and work as a graphic designer for the magazine *Mademoiselle.* Mature works, like *Untitled (Your Gaze Hits the Side of My Face)* (FIG. **28-44**), play with media layout techniques used in the mass media to sell consumer goods. But Kruger's huge word-and-photograph collages (often 4 by 6 feet in size) express the cultural attitudes embedded in commercial advertising. In *Untitled (Your Gaze Hits the Side of My Face),* she has targeted Feminist concerns by overlaying a ready-made photograph of the head of a classically beautiful female sculpture with a vertical row of text composed of seven words selected by the artist. They cannot be taken in with a single glance. Reading them is a staccato exercise, with an overlaid cumulative quality that delays understanding and intensifies the meaning (rather like reading a series of roadside billboards from a speeding car). The message in Kruger's piece reflects the interest of contemporary Feminist theorists in the way that much of Western art has been constructed to present female beauty for the enjoyment of a "male gaze."

28-44 BARBARA KRUGER, *Untitled (Your Gaze Hits the Side of My Face),* 1985–1987. Collage.

The "male gaze" is painfully deflected in the work of CINDY SHERMAN (b. 1954), who initially established her reputation as a photographer of self-portraits, but more recently has been grouping and photographing plastic anatomical dummies and body parts, such as would be used in medical school instruction. These bear initial resemblance to dismembered female corpses gruesomely exposed (FIG. **28-45**). The impact is not lessened by closer inspection. The placement and emphasis of the plastic forms communicate unmistakably Sherman's indignation at the exploitation of women's bodies in pornography. Her ironic, pseudopornographic posing of the figure stimulates not an erotic response, but one of horror and revulsion, a harsh lesson for the voyeuristic and prurient male. The concept clearly determines the expressive distortions of the forms, and Sherman's art can be classified as both Conceptualist and Expressionist, with more than a touch of Surrealism.

New Expressionism

The Modernist dialogue between Purist Formalism on the one hand, and Expressionism—Abstract or Figural—on the other hand, continues in these Postmodern decades. Formalism, which had seemed to bring art to an end by excluding all reference to anything but itself and the process of making it, has been reacted against by artists who wish to preserve communication through expressive representation of the external world, the world as we ordinarily perceive it. This is the world full of conflict and stress, trial and anxiety, that is the stage upon which, since the beginning of humanity, has been enacted a drama recorded in the history of art as we have reviewed it. Artists who still wish to record any of the thousands of scenes and predicaments that make up the human drama, and to express their emotional responses and their own participation in it, can resort to the age-old imagery of the human figure and to a variety of media to make their point.

The stoic, everyday toughness of the human spirit is the subject of figurative works by the Polish fiber artist MAGDALENA ABAKANOWICZ (b. 1930). A leader in the recent exploration in sculpture of the expressive powers of weaving techniques, Abakanowicz gained fame with experimental, freestanding pieces in both abstract and figurative modes. For Abakanowicz, fiber materials are deeply symbolic:

> I see fiber as the basic element constructing the organic world on our planet, as the greatest mystery of our environment. It is from fiber that all living organisms are built—the tissues of plants and ourselves. . . . Fabric is our covering and our attire. Made with our hands, it is a record of our souls.*

To all of her work, this artist brings the experiences of her early life as a member of an aristocratic family disturbed

*In Mary Jane Jacob, *Magdalena Abakanowicz* (New York: Abbeville, 1982), p. 94.

28-45 CINDY SHERMAN, untitled, 1992. Color photograph, 45″ × 68″.

by the dislocations of World War II and its aftermath. Initially attracted to weaving as a medium that would adapt well to being used in the small space she had available for a studio, Abakanowicz gradually developed huge abstract hangings, called *Abakans*, which suggest organic spaces as well as giant pieces of clothing. She returned to a smaller scale with works based on human forms—*Heads*, *Seated Figures*, and *Backs*—multiplying each type for exhibition in groups as symbols for the individual in society, lost in the crowd yet retaining some distinctiveness. This impression is especially powerful in an installation of *Backs* (FIG. **28-46**), each piece of which was made by pressing layers of natural organic fibers into plaster mold depicting the slumping shoulders, back, and arms of a figure of indeterminate sex, which rests legless directly on the floor. The repeated pose of the figures in Backs suggests meditation, submission, and anticipation. Although made from a single mold, the figures achieve a touching sense of individuality by means of the slightly different posture each assumed as the material

28-46 MAGDALENA ABAKANOWICZ, artist with *Backs,* at the Musée d'Art Moderne de la Ville de Paris, 1982.

dried and as a result of the different pattern of fiber texture imprinting on each.

The rough-cut power in the work of a trained painter like the American artist LEON GOLUB (b. 1923) can express a seemingly brutal vision of contemporary life, through a sophisticated reading of the raw data of the news media. In the 1960s, Golub painted mythic battles between crudely rendered groups of naked giants inspired by ancient Hellenistic reliefs. The work for which he is best known, however, deals with the violent events of our own time— the implied narratives we have learned to read in news photos of anonymous characters participating in the brutalities of street violence, terrorism, and torture. Paintings in Golub's *Assassins* and *Mercenaries* series suggest not specific stories, but a condition of being. As the artist has said:

> Through media we are under constant, invasive bombardment of images—from all over—and we often have to take evasive action to avoid discomforting recognitions. . . . The work [of art] should have an edge, veering between what is visually and cognitively acceptable and what might stretch these limits as we encounter or try to visualize the real products of the uses of power.*

Mercenaries (IV) (FIG. **28-47**) is a huge canvas that represents a mysterious tableau in which three mercenaries (tough, freelance, military professionals willing to fight, for

*In Richard Marshall and Robert Mapplethorpe, *50 New York Artists* (San Francisco: Chronicle Books, 1986), pp. 48–49.

28-47 LEON GOLUB, *Mercenaries (IV)* 1980. Acrylic on linen, 10' × 19'2". The Saatchi Collection, London.

a price, for any political cause) cluster at the far side of the canvas, in the process of reacting with tense physical gestures to something being said by one of the two other mercenaries standing at the far left. The dark uniforms and skin tones of the four black fighters flatten their figures and make them stand out against the searing, flat red background, which seems to push their forms forward toward the picture plane and becomes an echoing void in the space between the two groups. The menacing figures loom over the viewer. Golub has painted them as if our eyes are level with their knees, placing the men so close to the front that their feet are cut off by the painting's lower edge; we are trapped with them in the painting's compressed space. Our gaze is drawn repeatedly to the scarred, light tones of the white leader's skin and to the weapons, modeled with shadow and gleaming highlights, which contrast with the harshly scraped, flattened surfaces of the figures. The feeling of peril confronts the viewer mercilessly; we become one with all the victims who have been caught by the political battles of our age.

History and myth as bearers of the troubled experience of humanity inspired the German artist Anselm Kiefer (b. 1945) to develop a personal iconography that refers to his country's mythic past, its more turbulent twentieth-century history, and the vital participation of human beings in all of that history. Kiefer noted that he paints in layers: "Each layer shines through and so I work according to a kind of 'inverted archeological' principle." In later works, the layers may be tangible (crusted with paint and materials like straw and wood), as well as metal. Kiefer's earlier paintings, like *Vater, Sohn, Heiliger Geist (Father, Son, Holy Ghost)*, (FIG. **28-48**), are large and relatively thinly painted, but they contain multiple strands of the symbols and themes important to him. In *Vater, Sohn, Heiliger Geist*, three sketchy chairs sit in a bare, wood-paneled room patterned after the attic studio in an old schoolhouse used by Kiefer at the time this work was painted. Hovering within each seat is a briskly burning flame. Below the scene in the room in a second, slightly larger canvas, containing a view through densely packed rows of almost dead tree trunks that stand in a deserted forest. Steep perspective and carefully rendered wood grain transform the attic room into a vast hall. Rough, handwritten words—"*Vater, Sohn, hl.* [for *heiliger*] *Geist*"—scrawled across the top of the forest scene identify the three chairs/flames as members of the traditional Christian Trinity: "Father, Son, Holy Ghost." The forest scene, the bare room, the flames, and the words all call up associations in the viewer's mind. Memory joins with the viewing of the canvas in the present to create layers of experience for the observer. The jump between the canvases, the sketchy forms, and the unevenly brushed paint surfaces all heighten the feeling of flux related to Kiefer's belief that humans function at full power only when connected with the ongoing processes of history: "History for me is like the burning of coal, it is like a material. History is a warehouse of energy." The energy is produced, like that

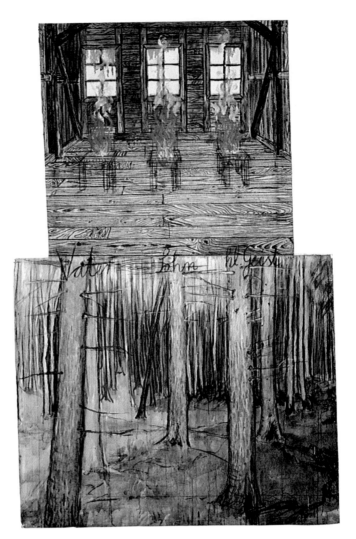

28-48   Anselm Kiefer, *Vater, Sohn, Heiliger Geist (Father, Son, Holy Ghost)*, 1973. Oil, charcoal, synthetic resin on burlap, 9'6" × 6'2¼". Courtesy Marian Goodman Gallery, New York.

created when flammable materials burn, by an "exchange of materials." In this painting, the wooden walls, chairs, and trees are all potential sources of energy for the spirit flames that govern the future.

The figural scarcely appears in the art of Julian Schnabel (b. 1951), which is in effect a forceful restatement of the premises of Abstract Expressionism; although, in executing his works, Schnabel experiments widely with materials and supports—from fragmented china plates bonded to wood, to paint on velvet and tarpaulin. These emphatic physical presences, and the interest in experiment with materials, smacks also of the concerns of the Formalists. *The Walk Home* (FIG. **28-49**) is a vast mosaic of broken crockery painted and glued to a wooden support. Superficially, it recalls the dripping method of Pollock (FIG. 28-4) and the black slashes of Kline (28-5). The thickly impacted, jagged surface deflects the artist's hand, so that an element of the random and automatic enters the painting process. The thick, mosaic-like texture is an amalgamation of media, bringing together painting, mosaic, and low-relief sculpture. In effect, Schnabel reclaims older media for his expressionistic method, which considerably amplifies his bold and distinctive statement.

Schnabel's mixing of media raises the area upon which the artist works into a shallow projection. The mixed-media pieces of the American artist JUDY PFAFF (b. 1946) expand it

into the full three dimensions of a fragile, tentlike architecture. Works like *Rock/Paper/Scissors* (FIG. **28-50**) have the quality of an exploded Abstract Expressionist painting that has taken over a whole interior space. The title refers to a children's game that is played with hand-symbols for "rock," "paper," and "scissors," in which each symbol is able to "conquer" one of the others; chance alone creates a tied

28-49   JULIAN SCHNABEL, *The Walk Home*, 1984–1985. Oil, plates, copper, bronze, fiberglass, and bondo on wood, 9'3" × 19'4". Eli Broad Family Foundation and the Pace Gallery, New York.

28-50   JUDY PFAFF, *Rock/Paper/Scissors*, 1982. Mixed media, temporary installation, Albright-Knox Art Gallery, Buffalo, New York.

score between the players. Pfaff's *Rock/Paper/Scissors,* thus, might be considered a metaphor for the Cold War or for the complex social maneuvering of modern urban life. The exuberant, overall clutter of Pfaff's installation counteracts such a reading, however, by evoking such subjects as the sights of a New Year's Eve party or of a giant kaleidoscope. Yet, above all, the forms in *Rock/Paper/Scissors,* as well as in all of Pfaff's installation works, remain resolutely nonobjective. The main "subject" of *Rock/Paper/Scissors* (like that in a painting by Pollock) is the variety and impact of the materials, shapes, and colors, a brilliant reflection of Pfaff's stated interest "in opening up the language of sculpture as far and as wide as [she] can . . . in trying to include all things that are permissible in painting but absent in sculpture."

Installations like *Rock/Paper/Scissors* are planned to activate a certain space temporarily and to vanish at the end of the special occasion or exhibition that gave them birth. Even the works that Pfaff creates for specific museum collections occupy so much space that they are designed to be taken down and stored when the space is needed for other exhibitions. Each time a Pfaff work is in place, however, it provides the viewer with an exuberant and festive sight, like a modern-day descendant of a Matisse painting expanded to a scale that can enfold the viewer in its joyous midst.

Continuing Formalism

Some critics call the abstract/non-objective art of the 1980s and 1990s *Post-minimal,* noting the readiness of Formalist artists to refer through their work to a world beyond the work itself. Recent Formalism, though it excludes imagery,

produces work that permits, even encourages, associative responses on the part of the viewer. An elegant example of this approach is a mural painting by the Canadian-born artist DOROTHEA ROCKBURNE (b. 1934), who is willing to give more than a hint about how the work is to be understood. *Sensor III* (FIG. **28-51**) is a visual metaphor that spans space and time. The width of the wall itself is the here and now; the openness of the wall area refers back in time to the latitude, color, and tone of ancient Roman wall spaces and their slender, ornamental motifs (FIGS. 7-18 to 7-25). Upon this foundation meaning, other levels of meaning can be raised. The artist herself suggests that the physics of light can be visualized in the long, looping and intertwining trajectories of subatomic particles, as they curve and spin in electromagnetic fields. Three simple colors fill the main regions—blue and turquoise in the wing panels and a golden yellow in the center. These are repeatedly crossed by a graceful, "celestial," tracery of light and dark blue and maroon lines. The control of the forms, colors, and especially the long, sinuous lines requires the utmost in technical discipline. This is one with the management of the themes, which include yet another metaphor, that of cosmic harmony. The reverential, even religious overtones to be felt in this work compose a hymn of affirmation at a time when the culture is corroded with cynicism and the environment tormented by bad sound.

A corresponding reassurance of value is to be found in the sculpture of the African-American artist MARTIN PURYEAR (b. 1941), who provides a stimulating new union of traditional media and technique with abstract form. One of his recent works, *Thicket* (FIG. **28-52**), is not a representation of the thing the title names, a "thicket," a dense growth of

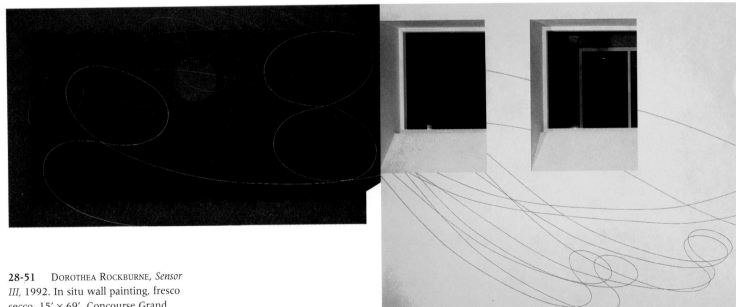

28-51 DOROTHEA ROCKBURNE, *Sensor III,* 1992. In situ wall painting, fresco secco, 15' × 69'. Concourse Grand Stairway, Hilton Hotel, San Jose, California.

intertwined and twisted roots and branches, like a hedgerow. It is a singular construction made of a criss-crossed interlocking of sturdy struts doweled together, a completely independent object which, unlike a minimalist piece, insistently refers beyond itself and stimulates our imaginations to reach for what it refers to. Thus, *Thicket* could be the section of a complex bracing system, a cage-like puzzle that could be taken apart and reassembled, or a three-dimensional model of a problem in logic. Its indeterminacy of meaning resonates with the contemporary Deconstructionist theory of the indeterminacy of all language. On the other hand, the method of construction, unlike the meaning of the constructed, is perfectly determinate and visible and belongs to the ancient crafts of carpentry, joinery, cabinetmaking, and shipbuilding. Unaffected by the still current and invidious distinction between art and craft, Puryear reveals in the cutting, joining, and finish of his wooden material the mastery achieved by a slow, painstaking, and experienced practice. After more than a century, he reasserts the moral as well as esthetic value of the unique, hand-crafted objects in a world of mass-produced and machined production.

Puryear acknowledges the many sources of his inspiration, especially the African. As he recently observed:

> I acknowledge and revere the power of ceremonial objects from Africa, but what I mostly own are objects of use—things not deliberately charged for ritual or magical purpose, yet nevertheless transcending function to achieve enormous visual power in their own right. I'm especially interested in the West African textile traditions of the Ewe and Asante peoples. Their strip-woven cloths have a strong

28-52 MARTIN PURYEAR, *Thicket*, 1990. Basswood and cypress, 67″ × 62″ × 17″. The Seattle Art Museum, gift of Agnes Gund.

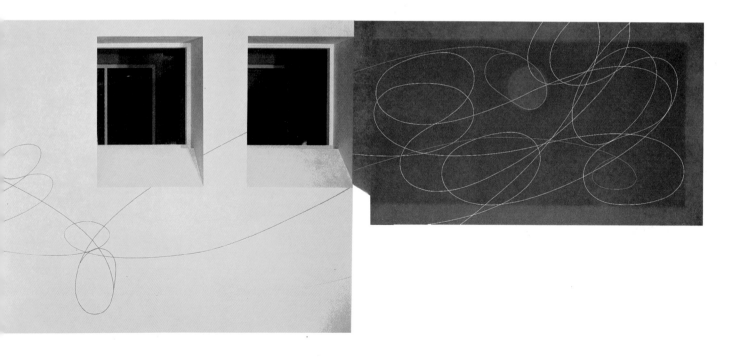

repetitive pattern, as insistent as a drumbeat, combined with startling and constant inventions within the regular rhythm, like good jazz.*

Pictorialism

A Postmodern approach we might call *Pictorialism* sets aside Modernist Formalism, Expressionism, and Realism in favor of picture-making, where idea and subject matter determine what the picture will look like. Taking a cue from conceptualism, the artist begins with the *idea,* and the picture follows; unlike conceptualism, the end result is a framed and painted picture with figures in pictorial space, not an array of letters, symbols, images, and artifacts. Formalism, Expressionism, and conventional Realism *begin* with a "real world out there," no matter how far the artists analytically reduce it, emotionally express it, or faithfully copy its appearance. Pictorialism *begins* with ideas that already organize the "real world" into images corresponding with the artist's concepts and not with a presumed "reality." This is the very reverse of Modernist Realism (culminating in Superrealism), which began with Courbet and Manet, for whom realism meant the recording of "reality" in terms of the present modern age and environment; the whole iconography of Christian or Classical Tradition was rejected, along with its forms. Courbet bids the Tradition goodbye with: "Show me an angel, and I'll paint one!" The new pictorial artist replies: "I *know* what an angel is, *I've seen it in pictures,* and I'll paint you one, never inquiring whether or not it is *real.*" In this respect, the pictorial artist is like the masters of religious art worldwide, who made images of all sorts of beings without having seen them except in other pictures, mosaics, or statues. The difference is that, for these masters, angels and other beings, natural or supernatural, were a part of their reality, while for the Postmodern Pictorialist it makes no difference whether such beings exist. The Pictorialist does not draw images by direct observation of the real world, but from images already made of it by the photograph and reproduced by the billions in the visual media. Thus, such artists make their pictures out of other pictures, which, taken together, make an immense, vernacular iconography of modern life. As writers compose their texts with a vocabulary of conventionally meaningful words, pictorial artists compose their pictures with a vocabulary of conventional images perfectly familiar to the public and as readable as the written text in a magazine.

As a matter of fact, what is real for people today is what has been certified in the photo-record, so much so that they can identify, by familiarity with that record, what is and what happens in the real world. Photo-images determine seeing by identifying the seen; the image becomes the reality, as it does for those dwelling in Plato's cave. Spectators reporting some striking event exclaim: "It was just like on TV!" In political publicity it is not the reality of the candidate that counts, it's the "image" of the candidate constructed by public-relations teams.

Thus, the Pictorial artist is content with the image, and says nothing about any presumed reality behind or beyond it. The perpetual interplay and shifting relationships of vernacular images are the concern and sole subject. Combinations, arrangements, and rearrangements of images, in limitless variety of order and context, are used to express a limitless variety of ideas and meanings. Pictorialism reinvents the picture by restoring it solely to image making, without requiring it to represent "reality" in the Modernist or any other sense.

The primacy of idea and image over representation of "reality," and the indeterminacy of meaning, which characterize the pictorial approach, harmonize with two Postmodern phenomena: the critical philosophy of *deconstruction,* and the "post-photographic" device of digital image-making. The effects of these cast doubts respectively on the determinacy of meaning in language and the reliability of the photo-record of reality. Meaning, truth, and reality are not fixed, but indeterminate, depending upon ever-changing convention and relativity of viewpoint. The meanings of texts, as well as the words in them, change. The intentions of their authors are never certain; or are, in fact, caused by, or expressions of, forces and factors of a sociopolitical kind of which the authors are unaware. Photographs are easily altered, so their reliability as evidence can be challenged. Digital-imaging by computer can produce convincing images of *anything* and in endless combinations. The "reality" from which Modernism took its departure—and even its image—is now dissolving.

With this in mind we can approach the pictorial art of MARK TANSEY (b. 1949), prepared to some degree for the ambiguities and paradoxes that crowd his deceptively photographic paintings. The photographic look is not surprising, since Tansey works from photographs—not his own, like the Superrealist's—rather than directly from nature. He possesses a vast archive of photo images, reproductions cut from newspapers, magazines, and castoff publications of all sorts, which supplies thousands of images for his researches. These he can sort, arrange, combine, alter to fit a revolving, adjustable catalogue of ideas, which he has constructed to serve as a kind of generator of iconography. The matching of idea with an appropriate image is the gist of his pictorial method.

His *Innocent Eye Test* (FIG. **28-53**) illustrates some characteristic features of that method. The "innocent eye," a term first used by John Ruskin, the eminent nineteenth-century English art critic ,* referred to the ideal condition for view-

---

*"African Art-Life," *Art News,* May, 1994, p. 96.

*In Roger Shattuck, *The Innocent Eye* (New York: Washington Square Press, 1960, 1986), p. 415. This study is a brilliant early attack on Modernism.

28-53 MARK TANSEY, *Innocent Eye Test*, 1981. Oil on canvas, 6'6" × 10'. The Metropolitan Museum of Art, New York, promised gift of Charles Cowles.

ing art, much as a child who might see art without preconception for what it actually is; or a blind man, who sees the world for the first time. For Modernism, this would mean seeing art essentially as line, shape, and color, without the falsifications of representation. The "eye test" is something familiar to all of us. For a truly "innocent eye" to be tested we might resort to a non-human subject—in this case, a cow.

Next, we have the scene of the test, a gallery in a museum. Museum curators, professing the ideal of "innocent eye" viewing, arrange an experiment, drawing aside a curtain* to confront the animal with a painting of a cow and a young bull, an actual work by the seventeenth-century Dutch painter Paulus Potter. Farther along the wall there is a Monet painting of a haystack, another item that might be of interest to the cow. (Significantly, the two paintings are not in the same museum; for the Pictorialist, that is not

*Tansey alludes here to a famous story related by the ancient author Pliny. An artist, vying with his competitors, painted a curtain so illusionistically on a wall that when visitors to his studio saw it, they asked him to draw it aside.

important.) The group at the left, one of them prudently armed with a mop, is coolly objective and confident; assistants at the right adjust the Potter canvas and take notes. The whole scene is completely implausible, yet convincingly recorded as if it had taken place. It is a picture of what never happened, faithfully rendered in every detail.

The figures are painted in monotone, the tonality associated with old rotogravure reproductions in newspapers. Tansey paints monochromatically not only to stress the photographic origins of his images, but to bring out texture, which he considers the trace of touch and of time. Color would minimize this, and for the artist's purpose it is not essential.

Photography almost from its beginning had attempted to achieve the pictorial effects of painting by printing multiple negatives on a single paper. H. P. Robinson (1830–1901) produced many of these "composition pictures," and wrote a popular work that went through many editions, *Pictorial Effect in Photography* (1869); we have seen a relatively simple example of photo-pictorialism in the work of Gertrude Käsebier (FIG. 26-54). The motion picture, with its

28-54 JEFF WALL, *Vampire's Picnic*, 1991. Cibachrome transparency, fluorescent light, and display case, 7'6" × 11'. Collection of the National Gallery of Canada, Ottawa.

succession of single images in time, replaced in public attention the spatial art of the composition picture. The Canadian artist JEFF WALL (b. 1946) returns to it, using today's greatly advanced reproductive technology. He records his complex arrangements of figures on a large transparency, which he exhibits in a fluorescent-lighted display box. The artist can alter the composition as he pleases, to suit his concept. Again, as with Tansey's work, the idea comes first, though Wall works with light rather than with the brush. The flexibility of the medium allows him the freedom to bring together disparate and paradoxical images and settings and to develop a personal iconography, much as Tansey's pictorial method does. Art-historically as well as studio trained, Wall composes in line with the Tradition, though in no sense is he bound by it. For example, his *Vampire's Picnic* (FIG. **28-54**) could call to mind Giovanni Bellini's *Feast of the Gods* (FIG. 22-57), though Wall's picture is far away in time and culture and radically different in context and spirit. His context is the contemporary suburb and its social peculiarities and predicaments, which he here presents ironically and rather shockingly. What at first appears to be the end of a yard party of affluent suburbanites in various stages of substance abuse, at closer inspection is a collection of casualties of vampire cannibalism, most of them passed out and pros-trate. They are dressed in modish contemporary fashion, though the central figure is that of a nude old man orating drunkenly. Here and there are splashes of blood, notably on the white dress of the demure hostess at the left. The pas-toral Bacchanals of Venetian painting, that take place in verdant groves, are transformed here into a sinister

suburban atrocity occurring among dead trees before a dilapidated shack. Pictorialism, whether in painting or pho-tography, gives the artist ample opportunity to compose intricate and arresting views, both real and unreal, into contemporary life. With the new resources of image-making, the still picture has virtues of its own which can match, or even rival, those of the temporal arts of movies, television, and video.

Computer Art and Video Art

While some new technologies were revolutionizing the way artists could work with pictorial space, other technolo-gies, especially that of computer graphics, were transform-ing the ways in which artists could create and manipulate illusionistic three-dimensional forms. Computer graphics uses light to make images, and like photography, can incorporate specially recorded camera images. Computer graphics allows the artist to work with wholly invented forms, as a painter can.

The medium of computer graphics was developed during the 1960s and 1970s and opened up new possibilities for both abstract and figurative art. Computer graphics oper-ates by means of electronic programs that divide the surface of the cathode-ray tube (CRT) of the computer monitor into a grid of tiny boxes called "picture elements" (pixels), which individually can be addressed electronically to create a design, much as knitting or weaving patterns use a grid-ded matrix as a guide for making a design in fabric. Once created, parts of a computer-graphic design can be changed quickly through the operation of an electronic program,

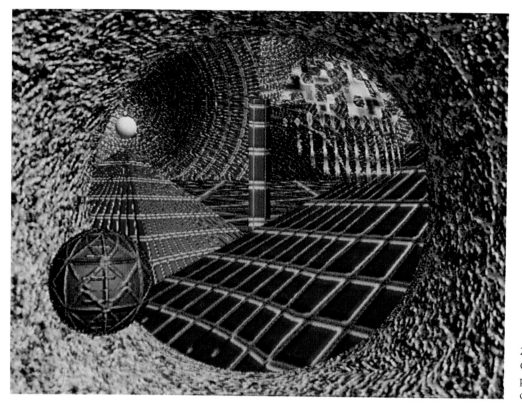

28-55 DAVID EM, *Nora,* 1979. Computer-generated color photograph, 17″ × 23″. Private collection.

allowing the artist to revise or duplicate shapes in the design and to manipulate, at will, the color, texture, size, number, and position of any desired detail. A computer-graphic picture is displayed in luminous color on the cathode-ray tube; the effect suggests a view into a vast world that exists inside the tube.

One of the best-known artists working in this electronic painting mode is DAVID EM (b. 1952), who uses what he terms *computer imaging* to fashion fantastic imaginary landscapes that have an eerily believable existence within the "window" of the computer monitor. As former artist-in-residence at the California Institute of Technology's Jet Propulsion Laboratory, Em created brilliantly colored scenes of alien worlds using the laboratory's advanced computer graphic equipment. He also had access to software programs developed to create computer-graphic simulations of NASA missions in outer space. Creating images with the computer allows Em great flexibility in manipulating simple geometric shapes—shrinking or enlarging them, stretching or reversing them, repeating them, adding texture to their surfaces, and creating the illusion of light and shadow. In images like *Nora* (FIG. **28-55**), Em created futuristic geometric versions of Surrealistic dreamscapes in which the forms seem familiar and strange at the same time. The illusion of space in these works is immensely vivid and seductive. It almost seems as if one could wander through the tubelike foreground "frame" and up the inclined foreground plane or hop aboard the hovering globe at the lower left for a journey through the strange patterns and textures of this mysterious labyrinthine setting.

SONIA LANDY SHERIDAN (b. 1925) is one of the most inventive artists to combine, in a single computer-graphic work, images made by an electronic camera and those drawn by hand. Sheridan finds the computer-graphic medium to be a powerful means of providing psychological and conceptual insights into the human experience. From her days studying French and art in grade school, Sheridan has been fascinated with the ways in which both verbal and visual languages work. Although she trained as a painter and printmaker, she holds a strong belief (like Moholy-Nagy) that art and science belong together. In the mid-1960s, her interest led her to initiate a series of collaborations with research scientists to explore artistic uses for technological media. She brought this approach to the Generative Systems Program, which she founded at the School of the Art Institute of Chicago in 1970 to help students investigate the artistic potential of technological tools. Sheridan's personal work includes art created with diffraction gratings,* and a variety of copy machines, early fax machines, and computer graphics. *Drawing in Time: My New Black Book*

---

*Diffraction gratings, used mainly in scientific experimentation, are sheets of glass, plastic, or metal that are inscribed with grids whose lines diffract any light directed at the gridded surface and break this light up into its color spectra so that the rays may be accurately measured.

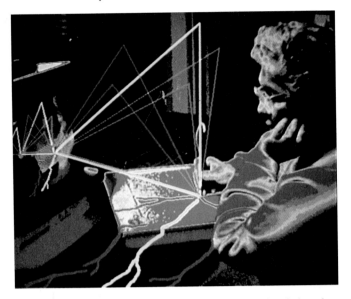

28-56 Sonia Landy Sheridan, *Drawing in Time: My New Black Book No. 2*, 1982. Easel (John Dunn Software), Cromemco Z-2D hardware, 5¼" computer disc and in multiple dimensions as photographs. Artist's collection.

No. 2 (FIG. **28-56**) is one of the works done with Easel, the versatile computer-graphics program designed by one of Sheridan's ex-students, John Dunn, to run on a computer. On this small desktop system, as on the more complex system used by Em, the artist has immense control over manipulation of color, size, shape, and texture. Sheridan can mix hand-drawn shapes with those captured by a video camera or use each kind of image alone.

Initially, the medium of video was available only in commercial television studios and only occasionally accessible to artists. With the invention of relatively inexpensive portable video-recording equipment and electronic devices that allow the manipulation of the recorded video material, artists began to explore in earnest the particularly expressive possibilities of this new medium. In its basic form, video technology uses a special motion-picture camera to capture images from the world and to translate them into electronic data that can be displayed on a video monitor or television screen. Video pictures resemble photographs in the amount of detail they contain, but like computer graphics, a video image is displayed as a series of points of light on a grid, giving the impression of soft focus. A viewer looking at television or video art is not aware of the surface of the monitor; instead, fulfilling the Renaissance ideal, we concentrate on the image and look through the glass surface, as through a window, into the "space" beyond. Video images combine the realism of photography with the sense that the subjects are moving in "real time" in a deep space "inside" the monitor.

When video introduced the possibility of doing such manipulation in real-time, artists like the Korean-born,

New York-based videographer Nam June Paik (b. 1932) were eager to work with the medium. Inspired by the ideas of American composer John Cage and after studying music performance, art history, and Eastern philosophy in Korea and Japan, Paik worked with electronic music in Germany in the late 1950s before turning to performances using modified television sets. In 1965, relocated to New York City, Paik acquired the first inexpensive video recorder sold in Manhattan (the Sony Porta-Pak) and immediately recorded everything he saw out the window of his taxi on the return trip to his studio downtown. Stints as artist-in-residence at television stations WGBH in Boston and WNET in New York allowed Paik to experiment with the most advanced broadcast video technology, and a grant permitted him to collaborate with the gifted Japanese engineer-inventor Shuya Abe in the development of a video synthesizer—a special instrument that allows the artist to manipulate and change the electronic video information in various ways, causing images or parts of images to stretch, shrink, change color, or break up. Using the synthesizer, the artist also can layer images, inset one image into another, or merge images from various cameras with those from videotape recorders to make a single, visual, kaleidoscopic "time-collage." This kind of compositional freedom allowed Paik to combine his interests in the ideas of Cage, painting, music, Eastern philosophy, global politics for survival, humanized technology, and cybernetics.

Paik's best-known video work, *Global Groove* (FIG. **28-57**), combines in quick succession fragmented sequences of female tap dancers, poet Allen Ginsberg reading his work, a performance in which cellist Charlotte Moorman uses a man's back as her instrument, Pepsi commercials from Japanese television, Korean drummers, and a shot of the Living Theatre group performing a controversial piece called *Paradise Now*. Commissioned originally to

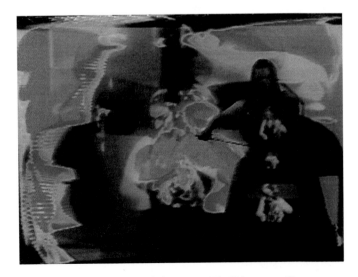

28-57 Nam June Paik, *Global Groove*, 1973. Videotape still.

be broadcast over United Nations satellite, the cascade of imagery in *Global Groove* was intended to give viewers a glimpse of the rich worldwide television menu Paik had predicted would be ours in the future.

Paik called his videotape works *physical music* and said that his musical background made him able to understand time better than video artists trained in painting or sculpture. As critic Jonathan Price reported, Paik considered the effect on the viewer of his kind of video narrative to be similar to both the style of writing in James Joyce's *Finnegan's Wake* and to "a classical Taoist way of meditation; by becoming aware of everything going on in the present, you discover eternity right now."* James Joyce developed his writing style to express the layering of thought, feeling, and experience of the exterior physical world made apparent to us through the work of psychologists and physical scientists. Nam June Paik used the methods of new technology to extend this kind of composition into the visual world.

Memorial and Documentary Art

It is appropriate that before we consider the cosmopolitan architecture of the later twentieth century we conclude our history of the sculptural and pictorial media with two works that celebrate the enduring virtues of courage and self-sacrifice. One of them, the Vietnam Memorial in Washington, D.C. (FIG. **28-58**) is made of enduring stone

*Jonathan Price, *Video Visions: A Medium Discovers Itself* (New York: New American Library, 1977), pp. 128–129.

28-58   MAYA YING LIN, Vietnam Veterans Memorial, Washington, D.C., 1981–1983. Black Granite, each wing 246′ long.

the other, a telephoto snapshot of an incident from the Tiananmen uprising (FIG. 28-59) in Beijing, June 1989, is a fragile transparency of a newsprint reproduction. The two are at opposite ends of the span of media from which the visual arts are made: granite, as ancient as Egypt and Mesopotamia, sensitized film, as recent almost as the present day.

The ancient Greeks were accustomed to carving memorial inscriptions on stone stelae, many as epitaphs for soldiers who had died in battle. The most famous of these epitaphs was written by the poet Simonides, to be inscribed in honor of the Lacedemonians (Spartans) who had fallen at Thermopylae (480 B.C.) during the Persian wars. For its brief, simple, and touching eloquence it has no rival:

Stranger, go tell the Lacedemonians that we lie here in obedience to their command.

Thermopylae was a defeat for the Greeks, as Vietnam was for the Americans, but the spirit of dedication is much the same, and all the more poignant. It has not been dimmed by time.*

An immense, dedicatory stela, the Vietnam Memorial, the work of MAYA YING LIN (b. 1960), is located on the Mall in Washington D.C. It consists of a long wall constructed of seventy slabs of highly polished granite (FIG. 28-58). The wall bends in the middle to form two triangular wings that widen as they descend into the earth from a shallow height at the outer corners toward a depth of over 100 feet at their joint. Carved into the face of the wall are the names of all of the Americans who died in the Vietnam conflict, listed chronologically in the order of their deaths. The slabs are numbered and directories containing alphabetical lists of the names are placed at the entrances to the site so visitors can find the memorial location of a loved one. Clearly, Lin understands the resonant power of a name to signify a person. Those who lost relatives and friends visit the wall to linger over a particular name, making paper rubbings of it and leaving photographs, mementos, and flowers at its base as tributes. But all who come are filled with the enormity of the loss as the columns of names unroll as one walks along the adjacent path. Unlike the usual monument, the names carved here do not vanish into the comfort of a list ordered by rank or alphabetical placement. Each life lost in Vietnam has equal importance, equal value. Furthermore, as visitors move along the wall, its highly polished surface acts as a mirror, joining viewers with those who died. Rare is the visitor to this monument who is not drawn into silent meditation on the immeasurable cost of human life lost in the Vietnam conflict. The power of the wall to heal has

*The modern poet A. E. Housman expands the theme of dead youth at the time of World War I:

Here dead we lie, because we did not choose
To live, and shame the land from which we sprung.
Life, to be sure, is nothing much to lose,
But young men think it is, and we were young.

been so great that replicas of the panels have been made and sent on tour throughout the country; at each stop this traveling monument attracts crowds who come to make connections with the silent rows of names.*

The year 1989 was one of the most fateful in the history of the twentieth century. It saw the collapse of the communist regimes of Central Europe and of the Soviet Union. But it also saw a massive suppression of dissent in Communist China, centered in Tiananmen Square in the heart of the capital city of Beijing. Here, an encampment of thousands of students and workers, who defied the authorities for several weeks, demanding liberty, civil rights, and an end of the autocratic communist system, was broken up by the tank-led government army. On June 4 and 5, hundreds were killed and injured; later, thousands were rounded up and imprisoned. The media brought the whole world to the scene, and broadcast the cries of the unarmed, desperate young people crouching under the merciless attack:

> Butchers! Executioners! Murderers! . . . They are murdering us! We are the common people! We had no weapons! We came in peace. . . . The People's Liberation Army has trained its guns on the people. . . . See the blood of the Chinese people on the streets of Beijing! . . . Tell all the world this is the true face of our country!"

Of all the pictures transmitted by the media—television, movies, and the printed press—one stands out, an awe-inspiring image of defiant heroism (FIG. **28-59**). An unknown man singly confronts a whole column of heavy tanks on their advance against his comrades. (A student grasps a foreign reporter by the arm: "For thousands of years the world and the people of China thought the Chinese weak—weak of body, weak of spirit. Now we are showing the world and our own people that we are brave!")

This picture, like the Vietnam Wall, exemplifies that ultimate and supreme exertion of the human spirit, always rare, and especially so in times of danger. While both works carry powerful moral messages that are unmistakable, they are also reminders that at the end of the twentieth century we may have to summon such moral force again.

---

*When Lin's winning design was first announced, one group of Vietnam veterans felt that it was not a suitable memorial for their lost comrades. They lobbied successfully for an additional monument of three naturalistically modeled bronze fighting men, representing the branches of the military service that were most active in the conflict. These figures stand on the Mall in a nearby grove of trees and look toward Lin's memorial. More recently, the nurses who served in Vietnam won the addition of a fourth figure, representing the women who lost their lives. Curiously, these figures draw fewer visitors than the wall, perhaps because they are more in the tradition of monuments to be looked at, whereas Lin's memorial invites its visitors to engage in active participation with its information and its symbolism.

28-59 *Tiananmen Square, June 6, 1989,* Associated Press Photo.

MODERNISM AND POSTMODERNISM IN ARCHITECTURE

Just as painters and sculptors in the earlier twentieth century wanted to purify art of Traditional representation and to reduce it by abstraction to its elementary forms and functions, so the architects wanted to "purify" architecture of ornament and the trappings of the Traditional styles in order to reveal the unadorned structure and function of a building. Both were concerned with a formalism that made a virtue of simplicity, favoring geometrical shape and composition. At first, rectilinear and cubic formalism prevailed, and then the curvilinear. We have described the Abstract Formalism of painting and sculpture as Geometric and Organic; Frank Lloyd Wright described his own architecture as "Organic." The two kinds of formalism balance each other during the earlier century, and the esthetic kinship of Modernist art and architecture is seen in the Bauhaus, De Stijl (Rietveld-Mondrian), Purism (Le Corbusier-Leger), and Constructivism (Malevich, Tatlin, Gabo). Modernism is challenged in the later century by Pop Art and Postmodernism in painting and sculpture and by Postmodernist Deconstruction in architecture. Postmodernism rejects the rigid formalism of the Modernist in favor of a permissive theory that encourages free formal invention and experiment.

At mid-century the Modernist balance of Geometrical and Organic Formalism is still prominent. Architects with long careers behind them, like Frank Lloyd Wright and Le Corbusier, invested many of their buildings during the post-1940 period with powerful organic sculptural qualities.

The long, incredibly productive career of Frank Lloyd Wright ended with his design for the Solomon R.

28-60   FRANK LLOYD WRIGHT, Solomon R. Guggenheim Museum, New York, 1943–1959 (exterior view from the north).

Guggenheim Museum (FIGS. **28-60** and **28-61**), which was built in New York City between 1943 and 1959. Here, using reinforced concrete almost as a sculptor might use resilient clay, Wright designed a structure inspired by the spiral of a snail's shell.

Wright had introduced curves and circles into some of his plans in the 1930s, and as the architectural historian Peter Blake noted: "The spiral was the next logical step; it is the circle brought into the third and fourth dimensions."* Inside the building, the shape of the shell expands toward the top, and a winding interior ramp spirals to connect the gallery bays, which are illuminated by a strip of skylight embedded in the museum's outer wall. Visitors can stroll up the ramp or be brought by elevator to the top of the building and proceed down the gently inclined walkway, viewing the works of art displayed along the way. Thick walls and the solid organic shape give the building the sense of turning in on itself, with the long viewing area opening onto a 90-foot central well of space that seems a sheltered environment secure from the bustling city outside.

The startling forms of Le Corbusier's Notre Dame du Haut (FIG. **28-62**), completed in 1955 at Ronchamp, France, challenge the viewer in their fusion of architecture and sculpture in a single expression. This small chapel on a

*Peter Blake, *Frank Lloyd Wright* (Hammondsworth, Middlesex: Penguin Books, 1960), p. 115.

28-61   Interior of the Solomon R. Guggenheim Museum.

28-62 Le Corbusier, Notre
Dame du Haut, Ronchamp,
France, 1950–1955.

28-63 Interior of Notre
Dame du Haut.

pilgrimage site in the Vosges mountains was designed to replace a building destroyed in World War II. The monumental impression of Notre Dame du Haut seen from afar is somewhat deceptive. Although one massive exterior wall contains a pulpit facing a spacious outdoor area for large-scale, open-air services on holy days, the interior holds at most two hundred people. The intimate scale, stark, heavy walls, and mysterious illumination (jewel tones cast from the deeply recessed stained-glass windows) give this space (FIG. **28-63**) an aura reminiscent of a sacred cave or a medieval monastery.

The structure of Notre Dame du Haut may look free-form to the untrained eye, but it is actually based, like the medieval cathedral, on an underlying mathematical system. The fabric was formed from a frame of steel and metal mesh, which was sprayed with concrete and painted white, except for two interior private chapel niches with colored walls, and the roof, which was left unpainted to darken naturally with the passage of time. The quality of mystery in the interior space is intensified by the way the roof is elevated above the walls on a series of nearly invisible blocks, which has the effect of making the roof appear to float freely above the sanctuary. Le Corbusier's preliminary sketches for the building indicate that he linked the design with the shape of praying hands, the wings of a dove (representing both peace and the Holy Spirit), and the prow of a ship (reminding us that the Latin word used for the main gathering place in Christian churches is *nave*—meaning "ship"). The artist envisioned that in these powerful sculptural solids and voids, human beings could find new values—new interpretations of their sacred beliefs and of their natural environment.

The opera house in Sydney, Australia (FIG. **28-64**), the design of the Danish architect JOERN UTZON (b. 1918) is a bold composition of organic forms on a colossal scale. Utzon worked briefly with Frank Lloyd Wright at Taliesin, and the style of the Sydney Opera House resonates distantly with the essay in sculpturesque curvature that is the Guggenheim Museum. Two clusters of immense concrete shells, elliptical paraboloids, rise from massive platforms; Utzon was especially taken with the platform architecture of Meso-America, which he regarded as "the backbone of architectural composition" (FIGS. 17-6 and 17-15). Recalling at first the ogival shapes of Gothic vaults, the shells also suggest both the buoyancy of the wings of sea birds and the sails of the tall ships that brought European settlers to Australia in the eighteenth and nineteenth centuries. These architectural metaphors are appropriate to the sea-girt harbor that surrounds Bennelong Point, upon the bedrock foundations of which the building is raised. The matching of the structure with its site and atmosphere is a special objective of Organic architectural practice.

The building is not only a monument of civic pride, but functions as the cultural center of the city. In addition to

28-64 JOERN UTZON, Sydney Opera House, 1959–1972. Reinforced concrete, height of highest shell 200'.

the opera auditorium that gives it its name, the building houses auxiliary halls and rooms for concerts, the performing arts, motion pictures, lectures, art exhibitions, conventions, and all the "high" and mass cultural life that define the recreational scope of the modern metropolis.

The structure was long in building. Utzon's design was controversial, and from the beginning required constructional technology that was not yet available to meet the requirements of its daring innovations. Utzon left the project in 1966, and it was completed by Australian architects in 1972. Today it is accepted as a defining symbol of the city of Sydney, as emblematic of the ever-increasing democratization of culture, and as a world-renowned achievement of the Organic mode in Modernist formalism.

For Geometrical Formalism, in contrast with Organic, the "purest" form created in post–World War II architecture is undoubtedly the rectilinear glass and bronze tower in Manhattan (FIG. **28-65**) designed for the Seagram Company by Mies van der Rohe and PHILIP JOHNSON (b. 1906). By the time this structure was built (1956–1958), the concrete, steel, and glass towers of the Functional International Style, which had been pioneered in the works of Louis Sullivan (FIG. 26-97) and in Mies van der Rohe's own model for glass skyscrapers (FIG. 27-12), had become a familiar sight in cities all over the world. Appealing in its structural logic and clarity, the style, although often vulgarized, was easily emulated and quickly became the norm for postwar, commercial high-rise buildings. The Seagram Building still stands as a perfect statement of the best aspects of the Functional International Style. The architects deliberately designed the building as a thin shaft, leaving the front quarter of the structure's mid-town site as an open pedestrian plaza. The tower appears to rise from the pavement

28-65   LUDWIG MIES VAN DER ROHE and PHILIP JOHNSON, Seagram Building, New York, 1956–1958.

28-66   PHILIP JOHNSON and JOHN BURGEE with Simmons Architects; associated architects, a model of the AT&T Building, New York, 1978–1984.

on stilts; even the recessed lobby is surrounded by glass walls. The bronze metal and the gray glass windows give the building a richness found in few of its neighbors. Every detail, inside and out, was carefully planned to create an elegant whole; even the interior and exterior lighting were planned to make the edifice an effective sight by day or by night.

Out of the social and cultural turmoil of the 1960s came new trends in art and art criticism that, as we have seen, challenged the authority of Modernism. One of the most startling shifts of style in twentieth-century architecture was made by Philip Johnson himself, who changed over—abruptly, it would seem—from the severe, Geometric Formalism of the Seagram Building to the classicizing transformation of it in his AT&T (American Telegraph and Telephone Co.) Tower in New York (FIG. **28-66**). The latter

structure has powerfully helped to turn architectural taste and practice away from Modernism to Postmodernism—away from Organic "concrete sculpture" and the Geometric "glass box" to elaborate shapes, motifs, and silhouettes freely adapted from historical styles. Historicism and eclecticism of style, abominated by Modernism, again becomes acceptable and routine.

The 660-foot-high slab of the AT&T Tower, sheathed in granite, reduces the window space to some thirty percent of the building—so much for the ideal of the tower of glass! The design of its exterior elevation is classically tri-partite, having an arcaded base and arched portal, a tall, shaftlike body articulated by slender mullions, and a crowning pediment broken by an *orbiculum* (a disc-like opening). The arrangement is a reference to the base-column-entablature system of ancient Greek structures and Renaissance elevations (FIGS. 5-47, 21-39, 21-40). More specifically, the pediment, indented by the circular space, resembles the crown of a typical, eighteenth-century Chippendale high chest of drawers, familiar as "colonial" in any furniture store. It rises among the monotonously flat-topped glass towers of the New York skyline as an ironic rebuke to the rigid uniformity of Modernist architecture; Modernist critics were not at all amused, and controversy raged over the legitimacy and integrity of the design. The AT&T Building, however, seems to be related in its originality and bold departure from convention to the much earlier, and now respected, Chrysler Building (FIG. 27-7).

Philip Johnson at first endorsed, then disapproved of, a building that rode considerably farther on the wave of Postmodernism than did his own AT&T tower. The Portland (Oregon) Building (FIG. **28-67**), the work of MICHAEL GRAVES (b. 1934), of much smaller scale, reasserts the wall and its horizontality against the verticality of the tall, fenestrated shaft. Graves favors the solidity and stability of the square, which he makes the main body of his composition (and echoes in the windows), resting upon a wider base, and carrying a set-back penthouse crown. Two paired facades are opened by narrow vertical windows tying together seven stories. On one pair of facades, these support capital-like, large hoods; on the other, a frieze of stylized Baroque roundels tied by bands. A huge, painted keystone motif joins five upper levels on one facade pair, and painted surfaces further define the base, body, and penthouse levels. The assertion of the wall, the miniature square windows, and the painted polychromy define the surfaces as preeminently mural and carry a rather complex

symbolic program. Neither wall, nor color painting, nor symbolic reference could be welcome to the Modernist purist. These features, taken together, raised even a greater storm of adverse criticism than that which greeted the Sydney Opera House and the AT&T Tower. Graves's Portland Building was denounced variously as "an enlarged jukebox," an "oversized Christmas package," a "marzipan monstrosity," a "histrionic masquerade," and a kind of "pop surrealism." Yet others approvingly noted its Classical references as constituting a "symbolic temple," and praised the building as a courageous architectural adventure. City officials and citizens joined architectural critics in commending or blaming the architect. At present, the Portland Building, like the AT&T Tower, has come to be regarded as an early marker of Postmodernist innovation.

It is important to note here the widening participation of the public in the judging of new architecture as an indication of an increasing awareness of the new, popular uses of the urban environment, There is the feeling among many that building design is not the worse for borrowing from the lively, if more or less garish, bric-a-brac of pop culture. The night-lit dazzle of entertainment sites like Las Vegas, or the carnival colors, costumes and fantasy of theme park props, might just as well serve as inspiration for the designers of civic architecture. The Portland Building could seem to many observers a vindication of architectural populism against the pretension of Modernist elitism. Pop art and architecture together could assert the validity of popular taste and the relativity of contemporary esthetic values, whether or not they lead—as apparently they are leading—to a Postmodern redefinition of the arts altogether.

28-67 MICHAEL GRAVES, The Portland Building, Portland, Oregon, 1980.

28-68   RICHARD ROGERS and RENZO PIANO, Georges Pompidou National Center of Art and Culture (the "Beaubourg"), Paris, 1977.

To meet an internationally popular demand for culture as entertainment, an architecture of the people and for the people rises, with or without approval of official criticism. Almost any design approach may be tried. In Paris, the short-lived partnership of British architect RICHARD ROGERS (b. 1933) and Italian architect RENZO PIANO (b. 1937) resulted in the use of motifs and techniques from ordinary industrial buildings in the design for the Georges Pompidou National Center of Art and Culture, known popularly as the "Beaubourg" (FIG. **28-68**). The anatomy of this six-level building, which opened in 1977, is fully exposed, rather like an updated version of the Crystal Palace (FIG. 26-94). However, in the case of the Pompidou Center, the structure's "metabolism" is also visible. Pipes, ducts, tubes, and corridors are coded in color according to function (red for the movement of people; green, for water; blue, for air-conditioning; yellow, for electricity), much as in a sophisticated factory. Critics who deplore the Beaubourg's vernacular qualities have pointed out that its exposed entrails require excessive maintenance to protect them from the elements and disparagingly refer to the complex as a "cultural supermarket." Nevertheless, the building has been popular with people since it opened. The flexible interior spaces and the colorful "archigraphic" revelation of the structural body provide a festive environment for the great crowds that flow through the building, enjoying its art galleries, industrial design center, library, science and music centers, conference rooms, research and archival facilities, movie theaters, rest areas, and restaurant (which looks down and through the building to the terraces outside). The sloping plaza in front of the main entrance has become part of the local scene. This "square" is filled with peddlers, street performers, Parisians, and tourists at almost all hours of the day and night. The kind of secular activity that once

took place in the open spaces in front of cathedral entrances interestingly has shifted here to a center for culture and popular entertainment—perhaps the things shared now by the largest number of people. As a former director of the Beaubourg, K. G. Pontus-Hultén said:

> If the hallowed, cult-like calm of the traditional museum has been lost, so much the better. . . . We are moving toward a society where art will play a great role, which is why this museum is open to disciplines that were once excluded by museums and which is why it is open to the largest possible public.*

To accommodate the "largest possible public," and to make room for its ever-expanding collections, the directors of the National Gallery in Washington called for an eastern addition to the handsome Jeffersonian Neoclassical building by J. R. Pope, designed and built between 1937 and 1941. The award-winning design for the East Building was the work of I. M. (IEOH MING) PEI (b. 1917), an American architect born in China. Pei was the pupil of Walter Gropius, master of the Bauhaus (FIG. 27-8), when Gropius was teaching at Harvard in the forties. Pei's Geometrical Formalism and mastery of the "hard materials"—stone, concrete, steel, and glass—show the direct influence of Gropius; but his complex, dramatic grouping of units, and his close attention to the "context" of the building (that is, its physical and architectural environment) are distinctively his own.

For example, the new East Building was designed to complement the older West Building (FIG. **28-69**) by aligning with its axis (the two structures are connected by an underground, moving walkway) and by wearing a facing of the same pink Tennessee marble that adorns the older structure. In Pei's design, the awkward building site became a virtue made of necessity, somewhat as the Campidoglio (FIG. 22-29) had in the hands of Michelangelo. Pei ingeniously maximized his use of the difficult site by bisecting

*K. G. Pontus-Hultén, *Architectural Record* (February 1978) p. 103.

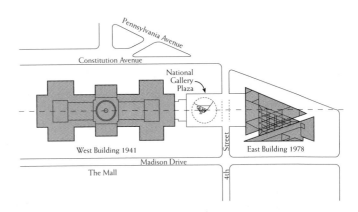

28-69   **Plan showing the relationship of the East Building of the National Gallery, designed by I. M. PEI, to the earlier West Building.**

and as the large public area necessary to accommodate crowds of people for the special events that are a part of the museum's role in the Washington social scene. The glass tetrahedra of the skylight (FIG. **28-70**), with their complex tracery of frames, seem to change, multiply, and create shapes as one moves. The experience of fluid space and transformation of form is intensified by the Alexander Calder mobile that hangs majestically above the courtyard. Bridges, escalators, and stairways casually connect the central space with numerous irregularly shaped and randomly placed galleries, which range in size from those intimate enough to show very small pictures to those ample enough to accommodate the largest canvases of the New York School. The whole structure is a marvel of coherence and order and a triumph of craftsmanship down to the least detail.

The transparency of the structural scheme of the Beaubourg, with all the visually exciting display of its colored vitals; and the Geometric Formalism and ingenious complexity of the East Building; are in striking contrast with the simplicity and serenity of the Kimbell Art Museum in Fort Worth, Texas (FIG. **28-71**). Its designer, LOUIS KAHN (1901–1974), was one of America's foremost architects, and the Kimbell Art Museum is an American masterpiece, worthy of a great tradition. Working within Modernism's conceptual frame of functional and structural integrity, exclusion of ornament, and truth to materials, Kahn remained unattached to any school or movement, producing a style markedly his own. What distinguishes his architecture is the special attention he gives to volume and light

28-70   I. M. PEI, interior of the East Building of the National Gallery, showing mobile by ALEXANDER CALDER.

the trapezoid into a large isosceles triangle and a smaller right triangle. The larger triangle, with its diamond-shaped towers, provides exhibition space; the smaller, with its dramatic wedge shape (the walls meet in a sharp nineteen-degree angle), provides space for art-historical research. The two are unified by a vast, faceted skylight 80 feet above a spacious courtyard six levels high. The great central courtyard was designed both as an internal reception "piazza"

28-71   LOUIS KAHN, Kimbell Art Museum, Fort Worth, Texas, 1972 (view from the southwest).

28-72 Gallery interior, Kimbell Art Museum, Fort Worth.

as its primary elements. He thought of his buildings as groups or "societies" of rooms, subtly illuminated by daylight. The Kimbell Art Museum is an association of long "rooms" or halls, barrel vaulted, (FIG. **28-72**), with light admitted from garden spaces, and from slit-like apertures above the arcs of the vaults. The cool diffusion of the light, and the curvature of the enclosing vaults, shape the space of the halls into almost tangible substance.

The elemental trabeated architecture of ancient Greece and the just as elemental arcuated and vaulted architecture of Rome were Kahn's inspiration from the past. Without special quotation from them, without specific historical reference, he re-creates an ancient spirit of simplicity, clarity, and stability of structure peculiarly restful and reassuring in an age of strident stylistic confusion. Kahn's work is both Classical and Modern, in effect, a modern classic.

Postmodernism

Though built in the early seventies, Kahn's Kimbell Art Museum is still firmly Modernist, as is Pei's East Building of the National Gallery, an echo of Bauhaus Formalism. On the other hand, Philip Johnson's AT&T Tower and Graves's Portland Building are transitional to a new approach. Though they retain much of Modernist design, they draw inspiration from historical styles. This historicism is a principle feature of what is now called Postmodern architecture.

A clean break with Modernism is conspicuous in the work of CHARLES MOORE (b. 1925). Taking advantage of a surge of interest in urban planning and renewal to suit popular convenience, an interest that rapidly produced shopping malls, industrial parks, high-rise hotels, convention centers, and public squares, Moore designed the Piazza d'Italia in New Orleans (FIG. **28-73**). Here he is mindful of both environment and cultural context. The Piazza is dedicated to the Italian colony of New Orleans, and Moore's use of Classical models for its design is meaningful in its direct reference to the Mediterranean origin of Italians and to a region, strewn with Greek and Roman ruins, that evokes ancient cultural reminiscences.

Backed up against a contemporary high-rise and set off from urban traffic patterns, the Piazza d'Italia can be reached on foot from three sides, through gateways of varied design. The approaches lead to an open, circular area partially formed by short segments of colonnades arranged in staggered, concentric arcs, which direct the eye to the composition's focal point: an exedra (FIG. **28-74**) on a raised platform that serves as rostrum during the annual festivities of St. Joseph's Day. The Piazza's pavement is inlaid with the map of Italy, in which Sicily, the place of origin of the Italian colony's majority, is centrally placed. From there, the Italian boot moves in the direction of the steps that ascend the rostrum and that, geographically, correspond to the Alps.

The Piazza's most immediate historical reference is to the Greek agora or the Roman forum; on the other hand, its circular form refers to the ideal geometric figure of the Renaissance. The irregular placement of the concentrically arranged colonnade fragments inserts a note of instability into the design that is reminiscent of Mannerism; and illusionistic devices, like the continuation of the Piazza's pavement design (apparently through a building and out into the street), are Baroque in character. All of the Classical orders are represented—some with whimsical modifications: fluting defined by rising jets of water; water falling

28-73 CHARLES MOORE, model of the Piazza d'Italia, New Orleans, Louisiana, 1976–1980.

from metopes (Moore calls these "wetopes") and spouting from the mouths of the architect's relief that have been set into spandrels. Twentieth-century touches are provided in the form of stainless-steel columns and capitals, neon collars around the necks of columns, and the framing of various features of the exedra with neon lights.

In sum, the design of the Piazza d'Italia is a complex conglomerate of symbolic, historical, and geographical allusions—some overt, others hidden—assembled for visual effect and not without humor. The Piazza's specific purpose is to give identity (or, to use a favorite Postmodern expression, a "heart") to the Italian community of New Orleans. Its more general purpose is to revitalize an urban area by becoming a focal point and an architectural setting for the social activities of the neighborhood residents. It remains to be seen if it can fulfill this expectation or if it will become just another curiosity and tourist attraction.

Historical eclecticism, symbolism, allusions, and references to contemporary values and icons are admitted and encouraged by Postmodernism. An early promoter of Postmodernist thinking, ROBERT VENTURI (b. 1925) notes the "richness and ambiguity of modern contemporary experience." In a trail-blazing book, *Complexity and Contradiction in Architecture* (1966), Venturi declares:

> Architects can no longer afford to be intimidated by the puritanically moral language of orthodox Modern architecture. . . . A valid architecture evokes many levels of meaning and combinations of focus; its space and its elements become readable and workable in several ways at once.

28-74 Piazza d'Italia, view of the exedra.

28-75 ROBERT VENTURI, Rauch and Scott Brown, house in Delaware, 1978–1983. West elevation.

Against a fundamental axiom of Modernism, that the form of a building must arise directly and logically from the facts of its function and structure, Venturi asserts that the form should be *separate* from the functional and structural facts; and that the forms, decorative and symbolic of everyday life, should enwrap the structural core. In another book, *Learning from Las Vegas* (1972), Venturi advises the architect to take popular, vernacular architecture on its own terms, and not dismiss it as contemptible. Here we find, at least in theory, a correlation of Postmodern architecture with Pop Art.

Venturi's own designs for houses show him adapting historical as well as contemporary styles to suit his symbolic and expressive purpose. He does not actually work in historical style, but somewhat ironically selects and exaggerates the formal traits that identify it. Thus, for a residence in Delaware (FIG. **28-75**) Venturi respects the countryside setting and its eighteenth-century history by recalling the stone-based, barnlike, low-profile farm dwellings, their shingled roofs and double-hung, multipaned windows. He fronts the house with an amusingly "cut-out" and asymmetrical parody of a Neoclassical portico. A building by Venturi is, in his own words, a kind of "decorated shed."

Deconstruction

In the later decades of the century, art critics have taken a commanding role, such that the categorizing of movements and the interpretation and evaluation of monuments has become a kind of monitoring, gate-keeping activity, that determines as well as describes what is going on in the

world of the arts. *Critical Theory* views art and architecture, as well as literature and the other humanities, as intellectual products or "constructs" of a culture, which unconsciously suppress or conceal the actual assumptions of the culture, primarily the values of those who are politically in control. When revealed by analysis, the facts behind these constructs explain what the art works are really about. The kind of analysis used by Critical Theory is called *deconstruction*, after a method developed by French intellectuals, notably Michel Foucault and Jacques Derrida, in the 1960s and 1970s. For deconstructionists, all constructs are "texts." These "texts" can be read in a variety of ways; there are no fixed or uniform meanings that can be finally agreed upon; any readings can be valid, and readings will differ from time to time, place to place, and person to person. Further, texts are cultural products; and the way they signify, and what they signify, are entirely conventional; they can refer to nothing outside of themselves, only to other texts. Thus, there is no extra-textual "reality" to be referred to.

The agenda of Critical Theory and its strategy of deconstructive analysis are primarily political and social; the ultimate aim is to effect political and social change. As such, Critical Theorists seek to uncover the "facts" of power, privilege, and prejudice that underlie the constructs of any given culture, all of which are suspect of concealment and must be "interrogated" and unmasked, that is, "deconstructed." (But of course the "facts" disclosed by deconstructive reading of "texts" are themselves "texts," for, as we have just noted, there is no "reality" to be known other than that of "texts." This apparent contradiction is dismissed by deconstructionist critics as just another "construct.")

Some examples may serve to clarify deconstructive analysis. A Feminist critic might deconstruct a picture of a female nude as revealing the subordination of women in a patriarchal society, or as presenting a victim of the prurient "male gaze" (FIG. 28-44). An ethnically committed critic might deconstruct the term "primitive" as a post-colonial, derogatory epithet, when applied to African or Oceanic art. A class-conscious critic might deconstruct "fine" art as the elitist product of an unfair social system.

Though there may be little agreement among Critical Theorists with respect to any firm definition of their philosophy and method—since in principle they are opposed to firm definitions—they share a skeptical suspicion of all traditional truth claims and value standards, all hierarchical authority and institutions. For them deconstructionism means the destabilization of established meanings, definitions, and interpretations, and the encouragement of subjectivity and individual differences. This means liberation from all binding obligations to the demands of customary precept and practice in art and life and the cultivation of free creativity. Rules and canons are limiting obstructions to the free play of artistic imagination. It is the job of the artist to be a creator of new forms, absolutely independent of traditional or contemporary constraint. Representation in art is such an obstruction and should be shunned altogether as in essence false to human experience and a mask for the dishonesty of society.

Deconstruction in architecture proposes, above all, to *disorient* the observer. To this end, the conventional categories of architecture are set aside and our expectations based upon them upset. Order, harmony, balance, symmetry, regularity, clarity, consistency, continuity, completeness are replaced by their negatives: disorder, dissonance, and so forth. We are meant to be confused by a haphazardry of volumes, masses, planes, borders, lighting, locations, directions, spatial relations, and disguised structural facts. According to deconstructionist theory, it is the very *absence* of the assurances given us by habit and by the traditional categories of architecture that create the *presence* of a "deconstructed" building. A contemporary critic entitles an essay on the subject: "Deconstruction: The Pleasures of Absence."*

The Postmodernism of Philip Johnson, Michael Graves, Charles Moore, and Robert Venturi, with its respect for the architectural categories, and for Classicism in style, is not at all to the liking of the Canadian-born American architect FRANK GEHRY (b. 1929), who pokes deconstructionist fun at it. Referring to his restaurant building in Kobe, Japan, which is in the shape of a giant fish, Gehry suggests that there is no basis whatever for choice of one architectural style over another:

> If everybody is going to say that [Postmodern] Classicism is perfection, then I'm going to say fish is perfection, so why not copy fish? And then I'll be damned if I don't find reasons to reinforce why the fish is important and more interesting than Classicism. That's intuitive. Intuition and free invention are what count.†

Gehry, trained in sculpture, and at different times a collaborator with Claes Oldenberg, Anthony Caro, and Donald Judd, works up his designs by constructing models and then cutting them up and arranging them until he has a satisfying composition. His Vitra Museum and Factory complex in Weil am Rhein, Germany, (FIGS. **28-76** and **28-77**)

*Charles Jencks, in A. Papdikis, C. Cooke, A Benjamin, *Deconstruction: Omnibus Volume* (New York: Rizzoli, 1989), p. 119.

†Ibid., p. 120.

28-76 FRANK GEHRY, The Vitra Museum and Factory complex, Weil am Rhein, Germany, 1989.

28-77   Interior of the Vitra Museum.

illustrate his intuitive way of working. The jumbled irregularity of the main masses, the profiles of which change dramatically with every change of the observer's position, appear like a collapsed or collapsing aggregate of units. The half-cylinder unit in the foreground seems to have been interrupted in the process of construction. The elevations of the aggregate do not reveal the scheme of the interior. The seemingly weightless screens, vaults, and volumes of the interior float and flow into one another, guided only by light and dark cues. Yet both exterior and interior have—even in integration and disintegration—the severely unadorned, geometric planes of Purist Abstraction. Deconstruction cannot help but work within the already established formalism it attempts to "deconstruct." Some critics, conscious of this fact, would designate Gehry's building as "neo-Modern."

More audacious in its dissolution of form, and farther along on the path of deconstruction, is the Hysolar Institute Building at the University of Stuttgart, Germany (FIG. **28-78**). Designed as a joint German–Saudi Arabian research project on the technology of solar energy, the building is

the work of GÜNTHER BEHNISCH (b. 1922), who is intent on denying here the possibility of space enclosure altogether, and whose apparently chaotic arrangement of the units defies easy analysis. The shapes of the Hysolar Institute's roof, walls, and windows seem to explode, avoiding any suggestion of clear, stable masses. There is not even a pastiche of vernacular or familiar forms appropriated from popular culture or earlier styles. Instead, Behnisch is aggressively playing with the whole concept of architecture and our relationship to it. The meaning of the building is dislocated by the building itself, and the viewer/inhabitant cannot avoid thinking about the nature of architecture and of building.

The ultimate deconstruction would deny the completeness, firmness, and stability of a building, showing it in the process of dilapidation—the very image of architectural impermanence and the impact upon it of the forces of the environment. This is the case with the so-called Indeterminate Facade of the Best Products Showroom in Houston, Texas (FIG. **28-79**), the work of a group called SITE (Sky, Stone, and Wines). The surprise effect of the

28-78 GÜNTER BEHNISCH, Hysolar Institute Building, University of Stuttgart, 1987.

28-79 SITE INC., Indeterminate Facade, brick and Sarabond mortar. Best Products Company, Houston, Texas. 1975.

28-80 KAZUO SHINOHARA, Centennial Anniversary Hall, Tokyo Institute of Technology, 1988. View from the north.

disintegrating facade is carefully contrived. The jagged roofline and the cascade of bricks falling from the huge gap in the wall never fail to astonish, even alarm, passersby seeing the building for the first time. Its builders refer to it as a work of "de-architecturalization," that calls for a thorough review and revision of all architectural assumptions and for a redefinition of architecture itself.

From this graphic annihilation of architecture there is bound to be a recoil. In the work of KAZUO SHINOHARA (b. 1925) we may find deconstructionist dislocations, but also agreements with earlier twentieth-century theory and practice. His Centennial Hall (FIG. **28-80**), built for the Institute of Technology in Tokyo, shows in its dominant forms a firm grip on both the Geometric and Organic Abstraction of Modernist style, even a reflection of Le Corbusier in the tower wings. The steady and strong influence of Modernism in late twentieth-century design is obvious, no matter the impulse to deconstruct it. Shinohara confesses the influence of the esthetics of the machine on his work, like the earlier Purists and Constructionists. But he also admits to the generating power of new ideas in architecture as the "anarchy of random noise" and "a new vital energy for city and architecture."*

*Quoted in Peter Cooke and Rosie Llewellen-Jones, *New Spirit in Architecture* (New York: Rizzolli, 1991), pp. 77–78.

FUNCTIONALISM AGAIN

The reassertion of architectural integrity with respect to its fundamental requirements of function and stability has been made in many contemporary buildings. Advanced technology has made possible new feats of construction to satisfy old demands. The office tower that originated in the days of Louis Sullivan to provide vertical space in the crowded, modern metropolis is an architectural type that still endures after a century of use. The role of the structural engineer is now even more conspicuous, and design is even more revealing of the bold features created by engineering ingenuity. Deconstruction, which tended to reduce architecture to a branch of sculptural, or even pictorial, art, yields to an architecture that increasingly appears to be but the esthetic form of the solution to an engineering problem.

A case in point is the Hong Kong and Shanghai Bank (FIG. **28-81**), built in Hong Kong by the American architect NORMAN FOSTER (b. 1935) and the engineering firm of Ove Arup. To build a stable foundation for the structure, the engineers first penetrated the loose, waterlogged subsoil to the granite bedrock some 250 feet below street level, creating a great concrete wall to enclose the site. Here they built a basement tunnel containing the water service lines for the building. The suspended, structural skeleton of the forty-three-story tower is fully visible on its north and south faces. The weight of the building is carried by eight huge masts aligned around the perimeter. The floors are hung from five enormous, aluminum-faced suspension trusses that form two-story-high triangles carrying the stresses of the floors to the masts.

In the credits of the Hong Kong and Shanghai Bank the architect's name is given first, a traditional courtesy, but the engineers' contribution suggests more than a merely secondary collaboration. Our technological age, bred as early as Paxton's Crystal Palace (FIG. 26-94), still speaks with commanding, expressive power above the noisy, doctrinal claims and counterclaims of modern architectural criticism.

28-81 NORMAN FOSTER and OVE ARUP, Engineers, The Hong Kong and Shanghai Bank, Hong Kong, 1988.

PRONUNCIATION GUIDE TO ARTISTS' NAMES

Artist's Name	Phonetic Pronunciation
Abakanowicz, Magdalena	ab-a-ʹkan-o-wits, mag-dŭ-ʹlā-nŭ
Achilles Painter	ŭ-ʹkil-ēz
Alberti, Leon Battista	al-ʹber-tē, lā-ʹon bat-ʹtēs-ta
Alexandros of Antioch-on-the-Meander	ă-lig-ʹzăn-dros of ʹăn-tē-ak *on the* mē-ʹăn-dŭr
Altdorfer, Albrecht	ʹalt-dor-fŭr, ʹal-breḵt
Ando Hiroshige	an-dō hē-rō-shē-ge
Andokides Painter	an-ʹdō-kē-dēs ʹ
Andrea del Castagno	an-ʹdrā-ŭ del ka-ʹstan-yō
Andrea del Sarto	an-ʹdrā-ŭ del ʹsar-tō
Angelico, Fra	an-ʹjā-lē-kō, fra
Anguissola, Sofonisba	ang-gwēs-ʹsō-lŭ, sō-fō-ʹnēz-ba
Anthemius of Tralles	ăn-ʹthē-mē-ŭs of trăl-ēz
Apollodorus of Damascus	ŭ-pal-ŭ-ʹdōr-ŭs of dŭ-ʹmăs-kŭs
Apollonios of Athens	ăp-ŭ-ʹlō-nē-ŭs of ʹăth-ŭnz
Āqā Mirak	a-ka ʹmē-rak
Arata Isozaki	a-ra-ta ē-sō-za-kē
Archipenko, Alexandr	ŭrḵ-ʹyēp-yŭn-kŭ (*or* ar-ki-ʹpyeng-kō), ŭl-yik-ʹsan-dŭr
Arnolfo di Cambio	ar-ʹnol-fō dē ʹkam-byō
Arp, Jean	arp, zhanⁿ
Arup, Ove	ʹă-rŭp, ʹō-vŭ
Asam, Cosmas Damian	ʹaz-am, ʹcos-mas dam-ʹyan
Asam, Egid Quirin	ʹaz-am, ā-ʹgēt kvē-ʹrēn
Atget, Jean-Eugène-Auguste	at-ʹzhe, zhanⁿ ö-ʹzhăn o-ʹgūst
Athanadorus	ŭ-thă-nŭ-ʹdor-ŭs
Balla, Giacomo	ʹbal-la, ʹja-kō-mō
Barlach, Ernst	ʹbar-laḵ, ʹernst
Barye, Antoine-Louis	ba-ʹrē, anⁿ-ʹtwan lwē
Bastien-Lepage, Jules	bas-tyanⁿ-lŭ-ʹpazh, zhŭl
Beardsley, Aubrey	ʹbi(ŭ)rdz-lē, ʹo-brē
Beckmann, Max	ʹbek-man, maks
Behnisch, Gunter	ʹben-ish, ʹgun-tŭ(r)
Bellini, Giovanni	bel-ʹlē-nē, jō-ʹvan-nē
Berlinghieri, Bonaventura	ber-ling-ʹgye-rē, bo-na-vanⁿ-ʹtū-ra
Bernini, Gianlorenzo	ber-ʹnē-nē, jan-lō-ʹren-zō
Bertoldo di Giovanni	ber-ʹtol-dō dē jō-ʹvan-nē
Beuys, Joseph	ʹbois, ʹyō-zef
Bihzad	bi-ʹzad
Boccioni, Umberto	bat-ʹchō-nē, ŭm-ʹber-tō
Bodmer, Karl	ʹbŏd-mŭr, karl
Boffrand, Germain	bo-ʹfranⁿ, zher-ʹmănⁿ
Bonheur, Rosa	bōⁿ-ʹŭr, ʹrō-zŭ
Borromini, Francesco	bōr-rō-ʹmē-nē, fran-ʹches-kō
Bosch, Hieronymus	ʹbos (*or* ʹbash, ʹbosh), hē-ŭ-ʹrō-nē-mus
Botticelli, Sandro	bot-ti-ʹchel-lē, ʹsan-drō
Boucher, François	bū-ʹshā, franⁿ-ʹswa
Bouguereau, Adolphe-William	bū-g(ŭ)-ʹrō, a-ʹdolf wēl-ʹyam
Bourgeois, Louise	būr-ʹzhwa, lwēz
Bouts, Dirk	ʹbauts, dirk
Bramante, Donato D'Angelo	bra-ʹman-tā, dō-ʹna-tō ʹdan-jā-lō
Brancusi, Constantin	ʹbran-kŭsh (*or* brăn-kū-zē), kon-stan-ʹtēn
Braque, Georges	brak, zhorzh
Broederlam, Melchior	ʹbrū-dŭr-lăm, ʹmel-ḵē-or
Bronzino	bron-ʹzē-nō
Bruegel, Pieter, the Elder	ʹbroi-gŭl, ʹpē-tŭr

Artist's Name	Phonetic Pronunciation
Brunelleschi, Filippo	brŭn-ŭl-ʹes-kē, fē-ʹlēp-pō
Buffalmacco, Buonamico	buf-fal-ʹmak-kō, bwon-ŭ-ʹmē-kō
Buffet, Bernard	bü-ʹfā, ber-ʹnar
Bunchō	bun-chō
Burgee, John	ʹbŭr-jē, jan
Caillebotte, Gustave	ka-y(ŭ)-ʹbot, gū-ʹstav
Callot, Jacques	kă-ʹlō, zhak
Campin, Robert	kanⁿ-ʹpenⁿ, rō-ʹber
Canaletto, Giovanni Antonio	ka-na-ʹlāt-tō, jō-ʹvan-nē an-ʹtōn-yō
Canova, Antonio	ka-ʹnō-va, an-ʹtōn-yō
Caradosso, Christoforo Foppa	kar-ŭ-ʹdos-sō, krē-ʹsto-fō-rō ʹfap-pa
Caravaggio	kar-ŭ-ʹvad-jō
Caro, Anthony	ʹka-rō, ʹăn-thŭ-nē
Carpeaux, Jean-Baptiste	kar-ʹpō, zhanⁿ bap-ʹtēst
Carracci, Agostino	ka(r)-ʹrat-chē, a-gŭ-ʹstē-nō
Carracci, Annibale	ka(r)-ʹrat-chē, an-ʹnē-bŭ-lā
Carracci, Lodovico	ka(r)-ʹrat-chē, lō-dō-ʹvē-kō
Carriera, Rosalba	kar-ʹye-ra, rō-ʹzal-ba
Cassatt, Mary	kŭ-ʹsăt
Cavallini, Pietro	ka-val-ʹlē-nē, ʹpye-trō
Celer	kē-lŭr
Cellini, Benvenuto	chel-ʹlē-nē, ben-vŭ-ʹnū-tō
Cézanne, Paul	sā-ʹzan, pōl
Chagall, Marc	shŭ-ʹgal, mark
Chardin, Jean-Baptiste-Siméon	shar-ʹdănⁿ, zhanⁿ bap-ʹtēst si-mā-ʹōⁿ
Chelles, Jean de	shel (*or* shey), zhanⁿ dŭ
Chirico, Giorgio de	ʹkir-i-kō, ʹjōr-jō dā
Chō Densu	chō dŭn-su
Christo	ʹkris-tō *or* ʹkrēs-tō
Christus, Petrus	ʹkris-tŭs, ʹpā-trŭs
Cimabue, Giovanni	chē-mŭ-ʹbū-ā, jō-ʹvan-nē
Clodion	klō-dē-ʹōⁿ
Clouet, Jean	klü-ʹe, zhanⁿ
Corot, Jean-Baptiste-Camille	kŭ-ʹrō, zhanⁿ bap-ʹtēst kŭ-ʹmēl
Correggio	kŭr-ʹred-jō
Courbet, Jean-Désiré-Gustave	kur-ʹbā, zhanⁿ de-zi-ʹrā gū-ʹstav
Coypel, Antoine	kwa-ʹpel, anⁿ-ʹtwan
Cranach, Lucas, the Elder	ʹkran-aḵ, ʹlū-kŭs
Cuvilliés, François de	kyū-vē-ʹyā, franⁿ-ʹswa dŭ
Daddi, Bernardo	ʹda-dē, ber-ʹnar-dō
Daguerre, Louis-Jacques-Mandé	da-ʹger, lwē zhak manⁿ-ʹdā
Dai Jin	dī jin
Dali, Salvador	ʹda-lē, sal-vŭ-ʹdōr [*also* da-ʹlē]
Dao Ji	dau jē
Daphnis of Miletos	ʹdăf-nis of mī-ʹlēt-ŭs
Daumier, Honoré	dō-ʹmyā, o-nor-ʹā
David, Jacques-Louis	da-ʹvēd, zhak lū-ʹē
De Kooning, Willem	dŭ-ʹkū-ning, ʹwil-ŭm
Degas, Edgar	dŭ-ʹga, ed-ʹgar
Delacroix, Eugène	del-ŭ-ʹk(r)wa, ö-ʹzhen
Delaroche, Paul	dŭ-la-ʹrosh, pōl
Delaunay, Robert	dŭ-lō-ʹnā, rō-ʹber
Della Robbia, Andrea	dăl-la ʹrob-bya, an-ʹdrā-ŭ
Della Robbia, Giovanni	dăl-la ʹrob-bya, jō-ʹvan-nē
Della Robbia, Girolamo	dăl-la ʹrob-bya, jē-ʹro-lam-ō
Della Robbia, Luca	dăl-la ʹrob-bya, ʹlū-ka
Derain, André	dŭ-ʹrănⁿ, an-ʹdrā
Desiderio da Settignano	de-si-ʹder-yō da set-tē-ʹnya-nō
Doesburg, Theo van	ʹdūs-bürgh, ʹtā-ō van
Domenichino	dō-mā-nē-ʹkē-nō
Domenico Veneziano	dō-ʹmā-ni-kō ve-net-ʹsya-nō
Donatello	do-nŭ-ʹtel-lō
Dong Qichang	dong chō-chang
Dong Yuan	dong yan
Dubuffet, Jean	dyü-bŭ-ʹfā, zhanⁿ
Duccio di Buoninsegna	ʹdŭt-chō dē bwo-nēn-ʹsā-nya

Artist's Name	Phonetic Pronunciation	Artist's Name	Phonetic Pronunciation
Duchamp, Marcel	dyū-'shan, mar-'sel	Holbein, Hans, the Younger	'hōl-bīn, hants
Dürer, Albrecht	'dü-rŭ(r), 'al-brekt	Honami Kōetsu	hō-na-mē kō-et-s(u)
Durieu, Eugène	dŭr-'yü, ö-'zhen	Honnecourt, Villard de	on-ŭ-'kŭr, vē-'lar (or vē-'yar) dŭ
Eadwine the Scribe	'ă-ŭd-'win-ŭ	Honthorst, Gerrit van	'hont-horst, 'gher-ŭt van
Eakins, Thomas	'ā-kŭnz	Horta, Victor	'hor-tŭ, 'vēk-tor
Eiffel, Alexandre-Gustave	e-'fel, 'al-ek-san-drŭ gū-'stav	Houdon, Jean-Antoine	ū-'dōn, zhan an-'twan
El Greco	āl 'grā-kō (also el 'gre-kō)	Huang Gongwang	hwang gong-wang
Epigonos	e-'pig-o-nos	Ikeno Taiga	i-kā-nō tī-gŭ
Ergotimos	er-'gō-ti-mos	Iktinos	ēk-'tē-nos
Ernst, Max	ernst, maks	Il Guercino	ēl gwer-'chē-nō
Euphronios	yu-'frō-nē-os	Imhotep	im-'hō-tep
Euthymides	yu-'thim-ŭ-dēz	Ingres, Jean-Auguste-Dominique	'ăn(ng)grŭ, zhan o-'gŭst do-mi-'nēk
Exekias	ek-'sek-yŭs	Isidorus of Miletus	iz-ŭ-'dōr-ŭs of mī-'lē-tŭs
Eyck, Hubert van	'īk, 'hū-bŭrt văn	Isoda Koryusai	i-sō-dŭ kōr-yu-sī
Eyck, Jan van	'īk, yan văn	Jing Hao	jing hau
Fan Kuan	fan kwan	Jōchō	jō-chō
Feuerbach, Anselm	'foi-ŭr-bak, 'an-selm	Jones, Inigo	jōnz, 'in-ŭ-gō
Fouquet, Jean	fö-'ke, zhan	Jouvin, Hippolyte	zhu-'văn, ē(p)-po-'lēt
Fragonard, Jean-Honoré	frăg-ŭ-'nar, zhan o-no-'rā	Ju Ran	jū ran
Frankenthaler, Helen	'frăng-kŭn-tha-lŭr, 'hel-ŭn	Juvara, Filippo	yū-'var-a, fē-'lēp-pō
Friedrich, Caspar David	'frēd-rik, kas-'par 'dav-ēt	Kahlo, Frida	'ka-lō, 'frē-da
Fuseli, Henry	'füs-lē (or 'fū-z(ŭ)-lē), 'hen-rē	Kahn, Louis	'kan, 'lū-ē
Gabo, Naum	'gab-ō, 'na-ūm	Kaigetsudō	kī-get-sud-ō
Gaddi, Taddeo	'gad-dē, tad-'de-ō	Kallikrates	kal-'ē-krŭ-tēz
Gainsborough, Thomas	'gānz-bŭr-ŭ	Kandinsky, Wassily	kăn-'din(t)-skē, vŭs-'yēl-yŭi
Garnier, J. L. Charles	gar-'nyā, sharl	Kanō Motonobu	ka-nō mō-tō-nō-bu
Gaudí, Antoni	gau-'dē, an-'tōn-ē	Kanō Sanraku	ka-nō san-ra-ku
Gauguin, Paul	gō-'găn, pōl	Kaō	kau
Gehry, Frank	'ge-rē	Kaprow, Allan	'kăp-rō, ăl-ŭn
Gelduinus, Bernardus	gel-'dwē-nŭs, bŭr-'nar-dŭs	Käsebier, Gertrude	'kās-ŭ-bēr, 'ger-trŭd(-ŭ)
Gentile da Fabriano	jen-'tē-lā da fab-rē-'an-ō	Katsushika Hokusai	ka-ts(ŭ)-sh(ē)-kŭ hō-k(ū)-sī
Gentileschi, Artemisia	jen-tē-'les-kē, art-ŭ-'miz-ē-ŭ	Kauffmann, Angelica	'kauf-man, ang-'gā-lē-ka
Gentileschi, Orazio	jen-tē-'les-kē, ō-'rat-syō	Kazuo Shinohara	ka-zū-ō shē-nō-har-a
Géricault, Théodore	zhe-ri-'kō, tā-ō-'dōr	Kenzo Tange	ken-zō tang-ge
Gérôme, Jean-Léon	zhā-'rōm, zhan lā-'on	Kiefer, Anselm	'kē-fŭr, 'an-selm
Ghiberti, Lorenzo	gē-'bert-ē, lō-'ren-zō	Kirchner, Ernst	'kirk-nŭ(r), ernst
Ghirlandaio, Domenico	gir-lŭn-'da-yō, dō-'men-i-kō	Kitagawa Utamaro	kē-ta-ga-wa ut-a-ma-rō
Giacometti, Alberto	jak-ŭ-'met-tē, al-'bert-ō	Klee, Paul	'klā, pōl
Giorgione da Castelfranco	jōr-'jō-nā da kas-tel-'frang-kō	Kleitias	'klē-tē-ŭs
Giotto di Bondone	'jot-tō dē bōn-'dō-nā	Klimt, Gustav	'klimt, 'gus-taf
Giovanni da Bologna	jō-'van-nē da bo-'lōn-yŭ	Kline, Franz	'klīn, fränz
Girardon, François	zhē-rar-'dōn, fran-'swa	Kokoschka, Oscar	'ko-kosh-ka, 'os-kar
Girodet-Trioson, Anne-Louis	zhē-rō-'de trē-ō-'sōn, an-'lwē	Kollwitz, Käthe	'kol-vits, 'ket-ŭ
Gislebertus	gēz-lā-'bert-tŭs	Kresilas	'kres-ŭ-las
Glykon of Athens	'glī-kon of 'ăth-ŭnz	L'Enfant, Pierre	lan-'fan, pyer
Gnosis	'nō-sŭs	La Tour, Georges de	la-'tŭr, zhorzh dŭ
Goes, Hugo van der	'gŭs, 'hyū-go văn dŭr	La Tour, Quentin de	la-'tŭr, kan-'tăn dŭ
Gogh, Vincent van	'gō, vin-'sent văn	Labrouste, Henri	la-'brŭst, an-'rē
Golub, Leon	'gol-ŭb, 'lē-an	Lange, Dorothea	lăng, dor-ŭ-'thē-ŭ
González, Julio	gōn-'sal-ās, 'hŭl-yō	Latrobe, Benjamin	lŭ-'trōb, 'ben-j(ŭ)-mŭn
Gossaert, Jan	'gos-art, yan	Le Brun, Charles	lŭ-'brŭnn, sharl
Goujon, Jean	gū-'zhōn, zhan	Le Corbusier	lŭ kor-byū-sē-'ā
Goya, Francisco José de	'goi-(y)ŭ, fran-'sis-kō hō-sā dā	Le Nain, Louis	lŭ-'năn, lwē
Gozzoli, Benozzo	got-'tsō-lē, bā-'not-tsō	Le Nôtre, André	lŭ-'nōtrŭ, an-'drā
Greenough, Horatio	'grē-nō, hŭ-'rā-sh(ē)-ō	Le Vau, Louis	lŭ-'vō, lwē
Greuze, Jean-Baptiste	grŭ(r)z (or gröz), zhan bap-'tēst	Léger, Fernand	lā-'zhā, fer-'nan
Gropius, Walter	'grō-pē-us (-ŭs), 'wol-tŭr	Lehmbruck, Wilhelm	'lām-bruk, 'vil-helm
Gros, Antoine-Jean	grō, an-'twan zhan	Leibl, Wilhelm	'lī-bŭl, 'vil-helm
Grünewald, Matthias	'grü-nŭ-valt, ma-'tē-as	Leochares	lē-'ak-ŭ-rēz
Gu Kaizih	gū kī-tsi	Leonardo da Vinci	lā-ō-'nar-dō da 'vēn-chē
Guarini, Guarino	'gwar-ē-nē, 'gwar-ē-nō		(or lē-ŭ-'nar-dō dŭ 'vin-chē)
Guo Xi	gwo shē	Lescot, Pierre	les-'kō, pyer
Hagesandros	hăg-ŭ-'săn-dros	Li Cheng	lē chŭng
Hals, Frans	hals, frants	Li Gonglin	lē gung-lin
Hardouin-Mansart, Jules	ar-'dwăn-man-sar, zhŭl	Liang Kai	lē-'ang 'kī
Hasegawa Tōhaku	has-e-ga-wa tō-ha-ku	Libon of Elis	'lī-bŭn of 'ē-lŭs
Hawes, Josiah Johnson	'hoz, jō-'zī-ŭ 'jan-sŭn	Lichtenstein, Roy	'lik-tŭn-stīn, 'roi
Heda, Willem Claez	'hā-da, 'vil-ŭm 'klas	Limbourg, Hennequin	'lim-burk, 'hen-(ŭ)-kăn
Herrera, Juan de	er-'rer-a, hwan dā	Limbourg, Herman	'lim-burk, 'her-man
Hesse, Eva	'hes, 'ē-vŭ	Limbourg, Pol	'lim-burk, pol
Hippodamos	hip-'ad-ŭ-mŭs	Lin, Maya Ying	lin, 'mī-ŭ yēng
Hishikawa Moronobu	hē-shē-ka-wa mō-rō-nō-bu	Lipchitz, Jacques	lēp-'shēts (or 'lip-shits), zhak

Artist's Name	Phonetic Pronunciation
Lippi, Filippino	'lēp-pē, fē-lēp-'pē-nō
Lippi, Fra Filippo	'lēp-pē, fra fē-'lēp-pō
Lochner, Stephan	'lok̲-nŭ(r), 'stä-fan
Longhena, Baldassare	lan-'gä-nŭ, bal-dŭ-'sar-ä
Lorenzetti, Ambrogio	lō-rent-'sät-tē, am-'brō-jō
Lorenzetti, Pietro	lō-rent-'sät-tē, 'pye-trō
Lorrain, Claude	lŭ-'răn, klōd
Luzarches, Robert de	lu-'zarsh, rō-'ber dŭ
Lysippos of Sikyon	lī-'sip-os of 'sik-ē-an
Ma Yuan	ma yü-an
Mabuse, Jan	ma-'bü-zŭ, yan
Machuca, Pedro	ma-'chü-ka, 'pä-drō
Maderno, Carlo	ma-'der-nō, 'kar-lō
Magritte, René	ma-'grēt, rŭ-'nā
Maiano, Giuliano da	ma-'ya-no, jūl-'yan-ō da
Maillol, Aristide	mī-'yōl, ar-ŭ-'stēd
Malevich, Kasimir	mŭl-'yāv-yich, 'kaz-ē-mēr
Manet, Édouard	ma-'nā, ā-'dwar
Mansart, François	man-'sar, fran-'swa
Mantegna, Andrea	man-'tān-yŭ, an-'drā-ŭ
Marc, Franz	mark, frants
Martini, Simone	mar-'tē-nē, sē-'mōn-ā
Maruyama Okyo	ma-rū-ya-ma ō-kyō
Masaccio	mŭ-'sat-chō
Masolino da Panicale	ma-sō-'lē-nō da pa-nē-'ka-lä
Matisse, Henri	ma-'tēs, an-'rē
Melozzo da Forli	mā-'lōt-tsō da for-'lē
Memling, Hans	mem-'ling, hants
Memmi, Lippo	'mem-mē, 'lip-pō
Metsys, Quentin	'met-sĭs, 'kvin-tŭn
Mi Fu	mē fū
Michelangelo Buonarroti	mē-kä-'lan-jä-lō bwo-nar-'rō-tē
Michelozzo di Bartolommeo	mē-kä-'lōt-tso dē bar-tō-lōm-'me-ō
Mies van der Rohe, Ludwig	mēs-van-dŭ-'rō(-ŭ), 'lud-vik
Millais, John Everett	mil-'ā, jan 'ev-(ŭ-)rŭt
Millet, Jean-François	mē-'yā (or mi-'lā), zhan fran-'swa
Minchō	min-chō
Miró, Joan	mē-'rō, zhu-'an
Mnesikles	(m-)'nes-i-klēz
Modigliani, Amedeo	mō-dēl-'ya-nē, am-ä-'de-ō
Moholy-Nagy, László	mō-'hō-lē-'na-zhē (or 'mo-hoi-nady), 'laz-lō
Mokuan Reien	mō-ku-an rā-en
Mondrian, Piet	'mon-drē-an, pāt (or pēt)
Monet, Claude	mō-'nā, 'klōd
Moreau, Gustave	mo-'rō, gü-'stav
Morisot, Berthe	mo-rē-'zō, bert
Munch, Edvard	'mungk, 'ed-vard
Mungarawai	mŭng-gŭ-'ra-wa
Muybridge, Eadweard	'mī-brij, 'ed-wŭrd
Nadar	na-dar
Nanni di Banco	'nan-nē dē 'bang-kō
Neumann, Balthasar	'noi-man, bal-tŭ-'zar
Ni Zan	nē tsan
Nièpce, Joseph Nicéphore	nyeps, zhō-'zef nē-sā-'fōr
Niobid Painter	nī-'ō-bid
Nolde, Emil	'nol-dŭ, 'ā-mēl
Novios Plautios	'nō-vē-ōs 'plau-tē-ōs
Ogata Kenzan	ō-ga-ta ken-zan
Ogata Kōrin	ō-ga-ta kō-rēn
Okumura Masanobu	ō-ku-mur-a ma-sa-nō-bu
Oldenburg, Claes	'ol-dŭn-burk̲, klas
Olowe of Ise	ō-lŭ-'wä of 'ē-sē
Onesimos	ō-'nes-ŭ-mōs
Orcagna, Andrea	ōr-'kan-ya, an-'drā-ŭ
Orozco, José Clemente	o-'rōs-kō, hō-'sā kle-'men-tā
Paik, Nam June	pīk, nam jūn
Paionios of Ephesos	pī-'ō-nē-ŭs of 'ef-ŭ-sŭs
Palladio, Andrea	pŭl-'la-dē-ō, an-'drā-ŭ
Pannini, Giovanni	pan-'nē-nē, jō-'van-nē
Parmigianino	par-mi-ja-'nē-nō

Artist's Name	Phonetic Pronunciation
Pei, Ieoh Ming	'pā, yŭ̄ ming
Perrault, Claude	pŭ-'rō, klōd
Perugino	per-ŭ-'jē-nō
Pfaff, Judy	'faf, 'jū-di
Phiale Painter	fē-'a-lā
Phidias	'fid-ē-ŭs
Philoxenos of Eretria	fŭ-'lak-sŭ-nŭs of er-ŭ-'trē-ŭ
Piano, Renzo	pē-'a-nō, 'ren-zō
Picasso, Pablo	pi-'kas-ō, 'pab-lō
Piero della Francesca	'pyer-ō dāl-ŭ fran-'ches-ka
Piranesi, Giovanni Battista	pē-ra-'nä-sē, jō-'van-nē bat-'tēs-ta
Pisano, Andrea	pē-'san-ō, an-'drä-ŭ
Pisano, Giovanni	pē-'san-ō, jō-'van-nē
Pisano, Nicola	pē-'san-ō, nē-'kō-la
Pissarro, Camille	pŭ-'sar-ō, ka-'mēl [or ka-mēy]
Plotinus	plō-'tī-nŭs
Pollaiuolo, Antonio	pōl-'lī-wō-lō, an-'tōn-yō
Pollock, Jackson	'pal-ŭk, 'jăk-sŭn
Polydoros of Rhodes	pal-i-'dor-os of 'rōdz
Polyeuktos	pal-ē-'yuk-tos
Polygnotos of Thasos	pal-ig-'nōt-os of 'tha-sos
Polykleitos	pal-i-'klīt-os
Pontormo, Jacopo da	pōn-'tor-mō, 'ya-kō-pō da
Porta, Giacomo della	'port-a, 'ja-kō-mō dāl-la
Poussin, Nicolas	pū-'săn, ni-kō-'la
Pozzo, Fra Andrea	'pōt-tsō, fra an-'drā-ŭ
Praxiteles	prak-'sit-(ŭ)l-ēz
Préault, Antoine-Auguste	prā-'ō, an-'twan o-'gŭst
Primaticcio, Francesco	prē-ma-'tēt-chō, fran-'ches-kō
Pucelle, Jean	pyū-'sel, zhan
Puget, Pierre	pyū-'zhä, pyer
Pugin, A. W. N.	'pyū-jin
Puvis de Chavannes, Pierre	pü-vē-d(ŭ)-sha-'van, pyer
Qi Baishi	chē bī-shi
Quarton, Enguerrand	kar-'tōn, an-ge-'ran
Raphael	'răf-ē-ŭl (or 'rä-fē-ŭl)
Rauschenberg, Robert	'rau-shŭn-bŭrg, 'rab-ŭrt
Redon, Odilon	rŭ-'dōn, ō-di-'lōn
Regnaudin, Thomas	reg-no-'dăn (or re-nyo-'dăn), to-'ma
Rembrandt van Rijn	'rem-brănt van 'rīn
Reni, Guido	'ren-ē, 'gwē-dō
Renoir, Auguste	ren-'war, o-'gŭst
Repin, Ilya	'ryä-pyin, il-'ya
Ribera, José (de)	rē-'bā-ra, hō-sā (dā)
Richter, Hans	'rik-tŭr, hănz
Riemenschneider, Tilman	'rē-mŭn-shnī-dŭr, 'til-man
Rietveld, Gerrit	'rēt-velt, 'gher-ŭt
Rigaud, Hyacinthe	rē-'gō, ē-ŭ-'sent (or ya-'sant)
Rodin, Auguste	rō-'dăn(n), o-'gŭst
Romano, Giulio	rō-'man-ō, 'jūl-yō
Rosa, Salvator	'ro-za, sal-va-'tōr
Rossellino, Antonio	rōs-sāl-'lē-nō, an-'tōn-yō
Rossellino, Bernardo	rōs-sāl-'lē-nō, ber-'nar-dō
Rosso Fiorentino	'rō-sō fyōr-ŭn-'tē-nō
Rouault, Georges	rŭ-'ō, zhorzh
Rousseau, Henri	rŭ-'sō, an-'rē
Rublëv, Andrei	rŭb-'lyof, an-'drā-(ē)
Rude, François	rüd, fran-'swa
Ruisdael, Jacob van	'rīz-dal, 'ya-kob van
Runge, Philipp Otto	'rung-ŭ, 'fē-lip 'o-tō
Ruscha, Edward	'rū-shä, 'ed-wŭrd
Saint-Gaudens, Augustus	sānt-'god-(ŭ)nz, ŭ-'gŭs-tŭs
Sangallo, Antonio da, the Younger	sang-'gal-lō, an-'tōn-yō da
Sangallo, Giuliano da	sang-'gal-lō, jūl-'yan-ō da
Sansovino, Andrea	san-sō-'vē-nō, an-'drä-ŭ
Sansovino, Jacopo	san-sō-'vē-nō, 'ya-kō-pō
Schnabel, Julian	'shnab-ŭl, 'jū-lē-ŭn
Schongauer, Martin	'shōn-gau-ŭr, 'mar-tēn
Schwitters, Kurt	'shvit-ŭrs, 'kurt
Senmut	sen-'mūt
Sesshū	ses-shu

Artist's Name	Phonetic Pronunciation	Artist's Name	Phonetic Pronunciation
Seurat, Georges	sŭ-'ra, zhorzh	Tournachon, Gaspard-Félix	tūr-na-'shōn, ga-'spar 'fā-lēks
Severini, Gino	sā-vā-'rē-nē, 'jē-nō	Traini, Francesco	tra-'ē-nē, fran-'ches-kō
Severus	sŭ-'vir-ŭs	Uccello, Paolo	ūt-'chel-lō, 'pau-lō
Shen Zhou	shŭn jō	Unkei	un-kā
Shūbun	shub-un	Utagawa Toyokuni	ut-a-ga-wa tō-yō-kun-ē
Signorelli, Luca	sē-nyō-'rel-lē, 'lū-ka	Utzon, Joern	'ut-zōn, 'yōr-(ŭ)n
Siloé, Gil de	sē-lō-'ā, hēl dā	Van Dyck, Anthony	văn-dĭk, an-'tō-nē
Sinan the Great	sŭ-'nan	Vanbrugh, John	'văn-brŭ (or văn-'brū), jan
Skopas of Paros	'skō-pŭs of 'păr-os	Vasarely, Victor	va-'sa-rŭ-lē, vēk-'tor
Sluter, Claus	'slū-tŭr, klaus	Vecelli, Tiziano	vŭ-'chel-lē, tēts-'ya-nō
Song Huizong	song hwā-tsong	Velázquez, Diego	vā-'las-kās, 'dyā-gō
Soufflot, Jacques-Germain	sŭ-'flō, zhak zher-'men	Venturi, Robert	ven-'tū-rē, 'rab-ŭrt
Southworth, Albert Sands	'sauth-wŭrth [also 'sŭth-ŭrth], 'ăl-bŭrt sănz	Vermeer, Jan	vŭr-'me(ŭ)r, yan
		Veronese, Paolo	ver-ŭ-'nā-sē, 'pau-lō
Spranger, Bartholomeus	'sprang-ŭr, bar-tō-lō-'mā-us	Verrocchio, Andrea del	vŭr-'rok-kyō, an-'drā-ŭ del
Stael, Nicolas de	stal, ni-kō-'la dŭ	Vigée-Lebrun, Élisabeth Louise	ve-zhā-lŭ-'brōn, ā-lē-za-'bet lwēz
Stieglitz, Alfred	'stēg-lŭts (or -lits), ăl-frŭd	Vignola, Giacomo da	vēn-'yō-lŭ, 'ja-kō-mō da
Stoss, Viet	'shtōs, 'vēt	Vignon, Pierre	vin-'yon, pyer
Su Dongpo	sŭ dong-po	Vitruvius	vŭ-'trū-vē-ŭs
Suzuki Harunobu	suz-uk-ē har-un-ō-bu	Wang Meng	wang mŭng
Takayoshi	ta-ka-yō-shē	Wang Wei	wang wā
Tatlin, Vladimir	'tat-lyin, vlŭ-'dyēm-yir	Warhol, Andy	'wor-hal, 'ăn-dē
Tawaraya Sōtatsu	ta-wa-ra-ya sō-(ō-)tat-s(u)	Watteau, Antoine	wa-'tō, an-'twan
Teerlinc, Lavinia	'tēr-lingk, lŭ-'vin-ē-ŭ	Wen Zhengming	wŭn jŭng-ming
Theodoros of Phokaia	thē-ō-'dor-os of fō-kā-ŭ	Weyden, Rogier van der	'vīd-ŭn, rō-'ghēr văn dŭr
Theotokópoulos, Doménikos	tā-o-to-'ko-pū-los, dō-'mān-ē-kŭs	Wiligelmus	vē-lē-'ghel-mūs
Tiepolo, Giambattista	tē-'ā-pŭ-lō, jam-bat-'tēs-ta	Witz, Conrad	'vits, 'kon-rat
Tinguely, Jean	'tăn-glŭ, zhan	Wolgemut, Michel	'vōl-gŭ-mūt, 'mik-ŭl
Tintoretto	tin-tŭ-'ret-ō	Wolvinius	wŭl-'vēn-yŭs
Titian	'tish-ŭn (or 'tē-shŭn)	Wu Daozi	ū dau-tsŭ
Toba Sōjō	tō-ba sō-jō	Wu Zhen	ū jŭn
Toledo, Juan Bautista de	tō-'lā-dō, hwan bau-'tēs-ta dā	Xia Gui	shya gwā
Tori Busshi	tō-rē bū-shē	Xu Beihong	shū bā-hong
Torii Kiyomasu	tō-rē-ē kē-yō-mas-u	Yan Liben	yan lē-bŭn
Torii Kiyonaga	tō-rē-ē kē-yō-nag-a	Yosa Buson	yō-sa bus-ōn
Torii Kiyonobu	tō-rē-ē kē-yō-nō-bu	Zhao Mengfu	jau mŭng-fū
Torii Kiyotada	tō-rē-ē kē-yō-ta-da	Zhou Jichang	jō jē-chang
Tosa Mitsunobu	tō-sa mēt-sun-ō-bu	Zhu Da	jū da
Tōshūsai Sharaku	tō-shus-ī sha-ra-ku	Zong Bing	tsong bing
Toulouse-Lautrec, Henri de	tū-lūz-lō-'trek, an-'rē dŭ	Zurbarán, Francisco de	sur-ba-'ran, fran-'sis-kō dā

GLOSSARY

Italicized terms in definitions are defined elsewhere in the glossary.

abacus—The uppermost portion of the *capital* of a *column*, usually a thin slab.

Abakans—Abstract woven hangings suggesting organic spaces as well as giant pieces of clothing made by Madgalena Abakanowicz.

Abstract Formalism—See *Suprematism*.

abstract—In painting and sculpture, emphasizing a derived, essential character that has only a stylized or symbolic visual reference to objects in nature.

acropolis—Literally, the "high city." In Greek architecture, the importance of the city temple was emphasized by building it on a hill above the city.

Action Painting—A type of *Gestural Abstractionism* (Abstract Expressionism or New York School) practiced by Jackson Pollock, in which the emphasis was on the heroic aspects of the artist's gesture in making art. Pollock stood on his canvases, pouring liquid paint in linear webs, and, in effect, incorporated his own physical nature into the components of the picture.

adobe—The clay used to make a kind of sun-dried mud brick of the same name; a building made of such brick.

additive—A kind of sculpture technique in which materials, e. g., clay, are built up or "added" to create form.

addorsed—Set back-to-back, especially as in heraldic design.

aerial perspective—See *perspective*.

agora—An open square or space used for public meetings or business in ancient Greek cities.

aisle—The portion of a church flanking the *nave* and separated from it by a row of *columns* or *piers*.

alabaster—A variety of gypsum or calcite of dense, fine texture, usually white, but also red, yellow, gray, and sometimes banded.

alla prima—A painting technique in which pigments are laid on in one application, with little or no drawing or underpainting.

altarpiece—A panel, painted or sculpted, situated above and behind an altar. See also *retable*.

Amazonomachy—In Greek mythology, the legendary battle between the Greeks and Amazons.

ambulatory—A covered walkway, outdoors (as in a *cloister*) or indoors; especially the passageway around the *apse* and the *choir* of a church.

amphiprostyle—The style of Greek building in which the *colonnade* was placed across both the front and back, but not along the sides.

amphitheater—Literally, a double theater. A Roman conception resembling two Greek theaters put together. The Roman *amphitheater* featured a continuous elliptical *cavea* around a central *arena*.

amphora—A two-handled, jar used for general storage purposes, usuallly to hold wine or oil.

Analytic Cubism—An art movement developed jointly by Pablo Picasso and Georges Braque in which the artists analyzed form from every possible vantage point to combine the various views into one pictorial whole.

anamorphic image—An image that must be viewed by some special means (such as a mirror) to be recognized.

anastasis—The Byzantine representation of the resurrection or the Harrowing of Hell.

andron—Dining room in a Greek house.

aniconic—Non-image representation.

animal style—A generic term for the characteristic ornamentation of artifacts worn and carried by nomadic peoples who, for almost two millennia (B.C. into A.D.) migrated between China and western Europe. The style is characterized by use of phantasms, like the dragon.

antae—The molded projecting ends of the walls forming the *pronaos* or *opisthodomos* of a Greek temple.

apadana—The great audience hall in ancient Persian palaces.

apotheosis—Elevated to the rank of gods or the ascent to heaven.

apotropaic—Capable of warding off evil.

apsara—In India, a nymph of the sky or air; in Chinese Buddhism, a heavenly maiden.

apse—A recess, usually singular and semi-circular, in the wall of a Roman *basilica* or at the east end of a Christian church.

arabesque—Literally, "Arabian-like." A flowing, intricate pattern derived from stylized organic motifs, usually floral, often arranged in symmetrical *palmette* designs; generally, an Islamic decorative motif.

arcade—A series of *arches* supported by *piers* or *columns*.

arch—A curved structural member that spans an opening and is generally composed of wedge-shaped blocks (*voussoirs*) that transmit the downward pressure laterally. A diaphragm arch is a transverse , wall-bearing arch that divides a *vault* or a ceiling into compartments, providing a kind of firebreak. See also *thrust*.

architrave—The *lintel* or lowest division of the *entablature*; sometimes called the epistyle.

archivolt—One of a series of concentric *moldings* on a Romanesque or a Gothic arch.

arcuated—Of *arch-column* construction.

arena—In a Roman *amphitheater*, the place where bloody gladiatorial combats and other boisterous events took place.

Arhats—Also *Bodhisattvas*. Buddhist holy persons who have achieved enlightenment and *nirvana* by suppression of all desire for earthly things.

arras—A kind of tapestry originating in Arras, a town in northeastern France.

ars—The technical knowledge and practical skill that made possible the building of Gothic churches. See also *scientia*.

ars geometria—The technical knowledge and practical skills of geometry that enabled architects, sculptors, and especially stained-glass artists to execute their designs, layouts, and assemblies. A sketchbook compiled by Villard de Honnecourt in the early 13th century demonstrates how artists of the time conceived of their work in terms of geometric form.

Art Brut—A term coined by Jean Dubuffet to characterize art that is genuine, untaught, coarse, even brutish.

Art Deco—Descended from *Art Nouveau*, this movement of the 1920s and 1930s sought to upgrade industrial design in competition with "fine art" and to work new materials into decorative patterns that could be either machined or hand-crafted. Characterized by "streamlined" design, elongated and symmetrical.

Art Nouveau—An early 20th-century art movement whose proponents tried to synthesize all the arts in an effort to create art based on natural forms that could be mass-produced by technologies of the industrial age.

ashlar masonry—Carefully cut and regularly shaped blocks of stone used in construction, fitted together without mortar.

assemblage—A three-dimensional composition made of various materials such as *found objects*, paper, wood, and cloth. See also *collage*.

atlantid—A male figure that functions as a supporting *column*. See also *caryatid*.

atlatl—Toltec "throw sticks."

Atmospheric or **aerial perspective**—See *perspective*.

atrium (pl. atria)—The court of a Roman house that is near the entrance and partly open to the sky. Also the open, colonnaded court in front of and attached to a Christian *basilica*.

attic—In architectural terminology, the uppermost story.

attribution—Assignment of a work to a maker or makers. Based on *documentary evidence*(i.e., signatures and dates on works and/or artist's own writings) and *internal evidence* (stylistic and iconographical analysis).

automatism—In painting, the process of yielding oneself to instinctive motions of the hands after establishing a set of conditions (such as size of paper or medium) within which a work is to be carried out.

avant-garde—Literally, the advance guard in a platoon. Artists who work in the most advanced stylistic expression. Also used as an adjective.

avatar—A manifestation of a deity incarnated in some visible form in which the deity performs a sacred function on earth. In Hinduism, an incarnation of a god.

avlu—A courtyard forming a summer extension of the *mosque* and surrounded by porticoes formed by domed squares.

axial plan—See *plan*.

baldacchino—A canopy on columns, frequently built over an altar. See also *ciborium*.

baptistery—The building next to a church, used for baptism.

barays—The large reservoirs laid out around Cambodian wats that served as means of transportation as well as irrigation. The reservoirs were connected by a network of canals.

baron—A feudal lord. See also *fief*.

Baroque—A blanket designation for the art of the period 1600 to 1750.

baroque—Ancient sculpture and architecture that appear to modern art historians to have strong stylistic affinities with 17th- and 18th-century monuments.

barrel or **tunnel vault**—See *vault*.

barroco—Portuguese for an irregularly shaped pearl, from which the word baroque probably comes.

bas-relief—See *relief*.

base—In Greek architecture, the lowest part of the Ionic column.

basilica—In Roman architecture, a public building for assemblies (especially tribunals), rectangular in plan with an entrance usually on a long side. In Christian architecture, an early church somewhat resembling the Roman basilica, usually entered from one end and with an *apse* at the other, creating an *axial plan*.

Bauhaus—A school of architecture in Germany in the 1920s under the aegis of Walter Gropius, whose mission was to give form to space by means of mastery of physical laws of statics, dynamics, optics, and acoustics. It stressed solutions to contemporary problems in housing, urban planning, and high-quality, utilitarian mass production.

beehive tomb—In Mycenaean architecture, beehive-shaped type of tomb covered by an earthen mound and constructed as a *corbeled vault*. See *tholos*.

ben-ben—A pyramidal stone; a *fetish* of the Egyptian god Re.

benizuri-e—A style of Japanese two-color printmaking in which the dominant pink contrasts with patches of pale green and still smaller areas of black to produce a strong color vibration despite the very limited palette.

besso—A modest Japanese country retreat.

bevel—See *chamfer*.

bhakti—In Buddhist thought, the adoration of a personalized deity (*Bodhisattva*) as a means of achieving unity with it. In Hinduism, the devout, selfless direction of all tasks and activities of life to the service of one god.

bilingual vases—Experimental Greek vases produced for a short time in the late sixth century B.C.; one side featured decoration in *red-figure technique*, the other *black-figure technique*.

black-figure technique—In early Greek pottery, the silhouetting of dark figures against a light background of natural, reddish clay.

blanc-de-chine—White china ware.

blind arcade (wall arcade)—An *arcade* having no actual openings, applied as decoration to a wall surface.

Bodhisattva—In Buddhist thought, one of the host of divinities provided to the *Buddha* to help him save humanity. A potential *Buddha*. See also *bhakti*.

bombé—Outwardly bowed.

bottega—A shop; the studio-shop of an Italian artist.

Buddha—The supreme enlightened being of Buddhism; an embodiment of divine wisdom and virtue. **Buddhist** (*adj.*).

burin—A pointed steel tool used for *engraving* or *incising*.

buttress—An exterior masonry structure that opposes the lateral thrust of an *arch* or a *vault*. A pier buttress is a solid mass of masonry; a flying buttress consists typically of an inclined member carried on an arch or a series of arches and a solid buttress to which it transmits lateral *thrust*.

caldarium—The hot-bath section of a Roman bathing establishment.

calligraphy—Handwriting or penmanship, especially elegant or "beautiful" writing as a decorative art.

calotype—Photographic process in which a positive image is made by shining light through a negative image onto a sheet of sensitized paper.

camera lucida—A device in which a small lens projects the image of an object downward onto a sheet of paper. Literally, "lighted room."

camera obscura—An ancestor of the modern camera in which a tiny pinhole, acting as a lens, projects an image on a screen, the wall of a room, or the ground-glass wall of a box; used by artists in the 17th, 18th, and early 19th centuries as an aid in drawing from nature. Literally, "dark room."

campaniform—Bell-shaped.

campanile—A bell tower of a church, usually, but not always, freestanding.

canon—Rule, i.e., of proportion. The ancient Greeks considered beauty to be a matter of "correct" proportion and sought a *canon* of proportion, in music and for the human figure.

canon law—The law system of the Church as opposed to civil or secular law.

capital—The uppermost member of a *column*, serving as a transition from the *shaft* to the *lintel*. The *capital* has two elements—the *echinus* and *abacus*—the forms of which vary with the order.

Capitolium—A shrine honoring Jupiter, Juno, and Minerva.

caravansary—An inn where caravans could rest.

cardo—The north–south road in a Roman town, intersecting the *decumanus* at right angles.

cartoon—In painting, a full-size preliminary drawing from which a painting is made. Before the modern era, cartoons were customarily worked out in complete detail; the design was then transferred to the working surface by coating the back with chalk and going over the lines with a stylus, or by pricking the lines and "pouncing" charcoal dust through the resulting holes.

caryatid—A female figure that functions as a supporting *column*. See also *atlantid*.

castrum—A Roman military encampment, famed for the precision with which it was planned and laid out.

catacombs—Subterranean networks of galleries and chambers designed as cemeteries for the burial of the dead.

catafalque—The framework that supports and surrounds a deceased person's body on a bier.

cathedra—Literally, the seat of the bishop, from which the word cathedral is derived.

cavea—The seating area in Greek and Roman theaters and amphitheaters. Literally, a hollow place or cavity.

celadon—A Chinese-Korean pottery glaze characterized by its mat gray-green color.

cella—An enclosed chamber (Greek—*naos*); the essential feature of a Classical temple, in which the cult statue usually stood.

cement—See *concrete*.

centaur—In Greek mythology, a fantastical creature, with the front or top half of a human and the back or bottom half of a horse.

centauromachy—In Greek mythology, the battle between the Greeks and *centaurs*.

central plan—See *plan*.

Ch'an—See *Zen*.

chaitya—An Indian rock-cut temple hall having a votive *stupa* at one end.

chakravartin—In India, the ideal king, the Universal Lord who ruled through goodness.

chamfer—The surface formed by cutting off a corner of a board or post; a bevel.

chancel—The elevated area at the altar end of a church reserved for the priest and choir.

chandi—A Javanese Buddhist temple.

chansons de geste—Epic songs, especially French.

Charuns—Etruscan death demons.

chateau fort—A Romanesque stone castle, surrounded by thick walls and moats, the seat and symbol of the authority of the medieval *baron*.

chatra—See *parasol* or *yasti*.

chevet—The east, or apsidal, end of a Gothic church, including *choir*, *ambulatory*, and radiating chapels.

chi/rho—The initial letters of Christ's name in Greek, and coming to stand as a monogram for Christ.

chiaroscuro—In drawing or panting, the treatment and use of light and dark, especially the gradations of light that produce the effect of *modeling*.

chigi—The crosspiece at the gables of Japanese shrine architecture.

chimera—A monster of Greek invention with the head and body of a lion and the tail of a serpent. A second head, that of a goat, grows out of one side of the body.

chiton—A Greek tunic, the essential (and often only) garment of both men and women, the other being the *himation* or *mantle*; a kind of cape.

choir—The space reserved for the clergy in the church, usually east of the *transept* but, in some instances, extending into the *nave*.

chroma—Of the two variables in color, the apparent amount of light reflected and the apparent purity, value and tonality represent lightness; chroma, saturation, and intensity represent purity.

chryselephantine—Fashioned of gold and ivory.

ciborium—A canopy, often freestanding and supported by four columns, erected over an altar; also, a covered cup used in the sacraments of the Christian Church. See *baldacchino*.

cinétisme—See *Kinetic Art*.

circles of confusion—A phenomenon appearing on out-of-focus negatives, observed by modern photographers.

cire perdue—The *lost-wax process*. A bronze-casting method in which a figure is modeled in wax and covered with clay; the whole is fired, melting away the wax and hardening the clay, which then becomes a mold for molten metal.

cista—A cylindrical container made of sheet bronze with cast handles and feet, often with elaborately engraved bodies, used for women's toilet articles.

Cizhou—A type of northern Chinese pottery characterized by subtle techniques of underglaze painting and incision of a design through a colored slip

clair de lune—A pale, silvery blue Chinese pottery glaze.

clerestory—The *fenestrated* part of a building that rises above the roofs of the other parts.

cloison—Literally, a partition. A cell made of metal wire or a narrow metal strip soldered edge-up to a metal base to hold enamel or other decorative materials.

cloisonné—A process of enameling employing *cloisons*.

cloister—A monastery courtyard, usually with covered walks or *ambulatories* along its sides.

cluster pier—See *compound pier*.

codex (pl. **codices**)—Separate pages of *vellum* or *parchment* bound together at one side and having a cover; the predecessor of the modern book. The *codex* superseded the *rotulus*. In Mesoamerica, a painted and inscribed book on long sheets of fig-bark paper or deerskin coated with plaster and folded into accordion-like pleats.

coffer—A sunken panel, often ornamental, in a *soffit*, a *vault*, or a ceiling.

collage—A composition made by combining on a flat surface various materials such as newspaper, wallpaper, printed text and illustrations, photographs, and cloth. See also *photomontage*.

colonnades—A series or row of *columns*, usually spanned by *lintels*.

colonnette—A small *column*.

color-field painters— A term used to describe the work Mark Rothko and other painters of the Abstract Expressionist or New York School who explored the optical and mystical effects of fields of color. Also known as Post-Painterly Abstractionists.

column—A vertical, weight-carrying architectural member, circular in cross-section and consisting of a base (sometimes omitted), a *shaft*, and a *capital*.

complementary colors—Those pairs of colors, such as red and green, that together embrace the entire spectrum. The complement of one of the three primary colors is a mixture of the other two. In pigments, they produce a neutral gray when mixed in the right proportions.

composite capital—An ornate combination of Ionic volutes and Corinthian acanthus leaves that became popular in Roman times.

composite view—See *twisted perspective*.

compound or **cluster pier**—A *pier* composed of a group or cluster of members, especially characteristic of Gothic architecture.

computer imaging—A medium developed during the 1960s and 1970s that uses computer programs and electronic light to make designs and images on the surface of a computer or television screen.

Conceptual art—Communicates message and meaning through more permanent media, two-dimensional or three-dimensional or both, often in combination with printed text. The primary purpose is to convey an idea or a concept with whatever visual means are available.

conches—Semi-circular half-domes.

concrete—A building material invented by the Romans and consisting of various proportions of lime mortar, volcanic sand, water, and small stones. From the Latin caementa, from which the English word cement is derived.

condottiere—A professional soldier employed by the Italian city-states in the early Renaissance.

connoisseur—An expert on works of art and the individual styles of artists.

Constructivism—A movement in art formulated by Naum Gabo in which he built up his sculptures piece by piece in space, instead of carving or modeling them in the traditional way. In this way the sculptor worked with volume of mass and volume of space as different materials.

consul—The elected representatives in Roman constitutional government, originally drawn only from among the *patricians*, or wealthy landowners.

contextuality—The causal relationships among artists, art work, and the society or culture that conditions them.

continuous narration—In painting or sculpture, the convention of the same figure appearing more than once in the same space at different stages in a story.

contrapposto—The disposition of the human figure in which one part is turned in opposition to another part (usually hips and legs one way, shoulders and chest another), creating a counter-positioning of the body about its central axis. Sometimes called weight shift because the weight of the body tends to be thrown to one foot, creating tension on one side and relaxation on the other.

corbel—A projecting wall member used as a support for some element in the superstructure. Also, courses of stone or brick in which each course projects beyond the one beneath it. Two such structures, meeting at the topmost course, create a corbeled arch.

corbel tables—Horizontal projections resting on *corbels*.

corbeled arch—See *corbel*.

corbeled vault—A *vault* formed by the piling of rocks in horizontal courses, cantilevered inward until the two walls meet in a pointed arch. No mortar is used, and the vault is held in place only by the weight of the blocks themselves, with smaller stones used as wedges.

Corinthian capital—A more ornate form than Doric or Ionic; it consists of a double row of acanthus leaves from which tendrils and flowers grow, wrapped around a bell-shaped *echinus*. Although this *capital* form is often cited as the distinguishing feature of the Corinthian order, there is, strictly speaking, no Corinthian order, but only this style of capital used in the Ionic order.

cornice—The projecting, crowning member of the *entablature* framing the *pediment;* also, any crowning projection.

Corpus Juris Civilis—Code of Civil Law; the codification of Roman law, supervised by Justinian, which became the foundation of the law systems of most European nations today.

cortile—In Renaissance architecture, an internal court surrounded by an arcade.

Cosmati—A group of 12th to 14th century craftsmen who worked in marble and mosaic, creating work (known as **Cosmato work**) characterized by inlays of gold and precious or semi-precious stones and finely cut marble in geometric patterns.

crenelated—Notched or indented, usually with respect to tops of walls, as in battlements.

cromlech—A circle of *monoliths*.

cross vault—See *vault*.

crossing—The space in a cruciform church formed by the intersection of the *nave* and the *transept*.

crossing square—The area in a church formed by the intersection (*crossing*) of a *nave* and a *transept* of equal width, often used as a standard measurement of interior proportion.

cruciform—Cross-shaped.

crypt—A vaulted space under part of a building, wholly or partly underground; in medieval churches, normally the portion under an *apse* or a *chevet*.

cubiculum (pl. **cubicula**)—A small cubicle or bedroom that opened onto the *atrium* of a Roman house. Also, a small room constructed in the wall of an Early Christian catacomb to serve as a mortuary chapel.

Cubism—See *Analytic* or *Synthetic Cubism*.

cultural constructs—In the reconstruction of the context of a work of art, experts consult the evidence of religion, science, technology, language, philosophy, and the arts to discover the thought patterns common to artists and their audiences.

culture—The collective characteristics by which a community identifies itself and by which it expects to be recognized and respected.

cuneiform—Literally, "wedge-shaped." A system of writing used in ancient Mesopotamia, the characters of which were wedge-shaped.

cupola—An exterior architectural feature composed of *drums* with shallow caps; a dome.

Cycladic art—The pre-Greek art of the Cycladic Islands.

Cyclopean—Gigantic, vast and rough, massive. Cyclopean masonry is a method of stone construction using large, irregular blocks without mortar. The huge unhewn and roughly cut blocks of stone were used to construct Bronze Age fortifications such as Tiryns and other Mycenaean sites.

cylinder seal—A cylindrical piece of stone usually about an inch or so in height, decorated with a design in *intaglio* (incised), so that a raised pattern was left when the seal was rolled over soft clay. In the ancient Near East documents, storage jars, and other important possessions were signed, sealed, and identified in this way.

Dada—An art movement that grew out of the absurdity and horror of World War I. *Dada* protested all art, modern or traditional, as well as the civilization that had produced it, to create an art of the absurd. Foremost among the Dadaists was Marcel Duchamp.

Daedalic—Refers to a Greek *orientalizing* style of the 7th century B.C. Characteristic of the style is the triangular flat-topped head framed by long strands of hair that form complementary triangles to that of the face.

daguerreotype—A photograph made by an early method on a plate of chemically treated metal; developed by Louis J. M. Daguerre.

damnatio memoriae—The Roman decree condemning those who ran afoul of the Senate to having their memorials demolished and their names erased from public inscriptions; the memory of them would be damned.

De Stijl—Dutch for "the style," a movement (and magazine) founded by Piet Mondrian and Theo van Doesburg.

deceptive cadence—In a horizontal scroll, the "false ending," which arrests the viewer's gaze by appearing to be the end of a narrative sequence, but which actually sets the stage for a culminating figure or scene.

deconstruction—A method of analysis proceeding by re-reading the received art-historical picture and showing where and how it is false to the realities of the cultures it attempts to explain and to the meanings of particular works of art.

découpage—A technique of decoration in which letters or images are cut out of paper or some such material and then pasted onto a surface.

decumanus—The east–west road in a Roman town, intersecting the *cardo* at right angles.

decursio—The ritual circling of a Roman funerary pyre.

demos—The Greek word meaning "the people," from which democracy is derived.

demotic—Late Egyptian writing

denarius—The standard Roman silver coin from which the word penny ultimately derives.

descriptive approach to representation—In artistic representation, that which is 'known' about an object is represented. To represent a human profile "descriptively" would require the artist to depict both eyes rather than just one.

devaraja—In Cambodia, the ideal king who was the Universal Lord and god-king in life and after death.

dhyani Buddha—A representation of *Buddha* in meditation, seated in yoga pose, expressing the tranquility of pure and perfect transcendence of the world.

di sotto in sù—A technique of representing perspective in ceiling painting. Literally, "from below upwards."

diaphragm arch—See *arch*.

dictator perpetuus—Dictator for life, the title awarded to Julius Caesar shortly before his death.

ding—A fine, white proto-porcelain used in Chinese pottery.

diorite—An extremely hard stone used in Mesopotamian and Egyptian art.

dipteral—The term used to describe the architectural feature of double *colonnades* around Greek temples. See also *peripteral*.

diptych—A two-paneled painting or *altarpiece*; also, an ancient Roman and Early Christian two-hinged carved writing tablet, or two ivory memorial panels.

disegno interno—"Inner design," a reference to the Platonic Idea which underlay the visible world.

documentary evidence—In *attributions* of works of art, this consists of contracts, signatures, and dates on works as well as the artist's own writings.

dolmen—Several large stones (*megaliths*) capped with a covering slab, erected in prehistoric times.

dome—A hemispheric *vault*; theoretically, an *arch* rotated on its vertical axis.

Donaustil—A 15th- to16th-century Northern Renaissance painting style that flourished along the Danube River from Regensburg eastward into Austria. The style formed around the depiction of landscape and stresses mood, sometimes heightened to passion.

Doric—One of the two systems (or *orders*) evolved for articulating the three units of the elevation of a Greek temple—the platform, the *colonnade*, and the superstructure (*entablature*). The Doric order is characterized by, i.e., capitals with funnel-shaped *echinuses*, columns without bases, and a frieze of *triglyphs* and *metopes*. See also *Ionic*.

douanier—In French, "customs collector," a term that came to be applied to Henri Rousseau, the French "primitive" painter.

dromos—The passage leading to a *beehive tomb*.

drum—The circular wall that supports a *dome*; also, one of the cylindrical stones of which a non-monolithic *shaft* of a *column* is made.

dry fresco—See *fresco*.

dry point—An engraving in which the design, instead of being cut into the plate with a *burin*, is scratched into the surface with a hard steel "pencil." The process is quicker and more spontaneous than standard engraving and lends itself to the creation of painterly effects. Its disadvantage is the fact that the plate wears out very quickly. See also *engraving, etching, intaglio*.

duomo—Italian for cathedral, from the dome that usually surmounts the cathedral.

Earth, Environmental, or Site Art—A kind of modernist art that constructs with natural or artificial materials monuments of great scale and minimal form. Permanent or impermanent, these works are intended to transform some section of the environment so as to assert its presence and importance as reworked by the hand of the artist.

echinus—In architecture, the convex element of a *capital* directly below the *abacus*.

écorché—A figure painted or sculptured to show the muscles of the body without skin.

elevation—In drawing and architecture, a geometric projection of a building on a plane perpendicular to the horizon; a vertical projection. A head-on view of an external or internal wall, showing its features and often other elements that would be visible beyond or before the wall.

emblema—The central section or motif of a *mosaic*.

embrasure—A *splayed* opening in a wall that enframes a doorway or a window.

encaustic—A painting technique in which pigment is mixed with wax and applied to the surface while hot.

engaged column—A column-like, nonfunctional form projecting from a wall and articulating it visually. See also *pilaster*.

engobe—A slip of finely sifted clay that originally is of the same color as the clay of the pot.

engraving—The process of incising a design in hard material, often a metal plate (usually copper); also, the print or impression made from such a plate. See also *dry point, etching, intaglio*.

entablature—The part of a building above the *columns* and below the roof or the upper story. The entablature has three parts: *architrave* or *epistyle*, *frieze*, and *pediment*.

entasis—A convex tapering (an apparent swelling) in the *shaft* of a column.

epistyle—See *architrave*.

escutcheon—An emblem bearing a coat of arms.

esthetic properties of works of art—The visual and tactile features of an object: form, shape, line, color, mass, and volume.

esthetics—The branch of philosophy devoted to theories about the nature of art and artistic expression. Also referring to such theories.

etching—A kind of *engraving* in which the design is incised in a layer of wax or varnish on a metal plate. The parts of the plate left exposed are then *etched* (slightly eaten away) by the acid in which the plate is immersed after incising. See also *dry point, engraving, intaglio*.

ethnocentrism—The tendency to explain and to judge artifacts from the perspective of one's own culture and to the detriment of other cultures.

ewer—A large pitcher.

exarch—A Byzantine governor of a foreign province.

exedra—Recessed area, usually semi-circular.

exemplum virtutis—Example or model of virtue.

Expressionism—A modernist art movement that was a manifestation of subjective feeling toward objective reality and the world of imagination. Characterized by bold, vigorous brushwork, emphatic line, and bright color. Two submovements within *Expressionism* were Die Brücke, in Dresden, and Der Blaue Reiter, in Munich.

extrados—The upper or outer surface of an *arch*. See *intrados*.

facade—Usually, the front of a building; also, the other sides when they are emphasized architecturally.

faïence—Earthenware or pottery, especially with highly colored design (from Faenza, Italy, a site of manufacture for such ware). Glazed earthenware.

fan vault—See *vault*

fauces—Literally, the throat of the house. In a Roman house, the narrow foyer leading to the *atrium*.

fauves—Literally, "wild beasts." An early 20th-century art movement led by Henri Matisse and characterized by wild, bright colors.

femmage—A kind of feminist sewn collage made by Miriam Schapiro in which she assembles fabrics, quilts, buttons, sequins, lace trim, and rick-rack to explore hidden metaphors for womanhood, using techniques historically associated with women's crafts (techniques and media not elevated to the status of fine art).

fenestration—The arrangement of the windows of a building.

fengshui—A Chinese notion of "wind and water", the breath of life, which is scattered by wind and must be stopped by water; thus the forces of wind and water must be adjusted in the orientation of Chinese architecture.

fetish—An object believed to possess magical powers, especially one capable of bringing to fruition its owner's plans; sometimes regarded as the abode of a supernatural power or spirit.

feudalism—The medieval political, social and economic system held together by the relationship of a liege-lord and vassal.

fibula—A decorative pin, usually used to fasten garments.

fictor—Latin for "sculptor."

fido—Latin for "to trust."

fief—The land owned by a medieval *baron*.

fin de siècle—Literally, the end of the century, a period at the end of the 19th century and just before World War I in which art and literature languished in a kind of malaise compounded of despondency, boredom, morbidity, and hypersensitivity to the esthetic.

First Style— The earliest style of Pompeiian mural painting. Also called the masonry style, because the aim of the artist was to imitate, using painted stucco relief, the appearance of costly marble panels.

flamboyant style—A Late Gothic style of architecture superseding the *rayonnant* style and named for the flamelike appearance of its pointed tracery.

flute or fluting—Vertical channeling, roughly semicircular in cross-section and used principally on *columns* and *pilasters*.

flying buttress—See *buttress*.

foreshortening—The use of *perspective* to represent in art the apparent visual contraction of an object that extends back in space at an angle to the perpendicular plane of sight.

formalism—Strict adherence to, or dependence on, stylized shapes and methods of composition.

forum—The public square or marketplace of an ancient Roman city.

found objects—Images, materials, or objects as found in the everyday environment that are appropriated into works of art.

Fourth Style—In Pompeiian mural painting, the Fourth Style marks a return to architectural illusionism, but the architectural vistas of the *Fourth Style* are irrational fantasies.

freedmen—In ancient and medieval society, the class which had been freed from servitude as opposed to having been born free.

freestanding sculpture—See *sculpture in the round*.

fresco—Painting on plaster, either dry (dry fresco or fresco secco) or wet (wet or true fresco). In the latter method, the pigments are mixed with water and become chemically bound to the plaster. Also, a painting executed in either method.

fresco secco—See *fresco*.

fret or **meander**—An ornament, usually in bands but also covering broad surfaces, consisting of interlocking geometric motifs. An ornamental pattern of contiguous straight lines joined usually at right angles.

frieze—The part of the *entablature* between the *architrave* and the *cornice*; also, any sculptured or ornamented band in a building, on furniture, etc.

frigidarium—The cold-bath section of a Roman bathing establishment.

frottage—A process of rubbing a crayon or other medium across paper placed over surfaces with strong and evocative texture pattern to combine patterns.

Futurism—A militant group of Italian poets, painters, and sculptors who regularly signed and issued manifestoes declaring revolution in art against all traditional tastes, values, and styles and embracing the modern age of steel and speed and the virtues of violence and war.

gable—See *pediment*.

garbha griha—Literally, "womb chamber." In Hindu temples, this is the *cella*, the inner sanctum, for the cult image or symbol, the holiest of places in the temple.

garth—The garden of a *cloister*.

genre—A style or category of art; also, a kind of painting realistically depicting scenes from everyday life.

gesso—Plaster mixed with a binding material and used for *reliefs* and as a *ground* for painting.

Gestural Abstractionism—Also known as Abstract Expressionism and *Action Painting*. A kind of abstract painting in which the gesture, or act of painting, is seen as heroic and the subject of art. Its most renowned proponent was Jackson Pollock.

gigantomachy—In Greek mythology, the battle between gods and giants.

glaze—A vitreous coating applied to pottery to seal and decorate the surface; it may be colored, transparent, or opaque, and glossy or *matte*. In oil painting, a thin, transparent, or semitransparent layer put over a color to alter it slightly.

glory—See *nimbus*.

glyph—A pictographic component of a pre-alphabetic system of writing, prominent in Mesoamerican inscriptions.

Golden Mean—Also known as the Golden Rule or Golden Section, a system of measuring in which units used to construct designs are subdivided into two parts in such a way that the longer subdivision is related to the length of the whole unit in the same proportion as the shorter subdivision is related to the longer subdivision. The *esthetic* appeal of these proportions has led artists of varying periods and cultures to employ them in determining basic dimensions.

gopuram—The massive, ornamented entrance structure of South Indian temple compounds.

gorget—Throat armor.

graver—A cutting tool used by engravers and sculptors.

Greek Cross—A cross in which all the arms are the same length.

grisaille—A monochrome painting done mainly in neutral grays to simulate sculpture.

groin—The edge formed by the intersection of two *vaults*.

groin or **cross vault**—Formed by the intersection at right angles of two barrel vaults of equal size. Lighter in appearance than the barrel vault, the groin vault requires *buttressing*. See *vault*.

grotteschi—Grotesque images used for ornament in architecture, especially in grottoes.

ground—A coating applied to a canvas or some other surface to prepare that surface for painting; also, background.

guang—A Chinese covered libation vessel.

guilloche—An architectural ornament that imitates braided ribbon, or that consists of interlaced, curving bands.

hallenkirche—A hall church. A type of Gothic design much favored in Germany in which the *aisles* rise to the same height as the *nave* section.

haniwa—Sculptured fired pottery tubes, modeled in human, animal, or other forms and placed around early (archaic) Japanese burial mounds.

Happenings—Loosely structured performances initiated in the 1960s, whose creators were trying to suggest the dynamic and confusing qualities of everyday life; most shared qualities of unexpectedness, variety, and wonder.

Hard-Edge Abstractionists—A movement within Abstract Expressionism or the New York School that rigidly excluded all reference to gesture, and incorporated smooth knife-edge geometric forms to express the notion that the meaning of painting should be its form and nothing else. Ellsworth Kelly is an example.

harmika—In Buddhist architecture, a square enclosure surmounting the dome of a *stupa*, from which arises the *yasti*.

hatching—A technique used in drawing, engraving, etc., in which fine lines are cut or drawn close together to achieve an effect of shading.

Hejira—The flight of Muhammad from Mecca to Medinet-en-Nabi ("City of the Prophet") in the year 622, the year Islam dates its beginnings.

Helladic art—The pre-Greek art of the Greek mainland (Hellas).

herm—A bust on a quadrangular pillar.

hieratic—A method of representation fixed by religious principles and ideas; also, the priestly supernaturalism disparaging matter and material values that prevailed throughout the Christian Middle Ages, especially in Orthodox Byzantium.

hieroglyphic—A system of writing using symbols or pictures; also one of the symbols.

high relief—See *relief*.

himation—A Greek *mantle* worn by men and women over the tunic and draped in various ways.

Hinayana—In Buddhist thought, the Lesser Vehicle to achieve *nirvana*.

Hippodamian plan—A city plan devised by Hippodamos of Miletos *c.* 466 B.C., in which a strict grid was imposed upon a site, regardless of the terrain, so that all streets would meet at right angles. A *Hippodamian plan* also called for separate quarters for public, private, and religious functions, so that such a city was logically as well as regularly planned.

historiated—Ornamented with representations, such as plants, animals, or human figures, that have a narrative—as distinct from a purely decorative—function. Historiated initial letters were a popular form of manuscript decoration in the Middle Ages.

horror vacui—Literally, fear of "empty space," a technique of design in which an entire surface is covered with pattern.

hôtel—A town house.

hubris—Human arrogance towards the gods.

hue—The name of a color. Pigment colors combine differently than colors of light. The primary colors (in pigment: blue, red and yellow; in light: blue, red, and green) together with the secondary colors (in pigment: green, orange, and violet; in light: cyan, magenta, and yellow) form the chief colors of the spectrum. See also *complementary colors*.

humanism—The philosophy that superseded scholasticism, characterized by its chief concern for human values and interests as distinct from, but not opposed to, the otherworldly values of religion.

hydria—An ancient Greek three-handled water pitcher.

hypaethral—A building having no pediment or roof, open to the sky.

hypostyle hall—In Egyptian architecture, a hall with a roof supported by columns.

icon—A portrait or image; especially in the Greek church, a panel with a painting of sacred personages that are objects of veneration. In the visual arts, a painting, a piece of sculpture, or even a building regarded as an object of veneration.

Iconoclasm—A period in 7th century Byzantium in which a series of calamities erupted, indirectly bringing about an imperial ban on images—the destruction of which we call *iconoclasm*. The destroyers of images were known as iconoclasts, while those who opposed such a ban were known as iconophiles or iconodules.

iconography—Literally, the "writing" of images, both the significance and study of them; the analytic study of the symbolic, often religious, meaning of objects, persons, or events depicted in works of art.

iconostasis—The large icon-bearing chancel screen that shuts off the sanctuary of a Byzantine church from the rest of the church. In eastern Christian churches, a screen or a partition, with doors and many *tiers* of *icons*, separating the sanctuary from the main body of the church.

idealization—The representation of things according to a preconception of ideal form or type; a kind of *esthetic* distortion to produce idealized forms. See also *realism*.

ideogram—A simple, picturelike sign filled with implicit meaning.

ikegobo—The Benin altar of the hand or arm, symbolizing the Benin king's powers of accomplishment.

illumination—Decoration with drawings (usually in gold, silver, and bright colors), especially of the initial letters of a manuscript.

imagines (sing. **imago**)—In ancient Rome, wax portraits of ancestors.

imam—The leader of collective worship in Muslim religious practices.

impasto—A style of painting in which the pigment is applied thickly or in heavy lumps, as in many of Rembrandt's paintings.

imperator—A Latin term meaning "commander in chief" from which we derive our word "emperor."

impluvium—In a Roman house, the basin located in the *atrium* that collected rainwater.

impost block—A stone with the shape of a truncated, inverted pyramid, placed between a *capital* and the *arch* that springs from it.

in antis—In Greek architecture, between the *antae*.

in situ—In place; in original position.

incising—Cutting into a surface with a sharp instrument; also, a method of decoration, especially on metal and pottery.

insula—In Roman architecture, a multistory apartment house, usually made of brick-faced *concrete;* also refers to an entire city block.

intaglio—A category of graphic technique in which the design is *incised,* so that the impression made is in *relief.* Used especially on gems, seals, and dies for coins, but also in the kinds of printing or printmaking in which the ink-bearing surface is depressed; also, an object so decorated. See also *dry point, engraving, etching.*

intarsia—Inlay work, primarily in wood and sometimes in mother-of-pearl, marble, etc..

interaxial—The distance between the center of one column drum and the center of the next.

intercolumniation—The space or the system of spacing between *columns* in a *colonnade.*

internal evidence—In *attributions* of works of art, what can be learned by stylistic and iconographical analysis, in comparison with other works, and by analysis of the physical properties of the medium itself.

International Style—A style of 13th–14th-century painting begun by Simone Martini, who adapted the French Gothic manner to Sienese art fused with influences from the north. This style appealed to the aristocracy because of its brilliant color, lavish costume, intricate ornament, and themes involving splendid processions of knights and ladies. Also a style of 20th-century architecture associated with Le Corbusier whose elegance of design came to influence the look of modern office buildings and skyscrapers.

intrados—The underside of an *arch* or a *vault.* See *extrados.*

Ionic—One of the two systems (or *orders*) evolved for articulating the three units of the elevation of a Greek temple, the platform, the *colonnade,* and the superstructure (*entablature*). The Ionic order is characterized by, i.e., volute capitals, columns with bases, and an uninterrupted frieze.

jamb—In architecture, the side posts of a doorway.

jataka—Tales of the lives of, or a scriptural account of the *Buddha.* See also *sutra.*

jihad—Holy war, participation and resultant death in which assures a faithful Muslim the reward of Paradise.

jomon—A type of Japanese decorative technique characterized by rope-like relief. *Jomon* means "rope decoration."

ka—In ancient Egypt, immortal human substance; the concept approximates the Western idea of the soul.

karma—In Vedic religions, the ethical consequence of a person's life, which determine his or her fate.

kermess—A festival celebrating a saint's day.

ketos—Greek for sea dragon.

key or **meander**—See *fret.*

keystone—The central, uppermost *voussoir* in an *arch.*

khutba—The sermon and act of allegiance by the Muslim community to its *imam* that takes place near the *qibla* wall.

Kinetic Art—A kind of moving art. Closely related to *Op Art* in its concern with the perception of motion by visual stimulus, it was a logical step to present objects that actually moved. Characteristic of the work of Alexander Calder and the *Constructivists.*

kivas—Large circular underground structures that are the spiritual and ceremonial centers of Pueblo Indian life.

kore (pl. **korai**)—Greek for "young woman."

koru—Maori decorative spiral motifs.

kouros (pl. **kouroi**)—Greek for "young man."

krater—An ancient Greek wide-mouthed bowl for mixing wine and water.

kufic—An early form of the Arabic alphabet.

kylix/cylix—An ancient Greek shallow drinking cup with two handles and a stem.

lakshanas—Distinguishing marks of the *Buddha.*

lamassu—In Assyrian art, genii guardians in the form of man-headed bulls.

lapis lazuli—A rich, ultramarine, semiprecious stone used for carving and as a source for pigment.

lekythoi—Flasks containing perfumed oil that were placed in Greek graves as offerings to the deceased.

lierne—A short *rib* that runs from one main rib of a *vault* to another.

linear perspective—See *perspective.*

lintel—A beam used to span an opening.

loculi—Openings in the walls of catacombs to receive the dead.

loggia—A gallery with an open *arcade* or a *colonnade* on one or both sides.

longitudinal plan—The *basilican* plan.

lost-wax process—See *cire perdue.*

lotiform capital—A capital in the form of a lotus petal.

low relief—See *bas-relief.*

lunette—A semi-circular opening (with the flat side down) in a wall over a door, a niche, or a window.

luster painting—An Islamic painting technique that gives a metallic sheen to a surface. Designs are based on motifs found in Islamic architectural decoration.

luster ware—A type of colored tile with a metallic sheen developed by the Abbasids in the 9th century at Samarra in Iraq.

lustral—Pertaining to rituals of purification.

luxuria—A 12th-century term for sensual pleasure.

machiocolation—An opening in the floor of an overhanging gallery through which the defenders of a castle dropped stones and boiling liquids on attackers.

madrasa—A higher theological college adjoining and often containing a *mosque.*

maestà—A depiction of the Virgin Mary as the Queen of Heaven enthroned in majesty amid choruses of angels and saints.

Mahayana—In Buddhist thought, the Great Vehicle to achieve *nirvana.*

makimono—A Japanese horizontal scroll.

malanggan—A type of New Ireland wood carving noted for bewildering intricacy, and characterized by generous use of openwork, sliverlike projections, and over-painting in minute geometric patterns that further subdivide the image, resulting in a splintered or fragmented and airy effect.

mana—Spiritual power.

mandala—A magic diagram of the cosmos, the wheel of life, and the cycle of being/becoming. Represents the three spheres of Buddhist cosmology: The Human Sphere of desire; the Bodhisattva Sphere of form; and the *Buddha* Sphere of Formlessness.

mandapa—A Hindu assembly hall, part of a temple.

mandara—*Mandala.*

mandorla—An almond-shaped *nimbus,* or *glory,* surrounding the figure of Christ or other sacred figure.

mantle—A sleeveless, protective outer garment or cloak. See *himation.*

mappa—The handkerchief thrown down as the ritual opening gesture for the beginning of *arena* games.

Marama—The Maori moon god.

masjid—See *mosque.*

Masonry Style—See *First Style.*

mastaba—Arabic for "bench." An ancient Egyptian rectangular brick or stone structure with sloping sides erected over a subterranean tomb chamber connected with the outside by a shaft, which provided the *ka* with access to the tomb.

matte (also **mat**)—In painting, pottery, and photography, a dull finish.

mausoleum—A central-plan, domed structure, built as a memorial.

Mbari house—Ceremonial houses filled with clay sculptures and paintings, honoring community deities of the Igbo tribe in Africa.

meander or **key**—See *fret.*

medium—The substance or agency in which an artist works; also, in painting, the vehicle (usually liquid) that carries the pigment.

megaliths—Literally, "great stone"; a large, roughly hewn stone used in the construction of monumental prehistoric structures: megalithic (adj.) See also *cromlech, dolmen, menhir.*

megaron—A rectangular hall, fronted by an open, two-columned porch, traditional in Greece since *Mycenaean* times. The large reception hall of the king in the palace of Tiryns.

memento mori—A reminder of human mortality, usually represented by a skull.

menhir—A prehistoric *monolith,* uncut or roughly cut, standing singly or with others in rows or circles.

menorah—The seven-branched candelabrum used in Jewish religious practices.

mens sana in corpore sano—Latin phrase meaning "a sound mind in a sound body."

Mesoamerica—The region that comprises Mexico, Guatemala, Belize, Honduras, and the Pacific coast of El Salvador.

Mesolithic—The "middle" prehistoric period, between the *Paleolithic* and the *Neolithic* ages.

metope—The panel between the *triglyphs* in a Doric frieze, often sculptured in *relief.*

mihrab—A semi-circular niche usually set into the *qibla* wall of a Muslim *mosque*, often surmounted by a dome over the bay in front to mark its location.

minaret—A distinctive feature of Muslim mosque architecture from which the *muezzin* calls the faithful to worship.

minbar—The pulpit on which an *imam* stands. It represents secular authority as well as a religious function.

Minimalism—A style of painting or sculpture that consists of a severe reduction of form to single, homogeneous units called "primary structures."

Minoan art—The pre-Greek art of Crete, named after the legendary King Minos of Knossos

mobiles—Sculptures with moving parts.

modeling—The shaping or fashioning of three-dimensional forms in a soft material, such as clay; also, the gradations of light and shade reflected from the surfaces of matter in space, or the illusion of such gradations produced by alterations of value in a drawing, painting, or print.

modern—In art, styles that are cut off from the past.

Modernism—A style or movement that understands the manifestation of progress to be in science and its achievements; it rejects the past, holding the idea that to live by past ideas and values is to regress.

module -A basic unit of which the dimensions of the major parts of a work are multiples. The principle is used in sculpture and other art forms, but it is most often employed in architecture, where the module may be the dimensions of an important part of a building, such as a *column*, or simply some commonly accepted unit of measurement (the centimeter or the inch, or, as with Le Corbusier, the average dimensions of the human figure).

modus francigenum—Latin for Frankish work; a term used by people in the 13th and 14th centuries to describe Gothic cathedrals.

molding—In architecture, a continuous, narrow surface (projecting or recessed, plain or ornamented) designed to break up a surface, to accent, or to decorate.

monolith—A column that is all in one piece (not composed of *drums*); a large, single block or piece of stone used in *megalithic* structures.

monumental—In art criticism, any work of art of grandeur and simplicity, regardless of its size.

mortise-and-tenon system—See *tenon*.

mosaic—Patterns or pictures made by embedding small pieces of stone or glass (*tesserae*) in cement on surfaces such as walls and floors; also, the technique of making such works.

moschophoros—Greek for calf-bearer.

mosque—A Muslim religious building. From *masjid*, meaning a place for bowing down.

mudra—A stylized and symbolic hand gesture of mystical significance, usually in representations of Hindu deities.

muezzin—The crier in the Muslim religion who calls the faithful to worship.

muhaqqaq—A style of Islamic calligraphy that fills the outer rectilinear frame of the *mihrab*.

mullah—An Islamic teacher.

mullion—A vertical member that divides a window or that separates one window from another.

mummification—A technique used by ancient Egyptians to preserve human bodies so that they

may serve as the eternal home of the immortal *ka*. .

muqarnas—Stucco decorations of Islamic buildings in which "stalactite"-like decorations break up the structural appearance of arches, transforming them into near-organic forms.

mural—A wall painting; a *fresco* is a type of mural medium and technique.

Muslim—One who is a believer in Islam.

Mycenaean—The late phase of *Helladic* art, named after the site of Mycenae.

Nabis—The Hebrew word for prophet. A group of *Symbolist* painters influenced by Paul Gauguin.

naos—See *cella*.

narrative composition—Elements in a work of art arranged in such a manner as to tell a story.

narthex—A porch or vestibule of a church, generally *colonnaded* or *arcaded* and preceding the *nave*.

natatio—In Roman baths, the swimming pool.

Naturalism—The doctrine that art should adhere as closely as possible to the appearance of the natural world. *Naturalism*, with varying degrees of fidelity to appearance, recurs in the history of Western art.

nave—The part of a church between the chief entrance and the *choir*, demarcated from *aisles* by *piers* or *columns*.

necking—A groove at the bottom of the Greek Doric *capital* between the *echinus* and the *flutes* that masks the junction of *capital* and *shaft*.

necropolis—A large burial area or cemetery; literally, a city of the dead.

nenfro—See *tufa*.

Neolithic—The "new" Stone Age, approximately 7000—3000 B.C.

Neoplasticism—A theory of art developed by Piet Mondrian to create a pure plastic art comprised of the simplest, least subjective, elements, primary colors, primary values, and primary directions (horizontal and vertical).

nimbus—A halo, aureole, or *glory* appearing around the head of a holy figure to signify divinity.

nirvana—In Buddhism and Hinduism, a blissful state brought about by absorption of the individual soul or consciousness into the supreme spirit.

nishiki-e—A style of Japanese printmaking called "brocade picture," a true polychrome print.

octafoliate—Eight-leafed design.

oculus—The round central opening or "eye" of a dome.

ogive—The diagonal *rib* of a Gothic *vault*; a pointed, or Gothic, *arch*. **ogival** (adj.)

omnivoyant—All-seeing.

one-point perspective—See *perspective*.

opere francigeno—Latin for in the Frankish manner, used to describe Gothic style buildings created outside of France.

opisthodomos—In Classical Greek architecture, a porch at the rear, set against the blank back wall of the cella.

Optical or Op Art—A kind of painting style in which precisely drafted patterns directly, even uncomfortably, affect visual perception.

optical approach to representation—In artistic representation, only that which is actually "seen" is represented, rather than what is

"known" (i.e., a human profile depicted optically would reveal only one eye, whereas a profile depicted "descriptively" would feature two eyes). See *descriptive approach to representation* .

opus modernum—Latin for modern work; a term used by people in the 13th and 14th centuries to describe Gothic cathedrals.

opus reticulatum—A method of facing concrete walls with lozenge-shaped bricks on stones to achieve a netlike ornamental surface pattern.

orans figures—In Early Christian art, figures represented with their hands raised in prayer.

orbiculum—A disc-like opening in a *pediment*.

orchestra—In Greek theaters, the circular piece of earth with a hard and level surface on which the ancient rites took place. Literally, it means dancing place.

order—In Classical architecture a style represented by a characteristic design of the *column* and its *entablature*. See also *superimposed order*.

Orientalizing—The early phase of Archaic Greek art, so named because of the adoption of forms and motifs from the ancient Near East and Egypt.

orrery—A special technological model to demonstrate the theory that the universe operates like a gigantic clockwork mechanism.

orthogonal—A line imagined to be behind and perpendicular to the picture plane; the *orthogonals* in a painting appear to recede toward a vanishing point on the horizon.

orthogonal plan—The imposition of a strict grid plan upon a site, regardless of the terrain, so that all streets meet at right angles. See also *Hippodamian plan*.

pagoda—A Chinese tower, usually associated with a temple, having a multiplicity of winged eaves; it is thought to be derived from the Indian *stupa*.

Paleolithic—The "old" Stone Age, before *c.* 7000 B.C.

palestra—A Roman exercise area, usually framed by a *colonnade*, often found in bathing establishments.

palette—In ancient Egypt, a slate slab used for ceremonial purposes, as in the *Palette of King Narmer*. A thin board with a thumb hole at one end on which an artist lays and mixes colors; any surface so used. Also, the colors or kinds of colors characteristically used by an artist.

palmette—A conventional, decorative ornament of ancient origin composed of radiating petals springing from a cuplike base.

pantomime—A method of representation used in Early Christian and medieval times which simplifies all meaning into body attitude and gesture.

Papatuanuku—The Maori earth mother.

papyrus—A plant native to Egypt and adjacent lands used to make paperlike writing material; also, the material or any writing on it.

parapet—A low, protective wall along the edge of a balcony or roof.

parasol—An umbrella atop a Chinese *pagoda*; a vestige of the chatra on an Indian *stupa*.

parchment—Lambskin prepared as a surface for painting or writing, one of the materials which comprised the leaves of a *codex*.

parekklesion—The side chapel in a Byzantine church.

passage grave—A burial chamber entered through a long, tunnel-like passage.

pastels—Chalk-like crayons made of ground color pigments mixed with water and a binding medium. They lend themselves to quick execution and sketching and offer a wide range of colors and subtle variations of tone, suitable for rendering nuances of value.

patricians—Wealthy landowners of the Roman Republic. Originally the *consuls* were elected from among these landowners.

Pax Augusta—See *Pax Romana*.

Pax Romana—The peace that Augustus established and that lasted for over two centuries under a succession of emperors.

Pax vobis—Latin for "Peace be unto you."

peachbloom—A pink dappled with green Chinese pottery glaze.

pediment—In Classical architecture, the triangular space (gable) at the end of a building, formed by the ends of the sloping roof above the *colonnade*; also, an ornamental feature having this shape.

pendant—Balancing.

pendentive—A concave, triangular piece of masonry (a triangular section of a hemisphere), four of which provide the transition from a square area to the circular base of a covering *dome*. Although they appear to be hanging (pendent) from the dome, they in fact support it.

peplos—A simple long woolen belted garment worn by Greek women that gives the female figure a columnar appearance.

peripteral colonnade—A *colonnade* or *peristyle*. See also *dipteral*.

peristyle—In Greek architecture, a *colonnade* all around the *cella* and its porch(es).

perpendicular style—The last English Gothic style, also known as Tudor, characterized by a strong vertical emphasis and dense thickets of ornamental vault ribs that serve entirely decorative functions.

persistence of vision—Retention in the brain for a fraction of a second of whatever the eye has seen; causes a rapid succession of images to merge one into the next, producing the illusion of continuous change and motion in media such as cinema.

perspective—A formula for projecting an illusion of the three-dimensional world onto a two-dimensional surface. In linear perspective, the most common type, all parallel lines or lines of projection seem to converge on one, two, or three points located with reference to the eye level of the viewer (the horizon line of the picture), known as vanishing points, and associated objects are rendered smaller the farther from the viewer they are intended to seem. Atmospheric or aerial perspective creates the illusion of distance by the greater diminution of color intensity, the shift in color toward an almost neutral blue, and the blurring of contours as the intended distance between eye and object increases.

petroglyphs—Engravings or incisings in rock.

photomontage—A composition made by fitting together pictures or parts of pictures, especially photographs. See also *collage*.

photoscreen—Technique employing photo processes to create stencil screens from graphic images, which then become part of complex printing or painting processes, as in the work of Robert Rauschenberg in his combine paintings.

physical music—A kind of video narrative made by Nam June Paik which comprises in quick succession fragmented sequences of a variety of media: dance, advertising, poetry, street scenes, etc.

piano nobile—The principal story (usually the second) in Renaissance buildings.

pictographs—A picture, usually stylized, that represents an idea; also, writing using such means; also painting on rock. See also *hieroglyphic*.

pictor—Latin for "painter."

Pictorial style—An early style of photography in which photographers desired to achieve effects of painting, using centered figures, framing devices, and soft focus. Gertrude Käsebier was a noted proponent of this style of photography.

Pictorialism—A *Postmodern* approach which sets aside *Modernist* formalism, *Expressionism*, and *Realism* in favor of picture-making, where idea and subject matter determine what the picture will look like. As in *Conceptual Art*, the artist begins with an idea and the picture follows.

pier—A vertical, freestanding masonry support.

pier buttress—See *buttress*.

pietà—A painted or sculpted representation of the Virgin Mary mourning over the body of Christ.

pietra serena—Literally, "serene stone," a type of gray stone used for its harmonious appearance when contrasted with stucco or other smooth finish in architecture.

pilaster—A flat, rectangular, vertical member projecting from a wall of which it forms a part. It usually has a *base* and a *capital* and is often *fluted*.

pillar—Usually a weight-carrying member, such as a *pier* or a *column*; sometimes an isolated, free-standing structure used for commemorative purposes.

pilotis—Thin steel or reinforced concrete posts used by architects in the early 20th century to support concrete roof and floor slabs, avoiding the need for load-bearing walls.

pinakotheke—The Greek word for picture gallery.

pitture metafisica—Literally, metaphysical painting. Exemplified by the work of Giorgio de Chirico, a precursor of *Surrealism*.

plan—The horizontal arrangement of the parts of a building or a drawing or a diagram showing such an arrangement as a horizontal *section*. In axial plan, the parts of a building are organized longitudinally, or along a given axis; in a central plan, the parts radiate from a central point.

Plateresque—A style of Late Gothic Spanish architecture derived from silversmithing, and characterized by its delicate execution of ornament.

plebeian—In the Roman Republic, the social class that included small farmers, merchants, and freed slaves.

plein-air—An approach to painting much favored by the Impressionists, in which artists sketch outdoors to achieve a quick impression of light, air and color. The sketches were then taken to the studio for reworking into more finished works of art.

plinth—The lowest member of a *base*; also a square slab at the base of a *column*.

pointed arch—See *ogive*.

polis (pl. **poleis**)—Independent city-states in ancient Greece.

polychrome—Done in several colors.

polyptych—An *altarpiece* made up of more than three sections.

pontifex maximus—A Latin term meaning "chief priest" of the state religion.

Pop Art—A term coined by British art critic Lawrence Alloway to refer to art that incorporated elements from popular culture, such as images from motion pictures, television, advertising, billboards, commodities, etc.

portico—A porch with a roof supported by *columns*; an entrance porch.

post-and-lintel system—A *trabeated* system of construction in which two posts support a *lintel*.

Post-Minimalist—A movement succeeding *Minimalism* in which the artists wanted to reintroduce a sense of visible process in the work. Using nontraditional sculptural materials like fiberglass, cord, and latex, artists such as Eva Hesse collapsed the pure forms of Minimal art.

Post-Painterly Abstraction—See *color-field painters*.

Postmodernism—A reaction against *Modernist* formalism, which is seen as elitist.

pottery—Objects (usually vessels) made of clay and hardened by firing.

Precisionists—A group of American painters whose work concentrated on portraying man-made environments in a clear and concise manner to express the beauty of the new world of perfect and precise machine forms. Charles Sheeler is an example.

predella—The narrow ledge on which an *altarpiece* rests on an altar.

princeps—A Latin term meaning "first citizen."

pronaos—The space in front of the *cella* or *naos* of a Greek temple.

propylaion (pl. **propylai**)—A gateway building leading to an open court preceding a Greek or Roman temple. The monumental entrance to the Acropolis in Athens.

proscenium—The part of the stage in front of the curtain. The stage of an ancient Greek or Roman theater.

prostyle—A style of Greek temple in which the *columns* stand in front of the *naos* and extend its full width.

provenance—Origin or source.

psalter—A book containing the Psalms of the Bible.

pseudoperipteral—In Roman architecture, a *pseudoperipteral* edifice has a series of engaged columns all around the sides and back of the *cella* to give the appearance of a *peripteral colonnade*.

purlins—Horizontal beams in a roof structure, parallel to the ridgepoles, resting on the main rafters and giving support to the secondary rafters.

purusha—Hindu for the primordial human being.

putto (pl. **putti**)—A young child, a favorite subject in Italian painting and sculpture.

pylon—The simple and massive gateway, with sloping walls, of an Egyptian temple.

qi—In Chinese artistic philosophy, the divine spirit of the Universe, apperception of which allows true artists to paint the truth beneath surface appearances.

qibla—In the Muslim religion, the direction (towards Mecca) the faithful turn when praying.

quadrant vault—Half-barrel vaults. See *vault*.

quadro riportato—A ceiling design in which painted scenes are arranged in panels resembling framed pictures transferred to the surface of a shallow, curved *vault*.

quatrefoil—A type of mosque architecture in which the forms assume the shape of a clover-leaf.

quoin—A large, sometimes *rusticated*, usually slightly projecting stone (or stones) that often form the corners of the exterior walls of masonry buildings.

Ra—The Maori sun god.

ragamalas—Hindu musical modes.

raigo—A Japanese depiction of the Buddha Amida descending through clouds amid a host of *Bodhisattvas*, welcoming deceased believers to his paradise.

raking cornice—The *cornice* on the sloping sides of a *pediment*.

rathas—Small, free-standing Hindu temples carved from huge boulders, found in Mahabalipuram, India.

rayonnant—Or "radiant" style of Gothic architecture, dominated the second half of the 13th century and was associated with the royal Paris court of Louis IX. Fundamental features of rayonnant style include bar tracery and stained glass.

realism—The representation of things according to their appearance in visible nature (without *idealization*). In the 19th century, an approach that supported the representation of the subject matter of everyday life in a realistic mode. Iconographically, 19th-century Realism is the subject matter of everyday life as seen by the artist.

red-figure technique—In later Greek pottery, the silhouetting of red figures against a black background; the reverse of the *black-figure technique*.

register—One of a series of superimposed bands in a pictorial narrative, or the particular levels on which motifs are placed.

Regula Sancti Benedicti—The rule established by Saint Benedict that became the standard by the 9th century for all Western monastic establishments. Monks who live by the rule or "regula" are known as regular clergy, while priests, living without a specific rule and subordinate to their bishops, are known as secular clergy.

relief—In sculpture, figures projecting from a background of which they are part. The degree of relief is designated high, low (bas), sunken (hollow), or *intaglio*. In the last, the backgrounds are not cut back, and the points in the highest relief are level with the original surface of the material being carved. See also *repoussé*.

relieving triangle—In a *corbeled arch*, the opening above the lintel that serves to lighten the weight to be carried by the *lintel* itself. The triangle that is formed is often filled with slabs decorated with sculptural programs.

relievo—*Relief*.

repoussé—Formed in *relief* by beating a metal plate from the back, leaving the impression on the face. The metal is hammered into a hollow mold of wood or some other pliable material and finished with a *graver*. See also *relief*.

reserve column—In Egyptian rock-cut and Etruscan subterranean tombs, a *column* that is hewn from the living rock and serves no supporting function.

respond—An engaged *column, pilaster,* or similar structure that either projects from a *compound pier* or some other supporting device or is bonded to a wall and carries one end of an *arch*, often at the end of an *arcade*. A nave arcade, for example, may have nine *pillars* and two *responds*. Vertical wall elements in *perpendicular style* architecture.

ressaut—The projection above each *capital* formed when engaged *columns* frame recessed *arches* and carry a flat *entablature*.

retable—An architectural screen or wall above and behind an altar, usually containing painting, sculpture, carving, or other decorations. See also *altarpiece*.

rhyton—An ancient Greek ceremonial drinking vessel with a base usually in the form of the head of an animal, a woman, or a mythological creature.

rib—A relatively slender, molded masonry *arch* that projects from a surface. In Gothic architecture, the *ribs* form the framework of the *vaulting*.

rib vault—Vaults in which the diagonal and transverse ribs compose a structural skeleton that partially supports the still fairly massive paneling between them.

Romanist—A 16th-century Northern Renaissance style characterized by a joining of Italian Mannerism with fanciful native interpretations of the Classical style to form a highly artificial, sometimes decorative, and often bizarre and chaotic style.

Rosetta Stone—An Egyptian artifact that gave scholars a key to deciphering *hieroglyphic* writing.

rotulus—The long manuscript scroll used by Egyptians, Greeks, Etruscans, and Romans; predecessor of the *codex*.

roundel—See *tondo*.

rusticate—To give a rustic appearance by roughening the surfaces and beveling the edges of stone blocks to emphasize the joints between them. A technique popular during the Renaissance, especially for stone courses at the ground-floor level.

sacra conversazione—Literally, "holy conversation," a style of *altarpiece* painting popular from the middle of the 15th century forward in which saints from different epochs are joined in a unified space and seem to be conversing either with each other or with the audience.

samsara—In Hindu belief, the rebirth of the soul into a succession of lives.

sarcophagus (pl. **sarcophagi**)—A coffin, usually of stone. From the Greek, "consumer of flesh."

sarsen—A form of sandstone used for the *megaliths* at Stonehenge.

satyr—A follower of Dionysos, represented as part human, part goat.

scarification—Decorative markings made with scars on the human body.

Schmerzensmann—Man of Sorrows, a favorite theme of Late Gothic German sculpture.

school—A chronological and stylistic classification of works of art with a stipulation of place.

scientia—The theory that underlay the building of Gothic churches. See also *ars*.

sculpture in the round—Freestanding figures, carved or modeled in three dimensions.

Second Style—In Pompeiian mural painting, from c. 80 B.C. the aim was to dissolve the confining walls of a room and replace them with the illusion of a three-dimensional world constructed in the artist's imagination.

section—In architecture, a diagram or representation of a part of a structure or building along an imaginary plane that passes through it vertically.

semiotics—A linguistic theory that has been applied to literary and artistic endeavors. *Semiotics* is concerned with the nature of signs, the fundamental elements in communication. All constructs are reducible to signs that communicate significance or meaning. The sign (the signifier) can be anything that signifies, and what it signifies (the signified) is its meaning.

senate—Literally, a council of elders. The legislative body in Roman constitutional government.

serdab—A small concealed chamber in an Egyptian tomb (*mastaba*) for the statue of the deceased.

serpentine (line)—The "S" curve, which was regarded by Hogarth as the line of beauty.

severe style—The earliest phase of Classical, sculpture, formal but not rigid in pose, emphasizing the principle of weight distribution.

severies—Thinly vaulted webs or panels between arches, a distinguishing feature of Gothic vaults.

sexpartite vaults—Vaults whose ribs spring from compound *piers*. The branching ribs divide the large square-vault compartment into six sections. See *vault*.

sfumato—A smokelike haziness that subtly softens outlines in painting; particularly applied to the painting of Leonardo and Correggio.

shaft—The part of a *column* between the *capital* and the *base*.

shoji—A translucent rice-paper-covered sliding screen that serves as a room divider in traditional Japanese houses.

sikhara—In Hindu temples, the tower above the shrine.

skene—In Greek theaters, the scene building that housed dressing rooms for the actors and also formed a backdrop for the plays.

skenographia—The Greek term for *perspective*, literally, "scene painting," which during the 5th century B.C. employed linear or single vanishing point perspective to create the illusion of depth.

skiagraphia—The Greek term for shading, literally "shadow painting," said to have been invented by Apollodoros, an Athenian painter of the 5th century B.C.

soak stain—A technique of painting pioneered by Helen Frankenthaler in which the artist drenches the fabric of raw canvas with fluid paint to achieve flowing, lyrical, painterly effects.

socle—A molded projection at the bottom of a wall or a *pier*, or beneath a pedestal or a *column* base.

soffit—The underside of an architectural member such as an *arch, lintel, cornice,* or stairway. See also *intrados*.

space—The bounded or boundless container of collections of objects.

spandrel—The roughly triangular space enclosed by the curves of adjacent *arches* and a horizontal member connecting their vertexes; also, the space enclosed by the curve of an *arch* and an enclosing right angle. The area between the arch proper and the framing *columns* and *entablature*.

Speculum Majus—Latin for The Great Mirror. Authored by Vincent of Beauvais, a scholar at the court of Louis IX, this was a comprehensive summary of medieval knowledge in which accounts of natural phenomena, scriptural themes, and moral philosophy serve a didactic religious purpose.

sphinx—A mythical Egyptian beast with the body of a lion and the head of a human.

splay—A large *bevel* or *chamfer*.

splayed—An opening (as in a wall) that is cut away diagonally so that the outer edges are farther apart than the inner edges. See also *embrasure*.

springing—The lowest stone of an *arch*, resting on the *impost block*.

square schematism—A church plan in which the crossing square is used as the module for all parts of the design. For example, in some Romanesque architecture each nave bay measures exactly one-half and each square in the aisles measures exactly one-quarter of a crossing square, and so on throughout the building.

squinch—An architectural device used as a transition from a square to a polygonal or circular base for a *dome*. It may be composed of *lintels*, *corbels*, or *arches*.

stanze—The Italian word for rooms.

statue column—See *atlantid* or *caryatid*.

stave—A wedge-shaped timber; vertically placed *staves* embellish the architectural features of the building.

stele—A carved stone slab used to mark graves and to commemorate historical events.

stiacciata or sciacciata—A kind of very low *relief*, originated by Donatello, that incorporates much of the illusionism of painting into carving, which in places is hardly more than a scratching of the surface.

stoa—In ancient Greek architecture, an open building with a roof supported by a row of *columns* parallel to the back wall. A covered *colonnade*.

strategos—A Greek general.

strigil—A scraper, used by Greek athletes to scrape oil from their bodies after exercising.

stringcourse—A horizontal *molding*, or band in masonry, ornamental but usually reflecting interior structure.

stucco—Fine plaster or cement used as a coating for walls or for decoration.

stupa—A large, mound-shaped Buddhist shrine.

stylobate—The uppermost course of the platform of a Greek temple, which supports the *columns*.

stylus—A needlelike tool used in *engraving* and *incising*.

subtractive—A kind of sculpture technique in which materials are taken away from the original mass, i.e., carving.

sue—A type of gray pottery emigrating from Korea to Japan in the archaic period.

superimposed orders—*Orders* of architecture that are placed one above another in an *arcaded* or *colonnaded* building, usually in the following sequence: Doric (the first story), Ionic, and Corinthian. Superimposed orders are found in later Greek architecture and were used widely by Roman and Renaissance builders.

Superrealist—A school of painting which emphasized making images of persons and things with scrupulous, photographic fidelity to optical fact.

Suprematism—A type of art formulated by Kazimir Malevich to convey his belief that the supreme reality in the world is pure feeling, which attaches to no object and thus calls for new, nonobjective forms in art—shapes not related to objects in the visible world. Also known as Abstract Formalism.

sura—Verses of the *Qur'an* (Koran).

Surrealism—A successor to *Dada*, *Surrealism* incorporated the improvisational nature of its predecessor into its exploration of the ways to express in art the world of dreams and the unconscious.

sutra—In Buddhism, an account of a sermon by or a dialogue involving the *Buddha*. A scriptural account of the *Buddha*. See also *jataka*.

Symbolists—In the late 19th century, a group of artists and poets who shared a view that the artist was not an imitator of nature but a creator who transformed the facts of nature into a symbol of the inner experience of that fact.

symmetria—Commensurability of parts. Polykleitos's treatise on his canon of proportions summarized the principle of symmetria.

Synthetic Cubism—In 1912 *Cubism* entered a new phase during which the style no longer relied on a decipherable relation to the visible world. In this new phase, called *Synthetic Cubism*, painting and drawings were constructed from objects and shapes cut from paper or other materials to represent parts of a subject in order to play visual games with variations on illusion and reality.

taberna—In Roman architecture, the single-room shop covered by a barrel vault.

Tane—Maori god of the forest.

Tangaroa—Maori god of the sea.

Tanginui—The Maori sky father.

tapa—Polynesian decorative bark cloth.

tatami—The traditional woven straw mat used for floor covering in Japanese architecture.

tattoo—A Polynesian word for the permanent decoration of human bodies.

Tawhiri-matea—The Maori god of the winds

te whanau puhi—The Maori children of the four winds.

technique—The technical process that artists employ to create form, as well as the distinctive, personal ways in which they handle their materials and tools.

tell—In Near Eastern archeology, a hill or a mound, usually an ancient site of habitation.

tempera—A technique of painting using pigment mixed with egg yolk, glue or casein; also the *medium* itself.

tenebrism—Painting in the "dark manner," using violent contrasts of light and dark, as in the work of Caravaggio.

tenon—A projection on the end of a piece of wood that is inserted into a corresponding hole (mortise) in another piece of wood to form a joint.

tepidarium—The warm bath section of a Roman bathing establishment.

terracotta—Hard-baked clay, used for sculpture and as a building material, may be *glazed* or painted.

terribilità—The notion of the sublime shadowed by the awesome and the fearful, often associated with Michelangelo and his works.

tesserae—Tiny stones or pieces of glass cut to desired shape and size to use in *mosaics* to create design and composition.

tetrarchy—Rule by four. A type of Roman government established in the late 3rd century A.D. by Diocletian in an attempt to share power with potential rivals.

texture—The quality of a surface (rough, smooth, hard, soft, shiny, dull) as revealed by light.

theatron—In Greek theaters, the slope overlooking the *orchestra* on which the spectators sat. Literally, the place for seeing.

Third Style—In Pompeiian mural painting, the style in which delicate linear fantasies were sketched on predominantly monochrome backgrounds.

tholos (pl. tholoi)—A circular structure, generally in Classical Greek style; also, in Aegean sculpture, a circular beehive-shaped tomb.

thrust—The outward force exerted by an *arch* or a *vault* that must be counterbalanced by *buttresses*.

tie-rods—Beams, bars or rods that tie parts of a building together.

tier—A series of architectural rows, layers, or ranks arranged above or behind one another.

togu na—The "head" and most important part of the Dogon anthropomorphized village. The name means "house of words," because the *togu na* is the place in which occur the deliberations vital to community welfare.

tokonoma—A shallow alcove in a Japanese teahouse which is used for a single adornment, i.e., a painting, or stylized flower arrangement.

Toltec—The Mayan word for "makers of things." The Toltecs invaded the Mayas from the north and contributed to the fall of the Classic Mayan civilizations. The Toltec capital flourished at Tula from about 900 to 1200.

tondo—A circular painting or *relief* sculpture.

torana—Gateway in the stone fence around a *stupa*, located at the cardinal points of the compass.

torii—Ceremonial gates leading to the inside of a Shinto shrine.

trabeated—Of *post-and-lintel* construction. Literally, "beamed" construction.

transept—The part of a *cruciform* church with an axis that crosses the main axis at right angles.

treasuries—In ancient Greece, small buildings set up for the safe storage of votive offerings.

tribune—In Romanesque church architecture, upper galleries built over the inner *aisles*.

triclinium—The dining room of a Roman house.

triforium—The bank of *arcades* below the *clerestory* that occupies the space corresponding to the exterior strip of wall covered by the sloping timber roof above the galleries. In a Gothic cathedral, the blind, *arcaded* gallery below the *clerestory*.

triglyph—A projecting, grooved member of a Doric *frieze* that alternates with *metopes*.

trilithons—A pair of *monoliths* topped with a *lintel*; found in *megalithic* structures.

triptych—A three-paneled painting or *altarpiece*.

trompe l'œil—A form of illusionistic painting that attempts to represent an object as existing in three dimensions at the surface of the painting; literally, "fools the eye."

trouvères—Minstrels of the chivalric age who sang secular music complimenting the sacred love of Our Lady (the Virgin Mary) by praising the worldly love of women and the pursuit of that love as the worthy occupation of the chivalrous knight.

true fresco—See *fresco*.

trumeau—In architecture, the *pillar* or center post supporting the lintel in the middle of the doorway.

Tudor—See *perpendicular style*.

tufa (nenfro)—A porous rock formed from deposits of springs.

tumulus (pl. **tumuli**)—Burial mounds; in Etruscan architecture, tumuli cover one or more subterranean multichambered tombs cut out of the local *tufa*.

tunnel vaults—Continuous, cut-stone barrel vaults.

Tuscan column—Also known as Etruscan column. Resemble Greek Doric columns, but made of wood, unfluted, and with bases. They were spaced more widely than were Greek columns.

Tusci—The ancient people who inhabited Etruria, or modern-day Tuscany.

twisted perspective—A convention of representation in which part of a figure is seen in profile and another part of the same figure frontally. Not strictly *optical* (organized from the perspective of a fixed viewpoint), but *descriptive*.

tympanum—The space enclosed by a *lintel* and an *arch* over a doorway; also, the recessed face of a *pediment*.

ukiyo-e—A style of Japanese *genre* painting ("pictures of the floating world") that influenced 19th-century Western art.

uomo universale—The "Universal" or Renaissance man, who is accomplished in many fields of endeavor. (Although women also attain this state, the word "uomo" is Italian for "man.")

urna—A whorl of hair, represented as a dot, between the brows of the *Buddha*. One of the *lakshanas* of the *Buddha*.

ushnisha—The knot of hair on the top of *Buddha*'s head. One of the *lakshana* of the *Buddha*.

ut pictura poesis— Latin for "As painting (goes), so poetry (goes)."

vault—A masonry roof or ceiling constructed on the *arch* principle. A barrel or tunnel vault, semicylindrical in cross-section is, in effect, a deep arch or an uninterrupted series of arches, one behind the other, over an oblong space. A quadrant vault is a half-barrel (tunnel) vault. A groin or cross vault is formed at the point at which two *barrel* (tunnel) vaults intersect at right angles. In a ribbed vault, there is a framework of ribs or arches under the intersections of the vaulting sections. A sexpartite vault is a rib vault with six panels. A fan vault is a development of *lierne* vaulting characteristic of English Perpendicular Gothic, in which radiating *ribs* form a fan-like pattern.

veduta—Type of naturalistic landscape and cityscape painting popular in 18th-century Venice. Literally, "view" painting.

velarium—In a Roman amphitheater, the cloth awning that could be rolled down from the top of the *cavea* to shield spectators from sun or rain.

vellum—Calfskin prepared as a surface for writing or painting, one of the materials which comprised the leaves of a *codex*.

veristic—True to natural appearance.

vestibule—See *portico*.

vignette—An image with a strong center that becomes less defined at its edges.

vihara—A Buddhist monastery, often cut into a hill.

vimana—In Hindu and Buddhist temples, the pyramidal tower above the shrine (composed of the *garbha griha* and the *sikhara*).

vita activa—In the Middle Ages, the two kinds of life that were open to monks, the *vita activa*, or active life, and the **vita contemplativa,** the religious life of contemplation.

volute—A spiral, scroll-like form characteristic of the Greek Ionic and the Roman Composite *capital*.

voussoir—A wedge-shaped block used in the construction of a true *arch*. The central voussoir, which sets the arch, is the *keystone*.

wall rib—The rib at the junction of the vault and the wall.

wat—A Buddhist monastery in Cambodia.

weight shift—See *contrapposto*.

wergild—A type of medieval recompense for criminal damages inflicted. Literally, "man-money" or "man-gold". The offender must compensate the victim or the victim's kinfolk with a payment in money or in kind.

westwork—A multistoried mass, including the *facade* and usually surmounted by towers, at the western end of a medieval church, principally in Germany.

wet fresco—See *fresco*.

white-ground technique—A Greek vase painting technique in which the pot was first covered with a slip of very fine white clay, over which black glaze was used to outline figures, and diluted brown, purple, red, and white were used to color them.

woodcut—A wooden block on the surface of which those parts not intended to print are cut away to a slight depth, leaving the design raised; also, the printed impression made with such a block Also known as woodblock.

yaksha/yakshi—Male and female Buddhist and Hindu divinities.

Yamato-e—A purely Japanese style of sophisticated and depersonalized painting created for the Fujiwara nobility.

yasti—In Buddhist architecture, the mast which arises from the dome of the *stupa*, *harmika*, and which is adorned with a series of chatras (umbrellas).

yingging—A type of Chinese pottery glaze characterized by a subtle pale blue color.

Zen—A *Buddhist* sect and its doctrine, emphasizing enlightenment through intuition and introspection rather than the study of scripture. In Chinese, Ch'an.

ziggurat—A roughly pyramidal platform for a template, built in ancient Mesopotamia, consisting of stages; each succeeding stage is stepped back from the one beneath.

zoopraxiscope—Device invented by Eadweard Muybridge, which he developed to project sequences of images (mounted on special glass plates) onto a screen in rapid succession, creating the illusion of motion pictures. See *persistence of vision*.

zullah—Shaded area along the central court of Muslim religious buildings.

BIBLIOGRAPHY

This supplementary list of books is intended to be comprehensive enough to satisfy the reading interests of the unspecialized student and general reader, as well as those of more advanced readers who wish to become acquainted with fields other than their own. The books listed range from works that are valuable primarily for their reproductions to those that are scholarly surveys of schools and periods. No entries for periodical articles appear, but a few of the periodicals that publish art-historical scholarship in English are noted.

SELECTED PERIODICALS

American Journal of Archaeology
Archaeology
The Art Bulletin
Art History
The Art Journal
The Burlington Magazine
Journal of the Society of Architectural Historians
Journal of the Warburg and Courtauld Institutes

REFERENCE BOOKS
AND GENERAL STUDIES

Arntzen, Etta, and Robert Rainwater. *Guide to the Literature of Art History.* Chicago: American Library Association/Art Book Company, 1981.

Bator, Paul M. *The International Trade in Art.* Chicago: University of Chicago Press, 1988.

Bindman, David, ed. *The Thames & Hudson Encyclopedia of British Art.* London: Thames & Hudson, 1988.

Broude, Norma, and Mary D. Garrard, eds. *The Expanding Discourse: Feminism and Art History.* New York: HarperCollins, 1992.

———. *Feminism and Art History: Questioning the Litany.* New York: Harper & Row, 1982.

Bryson, N. *Vision and Painting: The Logic of the Gaze.* New Haven: Yale University Press, 1983.

Chilvers, Ian, and Harold Osborne, eds. *The Oxford Dictionary of Art.* New York: Oxford University Press, 1988.

Christe, Yves, et al. *Art of the Christian World, 200–1500: A Handbook of Styles and Forms.* New York: Rizzoli, 1982.

Cummings, P., *Dictionary of Contemporary American Artists.* 6th ed. New York: St. Martin's Press, 1994.

Derrida, Jacques. *The Truth in Painting.* Chicago/London: University of Chicago Press, 1987.

Deepwell, K., ed. *New Feminist Art.* Manchester: Manchester University Press, 1994.

Encyclopedia of World Art. 15 vols. New York: Publisher's Guild, 1959–1968. Supplementary vols. 16, 1983; 17, 1987.

Fielding, Mantle. *Dictionary of American Painters, Sculptors, and Engravers.* 2nd rev. and enl. ed. Poughkeepsie, NY: Apollo, 1986.

Fleming, John, Hugh Honour, and Nikolaus Pevsner. *Penguin Dictionary of Architecture.* Baltimore: Penguin, 1980.

Fletcher, Sir Banister. *A History of Architecture.* 18th rev. ed. New York: Scribner, 1975.

Giedion, Siegfried. *The Beginnings of Architecture: The Eternal Present, a Contribution on Constancy and Change.* Princeton: Princeton University Press, 1981.

———. *Space, Time and Architecture: The Growth of a New Tradition.* 5th ed., rev. and enl. Cambridge: Harvard University Press, 1982.

Gombrich, Ernst Hans Josef. *Art and Illusion.* 5th ed. London: Phaidon, 1977.

Haggar, Reginald G. *A Dictionary of Art Terms: Architecture, Sculpture, Painting, and the Graphic Arts.* Poole, England: New Orchard Editions, 1984.

Hall, James. *Dictionary of Subjects and Symbols in Art.* 2nd rev. ed. London: J. Murray, 1979.

Harris, A. S. *Women Artists: 1550–1950.* Los Angeles: County Museum of Art; New York: Knopf, 1977.

Hauser, Arnold. *The Sociology of Art.* Chicago: University of Chicago Press, 1982.

Hind, Arthur M. *A History of Engraving and Etching from the Fifteenth Century to the Year 1914.* 3rd rev. ed. New York: Dover, 1963.

Holt, Elizabeth G., ed. *A Documentary History of Art.* 2nd ed. 2 vols. Princeton: Princeton University Press, 1981.

———. *Literary Sources of Art History.* Princeton: Princeton University Press, 1947.

Huyghe, René, ed. *Larousse Encyclopedia of Byzantine and Medieval Art.* New York: Prometheus Press, 1963; Excalibur Books, 1981.

———. *Larousse Encyclopedia of Renaissance and Baroque Art.* New York: Prometheus Press, 1964; Hamlyn/American (paperbound), 1976.

James, John, et al. *The Traveler's Key to Medieval France: A Guide to the Sacred Architecture of Medieval France.* New York: Knopf, 1986.

Janson, H. W., ed. *Sources and Documents in the History of Art Series.* Englewood Cliffs, NJ: Prentice-Hall, 1966.

Kostof, Spiro. *A History of Architecture: Settings and Rituals.* Oxford: Oxford University Press, 1985.

Kronenberger, Louis. *Atlantic Brief Lives: A Biographical Companion to the Arts.* Boston: Little, Brown, 1971.

Lucie-Smith, Edward. *The Thames & Hudson Dictionary of Art Terms.* London: Thames & Hudson, 1984.

Lutyk, Carol B. *The Adventure of Archaeology.* Washington DC: National Geographic, 1985, 1989.

Malraux, André; Salles, Georges; and Parrot, André, eds. *The Arts of Mankind.* 13 vols. New York: Golden Press, Odyssey Press, Braziller, 1961.

Murray, Peter, and Murray, Linda. *A Dictionary of Art and Artists.* New York: Penguin, 1976; (paperbound) 1984.

Myers, Bernard Samuel, ed. *Encyclopedia of Painting: Painters and Painting of the World from Prehistoric Times to the Present Day.* 4th rev. ed. New York: Crown, 1979.

———. *Encyclopedia of World Art,* Suppl. vol. 16. Palatine, IL: McGraw-Hill/The Publishers Guild, 1983. (Later edition available.)

Myers, Bernard S., and Myers, Shirley D., eds. *Dictionary of 20th-Century Art.* New York: McGraw-Hill, 1974.

Osborne, Harold, ed. *The Oxford Companion to 20th Century Art.* New York: Oxford University Press, 1981.

Pevsner, Nikolaus. *A History of Building Types.* 1979. Reprint. London: Thames & Hudson (paperbound), 1987.

———. *An Outline of European Architecture.* Baltimore: Penguin, 1960.

———. *An Outline of European Architecture.* 8th rev. ed. Baltimore: Penguin, 1974.

Pickover, C., ed. *Visions of the Future: Art, Technology and Computing in the Twenty-First Century.* New York: St. Martin's Press, 1994.

Pierson, William H., Jr., and Martha Davidson. eds. *Arts of the United States, A Pictorial Survey.* 1960. Reprint. Athens: University of Georgia Press, 1975.

Placzek, A. K., ed. *Macmillan Encyclopedia of Architects.* 4 vols. New York: Macmillan/Free Press, 1982.

Podro, Michael. *The Critical Historians of Art.* New Haven: Yale University Press, 1982.

Quick, John. *Artists' and Illustrators' Encyclopedia.* 2nd ed. New York: McGraw-Hill, 1977.

Ragghianti, C. L., ed. *Great Museums of the World.* 12 vols. New York: Newsweek/Mondadori, 1967.

Read, Herbert, and Nikos Stangos. eds. *The Thames & Hudson Dictionary of Art and Artists.* Rev. ed. London: Thames & Hudson, 1985.

Redig de Campos, D., ed. *Art Treasures of the Vatican.* New York: Park Lane, 1974.

Reid, Jane D. *The Oxford Guide to Classical Mythology in the Arts 1300–1990s.* 2 vols. New York: Oxford University Press, 1993.

Renfrew, Colin. *Archaeology: Theories, Methods, and Practices.* London: Thames & Hudson, 1991.

Rosenblum, Naomi. *A World History of Photography.* New York: Abbeville, 1984.

Rubenstein, Charlotte Streifer. *American Women Artists from Early Indian Times to the Present.* Boston: G. K. Hall/Avon Books, 1982.

Schiller, Gertrud. *Iconography of Christian Art.* 2 vols. Greenwich, CT: New York Graphic Society, 1971.

Smith, Alistair, ed. *The Larousse Dictionary of Painters.* New York: Larousse, 1981.

Smith, G. E. Kidder. *The Architecture of the United States: An Illustrated Guide to Buildings Open to the Public.* 3 vols. Garden City, NY: Doubleday/Anchor, 1981.

Snyder, James. *Medieval Art: Painting, Sculpture, and Architecture, 4th–14th Century.* New York: Abrams, 1989.

Steer, John, and Anthony White. *Atlas of Western Art History.* New York: Facts on File, 1994.

Stierlin, Henri. *Encyclopedia of World Architecture 1978.* 1978. Reprint. New York: Van Nostrand, Reinhold, 1983.

Stillwell, Richard, et al., eds., *The Princeton Encyclopedia of Classical Sites.* Princeton: Princeton University Press, 1976.

Stratton, Arthur. *The Orders of Architecture: Greek, Roman and Renaissance.* London: Studio, 1986.

Trachtenberg, Marvin, and Isabelle Hyman. *Architecture, from Prehistory to Post-Modernism.* New York: Abrams, 1986.

Tufts, Eleanor. *American Women Artists, Past and Present, A Selected Bibliographic Guide.* New York: Garland Publishers, 1984.

———. *Our Hidden Heritage, Five Centuries of Women Artists.* London: Paddington Press, 1974.

Turner, Jane, ed. *The Dictionary of Art.* 34 vols. New York: Grove Dictionaries, 1996.

Van Pelt, R., and C. Westfall. *Architectural Principles in the Age of Historicism.* New Haven: Yale University Press, 1991.

Waterhouse, Ellis. *The Dictionary of British 18th Century Painters in Oils and Crayons.* Woodbridge, England: Antique Collectors' Club, 1981.

Wilkins, David G. *Art Past, Art Present.* New York: Harry N. Abrams, 1994.

Wittkower, Rudolf. *Sculpture Processes and Principles.* New York: Harper & Row, 1977.

Wölfflin, Heinrich. *The Sense of Form in Art.* New York: Chelsea, 1958.

Young, William, ed. *A Dictionary of American Artists, Sculptors, and Engravers.* Cambridge, MA: W. Young, 1968.

CHAPTER 1 THE BIRTH OF ART

Bandi, Hans-Georg, Henri Breuil, et al. *The Art of the Stone Age: Forty Thousand Years of Rock Art.* 2nd ed. London: Methuen, 1970.

Bataille, Georges. *Lascaux: Prehistoric Painting or the Birth of Art.* Lausanne: Skira, 1980.

Breuil, Henri. *Four Hundred Centuries of Cave Art.* New York: Hacker, 1979. Reprint.

Graziosi, Paolo. *Paleolithic Art.* New York: McGraw-Hill, 1960.

Hawkes, Jacquetta. *The Atlas of Early Man.* New York: St. Martin's Press, 1976.

Kenyon, Kathleen M. *Digging Up Jericho.* New York: Praeger, 1974.

Kubba, Shamil A. A. *Mesopotamian Architecture and Town-planning: From the Mesolithic to the End of the Proto-historic Period.* Oxford: British Archaeological Reports 1987.

Leroi-Gourhan, André. *The Dawn of European Art: An Introduction to Paleolithic Cave Painting.* Cambridge: Cambridge University Press, 1982.

———. *Treasures of Prehistoric Art.* New York: Abrams, 1967.

Lewin, Roger. *In the Age of Mankind: A Smithsonian Book of Human Evolution.* Washington DC: Smithsonian Institution Books, 1988.

Marshack, Alexander. *The Roots of Civilization: The Cognitive Beginnings of Man's First Art, Symbol and Notation.* New York: McGraw-Hill, 1971.

Mellaart, James. *Çatal Hüyük: A Neolithic Town in Anatolia.* New York: McGraw-Hill, 1967.

———. *The Earliest Civilizations of the Near East.* New York: McGraw-Hill, 1965.

———. *The Neolithic of the Near East.* New York: Scribner, 1975.

Piggot, Stuart. *Ancient Europe.* Chicago: Aldine, 1966.

Pfeiffer, John E. *The Creative Explosion: An Inquiry into the Origins of Art and Religion.* New York: Harper & Row, 1982.

Powell, T. G. E. *Prehistoric Art.* New York: Praeger, 1966.

Renfrew, Colin, ed. *British Prehistory: A New Outline.* London: Noyes Press, 1975.

Sandars, Nancy K. *Prehistoric Art in Europe.* 2nd ed. New Haven: Yale University Press, 1985.

Sieveking, Ann. *The Cave Artists.* London: Thames & Hudson, 1979.

Trump, David H. *The Prehistory of the Mediterranean.* New Haven: Yale University Press, 1980. (Later edition available.)

Ucko, Peter J., and Andrée Rosenfeld. *Palaeolithic Cave Art.* New York: McGraw-Hill, 1967.

Wainwright, Geoffrey. *The Henge Monuments: Ceremony and Society in Prehistoric Britain.* London: Thames & Hudson, 1990.

Windels, Fernand. *The Lascaux Cave Paintings.* New York: Viking, 1950.

CHAPTER 2 ANCIENT NEAR EASTERN ART

Akurgal, Ekrem. *Art of the Hittites.* New York: Abrams, 1962.

Amiet, Pierre. *Art of the Ancient Near East.* New York: Abrams, 1980.

Amiet, Pierre, et al. *Art in the Ancient World: A Handbook of Styles and Forms.* New York: Rizzoli, 1981.

Culican, William. *The Medes and Persians.* London: Thames & Hudson, 1965; New York: Praeger, 1965.

Frankfort, Henri. *The Art and Architecture of the Ancient Orient.* Baltimore: Penguin, 1985.

Crawford, Harriet. *Sumer and the Sumerians.* Cambridge: Cambridge University Press, 1991.

Ghirshman, Roman. *Iran from Earliest Times to the Islamic Conquest.* New York: Penguin, 1978.

Groenewegen-Frankfort, H. A. *Arrest and Movement: An Essay on Space and Time in Representational Art of the Ancient Near East.* Cambridge, MA: Belknap Press, 1987.

Hinz, Walther. *The Lost World of Elam.* New York: New York University Press, 1973.

Kramer, Samuel N. *The Sumerians: Their History, Culture, and Character.* Chicago: University of Chicago Press, 1971.

Leick, Gwendolyn. *A Dictionary of Ancient Near Eastern Architecture.* New York: Routledge, 1988.

Lloyd, Seton. *The Archaeology of Mesopotamia: From the Old Stone Age to the Persian Conquest.* London: Thames & Hudson, 1984.

———. *The Art of the Ancient Near East.* New York: Praeger, 1969.

Lloyd, Seton, and Hans Wolfgang Muller. *Ancient Architecture: Mesopotamia, Egypt, Crete.* New York: Electa/Rizzoli, 1986.

Moortgat, Anton. *The Art of Ancient Mesopotamia.* New York: Phaidon, 1969.

Oates, Joan. *Babylon.* Rev. ed. London: Thames & Hudson. 1986.

Oppenheim, A. Leo. *Ancient Mesopotamia.* Rev. ed. Chicago: University of Chicago Press, 1977.

Paris, Pierre. *Manual of Ancient Sculpture.* Rev. and enl. ed. New Rochelle, NY: Caratzas, 1984.

Parrot, André. *The Arts of Assyria.* New York: Golden Press, 1961.

———. *Sumer: The Dawn of Art.* New York: Golden Press, 1961.

Pope, Arthur, and Phyllis Ackerman. *A Survey of Persian Art from Prehistoric Times to the Present.* London: Oxford University Press, 1977.

Porada, Edith, and R. H. Dyson. *The Art of Ancient Iran: Pre-Islamic Cultures.* Rev. ed. New York: Greystone Press, 1969.

Strommenger, Eva, and Hirmer, Max. *5000 Years of the Art of Mesopotamia.* New York: Abrams, 1964.

Wolf, Walther. *The Origins of Western Art: Egypt, Mesopotamia, the Aegean.* New York: Universe Books, 1989.

Woolley, C. Leonard. *The Art of the Middle East, Including Persia, Mesopotamia and Palestine.* New York: Crown, 1961.

———. *The Development of Sumerian Art.* Westport, CT: Greenwood Press, 1981.

———. *The Sumerians.* New York: Norton, 1965.

CHAPTER 3 EGYPTIAN ART

Aldred, Cyril. *The Development of Ancient Egyptian Art from 3200 to 1315 B.C.* 3 vols. London: Academy Edition, 1973.

———. *Egyptian Art in the Days of the Pharaohs, 3100–320 B.C.* London: Thames & Hudson, 1980.

———. *The Egyptians.* London: Thames & Hudson, 1987.

Arnold, Dieter. *Building in Egypt, Pharaonic Stone Masonry.* Oxford: Oxford University Press, 1991.

Badawy, Alexander. *A History of Egyptian Architecture.* 3 vols. Berkeley: University of California Press, 1973.

Baines, John, and Jaromir Malek. *Atlas of Ancient Egypt.* New York: Facts on File, 1980.

Davis, Whitney. *The Canonical Tradition in Ancient Egyptian Art.* Cambridge: Cambridge University Press, 1991.

Emery, Walter B. *Archaic Egypt.* Baltimore: Penguin, 1974.

Gardiner, Sir Alan Henderson. *Egypt of the Pharaohs.* London: Oxford University Press, 1978.

Lange, Kurt, with Max Hirmer. *Egypt: Architecture, Sculpture and Painting in Three Thousand Years.* 4th ed. London: Phaidon, 1968.

Lurker, Manfred. *The Gods and Symbols of Ancient Egypt: An Illustrated Dictionary.* New York: Thames & Hudson, 1984.

Mahdy, Christine, ed. *The World of the Pharaohs: A Complete Guide to Ancient Egypt.* London: Thames & Hudson, 1990.

Mekhitarian, Arpag. *Egyptian Painting.* New York: Skira, 1978.

Mendelsohn, Kurt. *The Riddle of the Pyramids.* New York: Thames & Hudson, 1986.

Robins, Gay. *Egyptian Painting and Relief.* Aylesbury, England: Shire Publications, 1986.

Romer, John. *Valley of the Kings.* New York: William Morrow, 1981.

Schäfer, Heinrich. *Principles of Egyptian Art.* Rev. reprint. Oxford: Aris and Phillips, 1986.

Smith, E. Baldwin. *Egyptian Architecture as Cultural Expression.* Watkins Glen, NY: American Life Foundation, 1968.

Smith, William Stevenson, and W. Simpson. *The Art and Architecture of Ancient Egypt.* Rev. ed. New Haven: Yale University Press, 1981.

Woldering, Irmgard. *Gods, Men and Pharaohs: The Glory of Egyptian Art.* New York: Abrams, 1967.

CHAPTER 4 AEGEAN ART

Betancourt, Philip, P. *A History of Minoan Pottery.* Princeton: Princeton University Press, 1965.

Cadogan, Gerald. *Palaces of Minoan Crete.* London: Methuen, 1980.

Chadwick, John. *The Mycenaean World.* New York: Cambridge University Press, 1976.

Cottrell, Arthur. *The Minoan World.* New York: Scribner, 1980.

Demargne, Pierre. *The Birth of Greek Art.* New York: Golden Press, 1964.

Doumas, Christos. *Thera, Pompeii of the Ancient Aegean: Excavations at Akrotiri, 1967–1979.* New York: Thames & Hudson, 1983.

Evans, Sir Arthur John. *The Palace of Minos.* 4 vols. 1921–1935. Reprint. New York: Biblo & Tannen, 1964.

Fitton, J. Lesley. *Cycladic Art.* Cambridge, MA: Harvard University Press.

Graham, James W. *The Palaces of Crete.* Princeton: Princeton University Press, 1987.

Hampe, Roland, and Erika Simon. *The Birth of Greek Art. From the Mycenaean to the Archaic Period.* Oxford: Oxford University Press, 1981.

Higgins, Reynold Alleyne. *Minoan and Mycenaean Art.* Rev. ed. New York: Oxford University Press, 1985.

Hood, Sinclair. *The Arts in Prehistoric Greece.* New Haven: Yale University Press.

Immerwahr, Sarah A. *Aegean Painting in the Bronze Age.* University Park, PA: Pennsylvania State University Press, 1990.

Marinatos, Spyridon, with Max Hirmer. *Crete and Mycenae.* London: Thames & Hudson, 1960.

Palmer, Leonard R. *Mycenaeans and Minoans.* 2nd rev. ed. 1963. Reprint. Westport, CT: Greenwood Press, 1980.

Pendlebury, John. *The Archeology of Crete.* London: Methuen, 1967.

Taylour, Lord William. *The Mycenaens.* London: Thames & Hudson, 1990.

Vermeule, Emily. *Greece in the Bronze Age.* Chicago: University of Chicago Press, 1972.

Wace, Alan. *Mycenae, an Archeological History and Guide.* New York: Biblo & Tannen, 1964.

Warren, Peter. *The Aegean Civilizations.* London: Elsevier-Phaidon, 1975.

CHAPTER 5 GREEK ART

Arias, Paolo. *A History of One Thousand Years of Greek Vase Painting.* New York: Abrams, 1962. (Later edition available.)

Ashmole, Bernard. *Architect and Sculptor in Classical Greece.* New York: New York University Press, 1972.

Beazley, John D. *The Development of the Attic Black-Figure.* Rev. ed. Berkeley: University of California Press, 1986.

Berve, Helmut, Gottfried Gruben, and Max Hirmir. *Greek Temples, Theatres, and Shrines.* New York: Abrams, 1963.

Bieber, Margarete. *Sculpture of the Hellenistic Age.* 1961. Reprint. New York: Hacker, 1980.

Biers, William. *The Archaeology of Greece.* Ithaca, NY: Cornell University Press, 1987.

Blumel, Carl. *Greek Sculptors at Work.* London: Phaidon, 1969.

Boardman, John. *Athenian Black Figure Vases.* New York: Thames & Hudson, 1974.

———. *Athenian Red Figure Vases: The Archaic Period.* New York: Thames & Hudson, 1988.

———. *Athenian Red Figure Vases: The Classical Period.* New York: Thames & Hudson, 1989.

———. *Greek Art.* Rev. ed. New York: Thames & Hudson, 1987.

———. *Greek Sculpture: The Archaic Period.* New York: Thames & Hudson, 1978.

———. *Greek Sculpture: The Classical Period: A Handbook.* London: Thames & Hudson, 1987.

Carpenter, Thomas H. *Art and Myth in Ancient Greece.* New York: Thames & Hudson, 1991.

Charbonneaux, Jean; Roland Martin; and François Villard. *Archaic Greek Art.* New York: Braziller, 1971.

———. *Classical Greek Art.* New York: Braziller, 1972.

———. *Hellenistic Art.* New York: Braziller, 1973.

Coldstream, J. Nicholas. *Geometric Greece.* New York: St. Martin's Press, 1977.

Cook, Robert M. *Greek Art: Its Development, Character and Influence.* Harmondsworth, England: Penguin, 1976.

Coulton, J. J. *Ancient Greek Architects at Work.* Ithaca, NY: Cornell University Press, 1982.

Dinsmoor, W. B. *The Architecture of Ancient Greece.* 3rd ed. New York: Norton, 1975.

Houser, Caroline. *Greek Monumental Bronze Sculpture.* London: 1983.

Hurwit, Jeffrey M. *The Art and Culture of Early Greece, 1100–480 B.C.* Ithaca, NY: Cornell University Press, 1985

Langlotz, Ernst, and Max Hirmer. *The Art of Magna Graecia. Greek Art in Southern Italy and Sicily.* New York: Abrams, 1965.

Lawrence, Arnold W., and R. A. Tomlinson. *Greek Architecture.* New Haven: Yale University Press, 1984.

Lullies, Reinhard, and Max Hirmer. *Greek Sculpture.* Rev. ed. New York: Abrams, 1960.

Martin, Roland. *Greek Architecture: Architecture of Crete, Greece, and the Greek World.* New York: Electa/Rizzoli, 1988.

Mattusch, Carol C. *Greek Bronze Statuary from the Beginnings through the Fifth Century B.C.* Ithaca, NY: Cornell University Press, 1988.

Onians, John. *Art and Thought in the Hellenistic Age: The Greek World View, 350–50 B.C.* London: Thames & Hudson, 1979.

Pedley, John Griffiths. *Greek Art and Archaeology.* Englewood Cliffs, NJ: Prentice Hall, 1993.

Pollitt, Jerome J. *The Ancient View of Greek Art.* New Haven: Yale University Press, 1974.

———. *Art and Experience in Classical Greece.* Cambridge: Cambridge University Press, 1972.

———. *Art in the Hellenistic Age.* Cambridge: Cambridge University Press, 1986.

———. *The Art of Ancient Greece: Sources and Documents.* New York: Cambridge University Press, 1990.

Richter, Gisela M. *A Handbook of Greek Art.* 9th ed. Oxford: Phaidon, 1987.

———. *The Portraits of the Greeks.* Rev. ed. Ithaca, NY: Cornell University Press, 1984.

———. *The Sculpture and Sculptors of the Greeks.* 4th ed. New Haven: Yale University Press, 1970.

Ridgway, Brunilde S. *The Archaic Style in Greek Sculpture.* Princeton: Princeton University Press, 1981.

———. *Fifth Century Styles in Greek Sculpture.* Princeton: Princeton University Press, 1981.

———. *Hellenistic Sculpture I: The Styles of ca. 331–200 B.C.* Madison: University of Wisconsin Press, 1990.

———. *The Severe Style in Greek Sculpture.* Princeton: Princeton University Press, 1970.

Robertson, Donald S. *Greek and Roman Architecture.* 2nd ed. Cambridge: Cambridge University Press, 1969.

Robertson, Martin. *The Art of Vase-Painting in Classical Athens.* Cambridge: Cambridge University Press, 1992.

———. *Greek Painting.* New York: Rizzoli, 1979.

———. *A History of Greek Art.* 2 vols. Cambridge: Cambridge University Press, 1976.

———. *A Shorter History of Greek Art.* Cambridge: Cambridge University Press, 1981.

Smith, R. R. R. *Hellenistic Sculpture.* New York: Thames & Hudson, 1991.

Stewart, Andrew. *Greek Sculpture.* 2 vols. New Haven: Yale University Press, 1990.

Travlos, John. *Pictorial Dictionary of Ancient Athens.* 1971. Reprint. New York: Hacker, 1980.

Wycherley, Richard E. *How the Greeks Built Cities.* New York: Norton, 1976.

CHAPTER 6 ETRUSCAN ART

Banti, Luisa. *The Etruscan Cities and Their Culture.* Berkeley: University of California Press, 1973.

Boethius, Axel. *Etruscan and Early Roman Architecture.* New Haven: Yale University Press, 1978.

Bonfante, Larissa, ed. *Etruscan Life and Afterlife. A Handbook of Etruscan Studies.* Detroit: Wayne State University Press, 1986.

Brendel, Otto J. *Etruscan Art.* New Haven: Yale University Press, 1978.

Mansuelli, Guido. *The Art of Etruria and Early Rome.* New York: Crown, 1965.

Pallottino, Massimo. *Etruscan Painting.* Geneva: Skira, 1953.

———. *The Etruscans.* Harmondsworth: Penguin, 1978.

Richardson, Emeline. *The Etruscans: Their Art and Civilization.* Chicago: University of Chicago Press, 1976.

Ridgway, David, and Francesca Ridgway, eds. *Italy before the Romans.* New York: Academic Press, 1979.

Sprenger, Maja, Gilda Bartoloni, and Max Hirmer. *The Etruscans: Their History, Art, and Architecture.* New York: Abrams, 1983.

CHAPTER 7 ROMAN ART

Andreae, Bernard. *The Art of Rome.* New York: Abrams, 1977.

Bianchi Bandinelli, Ranuccio. *Rome, the Center of Power.* New York: Braziller, 1970.

———. *Rome, the Late Empire.* New York: Braziller, 1971.

Brendel, Otto J. *Prolegomena to the Study of Roman Art.* New Haven: Yale University Press, 1979.

Clarke, John R. *The Houses of Roman Italy, 100 B.C.–A.D. 250.* Berkeley: University of California Press, 1991.

Hanfmann, George. *Roman Art.* Greenwich, CT: New York Graphic Society, 1964.

Hannestad, Niels. *Roman Art and Imperial Policy.* Aarhus, Denmark: Aarhus University Press, 1986.

Henig, Martin, ed. *A Handbook of Roman Art.* Ithaca, NY: Cornell University Press, 1983.

Kent, John P. C., and Max Hirmer. *Roman Coins.* New York: Abrams, 1978.

Kleiner, Diana E. E. *Roman Sculpture.* New Haven: Yale University Press, 1992.

Kraus, Theodor. *Pompeii and Herculaneum: The Living Cities of the Dead.* New York: Abrams, 1975.

Ling, Roger. *Roman Painting.* Cambridge: Cambridge University Press, 1991.

L'Orange, Hans Peter. *The Roman Empire: Art Forms and Civic Life.* New York: Rizzoli, 1985.

MacDonald, William L. *The Architecture of the Roman Empire I: An Introductory Study.* Rev. ed. New Haven: Yale University Press, 1982.

———. *The Architecture of the Roman Empire II: An Urban Appraisal.* New Haven: Yale University Press, 1986.

McKay, Alexander G. *Houses, Villas, and Palaces in the Roman World.* Ithaca, NY: Cornell University Press, 1975.

Maiuri, Amedeo. *Roman Painting.* Geneva: Skira, 1953.

Nash, Ernest. *Pictorial Dictionary of Ancient Rome.* 2 vols. New York: Hacker, 1981.

Pollitt, Jerome J. *The Art of Rome, 753 B.C.–A.D. 337.* Rev. ed. Cambridge: Cambridge University Press, 1983.

Ramage, Nancy H. and Andrew Ramage. *Roman Art: Romulus to Constantine.* Englewood Cliffs, NJ: Prentice Hall, 1991.

Richardson, Lawrence, Jr. *A New Topographical Dictionary of Ancient Rome.* Baltimore: Johns Hopkins University Press, 1992.

———. *Pompeii. An Architectural History.* Baltimore: Johns Hopkins University Press, 1988.

Robertson, Donald S. *Greek and Roman Architecture.* 2nd ed. Cambridge: Cambridge University Press, 1969.

Sear, Frank. *Roman Architecture.* Rev. ed. Ithaca, NY: Cornell University Press, 1989.

Smith, Earl Baldwin. *Architectural Symbolism of Imperial Rome and the Middle Ages.* Princeton: Princeton University Press, 1956.

———. *The Dome, a Study in the History of Ideas.* Princeton: Princeton University Press, 1971.

Strong, Donald, and Roger Ling. *Roman Art.* 2nd rev. ed. New Haven: Yale University Press, 1988.

Toynbee, Jocelyn M. C. *Death and Burial in the Roman World.* London: Thames & Hudson, 1971.

Ward-Perkins, John B. *Roman Architecture.* New York: Electa/Rizzoli, 1988.

———. *Roman Imperial Architecture.* 2nd integrated ed. New Haven: Yale University Press, 1981.

Zanker, Paul. *The Power of Images in the Age of Augustus.* Ann Arbor: University of Michigan Press, 1988.

CHAPTER 8 EARLY CHRISTIAN ART

Beckwith, John. *Early Christian and Byzantine Art.* New Haven: Yale University Press, 1980.

Brown, Peter. *The World of Late Antiquity.* London: Thames & Hudson, 1971.

Du Bourguet, Pierre. *Early Christian Art.* New York: William Morrow, 1971.

Gough, Michael. *The Origins of Christian Art.* New York: Praeger, 1973.

Grabar, André. *The Beginnings of Christian Art, 200–395.* London: Thames & Hudson, 1967.

———. *Christian Iconography.* Princeton: Princeton University Press, 1980.

Hutter, Irmgard. *Early Christian and Byzantine Art.* London: Herbert Press, 1988.

Krautheimer, Richard. *Rome, Profile of a City: 312–1308.* Princeton: Princeton University Press, 1980.

Krautheimer, Richard, and Slobodan Curcic. *Early Christian and Byzantine Architecture.* 4th rev. ed. New Haven: Yale University Press, 1986.

Lowrie, Walter S. *Art in the Early Church.* New York: Norton, 1969.

MacDonald, William L. *Early Christian and Byzantine Architecture.* New York: Braziller, 1963.

Mathews, Thomas, P. *The Clash of Gods: A Reinterpretation of Early Christian Art.* Princeton: Princeton University Press, 1993.

Milburn, Robert L. P. *Early Christian Art and Architecture.* Berkeley: University of California Press, 1988.

Perkins, Ann Louise. *The Art of Dura-Europos.* Oxford: Clarendon, 1973.

Schiller, Gertrud. *Iconography of Christian Art.* See Reference Books.

Volbach, Wolfgang. *Early Christian Mosaics, from the Fourth to the Seventh Centuries.* New York: Oxford University Press, 1946.

Volbach, Wolfgang, and Max Hirmer. *Early Christian Art.* New York: Abrams, 1962.

Weitzmann, Kurt. *Ancient Book Illumination.* Cambridge: Harvard University Press, 1959.

———. *Late Antique and Early Christian Book Illumination.* New York: Braziller, 1977.

Weitzmann, Kurt, ed. *Age of Spirituality. Late Antique and Early Christian Art, Third to Seventh Century.* New York: Metropolitan Museum of Art, 1979.

CHAPTER 9 BYZANTINE ART

Beckwith, John. *The Art of Constantinople: An Introduction to Byzantine Art (330–1453).* New York: Phaidon, 1968.

Chatzidakis, Manolis. *Byzantine and Early Medieval Painting.* New York: Viking, 1965.

Dalton, Ormonde M. *Byzantine Art and Archaeology.* New York: Dover, 1961.

Demus, Otto. *Byzantine Art and the West.* New York: New York University Press, 1970.

———. *The Mosaic Decoration of San Marco, Venice.* Chicago: University of Chicago Press, 1988.

Grabar, André. *Byzantine Painting.* New York: Rizzoli, 1979.

———. *The Golden Age of Justinian: From the Death of Theodosius to the Rise of Islam.* New York: Odyssey Press, 1967.

Grabar, André, and Manolis Chatzidakis. *Greek Mosaics of the Byzantine Period.* New York: New American Library, 1964.

Hamilton, George H. *The Art and Architecture of Russia.* 2nd ed. New York: Viking, 1983.

Hamilton, John A. *Byzantine Architecture and Decoration.* 1933. Freeport, NY: Books for Libraries/Arno Press, 1972.

Huyghe, René, ed. *Larousse Encyclopedia of Byzantine and Medieval Art.* See Reference Books.

Kitzinger, Ernst. *Byzantine Art in the Making.* Cambridge: Harvard University Press, 1977.

Maguire, Henry. *Art and Eloquence in Byzantium.* Princeton: Princeton University Press, 1981.

Mango, Cyril. *Byzantine Architecture.* New York: Electa/Rizzoli, 1985.

———. *Byzantium: The Empire of New Rome.* New York: Scribner's, 1980.

———. *Byzantium and Its Image: History and Culture of the Byzantine Empire and Its Heritage.* London: Variorum Reprints, 1984.

Meyer, Peter. *Byzantine Mosaics: Torcello, Venice, Monreale, Palermo.* London: Batsford, 1952.

Pelikan, J. *Imago Dei: The Byzantine Apologia for Icons.* Princeton: Princeton University Press, 1990.

Rice, David T. *The Appreciation of Byzantine Art.* London: Oxford University Press, 1972.

———. *The Art of Byzantium.* New York: Abrams, 1959.

———. *Byzantine Art.* London: Variorum Reprints, 1973.

———. *Byzantine Painting: The Last Phase.* New York: Dial Press, 1968.

Swift, Emerson H. *Hagia Sophia.* New York: Columbia University Press, 1980.

Von Simson, Otto G. *Sacred Fortress: Byzantine Art and Statecraft in Ravenna.* Princeton: Princeton University Press, 1986.

Walter, Christopher. *Art and Ritual of the Byzantine Church.* London: Variorum, 1982.

Weitzmann, Kurt. *Ancient Book Illumination.* Cambridge: Harvard University Press, 1959.

———. *Art in the Medieval West and Its Contacts with Byzantium.* London: Variorum, 1982.

———. *The Icon.* New York: Dorset Press (Mondadori), 1987.

———. *Illustrations in Roll and Codex.* Princeton: Princeton University Press, 1970.

Weitzmann, Kurt, et al. *The Icon.* New York: Knopf, 1982.

Weitzman, K., and G. Galavaris. *The Monastery of St. Catherine at Mt. Sinai.* Princeton: Princeton University Press, 1990.

CHAPTER 10 ISLAMIC ART

Arnold, Thomas W. *Painting in Islam.* New York: Dover, 1965.

Aslanapa, Oktay. *Turkish Art and Architecture.* London: Faber & Faber, 1971.

Atil, Esin. *Renaissance of Islam: Art of the Mamluks.* Washington, DC: Smithsonian Institution Press, 1981.

Badeau, John S., et. al., *The Genius of Arab Civilization: Source of Renaissance.* John Hays, ed. New York: New York University Press, 1975.

Beach, Milo Cleveland. *Early Mughal Painting.* Cambridge: Harvard University Press, 1987.

Blair, Sheila S. and Jonathan Bloom. *The Art and Architecture of Islam 1250–1800.* New Haven: Yale University Press, 1994.

Brend, Barbara. *Islamic Art.* Cambridge, MA: Harvard University Press, 1991.

Crespi, Gabriele. *The Arabs in Europe.* New York: Rizzoli, 1986.

Creswell, K. A. C. *A Short Account of Early Muslim Architecture.* Rev. and enl. ed. Aldershot, England: Scolar, 1989.

Ettinghausen, Richard. *Arab Painting.* Geneva: Skira, 1977.

———. *From Byzantium to Sasanian Iran and the Islamic World.* Leiden: Brill, 1972.

Ettinghausen, Richard, and Oleg Grabar. *The Art and Architecture of Islam, 650–1250.* New Haven: Yale University Press, 1992.

Golombek, Lisa, and Donald Wilber. *The Timurid Architecture of Iran and Turan.* 2 vols. Princeton: Princeton University Press, 1988.

Goodwin, Godfrey. *A History of Ottoman Architecture.* New York: Thames & Hudson, 1987.

Grabar, Oleg. *The Formation of Islamic Art.* Rev. and enl. ed. New Haven: Yale University Press, 1987.

Grover, Satish. *The Architecture of India: Islamic (727–1707).* New Delhi: Vikas, 1981.

Grunebaum, Gustave von. *Classical Islam: A History, 600–1258.* Chicago: Aldine, 1970.

Hoag, John D. *Islamic Architecture.* New York: Abrams, 1977; Rizzoli (paperbound), 1987.

Kühnel, Ernst. *Islamic Art and Architecture.* London: Bell, 1966.

Lane, Arthur. *Early Islamic Pottery, Mesopotamia, Egypt and Persia.* New York: Faber & Faber, 1965.

Levey, Michael. *The World of Ottoman Art.* New York: Scribner, 1975.

Lewis, Bernard, ed. *Islam and the Arab World.* New York: Knopf, 1976.

Rice, David T. *Islamic Art.* London: Thames & Hudson, 1975.

Robinson, Frank. *Atlas of the Islamic World.* Oxford: Equinox Ltd., 1982.

Schimmel, Annemarie. *Islam in India and Pakistan.* Leiden: Brill, 1982.

Schimmel, Annemarie, and Barbara Rivolta. *Islamic Calligraphy.* New York: Metropolitan Museum of Art Bulletin, Summer 1992, vol. 1, no. 1.

CHAPTER 11 EARLY MEDIEVAL ART IN THE WEST

Arnold, Bruce. *Irish Art: A Concise History.* Rev. ed. London: Thames & Hudson, 1989.

Beckwith, John. *Early Medieval Art: Carolingian, Ottonian, Romanesque.* New York: Oxford University Press, 1974.

Calkins, Robert G. *Illuminated Books of the Middle Ages.* Ithaca, NY: Cornell University Press, 1983.

Conant, Kenneth. *Carolingian and Romanesque Architecture 800–1200.* 4th ed. New Haven: Yale University Press, 1992.

Dodwell, C. R. *Anglo-Saxon Art: A New Perspective.* Ithaca, NY: Cornell University Press, 1992.

————. *The Pictorial Arts of the West 800–1200.* New Haven: Yale University Press, 1993.

Finlay, Ian. *Celtic Art: An Introduction.* London: Faber & Faber, 1973.

Goldschmidt, Adolf. *German Illumination.* New York: Hacker, 1970.

Grabar, André, and Carl Nordenfalk. *Early Medieval Painting from the Fourth to the Eleventh Century.* New York: Skira, 1967.

Harbison, Peter, et al. *Irish Art and Architecture from Prehistory to the Present.* London: Thames & Hudson, 1978.

Henderson, George. *Early Medieval Art.* Pelican Style and Civilization Series. New York: Penguin, 1972.

Henry, Françoise. *Irish Art During the Viking Invasions, 900–1020.* Ithaca, NY: Cornell University Press, 1970.

————. *Irish Art in the Early Christian Period, to 800.* Rev. ed. London: Methuen, 1965.

Hinks, Roger P. *Carolingian Art.* Ann Arbor: University of Michigan Press, 1974.

Klindt-Jensen, Ole, and David M. Wilson. *Viking Art.* 2nd ed. Minneapolis: University of Minnesota Press, 1980.

Laszlo, Gyula. *The Art of the Migration Period.* London: Allen Lane, 1974.

Leeds, Edward T. *Early Anglo-Saxon Art and Archaeology.* Westport, CT: Greenwood Press, 1971.

Lucas, A. T. *Treasures of Ireland: Irish Pagan and Early Christian Art.* New York: Viking, 1973.

Megaw, Ruth, and John V. Megaw. *Celtic Art: From Its Beginning to the Book of Kells.* London: Thames & Hudson, 1989.

Mütherich, Florentine, and J. E. Gaehde. *Carolingian Painting.* New York: Braziller, 1977.

Nordenfalk, Carl. *Celtic and Anglo-Saxon Painting: Book Illumination in the British Isles 600–800.* New York: Braziller, 1977.

Porter, Arthur K. *The Crosses and Culture of Ireland.* New York: Benjamin Blom, 1971.

Stokstad, Marilyn. *Medieval Art.* New York: Harper & Row, 1986.

Taylor, Harold M., and Joan Taylor. *Anglo-Saxon Architecture.* 2 vols. Cambridge: Cambridge University Press, 1981.

Wilson, David M., ed. *The Northern World: The History and Heritage of Northern Europe A.D. 400–1100.* New York: Abrams, 1980.

Zarnecki, George. *Art of the Medieval World.* New York: Abrams, 1976.

CHAPTER 12 ROMANESQUE ART

Clapham, Alfred W. *English Romanesque Architecture After the Conquest.* Oxford: Clarendon Press, 1964.

————. *Romanesque Architecture in Western Europe.* Oxford: Clarendon Press, 1959.

Conant, Kenneth John. *Carolingian and Romanesque Architecture, 800–1200.* 2nd integrated rev. ed. New York: Penguin, 1979.

Crichton, George H. *Romanesque Sculpture in Italy.* London: Routledge & Paul, 1954.

Decker, Heinrich. *Romanesque Art in Italy.* New York: Abrams, 1959.

Demus, Otto. *Romanesque Mural Painting.* New York: Abrams, 1959.

Deschamps, Paul. *French Sculpture of the Romanesque Period—Eleventh and Twelfth Centuries.* 1930. Reprint. New York: Hacker, 1972.

Dodwell, C. R. *Painting in Europe 800–1200.* Harmondsworth, England: Penguin, 1971.

Duby, Georges. *History of Medieval Art, 980–1440.* New York: Skira/Rizzoli, 1986.

Evans, Joan. *Art in Medieval France 987–1498.* Oxford: Clarendon Press, 1969.

Focillon, Henri. *The Art of the West in the Middle Ages.* Vol. 1. 2nd ed. London: Phaidon, 1969; Ithaca, NY: Cornell University Press (paperbound), 1980. (Later volume available.)

Gantner, Joseph, Marcel Pobé, and Jean Roubier. *Romanesque Art in France.* London: Thames & Hudson, 1956.

Gibbs-Smith, Charles H. *The Bayeux Tapestry.* London: Phaidon, 1973.

Grabar, André, and Carl Nordenfalk. *Romanesque Painting.* New York: Skira, 1958.

Hearn, Millard F. *Romanesque Sculpture in the Eleventh and Twelfth Centuries.* Ithaca, NY: Cornell University Press/Phaidon, 1981.

Holt, Elizabeth Gilmore, ed. *A Documentary History of Art, I: The Middle Ages.* Princeton: Princeton University Press, 1981.

Kubach, Hans E. *Romanesque Architecture.* New York: Rizzoli, 1988.

Kuenstler, Gustav, ed. *Romanesque Art in Europe.* New York: Norton, 1973.

Leisinger, Hermann. *Romanesque Bronzes: Church Portals in Mediaeval Europe.* New York: Praeger, 1957.

Male, Émile. *Art and Artists of the Middle Ages.* Redding Ridge, CT: Black Swan Books, 1986.

Michel, Paul H. *Romanesque Wall Paintings in France.* Paris: Éditions Chêne, 1949.

Morey, Charles R. *Medieval Art.* New York: Norton, 1970.

Nordenfalk, Carl. *Early Medieval Book Illumination.* New York: Rizzoli, 1988.

Porter, Arthur K. *Medieval Architecture.* 2 vols. 1909. Reprint. New York: Hacker, 1969.

————. *Romanesque Sculpture of the Pilgrimage Roads.* 1923. Reprint. New York: Hacker, 1969.

Rickert, Margaret. *Painting in Britain: The Middle Ages.* 2nd ed. Harmondsworth, England: Penguin, 1965.

Rivoira, Giovanni. *Lombardic Architecture: Its Origin, Development, and Derivatives.* 1933. Reprint. New York: Hacker, 1975.

Saalman, Howard. *Medieval Architecture: European Architecture 600–1200.* New York: Braziller, 1962.

Schapiro, Meyer. *Romanesque Art: Selected Papers.* London: Chatto & Windus, 1977; New York: Braziller, 1976.

Stoddard, Whitney. *Art and Architecture in Medieval France.* New York: Harper & Row, 1972.

Stone, Lawrence. *Sculpture in Britain: The Middle Ages.* New Haven: Yale University Press, 1972.

Swarzenski, Hanns. *Monuments of Romanesque Art.* Chicago: University of Chicago Press, 1974.

Webb, Geoffrey F. *Architecture in Britain: The Middle Ages.* Harmondsworth, England: Penguin, 1965.

Zarnecki, George. *Romanesque Art.* New York: Universe Books, 1971.

————. *Studies in Romanesque Sculpture.* London: Dorian Press, 1979.

CHAPTER 13 GOTHIC ART

Adams, Henry B. *Mont-Saint-Michel and Chartres.* New York: Cherokee, 1982.

Alexander, Jonathan J. G. *Medieval Illuminators and their Methods of Work.* New Haven/London: Yale University Press, 1992.

Arnold, Hugh. *Stained Glass of the Middle Ages in England and France.* London: A. & C. Black, 1956.

Arslan, Edoardo. *Gothic Architecture in Venice.* London: Phaidon, 1971.

Aubert, Marcel. *The Art of the High Gothic Era.* New York: Crown, 1965.

————. *Gothic Cathedrals of France and Their Treasures.* London: N. Kay, 1959.

Bony, Jean. *The English Decorated Style.* Ithaca, NY: Cornell University Press, 1979.

————. *French Gothic Architecture of the XII and XIII Centuries.* Berkeley: University of California Press, 1983.

Brandenburg, Alain Erlande. *Gothic Art.* New York: Harry N. Abrams, 1989.

Branner, Robert. *Chartres Cathedral.* New York: Norton, 1969.

————. *Gothic Architecture.* New York: Braziller, 1961.

Duby, George. *The Age of the Cathedrals.* Chicago: University of Chicago Press, 1981.

Dupont, Jacques, and Cesare Gnudi. *Gothic Painting.* New York: Rizzoli, 1979.

Evans, Joan. *Art in Medieval France 987–1498.* Oxford: Clarendon Press, 1969.

————. *The Flowering of the Middle Ages.* London: Thames & Hudson, 1985.

Favier, Jean. *The World of Chartres.* New York: Harry N. Abrams, 1990.

Fitchen, John. *The Construction of Gothic Cathedrals: A Study of Medieval Vault Erection.* Chicago: University of Chicago Press, 1977; Phoenix Books, 1981.

Focillon, Henri. *The Art of the West in the Middle Ages.* Vol. 2. Ithaca, NY: Cornell University Press, 1980.

Frankl, Paul. *Gothic Architecture.* Baltimore: Penguin, 1963.

————. *The Gothic Literary Sources and Interpretations.* Princeton: Princeton University Press, 1960.

Frisch, T. G. *Gothic Art 1140–c. 1450. Sources and documents in the History of Art Series* (H. W. Janson, ed.). Englewood Cliffs, NJ: Prentice Hall, 1971.

Grodecki, Louis. *Gothic Architecture.* New York: Electa/Rizzoli, 1985.

Huizinga, Johan. *The Waning of the Middle Ages.* 1924. Reprint. New York: St. Martin's Press, 1988.

Jantzen, Hans. *High Gothic: The Classic Cathedrals of Chartres, Reims, and Amiens.* Princeton: Princeton University Press, 1984.

Johnson, James. *The Radiance of Chartres.* New York: Random House, 1965.

Johnson, Paul. *British Cathedrals.* New York: William Morrow, 1980.

Katzenellenbogen, Adolf. *The Sculptural Programs of Chartres Cathedral.* Baltimore: Johns Hopkins Press, 1959.

Male, Émile. *The Gothic Image: Religious Art in the Twelfth Century.* Rev. ed. Princeton: Princeton University Press, 1978.

————. *Religious Art in France: The 13th Century—A Study of Medieval Iconography and Its Sources.* Princeton: Princeton University Press, 1984.

————. *Religious Art in France: The Late Middle Ages—A Study of Medieval Iconography and Its Sources.* Princeton: Princeton University Press, 1987.

Mark, Robert. *Experiments in Gothic Structure.* Cambridge: MIT Press, 1982.

Martindale, Andrew. *Gothic Art.* London: Thames & Hudson, 1985.

————. *The Rise of the Artist in the Middle Ages and Early Renaissance.* New York: McGraw-Hill, 1972.

Murray, S. B. *Beauvais Cathedral: Architecture of Transcendence.* Princeton: Princeton University Press, 1989.

Panofsky, Erwin. *Abbot Suger on the Abbey Church of St. Denis and Its Art Treasures.* 2nd ed. Princeton: Princeton University Press, 1979.

————. *Gothic Architecture and Scholasticism.* New York: Meridian Books, 1963.

Pevsner, Nikolaus. *The Buildings of England.* 46 vols. Harmondsworth, England: Penguin, 1951–1974.

Radding, Charles M., and William W. Clark. *Medieval Architecture, Medieval Learning.* New Haven: Yale University Press, 1992.

Sauerlander, Willibald, and Max Hirmer. *Gothic Sculpture in France 1140–1270.* New York: Abrams, 1973.

Sheridan, Ronald, and Anne Ross. *Gargoyles and Grotesques: Paganism in the Medieval Church.* Boston: New York Graphic Society, 1975.

Stoddard, Whitney. *Art and Architecture in Medieval France.* New York: HarperCollins, 1972.

Swaan, Wim. *The Late Middle Ages: Art and Architecture from 1350 to the Advent of the Renaissance.* Ithaca, NY: Cornell University Press, 1977.

Thompson, Daniel. *The Materials and Techniques of Medieval Painting.* New York: Dover, 1956.

Von Simson, Otto Georg. *The Gothic Cathedral: Origins of Gothic Architecture and the Medieval Concept of Order.* 3rd enl. ed. Princeton: Princeton University Press, 1988.

Wilson, Christopher. *The Gothic Cathedral.* London: Thames & Hudson, 1990.

Zarnecki, George. *Art of the Medieval World.* New York: Abrams, 1976.

CHAPTER 14 THE ART OF INDIAN ASIA

Acharya, Prasanna Kumar. *An Encyclopedia of Hindu Architecture.* 2nd ed. New Delhi: Oriental Books Reprint Corporation, 1979.

Archer, William G. *Indian Miniatures.* Greenwich, CT: New York Graphic Society, 1960.

————. *Indian Paintings from the Punjab Hills.* 2 vols. London: Sotheby Parke Bernet, 1973.

Asher, Frederick M. *The Art of Eastern India, 300–800.* Minneapolis: University of Minnesota Press, 1980.

Bachhofer, Ludwig. *Early Indian Sculpture.* 1929. Reprint. New York: Hacker, 1974.

Barrett, Douglas E. *Early Chola Bronzes.* Bombay: Bhulabhai Memorial Institute, 1965.

Barrett, Douglas E., and Basil Gray. *Painting of India.* Geneva: Skira, 1963.

Coomaraswamy, Ananda K. *History of Indian and Indonesian Art.* New York: Dover, 1985.

————. *Yaksas.* New Delhi: Munshiram Manaharlal, 1971.

Craven, Roy C. *Indian Art: A Concise History.* London: Thames & Hudson, 1985.

Dehejia, Vidya. *Early Buddhist Rock Temples.* Ithaca, NY: Cornell University Press, 1972.

Ghosh, Amalananda. *Ajanta Murals.* New Delhi: Archaeological Survey of India, 1967.

Ghosh, Sankar Prosad. *Hindu Religious Art and Architecture.* Delhi: D. K. Publications, 1982.

Gopinatha Rao, T. A. *Elements of Hindu Iconography.* 2nd ed. 4 vols. New York: Paragon, 1968.

Gray, Basil, ed. *The Arts of India.* Ithaca, NY: Cornell University Press/Phaidon, 1981.

Groslier, Bernard P., and Jacques Arthaud. *The Arts and Civilization of Angkor.* New York: Praeger, 1957.

Grover, Satish. *The Architecture of India: Buddhist and Hindu.* Sahibabad, Distt. Ghaziabad: Vikas, 1980.

Harle, James C. *The Art and Architecture of the Indian Subcontinent.* New Haven: Yale University Press, 1992.

Head, Raymond. *The Indian Style.* Boston: Allen and Unwin, 1986.

Huntington, Susan L, and John C. Huntington. *The Art of Ancient India: Buddhist, Hindu, Jain.* New York: Weatherhill, 1985.

Kramrisch, Stella. *The Art of India through the Ages.* Delhi: Motilal Banarsidass, 1987.

———. *The Hindu Temple.* 2 vols. Delhi: Motilal Banarsidass, 1991. (Original edition 1946.)

———. *Indian Sculpture.* The Heritage of India Series. London: Oxford University Press, 1933.

Krishna, Deva. *Temples of North India.* New Delhi: National Book Trust, 1969.

Lee, Sherman E. *Ancient Cambodian Sculpture.* New York: Intercultural Arts Press, 1970.

Manwani, S. N. *Evolution of Art and Architecture in Central India: With Special Reference to the Kalachuris of Ratanpur.* Delhi: Agam Kala Prakashan, 1988.

Meister, Michael W. *Encyclopedia of Indian Temple Architecture.* Philadelphia: University of Pennsylvania Press, 1983. Princeton: Princeton University Press, 1991 (4 vols.)

Munsterberg, Hugo. *Art of India and Southeast Asia.* New York: Abrams, 1970.

Rawson, Philip. *The Art of Southeast Asia.* New York: Praeger, 1967.

Rowland, Benjamin. *The Art and Architecture of India: Buddhist, Hindu, Jain.* Harmondsworth, England: Penguin, 1977.

Srinivasan, K. R. *Temples of South India.* New Delhi: National Book Trust, 1972.

Stutley, Margaret. *An Illustrated Dictionary of Hindu Iconography.* Boston: Routledge and Keegan Paul, 1985.

Welch, Stuart Cary. *India: Art and Culture, 1300–1900.* New York: Metropolitan Museum of Art/Holt, Rinehart & Winston, 1985.

Williams, Joanna Gottfried. *The Art of Gupta India: Empire and Province.* Princeton: Princeton University Press, 1982.

Zimmer, Heinrich, and Joseph Campbell, eds. *The Art of Indian Asia; Its Mythology and Transformations.* Bollingen Series 39. 2 vols. Princeton: Princeton University Press, 1983.

CHAPTER 15 THE ART OF CHINA AND KOREA

Bush, Susan, and Christian Murck, eds. *Theories of the Arts in China.* Princeton: Princeton University Press, 1983.

Blunden, Caroline, and Mark Elvin. *Cultural Atlas of China.* New York: Facts on File, 1983.

Cahill, James. *Chinese Painting.* New ed. Geneva: Skira, 1977; New York: Rizzoli, 1977.

Davidson, J. Leroy. *The Lotus Sutra in Chinese Art: A Study in Buddhist Art to the Year 1880.* New Haven: Yale University Press, 1954.

Han Zhongmin, and Hubert Delahaye. *A Journey through Ancient China.* New York: Gallery Books, 1985.

Hutt, Julia. *Understanding Far Eastern Art: A Complete Guide to the Arts of China, Japan, and Korea.* New York: Dutton, 1987.

Lee, Sherman E. *Chinese Landscape Painting.* Rev. ed. New York: HarperCollins, 1971.

———. *Past, Present, East and West.* New York: Braziller, 1983.

Liu, Lawrence. *Chinese Architecture.* New York: Rizzoli International, 1989.

Loehr, Max. *The Great Painters of China.* New York: Harper & Row, 1980.

———. *Ritual Vessels of Bronze Age China.* New York: Asia Society, 1968.

Mizuno, Seiichi. *Bronzes and Jades of Ancient China.* Tokyo: Nihon Keizai, 1959.

Munsterberg, Hugo. *Dictionary of Chinese and Japanese Art.* New York: Hacker, 1981.

———. *Symbolism in Ancient Chinese Art.* New York: Hacker, 1986.

Sickman, Lawrence C., and Alexander Soper. *The Art and Architecture of China.* 3rd ed. New Haven: Yale University Press, 1992.

Siren, Oswald. *Chinese Painting: Leading Masters and Principles.* New York: Hacker, 1973.

———. *Chinese Sculpture from the Fifth to the Fourteenth Centuries.* 4 vols. 1925. Reprint. New York: Hacker, 1970.

———. *A History of Later Chinese Painting.* 1938. Reprint. London: Medici Society, 1978.

Sullivan, Michael. *The Arts of China.* 3rd ed. Berkeley: University of California Press, 1984.

———. *The Birth of Landscape Painting in China.* Berkeley: University of California Press, 1962.

———. *A Short History of Chinese Art.* Berkeley: University of California Press, 1970.

Thorp, Robert L. *Son of Heaven: Imperial Arts of China.* Seattle: Son of Heaven Press, 1988.

Van Oort, H. A. *The Iconography of Chinese Buddhism in Traditional China.* Leiden: Brill, 1986.

Watson, William. *The Art of Dynastic China.* New York: Abrams, 1983.

———. *The Art of Dynastic China.* New York: Abrams, 1981.

Zo, Za-yong, and U Fan Lee. (John Bester, trans.) *Traditional Korean Painting: A Lost Art Rediscovered.* New York/Tokyo: Kodansha International, 1990.

CHAPTER 16 THE ART OF JAPAN

Akiyama, Terukazu. *Japanese Painting.* Geneva: Skira; New York: Rizzoli, 1977.

Cahill, James F. *Scholar Painters of Japan: The Nanga School.* New York: Ayer, 1979.

Drexler, Arthur. *The Architecture of Japan.* New York: Arno Press, 1966.

Eliseef, Danielle, and Vadime Eliseef. *The Art of Japan.* New York: Abrams, 1985.

Fontein, Jan, and M. C. Hickman, eds. *Zen Painting and Calligraphy.* Greenwich, CT: New York Graphic Society, 1970.

Kidder, J. Edward. *Art of Japan.* Milan: Mondadori Editore, 1985.

———. *Early Japanese Art.* London: Thames & Hudson, 1969.

———. *Japanese Temples: Sculpture, Painting, and Architecture.* Tokyo: Bijutsu Shuppansha, 1964.

Lee, Sherman E. *A History of Far Eastern Art.* New York: Abrams, 1982.

———. *Japanese Decorative Style.* New York: Harper & Row, 1972.

Neuer, Roni, and Herbert Ubertson. *Ukiyo-E; 250 Years of Japanese Art.* New York: Gallery Books, 1979.

Paine, Robert Treat, and Alexander Soper. *The Art and Architecture of Japan.* 3rd rev. ed. New Haven: Yale University Press, 1981.

Ragghiant, C. L. (Alberto Guiganino, ed.) *National Museum Tokyo.* New York: Newsweek Great Museums of the World, 1968.

Rosenfield, John M. *Japanese Art of the Heian Period, 749–1185.* New York: Asia Society, 1967.

Rosenfield, John M., and Shujiro Shimada. *Traditions of Japanese Art.* Cambridge: Fogg Art Museum, Harvard University, 1970.

Saunders, E. D. *Mudra: A Study of Symbolic Gestures in Japanese Buddhist Art.* Princeton: Princeton University Press, 1960.

Soper, Alexander. *The Evolution of Buddhist Architecture in Japan.* 1942. Reprint. New York: Hacker, 1978.

Stanley-Smith, Joan. *Japanese Art.* New York: Thames & Hudson, 1984.

Stern, Harold P. *Master Prints of Japan: Ukiyo-e Hanga.* New York: Abrams, 1969.

Sugiyama, Jiro. *Classic Buddhist Sculpture: The Tempyo Period.* New York: Kodansha/Harper & Row, 1982.

CHAPTER 17 THE NATIVE ARTS OF THE AMERICAS AND OCEANIA

Pre-Columbian Art of the Americas

Anderson, Richard L. *Art in Small-Scale Societies.* 2nd ed. Englewood Cliffs, NJ: Prentice-Hall, 1989.

Bennett, Wendell C. *Ancient Arts of the Andes.* New York: Museum of Modern Art/Arno Press, 1966.

Bernal, Ignacio. *The Olmec World.* Berkeley: University of California Press, 1977.

Burger, Richard, ed. *Early Ceremonial Architecture of the Andes.* Washington DC: Dumbarton Oaks, 1986.

Coe, Michael D. *The Maya.* 5th rev. ed. London: Thames & Hudson, 1994.

———. *Lords of the Underworld.* Princeton: Princeton University Press, 1978.

———. *Mexico.* 3rd ed. New York: Thames & Hudson, 1994.

Coe, Michael D., and R. A. Diehl. *In the Land of the Olmec.* 2 vols. Austin: University of Texas Press, 1980.

Coe, Michael, Dean Snow, and Elizabeth Benson. *Atlas of Ancient America.* New York: Facts on File, 1986.

Coe, William R. *Tikal: A Handbook of the Ancient Maya Ruins.* 3rd ed. Philadelphia: University Museum, University of Pennsylvania, 1970. (Later edition available.)

Emmerich, André. *Sweat of the Sun and Tears of the Moon: Gold and Silver in Pre-Columbian Art.* New York: Hacker, 1977.

Fash, William L. *Scribes, Warriors, and Kings.* London: Thames & Hudson, 1991.

Franch, José Alcina. *Pre-Columbian Art.* New York: Abrams, 1983.

Gasperini, Graziano, and Luisa Margolies. *Inca Architecture.* Bloomington: Indiana University Press, 1981.

Grieder, Terence. *Origins of Pre-Columbian Art.* Austin: University of Texas Press, 1982.

Heyden, Doris, and Paul Gendrop. *Pre-Columbian Architecture of Mesoamerica.* New York: Abrams, 1975.

Jones, Julie, ed. *Art of Precolumbian Gold. The Jan Mitchell Collection.* London: Weidenfeld & Nicolson, 1985.

Kubler, George. *The Art and Architecture of Ancient America: The Mexican, Maya, and Andean Peoples.* 3rd ed. New Haven: Yale University Press, 1992.

Lapiner, Alan C. *Pre-Columbian Art of South America.* New York: Abrams, 1976.

Lumbreras, Luis. *Peoples and Cultures of Ancient Peru.* Washington, DC: Smithsonian Institution Press, 1974.

Mason, John Alden. *The Ancient Civilizations of Peru.* Rev. ed. New York: Viking Penguin, 1988.

Miller, Mary Ellen. *The Art of Mesoamerica: From Olmec to Aztec.* New York: Thames & Hudson, 1986.

Paddock, John, ed. *Ancient Oaxaca: Discoveries in Mexican Archeology and History.* Stanford: Stanford University Press, 1970.

Pasztory, Esther. *Aztec Art.* New York: Abrams, 1983.

Proskouriakoff, Tatiana Avenirovna. *A Study of Classic Maya Sculpture.* Washington, DC: Carnegie Institute of Washington, 1950.

Robertson, Donald. *Pre-Columbian Architecture.* New York: Braziller, 1963.

Rowe, John H. *Chavín Art: An Inquiry into Its Form and Meaning.* New York: Museum of Primitive Art, 1962.

Sabloff, Jeremy A. *The Cities of Ancient Mexico.* New York: Thames & Hudson, 1989.

Schele, Linda, and David Freidel. *A Forest of Kings.* New York: Morrow, 1991.

Schele, Linda, and Mary Ellen Miller. *The Blood of Kings: Dynasty and Ritual in Maya Art.* New York: Braziller, 1986.

Sharer, Robert J. *The Ancient Maya.* 5th rev. ed. Stanford: Stanford University Press, 1994.

Steward, Julian H. *Handbook of the South American Indians.* 7 vols. New York: Cooper Square Publishers, 1963.

Stierlin, Henri. *Art of the Aztecs and Its Origins.* New York: Rizzoli, 1982.

———. *Art of the Incas and Its Origins.* New York: Rizzoli, 1984.

Stuart, Gene, and George Stuart. *Lost Kingdoms of the Maya,* Washington, DC: National Geographic Society, 1993.

Thompson, J. E. S. *Maya History and Religion.* Norman: University of Oklahoma Press, 1990.

Viole, Herman J. *After Columbus: The Smithsonian Chronicle of North American Indians.* Washington, DC: Orion Books, 1990.

Wauchope, Robert, ed. *Handbook of Middle American Indians.* 16 vols. Austin: University of Texas Press, 1964–1976.

Weaver, Muriel Porter. *The Aztecs, Maya, and their Predecessors: The Archaeology of Mesoamerica.* 2nd ed. New York: Academic Press, 1981.

North America

Boas, Franz. *Primitive Art.* 1927. Reprint. Magnolia, MA: Peter Smith, 1962.

Broder, Patricia Janis. *American Indian Painting and Sculpture.* New York: Abbeville Press, 1981.

Brose, David. *Ancient Art of the American Woodland Indians.* New York: Abrams, 1985.

Collins, Henry, et al. *The Far North: Two Thousand Years of American Eskimo and Indian Art*. Bloomington: Indiana University Press in association with the National Gallery of Art, Washington, DC, 1977.

Conn, Richard. *Circles of the World: Traditional Art of the Plains Indians*. Denver: Denver Art Museum, 1982.

Corbin, George A. *Native Arts of North America, Africa, and the South Pacific: An Introduction*. New York: Harper & Row, 1988.

Curtis, Edward S. *The North American Indian*. 30 vols. Cambridge: Cambridge University Press, 1907–1930. (Later reprint available.)

Ewers, John C. *Plains Indian Painting*. Stanford: Stanford University Press, 1939. (Later reprint available.)

Feder, Norman. *Two Hundred Years of North American Art*. New York: Praeger, 1972.

Feest, Christian F. *Native Arts of North America*. London: Thames & Hudson, 1992.

Grant, Campbell. *Rock Art of the American Indian*. 1967. Reprint. New York: Vistabooks, 1981.

Gunther, Erna. *Art in the Life of the Northwest Coast Indians*. Portland, OR: Portland Art Museum, 1966.

Holm, William. *Northwest Coast Indian Art*. Seattle: University of Washington Press, 1965.

Jonaitis, Aldona. *From the Land of the Totem Poles*. Seattle: University of Washington Press, 1988.

Kopper, Philip. *The Smithsonian Book of North American Indians*. Washington, DC: Smithsonian Books, 1986.

Murdock, George P., and Timothy O'Leary. *Ethnographic Bibliography of North America*. 4th ed. New Haven: Human Relations Area Files Press, 1972.

Ray, Dorothy J. *Artists of the Tundra and the Sea*. Seattle: University of Washington Press, 1980.

Ritchie, Carson I. A. *The Eskimo and His Art*. New York: St. Martin's Press, 1976.

Snow, Dean. *The Archaeology of North America/American Indians*. New York: Chelsea House, 1992.

Wardwell, Allen. *Ancient Eskimo Ivories of the Bering Strait*. New York: Rizzoli, 1986.

Whiteford, Andrew H. *North American Indian Arts*. New York: Golden Press, 1973.

Oceania

Barrow, Terence. *An Illustrated Guide to Maori Art*. Honolulu: University of Hawaii Press, 1984.

Barrow, Tui T. *Art and Life in Polynesia*. Rutland, VT: Charles E. Tuttle, 1973.

———. *Maori Wood Sculpture of New Zealand*. Rutland, VT: Charles E. Tuttle, 1970.

Bernot, Ronald M. *Australian Aboriginal Art*. New York: Macmillan, 1964.

Buck, Peter H. *Arts and Crafts of Hawaii*. Honolulu: Bishop Museum Press, 1964.

Dodd, Edward H. *Polynesian Art*. New York: Dodd, Mead, 1967.

Firth, Raymond. *Art and Life in New Guinea*. 1936. Reprint. New York: AMS Press, 1977.

Guiart, Jean. *Arts of the South Pacific*. New York: Golden Press, 1963.

Linton, Ralph, and Paul Wingert. *Arts of the South Seas*. 1946. Reprint. New York: Arno Press, 1972.

Newton, Douglas. *Art Styles of the Papuan Gulf*. New York: Museum of Primitive Art, 1961.

Rockefeller, Michael C. *The Asmat of New Guinea: The Journal of Michael Clark Rockefeller*. Greenwich, CT: New York Graphic Society, 1967.

Schmitz, Carl A. *Oceanic Art: Myth, Man and Image in the South Seas*. New York: Abrams, 1971.

Stubbs, Dacre. *Prehistoric Art of Australia*. New York: Scribner, 1975.

Taylor, Clyde R. H. *A Pacific Bibliography: Printed Matter Relating to the Native People of Polynesia, Melanesia, and Micronesia*. 2nd ed. Oxford: Clarendon Press, 1965.

CHAPTER 18 THE ARTS OF AFRICA

Ben-Amos, Paula. *The Art of Benin*. London: Thames & Hudson, 1980.

Bourgeois, Jean-Louis, and Carollee Pelos. *Spectacular Vernacular; The Adobe Tradition*. Chapter 11: "Stealing and Restoring Glory: Histories of the Great Mosques of Djenné." New York: Aperture, 1989.

Cole, H. M. *Icons: Ideals and Power in the Art of Africa*. Washington, DC: Smithsonian Institution Press for the National Museum of African Art, 1989.

Cole, H. M., and C. C. Aniakor. *Igbo Art: Community and Cosmos*. Los Angeles, Fowler Museum of Cultural History, 1984.

Cole, H. M., and Doran H. Ross. *The Arts of Ghana*. Los Angeles: Museum of Cultural History, UCLA, 1977.

Cornet, Joseph. *Art Royal Kuba*. Milan: Edizioni Sipiel, 1982.

Drewal, H. J., and J. Pemberton. *Yoruba: Nine Centuries of African Art and Thought*. New York: Center for African Art in association with Harry N. Abrams, 1989.

Ezra, Kate. *The Art of the Dogon: Selections from the Lester Wunderman Collection*. New York: Metropolitan Museum of Art/Harry N. Abrams, 1988.

———. *A Human Ideal in African Art: Bamana Figurative Sculpture*. New York: Metropolitan Museum of Art, 1986.

———. *Royal Art of Benin: The Perls Collection in the Metropolitan Museum of Art*. New York: Metropolitan Museum of Art, 1992.

Fraser, Douglas F., and H. M. Cole. eds. *African Art and Leadership*. Madison: University of Wisconsin Press, 1972.

Glaze, A. J. *Art and Death in a Senufo Village*. Bloomington: Indiana University Press, 1981.

Kasfir, Sidney L. *West African Masks and Cultural Systems*. Tervuren: Musee Royal de l'Afrique Centrale, 1988.

Kennedy, Jean. *New Currents, Ancient Rivers: Contemporary African Artists in a Generation of Change*. Washington, DC: Smithsonian Institution Press, 1992.

McGaffey, Wyatt, and Michael Harris. *Astonishment and Power (Kongo Art)*. Washington, DC: Smithsonian Institution Press, 1993.

McNaughton, Patrick R. *The Mande Blacksmiths: Knowledge, Power, and Art in West Africa*. Bloomington: Indiana University Press, 1988.

Nooter, Mary H. *Secrecy: African Art that Conceals and Reveals*. New York: Museum for African Art, 1993.

Roy, Christopher D. *Art and Life in Africa: Selections from the Stanley Collection*. Iowa City: University of Iowa Museum of Art, 1992.

Rubin, Arnold. *African Accumulative Sculpture*. New York: Pace Gallery, 1965.

Shaw, Thurstan. *Nigeria: Its Archaeology and Early History*. London: Thames & Hudson, 1978.

Sieber, Roy, and Roslyn A. Walker. *African Art in the Cycle of Life*. Washington, DC: Smithsonian Institution Press, 1987.

Vogel, Susan M. *For Spirits and Kings: African Art from the Tishman Collection*. New York: Metropolitan Museum of Art, 1981.

Vogel, Susan M. ed. *Art/Artifact: African Art in Anthropology Collections*. New York: TeNeues, 1988.

Vogel, Susan M. et al. *Africa Explores: Twentieth-Century African Art*. New York: TeNeues, 1990.

Willet, Frank F. *Ife in the History of West African Sculpture*. London: Thames & Hudson, 1969.

CHAPTER 19 LATE GOTHIC ART IN ITALY

Andrés, Glenn, et al. *The Art of Florence*. 2 vols. New York: Abbeville Press, 1988.

Antal, Frederick. *Florentine Painting and Its Social Background*. London: Keegan Paul, 1948.

Cole, Bruce. *Sienese Painting: From Its Origins to the Fifteenth Century*. New York: HarperCollins, 1987.

Cole, Bruce. *Italian Art, 1250–1550: The Relation of Renaissance Art to Life and Society*. New York: Harper & Row, 1987.

Fremantle, Richard. *Florentine Gothic Painters from Giotto to Masaccio: A Guide to Painting in and near Florence*. London: Secker & Warburg, 1975.

Hills, Paul. *The Light of Early Italian Painting*. New Haven: Yale University Press, 1987.

Meiss, Millard. *Painting in Florence and Siena after the Black Death*. Princeton: Princeton University Press, 1976.

Panofsky, Erwin. *Renaissance and Renascences in Western Art*. New York: HarperCollins, 1972.

Pope-Hennessy, John. *Introduction to Italian Sculpture*. 3rd ed. 3 vols. New York: Phaidon, 1986.

———. *Italian Gothic Sculpture*. 3rd ed. Oxford: Phaidon, 1986.

Schevill, Ferdinand. *The Medici*. New York: Harper & Row, 1960.

Smart, Alastair. *The Dawn of Italian Painting*. Ithaca, NY: Cornell University Press, 1978.

Stubblebine, James, ed. *Giotto: The Arena Chapel Frescoes*. New York: Norton, 1969.

———. *Assisi and the Rise of Vernacular Art*. New York: Harper & Row, 1985.

Van Marle, Raimond. *The Development of the Italian Schools of Painting*. 19 vols. 1923–1938. Reprint. New York: Hacker, 1970.

Venturi, Lionello, and Rosabianca Skira-Venturi. *Italian Painting: The Creators of the Renaissance*. 3 vols. Geneva: Skira, 1950–1952.

White, John. *Art and Architecture in Italy 1250–1400*. 3rd ed. New Haven: Yale University Press, 1993.

CHAPTER 20 FIFTEENTH-CENTURY ART IN NORTHERN EUROPE AND SPAIN

Chatelet, Albert. *Early Dutch Painting*. New York: W. S. Konecky, 1988.

Cuttler, Charles P. *Northern Painting from Pucelle to Bruegel*. New York: Holt, Rinehart & Winston, 1968.

Dhanens, E. *Hubert and Jan van Eyck*. New York: Tabaro Press (W. S. Konecky, Assoc.), 1980.

Friedlander, Max J. *Early Netherlandish Painting*. 14 vols. New York: Praeger/Phaidon, 1967–1976.

———. *From Van Eyck to Bruegel*. 3rd ed. Ithaca, NY: Cornell University Press, 1981.

Fuchs, Rudolph H. *Dutch Painting*. London: Thames & Hudson, 1978.

Hind, Arthur M. *History of Engraving and Etching from the Fifteenth Century to the Year 1914*. 3rd rev. ed. New York: Dover, 1963.

———. *An Introduction to a History of Woodcut*. New York: Dover, 1963.

Huizinga, Johan. *The Waning of the Middle Ages*. 1924. Reprint. New York: St. Martin's Press, 1988.

Meiss, Millard. *French Painting in the Time of Jean de Berry*. New York: Braziller, 1974.

———. *The "Très Riches Heures" of Jean, Duke of Berry*, Preface. New York: Braziller, 1969.

Müller, Theodor. *Sculpture in the Netherlands, Germany, France and Spain, 1400–1500*. New Haven: Yale University Press, 1986.

Panofsky, Erwin. *Early Netherlandish Painting*. Cambridge: Harvard University Press, 1953.

Prevenier, Walter, and Wim Blockmans. *The Burgundian Netherlands*. Cambridge: Cambridge University Press, 1986.

Seidel. L. *Jan van Eyck's Arnolfini Portrait*. New York/Cambridge: Cambridge University Press, 1993.

Snyder, James. *Northern Renaissance Art*. New York: Abrams, 1985.

Van Puyvelde, L. *Flemish Painting from the van Eycks to Metsys*. New York: McGraw-Hill, 1970.

Wolfthal, Diane. *The Beginnings of Netherlandish Canvas Painting, 1400–1530*. New York: Cambridge University Press, 1989.

CHAPTER 21 FIFTEENTH-CENTURY ITALIAN ART: THE EARLY RENAISSANCE

Baxandall, Michael. *Painting and Experience in Fifteenth Century Italy. A Primer in the Social History of Pictorial Style*. 2nd ed. New York: Oxford University Press, 1988.

Bennet, Bonnie A., and David G. Wilkins. *Donatello*. Oxford: Phaidon, 1984.

Berenson, Bernard. *The Italian Painters of the Renaissance*. Ithaca, NY: Phaidon/Cornell University Press, 1980.

———. *Italian Pictures of the Renaissance*. Ithaca, NY: Phaidon/Cornell University Press, 1980.

Blunt, Anthony. *Artistic Theory in Italy, 1450–1600*. Oxford: Clarendon Press, 1966.

Bober, Phyllis Pray, and Ruth Rubinstein. *Renaissance Artists and Antique Sculpture: A Handbook of Sources*. Oxford: Oxford University Press, 1986.

Borsook, Eve. *The Mural Painters of Tuscany*. New York: Oxford University Press, 1986.

Burckhardt, Jacob. *The Architecture of the Italian Renaissance*. Chicago: University of Chicago Press, 1987.

———. *The Civilization of the Renaissance in Italy*. 4th ed. 1867. Reprint. London: Phaidon, 1960.

Chastel, André. *The Age of Humanism*. New York: McGraw-Hill, 1964.

———. *A Chronicle of Italian Renaissance Painting*. Ithaca, NY: Cornell University Press, 1984.

———. *Studios and Styles of the Italian Renaissance*. New York: Braziller, 1971.

Cole, Bruce. *Masaccio and the Art of Early Renaissance Florence*. Bloomington: Indiana University Press, 1980.

———. *Piero della Francesca: Tradition and Innovation in Renaissance Art*. New York: Icon Editions, 1991.

Decker, Heinrich. *The Renaissance in Italy: Architecture, Sculpture, Frescoes*. New York: Viking, 1969.

De Wald, Ernest T. *Italian Painting, 1200–1600*. New York: Holt, Rinehart & Winston, 1961.

Earls, Irene. *Renaissance Art: A Topical Dictionary*. New York: Greenwood Press, 1987.

Edgerton, Samuel Y., Jr. *The Heritage of Giotto's Geometry: Art and Science on the Eve of the Scientific*

Revolution. Ithaca, NY: Cornell University Press, 1991.

————. *The Renaissance Rediscovery of Linear Perspective.* New York: Harper & Row, 1976.

Ferguson, Wallace K., et al. *The Renaissance.* New York: Henry Holt, 1940.

Gadol, Joan. *Leon Battista Alberti: Universal Man of the Early Renaissance.* Chicago: University of Chicago Press, 1969.

Gilbert, Creighton. *History of Renaissance Art throughout Europe.* New York: Abrams, 1973.

————. *Italian Art 1400–1500: Sources and Documents.* Englewood Cliffs, NJ: Prentice-Hall, 1970.

Godfrey, F. M. *Early Venetian Painters, 1415–1495.* London: Tiranti, 1954.

Goldthwaite, Richard A. *The Building of Renaissance Florence: An Economic and Social History.* Baltimore: Johns Hopkins University Press, 1980.

Gombrich, E. H. *Norm and Form: Studies in the Art of the Renaissance.* 4th ed. Oxford: Phaidon, 1985.

Hale, John R. *Italian Renaissance Painting from Masaccio to Titian.* New York: Dutton, 1977.

Hall, Marcia B. *Color and Meaning: Practice and Theory in Renaissance Painting.* Cambridge: Cambridge University Press, 1992.

Hartt, Frederick. *History of Italian Renaissance Art: Painting, Sculpture, Architecture.* 4th ed. rev. by David G. Wilkins. Englewood Cliffs, NJ: Prentice-Hall, 1994.

Helton, Tinsley, ed. *The Renaissance: A Reconsideration of the Theories and Interpretations of the Age.* Madison: University of Wisconsin Press, 1964.

Heydenreich, Ludwig H., and Wolfgang Lotz. *Architecture in Italy 1400–1600.* Harmondsworth, England: Penguin, 1974.

Holt, Elizabeth B. *A Documentary History of Art.* 2nd ed. Vol. 1. Garden City, NY: Doubleday, 1957.

Huyghe, René. *Larousse Encyclopedia of Renaissance and Baroque Art.* See Reference Books.

Janson, Horst W. *The Sculpture of Donatello.* 2 vols. Princeton: Princeton University Press, 1979.

Kempers, Bram. *Painting, Power, and Patronage: The Rise of the Professional Artist in the Italian Renaissance.* London: Penguin, 1992.

Krautheimer, Richard, and Trude Krautheimer-Hess. *Lorenzo Ghiberti.* Princeton: Princeton University Press, 1982.

Lieberman, Ralph. *Renaissance Architecture in Venice.* New York: Abbeville Press, 1982.

Lightbown, Ronald. *Mantegna.* Berkeley: University of California Press, 1986.

————. *Sandro Botticelli: Life and Work.* New York: Abbeville Press, 1989.

Lowry, Bates. *Renaissance Architecture.* New York: Braziller, 1962.

McAndrew, John. *Venetian Architecture of the Early Renaissance.* Cambridge: MIT Press, 1980.

Meiss, Millard. *The Painter's Choice, Problems in the Interpretation of Renaissance Art.* New York: HarperCollins, 1977.

Murray, Peter. *The Architecture of the Italian Renaissance.* Rev. ed. New York: Schocken, 1986.

————. *Renaissance Architecture.* New York: Electa/Rizzoli (paperbound), 1985.

Murray, Peter, and Linda Murray. *The Art of the Renaissance.* London: Thames & Hudson, 1985.

Olson, Roberta J. M. *Italian Renaissance Sculpture.* London: Thames & Hudson, 1992.

Panofsky, Erwin. *Renaissance and Renascences in Western Art.* New York: HarperCollins, 1972.

Pater, Walter. *The Renaissance: Studies in Art and Poetry.* Edited by D. L. Hill. Berkeley: University of California Press, 1980.

Pope-Hennessy, John. *An Introduction to Italian Sculpture.* 3rd ed. 3 vols. New York: Phaidon, 1986.

————. *Sienese Quattrocento Painting.* New York: Oxford University Press, 1947.

Schevill, Ferdinand. *The Medici.* New York: Harper & Row, 1960.

Seymour, Charles. *Sculpture in Italy, 1400–1500.* New Haven: Yale University Press, 1966.

Symonds, John Addington. *The Renaissance in Italy.* 7 vols. 1875–1886. Reprint. New York: Coronet Books, 1972.

Van Marle, Raimond. *The Development of the Italian Schools of Painting.* 19 vols. 1923–1938. Reprint. New York: Hacker, 1970.

Vasari, Giorgio. *The Lives of the Most Eminent Painters, Sculptors, and Architects, 1550–1568.* 3 vols. New York: Abrams, 1979.

Werkmeister, William H., ed.; Wallace Ferguson, et al. *Facets of the Renaissance.* New York: Harper & Row, 1963.

White, John. *The Birth and Rebirth of Pictorial Space.* 3rd ed. Boston: Faber & Faber, 1987.

Wilde, Johannes. *Venetian Art from Bellini to Titian.* Oxford: Clarendon Press, 1981.

Wittkower, Rudolf. *Architectural Principles in the Age of Humanism.* 4th ed. London: Academy, 1988.

CHAPTER 22 SIXTEENTH-CENTURY ITALIAN ART: THE HIGH RENAISSANCE AND MANNERISM

Ackerman, James S. *The Architecture of Michelangelo.* Rev. ed. Chicago: University of Chicago Press, 1986.

————. *Palladio.* New York: Penguin, 1978.

Bialostocki, Jan. *The Art of the Renaissance in Eastern Europe.* Ithaca, NY: Cornell University Press, 1976.

Blunt, Anthony. *Artistic Theory in Italy, 1450–1600.* London: Oxford University Press, 1975.

Briganti, Giuliano. *Italian Mannerism.* London: Thames & Hudson, 1962.

Castiglione, Baldassare. *Book of the Courtier.* 1528. Reprint. New York: Viking Penguin, 1976.

Cellini, Benvenuto. *Autobiography.* Reprint. New York: Random House, 1985.

Clark, Kenneth. *Leonardo da Vinci.* Rev. ed. London: Penguin, 1988.

DeTolnay, Charles, *Michelangelo,* Princeton, Princeton University Press, 1943–60. (5 vols.)

Freedberg, Sydney J. *Painting in Italy, 1500–1600.* New Haven: Yale University Press, 1990.

————. *Painting of the High Renaissance in Rome and Florence.* Rev. ed. New York: Hacker, 1985.

Friedlaender, Walter. *Mannerism and Anti-Mannerism in Italian Painting.* New York: Schocken, 1965.

Goffen, Rona. *Piety and Patronage in Renaissance Venice: Bellini, Titian, and the Franciscans.* New Haven: Yale University Press, 1986.

Hibbard, Howard. *Michelangelo.* 2nd ed. New York: Harper & Row 1985.

Holt, Elizabeth Gilmore, ed. *A Documentary History of Art.* Vol. 2, *Michelangelo and the Mannerists.* Rev. ed. Princeton: Princeton University Press, 1982.

Humfry, Peter. *Painting in Renaissance Venice.* New Haven: Yale University Press, 1995.

Huse, Norbert, and Wolfgang Wolters. *The Art of Renaissance Venice: Architecture, Sculpture, and Painting.* Chicago: University of Chicago Press, 1990.

Jones, Roger, and Nicholas Penney. *Raphael.* New Haven: Yale University Press, 1983.

Levey, Michael. *High Renaissance.* New York: Viking Penguin, 1978.

Murray, Linda. *The High Renaissance and Mannerism.* New York: Oxford University Press, 1977.

Partner, Peter. *Renaissance Rome, 1500–1559: A Portrait of a Society.* Berkeley: University of California Press, 1977.

Pedretti, Carlo. *Raphael: His Life and Work in the Splendors of the Italian Renaissance.* Florence: Giunti, 1989.

Pietrangeli, Carlo, et al. *The Sistine Chapel: The Art, the History, and the Restoration.* New York: Harmony Books, 1986.

Pope-Hennessy, John. *Cellini.* London: MacMillan, 1985.

————. *Italian High Renaissance and Baroque Sculpture.* 3rd ed. 3 vols. Oxford: Phaidon, 1986.

Rosand, David. *Painting in Cinquecento Venice: Titian, Veronese, Tintoretto.* New Haven: Yale University Press, 1982.

Shearman, John K. G. *Mannerism.* Baltimore: Penguin, 1978.

————. *Only Connect . . . Art and the Spectator in the Italian Renaissance.* Princeton: Princeton University Press, 1990.

Summers, David. *Michelangelo and the Language of Art.* Princeton: Princeton University Press, 1981.

Venturi, Lionello. *The Sixteenth Century: From Leonardo to El Greco.* New York: Skira, 1956.

Von Einem, Herbert. *Michelangelo.* London: Methuen, 1976.

Wölfflin, Heinrich. *The Art of the Italian Renaissance.* New York: Schocken, 1963.

————. *Classic Art: An Introduction to the Italian Renaissance.* 4th ed. Oxford: Phaidon, 1980.

Würtenberger, Franzsepp. *Mannerism: The European Style of the Sixteenth Century.* New York: Holt, Rinehart & Winston, 1963.

CHAPTER 23 SIXTEENTH-CENTURY ART IN NORTHERN EUROPE AND SPAIN

Baxendall, M. *The Limewood Sculptors of Renaissance Germany.* New Haven/London: Yale University Press, 1980.

Benesch, Otto. *Art of the Renaissance in Northern Europe.* Rev. ed. London: Phaidon, 1965.

————. *German Painting from Dürer to Holbein.* Geneva: Skira, 1966.

Blunt, Anthony. *Art and Architecture in France 1500–1700.* 4th ed. New Haven: Yale University Press, 1982.

Coulton, G. G. *The Fate of Medieval Art in the Renaissance and Reformation.* New York: Harper Torch Books, 1958.

Evans, Joan. *Monastic Architecture in France from the Renaissance to the Revolution.* New York: Hacker, 1980.

Gibson, W. S. *"Mirror of the Earth": The World Landscape in Sixteenth Century Flemish Painting.* Princeton: Princeton University Press, 1989.

Hitchcock, Henry-Russell. *German Renaissance Architecture.* Princeton: Princeton University Press. 1981.

Kaufmann, Thomas DaCosta. *The School of Prague.* Chicago: University of Chicago Press, 1988.

Kubler, G. *Building the Escorial.* Princeton: Princeton University Press, 1981.

Panofsky, Erwin. *The Life and Art of Albrecht Dürer.* 4th ed. Princeton: Princeton University Press, 1971.

Smith, Jeffrey C. *German Sculpture of the Later Renaissance c. 1520–1580.* Princeton: Princeton University Press, 1993.

Sullivan, M. A. *Bruegel's Peasants: Art and Audience in the Northern Renaissance.* New York/Cambridge: Cambridge University Press, 1994.

Waterhouse, Ellis. *The Dictionary of 16th and 17th Century British Painters.* Woodbridge, England. Antique Collectors' Club, 1988.

CHAPTER 24 BAROQUE ART

Alpers, Svetlana. *The Art of Describing: Dutch Art in the Seventeenth Century.* Chicago: University of Chicago Press, 1984.

Bazin, Germain. *Baroque and Rococo Art.* New York: Praeger, 1974.

Blunt, Anthony. *Art and Architecture in France: 1500 to 1700.* 4th ed. New Haven: Yale University Press, 1988.

Blunt, Anthony, ed. *Baroque and Rococo: Architecture and Decoration.* Cambridge: Harper & Row, 1982.

Brown, Jonathan. The Golden Age of Painting in Spain. New Haven: Yale University Press, 1991.

————. *Velázquez: Painter and Courtier.* New Haven: Yale University Press, 1986.

Engass, Robert, and Jonathan Brown. *Italy and Spain, 1600–1750: Sources and Documents.* Englewood Cliffs, NJ: Prentice Hall, 1970.

Fokker, Timon H. *Roman Baroque Art: The History of a Style.* London: Oxford University Press, 1938.

Freedberg, Sydney J. *Circa 1600: A Revolution of Style in Italian Painting.* Cambridge: Harvard University Press, 1983.

Gerson, Horst, and E. H. ter Kuile. *Art and Architecture in Belgium 1600–1800.* New York: Viking Penguin, 1978.

Haak, Bob. *The Golden Age: Dutch Painters of the Seventeenth Century.* London: Thames & Hudson, 1984.

Haskell, Francis. *Patrons and Painters: A Study in the Relations between Italian Art and Society in the Age of the Baroque.* New Haven: Yale University Press, 1980.

Held, Julius. *Rembrandt Studies.* Rev. ed. Princeton: Princeton University Press, 1991.

Held, Julius, and Donald Posner. *17th and 18th Century Art.* New York: Abrams, 1974.

Hempel, Eberhard. *Baroque Art and Architecture in Central Europe.* New York: Viking Penguin, 1977.

Hibbard, Howard. *Bernini.* Harmondsworth, England: Penguin, 1976.

————. *Caravaggio.* New York: Thames & Hudson, 1983.

————. *Carlo Maderno and Roman Architecture, 1580–1630.* London: Zwemmer, 1971.

Hinks, Roger P. *Michelangelo Merisi da Caravaggio.* London: Faber & Faber, 1953.

Howard, Deborah. *The Architectural History of Venice.* London: B. T. Batsford, 1981.

Huyghe, René, ed. *Larousse Encyclopedia of Renaissance and Baroque Art.* See Reference Books.

Kahr, Madlyn Millner. *Dutch Painting in the Seventeenth Century.* New York: Harper & Row, 1978.

————. *Velázquez: The Art of Painting.* New York: Harper & Row, 1976.

Kitson, Michael. *The Age of Baroque.* London: Hamlyn, 1976.

Krautheimer, Richard. *The Rome of Alexander VII, 1655–1677.* Princeton: Princeton University Press, 1985.

Lagerlöf, Margaretha R. *Ideal Landscape: Annibale Carracci, Nicolas Poussin and Claude Lorrain.* New Haven: Yale University Press, 1990.

Lees-Milne, James. *Baroque in Italy.* New York: Macmillan, 1960.

Martin, John R. *Baroque.* New York: Harper & Row, 1977.

Millon, Henry A. *Baroque and Rococo Architecture.* New York: Braziller, 1965.

Nicolson, Benedict. *The International Caravaggesque Movement.* Oxford: Phaidon, 1979.

Norberg-Schulz, Christian. *Baroque Architecture.* New York: Rizzoli, 1986.

———. *Late Baroque and Rococo Architecture.* New York: Electa/Rizzoli, 1985.

Pope-Hennessy, Sir John. *The Study and Criticism of Italian Sculpture.* New York: Metropolitan Museum, 1981.

Portoghesi, Paolo. *The Rome of Borromini.* London: Phaidon, 1972.

Powell, Nicolas. *From Baroque to Rococo: An Introduction to Austrian and German Architecture from 1580 to 1790.* London: Faber & Faber, 1959.

Rosenberg, Jakob. *Rembrandt.* 3rd ed. London: Phaidon, 1968.

Rosenberg, Jakob, Seymour Slive, and E. H. ter Kuile. *Dutch Art and Architecture, 1600–1800.* New Haven: Yale University Press, 1979.

Spear, Richard E. *Caravaggio and His Followers.* New York: Harper & Row, 1975.

Stechow, Wolfgang. *Dutch Landscape Painting of the 17th Century.* Oxford: Phaidon, 1981.

Summerson, Sir John. *Architecture in Britain: 1530–1830.* 7th rev. and enl. ed. New Haven: Yale University Press, 1983.

Tapie, Victor-Lucien. *The Age of Grandeur: Baroque Art and Architecture.* New York: Praeger, 1966.

Varriano, John. *Italian Baroque and Rococo Architecture.* New York: Oxford University Press, 1986.

Waterhouse, Ellis Kirkham. *Baroque Painting in Rome.* London: Phaidon, 1976.

———. *Italian Baroque Painting.* 2nd ed. London: Phaidon, 1969.

———. *Painting in Britain, 1530–1790.* 4th ed. New Haven: Yale University Press, 1979.

White, Christopher. *Peter Paul Rubens: Man and Artist.* New Haven: Yale University Press, 1987.

Wittkower, Rudolf. *Art and Architecture in Italy 1600–1750.* New Haven: Yale University Press, 1982.

———. *Gian Lorenzo Bernini: The Sculptor of the Roman Baroque.* 3rd rev. ed. Oxford: Phaidon, 1981.

Wölfflin, Heinrich. *Principles of Art History: The Problem of the Development of Style in Later Art.* 7th ed. New York: Dover, 1950.

———. *Renaissance and Baroque.* London: Collins, 1984.

Wright, Christopher. *The French Painters of the 17th Century.* New York: New York Graphic Society, 1986.

CHAPTER 25 THE EIGHTEENTH CENTURY: LATE BAROQUE AND ROCOCO, AND THE RISE OF ROMANTICISM

Arnason, H. H. *The Sculptures of Houdon.* New York: Oxford University Press, 1975.

Bacou, Roseline. *Piranesi: Etchings and Drawings.* Boston: New York Graphic Society, 1975.

Boime, A. *Art in the Age of Revolution, 1750–1800.* Chicago/London: University of Chicago Press, 1987.

Blunt, Anthony. *Art and Architecture in France, 1500–1700.* 2nd ed. Harmondsworth, England: Penguin, 1970.

Braham, Allan. *The Architecture of the French Enlightenment.* Berkeley: University of California Press, 1980.

Burchard, John, and Albert Bush-Brown. *The Architecture of America: A Social and Cultural History.* Boston: Little, Brown/The American Institute of Architects, 1965.

Chatelet, Albert, and Jacques Thuillier. *French Painting from Le Nain to Fragonard.* Geneva: Skira, 1964.

Cobban, Alfred, ed. *The Eighteenth Century: Europe in the Age of the Enlightenment.* New York: McGraw-Hill, 1969.

Conisbee, Philip. *Painting in Eighteenth-Century France.* Ithaca, NY: Phaidon/Cornell University Press, 1981.

Crow, Thomas E. *Painters and Public Life in Eighteenth-Century Paris.* New Haven: Yale University Press, 1985.

Cuzin, J.-P. *Fragonard: Life and Work.* New York: Abrams, 1988.

Davis, Terence. *The Gothick Taste.* Cranbury, NJ: Fairleigh Dickinson University Press, 1975.

Gaunt, W. *The Great Century of British Painting: Hogarth to Turner.* New York: Phaidon, 1971.

Hayes, John T. *Gainsborough: Paintings and Drawings.* London: Phaidon, 1975.

Herrmann, Luke. *British Landscape Painting of the Eighteenth Century.* New York: Oxford University Press, 1974.

Hitchcock, Henry Russell. *Rococo Architecture in Southern Germany.* London: Phaidon, 1968.

Holt, Elizabeth Gilmore, ed. *From the Classicists to the Impressionists: A Documentary History of Art and Architecture in the Nineteenth Century.* Garden City, NY: Anchor Books/Doubleday, 1966.

Irwin, David. *English Neoclassical Art.* London: Faber & Faber, 1966.

Kalnein, Wend Graf, and Michael Levey. *Art and Architecture of the Eighteenth Century in France.* New York: Viking/Pelican, 1973.

Kimball, Sidney F. *The Creation of the Rococo.* New York: W. W. Norton, 1964.

Levey, Michael. *Painting in Eighteenth-Century Venice.* Ithaca, NY: Phaidon/Cornell University Press, 1980.

———. *Rococo to Revolution: Major Trends in Eighteenth-Century Painting.* London: Thames & Hudson, 1966.

Millon, Henry A. *Baroque and Rococo Architecture.* New York: Braziller, 1961, 1965.

Norberg-Schulz, Christian. *Late Baroque and Rococo Architecture.* New York: Harry N. Abrams, 1974.

Pierson, William. *American Buildings and Their Architects: Vol. 1, The Colonial and Neo-Classical Style.* Garden City, NY: Doubleday, 1970.

Pignatti, Terisio. *The Age of Rococo.* New York: Hamlyn, 1969.

Powell, Nicolas. *From Baroque to Rococo: An Introduction to Austrian and German Architecture from 1580 to 1790.* London: Faber & Faber, 1959.

Raine, Kathleen. *William Blake.* New York: Oxford University Press, 1970.

Rosenblum, Robert. *Transformations in Late Eighteenth Century Art.* Princeton, NJ: Princeton University Press, 1970.

Roston, M. *Changing Perspectives in Literature and the Visual Arts, 1650–1820.* Princeton: Princeton University Press, 1990.

Rykwert, Joseph. *The First Moderns: Architects of the Eighteenth Century.* Cambridge, MA: MIT Press, 1983.

Schnapper, A. *David.* New York: Alpine Fine Arts, 1982.

Schwarz, Michael. *The Age of Rococo.* New York: Praeger, 1969.

Strachey, Lionel (trans.). *Memoirs of Madame Vigée Lebrun.* New York: Braziller, 1989.

Waterhouse, Ellis K. *Painting in Britain, 1530–1790.* 4th ed. New York: Penguin, 1978.

Whinney, Margaret Dickens. *English Art, 1625–1714.* Oxford, England: Clarendon Press, 1957.

———. *Sculpture in Britain, 1530–1830.* New Haven: Yale University Press, 1964.

Whinney, Margaret D., and Oliver Millar. *English Sculpture, 1720–1830.* London: H. M. Stationery Office, 1971.

Wittkower, Rudolf. *Art and Architecture in Italy, 1600–1750.* New York: Penguin, 1968.

Yolton, John W. *The Blackwell Companion to the Enlightenment.* Cambridge, MA: Oxford/Blackwell, 1992.

CHAPTER 26 THE NINETEENTH CENTURY: PLURALISM OF STYLE

Aslin, Elizabeth. *The Aesthetic Movement: Prelude to Art Nouveau.* New York: Frederick A. Praeger, 1977.

Baudelaire, Charles. *The Mirror of Art, Critical Studies.* Translated by Jonathan Mayne. Garden City, NY: Doubleday & Co., 1956.

Bisanz, R. M. *German Romanticism and Philipp Otto Runge.* De Kalb: Northern Illinois University Press, 1970.

Bischof, Ulrich. *Edvard Munch.* Köln (Cologne), Germany: Benedikt Taschen, 1988.

Boime, Albert. *The Academy and French Painting in the 19th Century.* London: Phaidon, 1971.

Bonnat, Jean. *Degas: His Life and Work.* New York: Tudor Publishing Company, 1965.

Borsch-Supan, H. *Caspar David Friedrich.* New York: Braziller, 1974.

Broun, Elizabeth. *Albert Pinkham Ryder.* Washington, DC: National Museum of American Art/Smithsonian Institutions, 1989.

Clark, Kenneth. *The Gothic Revival: An Essay in the History of Taste.* New York: Humanities Press, 1970.

Clay, Jean. *Romanticism.* New York: Phaidon, 1981.

Delacroix, Eugène. *The Journal of Eugène Delacroix.* Translated by Walter Pach. New York: Grove Press, 1937, 1948.

Dixon, Roger, and Stefen Muthesius. *Victorian Architecture.* London: Thames & Hudson, 1978.

Eitner, Lorenz. *Neo-Classicism and Romanticism 1750–1850: Sources and Documents on the History of Art.* 2 vols. Englewood Cliffs, NJ: Prentice-Hall, 1970.

Elsen, Albert. *Rodin.* New York: Museum of Modern Art, 1963.

Fliedl, Gottfried. *Gustav Klimt.* Köln (Cologne), Germany: Benedikt Taschen, 1989.

Friedlaender, Walter. *From David to Delacroix.* New York: Schocken Books, 1968.

Fusco, Peter, and H. W. Janson. *The Romantics to Rodin: French 19th-Century Sculpture from American Collections.* Los Angeles: Los Angeles County Art Museum/New York: Braziller, 1980.

Gerdts, William H. *American Impressionism.* New York: Abbeville Press, 1984.

Hamilton, George Heard. *Manet and His Critics.* New Haven, CT: Yale University Press, 1954.

Hanson, Anne Coffin. *Manet and the Modern Tradition.* New Haven, CT: Yale University Press, 1977.

Herbert, Robert L. *Impressionism: Art, Leisure, and Parisian Society.* New Haven: Yale University Press, 1988.

Hilton, Timothy. *The Pre-Raphaelites.* New York: Oxford University Press, 1970.

Holt, Elizabeth B. *From the Classicists to the Impressionists: Art and Architecture in the Nineteenth Century.* Garden City, NY: Doubleday/Anchor, 1966.

Honour, Hugh. *Neo-Classicism.* New York: Harper & Row, 1979.

———. *Romanticism.* New York: Harper & Row, 1979.

Janson, Horst W. *19th-Century Sculpture.* New York: Harry N. Abrams, 1985.

Jensen, Robert. *Marketing Modernism in Fin-de-Siècle Europe.* Princeton: Princeton University Press, 1994.

Leymarie, Jean. *French Painting in the Nineteenth Century.* Geneva: Skira, 1962.

Macaulay, James. *The Gothic Revival, 1745–1845.* Glasgow, Scotland: Blackie, 1975.

Middleton, Robin, ed. *The Beaux-Arts and Nineteenth-Century French Architecture.* Cambridge, MA: MIT Press, 1982.

Nochlin, Linda. *Gustave Courbet: A Study of Style and Society.* New York: Garland, 1976.

———. *Impressionism and Post-Impressionism, 1874–1904: Sources and Documents.* Englewood Cliffs, NJ: Prentice-Hall, 1966.

———. *Realism and Tradition in Art: Sources and Documents.* Englewood Cliffs, NJ: Prentice-Hall, 1966.

Novak, Barbara. *American Painting of the Nineteenth Century.* New York: Frederick A. Praeger, 1969.

Novotny, Fritz. *Painting and Sculpture in Europe: 1780–1880.* 2nd ed. New Haven: Yale University Press, 1978.

Pelles, Geraldine. *Art, Artists and Society: Origins of a Modern Dilemma: Painting in England and France, 1750–1850.* Englewood Cliffs, NJ: Prentice-Hall, 1963.

Pevsner, Nikolaus. *Pioneers of Modern Design.* Harmondsworth, England: Penguin, 1964.

Rewald, John. *The History of Impressionism.* New York: Museum of Modern Art, 1973.

———. *Post-Impressionism: From Van Gogh to Gauguin.* New York: Museum of Modern Art, 1956.

Rewald, John, Dore Ashton, and Harold Joachim. *Odilon Redon, Gustave Moreau, Rodolphe Bresdin.* New York: Museum of Modern Art, 1962.

Roberts, Keith. *The Impressionists and Post-Impressionists.* New York: E. P. Dutton, 1977.

Rosen, Charles, and Henri Zerner. *Romanticism and Realism: The Mythology of Nineteenth-Century Art.* London: Faber and Faber, 1984.

Rosenblum, Robert, and Horst W. Janson. *19th Century Art.* New York: Harry N. Abrams, 1984.

Russell, John. *Seurat.* New York: Frederick A. Praeger, 1965.

Sambrook, James, ed. *Pre-Raphaelitism: A Collection of Critical Essays.* Chicago: University of Chicago Press, 1974.

Schrade, Hubert. *German Romantic Painting.* New York: Harry N. Abrams, 1977.

Schapiro, Meyer. *Modern Art: 19th & 20th Centuries.* New York: Braziller, 1978.

Sloane, Joseph C. *French Painting Between the Past and the Present: Artists, Critics, and Traditions from 1848 to 1870.* Princeton, NJ: Princeton University Press, 1973.

Sullivan, Louis. *The Autobiography of an Idea.* New York: Dover, 1956.

Valsecchi, Marco. *Landscape Painting of the 19th Century.* Greenwich, CT: New York Graphic Society, 1971.

Van Gogh: A Self Portrait: Letters Revealing His Life as a Painter. Selected by W. H. Auden. New York: E. P. Dutton, 1963.

Vaughan, William. *German Romantic Painting.* New Haven, CT: Yale University Press, 1980.

Weisberg, Gabriel P. *The Realist Tradition: French Painting and Drawing, 1830–1900.* Cleveland: Cleveland Museum/Indiana University Press, 1980.

Wood, Christopher. *The Pre-Raphaelites.* New York: Viking Press, 1981.

CHAPTER 27 THE EARLY TWENTIETH CENTURY: THE ESTABLISHMENT OF MODERNIST ART

Ades, Dawn. *Dali and Surrealism.* New York: Harper & Row, 1982.

Anderson, Troels. *Malevich.* Amsterdam, Holland: Stedelijk Museum, 1970.

Antliff, Mark. *Cultural Politics and the Parisian Avant-Garde.* Princeton: Princeton University Press, 1993.

Apollinaire, Guillaume. *The Cubist Painters: Aesthetic Meditations, 1913.* New York: Wittenborn, 1970.

Barr, Alfred H., Jr. *Picasso: Fifty Years of His Art.* New York: Museum of Modern Art, 1946.

Bayer, Herbert, Walter Gropius, and Ise Gropius, eds. *Bauhaus 1919–1928.* Boston: Charles T. Branford, 1959.

Benevolo, Leonardo. *History of Modern Architecture.* 2 vols. Cambridge, MA. MIT Press, 1977.

Blake, Peter. *Frank Lloyd Wright.* Harmondsworth, Middlesex: Penguin Books, 1960.

———. *The Master Builder.* New York: W. W. Norton, 1976.

Boesinger, Willy, ed. *Le Corbusier.* New York: Frederick A. Praeger, 1972.

Breton, André. *Surrealism and Painting.* New York: Harper & Row, 1972.

Campbell, Mary Schmidt, David C. Driskell, David Lewis Levering, and Deborah Willis Ryan. *Harlem Renaissance: Art of Black America.* New York: The Studio Museum, Harlem/Harry N. Abrams, 1987.

Carls, Carl Dietrich. *Ernst Barlach.* London: Pall Mall Press, 1969.

Carrá, Massimo, Ewald Rathke, Caroline Tisdall, and Patrick Waldberg. *Metaphysical Art.* New York: Frederick A. Praeger, 1971.

Carter, Peter. *Mies van der Rohe at Work.* London: Pall Mall Press, 1974.

Cassou, Jean. *Chagall.* New York: Frederick A. Praeger, 1965.

Dupin, Jacques. *Alberto Giacometti.* Paris: Maeght Éditeur, 1963.

Duthuit, Georges. *The Fauvist Painters.* New York: Wittenborn, Schultz, 1950.

Edwards, Ehrlig. *Painted Walls of Mexico.* Austin: University of Texas Press, 1966.

Elderfield, John. *Kurt Schwitters.* New York: Museum of Modern Art/Thames & Hudson, 1985.

———. *The "Wild Beasts": Fauvism and Its Affinities.* New York: The Museum of Modern Art/Oxford University Press, 1976.

Elsen, Albert. *Origins of Modern Sculpture.* New York: Braziller, 1974.

Frampton, Kenneth. *A Critical History of Modern Architecture.* London: Thames & Hudson, 1985.

Friedman, Mildred, ed. *De Stijl: 1917–1931, Visions of Utopia.* Minneapolis: Walker Art Center/New York: Abbeville Press, 1982.

Fry, Edward, ed. *Cubism.* London: Thames & Hudson, 1966.

Geist, Sidney. *Constantin Brancusi, 1876–1957: A Retrospective Exhibition.* New York: Solomon R. Guggenheim Museum/Philadelphia: Philadelphia Museum of Art/Chicago: Chicago Art Institute, 1969.

George, Waldemar, and Dina Vierny. *Maillol.* London: Cory, Adams, and Mackay, 1965.

Gilot, François, and Carlton Lake. *Life with Picasso.* New York: McGraw-Hill, 1964.

Golding, John. *Cubism: A History and an Analysis, 1907–1914.* rev. ed. Boston: Boston Book & Art Shop, 1968.

Gowing, Lawrence. *Matisse.* New York: Oxford University Press, 1979.

Gray, Camilla. *The Russian Experiment in Art: 1863–1922.* New York: Harry N. Abrams, 1970.

Gray, Christopher. *Cubist Aesthetic Theories.* Baltimore: Johns Hopkins University Press 1953.

Grohmann, Will. *Kandinsky: Life and Work.* New York: Harry N. Abrams, 1958.

Gropius, Walter. *Scope of Total Architecture.* New York: Collier Books, 1962.

Haiko, Peter. *Architecture of the Early XX Century.* New York: Rizzoli, 1989.

Herrera, Hayden. *Frida: A Biography of Frida Kahlo.* New York: Harper & Row, 1983.

Hepworth, Barbara. *A Pictorial Autobiography.* London: The Tate Gallery, 1978.

Hof, August. *Wilhelm Lehmbruck.* London: Pall Mall Press, 1969.

Hunter, Sam. *American Art of the 20th Century.* New York: Harry N. Abrams, 1972.

Jaffé, Hans L. *De Stijl.* New York: Harry N. Abrams, 1971.

James, Philip. *Henry Moore on Sculpture.* New York: Viking Press, 1971.

Jean, Marcel. *The History of Surrealist Painting.* Translated by Simon Watson Taylor. New York: Grove Press, 1960.

Kahnweiler, Daniel H. *The Rise of Cubism.* New York: Wittenborn, Schultz, 1949.

Kandinsky, Wassily. *Concerning the Spiritual in Art.* Translated by M. T. H. Sadler. New York: Dover, 1977.

Kuspit, Donald. *The Cult of the Avant-Garde Artist.* Cambridge: Cambridge University Press, 1993.

Langaard, Johan H., and Reidar Revold. *Edvard Munch: Masterpieces from the Artist's Collection in the Munch Museum in Oslo.* New York: McGraw-Hill, 1964.

Le Corbusier. *The City of Tomorrow.* Cambridge, MA: MIT Press, 1971.

Levin, Gail. *Edward Hopper: The Art and the Artist.* New York: Whitney Museum of American Art/Norton, 1980.

Lodder, Christina. *Russian Constructivism.* New Haven: Yale University Press, 1983.

Martin, Marianne W. *Futurist Art and Theory.* Oxford: Clarendon Press, 1968.

Martinell, César. *Gaudí: His Life, His Theories, His Work.* Cambridge, MA: MIT Press, 1975.

Mashek, Joseph, ed. *Marcel Duchamp in Perspective.* Englewood Cliffs, NJ: Prentice-Hall, 1975.

Meltzer, Milton. *Dorothea Lange: A Photographer's Life.* New York: Farrar, Strauss, Giroux, 1978.

Moholy-Nagy, László. *Vision in Motion.* Chicago: Paul Theobald, 1969, first published in 1946.

Mondrian, Pieter Cornelius. *Plastic Art and Pure Plastic Art.* 3rd ed. New York: Wittenborn, Schultz, 1952.

Morse, John D., ed. *Ben Shahn.* London: Secker & Warburg, 1972.

Motherwell, Robert, ed. *The Dada Painters and Poets.* 2nd ed. Cambridge, MA: Harvard University Press.

Myers, Bernard S. *The German Expressionists: A Generation in Revolt.* New York: Frederick A. Praeger, 1956.

O'Keeffe, Georgia. *Georgia O'Keeffe.* New York: Penguin, 1977.

Osborne, Harold. *The Oxford Companion to Twentieth Century Art.* New York: Oxford University Press, 1981.

Overy, Paul. *De Stijl.* London: Studio Vista, 1969.

Passuth, Krisztina. *Moholy-Nagy.* New York: Thames & Hudson, 1985.

Peter, John. *Masters of Modern Architecture.* New York: Braziller, 1958.

Read, Herbert. *The Art of Jean Arp.* New York: Harry N. Abrams, 1968.

Read, Herbert, ed. *Surrealism.* New York: Frederick A. Praeger, 1971.

Richter, Hans. *Dada: Art and Anti-Art.* London: Thames & Hudson, 1961.

Rosenblum, Robert. *Cubism and Twentieth-Century Art.* New York: Harry N. Abrams, 1976.

Rubin, William S. *Dada and Surrealist Art.* New York: Harry N. Abrams, 1968.

———. *Dada, Surrealism and Their Heritage.* New York: Museum of Modern Art, 1968.

———. *Miró in the Collection of The Museum of Modern Art.* New York: Museum of Modern Art, 1973.

Rubin, William S., ed. *Pablo Picasso: A Retrospective.* New York: Museum of Modern Art/Boston: New York Graphic Society, 1980.

———. *"Primitivism" in 20th-Century Art: Affinity of the Tribal and the Modern.* 2 vols. New York: Museum of Modern Art, 1984.

Russell, John. *Max Ernst: Life and Work.* New York: Harry N. Abrams, 1967.

Schiff, Gert, ed. *Picasso in Perspective.* Englewood Cliffs, NJ: Prentice-Hall, 1976.

Schneede, Uwe M. *Surrealism.* New York: Harry N. Abrams, 1974.

Schwarz, Arturo. *The Complete Works of Marcel Duchamp.* London: Thames & Hudson, 1965.

———. *Man Ray: The Rigors of Imagination.* New York: Rizzoli, 1977.

Selz, Peter. *German Expressionist Painting.* 1957. reprint. Berkeley: University of California Press, 1974.

Selz, Peter, and Jean Dubuffet. *The Work of Jean Dubuffet.* New York: Museum of Modern Art, 1962.

Seuphor, Michel. *Piet Mondrian: Life and Work.* New York: Harry N. Abrams, 1956.

Shattuck, Roger, Henri Béhar, Mitchell Hoog, Carolyn Lauchner, and William Rubin. *Henri Rousseau.* New York: Museum of Modern Art, 1985.

Sharp, Dennis. *Twentieth Century Architecture: A Visual History.* New York: Facts on File, 1991.

Soby, James Thrall. *Georges Rouault: Paintings and Prints.* New York: Museum of Modern Art/Simon and Schuster, 1947.

Sotriffer, Kristian. *Expressionism and Fauvism.* New York: McGraw-Hill, 1972.

Speyer, James A. with Frederick Koeper. *Mies van der Rohe.* Chicago: Art Institute of Chicago, 1968.

Stephenson, Robert C., tr. *Orozco: An Autobiography.* Austin: University of Texas Press, 1962.

Stott, William. *Documentary Expression and Thirties America.* New York: Oxford University Press, 1973.

Taylor, Joshua C. *Futurism.* New York: Museum of Modern Art, 1961.

Troyen, Carol, and Erica E. Hirshler. *Charles Sheeler: Paintings and Drawings.* Boston: Museum of Fine Arts, 1987.

Tucker, William. *Early Modern Sculpture.* New York: Oxford University Press, 1974.

Vogt, Paul. *Expressionism: German Painting, 1905–1920.* New York: Harry N. Abrams, 1980.

Von Hartz, John. *August Sander.* Millerton, NY: Aperture, 1977.

Waldman, Diane. *Joseph Cornell.* New York: Braziller, 1977.

Wright, Frank Lloyd; Edgar Kaufmann, ed. *American Architecture.* New York: Horizon, 1955.

Wheat, Ellen Harkins. *Jacob Lawrence: American Painter.* Seattle: University of Washington Press, 1986.

CHAPTER 28 THE LATER TWENTIETH CENTURY

Albright, Thomas. *Art in the San Francisco Bay Area: 1945–1980.* Berkeley: University of California Press, 1985.

Alloway, Lawrence. *American Pop Art.* New York: Whitney Museum of American Art/Macmillan, 1974.

———. *Robert Rauschenberg.* Washington, DC: National Collection of Fine Arts/ Smithsonian Institutions, 1976.

———. *Topics in American Art Since 1945.* New York: W. W. Norton, 1975.

Amaya, Mario. *Pop Art and After.* New York: Viking Press, 1972.

Armes, Roy. *Patterns of Realism: A Study of Italian Neo-Realist Cinema.* New York: A. S. Barnes, 1971.

Battcock, Gregory, ed. *Minimal Art: A Critical Anthology.* New York: Studio Vista, 1969.

———. *The New Art: A Critical Anthology.* New York: E. P. Dutton, 1973.

———. *New Artists Video: A Critical Anthology.* New York: E. P. Dutton, 1978.

———. *Super Realism: A Critical Anthology.* New York: E. P. Dutton, 1975.

Battcock, Gregory, and Robert Nickas, eds. *The Art of Performance: A Critical Anthology.* New York: E. P. Dutton, 1984.

Beardsley, Richard. *Earthworks and Beyond: Contemporary Art in the Landscape.* New York: Abbeville Press, 1984.

Beardsley, John, and Jane Livingston. *Hispanic Art in the United States: Thirty Contemporary Painters and Sculptors.* Houston: Museum of Fine Arts/New York: Abbeville Press, 1987.

Benezra, Neal. *Martin Puryear.* Chicago: Chicago Art Institute, 1991.

Benthall, Jeremy. *Science and Technology in Art Today.* New York: Frederick A. Praeger, 1972.

Bourdon, David. *Christo.* New York: Harry N. Abrams, 1972.

Brion, Marcel, Sam Hunter, et al. *Art Since 1945.* New York: Harry N. Abrams, 1958.

Carmean, E. A., Jr., Elizabeth Rathbone, and Thomas B. Hess. *American Art at Mid-Century: The Subjects of the Artists.* Washington, DC: The National Gallery of Art, 1978.

Cassou, Jean, K. G. Hultèn-Pontus, and Sam Hunter, with statement by Nicolas Schöffer. *Two Kinetic Sculptors: Nicolas Schöffer and Jean Tinguely.* New York: Jewish Museum/October House, 1965.

Chicago, Judy. *The Dinner Party: A Symbol of Our Heritage.* Garden City, NY: Anchor Press/Doubleday, 1979.

Cockcroft, Eva, John Weber, and James Cockcroft. *Toward a People's Art.* New York: E. P. Dutton, 1977.

Cook, Peter. *New Spirit in Architecture.* New York: Rizzoli, 1990.

Crichton, Michael. *Jasper Johns.* New York: Whitney Museum of American Art/Harry N. Abrams, 1977.

Cummings, Paul. *Dictionary of Contemporary American Artists.* 3rd ed. New York: St. Martin's Press, 1977.

Danto, Arthur C. *Mark Tansey: Visions and Revisions.* New York: Abrams, 1992.

Davies, Hugh, and Sally Yard. *Francis Bacon.* New York: Abbeville Press, 1986.

Deken, Joseph. *Computer Images: State of the Art.* New York: Stewart, Tabori, and Chang Publishers, 1983.

Diamondstein, Barbaralee. *American Architecture Now.* New York: Rizzoli, 1980.

Diehl, Gaston, and Eileen B. Hennessey. *Vasarely.* New York: Crown Publishers, 1972.

Gilbert and George, and Carter Ratcliff. *Gilbert and George: The Complete Pictures, 1971–1985.* London: Thames & Hudson, 1986.

Goodman, Cynthia. *Digital Visions: Computers and Art.* New York: Harry N. Abrams, 1987.

Goodyear, Frank H., Jr. *Contemporary American Realism Since 1960.* Boston: New York Graphic Society, 1981.

Gordon, John. *Louise Nevelson.* New York: Whitney Museum of American Art, 1967.

Gough, Harry F. *The Vital Gesture: Franz Kline.* Cincinnati: Cincinnati Art Museum/New York: Abbeville Press, 1985.

Graham, Peter. *The New Wave.* Garden City, NY: Doubleday, 1968.

Gray, Cleve, ed. *David Smith on David Smith: Sculpture and Writings.* London: Thames & Hudson, 1968.

Hamilton, Richard. *Collected Words 1953–1982.* London: Thames & Hudson, 1982.

Hertz, Richard, ed. *Theories of Contemporary Art.* Englewood Cliffs, NJ: Prentice-Hall, 1985.

Hess, Thomas B. *Barnett Newman.* New York: Walker and Company, 1969.

———. *Willem de Kooning.* New York: Museum of Modern Art, 1968.

Jacob, Mary Jane. *Magdalena Abakanowicz.* New York: Abbeville Press, 1982.

Jacobus, John. *Twentieth-Century Architecture: The Middle Years, 1940–1964.* New York: Frederick A. Praeger, 1966.

Jencks, Charles. *Architecture 2000: Prediction and Methods.* New York: Frederick A. Praeger, 1971.

———. *The Language of Postmodern Architecture.* New York: Rizzoli, 1977 (1981).

Kaprow, Allan. *Assemblage, Environments, and Happenings.* New York: Harry N. Abrams, 1966.

Kepes, Georgy. *Arts of the Environment.* New York: Braziller, 1970.

Kirby, Michael. *Happenings.* New York: E. P. Dutton, 1966.

Lippard, Lucy R. *Eva Hesse.* New York: New York University Press, 1976.

Lippard, Lucy R., ed. *Pop Art.* New York: Frederick A. Praeger, 1966.

———, ed. *Six Years: The Dematerialization of the Art Object from 1966 to 1972.* New York: Frederick A. Praeger, 1973.

Livingstone, Marco. *David Hockney.* London: Thames & Hudson, 1981.

Lovejoy, Margot. *Postmodern Currents: Art and Artists in the Age of the Electronic Media.* Ann Arbor, MI: UMI Research Press, 1989.

Lucie-Smith, Edward. *Art Now.* Edison, NJ: Wellfleet Press, 1989.

———. *Movements Since 1945.* new rev. ed. New York: Thames & Hudson, 1984.

Marder, Tod A. *The Critical Edge: Controversy in Recent American Architecture.* New Brunswick, NJ: Rutgers University Press, 1980.

McShine, Kynaston. *Andy Warhol: A Retrospective.* New York: Museum of Modern Art, 1989.

———. *An International Survey of Recent Painting and Sculpture.* New York: Museum of Modern Art, 1984.

Meyer, Ursula. *Conceptual Art.* New York: E. P. Dutton, 1972.

Mitchell, William J. *The Reconfigured Eye: Visual Truth in the Post-Photographic Era.* Cambridge, MA: MIT Press, 1992.

Nervi, Pier Luigi. *Aesthetics and Technology in Building.* Cambridge, MA: Harvard University Press, 1965.

Norris, Christopher, and Benjamin, Andres. *What Is Deconstruction?* New York: St. Martin's, 1988.

O'Connor, Francis V. *Jackson Pollock.* New York: Museum of Modern Art, 1967.

O'Hara, Frank. *Robert Motherwell.* New York: Museum of Modern Art, 1965.

Papadakis, Andreas. *Deconstruction: Omnibus Volume.* New York: Rizzoli, 1989.

Price, Jonathan. *Video Visions: A Medium Discovers Itself.* New York: New American Library, 1977.

Reichardt, Jasia, ed. *Cybernetics, Art & Ideas.* Greenwich, CT: New York Graphics Society, 1971.

Risatti, Howard, ed. *Postmodern Perspectives.* Englewood Cliffs, NJ: Prentice-Hall, 1990.

Robbins, Corinne. *The Pluralist Era: American Art, 1968–1981.* New York: Harper & Row, 1984.

Rose, Barbara. *Claes Oldenburg.* New York: Museum of Modern Art, 1970.

———. *Frankenthaler.* New York: Harry N. Abrams, 1975.

Rosenberg, Harold. *The Tradition of the New.* New York: Horizon Press, 1959.

Russell, John. *Francis Bacon.* London: Thames & Hudson, 1971.

Russell, John, and Suzi Gablik. *Pop Art Redefined.* New York: Frederick A. Praeger, 1969.

Sandler, Irving. *The Triumph of American Painting: A History of Abstract Expressionism.* New York: Frederick A. Praeger, 1970.

Schneider, Ira, and Beryl Korot. *Video Art: An Anthology.* New York: Harcourt Brace Jovanovich, 1976.

Seitz, William C. *Abstract Expressionist Painting in America.* Cambridge, MA: Harvard University Press, 1983.

Sitney, P. Adams. *Visionary Film: The American Avant-Garde.* New York: Oxford University Press, 1974.

Smagula, Howard. *Currents: Contemporary Directions in the Visual Arts.* 2nd ed. Englewood Cliffs, NJ: Prentice-Hall, 1989.

Smith, Patrick S. *Andy Warhol's Art and Films.* Ann Arbor, MI: UMI Research Press, 1986.

Smithson, Robert. *The Writings of Robert Smithson.* Edited by Nancy Holt. New York: New York University Press, 1975.

Solomon, Alan. *Jasper Johns.* New York: The Jewish Museum, 1964.

Sonfist, Alan, ed. *Art in the Landscape: A Critical Anthology of Environmental Art.* New York: E. P. Dutton, 1983.

Stangos, Nikos. *Concepts of Modern Art.* 2nd ed. New York: Harper & Row, 1985.

Stern, Robert A. M. *Modern Classicism.* New York: Rizzoli, 1988.

Tisdall, Carolyn. *Joseph Beuys.* New York: Solomon R. Guggenheim Museum, 1979.

Tomkins, Calvin. *The Scene Reports on Post-Modern Art.* New York: Viking Press, 1976.

Tuchman, Maurice. *American Sculpture of the Sixties.* Los Angeles: Los Angeles County Museum of Art, 1967.

Venturi, Robert, Denise Scott-Brown, and Steven Isehour. *Learning from Las Vegas.* Cambridge, MA: MIT Press, 1972.

Waldman, Diane. *Mark Rothko, 1903–1970: A Retrospective.* New York: Solomon R. Guggenheim Museum, 1978.

Wallis, Brian, ed. *Art After Modernism: Rethinking Representation.* New York: New Museum of Contemporary Art in association with David R. Godine, 1984.

Watson-Jones, Virginia. *Contemporary American Women Sculptors.* Phoenix: Oryx Press, 1986.

Wye, Deborah. *Louise Bourgeois.* New York: Museum of Modern Art, 1982.

BOOKS SPANNING THE EIGHTEENTH, NINETEENTH, AND TWENTIETH CENTURIES

Ades, Dawn. *Art in Latin America: The Modern Era, 1820–1980.* London: The Hayward Gallery, 1989.

Antreasian, Garo, and Clinton Adams. *The Tamarind Book of Lithography: Art and Techniques.* Los Angeles: Tamarind Workshop and New York: Harry N. Abrams, 1971.

Armstrong, John, Wayne Craven, and Norma Feder, et al. *200 Years of American Sculpture.* New York: Whitney Museum of American Art/Boston: David R. Godine, 1976.

Brown, Milton, Sam Hunter, and John Jacobus. *American Art: Painting, Sculpture, Architecture, Decorative Arts, Photography.* New York: Harry N. Abrams, 1979.

Chipp, Herschel. *Theories of Modern Art.* Berkeley: University of California Press, 1968.

Coke, Van Deren. *The Painter and the Photograph From Delacroix to Warhol.* rev. and enl. ed. Albuquerque: University of New Mexico Press, 1972.

Collins, Peter. *Changing Ideals in Modern Architecture, 1750–1950.* London: Faber & Faber, 1971.

Condit, Carl W. *The Rise of the Skyscraper: Portrait of the Times and Career of Influential Architects.* Chicago: University of Chicago Press, 1952.

Driskell, David C. *Two Centuries of Black American Art.* Los Angeles: Los Angeles County Museum of Art/New York: Alfred A. Knopf, 1976.

Elsen, Albert. *Origins of Modern Sculpture.* New York: Braziller, 1974.

Fine, Sylvia Honig. *Women and Art: A History of Women Painters and Sculptors from the Renaissance to the 20th Century.* Montclair, NJ: Alanheld and Schram, 1978.

Flexner, James Thomas. *America's Old Masters.* New York: McGraw-Hill, 1982.

Giedion, Siegfried. *Mechanization Takes Command: A Contribution to Anonymous History.* New York: Norton, 1948.

———. *Space, Time and Architecture: The Growth of a New Tradition.* 4th ed. Cambridge, MA: Harvard University Press, 1965.

Goldwater, Robert, and Marco Treves, eds. *Artists on Art.* 3rd ed. New York: Pantheon, 1958.

Greenough, Sarah, Joel Snyder, David Travis, and Colin Westerbeck. *On the Art of Fixing a Shadow: One Hundred and Fifty Years of Photography.* Washington, DC: The National Gallery of Art/Chicago: The Art Institute of Chicago, 1989.

Hamilton, George Heard. *Nineteenth- and Twentieth-Century Art.* Englewood Cliffs, NJ: Prentice-Hall, 1972.

Hammacher, A. M. *The Evolution of Modern Sculpture: Tradition and Innovation.* New York: Harry N. Abrams, 1969.

Hitchcock, Henry-Russell. *Architecture: Nineteenth and Twentieth Centuries.* 4th ed. New Haven: Yale University Press, 1977.

Hopkins, H. J. *A Span of Bridges.* Newton Abbot, Devon, England: David & Charles, 1970.

Hunter, Sam. *Modern French Painting, 1855–1956.* New York: Dell, 1966.

Irving, Donald J. *Sculpture: Material and Process.* New York: Van Nostrand Reinhold, 1970.

Kaufmann, Edgar, Jr., ed. *The Rise of an American Architecture.* New York: Metropolitan Museum of Art/Frederick A. Praeger, 1970.

Klingender, Francis Donald and Elton, Arthur ed. and rev. *Art and the Industrial Revolution.* London: Evelyn, Adams and MacKay, 1968.

Licht, Fred. *Sculpture, Nineteenth and Twentieth Centuries.* Greenwich, CT: New York Graphic Society, 1967.

Loyer, Francois. *Architecture of the Industrial Age.* New York: Rizzoli, 1983.

McCoubrey, John W. *American Art, 1700–1960: Sources and Documents.* Englewood Cliffs, NJ: Prentice-Hall, 1965.

Mason, Jerry, ed. *International Center of Photography Encyclopedia of Photography.* New York: Crown Publishers, 1984.

Newhall, Beaumont. *The History of Photography.* New York: The Museum of Modern Art, 1982.

Pehnt, Wolfgang. *Encyclopedia of Modern Architecture.* New York: Harry N. Abrams, 1964.

Peterdi, Gabor. *Printmaking: Methods Old and New.* New York: Macmillan, 1961.

Phillipe, Robert. *Political Graphics: Art as a Weapon.* New York: Abbeville Press, 1980.

Pierson, William. *American Buildings and Their Architects: Technology and the Picturesque.* Vol. 2. Garden City, NY: Doubleday, 1978.

Risebero, Bill. *Modern Architecture and Design: An Alternative History.* Cambridge: MIT Press, 1983.

Rosenblum, Robert. *Modern Painting and the Northern Romantic Tradition: Friedrich to Rothko.* New York: Harper & Row, 1975.

Ross, John, and Clare Romano. *The Complete Printmaker.* New York: The Free Press, 1972.

Ross, Stephen David, ed. *Art and Its Significance: An Anthology of Aesthetic Theory.* Albany, NY: SUNY Press, 1987.

Sachs, Paul, Jr. *Modern Prints and Drawings: A Guide to a Better Understanding of Modern Draughtsmanship.* New York: Alfred A. Knopf, 1954.

Scharf, Aaron. *Art and Photography.* Baltimore, MD: Penguin Books, 1974.

Scully, Vincent. *American Architecture and Urbanism.* New York: Frederick A. Praeger, 1969.

Selz, Peter; Michelson, Annette, tr. *Modern Sculpture: Origins and Evolution.* London: Heinemann, 1963.

Seuphor, Michel. *The Sculpture of this Century.* New York: Braziller, 1960.

Shikes, Ralph E. *The Indignant Eye: The Artist as Social Critic, from the Renaissance to Picasso.* Boston: Banion Press, 1969.

Slatkin, Wendy. *Women Artists in History: From Antiquity to the 20th Century.* 2nd ed. Englewood Cliffs, NJ: Prentice-Hall, 1985.

Spencer, Harold. *American Art: Readings from the Colonial Era to the Present.* New York: Charles Scribner's Sons, 1980.

Summerson, Sir John. *Architecture in Britain: 1530–1830.* 7th rev. and enl. ed. Baltimore: Penguin, 1983.

Sypher, Wylie. *Rococo to Cubism in Art and Literature.* New York: Random House, 1960.

Szarkowski, John. *Photography Until Now.* New York: Museum of Modern Art, 1989.

Thorndike, Joseph, Jr. *Three Centuries of Notable American Architects.* New York: American Heritage, 1981.

Weaver, Mike. *The Art of Photography: 1839–1989.* New Haven, CT: Yale University Press, 1989.

Whiffen, Marcus, and Frederick Koeper. *American Architecture, 1607–1976.* Cambridge: MIT Press, 1983.

Wilmerding, John. *American Art.* Harmondsworth, England: Penguin, 1976.

————. *The Genius of American Painting.* London: Weidenfeld & Nicolson, 1973.

Wilson, Simon. *Holbein to Hockney: A History of British Art.* London: The Tate Gallery & The Bodley Head, 1979.

BOOKS SPANNING THE WHOLE OF THE TWENTIETH CENTURY

Ades, Dawn. *Photomontage.* Rev. and enl. ed. London: Thames & Hudson, 1976.

Andersen, Wayne. *American Sculpture in Process: 1930–1970.* Boston: New York Graphic Society, 1975.

Arnason, H. H. *History of Modern Art: Painting, Sculpture, Architecture.* 3rd rev. and enl. ed. Englewood Cliffs, NJ: Prentice-Hall 1988.

Ashton, Dore. *Twentieth-Century Artists on Art.* New York: Pantheon Books, 1985.

Banham, Reyner. *Guide to Modern Architecture.* Princeton, NJ: D. Van Nostrand, 1962.

Burnham, Jack. *Beyond Modern Sculpture. The Effects of Science and Technology on the Sculpture of This Century.* New York: Braziller, 1968.

Castelman, Riva. *Prints of the 20th Century: A History.* New York: Oxford University Press, 1985.

Compton, Susan, ed. *British Art in the 20th Century.* London: Royal Academy of Arts/Berlin: Prestel Verlag, 1986.

Curtis, David. *Experimental Cinema: A Fifty-Year Evolution.* New York: Dell, 1971.

Davis, Douglas. *Art and the Future: A History/Prophecy of the Collaboration Between Scientists, Technology and the Arts.* New York: Frederick A. Praeger, 1973.

Frascina, Francis, and Charles Harrison, eds. *Modern Art and Modernism: A Critical Anthology.* New York: Harper & Row, 1982.

Haftmann, Werner. *Painting in the Twentieth Century.* New York: Frederick A. Praeger, 1960.

Hamlin, Talbot F., ed. *Forms and Functions of Twentieth-Century Architecture.* 4 vols. New York: Columbia University Press, 1952.

Hatje, Gerd, ed. *Encyclopedia of Modern Architecture.* London: Thames & Hudson, 1963.

Herbert, Robert L., ed. *Modern Artists on Art.* Englewood Cliffs, NJ: Prentice-Hall, 1964.

Hertz, Richard, and Norman M. Klein, eds. *Twentieth-Century Art Theory: Urbanism, Politics, and Mass Culture.* Englewood Cliffs, NJ: Prentice-Hall, 1990.

Hunter, Sam, and John Jacobus. *Modern Art: Painting, Sculpture, and Architecture.* New York: Harry N. Abrams, 1985.

Hunter, Sam. *Modern American Painting and Sculpture.* New York: Dell, 1959.

Jencks, Charles. *Modern Movements in Architecture.* Garden City, NY: Anchor Press/ Doubleday, 1973.

Joachimides, Christos. M., Norma Rosenthal, and Wieland Schmied, eds. *German Art in the 20th Century: Painting and Sculpture, 1905–1985.* Munich: Prestel-Verlag, 1985.

Kraus, Rosalind E. *Passages in Modern Sculpture.* Cambridge, MA: MIT Press, 1981.

Lynton, Norbert. *The Story of Modern Art.* 2nd ed. Englewood Cliffs, NJ: Prentice-Hall, 1989.

Phaidon Dictionary of Twentieth-Century Art. Oxford: Phaidon Press, 1973.

Phillips, Gene D. *The Movie Makers: Artists in an Industry.* Chicago: Nelson-Hall, 1973.

Pontus-Hultén, K. G. *The Machine as Seen at the End of the Mechanical Age.* New York: Museum of Modern Art, 1968.

Popper, Frank, et. al. *Electra: Electricity and Electronics in the Art of the 20th Century.* Paris: Musée d'art moderne de Paris, 1983.

————. *Origins and Development of Kinetic Art.* Translated by Stephne Benn. Greenwich, CT: New York Graphic Society, 1968.

Raynal, Maurice. *History of Modern Painting.* 3 vols. Geneva: Skira, 1949–1950.

Read, Herbert. *Concise History of Modern Painting.* 3rd ed. New York: Frederick A. Praeger, 1975.

————. *A Concise History of Modern Sculpture.* rev. and enl. ed. New York: Frederick A. Praeger, 1964.

Rickey, George. *Constructivism: Origins and Evolution.* New York: Braziller, 1967.

Ritchie, Andrew Carnduff, ed. *German Art of the Twentieth Century.* New York: Museum of Modern Art, 1957.

————. *Sculpture of the Twentieth Century.* New York: The Museum of Modern Art, n.d.

Rose, Barbara. *American Art Since 1900.* rev. ed. New York: Frederick A. Praeger, 1975.

Russell, John. *The Meanings of Modern Art.* New York: Museum of Modern Art/Thames & Hudson, 1981.

Scully, Vincent. *American Architecture and Urbanism.* New York: Frederick A. Praeger, 1969.

————. *Modern Architecture.* rev. ed. New York: Braziller, 1974.

Sharp, Dennis. *Twentieth Century Architecture: A Visual Survey.* New York: Facts on File. 1991.

Spalding, Francis. *British Art Since 1900.* London: Thames & Hudson, 1986.

Tomkins, Calvin. *The Bride and the Bachelors, Five Masters of the Avant-Garde.* New York: Viking Press, 1968.

Tuchman, Maurice, and Judi Freeman, eds. *The Spiritual in Art: Abstract Painting, 1890–1985.* Los Angeles: Los Angeles County Art Museum/New York: Abbeville Press, 1986.

Wescher, Herta. *Collage.* Translated by Robert E. Wolf. New York: Harry N. Abrams, 1968.

Whittick, Arnold. *European Architecture in the Twentieth Century.* Aylesbury, England: Leonard Hill , 1974.

ACKNOWLEDGMENTS

The authors and publisher are grateful to the proprietors and custodians of various works of art for photographs of these works and permission to reproduce them in this book. Sources not included in the captions are listed here.

KEY TO ABBREVIATIONS

AA&A	The Ancient Art & Architecture Collection
AL	Fratelli Alinari
AR	Art Resource
BPK	Bildarchiv Preussischer Kulturbesitz
Bulloz	J. E. Bulloz, Paris
Canali	Canali Photobank, Italy
Fototeca	Fototeca Unione at the American Academy, Rome
Gir	Giraudon
Harding	Robert Harding Picture Library, London
Hinz	Colorphoto Hans Hinz
Hir	Hirmer Fotoarchiv, Munich
Mar	Bildarchiv Foto Marburg
MAS	Appliaciones y Reproducciones MAS, Barcelona
NYPL	New York Public Library
PRI	Photo Researchers, Inc., New York
R.M.N.	Photo, Réunion des Musées Nationaux
Scala	Scala Fine Art Publishers
Summerfield	Summerfield Press, Ltd

Note: All references in the following credits are to figure numbers unless otherwise indicated.

Cover, Vol. I paperbound—Erich Lessing/AR. Frontispiece, Vol. I paperbound—R.M.N. **Introduction**—AL/AR: 4, 9, 10; © 1955, 1983, The New Yorker Magazine: 11; Hir: 12. **Part I**—Opening photograph Studio Pizzi/Summerfield; black-and-white photograph Griffith Institute, Ashmolean Museum, Oxford. **Chapter 1**—Jean Vertut: 1, 5, 11; Robert Laborie: 2, 6; Hinz: 4; CNMHS/SPADEM: 7, 12; J.M. Arnaud/Musée d'Aquitaine: 9; Jean Dieuzaide: 10; MAS: 13; British School of Archaeology in Jerusalem: 14, 15; James Mellaart: 18; Arlette Mellaart: 19, 20; Aerofilms Limited: 21. **Chapter 2**—Staatliche Museen zu Berlin: 1; Erwin Böhm: 4; Hir: 5, 16, 17, 19, 22; Courtesy of The Oriental Institute of The University of Chicago: 6, 25; © photo Jean Mazenod, L'art antique du Proche-Orient, editions Citadelles & Mazenod, Paris: 7; Scala/AR: 12; R.M.N.: 13, 15, 27; The Mansell Collection: 20; Klaus Göken, 1992/BPK: 24; Gir/AR: 30; Sassoon/Harding: 31; Stolze: 33. **Chapter 3**—Hir: 2, 3, 6, 7, 8, 12, 13, 17, 18, 19, 20, 31, 36; Carolyn Brown/PRI: 4; Harding: 11, 29, 41, 42; R.M.N.: 15, 43; John G. Ross: 16; Mar/AR: 21, 27, 45; Wim Swaan: 23; John P. Stevens/AA&A: 26; Ron Sheridan/AA& A: 32; Jürgen Liepe/BPK: 33; Margarete Büsing/BPK: 37, 38, 39; Lee Boltin: 40. **Chapter 4**—Scala/AR: 1; Studio Kontos: 2, 7, 26; Photo by Raymond V. Schoder, © 1987 by Bolchazy-Carducci Publishers, Inc.: 3, 17; Wim Swaan: Hir: 6, 8, 10, 12, 14, 15, 18, 20, 23, 24, 25, 28; Nimatallah/AR: 9, 13; Hinz: 11; Leonard von Matt: 16; TAP: 27. **Chapter 5**—TAP: 1, 11, 72: Photograph by Schecter Lee: 2; Alison Frantz: 7, 35, 36, 57; R.M.N.: 8, 65, 93; Studio Kontos: 12, 13, 34, 40, 47, 73, 77, 88, 95; Summerfield: 16, 92; Vanni/AR: 19; Hir: 21, 39, 53, 56, 61, 62, 63, 70, 85, 94; AL/AR: 22(a), 42, 74; Scala/AR: 22(b), 38, 41, 58, 64, 98(a); Photo Vatican Museums: 23, 44, 68; Photo R.M.N./Duplicata: 25; Hinz: 26; Copyright A.C.L., Brussels: 27; Erich Lessing/AR: 28; Canali: 33, 79, 102; Mar/AR: 37, 83; German Archaeological Institute, Rome: 43, 75, 98(b); Photo by Raymond V. Schoder, © 1987 by Bolchazy-Carducci Publishers, Inc.: 45, 80; DAI, Athens. photo: G. Hellner: 55; Ronald Sheridan/AA&A: 60, 81; © 1981 M. Sarri/Photo Vatican Museums: 66, 71; Archivio I.G.D.A., Milano: 67; SANDAK/AR: 76; R. Hoddinott/AA&A: 78; Gian Berto Vanni/AR: 82; BPK: 86, 89, 90; Soprintendenza Archeologica, Rome: 91; Photo Chr. Koppermann: 97; © 1988 T. Okamura/Photo Vatican Museums: 101. **Chapter 6**—Hir: 1, 2, 4, 9, 10, 12, 17; David Lees: 3; German Archaeological Institute, Rome: 5, 11, 18; Fototeca: 6; Archivio I.G.D.A., Milano: 8; Photo Vatican Museums: 13; Scala/AR: 14;

Soprintendenza Archeologica per l'Etruria Meridionale: 15; AL/AR: 16. **Chapter 7**—Fototeca: 1, 13, 49, 51, 75; AL/AR: 2, 9, 14, 31, 32, 37, 41, 44, 45, 60, 62; German Archaeological Institute, Rome: 5, 6, 16, 33, 48, 52, 53, 55, 67, 73, 76, 79, 82, 86, 88; The American Numismatic Society, New York: 7, 93(a); The Whittlesey Foundation/ Aristide D. Caratzas, Publisher: 10; Ronald Sheridan/AA& A: 12; Photo Archives Skira, Geneva, Switzerland: 17; Canali: 18, 23, 24, 27, 34, 47; 63(b), 81, 90; Foto Biblioteca Apostolica Vaticana: 20; Scala/AR: 21, 26, 58, 65, 85; Madeline Grimoldi: 25; © M. Sarri/Photo Vatican Museums: 28; Photo Vatican Museums: 29, 64; Mar/AR: 35, 83; Oliver Benn/Tony Stone Images: 36; Leonard von Matt: 39, 40; © photo Jean Mazenod, L'art de l'ancienne Rome, Éditions Citadelles et Mazenod, Paris: 42; Summerfield: 43, 78; CNRS: 46; Israel Museum, Jerusalem/ D. Harris: 54; Cotton Coulson/Woodfin Camp: 57; Wim Swaan: 59; Ernani Orcorte/UTET: 61; Erich Lessing/AR: 63(a); De Masi/Canali: 66; Canali/On license of the Ministero per i Beni Culturali ed Ambientali: 69; Peter Muscato: 70; BPK: 71; Istituto Centrale per il Catalogo e la Documentazione, (ICCD): 87; Rheinisches Landesmuseum: 91, 92; Hir: 93(b). **Chapter 8**—Yale University Art Gallery, Dura-Europos Archive: 1; Fototeca & Benedettine di Priscilla, Rome: 3; Madeline Grimoldi: 4; Hir: 5, 6, 7, 10, 21, 23, 24, 27; AL/AR: 9, 14; Canali: 12; Andre Held: 13; Scala/AR: 15, 18, 19, 20; Anderson: 17; Foto Biblioteca Apostolica Vaticana: 25. **Part II** opening photograph—© photo Jean Mazenod, L'art gothique editions Citadelles & Mazenod, Paris. **Chapter 9**—Jean Dieuzaide: 1; Marvin Trachtenberg: 2; Hir: 4, 6, 12, 36; Scala/AR: 7, 13; AL/Gir: 8; Canali: 9, 10, 11, 16; Ronald Sheridan/AA& A: 14, 15; R.M.N.: 19; Alison Frantz: 20; Erich Lessing/AR: 23; Sostegni/Fotocielo: 24; Canali/Cameraphoto: 26, 30; HB Collection: 27; Studio Kontos: 28; Josephine Powell: 29; Enrico Ferorelli: 31; Sovfoto/Eastfoto: 32, 37; Courtesy of Dumbarton Oaks, Center for Byzantine Studies, Washington, D.C.: 33; Philip Craven/Harding: 34; Andre Held: 35; Reenie Schmerl Barrow: 38. **Chapter 10**—Yoram Lehmann, Jerusalem: 1; Ronald Sheridan/AA&A: 2, 5; Photo Archives Skira, Geneva, Switzerland: 3; Roger Wood/Continuum: 4, 18; Wim Swaan: 7, 11, 20, 22; MAS: 9; Douglas Dickins, FRPS: 10; HB Collection: 12; BPK: 14; Staatliche Museen zu Berlin: 15; By courtesy of the Israel Antiquities Authority: 16; Josephine Powell: 17; Linares/Yale University Photo Collection: 19; Russell A. Thompson: 23; Gir: 24; Anthony Kersting: 26; Photographer: Daniel McGrath: 27; Courtesy of Dr. Todd Disotell: 33. **Chapter 11**—Lee Boltin: 1; R.M.N.: 2(a); Bridgeman/AR: 2(b); Scala/AR: 5; Erich Lessing/AR: 6; Donato Pineider: 8; Mick Sharp: 10; University Museum of National Antiquities, Oslo, Norway: 11; University Museum of National Antiquities, Oslo, Norway. Eirik Irgens Johnsen: 12; Photo Zodiaque: 13; NYPL: 16; Summerfield: 19; Dr. Harold Busch: 22; Hir: 23; Mar/AR: 26, 29; HB Collection: 28; BPK: 30. **Chapter 12**—Ronald Sheridan/AA&A: 1; Jean Dieuzaide: 3, 23; Mar/AR: 5, 34; Hir: 8; HB Collection: 9; AL/AR: 10; Canali: 12, 19, 26; Bulloz: 13, 25, 27, 31, 33; W. S. Stoddard: 14; Anthony Kersting: 16; Fotocielo: 18; Scala/AR: 20; Ralph Lieberman: 21; Takashi Okamura/Abbeville Press, New York: 22; Emeric Feher © CNMHS/SPADEM: 28; Arch. Phot. Paris/SPADEM: 29; Gir: 30, 38; Lauros/Gir: 32, 35; Gir/AR: 36; Wim Swaan: 39. **Chapter 13**—HB Collection: 1, 3, 35; Harry Bliss, © National Geographic Society: 5; Mar/AR: 8, 18, 51, 53, 54, 55; Hir: 9, 11, 13, 23, 25; Bulloz: 10; Roger-Viollet: 14, 28; © photo Jean Mazenod, L'art gothique, éditions Citadelles & Mazenod, Paris: 15, 34; Aerofilms Limited: 16, 30, 31; Ralph Lieberman: 20, 22; Clarence Ward, Photographic Archives, National Gallery of Art, Washington, D.C.: 26, 49; Gir: 27, 36; Gir/AR: 29, 32, 33, 39; Rapho/PRI: 41;

Wim Swaan: 42; National Monuments Record: 44; RCHME Crown Copyright: 45, 46; Edwin Smith: 47; E.T. Archive: 48; Dr. Harold Busch/AR: 52; German Information Center: 57; Scala/AR: 58; Canali: 60, 61; AL/Canali: 62; Canali/Lensini, Italy: 63; George Holton/PRI: 64. **Part III** opening photograph—Justin Kerr; black-and-white photograph Eliot Elisofon. **Chapter 14**—Archeological Survey of India, Janpatch, New Delhi: 1, 2, 3, 4, 6, 8, 10, 12, 13, 15, 16, 17; Harding: 5, 7, 30; Joseph Szaszfai: 11; Photo by Edgar Oscar Parker, courtesy of the Visual Collections, Fine Arts Library, Harvard University: 14; David Tokeley/Harding: 18; Barnaby's Picture Library: 19; Gir/AR: 20; Douglas Dickins, FRPS: 21, 23, 33; HB Collection: 22; John Stevens/AA&A: 25; AR: 26; Werner Forman Archive/AR: 27; Eliot Elisofon/Life Magazine © Time Warner, Inc.: 28; R.M.N.: 31; Marie J. Mattson: 32. **Chapter 15**—Cultural Relics Publishing House, Beijing: 1, 2, 6; Chavannes: 7; Harding: 8, 27; Laurence G. Liu: 10, 11, 37, 39, 40, 41, 42; R.M.N.: 12, 30; HB Collection: 15; NYPL: 17; AR: 18: Tokyo National Museum: 23; Audrey R. Topping: 32; Edition d'Art, Paris: 35; Werner Forman Archive/AR: 43. **Chapter 16**—Kyoryokukai: 1, 16, 21; Courtesy of Jingu Shicho: 3; National Commission for Protection of Cultural Properties, Tokyo: 4, 11, 13; Sakamoto Photo Research Lab: 5, 9; Ogawa Kozo, Asukaen: 6, 7; From A History of Far Eastern Art by Sherman E. Lee, Harry N. Abrams, Inc.: 8, 10, 28, 29; Harding: 12(a); AR: 12(b); Wim Swaan: 17, 18; Shashinka Photo: 19, 23, 24, 25; Tokyo National Museum: 22; Photograph courtesy of the International Society for Educational Information, Inc.: 27; Japanese National Tourist Organization: 32. **Chapter 17**—Justin Kerr: 1, 7, 8, 9, 10, 13, 17, 28; Erich Lessing/AR: 2; Rene Millon, 1973: 4; Lee Boltin: 5; Photograph by Hillel Burger: 6, 34, 48; © 1988 Hillel Burger: 12; Foto Biblioteca Apostolica Vaticana: 14; Christopher Rennie/Harding: 15; Damm/ZEFA: 16; Wim Swaan: 18, 25, 35; American Museum of Natural History, New York: 20; Bill Ballenberg, © National Geographic Society: 21; Photo by Denis J. Nervig: 22; E. Hadingham: 23; ZEFA: 26; Douglas Dickins, FRPS: 27; Architectural Drawing Collection, University Art Museum, University of California, Santa Barbara: John Running: 36; Werner Forman Archive/AR: 31; From Karl von Steiner, Die Marquesaner und ihre Kunst I: 50; Photographer: Peter Horner: 52; Dr. George Kennedy, University of California, Los Angeles: 53; Helmut Jäger: 57; Hinz: 58; Meteorological Service of New Zealand Limited: 61. **Chapter 18**—H. M. Cole: 1, 22; © 1988 Rachel Hoffman: 2; Photograph by Roy Sieber, 1964: 3; National Commission for Museums and Monuments, Lagos: 4, 8, 9; Jean Dominique Lajoux: 6; T. K. Seligman: 7; James L. Stanfield, © National Geographic Society: 11; © Carollee Pelos, from Spectacular Vernacular: The Adobe Tradition: 12; © 1972, H. M. Cole: 14; Photograph by Eliot Elisofon, 1970: 15, 16; Photograph © by The Barnes Foundation: 20; © 1976, H. M. Cole: 21; Photograph by Philip Ravenhill, 1978: 25; Michel Huet/HOA-QUI, Paris: 27; Photo by Denis J. Nervig: 30; Frank Willett: 32; photograph by Henry John Drewal, 1978: 33; photograph by Philip Ravenhill, 1989: 34. **Part IV** opening photograph—Summerfield. **Chapter 19**—Canali: 1, 4, 5, 7, 18; Ralph Lieberman: 2, 12; AL/AR: 3, 14, 16; Scala/AR: 6, 8, 10, 19, 20, 21; Summerfield: 9, 15; Gir: 11; Takashi Okamura/Abbeville Press, New York: 13, 17; Anderson/AR: 22. **Chapter 20**—Gir/AR: 1; Inventaire général/SPA-DEM Jean-Luc DUTHU: 2, 3; Artothek: 5; Joseph S. Martin/Artothek: 6, 16; Photo by Richard Carafelli: 9; Paul Laes, Belgium: 13; Canali: 14; Summerfield: 15; © photo Jean Mazenod, L'art gothique, éditions Citadelles et Mazenod, Paris: 19; Jörg P. Anders/BPK: 20; R.M.N.: 21; Yves-Siza: 22; Photo Verlag Gundermann, Würzburg: 24; Jean Dieuzaide: 25; Luraine C. Tansey: 26.

Chapter 21—HB Collection: 1, 2; Ralph Lieberman: 3, 10, 13, 14, 17, 35, 36, 40, 42; Canali: 4, 8, 12, 19, 23, 24, 25, 28, 30, 32, 33, 34, 49, 52; Erich Lessing/AR: 22; Summerfield: 5, 27, 57; AL/AR: 6, 11, 43, 45, 46, 47, 50, 60, 62; Canali/Lensini, Italy: 7; Mar/AR: 9; Anderson/AR: 15, 21, 38, 51; Brogi/AR: 20; Scala/AR: 29, 58; © 1987 M. Sarri: 31; German Archaeological Institute, Rome: 39; Photo by Philip A. Charles: 48; Takashi Okamura/Abbeville Press, New York: 54; Bridgeman Art Library/AR: 55; Photo by Richard Carafelli: 56; © 1984 M. Sarri/Photo Vatican Museums: 59; Giovetti: 61.
Chapter 22—Scala/AR: 1, 13, 48, 59, 60, 65, 66; AL/AR: 3, 9, 34, 45; R.M.N./Duplicata: 4, 58; Canali: 6, 14, 16, 19, 35, 38, 61, 64; The British Architectural Library, RIBA, London: 10; Ralph Lieberman: 11, 27; Guidotti/Grimoldi: 12; © 1983 M. Sarri/PhotoVatican Museums: 15; R.M.N.: 17, 21, 22, 62; Canali/On license of Fabbrica di S. Pietro, Vatican: 18; Summerfield: 20, 39, 40; Nippon Television Network Corporation, Tokyo, 1994: 23, 26, 28; Photo Vatican Museums: 24; Bracchetti-Zigrossi/Photo Vatican Museums: 25; Rotkin, PFI: 29; Anderson/AR: 30, 36; Fototeca: 32; Gir/AR: 44; Edwin Smith: 46; AR: 47; Harry N. Abrams, Inc.: 50; Phyllis Dearborn Massar: 51, 53, 54; Canali/Cameraphoto: 55, 56, 67; Photo by Jose A. Naranjo: 57; Blauel-Gnamm/Artothek: 63.
Chapter 23—Artothek: 1; Photograph by Schecter Lee: 2; Gir/AR: 3, 4; Jörg P. Anders/BPK: 8, 14; Scala/AR: 11, 20; Studio Milar: 17; R.M.N.: 18; Lauros/Gir: 19; Gir: 21; Bulloz: 22; MAS: 23, 24, 25, 26; Lauros-Gir/AR: 27.
Chapter 24—Anderson/AR: 1, 13; Anthony Kersting: 2, 63, 72; Rotkin/P.F.I.: 3; Canali: 5, 7, 10, 16, 18, 21, 22, 23, 24; AL/AR: 8, 48; Summerfield: 11, 31, 44; G. E. Kidder Smith: 15, 17; Scala/AR: 19, 25, 29, 60; R.M.N./R.G. Ojeda: 26; © 1987 M. Sarri/PhotoVatican Museums: 27; Provinciebestuur van Antwerpen: 38; Blauel-Gnammf/Artothek: 39; Joachim Blauel/Artothek: 40; Artephot/Photo R.M.N.: 41; R.M.N./Duplicata: 43, 56, 69; Arch. Phot. Paris/SPADEM: 47; Novosti/Sovfoto: 49; Photo by Richard Carafelli: 50; Photograph © Mauritshuis, The Hague: 55; R.M.N.: 57, 70; Bulloz: 62; Aerofilms Limited: 64; NYPL: 65; Gir/AR: 66; HB Collection: 67; Roger-Viollet: 68; National Monuments Record: 71.
Chapter 25—Rapho/PRI: 1; British Stationery Office: 2; National Monuments Record: 3, 22; Anthony Kersting: 4, 5, 32; Hir: 7; AL/AR: 8; Scala/AR: 9; Ralph Lieberman: 10; Scala/AR: 11; R.M.N.: 12, 13, 27, 29, 49, 50; R.M.N./Duplicata: 14, 46; Bulloz; 18, 40; The British Library: 20; Summerfield: 25; Country Life Picture Library: 33, 38; Tate Gallery, London/AR: 35; The Collections of the Virginia State LIbrary & Archives: 42; Courtesy of the Library of Congress: 43; NYPL: 44; Photo: Ann Hutchison: 45.
Part V opening photograph—Lauros/Gir.
Chapter 26 map—R. R. Palmer, ed., *Atlas of World History*, Rand McNally, 1975. Permission granted by Reed Consumer Books, London.
Chapter 26—Arch. Phot. Paris/SPADEM: 1; AL/AR: 2, 26; AR: 3; R.M.N.: 4, 5, 6, 8, 12, 40, 55, 69; R.M.N./Duplicata: 13, 16, 17, 18, 37, 65; Gir/AR: 14, 35, 89; Elke Walford: 19, 44; Staatlich Museen zu Berlin: 20; Bulloz: 25; Brownlie/PRI: 27; Anthony Kersting: 28; Moreau/Arch. Phot. Paris/SPADEM: 29; Collection Société Francaise de Photographie, Paris: 31; Massachusetts Commandery Military Order of the Loyal Legion and the US Army Military History Institute: 34; Thomas Jefferson University Art Committee: 41; Novosti/Sovfoto: 45; © 1981 Sotheby's, Inc.: 46; Tate Gallery, London/AR: 49, 50, 70; Joachim Blauel/Artothek: 51; HB Collection: 59; Courtesy George Eastman House: 68; Michael Agee: 75; R.M.N./R.G. Ojeda: 81; Scala/AR: 86; Courtesy of the Library of Congress: 90; Lee Stalsworth: 91, 92; Mar/AR: 93; Photo: French Government Tourist Office: 95; Chicago Architectural Photography, Co.: 96; Ralph Lieberman: 97; Hedrich-Blessing photograph courtesy Chicago Historical Society: 98; The Preservation Society of Newport County/Newport Mansions: 99.
Chapter 27—Ralph Lieberman: 2; Chicago Architectural Photography, Co.: 3; Ezra Stoller © Esto: 5; © 1996 Estate of Gerrit Rietveld/Licensed by VAGA, New York, NY: 6; Cervin Robinson: 7; © 1995 ARS, NY/VG Bild-Kunst, Bonn: 9, 22, 23; Lucien Herve: 11; © 1995 ARS, NY/ADAGP, Paris: 13, 15, 28, 52, 53, 58, 59, 61, 70; Scala/AR © 1995 Succession H. Matisse, Paris/ARS, NY: 14; Erich Lessing/AR: 16; © 1995 ARS, NY/Pro Litteris, Zurich: 17; Elke Walford: 18; Photo: David Heald © 1995 ARS, NY/ADAGP, Paris: 21, 31, 33, 35, 39; © 1995 ARS, NY/VG Bild-Kunst, Bonn: 22, 23, 54, 60, 68; © 1995 ARS, NY/SPADEM, Paris: 24, 29, 34, 67, 71; HB Collection: 26; Martin Bühler, Basel © 1995 ARS, NY/ADAGP, Paris: 30; R.M.N.: 32 © 1995 ARS, NY/SPADEM, Paris; Photography by Sheldan C. Collins, NJ. © 1996 Estate of Stuart Davis/ Licensed by VAGA, New York, NY: 36; © 1995 ARS, NY/ADAGP/SPADEM, Paris: 38, 40, 63; Biff Henrich: 41; © 1996 Estate of Jacques Lipchitz/ Licensed by VAGA, New York, NY Courtesy, Marlborough Gallery: 43; Musee de L'Homme: 46; Tate Gallery, London/AR: 47, 55; Martin Bühler, Basel: 50; © 1996 Estate of Vladimir Tatlin/Licensed by VAGA, New York, NY: 51; Photo by Richard Carafelli © 1995 The Georgia O'Keeffe Foundation/ ARS, NY: 57; © 1996 Foundation Giorgio de Chirico/Licensed by VAGA, New York, NY: 62; © 1995 Demart Pro Arte, Geneva/ARS, NY: 64; Photo Hickey-Robertson © 1995 C. Herscovici, Brussels/ ARS, NY: 65; Schalkwijk/AR: 66; Photo: 1992 Peter Lauri, Bern © 1995 ARS, NY/VG Bild-Kunst, Bonn: 69; photography by Geoffrey Clements, NY. © 1996 Ben Shahn/Licensed by VAGA, New York, NY: 77; Photo: MAS © 1995 ARS, NY/SPADEM, Paris: 80.
Chapter 28—© 1995 ARS, NY/ADAGP, Paris: 1; Tate Gallery, London/AR © 1995 ARS, NY/ADAGP, Paris: 3; Lee Fatherree © 1995 The Pollock-Krasner Foundation/ARS, NY: 4; HB Collection: 5; © 1995 Willem de Kooning/ARS, NY: 6; photo by Edward Owen © 1995 ARS, NY/ADAGP, Paris: 7; 1985, Steve Sloman, NY © 1995 Kate Rothko-Prize & Christopher Rothko/ARS, NY: 9; © 1963 Ellsworth Kelly. Photo by Philipp Scholz Rittermann: 10; © 1995 Frank Stella/ARS, NY: 11; Photo courtesy André Emmerich Gallery, New York: 12; Photograph by Schecter Lee: 13; Photo: Lee Stalsworth 1995 © ARS, NY/ADAGP, Paris: 14; Photo by David Gahr © 1995 ARS, NY/ADAGP, Paris: 16; © 1995 John Chamberlain/ARS, NY: 18; © 1996 Louise Bourgeois/Licensed by VAGA, New York, NY: 19; © 1996 Estate of David Smith/ Licensed by VAGA, New York, NY: 20; Photograph by Rudolph Burckhardt. © 1996 Estate of Donald Judd/ Licensed by VAGA, New York, NY: 22; Photo by Gianfranco Gorgoni: 24; © 1983 Christo, photo: Wolfgang Volz: 25; © 1996 Richard Hamilton/ Licensed by VAGA, New York, NY: 26; David Hockney: 27; © 1996 Jasper Johns/Licensed by VAGA, New York, NY: 28; Rheinisches Bildarchiv © 1996 Jasper Johns/Licensed by VAGA, New York, NY: 29; Photo by: Graydon Wood, 1989. © 1996 Robert Rauschenberg/Licensed by VAGA, New York, NY: 30; Claes Oldenburg: 31; Roy Lichtenstein: 32; Tate Gallery, London/AR © 1995 The Andy Warhol Foundation for the Visual Arts/ARS, NY: 33; photo: Ron Jennings: 34; Photo by Anne Gold: 35; PaceWildenstein: 37; Photo courtesy Allan Stone Gallery. © 1996 Richard Estes/Licensed by VAGA, New York, NY Courtesy, Marlborough Gallery: 38; © 1995 ARS, NY/VG Bild-Kunst, Bonn: 39; Courtesy: Brooke Alexander, New York. Photo: D. James Dee: 40; © 1985 Gilbert & George; Courtesy Robert Miller Gallery, New York: 41; Judy Chicago, 1979; photo: Copyright Donald Woodman: 42; Courtesy Barbara Kruger: 44; Metro Pictures: 45; photo: Artur Starewicz, Warsaw. © 1996 Magdalena Abakanowicz/ Licensed by VAGA, New York, NY Courtesy, Marlborough Gallery: 46; Courtesy Ronald Feldman Fine Arts, New York: 47; Phillips/Schwab: 49; Photo by Robet McElroy. Courtesy André Emmerich Gallery, New York: 50; Photo: Office of Cultural Affairs, city of San Jose © 1995 Dorothea Rockburne/ARS, NY: 51; Paul Macapia: 52; © 1979 David Em: 55; Electronic Arts Intermix: 57; Peter Aaron/Esto: 58, 67; AP/Wide World Photos: 59; The Solomon R. Guggenheim Museum, New York, photo by Robert E. Mates: 60; The Solomon R. Guggenheim Museum: 61; Ralph Lieberman: 62; from *The New Churches of Europe* by G. E. Kidder Smith: 63; David Austen/Tony Stone Images: 64; Ezra Stoller © Esto: 65, 70; Richard Payne, Houston: 66; H. Armstrong Roberts: 68; Michael Bodycomb: 72; Deutches Architektur-Museum Archiv: 73; Michael Melford/The Image Bank: 74; Matt Wargo: 75; Peter Mauss/Esto: 76, 77; Photo: Christian Kandzia/Behnisch & Partner: 78; Photo courtesy of The Japan Architect © Shinkenchiku-sha: 80; Julian Calder/Tony Stone Images: 81.

ILLUSTRATION CREDITS

FIG. 1-3 From "The Archeology of Lascaux Cave," by Arlette Leroi-Gourhan. © 1982 Scientific American, Inc., all rights reserved.
FIGS. 1-16, 1-17 Arlette Mellaart.
FIG. 2-2 From E.S. Piggott, Ed., *The Dawn of Civilization*, London Thames and Hudson, 1961, pg. 70.
FIG. 2-3 From H. Frankfort, *The Art and Architecture of the Ancient Orient*, Harmondsworth and Baltimore: Penguin, 1970, p.69.
FIG. 2-18 © 1975 The Royal Institute of British Architects and the University of London, by permission of Athlone Press.
FIGS. 3-5(a), 4-4, 4-22, 8-11, 9-5 © Hir.
FIG. 3-5(b) From K. Lange and M. Hirmer, *Agypteu Architectur, Plastik, and Malerei in drei Jahrtausenden*, Munich, 1957. Used by permission of Phaidon Press and Hirmer Fotoarchiv.
FIGS. 3-22, 3-28, 7-74, 9-25, 13-59 From Sir Banister Fletcher, *A History of Architecture on the Comparative Method*, 17th ed., rev. by R. A. Cordingly, 1961. Used by permission of Athlone Press of the University of London and the British Architectural Library, Royal Institute of British Architects.
FIG. 4-21 From Alan J.B. Wace, *Mycenae*, Princeton University Press, 1949, Fig. 22.
FIG. 5-6 From J.G. Pedley, *Greek Art and Archaeology*, Prentice - Hall, 1993, Fig. 5.15.
FIG. 5-17 From Marvin Trachtenberg and Isabelle Hyman, *Architecture from Prehistoric to Post-Modernism/The Western Tradition*, Englewood Cliffs, NJ: Prentice Hall, 1986, p. 86, p. 293. Used by permission.
FIG. 5-18 From J. Charbonneaux, *Archaic Greek Art*, George Brazziller, Inc. 1971, Fig. 17.
FIG. 5-29 From H. Berve and G. Gruben, *Greek Temples, Theaters, and Shrines*, Harry N. Abrams, Inc., Fig. 41.
FIG. 5-46 Courtesy of the Agora Excavations, American School of Classical Studies, Athens.
FIG. 5-59 From H. Berve and G. Gruben, *Greek Temples, Theaters, and Shrines*, Harry N. Abrams, Inc., Fig. 66.
FIG. 5-84(a) From H. Berve and G. Gruben, *Greek Temples, Theaters, and Shrines*, Harry N. Abrams, Inc., Fig. 130.
FIGS. 7-3, 15-33 Editions Citadelles et Mazenod, Paris.
FIG. 7-4 From *A Concise History of Western Architecture* by Robert Furneaux Jordan, © 1969, by Harcourt Brace Jovanovich. Reproduced by permission of publisher.
FIG. 7-15 Verlag M. DuMont Schauberg.
FIG. 7-38 From J.B. Ward - Perkins, *Roman Architecture*, Adapted by permission of Electra Editrice, Milan.
FIG. 7-50 From Boethius, "Etruscan and Early Roman Architecture". © Yale University Press.
FIG. 7-84 After George M.A. Hanfamann, *Roman Art: A Survey of the Art of Imperial Rome*, A New York Graphic Society Book, by permission of Little Brown and Co.
FIG. 10-8 From G. Marcais *L'Architecture Musul mane d' Occident*. By permission of Arts et Metiers Grapohiques, Paris.
FIG. 10-13 From K.A.C. Creswell, *Early Muslim Architecture*. Adapted by permission of Clarendon Press/Oxford University Press.
FIG. 10-25 Plan drawn by Christopher Woodward.
FIG. 12-2 From H. Stierlin, *Die Architektur der Welt*, Vol. 1, p. 147, p. 188, © 1977 Hirmer Verlag, Munich.
FIGS. 12-4, 12-17 From Kenneth J. Conant, *Early Medieval Church Architecture*. Used by permission of Johns Hopkins Press.
FIG. 12-11 © AL/AR.
FIGS. 13-4, 13-6, 13-7 From Ernest Gall, *Gotische Kathedralen*, 1925. Used by permission of Klinkhardt and Biermann, publishers.
FIG. 13-19 Used by permission of Umschau Buchverlag, Frankfort.
FIG. 14-9 From Benjamin Rowland, *The Art and Architecture of India*, 1953 Penguin Books.
FIG. 14-29 Madeleine Giteau, "The Civilization of Angkor". Adapted by permission of Rizzoli International Publications.
FIGS. 15-34, 15-36, 15-38 © Laurence G. Liu.
FIG. 21-37 From Marvin Trachtenberg and Isabelle Hyman, *Architecture from Prehistoric to Post-Modernism/The Western Tradition*, Englewood Cliffs, NJ: Prentice Hall, 1986, p. 86, p. 293. Used by permission.
FIG. 21-41 From Nikolaus Pevsner, *An Outline of European Architecture*, 6th ed., 1960 Penguin Books Ltd., © Nikolaus Pevsner, 1943, 1960, 1963.
FIG. 24-20 By courtesy of Electa, Milano.
FIG. 27-10 Photo: Lucien Herve © 1995 ARS, NY/SPADEM, Paris.
FIG. 28-69 James A. Sugar © National Geographic Society.

INDEX

Page numbers in italics indicate illustrations.